ENCYCLOPEDIA OF
SCIENCE

AND TECHNOLOGY

ENCYCLOPEDIA OF

SCIENCE AND

Contributing Editors
Harold Morowitz, *George Mason University*
Paul Ceruzzi, *Smithsonian Institution*

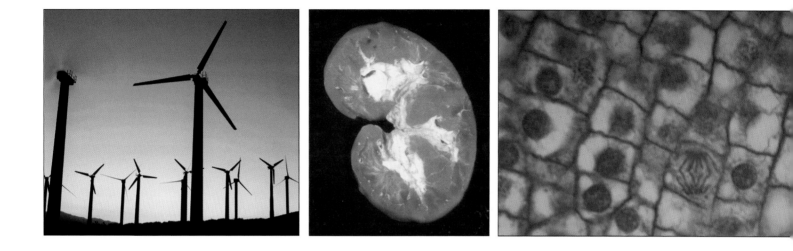

TECHNOLOGY

James Trefil, *General Editor*

Routledge
New York • London

Published in 2001 by
Routledge
29 West 35th Street
New York, NY 10001

Routledge is an imprint of Taylor & Francis Books, Inc.

Published in Great Britain by
Routledge
11 New Fetter Lane
London EC4P 4EE

Produced by The Reference Works, Inc.

Harold Rabinowitz, *Director*
Ross Mandel, *Executive Editor* • Douglas Heyman, *Managing Editor*

Editors
Rachel Soltis   Jenna Bagnini   Stephen Smith

Writers	*Production*	*Copy Editors*
Edward Edelson	Ilana Rabinowitz	Louise Weiss
Hartley Spatt	Daniel Vogel	Diane Root
Rachel Teitz	Anita Lovitt	Amy Fass
Elizabeth Bass	Vincent Arnone	Linda Reitman
Timothy Bay	Chanan Tigay	Trumbull Rogers
	Yisrael Tigay	Daniel Bubbeos
Line Editors	Hugo Sarago	
Ben Soskis		*Art*
Hartley Spatt		Eleanor Kwei
Ellen Catala	*Index*	Barbara Lipp
Richard Harth	Elliot Linzer	Tony O'Hara
Yossi Teitz		

Image Consultant Norman Curry, Corbis-Bettmann
Designed by Bob Antler, Antler Design Works

Library of Congress Cataloging-in-Publication Data

The encyclopedia of science and technology / James S. Trefil, general editor.
        p. cm.
   Includes bibliographical references and index.
   ISBN 0-415-93724-8 (alk. paper)
Science—Encyclopedias. 2. Technology—Encyclopedias. I. Trefil, James S., 1938-

   Q121 .E53 2001
   503—dc21   2001019983

1 0   9   8   7   6   5   4   3   2   1

Printed in the United States of America on acid-free paper.

ISBN:0-415-93724-8

HOW TO USE THIS BOOK

"It is doubtful that it will ever [again] be possible to assemble an encyclopedia that covers the breadth of all human knowledge." These words were written over ninety years ago on the occasion of the publication of a great encyclopedia. The sentiment reflected a sense that the sum of information about the natural world was about to explode, and indeed it did. Yet the encyclopedia form continued its popularity. The reason may be that the form is ideally suited for the kind of learning to which the modern reader has become accustomed and which approximates how learning is actually done: in small unconnected bits of information. In assembling this work, it was our intention not to cover every aspect of modern science: that early twentieth-century critic may, after all, have had a point. Instead we have brought to bear another development of the last half-century, the advent of high-quality science writing that is both entertaining and informative. For this, one could hardly have assembled editorial guidance better suited to the task of conveying the excitement of modern science than the General Editor and the advisory editors of this work.

A number of features will enhance the reader's experience in the pages that follow:

The Critical Path Feature. This feature appears above and below each article title in the form of the words "First see" and "Next see," respectively, each followed by the title of an entry in the work. This means that if the reader is interested in following the thread of the discipline back to its more fundamental subjects, see the article above the title. If one wishes to follow the argument forward and see the subject develop to a level, see the title listed below the title. It should thus (theoretically) be possible to gather

First see PERIODIC TABLE

Calcium Metabolism

Next see BONE AND BONE GROWTH

information on an entire discipline simply by following the "Critical Path" through it. The cross-referencing that appears throughout the text is complemented by many "Signpost" boxes,

placed at the end of many entries, in which the reader is not only apprised of other relevant articles, but is given some indication of what one can expect to find there. The article titles are also color-coded—blue for physical science; green for life science; and red for technology—to make it easier to follow an argument through the encyclopedia. Finally, an extensive index and bibliographies of available and accessible literature fill out the apparatus of this reference work.

Sidebars. Many entries contain sidebars consisting of observations of striking phenomena, interesting historical anecdotes of discovery, or reports on the cutting edge of current research. In both the text and the sidebars, it was our hope to make this work an enjoyable as well as a fascinating read.

Illustrations. The illustration program has been made extensive (almost beyond reason), but not at the expense of the words and the quality of the writing.

Scope and Tone. A further development of recent science is the acceptance of a sense of responsibility on the part of the scientist and on the part of society as a whole to use science to make the world a better place. Toward that end, the reader will often find a point of view or an attitude in the entries. Readers should realize that they are part of the ongoing discussion regarding the need to use science responsibly, an attitude that has increasingly become part of scientific discourse itself. If nothing else, it has become clear that neither scientist nor citizen ever ceases to bear the responsibility for research undertaken or underwritten. That is the spirit of the opinions expressed in the articles: the content, like all genuine discourse, recognizes the validity of other opinions and approaches even while forthrightly expressing positions.

Begin with the Introduction. The need for every person to be aware of the march of scientific disovery was never as clear as it is now, at the dawning of a new millenium. This is the orientation of the General Editor in the work's Introduction, and we urge the reader to begin the journey with Dr. Trefil's introductory remarks.

The Human Side of
SCIENCE and TECHNOLOGY

James Trefil, *General Editor*

A hundred years ago, at the dawning of the twentieth century, the world was very different from what it is now. People considered it the height of modernity to be able to travel across a continent by spending days on a coal-powered train. Life expectancy was barely half of what it is now, and diseases like diphtheria, pneumonia, and smallpox were major killers. Today, we routinely fly coast to coast in a matter of hours, and virtually the only smallpox virus left on the planet is kept under strict containment at a scientific laboratory, in case we need it to develop vaccines to combat it in the future.

Why is the world so different today than it was then? The answer is simple: over the past century, our knowledge of the way the universe works—what we call science—has grown enormously, and with it our ability to apply that knowledge to everyday problems—what we call technology—has changed the way we live. Science and technology touch every aspect of our lives, and this means that everyone, not just specialists, needs to know something about each of them. The entries in this encyclopedia are intended to provide enough information for readers to understand some of the main features of the science that affects our lives, without overwhelming readers with technical complexity.

And why have science and technology blossomed during this century? One reason has to do with the improved methods of communication between people. Someone thinking about a problem on one side of the world can influence and inspire someone thinking about the same problem on the other side of the world much more easily. The chance encounters in which a scientist receives the key bit of information or inspiration that leads to an advance in the field is now not so rare an occurrence as it was before. Scientists are brought together today by improved methods of transportation and communication, culminating in the Internet in which all of science—indeed, it seems, the entire world—is in constant and instant touch with one another. This is the felicitous irony of the twentieth century: the "wiring" of the world has improved communication between people and accelerated the pace of scientific discovery. For

this reason, we have tried to make the entries in this book readable and entertaining—to capture the sense of excitement scientists feel when, after many hours of painstaking work in the lab, at the computer, or at the blackboard, they are on the verge of a discovery or insight. For this is how science advances: with people talking to one another, be it at conferences, in the pages of a journal, on the phone, or by e-mail.

The Structure of the Scientific Enterprise. To interpret the entries, you need to have a sense of the way the scientific enterprise is structured and the way our ideas about the universe change. There are two bits of folklore about science that I have encountered during my career as an educator. On the one hand, there is the notion that science is essentially a set of answers—a secret book in which the initiated learn about unchanging and eternal Truth. On the other hand, there is the notion that somehow everything we know about the universe could change tomorrow—that the truths of science are completely ephemeral and have no firm roots in reality.

Science, however, is neither a completed book nor a set of temporary beliefs. Instead, it is something much more wonderful and human: a complex web of ideas, facts, philosophical concepts, history, and serendipity. I like to think of scientific knowledge as being somewhat analogous to the trunk of a tree. At the core is the heartwood, solid and unchanging. No matter how large the tree grows, this wood, the solid foundation of the entire structure, remains the same. Many of the central concepts of science are like this. Conceived decades or even centuries ago, they have been subjected to stringent scrutiny and testing for so long that the chances that they will turn out to be wrong are practically nil (though I wouldn't take bets on any of them). Like the heartwood of a giant oak, they support the entire structure of science and technology. Concepts connected with the conservation of energy, for example, are likely to remain an essential element of scientific thinking for a long time.

On the other hand, at the frontiers of scientific research, things are very different. Instead of permanence and solidity we have change and possibility. Like the outer layers of a tree, the research frontiers are where the growth occurs, when new science is added to the structure. In these new areas, a single fact or observation can (and often does) change our notions completely, for those notions are still being formed, still taking shape. I would be very surprised, for example, if everything written in the entries on cosmology or immunity were still accepted ten years from now. But even if that happens, it will be the result of a conversation involving many scientists from all over the world

What makes the tree of science special is that knowledge, once acquired, can be put to use to change the way human beings live. Modern medicine, for example, depends intimately on information about the details of the molecular machinery of living systems obtained over the past fifty years. Our far-flung information systems depend on scientific information about electromagnetic waves obtained over a century ago and on the understanding of new kinds of materials that may be only a few years old. As with the tree, the new growth rests solidly on the old.

Dance of the Scientists. It used to be that towering figures (Isaac Newton and James Clerk Maxwell, for example) could understand and dominate all the science of their time. Those days are long gone, however. Today, scientists specialize, both by field and by the kind of work they do. Some scientists study stars, others study cells, yet others atoms or quarks. Within each of these categories there are scientists who spend their time imagining what the universe might be like and converting their visions into hard mathematical predictions of the outcomes of experiments. These scientists are called theoreticians. At the same time, others actually do experiments to see which of the many possible universes that exist in the dreams of theoreticians we actually live in. These are the experimental or observational scientists.

Having been around a great many experimentalists and theoreticians, I never cease to be amazed how one group invariably thinks that it is the essential group in science and that the other is wholly dependent on it for their work. In truth, both groups are necessary and both continually feed off and give support to the other. The progress of science can be thought of as kind of a waltz through history between these two partners, the experimentalists and the theoreticians—first one leading, then the other. As solid science comes more and more to require a facility in both areas, the dance begins to look more like a tango, where both dancers are leading and following at the same time.

That balance between what we experimentally know because we've seen it (measured it, detected it, or tested it), and what we theoretically know because we think that's how it might be (must be, ought to be, or would be awfully nice if it were), is intrinsic to the advance of science. We've tried to capture this "dance" in paying as much attention to experiment as to theory throughout this work.

Backing Up the Truck. The entries in this book represent our best knowledge of the universe we live in. This knowledge is the basis for the technologies that have already changed our lives and will continue to do so in the future. It is knowledge everyone needs not only to understand the universe we live in, but to understand the headlines in tomorrow's paper. We've tried to bring this to our readers in a manner both engaging and entertaining. And after we backed up the truck, as it were, and delivered our encyclopedia, what did we do? We kept right on working—updating, elaborating, and expanding the material, not just for a future print edition, but with the the intention of making it available on the Web for our readers. It is our hope that every reader will become part of the discussion—the dance—in some way, beginning with a mature appreciation of contemporary science, its applications and its implications.

See you in cyberspace.

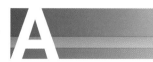

First see TEMPERATURE

Absolute Zero

Next see CRYOGENICS

The lowest temperature theoretically possible, corresponding to –459.67 degrees on the Fahrenheit scale and –273.15 degrees on the Celsius scale.

Absolute zero is the lowest temperature that is theoretically possible. It corresponds to a condition of minimum, or zero-point internal energy. That temperature is –459.67 degrees on the Fahrenheit scale and –273.15 degrees on the Celsius temperature scale. It is 0 on the Kelvin temperature scale, which uses the same degrees as the Celsius scale. Although absolute zero has not yet been reached, the techniques of cryogenics—the technology for creating temperatures below –200 degrees Celsius—have come close.

To produce these low temperatures, a coolant is treated in such a way that its entropy—the degree of disorder of the atoms or molecules in it—is reduced substantially. One way to ac-

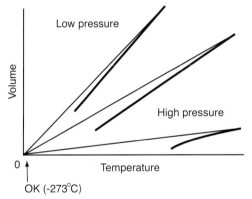

The concept of absolute zero arose from extending Charles's Law—the volume of a gas is directly proportional to its temperature—well below its range of applicability and noticing that T for zero volume for all gases converge at the same point.

complish this reduction is to compress a gas or to apply a magnetic field to certain salts. The heat produced by these methods is conducted away from the coolant. When the pressure applied to the gas or the strength of the magnetic field is reduced, substantial cooling results, to the point where gases become liquid. This temperature for hydrogen is about 20 degrees K (or –253 degrees C). Helium liquefies at 4.2 degrees K, then undergoes a marked change in properties at 2.178 degrees K; its viscosity, or frictional resistance, essentially disappears. Liquid helium can be cooled further, to about 0.7 degrees K; the rare isotope helium-3 can be cooled to about 0.04 degrees K by mixing it with the common isotope helium-4. Even lower temperatures, down to 0.00001 degrees K, can be achieved by demagnetization of paramagnetic salts such as iron alum.

Theoretical Limitations. The apparent failure to reach absolute zero can be explained by the quantum theory, which states that any subatomic particle that oscillates with a simple harmonic motion cannot have a stationary state at which it has zero kinetic energy. In addition, the

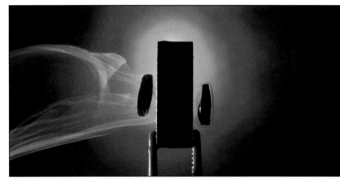

uncertainty principle—the statement that it is not possible to know both the position and the momentum of a particle with unlimited accuracy—entails that such a particle cannot be completely at rest, and thus at zero temperature, at exactly the centerpoint of its oscillations.

Near Absolute Zero. Materials exhibit unusual properties at temperatures close to absolute zero. Liquids (like liquid helium) lose their viscosity and become "superfluids," and metals are able to "superconduct" electric current with virtually no resistance. Superconductivity was first observed in 1911 in mercury frozen to 4.3 de-

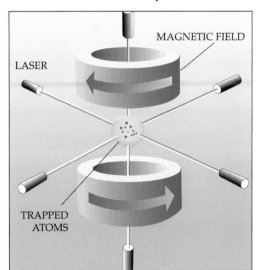

grees K. Other metals that exhibit superconductivity at temperatures near absolute zero include magnesium, cadmium, zinc, and aluminum.

Methods of achieving temperatures near absolute zero are described in CRYOGENICS *and* LIQUEFACTION. *The behavior of supercooled helium is described in* SUPERFLUID. *Theoretical considerations of very cold temperatures are found in* ENTROPY; HEAT; QUANTUM STATISTICS; *and* TEMPERATURE.

An electric current applied to a "warm" metal would dissipate as it heated the metal. Above, a supercooled superconductor retains an electric current and magnetically levitates metals without the continued input of energy.

Left, laser beams are used to trap a cloud of atoms, which are then held by magnetic fields generated by coils; the atoms are then cooled to near absolute zero.

Further Reading
Bernstein, Jeremy, *Three Degrees Above Zero: Bell Labs in the Information Age* (1984); Fairbank, J.D., *Near Zero: New Frontiers of Physics* (1988); Meredith, P.V.E., *Matter at Low Temperatures* (1989); Pobell, Frank, *Matter and Methods at Low Temperatures* (1992); Von Baeyer, Hans Christain, *Warmth Disperses and Time Passes: A History of Heat* (1999).

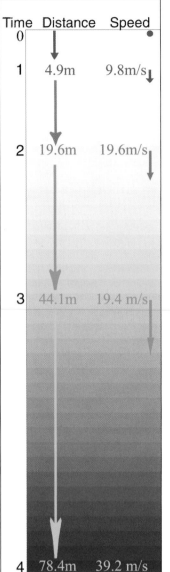

Time	Distance	Speed
0		
1	4.9m	9.8m/s
2	19.6m	19.6m/s
3	44.1m	19.4 m/s
4	78.4m	39.2 m/s

Above, the acceleration of a falling body during 4 seconds of free fall. The accelerometer in the space shuttle (below), though highly sensitive and reliable, still requires a separate device for each spatial dimension.

First see FORCE

Acceleration

Next see NEWTON'S LAWS

The rate at which the velocity of a body changes.

Acceleration is the rate of change of a moving body's velocity. Velocity has two components, speed and direction, and so a body's acceleration is altered by either a change in speed, a change in direction or both. For example, a ball that is being swung at the end of a rope at a constant speed is accelerating even though its speed does not change, because its direction is constantly changing. That acceleration is called centripetal or radial acceleration. The units in which acceleration is expressed include both velocity and time—for example, meters per second per second or feet per second per second. Suppose an automobile accelerates from 10 feet per second to 50 feet per second over a period of 10 seconds. Its acceleration is calculated by dividing 40 feet per second by 10 seconds, to give an acceleration of 4 feet per second per second. (*See* ROTATIONAL MOTION.)

Newton's second law of motion says that acceleration is the result of a force acting on a body. The acceleration a produced by a force F acting on a body of mass m is $a = F/m$. On Earth, the acceleration of a body near the Earth's surface due to gravity is about 9.8 meters per second per second, or about 32 feet per second per second. In aerospace ventures, the acceleration astronauts experience is sometimes expressed in terms of g, the force of gravity at Earth's surface. An acceleration of "3 g's" can cause an astronaut to black out. (*See* FORCE.)

Accelerometers. Acceleration is measured by a device called an accelerometer, the basic component of which is usually a heavy mass that moves only in one dimension and is supported by springs. An accelerometer measures the force involved in changing the velocity of a body with a given mass. The simplest accelerometer consists of just one weight and has a sliding electrical contact attached to it. As acceleration increases, the weight slips back and a higher voltage is generated. As acceleration decreases, the weight moves forward and a lower voltage is generated. Such an accelerometer can measure acceleration only in one dimension. In aircraft, a set of three accelerometers at right angles to each other is needed to monitor acceleration in all directions. Accelerometers are also able to measure acceleration with the use of a transducer that measures voltage change.

Accelerometers have been used to study the stresses that aircraft are subjected to and to study the ability of pilots to perform acrobatic maneuvers. They are also used to measure the pickup and braking power of automobiles and the load that tires or wheels experience when rounding curves. (*See* AUTOMOTIVE DESIGN.)

First see ATOM

Accelerator, Particle

Next see BUBBLE CHAMBER

A device for creating, propelling, accelerating, and directing atomic particles so that they may interact with each other and with matter and be studied.

A particle accelerator, sometimes called an "atom smasher," is an electromagnetic machine that produces beams of high-energy subatomic particles such as protons or electrons. These particle beams are used for studies in nuclear physics and, at very high energies, for studies of

The particle accelerator at Fermilab on the outskirts of Chicago. The main ring, the Tevatron, 1.3 miles in diameter, is actually underground and is marked by a service road. Particles begin their journey in the labs at left. They are brought to speed by the small "booster" ring near the lab, then injected into the main ring, where they are accelerated by two systems of powerful electromagnets, one on top of the other. The accelerated particles are then shot off to the labs (upper left), where they are detected, recorded, and analyzed by supercomputers.

elementary subatomic particles. The accepted energy unit for a particle accelerator is the MeV, or one million electron volts, the energy acquired by a charged particle when it traverses a potential of one million volts. The largest accelerators, capable of energies of trillions of electron volts, are located at Fermilab in the United States and at CERN laboratories in Switzerland. Particle accelerators can either be linear or circular.

The first particle accelerators, developed in the early 1930s, were the cyclotron, the voltage multiplier, and the electrostatic generator. They produced beams of photons and deuterons with energies of a few MeV. More advanced and higher-energy accelerators, such as the synchrotron, the synchrocyclotron, and the proton synchrotron, were developed in the late 1940s. Today's accelerators are in the multi-GeV (Giga-eV, or billion electron volts) energy range. They use the principle of multiple resonance acceleration, in which particles acquire ever higher energies by passing many times through an electric field with a low potential drop.

Some current accelerator types include:

—the cyclotron, in which ions are accelerated through circular paths of increasing radius (the acceleration is produced by having the ions move in resonance with an alternating electric field in a magnetic field of constant strength);

—the linear accelerator, or linac, in which particles pass through a series of cylindrical electrodes, increasing their energy with each pass.

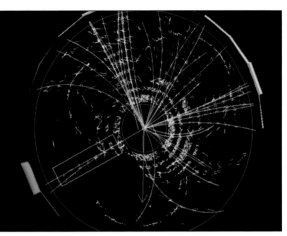

pulsing magnetic field. The proton synchrotron uses a pulsing ring magnet, with an applied frequency that is increased during the acceleration cycle.

There is an energy limit in cyclorotrons caused by relativistic effects. Synchrocyclotrons overcome that energy limit by modulating the applied radio frequency to match the decreasing orbital frequency that occurs at high energies. Much higher energies can be achieved, because magnets of significantly greater size can be used. Stable acceleration is obtained by controlling the passage of the accelerated particles, so that they remain in synchrony with the accelerating field for many thousand revolutions. Thus, a synchronous group of particles is accelerated steadily outward, with the individual charged particles in the group traversing circular paths of steadily increasing radius. The energy of such an accelerator is limited by the size and cost of the large solid-core magnets that are required.

Two operations are performed on accelerated particles: deflection and collision. Charged particles are deflected by strong electromagnetic fields, while neutral particles are unaffected. Above, the quadrupole magnet at SLAC (Stanford Linear Accelerator Center)—with two north poles and two south poles arranged so that like poles are opposite one another—used to focus the particle beam. Left, a computer display of a top quark event recorded and analyzed by the CDF detector at Fermilab. Computers now routinely analyze hundreds of thousands of particle events—a process that would have taken months of painstaking work—in minutes.

More detailed descriptions of important accelerator types are in CYCLOTRON; LINEAR ACCELERATOR; *and* SYNCHROTRON. *The chief detecting tool for accelerators is described in* BUBBLE CHAMBER; *the chief diagnostic tool in* SUPERCOMPUTER. *See also* BARYON; ELEMENTARY PARTICLE; LEPTON; *and* QUARK.

First see ATOM

Acids and Bases

Next see CHEMICAL REACTION

Many materials can be classified as either acids, bases, or neutral substances. Familiar acids include vinegar, citric acid, and certain bleaches. Common household bases include ammonia, baking soda, various detergents, and antacids.

Chemically speaking, an acid is any ionic compound whose cation (positively charged ion) is H^+, and a base is any ionic compound whose anion (negatively charged ion) is OH^-, the hydroxide ion. The Arrhenius definition of acids

CONTROVERSIES

The Superconducting Supercollider (SSC)

During the 1980s, the scientific community made a bold proposal for the construction of a "supercollider" some 52 miles long that would use superconducting magnets to create particle streams with enough energy to explore the structure of elementary particles. In 1993, with 14 miles of the underground tunnel for the SSC dug in Texas, the U.S. Congress stopped funding for what would have been the largest, most complex. . . and most costly scientific project in history. Physicists were forced to use existing accelerators more cleverly and focus on other areas of physics. The next advance in this field will be the inauguration of the Large Hadron Collider (LHC) in Geneva in 2005.

The synchrotron can accelerate either electrons or protons, using a pulsing magnetic field. The electron synchrotron uses a laminated, ring-shaped magnet to provide a guide field with a

Further Reading
Close, Frank, *The Particle Explosion* (1987); Close, F., *The Cosmic Onion: Quarks and the Nature of the Universe* (1986); Lee, S.Y., *Accelerator Physics* (1999); Pais, Abraham, *Inward Bound: Of Matter and Forces in the Physical World* (1988); Sutton, Christin, *The Particle Connection* (1984); Trefil, J., *From Atoms to Quarks: An Introduction to the Strange World of Particle Physics* (1994).

Litmus	OH	H	Universal indicator	Solution
Alkaline	0	14		Sodium hydroxide
	1	13		
	2	12		Limewater
	3	11		Washing soda
	4	10		
	5	9		Toothpaste / Borax
Neutral	6	8		Sodium bicarbonate
	7	7		Blood / Pure water / Fresh cow's milk
	8	6		Distilled water
	9	5		Ammonium sulfate
Acid	10	4		Soda water
	11	3		Vinegar
	12	2		Lemon juice
	13	1		Digestive juices in stomach
	14	0		Hydrochloric acid

In both the pH and pOH scales, pure water has a value of 7 and is considered neutral. When an antacid tablet is dropped in water, the mild citric acid in the tablet is neutralized by the sodium bicarbonate base, releasing carbon dioxide, which creates a "fizzing" effect. The main goal in relieving hyperacidity ("heartburn"), however, is the neutralization of stomach acids. Magnesium hydroxide ("milk of magnesia") is another base used to neutralize stomach acid.

and bases is that the compounds dissociate (separate) in water to produce these specific ions. Because the hydrogen atom originally consisted of simply one proton and one electron (which is now missing), the H^+ cation is really just a lone proton. Thus, the Brønsted-Lowry definition of acids and bases is that an acid functions as a proton donor and a base as a proton acceptor.

Indicators. Acid-base indicators are chemicals that turn specific colors in the presence of an acid or base. Some of the most common indicators are litmus, which is red in the presence of an acid and blue in the presence of a base, and phenolphthalein, which is colorless in the presence of an acid or neutral, and a bright purple in the presence of a base. Methyl red is red in the presence of a base or neutral, and yellow in the presence of an acid. (*See* CHEMICAL REACTION.)

Acidity or basicity are measured on the pH scale, which ranges from 0 to 14, with numbers less than 7 indicating an acid, 7 itself neutral, and more than 7 indicating a base. One can measure pH with an electric pH meter, or can simply dip specially treated strips of paper into the unknown substance and compare the resulting color to a pH chart. The pH scale indirectly measures the concentration of H^+ ions in a solution. To determine acidity or basicity, the relative amounts of ions are compared. If there are more H^+ ions than OH^- ions, the solution is acidic. If there are more OH^- ions, the solution is basic. If the concentrations are equal, the solution is neutral.

There is also a pOH scale that measures the concentrations of OH^- ions in solution. It is numerically the mirror image of the pH scale, also running from 0 to 14, but with numbers less than 7 indicating a base and numbers higher than 7 indicating an acid. Pure water is neutral. However, once an acid dissociates in solution, its H^+ combines with a molecule of water to form H_3O^+ (a hydronium ion), which means the water is acting as a proton acceptor. Since H_2O dissociates into both H^+ and OH^- ions, water can also act as a proton donor. A substance that can behave as either an acid (proton donor) or a base (proton acceptor) is called amphoteric. (*See* WATER.)

A strong acid is one that is a good proton donor, meaning it dissociates rapidly and its anion component does not easily recombine with the H^+. A weak acid is not a good proton donor. It is less likely to part with its proton and more likely to be reunited with it afterwards. The lower the pH number, the stronger the acid. Examples of strong acids include hydrochloric (HCl) and sulfuric (H_2SO_4) acids. Weak acids include acetic acid (vinegar) and citric acid.

A strong base is a good proton acceptor. It attracts the proton quickly and then holds onto it very well, and resists surrendering it. A weak base is not a very good proton acceptor. It is more hesitant about picking up the proton and then is more likely to simply let it go. The higher the pH number, the stronger the base. Examples of strong bases include milk of magnesia (magnesium hydroxide) and lye. Weak bases include ammonia (NH_3) dissolved in water.

Strength and Weakness. There is an obvious correlation between strong acids and weak bases. Both of them do not hold protons well and try to give them up at the first opportunity. There is also a connection between strong bases and weak acids. Both of them are better at holding onto protons than at letting them go. From these parallels arises the concept of acid-base conjugate pairs. A conjugate pair is two forms of the same molecule, one of which has a proton that the other one lacks. One member of the pair, the one with the proton, is the acid because it can function as a proton donor. Its conjugate or other half is the base, because it lacks a proton and can therefore act as a proton acceptor. If one member of a pair is strong, its conjugate is weak because they are essentially the same molecule.

Examples of conjugate pairs include:

Cl^- (base) + proton $\longrightarrow$ HCl (acid)
NH_3 (base) + proton $\longrightarrow$ NH_4^+ (acid)
H_2O (base) + proton $\longrightarrow$ H_3O^+ (acid)
OH^- (base) + proton $\longrightarrow$ H_2O (acid)

When an acid combines chemically with a base, they end up neutralizing each other. The H^+ of the acid combines with the OH^- of the base to form water. The other two ions, the cation from the base and the anion of the acid, combine to form a salt, which is an ordinary ionic compound without H^+ or OH^- ions. A chemical salt does not necessarily include sodium, although sodium is a cation in many compounds. (*See* SALTS.)

Uses. Acids play important roles in several life processes, notably in digestion. Many foods contain acids, and many industrial processes use acids. Sulfuric acid is used to make fertilizers, explosives, and dyes. Hydrochloric acid is used to clean metals and in the manufacture of many chemicals. Hydrofluoric acid (HF) is used in glass etching. (*See* DIGESTIVE CHEMISTRY.)

Bases also have many industrial uses. They are used in refining petroleum and in the manufacture of rayon, paper, and soap. Because bases neutralize acids, they are used in medications for upset stomachs. When dissolved in water, bases form electrolytes—ions that conduct electricity. (*See* ION; SOIL CHEMISTRY; *and* TITRATION.)

First see ACIDS AND BASES

Acid Rain

Next see AIR POLLUTION

A form of air pollution resulting from industrial and automobile activity that add aerosols of such substances as nitric acid and sulfuric acid to the air.

Acid rain first became prominent in the late 1950s, when Norwegian authorities correlated a decline in local fish populations with increased acidity of precipitation falling on rivers and lakes. Acid rain was considered a European problem until the 1970s, but measurements in the United States showed an increase in the acid concentration of lakes and rainfall in the Northeast.

Acidity is measured on the pH scale; unpolluted precipitation has a pH of 5.6. It is slightly acidic because atmospheric carbon dioxide dissolves in cloud droplets to form weak carbonic acid. In the Adirondack Mountains of New York, the pH levels of some lakes have been measured at 4 to 4.5, at least ten times more acid than normal. (*See* ACIDS AND BASES.)

Since the nitrogen and sulfur emissions that come from burning gasoline, coal, and oil can be transported over long distances in the atmosphere, regions far from major cities can be affected. For example, when sulfur compounds accumulate in the snow near lakes, the spring thaw can bring a short, devastating pulse of acidity. Efforts to reduce acid rain include emission controls on automobiles and on major industrial sources of emissions, such as electric power plants. (*See* AIR POLLUTION.)

First see SOUND

Acoustics

Next see ARCHITECTURAL ENGINEERING

The science that studies the production, properties, and effects of sound on physical surroundings.

One of the oldest sciences, acoustics was practiced in ancient Greece by such philosophers as Pythagoras and Euclid. While acoustics originally was limited to the study of audible sound in the air, its scope has been expanded to include mechanical waves and vibrations in all materials—solids, gases, and liquids—and waves of any frequency in these media. The unit of frequency of sound is the hertz (Hz), which is one cycle per second. (*See* WAVE.)

Sound Technology. Sound is produced by any change in pressure or stress that causes a local change in displacement or density of an elastic medium. In technological applications, a sound source is called a transducer. Standard transducers are electroacoustic—that is, they use electrical action to produce the mechanical vibrations that create sounds. An example is the electrodynamic speaker. It has a coil of wire in a magnetic field. An alternating current through the wire makes the coil oscillate, and its motion is transmitted to a membrane, whose vibrations are radiated as sound. Sound can be produced by other means, such as the flow of air over a rough surface or through a nozzle, as in a jet engine.

A sound wave transmits mechanical energy; the measure of this transmission is called the intensity of the sound. The unit used to describe in-

Above, the effects of acid rain are apparent in comparing tree branches from Germany's Black Forest far from (top) and near to (bottom) German industrial centers.

Modern concert halls, like the New Jersey Performing Arts Center, above, forgo having a stage proscenium, which directs the sound back at the performers. Instead, the design of the stage, the walls, and the ceiling projects most of the sound outward toward the audience.

tensity (sound levels) is the decibel, which is measured on a logarithmic scale: an increase or decrease of one decibel represents a tenfold increase or decrease in sound level. The logarithmic scale is particularly useful, because one decibel is about the smallest change in sound level that the human ear can detect. Conversational speech at a distance of one yard from the speaker has an intensity of about 60 decibels, while the intensity near a jet engine can be 140 decibels. Sounds over 90 decibels can damage the ear. Noise cancellation systems can reduce the intensity of mechanical sounds such as jet engine hum or traffic noise by 15 percent.

As for reception, the human ear generally does not hear sounds below 20 Hz, even those of high intensity. The upper limit for sound reception is about 20,000 Hz for younger people; this can drop to 10,000 Hz or even lower with advancing age. Frequencies above the audible range are called ultrasonic. Ultrasound in the gigabite (billion-hertz) range is put to use in signaling, metallurgy, and medicine. The unit of sound reception is the sone, which is defined as the loudness produced by a 1,000-Hz tone at an intensity of 40 decibels above the minimal audible threshold. (*See* EARS AND HEARING.)

Architectural Acoustics. Acoustics also describes the transmission of sound within a building such as an auditorium. Listening difficulties can occur in auditoriums because walls tend to be good reflectors of sound waves. For the best listening, there should be no intrusive echoes or resonances, and the reverberation time for sounds should be kept at an optimum. (Reverberation time is the time needed for a sound to decay to one millionth its original intensity.) The reverberation time should be less than one second for speech, from one to two seconds for chamber music and from two to almost four seconds for a large orchestra. (*See* SOUND.)

Echoes can be reduced by eliminating sweeping curved surfaces, which can focus sounds, by avoiding large plane surfaces, and by using sound-absorbing material. An excellent acoustic material may have a reflection coefficient—the percentage of sound that it reflects—as low as 0.1, while a highly reflective material such as concrete can have a reflection coefficient close to 1.

One way to minimize resonance is to avoid simple ratios for the main dimensions of an enclosure, reducing the reflection of sound waves. Reverberation time must be carefully calculated. If it is too long, speech will sound indistinct and music will not be heard clearly. If reverberation time is too short, music will sound wooden. Poorly contoured walls can create loud and soft spots in an auditorium. The audience also absorbs sound, which must be taken into account.

First see VALENCE

Actinides

Next see RADIOACTIVITY

The group of elements found in the seventh period (row) of the Periodic Table of the elements.

The actinides are a group of elements found in the seventh period (row) of the Periodic Table. The first element is actinium, the atomic number (Z) of which is 89. The fourteen elements following are called the actinoid series. Like the lanthanides, the actinides are classified as transition elements. They are also called group B metals, and are situated below the main section of the Periodic Table so that the table's columns do not get disrupted. (*See* PERIODIC TABLE.)

As transition elements, the actinides exhibit orbital overlap, a curious phenomenon of electron distribution. The electrons (negatively charged particles) of an atom are not located in the nucleus, but are arranged in discrete energy levels, each of which contains a specific number of sublevels, which in turn contain a specific number of orbitals. Proceeding outward from the nucleus, the levels grow progressively larger, with ever-increasing numbers of sublevels and orbitals. By the third and fourth levels, the energy levels are large enough to overlap with each other. This means electrons are being placed in farther levels while inner levels are not yet completely filled. In the actinides, the fifth level is not yet completely filled, but electrons are already found in the sixth and seventh levels.

The actinides behave much the same way as the lanthanides in terms of chemical reactions. However, all of the actinides are radioactive, meaning they have unstable nuclei. Uranium (Z = 92) is the last and largest naturally occurring element. All successive elements are synthetic and formed by bombarding other atoms with either alpha particles (helium nuclei consisting of two protons and two neutrons) or small nuclei from carbon and nitrogen.

First see MORPHOGENESIS

Adaptation

Next see NATURAL SELECTION

The ability of organisms to enhance over time their survivability in their environment.

When organisms have a heritable characteristic that makes them better able to survive and reproduce than others of their species, they pass it on to their offspring. Bolstered by the beneficial trait, each generation of offspring reproduces with enhanced success, spreading the trait throughout the population. Over time, this process of natural selection shapes the character-

Further Reading
Gross, Michael, *Life on the Edge: Amazing Creatures Thriving in Extreme Environments* (1998); Ulijaszek, S. J., *Human Adaptability: Past, Present, and Future* (1997); Wesson, Robert, *Beyond Natural Selection* (1993); Williams, G. C., *Adaptation and Natural Selection* (1996).

Nature provides many startling examples of adaptation, such as the giraffe gazelle, above, which, like the giraffe, is able to feed on the upper foliage and avoid the lower thorns; and the tree frog, below, able to use suction cups on its limbs to climb slippery logs.

istics of species to suit the circumstances of their lives. The traits that make organisms more fit in the evolutionary sense—that is, more likely to pass on their genes to future generations—are called adaptations. (*See* EVOLUTION.)

Mechanisms. While we often think of adaptation as requiring years to evolve, the process can be much quicker when environmental conditions change drastically. In one case, reported in the 1930s, a pasture was planted with a mix of grasses and legumes. Cattle were allowed to graze heavily on part of the pasture; the other part was left undisturbed. Three years later, the plant species in the grazed portion showed dwarf rambling growth patterns, rather than upright growth. Because the cattle had eaten the taller plants, only short members of these species had survived to reproduce.

Predator-prey relationships are responsible for many striking adaptations, including various forms of cryptic coloring. Unpalatable insect prey often have bright or distinctive markings—called aposematic coloration—that predators learn to avoid. In many cases, harmless prey develop similar markings that deceive predators, a phenomenon called Batesian mimicry.

In ecological adaptation, a species evolves to play a certain part in the environment, called its niche. The concept of niche covers many factors, including how, when, and where the organism gets food and reproduces; what physical conditions it can tolerate; and what conditions it prefers. By developing slightly different niches, species can avoid direct competition for resources. If two species feed on the same prey, one may hunt by day, one by night. Or each may seek the prey in a slightly different habitat—in an open meadow rather than underbrush, or even in different parts of the same tree.

First see DIGESTIVE CHEMISTRY

Addictive Disorders

Next see MENTAL DISORDERS

Disorders resulting from psychological and physiological dependence on, and a constant craving for, a chemical substance.

Alcohol dependence—a term preferred to "alcoholism"—is probably the most widespread addictive disorder. It is estimated that five million Americans—about one in 50—are alcohol-dependent, with another seven million nearly so.

Alcohol dependence develops in four stages that usually occur over a ten-year period, with a range of five to 25 years. The first stage occurs when a heavy social drinker develops a tolerance for alcohol, being able to drink more and more before experiencing any negative effects. In the next stage, heavier consumption of alcohol leads to memory lapses. This is followed by loss of control—the drinker is no longer able to discontinue drinking at will. The fourth and final stage is characterized by prolonged periods of intoxication, with noticeable mental and physical effects. These effects include aggressive behavior, loss of emotional control, frequent job changes, and neglect of personal appearance. Attempts to stop drinking often cause delirium with hallucinations, convulsions, and severe shakes. Physical effects include severe liver damage, gastritis, peptic ulcer, and an increased risk of cancer.

Drug dependence also has both psychological and physical aspects. The drugs that are most frequently associated with dependence include amphetamines, barbiturates, psychedelics such as LSD, and narcotics such as heroin and cocaine. Tobacco is sometimes considered an addictive substance because of its nicotine content.

Physical dependence occurs when the body has adapted to the presence of the drug, and severe physical and mental effects occur when the drug is not available. Mild withdrawal reactions include watery eyes, sweating, yawning, and sneezing. Severe withdrawal reactions include vomiting, uncontrollable trembling, cramps, mental confusion and, in the most severe cases, seizures and a lapse into coma. Withdrawal symptoms usually end if the drug is taken again.

Attempts to end alcohol dependence usually require medical and psychological treatments, which often include the help of others—such as the group Alcoholics Anonymous—who have had the same experience.

First see ORGANIC COMPOUNDS

Adenosine Triphosphate (ATP)

Next see MITOCHONDRIA

Some nucleic acids, such as deoxyribonucleic acid (DNA) and ribonucleic acid (RNA), function as the "keepers" of genetic information within a cell. Others, such as adenosine triphosphate (ATP), are used as energy "currency." Energy is expended every time a chemical reaction occurs. All reactions require a certain amount of activation energy to get started; once begun, some reactions will give off energy and others will require a steady input to continue. In living processes, the energy is measured in terms of molecules of ATP.

ATP Structure. Nucleic acids consist of nucleosides, which in turn consist of a sugar molecule, such as ribose or deoxyribose, and one of five nucleic "bases": adenine, guanine, cytosine, thymine, and uracil. When a phosphate group (PO_4) is added to the sugar-base complex, the nucleoside becomes a nucleotide.

The ATP nucleoside consists of ribose and adenine, which are together referred to as

ATP catalysis (right) begins when protons passing through the transmembrane protein—ATP synthase—cause the enzyme's core to rotate. The core's rotation brings about a change in the synthase molecule, which allows the enzyme to attach a phosphate ion to ADP. Paul Boyer and John Walker were awarded the 1997 Nobel Prize in chemistry for this discovery.

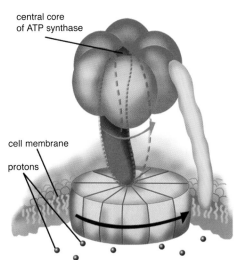

central core of ATP synthase

cell membrane

protons

"adenosine." The nucleotide is called "tri-phosphate" because there are three adjacent phosphate groups attached to the ribose. The third phosphate group is attached with an especially high-energy bond. It is this bond that acts as a temporary energy reservoir.

Function. When energy is required, the third phosphate group is detached from the nucleotide, thereby transforming the triphosphate ATP into adenosine diphosphate (ADP). The reaction is run by an enzyme known as ATPase. (All enzyme names end in "-ase," as all sugar names end in "-ose.") The process is easily reversible:

Adenosine-PO_4-PO_4-PO_4 $\longrightarrow$
Adenosine-PO_4-PO_4 + PO_4 + Energy

ADP can be broken down further by removing yet another phosphate group to form adenosine monophosphate (AMP).

This form of energy currency is the most "liquid" of assets, being more an immediate donor of energy rather than a means of long-term storage. Typically, an ATP molecule is used within a minute of its formation. The ATP turnover rate is high, relative to the stability of other types of molecules.

In Nature. Phototrophs, organisms that utilize light energy, "harvest" that energy to produce molecules of ATP, which is then used to produce glucose, in the process known as photosynthesis. All organism break down glucose, in the process known as cellular respiration, to produce energy that is stored as ATP.

Some cellular reactions require other triphosphate nucleic acids in addition to ATP. Guanosine triphosphate (GTP), cytidine triphosphate (CTP), and uridine triphosphate (UTP) function similarly, with the third phosphate group attached by a high-energy bond.

The chemistry of cellular digestion is described in PROTEIN METABOLISM *and* PROTEIN SYNTHESIS. *The movement of ATP through the cell is relevant to* CELLULAR MEMBRANES *and* TRANSPORT, CELLULAR. *Metabolic processes involving ATP are described in* MITOCHONDRIA *and* CYTOPLASM.

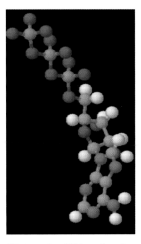

Above, the ATP molecule, consisting of (from bottom) adenine, ribose, and the three high-energy phosphate groups. ATP is responsible for bioluminescent phenomena in living organisms like fireflies and (below) algae.

Further Reading
de Duve, Christian, *A Guided Tour of the Living Cell* (1984); Goodsell, David S., *The Machinery of Life* (1998); Morowitz, Harold J., *Mayonnaise and the Origin of Life: Thoughts of Minds and Molecules* (1991).

of electrons between the two substances. The connection that occurs is a very weak attraction, similar to van der Waals forces, in which a temporary electron shift within a molecule results in its attraction to another one nearby. The type of adsorption, as well as the type of bond actually formed between adsorbate and substrate, can be determined by spectroscopic analysis. (*See* ION.)

An adsorbate can remain attached to the substrate indefinitely at low temperatures. If the temperature is increased, one of three things can happen: the adsorbate decomposes, resulting in the formation of new products; a reaction occurs resulting in the formation of new products; or the adsorbate desorbs from the surface and reverts to gaseous form. The desorbed material may be the original adsorbate itself or, in some cases, one of its isomers, a chemical "cousin" with the same formula but a different three-dimensional arrangement of atoms.

First see FLUID MECHANICS

At high speeds, minute variations in wing and flap design can result in dramatic differences in drag and lift. Above, a wing cross-section is tested.

Aerodynamics

Next see AIRCRAFT

The study of the motion of air and other gases in the atmosphere and their effect on stationary and moving objects, particularly aircraft and projectiles.

The science of aerodynamics is of relatively recent creation; both the diagnostic and theoretical tools for analyzing airflow were lacking and, in any case, human civilization had little need for a detailed understanding of the way in which air acted upon objects until the development of artillery. The effects of air in the higher velocities of cannon fire were clear from the start.

Properties of Air. Though usually invisible, air has weight—at sea level 0.0766 pounds per cubic foot—and must exert pressure in order to support the column of air above it. This means that air can be treated like any fluid and is subject to the principles developed by Daniel Bernoulli, a young contemporay of Newton who applied Newton's laws to fluid flow. Bernoulli's main result, encapsulated in Bernoulli's equation, was that the pressure exerted by a flowing fluid perpendicular to the fluid's flow is inversely proportional to the velocity of the fluid. This led to the invention of the airplane by the Englishman George Cayley, who engraved his (amazingly modern) design for an airplane on a silver medallion in 1799. (*See* FLUID MECHANICS.)

The principle of the airfoil is simple: a curved upper surface of a wing causes the air flowing above the wing to move faster and thus, by Bernoulli's principle, exert less pressure on the wing. The air under the wing thus exerts

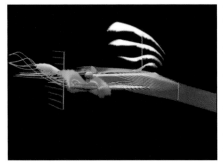

Above, a model for air flow around the Space Shuttle Orbiter is generated by computer. The computations are so complex that they require the use of a supercomputer.

Further Reading
Anderson, John, *Fundamentals of Aerodynamics* (1991); Anderson, John, *A History of Aerodynamics: Its Impact on Flying Machines* (1998); McCormick, Barnes W., *Aerodynamics, Aeronautics, and Flight Mechanics* (1994); Smith, H.C., *The Illustrated Guide to Aerodynamics* (1992).

Though models of aircraft can be productively tested in wind tunnels, there is no substitute for wind-tunnel tests of full-scale models like the Boeing 737 being tested, above, at NASA's Langley Field facility.

upward force on the wing and lifts it. Though the principle was simple enough, it would take more than a century before the Wright brothers were able to build a practical aircraft. The Wrights are, in fact, more important in aerodynamic history for their perfection of the chief tool used by aerodynamicists in the twentieth century, the wind tunnel, than for the invention of the airplane (an achievement others were on the verge of accomplishing at the time anyway).

Flow and Drag. With aircraft speeds climbing ever higher through the century (and through two world wars and the Cold War), the study of aerodynamics focused on the means of maintaining the even "laminar" flow of air over an airfoil at very high speeds when the flow tended to become turbulent. Here the wind tunnel was crucial, as the equations became too complex for standard Bernoullian analysis. In recent years, computer modeling of flight has helped designers create faster airplanes, but the wind tunnel has remained the chief tool for creating high performance aircraft.

Modern aerodynamic theory has its roots in the work of a British engineer, Osborne Reynolds, who published a seminal paper in 1883 on the transition in a flowing liquid from laminar to turbulent flow. He defined a parameter that related the properties of a liquid to the velocity and dimensions of an airfoil. This eventually became known as the Reynolds number; it predicted at what point the flow over an airfoil would become turbulent, and thus incapable of providing lift. All subsequent research, in spirit if not in substance, grew out of this kind of analysis and the work of Reynolds.

The basis of aerodynamic theory is discussed in NEWTON'S LAWS *and* FLUID MECHANICS. *Properties of air are discussed in* ATMOSPHERE. *Applications of aerodynamic principals are found in* AIRCRAFT, SUBSONIC AND SUPERSONIC *and in* JET PROPULSION.

Aggression and Territoriality

First see EMOTIONS

Next see ETHOLOGY

From threats, bluffs, and submissive acts to clan warfare, infanticide, and fights between sexual rivals, aggression and related behavior are prominent in animal life.

Darwin saw competition between individuals and species as a fundamental to the "struggle for existence." Since then, most students of animal behavior have continued to see aggressive behavior as part of a never-ending contest for the scarce resources that let animals survive and reproduce. In many species, these contests focus on territoriality—in which an animal, pair, or group has exclusive use of an area—and on dominance—a hierarchical system in which higher-ranking individuals dominate.

In recent years, some ethologists have emphasized a broader and more constructive role for aggression, seeing conflict and reconciliation as a powerful factor promoting social cohesion, especially in primate societies. Furthermore, studies in a range of species have made it clear that aggressive behavior is more variable and nuanced than once thought.

Violence Levels. The level of violence in territorial aggression varies widely. Among the lions of the Serengeti, unattached males sometimes invade a pride's territory and drive away or kill the pride's males. Male chimpanzees are known to kill males, infants, and older females in territorial clashes, although young females are allowed to move across territorial borders. However, few animals fight to the death. Many

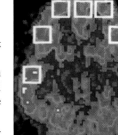

Controversial research attempts to correlate aggressive tendencies and individual brain chemistry. Above, a PET scan of the brain of an individual with an established history of aggressive behavior shows reduced levels of glucose metabolism in specific regions of the frontal cortex, indicated by arrows. How determinant such factors are remains an open question.

engage in nonlethal contests, such as roaring or teeth-baring matches, in which the animal who is less well equipped retreats.

Territoriality. Birds inspired the concept of territory, as established in Henry Eliot Howard's 1920 work, *Territory in Bird Life*. But the behavior had long been apparent: Aristotle noted that eagles need expansive living space and do not let other eagles live nearby. In 1772, the naturalist Gilbert White wrote that "during the amorous season" male birds became so "jealous" of one another that they would not share a hedge.

These perceptions have been confirmed by generations of study. Most bird species at some time establish a territory. These territories vary widely in size, permanence, and function. Some are used for mating, nesting, and feeding; some for only one or two of these activities. In territorial disputes, singing contests can go on for days until one party—usually the challenger—gives up. The combatants may also use threatening postures or displays, such as lifting a wing to flash a hidden patch of color.

Observers have often tried to draw lessons for human society from the study of animal aggression. Among the most notable was the controversial 1966 book, *On Aggression* by Konrad Lorenz, often called the father of ethology, which argued that aggression is, to a great extent, innate in humans and, unless vented, will erupt without provocation.

OBSERVATIONS

Swans at War

Few creatures seem as serene as swans gliding on a lake, but male swans are extremely territorial, fighting other swans for exclusive use of a lake without regard for the lake's size or abundance of resources. While the males are engaged in pitched battle, their necks intertwined as each attempts to mortally wound the other or pluck its flight feathers, other animals are quick to take advantage of the distraction. Other birds attempt to snatch eggs from the nests (the female swans wait anxiously nearby) and snapping turtles pull the hatchlings (or cygnets) underwater and drown them.

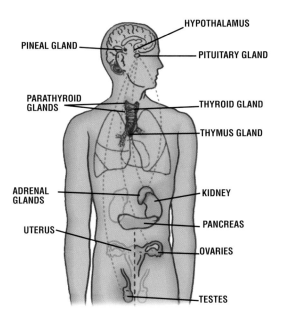

HYPOTHALAMUS

PINEAL GLAND

PITUITARY GLAND

PARATHYROID GLANDS

THYROID GLAND

THYMUS GLAND

ADRENAL GLANDS

KIDNEY

UTERUS

PANCREAS

OVARIES

TESTES

The principal hormones that direct aggressive behavior are secreted in a series of actuating and feedback mechanisms. The pituitary gland both sends and receives (epinephrine coming in; ACTH and others going out) hormonal triggers, as do other glands in the system.

First see CELL CYCLE

Aging

Next see POPULATION ECOLOGY

The stages of the human life cycle are birth, infancy, childhood, youth, maturity, old age, and death. A Greek myth tells the story of Tithonus, a mortal man who was the husband of Aurora, the Goddess of the Dawn. Aurora asked Zeus,

A wide range for life-spans is to be found among living things—from the tortoise (bottom), living 150-plus years; to the fruit fly (center), with a life span measured in weeks (though some bacteria have a normal life cycle measured in hours); and redwood sequoia trees that have life-spans measured in centuries.

the God of Thunder, to make Tithonus immortal, but neglected to ask that he stay young as well. Ultimately, he grew older and weaker with the passage of time even though he could not die.

Aging is a natural part of life and a constant one as well. It does not suddenly begin after a set number of years such as 40 or 65. It is rather an ongoing process that begins as soon as a newborn draws its first breath, or even earlier, at the embryonic state. With each passing moment, we are no longer as young as we once were. At first, our minds and bodies develop and advance until we reach our prime. Unfortunately, time does not stop there but continues marching on, inexorably, down the slope of decay.

Signs of Aging. The familiar signs of advancing age include changes in hair color, hair loss, and wrinkling of the skin due to the gradual loss of elasticity. Males experience enlargement of the prostate gland and a decrease in the number of viable sperm. Females stop ovulating and enter menopause. Impaired memory and reduced mental abilities are not due to increasing age itself but rather to diseases that occur with greater frequency during old age.

There is no body system that remains unaffected by aging. Other bodily changes include: an increase in blood pressure; hardening of the arteries; reduced efficiency of the heart's pumping action; a decrease in the number of taste buds; a decrease in lung elasticity; a decrease in basal metabolism rate; a decrease in visual and hearing acuity; a decline in speed and capacity of nerve impulse transmission; a loss of calcium in bones; and the calcification of joints.

For all our familiarity with aging and its effects, this phenomenon is still poorly understood and the primary determinants are unknown. It is not clear whether aging is determined by immunologic or hormonal changes throughout the body or by events occurring independently in various cells.

Aging Process. Individual cells age differently than a whole organism. Near the end of its life, a parent cell divides to form two daughter cells, each of which contains half the cellular contents of the parent, but a complete set of its own genetic information. At the moment of its division, the original cell has ceased to exist. However, as long as new generations of cells are being produced, the cell is, in a sense, immortal. Cellular aging is therefore associated with a cessation of the division process.

Individual cells go through a life cycle with specific stages, much as organisms do. The cell cycle is divided into the following phases: G1, S, G2, and M. Newly formed cells begin at G1, in which they rapidly grow until they reach full size and become differentiated or specialized. G1 is followed by S, or the synthesis stage, in which genetic material is replicated as the cell prepares to divide. G2 is a "gap," or resting phase, followed by the M phase in which division occurs.

Most cells can only divide a fixed number of times. Cultured embryonic cells divide approximately 50 times, whereas cells from a middle-aged individual divide only 20 times. If the nucleus of a young cell is transplanted into an old one, the cell will have the life span of a younger cell.

Non-Aging Cells. Immortal cells can divide indefinitely. Examples of immortal cells include epithelial cells, which cover all internal and external body surfaces; germ cells, which are precursors for sperm and eggs; and stem cells, which give rise to the blood cells. It has recently been discovered that the number of times a cell can divide depends upon the telomere, a structure attached to the chromosomes. With each successive division, the telomere is shortened, until it finally disappears. Immortal cells contain an enzyme called telomerase, which repairs the telomere and prevents its loss.

The existence of telomerase, and its possible inhibition or enhancement, has obvious implications in combating cancer as well as old age. Cancer cells, usually abnormal in some way, reproduce in an uncontrollable way and at the expense of other healthy cells nearby. Cancer cells contain high levels of the telomerase enzyme. Possible treatment therapies are being explored in which the enzyme is blocked. In recent experiments involving the enhancement of this enzyme, scientists have successfully enabled ordinary cells to keep on dividing long after they should be able to—in other words, creating cancer cells.

Much current research examines aging, with its accompanying deterioration and loss of function, in terms of a genetic disease rather than as a natural process. As an individual ages,

THE CUTTING EDGE

The Keys to Immortality

If cells undergoing cell division produced identical daughter cells, then cells would be immortal. But cells replicate only a finite number of times (a number known as the Hayflick limit), and until recently it was not clear why. Once it was realized that DNA replication required anchors on either side of gaps (called origins of replication), a new problem arose: how do the ends of DNA manage to get replicated? This question—known as the "end-replication" problem—is answered by telomeres, which add inert sequences to the chromosome just for replication purposes. Cell death—and the possible key to immortality—may thus be simply a matter of running out of telomeres.

there is a reduced ability to produce certain enzymes and antibodies, leading to various disorders. Cancer rates increase dramatically with age. In older people, epithelial cells are the main source of cancerous tumors.

Werner Syndrome and Hutchinson-Gilford progeria are both diseases involving premature aging. Hutchinson-Gilford strikes within the first decade of life, Werner Syndrome during adolescence. The gene for Werner Syndrome was recently identified and scientists expect this research to shed some light on the processes of normal aging.

Aging and Death. Aging inevitably leads to the end of life. The average life span of an organism varies widely among species, from the mayfly, which lives for only one day, to several species of tortoise that live more than 152 years.

In the past century, the human life span has been extended tremendously, to over 75 years, mainly due to medical advances and healthier living conditions. In the United States the fastest growing segment of the population is the over-85 group. Currently at 7 million, this group is projected to number about 25 million by 2050.

In rodents, caloric restriction has been shown to extend both average and maximal life spans. There is no evidence as of yet if this can extend life span in primates. Recent studies seem to indicate that there is a "natural limit" to the human life span of approximately 120 years, even with technological advances.

The normal processes of a cell are described in CELL *and* CELL CYCLE. *Damage to cells that may promote aging is described in* ANTI-OXIDANTS *and* MUTATION, GENETIC. *See also* DIFFERENTIATION, CELLULAR *and* DNA REPLICATION *for more on the mechanics of cellular aging.*

First see HIV

AIDS

Next see IMMUNE RESPONSE

Acquired immune deficiency syndrome, commonly known as AIDS, describes a collapse of the body's immune system as a result of infection by the human immunodeficiency virus (HIV).

Every year, from 1 to 5 percent of HIV-infected individuals develop AIDS. Most people who are

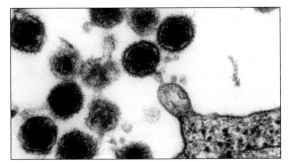

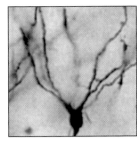
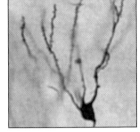

An element of aging is the loss of certain types of memory and mental acuity. Above, a comparison of dendrites of neurons from the hippocampus of a man in his forties (top) with those of a man of ninety (bottom) shows a loss of dendritic extension and strength, possibly the cause of mental aging phenomena.

Further Reading
Hayflick, Leonard, *How and Why We Age* (1996); Medina, John J., *The Clock of Ages* (1997); Olshansky, S. Jay, and Bruce, A. Carnes, *The Quest for Immortality: Science at the Frontiers of Aging* (2001); Orlock, Carol, *The End of Aging* (1995); Ricklefs, Robert E., *Aging: A Natural History* (1995).

infected with HIV do not immediately develop AIDS. In a few rare cases, the virus may disappear without causing the disease. In most cases, HIV weakens the body's immune system by destroying T4-lymphocytes, immune cells that regulate other lymphocytes that destroy disease-causing viruses and bacteria. With the T4-lymphocytes inactivated, these disease agents can multiply endlessly, eventually causing death.

Spread. AIDS was first observed in young homosexual men, who contracted the disease through sexual contact. Later, others were found to have the disease, particularly drug abusers who shared contaminated needles. AIDS can be spread through heterosexual sex, blood transfusions, and by a pregnant woman to her fetus.

Disease. After infection, some individuals may have no immediate symptoms. Others experience a short illness that resembles infectious mononucleosis. An HIV-infected person may have enlarged lymph glands and, as the infection continues, develop disorders such as skin inflammation, severe weight loss, diarrhea, fever, and a mouth infection (oral candidiasis or thrush).

AIDS opens the way for other infections that the immune system can no longer fight off. These infections include tuberculosis, herpes simplex, shingles, and salmonella. AIDS patients also have a high incidence of some cancers, including Kaposi's sarcoma and brain lymphoma. Major infections that develop include pneumocystic pneumonia, toxoplasmosis, cytomegalovirus, candidiasis, herpes simplex, and cryptococcosis. HIV can affect the brain, causing dementia and other neurological disorders.

Treatment and Prevention. Various drugs have been developed to fight HIV by disrupting key chemical reactions. The oldest of these is AZT (zidovudine). However, the virus mutates rapidly and the drugs lose their effectiveness after a while. Newer, more promising medications include a class of drugs known as protease inhibitors, which arrest the progress of the virus and reduce viral loads to undetectable levels. A vaccine against HIV has not yet been developed.

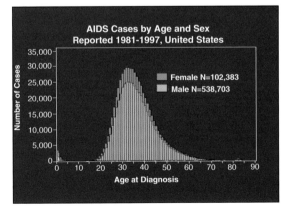

The insidious nature of AIDS lies in the very simple way the HIV virus "makes itself at home" in the human cell. At a certain point, having multiplied and exhausted a cell's resources, HIV spores are ejected (left) from the cell and seek new cells to victimize.

The HIV life cycle.
The virus (a) binds to the membrane of a cell (b) and deposits its genetic contents (c) into the cell. For reasons still unclear, this does not trigger an immune response; the cell "believes" the viral material belongs there. Soon an HIV enzyme transcribes viral RNA onto the cell's DNA (d), creating a provirus. Another enzyme, HIV protease, then attaches the provirus onto the cell's DNA and the cell proceeds to manufacture (e) new viral particles. The cell eventually becomes filled with HIV particles that exhaust and kill it, but not before budding from the cell (f) in search of new cells to infect.

Meanwhile, the HIV-1 virus prevents the body's immune cells from responding to the invasion by engaging them and in the process causing them to fuse into ineffective giant cells incapable of reaching where the real damage is being done. Inset, immune cells have been joined in the mucus of the adenoids forming a node of useless syncytia cells.

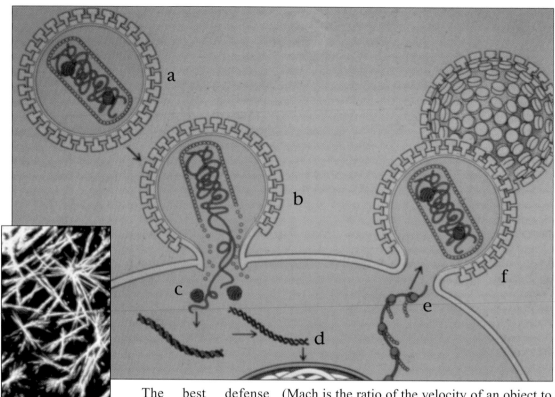

Further Reading
Eidson, Ted, *The AIDS Caregivers Handbook* (1993); Kubbler-Ross, Elisabeth, M.D., *AIDS: The Ultimate Challenge* (1999); Shilts, Randy, *And the Band Played on: Politics, People, and the AIDS Epidemic* (1988); Stine, Gerald J., *Acquired Immune Deficiency Syndrome: Biological, Medical, Social, and Legal Issues* (1998).

The best defense against AIDS is to avoid infection with HIV. Persons at risk of infection are told to reduce the number of their sexual partners and to use condoms and spermicidal jellies, which can inactivate the virus, in any sexual exchange. Users of intravenous drugs are warned never to share needles. Persons in high-risk groups should not donate blood or sperm; these now are routinely screened for the presence of HIV.

The HIV virus is not spread by casual contact, such as touching or hugging, by using the same cutlery or crockery, or by kissing with no exchange of saliva. People who donate blood are not at risk of infection, because sterile needles are always used to take blood.

More discussion of the virus that causes AIDS is in HIV; VIRAL GENETICS; *and* VIRUS. *The immune system is described in* AUTOIMMUNITY *and* IMMUNE RESPONSE. *Methods used to diagnose AIDS are described in* IMMUNOASSAY. *See also* EPIDEMIOLOGY.

First see AERODYNAMICS

Aircraft, Subsonic and Supersonic

Next see JET PROPULSION

Supersonic aircraft became possible with the development of jet and rocket engines. The speed of sound was first exceeded on October 14, 1947, when an American rocket-propelled airplane, the Bell X-1, reached Mach 1.06.

(Mach is the ratio of the velocity of an object to the velocity of sound; at sea level, Mach 1 is 761 miles per hour.) Since then, speeds of Mach 5 and even higher have been attained.

Sonic "Barrier." A problem is faced by any supersonic aircraft that approaches the speed of sound. At transonic speeds, shock waves form over the wings, or airfoils, of the aircraft because the air in front of it becomes compressed. The shock waves angle out from the aircraft, just as bow waves angle out from a ship at sea, and the aircraft can be severely buffeted. However, the air becomes smooth again as soon as the aircraft passes through the speed of sound. A sonic boom that can be heard on the ground beneath the aircraft may occur at this point.

Wing Design. Wings that are swept back or have a delta arrowhead shape are the best for supersonic aircraft that fly at speeds up to Mach 1.4. An angled wing allows the aircraft better passage through the transonic range. A delta wing is a swept-back wing whose trailing edges have been filled in. This increases the wing area, which provides more lift for the aircraft.

At speeds higher than Mach 1.4, however, the drag of these wings increases greatly, until it exceeds the drag of an ordinary straight wing. Thus, an aircraft that has enough propulsive power to fly at speeds above Mach 2 generally will have straight wings. These differ from the wings of subsonic aircraft; they are much thinner and shorter.

The challenge of maintaining sufficient lift at supersonic speeds has centered on the boundary layer, the thin layer of air that is closest to the wings. All of the effects on the aircraft of air fric-

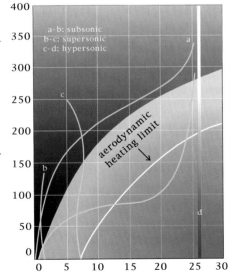

tion or drag occur in this small region. In the boundary layer, the velocity of the air changes to zero at the surface of the wing. Thus, air flow in the boundary layer can be simultaneously laminar—regular and parallel, promoting lift—or turbulent, decreasing lift and increasing drag. Aeronautical engineers have developed methods of conserving laminar flow in the boundary layer.

Heat. As an aircraft flies faster and faster in the supersonic range, heat can become a problem. The temperature of the air in the boundary layer of an aircraft flying at Mach 3 can be 600 degrees Fahrenheit. Temperatures in the tail pipe of the aircraft may reach 2,000 degrees, with the added heat of the exhaust. Ordinary aluminum alloys lose much of their strength at these temperatures, and so other alloys, many of them using titanium, are used for aircraft that fly at these speeds.

Theory. The theory of the airplane, or aerodynamics, deals with the way that a heavier-than-air aircraft gets enough lift to sustain its flight. The concepts behind this theory go back to Isaac Newton, whose first law of motion states that a body in motion will stay in motion and whose third law states that for every action there is an equal and opposite reaction, and to Daniel Bernoulli, who stated that an increase in the velocity of air reduces its pressure.

Lift. The surface of an airplane's wing, rudder, or propeller blade makes use of all these concepts. To obtain lift, an aircraft wing is shaped so that it allows a streamlined flow of air over it and under it. The air that flows under the wing of a moving airplane produces a lifting effect that is basically the same as the effect that sustains a kite in the air. This lifting effect, caused by the positive pressure on the underside of the wing, is responsible for about 30 percent of the lift of a normal

airfoil. The air that passes over the top of the wing produces the rest of the lift by negative pressure. Most aircraft wings have a camber, or curve, that causes the top of the wing to have a greater curvature than the bottom of the wing. Thus, the air that passes over the top of the wing has to travel a greater distance than the air passing under the bottom in the same amount of time. It thus has a greater velocity and, according to Bernoulli's theorem, a lower pressure on top of the wing than on the bottom. This difference in pressure between the top and the bottom of a wing is responsible for about 70 percent of the total lift that keeps an airplane in flight.

Drag. In order to stay in flight, an airplane must overcome the drag, the total force of the air that acts against the airplane's path of flight. There are two types of drag. One, called induced drag, is caused by the deflection of air around the wing. It can be reduced by having a short, wide wing, but this also reduces the speed of the airplane. The second kind of drag, profile drag, is caused by such factors as the friction of the air that flows along the surface of the aircraft and by the turbulent wake that is created by an airplane in flight. There is a third kind of drag, wave drag, that affects only airplanes flying faster than the speed of sound, caused by the shock wave that forms as an airplane achieves supersonic speeds.

One of the conditions that affects the relationship between the lift and the drag of an airplane is the airplane's angle of attack, which is the angle between the wing chord, the degree of slant of the wing, and the flight path of the airplane. When the angle of attack is increased, as when an airplane climbs, lift is increased to cause the airplane to climb. But the drag on the airplane is increased at the same time. The engineers who design a wing must therefore ensure that the maximum amount of lift and minimum amount of drag is caused by a change in the airplane's angle of attack. But as the angle of attack is increased, there comes a point when the smooth flow of air over the wing becomes disrupted to the extent that it can no longer provide the necessary lift. The aircraft can then stall, so that the controls are no longer effective and the airplane can go into a spiral or spin.

Improving Stability. Aircraft in normal flight can also become unstable, if the air through which it flies is in turbulent motion. An airplane thus has a horizontal stabilizer, a small wing that is part of the tail assembly. If the nose of the airplane goes down, the lifting action of the tail goes down, so that the tail of the aircraft moves downward, restoring a level path of flight. Airplanes also have a tendency to roll. The

Above, left, an early NACA (1925) aircraft with innovations in streamlining and fuselage design. Top, right, a computer simulation of the heat signature of the experimental Hyper-X space aircraft. Above, right, the X-29 forward swept jet fighter—an aircraft almost too maneuverable for a human to fly. Above, the SR-71B "Blackbird," reputed to be the fastest aircraft ever built. Below, the aerodynamic domains of flight.

altitude (thousands of feet)

a-b: subsonic
b-c: supersonic
c-d: hypersonic

aerodynamic heating limit

speed (thousands of feet per second)

design feature that reduces that tendency is a slight upward slope of the wings from the fuselage to their tip, called dihedral. When one wing goes down, dihedral causes it to develop more lift, so that the roll of the airplane is reduced. There are many other design features that assure a straight, even flight for airplanes in common commercial and military use.

The theoretical foundations of subsonic and supersonic flight are discussed in AERODYNAMICS *and* FLUID MECHANICS. *Propulsion systems for aircraft are discussed in* JET PROPULSION *and* PROPULSION. *See* ALLOY *for more on materials;* AVIONICS *for more on aircraft systems; and* LUBRICANTS *and* SYNTHETICS *for more on lubricants and fuels.*

Further Reading
Anderson, John D., *Introduction to Flight* (1988); Bilstein, Roger E., *Flight in America* (1994); Boyne, Walter J., *The Smithsonian Book of Flight* (1987); Crouch, Tom D., *The Bishop's Boys: A Life of Wilbur and Orville Wright* (1990); Rabinowitz, Harold, *Conquer the Sky: Great Moments in Aviation* (1996).

First see ATMOSPHERE

Air Pollution

Next see CHLOROFLUOROCARBONS

Air pollution is often divided into four basic categories: turbidity, caused by particulate matter; acid rain, caused by oxides of nitrogen and sulfur; the threat to the ozone layer; and a rising level of carbon dioxide. Each of these represents a potential danger to the Earth's ecosystem .

Before the twentieth century, turbidity represented the most dangerous form of air pollution. Volcanoes eject tons of sulfur-laden ash and dust into the atmosphere, cutting down on solar heating and precipitating out of the air in the form of acid rain. The explosion of Mount Krakatoa in 1883 emitted some 50 million tons of debris. When humans started burning wood and coal for heating, cooking, and industrial

uses, the volume of ash and dust increased exponentially, often producing "killer fogs," mists laden with unburned silicates and sulfuric acid. Today, most coal burning is centralized in large power plants, where stack scrubbers control particulate emissions, although Eastern Europe still faces severe turbidity problems.

Acid Rain. Acid rain is also a pollutant of historic proportions. Sulfuric and nitrous compounds released into the air are broken down by sunlight, combine with water vapor, and produce acids that precipitate onto lakes and vegetation below. Some 50 million tons of sulfur dioxide and nitrogen oxides are spewed into the atmosphere yearly from sources in the United States alone. Canada and the American Northeast, which lie downwind from the industrial region of the American Midwest, have been heavy sufferers from this problem.

Ozone. Earth's surface is protected from the harshness of ultraviolet radiation by the ozone

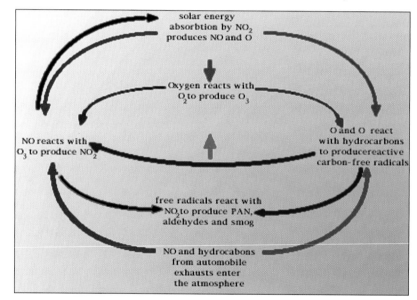

solar energy absorbtion by NO_2 produces NO and O

Oxygen reacts with O_2 to produce O_3

NO reacts with O_3 to produce NO_2

O and O react with hydrocarbons to produce reactive carbon-free radicals

free radicals react with NO_2 to produce PAN, aldehydes and smog

NO and hydrocabons from automobile exhausts enter the atmosphere

Above, the urban system that results in the formation of smog. The cycle begins when very small amounts of nitrous oxide in automobile exhaust combine with oxygen to form nitrous dioxide, which then provides the oxygen that combines with hydrocarbons in the air to produce smog.

layer in the stratosphere. Ozone absorbs UV-B radiation, which decomposes it into normal oxygen; at the same time, normal oxygen absorbs UV-C radiation and recombines into ozone. Thus both forms of ultraviolet radiation are absorbed in the upper atmosphere, where they cannot damage our fragile ecosystems. However, the use of chlorofluorocarbons (CFCs) beginning in the 1930s released millions of tons of this chemical into our atmosphere; some of it found its way into the ozone layer, where it has begun an insidious process of ozone depletion. Although CFCs have been banned worldwide, they remain in use as refrigerants. Since each molecule can last anywhere from 40 to 100 years, this represents a continuing threat to this vital protective layer of our atmosphere.

Greenhouse Challenge. The final form of air pollution that threatens Earth is a long-term rise in carbon dioxide, a by-product of all forms

TOOLS

The Mini-Sniffer

The Mini-Sniffer is a remote-controlled propeller-driven vehicle developed by NASA researchers to sample the pollution in the upper atmosphere. The original Mini-Sniffer was propelled by a small air-breathing engine, while a later version employed a non-airbreathing hydrazine engine for higher altitude capabilities. A large propeller was employed because of its effectiveness in the thin upper atmosphere. The Mini-Sniffer was an early attempt by NASA to monitor the Earth's upper atmosphere and was also considered for planetary atmospheric sampling flights over Mars.

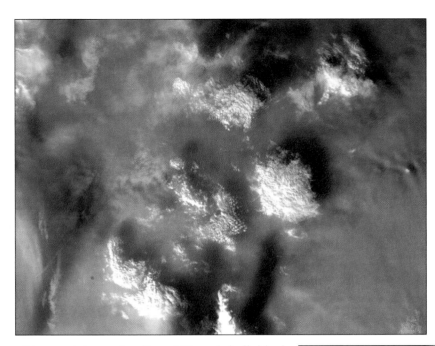

Left, photograph of Lake Toba, Indonesia, taken by Space Shuttle Atlantis on September 27, 1997. The photograph shows the smoke and dust thrown into the atmosphere by brush fires set anually to clear the terrain. However, the El Niño effect seen in 1997 and 1998 held back the rains that normally put these fires out.

First see RADAR

Air Traffic Control

Next see AIRCRAFT

Air traffic control (ATC) systems monitor the approach, takeoff, and landing of aircraft at most airports in the United States and other countries. Air traffic control relies on radar to track the flight of aircraft. This equipment is designated as terminal radar approach control, or tracons. There are hundreds of such tracons at both military and civilian airports throughout the United States. The information gathered by radar sweeps is processed by computers and is displayed on video screens that are manned by air traffic controllers, who guide aircraft in their approach to the landing site. If a lapse in the system causes the air traffic network to lose track of an aircraft in flight, a shrill alarm is sounded, and flashing lights indicate the source of the problem.

During the first few years of the twenty-first century, the United States is preparing to install a new system, called the Standard Terminal Automation System, or STARS, throughout the continent's airport system. The first step in switching to STARS is replacement of the air traffic controllers' old video screens with newer, better screens. Existing computers will continue to process the radar data until new software is written for a new generation of computers.

The STARS Early Display Configuration (EDC) was installed and acheived initial opertional capability first at El Paso, Texas, in December 1999 and later at Syracuse, New York, in January 2000. (*See* AIRCRAFT; AVIONICS.)

First see ORGANIC COMPOUNDS

Alcohol

Next see DISTILLATION

Alcohols are an important category of organic compounds. They are used as industrial materials, laboratory reagents, and solvents. And, of course, alcohols have been famous since the beginning of recorded history as medicinal and intoxicating agents. (*See* DISTILLATION.)

Alcohols have characteristic odors and

of incomplete combustion. Although individual automobiles emit relatively small amounts of carbon dioxide, for example, the total daily worldwide emission of carbon dioxide by cars and trucks reaches thousands of tons; burning fossil fuels generates more than 5 billion tons of carbon dioxide each year. Simultaneously, the world's forests, which absorb carbon dioxide and emit oxygen, are being destroyed by a combination of deliberate processes such as the burning of the Amazon rain forest, and unintended processes such as acid rain; the oceans, which also absorb carbon dioxide, cannot keep pace with more than half the yearly inflow.

Carbon dioxide is not harmful in itself, but it is the main cause of the greenhouse effect, or global warming. Solar radiation is transmitted to the surface of the Earth at a wavelength that is not absorbed by gases in the atmosphere, but when that heat is reradiated back into space—on a clear night, for example—it occurs at a wavelength which is intercepted by the so-called "greenhouse gases," of which carbon dioxide is the most abundant. Without this blanket of heat-absorbing gas, the Earth would be too cold to sustain life. But in 1903, S. Arrhenius recognized that as the level of carbon dioxide rose, the heat absorbed would rise even faster, leading to a rise in Earth's temperature. He estimated that a doubling of carbon dioxide levels could raise temperatures by 4 degrees C; for comparison, during the last ice age temperatures changed by only 5 to 10 degrees C.

The mechanics of the atmosphere are described in ATMOSPHERE *and* VOLCANO. *Specific forms of air pollution are further discussed in* ACID RAIN; GLOBAL WARMING; *and* OZONE LAYER. *See also* CARTOGRAPHY *and* REMOTE SENSING *for discussion of means of measuring and evaluating air pollution.*

Top, a typical console has an air traffic controller responsible for from 20 to 40 aircraft at any given moment, especially near the busier airports. Bottom, the nerve center of an ATC center is highly charged as the safety of thousands of passengers depends on an effective system.

Further Reading
Lipfert, Frederick W., *Air Pollution and Community Health: A Critical Review and Data Sourcebook* (1997); Turco, Richard P., *Earth Under Siege: Air Pollution and Global Change* (1997); Warner, Cecil F., *Air Pollution: Its Origin and Control* (1997).

sharp tastes. They are produced in nature by a process known as fermentation, as a by-product of the metabolic reactions in which anaerobic (without oxygen) organisms break down sugar in order to produce energy. The alcohol is removed from the fermented mixture by distillation, in which the liquids are heated and the vapors condensed. Since alcohol has a much lower boiling point than water, it will vaporize first and can therefore easily be separated. (Distillation is used to separate and purify many different organic and inorganic compounds, not just alcohol.)

In the lab, alcohols can be prepared from many different classes of compounds and in turn be transformed into still others, making them an important synthetic intermediary.

Methanol. Wood alcohol, also called methanol or methyl alcohol, was originally prepared by the dry distillation of wood, but is currently produced from carbon dioxide and hydrogen. It is highly toxic if ingested, attacking the nervous system and resulting in blindness and death. Grain alcohol, also known as ethanol or ethyl alcohol, is the alcohol found in beverages and materials meant for internal consumption. Ethanol is also used in industrial processes; when designated for this purpose, it is usually denatured, meaning toxic or otherwise unappetizing chemicals are added to it. Undenatured, pure ethanol is not classified as a poisonous substance, but acts upon the central nervous system as well and can have harmful effects if ingested

Model of ethanol (C_2H_5OH) molecule, made-up of two carbon, one oxygen, and six hydrogen atoms.

by pregnant women, children, and any individuals who consume excessive amounts. (*See* POISON *and* TOXICOLOGY.)

Molecular Structure. All alcohols contain the elements carbon, hydrogen, and oxygen. Structurally, the carbons link to each other to form long chains, with hydrogen atoms attached on the sides. What transforms an ordinary hydrocarbon chain such as this into an alcohol is the presence of a functional group, hydroxyl (OH), which replaces one of the hydrogen atoms bonded to the carbon chain. The hydroxyl group is connected by a covalent bond (electrons are shared between atoms). It is important to distinguish between the hydroxyl group found in alcohols and the OH-group found in certain inorganic compounds, as the latter group is connected to its molecule by means of an ionic bond (electrons are gained or lost). This means that alcohols do not dissociate (separate) in water to form hydroxide ions, while the inorganic compounds that contain hydroxyl groups do. Even though they do not dissociate, the lower molecular weight alcohols are water-soluble. (*See* SOLVATION.)

A monohydroxyl alcohol is an alcohol in which there is only one hydroxyl group per molecule. Examples include methyl and ethyl alcohols. (*See* ALDEHYDES.)

Types. Alcohols can be classified as either primary, secondary, or tertiary alcohols, depending on the number of carbon atoms directly bonded to the carbon atom holding the functional group. A primary alcohol has only one other carbon atom bonded to the hydroxyl carbon, or has the group at the end of the hydrocarbon chain. A secondary alcohol has two carbon atoms attached to the hydroxyl carbon, and a tertiary alcohol has three carbon atoms attached to it.

There are also behavioral distinctions among the three types of alcohols, in terms of what new organic products are formed when the alcohol undergoes oxidation. Primary alcohols will form aldehydes and organic acids, secondary alcohols form ketones, and tertiary alcohols can only be oxidized by very strong oxidizing agents which cause them to break down into smaller molecules. (*See* OXIDIZING AGENT.)

The distillation of alcoholic beverages is one of the world's largest industries, practiced virtually since the beginning of recorded history. At right, a 13th-century illustration shows all the basic elements of the process. Whiskey is produced by twice distilling the liquid mixture of barley and hot water (called wort).

Aldehydes

First see ALCOHOL

Next see OXIDIZING AGENT

A family of organic compounds characterized by a -CHO group. Ketones are similar, but characterized by a carbonyl (C=O) group.

Aldehydes and ketones are two very closely related molecules. They are special types of hydrocarbon chains—long-linked chains of carbon atoms with attached hydrogens—that contain a functional group. The particular group that both aldehydes and ketones share is the carbonyl group—a carbon atom connected to an oxygen atom with a double bond. The placement of the functional group determines which specific molecule has been formed. In an aldehyde, the carbonyl is found at the end of the chain, and in a ketone it is located in the middle and attached to a non-terminal carbon atom. Aldehydes can easily be converted into ketones and ketones into aldehydes.

Aldehydes have very strong odors, compared to ketones whose odors are somewhat milder. Aldehydes are easily oxidized to organic acids and therefore are often used to identify unknown compounds or to look for the presence of a specific chemical within a substance. For example, Benedict's solution is used to detect the presence of sugar in urine.

Formaldehyde. Among the more prominent aldehydes are formaldehyde, also known as methanal because it is formed from the hydrocarbon methane, and acetaldehyde, also called ethanal because it is formed from the hydrocarbon ethane. Formaldehyde is used for the preservation of animal tissue and as a disinfectant, and it is one of the starting materials in the production of rayon and plastics. Acetaldehyde is used in the manufacture of dyes, rubber, and other organic compounds.

One other interesting application of formaldehyde is its use in the manufacture of mirrors. When formaldehyde is combined with a particular silver-ammonia complex upon a glass plate, metallic silver is freed and deposited onto the glass surface.

Ketones. The simplest, and most prominent ketone is acetone, a common chemical solvent. This particular property is quite familiar, as acetone is the active ingredient in nail polish remover.

See MIRRORS *and* PLASTICS *for more on the industrial use of aldehydes.* MEDICAL DIAGNOSTICS *contains material on the use of aldehydes, particularly ketones, in urinalysis. The chemistry of aldehydes is discussed in the entry on* HYDROCARBONS.

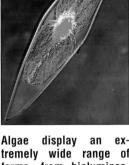

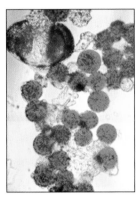

Algae display an extremely wide range of forms, from bioluminescent algae, above, to the red algae that cover melting snow, below.

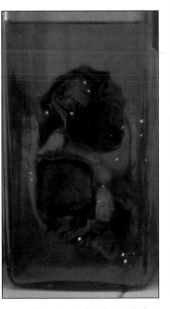

Above, a beaker of formaldehyde is used to preserve a biological specimen for future study.

Algae

First see EVOLUTION

Next see BIOREMEDIATION

Group of mostly aquatic, mostly photosynthetic organisms ranging from single-celled forms to complex seaweeds that can grow up to 30 yards long.

The ranks of algae include organisms that grow on the surface or at the bottom of saltwater or freshwater, in desert soil, on rocks or tree bark, within other plants, and even in the fur of polar bears. They appear as the simplest of one-celled plants, as colonies of cells, as filaments, and as multicellular plants with specialized cells analogous to the roots, stems, and leaves of higher plants. Various kinds of algae are responsible for pond scum; the toxic "red tide" that kills shellfish; the sushi-wrapping seaweed called nori; and the agar in which microbes are cultured in the laboratory.

Taken as a group, algae have been estimated to account for as much as 50 percent of all the photosynthesis on Earth, making them crucial to the maintenance of life. Much of this oxygen-producing activity is contributed by algae that are part of plankton, floating collections of small marine organisms. It has been estimated that 200,000 species of algae exist, although far fewer have been identified.

Taxonomy. Not surprisingly, algae are a taxonomic nightmare. They are generally classified into 10 or 15 major divisions, with more than a dozen proposed systems of classification. Most scientists agree that the blue-green algae (also called cyanobacteria) and the prochlorophytes are not plants but rather should be grouped with bacteria. These kinds of organisms are the only organisms known to be prokaryotic, meaning their nuclei are not bounded by a membrane. But authorities differ on whether other algae are part of the plant kingdom. As molecular analysis sheds more light on microbial evolution, some biologists have proposed that many (or all) other algae should be classed as protista (or protoctisa), along with protozoa, slime molds, and fungi; as chromista; or as members of more recently proposed kingdoms.

In the evolution of life on Earth, algae played crucial roles. Blue-green algae were among the first inhabitants of Earth, leaving fossils that have been dated at more than 3 billion years old. Their life in Precambrian seas was recorded in stromatolites, layered, rocklike structures of ancient algae and mud. Unlike most photosynthetic bacteria, but like land plants, algae (cyanobacteria) produce molecular oxygen as a by-product of photosynthesis. As a result, it is believed they produced the free oxygen that first began converting the planet's atmosphere, poisonous to animal life, to the one we know today. (In some

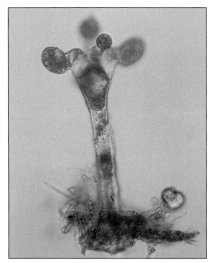

A sporangium, displaying an unusual complexity.

In areas where sunlight warms the surface of snow banks, red algae thrive, turning the snow red, particularly when pressed by a boot (right).

Further Reading

Barker, Rodney, *And the Waters Turned to Blood: The Ultimate Biological Threat* (1998); Cole, Kathleen M., *Biology of the Red Algae* (1990); Graham, Linda E., *Algae* (1999); Lembi, Carole A., *Algae and Human Affairs* (1988).

taxonomies, they are not even classified as algae for this reason.)

While cyanobacteria have only chlorophyll a, the prochlorophytes have both chlorophyll a and b, as higher plants do. Some biologists think these algae were the ancestors of most chloroplasts, the photosynthetic organelles of higher plants. It is thought they were incorporated through the process of endosymbiosis, in which one organism engulfs another. Many biologists suspect that charophytes, a green algae, were the precursor of the bryophytes, such as mosses and liverworts, and of the higher, fully terrestrial plants that arose later. (*See* EVOLUTION.)

Other Forms. Other common forms of algae include diatoms, microscopic organisms whose shell-like walls form the diatomaceous earth used in some filters; brown algae, which include many forms of seaweed and kelp; red algae, which include seaweed that are the source of agar, nori, and carageenans used to stabilize and suspend many processed foods.

Life Cycle. Sexual and asexual reproduction are both widespread among algae, with some distinctive sexual variations. Some unicellular algae, for instance, unite to function as gametes themselves. Some multicellular algae have gametangia, or gamete-producing structures, in which each cell produces a gamete. In the sex organs of land plants, by contrast, not all the cells are reproductive.

Many green, brown, and red algae have a life history that follows the patterns called alternation of generations: A plant that is diploid (with two sets of each chromosomes) produces spores that are haploid (with one set of each chromosome). Each spore develops asexually into a haploid plant, which produces haploid gametes. These unite sexually to form diploid zygotes, which grow into diploid plants.

The kingdom to which algae belong is discussed in PROTISTA. *The role algae may have played in the evolution of life is discussed in* EVOLUTION. *See also* MICROBIOLOGY *for more on the biological context of algae, and both* ASEXUAL REPRODUCTION *and* GAMETOGENESIS *for more on the reproductive systems of algae.*

First see SETS AND GROUPS

Algebra

Next see NUMBER

The result of the first great revolution in mathematics, it is the reduction of an arbitrary collection of arithmetic operations to a coherent set of rules.

Although the first steps in the direction of a modern algebra were taken as early as 250 C.E., by Diophantus of Alexandria, it was not recognized as a separate branch of mathematics until the ninth century, when Mohammed ibn Musa al-Khwarizmi wrote *Al-Jabr wal-Muqabalah*, a treatise on how to solve equations by isolating the unknown part on one side, and then solving the known operations on the other side. The first word of his title would pass into Western languages as standing for the whole. The modern symbology of algebra did not take shape for another nine centuries, when François Viète, René Descartes, Isaac Newton, and others finally agreed that "*x,*" "*y,*" and "*z*" would often represent the unknown quantities of algebra.

Algebra's main concern is the domain of numbers, and the performance of basic arithmetic operations on those numbers. There are four basic domains: natural numbers, the positive subset of what are commonly called integers; rational numbers, or fractions; real numbers, which fill in all the remaining gaps in the number line; and complex numbers, which have both a real and an imaginary component. There are only two basic operations: addition (+), which through the use of the minus sign (−) becomes subtraction; and multiplication (×), which through the use of the inverse (÷) becomes division. Multiplication takes precedence over addition, so in any equation multiplication or division is performed before addition or subtraction. A third operation is commonly added to these two, the deriving of square and cube roots, which takes precedence over both.

Algebraic Laws. Algebraic operations are characterized by three basic laws: the commutative law, the associative law, and the distributive law. The commutative law states that the order in which addition is performed or the order in which multiplication is performed does not change the result: $6 + 3 = 3 + 6$ and $6 \times 3 = 3 \times 6$. The associative law goes on to state that numbers can also be grouped in any way desired: $6 + 3 + 4$ can be grouped as $(6 + 3) + 4$, or it can be grouped as $6 + (3 + 4)$. The associative law also works for multiplication: $6 \times 3 \times 4$ can be computed as $(6 \times 3) \times 4$ or $6 \times (3 \times 4)$. The combination of these two laws yields the distributive law, which states that multiplication is distributive over addition: $6 \times (3 + 4)$ can also be written as $(6 \times 3) + (6 \times 4)$; thus a sum can be treated as a product, or a product treated as a sum.

Algebraic Expressions. Algebraic expressions are combinations of numbers and unknowns, arranged in significant groupings of the basic operations called polynomials. A polynomial is a sum (or difference) of terms, each of which is expressed as a product (or quotient); if the factors that make up a product are equal to one another, that term can be written as the exponent of the factor. Thus, the formula $3x^2 + 5x - 4y^2 + 8y + 1$ is a more convenient form of $(3)(x)(x) + (5)(x) + (-4)(y)(y) + (8)(y) + 1$. Polynomials like this that contain a squared term are called quadratic. Polynomials always follow the distributive law, so that $(x^2 - 4x + 4) \times (x - 1) = (x) \times (x^2 - 4x + 4) - (1) \times (x^2 - 4x + 4) = x^3 - 4x^2 + 4x - x^2 + 4x - 4 = x^3 - 5x^2 + 8x - 4$. Identifying the factors—like $(x - 1)$—in a given expression is one of the most critical maneuvers in algebra. Taking the example one step further, $(x^2 - 4x + 4)$ can itself be factored into $(x - 2)$ and $(x - 2)$; thereby one determines the critical values of x—those that will produce 0 in the resulting polynomial: in this case, 1 and 2. The assertion that every polynomial can be factored into linear factors—although the roots of those factors may be complex—is called the Fundamental Theorem of Algebra. This theorem is the foundation of algebraic equations.

The next step in developing a logic of algebra is to examine the result of division with polynomials. The division of one integer by another results in a rational number; correspondingly, the division of one polynomial by another results in a rational expression—as long as the dividend is not at its critical value, since division by zero is not allowed. Moreover, since taking square and cube roots is commonly accepted as an elementary operation in algebra, sometimes the result is an irrational number, leading to an irrational expression; if the irrational number is in the denominator of a fraction, it must be rationalized. In the same way, complex numbers are introduced into algebraic expressions and manipulated according to the above rules. Finally, although the algebraic field is usually a finite sequence, leading to discussion of the limit, in many cases (particularly where one is dealing with a geometric rather than an arithmetic series) the field may be infinite.

Applications. Solutions to problems in algebra have led to the creation of entirely new areas of mathematical thought. First among them is linear algebra, closely related to finite math; linear algebra focuses on finding solutions to simultaneous algebraic equations, either through vector representation or through matrices. Other aspects of algebra which have developed into separate fields of study include group theory; field theory, which extends algebra's ability to manipulate rational numbers into the real and complex fields; and homological algebra, which connects algebra to topology.

One of the most important branches of modern algebra is Boolean algebra, invented by George Boole in 1850 and extended by John Venn in 1881. Boole posited that polynomial expressions could be built up not through arithmetical operands but through logical ones: union ("and"), intersection ("or"), inverse ("not"), et al. Because Boolean algebra and binary coding are binary in nature, they have proven ideal for computer software design; all computer systems rely on Boolean logic and binary field coding to process information.

Algebraic Equations. Algebraic equations are commonly separated into three categories: linear, quadratic, and polynomial. Technically, the first two are special cases of a polynomial, which defines all equations:

$$f(x) = a_0 x^n + a_1 x^{n-1} + ... + a_{n-1} x + a_n = 0$$

A linear equation contains only the last two items in the series: $ax + b = 0$, while a quadratic equation contains three items: $ax^2 + bx + c = 0$. The goal of all algebraic equations is the same: To manipulate a given equation so that one side equals zero, and then to solve for some number or set of numbers that, when introduced into the equation, causes the other side to equal zero. That set of numbers is commonly termed the solution of the equation.

Solving Algebraic Equations. Mathematicians are often interested in whether a given algebraic equation can be solved using only elementary operations (addition and subtraction, multiplication and division, square and cube roots), in which case it is called a rational solution, and particularly whether the solution can be represented geometrically. More advanced algebra treats the symmetric functions of the roots of a given equation, which attempt to resolve the paradox that the solution to an algebraic equation demands an extension of the original field. This is a direct outgrowth of the fundamental theorem of algebra, which states that any polynomial equation of degree (n) must have at least (n) so-

Above, a 16th-century text by Johann Schoener from his *Algorithmus Demonstratus*, on the solution of algebraic equations.

TOOLS

Diophantus' Tomb

The following epitaph, written for Diophantus, took the form of a classic algebraic equation: "This tomb holds Diophantus. Ah, what a marvel! And the tomb tells scientifically the measure of his life. God vouchsafed that he should be a boy for the sixth part of his life; when a twelfth was added, his cheeks acquired a beard; He kindled for him the light of marriage after a seventh, and in the fifth year after his marriage, He granted him a son. Alas! When he had reached the measure of half his father's life, the chill grave took him. After consoling his grief by this science of numbers for four years, Diophantus reached the end of his life." How old was Diophantus when he died?

(Answer: 84)

---

lutions, but the solution to a real-number equation will typically contain complex numbers. Thus, whereas the roots to an equation themselves lie outside the original field, the symmetric functions of the roots always lie in the same coefficient field as the original equation. Further work with polynomials leads into the field of algebraic geometry.

Many students fear algebra because of the dreaded quadratic formula, a shortcut route to the solution of quadratic equations which took centuries to work out:

$$x = -b \pm \sqrt{(b^2 - 4ac)} / 2a$$

If the expression $(b^2 - 4ac)$ equals zero, there is only one solution; if it is negative, there are two complex solutions; and if it is positive there are two real solutions. Therefore, $(b^2 - 4ac)$ is called the discriminant. Quadratic equations find applications in fields from hydrodynamics to ballistics.

A more fruitful field for practical applications has been the linear equation or, more precisely, the method by which simultaneous linear equations are established, linking multiple variables ($ax + by + c = 0$), and then solving them using linear programming or matrix algebra. This approach, first codified by Gabriel Cramer in 1750, uses the relationship between determinants of two matrices to solve for two or three variables at once; more complex equations are solved by the simplex method, or recursively. Simultaneous linear equations are set up to solve problems in areas ranging from manufacturing, marketing, and personnel management to investment and menu planning.

Broad topics in algebra are covered in NUMBER THEORY *and in* SETS AND GROUPS. *More detailed subjects are covered in* CATEGORY THEORY; COMPLEX NUMBERS; *and* GÖDEL'S THEOREM. *A discussion of perhaps the most famous problem in the history of algebra (and recently solved) is found in* FERMAT'S LAST THEOREM.

First see ALGEBRA

Algorithm

Next see COMPUTER PROGRAM

A set of operations that, when completed in sequence, invariably generates a single solution for a particular, well-defined problem.

For thousands of years, mathematicians have invented algorithms to solve difficult equations, devise complex geometrical forms, and even to simplify everyday problems. The term can be traced back to the ninth-century Persian mathematician Muhammed ibn Musa al-Khwarizmi, whose name was the basis for the word algorithm. Today, all programs that run on computers are algorithms and the theory and design of algo-

Further Reading
Boyer, Carl B., et al., *A History of Mathematics* (1989); Dunham, William, *Journey Through Genius: The Great Theorems of Mathematics* (1991); Friedberg, Richard, *An Adventurer's Guide to Number Theory* (1994); Hersh, Reuben, *What Is Mathematics Really?* (1999); Hoffman, Paul, *Archimedes' Revenge: The Joys and Perils of Mathematics* (1997); Kline, Morris, *Mathematics: The Loss of Certainty* (1982).

Further Reading
Berlinski, D., *The Advent of the Algorithm* (2000); Ceri, S., *The Art and Craft of Computing* (1997); Ceruzzi, P., *A History of Modern Computing* (1998); Goldstine, H. H., *The Computer from Pascal to Von Neumann* (1993); Dewdney, A. K., *The Turing Omnibus* (1993).

rithms constitute a large portion of the study of computer science. The application of the concept of algorithm to the problems of digital computing was promulgated by Alan Turing and John von Neumann.

Algorithms are set apart from other problem-solving methods by the fact that an algorithm has an exact solution based on a given set of initial conditions. An easy way to understand what this means is to compare the difference between a set of directions for assembling a bicycle and a cake recipe. The bicycle directions are algorithmic in nature: by correctly following the directions step by step one will invariably wind up with a complete bicycle, no matter how many attempts are made. However, even though a recipe contains step-by-step directions, each attempt will produce a somewhat different cake. This differentiation in the outcome of a non-algorithmic instruction set can be attributed to the inexact nature of the steps as well as the variation inherent in each recipe attempt (i.e., oven type/temperature; altitude; ingredients).

Uses for Algorithms. While there are a number of problems for which an algorithmic approach has proved unsuitable, algorithms are exceptionally useful for problems that have clearly defined operands and initial conditions. Perhaps one of the most famous algorithms in the history of mathematics was one that Euclid described over 2,000 years ago to determine greatest common divisors. This same algorithm is still used in many computer programs.

Algorithms are used to compute square roots, matrix determinants, numerical integration, derivatives, and all trigonometric functions. But the use of algorithms is not only confined to mathematics. Word processors use algorithms to compute line breaks, perform spelling checks, and compute font sizes. On the Internet, algorithms drive search engines that use sorting and hunting techniques to find information quickly. Computers take raw data from medical equipment and convert them to graphic, easy-to-understand forms that doctors can use to diagnose patients. Astronomers use algorithms to convert the data that they collect into a comprehensible form.

Genetic Algorithms. In genetic algorithms, data strings representing possible values in a search are treated like chromosomes and are recombined with other data strings and sometimes mutated. As in evolution, the search is optimized by combining the "fittest" data strings with the best search results to provide a new population of improved search results.

A theoretical application of algorithms is discussed in TURING MACHINE *and* VON NEUMANN MACHINE. *Practical applications of algorithms are discussed in* COMPUTER, DIGITAL; EXPERT SYSTEMS; *and* OPERATIONS RESEARCH. *Related information is to be found in* PROGRAM, COMPUTER *and* ROBOTICS.

First see METAL

Alkali Metals and Alkaline Earth Metals

Next see ELECTRONEGATIVITY

The alkali metals are the first group on the Periodic Table, numbered IA. Members of this family include lithium, sodium, potassium, as well as the less-known and rarer rubidium, cesium, and francium. Although often depicted in the same column as these others, hydrogen is not a member of this family. As might be expected, being in the same family, all alkali metals share important chemical properties and behavior.

Alkali metals are not very electronegative, meaning they do not strongly attract electrons. In fact, they have trouble holding onto their own valence electrons, let alone being capable of taking electrons away from another atom. They will lose their single valence electron and are transformed into positively charged ions, or cations. These cations are attracted to anions and form ionic bonds. Because they only have one electron to dispose of, the alkali metals are the most reactive of all the metals on the Periodic Table.

Properties. Many of these elements can be distinguished from each other by means of their flame signature. When highly reactive metals are heated in a fire, the electrons obtain additional energy and jump to a higher energy level. They almost immediately lose this additional energy in the form of a wavelength of visible light and thus the flame color changes momentarily. Lithium produces a bright orange-red flame and sodium a yellow-orange one. Potassium's flame is lavender. The colors are determined by how much energy the electrons absorbed.

Although sodium chloride is commonly referred to as salt, the actual definition of salt is any ionic compound made up of a cation other than H^+ and an anion other than OH^-. Therefore, sodium is just one possible component of a salt. Any other metal can be substituted.

All of the alkali metals can act as electrolytes in solution, meaning that they conduct electricity. Many of these elements are found in alkaline batteries. Lithium in particular is found in many types of batteries. (*See* BATTERIES.)

Lithium is also an important component of several drugs used to treat mental illness.

Alkaline Earth Metals. The alkaline earth metals are the second group on the left of the Periodic Table, numbered IIA. Members of this family include beryllium, magnesium, calcium, strontium, barium, and radium. The name of this family indicates a relationship to the first family of metals, the alkali metals (group IA), and also that these elements, when combined with oxygen or water, form compounds with a basic pH.

Like alkali metals, alkaline earth metals are not very electronegative. They have only two valence electrons, and will lose them to become positively charged ions, or cations. These cations are attracted to anions and form ionic bonds. Alkaline earth metals are highly reactive, if not quite so much as group IA elements.

Properties. Like the alkali metals, many of these elements also exhibit a particular flame signature. Calcium produces an orange flame, strontium a deep crimson, magnesium bright white, and barium a jade green. When highly reactive metals are heated in a fire, the electrons obtain additional energy and jump to a higher energy level. They almost immediately lose this additional energy in the form of a wavelength of

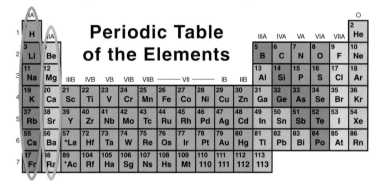

visible light and thus the flame color changes momentarily. The colors are determined by how much energy the electrons absorbed.

As with group IA elements, these metals will form cations (positively charged ions), which will act as electrolytes in solution and conduct electricity. Many of these elements are used in alkaline batteries. Calcium is an extremely important element in living systems, as it is a major component of bone and teeth, and is used for impulse transmission in muscles and nerves.

Barium is used as an internal imaging dye as an aid to x-rays of the gastrointestinal system.

After natural radioactivity was discovered, Marie Curie identified the element radium. Radium gives off radiation at a rate two million times as great as uranium. After the discovery of radium, many other radioactive elements were found, many of them isotopes of naturally occurring elements and others among the transuranic (synthetic) elements. (*See* RADIOACTIVITY.)

Above, a periodic table showing the alkali metals circled in blue, and the alkaline earth metals circled in red.

First see HALOGENS

Alkyl Halides

Next see HYDROCARBON

Long-chained hydrocarbons in which one of the hydrogen atoms has been replaced with a halogen.

In alkyl halide hydrocarbons, halogens, which include fluorine, chlorine, bromine, and iodine, act as a functional group on the hydrocarbon chain, and in turn can be converted into other

Trichloroethane

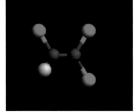

functional groups. The hydrocarbon chains can have multiple substitutions of halogens for hydrogens at the same time. Different types of halogens can be found on the same molecule. (*See* HALOGENS; HYDROCARBON.)

The lowest weight alkyl halides are gases at room temperature, with the rest being liquids. The difference depends more on the weight of the individual halogen atom used than on the size of the hydrocarbon chain.

Alkyl halides do not dissolve in water, but are soluble in most organic solvents. They vary greatly in stability, with fluorine compounds being the most unstable. One alkyl halide that contains chlorine, chloroform, decomposes when it is exposed to light. Bromides and iodides are also light-sensitive and turn brown when exposed. (*See* PHOTOCHEMISTRY.)

Alkyl halides are used as industrial solvents. Carbon tetrachloride was once a popular dry-cleaning agent, but is no longer in widespread use as it was found to cause liver damage. Chloroform was once used as an anesthetic but also fell into disfavor as a suspected carcinogen. Ethyl chloride is still used as a topical anesthetic. Other alkyl halides are used as pesticides.

Chlorine is generally used more frequently in alkyl halides than bromine or iodine due to cost. Chlorofluorocarbons (CFCs) are used for a variety of purposes, from manufacturing to refrigerants to aerosol propellants. Unfortunately, they have been found to have a deleterious effect on the atmosphere, particularly the ozone layer. CFCs are released into the lower atmosphere and, because they are insoluble in water, do not "wash out" in rain. Eventually they work their way to the upper atmosphere where they interact with ozone and break it down—which is why CFC use is being phased out. (*See* OZONE LAYER.)

First see IMMUNE RESPONSE

Allergy

Next see ANTIGEN PRESENTING CELL

An inappropriate or exaggerated response of the body's immune system to an otherwise harmless substance, such as a grain of pollen.

Usually, the immune system defends the body against dangerous organisms such as bacteria and viruses by recognizing the unusual proteins they contain and forming antibodies and lymphocytes, white blood cells, to attack the organisms that contain them. In an allergic response, antibodies and lymphocytes are formed inappropriately against substances called allergens. About one person in eight will have an allergic reaction to one or another allergen. The reason why allergies occur is not known, although a genetic factor appears to be involved.

Allergy Types. The most common kinds of allergies, called anaphylactic or immediate hypersensitivity, are displayed against pollens, grasses, animal skin and hair, house dust, mites, and some drugs and foods. The most common food allergens are in eggs, milk, shellfish, dried fruit, and nuts. Hay fever, perhaps the most widespread allergy, is incorrectly named, since the reaction is not against anything in hay, but against some kinds of pollen.

When an allergic person encounters one of these allergens, the immune system releases antibodies in a family called immunoglobulin E (IgE), which are found in specialized mast cells that exist in the lungs, upper respiratory tract, and other parts of the body. IgE, in turn, causes the release of several body chemicals that cause the symptoms of an allergic reaction. Perhaps the most common of these chemicals is histamine. It can cause muscle spasms, cause blood vessels to dilate, and cause fluids to leak into tissues. The resulting symptoms include itchy and swollen skin, inflammation of the upper respiratory tract, compulsive sneezing, eye inflammation, and even vomiting and diarrhea when the intestinal tract is affected.

Treatment. The treatment for such allergies can start with antihistamine drugs. Many antihistamine drugs also cause drowsiness, but some that do not affect attention are available. Drug treatment can also include cromolyn sodium and corticosteroid creams. These steroids can be used regularly to prevent allergic symptoms from developing, but they can cause skin damage over the long run. Another kind of treatment is immunotherapy, in which larger and larger doses of an allergen are given to promote the development of protective antibodies that will block future allergic reactions. Immunotherapy requires two to three years of treatment and is effective only two-thirds of the time.

Severe Responses. There are other, more severe forms of allergic response. One form is responsible for autoimmune disease, in which the body attacks its own tissue, including red blood cells. In another form, antibodies combine

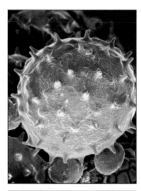

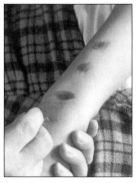

Common allergies include pollen grains (top) and dust mites (center). The "patch" test (bottom) is used to determine if a patient is allergic. Below, the physiological chain of the allergic response.

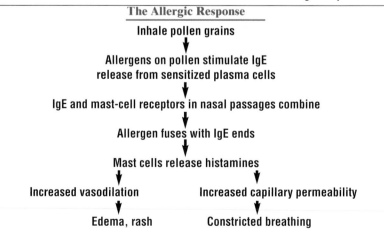

The Allergic Response

Inhale pollen grains
↓
Allergens on pollen stimulate IgE release from sensitized plasma cells
↓
IgE and mast-cell receptors in nasal passages combine
↓
Allergen fuses with IgE ends
↓
Mast cells release histamines
↓   ↓
Increased vasodilation   Increased capillary permeability
↓   ↓
Edema, rash   Constricted breathing

with antigens, forming particles called immunoplexes. These particles can become lodged in different tissues of the body, activating new immune responses that lead to tissue damage. The formation of immunoplexes is responsible for allergic alveolitis, a lung disease that results from exposure to the spores of some fungi. It also can cause skin swelling that follows the administration of booster vaccinations.

The mechanism of an allergy is based on material in IMMUNE RESPONSE. Also relevant is information in AUTOIMMUNITY; DISEASES, INFECTIOUS; and MEDICAL DIAGNOSTICS. See also ANTIGEN PRODUCING CELL and BLOOD TRANSFUSION for sidelights on related areas.

First see METAL

Alloy

Next see STEEL

A substance, usually metallic, that contains two or more metals, plus other substances, in a mixture.

Alloys have been known since virtually the beginning of recorded history; a prehistoric age, in fact, is known as the Bronze Age, denoting the advent of humankind's ability to smelt bronze, an alloy of copper and tin. Other well-known alloys include brass, an alloy of copper and zinc, and steel, an alloy of iron and carbon. Alloys have been created by mixing metals with semi-metals like arsenic and antimony and with non-metals like carbon and silicon.

Alloy Structure. The defining characteristic of an alloy is the effect the "alloying" substance (that which is added to the alloy's base) has on the alignment of the individual atoms. Alloys in which the alloying atoms are mixed randomly within and through the lattice structure of the base are called solid solutions, and they indeed resemble solutions in which one substance has dissolved into another. When the alloying material takes the place of base atoms at regular intervals, but the lattice structure of the mixture is unchanged, the alloy is called an intermetallic compound. When the alloying element joins the base atoms to create a new lattice structure, the alloy is called a multiphase alloy. As would be expected, solid solutions display the same basic characteristics of the base metal, but altered (sometimes improved, but as often not). Intermetallic compounds often take the properties of the base to extremes: material that is heat-resistant and hard, but also very brittle. Multiphase alloys are often so different from the base in their properties that there is little vestige of the base's properties in the new alloy.

Creating Alloys. Alloys are most often created during the molten stage of a metal, and the alloying element is usually added during the refinement process. Steel, for example, is made by introducing carbon from the coke used in the refinement of iron ore. There is, however, much variability here, and alloying elements are added at many (but very specific) points in the molten state of a metal. What type of alloy will result from any mixture has been found to depend very much on the manner in which the molten mixture was cooled. Rapid cooling does not give the alloying element enough chance to align properly, usually resulting in a solid solution. Slower cooling gives the atoms time (and energy) to align in a more orderly lattice. (*See* ALUMINUM.)

Alloys are also divided into ferrous (iron based) and non-ferrous, in which the base is usually copper, aluminum, or titanium. Titanium alloys have become particularly important for providing extreme durability (about that of steel) at very light weight (half of steel), both considerations in the construction of high-performance aircraft. But the alloys used in jet and rocket engines, especially in areas of intense heat and stress, are usually nickel- or cobalt-based. Alloys are often far less conductive of electricity and less reactive to living tissue than pure metals, which makes them ideal for use in prosthetic devices, pacemakers, and in dentistry.

First see ALLOY

Aluminum

Next see ANNEALING

Aluminum is produced by the Hall process, an electrolytic reduction technique that was invented in 1886 by an American scientist, Charles M. Hall. In this process, ore that contains the aluminum, most often bauxite, is first purified to form a substance called alumina, which contains both aluminum and oxygen. The alumina is placed in a bath of melted cryolite, whose constituents include fluorine and iron; fluorspar, a compound of calcium and fluorine, is added to lower the melting point. The cell in which this takes place is a rectangular steel tank that is lined with carbon and has carbon anodes for electrical current. Direct current is applied to melt the mixture in the cell, thus separating the alumina into oxygen and molten aluminum. The molten aluminum sinks to the bottom of the cell, where it is withdrawn at fixed intervals. The oxygen that is freed by the process attacks the anodes, causing the formation of carbon dioxide and carbon monoxide. Alumina is added as needed to keep the process going continually.

Uses. The elemental aluminum that is produced by the Hall process has many uses because of its light weight, tensile strength, and good conductivity of heat and electricity. Most notably, all of the modern aircraft that are flown by the military services and airlines have aluminum as their chief structural material.

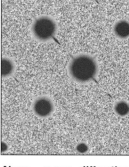

Above, x-ray diffraction pattern of a cobalt-nickel alloy, one of the toughest. The individual atoms align as if they were all the same element.

Nickel alloys are used in the high-temperature areas of a jet engine because they are able to withstand temperatures of many thousands of degrees.

When bauxite is melted down, it becomes a substance called alumina. When this is dissolved in a cryolite bath (above) and reduced by electrolysis, the result is aluminum.

First see NEURON

Alzheimer's Disease

Next see BRAIN

A condition of the brain that causes dementia, a progressive loss of mental ability.

The most common cause of dementia, Alzheimer's disease rarely occurs before age 60, but its incidence increases with age, so that it affects up to 30 percent of persons over the age of 85. Its cause is unknown, but there appears to be a genetic factor involved. The disease is more common in persons with Down's syndrome, and there is a family history of the disease in 15 percent of cases. In some families, there appears to be a dominant form of inheritance, in which children with one affected parent have a 50 percent chance of developing the disease.

Stages. There are three stages in most cases of Alzheimer's disease. In the first stage, the person becomes increasingly forgetful. Problems with remembering names and places can cause anxiety and depression, but the symptoms are so general that they often are ignored.

The second stage is a more severe kind of memory loss, particularly for recent occurrences. The person often remembers distant events, those that occurred in youth and young adulthood, but can forget a visitor who came the day before or a television show that was seen only a day or two earlier. Many persons become disoriented, so that they lose their way on streets that had been familiar or forget appointments. The ability to calculate numbers and to concentrate declines, as does the ability to find the proper word to complete a sentence or thought. This stage is accompanied by an increase in anxiety and unpredictable mood changes.

In the final stage, the disorientation and confusion of patients increases markedly. Many experience hallucinations and paranoid delusions, more commonly at night. In many cases, patients display the kind of primitive, involuntary reflexes that are seen in newborn babies, and become incontinent. While some patients become docile and helpless, others become more demanding of those around them, even behaving violently. There often is a neglect of personal hygiene, and perhaps purposeless wandering. As the disease progresses, the family can no longer care for the patient, and hospitalization becomes necessary. The patient becomes bedridden, and a combination of feeding problems, bedsores, and diseases such as pneumonia cuts life short.

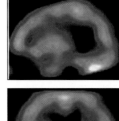
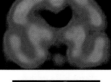
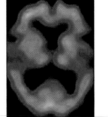

Above, though it is believed Alzheimer's disease is caused by local neural damage, MRI scans of the brain reveal that blood flow to the brain of an Alzheimer's sufferer (bottom) is restricted compared to normal blood flow (top and middle.)

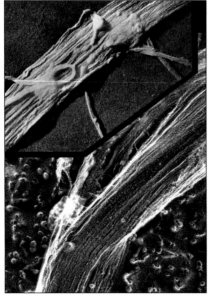

Both the axons (bottom) and the dendrites (top) of neurons in the brain of an Alzheimer's sufferer show signs of wear and plaque. Wear and plaque are also found in the normal brain (but to a lesser degree).

Diagnosis. Diagnosis generally depends entirely on the symptoms. An examination of the brain of a person with Alzheimer's with an EEG or magnetic resonance imaging will show reduced brain size; in addition, there is a loss of nerve cells and dendritic complexity that is apparent on microscopic examination. Autopsies further reveal characteristic protein plaques or "tangles" in the brain. Research in genetic indicators of the disease is ongoing.

Treatment. There is no specific drug or other treatment for Alzheimer's disease. Good nourishment, regular exercise, and keeping the patient occupied can help reduce anxiety and stress, both for the patient in early stages of the disease and for family members. The use of tranquilizing medicines can also ease the burden and help the patient sleep better, but no medication or other treatment to improve brain function has been found to be effective.

The physiological background of Alzheimer's disease can be found in NERVOUS SYSTEM *and* BRAIN, *where neuronal structures are discussed. Relevant information will also be found in* AGING; MENTAL DISORDERS; *and* PARKINSON'S DISEASE. *See also* MEMORY; NEURON; *and* NEUROTRANSMITTER.

First see ORGANIC COMPOUNDS

Amides

Next see POLYMER

A carboxylic acid is an organic compound that contains carboxyl (COOH) as its functional group. Under the proper pH conditions, the OH (hydroxyl) can lose its hydrogen, thereby acting as an acid. Because they are organic compounds and can act as an acid, carboxylic acids are known as organic acids. Organic acids are the basis of many other important compounds.

If the hydroxyl group as a whole is replaced by an amino group (NH_2), the resulting compound is called an amide. Amides in turn can be used as the starting point for still other compounds, as the hydrogen atoms can be replaced by alkyl (hydrocarbon) groups. This is very similar to the use of ammonia (NH_3) as a common "building block" for many organic compounds. Any or all of its three hydrogen atoms can be replaced by various alkyl groups to form more complex structures.

Polymers of amides are known as polyamides. The best known polyamides are nylon and Qiana, both used as textile fibers. Another polyamide, Nomex, is used as the insulating material on the space shuttles, between the heat-resistant ceramic tiles and the aluminum surface of the ship itself. Nomex is a very strong material and has a high melting point, which makes it suitable for this task.

First see MEDICAL DIAGNOSTICS

Amniocentesis

Next see BIRTH

A medical procedure in which fluids are extracted from the amniotic sac and examined for indications of the genetic and medical condition of the fetus.

Amniocentesis is a procedure that is done about the sixteenth week of pregnancy to detect possible disorders of the fetus. Guided by an ultrasound image, a needle is inserted into the amniotic sac, the membrane that contains the fetus, and a small amount of amniotic fluid is removed. Local anesthesia is often used, and an overnight stay in the hospital is not usually necessary.

Testing. A number of tests can be done on the fluid to detect conditions such as Down's syndrome, which affects the intelligence, and spina bifida, a congenital defect of the spinal cord. Cells from the fetus are in the amniotic fluid, and these can be grown in laboratory culture over a period of weeks to detect problems caused by abnormalities of the chromosomes, which carry the genetic information about the fetus.

In Down's syndrome, for example, an extra chromosome can be detected in the amniotic fluid. Amniocentesis can also detect other chromosomal abnormalities, metabolic disorders such as Tay-Sachs disease, sex-linked disorders such as hemophilia, and a variety of other problems, including respiratory distress syndrome, which are not discernible in the mother's blood or by any other disgnostic method.

Amniocentesis has become more common as the risk to mother and fetus has gone down; it is generally performed when the benefits of detecting a problem outweigh the risks of the procedure. Right and below, a local anesthetic is applied and an ultrasound wand provides a clear view of the fetus (bottom left) as a needle is inserted into the amniotic sac. It may soon become possible to retrieve the fetus' genetic information from a blood test of the mother, but the immunological barrier between the fetus and the mother may make complete prenatal diagnosis from maternal blood difficult.

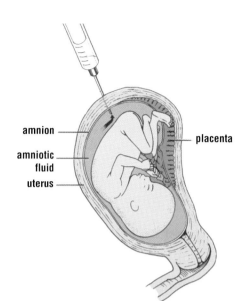

amnion
amniotic fluid
uterus
placenta

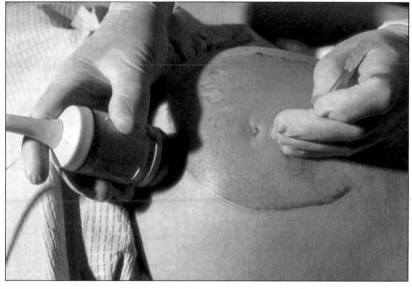

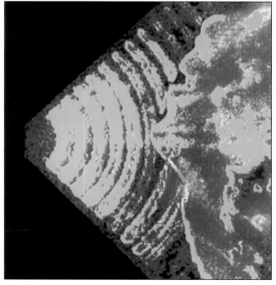

Risks of the Procedure. The risks of amniocentesis include miscarriage and fetal injury. These risks, however, are now so small that the procedure has become quite common; it is often strongly recommended for pregnancies in women who are over the age of 35 because the incidence of Down's syndrome and other complications rise with age.

The sex of a fetus can be determined during pregnancy using either amniocentesis or ultrasound procedures and expecting parents are now routinely given the choice of having that information before the baby's birth.

The biological background for amniocentesis can be found in BIRTH; EMBRYOLOGY; *and* MEDICAL DIAGNOSTICS. *Additional information is located in* RADIOLOGY; SICKLE CELL DISEASE; *and* GENETIC DISEASES.

Further Reading
Nightingale, E. O., *Before Birth: Prenatal Testing for Genetic Disease* (1990); Trent, R. J., *Handbook of Prenatal Diagnosis* (1995); Wexler, K., *Testing Women, Testing the Fetus* (1999); Wexler, K., *The ABC's of Prenatal Diagnosis* (1994).

Amphibians

First see REPTILE

Next see ECOLOGY

Animals that live on both land and water, characterized by glandular skin, larvae with gills, an adult stage with lungs, and eggs without amnions.

In the history of evolution, amphibians play a crucial role. As the link between fish and reptiles, and showing characteristics of both, they were the first animals to pull themselves out of the water and walk on land.

They became so numerous that the Carboniferous period (360 to 286 million years ago) is often called the Age of Amphibians. But by the end of the Triassic period, about 208 million years ago, most amphibians were extinct, displaced by reptiles. The only survivors were the immediate ancestors of today's amphibians: frogs and toads (order Anura), salamanders and newts (order Caudata) and the wormlike apodes or caecilians (order Gymnophiona).

Amphibians—the name is derived from the Greek for "living two lives"—typically hatch from eggs as aquatic larvae with gills and undergo metamorphosis, a series of physical changes that transforms them into terrestrial adults with lungs. Their hairless, mucus-covered skin also plays a role in respiration, as well as in maintaining water balance. Because the eggs lack a shell or amnion (a tough, protective membrane), they must be kept moist to prevent drying, a key survival disadvantage compared to reptiles. Amphibians have, however, evolved many exceptions to this pattern. Each order, for instance, has species whose eggs hatch as miniature adults, not larvae, and a few species that bear live young. Conversely, among salamanders,

At right, a longtail salamander (*Eurycea longicauda*), native to North America, has a tail nearly twice as long as its body. Below, a poison-arrow frog (*Dendrobates leucomelas*). The frog is so named for the poison it secretes that covers its skin. The poison is used as a defense against predators, who are alerted to the poison by the frog's colorful skin. More than 400 species of salamander and 2,000 species of frogs have been observed worldwide.

Life Cycle of the Frog. Clasping by the male (a) stimulates the female to lay up to 5,000 eggs, which the male fertilizes as they are laid. Three gel coats swell with water (b) as the first divisions begin (c) in 3 to 12 hours. An embryo develops (d) in 4 days, living on the yolk it packed in its gut, and hatches in 6 days (e) into a tadpole with external gills. By 11 days (f), an eye develops along with a cover for the gills. By 75 days, legs appear (g) and gills are replaced with lungs. By 90 days, the tail is nearly gone (h) and lungs nearly functional. A frog does not reach full maturity (i) until at least a year has passed.

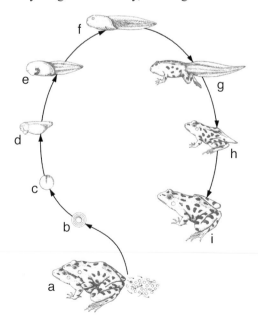

many species remain in the larval form throughout life or retain some larval characteristics.

Metamorphosis. Frogs provide the most dramatic examples of metamorphosis. In many species, the frog deposits hundreds or even thousands of eggs in ponds or streams. These hatch as tadpoles, which resemble fish— legless, with short oval bodies, long tails, and fins. They eat only plants and have a long, coiled intestine. After a period of time that varies with species, they make an abrupt transition: They grow hindlimbs and later forelimbs, they develop lungs, their skeleton turns from cartilage to bone, their intestines get shorter and thicker to prepare for life as carnivores, their eyes get bigger, they sprout eyelids, teeth, tongue, and skin glands. Their gills, tail, and fins disappear. As adults, they are noted for their powerful hindlimbs, leaping locomotion, and the male's insistent mating call. Even among frogs, however, there is much diversity: Some frogs live in trees and carry their eggs in a pouch on their back; others never leave the water. And although most species are tropical, they can be found in a wide range of climates and habitats.

Salamanders and apodes make more modest metamorphoses. Salamanders lose their external gills and tail fins and develop lungs and eyelids, but they have their four legs from the start. The apodes are limbless creatures that spend most of their lives burrowing underground and eating earthworms. They also lose external gills, as well as growing food-seeking tentacles, but their larval and adult forms are otherwise fairly similar. (*See* MORPHOGENESIS.)

Since the 1980s, ecologists have been concerned by sharp declines in the populations of many frog species around the world.

Analog Computer

First see ALGORITHM

Next see COMPUTER, DIGITAL

A machine that analyzes or models information based on a continuous flow of variable data.

Analog computers are differentiated from digital computers because, while digital computers operate through a system of binary computations based on Boolean algebra, analog computers operate through a system of physical or electronic operations, each one equivalent—an analogy—to its real-world counterpart. The first analog instruments were not even computers as such; they include the orrery, which modeled the action of the solar system, and the planetarium, which displayed the motion of the stars.

Early Days. The first analog instrument that can be recognized as a precursor of the computer was a tide-predicting machine designed by Lord Kelvin in 1876. Through a series of gears, wires, pulleys, and shafts he succeeded in modeling the relative effects of the moon's gravitation, friction of water against the sea floor, and changes in water velocity due to widening or narrowing of a given channel, and tracing the resulting water level at any given time on a continuous roll of paper. If one wanted to forecast the tides for a given period in the future, one simply ran the machine through the appropriate number of cycles. Of course, because each machine had to be constructed as an exact analogy to a specific harbor or channel, all results obtained by the analog computer were unique, applicable only to that time and place.

Such analog instruments were typically vast in size. In the 1930s a replica of the Zuyder Zee half the size of a basketball court was constructed in order to envision the effects of natural disasters on land-reclamation structures; as late as the 1960s, an analog replica of the Chesapeake Bay basin was constructed, large enough to sail model ships on.

The most famous analog computer was the Differential Analyzer, constructed by Vannevar Bush between 1928 and 1931; this complex machine was described by an early observer as a "tremendous maze of shafts, gears, motors, servos, etc." Despite its ability to solve a differential equation in seven variables in the then-astonishing period of fifteen to twenty minutes, the Differential Analyzer was not a true computer: it was neither digital nor electronic. Nevertheless, six of them were constructed, and with the coming of World War II they proved invaluable in computing ballistic artillery firing tables that might contain 3,000 entries each. In fact, so useful were they that an electronic differential analyzer was constructed at MIT, containing 2,000 tubes, thousands of relays, and 150

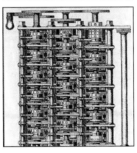

The earliest computers were analog machines. Above (from bottom), Charles Babbage's "Difference Engine" (1823) used a system of wheels and gears in building what was a large adding machine. Babbage went on to develop (1833) a similar machine with a stored program—the Analytical Engine—but built only a small model. One of the most ambitious analog computers was the Automatic Computing Engine (ACE), top, built in England shortly after World War II.

Further Reading

Augarten, Stan, *Bit by Bit: An Illustrated History of Computers* (1993); Ceruzzi, Paul, *A History of Modern Computing* (1998); Corada, James W., *Before the Computer: IBM, NCR, Burroughs, and Remington Rand and the Industry They Created, 1865-1956* (1983); Goldstine, Herman H., *The Computer from Pascal to Von Neumann* (1993); Greenia, M.W., *History of Computing: An Encyclopedia* (CD-2001).

motors. But with the coming of digital computers, it became clear that even electronic analog computers represented a dead end.

Current Uses. The major application of analog computing was, and remains today, in electrical engineering. As power generation grids extended across the United States in the 1920s, it proved impossible to deal mathematically with the resulting equations; but it was possible to construct ever-more complex models, containing thousands of resistors, capacitors, and inductors, which could prove the feasibility of the proposed project. In 1930, an AC Network Calculator was constructed at MIT which could be "programmed" to reflect the actual arrangement of any such power distribution grid.

Analog computers are still employed in engineering applications, using operational amplifiers, or op-amps. Op-amps are integrated circuits that perform basic operations, such as the differential amplifier, a basic part of the electrocardiogram. The most important op-amps for analog computation are the integrator, the summer, and the coefficient multiplier. For example, an automobile designer trying to determine the smoothest possible suspension system might formulate the relevant constraints as a complex differential equation; a complex series of separate iterations through different op-amps will then solve the equation.

Advantages. Analog computers actually offer several advantages. Because physical processes are being modeled electrically, time changes can be scaled to a slower pace, allowing each phase of a complex sequence to be studied and understood. The magnitude of processes can also be easily scaled up or down. Op-amps do, however, have their limitations. Because physical processes are being modeled electrically, there are failures of parallelism relating to voltage supply limits, which may distort output significantly by clipping; frequency response limits, which are related to gain-bandwidth product; offset voltages and currents; and the slew rate, which prevents output from keeping up with rapid changes in input.

Even in a growing digital environment, analog computing retains an important place. All voice and sound processing chips are necessarily analog; power management components are also analog; and of course every video-game player who has used a joystick to operate a game knows the advantage of analog systems at the machine-human interface.

Background information can be found in ALGORITHM *and* PROGRAM, COMPUTER. *Historically, analog computers played an important role in* CRYPTOGRAPHY *and in areas of* OPERATIONS RESEARCH. *Also, compare with* COMPUTER, DIGITAL.

First see HEART

Angioplasty

Next see CIRCULATORY SYSTEMS

A procedure in which a balloon is inserted into an artery to treat stenosis, a narrowing of a blood vessel or heart valve.

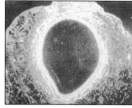

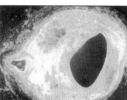

Above, top, a normal arterial cross-section, unobstructed by atherosclerotic plaque, as it is in the bottom photograph. Below, three phases of angioplasty.

Angioplasty is done to prevent a heart attack or other major medical problem. After a local anesthetic is injected, a hollow, flexible tube called a guide catheter is inserted into an artery of a leg or arm. Using a television display of an x-ray image, the physician guides the catheter to the area of obstruction. A smaller catheter with a balloon at its tip is then inserted through the guide catheter. When this catheter reaches the blockage, the balloon is inflated for about 30 seconds to widen the blood vessel. Several inflations and deflations are usually done. A stent, made of flexible wire mesh, is often inserted to ensure that the blood vessel remains open. The procedure generally takes between 30 and 90 minutes, and x-rays are done to determine how blood flow has improved. There is a risk that the procedure can damage the artery or valve, requiring immediate corrective surgery.

Candidates for angioplasty are patients who suffer angina, a pain that results from narrowed or blocked blood vessels, and who are not helped by drug treatment. Angioplasty can improve the condition of about two-thirds of such patients, but about a quarter of them may require additional angioplasty treatment after a year. The procedure is most effective in treating the iliac and femoral arteries, especially when the area of narrowing is not very large. (*See* HEART.)

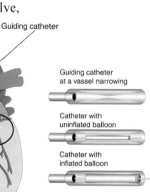

Aorta

Guiding catheter

Guiding catheter at a vassel narrowing

Catheter with uninflated balloon

Catheter with inflated balloon

Coronary arteries

BALLOON ANGIOPLASTY

First see PLANT

Angiosperms

Next see SEED

Plants that produce flowers, fruits, and seeds.

Most fruits, vegetables, grasses, shrubs, and trees are angiosperms, the flowering plants that have dominated terrestrial vegetation since the middle Cretaceous period about 100 million years ago. Currently, angiosperms number an estimated 250,000 species.

Flowering plants are thought to have descended from the other main group of seed

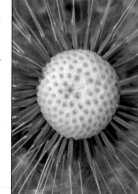

Above, a dandelion seedhead.

plants, the gymnosperms, the modern-day members of which include conifers (pine, fir, cedar, hemlock, larch), the ginkgo, and cycads. Gymnosperms generally have needle-like leaves and cones as reproductive structures. Fertilization of the ovules takes place on the scales of the female cone, and the ovule is shed from the surface of the cone as a seed.

By contrast, flowers are the reproductive organs of angiosperms. Their ovules are enclosed within carpels, which constitute the pistil at the center of a flower, and their seeds are enclosed within fruit that develop from the carpels. (*See* FLOWER *and* FRUIT.)

Angiosperms are the only organisms known to undergo "double fertilization." One sperm cell in a pollen grain unites with the egg to form the zygote. The other sperm fuses with the double-nucleated central cell in the female embryo sac, forming the endosperm, which serves as a food source for the embryo in the seed. Angiosperms are also distinguished from other plants by their large vascular systems and their reliance on insect pollinators, which are enticed by the color, nectar, or scent of their flowers.

Varieties. Angiosperms are generally divided into dicots and monocots. In monocots, which include grains, grasses, and spring bulbs, the embryos have a single leaf or cotyledon; vascular tissue is scattered in the stem; veins generally run in parallel lines; and petals, sepals, and stamens usually occur in threes or multiples of three. In dicots, which include the majority of flowering plants, the embryos have two leaves; vascular tissue is generally arranged in circular patterns; veins run in netlike patterns; and flower parts occur in multiples of four or five.

First see METAL

Annealing

Next see ALLOY

A heat treatment applied to metals.

Annealing is done for a variety of purposes. Most often it is to lessen the hardness of the metal, but annealing can also be done to change the microstructure of the metal or to achieve a specific set of physical or mechanical properties. In the annealing process, the metal is first heated to a predetermined temperature and then is allowed to cool to room temperature. For nonferrous metals—those that are not iron or steel—annealing usually is done to reduce the hardness of the metal after it has been processed without heating. The same is true for ferrous metals, but the process is somewhat different. For nonferrous metals, the heating is not drastic. For ferrous metals, the metal is heated to the point where the metal has a phase change—the structure of its atoms and molecules undergoes a change. Annealing is often an important step in the production of specific metal types.

For example, in the production of fine wires, there may be several intermediate annealing steps before the metal is drawn through fine openings to produce a wire with the desired properties. In some cases, annealing is the final production step to achieve a desired softened condition for a metal product. One major reason annealing is done is to reduce the dislocation density, or number of imperfections, in a metal sample or product after it has undergone cold working. Properly done, annealing can virtually eliminate the dislocation density caused by cold working.

First see ATOM

Antioxidants

Next see OXIDIZING AGENTS

Compounds that prevent free radicals from damaging a cell's structure.

Molecules are made up of atoms, which in turn contain smaller particles known as protons, neutrons, and electrons. Electrons, which are negatively charged, are located on the perimeter of the atom, in orbit around the center. The electrons are arranged in specific energy levels, with each level containing various sublevels and each sublevel containing at least one orbital, which can contain a fixed number of electrons.

A free radical is a compound with an unpaired electron in one of its orbitals. The atom tends strongly to fill its orbital which leads it to attract an electron from something else. The original free radical then becomes stable, but its donor is now short an electron and becomes a free radical in its own right.

DNA, which is the chemical of heredity, is highly susceptible to "attacks" of this sort. Genes control all the basic chemical reactions and activities of the cell, so genetic damage can result in altered cell functions. Free radicals have been implicated as major contributors to aging and degenerative diseases such as cancer.

Oxidation refers to the loss of electrons. The opposite reaction, the gaining of electrons, is called reduction. Oxygen itself can be transformed into several types of free radicals, such as the hydroxyl radical and the hydrogen peroxide radical. Free radicals can be generated by ozone, cigarette smoke, and other pollutants, and by chemicals such as herbicides and pesticides and by exposure to sunshine and x-rays.

Antioxidants are compounds that combat free radicals and prevent them from doing damage in the cell. Naturally occurring antioxidants include vitamins A, C, E, as well as the minerals zinc and selenium. These same materials are currently being studied for their role in combating cancer and stimulating the immune system.

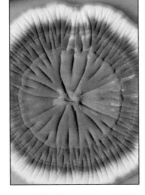

A mold colony from which the antibiotic penicillin is extracted.

Above, superoxide dismutase (SOD) are antioxidant metalloenzymes found in the mitochondria of many plants and animals.

First see BACTERIA

Antibiotics

Next see PHARMACOLOGY

Agents used to fight or prevent infections.

Most antiseptics are chemicals that are applied to the skin or to wounds to destroy bacteria and other microorganisms such as fungi that can cause infections, although heat, ionizing radiation, and ultraviolet light can also have an antiseptic effect. The most commonly used chemical antiseptics include iodine, hydrogen peroxide, and thimerosal. Open wounds generally are bathed with antiseptics in the form of fluids, while antiseptic creams are applied to wounds before they are dressed.

History. Modern antiseptics were developed in the nineteenth century by pioneers such as Ignatz Semmelweis in Hungary, Robert Koch in Germany, and Joseph Lister in England. It was Lister who pioneered the use of antiseptics in surgery, a major advance in modern medicine, while Semmelweis introduced the practice to childbirth, saving the lives of many mothers and newborn children.

Antibiotics are drugs used to treat infections caused by bacteria and other microorganisms. The first antibiotic was penicillin, whose antibacterial activity was recognized by Alexander Fleming in 1928. It became available as a drug in 1940 because of research and development work done in England by Howard Florey, a pathologist who was born in Australia, and Ernst Chain, a biochemist who was born in Germany. Like penicillin, the first generation of antibiotics were drugs that were derived from molds and fungi. Many of them are now made synthetically. Some antibiotics are effective against a limited range of bacteria. Others, called broad-spectrum antibiotics, can be used against many different infectious bacteria. A physician will choose an antibiotic for a patient based on both the type of bacteria causing the infection and the

THE CUTTING EDGE

The Antibacterial Fad

A host of substances formerly reserved for hospital environments—antiseptic agents like triclocarbon and benzalkonium chloride—have found their way into household soaps and detergents and even into toys, mattresses, and cutting boards. These substances do not prevent many common infections, but they do alter the bacterial balance, allowing microbes ordinarily unable to thrive to grow without competition from other bacteria. Many contain plasmids—segments of DNA—that confer resistance to antibacterial agents. Long-acting antiseptics may have the harmful and unintended effect of turning the home into a breeding ground for invulnerable microbes, much as hospitals have become infected with bacteria that antibiotics cannot eradicate.

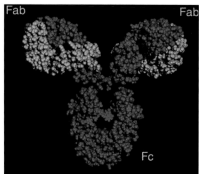

The human body is a battlefield in which adversaries wage an almost constant war. Two combatants (on opposite sides): above, an immuno-globulin-1 particle; below, a spherical human rhinovirus.

body site of the infection. The most effective choice is made by obtaining a sample of the infectious bacteria, growing them in the laboratory, and testing their sensitivity to different kinds of antibiotics.

Widespread use of an antibiotic can lead to emergence of strains of bacteria that are resistant to the effects of that drug. Resistance can develop when bacteria change genetically so that they begin to produce enzymes that break down the antibiotic. Resistance is most likely to develop in an individual patient if an antibiotic is used for a long period of time or if the patient does not take the medication as directed. When this happens, the physician can turn to a more powerful antibiotic that has stronger side effects. Most antibiotics can cause a rash, diarrhea, and nausea. Some patients experience an allergic reaction that results in swelling, itching, or breathing difficulties. One side effect of antibiotics is that they sometimes kill bacteria that are normal inhabitants of the body, allowing less friendly microbes such as fungi to grow out of control.

Some commonly used antibiotics are the aminoglycosides, such as gentamicin and streptomycin; the cephalosporins, such as ceflacor and cephalexin; the tetracyclines, such as doxycycline and oxytetracycline; and modern versions of penicillin, such as penicillin V and amoxicillin. Erythromycin and neomycin are other antibiotics that are in common use.

First see ANTIGEN-PRESENTING CELLS

Antibodies

Next see IMMUNE RESPONSE

Proteins manufactured by an immune system to ward off infectious invaders.

The immune system is designed to protect the body from invasion by foreign particles, known as infection, either with non-specific responses or specific responses. There are three main non-specific responses: inflammation—blood vessels in the infected region dilate, resulting in more fluid entering body tissues, which causes redness and swelling; fever—body temperature increases above normal in order to place the bacteria or viruses at a metabolic disadvantage; and increased white cell count—the number of white cells circulating in the bloodstream sharply increases in response to the presence of bacteria and other germs, which the white blood cells are designed to eliminate.

Specific responses involve the action of highly specialized types of white blood

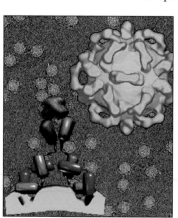

cells, the T- and B-lymphocytes. T cells are responsible for cellular immunity and destroy foreign cells. There are many different types of T cells, with each variety capable of responding to a specific type of antigen. (*See* T-LYMPHO-CYTE.)

B-lymphocytes are responsible for antibody immunity. A specific type of B cell responds to its particular antigen by becoming sensitized and dividing rapidly to produce hundreds of cells. Most of the new cells differentiate into plasma cells, which produce antibodies. Others become memory cells, in case the antigen is encountered again at a later date. (*See* B-LYMPH-OCYTE.)

B cells never leave the lymph nodes; only their antibodies circulate in the bloodstream. After the infection is over, some antibodies remain in circulation at a much lower concentration known as the basal level. (*See* BLOOD.)

Antibody proteins are also called immunoglobulins. They react with antigens to form a complex in much the same way that an enzyme combines with a substrate. Unlike enzymes, however, a "perfect fit" is not necessary for the formation of the antigen-antibody complex. Antibodies can function against antigens in one of three ways: they can form a complex with the antigen, which inactivates, but does not destroy, the antigen; they can form a complex with the antigen that makes the antigen more susceptible to a killer T cell; or they can form a complex with the antigen, which directly results in the destruction of the antigen. (*See* ANTIGEN.)

Immunities. Active immunity occurs when an individual has been exposed to an antigen and develops antibodies in response. Exposure to the antigen may come about as a result of having a disease, or receiving a vaccine against a particular disease. Many viral diseases, such as measles, mumps, and tetanus, can be prevented by receiving an inoculation. The shot contains weakened or killed versions of the virus, or antigens from its protein coat, which stimulate the body's immune system against it. Vaccinations are given in a set schedule during childhood and periodic boosters are sometimes required several years later to ensure continued immunity against the viral agent.

Passive immunity occurs when an individual receives someone else's antibodies against a disease. This provides temporary protection against the illness but will not result in permanent immunity. For example, a newborn baby receives antibodies from its mother's blood during pregnancy and is thus protected against various diseases during its first months of life. More antibodies are transmitted through the breast milk. However, the antibody levels eventually drop and the child must be exposed to the antigens and develop its own antibodies for permanent immunity. (*See* IMMUNIZATION.)

First see IMMUNE RESPONSE

Antigen-Presenting Cells

Next see ANTIBODIES

Molecules, usually proteins, that provoke an immune response.

An antigen provokes a primary immune response, which involves a rapid increase in the number of special types of white blood cells, called T- and B-lymphocytes. Once these cells are sensitized, or activated, they deal with the antigen-presenting cell in different ways. T cells destroy the invader by engulfing and digesting it. B cells produce antibodies, which form a complex with the antigen, either disabling it, killing it, or making it more susceptible to destruction by killer T cells. (*See* ALLERGY.)

After the antigen and the threat it represents have been neutralized, memory cells are left behind, enabling a secondary immune response to occur should that type of antigen ever be encountered again. (*See* B-LYMPHOCYTE.)

Antigens are primarily large molecules. Small molecules do not usually cause an immune response unless they are bound up with larger molecules, such as proteins. Thus viruses, which are usually small, often escape the immune system's network filtering. Only a small area on the surface of an antigen is recognized by an antibody. That specific region is called the antigenic determinant or epitope. An antigen may contain several epitopes, but they will not all equally stimulate the immune system. One or two epitopes are usually dominant.

First see ATOM

Antimatter

Next see ELEMENTARY PARTICLE

Antimatter consists of antiparticles—that is, subatomic particles that have the same mass as the particles that exist in the ordinary matter we see about us but have equal and opposite values of some other property or properties, such as electric charge. An example is the positron, the antiparticle of the electron. The positron has the same mass as the electron but a positive charge that is equal to the negative charge of the electron. In the same way, the antiproton has a negative charge that is equal to the positive charge of the proton. The neutron and antineutron, which do not have an electrical charge, differ in their magnetic moments, which is a measure of the strength of their magnetic field. In the neutron and antineutron, the magnetic moments are opposite in sign relative to their spins. The existence of antiparticles was predicted by P.A.M. Dirac in his formulation of relativistic quantum mechanics in 1931. (*See* QUANTUM MECHANICS.)

The first antiparticle to be discovered was the positron, whose existence was demonstrated in 1933. It was not until 1955 that the antiproton was produced in an accelerator. Work with accelerators has since confirmed the existence of antiparticles for virtually all the common particles. (*See* ACCELERATOR, PARTICLE.)

When a particle collides with its antiparticle, both the particle and the antiparticle are destroyed, and the energy created by their destruction is carried away by photons or other particles. When an electron collides with a positron, for example, the annihilation energy is carried away by two photons, each of which has an energy of 0.511 million electron volts. This amount of energy is equivalent to the rest-mass energies and the kinetic energies of the two annihilated particles. When nucleons such as the proton and antiproton collide, the annihilation energy is carried away by mesons.

Why Not Antimatter? It is possible to picture a world consisting of antimatter. In this world, there would be antihydrogen, with a positron orbiting the antiproton of the atom's nucleus. Antihydrogen has been created in the laboratory, and its spectrum has been shown to be identical with that of hydrogen.

As far as astronomers can tell, the universe appears to consist entirely of matter rather than antimatter. For example, when the solar wind sweeps through our solar system, there is no sign of the gamma rays that would be formed if any of the planets contained antimatter. Gamma-ray observations of our galaxy limit the antimatter content in interstellar gas to much less than one part in a billion. Observations of other galaxies that emit x-rays indicate that less than one part in 100,000 of that gas consists of antimatter. If antimatter did exist in the universe in the form of galaxies, those galaxies would have to be separated from ordinary-matter galaxies by distances many times the size of the galaxies. (*See* SYMMETRY IN NATURE.)

Top, Carl Anderson and the bubble chamber he used in 1932 to detect the positron. Bottom, the bubble-chamber tracks of cosmic rays photographed by Anderson, showing an electron curving one way in a strong magnetic field and another particle of the same mass curving in the opposite direction—the positron.

THE CUTTING EDGE

Where Is All the Antimatter?

The equations that led Paul Dirac to concoct antimatter demand that all matter and antimatter be created in pairs. This means that for every electron there must be a positron, and whole galaxies of antimatter should be swirling through space. When matter and antimatter come in contact, they annihilate each other, releasing gamma rays of a characteristic energy of 511 keV. But where are these bursts of gamma rays? This mystery was intensified when a Russian satellite discovered a powerful source of gamma rays with the tell-tale energy signature near the center of the Milky Way. The object, dubbed The Great Annihilator, spewed forth 50,000 times as much energy as the sun. But why the universe is so filled with matter and devoid of many Great Annihilators is still unclear.

First see BACTERIA

Archaebacteria

Next see PROKARYOTIC CELLS

A bacterial (or bacteria-like) organism thought to resemble the earliest life on Earth.

Scientists speculate that the Earth's earliest life-forms were archaebacteria, primitive unicellular organisms adapted to living in the extreme conditions existent at that time. Eventually, these gave rise to prokaryotes, cells lacking internal membranes, and eukaryotes, more "advanced" cells with internal membranes and compartmentalization. Although they appear to have been passed by in the evolutionary parade of life, archaebacteria are still present today.

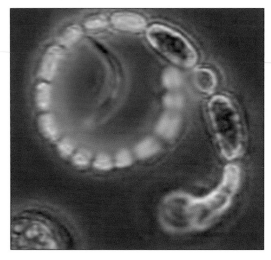

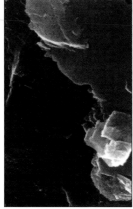

Despite their name, archaebacteria, also known as archaeans, are unlike most other bacteria. Their appearance is similar to bacteria, but they are different both biochemically and genetically. In some respects, particularly in gene organization and control of gene expression, archaeans appear to resemble eukaryotes more closely than they do other bacteria.

Archaeans inhabit some of the most extreme environments of Earth. Some live in or near deep sea vents where air and water pressures are very high and temperatures can exceed the boiling point of water. Others live in extremely alkaline or acidic waters or in high salt concentrations. Archaeans are not limited to extreme habitats; recent research indicates that they are quite abundant among plankton found in the sea.

Halobacteria. One type of archaean, halobacterium, which is halophilic ("salt-loving"), performs photosynthesis, the process by which an organism uses light energy to produce food. Usually, the organism in question is a plant or cell which contains chlorophyll, a green light-sensitive pigment. Halobacteria, however, contain a red pigment called bacteriorhodopsin, which is very similar to the light-detecting pigment rhodopsin found in the human retina.

Top and left, examples of prokaryotes—*Cyanophora paradoxa* and *Anabaena baltica*—that lay claim to being the first chapter of life on earth. Each is different enough from contemporary relatives to establish an evolutionary line that cuts off from the rest of the living world very early. At right, micro-fossil tubules found on rocks from Mars were thought to have been the remains of archaebacteria. Whether this is the case is still unresolved.

First see TEMPERATURE

Archaean Era

Next see CRYOGENICS

The earliest of the five eras of Earth's geological history, dating back more than 3 billion years.

The rocks of the Archaean era are largely igneous, formed from the solidification of hotter rocks such as magma or lava. The general characteristics of these rocks show that the earliest of them do not represent the even more ancient rocks that existed during the formation of the Earth's crust. While no major fossils have been discovered in Archaean rock formations, scientists have found carbonaceous rocks such as graphite that suggest that microbes existed during this era.

Evidence for the existence of living things more than 3 billion years old has been found in the rock structures called stromatolites, and fossil bacteria have been found in rocks 3.5 billion years old. But because of the lack of fossils, the structural complexity of Archaean rock formations, and the high degree of volcanism that occurred during that era, the evidence is difficult to decipher. The structural history of the Archaean era is thus not as well known as that of the periods that followed. Intercontinental correlation is particularly difficult.

The principal areas in which Archaean rock formations have been found are Canada, Finland, Scandinavia, Australia, Africa, and the northeastern part of South America. Many of these rocks contain rich ore deposits, especially of gold and silver, and so the search for ore deposits has been an important stimulus to the study of them, especially in Canada. The Archaean gave way to the Proterozoic era about 2.6 to 3 billion years ago.

First see CEMENT

Architectural Engineering

Next see HIGH-RISE CONSTRUCTION

Architectural engineering comes into play after the architect has chosen the site, the overall form, and the basic internal plan of a building. The engineering phase deals with details of structural design as well the choice of utilities for the building. In architectural engineering, the role of the architect can often overlap with that of the engineer. The design program for the architectural engineering effort begins with a study of the topography of the location, the bearing properties of the soil at that site, and the weather conditions to be expected in the area. Using this information, and working with the overall architectural plans, the engineer works to determine the details of the form that the structure will have. Among the elements that go into this planning are: the loads of the building and their distribution; the overall weight of the building; all the fixed elements of the building; and such environmental factors as the maximum amount of snow that could accumulate on the roof.

Civil. Civil engineers design bridges, dams, hydraulic piers, towers, and roadways, among other structures. The typical procedure starts with the determination of design criteria, such as the function of the building and establishment of the general layout that will meet its functional requirements. Several solutions are proposed, and the most appropriate design is chosen after all those that have been proposed are compared. The features that help determine the final decision include strength, function, economy, rigidity, and appearance.

Design. In the preliminary design stage, the loads of the structure are determined as accurately as possible. The preliminary building design is then analyzed in detail, so that the dimensions of the members making up the building structure and the way they are to be connected are determined. The loads that various structures are to bear cannot always be determined exactly. Such an exact determination is possible for a water tank, but the load of a parking garage, office building, or dance floor are not so precisely calculated.

Loads. There are two kinds of building loads—dead loads, which include permanent structures and details; and live loads, such as vehicles, people, office furniture, industrial equipment, and the like. Architectural engineering must also account for whether loads will be applied suddenly, as in the case of impacts, or whether they are permanent and static. If the weights and other building members that are recommended after studies by the architectural engineer differ from those of the initial plan made by the architect, the detailed design procedure must be continued until both the architect and the engineer have reached agreement.

Some feats of architectural engineering impress by sheer size, as is the case with the dramatic Seattle Space Needle, above. Others require great skill though small in size, as is the case with the inverted pyramid, below, left, in the courtyard of the Louvre Museum in Paris

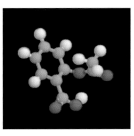

Above, chemical model for acetylsalicylic acid, better known as aspirin, an aromatic compound.

A number of varying and irregular loads usually have to be considered. One is wind load, the pressure that is exerted perpendicular to the external walls of the building by winds of varying force. This pressure usually is greater than ordinary atmospheric pressure on the windward side of the building, and negative, below atmospheric pressure, on the leeward side of a structure. In areas such as California, engineers may also have to consider the forces that might be exerted by an earthquake. In New York City, the engineer might have to consider the vibrational loads that a building is exposed to because of the presence of subway lines. Vibrational loads may also be experienced by a building that houses one or more large motors. The other forces that can affect structures include shrinkage, settlement, and other kinds of motion. The ultimate plan of both the architect and the building engineer is one designed to achieve maximum lifetime and minimum disturbance of a building under all foreseeable conditions of geological effects, weather, and seasonal effects.

First see ACIDS AND BASES

Aromatic Compounds

Next see HYDROCARBON

Hydrocarbons with ringed chemical structure.

The aromatic compounds, also known as arenes or the benzene series, are a type of hydrocarbon. A normal hydrocarbon is a long linked chain of carbon atoms with attached hydrogens. However, in the aromatic compounds, the end carbon atoms are attached, forming a cyclic compound. All members of this series are derivatives of the benzene molecule, a ring consisting of six carbon atoms connected by alternating double and single bonds. Many of these compounds have very strong or distinctive odors. Examples include naphthalene (the active ingredient in mothballs), cinnamon, vanilla, and wintergreen.

The single benzene rings can have attached groups such as halogens or hydroxyls, or they can be a functional group on another hydrocarbon chain. In addition, structures can form that are composed of multiple adjacent rings.

Benzene and many of its derivatives are very good solvents and so have many uses in the laboratory. Benzene itself is used as a starting material for various dyes. Many acid-base indicators, chemicals that change color depending on whether they are in a basic environment or an acidic one, are aromatic compounds. Some of the more well-known indicators are phenolphthalein, methyl orange, and litmus. Other products of the aromatic compounds include explosives, such as TNT, and the pesticide DDT, as well as aspirin and related drugs. (*See* EXPLOSIVES *and* HYDROCARBONS.)

Arthritis

First see Skeletal Systems

Arthritis and Rheumatism

Next see Autoimmunity

Arthritis and rheumatism are names for any inflammation of a joint that causes pain, redness, swelling, and stiffness.

Arthritis can involve one joint or a number of them, and its severity can vary from a mild pain to severe pain, with different effects on one or more joints.

Types. There are several types of arthritis. Osteo-arthritis, or degenerative arthritis, is caused by wear and tear over the years, and most often affects older people. Still's disease is a form of arthritis at the other end of the age scale. It is a juvenile arthritis that is most common in children under four, and it generally disappears in a few years. Rheumatoid arthritis is the most severe kind of inflammatory joint disease. It is an autoimmune disorder, in which the body's immune system mistakenly attacks normal tissue. Rheumatoid arthritis can cause marked deformity of joints, in addition to pain and stiffness. Infective arthritis is joint disease that occurs when bacteria from a nearby wound invade a joint, and ankylosing spondylitis is arthritis of the bones of the spine.

Treatment. There are specific treatments for each form of arthritis. For example, antibiotics can be used to treat infective arthritis, while both rheumatoid arthritis and osteoarthritis will respond favorably to treatment with anti-inflammatory drugs. If arthritis causes joints to become extremely painful or deformed, surgery may be required. One form of surgery is arthroplasty, in which the diseased joint is replaced by an artificial substitute. Another surgical treatment is arthrodesis, in which the affected bones of the joint are fused to manage the problem.

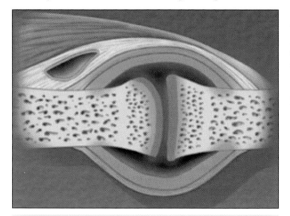

The human skeletal system is discussed in Bone and Bone Growth *and* Skeletal Systems. *For the biochemical aspects, see* Calcium. *The immunological aspects of arthritis are discussed in* Autoimmunity *and* Lupus. *See also* Aging *and* Surgery *for more on treatments.*

The hardware and software required to navigate across a room with simple obstacles has proven to be very complicated. Researchers have found that an insect-like design, such as that of Attila (below), a robot developed at MIT, containing a small computer and 150 sensors in each leg, has many advantages over other animal-like configurations. Attila used a neural net program to learn how to coordinate its motions and walk.

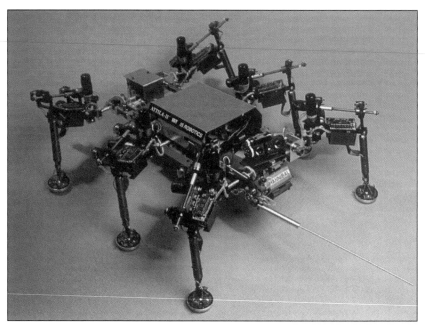

Left, a joint with rheumatoid arthritis. This form of arthritis involves the autoimmune system in that fluids are produced which inflame the joint and damage cartilage. Unlike osteoarthritis, the sufferer experiences pain in joints other than just those under physical stress.

Further Reading
Clark, Harold W., *Why Arthritis? Searching for the Cause and the Cure of Rheumatoid Disease* (1997); Scammell, Henry, *The New Arthritis Breakthrough* (1998); Shlotzhauer, Tammi L., et al., *Living With Rheumatoid Arthritis* (1995); Sundel, Robert P., *Rheumatoid Arthritis & Related Diseases* (1998).

First see Turing Machine

Artificial Intelligence

Next see Robotics

The subfield of computer science in which intelligent behavior is analyzed and computer systems are developed that are capable of emulating, mimicking, or generally exhibiting such behavior.

Even the most primitive machines must have led people to think about the similarities between human and machine thought processes. The first machines augmented human or animal muscles, but pre-industrial inventors also introduced devices that augmented or replaced the human intellect as well, such as windmills with self-regulating sails that adjusted for the intensity of the wind, or automatic float valves that maintained water in a tank at a desired level. These devices used the technique of feedback, whereby information about the machine's behavior—say, the level of water in a tank—is fed back to the input stage—in this case, the valve supplying water to the tank. By the nineteenth century, the development of machines that took on human capabilities had reached a high level. At each stage of these technical advances, there appeared as well philosophical and literary discussions of the implications of such work—the most famous perhaps being Mary Shelley's masterpiece, *Frankenstein*, written in 1818 (though the monster was not actually mechanical, but a resuscitated corpse).

Computers. The development of the digital computer in the twentieth century raised these philosophical questions at a much higher level. Here was a machine that could not only regulate itself according to changes in its physical envi-

44 • Encyclopedia of Science and Technology

ronment, but could also select courses of action based on the results of previous actions, and remember past actions and their consequences. In short, it could learn from experience, adapt to new conditions, and in some sense intelligently interact with its human creators.

The computers of the 1950s were fragile, bulky, and unreliable; their processing and memory capacities were hardly enough even to hint at such complex behavior. Nevertheless, the potential was there, and many computer scientists convened meetings, wrote papers, and began research programs directed at getting computers to perform such tasks. At a conference convened at Dartmouth College in 1956, Professor John McCarthy coined the term "artificial intelligence" (later shortened to AI) to describe this activity. One of his colleagues, Marvin Minsky, later defined the term to mean "the science of making machines do things that would require intelligence if done by men." The term "Artificial Intelligence" has been criticized by some as being vague and imprecise; yet it has persisted, perhaps because it nicely captures the imprecision and frustration encountered by investigators who try to undestand in an objecive way what most humans—even children—do effortlessly.

A few years later McCarthy developed the programming language "LISP" ("List Processing"), which made it easier to write programs that handled symbolic and logical problems, as opposed to the purely numerical problems most other computer languages were designed for. LISP remains the language of choice for AI researchers, although there are others, especially PROLOG, that are also popular. From that time, research in AI has been mainly a matter of writing programs in LISP for general-purpose computers. Some researchers build special-purpose hardware for specific applications, but the power and flexibility of modern commercial general-purpose computers usually is more than sufficient. That means, among other things, that artificial intelligence is primarily a matter of computer programming, albeit of a special type.

Robotics. A large branch of AI research, however, is concerned with robotics, especially with getting a robot to move across an ordinary landscape and avoid obstacles while recognizing desired objects. This research is of special interest to planetary scientists, who hope to develop such machines to explore Mars and the other bodies of the Solar System. Progress has been slow—one of the first things scientists found was that it takes a very large and sophisticated computer to navigate across a room as well as a toddler just learning to walk can do. The 2001 Mars mission planned to include a ground crawling vehicle known as Athena to search for rocks that might contian evidence of life or life remnants. Athena will likely be onboard for a 2005 Mars mission, while a simpler version will

AI applications in science fiction usually involve the creation of humanoid robots. At first depicted as inherently evil, as (below) in Fritz Lang's film, *Metropolis*, robots became more friendly in the Star Wars films (below, left). The android named Data in *Star Trek: The Next Generation* (left) often displays adolescent behavior.

be used to test the robot's agility in 2001.

Thus the field has evolved as a branch of academic computer science, with occasional forays into commercial products. The attempt to get computers to perform intelligent tasks has led to new, even revolutionary, insights into human psychology, and AI has given new life to philosophy as well. But AI research has not led to easier methods of programming computers, or to techniques of writing computer programs without errors—both very desirable ends that the marketplace would pay well for.

One of the ironies of AI is that as soon as one perfects a program that does what previously had been considered a task requiring intelli-

THE CUTTING EDGE

The Turing Test

Following his work as a cryptographer in World War II, Alan Turing turned his attention to establishing criteria of artificial intelligence. In 1950, he devised a test that bears his name. Imagine you are communicating with an entity you cannot hear or see via a terminal. Turing's belief was that machines will have achieved true intelligence when a computer running a program could fool you into believing a person was at the other end of the line. Turing was certain that by the year 2000, a computer would, during a five-minute conversation, fool the test-takers at least 30 percent of the time. So far, several programs—a therapy program called ELIZA and a "learning" program called SHRDLU—have made only slight inroads, in spite of rewards that have been offered for successful programs. In one test, after a computer was asked what a fur coat was made of (answer: fur), the program was betrayed by the answer to the question, what is a rain coat made of? The computer's answer: rain.

gence, computer scientists no longer think of it as important, and therefore it is no longer AI! In the early 1950s, computer scientists, including McCarthy, remarked that getting a computer to play a good game of chess would seem to penetrate to the very basis of human intelligence. Today chess programs are capable of beating any human player (on a good day), and pocket chess computers that sell for about 30 dollars play a respectable game. The result: chess is no longer considered an important topic among AI researchers. And philosophically, the existence of such machines has not led critics of AI to accept the assertion that computers some day will have an intelligence equal to or surpassing that of human beings.

Expert Systems. One branch of AI, called "Expert Systems," has had some commercial success. These systems consist of large, structured pools of data about a specific topic, say, locomotive maintenance, plus a set of rules of thumb acquired by interviewing, in this case, skilled locomotive mechanics and engineers. The result is a system the performance of which rivals and even in some cases exceeds human capabilities. The most famous fictional computer, HAL, of the 1968 Stanley Kubrick movie

2001: A Space Odyssey, was such an expert system, being able to diagnose and suggest repair procedures for the spacecraft on which it was a passenger. HAL's voice recognition and synthesis have also been achieved in reality, but HAL's emotional breakdown suggests a level of mentality that no computer today is even close to achieving. Researchers have neither agreed on how one might program a computer to do that, nor that such a program is even possible. The result is that AI remains a fascinating field for research, but one that always seems to raise more questions than it answers. Its principal contribution may be in telling humans more about who we are, than in providing us with the more prosaic benefits of computer technology.

> *Background material for Artificial Intelligence is found in* ALGORITHM; NEURAL NETWORK; OPERATING SYSTEM; *and* PROGRAM, COMPUTER. *Tools used in the discipline are discussed in* PATTERN *and* OCR RECOGNITION; SERVOMECHANISMS; *and* COMPUTER GRAPHICS. *Advanced issues are discussed in* EXPERT SYSTEMS; SUPERCOMPUTER; *and* VIRTUAL REALITY.

The Mars Rover, part of the Pathfinder mission that successfully landed on and explored Mars in July 1997. Navigating on the rock-strewn plain near the landing site was made possible by AI software. Yet, several times during the mission, the Rover required several hours of computing time and an occasional cybernetic boost from Earth to avoid obstacles.

Further Reading
Bailey, James, *After Thought: The Computer Challenge to Human Intelligence* (1997); Gershenfeld, Neil A., *When Things Start to Think* (1999); Kurzweil, Ray, *The Age of Spiritual Machines: When Computers Exceed Human Intelligence* (1999); Kurzweil, Ray, *The Age of Intelligent Machines* (1992); Paul, Gregory S., *Beyond Humanity: Cyberevolution and Future Minds* (1996).

First see COMPUTER, DIGITAL

ASCII

Next see PROGRAM, COMPUTER

Short for American Standard Code for Information Interchange—a code using binary numbers to represent letters and symbols.

In the development of the computer, one of the knottiest problems was figuring out how to enable each part of the computer system to communicate with the others, especially in the input/output (I/O) section. Early computer scientists had to agree on a code that would work efficiently both for the computer and for its human operators. The best-known such code is ASCII, developed in 1968. The code is based on the permutations of an eight-bit digital number, from 00000001 to 11111111, with seven bits used for information and one bit used for error checking. (*See* NUMBER.)

The original ASCII code started with 00100001, equivalent to 33, which represented the exclamation mark (!). After the basic punctuation, numbers began at 00110000, equivalent to zero (0); capital letters followed, beginning at 01000001 (65), and lowercase letters at 01100001 (97). Several additional punctuation marks were interspersed from decimal 58 to 63, and again from 91 to 96. The first 32 numbers were used for control characters, which translated early keyboard commands into machine language; this section of ASCII was, in effect, a primitive compiler. (*See* COMPILER.)

Almost immediately, objections arose because ASCII did not allow for foreign languages or technical applications. Thus an extended character set was introduced that incorporated the "parity" bit at the beginning of the number, allowing decimal equivalents up to 255. These spaces were filled with foreign-language symbols, mainly accented letters (through 167); with graphics symbols (through 223); and with technical symbols such as Greek letters and mathematical signs not included in the original character set. In the 1990's the Unicode 16-bit character set was developed to support characters of all major written languages.

First see PLANT

Asexual Reproduction

Next see REPRODUCTIVE SYSTEMS

Reproduction in which a single parent produces offspring without the fusion of separate genomes.

Asexual reproduction is widely seen in the plant world. It can foster a population explosion; when weeds run rampant, a form of asexual reproduction called vegetative reproduction is often involved. Most plants, however, can reproduce both sexually and asexually, and sexual union is generally the primary producer of the generations in nature. In producing cultivated plants, however, humans usually turn to vegetative propagation, such as grafting and layering, except when they are trying to develop new species. Because offspring are genetically identical to the parent plant, vegetative propagation ensures predictability and uniformity at the expense of genetic diversity and new adaptations. Asexual reproduction is particularly common among the lower plants such as algae and mosses, but is also seen among flowering plants.

Far left, anemones; left, hydra—both organisms that reproduce asexually

New plants can develop asexually from stems, roots, or leaves. Bulbs and corms, which are specialized, underground stems, commonly grow branch bulbs that grow into new plants once detached from the parent. The brittle, regular stems of numerous species sometimes break off and root, forming new individuals. Arching stems often root themselves when their tips touch the soil and sprout upright shoots, a process known as layering.

Stem cuttings—with rooting stimulated by the application of the plant hormone auxin—are the standard way of commercially propagating many shrubs and greenhouse plants. Similarly, grafting is the way most cultivated fruit trees and roses are propagated. In this process, a stem cutting from one plant, called the scion, is physically attached to another plant, called the stock, that has been stripped of all but its main stem and roots. If the species are well-matched, the graft heals, fusing the two plants.

Other Means. Some forms of asexual reproduction—collectively called apomixis—piggyback on the sexual process. They are not considered strictly vegetative since they involve reproductive, not vegetative, cells. In parthenogenesis, for in-stance, the egg develops into an embryo without being fertilized. Pollination is sometimes needed for the process to occur.

In another form of apomixis, non-egg cells in the ovule develop into embryos that become enclosed in seeds, either alone or alongside an embryo that resulted from a fertilized egg. Again, in some instances, pollination is necessary for the asexually formed embryo to mature. Apomixis is suspected of being widespread in tropical rainforests; many tropical trees with one-seeded fruit appear to produce multiple seedlings.

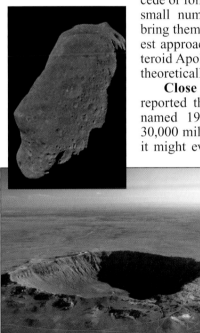

Above: top, Gaspara, an asteroid visited by space probe Galileo in 1993. Like most asteroids, Gaspara is irregularly shaped. Bottom, the Barrington Meteor Crater in Arizona, remnants of an impact of a relatively small meteor (some 30 yards across).

First see TEMPERATURE

Asteroids and Meteors

Next see CRYOGENICS

Smaller members of the solar system, some of which come close to Earth and a few of which strike Earth.

Many asteroids have diameters of a mile or less, but the largest known asteroid is Ceres, whose diameter is more than 600 miles. Astronomers estimate that there are perhaps 10 asteroids with diameters of greater than 200 miles and about 120 with diameters of a mile or more.

Most of the asteroids have orbits that keep them circling the sun. There is an "asteroid belt" about 2.2 to 2.5 astronomical units from the sun (an astronomical unit is the distance from Earth to the sun), between the orbits of Mars and Jupiter. A smaller group of asteroids—the Hilda group—orbit at about 4 astronomical units, a position that is in dynamical resonance with the orbit of Jupiter. Yet another group, the Trajan asteroids, are in the same orbit as Jupiter but precede or follow that planet by about 60 degrees. A small number of asteroids have orbits which bring them inside the orbit of Earth at their closest approach to the sun; one of them is the asteroid Apollo. An asteroid in such an orbit could theoretically impact with the Earth.

Close Encounter. In 1998, astronomers reported that they had discovered an asteroid, named 1997 XF11, that would pass within 30,000 miles of Earth in the year 2028, and that it might even collide with the earth. That estimate was revised to 600,000 miles after more study.

The most recent impact of a large asteroid, which occurred in Siberia in 1908, flattened trees over nearly 900 square miles and ignited forest fires, doing damage equivalent to that of a 15-megaton hydrogen bomb. That asteroid was estimated to be less than 100 yards across.

Asteroid Composition. Information about the composition of asteroids can be obtained by measuring their albedo—reflectivity—and the spectral composition of the light they reflect. These measurements show that the asteroid belt is highly structured, with asteroids of different types orbiting in specific bands. The composition of the asteroids indicates that they came into existence early in the formation of the solar system and have remained at or near their current locations since then. The types of asteroids include those designated C and D, which resemble carbonaceous chondrites (a type of meteorite), and S, which are stony asteroids.

Meteorites may derive from the asteroids. In general, their composition is the same as that of Earth and the other three innermost, or "terrestrial" planets. Officially, a meteorite is defined as an extraterrestrial object that strikes the earth. A meteor is the fireball that an incoming object makes before it strikes the earth. Such an object in space is called a meteoroid. If it is smaller than a grain of sand, it is called a micrometeorite. Meteorites are classified as iron, stony, and stony-iron. Iron meteorites contain 85 to 95 percent iron, stony-iron meteorites are 50 percent iron and 50 percent silicates. The most common kind of stony meteorites, the chondrites, consist of an aggregate of silicate particles. Carbonaceous chondrites are those that are richest in carbon compounds.

Planetary Bombardment. Evidence first seen on the moon and later verified by studies of Mars, Venus, and Mercury shows that all the terrestrial planets were bombarded by both asteroids and meteorites about four billion years ago. The bombardment diminished steadily, apparently because the debris created with the formation of planets of the solar system was being swept away. Some meteorites have survived the fireball phase of their entry into the earth's atmosphere, allowing study of their composition. The largest is the Hoba West meteorite, which was found in South Africa and has a mass of 45 to 60 tons. Four nickel-iron meteorites were discovered in Greenland early this century. The largest, called Ahnighito (the tent), weighs over 33 tons.

Recent Developments. Relatively recent events show that the impact of a meteorite can cause great damage. In 1947, for example, a brilliant fireball across the sky of Siberia preceded the impact of a meteorite that gouged out 100 craters, some of them 90 feet across, in an area of two square miles. More than 20 tons of iron meteorite fragments were later found.

In the United States, the largest crater caused by a meteorite impact is the Barringer Crater, near Winslow, Arizona. It is 4,265 feet across and 590 feet deep, with a rim that rises nearly 150 feet above ground level. More than 25 tons of iron meteorite fragments have been found, some of them more than four miles from the crater. The meteorite is believed to have struck Earth 120,000 years ago.

The place of asteroids in the evolution of solar systems is discussed in Solar Systems. *See also* Comet *and* Oort Cloud. *The connection between asteroid impact and mass extinctions is found in* Dinosaurs *and in* Extinction. *See also* Planets *and* Interstellar Medium.

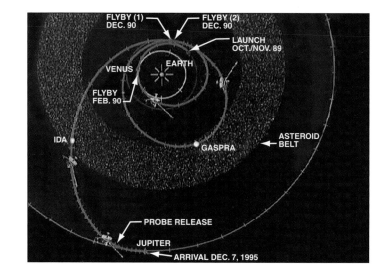

Above, the path of the Galileo space probe as it investigated the asteroid belt and several asteroids on its way to Jupiter.

Artist interpretation of the impact with Earth of the asteroid that created the Chicxulub crater in Mexico 65 million years ago. The event may have been responsible for the sudden demise of the dinosaurs.

Further Reading

Desonie, Dana, *Cosmic Collisions* (1996); Huggett, Richard, *Catastrophism: Asteroids, Comets and Other Dynamic Events in Earth History* (1998); Simon, Seymour, *Comets, Meteors, and Asteroids* (1994); Steel, Duncan, *Rogue Asteroids and Doomsday Comets: The Search for the Million Megaton Menace That Threatens Life on Earth* (1997).

First see Weather

Atmosphere

Next see Climatology

A thin layer of gas surrounding the solid body of the Earth.

The atmosphere we have today is not the one that existed when Earth was born. Earth's first atmosphere was filled with gases that were vented by volcanoes and other geological activities, but over the millennia it has been modified as light gases like helium and hydrogen were lost to space and living things produced oxygen. Today, Earth's atmosphere is approximately 80 percent nitrogen and 20 percent oxygen, with traces of carbon dioxide, water vapor, and other gases.

Air Pressure. Unlike water, air is highly compressible. This means that air near the surface, which has to support the column of air above it, has a much higher density than air farther up. If you are at sea level as you read this, the air in a column above one square inch of your skin weighs about 14.7 pounds. Your body must support this weight, although you are so used to it that you do not normally feel it. Because the weight of the column of air above a particular altitude pushes down on the air below it, most of the air in the atmosphere is quite close to the ground. Fifty percent of the air is found below an altitude of 3.4 miles (about 18,000 feet), and 99 percent lies below an altitude of 20 miles (about 100,000 feet).

The force exerted by the column of air above a point is normally measured in terms of the air pressure (pressure is defined to be the force exerted on a given surface divided by the area of the surface). At sea level, the pressure of air pushing down on mercury in one side of a U-shaped tube is enough to support the weight of a column of mercury 30 inches high on the other side. When a weather forecaster says that a "high" or a "low" is coming, he or she is referring to the pressure of the air. Similarly, the phrase "the mercury is rising (or falling)" refers to the height of a column of mercury that can be supported by the air in the new weather system.

Troposphere. The layer of air near the surface of Earth is called the troposphere (the name comes from the Greek word that means "change" or "turn"). Air in this layer is constantly churning around, rising and falling as it is heated and cools. It is in the troposphere that weather is generated. Because the bottom of the troposphere is constantly being warmed by contact with water and land, the temperature of the air falls as the altitude increases (this is why it is colder on mountaintops than in the neighboring lowlands). The troposphere extends between 6 and 10 miles (about 30,000–50,000 feet) up into the atmosphere.

Upper Atmosphere. Above the troposphere, and extending up to a height of about 30 miles (150,000 feet) is a region of thin air called the stratosphere. (The word comes from the Latin for "spread out"). One section of the stratosphere contains the ozone layer, which contains a relatively high concentration of ozone molecules. These molecules absorb ultraviolet radiation from the sun and hence play an important role in making the surface of the planet safe for living things. Because part of the sun's energy is absorbed high in the stratosphere, and because less and less survives to be absorbed in the stratosphere's lower regions, the temperature of the air actually rises as we go up in this region. Above the stratosphere are regions of progressively thinner air that eventually shade off into the vacuum of outer space.

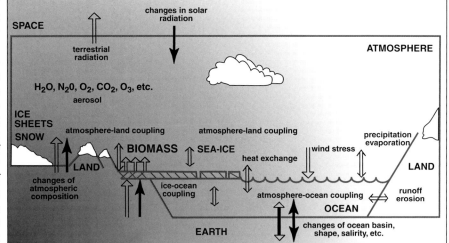

The interaction between land, ocean, and atmosphere involves the transport of heat, water, and land.

The composition of the atmosphere was not always oxygen rich. Air trapped in ice reveals an atmosphere composed preponderantly of carbon dioxide, which was conducive to the development of plant life.

into ice crystals, or through any of these processes in reverse. We measure the amount of water in the air by the quantity known as relative humidity, which is defined as the amount of water present in a sample divided by the amount of water that air at that temperature and pressure can hold. Air at high relative humidity is usually perceived as being uncomfortable, since perspiration cannot easily evaporate.

Each time water goes through a phase change, it either adds or extracts energy in the form of heat from its surroundings. The most common phase change in the atmosphere occurs when warm, moist air from the surface rises to higher altitude. In this case, the temperature drops and relative humidity of the air increases, even though no new water is added. When the relative humidity reaches 100 percent, the water starts to condense, in the form of water droplets, and a cloud begins to form.

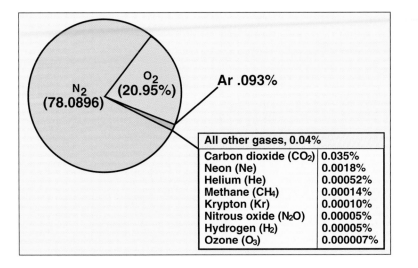

Atmospheric Water Vapor. Although water vapor represents a relatively small portion of the material in the atmosphere, it plays a very important role in the atmosphere's behavior. Water enters the atmosphere by evaporation, and while in the atmosphere it can undergo phase changes by condensing into water droplets, precipitating

Right, structure of the atmosphere.

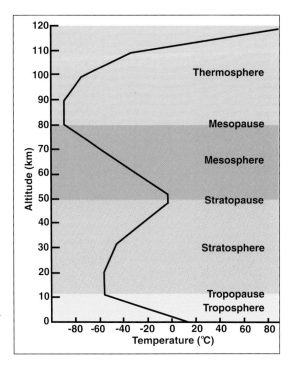

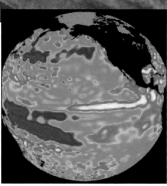

Above, a satellite photograph of the Indian subcontinent showing the lowlands of the Ganges valley on the left and the Tibetan plateau on the right. The darker area on the left is due almost entirely to air pollution: looking through just a few more miles of air accounts for the dramatic change in the color coming through from below. At right, a thermal image of the Earth shows the El Niño currents as they cut across the Pacific. The location and strength of the current is a major determinant of North American weather.

The type of cloud that results depends on the details of how the warm air rises. Puffy white cumulus clouds form as the result of the convection of small pockets of warm air. If large cumulus clouds rise to the top of the troposphere, they can expand and form thunderheads, or cumulo-nimbus clouds, which can produce severe storms. If air is lifted up over a large area (by an advancing weather front, for example), the result is a solid deck of stratus clouds—the sort of thing you see on gray, rainy days. Finally, air lifted very high by an approaching front will form the wispy filaments of cirrus clouds. Formed high in the troposphere, these clouds are usually made from ice crystals.

Further Reading
Firor, John, *The Changing Atmosphere: A Global Challenge* (1992); Holper, Paul, *Atmosphere: Weather, Climate, and Pollution* (1993); McCuen, Gary E., *Our Endangered Atmosphere: Global Warming and the Ozone Layer* (1993); Trefil, James, *Meditations at Sunset* (1987).

Weather phenomena in the atmosphere are discussed in WEATHER; WINDS AND CLOUDS; *and* CLIMATOLOGY. *Elements of the atmosphere are covered in* JET STREAM *and* OZONE LAYER. *Atmospheric phenomena are described in* AURORAS; HURRICANE AND TORNADO; *and* LIGHTNING AND THUNDER. *Issues regarding degradation of the atmosphere are discussed in* ACID RAIN; AIR POLLUTION; *and* GLOBAL WARMING. *See also* PLANETARY ATMOSPHERE.

First see PERIODIC TABLE

Atom

Next see NUCLEUS, ATOMIC

The smallest unit of matter that still has a chemical identity.

For a long time, the atom was also thought to be the smallest indivisible unit into which matter could be divided. but now we know that it consists of a small, heavy, positively charged nucleus around which light, negatively charged electrons circle in an orbit.

In 1911, Ernest Rutherford, a New Zealand physicist working in Manchester, performed an experiment that determined the structure of the atom. He directed a beam of radiation (think of it as a stream of subatomic bullets) at a thin gold foil. He found that, while 999 out of a thousand of his projectiles went through the foil or were scattered only slightly, one out of a thousand came bouncing back. He later explained that it was like shooting a pistol into a cloud of mist and having the bullet rebound. The only way to explain Rutherford's experiment was to assume that most of the mass of the atom was concentrated in a very small, dense body at the center. This body is called the nucleus.

Rutherford's Atom. The picture of the atom that resulted from Rutherford's work, then, had a superficial resemblance to the solar system. The positively charged nucleus sat at the center, and the negatively charged electrons moved around it in orbit, just as planets orbit the sun. In succeeding years, it was discovered that the primary constituents of the nucleus were particles called protons (which have a positive charge) and neutrons (which have no charge). In order for the atom to be electrically neutral, there have to be as many electrons in orbit as there are protons in the nucleus.

The atom is almost entirely empty space. If the nucleus of a carbon atom were the size of a bowling ball, then the six electrons around it would be equivalent to six grains of sand scattered over the county in which you reside. This fact has many consequences for the kind of combinations that can be formed between atoms. When two atoms come near each other, it is their outermost electrons that "see" each other first, and which therefore initiate chemical reactions. In the jargon of the chemist, the outermost electrons are called "valence electrons," and it is they that determine the chemical reactions in which the atom will participate.

One of the great triumphs of quantum mechanics in the early part of the 20th century was to come to an understanding about why different atoms have the chemical properties they do. In 1869, Russian scientist Dimitri Mendeleev noticed that if the chemical elements are

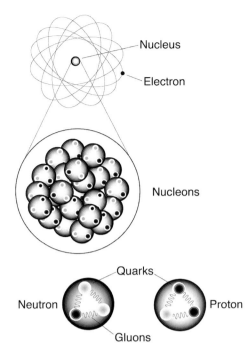

The story of physics in the twentieth century is the investigation of smaller and smaller structures of the atom and the basic constituents of matter.

arranged so that they read from left to right in order of increasing mass, then read down, the columns of the table group together substances with similar chemical properties. In Mendeleev's table, the first row has only two elements in it—hydrogen and helium. The next row has eight, beginning with lithium and going through to neon. The next row also has eight elements, starting with sodium argon, and subsequent rows have 18 and 32 elements in them. When Mendeleev first proposed this so-called Periodic Table of the Elements, there were several holes in it—places where elements should have fit, but for which no elements were known. It was in the course of searching for these missing elements that chemists in the nineteenth century came to discover the elements germanium and scandium. The great mystery of the Periodic Table, of course, was why atoms should arrange themselves in this particular way, and why the rows should have the numbers that they do.

Quantum Physics. It was not until the structure of the atom was discovered that one could begin to answer this question. The laws of quantum mechanics require that particles like electrons have a peculiar property: no two of them can occupy the same space. Like cars in a parking lot, once a particular parking space is occupied, no other car can use it. According to quantum mechanics, the innermost orbit of an atom has two "spaces" into which electrons can be put. Thus, the first two atoms in the periodic table (those that have one and two electrons) will fill up all the available spaces. This is why only

hydrogen and helium appear in the first row. The next atom, lithium, has three electrons in orbit, and, since two electrons fill up the innermost electron shell, the third electron must go into the next higher orbit. Thus, lithium will have two electrons in what is called a "closed shell" and one electron in the next orbit up.

The fact that lithium and hydrogen both have one valence electron means that they will combine with other atoms in similar ways. This is an example of why elements in the same column of the Periodic Table have similar chemical properties. The theory of quantum mechanics predicts that the next few rows in the table will have eight available spaces, which explains why there are eight elements in the next few rows. Thus, we can now say that quantum mechanics tells us how many valence electrons an element will have, and that the vast emptiness of the atom tells us that it is the valence electrons which will determine the chemical properties of the atom.

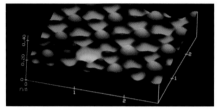

Finally, we should note that while atoms were a theoretical construct in the nineteenth century, today we routinely manipulate them in many different ways. It is even possible to trap an individual atom in magnetic and electrical fields and study its behavior over weeks and even months. Thus, for us, atoms are real, tangible things that can be handled and used.

The structure of the atom is explored in ATOMIC SHELL MODEL; NUCLEUS, ATOMIC; *and in* QUANTUM MECHANICS. *The constituents of the atom are described in* BARYON; BOSON; ELECTRON; LEPTON; NEUTRON; *and* PROTON. *Groupings of atoms are discussed in* CLUSTER, ATOM; *and* CHEMICAL REACTION. *The forces at work in the atom are covered in* ELECTROMAGNETIC FORCE *and in* NUCLEAR FORCES.

First see ATOM

Atoms can actually be observed with the help of a scanning tunneling microscope (STM). The (false-color) image above shows a single-atom defect in an iodine absorbate lattice on a platinum base.

Further Reading
Feinberg, Gerald, *What Is the World Made Of?* (1996); Pullman, Bernard, *The Atom in the History of Human Thought* (1998); Trefil, James, *From Atoms to Quarks: An Introduction to the Strange World of Particle Physics* (1994); Von Baeyer, Hans Christian, *Taming the Atom; The Emergence of the Visible Microworld* (1995).

Atomic Shell Model

Next see NUCLEUS, ATOMIC

A model of the atomic nucleus according to which the nucleus consists of a number of shells of particles, just as the electrons circling the nucleus are viewed as arranged in shells.

The atomic shell model of the nucleus assumes that each nucleon—proton or neutron—in a nucleus moves in a field that represents the average effect of its interactions with all the other nucleons. As a result of this assumption, we can consider that the nucleons are influenced only by a common "nuclear potential" that is characteristic of the nucleus as a whole and ignore specific interactions of one nucleon with another. We can say that there is a series of independent "particle states," the character of which is specified by nucleon energy and spin, and that each of these states can be occupied by each of the nucleons in accordance with the rules of quantum mechanics. (*See* QUANTUM MECHANICS.)

The result is an energy spectrum, in which there are nucleon groups, or shells, that have energy levels that are close together. Each group is separated from the other groups by large energy gaps. The model arranges nucleons in shells similar to the shells in which the electrons are arranged. Each nucleon is assigned an orbital l, a spin s, a total angular momentum j, and a magnetic quantum number. These four quantum numbers are used to describe the angular momentum of individual nucleons, in the same way that quantum numbers are used to describe the placing of electrons in the atom. According to the Pauli exclusion principle, only $2j + 1$ identical nucleons can occupy a level with total angular momentum.

An alternative picture of the nucleus, the liquid-drop model, pictures the nucleons in a constant state of motion, similar to the motion of the molecules of a liquid. The liquid-drop model gives a more vivid theoretical description of nuclear fission, but it has largely been replaced by the shell model. (*See* FISSION, NUCLEAR.)

First see DNA

Attenuation

Next see EXONS AND INTRONS

A regulatory mechanism for gene expression.

A structural gene is a sequence of DNA that begins with a promoter region, ends with a terminator region, and contains information for constructing a particular protein. A gene is "turned on" or expressed when it is being transcribed, meaning a molecule of RNA is formed to carry the information to the site where the protein will be assembled. This process is controlled by a series of regulator genes, which make up an operon. Transcription either occurs fully, or does not occur at all if the promoter region is blocked by an inhibitor. However, some prokaryote cells contain operons that allow only part of the gene sequence to be transcribed. This regulatory process is called attenuation.

The attenuator is a small terminator region located near the beginning of the gene sequence. Normally, transcription automatically stops when the terminator at the end of a gene sequence is reached. Transcription should therefore also stop much earlier, at the attenuator. However, some external factor causes the DNA molecule to change shape, allowing transcription to occur past this terminator region and the gene to be fully expressed. If this conformational change does not occur, transcription stops at

Further Reading
Asimov, Isaac, *Atom: Journey Across the Subatomic Cosmos* (1992); Born, Max, *Atomic Physics* (1998); Cox, P.A., *Introduction to Quantum Theory and Atomic Structure* (1996); Pais, A., *Inward Bound: Of Matter and Forces in the Physical World* (1988); Perrin, J., *Atoms* (1990).

Below, the Aurora Borealis over the Northern Hemisphere, the result of electrons originating in the sun being focused by the Earth's magnetic field and exciting oxygen and nitrogen in the atmosphere.

the attenuator, and the gene is only partially expressed. This affects the amount of protein product that will be formed.

Attenuation was discovered in the tryptophan operon, whose structural genes code for enzymes that convert chorismic acid to tryptophan. Whether or not transcription occurs past the attenuator depends on the amount of tryptophan present in the cell. (*See* DNA.)

First see MAGNETIC FIELD OF THE EARTH

Auroras

Next see SOLAR WIND

Luminosities of the night sky that occur chiefly in the regions near the poles.

Auroras are caused primarily by charged particles that approach the Earth from space at high speed and are deflected by the Earth's magnetic field into a ring. Spectroscopic studies show that the light of an aurora is emitted mostly by atoms and molecules of oxygen and nitrogen, with some emissions by hydrogen atoms. The Aurora Borealis, which occurs near the North Pole, is seen more frequently than the Aurora Australis, which occurs in southern polar regions.

The Aurora Borealis appears about 250 times a year in a zone that extends from Alaska through Greenland, Iceland, Norway, and Siberia, and then back to Alaska. Auroras occur less frequently south of this northern zone, but are brighter when they do occur. Perhaps once every ten years, the Aurora Borealis can be seen as far south as Mexico and southern Europe. The regions near the South Pole where auroras occur have not been mapped as well as those in the north. There is some evidence that displays of auroras can occur simultaneously in the northern and southern zones. (*See* SOLAR WIND.)

Magnitude. The brightness of individual parts of an aurora can range from very faint to very bright—so bright that the illumination of the ground in the region nearly equals what is achieved by the full moon. The shapes and forms of auroras include a vague, diffuse glow; an arc that extends across the sky; bands, with or without folds; patches or clouds whose brightness pulsates; and waves that sweep toward the earth, each lasting a fraction of a second. When an aurora is faint, it is nearly colorless. As it brightens, the first color to become evident usually is yellow-green. As brightness increases, red appears in rays, bands, and arcs. The brightest bands of an aurora may have a constantly changing pattern of blue, red, and green rays. Yellow and violet can sometimes be seen. Red light can be emitted by oxygen atoms and molecules of nitrogen, green light by oxygen, and blue light by single atoms of nitrogen.

The height of auroras above the earth has been measured in North America, Norway, and New Zealand. Most of the time, the lower border of an aurora is about 60 to 80 miles above the Earth's surface, with red arcs at 100 to 120 miles in space. Isolated rays may be even higher, extending up to 600 miles in space. Auroras occur most frequently when there is a large and active group of sunspots near the central meridian of the disk of the sun, particularly if a solar flare is emitted. On the Earth itself, magnetic storms, erratic variations of the planet's magnetic field, may occur at the same time. An aurora that is visible in the zone nearest the equator is always accompanied by an increase in the size of the simultaneous magnetic storm.

See MAGNETIC FIELD OF THE EARTH *for further information on the Earth's magnetic field. Also see* MAGNETISM *and* ELECTROMAGNETIC FORCE *for discussion of magnetic force. Relevant material is also found in* ATMOSPHERE; CHARGE AND CURRENT; ELECTRON; *and* SOLAR WIND.

Above, the Aurora Australis south of Australia, as seen from space. The glow of the moon is visible on the clouds, and the band of light following Earth's curvature is the luminescence of the atmosphere itself (called airglow).

Further Reading
Bone, N., *The Aurora* (1992); Davis, N., *Aurora Watcher's Handbook* (1992); Migdail, E., *Aurora: The Mysterious Northern Lights* (1995).

First see EVOLUTION

Australopithecus

Next see PRIMATE

The first recognizable hominids.

Members of the primate family that includes humans and human fossil ancestors appeared in Africa around 4 million years ago. In the 1970s, an archeological team in East Africa, headed by Mary Leakey, found fossilized footprints of hominids, which were dated at 3 to 3.75 million years old. Bones belonging to *Australopithecus*, believed to be the oldest known hominid, were discovered in the Great Rift Valley in eastern Africa in 1977. The most well-known *Australopithecus* fossil, discovered by Donald Johanson, is "Lucy," almost half of a complete female skeleton, thought to be between 3 and 4 million years old.

Lucy belonged to the species *Australopithecus afarensis* and had characteristics of both apes and humans. Lucy was only about a meter tall. Her skull and face were apelike, but her skeleton shows human characteristics and evidence that she walked upright on two legs. Her skull was much larger than that of an ape, indicating a larger brain, but there is no evidence of tool use. The Lucy fossil does prove, however, that brain size of early humans increased after the development of the ability to stand upright.

Other Discoveries. Different forms of *australopithecines*, other than *Australopithecus afarensis*, have been found in East and South Africa and dated to different times. *Australopithecus africanus* lived in southern Africa between 2.5 and 3 million years ago. *Australopithecus africanus* was about five feet tall and had a rounded skull and larger brain capacity than *Australopithecus afarensis*. *Australopithecus africanus* used simple stone tools and may have had meat as part of its diet.

Australopithecus robustus appeared even later, from 1.4 to 2.2 million years ago. *Australopithecus robustus* was larger than *Australopithecus africanus*. There are questions about descent relationships between the two groups as well as to modern humans. Some scientists believe *Australopithecus robustus* evolved from *Australopithecus africanus* in a separate line of descent from humans; others think humans did not evolve from any of the Australopithecines.

Skeletal Adaptations. All species of *Australopithecus* walked upright, judging from the structure of their hip and leg bones. They had relatively long arms, which may have been an adaptation to a tree-dwelling life, as the climate in Africa 4 million years ago was warm and favored abundant woodlands. Compared with prehominid fossils, Australopithecines have smaller canines, but the other teeth are still much

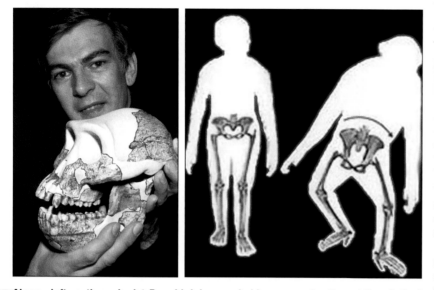

Above, left, anthropologist Donald Johanson holds a reconstruction of the skull of "Lucy," a hominid that shows indications of being an ancestor of modern humans. Discovered in 1974 in Hadar, Ethiopia, Lucy (the name taken from the title of a Beatles' song) lived some 3 to 3.5 million years ago. Lucy was probably one of several thousand of her species who roamed eastern Africa, but studies of modern mitochondrial DNA indicate the progeny of only one specimen survives to the present day. Above right, the skeleton of Lucy, at left, indicates she walked upright as a result of a genetic "redesign" of her hip (compared to chimps, at right).

larger and thicker than those of modern humans.

Adaptations and Migrations. Adaptive radiation (divergent evolution) of *Australopithecus* occurred between 2 and 2.5 million years ago. It is believed that the climate changed, becoming relatively cooler and drier, and this resulted in the transformation of the habitat from forest to open plains.

It is around this time that a new genus of hominid, *Homo*, appeared, which seemed to be better suited to the new conditions. *Australopithecus* did not vanish immediately, however. In eastern Africa, a large robust group of *Australopithecus boisei* lived at the same time as *Homo habilis*. In southern Africa, *Australopithecus robustus* and *Australopithecus africanus* possibly coexisted with *Homo habilis* and competed for resources.

Rival Primates. *Ramapithecus*, which was not a hominid, also originated in Africa, approximately 17 million years ago. *Ramapithecus* may be the common ancestor of both apes and humans, though recent DNA analysis indicates it departed from the evolutionary line that lead to modern humans.

Further Reading

Edey, Maitland, A., *Blueprints: Solving the Mystery of Evolution* (1990); Johanson, Donald C., *Lucy: The Beginnings of Humankind* (1990); Johanson, Donald, *From Lucy to Language* (1996); Lewin, Roger, *Bones of Contention: Controversies in the Search for Human Origins* (1997); Stringer, Christopher, *African Exodus: The Origins of Modern Humanity* (1997).

Background information is included in PRIMATES *and* HOMO SAPIENS. *Information on mitochondrial DNA is found in* MITOCHONDRIA *and* EXTRANUCLEAR INHERITANCE. *The mechanisms involved in evolution are described in* ADAPTATION; COEVOLUTION; EVOLUTION; NATURAL SELECTION; *and* SPECIATION.

First see BRAIN

Autism

Next see MENTAL DISORDERS

A condition in which children do not form normal relationships with others.

Autism occurs in about three of every 10,000 children and is nearly three more times more common in boys than in girls. The condition usually becomes evident in the first year of life. The precise cause is unknown, but it is believed to be a subtle form of brain damage. A quarter of autistic children have signs of a neurological disorder, and a third of them can develop epileptic seizures in their adolescent years.

Signs. The first sign of autism in the early months of life can be a failure to respond to parents, with resistance to being cuddled that can take the form of violent screaming when touched. As the child grows older, he or she does not form the usual relationships with parents or other children, generally playing alone and avoiding eye contact with people.

One outstanding feature of autism is an extreme resistance to change of any kind, with tantrums resulting from any attempt to change daily routines. An autistic child often develops an attachment to one idea or topic, causing difficulty in trying to teach new subjects. Autistic children often have a delay in speaking, with a lack of ability to understand speech or to copy speech or gestures. When an autistic child does speak, his or her speech is often immature and robot-like. There can be other abnormalities, such as sudden screaming fits and hyperactivity. There is no effective treatment, but family counseling and behavior therapy can help.

First see IMMUNE RESPONSE

Autoimmunity

Next see LUPUS

A condition in which the immune system regards the body's own tissue as foreign and attacks it.

Autoimmune diseases include rheumatoid arthritis, multiple sclerosis, and myasthenia gravis. Autoimmunity is due to an interlocking set of genetic, molecular, cellular, and environmental factors. Part of the explanation of the condition lies in the development of T cells—immune system cells that mature in the thymus.

Specifically, T cells learn to recognize two kinds of antigens. Type 1 antigens are carried by almost all cells, while type 2 antigens are carried by immune system cells, such as macrophages. T cells are trained to leave the body's type 1 antigens alone and to mobilize for attack when they spot a cell with a foreign type 1 antigen—one not made by the body's own cells—or the combination of a type 2 antigen and a foreign antigen on the surface of a macrophage or a similar cell.

One cause of autoimmune disease is believed to be the failure of some T cells to be trained properly. They come out of the thymus with a tendency to recognize the body's own type 1 antigens as foreign. It is believed that in most cases, it takes some kind of stimulus, such as infection by a virus, to make such a T cell attack the body's own tissue.

Genetic Factor. The genetics of the immune system is also a factor in autoimmunity. It has been found that some cells carry a kind of antigen that is made in the body but is recognized as foreign. It is not known why this happens, but when a cell that has such a foreign-seeming antigen picks up a truly foreign antigen, from a virus or bacterium, an attack by T cells is triggered.

There have been some promising developments in the study of autoimmunity and related diseases in recent years. For example, French researchers have reported that they were able to prevent, or at least delay, the development of Type 1 diabetes, which is classified as an autoimmune condition, by giving children the drug cyclosporine when the first symptoms appeared. Cyclosporine is a drug that is used to prevent rejection of transplanted tissues. It acts by neutralizing T cells. In the case of the children, it appeared to prevent T cells from attacking the body's insulin-producing cells, thus preventing the development of diabetes.

Left-handedness. Another line of research has linked autoimmunity to left-handedness. In the 1980s, it was found that learning disabilities such as dyslexia occur much more frequently in left-handed children than in right-handed children. It was also found that boys suffer learning disabilities more often than girls, and that anyone with a learning disability is more likely to have an immune disorder.

One explanation for these relationships starts with the fact that language function is controlled by the left side of the human brain. Should that hemisphere be damaged, not only would language disabilities such as dyslexia occur, but predominance would also be switched to the right hemisphere of the brain. If the autoimmune condition also is related to the body's levels of testosterone, the male sex hormone, boys would be more likely to be affected than girls. These theories have been tested in studies with mice who are bred to have autoimmune diseases, and confirmation has been obtained. However, the full dimension of autoimmune dysfunction and the diseases it can cause are still being explored.

Roster of Autoimmune Diseases. The list of autoimmune diseases once included only con-

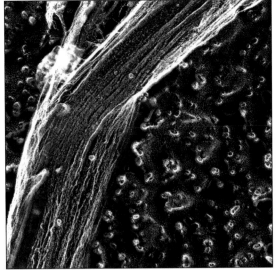

One possible cause for the demyelinization of nerve cells, left, that accompanies dystrophic diseases is that the body's immune system turns on itself, interpreting the nerve coatings that make the transmission of nerve impulses possible as foreign tissue.

ditions such as myasthenia gravis, in which some essential proteins of the muscle system are destroyed, and multiple sclerosis, in which the fatty sheath around the nerves is the target of the T-cell attack. The list has now been extended to include rheumatoid arthritis, which affects at least one of every 100 Americans, and Type 1 diabetes, in which the body fails to manufacture insulin. There may also be an autoimmune factor in Type 2 diabetes, in which the body cannot make proper use of insulin, but it is not a predominant factor in the condition.

The background for understanding autoimmunity is discussed in IMMUNE RESPONSE; GENETICS; *and* NERVOUS SYSTEM. *Direct applications of the science of autoimmunity are contained in* BLOOD TRANSFUSION *and* ORGAN TRANSPLANTATION. *Diseases where autoimmunity may play a role include* CYSTIC FIBROSIS; DIABETES; LUPUS; *and* MULTIPLE SCLEROSIS.

First see COMPUTER-AIDED DESIGN

Automotive Design

Next see HIGHWAY ENGINEERING

Automotive design involves all the components of a passenger car, a bus, or a truck. This design starts with the steel frame of an automobile, on which all the other elements of the car are assembled. An automobile frame is made of channel, I-beam, or tubular parts, mainly located horizontally, with beams between them providing rigidity.

The other elements of an automobile are:

—running gear, consisting of wheels, axles, brakes, a steering device, and suspension;

—propulsion, consisting of the engine and clutch, speed change gears, and drive shaft (almost all automobiles are propelled by internal combustion engines, either the Otto cycle type or a diesel);

—the body, which includes doors, glazing, interior fittings, and upholstery; and

—accessories and auxiliaries, such as the fuel tank, radiator, and defroster.

Frame Design. The design of the frame is of crucial importance, since all the other elements of an automobile depend on the frame. In the design process, the frame is subjected to a variety of stress tests—tensile, compressive, and torsional, or twist tests—that stimulate the stresses that the automobile can experience when it is driven on the uneven surfaces of the worst roads on which it is expected to be used. One major object of the design process is to keep the frame as light as possible, to decrease gasoline consumption and improve performance.

The side members of an automobile are usually steel channels whose depth varies according to the stresses that they will experience. In general, they are deepest at their midpoint and taper toward the front and rear. The side members are connected by I-beams that are perpendicular to them, but in some cases have an X shape to provide maximum rigidity. These members are welded and riveted together. Some buses use a so-called chassis-less construction, in which the trusses are incorporated into the body. Most modern automobiles use monocoque, or unitbody, construction, in which frame and body are designed as a single welded unit.

Running Gear. Almost all automobiles have four wheels. The distance between the front and back wheels is called the wheelbase, and the overall length of an automobile, bumper-to-bumper, may be as much as a third longer than the wheelbase. Inflatable tires are the standard, some of them with internal tubes to hold the air, some of them tubeless.

Brakes consist of shoes that expand internally to make contact with drums that are fixed rigidly to the wheels or pads that grip smooth discs attached to the wheels. The brakes can be activated by cables or by a hydraulic system that uses oil pressure acting on a piston whose movement is transferred to the cams of the brake shoes.

Steering. The most widely used types of steering gears are the screw-and-nut, worm-and-roller, and cam-and-lever. In each case, the first element in the name (screw, worm, or cam) is a part of the steering shaft that rotates when the driver moves the steering wheel, and the second element is the part that connects with the arm or level that positions the wheels. Power steering uses hydraulic pressure to reduce the effort needed to turn the automobile's wheels.

Automotive design in the future will have to devote significant attention to creating systems that are kinder to the environment, such as automobiles less reliant on fossil fuel.

Above, the "heads-up" cockpit of a modern fighter jet. Avionics' challenge is to maximize the efficiency of the system's most complex and irreplacable element: the pilot.

First see AIRCARFT

Avionics

Next see CYBERNETICS

The study and development of electronic devices and circuits to be used either on aircraft or on spacecraft.

The first airplanes required little in the way of instrumentation, since they flew at low speeds close to the ground. The first instruments to be used on aircraft displayed data on engine performance, such as oil pressure, the rate of fuel flow, and the revolutions per minute of the engine. New instruments had to be devised during and after World War I, as aircraft flew faster and higher. The simple magnetic compass was replaced by a more accurate instrument, the earth-inductor compass, which was based on measurements of changes in the Earth's magnetic field. Other instruments that were introduced at the time were the rate-of-turn indicator, the rate-of-climb indicator, the airspeed indicator, and the altimeter, which gave information about the height of the aircraft above the ground. These were followed by the artificial horizon, which used gyroscopes to measure the roll and pitch of the aircraft. The artificial horizon made night flights much easier, since the pilot no longer had to depend on sightings of the ground.

In the 1920s and 1930s, gyroscope-based instruments improved steadily. Major advances came during World War II, when the navigators in large bombers were positioned far from the cockpit. Devices to transmit instrument readings to the navigator were developed, and electrical indicators became the rule. Refinements continued steadily after the war, as the era of routine transcontinental flights opened.

Solid State. As in other areas of electronics, aircraft instrumentation moved from tube devices to solid-state device systems using transistors, and then to smaller and more accurate integrated circuits. The result was the installation of automatic control, navigation, and guidance systems that almost enable an aircraft to fly itself.

Computers have also been applied to the safety considerations of today's fast-moving aircraft. In supersonic flight, for example, computers integrate information from a wide range of instruments, giving the pilot data that is more immediate and easier to interpret.

See AIRCRAFT, SUBSONIC AND SUPERSONIC *for more on airplane systems. Additional relevant material is found in* COMPUTER GRAPHICS; ELECTRIC CIRCUITS; *and* VIRTUAL REALITY. *See also* ROBOTICS *and* SERVOMECHANISM *for other details.*

First see BLOOD

B-lymphocytes

Next see IMMUNE RESPONSE

One of two major classes of the white blood cells that are the principal actors in the body's immune defense system.

The role of B-lymphocytes in the body is to protect it against harmful invaders. These invaders, which include bacteria and viruses, activate the immune system because they contain foreign molecules called antigens. These antigens can activate the immune system to produce either T-lymphocytes or B-lymphocytes. When the B-lymphocytes are activated, they produce plasma cells, which in turn produce protective proteins called antibodies, which react on the antigens with specific agents.

The reaction of the B-lymphocyte antibodies with foreign antigens takes place in the bloodstream. This reaction either neutralizes foreign antigens by preventing them from entering the healthy cells of the body or starts the process of their destruction by making them susceptible to attack by macrophages—protective cells, the function of which is to engulf foreign invaders.

The immunity provided by the cells in the blood plasma is called humoral, a term that refers to their location in the body's fluids. The protection provided by T cells is called cellular, because it relies on activated cells. The antibodies that are produced by B-lymphocytes are made of a special kind of protein, called immunoglobulins. There are five kinds of immunoglobulins, classified by letter: immunoglobulin A (IgA), IgD, IgE, IgG, and IgM. The immunoglobulin that is of interest to allergy specialists is IgE, which is responsible for allergic reactions. (*See* ALLERGY.)

First see PROKARYOTIC CELLS

Bacteria

Next see DISEASES, INFECTIOUS

Microscopic, single-celled organisms, the nucleus of which is not a distinct organelle surrounded by a membrane.

Bacteria are the most ancient of the Earth's organisms, as well as the smallest, simplest, and most numerous form of cellular life. Fossil evidence indicates that organisms much like today's cyanobacteria existed 3.5 billion years ago and that bacteria remained Earth's only inhabitants for 2 billion years. Taken together, it has been calculated that Earth's bacteria would outweigh all other living organisms combined.

Although some bacteria synthesize food by photosynthesis or chemosynthesis, most feed off dead or living organic matter and have a role similar to that of fungi. Both kinds of organisms decompose Earth's dead plants and animals, an essential role that makes nitrogen, carbon, and other atoms available for recycling. Both kinds of organisms cause food spoilage and crop disease, are used to produce foods and antibiotics, and can cause human disease.

Some bacteria, however, have a life-giving role: They are the only organisms that can fix nitrogen—convert atmospheric nitrogen to a form usable by cells—a process that makes plant growth possible. Nitrogen-fixers include cyanobacteria (blue-green algae) and other photosynthetic bacteria, as well as symbiotic bacteria, chiefly rhizobium and bradyrhizobium, which form nodules on the roots of legumes.

Uniqueness of Bacteria. Bacteria are unique among living organisms in being prokaryotes, cells without an organized nucleus bounded by a nuclear envelope. Eukaryotes, which have such an envelope, have complex DNA-bearing chromosomes within their nucleus. Bacteria have a single long molecule of DNA

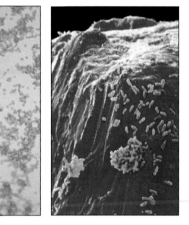

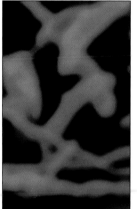

Bacteria are divided into three categories: coccis (above, left), or spherical cell; bacillus (above, center), or rod-shaped cell; and spirillum (above, right), or spiral-shaped cell. Top right, a colony of cocci and bacilli feeding.

arranged in a ring, sometimes called a bacterial chromosome, in an area of the cell called the nucleoid. Plasmids, small independent bits of circular DNA, may be present as well.

Bacteria reproduce asexually, not through mitosis, as do eukaryotes, but through fission. The DNA ring and sometimes some of the plasmids replicate themselves. Then the plasma membrane and cell wall form a wall between the copies, dividing the cell in the middle. The two cells usually separate, but sometimes they stay together and form chains.

Two Groups. Bacteria are divided into two major groups, which usually are considered separate kingdoms. The eubacteria, or "true bacteria," include all the commonly known bacteria and are the focus of this article. The archaebacteria ("ancient bacteria") differ from eubacteria in their metabolism and other features.

It has been estimated that more than 90 percent of all bacteria are either harmless or useful to humans; the human digestive tract, for instance, is rife with helpful bacteria. But as causes of human disease, they can be devastating: Anthrax, cholera, bacterial dysentery, gonorrhea, Legionnaires' disease, leprosy, bacterial meningitis, bacterial pneumonia, syphilis, tetanus, toxic shock, typhus, tuberculosis, typhoid fever, and whooping cough are all caused by bacteria. So are strep throat and staphylococcal skin infections such as boils and impetigo. Bacteria also cause botulism and many other forms of food poisoning.

Bacterial Damage. In the human body, bacteria do their damage in several ways. They may destroy tissue directly, overwhelm normal functioning by their sheer numbers, or produce toxins that kill cells. Exotoxins are released by living bacterial cells; endotoxins are released into the host when the bacterial cell dies.

Bacteria are classified in part by shape: Bacilli are rod-shaped, cocci are spherical, and spirilli are helical. They are also classified as gram-negative or gram-positive, depending on how they react to a dye called Gram's stain, which reflects the structure of their cell walls.

Many bacterial infections are spread by fecal contamination, others by sexual contact, coughing, or even sneezing. In industrialized countries, bacterial disease has been dramatically reduced by improved sanitation, immunization, and the development of antibiotics that are active against almost all bacteria. But in recent

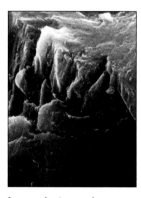

In an electron microscope image of a meteorite from Mars, above, there are several tiny structures that are possible microscopic fossils of primitive, bacteria-like organisms that may have lived on Mars more than 3.6 billion years ago. Organic molecules and mineral features were found suggesting biological activity and possible microscopic fossils such as these inside an ancient Martian meteorite. Subsequent analysis has raised questions about this conclusion.

to churn out insulin or other biological products.

Bacteria have long been used in food production, where they are essential in making yogurt, most cheeses, and vinegar. Now they are also being used to absorb toxins and other pollutants, and to kill agricultural pests. *Bacillus thuringiensis* (BT), effective against many caterpillars, is one of several bacterial pesticides that work without leaving toxins behind to pollute soil or streams.

Bacterial Genetics. The genome of a bacterium contains approximately 2,000 genes, a much smaller number than the 30,000 to 40,000 that compose the human genome. The complete genome of one type of bacteria, *E. coli*, was "mapped" (i.e., sequenced and individual genes identified), in 1997. (*See* GENOME, HUMAN.)

Bacteria often contain extrachromosomal elements known as *plasmids*, which are small circular "bits" of DNA. Plasmids are self-replicating and their number remains constant from generation to generation. The plasmids can either exist as separate units or can be integrated into the main chromosome. Once inserted, they are referred to as *episomes*, although the terms episomes and plasmids are often used interchangeably. Plasmids may be "transmitted" from one cell to another, thus allowing genes to be exchanged. Because of the genetic variation involved, the transfer of plasmids can be seen as a type of gene transfer in these primitive cells.

One of the most interesting aspects of bacterial genetics is the transformation of bacteria into miniature "factories" by means of genetic engineering. A gene contains information for constructing a particular protein. When a gene is activated, or turned on, its protein is produced. Recombinant DNA involves the introduction of foreign genes into another cell, complete with its control mechanism, in order to manufacture specific proteins.

Drug-Resistant Bacteria. Drug-resistant bacteria arise as a result of mutation or simply because of natural variation among a population. Once exposed to a drug, all susceptible organisms are killed off, leaving only resistant cells, which promptly reproduce. In this manner, a colony can change in a very short time to all-resistant bacteria. Drug resistance in bacteria is a growing problem, particularly for tuberculosis and staph infections. Overuse of antibiotics, as well as failure to complete a drug regimen properly, contribute to the problem. (*See* TUBERCULOSIS.)

THE CUTTING EDGE

Bacterial Genetics

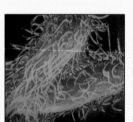

Bacteria have several means of transferring genetic information from one cell to another. One method is called conjugation, where a physical conduit is constructed between two bacterial cells and DNA is transferred from one cell to another. A second way is for a virus to inadvertently incorporate a piece of bacterial DNA into its own DNA, during replication (called transduction) and, upon injection of the viral DNA into another cell, the bacterial DNA goes along for the ride. This second method has proved useful in genetic engineering.

years, concern has risen because antibiotic-resistant strains of bacteria are increasing while more patients have immune systems that are weakened by immunosuppressive therapy or disease. At the same time, increased use of invasive treatments, such as those requiring catheters or implants, make patients more vulnerable to infection.

Using Bacteria. Ironically, most current antibiotics are derived from bacteria, and in recent years, some bacteria have become a key biological research tool. *E-coli* is considered the workhorse of genetic engineering. When the proper genes are inserted into it from other organisms, it can be used as a biological factory

Further Reading

Bacteria in Biology: Biotechnology and Medicine (1999); Baldry, Peter E., *Introduction to Bacteria,* (1976); Dale, J., *Molecular Genetics of Bacteria* (1998); Hess, D. J., *Can Bacteria Cause Cancer?* (2000); Singleton, Paul, et al., *Introduction to Bacteria* (1981).

See relevant material in ARCHAEBACTERIA; ASEXUAL REPRODUCTION; *and* DIGESTIVE CHEMISTRY. *The molecular genetics of bacteria is discussed in* DNA; MICROBIOLOGY; *and* PROKARYOTIC CELLS. *The role of bacteria in the ecosystem is discussed in* BIOREMEDIATION; EUTROPHICATION; *and* SOIL CHEMISTRY. *See also* GENETIC ENGINEERING *and* ANTIBIOTICS.

First see NUCLEUS, ATOMIC

Baryons

Next see ELEMENTARY PARTICLE

A group of subatomic particles, the subclasses of which are the nucleons and the hyperons.

Nucleons are the proton and neutron, the two particles of which the nuclei of atoms are made. There are also antinucleons, antiprotons, and antineurons. The hyperons include the lambda, the three sigma particles, the xi, and the omega. Baryons are grouped with the mesons, another kind of elementary particle, as hadrons, which denotes that they all interact through the strong or nuclear force. (*See* NUCLEAR FORCES.)

The two nucleons, proton and neutron, each have a mass about 1,840 times greater than the electron. The proton is the lightest baryon, with a mass of 838 million electron volts, or MeV. The neutron is the next heaviest baryon, with a mass of 1.293 MeV heavier than that of the proton.

The lambda is the lightest hyperon, with a mass 325 times that of the electron. It is an electrically neutral particle that usually decays into a nucleon and a pion. The three sigma particles each have the mass of 2,330 electrons. Charged sigmas have a lifetime measured in billionths of a second and decay mainly into nucleons and pions. The neutral sigma particle, however, decays much faster, producing a lambda and a photon. (*See* ELEMENTARY PARTICLE.)

Xi particles occur in both negatively charged and electrically neutral forms. A xi particle has the mass of 2,550 electrons and decays very quickly (a ten-billionth of a second).

The omega-minus particle has a mass of 3,300 electrons. It was discovered in 1964 at the Brookhaven National Laboratory in New York. (*See* ACCELERATOR PARTICLE.)

First see ELECTRICITY

Batteries and Fuel Cells

Next see AUTOMOTIVE DESIGN

Chemical means of obtaining electricity.

A battery produces electricity through chemical reactions known as redox reactions. Electrons are transferred from one substance to another. "Redox" refers to when the processes of reduction (one substance gains electrons) and oxidation (another substance loses electrons) occur simultaneously. Redox reactions are exothermic, meaning energy is produced. (*See* REDOX REACTIONS.) Scientists Luigi Galvani in 1780 and Alessandro Volta discovered in 1800 that an electric current is created when there is a flow of electrons or a movement of positive and negative ions along a path (ionic conduction).

A battery consists of two or more galvanic cells arranged to operate together. In a galvanic cell, each half of the redox reaction occurs at a separate electrode. The anode is the electrode where oxidation takes place and the cathode is the electrode where reduction takes place. Unlike an electrolytic cell, however, the cathode is positive and the anode is negative. Electrons are released by the half-reaction at the anode and travel through a conductor to the cathode where they are "taken up" by that electrode's half-reaction. Positive ions, or cations, accumulate at the anode, and negative ions, or anions, collect at the cathode. (*See* ION.)

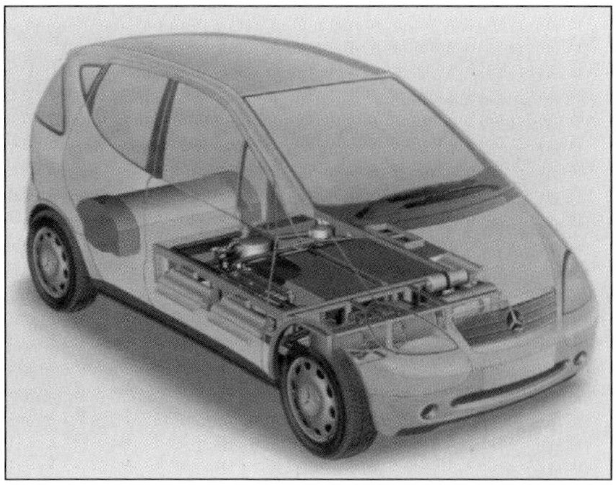

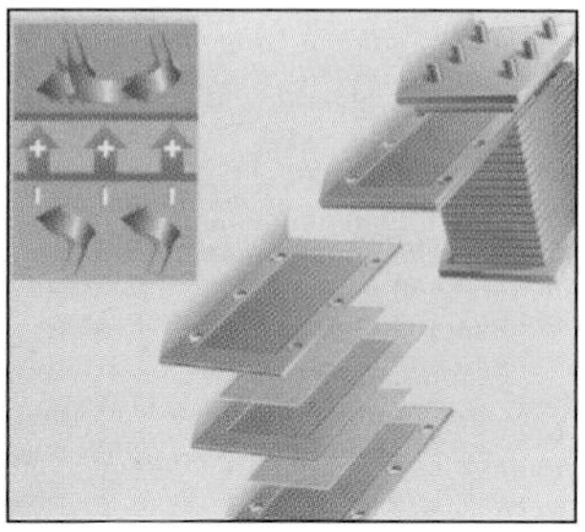

The fuel cell above was developed by Daimler-Benz and was incorporated into the world's first fuel cell vehicle (left). The vehicle, based on the Mercedes-Benz A-class, has the ability to generate hydrogen onboard, contributing to the drive system's low emissions.

The electrodes are made of metals, such as copper or zinc, with the more active metal acting as the anode and the less active one as the cathode. Surrounding these metals are electrolytes: solutions or solids containing the ions that conduct the electric current inside a cell.

Circuitry. The internal circuit is made up of the electrolytes through which the positive and negative ions flow. The external circuit is made up of the electrodes and their attached wires. The electrons that pass through the wire carry energy and can do work, such as lighting up a bulb or ringing a bell. The energy can be stored as long as the electrodes are not connected. (*See* ENERGY.)

The measure of the difference in electrical potential energy between two points in an electric current is known as electromotive force (emf) or voltage. An emf source producing a larger voltage forces a larger current through a circuit; an emf source producing a smaller voltage forces a smaller current through a circuit. Voltage is calculated by taking the difference between the reduction potentials of the two half-reactions that occur. Cell voltage is always a positive number, indicating that a spontaneous reaction is occurring. (*See* ELECTROMAGNETIC FORCE.)

Primary batteries, the most widely used, stop functioning when one of their chemicals is depleted. The three major types of dry primary batteries are carbon-zinc cells, alkaline cells, and mercury cells.

John Stuart Bell
(1928–1990).

Below, Arno Penzias and Robert Wilson stand next to the horn antenna they used to discover remnants of cosmic background radiation, the first direct evidence of the Big Bang. NASA's COBE instrument is a much more sophisticated radio telescope that is used to map the background radiation in the universe (below, right).

First see QUANTUM MECHANICS

Bell's Inequality

Next see UNCERTAINTY PRINCIPLE

Bell's inequality concerns the probabilities of two events both occurring in well-separated parts of a system. In 1964, Scottish physicist John Stuart Bell showed that quantum mechanics predicts a violation of the inequalities that are the consequences of local hidden variable theories. Bell was also able to demonstrate an observable discrepancy between quantum mechanics and any local hidden-variable theory. Experimental results are in agreement with the predictions of quantum mechanics, rather than those of local hidden-variables theories.

Bell's inequality, and the theorem based on it, is an important development in quantum mechanics. One reason is that the theorem makes it possible to design experiments that can test all the varieties of local hidden-variable theories, which propose that quantum mechanics may not be adequate to describe widely separated but correlated systems. That result would require a major revision of quantum mechanics. Several experiments have been designed and carried out in this area. They have given results that are in good agreement with quantum mechanics and that violate the predictions of local hidden-variable theories.

First see UNIVERSE

Big Bang Theory

Next see HUBBLE CONSTANT

Theory that a massive explosion marked the beginning of the universe as we know it.

We have known for some time that the universe is expanding, which means that it began at a specific point in the past. Today, however, scientists have gained unprecedented knowledge of the details of the early life of the universe—so much so that they can talk confidently about events that happened billions of years ago when the universe was less than a second old.

Hubble's Work. In 1927, astronomer Edwin Hubble, with an astronomy degree from the

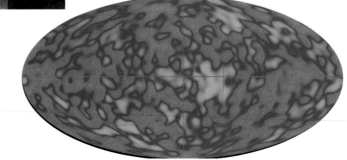

University of Chicago, went to the Mount Wilson Observatory in Los Angeles. Mount Wilson was equipped with a 100-inch telescope, at the time the world's most powerful instrument. Using it, Hubble was able to prove that matter in the universe is organized into separate galaxies separated by vast stretches of empty space. Furthermore, as he looked at the light emitted by atoms in stars from different galaxies, he noticed that it was somewhat redder than light emitted by those same atoms in the laboratory. Light that has been shifted toward the red has a longer wavelength than normal, and the stretching out of wavelengths occurs because the source of the light is moving away from the observer. This is the well-known "Doppler effect," the same thing that makes a car horn change pitch as the car drives by on the road. Hubble computed that the red shift he was observing was caused by the fact that the galaxies were moving away from Earth. Furthermore, he noted that the farther away the galaxies were, the greater the red shift was, i.e., the faster they were receding from us. He concluded that the universe is expanding—this is now referred to as the Hubble expansion. (*See* DOPPLER EFFECT.)

Here is an analogy to help explain the Hubble expansion: Imagine that there is some rising bread dough on a table in front of you. Suppose further that inside the bread dough are raisins. If you stood on a raisin, and you could see through the dough, you would see other raisins moving away from you. In fact, if one raisin were twice as far away as another, it would be moving away from you twice as fast, because there would be twice as much expanding dough between you and the second raisin. Imagine the universe is the bread dough and the raisins are the galaxies and you have a good picture of the universe in which we live. No matter which galaxy you are in, you see all other galaxies receding; the further away, the faster they move.

Now, if you further imagine looking at the frozen universe and then "running the film backwards," you can see that the current expansion implies that, sometime in the past, the universe began in a single event. The best estimate made thus far is that the time that has elapsed since that event is 12 billion years, give or take a few billion. The event that began the universe and the subsequent expansion is referred to by the phrase "Big Bang."

Back in Time. One way of measuring our knowledge about the evolution of the universe is to ask how far back along this track we can go. Going backward in time, we would see the universe and all the material in it being compressed into a smaller and smaller space. Eventually, some time about half a million years after the initial event, the temperature in this material was such that electrons would be stripped from atoms, and matter would be in the form of a plasma. Since light cannot move though a plasma, astronomers believe that galaxies could not have formed before this particular event. Any concentration of matter in a plasma would be blown apart by collisions with ambient radiation. (*See* PLASMA.)

Moving still farther back in time, we would see the universe become smaller and smaller. The next important event takes place about three minutes after the initial event. Before this time, if two elementary particles came together to form a nucleus, they would be moving so fast that subsequent collisions would knock it apart again. Thus, before this time there were no nuclei for atoms, but only a sea of elementary particles. After three minutes, on the other hand, the atoms of some light nuclei could form.

Nucleosynthesis. The formation of nuclei results from two competing effects: the temperature has to be low enough for them to stay together, but as time goes on, the expansion carries particles farther apart and makes collisions less likely. This means that there is a short window where nuclei can be formed, and only the very simplest nuclei (hydrogen, helium, and a little bit of lithium) could have formed during this time. All other elements, including the oxygen we breathe and the calcium in our bones, was made later, in supernovae.

Continuing our journey backward, we would see the universe as a sea of elementary particles colliding with one another at higher and higher energies, until we came to a time that is about 10 microseconds after the initial event. At this point, the energy of the particles would be so high that they would not stay together, but would be dissolved into their constituent quarks. Before 10 microseconds, in other words, no elementary particles existed, only quarks and leptons.

From this point back to the Big Bang, the situation becomes a little less clear. We know that there are four fundamental forces existing in the universe—the familiar forces of gravity and electricity, the strong force (which holds nuclei together), and the weak force (which is responsible for some kinds of radioactive decay). With matter broken down into its fundamental constituents, the next important milestone in our journey backward would involve the unification of these forces.

At one ten-billionth of a second after the initial event, the energies are high enough so that the weak and electromagnetic forces are uniform. In other words, before this time, there were only three fundamental forces acting in the universe—the strong force, gravitation, and the unified "electro-weak force"—and only after this time did the full complement of four emerge.

This time is important for another reason. At a few accelerators around the world—most notably at the Center for Nuclear Research (CERN) in Geneva Switzerland, and the Fermi-lab near Chicago, it is possible to accelerate protons and antiprotons to very high speeds. When these particles collide, for a brief fraction of a second the energy raises their temperature to what it might have been when the universe was one ten-billionth of a second old. Consequently, the unification of the electromagnetic and weak forces, and a number of other predictions that come from this theory, can thus be verified directly in a laboratory. (*See* UNIVERSE.)

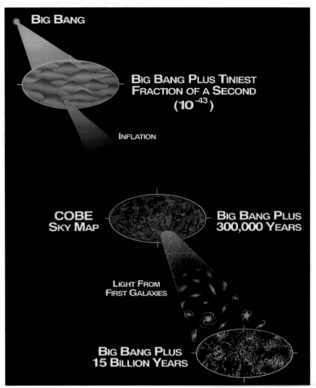

Near Point Zero. The next milestone occurs when the universe was 10^{-35} seconds old (that is, a decimal point followed by 34 zeroes and a one). At this time, it is theorized that the strong force unified with the electro-weak. Before this time, there were only two forces—gravitation and the unified force—and only after were there three forces.

Although these kinds of energies cannot be produced in a laboratory, predictions can be made about the universe based on our understanding of what should have happened then and comparing them to the universe we live in. A number of these predictions—that there should be so little antimatter around, for example—have been verified, so scientists have some confidence in the explanation. However, just as the previous milestone marked the frontier of our ability to explore the universe experimentally, this time marks the end of our ability to describe with any confidence the events that occurred involving elementary particles.

Planck Time. The last milestone would occur at 10^{-45} seconds. This is called the Planck

Above, an artistic depiction of crucial periods in the developing universe according to inflationary cosmology. From top left, a tiny fraction of a second after the Big Bang, to bottom right, 15 billion years later.

Further Reading
Guth, Alan H., *The Inflationary Universe: The Quest for a New Theory of Cosmic Origins* (1998); Lerner, E. J., *The Big Bang Never Happened* (1992); Schramm, David N., *The Big Bang and Other Explosions in Nuclear and Particle Astrophysics* (1996); Trefil, James, *The Moment of Creation: Big Bang Physics from Before the First Millisecond to the Present Universe* (1998); Weinberg, Steven, *The First Three Minutes: A Modern View of the Origin of the Universe* (1993).

Below, a comparison of the same area of sky (a double star) taken by the Hubble Space Telescope wide field planetary camera (bottom) and a ground-based image taken from Las Campanas Observatory, Carnegie Institute of Washington. From Earth, the double star can only be distinguised as a single star, but using the Hubble Space Telescope, astronomers have been able to discern that they are looking at a binary star.

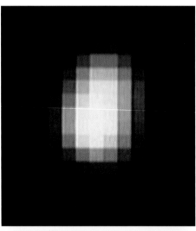

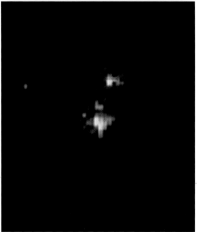

time, after one of the pioneers of quantum mechanics. At this point, we expect gravity to unify with the other forces, but we have no theory that describes how this could happen.

Background material for Big Bang cosmology is found in ELEMENTARY PARTICLE; GENERAL RELATIVITY; FORCE; GRAVITATION; NUCLEAR FORCES; *and* PLASMA. *Elements of the theory are discussed in* BLACK HOLES; HUBBLE CONSTANT; INTERSTELLAR MEDIUM; *and* NUCLEOSYNTHESIS. *See also* UNIVERSE.

First see STAR

Binary Stars

Next see PULSAR

Two stars orbiting around a common center of mass.

Binary stars were first described toward the end of the 18th century by the British astronomer William Herschel. Some pairs of stars appear to astronomers on Earth to be close together but actually have no physical connection—one may be much further from Earth than the other; these are called optical double stars. Other star pairs can be observed to move about each other; these are called visual double stars.

Astronomers usually cannot measure the motions of a pair with relation to the background, but they can measure the motion of one star about the other. This motion obeys Kepler's law, which states that the relative orbit of each star is an ellipse, with the other star at one focus of the ellipse. Detailed measurements of the orbits of a binary star can enable astronomers to determine the masses of the two stars. (*See* KEPLER'S LAWS.)

Some binary stars cannot be seen through a telescope, but can be identified by studying their light emissions through a spectroscope; these are called spectroscopic binary stars. When one star is moving away from an observer and the other star is moving toward the observer, the spectral lines of the first star will be shifted toward the red, while the spectral lines of the other will be shifted toward the blue. If an astronomer can look at the spectral lines of both stars in detail, the relative sizes of the orbits of the stars around the center of gravity can be found, which allows the calculation of the ratio of the masses of the two stars. The individual masses of the stars can be determined only if the inclination of the orbits to the line of sight is known.

This information enables astronomers to determine the true size of the orbits and the sum of the masses of the stars. In general, spectroscopic binaries are close, fast-moving pairs, while visual binaries are widely separated and slowly moving. (*See* SPECTROCOPY.)

Many binary stars have been found to have more than two components. About 40 percent of the stars in the vicinity of the solar system are binary or multiple systems. The shortest known period of rotation for a binary system is a few hours, while the longest known period is 10 million years. The separation of the components of binary star systems varies from very close to about 44,000 times the distance from Earth to the sun. Binary and multiple star systems are not believed to be caused by the capture of one star by another, but by the normal process of star birth from condensation of gas and dust.

First see EVOLUTION

Biodiversity

Next see SPECIATION

Short for "biological diversity," refers to the total genetic variation in the world—the total number of species on Earth.

The term "biodiversity" first came into wide usage in 1986, when it was used in the title of a meeting, the "National Forum on BioDiversity," sponsored by the Smithsonian Institution and the National Academy of Sciences. The forum drew 14,000 participants, including prominent biologists who spoke of "the species-extinction crisis" as a threat to civilization second only to the threat of nuclear war. By 1992, biodiversity was a central topic at the Rio de Janeiro environmental summit meeting. The term had become a battle cry for those seeking to protect the biosphere as it now exists—for to preserve biodiversity requires protecting the habitats in which species live and the climatic and atmospheric conditions to which they are adapted. As a concept, "preserving biodiversity" sets a broader agenda than environmentalists' earlier emphasis on saving individual species that happened to have been identified as endangered.

Understanding Biodiversity. Why does biodiversity matter? Reasons range from the practical to the cosmic. Species not yet identified may be rich sources of new and improved crops and medical treatments, with great impact on human well-being. Even obscure species can prove uniquely valuable in scientific research. But once species are gone, they can never be recovered. Tropical rain forests are hotbeds of biodiversity and help regulate climate; it has been estimated that eliminating the Amazon rain forest would reduce rainfall in the region by one-fourth and raise temperatures. If enough species

It is estimated that more than 30 million species exist on the planet, of which a vast majority are of the phylum arthropods (insects). Far left, a selection of beetles pinned on styrofoam. Left, a variety of scarab beetles. These specimens were prepared by the Institute for Biodiversity, a research organization in Costa Rica.

are destroyed, entire ecosystems might be destabilized, with catastrophic results.

The extent of current biodiversity is unknown. "We know more about the total numbers of atoms in the universe than about Earth's complement of species," biologist Norman Myers has written. Estimates of the number of species range from 5 million to more than 30 million. Conservation ecologists have estimated that species are being eliminated, largely through the destruction of tropical rainforests and other species-rich habitats, at a rate of one percent to 10 percent a decade, with some estimates as high as 30 percent. If one assumes there are 10 million species and an extinction rate of five percent a decade, then some 1.25 million species would have become extinct between 1975 and 2000. (*See* TROPICAL RAINFOREST.)

About 1.7 million species have been identified. But except for large mammals, birds, crop plants, and other groups important to humans, surprisingly little is known about most of them. What is their distribution and biology? How secure are they from extinction? Assuming there are 10 million species, biologist Nigel E. Stork has estimated that we know nothing about the distribution of 86 percent of them, and only seven percent are known from more than one locality. For less than half of one percent is the threat of extinction accurately known.

Intraspecies Biodiversity. Biodiversity is not confined to species. Within species are genetically distinct populations that contribute to biodiversity. Countless numbers of them are thought to have been destroyed by habitat destruction, making many surviving species far less genetically diverse than they once were. This is likely to make them more vulnerable to disease and less able to adapt to environmental challenges.

Biologist Paul R. Ehrlich and his colleagues have estimated that there are about 220 populations per species—which yields 2.2 billion populations globally, if one assumes 10 million species—and that 16 million populations within species are being destroyed each year in tropical forests alone. They warn that the consequences of these extinctions, unprecedented in the entire history of the Earth, are unknown.

THE CUTTING EDGE

How Much Life?

Species have been classified for hundreds of years, yet no one really knows how many are living on the planet today. It is estimated that there are approximately 100,000 species of fungi and 250,000 species of protocists. The largest group of all is composed of the insects—the phylum arthropod—of which there may be as many as 500,000. The literature lists 10,000 species of bacteria. However, some estimates of the number of species of bacteria are as large as ten times that number, since we can only catalog the bacterium that can be grown in culture. It has been estimated that 90 percent of the bacteria on the planet cannot grow on agar plates—the medium used most often in the laboratory—leaving only ten percent of the total population culturable, and therefore, only that portion of the total of the bacteria population known.

The range of life in Earth's biosphere is (merely) indicated by the entries BACTERIA; BIRDS; FISH; FUNGUS; MAMMALS; MICROBIOLOGY; *and* PLANT. *The systems aspects of life are discussed in* ECOLOGY; GAIA HYPOTHESIS; *and* POPULATION ECOLOGY. *Challenges to biodiversity are dealt with in* TROPICAL RAIN FOREST *and in* ACID RAIN; AIR POLLUTION; DEFORESTATION; DESERTIFICATION; EXTINCTION; *and* WATER POLLUTION. *See also* HAZARDOUS WASTE DISPOSAL.

Further Reading

Dobson, Andrew P., *Conservation and Biodiversity* (1998); Gould, Stephen Jay, *Wonderful Life: The Burgess Shale and the Nature of History* (1990); Perlman, Dan L., *Biodiversity: Exploring Values and Priorities in Conservation* (1997); Wilson, E. O., *Biodiversity* (1989); Wilson, Edward O., *The Diversity of Life* (1993).

Above, an anaerobic toluene degrader, a bacterium that breaks down toluene, a toxic component of gasoline.

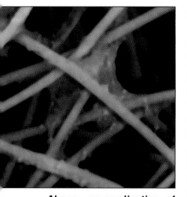

Biostratigraphic analysis requires an assessment of micropaleontological and kerogen content in rock material over a wide area.

First see BACTERIA

Bioremediation

Next see WATER POLLUTION

The use of bacteria or fungi to break down hazardous organic materials contaminating soil or water into harmless substances.

The advantages of bioremediation over other processes are twofold: unlike incineration, it requires little energy; and it can often be performed onsite with little permanent effect on the environment. (*See* ECOLOGY.)

Bioremediation has become popular in recent years because it offers a high success rate with petroleum products ranging from gasoline and waste oil to coal tar and creosote, as well as with chlorinated pesticides, solvents, and biphenyls (PCB). Bioremediation has also been applied to the by-products of heavy metal processing, such as at the Homestake Gold Mine in South Dakota, and to wood-processing operations. (*See* HAZARDOUS WASTE DISPOSAL.)

Methodologies. Bioremediation can be pursued by any of three methods: tank treatment, biopiles, and prepared beds. In tank treatment, a contaminated solution or slurry is pumped through a biofilm, which reduces contaminants to treatable solids. Biopiles typically involve removal of contaminated soil to a prepared berm, insertion of aeration lines, and covering of the pile to allow complete degradation. Prepared beds typically involve construction of extensive below-ground galleries, so that nutrients can be pumped through at one end and a recovery well can recycle the flow at the other. (*See* ALGAE and WATER POLLUTION.)

First see FOSSIL

Biostratigraphy

Next see Paleoecology

The study of the fossils found in various layers of Earth as they are excavated by scientists.

Studies of the fossils found in the different strata of a given area that is being excavated can be correlated with those of more distant areas and with the standard of the geological column. A correlation that is based on fossils that are used as indexes for such studies is called a biostratigraphic correlation. Finding such a correlation indicates that the layers in different areas were deposited at the same geological time, even though their lithology—the specific nature of their rocks—may be very different.

Zones. The basic unit of biostratigraphy is the zone. One or more biostratigraphic zones constitutes a series, and two or more such series form a system. All these terms refer to rocks the age of which can be specified. A different set of terms is used to refer to geological time itself. The length of time represented by a biostratigraphic stage is called an age, while the length of time that is represented by a series is called an epoch. The length of time represented by a system is called a period. Scientists use a variety of techniques to study not only the layers of rock in which fossils are found but also the fossils themselves, including those that may be too small to be detected by the naked eye. The resulting studies give an insight into the origin and evolution of Earth's living creatures.

First see PROTEIN

Biosynthetics

Next see PROTEIN SYNTHESIS

Organic compounds such as proteins and carbohydrates formed in the cells of living organisms.

The fundamental biosynthetic activity is photosynthesis, which occurs in the cells of green plants. Photosynthesis is believed to have evolved in the Precambrian era, about 4.7 billion years ago, as plants adjusted to the growing presence in the atmosphere of carbon dioxide, which was produced by even more primitive plants. Modern-day plants, using solar energy, transform such simple compounds as carbon dioxide and water into all the complex chemicals of life. (*See* PHOTOSYNTHESIS.)

Two key steps in photosynthesis take place in a fraction of a second and both steps are catalyzed by chlorophyll. In the first step, one key action is the splitting of water molecules so that their oxygen is eventually released. The second step involves the capture of energy from solar radiation, a reaction called photophosphorylation. Both steps require light to occur. Other steps in photosynthesis can take place with or without light, and are called dark reactions. A simple description of photosynthesis is that light provides the energy to transform water and carbon dioxide into carbohydrates with the release of oxygen. The carbohydrates produced in this way are used by cells that cannot perform photosynthesis, such as those plant cells that do not have chlorophyll, as well as all animal cells, including those of humans, which acquire these carbohydrates when the animal consumes food.

Growth and Biosynthesis. The growth of all organisms depends on a different form of biosynthesis in which new protein molecules are made in cellular activities that join the smaller molecules called amino acids to form the many proteins that not only serve as structural materials, but also carry out cellular functions. In particular, many proteins are classified as enzymes, molecules that serve as catalysts to promote other processes of cellular biosynthesis. Protein

Above, an application of biosynthetics. The plastic bioscaffolding for generating of new tissue. After the tissue is complete, the plastic biodegrades.

synthesis takes place on cellular subunits called ribosomes and is controlled by information carried by molecules of deoxyribonucleic acid, DNA, the genetic material that is found in the nucleus of a cell.

The formation of amino acids is a biosynthetic process that requires energy that is derived from the oxidation of other organic substances in the cell. In the biosynthesis of proteins, subunits called amino acids are linked together in highly specific sequences, with each protein intended for a specific function within the cell. Thus, the process of biosynthesis is usually different from the techniques used to synthesize such compounds in the laboratory. But it is often possible to induce a cell to produce a variant form of a natural protein, a form that has commercially or medically useful properties. One way in which this can be done is to provide an organism with unusual food materials. For example, cells of the mold penicillium have been induced to produce several different kinds of the antibiotic penicillin, each of which has different properties and thus can attack disease-causing bacteria in a different way.

First see ADAPTATION

Birds

Next see BIRDS, EVOLUTION OF

Also known as avians, birds are one of the five classes of vertebrates. They are warm-blooded, have feathers and wings, and lay eggs to reproduce.

How do birds fly? To begin with, their bodies have several features that have been adapted for flight. The long bones of the skeleton are very slender; many other skeletal "accessories" such as teeth have been lost. In place of marrow in most of the bones, there are cavities which contain air sacs, "auxiliary" lungs to increase the rate of respiration. Flying requires a great deal of energy, and birds have a double cycle of inhalation and exhalation compared to the "normal" breathing pattern of a mammal. The oxygen content of the blood is much higher as well. The shape of the wing is aerodynamically sound, allowing the bird to get enough lift to take off, as well as keeping the bird aloft.

In addition, the breastbone includes a structure known as the carina, shaped like the keel of a boat, to which the flight muscles are attached. Not all birds possess the carina, however. Those that do not—a group that includes ostriches, emus, and kiwis—are called ratites and are flightless. Perhaps the best known of the flightless birds is the penguin. Penguins are adapted for swimming. These adaptations include the secretion of an oily compound to make their feathers waterproof and a layer of fat under their skin to keep them from freezing in the cold waters of the Antarctic and southern Atlantic oceans where they are found. (*See* THERMAL REGULATION.)

Feather Coloration. Birds have distinct coloration patterns in their feathers, by which they are identified according to species. In many, the male is much more brilliantly colored than the female. For example, the sight of a male peacock is familiar, with his striking turquoise head and neck and large multicolored and patterned tail. Few observers notice the dull brown peahen nearby. Males compete with each other for the privilege of mating, and most females prefer the more strikingly colored males.

Mating often involves an elaborate courting ritual and "dance." In some species, the male builds a nest and then tries to lure a female to it. In others, once mating has already occurred, the pair builds the nest together. Nests are made of diverse types of materials, depending on species and what plants are available for use.

Eggs. Like reptiles, birds lay shelled eggs which are incubated and protected by one or both parents. There are some species of birds that mate for life, some where new pairings occur each year, and others in which the female may "set up housekeeping" with as many as three or four males, leaving each mate to incubate a separate clutch of eggs. After the eggs hatch, the nestlings are fed and protected by their parents until they are capable of leaving the nest.

Birds do not have teeth, but they have a diet that requires some type of grinding and mastication of food. The digestive system consists of a crop and gizzard in place of a stomach. The crop is a thin-walled sac for storage, and the gizzard is a muscular organ designed for grinding. The bird often swallows small stones and gravel which aid in the process. Birds have a structure known as the cloaca through which they excrete a semisolid nitrogenous waste. The cloaca is also used for reproductive purposes.

Bird Vision. The expression "eagle-eyed" refers to a very special feature of birds. The retina of the eye is lined with nerve cell receptors known as rods and cones. The fovea is an area where there is a very high concentration of cones, which gives shaper vision. Birds have a very large fovea, compared to other creatures. An eagle in the air can spot a mouse running along the ground several hundred feet below. In most species of birds, the eyes are located on the sides of the head rather than the front.

Although birds are endotherms, different species are still adapted to certain habitats and temperatures. There are thousands of different species of birds, some tropical, others subtropical, some adapted to very cold temperatures, and still others to temperate zones. In addition, there are species that follow regular migratory patterns, flying south for the winter and returning to cooler nesting grounds once spring arrives.

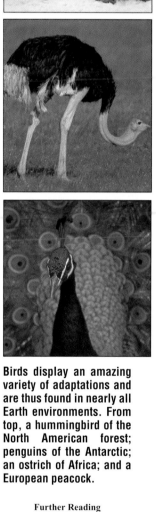

Birds display an amazing variety of adaptations and are thus found in nearly all Earth environments. From top, a hummingbird of the North American forest; penguins of the Antarctic; an ostrich of Africa; and a European peacock.

Further Reading
Attenborough, D., *The Life of Birds* (1998); Dengus, L., *The Mistaken Extinction* (1997); Shipman, P., *Taking Wing* (1998); *Stokes Guide to Bird Behavior* (1983).

First see BIRDS

Birds, Evolution of

Next see EXTINCTION

Birds are believed to have evolved from reptiles. One of the earliest birds was a creature called archaeopteryx, which lived 150 million years ago in the late Jurassic period. It had teeth and a long tail like a reptile, as well as feathers. The sternum, where flight muscles are attached, was small, and therefore this early bird may have been more of a glider than a flyer.

The first archaeopteryx fossil was discovered in Germany in 1855 and was originally thought to be a type of flying lizard known as a pterodactyl. Another specimen was found in 1861 and identified for what it truly was—a transition animal between dinosaurs and birds. However, archaeopteryx is not the ancestor of all living birds, just one important link in the evolutionary chain. Birds were not accepted as

The ability to survive a fall from a height—necessitated by a need for a vantage point to aid in the search of food—was a force of natural selection which drove the adaptation of flight. At right, an archaeopteryx fossil.

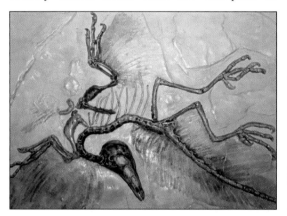

dinosaur descendants until the early 1970s but were believed to have possibly descended from another class of non-dinosaur reptiles like crocodilians. Today the issue is mostly which dinosaurs were the closest relatives of birds.

Many questions still remain regarding the connection between dinosaurs and birds. These questions include the earliest function of feathers, how endothermy ("warm-bloodedness"—being able to maintain a consistent body temperature) evolved, which group of theropods is the actual direct ancestor of birds, and why some bird groups survived the Cretaceous extinction of dinosaurs. (*See* BIRDS *and* DINOSAUR.)

First see CONCEPTION

Birth

Next see REPRODUCTIVE SYTEM

The emergence of viable offspring from a mother's body.

Delivery of human newborns has been a dangerous procedure throughout most of human history. The introduction of forceps into the process was a major advance in reducing infant mortality.

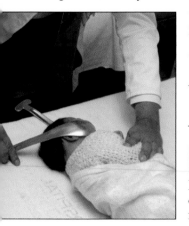

Birth, also known as parturition, occurs at various stages of newborn development. Some animals are born blind. Others, such as horses and cattle, can see and walk immediately after birth.

Phases. Parturition is generally considered to have three phases. In the first phase, the uterus and birth canal are prepared. The cervix softens and begins to efface (thin); receptors increase for oxytocin, a hormone that promotes uterine contractions, and the uterus, which had remained largely tranquil during pregnancy, begins to experience relatively weak and painless contractions of increasing frequency.

The second phase is active labor, in which forceful, coordinated contractions of the myometrium, the smooth-muscled walls of the uterus, force the offspring through the birth canal. This phase, which ends with delivery of the newborn and of the placenta, has been subdivided into the three stages of labor in humans. During Stage 1, the presenting part of the fetus, usually the head, descends into the mother's pelvis and the cervix fully dilates, opening to about four inches. Once the cervix is dilated, the fetal membranes usually rupture and the amniotic fluid drains out of the vagina. During Stage 2, contractions increase in strength and frequency, occurring every one to three minutes and exerting about 25 pounds of force on the fetus. As it wedges itself through the irregularly shaped birth canal, the fetus must flex, rotate, and extend its large head in order to fit. Stage 2 ends with delivery of the baby. Stage 3 ends with delivery of the placenta. (*See* EMBRYOLOGY.)

Compared to other normal human muscle contractions, uterine contractions are uniquely painful. The pain early in labor is thought to result from hypoxia—oxygen deprivation, as in angina pectoris—caused by compression of blood vessels in the uterine wall. Another explanation is that nerve ganglia in the cervix and lower uterus get compressed. Later, more severe pain results from cervical and perineal stretching and tearing or stretching in the birth canal.

The third phase of parturition involves recovery and lactation. The uterus returns to its pre-pregnancy size, which in humans can take four to six weeks. Some obstetrical authorities consider the third phase to last until fertility is restored, often not until breastfeeding ends.

The birth process varies in length, depending on species. In human first births, the preparatory phase generally lasts about eight hours, and active labor and delivery take about five hours more. The figures for subsequent human births are five hours and three hours, respectively. In horses, the preparatory phase takes about ten hours and the rest, half an hour.

In humans, there is evidence that the fetal adrenal gland plays a role in parturition, but it does not secrete extra cortisol before labor. Nor do progesterone levels fall—at least not until after the placenta has been delivered. But because progesterone withdrawal is the trigger for parturition in most mammals, researchers have pursued the possibility that some alternate form of progesterone deprivation may occur in humans, such as a reduced capacity for progesterone binding in the uterus of women at term or some antiprogestin produced in pregnancy. So far, this pursuit has failed to yield an answer.

It is known that a number of uterotonins—substances known to stimulate contractions in the uterus—form in increased amounts during labor. These include prostaglandins and oxytocin. They play a role in labor, although they do not seem to cause its initiation. In addition, estrogen levels increase dramatically throughout pregnancy, as estrogen forms in the placenta, and the estrogen-to-progesterone ratio increases in the last weeks of pregnancy. Adequate estrogen levels seem to be necessary for the timely onset of labor, but their exact role has yet to be uncovered. (*See* ENDOCRINE SYSTEM.)

Once labor begins, it appears likely that positive feedback mechanisms help intensify it. Stretching the cervix, for instance, is known to stimulate secretion of oxytocin, which promotes uterine contractions. As contractions push the fetus forward, its head stretches the cervix, which stimulates oxytocin production and uterine contractions, which pushes the fetus forward even more forcefully—a cycle of positive feedback that ends with delivery.

First see HEAT

Black Body Radiation

Next see QUANTUM MECHANICS

The electromagnetic radiation that is emitted by a hypothetical body that absorbs all the radiation that falls on it.

A hypothetical body that absorbed all radiation would be perfectly black when illuminated and thus would be invisible unless it obscured the existence of objects behind it. The closest approximation to a black body in the real world would be a small hole in the wall of an enclosure that is kept at a uniform temperature. In the laboratory, elongated metal cylinders with a narrow slit at one end are used for experiments.

Black bodies are of interest mainly because of the electromagnetic radiation they emit. That radiation extends over the whole range of wavelengths. The distribution of energy over this range has a characteristic form, with a maximum at one wavelength. The position of that maximum depends on the temperature of the black body; as its temperature goes up, the maximum wavelength shortens. The change in the distribution of the radiation is described by Wien's displacement law, formulated by Wilhelm Wien early in the twentieth century. Stefan's law states that the total energy radiated by a unit of surface area of a black body in a given period of time is

Above, the spectral distribution of tungsten is compared to the energy of an ideal black body at the identical temperature of 2450 K.

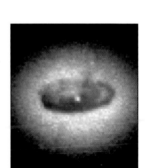

Above, an image spectrograph of galaxy NGC 4261 reveals (faintly) the twin gas jets theory requires, being jettisoned from the center of the black hole. Below, a drawing of the accretion disc believed to have been discovered in the constellation Cygnus.

proportional to the fourth power of that body's thermodynamic temperature. It was formulated by Joseph Stefan toward the end of the nineteenth century. (*See* ELECTROMAGNETIC WAVES.)

The radiation arises from the vibrations of atoms and molecules of the body. These vibrations are random, so that the speed and direction of the vibration of one atom is not related to those of any other atom. The motion of the atoms causes their electrons to emit radiation. If a black body is heated or struck by electromagnetic energy, that causes a change in the radiation emission of its electrons.

Place in History. Black body radiation is famous in the history of physics because it was the first of a series of phenomena that could be explained only by making a new set of assumptions about the laws that govern matter on the atomic level. The standard laws of mechanics and electromagnetism in the 19th century, when applied at that level, led to the conclusion that the amount of energy emitted by a black body would be infinitely high.

That picture was changed by Max Planck, who in 1901 proposed that instead of emitting radiation at any energy level, the electrons of atoms could emit or absorb energy only at certain wavelengths, based on the change they experience going from one set energy level to another. That proposal by Planck was thus the first to assume that energy is quantized—that is, transferred in packets called quanta. Calculations based on Planck's hypothesis agreed with the observed characteristics of black body radiation, which led to the adoption of the quantum theory of matter. (*See* ELECTROMAGNETISM; QUANTUM MECHANICS.)

First see GRAVITY

Black Hole

Next see GENERAL RELATIVITY

An object in space that has collapsed so much because of its gravitational mass that nothing can escape from it, not even light.

It is believed that one kind of black hole is formed by the gravitational collapse of massive stars toward the end of their lives. Under some circumstances, the collapse leads to the formation of a gravitational field that is strong enough to prevent the escape of all electromagnetic radiation, including visible light. The boundary of a black hole is called the event horizon; it is the surface at which the gravitational field reaches the critical limit that prevents the escape of all radiation. Therefore, events that occur inside this surface cannot be seen by outside observers.

Stellar Beginning. A black hole is the last stage in the life of a star that has 30 or more times the mass of our sun. Such a star maintains a balance between thermal expansion and gravitational contraction for most of its life; then, as the nuclear fuel is used up, it begins to contract. In a star up to about 1.5 times the mass of our sun, the contraction is stopped by the pressure of electrons, creating a white dwarf. In more massive stars, the collapse is stopped by the pressure of neutrons, creating a neutron star. The most massive stars continue to contract until their density becomes infinite.

The theory of black holes is based on general relativity, according to which a black hole can be described completely by three properties—its mass, its angular momentum, and its electrical charge. But the ultimate fate of matter inside the event horizon is not known. General relativity predicts that the center of a black hole is a singularity, a point at which all the presently known laws of physics break down. A new quantum theory of gravity would be needed to explain the properties of a singularity.

Objects believed to be black holes have been identified on the basis of their effect on the matter around them. For example, a black hole that is a member of a two-star system would capture matter from its neighboring star. That matter would form an accretion disc around the black hole, becoming compressed and heated to the point where it would emit x-rays. Astronomers may have sighted such a system in the constellation Cygnus. It consists of a supergiant star with an invisible companion whose mass is about ten times that of our sun, enough to form a black hole. Evidence for the existence of other black holes comes from the observation of the motion of gases and stars in the central region of our galaxy and other galaxies, and from the unusual emissions of quasars in several galaxies.

The background on the theory of black holes is found in GENERAL RELATIVITY *and* GRAVITY. *Additional information is contained in* GALAXY; HERTZSPRUNG-RUSSELL DIAGRAM; INTERSTELLAR MEDIUM; *and* STAR. *Regarding the search for black holes, see* INFRARED AND ULTRAVIOLET ASTRONOMY; RADIO ASTRONOMY; *and* X-RAY AND GAMMA RAY ASTRONOMY.

Above, simultaneous multiple records of galaxy NGC 4151, believed to contain a black hole at its center. Left: a spectral image showing the jets of oxygen being spewed from the center of the galaxy. Right: a wide-field image of oxygen emissions from the galaxy.

Further Reading
Ferris, T., *The Whole Shebang* (1998); Kaufman, W. J., and Freedman, R. A., *Universe* (1999); Trefil, J., *Space, Time, Infinity: The Smithsonian Views the Universe* (1993).

First see CIRCULATORY SYSTEMS

Blood

Next see BLOOD TYPE

A fluid matrix that bears blood cells and platelets, as well as electrolytes, hormones, and other substances throughout the body.

Blood circulates through the blood vessels carrying oxygen and nutrients to each cell in the body; taking waste products to the organs that will expel them; bearing hormones from the glands to their target cells; delivering immune-system cells to sites of infection; forming clots to plug holes in the vessels; and helping regulate the temperature and pH of the body.

Constituents of Blood. Plasma, the liquid portion of blood, is mostly water and contains a variety of proteins, including albumens and fibrinogen, which are needed for clotting. Plasma with the fibrinogen removed is called serum.

The most numerous cells in blood are red blood cells (erythrocytes), which make up almost half the average 5-liter blood volume in humans. In mammals, erythrocytes are small, round, and lacking a nucleus; in most other species they are nucleated. Erythrocytes are rich in hemoglobin, a red protein that combines easily with oxygen. Hemoglobin also binds with carbon monoxide. (*See* RESPIRATORY SYSTEMS.)

White blood cells (leukocytes) are rarer—by almost 1,000 to 1 in humans—and more varied. They are carried by the blood to sites of infection or inflammation to defend against infectious agents. There are six types of leukocytes in humans. Basophils and eosinophils secrete a variety of important substances. Neutrophils and monocytes engulf foreign cells to fight infection, a process called phagocytosis.

The remaining leukocytes are lymphocytes, which are responsible for acquired immunity, in which exposure to a foreign agent stimulates the body to attack it during later exposures. B-lymphocytes produce circulating antibodies, globulin molecules in the blood that attack an invading agent. T-lymphocytes become activated to destroy a foreign agent directly. Each B- and T-lymphocyte is programmed by the body to react to one specific agent, so there are millions of differently programmed lymphocytes waiting to be activated by a specific invader. In some cases, when B-lymphocytes are exposed to a foreign invader, they develop into yet another kind of leukocyte—plasma cells, which divide rapidly and churn out large amounts of immune globulin antibody for circulation in the blood.

Along with red and white blood cells, the final formed component of blood is platelets, small cellular fragments that play an important role in clotting. When a blood vessel is torn, platelets at the site swell and grow sticky, forming a plug to stop loss of blood. At the same time, the platelets release a variety of chemicals that promote clotting and constrict the vessel.

The composition of blood is covered in entries on B-LYMPHOCYTE *and* T-LYMPHOCYTE, *and in* GAMMA GLOBULIN; ANTIBODIES; *and* BLOOD TYPE. *Circulation of blood is covered in* CIRCULATORY SYSTEMS; HEART; *and* LYMPHATIC SYSTEMS. *Health concerns regarding blood are discussed in* AIDS; IMMUNIZATION AND VACCINATION; *and* SICKLE CELL DISEASE.

Further Reading
Gifford, N. L., *Common Blood Tests* (1999); Reshik, J., *Blood Saga: Hemophilia, AIDS, and the Survival of a Community* (1999); Starr, D., *Blood* (1998).

First see BLOOD

Blood Clotting

Next see LIVER

When human blood is shed, it quickly congeals into a mass of blood cells, platelets, and plasma trapped in a web of fibrin fibers. This clotting ability relies on a complex sequence of chemical reactions that override the anticoagulants that normally keep blood flowing. In the case of tiny holes that routinely develop in blood vessels, platelets form a platelet plug that seals the hole without clotting, but if the rupture is bigger, a clot forms. (*See* HEMOPHILIA.)

Mechanism. Reactions involving more than a dozen clotting factors take place that lead to the formation of prothrombin activator, the collective name for a complex of activated substances. This causes prothrombin, a plasma protein formed by the liver, to convert into thrombin, an enzyme that converts fibrinogen into fibrin. The fibrin fibers form a trap that catches platelets, blood cells, and plasma to form the clot. Within a few minutes, the clot begins to retract, expelling fluid from the trapped plasma and pulling together the torn edges of the blood vessel. (*See* BLOOD.)

The liver is crucial to blood clotting, since it forms prothrombin and most of the clotting factors; liver disease can cause a dangerous tendency to bleed. Inadequate amounts of any of the clotting factors can also cause abnormal bleeding: hemophilia A, classic hemophilia, is caused by a deficiency of Factor VIII; hemophilia B is caused by a deficiency of Factor IX. Platelets also play a crucial role: they accelerate the formation of thrombin, help constitute the clot itself, and are necessary for its retraction. (*See* LIVER.)

Abnormal clotting that blocks blood flow in crucial vessels can be responsible for catastrophic illness, including heart attack, stroke, and pulmonary embolism. (*See* HEART.)

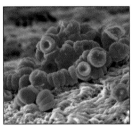

Above and top right, two views of red blood cells (erythrocytes) transporting oxygen and carbon dioxide through the body. The biconcave shape is an adaptation that maximizes the surface area for gas exchange.

Below, a mesh of the fibrin fibers forms around a wound, trapping blood cells, which prevents further blood loss and keeps out infections.

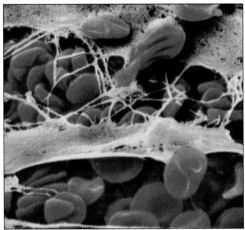

First see BLOOD

Blood Pressure

Next see CIRCULATORY SYSTEMS

The force exerted by blood in the main arteries. It rises and falls as the heart beats and as the body is at rest or in active motion.

Two kinds of blood pressure are measured by physicians. One is systolic pressure, the highest reading, which results when the two ventricles of the heart contract, sending blood out into the aorta, the large artery leading from the heart. The pressure that results with each contraction is felt as the pulse. Diastolic pressure is the reading that is obtained when the ventricles relax between heartbeats. There is still pressure, because flowing blood must overcome the resistance of all the small arteries throughout the body. Blood pressure that is too high can rupture a blood vessel, causing a stroke, so measurement of blood pressure is an essential part of a medical examination.

Readings. To measure blood pressure, a soft rubber cuff is wrapped around the upper part of the arm and is inflated until the flow of blood is stopped. The cuff is then deflated gradually, until the physician or attendant taking the measurement can hear the beat of the blood by listening with a stethoscope. That is the systolic pressure. The cuff is relaxed until blood flows steadily through the artery to obtain the diastolic pressure. Both systolic and diastolic pressure are expressed as millimeters of mercury, a tradition that arose because the earliest readings were obtained by using a glass column filled with mercury. A normal reading for a healthy young adult is about 110/75, while the reading for a healthy person over age 60 can be 130/90.

For discussion of health issues related to blood and blood pressure, see ANGIOPLASTY; ANTIBIOTICS; *and* STRESS. *Additional discussion of blood in the human physiology is contained in* NERVOUS SYSTEM; KIDNEYS AND EXCRETORY SYSTEMS; SURGERY; LIVER; LIPIDS; *and* LEUKEMIA. *See also* HEART.

First see BLOOD

Blood Transfusion

Next see BLOOD TYPE

The infusion of large amounts of blood or blood components, usually into an arm or vein.

Blood transfusion is most often done when there is a major loss of blood during a surgical procedure or because of an injury. Infants with hemolytic disease may receive an exchange transfusion, in which almost all of their blood is replaced. Patients with chronic anemia caused by conditions such as leukemia may need periodic transfusions. In any transfusion, the essential step is to be sure that the blood being given is of the same type as that of the recipient. Blood matching is done by taking a sample of the recipient's blood, identifying its type—A, B, AB, or O—and its Rh factor, positive or negative, and then mixing it with a sample of the donor blood to be sure that there are no adverse reactions.

In an ordinary transfusion, one unit of blood, about one pint, is transfused in one to four hours. If there is an emergency, such as rapid loss of blood after an accident, one unit may be given in minutes. The amount that is given depends on the amount of blood that has been lost by injury, surgery, or disease such as anemia. During the transfusion, there are regular readings of the recipient's temperature, pulse, and blood pressure. The transfusion can be stopped if there are signs of an adverse reaction. Because diseases such as AIDS and hepatitis B can be transmitted in blood, all donor blood is screened for the presence of infectious agents.

Further Reading
Feldschuh, J., *Safe Blood* (1998); Harmening, Denise, *Modern Blood Banking and Transfusion Practices* (1999); Starr, Douglas, *Blood: An Epic History of Medicine and Commerce* (1998); Vengelen-Tayler, Virginia, et al., eds., *Blood Group Systems: Rh* (1987).

First see BLOOD

Blood Type

Next see BLOOD TRANSFUSION

Classification of blood according to antigens present on the surface of red blood cells.

Human red blood cells have antigens on their cell membranes that can cause antigen-antibody reactions if mismatched blood is given in transfusion. Hundreds of antigens have been identified, but only about 30 occur commonly and only two groups of these antigens, which are more likely than others to cause blood transfusion reactions, are routinely checked before blood is transfused.

The first group—the ABO system—includes four blood types: A, B, AB, and O. People born with Type A blood antigens develop anti-B antibodies during the first year of life, while people with Type B blood develop anti-A antibodies. If a person with Type A blood receives a Type B transfusion, or vice versa, the

donor blood agglutinates, or clumps together, blocking small blood vessels. The agglutinated cells are eventually destroyed, releasing hemoglobin, which can cause jaundice and kidney failure. Because of their clumping effect, blood antigens are also called agglutinogens, and the antibodies are called agglutinins.

If A and B antigens are both present, the blood is type AB. AB can receive any type of blood because it does not contain antibodies against either A or B. If neither A nor B antigen is present, the blood is type O. The absence of antigens makes O the "universal donor," but it can receive only O blood because it contains both anti-A and anti-B antibodies. Among people of European ancestry, O and A are the predominant blood types. (*See* GENETICS.)

Rh Factor. The other blood group system important in transfusion is the Rh system, named for the rhesus monkey, in which it was first noted. Unlike the antibodies in the ABO system, antibodies to Rh antigen develop only after a person has been heavily exposed to the antigen, usually through transfusion or pregnancy. People are considered Rh positive if they have Rh antigen D; 85 percent of white people and 95 percent of African Americans possess the antigen.

Rh mismatches have their most dramatic effect in pregnancy, when the mother is Rh negative and the fetus is Rh positive. The mother can develop anti-Rh antibodies, which can cross the placenta and cause red blood cell agglutination in the fetus with fatal results. The more Rh-mismatched pregnancies a woman has, the more likely this reaction is to occur unless prevented by medical treatment.

OBSERVATIONS

The Blood-Brain Barrier

The concept of a barrier between the blood and the brain arose in the late nineteenth century when the German bacteriologist Paul Ehrlich observed that certain dyes administered intravenously to small animals stained all the organs except the brain. Ehrlich's interpretation of this was that the brain had a lower affinity for the dye than the other tissues, though some of the dye might have been expected to get through.

Ehrlich's student, Edwin E. Goldmann, injected the dye trypan blue directly into the cerebrospinal fluid of rabbits and dogs. The dye readily stained the entire brain but did not enter the bloodstream to stain the other internal organs. Goldmann concluded that the central nervous system is separated from the blood by a barrier of some kind.

Subsequent analysis showed that the brain is encased in a semipermeable lipid membrane that allows necessary substances into the brain and keeps other substances out. Thus, chemoanalysis, as well as chemotherapy, of the brain requires delivery of a brain-compatible carrier drug that can breach the blood-brain barrier.

First see MOLECULE

Bond, Chemical

Next see COVALENT SOLID

The attraction that attaches one atom to another.

Although atoms are the fundamental unit of matter as far as chemical identity is concerned, most of the materials we encounter do not involve single atoms, but atoms locked together into structures called molecules. In order to build molecules, it is necessary that atoms have a means of attaching themselves to one another. There are two general classes of bonds: those that involve movement of electrons between atoms and those that involve rearrangement of electrons within individual atoms without exchange. (*See* VALENCE.)

When two atoms are brought near each other, the outer (or valence) electrons of the two atoms can interact with each other. There are, essentially, three different kinds of bonds that can be formed by these electrons:

Ionic Bond. Consider an atom of sodium, which has one electron in its outer energy level, coming near an atom of chlorine, which has seven such electrons (or which, to make the statement in another way, lacks one electron to fill its outermost energy level). In this situation, an electron will move from the sodium to the chlorine, leaving behind a positively charged sodium and creating a negatively charged chlorine in the process. When this happens, ordinary electrical forces act to hold the two charged atoms together. Many crystals (like the ordinary table salt that results from the combination of sodium and chlorine we have just described) are held together by this kind of electrical force. It is called an ionic bond, because an atom (like sodium or chlorine) that has more or less than its usual number of electrons is called an ion. Many crystals and minerals contain ionic bonds.

Covalent Bond. When two atoms approach each other, often the lowest energy state available does not come from the permanent transfer of an electron, but from a process in which the two atoms share a pair of electrons. For example, if two carbon atoms, each with four electrons in its outer energy level, come together, one electron from each atom enters into the exchanged pair. The attraction created by this sharing is called a covalent bond. Many of the bonds that hold molecules together in living systems are of this type. (*See* ORGANIC COMPOUNDS.)

Metallic Bond. As the name implies, this type of bond is found in metals. It is created when each atom in a solid gives up one or more electrons, which are free to range throughout the material. The result is a system in which large, heavy ions are interspersed in a sea of electrons, like pieces of fruit in a gelatin mold. The electrons form a bond that holds the metal together in this situation, but they are also free to move in response to external electrical forces. This is why metals like copper are usually good conductors of electrical current. (*See* METAL.)

In addition to bonds created by the interactions of valence electrons, there are three ways in which atoms and molecules can be bonded together through the rearrangement of electrons without transfer.

Polar Molecules. In some molecules, the internal electrical forces are such that the electrons tend to congregate on one side of the molecules, leaving the other side with a positive charge. Overall, the molecule is still electrically neutral, but an atom approaching the molecule from the negative side will feel a force pushing its electrons away, while the compensating attraction of the (relatively far away) positive side will be much weaker. Consequently, the approaching atom will be polarized, with a positive charge located near the negative side of the original molecules. This will create an electrical bond between the two, even though both are electrically neutral. (*See* MOLECULE.)

The best known polar molecule is water, composed of two hydrogen atoms bound to one side of a single atom of oxygen. In the water molecule, the electrons tend to be located near the oxygen, leaving the hydrogen atoms with a positive charge. This is why water is such a good solvent—the polarization of the charges produces strong forces between the molecule and the atoms of any material put into it. As a result, the atoms of the material are pulled free and go into solution in the water. (*See* WATER.)

Hydrogen Bond. Because the electrons of hydrogen atoms tend to migrate when the hydrogen links to certain other atoms (oxygen or nitrogen, for example), it can act as a bridge to form another kind of bond. After the hydrogen has formed such a link and its electron has migrated, the positive charge left behind can attract another molecule or atom. In this situation, the hydrogen acts as a link between the two atoms or molecules to which it is attached. The bonds that hold the two sides of the double helix of DNA together are of this type. (*See* HYDROGEN.)

Van der Waals Bonds. This force is similar to that exerted by polar molecules in that it involves the rearrangement of electrons in atoms which remain electrically neutral, but differs in that that rearrangement is not permanent, as in the water molecule, but appears only when atoms come near each other. What can happen in such a situation is this: as two atoms approach each other, the electrons in each will be repelled by those in the other, causing each atom to become polarized. In some cases, the forces between the electrons and nuclei of the two atoms sum up to a net attraction, and a bond is formed. Van der Waals bonds tend to be relatively weak.

a

+

b

−

c

Two atoms (a) can form an ionic an bond (b) through the transfer of an electron from one to the other, or (c) a covalent bond by the sharing of an electron.

Further Reading
Emsley, J., *Molecules at an Exhibition* (1999); Hall, N., *The New Chemistry* (2000); Hoffman, R., *The Same and Not the Same* (1997); Stratham, P., *Mendeleev's Dream* (2001).

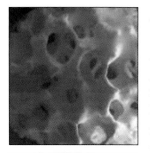

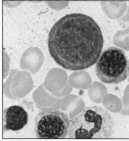

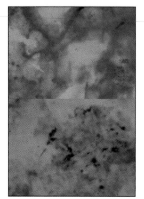

Above, top, the architectural form of bone tissue. Center, red blood cells are produced in the bone marrow. Below, interior structure of normal human bone.

Interior Bone Structure

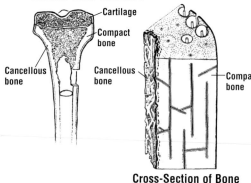

Cartilage
Compact bone
Cancellous bone
Cancellous bone
Compact bone

Cross-Section of Bone

First see SKELETAL SYSTEM

Bone and Bone Growth

Next see CALCIUM METABOLISM

Bone is a living tissue that grows throughout life, remodeling itself in young animals to provide greater space for internal organs, regenerating itself in mature animals to maintain its own strength, and serving as a repository of calcium and phosphate that can be drawn on to preserve the chemical balance of the body.

Competition. Bone consists of a matrix of collagen fibers, held together by a gelatinous medium called ground substance, and filled in with hydroxyapatite crystals, bone salts made up mostly of calcium and phosphate. In humans, bones contain more than 98 percent of the body's calcium and 66 percent of its phosphate. In its structure, bone is like reinforced concrete—the collagen fibers, like the steel of reinforced concrete, provide tensile strength, while the bones' salts, like the cement, sand and rock of concrete, provide compressional strength.

Bone Formation. Bone forms initially in one of two ways. In the typical vertebrate embryo, most of the skeleton forms as cartilage, and is replaced by bone—a process called endochondral ossification. In a long bone, such as in the arm or leg, the process begins in the middle of the shaft, called the diaphysis, and moves toward the two ends, called the epiphyses. New cartilage continues to be deposited as fast as old cartilage is replaced by bone, so the shaft grows while it is turning to bone. Eventually the process slows, with growth occurring only at the epiphyseal plate, a narrow band of cartilage between the shaft and each epiphysis. In mammals and birds, this process stops soon after sexual maturity when the epiphyseal plates turn to bone. But growth in diameter continues to take place, without thickening of the bone, as bone is deposited on the outer surface and eroded from the marrow cavity.

Membrane bones, found chiefly in the jaw, skull, and pectoral girdles, form without a cartilaginous precursor. Instead, collagen is excreted and bone crystals are deposited on that matrix. In either case, temporary spongy bone forms first. It later erodes and is replaced either by compact bone, permanent spongy bone, or a marrow cavity.

Even in a mature body, bone is continually being remodeled: Old bone is absorbed, or dissolved, and replaced by new bone. Large, multinucleated cells called osteoclasts eat away small tunnels in the bone, which are then filled in with new bone by osteoblasts, cells found on the outer surfaces of bones and in bone cavities. In an adult human, bone deposition occurs on about 4 percent of all surfaces at any given time. The new bone is deposited in concentric circles around a canal, called a haversian canal, through which blood vessels run to supply the bone cells with oxygen. Each unit of bone around a haversian canal is called an osteon.

Remodeling allows bones to thicken in response to stress; thus, weight-bearing bones grow stronger and sometimes change shape in response to particular stresses. Since bone grows weaker and more brittle with age, replacing it with new material maintains the overall strength of the bone. When a bone fractures, new bone forms quickly, as large numbers of new osteoblasts are produced. (*See* ADAPTATION.)

Several substances in the body stimulate bone growth: growth hormone; androgens; estrogens; and vitamin D. (*See* STEROID HORMONE.)

First see ELEMENT

Boron Group

Next see METAL

Group IIIA on the Periodic Table, known as the boron group, includes the elements boron, aluminum, gallium, indium, and thallium.

Group IIIA is not immediately adjacent to the IIA group, the alkaline earth metals, but is instead separated from them by the expanse of the transition metals. Group IIIA is the first family in which sharp variations in properties and behavior are seen among the members. In addition to these variations, IIIA is the first group to contain both metals and non-metals.

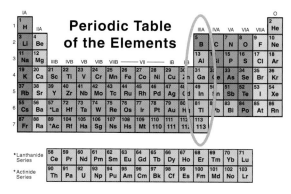

Boron is actually the only non-metal in this family, but the rest of the elements are on the border of the divide and so are more properly called metalloids, meaning they exhibit both metal and non-metal properties. All of the members of this group have three electrons (negatively charged particles) in their outermost (valence) energy levels.

Boron is located next to carbon and mimics

some of its properties. Boron forms covalent bonds, in which electrons are shared between atoms. Boron is capable of forming compounds analogous to hydrocarbons, the long-linked chains of carbon atoms with attached hydrogens. However, the smallest possible boron hydride unit consists of three atoms and has a difficult geometry with a tendency for structures to close in upon themselves. For this reason, boron cannot form the kinds of chains and rings that carbon does. The boron complexes are cosahedron fragments, with the crystalline state of boron consisting of 12 atoms and forming a complete cosahedron. (*See* CARBON; HYDROCARBONS.)

Aluminum is a very popular and well-known metal used in a variety of building and structural materials, as it is lightweight, yet strong. Aluminum is used in space shuttles, "tin" cans, and other containers, as well as in various foils. Aluminum exhibits mostly metallic properties in terms of luster, conductivity, and the ability to form ionic bonds, in which electrons are gained or lost. Aluminum is also capable of forming covalent bonds. Gallium, very similar to aluminum in terms of chemistry, is important in semiconductor fabrication. (*See* ALUMINUM.)

One other noteworthy element in this family is indium, which together with another element, antimony, is used in an array camera on the Hale telescope to photograph regions of space around certain types of stars.

First see ELEMENTARY PARTICLE

Bosons

Next see QUANTUM STATISTICS

Elementary particles that obey the Bose-Einstein statistics, which predict the probability that the energy levels of a set of elementary particles with integral spin will be distributed in a certain way.

The elementary particles that obey the statistics developed by Albert Einstein and Indian physicist S. N. Bose, include the photons, the pions, the kaons, and other mesons. Among the composite atomic systems that obey the Bose-Einstein rules are the hydrogen atom and the deuteron. Particles that do not obey the Bose-Einstein statistics are classified as fermions; all particles now known are either fermions or bosons. Wolfgang Pauli showed that there is a connection between the spin of a particle and its statistics—particles with spin expressed in integers are bosons and thus are not subject to the exclusion principle; particles with half-integer spins are fermions and are subject to the exclusion principle. Electrons thus are fermions while photons are bosons.

The weak force, which is responsible for radioactive decay, such as the decay of a neutron into a proton, an electron, and an antineutrino, is mediated by three intermediate vector bosons, designated W^+, W^-, and Z. These all have masses in the order of 100 giga-electron-volts, making them the heaviest known elementary particles. The discovery of these three intermediate vector bosons was made in 1983 at the CERN nuclear collider. That discovery confirmed the theory of the unification of the weak and electromagnetic interactions. (*See* NUCLEAR FORCES.)

The electromagnetic interaction between basic particles is mediated by the photon, which is also a massless vector boson. Finally, strong interactions between elementary particles are mediated by gluons, which are classified as massless vector bosons. The gluons that mediate strong interactions are confined to small regions of space and cannot be observed directly. But there is convincing evidence that gluons exist within the subatomic particles called hadrons, and that they can be emitted by these hadrons. Their emission results in observed jets of more hadrons.

Thus, all the interactions among elementary particles may be unified into one grand theory in which bosons mediate the weak, strong, and electromagnetic forces, and perhaps gravitational interactions as well. (*See* GRAND UNIFIED THEORIES.)

First see NEURON

Brain

Next see NERVOUS SYSTEMS

The mass of neural cells that regulate all mental and physical activity in animals.

The human brain is the most complex system known in the universe and the study of the brain remains one of the major challenges to science in the 21st century.

The major working element of the brain is a type of cell known as the neuron. Neurons come in many different shapes and sizes, but they all share some common features. They have a cell body, which contains the nucleus and other working parts of the cell. Leading away from the cell body are several extensions of fibers. The most striking of these is the axon, which carries outgoing signals. The axon can be quite long— some, for example, carry signals from the brain to the foot. Near the end of the axon the structure branches and each branch, in general, will connect to a different neuron. In addition to axons, neurons have other extensions, called dendrites, whose function it is to receive signals from other neurons. In the brain, each neuron may send signals to, and receive signals from, as many as 1,000 other cells.

Signals. The signals that travel down axons are not simple electrical currents, but involve a complicated flow of potassium and sodium ions

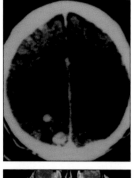

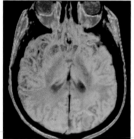

The diagnostic tools now available for brain medicine have made marked strides in the past two decades. Above, top, a CAT scan of a brain shows a lesion in the hindbrain; bottom, an MRI identifies the lesion as cancerous. A biopsy will have to be performed to determine whether the cancer is benign or malignant. The patient has felt no effects of the growth at this stage.

across the cell membrane. When the signal arrives at the end of an axon branch, it does not jump across like a spark. Instead, a spray of molecules known as neurotransmitters is emitted from the end of the "upstream" neuron. These molecules float across the gap between neurons and attach to special receptors on the "downstream" side. Each neuron takes the input from all of the signals that it receives and, by a process not yet understood, decides whether to send out a signal on its own or remain in a quiescent state.

Structure. The brain is made up of 100 billion or so neurons. (There are approximately as many neurons in the brain as there are stars in the Milky Way galaxy.) These neurons, with supporting cells, arteries, and veins are arranged in a specific set of structures inside the skull. The most common arrangements involve neurons clustered together in more or less globular units, called nuclei, and spead out in sheets, called cortices (the singular is cortex).

Each half of the brain is shaped something like a boxing glove with the thumb on the outside. At the base of the system, roughly at the place where the gloves lace up, are structures known as the brain stem and cerebellum, which are involved with regulating bodily functions. The brain stem, which is essentially a thickening at the end of the spinal column, is involved in processes like regulating breathing and heart rate, while the cerebellum controls unconscious bodily movements such as those that allow one to keep one's balance when bending over to pick something up.

Moving upward in the brain, roughly to the region of the palms of the boxing gloves, we come to the region known as the diencephalon, which is the main coordinating center of the brain. In this region is the thalamus, two small egg-shaped bundles of neurons that relay signals brought into the brain through the spinal cord to higher regions of the brain. Below the thalamus is a bundle of neurons called the hypothalamus, which is involved in basic functions such as pleasure, pain, hunger, thirst, and sex. The hypothalamus is connected to the pituitary gland, the master gland for the control of hormones in the endocrine system.

Grey Matter. The outer parts of the brain (corresponding to the padding in the boxing gloves) are the two cerebral hemispheres, which are connected by a thick sheath of nerve fibers. The very outermost layer of the hemispheres—the wrinkled "grey matter"—is the cerebral cortex. This is where most of the higher cognitive functions of the brain are located. The cerebral

hemispheres are divided into lobes, and each lobe, in turn, has many structures inside of it. The frontal lobes, located in the anterior part of each hemisphere, control conscious movement and many reasoning processes. The occipital lobe, located at the back of the brain, is where visual signals from the optic nerve are processed before they are sent forward.

Across the center of the brain are the parietal lobes, which deal with information about the state of the body. The temporal lobes, located on the sides of the brain (the thumbs of the boxing gloves), are the seats of learning, emotion, memory, and hearing.

Workings. It is important to realize that the brain is not like a computer, with a central processing unit that sends out orders in a neural chain of command. Instead, the brain consists of many highly specialized groups of neurons, each

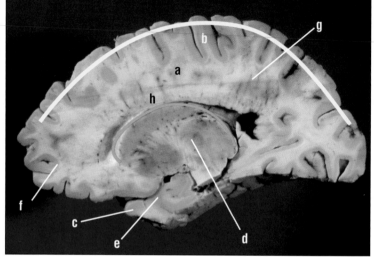

The Major Structures of the Human Brain.
The human brain has three major regions—the forebrain (to the right, above); the midbrain; and the hindbrain. The parts of the brain are: (a) cerebrum; (b) cortex layer (shown in yellow); (c) pineal gland; (d) thalamus; (e) hypothalamus; (f) frontal lobe; (g) parietal lobe; and (h) corpus calosum.

of which does one job very well. For example, in the occipital lobe there are some neurons that will fire only if there is a horizontal line in the visual field, others that will fire only if there is a vertical line, and still others that will fire only if there is a line tilted at a specific angle. The output of all of these specialized neurons is amalgamated, by a process not understood, to produce the picture of the world we see.

Brain Activity. The brain is intimately involved in virtually every event that takes place inside the body or in its interactions with the external environment. If the eyes are the windows of the soul, the brain is the seat of the mind—of thought, emotion, memory, and speech. (*See* SENSORY MECHANISMS.)

All sensations are experienced within the brain alone. The eyes do not see; they are simply sense organs, designed to pick up light stimuli and images. Only after the information is "processed" by the brain can vision be said to occur. The same can be said about hearing, taste, smell, touch, hunger, thirst, and temperature perception. If the brain is stimulated directly, either with drugs or physical probes, all of these sensations can be produced without any stimulus from the outside world.

Organization. The three main sections of the brain are the cerebrum, cerebellum, and brainstem. The cerebellum is chiefly involved in coordination and balance, and the brainstem deals with automatic functions such as heart rate and breathing. Most of the "higher" functions that we associate with the brain, such as speech, memory, and thought, take place in the cerebrum.

The cerebrum is divided into right and left hemispheres which are connected by a "bridge" known as the corpus callosum. Each hemisphere consists of four lobes: frontal, parietal, temporal, and occipital. The right hemisphere controls the left side of the body and the left hemisphere controls the right side of the body. One hemisphere is usually more dominant than the other, causing "handedness."

It is in the outer layer of the cerebrum, the cerebral cortex, that all of the activity takes place. The cortex is only two millimeters thick, yet contains numerous areas for sensory reception, motor control, and associative events. Researchers long ago "mapped out" the cerebrum in a broad manner, locating particular functions, such as memory, within a specific lobe. In recent years, the mapping process has been taking place on the cellular level.

Investigating the Brain. In the past, stroke and trauma victims were relied upon heavily to determine which activities were situated in which areas, drawing correlations between damaged sites and loss of functionality. Patient research still yields much meaningful information, but ethical constraints obviously restrict research in this area. With the advent of sophisticated imaging devices such as positron emission tomography (PET) and magnetic resonance imaging (MRI), researchers are able to study the brain at the organizational level, in terms of which neurons are activated and how they interact when called upon to perform a specific task.

Activated brain cells use more oxygen than cells at rest. The activated cells release nitric oxide into the blood, which in turn causes oxygen to be released from nearby capillaries. MRI can distinguish between oxygenated and deoxygenated blood and can therefore identify stimulated areas and specific circuits.

Subjects can be asked to perform specific tasks while undergoing MRI and researchers can see which areas "light up." The technique is sophisticated enough to distinguish the degree of stimulation. For example, more brain activity is seen when a subject produces a new thought than when a thought already known to the subject is repeated.

PET scans also show blood flow in the brain shifting to different locations, depending on which task is being performed. However, neither PET nor MRI measure nerve-cell activity directly, but simply track increased blood flow to a region where the nerve cells are activated. Unfortunately, the time it takes a nerve to transmit impulses is measured in milliseconds, whereas blood flow takes a second or more.

The messages sent by and to neurons are electrical in nature. Positive and negative ions are distributed in a specific pattern in and around the neural membrane. At a key signal, the ions migrate, causing a wave of depolarization to occur. A fully functioning brain can generate as much as 10 watts of electrical power.

The electrical activity of the brain is displayed in the form of brainwaves. There are four types of brainwaves, ranging from those signifying most activity to least: beta, alpha, theta, and delta.

Beta waves are a sign of arousal and a strongly engaged mind. Alpha waves represent non-arousal, in which an individual is at rest but still alert. Alpha waves are slower and higher in amplitude than beta waves. Theta waves are of even greater amplitude and slower frequency. A "daydreaming" state would be characteristic of these brain waves. During theta, an individual is in a state of mental relaxation and is able to free associate and think creatively. The lowest state of activity is found in delta, whose waves are of the greatest amplitude and slowest frequency. Deep, dreamless sleep is characteristic of delta.

Sleep. During sleep the brain is still quite active. Dreaming takes place during specific periods, during which rapid eye movements occur under closed lids. Because of this movement, the period is known as REM. Sleep is divided into 90-minute cycles, which alternate between REM and non-REM periods. When delta waves increase to the frequency of theta, active dreaming takes place.

Although one brainwave state may predominate at any given time, the remaining three brain states are present at all times, but at lower levels, almost as "background," or noise.

For all that we know about the brain, it is still the organ of greatest mystery in the body. Identifying physical structures of the brain is a

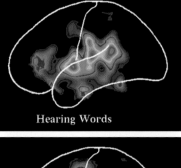

Hearing Words

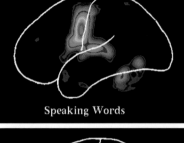

Speaking Words

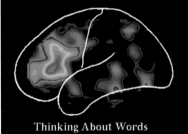

Thinking About Words

A PET scan of the brain during speech identifies blood concentrations at different points. Top, the primary auditory center is stimulated by hearing words spoken. Middle, the stimulation of the area of the brain that controls speech muscles is activated. Bottom, thinking about what was said or what to say stimulates the cerebral thought centers.

far cry from determining how the cells and networks work to form the human mind.

Further Reading
Blakemore, Colin, *Mechanics of the Mind* (1977); Ornstein, Robert, *The Amazing Brain* (1991); Pinker, Steven, *How the Mind Works* (1999); Restak, R., *The Brain* (1984); Rose, S. P., *The Conscious Brain* (1983).

For basic information regarding brain components, see NEURON; NERVOUS SYSTEMS; *and* BREATHING REGULATION. *Behavioral aspects and brain activity are central to* AGGRESSION; AGING; EMOTION; INSTINCT; SLEEP; *and* SENSORY MECHANISMS. *Brain disorders are covered in* ALZHEIMER'S DISEASE; AUTISM; EPILEPSY; *and* PARKINSON'S DISEASE.

First see RESPIRATORY SYSTEMS

Breathing Regulation

Next see NERVOUS SYSTEMS

Involuntary breathing is regulated by a complex interplay between elements of the neural system, muscles, and lungs. The respiratory control centers located in the medulla and pons of the brainstem generate the basic respiratory rhythm and activate the muscles that cause inhalation. Chemoreceptors in the medulla and the body sense changes in arterial levels of carbon dioxide, oxygen, and hydrogen ions (pH) and signal the respiratory control centers so they can adjust breathing to stabilize levels of these blood gases—the basic mission of respiration.

The result of these, and several less central factors, is a network of control that is extraordinarily sensitive, powerful, and flexible. During strenuous exercise, for instance, the body's consumption of oxygen and formation of carbon dioxide can increase 20-fold. But ventilation of the lungs increases in such close synchrony that the arterial levels of oxygen, carbon dioxide, and hydrogen ions remain almost exactly as they were at rest. In a low-oxygen environment, the system can acclimate itself so well that ventilation of the lungs increases 400-500 percent.

The brainstem's respiratory centers are composed of three major groups of neurons. Neurons of the dorsal medulla emit repetitive bursts of discharges that trigger inspiration. In normal breathing, the signal starts weakly and increases steadily for about two seconds, causing contraction of the diaphragm and intercostal muscles that move the rib cage up and out. The signal ends abruptly, the muscles relax, the rib cage falls back to its resting position, and the lungs recoil, a passive process that causes expiration. Then the inspiratory signal starts again.

The pneumotaxic center, located in the pons, sends signals to the inspiratory neurons that set their switch-off point. This affects the rate of breathing since the shorter the inspiration, the shorter the expiration.

The third major group of neurons, located in the ventrolateral medulla, come into play when greater than normal ventilation is needed; some boost inspiration, others expiration.

Rhythm Control. The respiratory centers are said to contain a central rhythm generator. It is thought to involve interplay between various neural groups of the medulla, but its nature and means of functioning have not been established.

To maintain the proper levels of oxygen, carbon dioxide, and pH—despite exertion, illness or altitude changes—the respiratory centers' signals vary in intensity. Central chemoreceptors, located in the medulla, signal other parts of the respiratory centers to respond to changes in carbon dioxide or hydrogen ions (pH) in the interstitial fluid of the medulla and the cerebrospinal fluid that bathes the brain. A rise in either chemical will trigger increased ventilation. If either falls, respiratory centers are depressed. If carbon dioxide falls enough, breathing will cease altogether.

It may seem counterintuitive, but in humans and other mammals, carbon dioxide—not oxygen—is the dominant factor that triggers changes in breathing. Carbon dioxide is a better trigger because its concentration in the blood and tissues closely reflects, in an inverse way, the degree of ventilation of the lung. By contrast, a hemoglobin buffer system ensures that oxygen will be delivered to the tissues in nearly normal amounts even when its concentration in the lungs varies widely. So oxygen pressure in the alveoli of the lung must fall well below normal to have an effect on breathing regulation.

Even very low oxygen levels do not stimulate the central chemoreceptors mentioned above, but they do stimulate the peripheral chemoreceptors. These are located in the carotid and aortic bodies, small collections of gland-like cells found near the arteries for which they are named. Signals from these receptors reach the medulla through the glossopharyngeal nerve, in the case of the carotid bodies, or the vagus nerve, in the case of the aortic bodies.

Below, the dynamics of breathing regulation. The effects of increased levels of PCO_2 (blue arrows) and decreased levels of PO_2 (red arrows).

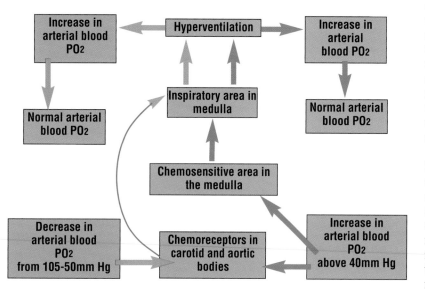

Increase in arterial blood PO_2

Hyperventilation

Increase in arterial blood PO_2

Normal arterial blood PO_2

Inspiratory area in medulla

Normal arterial blood PO_2

Chemosensitive area in the medulla

Decrease in arterial blood PO_2 from 105-50mm Hg

Chemoreceptors in carotid and aortic bodies

Increase in arterial blood PO_2 above 40mm Hg

Low oxygen levels, as perceived by the peripheral chemoreceptors, will lead to increased respiration. But normally, the effect is blunted because increased respiration causes carbon dioxide and hydrogen ions to fall, which in turn quickly depresses the respiratory centers. If, however, a person has a pulmonary disease, such as pneumonia, carbon dioxide and hydrogen ion levels may not necessarily fall when respiration increases. That means low oxygen levels can trigger a significant increase in ventilation without being short-circuited. (See CIRCULATORY SYSTEMS.)

Breathing Reflexes. In addition to these mechanisms, a number of reflexes are at work in regulating breathing. If the lungs become overinflated, stretch receptors in the walls of the bronchi and bronchioles stop inhalation by adjusting the switch-off threshold for the inspiratory neurons of the medulla. This process—called the Hering-Breuer inflation reflex—is similar in effect to that produced by the neurons of the pneumotaxic center. (See ALLERGY.)

Meanwhile, irritant receptors in the lung respond to dust, mucus, or other particles by causing coughing and sneezing. J receptors—named for their juxtaposition to the pulmonary capillaries—are stimulated by engorgement of the capillaries or pulmonary edema, a buildup of fluid commonly seen in congestive heart failure. J receptors are suspected of causing the feeling of breathlessness. (See HEART.)

First see FISSION, NUCLEAR

Breeder Reactor

Next see NUCLEAR POWER

A nuclear reactor that produces more fuel as it produces power.

A breeder reactor is one that produces more nuclear fuel than it consumes. This is done by surrounding the power-generating nuclear core, which consists of a fuel in which nuclear fission takes place, such as uranium-235, with a non-fissionable element, such as uranium-238, which is changed to a fissionable element when it is bombarded by neutrons coming from the core of the reactor. For example, the bombardment of neutrons changes atoms of uranium-238 to atoms of uranium-239, which decay to form neptunium-239 and then to form plutonium-239. By converting uranium-238, which is not usable in a nuclear reactor, to a fissionable material that can be used in a power-generating reactor, widespread use of such breeders can increase the available nuclear fuel by at least 60-fold.

Long thin stainless steel rods filled with uranium fuel are assembled in bundles and lowered into the reactor, where fission "breeds" more fuel.

Development of the breeder reactor began in the United States in 1951, when the U.S. Atomic Energy Commission inaugurated the experimental breeder reactor-1, EBR-1. (See NUCLEAR WEAPONS.) Construction of the second experimental reactor, EBR-2, was completed in 1963, when it went into long-term operation. The first commercial breeder reactor that was licensed for operation was the Enrico Fermi Fast Breeder Reactor, which went into operation in 1965 and was discontinued in 1972 because of safety concerns. Breeder reactor research is no longer pursued in the United States. (See HAZARDOUS WASTE.)

First see AUTOMOTIVE DESIGN

Bridge Design

Next see HIGHWAY ENGINEERING

Bridge design and construction go back to the earliest days of civilization. After the log or piece of wood used to cross a stream or gap, the simplest and oldest type is the pile-and-beam bridge, which consists of a series of wooden beams that support the deck of the bridge, with the ends of the beams driven into the bed of a stream or into the ground. These bridges were common by the time of the Roman Empire, and they still are all over the world for short spans on country roads or railroads.

A variation on the theme is the girder bridge, which is made of iron or steel. A girder that is supported just at its ends is a simple span, while one that has three or more supports is a continuous span. There are some girder bridges that are supported at just one end;

Above, the Golden Gate Bridge was the world's longest suspension bridge when it opened in 1937.

they are known as cantilever bridges.

Arch bridges, as the name implies, have a roadbed that is supported by an arch. The Romans built a number of arch bridges, made of stone. The arch that supports the bridge exerts both vertical and horizontal thrust, and therefore needs substantial support at both ends. Arch bridges are still being built, but the arch today generally is made of steel and concrete, because stone is too expensive. In the middle of the 19th century, the French developed the hinged arch, which has greater bearing ability.

Truss bridges were developed in the late 19th century. A truss is a metal framework that is specifically designed for greatest strength at the

Resonance can be a suspension bridge's worst enemy. Left, gusts of wind at just the right (or wrong) frequency caused the Tacoma Narrows Bridge to twist, undulate, and eventually collapse in 1940.

Further Reading

Gordon, J. E., *Structures: Or Why Things Don't Fall Down* (1988); Levy, M., *Why Buildings Fall Down* (1994); Petroski, H., *Engineers of Dreams* (1996).

points where the load on the bridge exerts the greatest pressure. If the deck of the bridge is at the top, it is a deck truss; if it is at the bottom, it is a through truss. Most movable bridges are truss spans.

A suspension bridge has two or more towers that have one or more flexible cables that support the bed of the bridge. The Chinese built suspension bridges as early as the sixth century, but they did not appear in Europe until the 18th century, with chains supporting the deck. Today's familiar suspension bridge, with wire cables supporting the deck, was introduced by the French in the middle of the 19th century. The use of cables allowed a great reduction in weight. Many famous bridges, including the Golden Gate Bridge in California and the George Washington Bridge linking New York and New Jersey, are suspension bridges. The rigidity of the deck that is hung from the cables is maintained by using stiffening trusses that run from side to side of the deck. The newest bridge design is the cable-stayed bridge, in which cables run diagonally from each segment over the tower, and back down to the opposite segment. Such bridges do not require massive anchors at either end of the span, and often can be built with only one tower.

Bridge Types. Other types of bridges include the swing bridge, which is pivoted on a central pier; the bascule, a descendant of the medieval drawbridge, whose segments can be pivoted so that they can be swung upward to allow ships to pass; the retractable bridge, whose segments can be moved on wheels; and the pontoon bridge, chiefly used for military purposes, which has a number of floating members that support the bed of the bridge.

Today's bridges are built on the basis of careful scientific and engineering studies. After the site of a new bridge has been chosen, studies are made of the topography, geology, and meteorology of the location. The most appropriate type of bridge is chosen on the basis of these studies. Bridge engineers calculate the loading capacity of the bridge on the basis of the anticipated traffic and the stresses exerted by wind and weather.

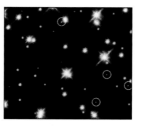

Above, white dwarf stars in the M4 galaxy.

Above, the brown dwarf Gliese 229B as seen by the Hubble Space Telescope.

An exact stress analysis is done to determine the tensile strength, compressive strength, and shearing strength of each member of the bridge structure; computers today play a major role in such calculations. For very large bridges, scale models may be built to verify the results of the studies. If the bridge is to be made of steel, samples of the steel are subjected to a variety of tests to be sure that they can carry the anticipated load with a satisfactory margin of safety. (*See* STEEL.)

First see STAR

Brown and White Dwarfs

Next see PLANETS, FORMATION OF

Brown dwarfs and white dwarfs are both small stars, but they differ greatly from one another. A brown dwarf is a body that never quite becomes a star, while a white dwarf is at a last stage in the evolution of an average-size star such as our sun.

Brown Dwarfs. A typical brown dwarf has a mass 8 percent or less than that of the sun. This mass is too small to generate the internal temperatures that will ignite the nuclear burning of hydrogen to release energy and light. A brown dwarf therefore contracts steadily, reaching a radius that depends on its mass and composition. For a star with a mass 7 percent that of the sun, the time required for this contraction is about one billion years; for brown dwarfs with smaller masses, the contraction time is less.

Once such a star has contracted completely, it simply becomes cooler over time, with steadily diminishing emissions of light and lowered internal temperatures. After 2 or 3 billion years, a typical brown dwarf will have a temperature of about 1,000° Centigrade and light emissions so small that the star is difficult to be observed from the Earth. These stars can be distinguished from white dwarfs because of their very cool surface temperatures and because their internal composition is essentially unchanged from the time of the star's formation—its interior still is about 75 percent hydrogen.

In many respects, the dividing line between brown dwarfs and large planets is not easy to determine. Jupiter, the largest planet in the solar system with a mass that is less than one percent of the mass of the sun, could be considered to be a brown dwarf because it is radiating at the expense of its internal energy. The mechanism of formation may be the only way that astronomers can distinguish between low-mass brown dwarfs and high-mass planets. (*See* JUPITER.)

White Dwarfs. A white dwarf, by contrast, starts its life as a star of ordinary size. It goes through a prolonged period of hydrogen burning, which is followed by another long period in which it burns the helium that is created by the burning of hydrogen. The star then evolves into a red giant, develops a core of carbon that is created by the burning of heavier and heavier elements, and eventually evolves into a white dwarf. Internally, such a white dwarf has reached the stage of electron degeneracy, which means that the density of electrons in its interior is so high that it is the determining feature of the star's interior.

The typical mass of the white dwarfs observed in the universe is between 60 and 80 percent of the mass of our sun. Their cores consist mostly of oxygen and carbon, with a thin layer of hydrogen on the outside. Internal temperatures are not high enough to burn nuclear fuel, and so the only energy source is the thermal energy of the ions in the interior of the star. A white dwarf at this stage still has billions of years of cooling ahead of it.

First see ATOM

Brownian Motion

Next see COLLOID

The continuous movement of microscopically small particles suspended in a fluid.

Brownian motion was first observed in 1827 by a British botanist, Robert Brown, looking at a suspension of pollen grains. Brown later showed that the phenomenon occurs in a suspension of any particles in that size range. Brownian motion was first thought to be the manifestation of some unknown vital force.

A full explanation of the effect was not given until 1905, when Albert Einstein did a mathematical analysis of the subject based on the statistical distribution of the velocity of large numbers of small particles. (Officially, Einstein was awarded the Nobel Prize for his explanation of Brownian motion and not for special relativity, which was still controversial.)

According to Einstein's explanation, the effect occurs because the surface of a particle immersed in fluid is bombarded on all sides by a multitude of molecules of that fluid, whose movements fluctuate constantly. If the bombardment was completely symmetrical, the tiny particle would not move at all. But the bombardment is not symmetrical. At any given mo-ment, the particle may get a bigger hit on one side, which makes it move in the opposite direction. But that hit is soon countered by other hits by molecules toward which the particle is directed. These tiny changes of motion go on endlessly. The larger the immersed particle, the greater the force of molecular hits that is required to set it in motion. Since large fluctuations in molecular movements are less common than small fluctuations, Brownian motion cannot occur in particles above microscopic size. (*See* ATOM.)

Further Reading
Chandrasekhar, S., *From White Dwarfs to Black Holes: The Legacy of S. Chandrasekhar* (1999); Jastrow, Robert, *Red Giants and White Dwarfs* (1990); Friedman, Herbert, *The Astronomer's Universe: Stars, Galaxies, and Cosmos* (1998); Szebehely, Victor G., *Adventures in Celestial Mechanics* (1998).

First see ACCELERATOR, PARTICLE

Bubble Chamber

Next see ELEMENTARY PARTICLE

A device used by physicists to record the trajectory of high-speed, electrically charged subatomic particles in particle accelerators.

The bubble chamber was invented in 1952 by American physicist Donald A. Glaser, who received the Nobel Prize for his achievement. A bubble chamber is a vessel filled with a transparent liquid so highly superheated that a moving ionized particle passing through it initiates boiling in the liquid along its path by knocking electrons out of some of the atoms that it encounters. The superheating of the liquid in the bubble chamber is done by suddenly reducing the pressure of the liquid to a point below which the liquid boils. During a brief period after this pressure reduction, the liquid will boil only where a charged particle passes through. A number of different liquids, including hydrogen at a temperature near absolute zero, have been used in bubble chambers. These chambers had an advantage over other detectors when they were introduced, since they could provide a pure absorber of radiation at the highest density then available and volumes up to 2 meters long.

Method. During the short time when tracks are present in a bubble chamber, they must be illuminated and photographed through glass or quartz windows. The chamber is usually illuminated by bulbs using xenon gas. The windows and camera lenses used must be of high optical quality, and they generally accommodate wide angles. Because the chamber may be as deep as 10 feet, photography requires a camera with a large depth of focus and a small aperture. These cameras generally use 35-millimeter or 70-millimeter film, which must be held absolutely flat to avoid distortion. Three or more stereo views of a particle's path through the chamber are photographed to make sure that the recorded particle path is accurate.

The particles from accelerators that pass through bubble chambers can be beams of protons, antiprotons, electrons, charged pi mesons, or charged K mesons. These particles are selected by arrays of magnets and electrostatic beam separators that act on a spray of many particles emerging from a target exposed to a primary circulating beam. Different arrangements can make possible exposure to gamma rays, neutrons, and neutrinos. Millions of pictures can be taken per experiment, for distribution to research groups that can study and analyze the nature of the events recorded by the photographs. Bubble chambers have largely been replaced by superior computer-assisted electronic detectors.

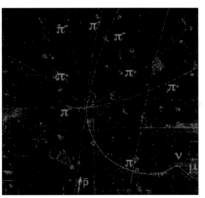

The analysis of complex bubble chamber tracks was once done with a magnifying glass, a strong light—and lots of time. Computers have taken over this laborious task, analyzing thousands of images in minutes.

First see CARBON

Buckminsterfullerenes

Next see NANOTECHNOLOGY

Molecules made up of clusters of 60 carbon atoms bonded together in a polyhedral structure consisting of hexagons and pentagons.

Buckminsterfullerenes (or fullerenes, for short) are named after Richard Buckminster Fuller, a twentieth-century American architect, because the molecular structure resembles that of the geodesic dome, which Fuller invented and which today is widely used. The buckminsterfullerene molecule was first identified in 1985, two years after Fuller's death. It was seen in the molecular products that came into existence when a high-powered laser was aimed at a target of graphite, a form of carbon. It

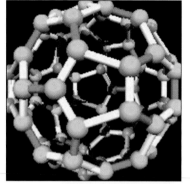

has since been found that fullerenes can also be made by creating an electric arc between two graphite electrodes in an atmosphere of an inert gas such as argon. It is this resulting molecule that is sometimes called a fullerene. A yellow crystalline solid form is also called a fullerite; it is not soluble in water but is soluble in benzene.

Derivative Molecules. Since fullerenes were first developed, a number of chemists have created derivatives of the original molecule. These derivatives are made by attaching any one of a number of organic groups to the carbon atoms on the buckyball sphere. It has also been found possible to produce novel enclosure compounds, which are made by trapping ions of one or another metal inside the carbon-60 sphere. Some of these enclosure compounds have semiconducting properties and so their use in modern electronic devices is being explored. When the electric-arc method of producing buckminsterfullerenes is used, a by-product is the production of a smaller number of fullerenes with different structures, such as carbon-70. These variations on the theme have structures that are less symmetrical than that of the buckyball.

Scientists have also been able to produce forms of carbon molecules in which the carbon atoms are linked so that they form a cylindrical framework, rather than a sphere. These carbon cylinders are called buckytubes, or nanotubes, because they have a diameter that is measured in nanometers, or billionths of a meter. Nanotubes open the possibility of using individual molecules as the structural basis for nanomachines.

Top, 82-year-old Richard Buckminster ("Bucky" to friends) Fuller poses in front of a geodesic dome of his design. Middle, a model of a carbon-60 fullerene. Because of his nickname, these structures are also known as "Buckyballs." Bottom, a computer model of buckytubes, used in nanotechnology.

The background for this emerging new technology is found in CRYSTAL *and* ARCHITECTURAL ENGINEERING. *Further relevant information is discussed in* CARBON; CLUSTER, ATOM; NANOTECHNOLOGY; *and* SOLID. *See also* BOND, CHEMICAL.

First see FORCE

Buoyancy

Next see UNDERWATER EXPLORATION

All buoyant vessels rely on Archimedes' principle, a relationship that was stated by that Greek scientist in the third century B.C.E. Archimedes said that if the weight of a body of a given volume is the same as the weight of the water it displaces, that body will float, with its top just at the level of the water surface. If the body weighs less than an equal body of water, it will float higher, displacing just enough water to equal its own weight.

The earliest vessels were built of wood, which is lighter than water, and the age of wooden vessels lasted into the nineteenth century. Large wooden vessels that carried crews and cargo could be built because they contained a large volume of air, which is much lighter than water. The steel hull of a modern ship is designed to resist the stresses that result from the pressure of the water in which it floats, the weight of the machinery, crew, and cargo that it carries, and the forces it experiences in rough seas. The hull is stiffened by bulkheads, internal structures that run both from side to side and from end to end of the ship. The hull is also designed to minimize resistance to the water through which it passes.

Submarines use a complex system of air and water tanks to maintain a neutral buoyancy, an exact balance between their weight and their displacement. The principle of buoyancy is the basis of all modern ship design, as it has been for many centuries. (*See* SUBMARINE TECHNOLOGY.)

The upward buoyant force of water never ceases to amaze as ships of enormous weight, like the Trident submarine, right, float by virtue of Archimedes' Principle.

Calcium Metabolism

Next see BONE AND BONE GROWTH

Calcium is an essential mineral in the body. In addition to its well-known role in causing bone rigidity and hardness, calcium-regulated functions in the body include: cell motility, muscle contractions, nerve impulse transmission, and hormonal responses. Calcium also plays a role in blood clotting. (*See* BONE AND BONE GROWTH.)

Blood Reactions. There is a continual series of interactions among the calcium levels in the blood, calcium found within a cell, and calcium stored in the bones. The parathyroid glands, together with vitamin D and calcitonin, are involved in calcium and phosphate metabolism in the body. They regulate the deposition and resorption of calcium and phosphate in bone. The blood levels of calcium and phosphate act, in turn, as feedback regulators of the secretion of parathyroid hormones and calcitonin.

Calcium absorption in the diet depends on the presence of calcium-binding proteins in the intestines. Calcium is deposited in the bone as tricalcium phosphate crystals which make bone rigid. Bone calcium is constantly being resorbed and redeposited. Several hundred milligrams of calcium are lost daily in the urine and feces.

The parathyroid hormones and vitamin D cause blood calcium levels to rise. The parathyroid hormones work by rapid short-acting stimulation of a "calcium pump" in bone to move calcium from bone fluid into the blood, and by long-lasting stimulation of osteoclasts, which break down bone, to release calcium and phosphate into the blood. (*See* BLOOD.)

Calcitonin rapidly lowers blood calcium and phosphate levels and inhibits osteoclast activity to prevent the loss of calcium and phosphate. Excess calcium in the blood can cause muscular weakness and a depressed central nervous system, and can also cause the heart to stop beating.

Muscles. The contraction of voluntary muscle is controlled by the calcium concentration in the cell. Before a contraction, when the cell is in a resting state, the concentration of calcium in the cytoplasm is very low. The calcium is sequestered within a structure known as the sarcoplasmic reticulum. When the nerve impulse arrives, calcium is released. Calcium acts as the intermediary between the nerve impulse and the muscle contraction by causing conformational changes in the molecules affecting the proteins that hook onto each other to cause a muscle contraction. Afterwards, a transport mechanism called the calcium pump moves the calcium back inside the sarcoplasmic reticulum.

In nerve impulse transmission, the release of the neurotransmitter acetylcholine depends on the presence of calcium in the extracellular fluid.

Calculus

Next see INTEGRAL CALCULUS

A mathematical technique for dealing with functions.

Calculus comes from the Latin word for "pebble," the primitive method of counting whose influence is also visible in the English word "calculation." It is most appropriate for this particular method, however, because calculus is based on the fragmentation of complex problems into infinitesimally small ("pebble"-sized) parts. The basic theory of calculus can be simply stated: although it is not always possible to understand the overall operation of a function, it is always possible to break it down into an infinite series of steps, each one occupying only a small portion of the total, and then to add these portions together to obtain the desired result.

Differential calculus allows one to visualize, or to calculate, the shape of a function at any moment. Integral calculus, which is its complement, allows one to visualize, or to calculate, areas and volumes defined by such shapes. Between them, these two forms of calculus allow one to answer complex questions in areas ranging from economics to aeronautics, engineering to medicine.

The Derivative. All forms of calculus are based on the concept of the derivative. A derivative is an instantaneous "snapshot" of a function at a given point in time. For example, an economist may measure median household income on a certain date; but that data alone is insufficient for analysis. The economist must take the first derivative of that income, representing the instantaneous rate of change in that income level—is household income climbing or falling?—and the second derivative, representing the rate of change of change—is household income climbing (or falling) faster (or slower) than it was on previous dates? Only by using calculus to discover these two additional aspects of the subject can the economist truly understand the significance of the data.

Some find it easier to approach calculus visually. Consider three lines: one is straight and horizontal, the second is straight and tilted upward to the right, while the third, a parabola, is curved upward. The derivative of the first function ($y = $ a constant c) is zero, so we can say that the function's rate of change is also zero. The derivative of the second function ($y = 2x + a$ constant c) is 2, which we can call the slope of the function at that point. Finally, the derivative of the third function ($y = x^2$) is $2x$, which shows that the slope of the function at that point is not only positive, but is still increasing as x increases; that is, the growth of y is accelerating. The typical problem faced in differential calculus is

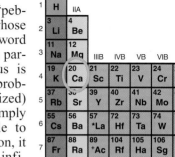

The position of calcium in the Periodic Table.

Gottfried Wilhelm Leibniz (1646-1716), a philosopher and self-taught mathematician, is famous for his development of integral and differential calculus independently of Newton.

Isaac Newton (1642-1727) developed calculus (independently of Leibniz) and applied it to the dynamics of bodies in *Principia Mathematica,* possibly the most important scientific treatise ever written. Below, a typical page from an 18th century edition of the *Principia.*

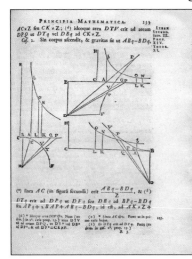

to determine the point at which the slope of the function is zero, indicating that the function has attained its maximum (or minimum) value; that is, the point at which a factory reaches maximum production, or a cannonball reaches a target the maximum distance away, or a homeowner reduces interest payments to a minimum.

The Antiderivative. Often, the information scientists or economists gather shows them the rate of change of a change; in this case, they must attempt to calculate the antiderivative, by which they can infer the underlying function. For example, scientists have been collecting data on world temperature patterns for a number of years; these data show an accelerating growth over the past three decades. From this information, an antiderivative function, called global warming, has been inferred. Other scientists warn that the rate of change has been calculated for just a short time span; they urge that more of the underlying function be confirmed before a worldwide alarm is raised.

This use of the antiderivative forms the basis of integral calculus, the complementary tool to differential calculus. Where a derivative determines the change, or slope, of a function at a given point, the antiderivative determines the area traced by the function. In this way, the work done by a pipeline pump, the force exerted by water built up behind a dam, or the value of corporate bonds years before their maturity date, can all be determined. This relationship between differentiation and integration is known as the Fundamental Theorem of Calculus.

History. Calculus operations were discovered by two great 17th-century geniuses, working alone and arriving at almost identical solutions at the same time: Isaac Newton and Gottfried Leibniz. There were differences between their concepts—Newton tended to stress the integrative side of calculus, while Leibniz stressed the differential aspect; Newton reduced his ideas to paper first, in 1669, while Leibnitz codified his ideas in a more systematic set of rules and formulas. There were four basic problems which motivated this work: understanding the exact relationship between acceleration, velocity, and distance; finding a line tangent to a curve; determining the maximum or minimum value of a function; and measuring curved lines, and the areas and volumes covered by them. The ability to solve these problems led to the scientific, and then to the industrial, revolutions.

Pedagogy. The teaching of calculus has changed greatly in recent years. The traditional method of teaching calculus, based on the use of paper and pencil, involved a great number of for-

mulas, graphical exercises, and drills in derivation and antiderivation. Such methods often succeed in direct proportion to the amount of energy and inspiration offered by the teacher, as in the highly publicized case of Jaime Escalante, a Los Angeles mathematics teacher whose so-called slower students proved to master calculus better than supposedly more advanced students in upper-class schools.

Nevertheless, much teaching of calculus now relies on the "Harvard" method, or C4L, which is based on problem solving with the help of calculators and computers, and relies less on inspirational lectures than on small, group-centered laboratory sessions. A critical aspect of this new method is the incorporation of reflection, in the form of journals and response papers, into what traditionally was thought of as a process demanding sheer memorization.

The background for calculus is found in FUNCTIONS *and* SETS AND GROUPS. *Further topics are covered in* DIFFERENTIAL EQUATIONS; INTEGRAL CALCULUS; *and* VECTORS AND TENSORS. *Special topics are discussed in* DIFFERENTIAL GEOMETRY; FOURIER ANALYSIS; *and* VARIATIONAL CALCULUS. *The tools of calculus permeate virtually every area of modern science and technology.*

Further Reading
Anton, Howard, *Calculus: A New Horizon* (1998); Apostol, Tom M., *Calculus* (1969); Berlinski, David, *A Tour of the Calculus* (1997); Boyer, Carl B., *History of the Calculus and Its Conceptual Development* (1989); Courant, Richard, *Differential and Integral Calculus* (1988).

First see HEAT

Calorimetry

Next see THERMOMETRY

The measurement of heat content and flow.

Contrary to popular opinion, a "calorie" is not a unit of fat; it is a unit of energy needed to perform a specific amount of work, namely raising the temperature of one gram of water by one degree Celsius. As can be imagined, this is a relatively small amount of energy. A food calorie is actually a kilocalorie (written as "Calorie"), or one thousand "small" calories. When food is consumed, our bodies break it down into its most basic nutrients; some are used for "building purposes" within the cells, others are converted to energy. The calorie content of food is actually how much energy can be obtained. One gram of carbohydrate or protein yields four calories, whereas one gram of fat yields nine calories.

Joules, a unit of mechanical work, are used as a measure of energy as well. An individual Joule, which is also defined in terms of the energy needed to raise the temperature of a gram of water by one degree Celsius, is smaller than a calorie. One calorie is equal to 4.18 Joules.

All chemical reactions are defined in terms of whether they ultimately give off energy or must continuously take in energy in order to occur. A reaction which gives off energy is called exothermic and one that requires energy is endothermic. Because of the Law of Conservation of Energy, which states that energy cannot be created or destroyed, we know that the energy involved in a reaction does not come from "nowhere," nor does it "disappear." What is occurring during a chemical reaction is an energy transfer between the reaction and its immediate environment. (*See* CHEMICAL REACTION.)

A calorimeter is an insulated container with water inside. The reaction takes place within the water chamber itself. The water temperature is measured both before the reaction occurs and afterwards. If the reaction is exothermic, the second water temperature will be higher than the first. If the reaction is endothermic, the second water temperature will be lower than the first. Because the amount of water in the chamber is known, the exact amount of energy gained or released in the reaction can then be determined. (*See also* REFRIGERATION.)

A simple calorimeter consists of: a sealed Dewar flask; a thermometer; a ringstirer; and an electrical resistance heater.

First see ATP

Calvin-Benson Cycle

Next see PHOTOSYNTHESIS

A description of the chemical processes involved in photosynthesis.

Photosynthesis consists of two kinds of reactions. "Light reactions" convert light energy into chemical form and store it in molecules like ATP and NADPH. "Dark reactions" use that stored energy to fix carbon dioxide, which means converting this low-energy inorganic compound into high-energy carbohydrates such as glucose.

The most common series of dark reactions are known as the Calvin cycle or the Calvin-Benson cycle, in honor of Melvin Calvin and Andrew Benson of the University of California at Berkeley. In the 1950s, they and colleagues traced the steps in the process by using the radioactive isotope carbon-14, which had recently become available. For his work, Calvin received the Nobel Prize in 1961.

Steps of Cycle. Each step in the Calvin cycle is catalyzed by a specific enzyme. First

The bedding within the Burgess Shale shows the sediment input that displays the sudden "Cambrian Explosion" in the lower layer

each molecule of carbon dioxide combines with a molecule of ribulose 1,5-biphosphate (RuBP), a five-carbon sugar. This results in an unstable six-carbon compound that splits to form two molecules of a three-carbon compound called 3-phosphoglycerate (PGA). The enzyme catalyzing this first reaction is RuBP carboxylase (Rubisco), which is the most abundant protein in the world, constituting much of the protein in actively photosynthesizing leaves.

The PGA is phosphorylated and reduced to a three-carbon sugar called glyceraldehyde 3-phosphate. Two molecules of this sugar must combine to synthesize glucose, a six-carbon sugar. Normally, glucose synthesized this way is quickly converted to sucrose, starch, or cellulose. The glyceraldehyde 3-phosphate can also be used to form lipids or amino acids.

It takes six carbon dioxide molecules (or six turns of the cycle) to produce 12 molecules of glyceraldehyde 3-phosphate, which yield one molecule of glucose. The remaining ten molecules of glyceraldehyde 3-phosphate are used to synthesize more RuBP for more turns of the cycle. Because it involves three carbon compounds, the Calvin cycle is also called the C3 photosynthetic pathway, and plants that fix carbon using it alone are called C3 plants. (*See* PLANTS *and* PHOTOSYNTHESIS.)

First see GEOLOGICAL TIME SCALE

Cambrian Diversification of Life

Next see LIFE, DEFINITION and ORIGIN OF

Nearly all of the major phyla of animals arose approximately 540 million years ago during the Cambrian period. Previously, protists, simple one-celled organisms, had slowly evolved into primitive multicellular creatures. Suddenly, from 540 million to 500 million years ago, adaptive radiation occurred, in which quickly developing organisms become widely distributed and formed complex life communities.

This period of rapid diversification is known as the "Cambrian Explosion." According to the fossil record, evolutionary changes occurred in as little as 5 million years—an astonishing rate. There are many theories about what caused these amazing events. (*See* EXTINCTION.)

A recent theory proposes that there was an abnormally rapid reorganization of the Earth's crust in the Cambrian period, much faster than ordinary continental drift. This theory is known as polar wander—the entire surface of the earth shifts relative to the interior. The climatic shifts triggered evolutionary change, as the rate of evolution is always higher during times of environmental stress. Established ecosystems became fragmented and began to undergo rapid changes.

The Calvin-Benson cycle. Each circuit of the Calvin-Benson cycle is driven by ATP and NADPH molecules produced by the energy provided by light. The end product of the process is to create one sugar molelcule that is used by the organism or cell as food.

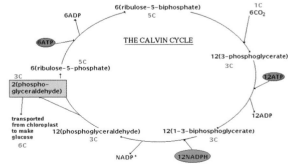

THE CALVIN CYCLE

6(ribulose–5–biphosphate)
5C

6ADP

6ATP

1C
6CO₂

6(ribulose–5–phosphate)
5C

12(3–phosphoglycerate)
3C

3C
2(phospho-
glyceraldehyde)

12ATP

transported
from chloroplast
to make
glucose
6C

12(phosphoglyceraldehyde)
3C

12ADP

12(1–3–biphosphoglycerate)
3C

NADP⁺

12NADPH

A wide variety of cameras have been produced for a variety of purposes, from personal recreation to scientific analysis. From top, the original box camera popular early in the century; a range-finder camera, in which the image was seen by the photographer through a lens above the lens to the film; a single-lens reflex, in which the photographer could see just what appeared on film; an early instant camera, capable of developing a photograph in the camera; and (below) a digital camera that produces images as digitized files. At right, a comparison between a camera system and that of the eye.

Camera

First see LENS

Next see REMOTE SENSING

An optical device for making still photographs or moving pictures, or the part of a television system that converts optical images into electronic signals for transmission.

Optical Camera. An optical camera, in simplest terms, consists of a lightproof box that has a lens at one end and a light-sensitive film or a plate at the other. The lens has a shutter that keeps light out. The lens, which generally has several elements, can be classified by f number, which is the ratio of its focal length (the distance from the lens center to the point of focus) to its diameter. To make an exposure, the shutter is opened to let a measured amount of light strike the film or plate. The length of time that the shutter is opened depends on the intensity of light, the sensitivity of the film or plate, and the aperture, or effective diameter, of the lens. In simple cameras, the aperture and shutter speed are controlled automatically. In more complex cameras, the shutter speed is adjusted on the basis of information gathered by an exposure meter, a photocell that measures the intensity of the available light.

In motion picture cameras, the shutter opens automatically as the film comes to rest behind the lens for each frame. A set number of frames,

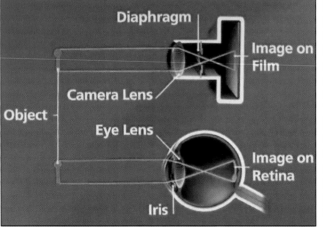

which can be 16, 18, 24, or 30, are exposed every second to create a moving image. When the film is projected at the proper speed, the illusion of motion is created because of the persistence of vision in the human eye.

In color photography, one common process uses a film with three layers of light-sensitive emulsion. Each layer responds to one of the three primary colors: red, yellow, and blue. When the film is developed, a black image is formed wherever the scene is blue. The white areas in this layer are dyed yellow, a comple-

mentary color to blue, and the black areas are bleached clean. A yellow filter between this layer and the next one, which is green-sensitive, prevents blue light from reaching the layer; the areas where no green light is present are dyed magenta. The final layer is red-sensitive, and is given a blue-green (cyan) image on the negative. When white light is shone through the three dye layers, the cyan dye subtracts red where it does not occur in the scene, the yellow dye subtracts blue, and the magenta dye subtracts green. The light that is transmitted through the negative thus reconstructs the colors of the original scene.

Television Camera. A television camera consists of a lens system that focuses light on the photosensitive part of the camera tube, causing a discharge in those parts of the tube that are struck by light. In a basic system, the image is focused on a mosaic of microscopically small cells on a thin sheet of mica that is backed by an electrically conductive material. The image that results when light strikes this mosaic is scanned from behind by a beam of electrons; the current of the beam varies as it passes over the light and dark areas. The signal that is picked up by the scanning beam is amplified electronically in the camera and is passed to a transmitter with signals that synchronize the transmission. The modern television system was made possible by the invention of the cathode-ray scanning tube and the iconoscope, the basic television tube, by V. K. Zworykin in the 1920s.

Color Television. In color television, the three primary colors are detected by three separate camera tubes. The information gathered by these three tubes is combined with sound and synchronization signals and is transmitted by technologies that differ from country to country; different systems are used in the United States, England, and France. When the signal reaches a television set, it is split again into the three primary colors. Each of these signals is fed to a separate electron gun in the cathode; each gun sends out a narrow, steady stream of electrons. The beam from each gun activates a set of phosphor dots that create color on the screen.

Digital cameras employ the basic technology of the television camera, transforming a visual image into three electronic signals corresponding to the primary colors. These signals can then be fed back into a video monitor or entered into a computer.

The basis of photography is discussed in PHOTOGRAPHY, CHEMISTRY OF; LENS; *and* OPTICS. *Further topics are found in* LIGHT; HOLOGRAPHY; *and* REFLECTION AND REFRACTION. *Important applications are discussed in* REMOTE SENSING. *See also* TELEVISION AND BROADCAST TECHNOLOGY.

First see DISEASE, THEORY OF

Cancer

Next see GENETIC ENGINEERING

A disease in which there is a dangerous unrestrained growth of cells in a body tissue or organ.

Cancer is now the second most common cause of death in the United States, led only by heart disease and causing one of every five deaths. Cancer is a malignant overgrowth of cells, distinguished from nonmalignant, or benign, tumors such as warts or lipomas that do not threaten life because their overgrowth is limited.

Cancer can develop in any part of the body, such as in the breasts, brain, pancreas, lungs, stomach, and skin. Cancer can also occur in the testes (for men) and ovaries (for women), on the tongue or lip, or in the nasal sinuses. The cancers that form in the cells of the bone marrow where blood cells are formed are called leukemias.

As a cancer in an organ or tissue grows, it spreads into the surrounding tissue, where it can block vital passageways, eat away at bones, and destroy nerves. It is also possible for a cancer to spread to other parts of the body, a process called metastasis. This occurs when malignant cells separate themselves from the original tumor and travel through the blood or the lymph to new locations, where they establish themselves and resume their uncontrolled growth.

Cancer occurs not only in humans but also in animals. Exposure to radiation or some chemicals can cause cancer, but most occur as an individual grows older. Anything that can cause cancer is called a carcinogen. Perhaps the best-known carcinogen is tobacco, which is estimated to cause 30 percent of cancers in the United States. A variety of carcinogens in different foods are estimated to cause about one cancer in three. The causes of 20 percent of cancers remain unknown.

Origins and Causes. Cancer seems to originate when the genes that control cell growth and division, the oncogenes, are somehow transformed so that their controlling elements are lost. That cancer-causing transformation can occur in a single cell. Once that cell's genes are changed, it begins to divide endlessly. In the process, the cancerous cells often lose their differentiation, the specialized form that distinguishes a normal cell an organ or tissue. Because they are no longer specialized, cancer cells escape from the normal controls of growth imposed by hormones and other body elements.

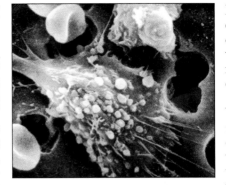

Above, the battle of cancer is often waged between the body's own immune system and the body's own cancerous cell.

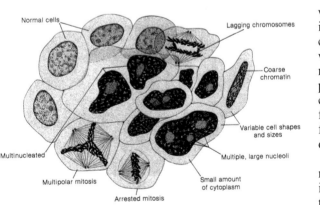

At an early stage, cancerous cells mingle with healthy cells.

Labels on figure: Normal cells; Lagging chromosomes; Coarse chromatin; Variable cell shapes and sizes; Multiple, large nucleoli; Small amount of cytoplasm; Arrested mitosis; Multipolar mitosis; Multinucleated

Further Reading

Hoffman, E.J., *Cancer and the Search for Selective Biochemical Inhibitors* (1999); Lodish, Harvey, et al., *Molecular Cell Biology* (1995); Markman, Maurice, *Basic Cancer Medicine* (1997); Weinberg, Robert A., *Genes and the Biology of Cancer* (1992).

It may take years for a cancer to cause symptoms that lead to its detection—a period during which the cancer can grow beyond the reach of surgical care and can establish many metastases.

Detection. Some cancers can be detected early by screening tests such as mammography and cytology tests such as the cervical smear test for cervical cancer. Chemical workers often undergo periodic urine cytology tests to detect the earliest signs of bladder cancer. But most cancers are detected only after the appearance of symptoms. The tests that are done to confirm the existence of a cancer include endoscopy, in which a tube with a viewing lens is used to examine organs where cancer is suspected; biopsy, in which a sample of tissue is removed and examined for the presence of abnormal cells; and chemical tests—such as looking for small amounts of blood in the feces that might indicate cancer of the intestinal tract.

Surgery is the primary treatment for most forms of cancer; it is often accompanied by radiation therapy or anticancer drugs to kill remaining cancer cells. The use of these drugs often causes severe side effects, because they attack not only the cancer cells but also normal cells and tissues, disrupting their activity.

THE CUTTING EDGE

Harvesting Taxol

In the 1980s, two studies revealed that Taxol, a drug derived from the bark of Pacific yew trees, is a potent agent in the fight against breast and ovarian cancer. But it takes 6,700 pounds of bark to produce one pound of the drug, and when in 1991 the Federal government ordered that 40,000 yews be reserved for Bristol-Myers Squibb, Taxol's producer, the Environmental Defense Fund filed suit to have the Pacific yew declared an endangered species. Finally, in 1999, the USDA announced success in culturing Taxol from laboratory-grown yew cells, a process that will be 100 times more productive and preserve the rapidly diminishing supply of Pacific yews in the old-growth forests of the Northwest.

The biology of cancer is discussed further in DISEASE, THEORY OF; LEUKEMIA; *and in* DISEASES, NON-INFECTIOUS. *Diagnosing cancer is discussed in* MEDICAL DIAGNOSTICS *and* MAMMOGRAPHY. *Treatments are discussed in* CHEMOTHERAPY; RADIOLOGY; *and* SURGERY. *Causes of cancer are discussed in* MUTAGENS AND CARCINOGENS *and* RADON. *Also see* GENE THERAPY.

First see CHARGE AND CURRRENT

Capacitor

Next See ELECTRIC CURRENT

A device used in electrical circuits for the temporary storage of electrical charge.

All capacitors contain two pieces of a material that conducts electricity, separated by a nonconducting material, or insulator. The oldest capacitor is the Leyden jar, which was developed in the Netherlands in the 1740s. It consists of a jar whose exterior and interior surfaces are coated with tin or aluminum foil (the conductors) separated by the glass wall of the jar, the nonconductor. Leyden jars today are used mostly for classroom demonstrations. The amount of charge that a capacitor can hold, its capacitance, depends on the area of the two conductors, their separation, and the dielectric constant of the insulator, its ability to prevent current flow.

Today, small capacitors are often made with metal foil plates as conductor and paraffin paper as the nonconductor, all rolled tightly into a cylinder to save space. They have a fixed capacity. Variable capacitors, such as those used in radio tuners, generally are made of metal vanes that are intermeshed and are separated only by air, which serves as the insulator.

Other Uses. Capacitors are used in computers (where they appear in both microscopic and macroscopic form), television sets, automobile ignition systems, recording devices, radio transmitters and receivers, and a large variety of other electrical systems. They can be made with metal foil, metal plates, tantalum, or other materials as the conductors; and plastics such as polystyrene, compressed gases, a vacuum, mica, or other insulators. (*See* ELECTRICAL CIRCUITS.)

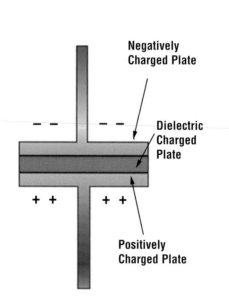

Negatively Charged Plate

Dielectric Charged Plate

Positively Charged Plate

A capacitor consists of two charged plates, one positive and one negative, with a dielectric wedged in between.

First see CARBON

Carbohydrates

Next see METABOLISM

A group of chemical compounds composed of carbon, hydrogen, and oxygen, which form a major energy source for animals—particularly for humans.

Carbohydrates, which contain the elements carbon, hydrogen, and oxygen, include sugars, starches, and cellulose. The carbon atoms are linked together, forming either straight chains or ring structures. Carbohydrates, particularly glucose, are a primary source of energy for all organisms. In addition, some carbohydrates, like cellulose, help form the building blocks of plant cells, primarily the cell wall.

Glucose. The basic sub-unit, or monomer, of a carbohydrate is the monosaccharide, or simple sugar. Examples of monosaccharides include glucose and fructose. Glucose is the universal food source, broken down chemically by all living cells to produce energy in the process known as cellular respiration. Fructose is the sugar found in fruits. Glucose and fructose are isomers, compounds with the same chemical formula but different three-dimensional structures. The formula for both of these monosaccharides is $C_6H_{12}O_6$ but the glucose structure is a hexagon-shaped ring and the fructose is a pentagon-shaped ring. (*See* BLOOD CHEMISTRY.)

Nomenclature. All sugar molecules have names that end in the suffix "-ose." Monosaccharides can be classified according to their number of carbon atoms, or by which functional groups they contain. Both glucose and fructose are hexoses, six-carbon sugars. Ribose and deoxyribose are pentoses, five-carbon sugars, found as components in nucleic acids such as deoxyribonucleic acid (DNA) and ribonucleic acid (RNA). Trioses, or three-carbon sugars, include glyceraldehyde and dihydroxyacetone. According to functional groups, glucose, ribose, and glyceraldehyde are all aldoses, meaning they contain an aldehyde group, and fructose and dihydroxyacetone are ketoses, meaning they contain a ketone group.

When two monosaccharides are chemically joined, they form a disaccharide. Examples of disaccharides include maltose, which consists of two glucose molecules, and sucrose, also known as "cane sugar," which is a glucose and a fructose. Disaccharides are used as the transport sugar in plants and some animals.

Three or more saccharides bonded together form a polysaccharide. Examples of these include starch and glycogen ("animal starch"), which is how the liver stores excess glucose. Starch, glycogen, and cellulose are all polymers of glucose. (*See* GLYCOLYSIS AND FERMENTATION.)

Role in Digestion. The human digestive tract can break down starch and glycogen but not cellulose. This is due to the different bond angles connecting the adjacent glucose units. Enzymes recognize the molecules and bonds they are supposed to work on according to their shape. Humans lack the specific enzyme to break down the cellulose "beta bonds." (Many mammals, however, are equipped with this enzyme and so can digest cellulose.) Pectin is also a polysaccharide found in plant cell walls. (*See* DIGESTION REGULATION *and* METABOLIC PATHWAYS.)

The exoskeletons of insects contain chitin, which is a polymer of modified monosaccharides. The basic sub-unit is a hexose, which also contains a nitrogen-containing group.

Carbon

First see PERIODIC TABLE

Next see BUCKMINSTERFULLERENE

Carbon, the sixth element on the Periodic Table, plays a very important role in the chemistry of living things. Carbon composes only 0.08 percent of Earth's crust, oceans, and atmosphere, but 18 percent of the human body. Carbon has a unique ability among elements to form bonds with itself leading to the formation of rings, straight chains, and branched chains, known as polymers. Millions of carbon compounds exist, the vast majority of which are organic compounds. (*See* ORGANIC COMPOUNDS.)

In order to understand carbon's prominent role, we must first discuss a few basic facts about the carbon atom. In the most common isotope of carbon, C_{12}, each atom is made up of six protons, six neutrons, and six electrons. Those six electrons are arranged in specific energy levels extending outward from the nucleus. The outermost occupied energy level, or valence shell, contains only four electrons instead of the maximum eight. It is the desire for a full valence shell that makes carbon so eager to form chemical bonds. Carbon will share electrons with up to four other atoms to achieve a stable octet, the most stable energy state possible for an atom. Carbon can share one pair of electrons with each of four other atoms (four single-covalent bonds, resulting in a tetrahedral-shaped molecule) or else two or three pairs (double- and triple-covalent bonds) with fewer atoms. Carbon will always end up with a total of four shared pairs of electrons, regardless of how many partners it has. This explains how several carbon atoms can link up with each other in so many ways.

Forms of Carbon. Besides C_{12}, other isotopes of carbon exist, among them C_{13} and C_{14}. The radioactivity of C_{14} is used as a tool to date excavated objects, in a process known as radiocarbon dating or carbon-14 dating. C_{14} has a half-life of 5,730 years. It is continuously being produced in the atmosphere as well as decomposing so the overall amount remains constant. C_{14} is used to date wood and cloth because only living plants maintain a constant C_{14} content in their molecules. Once the plant is dead, no more carbon is taken in so no new C_{14} is produced, and the C_{14} content begins to decrease.

Carbon in its pure elemental state (unbonded and therefore not part of a compound) exists in three main forms. There is the familiar dark carbon in the form of coal and graphite, diamond, and the newest member of the trio, fullerenes, or buckyballs (named after architect William Buckminster Fuller.)

In the diamond form, each carbon atom is bound to four other carbon atoms, creating a latticed crystal which appears colorless because the wavelengths of the visible light spectrum are too long to be absorbed and simply pass through. (A silicon crystal, by contrast, appears black because its lattice is capable of absorbing the entire visible spectrum.) Blue, yellow, pink, and other colored diamonds are contaminated with other elements. (*See* DIAMONDS.)

Buckyballs are a geometric structure consisting of 60 carbon atoms. Recently a new fullerene has been discovered, the nanotube, which is basically a buckyball stretched into a long slender tube of one million or more carbon atoms. These nanotubes can reversibly shift from one shape to another, giving rise to several potential applications. (*See* BUCKMINSTERFULLERENES.)

Carbon Dioxide. In addition to bonding well to itself, carbon also bonds easily with other non-metals. One of the resulting compounds is carbon dioxide, CO_2. (Carbon monoxide, CO, is produced as a result of incomplete combustion of hydrocarbons and is poisonous, if not fatal, to breathe.) In the carbon cycle, CO_2 and oxygen are recirculated throughout the environment. Producers such as trees take in CO_2 as a raw material and in return release oxygen. This oxygen is taken up by consumers who need it as a vital reactant to break down food to provide energy. As a result of this metabolic activity, CO_2 is released. When a living organism dies, decomposers break it down into its simplest chemical components and the carbon and other elements are returned to the soil and air.

CO_2 and Global Warming. Carbon dioxide normally makes up approximately 9 percent of atmospheric gases (a distant third behind nitrogen and oxygen). In recent years, CO_2 has received much unfavorable press as a greenhouse gas which may be contributing to global warming. When fossil fuels such as gasoline, coal, and oil (all of which are hydrocarbons) are

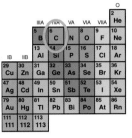

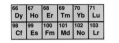

The position of carbon in the Periodic Table.

The Carbon Cycle.
The carbon cycle (below left) is necessary for life because there is only a finite amount of this precious element on Earth. Other critical elements are also circulated, but none with such rapidity as carbon. The vast amounts of carbon used by industry and the large percentage of carbon in the chemical composition of life demand constant monitoring of the cycle to make sure it never falls out of balance.

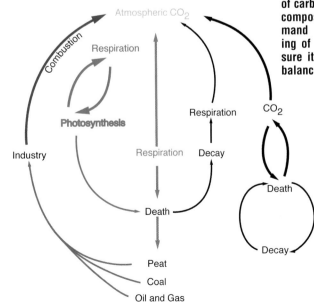

burned, several gases, chiefly among them carbon dioxide, are released into the atmosphere. The CO_2 acts as a blanket, trapping heat next to the earth's surface that would otherwise radiate back into space. Some of this additional CO_2 is of course taken up by plant life as part of the carbon cycle, but a great deal of it is not. In addition, fires in the tropical rain forest add more CO_2 to the environment while simultaneously removing some of the means by which it can be eliminated. (*See* GLOBAL WARMING.)

Various solutions have been proposed to somehow return the carbon back to the Earth. One proposal simply suggests growing more trees, estimating that 10 to 15 percent of the CO_2 problem could be solved this way. Another suggests pumping CO_2 into the ocean, which already contains at least 50 times more carbon than the atmosphere. Still other plans suggest pumping CO_2 into the ground, and of course, developing alternate fuels to eliminate the release of carbon entirely. In addition to the burning of fossil fuels, there is some concern about carbon-containing products that end up in landfills. Eventually, through oxidation or decomposition, all of these buried materials will eventually be released back to the atmosphere as CO_2 or methane (CH_4) which will make a significant contribution to the greenhouse effect.

The Case of the Missing Carbon. There is yet another interesting twist to the problem. Human beings release about 7 billion metric tons of carbon in the form of CO_2 into the atmosphere each year. However, the CO_2 content of the atmosphere rises annually by only 3.4 billion tons. Climatologists are trying to figure out what has happened to the missing CO_2, as this could bear directly on global warming. Many theories have been advanced, but as yet there is no conclusive answer. (*See* HYDROLOGIC CYCLE; ECOLOGY; *and* CLIMATOLOGY.)

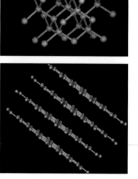

In the molecular arrangement of carbon in a diamond, top, the lattice produces a solid of incomparable hardness. In an organic compound, bottom, the carbon chain is easily broken.

Right, a graphic representation of the Carnot cycle. The work performed is proportional to the shaded area on the graph.

Carnot Cycle

Next see THERMODYNAMIC CYCLES

A series of changes, or stages, in the physical state of a gas in an idealized, perfectly efficient, reversible heat engine.

The Carnot cycle is an ideal cycle of operations that gives the maximum theoretical efficiency for any engine that utilizes heat, a category that ranges from steam engines to automobile motors. It was published in 1824 by Nicholas L. S. Carnot. (*See* HEAT; THERMODYNAMIC CYCLES.)

The Carnot cycle consists of several operations. In the first, the engine absorbs energy in the form of heat from a reservoir; in the case of a steam engine, the boiler is the reservoir. Work is done by the heat, which causes an expansion—in an automobile engine, the expansion drives a cylinder, and the temperature falls as a

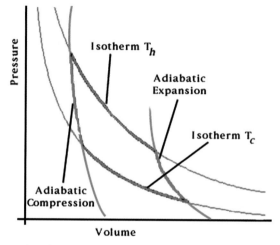

result. The next stage is compression, with heat given out—in the automobile engine, the cylinder moves back to its original position and heat is released to the atmosphere; in a steam engine the energy goes to a condenser. The net result is that a quantity of heat is taken from a hot source and some of that heat is imparted to something colder; the heat that is not imparted does work.

The Carnot cycle establishes the highest possible efficiency—measured by dividing the work that is done by the energy absorbed from the reservoir—for any heat engine. That efficiency is highest when the temperature of the heat source is as high as possible, compared to the heat of the surrounding environment.

Actual Engine Efficiency. In the real world, the efficiency of an engine never equals what is predicted by the Carnot cycle, because that efficiency is reduced by such factors as friction. Also, the phases are performed quasi-statically (very slowly) so that the ideal gas laws still apply. Thus it provides an absolute standard against which any heat engine can be judged.

OBSERVATIONS

From Carbon Atom to Life

One of the primary advantages of the carbon atom is its ability to form molecules with uniquely stable shapes, such as rings. For example, glucose, a basic sugar, is a ring of carbon atoms interspersed with oxygen and surrounded by a halo of hydrogen; it easily forms new bonds with water molecules in blood, thus offering instant energy to the body. But glucose molecules can also form long chains held together by ionic as well as covalent bonds, making them strong and water-resistant; in this form they are known as cellulose. Like bridge cables, hundreds of these cellulose chains are wound together first into microfibrils, and then into macrofibrils; it is these tough macrofibrils that form the walls of plant cells, making them strong enough to support the weight of all the cells above them. At their heart, a delicate fern and a California redwood both reflect the complex process of carbon atoms at work.

First see GEODETIC SURVEY

Cartography and Surveying

Next see REMOTE SENSING

Surveying is the science of determining the positions of points on the Earth's surface, and cartography is the making of maps that are based on the information gathered by surveying.

Surveying is believed to have been first practiced in ancient Egypt with the object of imposing taxes on the owners of farmland. Modern surveying began in the nineteenth century, with the expansion of technology and commerce. A number of methods of surveying are available, and the choice for a specific situation is based on the magnitude of the area to be surveyed and the purpose of the survey. All methods of surveying are based on direct linear measurements and the measurement of angles from which distances, directions, and heights can be determined. The instruments used for surveying start with those for measuring lengths—chains, tapes, or metal rods. A transit, or theodolite, is used for measuring horizontal and vertical angles. The transit commonly used for field work consists of a telescope that is mounted on a tripod and fitted with a pair of bubble-type levels and graduated circles that allow the surveyor to measure vertical and horizontal angles. Elevations and horizontal distances can be determined by triangulation, or by timing of laser beams.

Surveying Techniques. There are several kinds of surveying. In geodetic surveying, the purpose is to determine the nature of the Earth's surface over a large area, taking into account the curvature of the Earth. Small areas, in which curvature is not a factor, are mapped by plane surveying, which treats the area as a flat surface. For a large survey, observations are made of points that can be 30 to 40 miles apart. By measuring one line and observing the appropriate angles carefully, a systematic map can be made as a series of triangles. A topographical survey is used to determine the relative position of surface features that are then shown on a contour map.

Land surveying is used to get the precise location of parcels of land and to determine their dimensions and areas. Mine (or underground) surveying determines the way that mine shafts and tunnels are related to surface features. Engineering surveying includes the designation of the grades of land in a construction site. This is done for construction of highways, railroads, transmission lines, and similar facilities.

Aerial surveying is being used increasingly for such purposes as highway location, mapping remote areas, and making hydrographic and shore maps. Aerial surveying began in the mid-nineteenth century, at first from balloons and later through aerial photographs. For aerial surveys, the photographs are taken in strips, with each picture overlapping the one next to it. By using infrared photography, it is possible to produce accurate surveys of shorelines, since infrared radiation does not penetrate water. Color photography over water allows the determination of the underlying surface to a depth of at least 70 feet. Surveying from satellites relies on radar imaging, which is unaffected by clouds or darkness. The surface of Venus has been completely surveyed by the Magellan orbiter, which used radar to detect surface features through the planet's dense, sulfuric cloud cover.

The maps made on the basis of surveying include charts, which are intended for navigational purposes. The maps that can be prepared today include zenithal, or azimuthal, projections, in which points on the Earth's surface are transferred to a flat plane; and cylindrical projections, in which a cylinder can be constructed around the exterior of the globe, touching it at the equator. The best-known map made by this method is the Mercator projection, invented in Flanders in the 16th century, in which the space between parallels is determined by mathematical formulas rather than by geometric projection.

The earliest examples of cartography include a clay map dating back to about 1000 B.C.E.. The first world map is believed to have

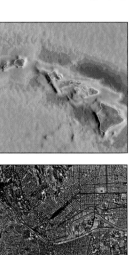

Three developments have vastly improved modern cartography: satellite photography; remote sensing techniques using gravitometric sensors, top, of the Hawaiian Islands; and the Global Positioning System (GPS), applied to the surveying of major cities.

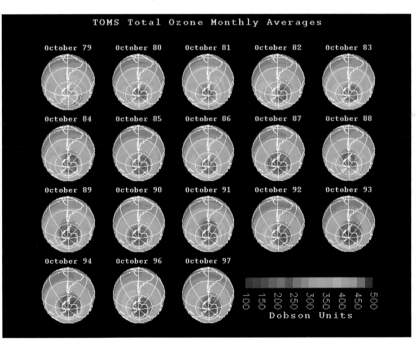

been made in the third century B.C.E. The modern era of cartography began in the 14th century, when major voyages of discovery stimulated the development of newer methods of mapmaking.

The foundations of the subject are discussed in DAMS; GEOMETRY; SPACE. *More details can be found in* COASTAL ENGINEERING; GEODETIC SURVEY; PETROLEUM PROS-PECTING. *Advanced subjects are in* HIGHWAY ENGINEERING; RADAR; REMOTE SENSING. *See also* VENUS.

Discovery of the erosion of Earth's ozone layer was an important achievement in cartography. In the comparative maps of the ozone hole developing over the South Pole, there was great reliance on known reference points, which were added to the data to give a global picture.

First see CHEMICAL REACTION

Catalyst

Next see SURFACE CHEMISTRY

A substance that alters—hastens or retards—the rate of a chemical reaction without being part of the reaction.

Chemical reactions are "spontaneous," meaning that when reactants are combined, a reaction begins and continues until all available reactants have been used up. Spontaneous simply means that the reaction will take place, but does not refer to the amount of time required. A spontaneous reaction may take place instantaneously or over ten years. The reaction can be speeded up, however, with the addition of a catalyst.

A common example of catalysis is the role water plays during the process of rust formation, as seen when leaving a piece of wet steel wool overnight. The gray, springy pad turns into an orange, powdery mass. The chemical name for rust is ferric oxide, Fe_2O_3, formed by the chemical combination of iron within the steel and oxygen from the air, a process which would normally take weeks. The presence of water accelerates this reaction.

In the Reaction. The catalyst itself is not affected by the reaction. It is not consumed in the process and can be used over and over again. Even though a catalyst speeds up a reaction that can occur on its own, it is incapable of causing a non-spontaneous reaction to occur. A catalyst will not affect the energy output of a reaction, nor the amount of products that can be produced or anything else except the amount of time required. A substance that catalyzes one reaction may not have any effect on another.

Reversibility. Some reactions are reversible, meaning reactants form products which then can be changed back into the original reactants. Catalysts speed up the rate of such a reaction in

catalysis occurs

no catalysis

Sometimes, the catalyst simply provides a setting where a reaction can take place. Above, top, an enzyme geometrically locks onto a sucrose molecule where water can interact with it and produce fructose. Bottom, where a molecule does not fit, the reaction does not occur.

Further Reading
Emsley, J., *The Elements* (1998); Emsley, J., *Molecules at an Exhibition: Portraits of Intriguing Materials in Everyday Life* (1998); Snyder, C. H., *The Extraordinary Chemistry of Ordinary Things* (1997); Sutton, M., *The Rise of Physical Chemistry* (1985).

both directions, bringing the system to a state of equilibrium.

A chemical reaction takes place in several small steps, which can occur either simultaneously or sequentially. The bonds holding the reactants together must be broken to allow the formation of new chemical bonds, and consequently new compounds. The slowest step of the mechanism is referred to as the rate-limiting step. An effective catalyst "targets" this step.

It is not enough to place reactants together for the reaction to occur. The molecules must actually collide with each other at the proper angle in order to react and recombine. Chemical reactions are either exothermic, meaning they cause energy to be released, or endothermic, meaning energy must be taken in. All reactions, whether or not they will ultimately give off energy, require activation energy to get started. The addition of a catalyst reduces the amount of activation energy needed, and subsequently the amount of time that the reaction will take.

Homogeneous catalysts are materials that are in the same state or phase as the reactants. Heterogeneous catalysts are solids that increase the rate of chemical reactions between gas or liquid molecules. The reactants adhere, or become attached, to the solid surface which "anchors" them in position. The most common examples of heterogeneous catalysts are metals, metal oxides, or metal sulfides, such as the platinum in an automobile's catalytic converter.

Enzymes, a specific type of protein, act as catalysts within cells. Their role is to lower the amount of activation energy needed so that chemical reactions required by the cell can occur under normal cellular environmental conditions regarding temperature and pH without compromising cellular life. Thus, chemical reactions cannot occur within a cell without an enzyme.

Elementary aspects of this subject are covered in CHEMICAL REACTION; COMBUSTION; OXIDIZING AGENT. *More information on particular aspects is contained in* COMBUSTION; ENZYME; SURFACE CHEMISTRY. *Further relevant information is contained in* ELECTROCHEMISTRY AND ELECTROPLATING *and* SOAPS AND DETERGENTS.

First see TOPOLOGY

Catastrophe Theory

Next see CHAOS

In most systems, continuous change of any variable leads to continuous changes in all related variables; however, not all systems are so stable. In unstable systems, a series of small changes in one variable may lead to discontinuous, large changes in the entire system. In a ship rolling in a heavy sea, the discontinuity is reached at the moment of capsizing; in an aerial walkway filled with people dancing, the discontinuity

---

THE CUTTING EDGE

Catalytic Converter

Catalytic converters are automotive emission control devices placed in the exhaust system to reduce carbon monoxide, nitrogen oxides, and hydrocarbons to inert compounds such as carbon dioxide, nitrogen, and water. The catalysts that promote these reactions are rare metals such as platinum, palladium, and rhodium, which help to reduce or remove oxygen atoms from nitrogen oxides while simultaneously helping to add oxygen to carbon monoxide; the results, nitrogen and carbon dioxide, are benign gases. But some environmentalists have expressed concern over our reliance on the catalytic converter, because the carbon dioxide it produces is a major "greenhouse gas" and therefore a contributor to global warming–though it is less than 0.06 percent of the total.

occurs at the moment when the steel fractures; if the system is a penitentiary under lockdown, the discontinuity is the first act of violence that begins the riot. These and related phenomena were first examined under the heading Catastrophe Theory by René Thom, Hassler Whitney, and Vladimir Arnold.

Catastrophe theory attempts to chart the behavior of the system up to its final discontinuity, by transforming the relevant physical equations into geometric ones, and relating them through differential geometry as if the equations were curves or plane surfaces. Catastrophe equations with only two relevant, or control, factors have been the most studied, because they can be charted as three-dimensional surfaces; the discontinuities are represented by sudden changes in the surface, known as "folds," "cusps," "umbilicals," and the like.

For systems with fewer than five control factors, only seven different catastrophes are possible: fold, cusp, swallowtail, butterfly, and three different forms of umbilical catastrophe. Once the relevant equations have been confirmed, the shape of the surface is mapped and the margins of hysteresis, where one becomes trapped within the fold or cusp, are identified; these margins represent the danger zones of the system.

For example, one might graph worker productivity as a resultant of two control factors, quality control and stress; each of these is subject to external manipulation, one through positive and the other through negative reinforcement. Over most of its surface, this graph would show that small increases in either control factor can lead to increases in productivity. However, at a certain point, the relatively smooth surface deforms, producing a cusp, within which any increase in stress or in quality control effort will result in a catastrophic loss of productivity.

The heart of catastrophe theory is the concept of punctuated equilibrium. So long as the control factors remain within the primary domain, the system will tend to stabilize at its primary equilibrium point: the center of gravity of the ship will remain over the keel. However, once the state of hysteresis is reached a secondary equilibrium point assumes dominance: the center of gravity of the ship is now under the keel. Escaping the cusp and regaining the original equilibrium point becomes extremely difficult, and often impossible. Once Humpty-Dumpty loses his equilibrium on top of the wall and falls into the secondary equilibrium of "scrambled egg," a whole kingdom of horses and men cannot restore him to his shell.

> *Related areas to be considered are* CALCULUS; EUCLIDEAN GEOMETRY; FUNCTION. *Other aspects of the subject are discussed in* DIFFERENTIAL GEOMETRY. *Related material can be found in* CHAOS AND COMPLEXITY *and* TOPOLOGY.

Above, three mathematical giants of the twentieth century. From top, René Thom and Vladimir Arnold, founders of catastrophe theory; and Saunders MacLane who, along with Samuel Eilenberg, founded category theory. Neither branch of mathematics has yet been applied to practical or physical problems to any great extent.

Further Reading
Brown, Courtney, *Chaos and Catastrophe Theories: Nonlinear Modeling in the Social Sciences* (1995); Saunders, Peter T., *An Introduction to Catastrophe Theory* (1980); Wassermann, G.S., *Catastrophe Theory* (1992); Wilson, Alan Geoffrey, *Catastrophe Theory and Bifurcation* (1984).

First see SETS AND GROUPS

Category Theory

Next see TOPOLOGY

Category theory is a branch of Sets and Groups, which is characterized by a "metamathematical" status. Where three different groups may be composed of integers, rational numbers, and complex numbers, a category would constitute a higher level of abstraction, being composed of all three related groups. Where sets and groups are defined by the values of the functions contained within them, categories are defined by morphisms, or compositions, by which one group can be mapped onto another. As a result of this conceptualization, mathematicians can observe profound correspondences among groups, rings, topological spaces, or other related concepts, through what are called functors. A functor defines the association of every object in one group with every object in the others, or associates a morphism in one ring with a morphism in every other one.

The vocabulary of categories and functors was first developed by American mathematicians Samuel Eilenberg and Saunders MacLane, in connection with their developing theory of naturality expressed in their paper, "General Theory of Natural Equivalences" (1945). Category theory provides a common ground for discussion of matters like the Cartesian products of sets, or Abelian groups, that would otherwise be unrelatable. This last category is the subject of homological algebra, which is important in modern topology. Category theory is also closely related to "Universal Algebra," a study initiated by James J. Sylvester in 1884, which has been superseded by the language of categories.

First see LASER

CD-ROM (Compact Disc)

Next see RECORDING TECHNOLOGY

A CD-ROM—"Compact Disc–Read Only Memory"—is a 4.75-inch piece of plastic, holding a spiral track some three miles long marked with pits and spacings (lands). As the disc spins at high speed, a laser beam reflects differently off the pits and spacings, producing a binary signal. At the 780-nm wavelength of a standard laser, 42,000 binary bits can be contained on each inch, making possible up to 650 megabytes of information on the three-mile data track.

Historical Development. Before disc technology was developed, the only reliable method of data storage was magnetic tape, which has several disadvantages: It is slow, because a tape reel must be physically unwound to the appropriate spot; it is unreliable, because areas of tape can become demagnetized; and it is subject to interference, because the writing and reading heads must touch the tape surface. CD-ROMs, with their permanent pits and lands protected by a layer of clear plastic and their laser readers at least one millimeter away from the surface, avoid all these problems.

How it Works. Each CD-ROM contains two laser-visible layers: a substrate coated with reflective material, and a non-reflective layer immediately below, formed when an argon-ion laser interacted with the original photosensitive material. Laser light reflects off the lands, and is scattered in the pits; each transition triggers a change in current in the CD reader's photodiode, read as a 1. The distance between these transitions registers as a series of 0's. Using what is

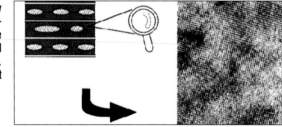

Right, a microscopic view of the surface of a CD-ROM. The area on the right is the coarse pitted area that scatters light. The area shown is about 30 millimeters wide.

commonly called Eight-To-Fourteen Modulation, 14 channel bits are translated into eight data bits, allowing the extra information to be used for error correction; it is this last feature that makes CD-ROM data especially reliable.

CD-ROMs now come in recordable and rewritable versions, known familiarly as CD-R and CD-RW. Using widely available packet writing software, files can be copied to CD, and with the rewritable version can be selectively overwritten; some software allows copying of both data and audio on the same disc. Thus such discs can be loaded with multimedia sales presentations that use current sales figures, or can be used repeatedly to back up important files.

CD-ROMs are being superseded by DVD-ROMs, which use digitized and compressed information storage to provide up to 5 gigabytes of data; future generations of DVD players will be able to read both sides of the disc, and focus on two levels, allowing 17 gigabytes of data storage. Combined with MPEG-2 video, which has four times the resolution of MPEG-1, DVD offers movies that are sharper than laser discs, with full digital audio. DVD-RAM, DVD–RW, and DVD+RW, recordable and rewritable versions, are also in development, but none share the format agreed to by the DVD Forum.

Further Reading
Benford, Tom, *Welcome to CD-ROM* (1993); Hall, Devra, *The CD-ROM Revolution* (1995); Smith, Greg M., *On a Silver Platter: CD-ROMs and the Promises of a New Technology* (1999); Williams, E.W., *The CD-ROM and Optical Disc Recording Systems* (1996).

Background material on CD-ROMs can be found in Computer, Digital; Laser; Light; Optics; *and* Reflection and Refraction. *More details can be found in* Polarized Light; Radio and Television Broadcasting; *and* Recording Technology. *Elementary aspects of this subject are covered in* Plastics *and* Telecommunications.

First see Life, Definition and Origin of

Cell

Next see Cell Cycle

The basic unit of life.

The cell is the basic unit of life; all organisms are composed of cells, whether one or many. The only noncellular entities are viruses, about which there has been an ongoing debate whether they can be classified as living things.

Some organisms are unicellular, made up of only a single cell. Examples of unicellular organisms include amoebae and bacteria. If an organism is made up of two or more cells it is multicellular. Examples of multicellular organisms include animals, fungi, and most plants.

A unicellular organism by definition must be self-sufficient, capable of carrying out all life activities, such as getting food, excreting wastes, "breathing" or exchanging oxygen for carbon dioxide, and reproducing. The cells of a multicellular organism employ division of labor. Each cell is highly specialized, performing only one specific task for the good of the whole. However, these cells lose their "independence," the ability to live on their own. A single human brain cell may be more complex than an amoeba, but the amoeba has one great advantage over a brain cell. It can survive by itself, whereas the brain cell cannot.

Within a multicellular organism, cells of identical structure and function form tissues. Tissues of similar structure and function within the same area make up a specific organ, and organs that perform the same general function make up a body system.

Cell Division. All organisms, whether unicellular or multicellular, begin life as a single cell. Growth for a unicellular organism involves the cell simply growing larger. A multicellular organism grows by producing more cells. The original cell divides to form two smaller, identical "daughter" cells. Each of its offspring contains half the cellular contents of its parent, but a complete set of its genetic information.

Once a cell divides, it no longer exists, but "lives on" through its daughter cells. There is a limit to the number of times a cell can divide, that is, the number of generations it can produce. This limit is imposed by the telomere, a structure found in the cell nucleus. With each subsequent division, the telomere is shortened until it finally disappears. "Immortal cells" are those that contain a special enzyme which repairs the telomere after each division. Immortal cells include skin cells; stem cells, from which the blood cells are derived; and germ cells, which give rise to sperm and eggs.

Physically, a cell is simply a blob of protoplasm, a jelly-like fluid made up of mostly water, plus some proteins, lipids, and dissolved ions. The protoplasm within a specific cell is referred to as the cytosol. Surrounding this fluid, and forming the outer boundary of the cell is the cell membrane, which serves to keep the cellular contents separate and discrete and to control traffic into and out of the cell.

Organelles. Embedded within the cytosol are the organelles, tiny structures which carry out all of the activities of the cell. The cytosol provides an aqueous environment in which the various metabolic activities can take place. The cytosol is delineated into various compartments by internal membranes which surround the organelles. Also found throughout the cytosol are the tiny structures that make up the cytoskeleton, the internal "scaffolding" which provides basic shape and support of the cell.

Cell Nucleus. Chief among the organelles is the nucleus, which controls all cellular functions. The nucleus contains the genetic information of the cell and therefore determines which chemical reactions are going to be carried out and at what times. Many organelles are surrounded by membranes while others appear simply to be membrane folds or sacs. These include the endoplasmic reticulum, the Golgi apparatus, and the vacuoles. Together they compose what is called the cytomembrane system.

The endoplasmic reticulum extends throughout the entire cytosol of the cell. "Rough" endoplasmic reticulum has ribosomes, the protein-synthesizing organelles, attached to its walls. "Smooth" endoplasmic reticulum does not have them. Most lipids are synthesized in the endoplasmic reticulum. The process of lipid trafficking, how other membranes "pick up" their lipid components from the endoplasmic reticulum, is not entirely understood.

Golgi Apparatus and Mitochondria. The Golgi apparatus is responsible for chemically modifying, sorting, and "packaging" various large molecules which are then delivered to other organelles or exported from the cell entirely. The Golgi "wraps" its products in vesicles, or "bubbles," formed from its own membrane sheets, which can move freely about the cell and penetrate through and fuse with other membranes.

Mitochondria are the "power plants" of the cell. They are the sites of cellular respiration, which is the process of breaking down glucose to produce energy in the form of adenosine triphosphate (AT). The mitochondria require

The Generalized Cell. There is much variation from cell to cell, even within a family of cells with the same function (just as there is in nearly all areas of life). But a eukariotic cell will generally have the following complement of organelles: (a) the smooth endoplasmic reticulum; (b) the nucleus; (c) the nucleolus; (d) a centriole; (e) a secretion granule; (f) a Golgi apparatus; (g) the nuclear envelope; (h) a mitochondrion; (i) a lysosome; (j) chromatin; (k) the cell membrane; (l) a microtubule; (m) the rough endoplasmic reticulum; (n) cytoplasm; (o) a ribosome.

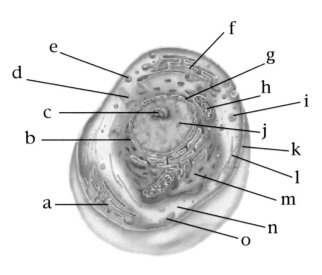

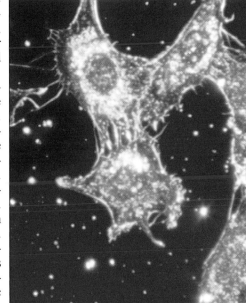

Cells can be said to lead lives: they move as if driven to perform certain functions, and they can suddenly destroy themselves (as above).

Further Reading
Harris, Henry, *The Birth of the Cell* (1999); Holbrook, Nikki J., *Cellular Aging and Cell Death* (1996); Lodish, Harvey, et al., *Molecular Cell Biology* (1995); Mather, Jennie P., *Introduction to Cell and Tissue Culture: Theory and Technique* (1998); Vogelstein, Bert, ed., *The Genetic Basis of Human Cancer* (1998).

oxygen for this process. Depending on its energy needs, a cell may contain anywhere from a few mitochondria to hundreds of them.

Plant and animal cells contain many of the same organelles. However, there are certain key differences between them. Animals lack plastids and a cell wall, a rigid structure located outside of the cell membrane which gives shape and support to the cell.

Categorizing Cells. Another way to classify cells is to categorize them as either prokaryotes or eukaryotes. Eukaryotic cells are much larger and more complex than prokaryotic cells. Although they contain many of the same organelles, as a general rule of thumb the eukaryotic version is bigger and more sophisticated than the prokaryotic one. Prokaryotes lack membrane-bound organelles and the internal compartmentalization found in eukaryotes. In addition, instead of a "true" nucleus, the prokaryote contains a single round chromosome that is not sequestered from the rest of the cytosol.

Evolution of Cells. Current theory believes that the first eukaryotic organisms were actually collections of prokaryotes that "banded together" in symbiotic relationships to form more complex cells. This is supported by the fact that mitochondria and plastids, among other organelles, have their own specialized DNA, as well as by the existence of membrane-bound organelles in eukaryotes and their lack in prokaryotes. Even earlier "protocells" are believed to be the forerunners of the first true cells, the archaea, which gave rise to prokaryotes.

Background material can be found in CELLULAR MEMBRANES; LIFE, DEFINITION AND ORIGIN OF; WATER IN LIVING CELLS. *More details can be found in* CELL CYCLE; EUKARYOTIC CELL; PROKARYOTIC CELL. *More information on particular aspects is contained in* AGING; ENDOPLASMIC RETICULUM AND GOLGI APPARATUS; GENETIC CODE; PROTEIN SYNTHESIS. *See also* MICROSCOPY.

First see CELL

Cell Cycle

Next see AGING

Most cells can only divide a fixed number of times. Others, known as "immortal cells," can keep on dividing for an unlimited number of generations. Examples of immortal cells include skin; germ cells, which are precursors for sperm and eggs; and stem cells, which give rise to the blood cells. The number of times a cell can divide depends upon the telomere, a structure attached to the chromosomes. With each successive division, the telomere is shortened, until it finally disappears. Immortal cells contain an enzyme called telomerase, which repairs the telomere and prevents its loss. (*See* CELL.)

The existence of telomerase, and its possible inhibition or enhancement, has obvious implications in combating cancer as well as old age. Cancer cells contain the telomerase enzyme, and possible treatment therapies are being explored in which the enzyme action is blocked. In experiments involving the enhancement of this enzyme, scientists have successfully enabled ordinary cells to keep on dividing long after they should be able to do so.

When a cell divides, the "parent" splits into two small, but equal, "daughter" cells. Cytokinesis is the division of the cytoplasm, the jellylike substance that makes up the cell and which contains the various organelles. Division of the cell nucleus itself, however, is not quite so simple.

The nucleus contains the chromosomes which are the genetic material. Each cell within the body, called a somite, must contain the same number of chromosomes and this number must be maintained from one cell generation to the next. Simply dividing the nucleus in half would result in a decrease in chromosome number and is therefore not an option.

Division. Mitosis refers to the events that take place in the nucleus of the cell prior to cell division. A copy is made of every chromosome in order to ensure that each new daughter cell receives a complete set and no chromosomes are "lost" from one generation to the next.

Chromosome number is referred to as "n." In humans, somites contain 46 chromosomes and are diploid or "2n," whereas gametes contain 23 chromosomes and are haploid or "1n." An individual begins as a single fertilized egg cell, called a zygote. The zygote is formed by the union of sperm and egg, a union primarily of chromosomes. In order to assure that the zygote and its resulting descendant cells contain the proper number of chromosomes, the gametes must all be haploid. The process used to create them is called meiosis. (*See* MITOSIS; MEIOSIS.)

(Meiosis differs from mitosis chiefly by having two cytoplasmic divisions, not one, and ultimately ends up with four haploid cells instead of two diploid ones.)

The cell cycle, which encompasses all of the stages of a cell's life, is made up of the following phases: G1, S, G2, and M. Newly formed cells begin at G1, in which they rapidly grow until they reach their full size and become differentiated or specialized. Depending on the type of cell, and how many generations of division have already elapsed, the length of G1 is highly variable. It may be the entire lifespan, a brief period, or anything in between. In a rapidly growing animal, the cell cycle can repeat every 18-24 hours, with G1 lasting between six to eight hours. G1 is followed by S, or the synthesis stage, in which the genetic material is replicated as the cell prepares to divide. S lasts only as long as is needed to copy all of the chromosomes, usually six to eight hours. G2 is a "gap" in the events, lasting three to four hours. The rest of mitosis occurs during the M phase and usually occurs in less than an hour.

The two key control points of the cell cycle are G1 and G2. At G1 a "commitment" is made somehow to enter the replication cycle which then automatically leads into the S phase. At the end of G2 another "decision" is made to enter the rest of the stages of mitosis. Between the M of one cell cycle and G1 of the next is a period called G0 in which the cell can withdraw from the replication cycle or can re-enter it. The actual activation events that occur are not well understood but are believed to involve various activator proteins. (*See* AGING; TRANSPORT, CELLULAR.)

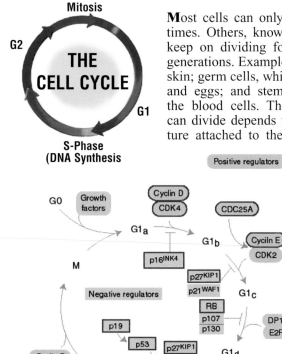

Cell Cycle. It has only recently become apparent that cells have internal clocks that trigger their activities, from phases in their replication to their death. The cycles pictured above are the results of those timing mechanisms. The exact nature of those mechanisms is still largely unknown.

THE CUTTING EDGE

The Death of a Cell

A cell can die in two ways: necrosis—usually the result of infection or injury—and apoptosis—the programmed death, sometimes called the "suicide," of the cell. Cells that undergo apoptosis include the cells lining the walls of internal organs such as the intestine and the uterus, which live a few days to a few weeks and then are discarded to make way for fresh cells; skin cells which die as they migrate towards the surface and ultimately create a protective layer over living tissue; and the lens of the eye, which during fetal development undergoes replacement with crystallin, a transparent protein. Apoptosis is being carefully studied because the failure of a cell to die at the end of its programmed life may offer clues to treating viruses and to preventing cancer.

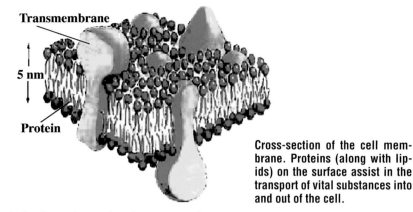

Cell Membrane

First see CELL

Next see CELLULAR SECRETION

A plasma tissue that surrounds all living cells.

All cells, regardless of type, are bounded by a plasma membrane. A membrane is a protein-lipid bi-layer, meaning it is composed of a double layer of phospholipids with various protein molecules "sandwiched in" and protruding off the sides of the membrane, making it asymmetrical. The phospholipids contain both hydrophobic ("water-hating") and hydrophilic ("water-loving") portions. Because of the water environment, the hydrophobic portions face inward.

Different types of membranes contain different proportions of proteins and lipids, giving them distinct physical properties. Many other types of molecules are present as well, such as cholesterol, which is usually found in animal membranes. Glycoproteins and glycolipids, formed by attaching sugar molecules to the proteins and lipids, respectively, play a role in intercellular recognition. Some large proteins also function as receptors which enable the cell to respond to changes in its environment.

Structure. The membrane structure is not rigid, but flexible enough so that the lipid and protein molecules can move with respect to each other. Thus, membranes are often referred to as "two-dimensional fluids." Lipid molecules do not usually move from one layer to another, but can exchange places within the same layer. Large, transmembrane proteins can "somersault" within the membrane, reversing which end is facing the interior of the cell and which the exterior. This ability is useful in transporting materials into or out of the cell. (*See* TRANSPORT, CELLULAR.)

Function. The plasma membrane acts as a "gatekeeper" for the cell, allowing only certain materials to pass through. The term for this selectiveness is semipermeability and is due to the structure of the membrane itself. The spaces between the membrane components are called pores; it is easier for small molecules to slip through than large ones. Charge also plays a role in determining what is permitted to pass through, as the phospholipids as well as the proteins contain various charged groups. A charged molecule attempting to cross the membrane will be repelled if it attempts to cross in an area of identical charge. Solubility also affects which materials are permitted to enter or leave.

Diffusion refers to the movement of materials from one side of the membrane to the other and follows a concentration gradient, that is, particles will cross from an area of greater concentration to an area of lower concentration until an equilibrium is reached in respect to both sides. In cases where an unequal concentration is

Cross-section of the cell membrane. Proteins (along with lipids) on the surface assist in the transport of vital substances into and out of the cell.

desired, or the molecules are too large to cross on their own, other forms of transport are used. Passive transport, also known as facilitated diffusion, involves the use of carrier molecules, usually membrane proteins, to "piggyback" materials. Active transport is similar, but requires the use of energy, as materials are being moved against the concentration gradient.

Cellular Automata

First see Brain

Next see PROGRAM, COMPUTER

Cellular automata were first proposed by John von Neumann, who theorized that a computer modeled on the human brain should, like the brain, be able to react to changes in thought and perception by "shifting gears." To do this, researcher Norman Margolus has built a series of eight-chip processors in which every element has a special ability to respond to changes in neighboring elements, achieving the speed of a supercomputer at about the cost of a conventional computer. (*See* NANOTECHNOLOGY.)

The CAM-8 computer at MIT's Laboratory for Computer Sciences, the latest cellular machine, can track heat diffusion in a complex solid, or air flow over an airplane wing, as effectively as a much larger computer because neighboring sequences of memory bits are linked to corresponding physical locations. As information is received, it is compared not only to the previous memory of that location but also to new data from nearby locations, and adjusted accordingly. There is a cost, however; cellular automata can only work this efficiently because they have been explicitly programmed on how to adjust their data, making cellular automata much harder to reprogram for new tasks. In effect, cellular automata are at the same stage as digital computers were in the late 1940s. (*See* SUPERCOMPUTER.)

Because each cell functions in conjunction with its immediate neighbors, device density in these machines is critical. Research is accordingly being pursued into transistorless automata, in which each cell is a "quantum dot" and output is controlled by a single electron.

John von Neumann, one of the most innovative thinkers of the 20th century.

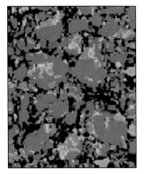

Microscopic image of the four types of particles that compose portland cement (each color representing a different substance).

First see SOLID

Cement

Next see COLLOID

Any substance used to make surfaces adhere, or that combines particles into a solid whole.

Cements can range from adhesive clay to bituminous asphalt. In practical terms, the word most often means portland cement, one of today's foremost building materials. The name comes from its resemblance to stone that was quarried in Portland, England. Portland cement is a pre-burned mixture of powdered limestone and clay that achieves a rock-like hardness when water is added. To make portland cement, limestone is ground into small particles, then clays and crushed rocks are added to provide a 25 percent silica content and 10 percent alumina content. The material is burned in a rotary kiln at temperatures well over 1,000 degrees Fahrenheit, converting the mixture into pellets. Gypsum is then added to slow the hardening process, and the resulting mixture is added to sand to make mortar, or to sand, gravel, and crushed rock to make concrete. When water is added to this mixture, solidification occurs in a series of complex chemical reactions.

Geologists still do not have a full understanding of this process. It is believed that each of the compounds in the mixture assumes a crystalline form when water is added, and that these crystals interlock to form the hardened cement. A variety of different cements can be made to meet special requirements of builders and engineers. When water is added, the cement sets in a few hours and achieves its ultimate hardness over a period of weeks. (*See* EPOXIES.)

First see GEOLOGICAL TIME SCALE

Cenozoic Era

Next see ICE AGE

The Cenozoic era began 70 million years ago, at the end of the Mesozoic era, and extends to the present time. Its name comes from the Greek ceno, for "recent," and zoic, for "life." The Cenozoic is also known as the Age of Mammals. During the opening period of the Cenozoic era, the Paleocene, most mammals were small, with short legs and small brains. Primitive primates, the ultimate ancestors of humans, were abundant, and species including the horses and rodents appeared and evolved.

As the continents rose during the Miocene and Pliocene eras, the climate became cooler and drier over much of the earth, so that forests shrank in area while the area of grasslands increased. Earth's temperatures were mild for most of the Cenozoic, but in its later phases, a trend to colder temperatures resulted in the

Glacial Ages of the Pleistocene era, a time that has seen the rise of the human species and which may not be over. Extensive ice caps appeared about one million years ago, and glaciers appeared on high mountains, even those near the equator. As the ice advanced and then retreated from the centers of its accumulation, it left glacial debris. That debris indicates that there have been four major ice advances separated by periods of relative warmth. The present is a period of active mountain building and volcanism.

First see FORCE

Centrifugal Force

Next see ROTATIONAL MOTION

Centrifugal force is a term that is used to explain the motion of an object that is moving in a curved path because of the force acting on it. It is actually nothing more than inertia. A simple example is a ball on the end of a string that a child is swinging around. The elastic tension in the rope that keeps the ball moving in a circle is called the centripetal force. If the rope breaks, the centripetal force is no longer acting and the ball flies off in a straight line. Centripetal force explains many other phenomena, including the rotation of the Earth around the sun, the orbiting of an artificial satellite around the Earth, and the rotation of an electron around the nucleus of an atom, which is controlled by the attraction between the negative charge of the electron and the positive charge of the nucleus. (*See* ATOM.)

Centrifugal force also affects a rider in an automobile that is going around a corner suddenly. That rider feels that he or she is being propelled outward by a force. In actuality, the rider is simply continuing to move in a straight line, The force that appears to be pushing outward is called the centrifugal force. Similarly, a satellite is balanced between gravitational pull and centrifugal force. Again, the satellite is trying to move in a straight line, but its path is bent by the gravitational attraction of the Earth. Centrifugal force is useful as an explanation, even though, in a sense, it does not actually exist.

First see CENTRIFUGAL FORCE

Centrifugation

Next see FILTRATION

A centrifuge is an instrument used to separate materials of different densities, to "settle" non-soluble solids such as precipitates at the bottom of a solution, or to remove excess moisture from a substance. The principle upon which a centrifuge operates is centrifugal force, in which a rotating body moves outward from the center as a result of inertia. (*See* CENTRIFUGAL FORCE.)

Liquids to be centrifuged are placed in special test tubes which are then sealed to avoid loss of material during the spinning process. The tubes are placed in slots within "buckets," which rotate at varied speeds for a preset length of time. It is important to arrange the tubes symmetrically to ensure that the load does not become unbalanced. If only a single item needs to be centrifuged, a tube of distilled water must be included on the opposite side for balance.

When centrifuging is used to separate several materials of different densities, special solutions are added in order to form a concentration gradient, in which the materials will form different bands along the sides of the tube, depending on their individual densities. The materials of greatest density will be found near the bottom, and those with lower densities will be found near the top. If the purpose of centrifuging is only to drive out excess moisture or to "spin down" a solid material, no additional solutions need to be added.

First see STAR

Cepheid Variable Stars

Next see PULSAR

Cepheid variable stars are supergiants with surface temperatures similar to that of the sun, but with a luminosity 500-30,000 times greater than that of the sun. Cepheids serve as standards by which many large distances in the universe can be determined, because the pulsations in their light emissions are correlated with their brightness—a fact that was established in the early 20th century by American astronomer Henrietta Leavitt. The longer the period of variation in its brightness, the brighter the Cepheid star, Leavitt found, and the period of variation can range from several days to several months. The brightness-period correlation thus allows determination of the absolute magnitude of a distant star, the magnitude that a star would have if it were just 10 parsecs—32.6 light years—from the Earth. Distance is then determined by the difference between the observed magnitude and the absolute magnitude. In this way the Cepheids have been used to calculate the distance to the Magellanic Cloud and the Andromeda Galaxy.

Since the original discovery, it has been found that the period-luminosity relationship is different for Cepheids in the arms of spiral galaxies and those in the nuclei of galaxies or globular clusters. This revision, determined by American astronomer Walter Baade, has helped to refine the value of the Hubble constant. Cepheids were named for their earliest-studied prototype, Delta Cephei. They are divided into two main subgroups: classical Cepheids, which are yellow supergiants and are rare, with periods that range from one to 50 days; and Type II Cepheids, whose light curves have broader maximums and which have periods of 12 to 20 days.

First see SOLID

Ceramics

Next see COATINGS AND FILMS

Ceramics are materials that are produced by treating nonmetallic, inorganic materials such as clay at high temperatures. Until recent decades, ceramics were primarily silica-based materials, but they now include graphite, oxides, carbides, borides, and nitrides. Most ceramics are manufactured, but some occur in nature. Diamond is a ceramic, and so are graphite, lava, mica, and marble. Fired clay products such as pottery are associated with the earliest days of mankind, and clay still is the basis of most commercial ceramic products. Ceramic products can be classified into two groups: sintered products, in which the starting materials are reduced to powder or a granular form and then are pressed or molded to the desired shape; and fused ceramics, which include glass, and which are produced by melting, without any premolding operation.

First see ELEMENTARY PARTICLES

Cerenkov Radiation

Next see ACCELERATOR, PARTICLE

Cerenkov radiation is the electromagnetic radiation emitted when an electrically charged particle travels through a medium at a velocity greater than the speed of light in that medium. It was first observed by Russian scientist Pavel A. Cerenkov in 1934. It is used in detectors for high-energy particle physics. The Cerenkov effect can been explained as the electromagnetic analog of the sonic boom made by aircraft traveling faster than the speed of sound in air. The radiation emitted by such a particle is due to the difference between the velocity of the particle and its associated electric and magnetic fields. The particle literally runs away from its own electromagnetic field.

In principle, even an electrically neutral particle such as a neutron will emit Cerenkov radiation, but because such a particle has an extremely small magnetic moment, the Cerenkov radiation it emits will be too small to measure. Typically, electrons traveling at relativistic speeds in water will emit 250 visible photons of light for every centimeter of travel. Because the effect is greater when the index of refraction of a medium is large, materials with high indexes of refraction are used in Cerenkov counters. These counters can be used either to select particles above a certain energy level, or to respond to particles of a particular velocity by detecting only light that is emitted at a predetermined angle from the direction of a beam of those particles. Such a counter can be used to select particles of a given test mass from all the particles in a beam.

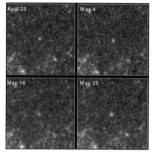

Above, the Cepheid variable in the Virgo cluster, going from peak to peak from April 23 to May 20.

Cerenkov radiation can be used to test the alignment of mirrors and optical configurations by selecting particles of known weight, charge, or speed. Above, Cerenkov radiation detectors are used to calibrate a laser-mirror optical bench.

First see THERMODYNAMICS

Chaos and Complexity

Next see FRACTALS

Three examples of seemingly unstructured phenomena that turn out to have complex but describable structures: smoke rising; a river meandering; and lighting striking the Earth through the atmosphere. One of the findings in the mathematical analysis of chaotic systems is that they display the same self-duplicating qualities of fractal images (a purely mathematical concept). At right, a detail of the fractal image known as the Lorenz Butterfly is repeated when the section of the detail of the Butterfly figure at far right is magnified.

The availability of computers in the late 20th century has allowed scientists to study subjects that they were simply unable to study before. One of the most important of these new areas has to do with the study of non-linear systems. To understand the difference between a linear and a non-linear system, think about a common rubber band. Pull on the rubber band with a given amount of force, it will stretch a predictable amount; pull it with twice the force, and it will stretch twice as far. This is a linear response—the amount of stretching is proportional to the amount of force. If, however, the rubber band is stretched too much, it will lose its elasticity, and from that point on, until it breaks, a very small force will cause a great deformation of the rubber band. In this instance, the rubber band is acting in a non-linear way.

There are many examples of non-linear systems in nature, and many of them are extremely important. For example, a turbulent flow in fluid—water in a pipe, blood in an artery—is often an example of a non-linear system.

Non-Linear Systems. The laws that govern systems like non-linear fluid flow have been known for a long time, but the equations are so complicated that they could not be solved by ordinary pencil-and-paper techniques. The availability of high-speed computers, however, has changed that, because given enough time and computing power, the solution to any equation can be found. Thus, the last quarter of the 20th century has been one in which one previously unexplored area of nature after another has been subjected to scientific inquiry.

In some cases, this kind of investigation has led to rather unexpected results—perhaps nowhere more so than in what are called "chaotic" systems. All chaotic systems are non-linear, but only some non-linear systems are chaotic.

An Example. To understand a chaotic system, imagine a stretch of white water on a river. If one starts a marker—a chip of wood, for example—at one particular point on the upstream side, it will flow down into the white water, move around erratically, and then come

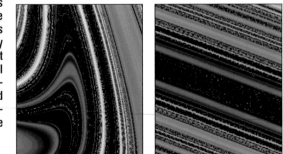

out somewhere on the other side. If one now puts another chip down very close to where the other one was placed, it too, will go into the white water, move around erratically, and come out on the other side. However, it will not necessarily come out anywhere near where the other chip did. In other words, a small change of initial condition (where the chip was placed) results in a large change in the final outcome. A system is defined to be chaotic if it has this kind of extreme sensitivity to initial conditions.

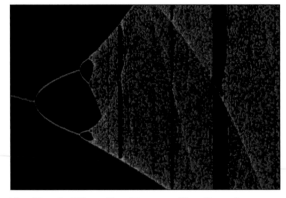

The Classic Bifurcation Diagram. **Chaotic systems can develop along several lines—first one, then one of two, then of four, etc.—until they deteriorate into many possible lines of development, some crossing over others. Predicting when that will happen is an important area of research in chaos and complexity theory.**

Predicting Chaos. It is sometimes argued that chaotic systems are unpredictable, but this is not strictly true. In fact, if you determine exactly where the woodchip starts on the upstream side of the white water, it can be determined exactly where it will land on the other side. The problem is, that, to get this kind of prediction, the initial conditions must be specified with infinite accuracy—which is impossible in practice. The nature of the chaotic system is such that if a mistake is made in the tenth or the fiftieth decimal place in describing where the chip is, the final result will be very different from that predicted. Thus, while predicting the outcome of a chaotic system is possible in principle, it is impossible in practice due to the level of accuracy required to define where the system starts.

The weather is often cited as a chaotic system. The most famous metaphor used to describe the nature of the weather is the so-called butterfly effect: The smallest possible effect—even the flapping of a butterfly's wings —can cause a system to have a much different outcome than it otherwise would have had. Thus, it may be said that "the flapping of a butterfly's wings in China will eventually cause a rainstorm in California." Not every butterfly will start a hurricane, of course, but the system is such that a small perturbation can be magnified many times, creating a cascading effect, just as a snowflake can, under the right conditions, start an avalanche.

Complex Systems. A much more common non-linear phenomenon is that of complexity. A complex system is one in which there are many agents—each interacting with the others. The agents in a complex system may be very simple—grains of sand in a pile, for example, interact by pushing on one another. The agents can also be quite complex— for example, both the free market (in which buyers and sellers interact with each other constantly), and the human brain (in which neurons signal to each other continuously)—are examples of complex systems. Because in the latter systems the agents change as a result of the actions of other agents, they are often called "complex adaptive systems."

The most important feature of complex systems is the appearance of what are called "emergent properties." Think of what happens as sand grains are added to a sandpile. For a while, the addition of each new grain causes the web of forces between one grain and the next throughout that pile to shift slightly. One reaches a point, however, where something totally new happens. Add the millionth grain (for example) and suddenly there is an avalanche. The avalanche is a new kind of behavior which can only appear when the sandpile reaches a certain level of complexity. If it takes a million sand grains to cause an avalanche, a single sand grain does not yield one-millionth of an avalanche.

The science of complexity is in its infancy. It is not known where it is going to lead, nor are the basic laws that govern complex systems known. For example, we do not know whether there are some properties that are shared by all complex systems, just because they are complex (all basketballs share the property of roundess, no matter where they were made or what game they are being used in). It is possible that when more is understood about such systems, we will see that there are connections between free markets, weather systems, the rhythms of the human heart, and the patterns in the human brain.

It is also possible that no such general laws will be discovered. After World War II, people who had worked on logistics and operations during the war began investigating whether there were properties associated with systems—that is, whether any system just by virtue of being a system, had certain kinds of properties. This turned out not to be the case. There are no general rules governing systems.

In any case, with the new abilities supplied by the digital computer, scientists are rapidly uncovering laws of all these complex systems.

Background material can be found in CATASTROPHE THEORY; DIFFERENTIAL GEOMETRY; FUNCTION. *More details can be found in* COMPUTER GRAPHICS; FRACTALS; TOPOLOGY. *Relevant information is contained in* KNOTS; METAMORPHIC ROCK; MOUNTAIN FORMATION; NEURAL NETWORKS; WEATHER FORECASTING.

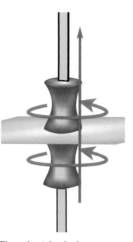

The electrical charge running through a wire creates a magnetic field that circles the wire in accordance with the "right-hand rule." If one places the right hand around the wire with the thumb pointing in the direction of the current, the fingers point in the direction of the mageneic field.

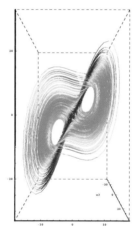

Above, a computer representation of the the Lorenz Butterfly.

Further Reading
Gleick, James, *Chaos: Making a New Science* (1988); Kauffman, Stuart, *At Home in the Universe: The Search for Laws of Self-Organization and Complexity* (1996); Ruelle, David, *Chance and Chaos* (1991); Stengers, Isabelle, *The End of Certainty: Time, Chaos, and the New Laws of Nature* (1997); Steward, Ian, *Does God Play Dice?: The Mathematics of Chaos* (1990); Waldrop, M. Mitchell, *Complexity: The Emerging Science at the Edge of Order and Chaos* (1993).

First see ELECTRON

Charge and Current

Next see ELECTRIC CIRCUIT

Electric current can be defined as the flow of electric charge caused by electromotive forces. More specifically, it is the time rate at which an electrical charge crosses a given surface. In metals, the current consists entirely of a flow of electrons. The current strength over a cross section of conducting material is the total amount of electrical charge that passes through that cross section of conductor in one second. A current I that passes through the cross section A has a current density of I/A. In direct currents, and in alternating currents of low frequency, the current density in a homogeneous conductor is uniform.

For a high-frequency alternating current, current tends to flow toward the surfaces of the conductor, in what is called the skin effect. In such a case, current density decreases in the interior of the conducting material. The ampere is the common unit of current strength. It is defined as the passage of one coulomb of charge in one second. The unit of charge of a single electron is 1.6 x 10-coulombs, and so one ampere is a flow of 6.2×10^{-19} electrons per second. In liquids and gases, both positive and negative charges may move to form a current.

In an electric discharge in a gas, for example, positively charged ions move toward the negative pole, the anode, and negatively charged ions move toward the positively charged pole, the cathode. In an electron tube, the current consists of a stream of electrons in a vacuum. In a mass spectrometer, the current consists of a flow of positive ions in a vacuum. Traditionally, the direction of current flow has been described as being from positive to negative. That description is still widely used, even though it is known that, in a metal, it is the electrons that move, and they flow from negative to positive.

James Clerk Maxwell, the British scientist, described a more subtle "displacement current." Maxwell realized that a variable electric field in space produces the same magnetic effect as a current whose density is proportional to the rate of change over time of that electric field. A displacement current can exist in empty space without any transfer of charge as long as the electric field keeps varying with time. An electric current produces a magnetic field around it and experiences a force when it is an externally generated magnetic field. Conversely, a changing magnetic field generates an electric current.

In early theories of electricity, the presence of positive or negative charge in a body was explained as the flow of two different fluids into or out of that body. For example, the charge created when a glass rod was rubbed with a piece of silk was explained as the flow of one fluid into the rod, and the charge noted when that glass rod touched a piece of metal was explained as the flow of a fluid out of the glass and into the metal. Benjamin Franklin was one of the first scientists who envisioned electricity as a single flow. The existence of electrons as the basic units of current was established in the 19th century by such scientists as H. A. Lorentz and J. J. Thompson. (*See* ELECTROMAGENTISM.)

First see METAL

Chelation

Next see SURFACE CHEMISTRY

A chelating agent is a type of ligand or coordination compound that bonds to metals. The total complex of metal and agent is referred to as a chelate.

Once a chelating agent has attached to the metal ion, it can act as a "scavenger" in removing traces of metals from water or other materials. Chelation therapy is used for ridding the human body of toxic amounts of minerals or heavy metals. In particular, lead poisoning is treated by chelating drugs which bind to the unwanted metals and dispose of them through the urine. Edentate disodium, known as EDTA, is a popular chelating agent. There are unverified claims that chelation therapy is also effective in treating cardiovascular diseases such as atherosclerosis and arteriosclerosis. (*See* HEART.)

Certain organic groups known as porphins are referred to as chelating groups. Porphins are flat organic molecules that have a metal atom bonded in the center. When iron is the atom involved, the porphin formed is heme, which is found in the protein hemoglobin. Hemoglobin is a major component of human red blood cells and is used to transport oxygen around the body. It is the iron atom in the heme that actually binds the oxygen molecule and then releases it as needed. (*See* BLOOD *and* RESPIRATORY SYSTEM.)

A related molecule, the cytochrome, also has iron in its center. Cytochromes are used by cells during the combustion of organic molecules, carbohydrates, and lipids, to produce energy in a process known as cellular respiration.

When an atom of magnesium is used in a porphin, the resulting molecule is chlorophyll, a light-sensitive pigment found in plants and used for photosynthesis, the process by which glucose is produced. (*See* PHOTOSYNTHESIS.)

First see PERIODIC TABLE OF THE ELEMENTS

Chemical Formula

Next see CHEMICAL REACTION

A chemical formula provides information on the composition of a compound—what elements it contains and how many atoms of that particular element are used, indicated by a subscript.

Subscripts are numbers written to the right of the element symbol and should not be confused with coefficients, the numbers written to the left of the whole formula and representing the number of molecules of the entire compound. For example, 6 H_2O means six molecules of water, with each individual molecule consisting of two atoms of hydrogen and one atom of oxygen.

Ionic Compounds. Ionic compounds consist of a positively charged ion, called a cation, and a negatively charged ion, called an anion. All atoms start out neutral, with an equal number of protons and electrons. Cations are formed when electrons are lost, and anions are formed when electrons are gained. The ions cling together by means of the attraction between their charges, resulting in an ionic bond. Molecular compounds are held together by covalent bonds, in which electrons are shared by neutral atoms.

Oppositely charged ions must be combined in the proper ratio to produce a neutral compound. If the numerical value of the cation matches the numerical value of the anion, one of each is all that is required to form a compound. For example, sodium (Na^{+1}) and chlorine (Cl^{-1}) combine to form sodium chloride, NaCl (also known as table salt). Barium (Ba^{+2}) and sulfur (S^{-2}), combine to form barium sulfide, BaS. However, if the values are not equal, differing numbers of each ion are needed. For example, if sodium is combined with sulfur, two cation units are required per anion and the resulting compound of sodium sulfide has the formula Na_2S. If aluminum (Al^{+3}) and sulfur are combined, the resulting compound of aluminum sulfide has the formula Al_2S_3.

Some metals, due to unique aspects in their electron arrangements, can form more than one type of ion. The most prominent examples are copper, iron, lead, and tin. Copper can be either +1 or +2, iron +2 or +3, and tin and lead either +2 or +4. Copper sulfide could therefore be written as either CuS or Cu_2S, depending upon which ion is used. In order to alleviate confusion, different names are used for different forms of ions. A copper ion whose charge is +1 is called either "cuprous" or "copper I," and the ion whose charge is +2 is "cupric" or "copper II." The pattern is maintained for the other metal ions, with the suffix -ous indicating the lower charge and -ic indicating the higher charge. The Roman numerals match the charge of the ion.

Ions may be monoatomic, consisting of a single atom that has gained or lost electrons, or polyatomic where two or more atoms are bonded together. Polyatomic ions include the ammonium ion, NH_4^{+1}, and the sulfate ion, SO_4^{-2}. These ions behave the same way as monoatomic ions do in forming compounds.

Molecular Compounds. Several different substances can be produced from the same combination of elements, depending on how many atoms of each are used. To distinguish among all of the different possible combinations, prefixes are used, such as mono-, di-, tri-, and tetra-. For example, a compound formed from carbon and oxygen containing one atom of each element is carbon monoxide, CO. If one carbon is used with two oxygens, carbon dioxide, CO_2, has been formed. The properties of the two substances are very different from each other, the difference being much more dramatic than one might suppose from the inclusion of just one additional atom of oxygen. Carbon monoxide is a poisonous gas, the inhalation of which can be life-threatening if not fatal, whereas carbon dioxide is a harmless gas produced continually in the human body as a by-product of energy production within the cells.

When writing the formula for an ionic compound, the cation is always written first. When writing the formula for a molecular compound, the less electronegative element (which does not attract electrons as easily) is always written first. The chemical formula of a molecular compound states the actual number of atoms used, whereas the empirical formula of an ionic compound simply states the lowest ratio of atoms of each element.

Binary Compounds. A compound consisting of just two elements is called a binary compound and all of the compound names end in the suffix -ide, regardless of whether they are ionic or molecular. Compounds consisting of three elements are known as ternary compounds. All inorganic ternary compounds are ionic. No prefixes are used in their names. Examples include sodium carbonate, Na_2CO_3, which is composed of sodium, Na^{+1}, and carbonate, CO_3^{-2}. If more than one polyatomic ion is required, it is placed in parentheses with the subscript written outside. For example, to form barium nitrate, one barium ion, Ba^{+2}, is combined with two nitrate ions, NO_3^{-1}. The formula for the compound is $Ba(NO_3)_2$.

Acids. Acids are ionic compounds whose cation is H^{+1}. They may be binary or ternary, depending on whether the anion is mono- or polyatomic. The acid name is derived from the anion. An anion whose name ends in -ide, such as chloride, Cl^{-1}, results in the formation of HCl, hydrochloric acid. An anion with a name ending in -ite, such as nitrite, NO_2^{-1}, results in the formation of HNO_3, nitrous acid. An anion with a name ending in -ate, such as sulfate, results in the formation of H_2SO_4, sulfuric acid.

Background material can be found in BOND, CHEMICAL; CHEMICAL REACTION; VALENCE. Advanced subjects are developed in ACIDS AND BASES; CATALYST; CHROMATOGRAPHY. Fundamental aspects of this subject are covered in ISOMERISM; ISOTOPE; PHOTOCHEMISTRY. See also specific processes—PHOTOSYNTHESIS; KREBS CYCLE; OX-REDOX REACTION—for chemical formulas in use.

First see CHEMICAL FORMULA

Chemical Reaction

Next see BOND, CHEMICAL

Chemistry studies the composition of matter and its interactions with other forms of matter and energy, producing either physical or chemical changes. A physical change is a change in the state or appearance of an object, such as the melting of ice into liquid water. A chemical change is a change in the composition of an object, such as iron turning into rust. In a chemical change, the end materials, called products, are completely different from the starting materials, known as reactants.

A chemical reaction describes the changes that are occurring. The reaction is recorded as an equation, showing the chemical formulas of the reactants and products, as well as the amounts of each material. An example of a chemical reaction would be: $2H_2 + O_2 \rightarrow 2H_2O$

Hydrogen and oxygen are the reactants, water the product. The arrow represents the chemical change that occurs. The small numbers written to the right of the element symbols are called subscripts and represent the number of atoms of each element used. The large numbers written to the left of a molecule are called coefficients and represent either the number of molecules or moles of a particular compound.

A mole is a way of describing and working with a large number of molecules at one time. Individual atoms and molecules are so small they can't be seen with the naked eye, nor even with a microscope. They are so small their masses can't be measured in grams, only in atomic mass units (amu). Just as the word "dozen" represents 12 of a given object at a time, the word "mole" represents 6.02×10^{23} units of an object.

A dozen marbles and a dozen baseballs are equal in number. However, the dozen baseballs weigh more than the dozen marbles, because each baseball weighs more than each marble. In the same way, moles refer to number, not mass. The importance of moles in chemistry lies in the fact that a mole acts as a "bridge" between the tiny masses measured in amu and "workable" masses measured in grams.

For example, one atom of hydrogen has a mass of 1 amu. Therefore, a mole of hydrogen atoms has a mass of 1 gram. One oxygen atom has a mass of 16 amu, so one mole of oxygen atoms has a mass of 16 grams. A single molecule of water contains two atoms of hydrogen and one atom of oxygen, equaling 18 amu. Thus a mole of water molecules has a mass of 18 grams. The amount of water formed in the reaction written above is two moles, with a mass of 36 grams.

The Law of Conservation of Matter states that matter cannot be created or destroyed, only turned into other forms of matter and energy.

Further Reading
Atkins, P., *The Periodic Kingdom* (1997); Brock, William H., *The Chemical Tree* (2000); Cobb, Cathy, *Creations of Fire* (1995); Hoffman, Roald, *The Same and Not the Same* (1997).

During a chemical reaction, the original reactants are recombined in order to form the products. In the same vein, the products are not created from thin air. They are formed by atoms that had previously been part of something else. A chemical equation must therefore always be balanced, containing the same number of atoms of an element on one side of the reaction arrow as on the other. (*See* CHEMICAL FORMULA.)

All chemical reactions, regardless of type, require a small amount of energy to get started. This activation energy breaks the chemical bonds holding together the reactants so that they may recombine and form new bonds. Energy is released when chemical bonds are broken, and energy is required to form new bonds. If more energy is released by breaking old bonds than is needed to form new ones, the reaction is exothermic. If the amount of energy released is less than what is required to form new ones, the reaction is endothermic. Thus, there is an energy transfer between the reaction and its immediate environment. The energy given off by an exothermic reaction is absorbed by its surroundings. An endothermic reaction absorbs energy from its immediate environment.

Types of Chemical Reactions. Chemical reactions are categorized according to what occurs during the change and the types of materials produced. Many reactions can be classified as redox reactions, because there is a transfer of electrons from one material to another; reduction refers to gaining electrons, whereas oxidation refers to the loss of electrons.

Other types of chemical reactions include:
1. Precipitation—Two aqueous solutions react to form a non-soluble solid;
2. Displacement—ionic compounds dissociate and re-form with different "partners" in one of two ways;
a. single displacement—only one ion moves, as in: $2NaCl + Br_2 \longrightarrow 2NaBr + Cl_2$
b. double displacement—two ionic compounds trade ions, as in:
$$NaCl + LiF \longrightarrow NaF + LiCl;$$
3. Synthesis—combining elements to form a compound, or going from simple compounds to more complex ones;
4. Decomposition—breaking a compound down into its component elements, or going from a complex compound to a simpler one;
5. Acid-Base—an acid reacts with a base to form salt and water;
6. Oxidation—a chemical combination with oxygen, which can occur in two ways:
a. non-combustion—no release of energy;
b. combustion—with a release of energy, usually "burning," but may be explosive.

Spontaneous Reactions. A spontaneous reaction is one that occurs naturally. Spon-tane-ity, however, has nothing to do with how much time it takes for the reaction to occur. As long as it can happen, the reaction is called spontaneous, and one of the following events will occur:
—formation of a precipitate;
—formation of water;
—formation of a gas; or
—transfer of electrons.

Chemical reactions do not occur all at once, but by individual steps. An example is the following reaction, in which sodium chloride (NaCl) and potassium bromide (KBr) react to form sodium bromide (NaBr) and potassium chloride (KCl). This reaction involves double displacement, in which the reactants, both of which are ionic compounds, separate into their individual ions. Those ions then recombine differently to form the products.

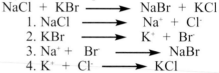

$$NaCl + KBr \longrightarrow NaBr + KCl$$
1. $NaCl \longrightarrow Na^+ + Cl^-$
2. $KBr \longrightarrow K^+ + Br^-$
3. $Na^+ + Br^- \longrightarrow NaBr$
4. $K^+ + Cl^- \longrightarrow KCl$

Step (1) shows the breakdown of sodium chloride and step (2) shows the breakdown of potassium bromide. Both of these steps are simultaneous; they can occur independently of each other. Steps (3) and (4) show the ions recombining into new products. These last two steps are also simultaneous. However, the first two steps must occur before the last two; they are sequential. (*See* ION; SALTS.)

The rate of a reaction refers to how much product is produced in how much time. It is dependent on the nature and concentration of the reactants, the temperature, and the presence or absence of a catalyst. The reactants themselves sometimes determine the rate of reaction. In order to react, molecules must physically collide with each other. If the concentration is high, collisions will occur sooner and the reaction will happen faster. Higher temperatures make more energy available to get the reaction started. Lower temperatures will slow the reaction down.

A catalyst speeds up a chemical reaction by lowering the amount of activation energy needed. A common example is the role of water in rust. Rust is formed by the combination of iron with oxygen in the air. If kept dry, steel wool will stay rust-free for a relatively long period of time. However, a wet piece of steel wool will rust within hours. The water "traps" oxygen, bringing it into closer proximity with the iron. A catalyst cannot cause a non-spontaneous reaction to occur. In addition, a material that acts as a catalyst for one type of reaction may have no effect on another. (*See* CATALYST.)

Chemical reactions are not simply events occurring in a laboratory. Every process of the world around us, every activity in which an organism engages to stay alive, comes down to a series of chemical reactions that occur on the molecular level. (*See* ORGANIC COMPOUNDS.)

Chemotherapy

First see PHARMACOLOGY

Next see CANCER

Chemotherapy usually refers to treatment of various types of cancer with drugs, but the word can also be used to describe the drug treatment of infectious diseases. Infections that are caused by bacteria are treated with antibiotics, of which a wide variety are available. Some antibiotics are bacteriostatic, which means that they do not kill the bacteria but stop their growth so that the body's immune defense system can destroy them. Others are bactericidal, killing the bacteria directly. Infections caused by viruses can be treated with antiviral drugs, but their effectiveness is limited because viruses live within cells, and there is a danger of damaging the cells as well as the viruses. Infections caused by fungi, such as athlete's foot and candidiasis, can be treated with antifungal drugs. (*See* CANCER.)

Cancer Treatments. In cancer chemotherapy, many of the drugs that are used are cytotoxic, meaning that they kill cancer cells selectively, doing little or no damage to normal, nonmalignant cells of the body. These drugs prevent the cancer cells from growing and dividing, often by damaging the genetic material of the cells. Others attack cancer cells by interfering with the chemical mechanisms by which they grow.

The commonly used cytotoxic drugs include chlorambucil, cyclophosphamide, doxorubicin, fluoracil, melphalan, mercaptopurine, and methotrexate. Each is used against different kinds of cancer. Methotrexate, for example, is given for lymphoma, some forms of leukemia, and cancers of the breast, uterus, ovary, lung, bladder, and testes. Mercaptopurine is also used to treat leukemia and lymphoma, while fluoracil is used against cancers of the breast, bladder, ovary, intestine, and stomach. Combination chemotherapy can be administered against some forms of cancer. The drugs that are given to a specific patient depend not only on the kind of cancer being treated but also on the general health of the patient and the stage at which the cancer is detected. Chemotherapy is sometimes given in combination with other forms of treatment, such as radiation therapy and surgery.

Hormonal Therapies. Another kind of cancer chemotherapy is based on the knowledge that the body's normal sex hormones can stimulate the growth of some kinds of cancer. For example, the sex hormone estrogen can increase the growth rate of some breast cancers. Anticancer drugs that are based on this knowledge are substances that are related to the hormones and block their harmful activity. Sex hormone therapy is not limited to cancers of women. Diethylstilbestrol, an estrogen drug, is used to treat cancer of the prostate, an organ found only in men. In addition to diethylstilbestrol, other commonly used sex hormone cancer drugs include aminoglutethimide, ethyinyl estriadol, megestrol, nandrolone, and tamoxifen.

Side Effects. Anticancer drugs inevitably cause side effects. In the early stages of treatment, the patient may experience vomiting, nau-

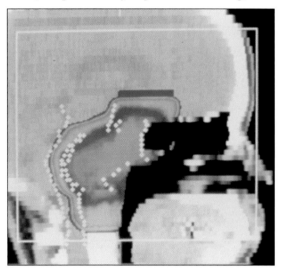

sea, and diarrhea. Some drugs cause severe hair loss, or alopecia. Others can cause anemia because they reduce the production of blood cells by the bone marrow. This can lead to increased susceptibility to infection and abnormal bleeding. Physicians treating cancer patients try to limit these side effects by giving these drugs over brief periods, allowing normal cells to recover from the adverse effects of the drugs before the next round of treatment begins.

A cancerous growth is highlighted in the scan at left. The negative effects of many cancer therapies makes careful and quick evaluation of a particular therapy's effectiveness important to a patient's well-being.

Further Reading
Hoffman, E.J., *Cancer and the Search for Selective Biochemical Inhibitors* (1999); Lodish, Harvey, et al., *Molecular Cell Biology* (1995); Markman, Maurice, *Basic Cancer Medicine* (1997); Weinberg, Robert A., *Genes and the Biology of Cancer* (1992).

First see DISEASE, INFECTIOUS

Chicken Pox

Next see HERPES

A mild but highly contagious disease caused by a virus belonging to the herpes group.

Chicken pox, or varicella, is a disease found mainly in children under the age of ten; less than five percent of cases occur in people over 15. One infection usually gives the victim immunity for life. The virus's incubation period can be up to three weeks. The first symptoms are small blister-like lesions on the torso that soon make their way to the limbs and face. Other than the itching, which can be somewhat soothed by lotion, the only other discomfort the patient will experience is a fever. The symptoms recede in about a week, although the patient remains infectious until the last blister disappears. A related virus is the cause of shingles.

The United States Food and Drug Administration approved a chickenpox vaccine in 1995 that was determined to be up to 90 percent effective. (*See* DISEASES, INFECTIOUS.)

First see AIR POLLUTION

Chlorofluorocarbon (CFC)

Next see OZONE LAYER

Chlorofluorocarbons (CFCs) are synthetic chemicals, widely used as refrigerants, cleaning agents, and propellants, that have been found to contribute to ozone depletion and have therefore been limited by a series of international treaties. Ironically, the same properties that made CFC—commonly known by a trade name, Freon—effective in its industrial applications are what make CFCs so destructive.

CFC was first developed in the 1930s, when a gas that was chemically inert, nonflammable, and harmless to humans was sought for use in

The effects of chlorofluorocarbons on the atmosphere were unknown when the chemicals were first used in aerosol cans and as refrigerants. Above, cans awaiting safe disposal in California—but much CFC remains.

refrigeration and air conditioning, industries which were burgeoning with the spread of electrification. Its inertness gradually made CFC even more prized, as it could be used in the production of plastic foam products, and in the manufacture of electronic components, without leaving any traces behind. Finally, and most menacingly, CFC found wide use as the propellant gas in aerosol sprays, since it would not react with the product being sprayed.

By the 1970s, almost a million tons of CFCs were entering the atmosphere each year. Although CFC is a relatively heavy molecule, over the course of six to eight years, any given CFC molecule has an even chance of circulating as high as the stratosphere; when it is exposed to ultraviolet radiation, it breaks down. The chlorine atoms released by this process are highly reactive, particularly to ozone molecules, which they can break down to normal oxygen in a

chain reaction. The discoverers of this process, S. Rowland and M. Molina, estimated that as much as 40 percent of the ozone layer could be destroyed by free chlorine atoms released from CFC in the upper atmosphere over the course of a century; for their work, Rowland and Molina shared the Nobel Prize in 1995. (*See* AIR POLLUTION; OZONE LAYER.)

Montreal Protocol. In 1987, the Montreal Protocol of Substances That Deplete the Ozone Layer was signed by 43 countries, promising to cut CFC production in half. This protocol has now been signed by 163 nations. By 1995, production of CFC had been cut in half, but that still meant a million tons produced. The growth rate of CFC-11 has now ceased, although it is still widely used in foreign manufacturing, and the growth rate of CFC-12, a longer-lived molecule, has dropped by 50 percent; it is the only CFC still produced in the United States, mainly to service the 90 million automobiles that cannot use non-CFC refrigerants. The last form of CFC, CFC-13, has also been replaced by substitute hydrofluorocarbons such as R-134a; these chlorine-free gases are somewhat more toxic and even longer-lasting than their chlorinated counterparts, but their ozone depletion is one-twentieth that of CFC. Disposal of CFC remains a vital environmental issue, although a new technique using sodium oxalate, a natural substance found in rhubarb leaves, holds promise.

First see PLANT

Chloroplast

Next see PHOTSYNTHESIS

Site of photosynthesis within a plant cell.

The chloroplast is the site of photosynthesis within a cell. Photosynthesis is the process of using light energy to produce simple sugars such as glucose. In order to carry out this process, an organism needs a light-sensitive pigment, such as chlorophyll, to convert the energy from sunlight into chemical energy (ATP and NADH) to be utilized in the cellular chemical reactions.

A chloroplast is 5 microns in length and has a double membrane covering, similar to mito-

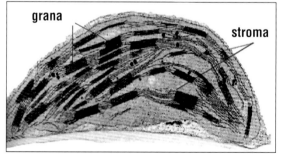

Above, the chloroplast, site in the plant cell of the process of photosynthesis. The grana are stacked corpuscles that carry the chlorophyl-bearing thylakoids.

chondria which are the site of cellular respiration, the "mirror image" reaction of photosynthesis. Chloroplasts contain large amounts of chlorophyll, a greenish pigment. The chlorophyll is located in structures known as thylakoid discs, which in turn are arranged in stacks called grana. The chemical reactions corresponding to the first half of photosynthesis, known as the Light Reaction, occur within the grana. The grana are surrounded by a viscous liquid called stroma, which is where the rest of the photosynthesis reactions, known as the Dark Reaction, take place. (*See* PHOTOSYNTHESIS.)

Within a leaf, the vast majority of chloroplasts are located in the palisade layer; therefore the majority of photosynthesis takes place there. Some chloroplasts are also present in the spongy layer. (*See* PLANT.)

Chloroplasts are a type of organelle known as plastids. Other plastids include chromoplasts and leukoplasts. Chromoplasts (from *chromos*, Greek for color) contain other colored pigments such as anthocyanins (reddish-purple), xanthophylls (yellow), xylenes (yellow), and carotenes (orange). These pigments are responsible for the colors of autumn foliage. They are present during the majority of the growing season, but are "invisible" due to the vast amount of chlorophyll also present. It is only when the chloroplasts die and the chlorophyll disappears that the other colors emerge. Leukoplasts (*leukos*, white) are used for storing starch and do not contain any colored pigments. (*See* CHLOROPLAST PIGMENTATION.)

Chloroplasts are one of the few organelles, aside from the nucleus, that contain their own DNA. (*See* EXTRANUCLEAR INHERITANCE.)

First see CHLOROPLAST

Chloroplast Pigmentation

Next see PLANT HORMONES

The pigments of chloroplasts are the receptors of light energy that transform CO_2 and H_2O into O_2 and sugar through the process of photosynthesis. Chief among them is chlorophyll, the pigment that makes leaves green by absorbing light in the violet, blue, and red wavelengths.

Chlorophyll-a is bluish green and is found in all photosynthetic plants and in the cyanobacteria, or blue-green algae. Chlorophyll-b, which makes up about one-quarter of the chlorophyll in green plants, is yellowish green and thus broadens the range of light available for photosynthesis. It is considered an accessory pigment: when it absorbs light, it transfers the energy to chlorophyll-a, which then converts it into chemical energy. Other forms of chlorophyll are found in some algae and photosynthetic bacteria.

Like chlorophyll-b, two other kinds of pigments—the carotenoids and the phycobilins—are accessory pigments that transfer their energy

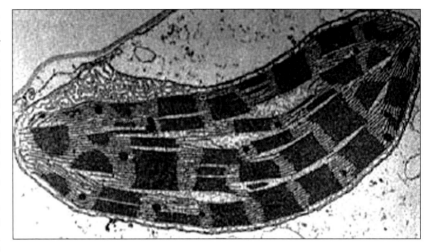

to chlorophyll-a. The carotenoids are red, orange, or yellow. Two groups of these pigments—carotenes and xanthophylls—are usually present in all chloroplasts. The phycobilins are blue or red pigments found in the cyanobacteria and in red algae.

In green plants, the pigments are grouped together in the chloroplasts into two varieties of photosynthetic units, designated photosystem I and photosystem II. Each system includes 250 to 400 pigment molecules, including chlorophyll-a, chlorophyll-b, and carotenoids. One small group of special chlorophyll-a molecules in each unit acts as a reaction center. When a photon of light strikes a pigment molecule, its energy excites an electron in the molecule, which moves up to a higher, less stable energy level. This excited state is passed from one pigment molecule to another until it reaches the reaction center, where it is converted into chemical energy.

Background material can be found in CELL; CHLOROPLAST; PLANT. *Advanced subjects are developed in* CALVIN-BENSON CYCLE; PHOTOSYNTHESIS; PLANT HORMONES. *More information on particular aspects is contained in* GROWTH REGULATION IN PLANTS *and* TROPICAL RAIN FOREST.

First see DIGESTIVE SYSTEM

Cholera

Next see DISEASES, INFECTIOUS

An infection of the small intestine that is caused by the bacterium called *Vibrio cholerae*.

Cholera causes a watery diarrhea that, left untreated, can result in rapid and severe loss of body fluid, a dehydration that can be fatal. Cholera is acquired by eating food or drinking water that is contaminated with the infectious agent. The disease has been known for many centuries in the northeastern part of India. When trade routes to India were opened in the 19th century, cholera spread rapidly throughout the world, causing epidemics that killed millions

Chloroplasts take up so much of a plant cell that there is barely enough room for other organelles. In the electron micrograph above, mitochondria and other structures are crushed into the upper left corner of the cell.

Further Reading
Argyroudi-Akoyunoglou, T., *The Chloroplast: From Molecular Biology to Biotechnology* (1999); Dicosmo, Frank, *Plant Cell Culture Secondary Metabolism: Toward Industrial Application* (1996); Hoober, J.K., *Chloroplasts* (1984); Nobel, Park S., *Physicochemical and Environmental Plant Physiology* (1999); Rashid, A., *Cell Physiology and Genetics of Higher Plants* (1998).

of people. The symptoms of cholera appear one to five days after infection, most notably diarrhea that is often accompanied by vomiting. The fluid lost in diarrhea must be replaced quickly to avoid death, and the replacement fluid must include appropriate amounts of the salts and sugar normally found in the body. Antibiotics such as tetracycline can lessen the attacks of diarrhea and help prevent the spread of the infectious agents to other people. Complete recovery is possible over a period of days with rehydration therapy.

Cholera can be prevented by adequate sanitation, which prevents drinking water from being contaminated by sewage. Travelers to infested areas are advised to boil the local water before drinking it or to rely on bottled water. There is a vaccine for cholera, but the protection it gives lasts only for a few months, and precautions about drinking water still must be obeyed. Travelers to areas where cholera is prevalent are advised to check vaccination requirements before a trip. (*See* WATER POLLUTION.)

First see CHROMOSOME

Chromatin

Next see MITOSIS

Conglomeration of DNA and protein found within the nucleus of a cell prior to cell division.

Chromosomal material in the cell is very long and thin, and resembles tangled strands of spaghetti rather than distinct and separate chromosomes. Before the cell can divide, mitosis must occur. A copy is made of every chromosome in order to ensure that each new daughter cell receives a complete set and no chromosomes are "lost" from one generation to the next. The first stage of mitosis is called interphase, and it is during this time that the replication of all genetic material occurs. Only chromatin is visible during interphase. It is not until the next stage, called prophase, that the chromosomes can be seen clearly as pairs.

Within the chromatin, most DNA sequences are inaccessible and inactive. The basic unit of chromatin is the nucleosome, which consists of approximately 200 base pairs of DNA "wrapped around" specific proteins known as histones. Nucleosomes are in turn organized into fibers which are 30 nanometers in diameter. The DNA exhibits "supercoiling" and other forms of folding and packing in order to "fit" the chromosome structure.

Chromatin was originally identified in the cell by its reaction to chemical dyes that stain for DNA. The name for both chromatin and chromosome comes from the Greek word *chroma*, which means color. (*See* CHROMOSOME; DNA REPLICATION; CELL CYCLE; *and* MITOSIS.)

Two views of the solenoid model of chromatin. The string of nucleosomes (blue in the bottom image) are coiled in a helical ladder around histone discs (red), and the ladder is coiled again around a long histone axis (top image).

First see FILTRATION

Chromatography

Next see ELECTROPHORESIS

A process used to separate materials from one another, due to a difference in phase distribution.

Materials can exist in three phases: solid, liquid, or gas. During chromatography, one component of a mixture is captured while the other components flow past. Chromatography comes from *chroma*, the Greek word for color, because extraction of the different materials from the mixture often results in the appearance of different spots or bands of color. The major types of chromatography are: column; thin-layer (TLC); and high-pressure liquid (HPLC)—all of which are characterized by liquid-solid phase interactions. In addition, gas chromatography (GC, or GLPC for gas-liquid partition) involves a mobile gas phase and a stationary liquid phase. Paper chromatography involves a liquid-liquid multiple extraction process.

Methods. Column chromatography, as the name implies, involves the use of a tall glass column which is packed with finely divided solids such as alumina or silica gel. The mixture is applied at the top and a liquid solvent is used to "wash" the components down the length of the column. Different materials travel at different rates because they cling with different intensities to the packing materials. With colored compounds, a series of varicolored bands will form. TLC and paper chromatography are horizontal versions of column chromatography. A solid adsorbent is spread in a thin layer on a ridged glass or plastic plate, or on a paper strip. A drop of the mixture is placed at one end along with the solvent and the components of the mixture separate and settle into different spots.

HPLC closely resembles column chromatography. The major differences are that the packing materials are much more densely packed within the column, and a pump is used so the extraction process is done under high pressure. This is important where the liquids involved have slow diffusion rates. The increased pressure enables the liquid components to be evaporated out in separate units.

Gas chromatography is used to separate volatile compounds whose boiling points differ from each other by less than 0.5°C. It has for all intents and purposes largely replaced fractional distillation (another popular extraction method) for separations and purifications on a small scale. The mixture to be separated is vaporized and carried along the column by a carrier gas, which is an inert gas such as nitrogen or helium. The lower volatile liquids will be trapped along the packing material, so a partitioning occurs between the gas and liquid phases.

Chromosome

First see GENE

Next see DNA REPLICATION

Location of the genetic material of a cell

The genetic material of a cell is "packaged" into distinct structures known as chromosomes. The word chromosome comes from the Greek *chroma,* meaning color, as the structures absorb dye readily and are thus easily identifiable within the cell. A chromosome consists of a very long molecule of DNA wrapped up in an equal mass of proteins. Prokaryotes, which are very primitive cells such as bacteria and blue-green algae, have only a single round chromosome which is not partitioned off in any way from the rest of the cellular contents. Eukaryotes, more advanced cells, have pairs of homologous chromosomes located in the nucleus. Human cells have 46 chromosomes, arranged in 23 pairs. Of these pairs, 22 are autosomes, or "regular" chromosomes. The remaining pair are the two sex chromosomes—XX for females; XY for males.

Genes. A gene is a segment of DNA which contains information for constructing a particular protein. There are approximately 30,000-40,000 genes, made up of 3 billion DNA base pairs, in the human genome. Each chromosome contains much more than just one gene. Genes found together on the same chromosome are said to be linked and are usually inherited together.

Each individual carries two genes for a particular trait. During meiosis, the production of gametes such as sperm and eggs, homologous chromosomes separate from each other so that each resulting gamete has only half the chromosomes, and consequently half the genes, of a regular cell. (*See* MITOSIS *and* MEIOSIS.)

A karyotype is the pattern of the chromosomes within the cell. The karyotype of fetal cells obtained from amniocentesis can be analyzed to detect genetic abnormalities, such as Down's syndrome. Identification of the sex chromosomes also reveals the baby's sex.

Errors. Sometimes mistakes occur during meiosis and a particular gamete receives two copies of a chromosome. If used in reproduction, the result will be a cell containing a chromosome in triplicate, a condition known as trisomy. Down's syndrome results from trisomy 21, the presence of three copies of chromosome number 21.

Uniparental disomy refers to a cell which receives both copies of a chromosome from one parent and none from the other. It is believed that disomy results from a trisomy condition followed by the "loss" of one of the triplet chromosomes. (*See* MUTATION, GENETIC.)

Imprinting. Genetic imprinting refers to the difference in phenotype depending upon which parent contributed the genetic material. In an "imprinted region" of the chromosome, only one copy of the gene is expressed. The other has been inactivated and is "genetically silent." The inactivation occurs only in the chromosomes inherited from a parent of one sex, but not when inherited from the other. Genetic imprinting appears to be a way of regulating gene expression. Studies have shown that both maternal and paternal genetic material are essential for normal development and that the different parental "contributions" produce different phenotypes.

Inheritance. Mendel's second law of genetic inheritance states that independent assortment occurs, meaning the inheritance of a specific allele (the form a gene may take, either dominant or recessive) for one trait occurs independent of the inheritance of a specific allele for another trait. However, this is only true if the genes for the traits being studied are located on separate chromosomes. (*See* GENETICS.)

Genetic linkage can be tinkered with, however, due to a phenomenon known as crossing-over. During the early stages of meiosis, when the chromosomes are pairing up, homologous chromosomes often exchange pieces of themselves. Genes for particular traits will still be found on the same chromosome, but the specific alleles that are inherited together may be different. Crossing over occurs very frequently; in fact, the frequency is used as a tool to construct a genetic map of the chromosome, for the closer the gene loci, the higher rate of crossing over.

Mapping. Mapping of the chromosomes involves identification of the various genes found in the different regions of the chromosome. By sequencing the DNA and correlating a sequence

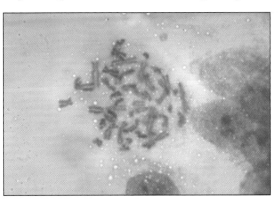

Left, the chromosomes of a human cell undergoing mitosis. The process is not as orderly as textbook drawings would have one believe, yet every step in the complex process is carefully monitored and directed by the structures of the cell.

with a known protein, scientists are able to identify the genes for particular traits. The Human Genome Project, begun in 1990 and with a rough draft completed in 2001, is concerned with sequencing and deciphering the entire genetic code. The genes for specific traits are being discovered and identified on a regular basis.

The chromosomes can only be seen as distinct pairs during cell reproduction. Mitosis refers to the copying of each chromosome prior to cell division, to assure that each new "daughter" cell receives a complete set of chromosomes. Prior to mitosis, the genetic material in the cell is called chromatin, and closely resembles long tangled strands of spaghetti.

Within the chromatin, most DNA sequences are inaccessible and inactive. The basic unit of chromatin is the nucleosome, which consists of approximately 200 base pairs of DNA "wrapped around" specific proteins known as histones. Nucleosomes are in turn organized into fibers which are 30 nanometers (10^{-9} meters) in diameter. The DNA exhibits "supercoiling" and other forms of folding and packing in order to fit the chromosome structure. (*See* GENOME, HUMAN.)

First see CELL MEMBRANE

Cilia, Flagella, Basal Bodies, and Centrioles

Next see CELL

Cilia are microscopic hairs on the outside of a cell membrane, used for locomotion. Flagella are similar to cilia, but are longer and most cells that contain them usually have only one or two at most, as opposed to cilia which may number in the hundreds. Cilia cause the cell to move by beating back and forth like the oars on a rowboat. Flagella whip around like a propeller.

Internally, cilia and flagella are composed of tiny structures called microtubules. These are arranged in a specific pattern: nine pairs of tubules around the perimeter of the shaft and a single pair in the center. This is known as the "9-2" arrangement. Some flagella have microtubules arranged in triplets instead of pairs.

Cells lining the interior of the human respiratory tract contain cilia whose job is to remove the mucus coating (there to trap dirt and germs and prevent their further entry) by sweeping it to the back of the throat to be swallowed. In addition, the inner ear houses a structure called the cochlea, which contains cilia. These cilia bend in a specific way according to the vibrations that have been transmitted to them. It is this bending that signals the auditory nerve to send a message to the brain so hearing can occur.

Both cilia and flagella are formed from basal bodies, which are cylinder-shaped structures. Basal bodies contain nine triplets of microtubules but no central pair.

Centrioles have the same internal structure as basal bodies. Centrioles play some role in mitosis, the process undergone by the nucleus of a cell before it divides, but the exact nature of that role is unclear. It is currently believed to be involved with the spindle, the set of fibers concerned with organizing and manipulating chromosomes. In animal cells, the centrioles are found within structures known as centrosomes, which organize microtubules to form the spindle. Other cells contain centrosomes without centrioles. (*See* CELL *and* CELL CYCLE.)

A newly formed cell contains two centrioles, "inherited" from the original parent cell. During interphase, the centrioles reproduce, so there are four altogether when the cell begins mitosis and the process of cell division.

First see HEART

Circulatory Systems

Next see BLOOD PRESSURE

Pumped by the heart through a dense web of tubes—from the mighty aorta to capillaries only a cell wide—the blood carries its chemical traffic to every part of the vertebrate body with an efficiency that would be the envy of many a transportation planner.

This cardiovascular circulatory system brings nutrients, water, oxygen, hormones, and antibodies to the cells and carries away carbon dioxide and other waste products. It also plays an important role in regulating body temperature. A second, less familiar circulatory network—the lymphatic system—filters bacteria from the tissues, removes excess fluid between cells, and retrieves protein that has escaped the bloodstream in the capillaries.

Two Types of Circulation. In most vertebrates, including mammals and birds, the cardiovascular circulation consists of two closed loops that begin and end at the heart. Pulmonary, or lesser, circulation pumps unoxygenated blood to the lungs to pick up oxygen. Systemic, or greater, circulation pumps oxygenated blood around the body. Arteries carry the blood away from the heart; veins carry it back.

In systemic circulation, the heart pumps the blood out through a large artery called the aorta (in reptiles, through two aortic trunks), which branch into smaller arteries, divide into still-smaller arterioles, and finally bcome microscopic capillaries. The main work of the circulatory system—the exchange of oxygen, nutrients, and other materials—takes place in the capillary beds, chiefly by diffusion. The capillaries are so

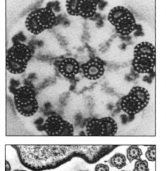
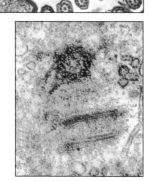

Above, some of the complex structures that make a living cell work (from top): a micrograph of the cross-section of a cilium, showing the two arms that are driven to oscillate by ATP; the basal bodies that direct the movement of the cilia; the structure of the centrioles, composed of microtubules, and responsible for forming the structure that organizes the chromosomes (the spindle apparatus) during mitosis; and finally, flagella on a microbial cell.

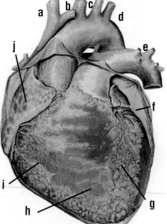

The human heart.
(a) superior vena cava;
(b) brachiocephalic artery;
(c) left common carotid artery;
(d) left subclavian artery;
(e) pulmonary trunk;
(f) left auricle;
(g) left ventricle;
(h) right venticle;
(i) right auricle;
(j) right atrium.

numerous that, taken together, they would form the largest organ in the body; in humans, a route over 100 km long. The body does not contain enough blood to fill all the capillaries at once, so blood gets directed to those with the greatest need—capillaries in a hard-working muscle, for instance. The remaining tiny vessels are shut off by precapillary sphincters, rings of muscle at the base of most capillaries. The capillaries converge to form venules, which merge to form veins, culminating in large veins that return blood to the heart. In humans, the veins reaching the heart are the superior or anterior vena cava, which drains the head, neck, and arms, and the inferior or posterior vena cava, which drains the rest of the body.

Blood in capillaries of the intestinal walls takes a detour from this route, traveling into the portal vein and then the liver, where it enters a network of tiny channels that process digested nutrients and toxic substances. The liver separately receives oxygenated blood through the hepatic artery. The two pools of blood mix in the liver and leave through the hepatic vein, which feeds into the inferior vena cava.

Blood Pressure. The nature of the blood flow through the body varies widely. Blood leaves the heart under considerable pressure and surging with the beat of the heart muscle; the arteries that carry it away generally have thick, elastic walls containing smooth muscle. As a result of friction between the blood and the vessel walls, blood pressure decreases as the blood gets farther from the heart. It falls rapidly in the arterioles and capillaries and reaches its lowest point in the veins, just before returning to the heart. This pressure gradient is necessary since blood can flow only from an area of higher pressure to one of lower pressure.

In humans, blood pressure usually is measured in the brachial artery of the upper arm. A typical normal pressure is 120 mm Hg during systole, when the ventricles contract to eject the blood, and 80 mm Hg during diastole, the relaxation phase that follows. By the time blood reaches the thin-walled, collapsible veins, its flow is no longer surging but smooth, and the pressure from the heart is no longer enough to keep it flowing. The moving muscles of the body compress the veins, forcing the blood onward while valves in the veins prevent it from flowing backward. The expansion of the chest during breathing lowers pressure in the thorax, creating another pressure gradient that encourages blood flow back to the heart.

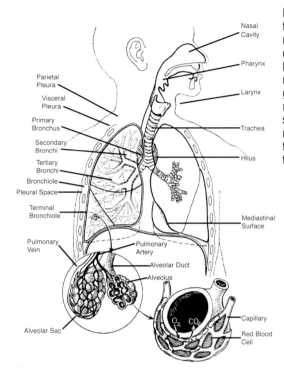

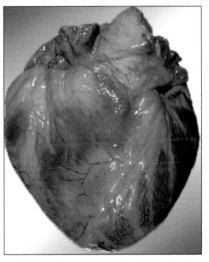

The human heart (preserved specimen).

Left, the respiratory system is integrally connected to the cardiovascular system. Air is inhaled into the lungs and reaches the alveoli. Oxygen diffuses through the membranes of the alveolar sacs and is picked up by red blood cells, which are then pumped throughout the body.

Thermal Regulation. Circulation also helps to heat or cool animals. Major arteries and veins to the extremities generally lie next to each other to foster heat conservation through countercurrent exchange: warm arterial blood coming from the center of the body transfers some of its heat to the cold, venous blood returning from the body's periphery. To maximize this heat exchange, some arctic mammals have veins that cluster around an artery in their extremities, a feature called the *rete mirabile* or "wonderful network."

Conversely, when a body needs to cool off, blood can be shunted to the skin to radiate heat and to be cooled by the evaporation of sweat. In animals that do not sweat, blood may be cooled in the capillaries of the mouth by panting. In dogs, for example, which generally have sweat glands only in their tongues, the cooled blood enters the carotid rete, a bed of capillaries where it cools arterial blood bound for the brain.

Background material can be found in BLOOD; BONE AND BONE GROWTH; HEART; MUSCLE. *Advanced subjects are developed in* ANGIOPLASTY; BLOOD PRESSURE; LEUKEMIA. *Additional relevant information is contained in* AMNIOCENTESIS; CHEMOTHERAPY; FLUID MECHANICS; HEMOPHILIA; LIPOPROTEINS.

Further Reading
DeBakey, Michael E., Gotto, Antonio., *The New Living Heart* (1997); Des Jardins, Terry, *Cardiopulmonary Anatomy & Physiology: Essentials for Respiratory Care* (1993); Mohrman, David E., et al., *Cardiovascular Physiology* (1991); Opie, Lionel H., *The Heart: Physiology, from Cell to Circulation* (1998); Vogel, Steven, *Vital Circuits: On Pumps, Pipes, and the Workings of Circulatory Systems* (1993).

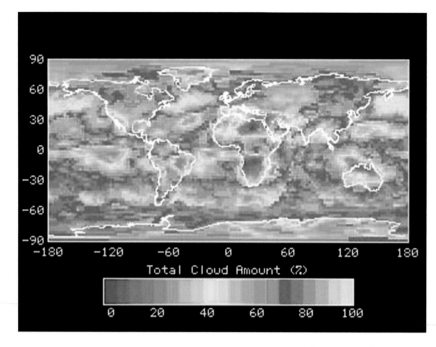

Total Cloud Amount (%)

First see WEATHER

Climatology

Next see GLOBAL WARMING

Climatology is the study of the weather conditions in different regions. In addition to the presentation of climatic data, climatography, it includes the analysis of the causes of climatic differences, a field called physical climatology; and the application of climatic data to solving specific problems, or applied climatology. Some climatologists study fossil remains, rock layers, and other such evidence to describe the climates of very ancient times, a field known as paleoclimatology. There are further subdivisions. One is agricultural climatology, which deals not only with farming but with the effects of climate on human health. Two other fields are synoptic and dynamic climatology, which deal with the relationships between the atmosphere and climate.

The permanent factors that govern the nature of the climate of a given region of the earth are called climatic controls. They include the solar radiation received by that region, its distribution of land and water masses, its elevation and large-scale topography, and the ocean currents that influence its weather. The general circulation of the main wind systems of a region is regarded as a secondary factor.

The general overall climate of a very large region is known as the macroclimate. Small areas within that region may display mesoclimates; such areas can include small valleys, forest clearings, and open spaces in cities. The Greeks were the earliest to divide each hemisphere of Earth into summerless, intermediate, and winterless zones, labels that were later

Satellite sensing allows for careful assembly of records for climatological studies, such as the record of mean rainfall and cloud cover, above, for the month of June 1991.

Further Reading
Chorley, Richard, *Atmosphere, Weather and Climate* (1998); Graedel, Thomas E., *Atmosphere, Climate, and Change* (1997); Oort, Abraham H., *Physics of Climate* (1992); Trefil, James, *A Scientist at the Seashore* (1984); Trenberth, Kevin E., *Climate System Modeling* (1993).

changed to torrid, temperate, and frigid. Starting in the 19th century, a number of different climate classification systems were introduced, still in use today. The most widely used system was developed by Wladimir Peter Köppean in 1918. It identifies the following climates:

Continental Climates are the conditions that prevail in the interior of land masses of continental size. Continental climates are marked by large ranges of temperature, year-to-year, day-to-day, and seasonal. They also generally have low relative humidity and moderate or small and irregular rainfall. At their extremes, continental climates give rise to deserts. The annual extremes of temperature during the year occur soon after the solstices, in June and December, when the sun is on the points of the ecliptic furthest from the equator.

Maritime Climates are predominantly under the influence of the oceans. Such climates occur on islands and on the western coasts of continents in the middle latitudes. They extend inland until they reach a natural barrier such as a mountain range, when they become continental. Marine climates have small temperature ranges, with temperature extremes occurring a month or two after the solstices.

Mountain Climates are different from those of lower-lying areas, primarily because their air becomes thinner with altitude, which causes reduced oxygen availability, lower temperatures, and increased exposure to sunlight. On many tropical mountains, there is a dense forest region that extends to the level of cloud height.

Temperate Climates are the variable climates of the middle latitudes. They include a number of subdivisions, such as temperate rainy and snow forest. Much of the continental United States has a temperate climate.

Tropical Climates are generally found in regions close to the equator. They are characterized by high temperatures and heavy rainfall for most or part of the year. Different tropical climates include tropical rainy, tropical monsoon, and tropical savannah.

Polar Climates (sometimes called arctic climates) occur where temperatures are so low that the annual accumulation of snow or ice exceeds the annual rate of removal. Examples include Greenland, Antarctica, and parts of Alaska. In these regions, the temperature during the warmest months never rises above the freezing point of water. The different kinds of polar climates include tundra, snow forest, and perpetual frost climates.

Related areas to be considered are ATMOSPHERE; WEATHER; WEATHER FORECASTING; WINDS AND CLOUDS. *Advanced subjects are developed in* GLOBAL WARMING; HURRICANES AND TORNADOES; OZONE LAYER. *Relevant information is contained in* ACID RAIN; CHAOS AND COMPLEXITY; OCEANOGRAPHY; VOLCANO.

Cloning

First see GENETICS

Next see RECOMBINANT DNA

Cloning refers to the stimulation of a somite, an ordinary body cell, to develop into a whole new organism. The cell divides rapidly (a process known as cleavage) and as the number of cells increases, a hollow ball is formed. Eventually there is the formation of two additional cell layers from which all organs and body systems arise. Normally, it is an egg cell which develops in such a manner. The egg is usually fertilized, but can in some cases develop without the benefit of a sperm. The term for this is parthenogenesis, which occurs among bees along with conventional methods of reproduction.

Background. Cloning has fascinated and disturbed scientists, and virtually everyone else, for more than 30 years. Popular fiction and movies have explored the idea of cloning famous, or infamous, individuals. Early experiments proved the feasibility of cloning, in the sense that all body cells contain the same genetic information. Success was first achieved with cloning from embryonic cells, the earlier the better. Although cells retained all of their information, somehow the genes became more "inaccessible" the older the cell was, i.e., the more specialized and differentiated the cell became. In the late 1960s, Dr. John Gurdon worked with frogs and established that adult cells could be "encouraged" to develop into tadpoles (but not further) and that embryo cells could develop into adult frogs.

Cloning mammals was much more difficult, but was eventually accomplished. Once again, a final barrier existed, the problem of being able to clone from adult cells or even more advanced embryo cells. As the world knows, this was overcome with the birth of Dolly, a sheep cloned in 1996 from an adult mammary cell, by Scottish researcher Ian Wilmut.

The cloning of human cells has raised many ethical issues, which has caused reasearchers to proceed with caution. In many experiments already conducted, cells that had been cloned were aborted before significant differentiation could take place.

Above, the halving of a calf egg by physically dividing the egg with a micro-scalpel. This "twinning" of the egg was an important step on the road to cloning. Below, Dolly.

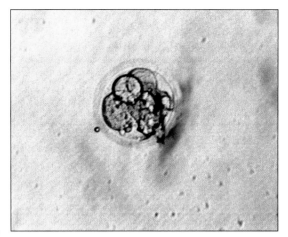

Method. The method used for cloning is as follows: an egg cell, whose own nucleus has been removed, is fused with an adult cell. The adult genes "take over" the egg cell and cause it to develop into a whole organism. The method is relatively inexact and results are less than guaranteed. Dr. Wilmut's team began with 277 udder cells, but only 29 of them developed into embryos. Of those, only Dolly was born.

Twins. Clones are "identical twins" in that they contain identical genetic information. But a clone is not the same individual, any more than conventional identical twins are. It takes more than just genes to create the sum total of an organism; the environment in which those genes are expressed is equally important. The genetic material replicated in each cell of the new organism comes from the donor cell and, therefore, the "parent" of a clone is the genetic donor. A woman pregnant with a clone of herself is not going to give birth to another "self," but rather to her identical twin. She is not her own parent, but the parent of her twin, which is still a unique circumstance. (*See* GENETIC ENGINEERING.)

Related to, but not quite the same, is the "twinning" of embryo cells to create new organisms. This involves separating the cells of an embryo, at a relatively early stage, so that each newly independent unit will develop into a whole new organism. In nature, identical twins are formed when this process happens during the early stages of cleavage. Experiments in twinning have been successful in mammals and even in primates such as monkeys.

The term clone also refers to a group of cells or molecules descended from and identical to an original ancestor. Scientists often use cloned cells to establish cell lines for use in studies in molecular genetics or immunology.

Therapy. A cloning vector is a vehicle for inserting new genes into a cell. The vehicle used is usually a virus or a plasmid—a small circular piece of extrachromosomal DNA found in bacteria. Cloning vectors are often used in recombinant DNA work as well as in attempts at gene therapy, correcting or replacing defective genes.

THE CUTTING EDGE

Hello, Dolly

To produce Dolly, the first cloned mammal, Dr. Ian Wilmut of the Roslin Institute transferred the nuclei of nearly three hundred cells from mature sheep into the eggs of other sheep, hoping to produce a genetic duplicate of one donor. The key to his success was that he starved the cells for five days before transferring their nuclei into the recipient eggs, making them ready to initiate new growth. Dolly's life span will probably be shorter than her mother's, because the ends of her chromosomes, their telomeres, show wear and tear equivalent to the six-year-old sheep who was her genetic mother. However, Dolly's first lamb has normal chromosome ends, implying that clones will not pass on such inherited flaws.

First see ATOM

Cluster, Atomic

Next see BUCKMINSTERFULLERENE

An assemblage of atoms (or molecules), often on a surface, that are weakly bound together.

An atomic cluster can contain as few as two atoms, or as many as the many billions that are contained in a large-scale object or celestial body. The general classification of matter into three states—gas, liquid, solid—and the possible inclusion of a fourth state, namely, a plasma (a highly ionized aggregate of atoms) is challenged by the observation of a possible fifth state: the atomic cluster. One might ordinarily regard this as no state of matter at all—the atoms are not bound by electromagnetic force and they do not interact kinetically. In what sense, then, can the haphazard assembly of atoms be a state of matter worthy of study?

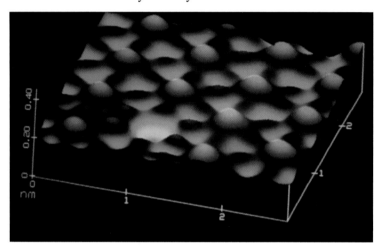

Above, a scanning tunnel microscope (STM) image shows an imperfection in yellow in the structure of an iodine adsorbate lattice (false-colored purple) on a platinum base (green). The bonds that hold the platinum substrate in place are strong, but the iodine atoms are loosely embedded and bound to one another, approximating a cluster of atoms.

Further Reading

Feinberg, Gerald, *What Is the World Made Of?* (1996); Pullman, Bernard, *The Atom in the History of Human Thought* (1998); Trefil, James, *From Atoms to Quarks: An Introduction to the Strange World of Particle Physics* (1994); Von Baeyer, Hans Christian, *Taming the Atom; The Emergence of the Visible Microworld* (1995).

Accumulated Forces. The bulk presented by an atom, the very slight gravitational force it exerts, and the nearly as slight kinetic interaction created by random (one might say "accidental") collisions between atoms, when added to the light electromagnetic bonding that exists between the atoms, all become significant when there are large numbers of atoms involved. Also, when a gas or liquid encounters a cluster and "enters" it, interesting phenomena take place that serve as models for what happens in the instellar medium of outerspace and in the bloodstream. Since many catalysts operate in a chemical reaction by offering a geometrical setting for a reaction to take place, without interacting chemically with the reactants, a cluster offers a model for large-scale catalytic action.

Carbon Clusters. By far the most work done in recent years on atomic clusters has been for the element carbon. The best known of this class is the C60 molecule known as the buckminster-fullerene, in which carbon atoms are held loosely in a soccer-ball configuration. The structure displays great strength while allowing other sub-stances to enter into the structure and mingle with it, two activities that are mutually exclusive for other states of matter.

Carbon clusters have been observed (using spectral analysis) in the vicinity of stars and in the tails of comets. The bonds in these aggregates are too weak to form a lattice structure, but covalent bonds do form between neighboring atoms. The effect is to create a mass of matter that has the appearance of a coherent mass, but is so loosely bound as to be virtually transparent to particles and radiation passing through. (An analogy has been drawn to children's play areas that consist of a room filled to the brim with plastic balls. The balls offer buoyant support and impede the progress of the children—as well as offering the opportunity to through themselves about safely—but the balls do not interact.)

Producing Clusters. As one would imagine, producing clusters can be a difficult undertaking. Because atoms and elements are inclined to interact with one another forming a chemical bond, bringing atoms and molecules together in such a way that they form a very slight bond and yet display a discernable structure with macroscopic qualities can be a difficult task. The key to successful production of clusters has been the environment in which they are produced: adiabatic (thoroughly sealed, thermally) expansion of a gas from a high pressure to a vaccum has proven effective. But these methods are not common processes in nature, so that how clusters are created in the natural world—and why they are so widespread—remains a mystery.

Applications. While the study of clusters is in its infancy—and the subject by its very nature offers researchers little onto which to anchor a theory or a research program—the widespread appearance of this form of matter throughout the universe may make the subject of atomic clusters a robust area of investigation. Three of the more promising avenues include:

—The delivery of medications may be more effectively carried out at the cellular level by an atomic cluster.

—Metallurgical processes may benefit from the use of cluster techniques. Metals characteristically respond to catalycized processes, so that a metal-soaked atomic cluster may undergo such reactions faster and more efficiently.

—Chemical processes, especially those involved in combustion, rely heavily on surface chemical qualities. A cluster "solution" of fuel would expose greater surface areas of combustants and offer the possibility of increased power and efficiency for jet and rocket fuels.

Background material can be found in ATOM; BOND, CHEMICAL; CHEMICAL REACTION; VALENCE. *Advanced subjects are developed in* ACIDS AND BASES; CATALYST; GASES, BEHAVIOR OF. *Fundamental aspects of this subject are covered in* ISOMERISM; COLLOID; SURFACE CHEMISTRY.

First see SOIL CHEMISTRY

Coastal Engineering

Next see DAMS

Coastal Engineering and Erosion Control have changed dramatically in recent decades. The U.S. Army Corps of Engineers, which was charged with the responsibility for America's coastlines in 1824, has for a century pursued an aggressive policy of rigid containment and retention of rivers, inlets, and ocean beaches. Perhaps its most spectacular triumph was a 17-foot seawall built in 1900 to protect Galveston, Texas. However, starting in 1972, the National Parks Service has adopted a more flexible approach to coastal engineering, which is beginning to show promising results.

Coastal Erosion. It is the nature of coastlines to erode; wind, currents, and storms scour away far more sand than can be replenished by deposits of sediment. Over the past 18,000 years, Earth's seas have been rising at about one foot per century, increasing the effect of erosion; global warming has increased this rate slightly. If people did not build structures on or near the shoreline, these inevitable changes would have no long-term effect; but with the development of civilization, human desires to secure their possessions have begun to clash with the shoreline's desire to shift. (*See* GEOMORPHOLOGY.)

Responses. The most common response to shoreline erosion is hard stabilization through the use of groins, jetties, and seawalls to protect beachfront property. Lt. Robert E. Lee built a series of jetties at Fort Moultrie, S.C., in 1829. Their drawback is that they only protect land to one side: upstream, or upcurrent in the case of groins and jetties, landward in the case of seawalls. Whatever is on the other side is given up to the encroaching sea. The flow of sand can be predicted by computer programs such as GENESIS and SBEACH, but so far inaccurately.

Thus, some states, including Maine and the Carolinas, promote soft stabilization, using techniques such as beach replenishment and dune emplantation. These techniques, less expensive and far less destructive of the coastal environment than jetties and seawalls, nevertheless are at best temporary stopgaps. Replenishment of Miami Beach, performed in 1981, lasted until the late 1990s before further repairs were needed; on the other hand, replenishment of the beach at Ocean City, N.J., has had to be repeated forty times since 1951, with one project disappearing in just two and a half months.

Relocation. The final option, structural relocation, has often been chosen by individual property owners. Famous cases include the moving of New York City's Brighton Beach Hotel in 1888, and the relocation of the Block Island Lighthouse in 1996. However, once large steel and concrete structures such as hotels, highways, and bridges have been erected, this option becomes impossible to contemplate; hard stabilization thus becomes the only choice.

First see METAL

Coatings and Films

Next see PLASTIC

Coatings and films are materials that are used to cover or protect a surface. A coating is a protective layer that changes the properties or utility of the material it covers, while a film is a material that is cast or extruded so that it forms a thin, usually transparent or translucent, flexible membrane. Films usually consist of plastics, while a large variety of materials are used as coatings. For example, glass has long been used to coat the interiors of hot-water heaters, while ceramic coatings are common on tiles, porcelain, and metal wall panels. (*See* CERAMICS.)

The coatings used to protect space vehicles as they reenter Earth's atmosphere consist of multiple layers of glass, ceramic, or plastic that absorb the heat of reentry by disintegrating. Synthetic rubbers such as chlorosulfonated polyethylene are used to coat fabrics that are utilized as firewalls in aircraft, inflated structures such as radar domes, and diaphragms in fuel pumps. Plastic films are used as laminated coatings over metal, wood, and other materials.

For example, a polyvinyl fluoride coating applied to steel or aluminum that is used in construction is more durable than paint and has greater resistance to ultraviolet light and the effects of weather conditions. The metallized films that are applied to the decorative trim on automobiles prevent rusting and other damage, while plastic resins that have chemical inertness, resistance to heat, and antisticking properties are applied not only to industrial equipment but also to household items such as frying pans, where the antisticking property reduces the need for grease and fats in cooking. (*See* METALLURGY.)

First see EVOLUTION

Coevolution

Next see SPECIATION

The phenomenon where one species acts as a selective force to directly influence the evolution of another species.

Nature supplies many examples of genetically disparate species that are ecologically intimate, bonded as predator and prey, parasite and host, competitors, or partners in a mutually beneficial relationship. (*See* COMPETITION AND ALTRUISM.)

Ecologist Paul Ehrlich and botanist Peter Raven first proposed the term coevolution in 1965, after studying the interplay of butterfly

An especially heavy surf pounds the northern shore of the island of Oahu, Hawaii. Containing coastal erosion is very important for islands like Oahu, where the shore constitutes a significant proportion of the total land area.

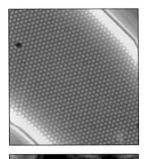

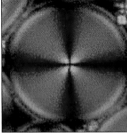

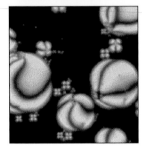

Above, examples of colloids. From top, polystyrene balls of diameter 0.8 microns trapped between two layers; a large drop of a liquid crystal that contains a water droplet at its center; drops of several liquid crystals with water droplets inside.

Further Reading

Ehrlich, Paul, *Science of Ecology* (1987); Raven, Peter, *Environment* (2001); Thiele, Leslie P., *Environmentalism for a New Millennium* (1999); Wills, C., *Yellow Fever, Black Goddess: The Coevolution of People and Plagues* (1997).

caterpillars and the plants they feed on. They hypothesized that noxious compounds found in plants, such as milkweed, are not waste products, as was widely thought, but chemical defenses against insect predators. Plants that develop such defenses, through a random mutation, outsurvive others of their species and pass on their defensive abilities. Eventually, a genetic mutation arises among the predators, allowing some to tolerate the plant's poison. These thrive, allowing the beneficial feature to spread in later generations of the species. The caterpillars of monarch and queen butterflies, for instance, are immune to milkweed toxins. Each side in the predator-prey relationship has evolved in response to the other. Ehrlich and Raven concluded that this kind of evolutionary interplay is largely responsible for the feeding patterns of various kinds of caterpillars.

Narrow Specialization. Coevolution between two species can lead to narrow specialization. Many parasites become so specialized that they can survive only in a specific host or a specific succession of hosts. For instance, the blood fluke that causes the common human disease schistosomiasis must spend part of its life cycle in a human and part in a snail.

More general adaptation, called diffuse coevolution, involves traits developing in a number of species in response to traits that arise in several other species. For example, a number of predators in an ecological community might evolve greater speed, and the prey they compete for might evolve keener senses. The coevolved traits in such cases are not highly specific. If circumstances change, and predator and prey each face different adversaries, these traits are likely to remain as useful. (*See* POPULATION ECOLOGY.)

Techniques. Coevolution in prey and predator has been likened to an ecological arms race in which the prey needs to stay one step ahead. Besides chemical weapons, which can include noxious odors as well as toxic tissue and venom, cryptic coloring is common among both prey and predator. This can range from camouflage, in which a species blends with its surroundings, to warning coloration, in which a species advertises its chemical defenses by a characteristic color pattern. In false mimicry, a prey species may come to resemble a species that is fiercer or less palatable, while a predator may take on the coloration or behavior of its prey so it can approach or even attract its unsuspecting victim. Coevolution can also shape the life cycle. In prey species as diverse as caribou and cicadas, individuals' reproduction is synchronized. So many offspring are produced at one time that predators simply can't consume them all.

In this evolutionary back-and-forth, natural selection tends to give prey the edge because of what has been called the life-dinner principle. When a fox chases a rabbit, the fox is running for its dinner; if it loses, it can still go on to reproduce. But the rabbit runs for its life; if it tires or stumbles, it will never reproduce again.

First see SOLVATION AND PRECIPITATION

Colloid

Next see CLUSTER, ATOMIC

A colloid is a mixture that in some ways closely resembles a solution or suspension, and in other ways is very different. In a solution, particles are dispersed within another material, called a solvent, to make a uniform mixture. Once dissolved, the particles cannot be separated out of a solution by any conventional means, even with a filter. In a suspension, the dissolved particles are larger than individual molecules. The mixture is only a temporary one; the particles can be filtered out, and if left undisturbed will eventually settle to the bottom. A suspension has a cloudy appearance while solutions are clear.

In a colloid, the suspended particles are smaller than those in an ordinary suspension, but larger than the particles in a solution. Colloidal particles cannot be filtered out and will not "settle" out. A colloid will last indefinitely if left undisturbed. (*See* LIQUID.)

Sols and Gels. A colloid can exist as a sol or a gel. For example, gelatin is a colloid in sol form when the particles are uniformly dispersed in warm water, and it behaves very much like a liquid. The gel form occurs when the above mixture is chilled. The particles join together to form a three-dimensional matrix (network) "trapping" the surrounding water molecules. The colloid now has a semisolid consistency.

Because of their water-trapping ability, gels are an important part of recent innovations in diaper technology and other related products. The flexible matrix provided by a gel is useful in other materials, such as sneaker soles.

Colloidal crystals are formed when the ordered arrays of suspended particles in certain fluids give those fluids the properties of a crystal. Some colloidal crystals display unique properties which can be used to create new materials. Shaking a colloidal crystal disrupts its "order," although it retains the density and temperature of its crystalline state. The result is a supercooled fluid in which various stages of crystallization can be seen. (*See* BROWNIAN MOTION.)

First see CHEMICAL REACTION

Combustion

Next see OXIDIZING AGENTS

Oxidation is a reaction in which something is chemically combined with oxygen. Oxidation refers to a loss of electrons; reduction refers to a gain of electrons. The compound combining with oxygen loses electrons to the oxygen, which in turn becomes reduced. Oxidation and reduction must always occur together, with the electrons lost by one entity being "picked up" by the other. (*See* OXIDIZING AGENTS.)

A common example of oxidation is the rusting of iron. Oxidation is an exothermic reaction, causing energy to be given off. Usually oxidation is a relatively slow process and so the energy is emitted gradually. Combustion is an oxidation reaction that produces so much heat so rapidly that a flame or explosion results.

Rapid Oxidation. Combustion is used to produce heat or electricity. Fuels may be either solids, liquids, or gases. Whichever state it is in, the fuel must first be vaporized, or converted to a gas, before it can burn. The temperature required for the combustion to begin is called the ignition temperature. The energy given off by the reaction is called the heat of combustion. Variations in their ignition temperatures and heats of combustion determine how and what different fuels are used for. The most common types of fuel are oil, gasoline, and coal.

During the combustion process, hydrocarbons (long-linked chains of carbon atoms with attached hydrogens) are broken down in the presence of oxygen to form carbon dioxide and water, or just carbon dioxide. Complete combustion means that the hydrocarbon has been completely broken down. Incomplete combustion means the reaction has not occurred fully and results in the formation of carbon monoxide instead of carbon dioxide. Carbon monoxide is an odorless, colorless gas that is poisonous and dangerous to inhale. This is why it can be fatal to breathe in car exhaust fumes in an enclosed area such as a garage and why home heating furnaces should be regularly cleaned and maintained. Whether or not combustion is complete depends on the temperature and the amount of oxygen present. Greater oxygen concentrations and higher temperatures result in a more complete combustion reaction.

In a power plant, fuel such as coal or oil is used indirectly to produce electricity. The fuel itself is burned in a combustion chamber and the heat produced is used to change water into steam. The steam is then used to drive a turbine which actually produces the electricity.

Although combustion is a type of oxidation reaction, oxygen itself does not necessarily have to be involved. An oxidation reaction is any reaction in which a compound loses electrons to some other substance. In some cases, fluorine or chlorine can be substituted for oxygen in the combustion process.

Combustion should also not be thought of solely in terms of electricity and power stations. Living cells use the combustion of glucose ($C_6H_{12}O_6$) to produce energy for metabolic activities. This combustion can occur with or without the presence of oxygen, depending on the type of cell involved. (*See* METABOLISM.)

Spontaneous combustion occurs when a substance suddenly ignites and burns without having been exposed to a flame. This occurs when a substance undergoing an exothermic reaction retains heat due to poor air circulation. The temperature of the substance rises and the oxidation process speeds up, producing even more heat. This cycle continues until the material bursts into flame. Spontaneous combustion occurs most commonly in large piles of rags or papers, or in large accumulations of fuel where the temperature is not carefully monitored.

First see SOLAR SYSTEMS

Comet

Next see OORT CLOUD

A body that orbits the sun in an elongated ellipse.

Comets usually orbit the sun in very eccentric ellipses, although some of them have orbits that are in the shape of hyperbolas. Some comets have orbits that bring them closer to the sun than Mercury, the innermost planet. As they approach the sun, comets can develop tails that can be millions of miles long; some develop more than one tail. The tail of a comet always points away from the sun, so that when a comet goes out into space, its tail precedes it. Cometary tails are believed to be shaped by the solar wind, the electrically charged material thrown out by the sun.

There are about 100 short-period comets, whose orbits generally are associat-

Further Reading
Frankel, Charles, *The End of the Dinosaurs* (1999); Lewis, John L., *Comet and Asteroid Impact Hazards* (1999); Levy, David H., *Impact Jupiter* (1997); Levy, David H., *Skywatching* (1995); Sagan, Carl, *Comet* (1997).

A fireworks display requires just the right chemical mixture to produce bursts of brilliant color.

OBSERVATIONS

Fireworks

Fireworks have brought entertainment to spectators for a thousand years, but the exact chemical formulas necessary to produce such brilliant colors and dazzling starbursts remain closely guarded secrets. Researchers have, however, revealed some of the science underlying pyrotechnic art. A predetermined number of seconds after a fireworks canister has been launched into the air, a charge of black powder explodes; the heat of that explosion ignites the secret mixture, creating compounds like strontium chloride, barium chloride, and copper chloride. As the explosion subsides, each of these compounds emits photons at a characteristic wavelength, producing red, green, and blue light respectively; similarly, yellow and white are produced by the vaporization of sodium and aluminum.

ed with the orbit of Jupiter. The shortest known period is of Comet Enke, one of 40 comets that make up what is known as the Jupiter family; its period is 3.3 years. Long-period comets are far more numerous and generally are much more massive than short-period comets, which may be the remains of long-period comets deflected by the gravitational pull of Jupiter into smaller orbits. It is believed that these comets eventually will decay into meteor streams.

Composition. Studies of the light from comets show the presence of carbon, hydrogen, nitrogen, and oxygen, as well as molecules made of these elements. Comets that pass extremely close to the sun also have light emissions indicating the presence of sodium, and sometimes of magnesium, nickel, and iron.

Most of the mass of a comet is contained in the head, or nucleus, which can be less than a

Three recent encounters with comets. Above, the Comet Hale-Bopp as seen from the Space Shuttle Columbia, April 4, 1997.

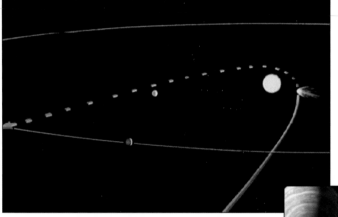

The passage of the Comet Kohoutek in the winter of 1973 provided a brilliant display. Above, the path of the comet shown relative to the sun, Venus, and Earth. Right, depiction of the collision of Comet Shoemaker-Levy into Jupiter in July 1994 provided a reminder of the potential danger from cometary collision with the Earth.

mile across or many miles in diameter. The nucleus of a comet consists primarily of ice and frozen gases, which are mixed with smaller amounts of meteoric material. The nucleus is surrounded by a bright area called the coma, which is many miles in diameter and is composed of gases erupting from the nucleus as well as small particles emitted from the nucleus.

History. In Greco-Roman times, it was generally believed that comets existed in the upper portion of the Earth's atmosphere. By the sixteenth century, astronomers such as Tycho Brahe found that comets were far more distant than the moon. Isaac Newton believed that each comet seen from Earth was appearing for the first time, but in the late seventeenth century, Edmund Halley proposed that comets make full orbits around the sun. Halley is best known for his prediction that the comet seen in 1680 would return to view in 1758. Halley's Comet is the brightest of all recurring comets, and there are records of

its appearance dating back to 240 B.C.E. It last appeared in 1986. (*See* EXTINCTION.)

Background material can be found in SOLAR SYSTEM; KEPLER'S LAWS; ASTEROIDS AND METEORS. *Advanced subjects are developed in* OORT CLOUD; PLANETS, FORMATION OF; LIFE, DEFINITION AND ORIGINS OF. *Other aspects of this subject are covered in* EXTINCTION *and* DINOSAURS, EXTINCTION OF.

First see DISEASE, INFECTIOUS

Common Cold

Next see INFLUENZA

The common cold is an infection of the mucus membranes of the nose and throat that causes a runny nose and can also bring on a sore throat and headaches. A cold results from infection with one of about 200 viruses in the coronavirus and rhinovirus families. Most colds begin when someone breathes in water droplets that have been coughed or sneezed out by an infected person and that contain a cold virus. Colds can also be contracted by body contact or by handling infected objects. (*See* DISEASE, INFECTIOUS.)

Most colds start with sneezing and a runny nose. The fluid that runs from the nose can become thicker and turn yellow or green over the next days, and the infected person can have watery eyes, a cough, a mild fever, aches of the muscles and bones, and a headache. Most colds clear up with little or no treatment in a week or two. Some can spread beyond the respiratory tract, requiring a visit to a doctor, but most can be handled by treating the symptoms with aspirin and other over-the-counter drugs.

Colds are most common in children, who can contract ten or more in a year, mostly in the winter. The incidence decreases with age, as an individual's immune system builds resistance to common cold viruses. Young adults may have one or two colds a year, and older adults may have none. Many ways of preventing colds, such as taking vitamin C, a prescription advanced by Linus Pauling, have been proposed, but none have been unequivocally shown to be effective.

Below, Linus Pauling, holding symbols of his advocacy of a cure for the common cold: an orange (source of vitamin C) and a model of ascorbic acid.

First see ETHOLOGY

Communication in Nature

Next see PHEROMONES

Animals communicate by chemical signals, sound, visual display, and touch. Most commonly, they advertise their identity and sexual availability to potential mates, warn of danger or threaten aggression. Their ability to signal others of their species, in particular, is a keystone of social organization. But even relatively simple organisms like slime molds communicate, using chemicals called pheromones to find each other for reproduction.

Animal communications vary widely in their specificity. It is important that mating calls be species-specific so that only an appropriate mate will respond. To prevent mistakes in identity, courtship may require a succession of signals to be used in a set order. Communication between parents or offspring sometimes needs to be specific to the individual as well; birds, for instance, sing the song of their species but with individual variations. On the other hand, it may

A great deal of interspecies communication takes place in ritualized grooming, as with these vervet monkeys.

be unimportant or even undesirable for a warning cry to identify the species of its source. Yet signals must be clearly enough differentiated so that, for instance, a warning cry will not be confused with a sexual invitation. The vervet monkey goes so far as to have separate cries to warn of snakes, leopards, or eagles; its listeners react to each call with a different action.

Chemical Signals. Each medium has its own strengths and weaknesses. Communication through pheromones, scent, and taste is thought to be the oldest and most common, and it can be said that even separate cells within an organism communicate by chemical means. Chemicals are used to signal sexual availability by moths, beetles, and some mammals. Social insects, such as ants, have an array of chemical signals used for warning of danger and marking trails, as well as regulating sexual conduct. Many territorial male mammals use them to mark their turf. (*See* PHEROMONES; MAMMALS.)

Chemical signals last for a long time, but they cannot be turned on and off quickly, as sound can. Auditory signals have other advantages—through changes in pitch, loudness, and rhythm, they offer inexhaustible variety, as proven by birds and humans, the virtuosos of auditory communication. Among some birds, alarm cries have auditory characteristics that make them particularly hard to trace to their

source, so the sentinel can elude the bird of prey. Among crickets and frogs, it is not pitch that is significant but the pattern of intervals between pulses of sound.

Visual Signals. A similar pulsed signal, but a visual one, is produced by fireflies. Other visual signals range from permanent markers of sex or species, such as plumage patterns, to facial expressions, postural cues, and body motions, like the wagging tail of a dog. (*See* INSTINCT.)

Language. Animals as different as a chimpanzee and a grey parrot have been taught elements of human language. In nature, aside from human speech, probably the most notable communication system is the waggle dance that honey bees use to inform their hive mates of the distance and direction of particularly good food sources. The angle of the central portion of the dance corresponds to the direction of the food in relation to the sun. The orientation of the bee's body and the sound from its vibrating wings represents roughly the direction and distance to the food. Extraordinary as this ability is, it does not have the flexibility of language.

First see ETHOLOGY

Competition and Altruism

Next see AGGRESSION AND TERRITORIALITY

Competition occurs when individuals of the same or different species strive to secure for themselves scarce resources that are essential for survival or reproduction. Plants may compete for light in a forest, animals for food or breeding territories. Traditionally, competition has been seen as a key factor in evolution, promoting the survival of the fittest and the formation of new species, as well as regulating population density within species. In recent years, however, some in the field have emphasized the role of chance, rather than competition, in evolution and have given increased attention to altruism and social cooperation within species. (*See* EMOTIONS.)

Among Individuals. Competition among individuals generally follows one of two patterns. In scramble or resource competition, common among invertebrates and plants, the rivals compete directly for the resource at issue. Each gets a reduced share of the resource and may grow more slowly and reproduce less. In cases of extreme scarcity or population density, almost all the individuals may die or fail to reproduce. In contest or interference competition, common among mammals and birds, individuals attack each other, although often physical conflict becomes ritualized into threatening displays. Stronger individuals get a full share of the resource—a breeding territory of their own, or a satiating meal—while weaker ones get nothing.

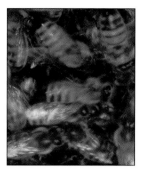

It was believed that bees communicate detailed information to one another through the particulars of their "dance" or flight. Above, a tagged bee communicates to others about the location of a source of nectar. It now seems apparent that the information is not the exact location of the treasure, but simply a call to "follow me!" Below, two striking instances of animal communication: top, the display of the peacock as part of his mating behavior; and, bottom, a dolphin, which shows signs of having the second most sophisticated language in the animal kingdom.

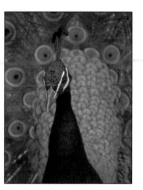

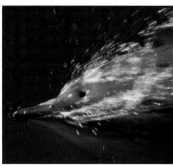

The losers in such competition may survive but often leave the group and fail to reproduce.

Among Groups. Competition between populations of different species inhibits or harms both parties. It can, however, lead to coexistence, in which species partition resources. Birds in the same habitat, for instance, may feed on different sizes of seeds, feed at different times, or occupy different parts of a tree. Interspecies competition can also lead to competitive exclusion, in which one population dies out or is forced to leave the habitat. The competition exclusion principle, also known as Gause's principle, holds that two species cannot coexist if they occupy the same ecological niche—meaning, if they compete in every way by occupying the same habitat and having the same ecological requirements. (See COEVOLUTION.)

When closely related species occupy the same habitat, competition can have another result: It can promote the evolution of new characteristics that make the species more different, minimizing the competition between them. New species eventually can arise. This kind of evolution, called character displacement, is famously

---

THE CUTTING EDGE

Competition and Cooperation

Competition is not the universal pattern in nature; several animal species engage in what has been termed "reciprocal altruism." For example, among several species, one member of the group will stand guard against predators while the others feed; in exchange, they will leave some of the best food for the guard. Among vampire bats, those who return to the nesting site hungry are fed by those who have been successful; the weakest are fed first. Vervet monkeys can devote hours to picking lice and ticks out of the hair of other monkeys, in the expectation that the same will be done for them later. Such examples imply that animals recognize one another as individuals more than previously thought.

---

seen among Darwin's finches on the Galapagos Islands, where Darwin did much of his research. The seed-eating species have evolved different-sized beaks so that different species feed on different-sized seeds. David Lack has shown that when small and medium ground finches coexist on an island, their beak sizes are clearly differentiated. But when only one of those species lives on an island, free of competition from the other, its beak is of an intermediate size.

Theories of competition largely reflect the biological truism that each organism acts to preserve its own life and ability to reproduce. In recent years, a great deal of attention has been given to behavior that appears to violate that rule. Altruistic behavior—in which an organism gives up its chance to reproduce, risks its life, or restricts its consumption of resources, apparently to help others of its species—turns out to be

Further Reading

Dawkins, Richard, *The Selfish Gene* (1990); Ledoux, Joseph, *The Emotional Brain* (1998); Lorenz, Konrad, *On Aggression* (1997); Wilson, E. O., *On Human Nature* (1988).

quite common. Bees spend their lives caring for the offspring of their queen and often die defending the hive; primates share food and groom each other; many animals, such as wolves, assist the breeding pair in their social unit without breeding themselves; many others, such as ground squirrels, risk their lives to warn others that a predator is near. Such behavior seems to violate the rules of natural selection. How can the genes for such altruistic behavior survive when the organisms that practice it are less likely to reproduce? (See ADAPTATION.)

Kin Selection. Much of the answer is believed to lie in the concept of kin selection. Genes for altruistic behavior will survive if those who benefit from the altruism also carry the genes. That is most likely to be the case if the altruist and the beneficiaries are genetically similar—in other words, if they're kin, the closer the better. By increasing the survival of kin, altruistic behavior can increase the number of copies of the altruism genes that make it into the next generation. In terms of natural selection, it does not matter which individual carries the genes, only that the genes are reproduced.

Altruism does occur among animals who are not apparently related. This is usually explained as reciprocal altruism. Each party helps the other at different times, increasing the possibility of survival for both. (See AGGRESSION.)

First see COMPUTER, DIGITAL

Compiler

Next see OPERATING SYSTEMS

A means of translating the language of a computer program into a binary code a computer can read.

The first digital computers had extremely large requirements, not only in space but in time. Although the first true computer could process six mathematical operations in a single second, and subsequent computers could process a thousand complete transactions in the same time span, they required months and sometimes even years to be programmed to that level of efficiency. For example, the SAGE system of early-warning radar, developed in the late 1950s but not fully deployed until 1963, demanded 1,800 person-years of effort merely to write its programs; the total exceeded 1 million lines of binary code, each one containing a string of 18 zeros and ones. (See COMPUTER, DIGITAL.)

A useful programming language must resemble ordinary language—whether that language is English or algebra; but it is also necessary to develop a means of converting that language into the binary code that computers can read. This is done through the compiler.

Background. The first compiler, named because it compiled, or put together, the pieces of code named by the individual "words" of the programming language, was developed by Grace Hopper in the early 1950s. She called it the A-O Compiler. The first usable compiler was developed in parallel with the first successful language, FORTRAN, and it needed 18,000 lines of instruction to translate back and forth from machine language to human language; the compiler for FORTRAN II demanded 50,000 lines of instruction, or code; today's compilers routinely process a million lines of code.

The compiler must also translate binary code back into a form that is readable by the user; the best-known such code is the American Standard Code for Information Interchange, or ASCII. This code is based on the permutations of an eight-bit digital number, from 00000001 to 11111111, representing 196 different letters, numerals, punctuation marks, mathematical symbols, and printer and keyboard commands. A more recent code, Unicode, is based on permutations of a 16-bit number. (*See* ASCII.)

The compiler interface remains an area of innovation, particularly as the Internet, where different operating systems must communicate with each other, has become more commonly used. The rapid advance of Java programming language has been made possible in part because it incorporates a "virtual" compiler, making it able to operate within any operating system. (*See* OPERATING SYSTEM.)

First see GENE

Complementation and Allelism

Next see GENETICS

An allele is the form a gene may take. One version of the gene may be dominant, meaning it is the one that is expressed, whereas the other is recessive or "covered up" and not apparent in the physical expression, or phenotype, of the trait. Some genes have co-dominant alleles, which when found together are equally expressed. An organism has two copies of a gene for a specific trait, located on homologous (paired) chromosomes. (*See* CHROMOSOME.)

On the molecular level, genes are actually segments of DNA which contain information on how to construct a particular protein. The "one gene one polypeptide" theory states that each gene is highly specific, corresponding to a single protein. In many cases, several genes work in concert, each responsible for a particular segment of a complex protein. A single genetic unit is referred to as a cistron. (*See* DNA.)

"Wild type" refers to a cell with normal genes, in which there are no mutations present. Instead of testing the genes directly, the gene product, or protein, is analyzed. A mutation results in an abnormal protein.

Mutations can be caused by the insertion or deletion of either a whole or partial gene sequence. Complementation refers to the ability of independent, or nonallelic genes, to overcome a mutation and result in the wild phenotype once again. Complementation is generally seen in two mutants, each of which has something the other specifically lacks. They pool their resources, in this case, their gene sequences, to come up with a combination in which each of their individual mutations has been canceled out. The situation can be compared to a blind man with good legs carrying and being directed by a man with bad legs and perfect vision. (*See* MUTATION.)

A complementation assay is used to identify the gene component that has been inactivated by a particular mutation. The complementation group refers to a series of mutations that are unable to complement each other when tested in different paired combinations.

First see NUMBER

Complex Numbers

Next see DIFFERENTIAL GEOMETRY

Numbers having both real and imaginary componenets.

Complex numbers are written in the form $a + ib$, where a and b are real and i is "imaginary," so that ib is also imaginary. The imaginary number i, symbolizing the square root of -1 ($\sqrt{-1}$), was first proposed as a useful mathematical tool by Hieronymus Cardan in 1545.

Although medieval mathematicians in both Europe and India had rejected the idea that a negative number could have a square root, Cardan managed to solve a classic problem (Are there two numbers whose sum is 10 and whose product is 40?) when he realized that the problem worked for $(5 + \sqrt{-15})$ and $(5 - \sqrt{-15})$, numbers that he himself called "meaningless... impossible...fictitious...imaginary." Twenty-five years later, R. Bombelli reached a similar impossible result, $(2 + \sqrt{-1})$ and $(2 - \sqrt{-1})$, for the classic problem $x^3 = 15x + 4$. Rather than dismiss his results as fantastic, however, Bombelli subjected them to the standard algebraic tests, and was astonished to find that they passed every one: complex numbers are commutative, associative, and distributive. (*See* ALGEBRA.)

Purpose. The primary benefit of the invention of complex numbers was the fulfillment of what has come to be called the Fundamental Theorem of Algebra: every algebraic equation possesses at least one solution, whether real or complex. Although this theorem was not proved until 1896, its validity was assumed throughout the nineteenth century, and led to significant secondary breakthroughs. For example, Gauss' 1831 study of the relationship between Cartesian geometry and complex numbers, showing that "just as objective an existence can be assigned to imaginary as to negative quantities."

The key was to recognize that a complex number can be treated as a vector on a graph whose axes are the number's real and imaginary components. Thus the magnitude of the complex number, which is the square root of the sum of the squares of its two coefficients, becomes a vector quantity called the modulus. It was only a short step from graphing complex numbers on a Cartesian plane to graphing them on a polar coordinate plane. By redefining the coefficients as cosine and sine of a given angle ø, one can plot the complex number as a point on a circular graph; as ø becomes larger, the point will move in a counterclockwise direction, returning to its origin with every change of 2π. This point can also be seen as a vector, whose angle ø becomes known on this view as the argument of the complex number. The modulus and argument completely determine the complex number.

The ability to graph complex numbers not only enabled them to be incorporated into traditional algebraic and geometric calculations, it also created a geometric way of visualizing multiplication. This in turn led in this century to a whole family of new operations, which became the heart of vector analysis, matrices, and differential geometry. (*See* VECTORS AND TENSORS; DIFFERENTIAL GEOMETRY.)

First see NUMBER

Computer, Digital

Next see COMPILER

A computational device that operates on data expressed in binary notation—only two digits (0 and 1) are used to describe the entire set of real numbers rather than the ten (0 to 9) used in decimal notation.

Digital computers are distinguished from analog computers based on the type of data on which they perform calculations. An easy way to understand the difference between the two is to think about how a computer would store the data associated with a graph. Digital computers operate on discrete data sets—a line in the graph would be represented by a series of numbers corresponding to the coordinates of the line. An analog computer might represent the same line as an algebraic equation. Digital computers operate on pieces of information called bits. A bit can be either a 1 or a 0 (on or off). A set of eight bits represents a byte—usually considered to be the smallest piece of information in a digital computer. One byte can represent either a number, letter, or part of an image.

Most modern computers are digital, as they can perform extremely accurate numerical calculations in a very short time. This has proved useful for scientists and mathematicians in solving complex problems. But it has also spawned a

Above, the ENIAC computer in the basement of the Moore School on the campus of the University of Pennsylvania. The technician is entering a number on one of three function tables. (Keyboards for entering data came much later.)

Below, an image that will increasingly become out of date: a contemporary desktop computer, opened to reveal its inner working. Bottom, the central processor of a desktop computer, showing the organization of the components, an expression of the system's architecture.

secondary commercial market for entertainment and business programs.

Computer Architecture. The different parts of a computer taken as a whole are termed the computer's architecture. The main core of the computer is called the central processing unit, or CPU. The CPU performs the majority of the calculations that are required of the computer.

Memory. There are two different types of memory in a computer, RAM and ROM. RAM—random access memory—does not have to be read sequentially, allowing the computer to jump around and find what it is looking for more efficiently. Most types of computer storage, including hard disks and CD-ROMS, are random access. However, the term RAM has come to be associated with the main working memory the computer uses to run programs. ROM stands for "read only memory" since it is a type of storage that cannot be changed once it has been set by the manufacturer.

Data Storage. There are several types of media that the computer uses to store data. Hard disk drives, floppy disk drives, and CD-ROMs, all are random access devices. Hard disks are large fixed-storage devices made up of several platters coated with magnetic material that is used to represent the 0's and 1's that the computer understands. Floppy disks are usually 3.5" square and have a single thin magnetic "floppy" disk inside. Floppies cannot hold large amounts of data as do hard disks, but they can be used to transfer information from computer to computer easily due to their small size and transportability. CD-ROMs hold large amounts of information, are removable, and are very reliable, as they are based on optical rather than magnetic technology. However, CD-ROMs are generally fairly slow and are fast being replaced by a newer type of optical technology, DVD-ROM, which promises to store four to ten times as much information on one disk. (*See* PROGRAM, COMPUTER.)

Computer Graphics

First see COMPUTER, DIGITAL

Next see FRACTAL

Computer graphics began with a computer game called Pong, designed by Al Alcorn and Nolan Bushnell in 1972. Two paddles moved up and down on either side of a screen, attempting to intercept a moving dot of light and send it back across the screen. From this humble beginning came Atari, then Nintendo, then Sega and Sony—a $3 billion a year business in video games alone.

These early games relied on bit-mapped graphics, in which images were stored as patterns of pixels (for picture elements) illuminating shapes on a screen; such graphics had to be refreshed often in order to give the illusion of movement, and even then diagonal lines came out looking jagged because not enough pixels could be activated (this is one reason that scan rates for computers are twice that for televisions). Game development soon drove the transition to vector graphics, in which images were stored as mathematical representations; although this demanded greater processor capacity, the revolution in computer speed and size soon made vector graphics the industry standard. (*See* CARTOGRAPHY.)

Applications. Computer graphics may have been driven by the desire of youthful computer programmers to devise ever more complicated video games to play, but they have flourished because of their very important applications in education, business, government, and industry. Using projective geometry, software has been developed that covers everything from the heavens—a Digital Sky Survey has mapped all visible celestial objects—to Earth. Geographic Information Systems (GIS) technology is capable of mapping every curb, manhole cover, light pole, and pothole in an urban district and presenting the information in overhead and topographical elevations.

3-D. One of the greatest challenges that computer graphics researchers had to solve was the creation of stereoscopic (or 3-D) images on a two-dimensional computer screen. An innovation known as raster optics, which relied on single-point perspective, was the first breakthrough; but raster images could not be re-sized without distortion. It was followed by vector graphics programs like Catia (Computer-Assisted Three-Dimensional Interactive Analysis), able to rotate objects in space and view them from multiple-point perspectives. Computer medical software now has the ability to catalog MRI images of tumors according to size, shape, texture, and location in the body, and use this 3-D database to perform initial screenings on x-rays of new patients. Some imaging software can take a scanned image and filter it in multiple ways—add noise, stylize, distort, sharpen, render, etc.—to create anything from marketing presentations to works of art. Features originally designed for gaming, like the Accelerated Graphics Port and Positional 3-D Audio, have made their way into everyday use.

First see COMPUTER, DIGITAL

Computer-Aided Design

Next see AIRCRAFT, SUBSONIC AND SUPERSONIC

Computer-Aided Design (CAD) is one of the fastest-growing computer applications today. CAD has become an essential feature of the automotive industry, textiles, jewelry design, architecture and landscape design, medicine, and urban planning. CAD has had a direct impact on the way we design, evaluate, and build items that can fit on a fingernail, and those that stretch a mile.

On the smallest scale, CAD is essential for building the complex integrated circuits that make up computers themselves. At the other end of the scale, CAD was recently used in the design of the new Bay Bridge between San Francisco and Oakland, California. Twelve different computer-generated designs, complete with elevations and renderings of approaches, were presented to the people of the Bay Area, and the voters chose the final design. The components of the Boeing 777, the first commercial airplane to be designed totally through CAD procedures, fit together without a flaw when finally produced.

CAD grew out of a 1950s innovation in machine tool design called computer numerical control, in which machines are programmed for all the operations needed to transform a block of metal into a finished, machined part. Because the process is based on digital transformation of information, once computer graphics had advanced sufficiently to represent a three-dimensional part on a two-dimensional screen, it became possible to design such machined parts directly on the computer screen, then feed the

Further Reading
Foley, James, *Computer Graphics* (1998); Mandelbrot, Benoit, *Fractal Geometry of Nature* (1988); Pickover, Clifford A., *Chaos and Fractals: A Computer Graphical Journey* (1998).

Computer modeling is critical for the design of supersonic aircraft, which are difficult to test using the conventional wind-tunnel methods. Below, computer model for the heat stress the body of a suborbital supersonic transport aircaft is likely to encounter upon reentry into the atmosphere.

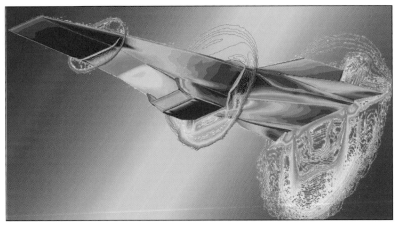

appropriate digitized data to the CNC machine tools. The most advanced CAD software used today is called Catia, for Computer-Assisted Three-Dimensional Interactive Analysis.

Unfortunately, the majority of metal and plastic parts are not machined; they are cast and stamped, requiring the creation of molds and dies. Some molds are still produced using the "lost wax" method of casting, which is a technology that dates back to the ancient Egyptians. To speed up this critical phase of the design process, CAD researchers have introduced rapid prototyping, in which stereo lithography and 3-D printers are used to construct physical models directly from the CAD screen.

Rapid manufacturing employs a 3-D printer to fabricate actual products. This process has been used to construct ceramic air filters ten times more efficient than contemporary filters, and metal parts created from powdered steel and bronze. With the development of a 1,000-watt neodymium YAG laser by Sandia National Laboratories, even stainless steel, nickel, and tungsten alloys can be manufactured without human intervention between the CAD designer and the final customer. (*See* PRINTING.)

First see REPRODUCTIVE SYSTEMS

Conception

Next see BIRTH

The fertilization of an egg by a sperm cell.

At the heart of sexual reproduction is conception, the merging of a sperm with an egg to form a genetically unique cell that will develop into a new individual. This process of fertilization occurs externally in most fish, amphibians, and aquatic invertebrates: both male and female gametes, or sex cells, are shed into the water, often in large numbers to improve the chances they will meet. For the same reason, many animals, including the much-studied sea urchins (echinoderms), synchronize their release of eggs and sperm by sensing fluids released during spawning by other members of their species. In such cases, one individual can trigger "epidemic spawning" in an area. Various species use other means as well to improve the odds of a matchup. One common type of algae, for instance, releases eggs and sperm only when the surrounding waters are calm, as indicated by a low level of dissolved inorganic carbon.

Most land animals, including insects, use internal fertilization, in which sperm are deposited in the egg-bearing reproductive tract of the female. Since the tract is coated with fluid, internal fertilization also occurs in an essentially aquatic environment. The zygote, or fertilized egg, that results may either remain within the female's body for embryonic development or be released within a shell to develop.

A 400-times magnification of a human egg surrounded and "besieged" by sperm cells.

Animal Conception. For animals to conceive, egg and sperm must undergo a complex set of chemical changes that are only partially understood but appear similar in many respects across species. In humans, eggs mature only after the onset of menstruation. Six to 12 begin the process in each menstrual cycle, but only one, or occasionally two, leave the ovary each month. By then, the egg—also called the ovum or oocyte—has been enclosed in a poetically named set of barriers: the zona pellucida, a thick coat made of a carbohydrate protein complex, and the corona radiata, a retinue of granulosa cells that surround the ovum like tiny tugboats and appear to play a role in its transport. Aided by tubal contractions and the action of cilia, the ovum is collected by the adhesive fimbria of the fallopian tube, the fringed, open end of the tube that waves across the ovary. When the egg reaches the ampullary-isthmic junction. a bend in the tube, it is held for one to two days. That is where fertilization occurs.

Human Conception. In humans, about 400 million sperm are released in a single ejaculation, but only a few thousand ever reach the right region of the fallopian tube, with the first arriving in about ten minutes. As in most species, human sperm undergoes a process called capacitation in the female reproductive tract. This makes possible the sperm's crucial acrosome reaction, in which its membrane fuses with that of the egg. The nature of capacitation is still being elucidated, but it is thought to involve removing inhibitory agents that keep sperm inactive in the male genital ducts, and removing excess cholesterol from the membrane covering the acrosome, the cap-like structure at the head of the sperm. With the membrane weakened, calcium ions pour in and give the sperm's tail, or flagellum, a powerful whipping motion that increases its swimming speed.

The membrane of the acrosome fuses with the cell membrane at the head of the sperm. This causes the acrosome to release enzymes, including hyaluronidase, which dissolves the bonds between the granulosa cells, allowing the sperm cell to reach the zona pellucida. The membrane at the head of the sperm binds with a receptor in the zona pellucida, then the acrosome membrane dissolves rapidly, releasing more acrosomal enzymes. These open a path for the sperm into the zona. Within 30 minutes the membrane of the sperm head fuses with that of the ovum. The sperm genetic material enters the egg cell and forms the male pronucleus, which contains a haploid complement of chromosomes, half the normal human complement of 23 pairs.

Penetration of the zona pellucida triggers the final stage of meiosis in the egg, a special form of cell division that leaves the egg, too, with a haploid complement of chromosomes in its pronucleus. The male and female pronuclei move toward the center of the cell, their chromosomes replicate, and the cell divides and forms two blastomeres, each with a full set of 23 pairs of chromosomes, half from the female and half from the male.

Within seconds of the first sperm entering the zona pellucida, another important event takes place: calcium ions diffuse into the ovum, causing release of cortical granules that permeate the zona pellucida, preventing additional sperm from entering. Most species have some mechanism to prevent more than one sperm from entering the egg cell.

After fertilization in humans, it takes about seven days for the zygote to reach the uterus and implant in its wall. By then it has become a blastocyst, a hollow sphere of cells. In some mammals, weeks or even months can pass before implantation occurs.

A sperm attaches to the egg and triggers a chemical response that allows it to bind to the membrane and enter the cell, while other sperm cells are kept out by the secretion of a protein that bars them from attaching to the cell.

THE CUTTING EDGE

Future Contraception

Science is beginning to offer a wider range of methods of contraception. For men, doctors are developing an injection that combines androgen—a male hormone—and progestin—a female steroid—to effectively stop sperm production for as long as three months. Contraceptive vaccines and drugs that target the epididymides, where sperm mature, are also under investigation. Women, who already take hormonal contraceptives in the form of pills or implants, will have new spermicides available to them, at least one of which offers hope of protecting against chlamydia, the most common sexually transmitted disease. Just beyond the horizon is a once-a-month contraceptive pill.

Related areas to be considered are BIRTH; REPRODUCTIVE SYSTEMS; SEX; SEXUAL STRATEGIES. *Advanced subjects are developed in* AMNIOCENTESIS; POPULATION ECOLOGY; EPIDEMIOLOGY; GENETIC DISEASES. *Relevant information is contained in* BLOOD; DISEASES, INFECTIOUS; AIDS; EMBRYOLOGY; SYPHILIS AND GONORRHEA.

Further Reading
Jones, Richard E., *Human Reproductive Biology* (1997); Sparks, John, *Battle of the Sexes: The Natural History of Sex* (1999); Stoppard, Miriam, *Conception, Pregnancy and Birth* (1993).

First see INSTINCT

Conditioning

Next see ETHOLOGY

A form of learning in which a subject associates a particular stimulus with a specific outcome, leading it to behave in new ways.

Classical conditioning, discovered by Ivan Pavlov, relies on an unconditioned or instinctively recognized stimulus that always provokes an unconditioned or innate response. The unconditioned stimulus is repeatedly paired with another stimulus, called the conditioned stimulus. After enough repetition, the new stimulus by itself is able to provoke the response, which is then called the conditioned response.

In his experiments, Ivan Pavlov measured dog salivation—the unconditioned response—when exposed to food, the unconditioned stimulus. Then he rang a bell or flashed a light—the conditioned stimulus—just before presenting the food. After some repetition, the bell or light triggered salivation by itself. This was the conditioned response. In nature, classic conditioning can lead animals to seek out conditions associated with food in the past. If ducks in a pond have been fed by people, for instance, they will race to converge on any person who approaches the shore. Classic conditioning can work negatively as well, teaching an animal to take defensive measures at the first sign of danger.

Another form of associative learning, called operant conditioning or trial-and-error learning, is more common in nature. In operant conditioning, an animal learns to associate rewards or punishments with its own actions, rather than with an outside stimulus. The animal then tends to repeat the actions that get a good response and avoid those that end in trouble. By this means, for instance, animals learn the most efficient and least painful ways to procure their food, whether it involves opening a new kind of seed or catching a new kind of prey.

The most famous experimental example of operant conditioning involves a rat in a Skinner box (named for psychologist B.F. Skinner) who pushes a lever by accident and gets a pellet of food. Through repetition, the rat learns that pushing the lever always brings food and begins intentionally pushing it. "Shaping" can speed the learning process: at first, the rat is rewarded for merely coming near the lever, then only for touching the lever, finally only for pushing it. (*See* ADAPTATION; HABITUATION; IMPRINTING.)

First see CHARGE AND CURRENT

Conductors and Resistors

Next see ELECTRIC CIRCUIT

A conductor is a material that readily permits the passage of electric current when placed between terminals that have different electric potentials. A resistor is a material that offers resistance to the passage of the current in an electric circuit.

The effectiveness of a conductor, its conductivity, is the ratio of current density to the applied electric field. The best conductors are metals—aluminum, copper, silver, mercury, platinum, etc. Copper and aluminum are the conductors that are most commonly used in everyday electric circuits. Copper is the conductor that is found in most household circuits, while aluminum generally is used in high-voltage transmission lines, where its light weight is an important advantage. Steel, which does not have the high conductivity of copper or aluminum, is used where strength and resistance to wear is important, as in the third rail of electrified railroads. The resistance of a material is defined as its resistivity multiplied by its length and divided by its cross-sectional area. If we express area in circular mils and length in feet, the resistivity of copper is 10.5; of aluminum, 17.8, and of iron, 58. All these resistivity constants apply only to an ambient temperature of 20°C; resistivity and conductivity change with temperature. In common practice, resistance is put to practical use. For example, the wire inside an incandescent light bulb is a resistor; its resistance causes the wire to get hot and give off light.

First see ENERGY

Conservation Laws in Nature

Next see SYMMETRY IN NATURE

Further Reading
Barrow, John, D., *The Left Hand of Creation* (1994); Elkana, Yehuda, *The Discovery of the Conservation of Energy* (1989); Feynman, R. P., *The Character of Physical Law* (1983); Trefil, James, *The Unexpected Vista* (1983); Weyl, Hermann, *Symmetry* (1989); Wil-czek, F., *Longing for the Harmonies* (1988).

Conservation laws in nature state that some physical quantity remains constant during interactions or processes in an isolated system. Some laws of conservation date to the earliest days of science, but modification of a law is always possible as new knowledge comes to light. Probably the most famous such modification occurred when Albert Einstein established that energy and mass are equivalent, a finding expressed in the famous formula $E=mc^2$. Until then, there had been two separate laws. One of them stated that the amount of mass in an isolated system was always conserved; the other stated that the amount of energy in an isolated system was always conserved.

The law of conservation of energy today is described as a special case of the conservation of mass-energy. It plays a fundamental role in thermodynamics, and thus is called the First Law of Thermodynamics. In its most general form, the law states that any change in the internal energy of a system will be equal to the energy flow from the surroundings of the system.

Other Conservation Laws. The law of the conservation of mechanical energy states that in a conservative system, the mechanical energy, which is equal to the sum of the kinetic energy and the potential energy, always equals a constant. That constant is determined by the initial conditions of the motion of the system.

The law of conservation of momentum states that for a dynamic system consisting of a number of masses m with a number of position vectors r, the total momentum of the system remains constant. The law of momentum is fundamental in physics.

The law of conservation of charge is of fundamental importance in the field of particle physics, and can be stated simply: the total charge of a system always remains constant. There are several conservation principles included in this law. One states that the number of baryons—protons, neutrons, or heavier particles and their antiparticles—always remains constant. Another states that the number of leptons—electrons, neutrinos, muons, and their antiparticles—always remains constant. Other properties of subatomic particles are believed to be related by laws of conservation, but the nature of these properties and the laws that describe them are not yet clear.

Other Conserved Quantities. Other properties of matter once were believed to be subject to conservation laws, but no longer are. These properties include space inversion, charge conjugation, and time reversals, which are associated with all physical processes. The most commonly used member of this group of properties is parity, which is also called space inversion. In an atomic sample that emits electromagnetic radiation, as long as that radiation has negative parity, the system as a whole will conserve parity. However, in weak subatomic interactions such as beta decay, the emitted beta radiation changes from positive to negative (or vice versa) so parity is not conserved. Another way of looking at this is that the "handedness" of a process at the subatomic level is not conserved: a mirror image of the process does not obey the same laws or follow the same path.

Related areas to be considered are ENERGY; SCIENTIFIC METHOD; SYMMETRY IN NATURE. *More details on conservation can be found in* CHARGE AND CURRENT; ENTROPY; UNCERTAINTY PRINCIPLE. *Foundational aspects of this subject are covered in* BELL'S INEQUALITY; GRAND UNIFICATION THEORIES; QUANTUM ELECTRODYNAMICS.

First see GEOLOGICAL TIME SCALE

Continents, Formation of

Next see PLATE TECTONICS

The formation of the Earth's continents took place several billion years ago. They have been evolving ever since, an evolutionary process that continues because of such geological phenomena as continental drift. Formally, a continent is defined as any of the major connected land masses of the Earth. (*See* GEOMORPHOLOGY.)

It is often said that there are seven continents, but some geologists list the European and Asian land mass as a single continent, Eurasia. The continental crust has an average thickness of 20 miles (the depth at which the Mohorovicic discontinuity is found), compared to a three-mile thickness for the crust underlying the oceans. The continents cover an area of about 50 million square miles, and their total mass amounts to about 1 billion cubic miles.

One of the most cherished scientific principles is the conservation of mass and energy, but the possibility that new matter and energy is entering our universe through a "worm hole" at the center of a black hole puts even that principle on shaky ground.

At the present rate with which lava is extruded from the depths of the earth, it would take some 3 billion years to accumulate this volume, which corresponds to the age of the earliest rocks (about 3.8 billion years). Estimates of the average composition of the rocks of the continents vary between 59 percent and 65 percent silica—roughly the same composition as the most common forms of lava. Thus, continents probably developed by the extrusion of volcanic rocks, the erosion of these rocks to form sediments, and the metamorphism of these sedimentary layers by stresses and forces within the crust. The belief that the continents have grown in this manner is supported by the existence of continental shields, which appear to consist of the roots of former mountain ranges that have eroded over time to common plains.

Tectonics. Plate tectonics describes the Earth's surface as consisting of eight major plates and a variable number of small plates. Most of these major plates include both continental and oceanic sectors. The continents have two kinds of margins at their edges, active and passive. A margin is said to be active when it coincides with transform boundaries, as along the Pacific coasts of the Americas. Margins are passive when they lie within a plate; examples are the continental margins that border the Atlantic Ocean. Active continental margins are characterized by narrow borderlands and slopes, by the presence of active volcanoes, by seismicity—the occurrence of earthquakes—and the presence of ore deposits that contain both precious metals and uranium. Passive continental margins have wide continental shelves underlaid by thick wedges of sedimentary rock and by salt domes, which often contain oil reservoirs. Passive margins have little seismic or volcanic activity. (*See* MOUNTAIN FORMATION.)

The continental shield is the broad plain that lies over the 600 million-year-old layer of Precambrian rock. This shield forms a large part of the mass of all of the continents. Each continent can be divided into three sections: the shield, young coastal plains, and mountains, which are only moderately old. Except in Africa and Asia, the continental shield is only a few hundred feet above sea level. Nevertheless, continental shields are only partially exposed to the atmosphere. In the parts that are not exposed, old metamorphic rocks lie under sedimentary rocks, whose depth can vary from a few hundred feet to a few thousand feet. The term "shield" is sometimes used to refer only to the part that is exposed, as in references to the Canadian Shield. Recent geological mapping and the use of radioactive methods for determining the ages of rock have found that shields can be divided into regions called provinces, which have different ages. These provinces are sharply separated from one another by major systems of geological

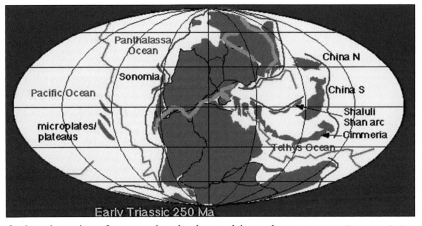

Early Triassic 250 Ma

faults; deposits of ore tend to be located in and around these faults. The oldest segments of continents are more than 2 billion years old. They have a heavy concentration of volcanic rock and are called continental nuclei.

The evolution of the continents occurs primarily at the boundaries where crustal plates come into contact. At these boundaries, plates can grow, jam against one another, move in relation to one another, and have a number of other activities that cause the continents to become smaller or larger and to change slightly in shape. These changes are small measured by human standards, but they are significant in the continuing evolution of the continents over millions and billions of years. (*See* PLATE TECTONICS.)

First see OPERATING SYSTEMS

Control Systems

Next see SERVOMECHANISMS

Early in the development of civilization, people were seldom afraid of machines; but they were afraid of what machines could do if people lost control of them. The stories of Icarus, unable to control his wings, and of the Sorcerer's Apprentice, unable to control his magic broom and buckets, testify to this continuing fear that our ability to produce technology tends to outrun our ability to manage it. Thus one of the great challenges in the history of technology has been the development of control systems.

Feedback. The heart of control is the principle of feedback. As a machine changes speed, it needs a control system that will sense the gap between the desired speed and the actual speed, adjusting accordingly. The first mechanical feedback device was a speed governor invented by James Watt to control his steam engine. As the machine speeded up, the balls on the speed governor rotated faster, centrifugal force pushed them farther from their axis, so the sleeve to which they were attached rose past a valve and released excess steam; with less steam pressure in the cylinder the machine ran more slowly, the balls rotated with less centrifugal force, and the valve was covered. Similar systems include the

Land mass (in green) that was above the waters of the ocean 250 million years ago. The shapes of what would become continents are outlined.

Further Reading
Condie, Kent C., *Plate Tectonics* (1997); McPhee, John A., *Annals of the Former World* (2000); Moores, Eldridge M., *Tectonics* (1995); Skinner, B. J., *The Dynamic Earth* (1995).

thermostat in an air conditioner, the cruise control in an automobile, and the coverage regulator on a lawn sprinkler.

However, thermostats set with limits that are too narrow will cycle on and off repetitively. The solution, developed by Lofti Zadeh in 1964, is fuzzy logic, based on a mathematical concept called set theory. Sets demand that every object must be either in or out of the set; fuzzy logic states that objects can belong fractionally. As applied to computers, based on binary logic gates, it demands the introduction of "sieves" instead. These sieves, mounted on special fuzzy chips, can be definitional (voice recognition), generational (computer poetry), relational (fuzzy thermostats), or decisional (robot navigation).

The first fuzzy control system was introduced at a Danish cement plant in 1978. Fuzzy control systems now operate a one-button washing machine that automatically selects the proper wash and rinse cycles, a camcorder that records a stable picture even when the camera is bouncing, an entire Japanese subway system—at a ten percent fuel saving—and the Air Force's new F-22 jet fighter, an airplane which could not fly without its computerized control system.

Special topics in this area are found in ANALOG COMPUTER; COMPUTER, DIGITAL; COMPILER. *Advanced subjects are developed in* OPERATIONS RESEARCH; SERVOMECHANISM; TELECOMMUNICATIONS. *Additional aspects of this subject are covered in* ARTIFICIAL INTELLIGENCE *and* EXPERT SYSTEM.

First see ROTATIONAL MOTION

Coriolis Force

Next see HURRICANES AND TORNADOS

The effect of Earth's rotation on all objects on its surface as well as on the atmosphere.

Suppose a bullet is fired toward the south from the North Pole. If the Earth were not rotating, the bullet would move directly southward, and its motion could be described by Newton's laws of motion, which allow us to calculate motion in a system that is moving at constant velocity with respect to the fixed stars. But because the Earth is rotating toward the east, the bullet would appear to be moving toward the west as well as toward the south. The complete motion of the bullet can be described in terms of a Coriolis force whose strength is proportional to the mass of the bullet, its velocity, and the rate of rotation of the frame of reference—in this case, the Earth. A simpler example would be an attempt to draw a straight line outward from the center of a rotating disk. A truly straight line would be curved because of the rotation of the disk.

The Coriolis effect accounts for the circulation of air in cyclones and other weather systems. The Coriolis force is proportional to the

The rotational motion of hurricanes is due to the Coriolus force that twists the air moving from high to low pressure in the eye of the storm.

sine of the latitude multiplied by the speed of the wind. In the northern hemisphere, the Coriolis effect causes the air to blow counterclockwise around a low-pressure system; in the southern hemisphere, air flow is clockwise. Coriolis forces explain why weather systems in the United States move from the west to the east.

First see TELESCOPE

Cosmic Rays

Next see MESONS

Cosmic rays are high-energy particles that constantly bombard Earth's atmosphere. Some originate in the sun, some in our galaxy, and some are believed to come from other galaxies. The primary cosmic rays that strike the outer atmosphere consist mostly of protons but also include some alpha particles (helium nuclei), a variety of heavier atomic nuclei, gamma rays, and electrons. The electrons are believed to result from the collision of cosmic ray particles with atomic nuclei in the interstellar medium. When these various cosmic ray particles collide with atoms in the upper atmosphere, the result is a shower of fundamental particles, including electrons, neutrons, muons, and mesons.

The discovery of cosmic rays began with radiation measurements made during high-altitude balloon flights in 1910 by V. F. Hess. Their existence was confirmed by the American physicist Robert A. Millikan, who coined the name for them in 1927. (*See* RADIO ASTRONOMY.)

Varieties. It is sometimes convenient to distinguish between solar cosmic rays, which come from the sun, and galactic cosmic rays. These differ in one important respect. The average and maximum energy of the protons in galactic cosmic rays are much higher than the energy of the protons in solar rays. In addition, the flux of solar cosmic rays varies, increasing with such events as solar flares, while the flux of galactic cosmic rays remains constant. The periods of variations are one day, 27 days, and approximately 11 years. The first period is clearly related to the Earth's rotation relative to the sun. The second is related to the rotation of the sun, which brings more active regions to face Earth every 27 days. The 11-year cycle is of special interest because it has been found that the inten-

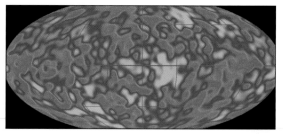

The cosmic ray background radiation for the entire sky, remnant of the Big Bang, at a temperature of 18 x 10⁻⁵ K.

sity of galactic cosmic rays is inversely proportional to the number of sunspots, meaning that galactic cosmic rays are most intense when the sun is least active, and vice versa. A cause for this effect was found in 1960, when a solar flare occurred during the mission of the Pioneer V space probe. About 20 hours later, the spacecraft recorded the passing of a plasma cloud from the sun moving at 1,200 miles per second and a decrease in the intensity of galactic cosmic rays; a small decrease was measured on earth a few hours later, accompanied by a geomagnetic storm. These observations showed that changes in the magnetic field around Earth decrease the intensity of galactic cosmic rays.

When cosmic rays enter the atmosphere, they collide with the nuclei of air molecules, mostly oxygen and nitrogen, between 10 and 20 miles above Earth's surface. Some of these cosmic ray particles have energies of many billions of electron volts, but most have energies in the range of a few hundred million to perhaps 10 billion electron volts. A high-energy proton of galactic origin can cause complete disintegration of an atmospheric molecule, producing a shower of protons, neutrons, and mesons. These, in turn, can cause the disintegration of other air molecules in a chain that continues until the energies become too low to cause disintegrations. Between 10 and 20 such particles bombard every square inch of the Earth's surface every minute. (*See* SCINTILLATORS.)

Cosmic Ray Astronomy. Cosmic ray astronomy is the study of high-energy particles that fall on Earth from space or interact with meteorites in outer space. Primary cosmic rays consist of nuclei of the most abundant elements, primarily protons. The less energetic of these cosmic rays, with energies up to 10 billion electron volts, are believed to be emitted by the sun. More energetic cosmic rays are believed to originate elsewhere in the galaxy. Asronomers study primary cosmic rays by measuring the secondary particles that they produce when they collide with oxygen and nitrogen nuclei in the

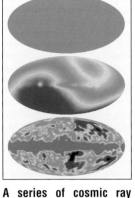

A series of cosmic ray whole sky measurements for different energies (temperatures). The measurements confirm that the universe is awash with a great deal of radiation, suggesting that the concept of a vacuum may be an unrealizable idealization.

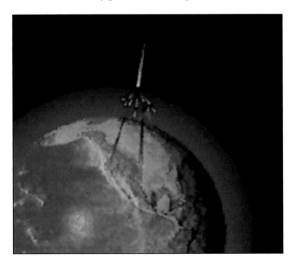

When a proton from outer space hits the Earth's atmosphere, it produces a number of particles. One, a muon (shown in red), lives long enough to reach the Earth's surface. Scintillation counters record the muons at different locations—but how do they know they are recording muons from the same proton collision? The clocks of the scintillators are so finely synchronized that they can determine simultaneity to one part in a trillion. The assumption is that muons that reach the Earth at exactly the same time are products of the same proton collision.

atmosphere. Astronomers can obtain more information about primary cosmic rays by studying the results of their interactions with meteorites in space. Most of the cosmogenic products in meteorites are made by high-energy galactic cosmic rays, but some are produced by solar cosmic rays. These products include radioactive elements with a wide range of half-lives, stable isotopes that are rare in meteorites, such as noble gases, and tracks that are caused by radiation damage. The cosmic ray record in meteorites shows that cosmic rays of the past were not very different from those of the present time, although the intensity of cosmic ray emissions has varied greatly. By studying the exposure history of meteorites to cosmic rays, astronomers can get information about the recent evolution of meteorites and other objects in space.

First see SOLID

Covalent Solid

Next see CRYSTAL

Crystals are solids which are made up of highly ordered, repetitive units that form a specific pattern or lattice. The actual type of crystal depends upon the atoms or molecules in the arrangement and the attractive forces holding them together. Within a covalent network solid, the repeating units are atoms and the attractive forces between them are covalent bonds, in which electrons are shared between atoms.

Both hydrogen bonds and van der Waals forces are based on electrostatic force, the attraction between opposite charges. In these situations, the opposite charges are found on neighboring molecules, causing those molecules to be held together. (*See* BOND, CHEMICAL.)

Bonds. Hydrogen bonding refers to the attraction between a hydrogen atom in one molecule and an atom on a different molecule. There is no movement of electrons between them, as in conventional bonding. Hydrogen bonds—found in all states of water—are responsible for many of its properties as a liquid, such as surface tension. Within a crystal of ice, the solid phase of water, each molecule of H_2O is connected to four other molecules to form the lattice.

Solid Forces. Van der Waals forces are caused by a temporary electron shift within a group of molecules, transforming them into dipoles. Nearby molecules align themselves so that their oppositely charged ends are adjacent. Electrostatic force between the oppositely charged ends of different molecules causes them to be linked together and results in a covalent solid. Van der Waals attractions are constantly forming, breaking, and re-forming within the solid. Covalent solids have relatively low melting points due to the weak forces holding them together. (*See* SURFACE CHEMISTRY.)

Diamond and graphite, both of which consist of carbon atoms linked in a vast array, are examples of such solids. In diamond, each carbon atom is linked to four other carbon atoms arranged in a tetrahedral shape. The C-C bonds extend across the whole crystal lattice, making the entire crystal one single large molecule.

Graphite is made up of a large number of flat molecules stacked loosely atop one another, which gives graphite its slippery properties and ability to act as a lubricant. (*See* CARBON.)

First see GEOLOGICAL TIME SCALE

Cretaceous-Tertiary (K-T) Boundary

Next see EVOLUTION

The Cretaceous-Tertiary Boundary is the geological time of transition from the Cretaceous period, which began perhaps 150 million years ago, to the modern, or Cenozoic era, which began about 65 million years ago and in which we now live. The term "Tertiary" has been largely abandoned but reference is still made to the K-T Boundary, K standing for the German word *Kriede,* referring to the Cretaceous.

The first period of the Tertiary era was the Paleocene, which lasted for about 10 million years. That period is chiefly remarkable for the extinction of the dinosaurs. The reasons for the extinction of the dinosaurs are not clearly understood; scientists studying the Cretaceous-Tertiary Boundary have found unusual concentrations of a number of elements, such as iridium, osmium, gold, and platinum. Because meteorites are rich in these elements, the findings imply that a meteorite struck the Earth, killing off not only the dinosaurs but also many other creatures. This theory is a leading explanation for the changes that occur at the K-T Boundary.

Background material can be found in GEOLOGY, ARCHAEOLOGICAL; GEOLOGY, GEOLOGICAL TIME SCALE; *Further developments are discussed in* BIOSTRATIGRAPHY; MESOZOIC ERA; SEISMICS. *Special topics in this area are found in* PALEOZOIC ERA; PANGAEA; UNFORMITARIANISM; ASTEROIDS AND METEORS; COMETS; EXTINCTION.

First see TEMPERATURE

Cryogenics

Next see ABSOLUTE ZERO

The branch of physics that deals with the behavior of matter at very low temperatures—less than −200 degrees Celsius—and with the techniques of achieving those low temperatures.

The first step in achieving low cryogenic temperatures is to treat a coolant in such a way as to reduce its entropy—the statistical expression of the heat-caused disorder of its atoms or molecules. One way to achieve this reduction in temperature is to start by compressing a gas; another technique is to apply a magnetic field to certain salts. Both these methods produce heat, which is then conducted away from the coolant material. The next step is to reduce whatever has produced the heat that is conducted away—the compression or the magnetic field—so that extreme cooling results. Gases can be used as coolants only until they reach the point where they become liquefied. This temperature is about 253 degrees below zero Celsius for hydrogen and about 270 degrees below zero Celsius for helium. However, if the vapor pressure over helium is reduced or other techniques are used to treat helium, temperatures within a fraction of a degree of absolute zero can be achieved.

Processes. One method of achieving very low temperatures is adiabatic demagnetization. A paramagnetic substance—one whose atoms or molecules become aligned in a magnetic field—can be subjected to such a magnetic field and then demagnetized. At temperatures within a degree or two of absolute zero, this technique can achieve a reduction of a large fraction of a degree—a reduction that is significant at such a temperature. Temperatures as low as one-millionth of a degree have been reached by carrying out two successive demagnetizations of paramagnetic salts in the same temperature-lowering device. The first stage in this cryogenic process is an ordinary demagnetization from the temperature of liquid helium. A second sample of the salt is then cooled in a magnetic field by the first sample, and is demagnetized in its turn. The lowest temperatures can be achieved by using such a technique on atomic nuclei, rather than on whole atoms. (*See* REFRIGERATION.)

Cryogenics is also concerned with the techniques of making measurements and conducting

The K-T boundary. Below (bottom), amid boulders that lie at the base of a cliff in Zumaya, Spain, a thin band of gray clay is apparent—and found virtually worldwide —marking the boundary between the Cretaceous and Tertiary periods. Top, a sample of the K-T boundary layer. The iridium and shocked quartz found in the uppermost section first alerted researchers to the possibility of an asteroid impact being responsible for the sudden extinction of a large segment of the biosphere during this period.

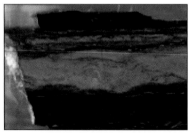

investigations of materials at these temperatures. Cryostats, assembled units of equipment that are commercially available and are specifically designed for low-temperature research, can commonly maintain temperatures within a fraction of a degree of absolute zero. Operation of cryostats often hinges on superconductivity, an electrical phenomenon that occurs in some materials at very low temperatures. (*See* SUPERCONDUCTOR.)

A metal through which heat passes easily at ordinary temperatures can become a heat insulator at superconducting temperatures. Some experiments and observations in cryogenics have been done in outer space, where temperatures are far below those found on Earth.

First see COMPUTER, DIGITAL

Cryptography

Next see ARTIFICIAL INTELLIGENCE

The study of the creation, transmission, and deciphering of (secret) codes.

Cryptography and secrecy became pressing issues in the twentieth century, with the introduction of electronic media for sending and receiving messages. The technology of warfare also played a part in the development of this science; airplanes and submarines must communicate information and receive orders, but are vulnerable if their positions are thereby revealed.

Basic Code. Most codes rely on substitution; for every letter of the alphabet a different letter is chosen, in a one-to-one matching. The simplest codes merely shift the letters: a-m, b-n, c-o, d-p, and so on. More complicated systems use a system known as transposition, in which each letter is matched with some other letter by random number generation, or by a previously agreed transposition chart. The most secure code uses the one-time pad. The sender transforms letters into numbers, then adds a series of random digits to the result; the recipient subtracts the appropriate digits, transforms the resulting numbers back to letters, and reads the message. Of course, if sender and recipient are not "on the same page," the message is forever lost.

The theoretical strengths of most codes are, unfortunately, matched by the practical weaknesses of most cryptographic systems. As Waldemar Werther, a German cryptanalyst, has said: "The security of a cipher lies less with the cleverness of the inventor than with the stupidity of the men who are using it." For example, in World War II the Germans would often field-test a new code cipher by sending the equivalent of "A bird in the hand is worth two in the bush," or an outpost's most common message would be "Nothing to report"—so the necessary code key was routinely, inadvertently handed out.

Computer Cryptography. The development of computers made code-breaking much more efficient. The Enigma code machine used by Germany during World War II was broken with information supplied by a Polish political refugee. When the Germans changed settings, however, it took days before the English could decipher new messages. Alan Turing was put in charge of building a computer that could search all possible permutations; the result was the Colossus, the fastest computer built before 1950, hard-wired so that it could only break codes.

Modern codes must withstand high-speed analysis by supercomputers, demanding special methods of encryption. Financial information sent over the Internet usually employs RSA encoding, developed in 1977, in which a very large key number (from 10 to 400 digits long) is mixed into the message in such a way that only the two prime numbers that, when multiplied, create the key number can resolve the message.

A recent development in cryptography is public key cryptography, in which a message is encoded by one key and is later deciphered by its unique counterpart. One of the keys is known only to the owner and the other is publicly available. A message intended for a specific recipient can be encoded by the recipient's public key so that only he can read the message by using his private key. Also, the user can encode a message with his private key; it can be deciphered only by applying his public key, comfirming that the message originated from the user.

THE CUTTING EDGE

Quantum Cryptography

The newest process under development is quantum cryptography, which relies on Heisenberg's Uncertainty Principle. According to Heisenberg, any energy used to determine a subatomic particle's position will change its velocity. In the case of messages stored as variation in polarization states, energy used to measure each photon's polarization will garble the intended message, revealing tampering. A second process takes advantage of optical interference, focusing on each photon's phase; bends in the optical fiber can change photon polarization, but they do not affect phase. A third variation involves sending polarized photons through the open air, employing interference effects. So far, these techniques are limited to distances of 20 miles or less. However, the advantages are great, since quantum cryptography promises the ability to send both message and key simultaneously, overcoming the greatest challenge to secure transmission of information.

The foundations of the subject are discussed in ALGORITHM; COMPUTER, DIGITAL; NUMBER; *and* PROGRAM, COMPUTER. *More details can be found in* ALGEBRA; ARTIFICIAL INTELLIGENCE; NEURAL NETWORK. *Advanced subjects are developed in* COMPUTER VIRUS; SUPERCOMPUTER; TURING MACHINE.

Further Reading
Atkins, P. W., *The Second Law* (1994); Dugdale, T. S., *Entropy and its Physical Meaning* (1996); Shochtman, Tom, *Absolute Zero and the Conquest of Cold* (1999); Von Bayer, H. C., *Warmth Disperses and Time Passes: A History of Heat* (1999).

Further Reading
Bauer, Friedrich, *Decrypted Secrets* (1997); Hinsley, F. H., *Codebreakers: The Inside Story of Bletchley Park* (1996); Kahn, David, *The Codebreakers* (1996); Newton, David E., *Encyclopedia of Cryptology* (1997).

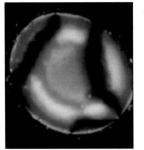

Above, a droplet of a liquid crystal.

Above, glasses equipped with liquid crystal lenses flicker independently between clear and dark every 1/30th of a second. When coordinated with an image on a computer monitor, the effect is a full-color stereoscopic (3-dimensional) image.

Above, the crystalline structure of three common substances.

First see MOLECULE

Crystal

Next see SOLID

A solid in which the atoms or molecules are arranged in an ordered, repeating pattern.

The basic unit of a crystal is called the unit cell, and the pattern is referred to as a crystal lattice. There are two atoms per unit cell in body-centered cells that have an additional lattice point in the center. In a face-centered cell, there are one or more lattice points centered in the faces, besides the points at the corners.

The Lattice. The type of crystal formed depends on the basic units that make up the lattice. In ionic crystals, the repeating units are positively and negatively charged atoms known as ions and are held together by electrostatic force, or the attraction between opposite charges. (*See* ELECTROMAGNETIC FORCE.)

In molecular crystals, the repeating units are molecules and the attractive forces holding them together are weak interactions such as hydrogen bonds or Van der Waals forces (which are both based on electrostatic attraction between molecules). In covalent network solids, the attractive forces are chemical bonds between atoms, such as the carbon-carbon bonds found in diamond and graphite. Metallic solids are composed only of metal atoms. A metal atom does not hold onto its electrons very well. As a result, the electrons move easily from one atom to another, holding the positive metal ions together. This is known as a metallic bond, and is what gives metals their hardness and ability to act as conductors.

Dimensions. The size of individual crystals varies greatly and is related to how quickly the crystals form and grow. Slower growth results in larger crystals. A powder consists of a heap of tiny crystals. Crystals also come in a variety of shapes, which depend on the type of atoms or molecules themselves and whether growth occurs horizontally or vertically.

Types of Crystals. There are seven types of simple unit cells, ranging from cubic, which has all sides equal and all angles at 90º, to triclinic, which has all unequal sides and unequal angles that are not 90º. The other types are combinations of equal and unequal sides and angles.

Crystals can also be visualized as spheres, stacked like cannonballs. Hexagonal closest-packing consists of multiple layers of spheres stacked on top of each other with identical alternating layers. In cubic closest-packing, the pattern of layers atop each other does not repeat until the fourth layer. Cubic closest-packing corresponds to face-centered cubic unit cells, as this is the closest regular packing arrangement possible for spheres of equal size. The advantage of having a closest-packed arrangement is the max-

imization of attractive forces because of the large number of neighboring atoms with which to interact. Each sphere has 12 "nearest neighbors," and less than 26 percent of the volume is empty space. Some metals exhibit hexagonal closest-packing crystal structures, whereas others have cubic closest-packed. Noble gases and hydrogen exhibit cubic closest-packing at very low temperatures. (*See* NOBLE GASES.)

Paracrystals. Crystals represent a long-range ordered structure; liquids represent long-range disorder. When water freezes to form ice, the necessary pattern slowly forms around a small ice crystal, or seed. Liquid crystals are materials that do not go straight from a liquid to a solid phase. They are observed in substances composed of long-chain molecules which are easily tangled and disordered. The partially ordered arrangement between liquids and solids is called the paracrystalline state and is a distinct phase like a solid or liquid. The transitions from a crystal to a liquid crystal to an actual liquid are comparable to melting or freezing. Liquid crystals can flow and mix readily, but maintain an ordered arrangement. (*See* BOND, CHEMICAL.)

Liquid Crystals. Liquid crystals are used in some digital watches and calculators. A thin film of liquid crystal is placed between two pieces of glass, one of which is coated with a conducting material. The liquid crystal molecules are polar (the ends are oppositely charged), so an electrical current aligns them to form a number or letter. (*See* COVALENT SOLID.)

First see X-RAY

CT and PET Scans

Next see MEDICAL DIAGNOSTICS

CT and PET scanners are two devices for viewing the internal structures of the human body. CT scanning (CT stands for computed tomography) uses an extremely thin beam of x-rays. This beam is directed through the part of the body that is being examined. Different types of tissue, such as bones or fluid, absorb different amounts of the x-rays in the beam. The intensity of the beam that emerges from the body is measured by an x-ray detector. The various tissues appear as different shades of gray on the scanning device. The beam that has passed through bone produces a segment of the image that is white, while the beam that has passed through air within the body is at the opposite end of the spectrum and produces an image that is black.

How It's Done. Scanning with CT is done with detectors that record measurements from thousands of angles while the person being examined lies on a special table. The measurements are made automatically, and the information is then processed by a computer program to create a composite, three-dimensional representation of the body. The physician doing the examination can select any "slice" or two-dimensional plane from this representation and have it displayed on a cathode ray tube for close inspection. Photographs of the images can also be made for further analysis.

A major advantage of CT scanning is that it shows the soft tissues of the body's internal structure much better than conventional x-rays. The technique thus can reduce the need for exploratory surgery or other invasive diagnostic measures. CT scanning is particularly useful for clear images of the brain and its disorders, such as strokes, tumors, hemorrhages, abscesses, swelling, fluid accumulation, and dead brain tissue. It is even possible for CT scanning to distinguish between tumors that are malignant and those that are benign, because they have different densities that show up on the CT scan image. CT scanning thus has helped revolutionize diagnosis in neurology and neurosurgery, as well as other medical specialties. (*See* SURGERY.)

For example, a CT scan of the spine may be done to diagnose damage or lesions, or to monitor the effects of spinal surgery or therapy. A CT scan of the liver may be done to detect liver disease, to distinguish between the various types of jaundice, or to detect suspected blood clots after an injury to the abdomen. A CT scan of the pancreas can be done to detect or evaluate pancreatitis or to detect other disorders, including pancreatic cancer. A CT scan of the skeleton can be done to check for the presence of bone tumors, to diagnose joint abnormalities when other methods are not adequate, and to give a physician an overall view of the patient's bones and joints.

PET Scan. PET scanning uses an engineered version of molecules that are normally found in the human body. Chemists can make synthetic versions of some of these models that include radioisotopes that emit positrons, which are the antiparticles that correspond to electrons. While an electron carries a negative electric charge, a positron carries a positive charge. The emission of such positive charges makes it possible to take pictures showing the distribution within the body of molecules such as glucose, a form of sugar, and a number of other common molecules, including water. (*See* ANTIMATTER.)

One positron-emitting molecule used in PET scanning is fluorine-18 fluoro-dexyglucose, FDG for short, which is taken up by a number of body organs and tumors because it is chemically similar to glucose. This molecule can make it possible to identify some tumors when other methods, such as CT scanning, have failed. FDG can also be used to obtain images of the heart and the brain for diagnosing problems other than tumors. PET scans require special cameras. The images are obtained soon after the FDG, or another radiopharmaceutical, is injected into the body, usually through a vein in the arm. The patient does not require special care after the procedure is done. A drawback of PET scanning is that it is very expensive. Its high cost has tended to limit its use, but it has already provided valuable information about the brain to both neurologists and brain scientists. (*See* BRAIN.)

First see CONTROL SYSTEMS

Cybernetics

Next see ARTIFICIAL INTELLIGENCE (AI)

The study of how systems evolve and learn, as well as how they manage themselves.

There has always been a connection between the work of scientists and the waging of war. During World War II this connection became a direct and powerful one. The physicists' role in developing the atomic bomb is well-known, but just as important was the work done by mathematicians, electrical engineers, and physicists in the field of fire control: the directing of guns, especially anti-aircraft guns aimed at fast-moving enemy airplanes. Among those involved was an MIT mathematician named Norbert Wiener (1895–1964), who, besides having a gift for mathematics, was also articulate, well-read, and vocal in his beliefs.

Wiener recognized that the theories developed for fire control were also relevant to a wide range of problems, such as the transmission of signals over telephone or radio channels, the operation of the animal nervous system, and the control of automatic production machinery. In a widely read book published in 1948, he coined the term "cybernetics" to bring all these topics under one rubric. He defined the word, which he derived from the Greek (from which also comes the English word "govern"), as the science of communication and control in the animal and the machine. A few years later he wrote a popular version, *The Human Use of Human Beings*, which also found a wide audience.

The notion of cybernetics fit well with the emerging idea that the inventions of the 1940s were about to transform society in ways undreamt of a few short decades before. To the public it was at the time kin to "automation"—another term—that promised a world in which

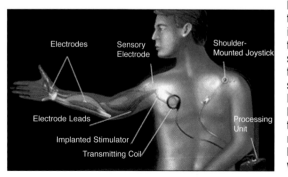

Left, a cybernetic system—the "Freehand" system—involves combining electronic prosthesis, neural stimulation, and conventional transplantation to restore use of a paralyzed limb. Such systems have been staples of science fiction for decades, but implementation of a practical cybernetic scheme has proven difficult.

automatic machines would direct other machines to produce an abundance of material goods for all human beings, with little or none of the drudgery associated with assembly-line work. Wiener developed theories, such as the theory of feedback mechanisms, which he hoped could solve some of the technical problems in constructing automatic machines that could regulate themselves.

At the same time Wiener hoped his writing could help frame the issues without resorting to either the extreme of promising an instant Utopia on Earth or a world plagued by mass unemployment and loss of a skilled society.

Cybernetics also spoke to an understanding of the animal nervous system, postulating that one might consider the brain as a collection of individual neurons that behave much like the binary circuits of a digital computer. Ironically, subsequent research showed that this concept was not correct, but the analogy had a strong effect on biologists, driving them toward a more mathematical and rigorous basis for their own work, and on computer engineers, leading them to think of their creations more as information processing machines than as electronic circuits.

As a mathematician at MIT, Wiener was well acquainted with the digital computer projects there in the late 1940s and 1950s. He submitted a proposal for a digital computer early in this period, but it was never built. Cybernetics implied using computers to handle the controlling functions, but for Wiener these could just as easily be analog as digital computers. Perhaps for that reason, as digital computers came of age and began doing some of the things Wiener predicted, it was not his theories that guided these researchers, but rather those of others. The term "cybernetics" gained currency in the Soviet Union, where it was enthusiastically adopted as a tool to aid in planning a socialist, technology-based economy. In the United States, however, computer researchers by 1960 preferred terms like "artificial intelligence" and "computer science."

Further Reading
Kayles, N. Katherine, *How We Became Posthuman: Virtual Bodies in Cybernetics, Literature, and Informatics* (1999); Shannon, Claude, *Mathematical Theory of Communication* (1963); von Neumann, J., *The Computer and the Brain* (1958); Wiener, Norbert, *The Human Use of Human Beings: Cybernetics and Society* (1988); Wiener, Norbert, *Cybernetics* (1986).

Elementary aspects of this subject are covered in CONTROL SYSTEMS; PROSTHETICS; SERVOMECHANISM. *More information on particular aspects is contained in* ARTIFICIAL INTELLIGENCE; CELLULAR AUTOMATA; ROBOTICS. *Relevant information is contained in* EXPERT SYSTEM; NEURAL NETWORK; VIRTUAL REALITY.

First see HYDROCARBON

Cyclic Compounds

Next see AROMATIC COMPOUNDS

Hydrocarbon chains in which the carbon ends are bonded together to form a closed ring structure.

Each carbon atom in a cyclic compound is a "corner" of the resulting geometric shape. Therefore, a chain consisting of three carbons will form a triangle, four a square, five a pentagon, and six a hexagon. Sometimes an oxygen atom is present in the hydrocarbon chain as well, displacing one of the carbon atoms to the outside of the ring. (*See* CARBON *and* HYDROCARBON.)

Two Groups. The two main groups of cyclic hydrocarbons are alicyclic hydrocarbons and the aromatic compounds. Alicyclic hydrocarbons are "circular" versions of three classes of hydrocarbons: alkanes (all carbons are connected by single bonds only), alkenes (one pair of carbon atoms is connected by a double bond), and alkadienes (two pairs of carbon atoms are connected by double bonds). The aromatic compounds are all derivatives of benzene, a ring consisting of six carbon atoms linked by alternating double and single bonds. (*See* AROMATIC COMPOUND.)

Ring structures are found in other types of molecules, such as sugars, lipids, and nucleic acids. Glucose, which has six carbon atoms, is most commonly seen as a hexagonal ring, and its isomer (same chemical formula, different structure) fructose as a pentagonal ring. Deoxyribose and ribose also form pentagonal rings. (*See* ORGANIC COMPOUNDS.)

Most DNA and RNA components are made up of rings. The molecules adenine, guanine, thymine, cytosine, and uracil are "nucleic bases" whose sequence determines a particular gene. Adenine and guanine are purines, double-ringed structures, while thymine, cytosine, and uracil are pyrimidines, single rings. (*See* DNA.)

DNA and RNA are found almost exclusively as straight chains, but one related nucleic acid, adenosine monophosphate (AMP), is also found as a cyclic compound, called cAMP. The "normal" structure for AMP consists of a sugar molecule bonded on either side to adenine and a phosphate group (PO_4). The phosphate group is usually only attached in one place on the sugar molecule, but in cAMP it is attached in two places, forming a loop. cAMP plays an important role in various metabolic reactions.

Steroids, a category of lipids, which includes cholesterol and some of the sex hormones like testosterone, have intricate structures consisting of interlocking rings. (*See* LIPIDS.)

First see ACCELERATOR, PARTICLE

Cyclotron

Next see SYNCHROTRON

The cyclotron was first conceived by Ernest O. Lawrence in 1929 and developed by Lawrence and his colleagues at the University of California in the 1930s. Their aim was to impart high energies to ionized atoms without the need for very high voltages. The principal components included a direct-current electromagnet with circular pole pieces that had a magnetic gap that was small compared to their diameter.

The electromagnet thus produced a nearly uniform, symmetrical magnetic field. Two hollow, flat electrodes were placed in a magnet gap, open toward each other. Because the first electrodes had shapes resembling a capital D, cyclotron electrodes are still called dees, even though many now have different shapes. An electric field was produced across the dee gap and was driven by an oscillator that produced a constant radio frequency. When the cyclotron went into operation, positively charged ions of

mass M and charge q were released from a source near the center of the gap between the faces of the magnetic poles and the gap between the dees. Each ion was accelerated toward the negatively charged dee so that it entered the hollow cavity of the dee, a region that has no electric field but does have a magnetic field that acts on the charged particle. This magnetic force bends the charged particle into a curved path. If the frequency of the oscillator and the strength of the magnetic field are adjusted properly, the ions pick up acceleration every time they pass through the gap between the dees. Because the ions pick up kinetic energy and velocity each time they pass through the gap, they travel in curved paths that are successively larger, until they reach the target. (*See* ELECTROMAGNETISM.*)

Current Use. Cyclotrons are still widely used to study nuclear reactions and to make some elements radioactive. But there is a limit to the energy that can be imparted to a particle by such a machine. When a proton achieves an energy of 5 MeV, it is moving at one-tenth the speed of light, which means that the effects of relativistic mechanics begin to cause the particle to gain mass, which decreases its speed. Since the radius of curvature and the frequency of the cyclotron depend on the mass of the ion that is being accelerated, there is an effective upper limit on the operations of a fixed-frequency cyclotron.

The first machines to overcome this energy barrier were the frequency-modulated cyclo-

Machines associated with nuclear physics research are thought of as very large, but above is a "table-top" cyclotron in use at the University of California at Berkeley. Left, the 184-inch cyclotron at Oak Ridge, Tennessee, at its inauguration in October 1941 (in a photograph that was not made public until 1981).

Cystic Fibrosis.
The mechanism of the cell in allowing chlorides into the cell, regulating the pH of the cell and maintaining the proper balance of salt and water. The mutation of the CF gene impairs the production of a substance known as cystic fibrosis transmembrane conductance regulator (CFTR), which, in turn, forms a chloride-permeable channel in the cell membrane. The movement of chlorides across the mebrane depends on cleaving onto ATP as it is transported into the cell. The absence of a particular protein confuses the regulatory mechanism, and the connection (and hence the transferrance) never takes place. Much about the mechanisms involved is still unknown, however.

trons, or synchrocyclotrons, which adjust the frequency of the oscillator as the speed and mass of the particle being accelerated increase. Other cyclotrons, developed after World War II, include the electron synchrotron and the proton synchrotron. They produce their particle beams in pulses, rather than continually.

There have been a number of other variations on the basic theme of the cyclotron. Well over 100 cyclotrons today are in operation in more than two dozen countries. In addition to applications in physics, they are used for studies in other sciences, such as chemistry, and to produce radioisotopes for medical and industrial applications. (*See* LINEAR ACCELERATOR.*)

First see GENETIC DISEASES

Cystic Fibrosis

Next see GENE THERAPY

A genetic (inherited) disease that limits the ability of cells to absorb fats and other nutrients from food and that causes chronic lung infections.

Cystic fibrosis (CF) is a recessive disease; a person must inherit two CF genes, one from each parent, to develop the disease. Those who have just one copy of the CF gene usually suffer no ill effects and often are unaware that they are carriers of the disease. The CF gene is rare in nonwhites, but about one white American in 22 is believed to be a carrier. CF appears to interfere with the normal functioning of several glands. One of them is the pancreas, which loses its ability to produce enzymes that are essential for the digestion of fats. Some glands that line the bronchial tubes also malfunction, producing excessive, unusually thick mucous that weakens the resistance to chronic lung infections.

Symptoms. The disease usually becomes evident in early childhood, when the affected child passes stools that are greasy and have an unusually foul smell. The child also suffers frequent chest infections such as bronchitis and pneumonia,

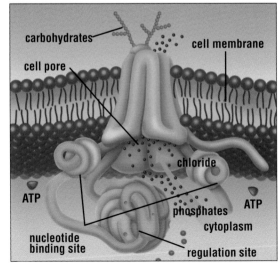

which usually cause permanent damage to the lungs. Growth is stunted in many sufferers. Males are usually sterile, but females are not.

Treatment. Treatment generally requires specialized centers, and starts with the daily replacement of pancreatic enzymes, which are

---

THE CUTTING EDGE

Gene Hunting

The defective gene that causes cystic fibrosis is known as the CFTR gene, for "cystic fibrosis transmembrane conductance regulator." With a normal CFTR gene, the water in a person's body is able to maintain an appropriate proportion of salt; with the defective gene, chlorides fail to cross the cell membranes, and sodium collects. In the lungs, the resulting mucus traps bacteria; in the intestines, it blocks the movement of digestive enzymes; and in the nasal passages it creates a high-salt environment which decimates the substances that normally offer a protective barrier against air-borne invaders. As a genetic disease, screening would help identify potential sufferers, but more than four hundred types of defective CFTR genes exist, making it extremely difficult to identify the single defect that is responsible for 70 percent of CF cases.

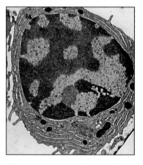

The inside of the cell is filled with a jelly-like substance in which the organelles are embedded, and through which all messenger molecules travel. Below, the cytoskeleton extends to allow the cell to move like an amoeba. Opposite, a micrograph of the cytoskeleton, the structure that gives the cell some solidity, but also the porous substance that allows the business and traffic of life to take place.

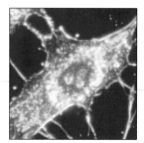

taken with meals, a calorie and protein-rich diet, and supplemental vitamins. In spite of treatment, however, most CF patients currently suffer major lung damage and have shortened life expectancies. (*See* RESPIRATORY SYSTEMS.)

First see CELL

Cytoplasm

Next see CYTOSKELETON

The entire contents of a cell, with the exception of the nucleus.

The cell is filled with a jelly-like material called cytosol, sometimes referred to as protoplasm. The cytosol in turn contains the various organelles of the cell, in an arrangement known as the "fluid-mosaic model." This model can best be envisioned as a gelatin mold (the cytosol) in which fruit slices (the organelles) have been suspended. The cytosol itself consists mostly of water and several proteins, enzymes, and dissolved ions. (*See* PROTEIN METABOLISM.)

The cytosol provides an aqueous environment in the cell in which the various metabolic activities can take place. The cytosol is delineated into various compartments by internal membranes, which surround the organelles and are also honeycombed through with the tiny structures which make up the cytoskeleton, the internal scaffolding that provides basic shape and support of the cell. (*See* CELL MEMBRANE.)

When cells divide in order to reproduce, the nucleus and its contents must be dealt with first, in a process known as mitosis. It is essential to ensure that each new "daughter" cell receives a full set of chromosomes. Afterwards, division of the cytoplasm, called cytokinesis, can occur. The cytoplasm and all of its contents are simply divided into two portions, half going to one new daughter cell and half going to the other.

To produce somites, ordinary body cells, only one cytoplasmic division occurs, resulting in the formation of two new cells. The production of gametes, or sex cells, is more elaborate and requires two cytoplasmic divisions. During sperm production all cytoplasmic divisions are equal, with the result being the formation of four small cells called spermatids. However, during egg production, the cytoplasm is divided unevenly, with the result being the formation of only a single, large ovum. The zygote, which is formed by the union of sperm and egg and gives rise to all of the cells forming the new organism, thus receives the majority of its cytoplasm from the maternal parent. (*See* MITOSIS.)

First see CYTOPLASM

Cytoskeleton

Next see CILIA, FLAGELLA, BASAL BODIES, AND CENTRIOLES

The interior of a cell is honeycombed through with thousands of tiny tubes, called microtubules, and tiny threads, called microfilaments; together these form the cytoskeleton. Both microtubules and microfilaments are composed of proteins, primarily tubulin. Each microtubule is only 25 nanometers thick, with the microfilaments being even thinner. They are much smaller individually than any other organelle in the cell, yet together form a network that acts as a scaffolding for the cell, providing support as well as giving it its shape. (*See* CELL.)

The protein content of the cytoskeleton is responsible for the jelly-like consistency of the cytosol, the material filling the cell. The cytoskeleton is classified as an organelle in its own right, but also as a cytosol component.

The cytoskeleton plays a role in the cell locomotion, allowing cells to "crawl" forward (like the compression of a spring followed by its release). The cytoskeleton is also responsible for muscle contraction and for the way vertebrate embryos change shape during their development. The cytoskeleton anchors the various organelles in place, yet also provides the mechanism for the mobile organelles to move within the interior of the cell. (*See* LOCOMOTION.)

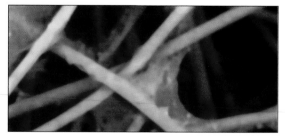

Dams

First see SOIL CHEMISTRY

Next see ARCHITECTURAL ENGINEERING

Dams are structural barriers built to contain or control the flow of bodies of water, to divert their flow, to facilitate navigation, to store water for irrigation or city supplies, or to raise the level of a body of water for use in power generation.

The earliest known dam was built on the Nile River in Egypt about 2900 B.C.E. Most modern dams serve more than one function and are often classified by the type of material used to build them.

Types of Dams. There are two major types of dams: rock-fill and earthen. Rock-fill dams are embankments of loose rock that have either a watertight upstream face built of concrete or a watertight core. They generally are built where a large amount of suitable rock is available, so that a minimum amount of transport is needed.

Above, the ruins of the Malpassart Dam. Below, Hoover Dam, using the geological formation for support.

Earthen dams can be constructed in several ways. One type is the earth-fill dam: a simple embankment of earth that is firmly compacted. Another type has a watertight core and perhaps a concrete wall. Masonry or concrete dams usually are built to block streams in narrow gorges. The highest may rise to 1,000 feet.

Gravity dams hold back water by their own weight. A gravity dam may be solid, sloping downstream with a thick base, or buttressed, sloping upstream and strengthened by buttresses that transfer dead weight sideways, thus necessitating less concrete or other structural material.

Arch dams have one or more arches pointing upstream. They are often built in a canyon, transferring some of the dead weight of the contained water to the walls of the canyon.

Individual dams may use more than one of these construction types. The Hoover Dam, for example, built in 1936 on the Colorado River, is a combination of arch- and gravity-types.

During construction, temporary coffer dams may be built to keep water away from the construction site. For purposes of river control, a series of dams built to an overall plan may have to be erected. Major problems encountered by dams are leakage under the foundation; partial failure of the structure resulting in cracks through which water can leak; and the accumulation of silt in the reservoir behind the dam, which erodes the structure. (*See* CEMENT.)

First see ACID RAIN

Deforestation

Next see DESERTIFICATION

Ever since agriculture was developed 10,000 years ago, humans have been turning forests into farmland. It is estimated that one-third of Earth's original forests have been eliminated, and deforestation continues at an alarming pace. The loss of forests represents the loss of the Earth's most species-rich habitats and its richest pool of biodiversity. (*See* BIODIVERSITY.)

Tropical Rain Forests. Most concern has focused on the destruction of the tropical rain forests, believed to harbor more than half of all plant and animal species in the world, many found nowhere else. It is estimated that tropical rain forests once covered about 14 percent of the Earth's land; today the figure is estimated at 6 percent. In Madagascar, an island teeming with unique species, 80 percent of the rain forest and 50 percent of its species have disappeared as a desperately poor population creates farmland and pastures. It has been estimated that if the Amazon rain forest were reduced to only the areas already set aside as reserves and parks, about two-thirds of all its species of plants and birds would disappear.

Temperate forests are also shrinking, through a combination of intentional clearing and pollution. Some of the most severe deforestation has taken place in China and in Siberia.

Natural Cycles. Besides being important habitats, forests are important elements in the cycling of water and nutrients. Deforestation throws some of these processes out of balance by causing land erosion, flooding, and a runoff of nutrients into streams and lakes. This causes eutrophication—overnourishing of lakes that degrades water quality. The effect is multiplied when erosion reduces the fertility of the land, requiring fertilizers, the runoff from which adds to the nutrient overload in nearby water.

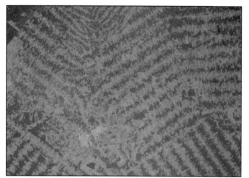

Above, a mechanized logging operation in Caribou, Maine. The introduction of such methods has increased the per-logger productivity (the amount of forestland cleared) by a factor of ten.

Forests play a major role in recycling rainwater into the atmosphere to fall again as rain. It has been estimated that clearing the Amazon rain forest would cut rainfall in the region by about 25 percent and raise temperatures about 3 degrees Celsius. While the local effects would obviously be severe, a change of that magnitude would probably have an effect on global climate as well. Forests also play a major role in removing carbon dioxide from the atmosphere in order to use it in photosynthesis. As forests are cleared, the carbon dioxide level in the atmosphere rises, contributing to the global greenhouse effect that many scientists believe has already started to cause global warming.

First see BONE AND BONE GROWTH

Dentistry

Next see INGESTION

A health profession that deals with the teeth and the body tissues around them.

Dentists work to diagnose, treat, and prevent diseases, injuries, decay, and malformations of the teeth, gums, and jaws. That work begins with the dental examination, which is recommended as a normal procedure for every person at least once a year. During the examination, the dentist starts the procedure by asking about the person's general health and dental health. The structures around the mouth, such as the temporomandibular joint, are examined to detect any abnormalities. The next step is to examine the teeth, looking for any cavities that have developed since the last examination and for teeth that may be missing, rotated, or otherwise out of normal position. Existing fillings and crowns are examined for signs of degeneration; and the gums are inspected for indications of disease, such as gingivitis and periodontitis, two types of inflammation.

The dentist checks for the presence of tartar and plaque, deposits that may lead to loss of teeth. Dental x-rays are taken if necessary. They can show defects of the teeth and the surrounding tissues not visible to the eye. If a cavity caused by decay or chipping is found, it is treated by removing soft material with a scoop and harder material with a high-speed drill, to produce an opening that will be filled, usually by amalgam, a metal alloy consisting of mercury and one or more other metals. This work is normally done after a local anesthetic is injected to prevent pain. If circumstances warrant greater expertise, the dentist will refer the patient to specialists such as an orthodontist, prosthodontist, endodontist, or periodontist.

Flouridation. Public dental health has been improved by fluoridation, the addition of a small amount of fluoride to water supplies to prevent cavities. More than 60 percent of the U.S. water supplies have been fluoridated since the practice began in the 1940s. It has been shown that children who drink fluoridated water from birth have 65 percent fewer cavities than those drinking water with less than the recommended amount of fluoride. (*See* TEETH.)

First see DEFORESTATION

Desertification

Next see BIODIVERSITY

The transformation through human activities of fertile forests or plains land into arid, unusable land.

There are two basic kinds of desertification. One results from the agricultural overuse of cleared land, particularly in areas of low rainfall. This overuse sets in motion a chain, creating dust storms that reduce rainfall. A classic example is the American Dust Bowl—an area covering hundreds of thousands of square miles of land in the Great Plains region—during the 1930s. From 1910 through the 1920s, farmers plowed up grassland to plant wheat. A severe drought that developed in the early 1930s killed vegetation, and high winds blew away the topsoil. Federal action was necessary to rehabilitate the land. In ancient times, similar activity is believed to have increased the aridity of much of the land stretching from the southern Mediterranean to Afghanistan. Some semiarid regions of India and Pakistan may now be in danger.

Responses and Solutions. The situation is not irretrievable, however; the desert-causing process can be reversed. In particular, it has been shown that prevention of overgrazing by sheep and other animals can increase the vegetative cover of land, restoring its fertility.

"Slash-and-Burn." A second type of desertification is caused by human plundering of the

Above, the rapid transformation of the rain forest of Brazil is apparent in three satellite photographs taken at the same season in (from left) 1975, 1985, and 1996.

tropical rain forest through such practices as "slash-and-burn" agriculture, in which small areas of the jungle are cut down and burned, the ashes enabling primitive farming for a few years. The cleared land, however, then becomes infertile and uncultivatable. The farmer moves on to an adjacent area, where the process is repeated. The forest in the first area never recovers, because the soil is now as unsuitable for trees and other jungle vegetation as it is for crops. The surface albedo—a measure of how much sunlight is reflected—has been changed for the worse, as has the soil's water-retaining property.

Pictures taken by orbiting satellites have demonstrated major desertification-promoting changes in the Amazon Basin of South America in recent decades. In addition to their effect on the tropical forest, these changes are also expected to affect the climate of the earth as a whole. The fires of "slash-and-burn" agriculture can also be major contributors to air pollution, on a scale equal to the emissions of industrial sources. (*See* DEFORESTATION.)

First see BLOOD

Dialysis

Next see KIDNEY AND EXCRETORY SYSTEM

An artificial means of removing waste products and excess fluids from the body.

Dialysis is resorted to when the kidneys can no longer perform their function and when kidney transplantation is not possible. There are two methods of dialysis: hemodialysis and peritoneal dialysis. Hemodialysis removes the chemical wastes and extra fluid by filtering the blood through an artificial kidney, or dialyzer. In order to perform hemodialysis, the bloodstream must be accessed, usually through an arm or leg.

Procedure. During hemodialysis, a fistula, a connection between an artery and a vein, is made or a tube may be inserted between an artery and a vein. Persons on hemodialysis spend from 6 to 12 hours connected to an artificial kidney machine each week. Blood is pumped into the machine, which has a set of membranes that allow the waste products to filter through them and be removed. No more than a cupful of blood is outside the body at any one time.

The other method, peritoneal dialysis, uses the body's own peritoneal cavity, located in the abdomen, to filter wastes out of the blood. The peritoneal cavity has an extensive network of small blood vessels that can remove the impurities. To do peritoneal dialysis, a catheter is inserted into the abdomen, and dialysis solution is pumped into and drained out of the peritoneal cavity. The impurities pass from the small blood vessels into the dialysis solution, thereby removing them from the body. In some cases, this can be done at home. (*See* OSMOSIS.)

First see CARBON

Diamond

Next see CRYSTAL

A form of carbon in which the crystal lattice structure is perfectly regular.

Diamonds are minerals consisting essentially of pure carbon. Their carbon atoms have a crystal arrangement that makes the stones extremely hard, yet brittle. Diamonds are formed under the extremely high pressures that exist deep underground, and are brought to the surface when the basalt formations in which they exist move toward the surface. Important diamond deposits are found in Africa and India; South Africa in particular is known for its diamond fields. There are some small diamond fields in the U.S.

Most diamonds are faint yellow or brown, but they may be colorless, very pale blue or, in rare cases, bright yellow, green, pink, orange, or a different color. The reason a diamond is extraordinarily bright after it is cut is that it has a very high refractive index, which means that it transmits light at a very high speed. (*See* CARBON; CRYSTAL.)

Diamond crystals found in nature range in size from microscopically small to as much as several pounds. The unit of measurement for diamonds is the carat, equal to one-fifth of a gram; most diamonds weigh less than one carat.

Diamonds are cut and polished on a rapidly revolving, soft cast-iron fixture covered with diamond dust. They can be cut only in certain directions, depending on the areas of softness found in a given stone. Synthetic diamonds have been produced in recent years, but these are very small and are used for industrial purposes.

Above, the Light of Peace, among the largest diamonds in the world.

First see INTERNAL COMBUSTION ENGINE

Diesel Engine

Next see AUTOMOTIVE ENGINEERING

The diesel engine is an internal-combustion engine used to power many heavy vehicles, mostly trucks, but also some cars. It was developed in 1896 by German inventor Rudolf Diesel. Unlike the four-stroke Otto engine, which is found in most automobiles, the diesel engine does not have spark plugs to ignite its fuel. Instead, the fuel is ignited by the heat produced when air is compressed within the diesel engine's cylinder.

The operation of a diesel engine can be described in five steps. First, air is drawn or forced into the cylinder of the engine. Then, the air in the cylinder is compressed to create very high pressure and an elevated temperature.

Rudolf Diesel (1858–1913)

Diesel Engine Cycle

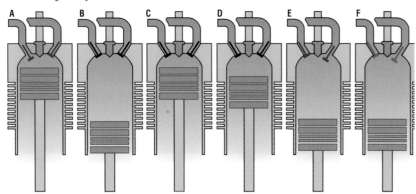

Above, the cycle of the diesel engine. Air enters as the piston descends from A to B. The air is then compressed from B to C as fuel is sprayed in. An ignition takes place when the piston is at its highest point, C, powering the piston downward to E. At that point, the exhaust valve opens and the products of the combustion are expelled in step F, after which the piston and cylinder return to step A.

Third, fuel is injected into the cylinder, where it is ignited when it comes in contact with the hot compressed air. In the fourth step, the hot, high-pressure fuel-air mixture expands against the cylinder, pushing it and thus transferring energy to it. It is this movement that is the driving force of the diesel engine. In the fifth step, the gases that are left in the cylinder are blown out, so that the cylinder is ready for the next five-step cycle.

In most diesel engines, the movement of the piston is converted into rotary motion by means of a connecting rod and crank. Diesel engines can be classified by the number of cylinders they have, and by the arrangement of their cylinders—in-line, radial, or V-shaped.

First see CALCULUS

Differential Equations

Next see DIFFERENTIAL GEOMETRY

Mathematical formulas that describe functions in terms of their change over time, and the attempt to derive solutions to them.

A differential equation is a mathematical way of describing change over time. Differential equations are used to predict population growth, or they may be used to describe decay of radioactive isotopes in carbon-14 dating; they may even refer to variation over time, as when differential equations compute repayment schedules for different home-mortgage opportunities in order to determine which offer to pursue.

Second-Order Differential Equations. Differential equations may also occur in a more complex form, known as second-order differential equations (even higher-order equations are possible, but cannot usually be solved unless they are linear). In these, the solution demands change not only with respect to time, but also with respect to other variables. The best-known second-order differential equation is Newton's second law of motion, in which position, force, and time affect velocity. (*See* NEWTON'S LAWS.)

A complex differential equation is linear if none of its dependent variables is accompanied by an exponent value; that is, the primary variable may be written with a superscript that is positive or negative, integral or fractional, even complex (x^2, $x^{-1/3}$, even x^{n-2}), but the function $y(x)$ may not have an exponent. When this is the case, and the coefficients are all constants, the differential equation can be reduced to an algebraic equivalent through what is called the Laplace transform, and it can be solved without the use of any calculus operations. If the coefficients are also variables, the differential equation can only be solved by what is known as the Power-series method. This method has been used to provide independent confirmation of many classical theories, such as Euclid's original geometrical formulations. (*See* FUNCTIONS.)

Where a differential equation represents a function of two or more independent variables, it is likely that it will contain one or more partial derivatives; such equations are called partial differential equations. Problems in heat diffusion, electrostatics, fluid flow, and vibration often fall into the partial differential form, because they concern effects over time on three-dimensional objects whose surfaces and volumes are incompletely defined.

History. The earliest formal inquiry into partial differential equations, written by Jean Le Rond d'Alembert (1717–83), concerned the musical tone generated by a string plucked at a certain point, and its duration. His paper was quickly followed by a series of further analyses of music, by such figures in the history of mathematics as Leonhard Euler (1707–1783), Daniel Bernoulli (1700–1782), Joseph-Louis Lagrange (1736–1813), and Herman von Helmholtz (1821–1894). The issue was not conclusively settled until 1822, when Joseph Fourier (1768–1830) discovered the Fourier series.

Partial differential equations highlight the need for an effective method of mathematical modeling. That is, real-world situations must be analyzed to determine all the functional variables at work in them; each variable must be charted and predicted, and the relevant data entered into the model; the model must be solved, or at least analyzed; and the results obtained from the model must be judged against the real-world situations which impelled its original construction.

Had such analysis been performed during the design of the Tacoma Narrows Bridge in 1940, its collapse from aerodynamic stall flutter response might never have occurred. (*See* AERODYNAMICS; BRIDGE DESIGN.)

First see EUCLIDEAN GEOMETRY

Differential Geometry

Next see DIFFERENTIAL EQUATIONS

Differential geometry is the study of the structure of stationary objects. Curves and surfaces of most objects vary from point to point, and therefore cannot be analyzed by traditional geometric means.

Clockmaking. The first successes in differential geometry were attained by clockmakers seeking to achieve perfectly regular pendulums, and by mapmakers seeking to achieve flat representations of a round Earth. Christian Huygens determined as early as 1673 that a figure called a cycloid would allow a pendulum to swing in exactly the same time, whether the amplitude of its swing was large or small. Seventy years later, Alexis-Claude Clairaut analyzed the oblate spheroid form that the Earth assumes as a result of rotational and gravitational forces. By 1771, Leonhard Euler had worked out a mathematical method of, as he put it, "unfolding" the surface of a solid into a plane, and had constructed a flat map of Russia. But in 1775, he admitted that, with the methods available in his time, a sphere could be mapped conformably, but not congruently, into a plane.

Gauss. The next phase in the development of differential geometry was made by Christian Gauss in 1827. He worked out many solutions to the problem of finding geodesics, or straight lines, between points on curved surfaces; this was important because on the surface of the Earth there is no visible straight line to provide the shortest distance between any two points. As anyone who has passed over Greenland while flying from New York to London knows, solutions to problems of geodesics are not always obvious. As a corollary, Gauss recognized that the surface of a curved body can be considered as a space in itself; straight lines from one point to another on that surface would be geodesics, or curved. Non-Euclidean geometry, a basis for much of modern physics, had been born.

Reimann. The originator of non-Euclidean geometry was Georg Riemann, a student of Gauss. Riemann determined that a space of however many dimensions, not just its surface, can be seen as curved. He even developed a formula by which one could predict the exact curvature of any given space.

Once it was possible to employ differential geometry to treat a curved space, it also became possible to perceive space itself as curved. Classical physics had treated all matter as particulate, but modern physics perceives matter as only sometimes particulate; at other times matter is like a wave—and a wave is a curved surface. Thus, differential geometry has allowed contemporary physicists to develop a wave theory of matter, which relies on differential geometry for its analysis and explication.

Background material is found in ALGEBRA; EUCLIDEAN GEOMETRY; FUNCTIONS. *Other aspects of the subject are discussed in* CALCULUS; DIFFERENTIAL EQUATIONS; VECTORS AND TENSORS. *Related material and applications can be found in* CATASTROPHE THEORY; NON-EUCLIDEAN GEOMETRY; TOPOLOGY.

First see CELL CYCLE

Differentiation, Cellular

Next see EMBRYOLOGY

The primary difference between unicellular organisms and cells from a multicellular organism is the degree of cellular specialization. A unicellular organism is very generalized and able to perform a variety of activities, whereas a cell from a multicellular organism is highly specialized and performs only one task.

A multicellular organism starts out as a single cell and immediately begins to divide to produce more cells. As more cells develop, they form a hollow, ball-shaped structure, called a blastosphere. Some of the cells then begin migrating inward, a process called invagination, to form two cell layers instead of one. The outer layer is called the ectoderm and the inner layer the endoderm. The process is repeated to form a third layer, the mesoderm. All body systems will arise from these three cellular layers.

At this point, the cells differentiate—they become different from one another. Tissues are made up of cells, all of which have the same structure and function and are located in the same specific area. Within a cell layer, vastly different systems arise; even within each layer distinct organs composed of different tissues are formed as well. How do cells know what type of tissue they are going to form? More fundamentally, how can cells become so different if they all started out from one "ancestral" cell, and all still contain exactly the same genetic material?

"Embryonic induction" refers to the observation that cells differentiate according to where they are located. It is believed that cells communicate with each other, probably by means of chemical messengers. Early experiments with developing tadpole embryos involved transplanting cells from the tail region to the head. Instead of developing into tail cells, the transplanted cells assumed the identity of their new neighbors. When "future" eye cells were transplanted to the tail region, the tadpole did not develop eyes on its tail. Once again, the cells "assimilated" into their new surroundings.

Genetic Basis. Genes are segments of DNA that contain information for constructing a particular protein. Depending upon which proteins are produced, different chemical reactions can take place in the cell. It is these reactions on the molecular level that distinguish cells from each other by both structure and function. Even though all cells of the body contain the same genes, not all genes are active in all of the cells. During the very early stages of development, all genes are turned on full force because the cell must rapidly reproduce. But soon cells start to specialize and some genes are turned off. (*See* IMPRINTING, GENETIC; EXONS AND INTRONS.)

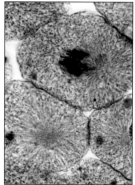

Above, fertilized human cells after two divisions. Each of these cells will develop into a different part of the embryo, but what distinguishes one from the others (how does the cell "know" what it is supposed to become?) is a subject of intense current investigation.

Further Reading
Darnell, J., *Molecular Cell Biology* (1990); de Duve, Christian, *A Guided Tour of the Living Cell* (1984); Pomerai, D., *From Gene to Animal* (1985); Gould, Stephen J., *Ontogeny and Phylogeny* (1977); Judson, Horace F., *The Eighth Day of Creation* (1979).

First see LIGHT

Diffraction

Next see OPTICS

The spreading or bending of waves as they pass through an opening or around the edge of a barrier.

Diffraction effects occur in all types of waves, including light rays, sound waves, water waves, and all kinds of electromagnetic radiation, such as x-rays and radio waves. Diffraction limits the sharpness of images formed by lenses or mirrors, because even the sharpest lines of these images are blurred. Diffraction effects in sound waves are more easily noticed than those in light waves because diffracted waves interfere with one another, producing regions of stronger and weaker waves. The phenomenon of diffraction was first noticed in the seventeenth century by Francesco Grimaldi. His observations gave major support to the wave theory of light. (*See* X-RAY DIFFRACTION.)

The diffraction effect is applied in the design of diffraction gratings, used in spectrographs and spectroscopes for the analysis of light beams. A diffraction grating has a very large number of parallel lines ruled in it, perhaps 1,000 per millimeter. Light that is diffracted by these lines breaks up into characteristic patterns. X-ray diffraction techniques can be used to experimentally determine the structure of crystals, while microwave diffraction studies have helped to develop refined radar systems.

Diffraction effects can also be observed in fast-moving particles, such as neutrons and electrons. Neutron diffraction is thus an important tool in nuclear physics. (*See* INTERFERENCE.)

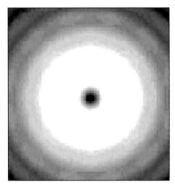

Above, the diffraction of light by a Fresnel lens. As a result of the diffraction, the light is "warmer," making such lenses more suitable for spotlights and in lighthouses.

First see BROWNIAN MOTION

Diffusion

Next see MAXWELL-BOLTZMANN DISTRIBUTION

The process by which the particles of a substance spread throughout another material, as a result of the random motion of the molecules.

Diffusion occurs in gases, liquids, and solids. The rate of diffusion of a gas depends on its molecular mass or density. The higher the mass or density, the slower the rate. During a chemical reaction, diffusion can replenish gaseous reactants, thus affecting the rate of that reaction.

In biology, diffusion refers to the movement of particles across a membrane. Materials follow a concentration gradient, traveling from an area of higher concentration to an area of lower concentration until there is an equal amount on both sides of the membrane. The ability of a particle to diffuse depends upon the following properties: size, charge, and solubility, resulting from the physical makeup of the membrane itself.

Smaller particles can traverse the membrane easier than larger ones, since they have a better chance of slipping through the pores and around the constituent molecules. If a particle has an electrical charge, it can only cross the membrane in an oppositely charged area. If the particle is fat-soluble, it will have an easier time crossing the membrane's lipid areas. (*See* LIPIDS.)

Osmosis refers specifically to the diffusion of water; water molecules always move toward the side with a higher concentration of solid particles. The area with the higher concentration is said to be hypertonic in relation to the other side. Water continually moves to the hypertonic area, which is why a high concentration of salt causes water retention. (*See* OSMOSIS.)

Many important bodily functions depend upon diffusion between cells. The blood transports materials throughout the body, including nutrients and oxygen, which must be taken in by these cells. In return, the blood absorbs waste materials, such as urea and carbon dioxide, from the body cells. The transfers occur primarily by diffusion. The electrical impulses by which muscle and nerve cells function also depend upon the diffusion of various ions in and out of their cell membranes. (*See* WATER IN LIVING CELLS.)

First see INGESTION

Digestion

Next see DIGESTION REGULATION

The mechanical and chemical breakdown of food into smaller, simpler units that can then be utilized by the cells of a living organism.

Mechanical digestion refers to tearing, grinding, and chewing food into smaller pieces. Chemical digestion refers to the breakdown of carbohydrates into simple sugars, proteins into amino acids, and fats into fatty acids. Enzymes are required for chemical digestion. (*See* DIGESTION REGULATION *for references to related entries.*)

Microorganisms, consisting of just a single cell, do not have separate organs making up various body systems, but rather have small structures known as organelles. In terms of digestion, these organisms have an organelle called a food vacuole, which is a membrane-enclosed sac that secretes digestive enzymes. (*See* INGESTION.)

The Alimementary Canal. The digestive tract, also called the alimentary canal, is basically a long tube with an opening to admit food and an opening to expel wastes. The basic arrangement for humans consists of a mouth or oral cavity, pharynx (throat), esophagus, stomach, intestines, and anus or cloaca.

Animals are consumers; they cannot produce their own food but must consume other organisms in order to produce energy. Some animals are filter feeders: plankton and other small organisms flow into their oral cavities as water enters and are "filtered" or strained out. Primitive creatures such as sponges, which consist of just one cell layer, are filter feeders, as are more complex vertebrates, such as baleen whales. These whales strain literally tons of creatures from the water each day and must do so continuously in order to obtain sufficient food.

The Mouth. The oral cavity contains the teeth, tongue, and salivary glands. The function of the teeth is to tear and grind food. Some organisms, notably amphibians and birds, do not have teeth and therefore must either digest their food whole or employ some other method of mechanical digestion. Snakes have teeth, but for the purpose of injecting their prey with venom, not for chewing. They, too, must digest their prey whole. Some birds, like annelids, have a crop and a gizzard in place of a stomach, where grinding of the food takes place. The tongue serves to manipulate the food as it is being chewed and to propel it to the back of the throat for swallowing. Salivary glands produce saliva which moistens the food, making it easier to swallow, as well as providing a digestive enzyme, amylase, to begin the breakdown of starch. (*See* DENTISTRY.)

The esophagus is simply a conduit between mouth and stomach. No digestion occurs here, but mucus is added to food, making it easier to swallow—the last voluntary act of digestion. From that point on, the food moves automatically through the rest of the alimentary canal, in assembly-line fashion. This movement is caused by a series of rhythmic contractions known as peristalsis. (*See* MUSCLE.)

The Stomach. In the stomach, protein digestion begins, and a great deal of mechanical digestion occurs there as well. The stomach environment is highly acidic because of the pH requirement for gastric enzymes to function. Afterwards, the stomach contents pass into the small intestine, where the majority of digestion takes place. (*See* ACID AND BASE.)

The Intestines. The small intestine not only produces its own enzymes for the digestion of food, but also receives enzymes from other organs that contribute to digestion, though the food does not pass through their interior. The liver produces bile, for the emulsion of fats. Bile is stored in the gall bladder and passes through the bile duct into the small intestine. Later, the liver plays a role in digestion as well, as the nutrients are sent there for further processing before general distribution throughout the body. The pancreas produces pancreatic juices, enzymes for the breakdown of fats, proteins, and carbohydrates. These enzymes also pass through a duct into the small intestine.

The last region of the small intestine is where nutrients are absorbed into the bloodstream, through small fingerlike projections known as villi. After this point, digestion is finished, but the digestive system is not. In the large intestine, excess water is removed and absorbed back into the bloodstream. The remaining material, consisting mostly of undigested food, fiber, mucus, and bile salts (left after bile has done its job), are consolidated into feces, which are stored temporarily in the rectum before being expelled from the body.

The "gut" of every creature is teeming with bacteria that live in a mutually beneficial relationship. The bacteria are provided with a sheltered environment and access to nutrients; in return they aid in digestion. It is because of this relationship that travelers may become sick upon ingesting foreign water and food— the local bacteria are not compatible with the bacteria already residing in their intestines.

Each species has various adaptations in digestion to suit its diet and needs. The type and number of teeth reflects "specialization" according to organism, as do the enzymes present. For example, humans cannot digest fiber, plant cellulose, because our bodies lack the specific enzymes needed to break it down. Termites, on the other hand, and grazing animals, such as cows, either have this enzyme, or get it through a symbiotic relationship with an organism that does produce it. (*See* METABOLIC PATHWAYS.)

First see DIGESTION

Digestion Regulation

Next see DIGESTIVE CHEMISTRY

Most food consists of large molecules that must be broken down into their small constituent parts in order to be absorbed and used by the body. This work of chemical disassembly—digestion—is accomplished mainly by a large array of digestive enzymes, often aided by mechanical processes that break or grind down the food to allow the enzymes full access.

In primitive animals, such as coelenterates (jellyfish), and other more complex organisms, such as bivalves, that feed on microscopic particles, digestion takes place within the cells, in

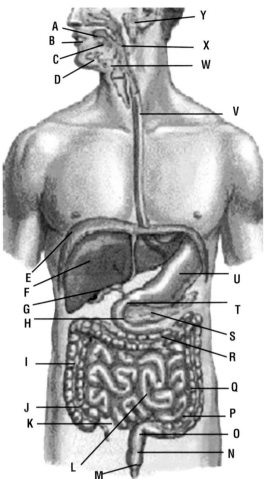

The human digestive system. Food enters the oral cavity (A) where it is broken down by the teeth (B), tongue (C), sublingual gland (D), parotid gland (Y), and submandibular gland (W). The food is introduced by the pharynx (X) to the esophagus (V), which transports it to the stomach (U). There the food is further processed and it is passed to the small intestine (L), where it is further broken down by secretions from the pancreas (S), liver (F), and gall bladder (G). In the small intestine, nutrients are absorbed by the villi. Material not fit for absorbtion goes to the cecum (J), past the appendix (K), and into the large intestines (I, R, and Q), until it is ejected from the body through the sigmoid colon (P), the rectum (O), and the anal canal (M).

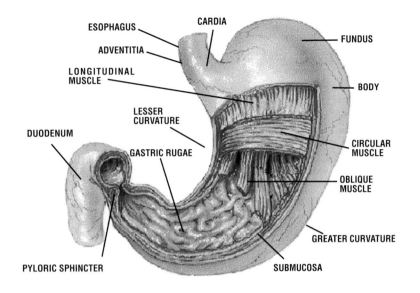

The human stomach.

Further Reading
Chivers, D. J., *The Digestive System in Animals: Food, Form, and Function* (1994); Church, D. C., *The Ruminant Animal* (1993); Clayman, C., *A Healthy Digestion* (1992); Johnson, Leonard, *Gastrointestinal Physiology* (2001).

vacuoles or chambers devoted to this purpose. But in vertebrates, and in many invertebrates, digestion is an extracellular event, taking place in the organs of a specialized digestive tract.

Enzymatic Control. In humans and other mammals, complex controls involving neural and hormonal systems are required to coat the digestive tract with slippery, protective mucus. The food moves along by muscular contraction, exposed to the right amounts of enzymes, acid, bicarbonate, and other substances at the right times. These controls involve the sympathetic and parasympathetic nervous systems, as well as the enteric nervous system, which is located in the digestive tract.

In humans, the first of these enzymes is amylase, or ptyalin, which starts the digestion of carbohydrates. It is secreted in the saliva by the parotid, submandibular, and sublingual glands. The salivary glands are controlled mainly by parasympathetic nervous signals from nuclei in the brain stem that are stimulated by sensations of taste and touch in the mouth. Sour tastes and smooth textures excite them more than the sweet and the rough. The glands also respond to higher neural centers—witness the fact that a favorite food makes the mouth water more than one that is disliked. Reflexes from the stomach and small intestine can also stimulate salivation during periods of nausea.

The regulation of acid in the stomach provides an example of how complex the digestive control mechanisms are. Enzyme-secreting glands in the stomach are activated by two sets of neural signals: Some are carried by the vagus nerves from the limbic system in the brain, stimulated by the smell or taste of food. Others result from reflexes in the enteric nervous system in the stomach wall, triggered by stomach distention and by the presence of acid or protein.

There are two types of stomach glands. In the gastric (or oxyntic) glands, parietal cells secrete hydrochloric acid, and peptic or chief cells secrete pepsinogen. If hydrochloric acid is present, pepsinogen is converted into pepsin, an enzyme that begins to break down proteins. Pepsin, in turn, activates more pepsinogen. But without sufficient acid, that chain reaction does not begin and protein digestion cannot take place. In the pyloric glands, cells secrete the important hormone gastrin, which is absorbed into the blood and carried to the gastric glands. If histamine and the neurotransmitter acetylcholine are also present, the gastrin stimulates a bountiful release of acid. Histamine is normally present. Acetylcholine is released by the stimulation of the vagus nerve and the enteric reflexes.

When the gastric juices become too acidic—with a pH below 3.0—the secretion of gastrin is inhibited, protecting the stomach and preserving the optimum pH for the peptic enzymes. In addition, if food is present in the small intestine, signals are transmitted from the enteric nervous system, the vagus nerve, and the sympathetic nervous system to depress secretions in the stomach. This prevents food from reaching an intestine that is already occupied.

Most digestion, as well as absorption of nutrients, takes place in the small intestine. Ducts from the pancreas, liver, and gallbladder deliver enzymes to digest protein, carbohydrates, fat, and nucleic acid, as well as bile to emulsify fat. Intestinal glands also secrete enzymes that continue the digestive process.

> *Background material can be found in* DIGESTION; DIGESTIVE CHEMISTRY; DIGESTIVE SYSTEMS. *More details about digestion can be found in* ENZYMES; NUTRITION; SECRETION, CELLULAR. *Foundational aspects of this subject are covered in* ANTIOXIDANTS; PANCREAS; PROTEIN METABOLISM. *See also* ENDOCRINE SYSTEMS IN VERTEBRATES; LIVER; BACTERIA; INGESTION.

First see DIGESTION

Digestive Chemistry

Next see DIGESTION REGULATION

Chemical digestion is the breakdown of materials into smaller, more basic units by means of disrupting chemical bonds. Carbohydrates such as starch are broken down into simple sugars, called monosaccharides and disaccharides; proteins are transformed into amino acids; and fats into fatty acids. These units are absorbed into the bloodstream and can be absorbed by body cells for use in various cellular reactions.

The Role of Enzymes. The chemical breakdown is performed by enzymes—protein molecules that catalyze the various cellular chemical reactions so they can occur under normal body conditions of temperature and pH. Many such enzymes exist in inactive form and must first be activated in order to work. The inactive precursor of an enzyme is called a zymogen or proenzyme. These are activated by the cleavage of one or more specific bonds, which free the component amino acids and allow them to assume a different shape. It is the new conformation that allows the enzyme to function. Examples of proenzymes include pepsinogen, a stomach enzyme that converts to pepsin, and trypsinogen, a pancreatic enzyme that converts to trypsin. This is an important control mechanism to insure that enzymes will not work when the desired material or substrate is absent.

Enzyme-Producing Glands. The major enzyme-producing organs are the salivary glands, stomach, pancreas, liver, and small intestines. The salivary gland enzyme is salivary amylase, which catalyzes the breakdown of starch. Pepsinogen, produced by the stomach, is converted to the active form, pepsin, in the presence of gastric acid, and catalyzes the breakdown of protein.

Pancreatic enzymes include trypsin, chymotrypsin, lipase, and amylase for the breakdown of proteins, fats, and starch, respectively. The intestinal enzymes include disaccharidases, which further break down simple sugars, peptidases, which further break down proteins, and more lipase for the breakdown of fats. Each of these enzymes has a particular pH requirement to insure optimum function. The stomach enzymes require an acidic environment; others require neutral to basic conditions.

System Control. The release of digestive enzymes is controlled by the nervous system as well as by various hormones such as gastrin, which enhances the secretion of the stomach enzymes. The release of stomach enzymes is inhibited when the pH falls below 2. This in turn inhibits the release of gastrin, allowing the pH to rise to the optimum pH (2-3) for the enzymes to function most efficiently.

This type of control is known as negative feedback. Cholecystokinin (CCK) is the hormone that controls the release of intestinal enzymes. Another hormone, secretin, helps to neutralize the highly acidic material that enters the small intestine. Both CCK and secretin are responsible for the release of bile from the liver, which assists in the breakdown of fat.

The end results of the digestive processes, namely the simple sugars, amino acids, and fatty acids, are absorbed into the bloodstream from the small intestine via various types of active transport that take place in the villi.

Background material on digestive processes can be found in DIGESTION; DIGESTION REGULATION; DIGESTIVE SYSTEMS. *More details on digestion can be found in* CARBOHYDRATES; LIPIDS; METABOLISM. *More information on particular aspects of digestion is contained in* PROTEIN METABOLISM; STEROID HORMONES; STRESS.

First see DIGESTION

Digestive Systems, Animal and Human

Next see DIGESTION REGULATION

In most animals, the digestive system is a tube, straight or, more commonly, coiled, stretching from mouth to anus or vent and divided into specialized regions: oral cavity, pharynx, esophagus, stomach, and intestine. Along this muscular, mucus-coated tract, food is temporarily stored, mechanically broken up, and chemically broken down. Nutrients are absorbed, water is reabsorbed, and waste is expelled. Assisting in the process are a number of accessory organs, chiefly the tongue, teeth, oral glands, pancreas, liver, and gall bladder.

Within that shared structure, digestive systems vary, depending largely on the organism's diet. Unlike meat, plant cells are enclosed in cellulose cell walls that cannot be digested by the usual enzymes. As a result, the digestive systems of herbivores, animals that eat only plants, have a number of elaborations. These may include gizzards, multichambered stomachs, and ceca or diverticuli—blind pouches opening off the digestive tract where bacteria work to break down the cellulose.

In the Mouth. In many species, such as bats, toads, and woodpeckers, the tongue plays a prominent role in the capture of food. In others, including humans, the tongue manipulates food as it is being crushed by the teeth, mixes it with the secretions of the mouth, helps form it into a mass, and pushes it back to be swallowed.

Oral glands typically secrete mucus and other fluids that lubricate food and allow taste buds to function. In some species, the secretions include venom to tranquillize or kill prey. In mammals, the mix of secretions is called saliva and usually includes an enzyme called amylase or ptyalin, which begins to digest carbohydrates.

In mammals and adult amphibians, the pharynx or throat leads not only to the esophagus but also to the glottis, the opening to the trachea or airway. Reflexes cause the glottis to be blocked during swallowing to prevent choking. Starting in the esophagus, the tube leading to the stomach, food is propelled through the digestive tract by peristalsis, waves of muscle contractions in the gut wall.

To the Stomach. The stomach, which is U- or J-shaped in most animals, is a muscular sac that churns food, breaking it into smaller pieces. In its lining, glands secrete gastric juice, a mixture of enzymes such as pepsin, which digests protein, and hydrochloric acid, which activates the pepsin. In birds, the stomach is composed of a proventriculus, which secretes digestive enzymes, followed by a gizzard, a chamber lined

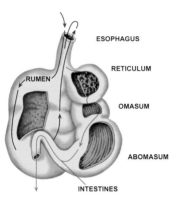

ESOPHAGUS

RETICULUM

RUMEN

OMASUM

ABOMASUM

INTESTINES

The ruminant stomach is perfectly adapted to the ruminant's behavior patterns. Food passes first to the rumen (directly or through the reticulum) and is then returned to the mouth for rechewing (or "rumination"). The food then follows the path indicated by the red arrow into the final digestion system. The system is adapted for animals that graze for long sustained periods, depending on covering a wide area over a long period of time.

Further Reading
Bastian, Glenn F., *An Illustrated Review of the Digestive System* (1994); Bolt, Robert J., *The Digestive System* (1983); Chey, William Y., ed., *Functional Disorders of the Digestive Tract* (1983); Dobson, A. and M., eds., *Aspects of Digestive Physiology in Ruminants* (1988).

with a hard membrane that grinds the food, sometimes using pebbles that have been swallowed.

Specialized Stomachs. The most specialized stomachs are found in cows and other ruminant animals that live on grasses and grains. In a cow's four-chambered stomach, grasses enter the rumen first, where they mix with mucus and cellulase, a cellulose-digesting enzyme secreted by bacteria that live in the organ. After fermenting, they pass into the smaller reticulum, where they are shaped into small bolluses, or cuds. They are regurgitated, chewed again, and swallowed—a sequence that may be repeated several times. Eventually, the pulpy cud passes into the omasum, a holding chamber, and then into the abomasum, where pepsin and hydrochloric acid become active.

After the Stomach. When the stomach, human or otherwise, has finished its work, the food has been transformed into an acidic, soupy mixture called chyme. Its acidity triggers reflexes that relax the pyloric sphincter at the end of the stomach, allowing the chyme to pass into the duodenum, the first section of the intestine. In all vertebrates, the intestine is the site of most digestion and absorption of nutrients. Fish generally have a single, fairly straight intestine. Mammals, birds, and reptiles have large and small intestines, the latter often coiled to increase its absorptive surface area.

Ducts from the pancreas, liver, and gall bladder enter the duodenum, carrying enzymes to digest protein, carbohydrates, fat, and nucleic acid, as well as bile to emulsify fat. In addition, intestinal glands secrete the enzymes sucrase, maltase, isomaltase, and lactase to complete digestion of starches, as well as several peptidases to complete digestion of proteins, and intestinal lipase to help with digestion of fat. Cells called enterocytes secrete large amounts of watery fluid that help the absorption of nutrients into the villi, fingerlike projections that line the small intestine and increase its surface area for absorption.

The large intestine is less likely to be coiled. In humans, it is about five feet long and bends around the coils of the small intestine. In birds and mammals that eat fibrous plants, it often has ceca; in some cases, they may hold more than the large intestine itself. The koala, which eats mostly eucalyptus leaves, has a cecum that can be six feet long. Leaves ferment there as long as a week. Humans have one cecum. Tapering into the appendix, it is located at the juncture of the small and large intestines and has no known role in digestion.

Background material can be found in NUTRITION; DIGESTION; DIGESTION REGULATION. *More details can be found in* DENTISTRY; LIVER; VITAMINS AND MINERALS. *Additional information is contained in* ALLERGY; ECOLOGY; PREDATION. *Many entries on anatomical systems contain material in which animal and human systems are compared.*

First see Reptiles

Dinosaur

Next see Ecology

The dinosaur era lasted for 160 million years. During that time, dinosaurs were the dominant form of animal life on Earth. Since the discovery of their fossils in the early 1800s, they have continued to stimulate our fascination with the planet Earth's ancient history.

The dinosaurs lived during most of the Mesozoic era, popularly referred to as the Age of Reptiles or the Age of Dinosaurs. The Mesozoic is divided into three main periods:

—the **Triassic,** which extended from 240 to 205 million years ago;

—the **Jurassic,** which extended from 205 to 138 million years ago; and

—the **Cretaceous,** which extended from 138 to 65 million years ago.

Dinosaurs first appeared 230 million years ago and occupied all types of habitats. They died out suddenly 65 million years ago, at the end of the Cretaceous period. The cause is believed to have been a major meteor impact that created an immense cloud of dust, altering the climate of the entire planet and causing mass extinctions.

Appearance. Dinosaurs had skin and teeth similar to modern reptiles. Many were bipeds, walking on their hind legs, with hip structures suggestive of birds. Some dinosaurs were herbivores (plant-eaters), and others were carnivores (flesh-eaters) or omnivores (eating both) that probably preyed on other dinosaurs.

Dinosaurs were a type of archosaur. The archosaurs included non-dinosaurs as well, namely crocodilians, such as alligators and crocodiles, and pterosaurs, which were winged reptiles. The pterosaurs had wing membranes, possibly for gliding, but no feathers.

Dinosaurs have popularly been thought of as ectothermic, or cold-blooded, like modern reptiles, unable to regulate their body temperatures. However, there is some evidence that at least some of the dinosaurs were endothermic, warm-blooded, like modern-day birds and mammals.

More than twenty types of dinosaurs may have occupied the same area at the same time. Some lived in herds, whereas others were solitary or traveled in much smaller groups. Dinosaurs may have been brightly colored, much like many reptiles and birds today. Coloration may have been a key to attracting mates.

Dinosaurs used to be thought of as sluggish and relatively stupid creatures, based on their status as ectotherms with very small brain cases, indicating the presence of tiny brains. However, the prevailing opinion is changing, with the new discoveries of dinosaur nests and eggs, which have opened the possibility that dinosaurs engaged in much of the same parenting behavior as is seen in present-day birds.

Fossils of dinosaurs have been found on all continents, suggesting that during the Mesozoic era all of the continents were joined together as one large land mass. The first dinosaur bones were found in 1818, but it wasn't until 1841 that they were assigned their own special group called Dinosauria.

Classification. True dinosaurs are divided into two major categories, based on their hipbone structures. Ornithischians are those whose structures most closely resembled birds; saurischians are those who most closely resembled lizards. The name dinosaur means "terrible lizard," but they were not lizards and not all of them were terrible predators.

Ornithischians were all herbivores and had beaklike bones in front of their lower jaws, as well as bony skin plates. During the Cretaceous period they were the most prominent plant-eaters.

The five types of ornithischians were:
1. stegosaurs, which included the stegosaurus;
2. ankylosaurs, the most heavily armored dinosaurs;
3. ornithopods, one of which, the iguanodon, was the first dinosaur discovered;
4. pachycephalosaurs, or "dome-headed";
5. ceratopsians, which had horns, and included the triceratops.

The most "advanced" dinosaurs were the hadrosaurs, duck-billed dinosaurs, which were types of ornithopods. Many of them had crests on their skulls which recent research indicates could have been used to make a honking noise, perhaps for communication purposes. The saurischians included the largest and fiercest dinosaurs ever to have lived. They were divided into two main groups, the sauropodomorphs and the theropods.

The herbivorous sauropodomorphs were as much as 150 feet in length. One of the best-known dinosaurs, apatosaurus (previously called brontosaurus) belonged to this group.

The theropods were carnivores and walked on two legs. They included the allosaurs, the main meat-eaters of the Jurassic period, which reached between 30 and 40 feet in length, and the ceratosaurs, small active predators that lived at the beginning of the Age of Dinosaurs.

Tyrannosaurus. The tyrannosaurs were theropods that lived during the second half of the Cretaceous period. The largest species was Tyrannosaurus rex (T. rex), perhaps the fiercest known predator. In recent years the image of T. rex has undergone some changes, particularly regarding posture. T. rex is no longer believed to have stood completely upright, dragging its tail along the ground, although it was bipedal. The forearms are much too small to have been used for locomotion, although it is unknown just what precisely their function was. Recently, fossilized bones have been found of another predator that may have been even larger than T. rex, but with a smaller brain.

Deinonychus and velociraptors were smaller carnivores, approximately 6 feet high, and very ferocious. Perhaps the most intelligent carnivore was the troodon, a small biped that lived during the late Cretaceous.

There was a rapid "explosion" of many types of giant carnivore toward the end of the dinosaur age.

Fate of the Dinosaurs. Birds are believed to have evolved from small theropods. The fossil of a creature called archaeopteryx provides strong evidence for this theory, as it closely resembles theropod dinosaurs in terms of its teeth, long tail, presence of abdominal ribs, and three digits on each hand—all of which are features absent in birds. It also has birdlike features, including the presence of a wishbone, an opposable "big toe" for perching, and a distinct impression of feathers around the forelimbs and tail. Recently, the discovery in Liaoning Province in China of a bipedal dinosaur that appears to have had feathers has added further evidence for this theory.

Two theories regarding the evolution of birds are the cursorial and arboreal. The cursorial theory states that small, fast, theropod dinosaurs were "protobirds," runners that flapped their wings to increase speed. An opposing view is the arboreal theory, according to which protobirds evolved from another group of reptiles related to dinosaurs. (*See* BIRDS, EVOLUTION OF.)

The fossil record has provided us with all we know about dinosaurs, but there are still many gaps in our understanding. There is no doubt that dinosaurs will continue to be the objects of much speculation and fascination.

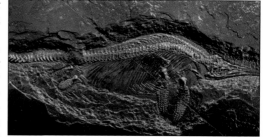

Above, an icthyosaurus fossil shows a mother with five unborn young. The icthyosaur was a precursor of the dinosaurs, becoming extinct 66 million years before dinosaurs roamed the Earth.

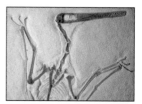

Above, top, fossil of a pterodactylus dinosaur from the late Jurassic era. Above, a paleontologist inspects the fossil remains of albertosaurus, a dinosaur nearly as large as a T. rex, which stalked the late Cretaceous swamps of Canada. At left are models of two dinosaurs. Far left: a dilophosaurus, a forest dweller; and at left, a styracosaurus, the main competitor (and prey) of the albertosaurus.

Background material on the age of dinosaurs can be found in FOSSIL; GEOLOGICAL TIME SCALE; JURASSIC PERIOD. *Advanced subjects are developed in* CAMBRIAN DIVERSIFICATION OF LIFE; EVOLUTION; ICE AGE. *Other aspects of this subject, including questions regarding the fate and progeny of dinosaurs, are covered in* BIRDS, EVOLUTION OF; DINOSAURS, EXTINCTION OF; EXTINCTION.

Further Reading
Fastovsky, David E., et al., *The Evolution and Extinction of the Dinosaurs* (1996); Gould, Stephen Jay, *Bully for Brontosaurus* (1992); Gould, Stephen Jay, *Dinosaur in a Haystack* (1997); Wilford, John Noble, *The Riddle of the Dinaosaurs* (1987).

Sometimes, only dinosaur footprints, like the ones above in Arizona, survive.

Dinosaur bone fossils have been a mainstay at natural history museums for decades.

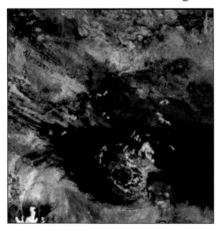

Above, an image of the Roter Kamm impact crater in southwest Namibia, the result of a meteor that collided with Earth some 5 million years ago.

First see EXTINCTION

Dinosaurs, Extinction of

Next see CRETACEOUS-TERTIARY BOUNDARY

Approximately 65 million years ago, more than half of all known species suddenly disappeared, including the dinosaurs. Sediment from the layer of rock at the boundary between the Cretaceous and Tertiary time periods (K-T) contains the element iridium, which is relatively rare on Earth but common in meteorites. Drs. Luis and Walter Alvarez put forth the Impact Theory of Extinction, hypothesizing that a large meteorite (over 6 miles in diameter) struck the planet and kicked up a tremendous cloud of dust which caused major climatic changes. Species that could not adapt to these changes died out. The Impact Theory, first proposed in the late 1970s, has gained acceptance with the recent discovery of an impact crater in Chicxulub, Mexico; the crater is approximately the correct size and age predicted by Alvarez's Theory. Because of this discovery, an asteroid impact is currently the most widely accepted explanation of extinction among scientists.

Another theory for the cause of mass extinctions, proposed at the same time as the Impact Theory, is the massive eruption of the Deccan Traps volcanoes in India. These eruptions caused the release of large amounts of carbon dioxide, causing greenhouse-effect changes to the climate. There is geological evidence of climatic warming at the time of the eruptions.

Other theories have been put forward regarding the extinction of the dinosaurs, including ozone depletion. Volcanic eruptions at the time also released large amounts of gases into the atmosphere which affected the ozone layer, allowing increased amounts of ultraviolet rays to percolate through. Dinosaurs and other reptiles may have been more susceptible to damage than were mammals. Another possibility is that something happened to cause the dinosaurs to produce eggshells of a very inferior quality, too thin-walled to be of much protection to the developing organism within, which consequently died.

Background information on the extinction of the dinosaurs can be found in DINOSAUR; EVOLUTION; EXTINCTION; POPULATION ECOLOGY. *Other aspects of the subject are discussed in* ASTEROIDS AND METEORS *and* OZONE LAYER. *See also* BIRDS, EVOLUTION OF.

First see SEMICONDUCTOR

Diodes and Photodiodes

Next see TRANSISTOR

Diodes and photodiodes are semiconductor products designed to take advantage of the rectifier effect of the p-n junction. The first rectifier was invented by John A. Fleming in 1904, using vacuum-tube technology: a stream of electrons flowed from a hot electrode to a cold one, but could not flow back. Although he named his invention an "oscillation valve," it came to be called a diode. The rectifying effect was duplicated with semiconductor materials by William Shockley, Walter Brattain, and John Bardeen in 1947, when they invented the transistor. All modern diodes and photodiodes are semiconductor-based. (*See* P-N JUNCTION; TRANSISTOR.)

As AC current flows into a diode, it excites electrons on one side of the junction, or boundary between two slightly different semiconductor materials, while it excites "holes" on the other side of the junction; the result is a current, but one which flows in a single direction. Simple diodes of this kind are used in applications as mundane as the alternator in an automobile. In addition, any diode junction will act as a photodetector: light will excite electrons and "holes" in the same way as a current does, creating either a voltage flow or a frequency. Infrared alarm systems are all photodiode-based. (*See* ELECTRIC CIRCUIT.)

This process can also be reversed, resulting in a light-emitting diode (LED). Since a specific material emits coherent light at a single wavelength, an LED can be used to power a laser; joined in series, laser diodes can create enormous power, which can be delivered through fiber-optics to a precise site for applications ranging from microsurgery to welding. Laser diodes are also used in communications, robotics, and spectroscopy. (*See* CRYSTAL.)

First see POISON AND TOXICOLOGY

Dioxins

Next see MUTAGEN AND CARCINOGEN

Dioxin is one of the most toxic of all synthetic substances. Technically, a dioxin is any molecule constructed with two benzene rings linked by two oxygen atoms; there are 75 possible isomers, depending on which ions—typically chlorine—attach to this structure and at which points. The most toxic is called 2,3,7,8-TCDD. Dioxin is chemically stable, insoluble in water, but soluble in oils; thus rainwater will tend not to dilute or break it down, but it is easily absorbed into the fatty tissues of animals. It is fatal to some species of mammals at levels of five parts per trillion. (*See* WATER POLLUTION.)

Sources. Dioxin occurs as an unintended byproduct in the manufacture of herbicides and the antibacterial formula hexachlorophene, and even occurs in waste oils. The spraying of waste oil in Missouri in 1971 led to hundreds of animal deaths, numerous illnesses, and ultimately the evacuation of several communities. Spraying of Agent Orange, a defoliant, during the Vietnam War led to a class-action suit containing some 250,000 members, which was eventually settled for $180 million. (*See* CANCER.)

Experience with short-term dioxin exposure since the Vietnam War, in the form of workers accidentally exposed to the compound, has shown surprisingly few adverse effects beyond severe acne formation. Dioxin in humans appears to bind to a receptor protein, which limits accumulation of the dioxin in cell nuclei and thus in turn limits genetic damage. Nevertheless, long-term exposure to dioxin remains extremely dangerous; a 1991 report revealed that workers exposed to the substance over long periods suffered significant increases in cancer rates.

First see DISEASES, INFECTIOUS

Disease, Theory of

Next see DISEASES, NONINFECTIOUS

Disease refers to a breakdown in the normal functioning of the body systems. Over time many theories have been advanced as to the cause of these malfunctions and different attempts have been made at treatment. During the Middle Ages, a common belief was that the body contained four "humors," linked to the four major bodily fluids as well as to the four elements of earth, fire, water, and air. Disease was thought to be caused by an imbalance of these humors. Cures were aimed at restoring this balance, as well as driving out the malign influences that were responsible for the disease. Medical science has fortunately advanced beyond this and other primitive stages of diagnosis and treatment. We now know that most diseases are caused by microorganisms such as bacteria, fungi, viruses, protozoa, worms, and other parasites. Disease can also occur when the body begins attacking its own tissues.

Circumstances often blamed for illness, such as going outside with wet hair, or being under stress, do not by themselves cause a person to get sick. However, they can help lower the body's resistance to disease and make it easier to pick up an opportunistic infection.

The word "germ" can refer to any of the infectious agents mentioned above. The term "microbe" can refer to any microscopic organism. However, it is important to note that the terms bacteria and virus are not interchangeable but refer specifically to distinct types of organisms. Viruses are non-cellular, which makes them different from all other living things.

Analysis. A disease actually consists of two parts: the damage inflicted by the infectious agent and the body's response to it. The skin is the body's first line of defense against infection. As long as the skin remains unbroken, it is a solid barrier that is impenetrable. The regular body openings—the eyes, ears, nostrils, mouth, urethra, anus, and vagina—are lined with mucus or other fluids, such as wax or tears, to wash away or trap any particles that enter. However, if a break occurs in the skin, resulting in a cut or a sore, invaders can easily enter the bloodstream and from there travel anywhere in the body.

Responses. The body reacts to infection with nonspecific responses such as inflammation, fever, and an increased white-cell count. Blood vessels in the infected region dilate and the capillary walls become more permeable, resulting in more fluid entering body tissues. The entire area exhibits redness and swelling. Congestion is caused by the accumulation of fluid in body tissues. In addition, mucus production is increased to "wash away" infectious agents.

A fever is defined as an elevated body temperature. The body does this to put any invading bacteria or viruses at a metabolic disadvantage. Therefore, it is not essential and may even be counterproductive to force the body temperature down prematurely, unless it is dangerously high.

White blood cells are designed to consume invading germs and bacteria. When an infection is present, the number of white cells circulating in the bloodstream sharply increases. Depending on the specific type of white cell, some of these cells are able to consume between 20 and 100 bacteria during their lifespan.

Bacterial. Diseases caused by bacteria include tuberculosis, typhus, diphtheria, tetanus, and streptococcal infections. Prior to the development of antibiotics, these were serious diseases that were often fatal. However, they can still lead to complications or death even now if left untreated. In addition, the emergence of drug-resistant strains of bacteria has led to fears that these diseases may regain their once-deadly status.

Viral. Diseases caused by viruses include chicken pox, poliomyelitis, measles, hepatitis, and the common cold. Many viral diseases can be prevented entirely with inoculations. Vaccines stimulate the body's own immune system into developing antibodies to fight the disease. Once exposed, the immune system is primed and ready to fight the attackers. "Memory cells" remain in the event the infectious agent makes another appearance.

Due to an aggressive program of inoculation, smallpox has been completely eradicated as a disease. Polio is under control in the Western Hemisphere, with a very small number of cases reported each year. There is, however, still no cure or prevention for the common cold.

Other Sources. Fungal diseases include athlete's foot and ringworm. Diseases caused by parasitic worms include trichinosis, hookworm, and tapeworm.

Spread of Disease. Diseases are spread in different ways. Many germs are hardy enough to be airborne and can be spread through droplets released by sneezing or coughing, or by other casual contact. Proper hygiene is essential to limit their spread. Hand washing is particularly important. Other diseases are transmitted only through bodily fluids such as blood, semen, vaginal secretions, and breast milk.

Some methods of transmission involve insects as an intermediary host for the infection. Malaria is carried by the female Anopheles mosquito. The disease is actually caused by a protozoan; the mosquito simply serves as the source of transmission. Yellow fever is carried by another type of mosquito, the Aedes.

Bubonic plague is caused by a bacterium carried by fleas. Flea bites transmit the disease to other animals as well as humans. Rats historically provided a host for infected fleas. During the Middle Ages, approximately one-third of the European population died of this plague.

Typhus is carried by body lice. The actual infectious agent is a rickettsia, an organism that is larger than a virus but smaller than a bacterium. African sleeping sickness is carried by the tsetse fly, but the organism causing the disease is a protozoan. Lyme disease, first seen in large numbers in the town of Lyme, Connecticut, is caused by a bacterium carried by deer ticks.

Types of Diseases. Sexually transmitted diseases, also called venereal disease, are spread through sexual intercourse. This disease category includes syphilis, gonorrhea, herpes, and chlamydia. Some of these are bacterial, whereas others are viral. If left untreated, they can lead to severe complications or even death. A pregnant woman can pass the disease on to her fetus, resulting in physical or mental defects or even a miscarriage or stillbirth.

Autoimmune diseases affect the immune system functions. In some cases, the immune system begins to attack normal body tissue, somehow mistaking it for an infectious agent. In other diseases, most notably AIDS, the immune system itself is attacked and weakened, leaving the body defenseless against infection.

Treatment. Depending upon the cause of a particular disease, treatment can vary. Antibiotics are aimed at disrupting the metabolic activities of bacteria. They are, however, not effective against viral diseases. Overuse of antibiotics in our society has lead to the development of resistant strains of bacteria.

Many treatments are not designed to cure a particular condition, but to alleviate the symptoms and make the patient more comfortable while the immune system battles the infection.

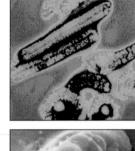

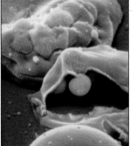

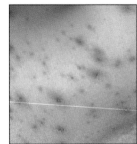

Many forms of disease confront all living beings. Above, three main varieties (from top): the bacterium that causes Legionnaire's Disease; the malaria protozon inside a red blood cell it has ravaged; and the scabs of chicken pox, caused by a virus. Of the three, the virus has (for the time being) proven the most stubborn and resistant to pharmacological remedies.

Heart disease, cancer, and genetically inherited conditions are not caused by germs. In the case of heart disease and cancer, diet and exercise can help somewhat in terms of prevention and treatment. Scientists are attempting now to treat genetic diseases by replacing faulty genes. The difficulty lies in getting the new genes to the proper place and, once there, getting them to function properly. There has been very limited success in this type of treatment so far.

Not all diseases can be cured completely. Treatment in these cases is aimed at controlling the disease, enabling the patient to live as normal a life as possible, albeit with a chronic condition. Diabetes is an example of a "maintainable" disease. Use of insulin and careful monitoring of blood sugar levels enable patients to lead a normal life. Recent advances with protease inhibitors have given researchers hope that AIDS can be moved to this category as well.

Background material on disease can be found in BACTERIA; DISEASES, INFECTIOUS; DISEASES, NONINFECTIOUS. *Advanced subjects relating to disease are developed in* COMMON COLD; IMMUNE RESPONSE; PHAMACOLOGY. *More information on particular aspects of disease is contained in:* ALLERGY; CANCER; VIRAL DISEASES, EXOTIC.

First see DISEASE, THEORY OF

Diseases, Infectious

Next see DISEASE, NONINFECTIOUS

Infectious diseases are illnesses that are caused by microorganisms. The most important of these organisms are the bacteria, viruses, and fungi; others are the rickettsiae, chlamydiae, and mycoplasmas. Some infectious diseases are caused by more complex organisms, such as protozoa, worms, and flukes. In the past century, most infectious diseases have become much less of a medical problem in developed countries, such as the United States, because of a number of developments. One of them is improved living conditions, such as better sanitation, cleaner water supples, better housing, pest control, and quarantine conditions. Another is the development of effective drugs for treating infections, such as antibiotics. In addition, vaccines now are commonly used to prevent a number of diseases, such as poliomyelitis, measles, mumps, rubella, diphtheria, and typhoid fever, to mention some of the most common. Better overall health, including better nutrition, is another important preventive development.

The AIDS Crisis. Nevertheless, some infectious diseases present a continuing hazard. Probably the best-known of these is acquired immune deficiency syndrome, AIDS, caused by the human immunodeficiency virus, HIV, which made its appearance in the U.S. in the 1980s. HIV is most often spread by sexual contact or use of contaminated needles. In less developed countries, poor living conditions and lack of substantial medical services are among the factors that make infectious diseases a continuing threat.

Today, AIDS heads the list of important infectious diseases in developed countries. Its symptoms include fever, severe weight loss, diarrhea, fatigue, and swollen lymph glands. There are now several drugs that can prolong the lives of persons infected with HIV, but no cure for AIDS is in sight.

Different infectious diseases cause a variety of symptoms. These result from the damage that the infectious microorganisms cause to the cells and tissues of the body and by the efforts of the body's defenses, most notably the immune system, to fight the infectious agent. Fever is one of the most common symptoms of an infection. Others include a skin rash, diarrhea, or a cough. The diagnosis of an infectious disease depends partly on the symptoms that it causes and also on identification of the infectious microorganism. Tests to determine the causative agent include growing it in a laboratory culture, examining a sample of blood or body tissue under a microscope, and laboratory tests to detect antibodies—proteins that the immune system produces to defend against specific bacteria, viruses, or other infection-causing agents.

Incubation. One problem in the medical treatment of infectious diseases is that there is always a gap in time, called the incubation period, that occurs after the infectious agents enter the body and the first symptoms of the disease appear. The incubation period for some diseases is only a few hours, but for others it can be days, weeks, or even years. During this period, the infected person can pass the disease-causing microorganism to other people, who in turn can transmit it to even more. Because of this, an epidemic can become established before medical authorities are aware of the spread of the disease. This was the case with AIDS, which can have a very long incubation period.

At the other extreme of severity from AIDS is the common cold, which is caused by a number of different viruses, including rhinoviruses and coronaviruses. These viruses are spread by airborne droplets spread when someone coughs or sneezes. The symptoms of the common cold include chills, sneezing, coughing, runny nose, and muscle aches. Treated or untreated, the cold runs its course in a few days.

A more deadly infectious disease that causes many of the same symptoms is influenza. It, too, is caused by several kinds of virus, which are classified into three broad groups and usually spread by the same kind of airborne droplets that carry the cold viruses. The incubation period for influenza is one to three days.

Prevention and Vaccination. One disease that was a major worry in previous years but has been vanquished in developed countries by the widespread use of vaccines is poliomyelitis—infantile paralysis, as it once was called. In its mildest form, polio causes only a sore throat, headache, and vomiting, but its most severe form results in paralysis. There is still no effective treatment for poliomyelitis; prevention is the first line of defense. The same is true of rabies, caused by a virus transmitted by the bite of an infected animal; an effective vaccine prevents infection by this disease.

Background material on infectious diseases can be found in BACTERIA; BLOOD; DISEASES, NONINFECTIOUS; DISEASES, THEORY OF. *Advanced subjects regarding defense and treatment are developed in* ANTIBIOTICS; GAMMA GLOBULIN; IMMUNE RESPONSE. *Additional relevant information is contained in* AIDS; COMMON COLD; INFLUENZA.

First see DISEASE, THEORY OF

Diseases, Noninfectious

Next see GENETIC DISEASES

Until the middle decades of this century, medical attention in the United States and other developed countries was focused primarily on diseases caused by infectious agents, bacteria, and viruses. Today, most of these diseases (with the notable exception of AIDS, acquired immune deficiency syndrome) have been conquered through the development of vaccines, antibiotics, and antiviral drugs; attention has turned to diseases of noninfectious causation—heart disease, stroke, cancer, diabetes, arthritis, and the like.

Heart Disease. Heart disease leads the list, since it is the leading cause of death in developed nations, such as the United States. There are infectious diseases of the heart, such as myocarditis, but these are overshadowed by atherosclerosis, a narrowing of the heart arteries due to deposits of fatty material, which can lead to angina pectoris—pain in the chest and arms due to an insufficient supply of oxygen for the heart muscle—or myocardial infarction, commonly called a heart attack, in which part of the heart muscle dies because of lack of oxygen. Another noninfectious disease of the heart is cardiomyopathy, in which blood circulation is slowed because the blood-propelling force of heart contractions is reduced as a result of weakness of the heart muscle. There are a variety of other noninfectious heart conditions, including arrythmia, an abnormal heartbeat; cor pulmonale, a failure of the right side of the heart; and heart failure, in which the heart does not pump enough blood to meet the body's needs.

Closely related to these heart conditions are diseases of the blood vessels. The most damaging of these is stroke, in which brain damage is caused by an interruption of its blood supply or leakage of blood from the arteries or veins. A stroke is fatal in about one-third of cases. In the

Further Reading
Biddle, Wayne, *A Field Guide to Germs* (1996); Garrett, Laurie, *The Coming Plague* (1995); Kendall, Marion D., *Dying to Live: How Our Bodies Fight Disease* (1998); Knutson, Roger, *Fearsome Fauna* (1999); Olshaker, Mark, *Virus Hunter* (1998); Preston, Richard, *The Hot Zone* (1995).

other cases, damage to a specific part of the brain causes a loss of function in the part of the body controlled by that brain segment. There can be a loss of bodily sensation, movement, or other function, such as speech and language ability, a condition called aphasia. (*See* BLOOD.)

Cancer. The second most common cause of death in the United States and other developed countries, cancer is also a noninfectious disease. There are suspicions that some cases of cancer can be caused by viruses, but those conjectures remain unproven. Cancer begins when the normal genes, called oncogenes, which control the growth and multiplication of cells, are transformed by agents called carcinogens. Radiation is one carcinogen, as are many chemicals. Other carcinogens include tobacco smoke, alcohol, and some natural constituents of food. When cells are transformed by a carcinogen, they begin to divide and grow without the normal mechanisms that keep their growth under control. These cancerous cells generally lose their ability to perform their specialized functions, becoming nothing more than parasites. The original cancerous growth may send out colonies, called metastases, that begin to grow in other parts of the body. Early detection of cancer is essential for treatment, including drug therapy and surgery, that can lead to a cure.

Diabetes. Another major noninfectious disease is diabetes mellitus, in which the pancreas stops producing enough insulin, the hormone that is needed for cells to absorb the sugar glucose that supplies their energy needs. There are two forms of diabetes. The most severe form is Type 1, or insulin-dependent diabetes, in which insulin production stops totally. It often develops early, by the age of fifteen or sixteen. A person with insulin-dependent diabetes requires regular injections of insulin to maintain life. Type 2, or noninsulin-dependent diabetes, usually occurs gradually after the age of forty and results in the production of insufficient amounts of insulin. Type 2 diabetes often can be treated with a combination of weight reduction, dietary measures, and oral medicines.

Arthritis. Another major noninfectious disease is arthritis, which occurs in several forms. In each form, there is joint inflammation that results in pain, swelling, stiffness, redness, and often joint damage. The most common form is osteoarthritis, which generally occurs in middle age and is caused by wear and tear on one or more joints. A more severe form is rheumatoid arthritis, an autoimmune disorder in which the body's immune defense system mistakenly attacks the joints, causing severe pain, inflammation, stiffness, and deformity. These and other forms of noninfectious arthritis can be treated with anti-inflammatory drugs and other medications. In severe cases, surgery to replace or repair damaged joints may be necessary.

Allergy. Another noninfectious condition that affects millions of people is allergy. It occurs when the immune system mistakenly reacts against a harmless substance, such as pollen. The list of noninfectious diseases is a long one, but those listed above are among the major problems that concern modern medicine.

> *Related areas are discussed in* DISEASE, THEORY OF; DNA; GENETIC ENGINEERING. *Advanced subjects are developed in* CANCER; MUTAGENS AND CARCINOGENS; SEX LINKAGES. *Additional relevant information is contained in* AGING; GENE THERAPY; STRESS.

First see CHROMATOGRAPHY

Distillation

Next see ALCOHOL

The process of separating a mixture of substances from one another by taking advantage of their different boiling points.

The substances involved in distillation can be all liquids or a combination of liquids and solids. There are three main types of distillation: simple, fractional, and vacuum.

Simple distillation allows the separation of a pure liquid from nonvolatile substances. As a desired liquid boils, its vapors are caught in a condensation chamber where it reverts to a liquid state; the remaining substances are left behind. Simple distillation can also be used for a mixture of volatile liquids whose boiling points differ by more than 20 to 30 degrees Celsius.

Fractional distillation is used for mixtures of liquids whose boiling points are too close to be separated by ordinary simple distillation. Fractional distillation adds packing material in the column through which the vapors rise. The packing in the column consists of an inert material with a large surface area, such as glass beads, metal or ceramic pieces, or a mesh. The role of the packing material is to "trap" the rising vapors, allowing them to condense and then fall back into the distillation chamber. Uncondensed vapor rises higher and higher in the column and undergoes a repeated series of condensations and revaporizations, equivalent to performing a number of simple distillations within the column. The vapor produced contains an increasingly higher percentage of the more volatile component, while the condensate has a greater percentage of the less volatile component. It is important to maintain a temperature gradient along the column in order for this to occur most efficiently. The temper-

The basics of the distillation process have remained unchanged for centuries (above, a medieval document explains the process), and the distiller's art has been valued in virtually every society. Below, the copper pot still of the Glenlivet Distillery, makers of outstanding Scotch whisky.

ature must be greatest at the bottom of the column, equal to the boiling temperature of the mixture, and lowest at the top of column, equal to the boiling temperature of the more volatile liquid.

Vacuum distillation is used to carry out distillations at less than atmospheric pressure. The lower the pressure, the lower the boiling point of a material will be. This becomes important in the case of compounds of high molecular weight which may decompose, oxidize, or undergo molecular rearrangement before reaching their actual boiling temperatures. Atmospheric pressure is measured at 760 torr. At a pressure of 25 torr, the boiling point of something that would normally be 250 to 300 degrees Celsius is lowered by 100 to 125 degrees Celsius. Below 25 torr, the boiling point is lowered by ten degrees Celsius each time the pressure is cut in half.

In vacuum distillation, the volume of vapor formed is dependent on the pressure; also serious bumping, splashing, and splattering of the mixture can occur. It is important to maintain a slow and steady rate of distillation and avoid "superheating" the mixture. Often fractional and vacuum distillation apparatus are set up with multiple receiving chambers for the different vapors.

Finally, steam distillation is used to remove insoluble volatile liquids or solid organic compounds from nonvolatile compounds. This technique is not applicable to substances that react with water or decompose on prolonged contact with steam or hot water.

First see GENETICS

DNA

Next see DNA REPLICATION

Deoxyribonucleic acid (DNA) is the chemical of life, the stuff that genes are made of. Genes are the units of heredity that determine the characteristics of an organism. Each gene contains information for a particular protein. Different chemical reactions take place within the cell, based upon which proteins are being produced at any given time. It is these chemical reactions which affect our characteristics beyond the molecular level.

DNA is a universal molecule, found in every organism, whether it is a microbe, plant, or animal. Its chemical content is remarkably consistent; the major difference between the genome of one species and another is in the number of genes. Even viruses, which are not made up of cells, contain either DNA or its chemical "cousin" ribonucleic acid (RNA) as their genetic material. (*See* RNA.)

Structure. DNA is a nucleic acid, the most complex of major biological compounds. The basic unit of a nucleic acid is the nucleoside which in turn consists of a sugar molecule, either ribose or deoxyribose, and one of five nucleic bases: adenine, guanine, cytosine, thymine, and uracil. Adenine and guanine are both types of purines, which are double-ringed structures. Cytosine, thymine, and uracil are all types of pyrimidines, which are single-ringed structures.

Nucleosides that also have a phosphate group (PO_4) attached to the sugar molecule are called nucleotides. Individual nucleotides, those not incorporated into a polynucleotide chain, have three adjacent phosphate groups linked to the sugar.

To incorporate a new nucleotide into the growing chain, the "incoming" nucleotide drops its outer two phosphate groups and forms a bond between its remaining PO_4 and the sugar molecule of the nucleotide preceding it in the chain. The polynucleotide chain itself consists of alternating sugar and phosphate groups forming a "backbone" with the bases protruding off the sugar molecules.

DNA consists of two such polynucleotide chains running "antiparallel," or in opposite directions. The famous "double helix" configuration of DNA is actually a twisted version of the "ladder" formed by the two chains, with the "sides" of the ladder formed by the alternating sugars and phosphates. The "rungs" consist of pairs of bases, known as Watson-Crick base pairs after their discoverers, James Watson and Francis Crick.

In Watson-Crick base pairs, a purine is always found together with a pyrimidine, in order to guarantee a uniform width throughout the DNA double helix. The pairs are held together with hydrogen bonds, relatively weak forms of intermolecular bonding, in order to facilitate the "unzipping" of the DNA so that it can perform its functions. Adenine is paired either with thymine (in DNA) or uracil (in RNA) by means of two hydrogen bonds. The guanine-cytosine pair is held together by three hydrogen bonds.

DNA and RNA. In terms of structure, there are three major differences between DNA and RNA:

1. DNA is found as a duplex. RNA is primarily a single strand, although it can form a duplex by base-pairing along its own length, with another RNA strand or with a single DNA strand.
2. DNA contains deoxyribose as its sugar and RNA contains ribose.
3. DNA contains thymine and RNA contains uracil. Thymine and uracil are chemically identical, but thymine has an additional methyl group (CH_3) attached to its ring.

The majority of DNA molecules are "right-handed," meaning the turns of the double helix run clockwise. Each base pair is rotated approximately 36 degrees around the axis of the helix and therefore every 10 base pairs represent a full

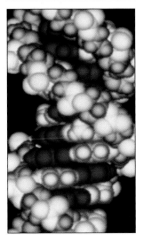

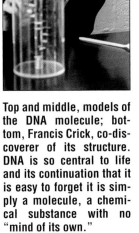

Top and middle, models of the DNA molecule; bottom, Francis Crick, co-discoverer of its structure. DNA is so central to life and its continuation that it is easy to forget it is simply a molecule, a chemical substance with no "mind of its own."

turn of the structure. The duplex structure is not immutable; the two strands separate temporarily in order for the DNA to be replicated or to allow gene expression to occur.

An individual chromosome consists of a very long molecule of DNA, wrapped up in an equal mass of proteins. Unless the cell is actively preparing to divide, the chromosomes are not seen as distinct units, but rather a tangled mass called chromatin. Within the chromatin, most DNA sequences are inaccessible and inactive. The basic unit of chromatin is the nucleosome, which consists of approximately 200 base pairs of DNA wrapped around specific proteins known as histones. Nucleosomes are in turn organized into fibers which are 30 nanometers in diameter. The DNA exhibits "supercoiling" and other forms of folding and packing in order to "fit" the chromosome structure.

Prior to cell division, all of the DNA in the nucleus must be replicated in order to ensure that each resulting "daughter cell" contains a complete set of DNA. The "parent" DNA molecule gives rise to two identical daughter molecules.

Replication. DNA replication is semiconservative; each daughter molecule contains one strand of the original parent molecule and one completely "new" strand. Three enzymes "mastermind" the process. The DNA double helix unwinds due to the action of DNA polymerase I. DNA polymerase III then pairs nucleotides against the parental strands at the newly formed replication fork to form two daughter duplexes. This is followed by ligase linking the adjacent nucleotides, sugar to phosphate, to form the "backbone" of the DNA molecules. Ligase also removes any incorrectly paired bases.

A gene is found along one or the other strand of the DNA duplex, and begins with a specific sequence known as the promoter region and ends with the terminator region. A structural gene contains information for the amino acid sequence of a protein. This information is "transcribed" to form a molecule of messenger RNA (mRNA) which is in turn "translated" to form a protein. The product of a regulatory gene controls the expression of structural genes, either allowing transcription to take place or else blocking it.

Exons and introns are segments found within genes. Exons are the segments which correspond to the "useful" part, whereas introns are non-coding segments interrupting the main body of a gene. Introns are "spliced out" of the sequence during post-transcription modification and are no longer present when the mRNA is translated to form the actual protein. It is unknown why introns exist at all, or why they are only present within eukaryotic DNA and not prokaryotic (bacteria and blue-green algae). A current theory proposes that perhaps introns are vestigial remnants of our evolutionary past.

DNA Fingerprinting. DNA fingerprinting is a method of determining whether a biological sample, such as a piece of flesh or a drop of blood, comes from a given individual. To perform DNA fingerprinting, DNA is first taken from an evidence sample and from the blood of a suspect. The DNA samples are then chopped into millions of pieces. This is done by using restriction enzymes, a molecule that cuts the DNA molecule at places where a known sequence of the sub-units of DNA occur. These fragments are then separated by the technique called gel electrophoresis, which is based on the different sizes and electric charges of the fragments. Each sample is loaded at the top of a lane of a special gel and is subjected to an electric field that causes DNA fragments to migrate at different speeds. At the end of the process, the DNA fragments in each lane are transferred to a special membrane and fixed in place so that they can be analyzed. (*See* ELETROPHORESIS.)

The analysis is done by using a radioactive probe that contains a short sequence of DNA. This radioactive probe is washed over the membrane, and it binds to DNA fragments whose composition matches it. The membrane is then exposed to x-ray film overnight to see the locations where the radioactive probe has bound. These locations are marked by dark horizontal bands on the film, which is called an electroradiogram. The bands constitute the DNA pattern for the locus that is being examined. For each locus, the investigator compares whether the DNA patterns of the sample—the exact number and positions of the bands—match those of the white cells in the blood of the suspect. (Red blood cells cannot be used because they do not carry DNA.)

If the patterns do not match, it is clear that they must come from different sources. But if the patterns do match at every locus, they may have come from the same source—although there is a possibility that they came from different people who happen to have the same patterns at these loci. If matches are found at a number of loci, the chances that the sample came from the suspect is increased. The number of loci that are necessary to establish a match depends on the degree of variability at each locus. To maximize

DNA fingerprinting was discovered quite by accident by University of Leicester (England) geneticist Alec J. Jeffreys in 1984. The basic theory is that the process of electrophoresis can yield a sequence of stains that are uniquely determined by the genetic makeup of the sample tested. The great care that needs to be applied and the complicated nature of the process has made the use of the technique difficult to apply in courts of law. Several cases, however, have made headlines in which DNA fingerprinting was decisive: the technique was used to verify the death of Nazi war criminal Josef Mengele and to discredit the claims of several women who claimed to be the daughter of Tsar Nicholas.

In the diagram below, the full display of a donor's DNA at left shares lines with another set at right, making it possible that the two are related.

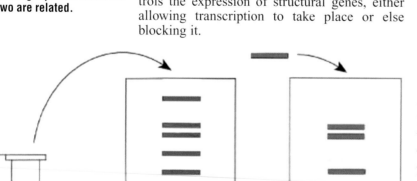

the matching ability of DNA fingerprinting, forensic analysts work with segments of DNA called variable number of tandem repeat (VNTR) loci, which tend to be highly individualized.

DNA fingerprinting was first admitted as evidence in a court in 1988, in a Florida trial. The following year, the Federal Bureau of Investigation began to use the technology in its own laboratories, and to do DNA fingerprinting for state police departments. While the technique has become widely accepted, there still is the possibility of error because of the damage that a tissue sample from which DNA is extracted may have experienced before it was analyzed. (*See* FORENSIC SCIENCE.)

DNA Hybridization. DNA hybridization is a procedure in which two single strands of DNA, the genetic molecule, are made to meet and match up. The technique allows researchers to look for genes that are present in different organisms but have an evolutionary relationship to each other, even if that relationship is distant. The first step is to break apart the two strands of a DNA molecule into two single strands. This is done chemically or by heat. The two strands are remarkably specific. When they are mixed with a large number of DNA molecules, only a few of which may be related to them, the strands will eventually come into contact with, and bond to, a complementary segment of DNA, thus recreating the double helix of a normal DNA molecule.

When such a hybridization experiment is being performed, the conditions can be altered so that the chances of finding a match can be made more or less probable. Under the more stringent conditions, the DNA molecule will match only with a strand that matches it exactly, while under less stringent conditions the molecule will match with a strand that may be somewhat different from it.

For example, under stringent conditions a bit of human DNA will match only with a sample of human DNA, but if the stringency is reduced it can match with a sample of monkey DNA. If conditions are eased even more, human DNA can match with DNA from a bird or a reptile. The amount of matching under different conditions thus shows the genetic relationship of various organisms.

Special topics in this area are found in CELL CYCLE; RNA; GENETICS. *Advanced subjects are developed in* DNA SEQUENCING; EXTRANUCLEAR INHERITANCE; PROTEIN SYNTHESIS. *More complex aspects of this subject are covered in* POLYMERASE CHAIN REACTION (PCR) *and* VIRAL GENETICS. *See also* CENTRIFUGATION; CHROMATOGRAPHY; ELECTROPHORESIS; SPECTROSCOPY.

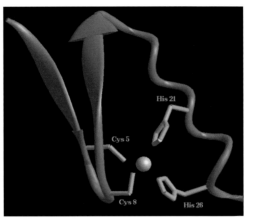

The helical three-dimensional shape of DNA provides a tricky binding surface for other proteins to adhere to. Researchers have shown that approximately 80% of the DNA binding domains fall into three classes: the helix-turn-helix (HTH), zinc-finger (above), and the leucine zipper.

Further Reading
Crick, Francis R.C., *What Mad Pursuit* (1988); de Duve, Christian, *A Guided Tour of the Living Cell* (1987); Judson, Horace F., *The Eighth Day of Creation* (1979); Pollack, Robert, *Signs of Life* (1994); Watson, James D., et al., *Molecular Biology of the Gene* (1987); Watson, James D., *The Double Helix* (1968).

First see DNA

DNA Replication

Next see DNA SEQUENCING

The genetic material of a cell is made up of DNA. This remarkable chemical is actually one long molecule, consisting of smaller units called nucleotides. Each nucleotide is made up of a sugar molecule called deoxyribose, a phosphate group (PO_4), and one of four nucleic bases: adenine (A), guanine (G), cytosine (C) and thymine (T). Unattached nucleotides have three adjacent phosphate groups linked to the sugar.

To incorporate a new nucleotide into a chain, the "incoming" nucleotide drops its outer two phosphate groups and forms a bond between its remaining PO_4 and the sugar molecule of the nucleotide preceding it in the chain. The polynucleotide chain itself consists of alternating sugar and phosphate groups, which form a "backbone" with the bases protruding off of the sugar molecules.

The Double Helix. DNA consists of two such polynucleotide chains running "anti-parallel," or in opposite directions: the famous "double helix" shape of DNA, actually a twisted version of the "ladder" formed by the two chains, with the "sides" of the ladder formed by the alternating sugars and phosphates; and the "rungs," consisting of pairs of bases, known as Watson-Crick base pairs after their discoverers, James Watson and Francis Crick. Adenine always pairs with thymine, and guanine with cytosine. The pairs are held together with hydrogen bonds, relatively weak forms of intermolecular bonding, in order to facilitate the "unzipping" of the DNA in order to replicate itself or to perform its functions. There are two hydrogen bonds between each A-T pair and three between each G-C pair.

Prior to cell division, all of the DNA in the nucleus must be replicated in order to ensure that each resulting "daughter cell" contains a complete set of DNA. The "parent" DNA molecule gives rise to two identical daughter molecules.

DNA replication is semiconservative; each daughter molecule contains one strand of the original parent molecule and one completely "new" strand. Three enzymes "mastermind" the process. The DNA double helix unwinds due to the action of DNA polymerase I. DNA polymerase III then pairs nucleotides against the parental strands at the newly formed replication fork to form two daughter duplexes. This is followed by ligase linking the adjacent nucleotides, sugar to phosphate, to form the "backbone" of the DNA molecules. Ligase also removes any incorrectly paired bases.

In the early days of DNA study, it was unclear how the parental strands were incorporated into the new daughter molecules. Three

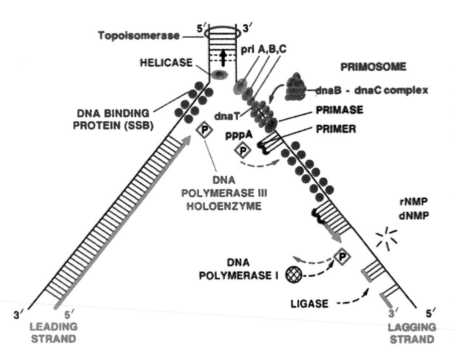

Topoisomerase
HELICASE
pri A,B,C
PRIMOSOME
DNA BINDING PROTEIN (SSB)
dnaB - dnaC complex
PRIMASE
dnaT
PRIMER
pppA
DNA POLYMERASE III HOLOENZYME
rNMP
dNMP
DNA POLYMERASE I
LIGASE
LEADING STRAND
LAGGING STRAND

DNA replication—a schematic representation. The older notion that the DNA strand unzips and is matched in a linear fashion turned to be an oversimplification. Replication takes place in several locations and even there the process seems to be operating on several base pairs at once. How the molecule keeps track of the "bookkeeping" so perfectly is the subject of ongoing research.

theories on replication were advanced: totally conservative, in which one daughter molecule consists of both parental strands, and the other of two new strands; semiconservative, as described above; and unconserved, in which the two strands of each daughter molecule contain some parental material and some new, in a random distribution.

A Confirming Experiment. An experiment was performed by scientists Meselson and Stahl to determine which of the scenarios was correct. The cells bearing the DNA were grown in a medium containing a "heavy" isotope of nitrogen, N_{15}, which would be incorporated into the DNA molecules. Spinning in a centrifuge (which separates materials according to their respective densities) produced only one band of DNA. After one generation the DNA was replicated in a lighter density medium. A single band of DNA was once again produced by centrifuging—but this band was of a lighter density than the previous generation, confirming the presence of daughter molecules made up of one heavy strand and one light.

After a second generation, two bands of DNA were produced after centrifuging, one of the hybrid density and one of light. This confirmed the presence of two daughter molecules that were hybrids of light and heavy, and two others that only contained light.

Special topics in this area are found in CELL CYCLE; DNA; GENETICS. *Advanced subjects are developed in* DNA SEQUENCING; EXTRANUCLEAR INHERITANCE; PROTEIN SYNTHESIS. *Elementary aspects of this subject are covered in* POLYMERASE CHAIN REACTION (PCR); VIRAL GENETICS.

First see GENE

DNA Sequencing

Next see DNA

Genes are segments of DNA that contain information for constructing a particular protein. DNA itself is a long chain of nucleotides, each of which consists of a sugar molecule, a phosphate group (PO_4), and one of four bases: adenine (A), guanine (G), thymine (T), and cytosine (C). Sequencing DNA involves deciphering the pattern of the bases that appear in the DNA molecule. Mapping a chromosome refers to identifying the location of the various genes along its length. The most detailed physical map is the complete sequence of the DNA composing it.

Structural genes contain information for making proteins, whereas regulator genes control the expression of the structural genes. However, not all of the DNA corresponds to specific genes in eukaryotic cells (a set excluding bacteria and blue-green algae). Exons are the segments that correspond to the "useful" part, whereas introns are non-translated segments interrupting the main body of a gene. To produce a protein, a copy of the DNA information is made in the form of RNA that is the actual molecule used. Both exons and introns are faithfully copied over and included in the RNA sequence, although the introns are "spliced out" of the sequence during a later step of protein synthesis. It is unknown why introns exist. (*See* EXONS.)

Base Reactions. In sequencing, the DNA molecule is treated with four separate reactions, each of which is specific for a particular base. The DNA is broken down into several small fragments, each of which terminates at a position corresponding to a specific base. Gel electrophoresis is used to separate the fragments. They are deposited on a gel submerged in a salt solution capable of conducting electricity. The DNA has a negative charge due to its phosphate groups. An electric current is passed through the gel, causing the segments to move towards the positively charged end. Large fragments move more slowly than small ones. Over time, the fragments will have moved far enough apart that they can be easily distinguished from each other. (*See* ELECTROPHORESIS.)

Either chemical or enzymatic methods can be used for sequencing. In each case, several DNA fragments are produced which are identical at one labeled end, but differ in length by single bases. Four series of fragments are produced, one for each possible base. The chemical method involves breaking the chain at a particular base. The enzyme method involves synthesizing DNA and terminating the new chain at a particular base. The use of overlapping fragments ensures that no parts of the sequence are omitted.

First see WAVE

Doppler Effect

Next see HUBBLE CONSTANT

The apparent change in the observed frequency of sound, light, and other waves that results from the relative motion of the wave source and an observer.

An example of the Doppler effect is the drop in pitch of a train whistle as the train passes. It was first described in 1842 by Christian Johann Doppler, an Austrian physicist, to explain the coloration of stars. To understand the Doppler shift, suppose a person P observes or hears waves from a source S. If P and S are both stationary, the number of waves perceived by P is the same as the number emitted by S. But the number of wave crests perceived by P will increase if the person moves toward the source and will decrease if the person moves away from the source.

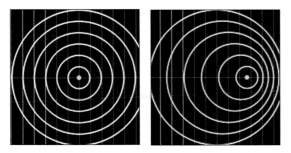

The Doppler effect is commonly experienced by listening to a train whistle or an automobile horn as it passes. Above at left, the sound is of the same wavelength in all directions when it is stationary; at right, the wavelength is longer, sounding lower to those left behind and higher to those the sound is approaching.

Radar systems today use the Doppler effect to distinguish between targets that are stationary and those that are moving, and to provide information about the speed of moving objects by measuring the frequency shift between the radiation emitted by the radar system and the radiation that is reflected.

The Red Shift. Astronomers determine how rapidly stars or other celestial objects are approaching or receding from the Earth by applying the Doppler effect. The expansion of the universe is measured by a red shift, which displaces waves in the visual spectrum toward the longer wavelengths, such as red.

A two-star system that appears to be one star can sometimes be identified by the Doppler effect produced as one star approaches the Earth while the other recedes from it.

Further developments in the field are discussed in LIGHT; SOUND; WAVE. *More details can be found in* BIG BANG COSMOLOGY; OPTICS; PHONON. *Relevant information is contained in* LIGHT, SPEED OF; RADAR; UNIVERSE, LARGE-SCALE STRUCTURE OF.

First see SOIL CHEMISTRY

Dormancy

Next see DESRTIFICATION

In regions with seasonal temperature variation, the seeds of most plants and the buds of perennials go through a period of dormancy in which metabolic activity is shut down. This ensures that seeds will not germinate or that buds will not begin to grow in the autumn, when the onset of winter would make survival difficult.

Some inactive seeds or buds are said to be quiescent, not dormant. They will begin to grow whenever conditions become favorable—warm and wet enough, in the case of a winter warm spell. A dormant plant, by contrast, will begin to grow only after experiencing specific environmental cues. In temperate regions, for instance, dormancy in many species will not end until the plants undergo a period of chilling or freezing. Many fruit trees and ornamental plants require weeks of rest at temperatures below about 45 degrees Fahrenheit (7 degrees Celsius) before their buds or seeds will begin to develop. In many cases, this period enables embryos to mature, a process called after-ripening. (*See* SEED.)

To break dormancy, other plants may require light or darkness, scorching by fire, ingestion by an animal, or abrasion of a hard seed coat to admit water or oxygen. In a desert setting, relatively heavy rainfall—enough to establish the seedling—may be necessary to wash away germination inhibitors in the seed coat and allow it to grow. The plant hormone abscissic acid is among growth inhibitors found in many seed coats. Two other hormones, gibberellin and ethylene, may play a role in breaking dormancy. (*See* CLOCKS, BIOLOGICAL.)

Some seeds routinely remain dormant for years, and great feats of viability have been reported in special cases. Dormant seeds of the lotus, for instance, have been induced to germinate hundreds of years after they began their long period of dormancy.

Ears and Hearing

Next see SENSORY MECHANISMS

A highly complex organ of hearing and balance, the mammalian ear has three parts—the outer, middle, and inner ear. All three are involved in sending information to the brain about the pitch, loudness, and direction of sound waves in the air. The inner ear, with its labyrinthine canals, is involved in monitoring how the body is oriented in space. Although birds and some frogs and reptiles have features of the middle ear, only the basic structures of the inner ear are common to all vertebrates.

Maintenance of balance appears to be the oldest function of the ear, which is thought to have evolved from the lateral-line system of fish. This system lets fish orient their bodies by perceiving changes in the motion of water around them. In both the ear and the lateral-line system, the sensory receptors are hair cells embedded with hairs called stereocilia. Their minute movements, caused by movements of a surrounding fluid, trigger nerve impulses to the brain.

In mammals, sound is directed by the external ear, called the pinna, and travels through the ear canal to the eardrum (the tympanic membrane), a thin membrane between the outer and middle ear. From the inner side of the eardrum, three bones called ossicles convert the sound waves to mechanical energy and transmit it across the air-filled cavity of the middle ear to the fluid-filled inner ear. The three bones are named for their shape—the malleus (hammer), incus (anvil), and stapes (stirrups). Together they amplify the force of the sound, the pressure exerted by the sound waves; in humans, the increase is 22-fold. The stapes transfers this force to the inner ear by pressing against the cochlear fluid at the oval window, the opening into the inner ear. Amphibians, birds, and reptiles have only a single ossicle, the columella.

The eustachian tube links the middle ear to the back of the throat. When the tube is opened by yawning or swallowing, air can enter the ear to equalize the pressure on both sides of the eardrum—often with the pop familiar to airline travelers. The eustachian tube is also the route by which respiratory infections migrate to the middle ear, a sequence common in children.

Inner Ear. The fluid-filled inner ear (labyrinth) contains the cochlea, the coiled, snail-shaped organ of hearing in mammals. In other vertebrates, a shorter, straighter canal, the lagena, takes its place. The cochlea consists of three tubes coiled together and separated by membranes. One of these, the basilar membrane, holds the organ of Corti, a series of receptor hair cells. The minute stereocilia project upward from the hair cells and touch a gel coating the nearby tectorial membrane. When the basilar membrane vibrates in response to sound, the hairs oscillate back and forth against the tectorial membrane. This excitation is converted to nerve impulses that are transmitted to the brain.

Sounds of different frequencies—perceived by humans as different pitches—resonate at different points along the basilar membrane, which contains stiff fibers that can vibrate like the reeds of a woodwind. The fibers get longer and thinner as they get farther from the oval window. As a result, high-frequency sounds resonate close to the start of the cochlea, while low frequencies resonate farther along.

Brain Pathways. Nerve pathways from the ear take a complex route through the brain, with left and right pathways crossing at least three times before reaching the brain's auditory cortex. Mammals commonly can hear sound, if it is loud enough, over a wide frequency range, from 20 to 20,000 Hz. Dogs can hear sounds at 40,000 Hz, and some aquatic and flying mammals use much higher frequencies for echolocation. At the lower extreme, elephants and some whales can hear sounds as low as 12 Hz.

Balance and Equilibrium. The organs of balance are also located in the inner ear. Three semicircular canals, arranged at right angles to each other so they cover the three planes of space, are connected to two chambers, the utricle and the saccule. Movement of the head causes the fluid in these structures to move in various ways. This excites the hair cells, which trigger nerve impulses to the brain containing information on the position of the head in space.

Background material can be found in BRAIN; SENSORY MECHANISMS; SOUND. Further developments in the field are discussed in ACOUSTICS; NERVOUS SYSTEM; RECORDING TECHNOLOGY. Special topics in this area are found in DOPPLER EFFECT and LOCOMOTION.

The Human Ear.
The ear is divided into three sections: The outer ear, which consists of (a) helix, (b) auricle, (c) outer ear canal, and (d) earlobe; the middle ear, which consists of (e) eardrum (tympanic membrane), and (f) auditory ossicles; and the inner ear, which consists of (g) auditory tube, (h) tympanic cavity, (i) oval window, (j) temporal bone, (k) cochlea, (l) cochlea nerve, (m) vesticular nerve, and (n) semicircular canal.

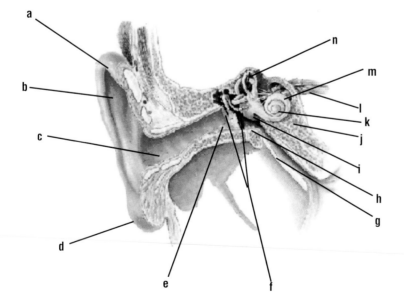

Earth

First see SOLAR SYSTEM

Next see GAIA HYPOTHESIS

The Earth, our home, is the fifth largest planet of the solar system, the third from the sun and the only one known to support life. Its diameter is 7,926.68 miles at the equator and 7,899.98 miles between the poles. The difference is caused by the rotation of Earth, which exerts a centrifugal force that results in a slight bulge. There is a difference of about 13 miles between the highest points on the Earth—mountains that are 29,000 feet above sea level—and the lowest, ocean depths of about 36,000 feet. The mean density of the Earth's mass is about 5.5 times that of water. Since the crust, the mass of solid matter near the surface, has a mean density 2.7 times that of water, the core of the Earth is estimated to have a density of 10 or 12 times that of water, about that of iron or nickel-iron.

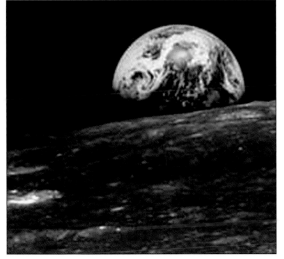

The Earth's Surface. Almost 70 percent of the Earth's surface area of 197 million square miles is covered by water. Most of the 56 million square miles of land are concentrated in the continents—seven in all (unless Eurasia is listed as a single continent). These ratios of land to water reflect what exists today; geologists have found that the oceans covered greater area in the past. The waters of the Earth are called the hydrosphere and the crust of the Earth is called the lithosphere. The lithosphere is being changed constantly by thrusting, folding, faulting, and upward or downward movements, as well as by volcanic activity caused by Earth's internal heat and by erosion caused by rainfall. The Earth may well be unique among the planets of the solar system in the variety and strength of these activities. For example, continental drift, the process by which islands and continents move relative to one another across the face of a planet, is much more pronounced on the Earth than on any other

planet. (*See* FAULTS, FOLDS, AND JOINTS.)

Inside the Earth. The internal structure of the Earth is believed to be composed of three well-defined zones that have different densities and are made of different kinds of material. Overall, the mass of the Earth has been set at 6.6 billion trillion trillion trillion tons, and its mean density about 5.5 times that of water. The innermost part of the Earth, the core, has a diameter of about 4,320 miles and is made of rock with a density 10 to 12 times that of water, roughly the same density as nickel-iron. Pressure at the core is believed to be 5 million times greater than atmospheric pressure. The core may be entirely fluid, but it may have a solid inner portion about 1,600 miles in diameter, with an outer fluid portion. The existence of such a solid core is suggested by the observation that secondary seismic waves, which can penetrate fluids, do not pass through the core.

Lying above the core is the the mantle. It is 1,782 miles thick and has a density 3.3 times

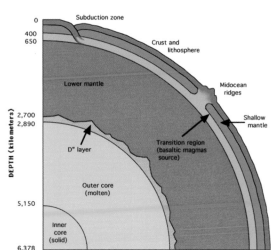

greater than water. The mantle is rigid enough to allow all seismic waves to pass through it. But the rock of the mantle may also have some plasticity, because of the enormous pressures that exist within it. These pressures could be great enough to cause the rock to flow, perhaps in convective currents. Most geologists believe that there are several zones within the mantle. The outermost is believed to be composed of a rock similar to olivine, iron-magnesium silicate. Nearer the core, under increasing pressure, both the density of the rock and its iron content increase dramatically.

The Earth's Crust. The Earth's crust is composed of much less dense rock, such as sima, which is mostly silica with a high percentage of iron and magnesium, and sial, which has a lower content of iron and magnesium. The border between the crust and the mantle is called the Mohorovicic Discontinuity, or the Moho, after its discoverer. The Moho lies about three

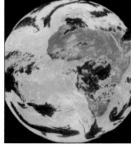

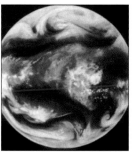

As seen from space (top) in the visible light range, the Earth is a beautiful blue marble in the blackness of space, but shows no signs of life. Seen in infrared (middle), the temperature differences between the oceans and the ground are apparent, and a world with land mass amid oceans becomes observable. In the bottom image, however, taken in the near infrared range and thus reflecting the carbon dioxide and water vapor of the upper atmosphere, the ground planet below is obscured, not unlike nearly all images of Venus, indicating an already serious greenhouse effect under way. At left, a schematic of the composition of the Earth, and at far left, an Earthrise as seen on the moon, reported by astronauts to be one of the most magnificent sights in the solar system.

First see EARTH

Earthquake

Next see PLATE TECTONICS

THE CUTTING EDGE

Is the Earth Expanding?

Some geologists suspect that the Earth may be expanding. According to observations of plate tectonics, all the continents are moving away from Antarctica; but those same observations show that they are also moving away from Africa. Further observations show that the Arctic Ocean is expanding, as is the circumference of the Pacific Ocean. One explanation, offered by Professor S. Warren Casey of Tasmania and his colleagues, is that the Earth itself is expanding, perhaps because the core of the Earth is so hot that it exists as a plasma. In the past 700 million years that plasma has begun to cool down and convert to normal atomic form, expanding as it cools. The change is so slight, however, that it may take decades of precise measurement before we know for sure.

miles beneath the ocean floor and from 15 to 40 miles under the continents. It is marked by a sharp change in the velocity of seismic waves. Beneath the oceans, the crust consists almost entirely of sima. The crust beneath the continents has a thin layer of sima surrounded by a thicker layer of sila. The great mountain ranges represent the thickest portion of the crust.

The Atmosphere. The Earth's water and land mass is surrounded by an atmosphere whose composition is 78.08 percent nitrogen, 20.95 percent oxygen, 0.94 percent argon and other rare gases, and 0.03 percent carbon dioxide. This composition is consistent to an altitude of 30 miles or more above the surface. The water vapor content of the atmosphere ranges from more than 5 percent in the tropics to less than 0.001 percent in the polar regions.

The layer of the atmosphere closest to the Earth's surface, the troposphere, contains about 75 percent of the mass of the atmosphere and more than nine-tenths of its water vapor, dust, and smoke. The troposphere is the turbulent part of the atmosphere. The disturbances that occur within the troposphere range from thunderstorms that are less than a mile in diameter to major storms that can cover hundreds of thousands of square miles. The principal wind systems of the troposphere are caused by the movement of warm air from the equator to the poles. This movement in the lower troposphere is modified by surface friction and the Earth's rotation, causing what are called primary wind belts. These include the trade winds, which extend from the equator to 30° north and south; the westerlies, which lie between 30° and 60° latitude; and the polar easterlies, from latitude 60° to the poles.

The foundations of the subject are discussed in GEOLOGY; PLANET; SEISMOLOGY. *More details can be found in* ATMOSPHERE; EARTHQUAKE; GEOSYNCLINE. *Advanced topics in Earth Science are developed in* GEODETIC SURVEY; PLATE TECTONICS; REMOTE SENSING. *See also* FAULTS, FOLDS, AND JOINTS *and* GEOMORPHOLOGY.

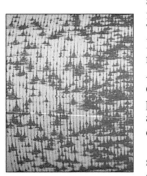

Increased seismic activity is recorded on seismographic equipment (above) during an eruption of Mount St. Helens.

Further Reading
Earthquakes and Geological Discovery (1993); Bolt, Bruce A., *Earthquakes* (1999); Hernon, Peter, *8.4* (1999); Levy, Matthys, *Why the Earth Quakes: The Story of Earthquakes and Volcanoes* (1995); Sieh, Kerry, *The Earth in Turmoil: Earthquakes, Volcanoes, and Their Impact* (1998).

Billions of years ago, when Earth cooled, the lithosphere (the level just beneath the crust) broke into several floating land masses. These "plates" are in a constant state of motion, relentlessly grinding and pushing up against each other—sometimes even climbing over one another. This movement is caused by convection currents—the force created by heated particles that rise up through the Earth's mantle. As the tectonic plates are sliding on these currents and colliding with each other, they are also resisting each other through friction. Two rocks floating down a river that is too narrow for them to pass will collide until one breaks apart or rises over the other. This asimilar movement of plates has been going on for eons and explains why the present-day continents would fit together like pieces of a puzzle if they were somehow reunited.

At one the point in Earth's history, the continents were all one mass, often referred to as Pangaea. Several rifts formed and the massive Pangaea began to break apart into what are now continents. This movement continued for more than 150 million years and, as a result, the constant pushing and pulling of the Earth's crust formed mountain ranges such as the Himalayas. These spectacular peaks were formed when India broke off from Madagascar and began moving north. India finally collided with the Asian continent and was forced under it at its edge. The immense force that was generated pushed the Himalayas to their dizzying heights; and they are, in fact, still rising today at the rate of two inches a year.

The point at which these continental plates slide by each other is called a transform boundary. It is at this point that earthquakes and volcanoes most commonly occur. When the friction between plates builds up and the stress level at the edge of the plates becomes too high, friction is overcome, the plates finally give and an earthquake is the result.

Measuring Earthquakes. Seismic waves are the bursts of energy created by an earthquake (or an explosion). There are two kinds of seismic waves: body waves and surface waves. Body waves travel through the Earth's interior, while surface waves, as their name implies, travel through the surface of the Earth's crust and are felt on the surface as earthquakes. The Richter scale uses the measurement of seismic waves to calculate the magnitude of an earthquake. The magnitude is a function of the amount of energy released in the form of ground waves, which are measured by a seismograph. Each whole number on the Richter scale represents a tenfold

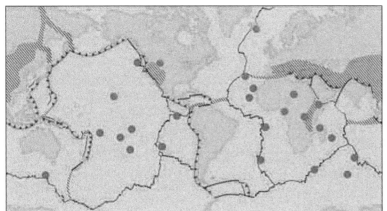

Earthquake zones are marked by the boundaries of the Earth's plates; hot spots of increased earthquake activity are marked in purple. Volcanic activity is indicated by orange dots.

increase in magnitude. However, this does not mean that a magnitude 6 quake has 10 times the energy of a magnitude 5 quake. Various measuring devices and calculations have determined that one magnitude is equal to an approximately 30-fold increase in energy output. Therefore, the energy produced by an earthquake of magnitude 8 would be at least 1 million times as much as one with a magnitude of 4. To put the Richter scale in perspective: magnitude 6 quakes take place daily, while magnitude 8 quakes take place only once a year. Today, the Richter scale has largely been replaced by direct measurement of earthquake magnitude.

Elementary aspects of this subject are covered in EARTH; PLANET, INTERIOR OF; PLATE TECTONICS. *More information on particular aspects of earthquakes is contained in* CONTINENTS, FORMATION OF; FAULTS, FOLDS AND JOINTS. *Additional relevant information is also contained in* SEDIMENTARY ROCK GEOLOGY; SEISMICS; SEISMOLOGY.

First see MOON

Eclipse

Next see SATELLITE, PLANETARY

The total or partial obscuring of light from one celestial body to another celestial body when the latter passes behind or through the shadow of a third body.

A lunar eclipse occurs when the centers of the sun, the Earth, and moon are in a straight line, or nearly so. If the orbits of the sun, moon, and Earth were in the same plane, there would be a lunar eclipse at each full moon. But because the orbit of the moon is tilted somewhat, a lunar eclipse occurs only when the moon's orbit intersects the ecliptic—the great circle in which the plane of Earth's orbit lies during a full moon. In a total eclipse, the moon is totally covered by the umbra, the dense inner part of the shadow cast by the Earth. In a partial eclipse, part of the moon's surface remains illuminated by the sun. In a penumbral eclipse, the brightness of the moon is dimmed partially as it passes through the penumbra, the light, outer part of the Earth's shadow.

A solar eclipse takes place when the sun, moon, and Earth are nearly in a straight line, so that the shadow of the moon falls on the Earth. Solar eclipses occur only at times of the new moon. During this type of eclipse, observers on Earth see the apparent disk of the moon projected against the sun.

A solar eclipse is total if the shadow hides the sun entirely and partial if part of the sun remains visible from the Earth. In an annular eclipse, the shadow of the moon does not cover the sun entirely, so that the edge of the sun is visible as a ring of light. A solar eclipse lasts about seven minutes at most; many eclipses are much shorter. Just before the sun is eclipsed, some rays of sunlight seem to circle the sun in what is called a diamond ring.

Total Eclipse. When the eclipse is total, the solar prominences and corona, normally lost in the sun's glare, can be seen. Great care must be taken to avoid eye damage when observing a solar eclipse. Viewing the eclipse through heavily smoked glasses or dark photographic film is recommended. Viewing the sun directly for even a brief time without such eye-protecting measures can cause permanent eye damage, or even blindness.

Astronomers have observed eclipses of other bodies within the solar system. The four moons of Jupiter—Io, Europa, Ganymede, and Callisto—undergo eclipses similar to earthly lunar eclipses. Because Jupiter is much larger than the Earth and thus casts a much larger shadow, eclipses of Io, Europa, and Ganymede occur at each revolution around the planet. Callisto experiences fewer eclipses because its orbit is inclined somewhat to the plane of Jupiter's orbit. Interstellar observation is approaching the point where eclipses in remote reaches of space can be observed on Earth.

Related areas to be considered are MOON; SOLAR SYSTEM; SUN. *Other aspects of the subject are discussed in* PLANETARY SATELLITE; *and* TELESCOPE. *Related material can be found in* PLANET, FORMATION OF.

Further Reading
Bolt, Bruce A., *Earthquakes* (1999); Levy, Matthys, *Why the Earth Quakes* (1995); Meehan, Richard, *The Atom and the Fault* (1984); Prager, Ellen, *Furious Earth* (1999); Sieh, Kerry, *Earth in Turmoil* (1999).

The "diamond ring" effect (also known as Bailey's Beads) is caused by sunlight shining through the rifts and valleys on the moon's surface.

Further Reading
Brewer, Bryan, Eclipse (1991); Brunier, Serge, *Glorious Eclipses: Their Past, Present, and Future* (2001); Harrington, Philip S., *Eclipse!* (1997); Levy, David, *Eclipse: Voyage to Darkness and Light* (2000); Littman, Mark, *Totality: Eclipses of the Sun* (1999).

First see COMPETITION AND ALTRUISM

Ecology

Next see POPULATION ECOLOGY

The study of all living things and their interactions with each other and their environment.

No living thing exists in isolation, but occupies a specific environmental niche or habitat. A population consists of several individuals of the same species occupying the same habitat. If different interacting populations occupy the same area, they are known as a community.

Every community consists of producers, consumers, and decomposers. A producer is an autotroph or self-feeder. Most producers contain chlorophyll, a green, light-sensitive pigment which enables them to manufacture glucose through the process of photosynthesis. Consumers are organisms that are called heterotrophs. They cannot produce their own glucose, the universal food source, and therefore eat other organisms in order to satisfy their energy needs. Consumers that eat producers exclusively are called herbivores. Consumers that eat other consumers are called carnivores. Organisms which eat both plants and animals are called omnivores.

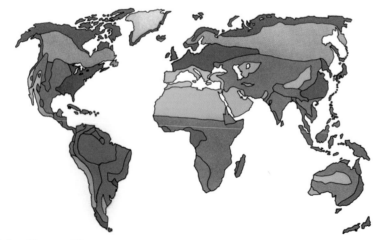

The Major Biomes. Eleven distinct biomes are marked off in the map above—from the polar ice-cap and the tundra in the north to the deserts and tropical rain forests near the equator. But there are, in fact, many biomes, with many of them intersecting neighboring areas.

Decomposers are bacteria that break the body down into its basic chemicals. In this way, they are returned to the environment and the cycle can begin again with a different producer drawing nutrients from the soil.

Interrelationships. Symbiosis, also called mutualism, refers to two organisms living in a mutually beneficial relationship. A common example is a lichen, which consists of an alga (a simple plant) and a fungus. The alga, a producer, provides food. The fungus in turn provides water and protection.

Parasitism occurs when one organism takes advantage of another, reaping all the benefits and providing nothing in return but harm. A tapeworm is an example of a parasitic organism.

It attaches itself to the inner intestinal lining and takes nutrients away from its host, as well as using the intestine as a secure area to reproduce. Viruses are the ultimate parasite, requiring host cells to help them do all their activities, including reproduction. A successful parasite does not kill its host too rapidly, lest it be harmed as well.

In commensalism, only one organism profits from the relationship. The other receives no benefits, but is not harmed. An example is the remora fish, which attaches itself to the underside of a shark and feeds on food scraps left over from the shark's meals. The shark does not suffer as a result of its guest's freeloading.

Life Cycles. A food chain begins with a producer, such as grass. The producer is eaten by a primary consumer, such as a mouse, which in turn is eaten by a secondary consumer, such as an owl. The food chain can continue to extend to several levels of consumers but eventually ends with a decomposer. Food chains can be terrestrial or aquatic. The intersection of two or more food chains constitutes a food web.

Ecosystems. An ecosystem is a self-sustaining community of plants and animals. In this system, matter is transferred and recycled. Water, carbon, oxygen, hydrogen, and nitrogen are all recirculated. Only energy needs to be continually added. Proceeding through the trophic levels of a food chain, less energy is obtained with each successive level. A great deal is lost through the expenditure of energy to obtain food and through heat. In an idealized energy pyramid, 10 percent of the energy available at each level is available at the next. In an actual ecosystem the productivity varies depending on the organisms.

All living things require oxygen in order to perform cellular respiration, the process of breaking down glucose to obtain energy. In return, all living things give off carbon dioxide as a byproduct of respiration. Producers require carbon dioxide in order to perform photosynthesis and in return give off oxygen as a byproduct. In this way, carbon dioxide and oxygen circulate throughout the ecosystem.

The water cycle consists of water from streams, rivers, and oceans evaporating into the atmosphere, where it condenses as water vapor to form clouds. When the clouds reach a certain saturation point, they release moisture in the form of precipitation returning water to the land.

The basic metabolic activities of all cells result in the formation of nitrogenous wastes. Some of these deposits are used by plants and incorporated into their cells. As the plants themselves either die and decompose or are eaten by animals which then decompose, the nitrogen is returned to the soil.

Species. A species is defined as a group of nearly identical organisms all capable of interbreeding. If two different species occupy the same ecological niche, they will compete with each other for nutritional resources. The species that reproduces faster eventually eliminates its competitor.

Communities change as the environment changes. Ecological succession refers to one community being supplanted by another as conditions change. Succession ultimately leads to a climax community, which is stable and undergoes little or no further change.

Biomes. A biome is a major ecological grouping of organisms within specific climate zones. Biomes are distinguished from one another on the basis of temperature and the amount of rainfall and solar radiation.

The major land biomes are:

1. tundra—the treeless region in the north with an arctic climate, where the underlying layer of soil is permanently frozen;
2. taiga—the northernmost forest below the tundra across Europe, Asia, and North America;
3. temperate deciduous forest—the eastern United States, England, and central Europe, containing trees that seasonally shed their leaves;
4. tropical rain forests—regions of high temperature and ample rainfall;
5. grasslands—also called savanna, receiving less rain than deciduous forests; and
6. deserts—the most arid region, with hot days and cold nights.

Aquatic biomes are either marine, referring to oceans and other bodies of salt water, or freshwater, such as lakes and rivers. Plankton—microscopic organisms such as algae and protozoa—are the starting point of aquatic food chains.

Background material can be found in ADAPTATION; EVOLUTION; HOMEOSTASIS. *More details can be found in* COEVOLUTION; DEFORESTATION; DESERTIFICATION. *Advanced aspects of this subject are covered in* BIODIVERSITY; GAIA HYPOTHESIS; POPULATION ECOLOGY; SPECIATION.

First see ELECTROMAGNETIC FORCE

Electric and Magnetic Fields

Next see ELECTROMAGNETISM

Forces created by the presence of an electric current, an electric charge, or a magnet.

The existence of an electric field is made known by its effect on another electric charge, and the existence of a magnetic field can be made known by its effect on another magnet. In 1785, French scientist Charles Augustin de Coulomb determined that the force of attraction between unlike electric charges in an electric field or the force of repulsion between two like charges is inversely proportional to the square of the distance between them and directly proportional to

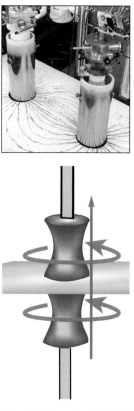

Top, electromagnetic field lines of force are formed by current in superconductors. Bottom, the magnetic field around a wire carrying a current.

Further Reading

Danson, F. Mark, *Advances in Environmental Remote Sensing* (1995); Gurney, W.S.C., *Ecological Dynamics* (1998); Katz, William B., *ABCs of Environmental Science* (1998); Newman, Edward I., *Applied Ecology* (1993).

the magnitude of the charges. Coulomb later verified that an analogous law of repulsion and attraction applies to two magnetic poles.

A field around a magnet or an electric current will deflect a small magnet, such as a compass needle, in a particular direction when it is placed in such a field. The direction in which the north pole of the magnet points is by convention called the direction of the field. The direction of the field generally follows curved lines of force. If the field is caused by the electrical current in a conducting material, the lines of force form completely closed curves that enclose the conductor. If the field is caused by the presence of a magnet, the lines of force appear to enter the magnet at its south pole and emerge at its north pole, presumably running through the magnet.

Electric Potential. An electric potential exists at every point of an electric field. This potential is defined as the work done by moving a unit positive charge from a specified location—sometimes an infinite distance, sometimes Earth's surface—to the specific point in the electric field. Similarly, a magnetic potential exists at every point of a magnetic field, measured by the work that is needed to move a unit magnetic pole from one point in the field to another. This difference is sometimes called a magnetomotive force. It is analogous to the electromotive force, the difference between the terminals of a device that is used to supply an electric current, such as a battery.

The lines of intensity of a magnetic field that forms around a wire carrying an electric current are circular, in a plane perpendicular to the axis of the wire. The direction of these lines of force is determined by what is called the right-hand rule: when the right hand grasps the wire, with the thumb pointing in the direction of the current flow, the fingers encircling the wire describe the direction of the lines of force of the magnetic field. In a circular helix of current-carrying wire—often called a solenoid—an axial magnetic field is produced. Then the right-hand rule points in the direction of the solenoid's north pole. This is a basic electromagnet.

The force on a stationary positive charge in an electric field is defined as the electric field vector. When the ratio of force to charge in the field is not constant, the field vector is defined as the limit of the ratio when the change approaches zero measured in volts per meter. The electric field vector is sometimes called the electric field intensity, but the term "field strength" is preferred because intensity, when used in the areas of optics and radiation, implies a unit of power.

Earth's Two Magnetic Fields. Just as Earth has a magnetic field that makes compass needles point north, there is an electric field around Earth—the atmospheric electric field. In areas of fair weather, the strength of this field near

**Michael Faraday
(1791–1867)**

Earth's surface is about 100 volts per meter and decreases with altitude. At an elevation of 6 miles about Earth's surface, for example, its strength is about 5 volts per meter. The atmospheric electric field is directed vertically, and drives positive charges towards Earth's surface. Electrical disturbances such as thunderstorms can greatly affect this field, even reversing it.

Background material on electric and magnetic fields can be found in CHARGE AND CURRENT; ELECTRICITY; MAGNETISM. *More details can be found in* INDUCTION. *More information on particular aspects of this subject is contained in* ELECTROMAGNETISM; ELECTROMAGNETIC WAVES; MAXWELL'S EQUATIONS.

First see CHARGE AND CURRENT

Electric Circuit

Next see ELECTRIC CIRCUITS, APPLICATIONS OF

A closed path that conveys an electric current through a conducting material.

An electric circuit can be made of ionized gases or ionized liquids, but metals are most commonly used. The current (expressed as I), the voltage (V), and the resistance (R) of an electric circuit obey Ohm's law, developed by nineteenth-century German physicist, Georg Simon Ohm: $I = V/R$ (or, equivalently, $V = I \times R$).

The simplest electric circuit consists of a source of electricity such as a battery and a conducting material such as a wire. Current flows from the positive terminal of the battery through the wire to the negative terminal. A resistor such as a light bulb can be added to the circuit, as can a switch that can open the wire. Current flowing through the wire will light the bulb unless the switch is used to cut the circuit. If two or more resistors are connected to a single wire that makes up a circuit, they are said to be in series. If another wire is added so that the electricity can flow through both wires, the circuit is said to be parallel. One branch of a parallel circuit can be turned off, and current will continue to flow through the other branch or branches. The current that flows through each branch is in inverse relationship to the resistance of that branch; the greater the resistance, the lower is the flow of current.

Mathematically, the total resistance of a current through a parallel circuit with two branches is expressed by the formula $I = R_1 + R_2$. Other terms used to describe an electric circuit include Kirchoff's laws, developed by German physicist Gustav Kirchoff, which state that the algebraic sum of the currents at any junction of a circuit is zero, and that the algebraic sum of the electromagnetic force (the voltage of the circuit) and the decrease in potential due to resistance in any closed path of an electric circuit is zero. If we apply Kirchoff's first law to a point on a circuit with two branches, we would say that the current

flowing into that point, I_t, is equal to the current flowing out of the two branches, $I_t - I_1 - I_2 = 0$. If we apply Kirchoff's second law to that circuit, we would say mathematically that $emf - I_1R_1 - I_1I_2 = 0$, which is the same as saying that $I_1I_2 - I_1I_2 = 0$. Kirchoff's second law is important for any circuit with more than one source of electricity. It says that the total current in any part of such a network equals the sum of all the currents that are produced by each source.

Electric circuits can be direct, with current flowing in one direction, or alternating, in which the current reverses flow at regular intervals. A frequency of 60 cycles per second has been made standard for the United States, but other frequencies have been adopted by other countries. Alternating current is used almost exclusively by the power industry, because its voltage can be increased or decreased easily by a transformer, which is not possible with direct current. The mathematical analysis of alternating currents is difficult because the values of both voltage and current change in both magnitude and direction. Variations of Ohm's laws are used to make such an analysis. (*See* ELECTRIC CIRCUITS, APPLICATIONS OF.)

First see ELECTRIC CIRCUIT

Electric Circuits, Applications of

Next see ELECTRICITY AND ELECTRICAL ENGINEERING

An electrical circuit in its most basic form consists of three components: an electric power source, a load or resistance, and a means of conducting the electricity from source to load and back again. Such circuits were analyzed systematically for the first time by Gustav Kirchoff (1824–1887), whose laws on current and voltage form the basis of all circuit analysis.

Kirchoff showed that electric charges are always conserved, so that the left and right headlights on a car will each consume exactly half the available current; he also showed that the work associated with creating electrical energy must always be exactly matched by the work consumed in dissipating that energy, so that the headlights and their associated wiring must convert all the voltage supplied to them into heat or light. The product of the voltage and the current equals the power of the circuit.

The second major contributor to the theory of electrical circuits was G. S. Ohm, who discovered the relationship between voltage (V), current (I), and resistance (R): $V = I \times R$. That is, the free movement of electrons through any given material is restricted by the size or atomic structure of that material; a large copper wire, generally called a conductor, offers very little resistance to electrons, while a thin sheet of mica offers a great deal of resistance and is generally called an insulator. A third category of material sharing characteristics of both materials, called a semiconductor, has proved to be the key to development of transistors and other modern electronic systems.

In addition to their power sources and the various resistors, capacitors, and inductors that compose them, all electrical circuits are defined by the ways in which these components are organized. A branch, for example, is any portion of a circuit with two terminals connected to it; when these terminals are clearly marked on a battery, all components have a means for current to flow in and a means for it to flow out. A node is a junction of two or more branches, as where a single current in an automobile operates the headlights, the running lights, and the turn lights. A loop is a connected path starting at one terminal of a branch and ending at the opposite terminal; a loop may enclose a smaller loop, or it may be the smallest possible, in which case it is called a mesh. The loop from the battery to a given instrument panel light would constitute a mesh, as would the loop from the battery through the brake pedal to the brake lights. The most important measurements in analysis of such circuits include the node voltages and the branch currents.

AC Circuits. In alternating current (AC) circuits, which are the most common type, the power sources are sinusoidal—that is, voltage is a function of time, and therefore is susceptible to Fourier analysis, a powerful mathematical tool for simplifying complex electrical circuits into phasor circuits, then using superposition to analyze them. In addition, the energy-storage effects of capacitors and inductors sometimes necessitate the use of a mathematical analysis known as Thévenin equivalent analysis. Since 1948, the discovery of the p-n junction has led to the development of electronic circuits, based on diodes, transistors, amplifiers, and filters. Such circuits, operating at high speed, enable modern electronic devices to use feedback and sampling to perform digital circuit analysis, the basis of programmable logic devices.

Digital Logic Circuitry. The most important type of electrical circuit today is the digital logic circuit, the heart of the computer. For example, every automobile has an air-flow sensor that tracks the amount of air entering each cylinder, and then computes the proper amount of fuel to inject into that cylinder to minimize emissions. One way would be to divide the mass of air by 14.7 (the stoichiometric value), then divide that amount by the rate at which the injector can emit fuel, to find a unique answer to each instant's problem; but that relatively time-consuming process would create an unacceptable delay in providing fuel to the cylinder. Therefore a digital logic circuit, in the form of an erasable

programmable read-only memory (EPROM), stores all possible air-mass values along with precomputed values for the corresponding fuel mass and the time the fuel injector valve must remain open to achieve that mass, in what is called a look-up table.

First see ELECTRIC CIRCUITS, APPLICATIONS OF

Electricity and Electrical Engineering

Next see MOTORS AND GENERATORS

Electricity and electrical engineering are both the foundation and keystone of the twentieth century. Without electricity our world would be more heavily polluted, would communicate and operate at much slower speeds, and would probably be far more centralized than it is; there would be no electrical equipment, no electronic devices, and probably not even works like this encyclopedia, the articles for which were all written on computer, typeset by computer, and printed on computer-controlled machinery.

The knowledge of electricity goes back to the 18th century, with the discoveries of Galvani, Volta, and Franklin; but its utilization did not begin until the 1820s, when the basic scientific discoveries that would make electrical engineering possible were made: Ampère's law, Faraday's law, and Ohm's law. The only valuable application of electricity perfected before 1865, when James Clerk Maxwell brought all electromagnetic laws together in one set of mathematical formulas, was a machine that interrupted a continuous electric circuit to produce dots and dashes on a paper tape run under an electromagnet—the telegraph. Developed by Samuel F. B. Morse in the 1830s, telegraphy grew so rapidly that by 1875 there were 250,000 miles of telegraph lines in the United States alone and 100,000 miles of undersea telegraph cables linking the world.

Further Reading
Bogart, T. F., *Electric Circuits* (1992); Dorf, R. C., *Introduction to Electric Circuits* (2000); Kubala, T. S., *Electricity* (2001); Robbins, Alan H., *Circuit Analysis: Theory and Practice* (1999).

Below, an AC electric generator. Both motors and generators operate by an application of a law that bears Faraday's name. A changing magnetic field induces a current in a conductor. If a turbine turns a conducting wire in a magnetic field, a current is induced in the wire. If a current flows through a wire loop creating a magnetic field of its own in the presence of another (natural) magnetic field, the wire is forced to move so that the total magnetic field flowing through the loop remains a constant.

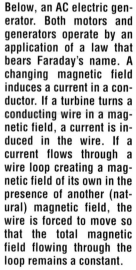

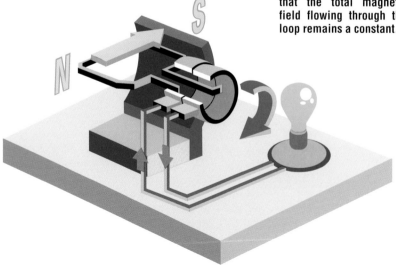

Electrical Generation. The telegraph had to be powered by batteries; electrical generators were not developed until the late 1860s, and electric motors a few years after that. Furthermore, these early electrical applications were based on direct current or DC; Thomas Edison committed his entire resources to DC power in the 1880s, nearly ruining himself in the process. The problem was that DC power could not be transmitted more than a mile without prohibitive cost. Real utilization of electric power had to wait for the invention of practical alternating current motors and generators, which was accomplished by Nikola Tesla in the late 1880s.

With the development of practical electric power generating equipment, a rush began to electrify vast areas of the globe. Most notable among these efforts was the Tennessee Valley Authority (TVA), a 1930s project to bring hydroelectric power to the American Southeast; by 1945 the TVA provided 2.5 million kW, rising to 17 million kW by 1975, along with a reduction in electric rates of up to 80 percent. Electricity was also generated by nuclear power plants, constructed around the world between 1957 and 1979, but a series of near-disasters from Three Mile Island to Chernobyl ended this phase.

Electrical engineering retained two aspects throughout the twentieth century: on the one hand, it sought new means of creating power, through electrical generation and amplification; on the other hand, it sought new means of using electricity for communication, through such media as the telephone, radio, and television, as well as media using other portions of the electromagnetic spectrum, such as radar and lasers. Perhaps its greatest accomplishment was the personalizing of electricity. From an industry centered on metal refining, city lighting, and commuter railways, electrical engineering now centers on cellular telephones, computers, and GPS locators. It is this individual application of electrical power, multiplied around the world five billion times, that will characterize the twenty first century. This new focus was achieved through a transformation from electricity to electronics.

Electronics. Electronics can be said to have begun in 1895, when W. Roentgen discovered x-rays and developed machinery to utilize them. Researchers soon learned that electricity generated by, and flowing within, semiconductors offered more potential than copper-based electricity. The invention of the transistor in 1947, and the subsequent invention of integrated circuits in 1958–1959, turned attention from making electricity span great distances, to making it span the distance between two atoms in a crystal lattice. The result was not merely miniaturization and high efficiency—it was a transformation of society. The computer has made possible vast gains in industrial productivity and global

communication; moreover, the "smart chip" has made possible achievements ranging from cars that emit far fewer pollutants to credit cards that carry not only banking information but also personal identification, professional attachments, and even records of private interests.

Background material on electrical engineering can be found in CHARGE AND CURRENT; ELECTRIC CIRCUIT; INSULATOR. *More details can be found in* CONDUCTORS AND INSULATORS; ELECTRIC CIRCUIT; ELECTRIC CIRCUITS, APPLICATIONS OF; MOTORS AND GENERATORS; TRANSFORMERS. *Additional relevant information is contained in* DIODE AND PHOTODIODE; TRANSISTOR.

First see ELECTRICITY AND ELECTRICAL ENGINEERING

Electrochemistry and Electroplating

Next see ELECTRON AFFINITY

An electric current refers to the flow of electric charges. One type of electric current is metallic conduction, as found in power lines and transistors. Another type of electric current is ionic conduction, which refers to the movement of positive and negative ions along a path. During electrolysis, electric current is carried by electrons in metals and by ions dissolved in solution. Electrons and ions do not flow spontaneously through a conductor. Electric forces, such as batteries, are needed to get the process started. With a battery, one terminal or electrode has an excess of negative charges and the other has an excess of positive charges. The negative electrode repels electrons, which are negatively charged, and the positive terminal attracts them, resulting in a continuous flow of electrons, known as direct current. (*See* ELECTRON EMISSIONS.)

A separate chemical reaction occurs at each electrode. When direct current is passed through an electrolyte solution, positive ions, or cations, are attracted to the negative electrode and gain electrons. Negative ions, or anions, are attracted to the positive electrode and lose electrons. The electrode where the cations gain electrons (become reduced) is called the cathode. The electrode where the anions lose electrons (become oxidized) is called the anode. The electrodes themselves are usually inactive materials such as platinum and graphite.

A complete electrical circuit is operating during electrolysis. The external circuit current is the flow of electrons; the flow of ions is the internal circuit current.

Electroplating. Electroplating involves the use of electrolysis to coat a material with a layer of metal. This is done to increase the value of the base material, improve its appearance, or protect against corrosion. A common example is silver plated cutlery or candlesticks that are made of a less expensive metal.

The object to be plated must be able to con-

A Simple Idea

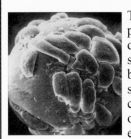

The best-known form of electrochemistry is probably xerography, which relies on photoconductive materials such as selenium. In the dark, selenium is an insulator; but when exposed to bright light, its electrons shift into an excited state, and it becomes a conductor. In a photocopier, an image of the document is projected onto the surface of a rotating drum; light causes the surface to become conductive, and it loses its charge in the light areas. Next, toner (small grains to which dry ink adheres—a micrograph of a grain with ink is shown at left) is applied, adhering by electrostatic force only to the dark parts of the image; the particles are then transferred to a sheet of paper, and fused together by heat. In a laser printer, the image is projected by a laser beam, which creates greater contrast between areas of light and dark, resulting in crisper printing.

duct an electric current. If it is a nonconductor, it is dusted with graphite. The object is then placed in a solution containing dissolved ions of the plating metal, such as silver nitrate, $AgNO_3$, which separates into silver cations $Ag+$ and nitrate anions NO_3^-. Metal cyanides are often used in electroplating solutions because they produce a more even coating.

The object to be plated is connected to the cathode, giving it a negative charge. A bar of the plating metal is used as the anode. When the current is on, positive metal ions in solution are attracted to the object. As the metal ions contact the object, they become reduced to neutral atoms, which are deposited on it. Gradually the metal bar becomes oxidized and dissolves into the solution, thereby replenishing the ions being removed for the coating. (*See* ELECTROMETALLURGY.)

First see ELECTRIC AND MAGNETIC FIELDS

Electromagnetic Force

Next see ELECTROMAGNETISM

The force produced by an electromagnetic wave as it travels through space.

In 1831 British scientist Michael Faraday found that when he set up an electric circuit, a change in the current carried by the circuit caused a change in the magnetic field surrounding the current, and this change carried an electromagnetic force.

The discovery was almost accidental; it occurred when Faraday put a bar magnet into a coil that was connected with a galvanometer, an instrument for measuring electric current, and noticed that there was a momentary deflection of the galvanometer's needle. Faraday found that the magnitude of the electromagnetic force is proportional to the rate of variation of the electrical flux through the circuit. If we represent the number of turns of the wire of a circuit as N, the flux through the wire as F, and the rate of change as d, then the electromagnetic force E generated by a circuit can be expressed by the formula $E = N \times dF/dt$. The units of this force are volts.

An American physicist, Joseph Henry, discovered the same effect about the same time as Faraday. Henry wound a few turns of an insulated wire around an iron keeper that was placed across the poles of a large electromagnet. Henry then connected the turns of wire to a galvanometer. Like Faraday, he observed that the needle of the galvanometer was deflected when the current in the electromagnet was being turned off and on, but that there was no deflection when the current was steady.

Henry also observed the effect called self-induction. He found that a long piece of wire produced a larger spark than a short wire when its contact with a battery was broken, and that the intensity of the spark was intensified if the wire was wound into a tight coil. Henry concluded that an electromagnetic force was induced in the coil because of the variation of the magnetic field in the coil.

Maxwell's Formulation. Another way to view electromagnetic force is to picture an electrical conductor moving through a magnetic field, or a magnetic field that is passing over a conductor in such a way that the conductor cuts across the magnetic lines of force. In this case, the electrical current in the conductor is subjected to a force that is at right angles to the electrical field and to the motion of the conductor or magnetic field. James Clerk Maxwell generalized this finding, saying that when magnetic lines of force move sideways, their movement produces an electric field at right angles to the magnetic lines and their direction of motion.

The practical consequences of the discovery of electromagnetic force have been enormous. It has been applied to the development of electrical generators, the telephone, the transformer, electric motors, and all electric appliances used at home and at work. The basic units of electricity and inductance, the volt and the henry, are defined in terms of electromagnetic force. The volt is defined as the steady potential difference that exists across a conductor that carries a current of one ampere and dissipates thermal energy at the rate of one watt. The henry is defined as the inductance of a coil in which an electromagnetic force of one volt changes the current in that coil at the rate of one ampere per second.

Joseph Henry's discovery of self-induction led to the triumph of alternating current electric power transmission, by enabling the invention of practical transformers. In a vacuum, the linkage through one circuit caused by a steady electric current in a neighboring circuit is the same as the linkage through the first circuit that is caused by a steady current in the other circuit. In other words, the mutual inductance of the two circuits is the same no matter which is the primary circuit. If two circuits are closely coupled and have high self-inductance, and an alternating electromagnetic force is applied to one circuit, the resulting alternating current induces an electromagnetic force in the other circuit proportional to the number of turns of wire in both circuits, stepping voltage up or down as needed.

Background material can be found in CHARGE AND CURRENT; ELECTRIC AND MAGNETIC FIELDS; FORCE. *Advanced subjects are developed in* ELECTRICITY AND ELECTRICAL ENGINEERING; ELECTRON EMMISSIONS. *Theoretical aspects of this subject are covered in* ELECTROMAGNETISM; ELECTRON AFFINITY; ELECTRONEGATIVITY.

First see WAVE

Electromagnetic Waves

Next see MAXWELL'S EQUATIONS

Waves that carry radiant energy through space, and can transfer that energy to matter.

Electromagnetic waves include not only light waves, radio waves, and x-rays, but also infrared waves, which carry heat. Electromagnetic waves are classified by their frequency—the number of cycles per second—and their length.

Electromagnetic waves can be pictured as a series of crests and troughs occurring at certain frequencies; wavelength is the distance between two adjacent crests. They are transverse waves, and thus can be pictured in terms of a rope shaken up and down: the waves created by that motion travel along its length. "Electromagnetic" means that every wave has an electrical and a magnetic component. The electric and magnetic fields of such a wave are both perpendicular to the direction in which the wave moves and to each other. (*See* ELECTRIC AND MAGNETIC FIELDS.)

Among the nineteenth-century scientists who contributed to the discovery of electromagnetic waves were Michael Faraday, James Clerk Maxwell, and H. C. Oersted. It was Oersted who first established in 1819 the relationship between the electric current and the accompanying magnetic field.

The longest electromagnetic waves are the waves that carry the alternating current that runs television sets, lights, and household appliances. Alternating current, the wavelength of which is long, is produced in generating plants, by a metal coil that rotates in a magnetic field. Wavelength is customarily measured in centimeters (one centimeter being equal roughly to four-tenths of an inch.) The electromagnetic waves of alternating current are about 10^7 centimeters long. (*See* ELECTRIC CIRCUIT.)

Radio and Television. Radio waves, used in communications, range in length from 10^3 to nearly 10^7 centimeters. When transmitted from a radio station, they reach our homes when they are reflected by the upper atmosphere.

Television sets receive ultra-high-frequency radio waves (also used in radar). They range in length from 10^{-1} centimeters to 10^3 centimeters. (*See* RADIO AND TELEVISION BROADCASTING.)

Infrared rays range in length from a 10^{-1} centimeters to 10^{-4} centimeters. They are generated by heat lamps and are also used in special photography and industrial drying equipment.

Visible light has wavelengths ranging from 10^{-6} to 10^{-4} centimeters. It enables us to see the world around us, and is used in photography and in some chemical reactions.

Ultraviolet light has wavelengths ranging from 10^{-7} centimeters to 10^{-6} centimeters. It is used in photography and in chemical reactions.

X-rays have wavelengths of 10^{-10} centimeters to 10^{-7} centimeters. Their most prominent use is in medical testing. (*See* X-RAYS.)

Gamma rays have wavelengths as small as 10^{-11} centimeters. They also are used in medicine, and are applied to the investigation of the subatomic world. (*See* GAMMA RAYS.)

The shortest electromagnetic waves, with lengths shorter than a hundred-billionth of a centimeter, arrive on Earth from space, presumably emitted by solar flares and other cosmic phenomena. On Earth, they are applied in physics, to study interactions in the atomic nucleus and subatomic particles. (*See* COSMIC RAYS.)

First see ELECTROMAGNETIC FORCE

Electromagnetism

Next see GAUGE THEORY

The study of electric and magnetic fields and their interaction with electric charges and electric currents.

When electric forces and magnetic forces were first studied, it was thought that they were separate entities. The discovery that they are related began in 1819, when Hans Christian Oersted, a Danish physicist, found that if a wire carrying an electric current is placed parallel to a compass needle, the needle will turn at a right angle to the direction of the current. The intensity of this magnetic effect of a current-carrying wire can be raised in several ways: by increasing the current running through the wire; by winding the conducting wire in a helix, called a solenoid; or by inserting an iron core in the center of the coil. (*See* INDUCTORS.)

The Right-Hand Rule. The direction of the magnetic field around a current-carrying wire can be determined by what is called the right-hand rule. If the conducting wire is grasped by the right hand, with the thumb pointing in the direction in which the current flows in the positive-to-negative direction, the fingers curl in the direction of the magnetic field. The polarity of

Considering that the power of a lightning flash was apparent since antiquity (and the force of gravity is an abstraction), it is remarkable that progress in understanding electricity and the electrical nature of lightning had to wait for the genius of investigators like Franklin and Faraday.

the solenoid, or electromagnet, can be determined by another right-hand rule. If the wire carrying the current of the electromagnet is grasped with the right hand with the fingers pointing in the direction of current flow, the thumb, when extended, points in the direction of the north pole of the magnetic field.

The magnetic force of an electromagnet, also called the flux density of magnetic induction, can be expressed in terms of the number of lines of force per centimeter, a unit called the gauss. A magnetic field, in turn, can influence the flow of electric current through a wire. When that wire is placed at a right angle to a magnetic field, the wire will move in a direction perpendicular both to the direction of the current that it carries and the direction of the magnetic field. The direction of the force exerted by the magnetic field on the wire can be determined by extending the thumb, index finger, and middle fingers of the right hand at right angles to one another, with the index finger pointing along the field and the middle finger pointing in the direction of the current. The thumb then indicates the direction of the force that is exerted on the current-carrying wire. This principle formed the basis of a famous 1909 experiment by Robert A. Millikan.

The principles of electromagnetism are the basis of almost all the electric devices used today, from television picture tubes to cyclotrons used by physicists, to mention just two.

Background material can be found in CHARGE AND CURRENT; ELECTRIC AND MAGNETIC FIELDS; INDUCTORS. *Advanced subjects are developed in* ELECTROMAGNETIC FORCE; ELECTROMAGNETIC WAVES. *More information on particular aspects of this subject is contained in* MAXWELL'S EQUATIONS *and* CONSERVATION LAWS IN NATURE. *Important tools for the study of electromagnetism are* CALCULUS *and* VECTORS AND TENSORS.

First see METAL

Electrometallurgy

Next see ELECTROCHEMISTRY AND ELECTROPLATING

Electrometallurgy and hydrometallurgy are two techniques that are used in metallurgy, which is concerned with extracting metals from ores, refining them, purifying them, and preparing them for use. Metallurgy also involves the study of the structure and physical properties of pure metals and alloys.

While some metals such as gold and silver can be found uncombined with other elements in nature, most metals occur as minerals—that is, in chemical combination with nonmetallic elements. When the combination is such that the extraction of a metal from such a mineral is economically attractive, the combination is called an ore. The technique of producing metals from ores is called process metallurgy or extraction

James Clerk Maxwell (1831–1879)

Further Reading
Dubroff, Richard E., *Electromagnetic Concepts and Applications* (1996); Phillips, W. R., *Electromagnetism,* (1991); Plonus, Martin A., *Applied Electromagnetics* (1978); Vanderlinde, Jack, *Classical Electromagnetic Theory* (1993).

An electron track in a bubble chamber.

metallurgy. A different branch of the technology, fabrication metallurgy, is concerned with the processes by which raw metals are made into alloys, sheets, wires, and other products. Yet another branch is physical metallurgy, concerned with the ways metals and alloys are worked mechanically, their heat treatment, and their testing. Physical metallurgy begins with the dressing of ore, using physical methods such as crushing, grinding, and separation by gravity to separate the various minerals that are found in a specific ore. (*See* STEEL AND WELDING.)

The next stage of physical metallurgy is the use of chemical activities such as electrometallurgy and hydrometallurgy to separate the metallic part of the ore from the undesirable nonmetallic segments. The method used in this stage depends on the chemical nature of the mineral compound—for example, whether it is an oxide or a sulfide, whether it is soluble in acid, and so on. Hydrometallurgy uses chemical reactions in aqueous solutions to extract a metal from its ore. Electrometallurgy uses electricity to separate the metal from the other elements in a compound.

Another branch of metallurgy, pyrometallurgy, covers roasting, smelting, and other high-temperature chemical reactions. Pyrometallurgy has the advantage of giving fast reactions and yielding a molten or gaseous product that can easily be separated from unwanted components. The extracted metal may need further refining or purifying; electrometallurgy can be used again at this stage. The molten metal that is produced may then be cast by pouring it into a mold or forming it into ingots. (*See* METALLURGY.)

First see ATOM

Electron

Next see ELEMENTARY PARTICLE

An electron is a subatomic particle; it was the first to be discovered. It has a very small mass, carries one unit of electric charge, and spins continually on an axis that passes through it, thus creating a magnetic field in its immediate vicinity. By convention, the electric charge of an electron is described as negative, while the charge on a proton is described as positive. The creation of this magnetic field around an electron is explained by the law of electromagnetism, which states that any moving electrical charge produces such a magnetic field.

The electron belongs to a class of elementary particles called leptons, which exert a force called the weak nuclear force. This force is stronger than the gravitational force between masses but weaker than the electrical force associated with positive and negative charges. The electron is not affected by the strong nuclear force, which holds the protons and neutrons of the atomic nucleus together.

It is the number, motion, and spin of electrons around the atomic nucleus that create magnetic effects for atoms. For example, if a majority of the electrons in the atom spin in one direction, that atom will have a net magnetic field.

The charge carried by an electron was determined in 1909 by American physicist R. A. Millikan, in what has become known as the oil-drop experiment. Millikan studied the movement of small electrically charged droplets of oil as they fell through electric fields. Since he knew the strength of the fields and the mass of the oil drops, Millikan could calculate the charge on each drop. He determined that they were all multiples of a basic charge, the charge on a single electron. The charge on an electron is expressed today as 1.60207×10^{-19} coulomb.

Quantum Numbers. An electron in orbit around an atomic nucleus is assigned a quantum number, m. This quantum number has two possible values, $+1/2$ and $-1/2$, corresponding to the direction of spin of the electron. Other quantum numbers describe the electron's energy level, orbital momentum, and magnetic momentum; together they provide a complete quantum description of the electron's behavior.

Each atom of a chemical element is defined by the number of protons in its nucleus and the number of electrons surrounding its nucleus; there is one electron for each proton. The electrons of an atom are arranged in shells around the nucleus. In general, the innermost shells of an atom are filled first, but there are exceptions in the case of some of the heavier elements. Interactions between the electrons in the outermost shells are responsible for chemical, physical, and biological phenomena, such as the formation of a molecule by ionic interactions.

Electricity. If energy is supplied to an appropriate material it can be made to release electrons, creating an electric current. This phenomenon is responsible for the vast complex of electric and electronic devices that are integral parts of our everyday lives—from the light bulb to the computer. The original unit of electronic systems was the electron tube, in which electrons or ions were made to flow between electrodes, creating electric currents that could be varied to create the desired results. Electron tubes now have been replaced by solid-state devices such as transistors and integrated circuits. The principle is still the same, however: a desired result, such as magnification of an ingoing or outgoing signal, is produced by the carefully controlled passage of electrons.

Further Reading
Close, F .E., *The Cosmic Onion: Quarks and the Nature of the Universe* (1986); Griffiths, D., *Introduction to Elementary Particles* (1987); McDaniel, E. W., *Atomic Collisions: Electron and Photon Projectiles* (1989); Rolnick, W. B., *The Fundamental Particles and their Interactions* (1994).

Background material regarding electrons can be found in ATOM; NEUTRON; PROTON. *Advanced subjects are developed in* ATOMIC SHELL MODEL; EXCLUSION PRINCIPLE; QUANTUM MECHANICS; VALENCE. *Additional relevant information is contained in* ELECTRON AFFINITY; ELEMENTARY PARTICLES; QUANTUM ELECTRODYNAMICS. *See also* RECORDING TECHNOLOGY *and* ELECTRICAL ENGINEERING.

First see ATOM

Electron Affinity

Next see ELECTRON

All atoms contain three subatomic particles: protons (positively charged), neutrons (no charge), and electrons (negatively charged). The protons and neutrons make up the nucleus, while the electrons orbit outside in discrete energy levels. Each principal energy level contains a specific number of sublevels, which in turn contain a specific number of orbitals. An orbital can hold a maximum of two electrons. The number of electrons per principal energy level is therefore dependent on the number of sublevels and orbitals it contains. The total arrangement of all the electrons within the orbitals, sublevels, and energy levels is known as the electron configuration. The outermost energy level that contains electrons is called the valence shell. All atoms desire a full valence shell in order to reach their most stable state. With the exception of the noble gases, however, this state does not occur naturally. One method of achieving this goal is to attract electrons from other atoms.

Anions. When an atom of a gas obtains an additional electron and becomes a negative ion (anion), the energy change that accompanies this transformation is known as the electron affinity (EA). If there is a convenient place to put this electron, such as a partially filled orbital within a partially filled level, the atom benefits by gaining the electron, it saves energy with this addition and has a positive EA. If such a niche does not exist, however, the transaction costs the atom energy, and there will be a negative EA.

The EA is generally consistent within each family of elements. Noble gases have a negative EA because they already have full valence shells, and the added electron would have to go into the next highest energy level. Halogens have the highest positive EA because they need only one more electron to fill their valence shells.

Lithium and sodium, both of which have only one valence electron, have moderate EA. Beryllium and magnesium, both of which have only two valence electrons, have negative or near zero EA. Nitrogen and phosphorus—both nonmetals only a few electrons short of a full valence shell—have low EA. (*See* VALENCE.)

First see ELECTRON

Electronegativity

Next see VALENCE

How strongly an atom attracts electrons—not only its own, but those belonging to other atoms as well.

All atoms desire a full complement of electrons in their outermost (valence) energy level, because that enables the atoms to be in their most stable energy state. With the exception of the noble gases, this condition does not exist naturally. Atoms attempt to complete their valence shells by a variety of means, either luring electrons away from other atoms in an ionic bond, or else sharing them in a covalent bond.

Bonding. The type of bond formed depends on the electronegativity values of the atoms involved. If the difference between the relative values is slight, the bond is covalent. If the difference is larger, the bond will still be covalent, but the atom with the greater electronegativity will monopolize the electrons, thus giving the bond a dipole character. This is known as a polar bond. If the discrepancy is very great, the bond will be ionic. (*See* ION; IONIC SOLID.)

Removal of an electron from its original atom requires a certain amount of energy, known as ionization energy because both atoms involved in the transaction become ions. With each subsequent lost electron, the atom becomes increasingly positive, and it becomes harder and harder to remove additional electrons. By the time the third electron is lost, the amount of ionization energy involved is so great that further removals become impossible. For this reason, atoms lacking three or fewer electrons in their valence shell are more electronegative and tend to gain electrons, whereas atoms with only one to three valence electrons are "electropositive" and tend to lose electrons.

Nonmetals are much more electronegative than metals. A bond between a metal and a nonmetal atom will thus be ionic. A bond between two nonmetals will be covalent, but may be polar, depending on the electronegativity values.

Patterns. Electronegativity follows a distinct pattern across the Periodic Table. Within a family (column), electronegativity is greatest at the top and weakest at the bottom due to the increasing number of energy levels, therefore increasing the distance of the valence electrons from the nucleus. Within a period (row), electronegativity is greater farther to the right, as the atomic nuclei are growing larger.

The noble gases are the most electronegative of all elements. They already have a full valence shell, so any attempt to remove an electron would "cost" a great deal of energy. The next most electronegative elements are fluorine, oxygen, and chlorine. The least electronegative elements are cesium and francium.

First see ELECTRON

Electron Emissions

Next see RADIO AND TELEVISION BROADCASTING

Electron emissions from surfaces were first discovered in the early 1800s, when Johann Wolfgang von Goethe recorded that certain substances, called "Bologna stones," gave off light when exposed to blue light, but not when exposed to red light. Over the next hundred years, researchers discovered other strange effects of light, such as the way certain rare metals emitted electricity when struck by light. But no one knew why, until Max Planck created the quantum theory: electrons surrounding the nucleus of an atom can occupy only a few widely separated energy levels, and to move from one level to another they must absorb, or emit, energy. (*See* LIGHT.)

Finally, in 1905, an obscure Swiss postal clerk named Albert Einstein used quantum theory to solve the photoelectric effect, as it is now called. Red light, it turned out, simply did not supply enough energy to cause electrons to change orbits, so the Bologna stones did not fluoresce in red light, although they might absorb enough energy to grow a little warmer. Blue light, however, had sufficient energy to shake electrons loose. (*See* SPECTROSCOPY.)

One of the first applications of this effect was the development in the 1920s of a camera using photoelectric cells rather than film emulsion to capture pictures involving action, and of a way of displaying such images through the electrical excitation of fluorescent patterns. Vladimir Zworykin called these inventions an iconoscope and a kinescope; we call them television. Today, the photoelectric effect is at the heart of transistor technology, photovoltaic technology, and solid state physics. (*See entries under each of these titles.*)

First see MICROSCOPY

Electron Microscopy

Next see SCANNING TUNNEL MICROSCOPY

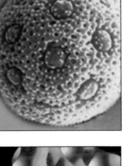

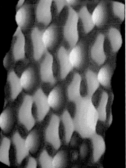

Electron microscopy has opened a microscopic world that could scarcely be imagined. Above, top, an electron micrograph of a pollen grain; bottom, a scanning tunnel microscopic (STM) image of iodine molecules on a platinum bed.

Electron microscopy takes advantage of the fact that electrons, like other elementary particles, behave like waves as well as particles. Because they have wavelengths that are much shorter than those of visible light, electrons can be used to study objects that are too small to be seen through ordinary microscopes. For example, an electron that is accelerated by a force of 50,000 volts has a wavelength that is 100,000 times shorter than that of green light. Because electrons carry an electric charge, they can be deflected by electric or magnetic fields, which allows them to be focused in the same way that a glass lens focuses a beam of light.

An electron microscope starts with the generation of electrons in what is called an electron gun, conssisting of a filament made of tungsten that is heated to a very high temperature, which makes the filament give off electrons. These electrons then pass through a vacuum chamber, where they are focused by circular and symmetrical magnetic fields, generated by circular coils through which a constant electric current flows. In the transmission-type electron microscope, sharp contrasts in the image are created by variations in the degree to which the accelerated electrons are scattered by the atoms of the sample that is being examined. This image can be observed on a fluorescent screen or recorded on a photographic plate positioned at the bottom of the microscope.

The magnification an electron microscope can attain is one million times the size of the specimen being studied, although magnifications between 200 and 20,000 are more common. The amount of magnification is limited by aberrations in the system of lenses used to focus the electron beam. These lenses do not have the same degree of accuracy as those used in light microscopes, but they do provide otherwise unobtainable images for a number of fields of science, including biology, bacteriology, chemistry, metallurgy, and crystallography.

More recently developed instruments include the scanning electron microscope, in which a beam of electrons is passed over the sample being studied, and the scanning transmission electron microscope, in which manipulation of the beam of electrons produces better-images of objects or surfaces under examination.

Related material is found in CELL; MICROBIOLOGY; MICROSCOPE. *Advanced subjects are developed in* FIBER-OPTICS; MEDICAL DIAGNOSTICS. *Relevant information is contained in* CT AND PET SCANS; PIEZOELECTRICITY; SCANNING TUNNEL MICROSCOPY.

First see CHROMATOGRAPHY

Electrophoresis

Next see DNA

A technique used to make a physical map of DNA at the molecular level.

DNA is a long molecule consisting of individual nucleotides, each containing a sugar molecule, a phosphate group, and a nucleic base. The four bases are adenine (A), guanine (G), thymine (T) and cytosine (C). Different gene sequences are determined by the pattern of these nucleic bases.

Technique. The DNA is broken apart at pre-determined points by the use of restriction enzymes that cut at specific sequences. Some enzymes recognize and cut at five specific bases, others at three or four bases, and still others at six or seven. Depending on the enzyme used, fragments of different lengths are created. The largest yet fewest fragments are generated by enzymes recognizing a six- or seven- base sequence, while the smallest and most numerous fragments are produced by enzymes recognizing a three- or four-base sequence. Two or more enzymes are used at the same time, so there will be overlapping fragments. The "double digest" method and overlapping fragments allow for a very detailed map. Sometimes end-labeling is also used, in which radioactive groups are added to the ends of segments to make them stand out even more. The segments will then be separated according to size with gel electrophoresis.

The solution containing the DNA sample mixed with the restriction enzymes is called a restriction digest. A blue dye is added to make the DNA fragments more visible, and then the restriction digest is deposited on a gel made of either agarosa or polyacrylamide. The gel is submerged in a salt solution capable of conducting electricity. The DNA molecule itself has a negative charge due to its phosphate groups. An electric current is passed through the gel, causing the fragments to move toward the positively charged end. How far the fragments get depends on their relative size; large fragments move more slowly than small ones. Over time, the fragments separate from each other.

The movement across the gel produces a series of bands that correspond to a specific fragment. The gel is calibrated by running a control, a mixture of standard fragments of known size, called markers, which are used for comparison. This defines the relationship between fragment length and the distance traveled.

The salt solution containing the gel contains a dye called ethidium bromide, which binds tightly to the DNA molecules. Ethidium bromide is colorless under normal light but turns pale orange in the presence of ultraviolet (UV) light. Once the gel has finished running, it is exposed to UV light and photographed. The resulting film shows clearly the DNA restriction fragment bands. The gel itself can then be discarded or the DNA fragments isolated for further manipulation. (*See* FORENSIC SCIENCE.)

First see ACCELERATOR, PARTICLE

Elementary Particle

Next see STANDARD MODEL

A particle—a constituent of matter—considered not to be comprised of other, more fundamental entities or particles. Some elementary particles, however, will be called that even after they are found (or thought) to be made of other things.

The first person who recorded his thoughts about the basic structure of matter was the Greek philosopher Democritus (c. 460–c. 370 B.C.E.). He asked a very profound question—what are the basic building blocks with which the entire physical universe is constructed? That he asked the question is in itself interesting, but the way he went about answering it was even more interesting. He began thinking about what would happen if one were to take the sharpest knife

Below, the process of gel electrophoresis is a routine procedure in many life science laboratories. The doubts regarding the reliability of DNA (genetic) fingerprinting, which uses this process, are at odds with the confidence the laboratory community has in the procedure.

imaginable and began slicing an object. One could cut the object, then take one half and cut it in half, then cut one of the quarters in half. He argued that if one kept cutting, one would eventually come to a piece of matter that could not be cut or divided. He gave this the Greek name "atom," a word which loosely means "that which cannot be divided."

Nineteenth-Century Theories. The only thing that survived of this original atomic theory of the Greeks was the Greek word "atom" itself. Then, in the early nineteenth century, the British chemist John Dalton published a book entitled *A New System of Chemical Philosophy*. In it, he compiled much of the new chemical knowledge that was being gathered in his day, and came up with a theory very close to what Democritus must have conceived.

For example, chemists knew that there were materials called elements (like carbon and aluminum) that could not be broken down by any chemical reactions. They also knew that there were many materials (such as wood, cloth, and rocks) that could be broken down by chemical means. Wood, for example, could be burned and reduced to carbon and various gases. Chemists also knew that these elements appeared in certain compounds in definite proportions. Water, for example, always contained one part of hydrogen by weight and one part of oxygen, no matter where the water came from.

Dalton proposed that the way to understand these and many of the regularities was to suppose that the smooth, continuous material that we perceive with our senses is in fact made up of fundamental entities. He called these entities *atoms*, using the word that had originally been coined by Democritus. Unlike Democritus' work, however, Dalton's work rested firmly on scientific experiment.

His fundamental hypothesis was that, for each of the known chemical elements, there was a different kind of atom, and that all other kinds of materials were simply different kinds of atoms hooked together—what we would call today a molecule. Dalton really did think of his atoms as being indivisible. Some of his sketches show his visualization of compounds resembling stacks of cannonballs.

To a Modern Theory. With Dalton, then, we come to the modern atomic theory. In this theory, the elementary particles—the fundamental building blocks of the universe—are atoms. Just as it is possible to make many different kinds of buildings from the same set of bricks, it is possible to make many kinds of materials from the same set of atoms. In this way, modern atomic theory reduced the complexity of nature. Even if there were a bewildering number of materials in nature, there would be only a small number of atoms.

Twentieth-Century Theories. Throughout

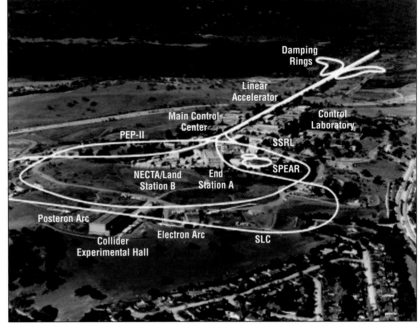

the nineteenth century, there was a continuing debate among scientists and philosophers about whether atoms were "real" or simply a convenient mathematical fiction. This debate was not resolved until the early twentieth century, when Albert Einstein worked out the theory of Brownian motion. Einstein showed that the motion of tiny particles was due to a statistical effect—that at any given moment more atoms were hitting one side of a particle than the other. The erratic path of each particle corresponded to these fluctuations at the atomic level. This pretty much resolved the debate, since it is hard to picture a mental construct causing a particle to move.

By the end of the nineteenth century, however, the notion of indivisible atoms was beginning to run into problems. For one thing, the electron had been discovered. Since electrons clearly came from atoms, the atom itself must have a structure. In 1911, Ernest Rutherford, a New Zealand physicist working in Manchester, performed an experiment that settled the structure of the atom once and for all. He directed a beam of radiation (think of it as a stream of subatomic bullets) at thin gold foil. He found that, while 999 out of 1,000 of his projectiles went through the foil or were scattered only slightly, one out of 1,000 came bouncing back at him. He later explained that it was like shooting a pistol into a cloud of mist and having a bullet come bouncing back. The most plausible explanation of Rutherford's experiment was to assume that most of the mass of the atom was concentrated in a very small dense body at the center. This body is called the nucleus.

Above, the Stanford Linear Accelerator (SLAC) facility has become one of the premier research laboratories in particle physics in the world.

Above, tracks of charged particles in an early bubble chamber photograph. Knowing the potential through which the particle was accelerated provides values for the particle's speed; and knowing the strength of the magnetic fields that curve the particle's path yields values for the particle's quantum numbers.

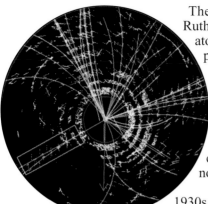

Above, the image that confirmed the existence of quarks, taken at the CERN laboratories in Switzerland in 1981.

The picture that resulted from Rutherford's work, then, was that the atom resembled the solar system. The positively charged nucleus sat at the center, and the negatively charged electrons moved around it in orbit. In succeeding years, it was discovered that the primary constituents of the nucleus were particles called the proton (which has a positive charge) and the neutron (which has no charge).

The Particle Zoo. Starting in the 1930s, physicists studying extremely high-energy rays discovered that there are not only protons and neutrons inside the nucleus, but literally hundreds of elementary particles as well, whizzing around, being emitted and absorbed and, in the process, holding the nucleus together. Today we know of at least 200 such particles. The particles that exist inside the nucleus of an atom are called "hadrons," from the Greek for "strongly interacting ones." Particles like the electron that do not exist inside the nucleus of an atom are called "leptons," from the Greek for "weakly interacting ones."

Enter the Quark. In 1963, the American physicists George Zweig and Murray Gell-Mann, working independently, proposed that even though the world of elementary particles had become complex, there was, one layer down, a world of simplicity. They suggested that all the elementary particles that exist inside the nucleus—protons, neutrons, and all the other 200 particles—were not themselves elementary, but consisted of things more elementary still. These truly elementary particles are called quarks (the name comes from a line in *Finnegan's Wake*). We have discovered evidence for six different kinds of quarks in the world. According to the quark model, all hadrons are made up of these six fundamental kinds of quarks (physicists use the word "flavor" to distinguish among quarks). There are also six leptons, a number that includes the electron.

Today's view. The basic structure of matter is organized by the six flavors of quarks which, taken together, make up the various hadrons. The hadrons make up the nuclei of atoms. These nuclei, along with the addition of electrons (in their orbitals) comprise the hundreds of different atoms. Atoms, in the form of the elements of the periodic table, are put together to construct all the matter in the universe. In this way, we have returned to a kind of simplicity that Democritus would no doubt have appreciated.

Further Reading
Close, F. E., *The Cosmic Onion: Quarks and the Nature of the Universe* (1986); Griffiths, D., *Introduction to Elementary Particles* (1987); Hughes, I. S., *Elementary Particles* (1991); Trefil, James, *From Atoms to Quarks* (1998).

Related areas and background is found in ATOM; NUCLEUS, ATOMIC; PROTON. *More details on this subject can be found in* ATOMIC SHELL MODEL; STANDARD MODEL. *Fundamental aspects of this subject are covered in* ACCELERATOR, PARTICLE; RADIOACTIVITY; WIMP (WEAKLY INTERACTING MASSIVE PARTICLE).

First see PERIODIC TABLE OF THE ELEMENTS

Elements, Distribution of

Next see NUCLEOSYNTHESIS

The distribution and evolution of the elements on the Earth are the subject of geochemistry, a branch of geology. But the study of the origin of the elements is part of astrophysics. All elements heavier than hydrogen, the lightest, are believed to have originated in stars, where temperatures and pressures are high enough to fuse two hydrogen nuclei, forming one helium nucleus, then fusing those helium nuclei to form heavier elements, which in turn form successively heavier elements. Star explosions, novas, and supernovas expel those atoms into space, where they become parts of the planets around the star.

Geologists have determined that the Earth has a core consisting largely of molten nickel-iron, with an intermediate shell called the mantle and an outer crust called the lithosphere. That determination was greatly influenced by the study of the meteorites that have struck the Earth. Studies of the Earth's crust have determined the chemical composition of the rocks that make up most of its mass. About 99.5 percent of the crust is made up of 11 elements, combined in various ways. In order of their abundance, those elements are oxygen (46.7 percent), silicon (27.7 percent), aluminum (8 percent), iron (5 percent), calcium (3.6 percent), sodium (2.8 percent), potassium (2.6 percent), magnesium (2.1 percent), titanium (0.63 percent), hydrogen (0.14 percent), phosphorus (0.13 percent), and carbon (0.094 percent). Most of the rocks of the lithosphere are silicates—silicon compounds—or aluminosilicates containing five elements: iron, calcium, sodium, potassium, and magnesium. The features that geochemists find of special interest include the high percentage of silicon and elements similar to silicon (aluminum, titanium, germanium), the relatively high concentration of iron, and the fact that, in most cases, elements with even-numbered atomic weights are more abundant than the odd-numbered elements that adjoin them in the Periodic Table.

Studies of the distribution of elements in the various mineral phases of rocks are the subject of the relatively new field of crystal chemistry. These studies have provided valuable information about the chemical reactions that take place in the Earth's crust. Among other information, crystal chemistry can illuminate the temperatures and/or pressures at which various minerals are formed. Chemical analysis of the Earth's atmosphere and of its organic matter, when combined with such studies of water and rock materials, have enabled geochemists to achieve a better understanding of the complicated interplay between the atmosphere, hydrosphere, lithosphere, and biosphere. (*See* ATMOSPHERE.)

Embryology

First see CONCEPPTION

Next see BIRTH

The study of the development of an embryo into an organism capable of living independently.

In the beginning of life, there is a single cell, the fertilized egg known as a zygote. The zygote divides several times until a ball of cells, the blastula, is formed. The blastula is a hollow structure, one cell layer thick. A portion of its cells make up the embryo and the rest form the embryonic membranes that help provide the embryo with all its needs.

The blastula develops into the gastrula, with two cell layers, through the process of invagination, an inward migration of cells. These cell layers are the ectoderm (outer) and the endoderm (inner). A third cell layer, the mesoderm, eventually forms between them through the same process. From these three cell layers arise all body systems and structures:

—ectoderm: central nervous system, skin;

—mesoderm: skeleton, muscles, reproductive, endocrine, and excretory systems;

—and endoderm: digestive system, lungs.

Cells that have the same structure and function and are located in the same area make up a tissue. Tissues located together, with the same general function, make up an organ. Organs with related functionality make up a system. For example, an individual cell that secretes a particular acidic enzyme, together with other cells of its type nearby, form a specific gastric tissue. Other tissues, which have cells that secrete other digestive enzymes, together make up the stomach, which in turn is one of several organs of the digestive system.

Differentiation. How do the cells "know" what kind of tissue to develop into? Somehow, probably through chemical messengers, the cells communicate with each other. Tissues develop in certain ways based upon which other tissues are nearby. This process is known as embryonic induction. Experiments have shown that it is location that directs the development process. Scientists have "rearranged" cells of early frog embryos. Cells that should have developed into eyes, upon being moved to the tail region, instead developed into more tail tissue. Cells from the tail, upon being transplanted to the head region, developed into tissue normally found on the head.

The amazing fact is that all of the diverse cells of the body originated from a single cell. Genes, composed of DNA, control all cellular activity, yet all body cells contain exactly the same genes, regardless of whether they are bone, skin, muscle, or nervous tissue, with vastly different appearances and functions. The reason for this is that during the early stages of development, during the rapid rounds of cell division and the formation of the early embryonic layers, all of the genes are "turned on full blast." Gradually, as enough cells have been formed and begin organizing into tissues, the cells begin to specialize

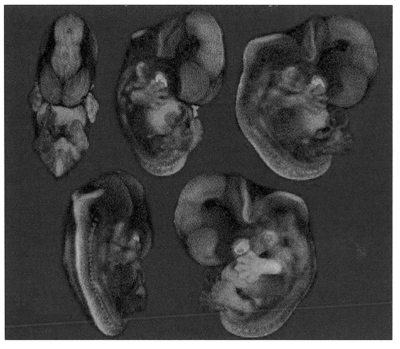

and differentiate. Some of the genes are now permanently inactive, whereas others are permanently active.

These cells are now known as adult cells, because they have become specialized. Much is still unknown about the controls that sculpt specialized tissues and organs from an undifferentiated mass of cells. In cloning mammals from adult cells, scientists have succeeded in resetting the cells' DNA to an earlier stage of development, in order to stimulate the development of a new organism.

Cancer Studies. There are links between embryology and cancer studies as well. Cancer is defined as uncontrolled cell growth at the expense of other normal cells nearby. It is almost as if the cancerous cell has reverted to its embryonic stage and begins rapidly dividing, even though the time for such activity is long past. The cells produced, abnormal in their functionality, are as mobile as early embryonic cells, capable of migrating elsewhere in the body and causing other cells to become cancerous as well. As scientists unravel the mysteries of embryology, there are certain to be some applications in combating cancer as well.

Special topics in this area are found in BIRTH; CONCEPTION; REPRODUCTIVE SYSTEMS. *Advanced subjects in embryology are developed in* BIRDS; CELL DIFFERENTIATION; MAMMALS. *Fundamental aspects of this subject are covered in* AMNIOCENTESIS; MORPHOGENESIS; PHYLOGENY.

An MRI gallery of a human embryo at seven weeks. By this stage, nearly all the cell differentiation has taken place, and the cells are focused on developing into the organs for which they are programmed.

Further Reading
Bensadoun, Paula D., *Life Before Birth: The Challenges of Fetal Development* (1996); Flanagan, Geraldine Lux, *The First Nine Months of Life* (1982); Moore, Keith L., *Before We Are Born: Essentials of Embryology and Birth Defects* (1998); Moore, Keith L., *The Developing Human: Clinically Oriented Embryology* (1998); Sadler, T. W., *Langman's Medical Embryology* (1995).

First see INSTINCTS

Emotions

Next see AGGRESSION AND TERRITORIALITY

The troublesome emotions—anger, fear, aggressiveness, despair—have drawn most of science's attention as it attempts to find a biological basis of mood and feeling. The search has brought a growing appreciation of the widespread and interrelated effects of neurotransmitters, such as seratonin and dopamine, and hormones, such as estrogens and androgens, in affecting emotion. In fact, whole classes of psychiatric illness or personality type once attributed to psychological, cognitive, or moral problems are now seen as primarily biochemical conditions that should be chemically correctable. Researchers are seeking genetic components of mental states. This has raised some concern that simplistic interpretations could cause people to be labeled, in effect, "born criminals."

Pharmacology. Even though the biological mechanisms of emotion are not fully understood, current knowledge is being widely applied. Among the most-prescribed drugs in the United States are Prozac™ (fluoxetine) and other antidepressants of the class called selective seratonin reuptake inhibitors, which elevate mood by allowing seratonin to remain active longer in the brain. These not only appear to lift depression and alleviate panic, but also to reduce impulsive aggressive behavior, independent of changes in depression. A variety of studies have found that the major metabolite of seratonin—5-HIAA—is lower in people who have a history of violence.

Another major class of antidepressants—known as the MAOIs, which includes such drugs as Parnate—also increases the activity of seratonin, as well as other neurotransmitters. These drugs inhibit an enzyme called MAO (monoamine oxidase) that breaks down seratonin, dopamine, and noradrenaline in the brain.

Estrogen, the hormone that stimulates sexual characteristics and regulates fertility in women, affects emotion by acting on the neurotransmitter system in a different way. It stimulates increases in dopamine and seratonin receptors in several areas of the brain that help control emotion, mood, and cognition. When given as therapy, estrogen has been found to alleviate depression in menopausal women, and to prevent it in those with a history of postpartum and premenstrual syndrome depression.

The areas of the brain most closely associated with emotion are known collectively as the limbic system. This includes the hypothalamus, amygdala, septal areas, hippocampus, and prefrontal cortex. Electrical stimulation of some of these areas in animals yields obvious signs of rage or pleasure. In general, the brain's right hemisphere tends to be concerned with negative emotions and arousal, while the left deals with positive emotions and inhibiting arousal.

Experiments. In animal experiments, the small, almond-shaped amygdala seems especially important in allowing an animal to interpret its world emotionally—is an approaching stranger to be feared? In both rats and humans, the amygdala is thought to be essential for learning and expressing conditioned fear.

In experiments in which a tone was paired with a shock to condition fear in rats, Joseph LeDoux found that the tone was conveyed by two different routes to the amygdala. One route went through the auditory cortex and prefrontal association areas. The other, which bypassed these stops, was faster and more direct. When the rat's auditory cortex was destroyed, it still responded with fear to a tone it could not hear. The conditioning, it appeared, took place in the brain below the cortex. In the wild, this system would allow the rat to react to a possible threat before its brain could fully evaluate the stimulus as dangerous or not. The survival value of such a system is obvious. But, as noted by Richard Restak, it may also help explain why phobias can be so resistant to treatment by rational means.

Further developments in the field are discussed in ADAPTATION; BRAIN; INSTINCT. *More details can be found in* AGGRESSION AND TERRITORIALITY; ETHOLOGY; REFLEXES; STRESS. *Additional relevant information is contained in* ADDICTIVE DISORDERS; AUTISM; MENTAL DISORDERS; SCHIZOPHRENIA. *See also* ENDOCRINE SYSTEM; NERVOUS SYSTEMS; NEUROTRANSMITTERS.

Further Reading
Damasio, Antonio, R., *The Feeling of What Happens: Body and Emotion in the Making of Consciousness* (2000); Johnston, Victor S., *Why We Feel: The Science of Human Emotions* (2000); Le Doux, Joseph, *The Emotional Brain* (1998); Sternberg, Esther M., *The Balance Within* (2000).

First see VIRUS

Encephalitis

Next see VIRAL DISEASES

A viral infection that causes inflammation of the brain. It may also affect the meninges, the membranes that encase the brain.

The most common virus in cases of encephalitis is the herpes simplex virus, type 1, which also can produce cold sores. Infection with HIV, the human immunodeficiency virus responsible for AIDS, may also cause encephalitis. The disease may also be a side effect of other viral infections, such as measles and mumps.

The first symptoms of encephalitis usually are fever, headache, and lethargy. These are usually followed by confusion, hallucinations, partial paralysis, and disturbances of speech, memory, vision, and eye movement. Coma and epileptic seizures may occur in some patients. If the meninges are infected, there can be neck stiffness and an unusual sensitivity to light. Diagnosis of the disease may require an electroencephalogram, to measure brain activity, and a lumbar puncture, in which fluid is taken from the spinal column for analysis. In severe cases, doctors may perform a brain biopsy, removing a small amount of brain tissue for analysis. If the encephalitis is caused by the herpes simplex virus, it can be treated successfully with acyclovir, an antiviral drug given by intravenous drip. Treatment for other viruses that cause encephalitis is less effective, and the patient may experience brain damage, impairment of mental function, disturbances of behavior, and even persistent epilepsy. In some of these cases, encephalitis can be fatal. (*See* VIRAL DISEASES.)

First see ENZYME

Endocrine System

Next see DIGESTION REGULATION

The endocrine system is made up of ductless glands that secrete hormones, chemical messengers that travel through the bloodstream to regulate the activity of other cells. Along with the nervous system, with which it interacts, the endocrine system regulates almost all metabolic activities, helps determine the pace of growth, controls every step of reproduction, and is crucial to homeostasis, the process of maintaining a stable internal environment—blood pressure, fluid balance, and the like—so that cells can function at maximum efficiency.

The system characteristically works through feedback mechanisms, usually negative feedback. For instance, when thyroxine, a thyroid hormone, is at low levels in the blood, the pituitary gland releases a thyroid-stimulating hormone. This causes a rise in thyroxine, which in turn inhibits the pituitary from releasing more thyroid-stimulating hormone.

An antagonistic system—with a finely tuned interplay between stimulating and inhibiting factors—is typical of the endocrine system. For instance, the important task of maintaining blood glucose levels within a narrow range requires not only insulin, which lowers glucose in the bloodstream, but glucagon, which raises it. At least four other hormones also raise blood glucose levels, while others affect the release of insulin or glucagon or alter the appetite.

Biorhythms also play a role in the release of hormones. Cycles may be daily, as with cortisol secretion; monthly, as with menstruation; or seasonal, as with changes in thyroxine production. (*See* CELL CYCLE.)

In lower vertebrates, endocrine tissue is often diffuse. Even in higher vertebrates, including humans, some endocrine cells are found within the liver, kidney, and digestive tract. But in tetrapods (four-legged animals), most of the endocrine system is concentrated in discrete organs—the principal ones being the pituitary, thyroid, parathyroids, adrenals, pancreas, ovaries, and testes. The organs are diverse in origin and are not anatomically linked.

Chemistry. Most hormones are either polypeptides, composed of long chains of amino acids; amines, derived from amino acids; or glycoproteins, composed of large proteins and carbohydrates. The hormones of the adrenal cortex, such as cortisol, and of the gonads, such as testosterone, are steroids—lipids synthesized from cholesterol. (*See* STEROID HORMONES.)

Hormones are generally released into the bloodstream but affect only those cells that have the right receptors. Some receptors, such as those for insulin, are found throughout the body; others are more narrowly distributed. Many hormones, such as estrogens or testosterone, have multiple and diverse effects. Some can bind to another hormone's receptors, blocking its action; this blocking potential is the basis of some drugs as well. (*See* BLOOD.)

Endocrine effects tend to be slower and more sustained than the effects produced by the nervous system, but the two systems are closely intertwined. The brain influences the rate of most hormonal secretions, and most hormones influence brain activity. Both nerve and endocrine cells release chemicals that react with receptors in target cells—and in many cases, the chemicals are identical, even if they are called neurotransmitters when synthesized by nerve cells and hormones when secreted by endocrine

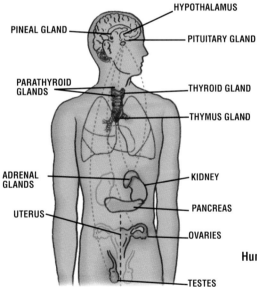

Human endocrine system.

glands. In addition, some nerve terminals release hormones into the circulation, just as endocrine glands do, a process called neurosecretion.

The Master Gland. Nowhere is the connection clearer than in the interplay between the hypothalamus region of the brain and the pituitary gland, sometimes called the master gland of the endocrine system. Together they regulate much of the rest of the endocrine system. The pituitary has two lobes, the anterior and the posterior, which are connected by a stalk to the hypothalamus. The posterior lobe (also called the neurohypophysis) releases two hormones—oxytocin, which causes the uterus to contract in labor, and vasopressin (also called antidiuretic hormone, ADH), which affects fluid balance by stimulating the kidneys to reabsorb more water. These hormones actually are produced by nerve cells in the hypothalamus, which delivers them through the stalk to the posterior lobe for storage. The hypothalamus eventually triggers their release as well. (*See* KIDNEYS AND EXCRETORY SYSTEMS *and* THYROID GLAND.)

In addition, the hypothalamus regulates the many important hormones produced by the pituitary's anterior lobe (also called the adenohypophysis). These include growth hormone (GH), whose metabolic effects make it crucial to normal growth; and prolactin, which stimulates milk production and plays other roles in reproduction, metabolism, and fluid balance. The anterior lobe also produces hormones that stimulate other glands: thyroid-stimulating hormone (TSH); adrenocorticotropic hormone (ACTH), which stimulates the adrenal cortex; follicle-stimulating hormone (FSH), and luteinizing hormone (LH), which stimulate the gonads.

The hypothalamus, meanwhile, stimulates the stimulator—it produces releasing hormones that spur production of each of these pituitary hormones. In a few cases, the hypothalamus produces inhibiting hormones as well. The hypothalamus hormones, in turn, are under feedback control. If the adrenal cortex, for instance, produces more hormone, then the hypothalamus produces less corticotropic releasing hormone, which means the pituitary produces less ACTH to stimulate the adrenal cortex.

Adrenal Glands. The two adrenal glands, which lie on top of the kidneys in humans, have separate components in mammals. The medulla, the core of the gland, secretes adrenaline and noradrenalin (also called epinephrine and norepinephrine), hormones that produce the "fight or flight" response. They quicken the heartbeat and increase blood pressure, oxygen consumption, blood glucose levels, and blood flow to the heart and skeletal muscles.

The adrenal cortex, the outer part of the gland, produces steroid hormones that are essential to life in vertebrates. These include cortisone and other glucocorticoids that raise blood-sugar levels while regulating protein and carbohydrate metabolism, and mineralocorticoids, such as aldosterone, which play a role in controlling blood pressure, blood volume, and salt balance.

The thyroid, located in the neck, is a single gland in humans, but occurs in pairs in most vertebrates. It produces two hormones that elevate the basal metabolism rate and help metabolize protein. Low levels lead to mental and physical lethargy and if untreated at birth, can cause cretinism, stunting size, intelligence, and sexual development. In mammals, the thyroid also pro-

duces calcitonin, which prevents the accumulation of high levels of calcium in the blood. In lower vertebrates, calcitonin is secreted by the ultimobranchial glands.

The parathyroids are small glands embedded in the thyroid. Their hormone acts as a calcitonin antagonist, stimulating the release of calcium from bones into the blood. (*See* THYROID.)

Important digestive hormones—gastrin, secretin, and cholecystokinin—are produced by the epithelial cells lining the stomach and duodenum. The thymus, an organ located in front of the aorta, secretes thymosin, which stimulates immune system cells. The pineal gland, a small lobe in the brain, produces melatonin, which affects the pituitary's secretion of gonadotropins, apparently in response to light. (*See* DIGESTION *and* METABOLIC PATHWAYS.)

Further Reading
Kascoh, B., *Endocrine Physiology* (2000); Litwack, Gerald, *Hormones* (1997); Nuland, Sherwin, *The Wisdom of the Body* (1992); Sternberg, Esther M., *The Balance Within* (2000); Vines, Gail, *Raging Hormones* (1994).

First see CELL

Endoplasmic Reticulum and Golgi Apparatus

Next see MITOSIS

The endoplasmic reticulum (ER) and Golgi apparatus are two cellular organelles that are composed largely of membranes. Together with the various types of vacuoles, membrane-bound sacs used for storage and related activities, they comprise the cytomembrane system. The ER and Golgi apparatus work together in protein trafficking, sorting and directing proteins to their final destinations.

The ER is a network of membrane tubes used for intracellular transport. It extends throughout the entire cytosol of the cell. "Rough" endoplasmic reticulum has ribosomes, the protein-synthesizing organelles, attached to its walls. "Smooth" endoplasmic reticulum does not have them. Most lipids are synthesized in the ER. The process of lipid trafficking—how other membranes "pick up" their lipid components from the ER—is not entirely understood.

Golgi Apparatus. The Golgi apparatus, or body, is a stack of flat membranes that functions as the "factory" of the cell. It is responsible for chemically modifying, sorting, and packaging various large molecules, which are then delivered to other organelles or exported from the cell entirely. A Golgi body wraps its products in vesicles, membrane-bonded fluids formed from its own membrane sheets, which can move freely about the cell and penetrate through and fuse with other membranes.

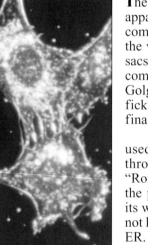

Electron micrograph of the Golgi apparatus in the center of the photograph. The Golgi apparatus seems to serve as a clearing house for substances being exchanged between the endoplasmic and exoplasmic domains. The structure is named after Camillo Golgi (1843-1926), who shared the 1906 Nobel Prize for his work on the structure of the nervous system.

Background material can be found in CELL; CYTOPLASM; WATER IN LIVING CELLS. *Further developments in the field are discussed in* BASAL BODIES AND CENTRIOLES; CELL MEMBRANE; CILIA; FLAGELLA; METABOLISM. *Special topics in this area are found in* CYTOSKELETON; MITOCHONDRIA; MICROSCOPY.

Energy

First see FORCE

Next see ENERGY, ALTERNATIVE

The ability to do work.

Energy is most broadly defined as the ability to do work. When a force moves an object, the work that is done is the product of the average value of the force along the direction of motion and the distance that the object is moved. The energy of any body is the sum of its kinetic, potential, and rest-mass energy. (*See* SPECIAL RELATIVITY.)

Form of Energy. Kinetic energy is measured by the mass of an object and the speed with which it moves. The faster an object moves and the more massive it is, the more kinetic energy the object has. The kinetic energy of a body of a mass m, moving with a velocity v, is $1/2mv^2$.

Potential energy is defined by the position of an object at rest in a force field, such as gravity. When a book is lifted off a table, for example, the book gains potential energy by virtue of its new position. If the book is dropped onto the table, the drop releases as much energy as was created when the book was lifted. Every object has the lowest potential energy consistent with the constraints on it. The potential energy of the book would thus be increased if it were dropped onto the floor rather than the table.

An important form of potential energy is associated with the electromagnetic forces between the nuclei of atoms and the electrons that circle the atomic nucleus. Electrons are attracted toward the nucleus because they have a negative charge while the nucleus has a positive charge, but they continue to circle the nucleus in orbits fixed by the laws of quantum mechanics. When an electron does fall from an outer orbit to one that is closer to the nucleus, it releases some potential energy, usually in the form of light. When molecules, which are collections of atoms, collide, their nuclei and electrons are rearranged into a configuration with the lowest possible potential energy. If the potential energy of the new arrangement is lower than that of the previous arrangement, potential energy is released. This is what happens when fuel is burned: the oxygen atoms of the air combine with the atoms of the fuel to release energy. In the human body, oxygen atoms combine with sugar atoms to release the energy that enables the body to do work. (*See* FOSSIL FUEL POWER.)

Internal energy is the sum of all the potential energies of the electrons and nuclei of a body, plus the potential energies of the molecules in the force fields of all the other molecules, plus the kinetic energies associated with the thermal motion of the molecules. Internal energy exists because no molecules are ever at rest. Molecules of a body or a liquid vibrate about their equilibrium positions, while molecules of a gas move through space. While the movement of each molecule is random, the total energy associated with all their movements can be measured. This internal energy is related to the temperature of a body or gas. When two bodies or gases at different temperatures come into contact, the system with the higher temperature transfers internal energy to the one at lower temperature until the difference disappears. This transfer is made by collisions between molecules. The transfer of internal energy from one system to another is called heat-flow energy. For example, the energy created by the combustion of a stove's fuel is transferred to the walls of the stove as heat, and to the food that is being cooked as chemcial reactions. (*See* HEAT.)

Our Energy Future. The possibility of converting one form of energy into another—the chemical energy of fossil fuel, say, into the mechanical energy that drives electric generators and machines —is responsible for the growth of industry in this century. But as the graph below shows, that system has limitations that could prove disastrous.

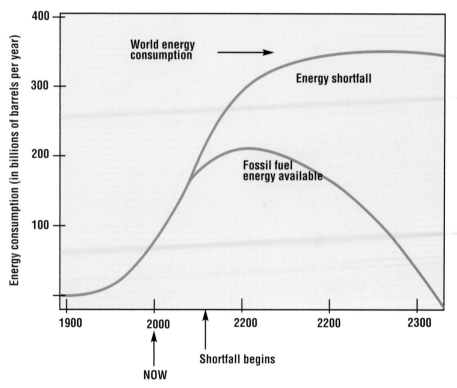

PROJECTED ENERGY SHORTFALL

In 1900, a fundamental property of energy was discovered: it is quantized—that is, energy is transferred from one system to another in very small packets, called quanta. In an atom, for example, electrons can only have orbits that correspond to quanta of energy. When this energy is transferred outside the atom, the transfer is made in the quanta that permit electrons of the atom to move from one orbit to another. This quantum property of energy is not observable in everyday life because individual quanta are very small, but it can be measured on the atomic level.

Energy is one of the few conserved quantities in nature. While it can be changed from one form to another or transferred from one system

Further Reading
Aubrecht, Gordon J., *Energy* (1994); Caneva, Kenneth L., *Robert Mayer and the Conservation of Energy* (1993); Hiebert, Erwin N., *Historical Roots of the Priciple of the Conservation of Energy* (1981); Ramage, Janet, *Energy: A Guidebook* (1997); Ricketts, Jana, *Energy and Environmental Visions for the New Millennium* (1998).

to another, it cannot be created or destroyed. The law of the conservation of mass-energy says that any collection of objects isolated from the rest of the universe can neither gain nor lose total energy, regardless of how the objects interact with one another. (*See* CONSERVATION LAWS.)

First see ENERGY

Energy, Alternative

Next see DESERTIFICATION

Alternative sources of energy are those that do not use fossil fuels such as coal and oil. These alternate sources often rely on energy provided by nature. Major alternative energy sources include geothermal energy, wind power, tidal power, and solar energy. About 8 percent of our total energy use comes from alternative sources.

Geothermal energy has been used for centuries; the Romans built communal baths over hot springs. The warmth generated below the Earth's surface can be used to generate power through steam turbines and thermocouple generators. The United States currently has a geothermal capacity of 2,700 megawatts per day.

Wind power has also been harnessed for centuries; the picturesque windmills of the Netherlands are examples. In the United States, thousands of small wind generators were in operation on farms until the early 1940s, when the rural electrification program of the federal government was one of the factors that led to their abandonment. Complete sets of hardware that combine wind generators and electric storage batteries with a capacity of 1,000 kilowatt-hours are available commercially. The winds available in the United States could generate several billion kilowatt-hours of electricity. Wind generators installed all over the entire state of North Dakota could provide more than one-third of the nation's energy needs.

Tidal power systems use the energy of inflowing and outflowing tidal waters to turn turbines that generate electricity. Among such systems in operation is the Rance development in northeastern France, completed in 1967 with a total capacity of 240,000 kilowatts per day. Areas where tidal ranges are the largest are the best locations for tidal power systems. These areas include the Bay of Fundy in Canada and the Gulf of California in Mexico.

Solar Energy. Solar energy systems capture the energy in sunlight. Three methods are used to generate solar-electric power: the solar-thermal distributed receiver system (STDS), the solar-thermal central receiver system (STCRS), and the photovoltaic system (PVS).

In the STDS, solar energy is absorbed by flat-plate collectors or parabolic-trough concentrators. Both use the heat gathered in this way to generate electricity by turning a turbine. A flat-

Sources of alternative energy that are being developed include (from top left, clockwise): wind power (in the desert area of California); nuclear power (a cooling tower of a nuclear power plant in Missouri); solar energy (on a solar power farm in Hesperia, California); and geothermal energy (being "mined" in northern California).

Further Reading
Beattie, Donald A., *History and Overview of Solar Heat Technologies* (1997); Crowther, Richard L., *Sun/Earth: Alternative Energy Design for Architecture* (1983); Schaeffer, John, *The Real Goods Solar Living Sourcebook: The Complete Guide to Renewable Energy Technology and Sustainable Living* (1999); Seymour, Richard J., *Ocean Energy Recovery: The State of the Art* (1992).

plate collector operates at turbine inlet temperatures of 120° to 260° Fahrenheit. A parabolic trough concentrator focuses the sunlight it receives on a heat pipe carrying a working fluid, and achieves temperatures of 300° to 530° Fahrenheit at the turbine inlet. Because a higher temperature means higher efficiency and the need for less land to be covered by collectors, the parabolic trough concentrator can generate more electricity, but it is more expensive than flat-plate collectors.

In the STCRS, sunlight is concentrated on a receiver by a large number of heliostats, mirrors that follow the sun throughout the day. The receiver is a heater located on top of a tower. The power output depends on the area of the array of collectors; this area also determines the height of the tower on which the receiver is mounted. The horizontal distance of the mirror that is farthest from the foot of the tower is about twice the height of the tower.

In the photovoltaic system, solar cells are used to generate direct-current electricity. In most cases, this must be converted to alternating current. The principal advantage of the photovoltaic system is that it does not require moving parts and does not need cooling equipment. Its major disadvantage is its low efficiency. A photovoltaic system converts less than 20 percent of the sunlight it receives into electric power.

The foundations of the subject are discussed in ENERGY; FOSSIL FUEL POWER. *More details can be found in* FUSION, NUCLEAR; GEOTHERMAL ENERGY; NUCLEAR POWER; SOLAR ENERGY. *Advanced subjects are developed in* FUSION, NUCLEAR; HAZARDOUS WASTE DISPOSAL. *See also* SUPERCONDUCTOR.

Energy, Equivalence of Mass and

First see ENERGY

Next see SPECIAL RELATIVITY

The equivalence of mass and energy, described by Albert Einstein in 1905 as part of the special theory of relativity, states that the mass of a body is a measure of its total energy content. The most familiar expression of this statement is the equation $E=mc^2$, where E is energy, m is mass, and c is the speed of light. Perhaps the most impressive result of this principle is that it is possible to utilize some of the mass of a system and convert it to energy. This is done in nuclear weapons, such as the atomic bomb, and for peaceful purposes in nuclear reactors that generate electricity. The energy released by one fissioning atom of uranium is about 2.5 million times greater than that from the chemical combustion of a carbon atom.

Symmetry. Conversely, it is possible to create actual mass by converting kinetic energy. This process is put to practical use in the experimental tools of high-energy physics. For example, a proton traveling at a very high speed can be made to collide with another proton that is at rest. The result is the creation of another subatomic particle, a pion or a meson, by conversion of the energy of the other two particles. The mass-energy equivalence violates one of the major tenets of classical physics, which upholds the principle that mass is always conserved. In special relativity, neither mass nor energy is conserved, because each can be converted into the other. What is conserved is the system's rest-frame total energy, which combines the rest-mass of the system with the energy of each constituent, which equals mc^2 for the total system.

Another aspect of the principle is that in the rest frame of any system, any form of normal energy—thermal (heat), kinetic, chemical, or nuclear—has a mass associated with it. At low velocities, the mass of the system has the properties of inertia and gravitational interactions that are identical or nearly identical with the predictions of classical Newtonian physics. At high velocities, the dynamic and gravitational properties of the system must be determined by applying the principles of both special and general relativity to the mass in motion.

Speed Limit. The principle of mass-energy equivalence also sets a limit on the velocity that any body can achieve. At the speed of light, the mass of a particle would become infinite. Thus, while particles can approach the speed of light, and massless particles can travel at the speed of light, no particle with mass can reach the speed of light. Whether a particle can travel faster than light is currently under investigation; such particles, if they existed, would be called tachyons.

Albert Einstein (1879–1955)

Further Reading
Goldstein, Martin, *The Refrigerator and the Universe: Understanding the Laws of Energy (1997)*; Morowitz, Harold J., *The Thermodynamics of Pizza* (1992); Morowitz, Harold J., *Entropy and the Magic Flute* (1993); Trefil, James, *The Unexpected Vista* (1983); Von Baeyer, Hans Christian, *Maxwell's Demon: Why Warmth Disperses and Time Passes* (1998)

Entropy

First see ENERGY

Next see PHASE

The thermodynamic quantity that describes the degree of disorder in a physical system.

In thermodynamics, entropy (symbol S) is related to the absolute temperature, pressure, and volume of a substance. Entropy increases whenever the internal disorder of a physical sample increases or when its store of free or available energy decreases. When a system experiences a reversible change, the accompanying entropy change is equal to the amount of energy transferred to the system by heat divided by the temperature at which the change occurs. The change can be expressed by the formula $S=Q/T$, where Q is the amount of heat energy that is transferred and T is the absolute temperature at which the transfer takes place. If a mass of matter is cooled, its entropy increases. In general, however, irreversible changes are accompanied by an increase in entropy.

The total entropy of a substance in its standard state is defined as its standard entropy. For example, the standard state of a gas on Earth is defined as one atmosphere of pressure at a specified temperature, and its standard entropy is the change that occurs when the gas is put under zero pressure or when the pressure is changed from one atmosphere to zero.

The absolute entropy of a substance cannot be determined; only a change in entropy has real meaning. The value of the change of S is not affected by the path by which energy is transferred, but only by the starting and finishing states of the system that is being studied. One example of a reduction of entropy is the liquefaction of gas under high pressure. The heat generated by the gas as it becomes liquid is removed to a cooler surrounding. A more common example is the increase in entropy that occurs when ice is melted to form water; the disorder of the water molecules, and hence the entropy of the sample, increases.

The Second Law. The principle of entropy is another way to state the second law of thermodynamics: if any isolated physical system is left to itself and allowed to distribute its energy in its own way, the system's entropy always increases and the system's available energy decreases.

The concept of entropy can be applied to the universe as a whole. If the universe is considered to be a closed system, the fact that it is expanding indicates that its energy is decreasing and its entropy increasing. If the entropy of the universe reached a maximum, all samples of matter would be at a uniform temperature, and no energy would be available to do work. This state would be described as the heat death of the universe.

First see PROTEIN METABOLISM

Enzymes

Next see DIGESTION REGULATION

Proteins that act as catalysts in the cell, regulating chemical reactions.

Enzymes are highly specific and can only be involved in one chemical reaction. If the reaction is reversible, the enzyme can catalyze in either direction. Most enzyme names end in *ase*.

Like other catalysts, enzymes speed up chemical reactions by lowering the amount of activation energy necessary to start the reaction, making it possible for a reaction to occur under normal cellular conditions of temperature and pH. An enzyme does not affect the energy output of a reaction, nor can it cause an impossible reaction to occur. The enzyme is not affected in any way or "used up" by the reaction; it may be used over and over again.

Active Sites. For a reaction to occur, the reactants must collide at the proper angle. Enzymes bring the reactants, called substrates, together by binding with them. The "active site" of the enzyme is designed specifically to fit a particular substrate. Depending on the reaction the enzyme is meant for, it may have more than one active site to accommodate the various substrates. Once the enzyme-substrate complex has formed, the reaction occurs and the products are released. The interaction between an enzyme and its substrate is described by the "lock and key theory," because the active site and substrate fit together just as a key fits a particular lock.

Inactive Enzymes. Many enzymes exist in inactive form and must first be activated in order to work. The inactive precursor of an enzyme is called a zymogen or proenzyme. They are activated by the cleavage of one or more specific bonds that free up the component amino acids and allow them to assume a different shape. It is the new conformation that allows the enzyme to function. Examples of proenzymes include pepsinogen, a stomach enzyme that is converted to pepsin in the presence of hydrochloric acid. This is an important control mechanism ensuring that the enzyme will not activate when its substrate is not present.

The turnover rate of an enzyme is the number of molecules of substrate that can be handled per second. An average enzyme has a turnover rate of approximately 10^8. A fast enzyme can have a turnover rate of 10^{15}. The turnover rate of an enzyme is affected by the temperature, pH, and presence or absence of an inhibitor.

Each enzyme has an optimum temperature and pH. Straying too far from that optimum can cause the enzyme to become denatured, or literally "bent out of shape." Since an enzyme's shape determines which substrates and reactions

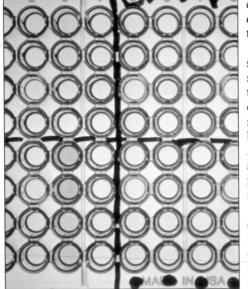

ELISSA Assay Test Plate. Above, an enzyme-lined immunoabsorbant assay (ELISA) plate, a test that can detect small quantities of antigens and antibodies—HTLV-III viral antibodies in this case. The positive reaction is indicated by the dark brown color of the horseradish-based gel at lower left.

it is involved in, changing the shape seriously undermines the ability of the enzyme to perform. Up to that point, however, an increase in ten degrees Celsius will cause the turnover rate to double.

An inhibitor is a molecule shaped enough like the substrate to offer serious competition for the active site of an enzyme. As long as the active site is occupied by the inhibitor, the turnover rate is zero. A temporary inhibitor eventually leaves the active site; a permanent inhibitor permanently disables an enzyme.

Coenzymes. Small molecules that assist an enzyme are knowns as coenzymes. Many coenzymes are molecules called vitamins, such as niacin and riboflavin, which are involved in many of the steps of cellular respiration, the process by which cells obtain energy. Coenzymes are not depleted by their reactions, and are less specific to a particular reaction than are enzymes.

Ribozymes are small segments of ribonucleic acid (RNA) involved in catalytic activities. Some RNA catalysts work on separate substrates, while others are intramolecular and perform either autocleavage (self-cutting) or autosplicing (self-joining) along their own structure.

OBSERVATIONS

Smooth as Silk

The most remarkable property of enzymes is their ability to catalyze the transformation of complex proteins into simpler, more usable components, or conversely to assist in the creation of large-scale polypeptide chains. Perhaps the best known of these is the protein fibroin, the basic constituent of silk and spider webs. This protein, which is made up of some three thousand amino acids, is built up by enzymes in the silkworm into a structure called a beta sheet, which is smooth on one side and rough on the other; thus it is both strong, because of the bonding between adjacent rough sides, and flexible, because of the weak interactions of the smooth sides. The fibroin is then stretched by the act of spinning, completing the process that results in silk fiber.

Further Reading
Bugg, Timothy D., *An Introduction to Enzyme and Coenzyme Chemistry* (1997); Hirs, G. H. W., ed., *Enzyme Structure* (1973); Page, M., *Enzyme Mechanisms* (1987); Suckling, C. J., *Enzyme Chemistry* (1998).

Elementary aspects of this subject are covered in CATALYST; CHEMICAL REACTION; ENDOCRINE SYSTEM; METABOLISM. *More information on particular aspects is contained in* CIRCULATORY SYSTEMS; DIGESTIVE CHEMISTRY; LIPIDS. *Relevant information on enzymes is contained in* PROTEIN METABOLISM; PROTEIN SYNTHESIS; SECRETION, CELLULAR.

First see DISEASE, THEORY OF

Epidemiology

Next see POPULATION ECOLOGY

The branch of medicine concerned with the study of disease in its natural surroundings as it affects communities of people rather than individuals.

The primary concern of epidemiology was traditionally infectious diseases, such as measles, mumps, cholera, and plague, but in recent decades it has been extended to noninfectious diseases common in a given society, such as cancer and heart disease in the United States and other developed countries. The principles of epidemiology start with the selection of the population or populations to be studied. In the case of heart disease, for example, the epidemiologist may compare men with women, or young men with older men. The members of the population or populations being studied are carefully counted, and the characteristics of the overall population are carefully defined. These characteristics may include sex, age, race, occupation, social class, marital status, employment status, and the like—whatever characteristics seem important in the study of a given disease.

The epidemiologist then measures the incidence of the disorder in two ways. One measurement is of incidence—the number of new cases of the condition per week, month, or year. The other measurement is prevalence—the number of persons in the population who have the disease at any given time. The two measurements together provide a statistical record that is often enough to give valuable information about many diseases.

Epidemiologists have found that groups of people who spend most or all of their lives in a carefully defined area can give more valuable information about a given condition than persons who move about into different areas, which means that their environment changes over years or decades. One example of an epidemiological finding based on this principle was the study of cancer of the esophagus in residents of a certain area of China where the incidence was high. By comparing the incidence in these areas with that in other areas and then looking at the characteristics of the area and the population—diet, for example—information about possible causes of the disease can be obtained.

One field that has proved to be of growing value is comparative epidemiology, which is being applied to the diseases that are common in modern, industrialized societies such as the United States—heart disease, cancer, and the like. In comparative epidemiology, two or more groups are chosen for study. The choice is made on the basis of group characteristics that may affect the incidence of a disease—smoking in relation to the incidence of lung cancer, or diet in relation to the incidence of heart disease, for example. In the first instance, the epidemiologist may compare a group of persons who smoke cigarettes with a nonsmoking group. In the second instance, a group eating a low-fat diet may be compared with a group whose diet is based on meat. Great care is taken to make the two groups as alike as possible with regard to all their other characteristics. Another approach in comparative epidemiology is to compare a group of persons who have a given condition, such as high blood pressure, with a group that does not have the condition. The object of the comparison is to single out characteristics that are associated with the condition being studied—being overweight in the case of high blood pressure, for example.

It must be kept in mind, however, that the links between characteristics and incidence of a condition that are detected by comparative epidemiology are not always indicators of the cause of a condition. For example, epidemiologists can say that the incidence of heart disease is higher in countries like the United States, where ownership of television sets and automobiles is high, than in countries where these objects are less common. But epidemiology does not say that owning a car or a television set is a cause of heart disease; ownership instead is an indicator of other characteristics that are connected with the disease, such as lack of exercise. Overall, however, epidemiology has provided extremely valuable information about the causes of many diseases, and hence about steps that can be taken to prevent them.

Further Reading
Bray, R. S., *Armies of Pestilence* (1998); Karlen, Arno, *Biography of a Germ* (2000); Kolata, Gina, *Flu* (1999); Zimmer, Carl, *Parasite Rex* (2000).

First see BRAIN

Epilepsy

Next see NERVOUS SYSTEMS

A condition that causes recurrent seizures, caused by temporary abnormalities in the normally regulated and orderly electrical activity of the brain.

One of every 200 Americans suffers from epilepsy. The disorder usually becomes evident in childhood or adolescence. It may last a lifetime, but it can disappear with age in some people. There are two broad types of epileptic seizures—generalized and partial. There are two kinds of generalized seizures, grand mal and petit mal. An epileptic who experiences a grand mal seizure falls unconscious, the body stiffening, then twitching or jerking uncontrollably. As the seizure ends, bowel and bladder control may be lost. Status epilepticus, a prolonged grand mal seizure, can be fatal. Petit mal seizures are much less severe. Partial seizures can be simple or complex. The person remains conscious during a

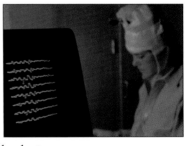

Brain feedback techniques (above) have joined medication as treatment for epilepsy.

simple seizure but loses consciousness when the seizure is complex. Both kinds of partial seizure may eventually involve the entire brain, becoming grand mal seizures.

Physicians diagnose epilepsy by physical examination and an electroencephalogram, (EEG), which records the brain's electrical activity. The basic treatment for epilepsy is administration of anticonvulsant drugs, which usually lessen the frequency of seizures. If a patient has not experienced seizures for several years, drug treatment may be suspended to determine if the condition has corrected itself.

First see POLYMER

Epoxies

Next see COATINGS AND FILMS

Epoxies, elastomers, and resins are materials widely used in industry and for home products. An epoxy is a thermoplastic polymer, one that can be shaped by heating. Epoxies are useful because they are strong, inert, and adhesive substances that are also good insulators. They are mixed with fillers and plasticizers and are used for construction, as bonding material, and as protective coating for many kinds of surfaces.

An elastomer is any polymer suitable for use as a synthetic rubber. The main types of elastomers include polymers of butadiene alone, butadiene combined with either styrene or nitrile, ethylene combined with propylene, and polymers of isobutylene and silicones. Another elastomer is latex, natural or synthetic, which is used in products ranging from tires to shoes, rainwear, belts, hoses, and insulation. A resin is a high molecular-weight substance that generally is gummy or tacky in a given temperature range. Resins obtained from natural sources include shellac (from insects), rosin (from pine trees), and Congo copal.

Synthetic resins include a wide variety of plastics currently available; in fact, the distinction between a plastic and a resin is often difficult to determine. The first partially synthetic resins were made in 1862 using nitrocellulose, vegetable oils, and camphor. The first completely synthetic resin was Bakelite, developed in 1910 from phenol and formaldehyde by Leo Baekeland. The rapid development of polymer science in the twentieth century has stimulated the invention of a wide range of synthetic resins. (*See* SYNTHETICS.)

First see GRAVITY

Equivalence Principle

Next see GENERAL RELATIVITY

The equivalence principle was proposed by Albert Einstein as he developed the general theory of relativity. Newton proposed that the gravitational mass of a body determines the strength of the gravitational force between massive bodies, while inertial mass measures the resistance of a body to forces imposed upon it. Einstein was struck by the constancy of the ratio of inertial mass to gravitational mass of all material bodies. Galileo had been the first to observe the constancy of the relationship between the two kinds of mass, when he showed that the acceleration experienced by objects in the Earth's gravitational field was independent of their mass.

Local Agreement. By the end of the nineteenth century, the inertial and gravitational masses of bodies were shown to be identical with an accuracy of one part in ten million. While there was no explanation of the constancy of the two masses, Einstein proposed that it was impossible to distinguish locally—in a small region of space-time—between the effects of inertial and gravitational mass on material bodies. For example, an observer in an elevator going upward with an acceleration equal to that produced by the gravitational pull of the Earth would see any object that was dropped fall to the floor of the elevator in exactly the same way that it would fall to Earth. In both cases, the acceleration of the objects would be independent of their mass. (*See* GRAVITY.)

Einstein then proposed that it is impossible to distinguish between the effect of inertia and the effect of gravity. This is the equivalence principle. It states, in effect, that inertial forces are gravitational in origin. Having assumed that inertial forces have a physical character, Einstein could formulate the principle of general relativity, which states that the laws of nature apply equally to inertial and non-inertial bodies. Observers simply cannot tell whether they are in a non-inertial system, or in a gravitational field.

Consequences of the Principle. One consequence of the principle is that a beam of light would appear to be bent in a gravitational field just as it would appear to be bent to an observer in an accelerating elevator. This required a change in the part of the special theory of relativity that dealt with relativistic space-time.

Another consequence was that if the effects of inertia and gravity are indistinguishable from one another, then one object could be used to characterize both effects. Since there is a specific metric responsible for the inertial effects that are observed in special relativity, then the same metric should be associated with the gravitational field. The metric must thus be a dynamical object, while the laws of motion of special relativity were absolute, not dynamical. (*See* SPACE-TIME; *and* SPECIAL RELATIVITY.)

Einstein then argued that all motion should be relative, which is why the theory is called the general theory of relativity—it applies to all objects. (*See* GENERAL RELATIVITY.)

First see STATISTICS

Error Analysis

Next see CATASTROPHE THEORY

Error analysis is a necessity in all precision work. Error creeps into work in two ways: systematically, through relatively predictable biases in equipment or procedure, and randomly, through fluctuations in the environment or human fallibility. Systematic error can usually be identified and corrected, as was done with the flaws in the Hubble Space Telescope; random error can also be identified through statistics.

The most common technique of error analysis is the use of the standard deviation:

$$s = [\Sigma (x_i - a)^2 / N - 1]^{1/2}$$

The standard deviation is the square root of the sum of the squares of the individual deviations divided by one less than the number of repetitions. The number is reduced by one to correct for the use of a sample rather than the total population. The standard deviation is the basis for error analysis because more than two-thirds of results of any given measurement will normally fall within one standard deviation of the mean. Random errors that might otherwise skew results can often be excluded from consideration if, when plotted on the curve, they fall more than two standard deviations from the mean.

A second form of error analysis is the use of the variance, which is the square of the standard deviation. When a process involves a number of stages, at each of which error may be introduced, the total random error can be obtained by adding the variance for each stage, then taking the square root of the sum. A similar process is used for identifying elements and estimating the risk of catastrophic failure in a complex system, such as a nuclear power plant.

First see ALCOHOL

Esters

Next see SYNTHETICS

Compounds formed when either organic or inorganic acids react with alcohol.

The process that produces esters is called esterification; it can also be easily reversed. Esters made from organic acids of low molecular weight are colorless liquids with pleasant fruity odors. In fact, most of the odors we associate with various fruits and flowers are caused by the presence of esters. Bananas and oranges contain the esters n-amyl acetate and n-octyl acetate, respectively. Many esters are used in the production of perfumes and artificial flavorings. Fats are glycerol esters made with organic acids of high molecular weight. (*See* ALCOHOL.)

Polyesters, common synthetic fibers, are polymers (very long chains) of repeated units of different types of esters. Some polyesters, such as Dacron and Terylene, are used as textiles. Mylar is a polyester used in the production of audio and video tapes. (*See* SYNTHETIC FIBER.)

Another prominent ester is nitroglycerin, an oily liquid that explodes easily when heated or shaken. Because of its relative instability, it is often combined with wood pulp to form dynamite, which is easier to handle and store, while still retaining explosive properties. Another important ester is acetylsalicylic acid, the active ingredient in aspirin.

First see ORGANIC COMPOUNDS

Ethers

Next see SURGERY

Organic oxide compounds that have an oxygen atom bonded between two carbon atoms in a chain.

The best known ether molecule is diethyl ether, also known as ethyl ether or just plain ether, which has a distinctive sweet odor. Once widely used as an anesthetic, it has been mostly replaced by other chemical compounds in recent years. Problems with the use of ether include its high flammability (due to a very low boiling point) and its tendency to irritate the respiratory tract and cause nausea in patients.

Ethers are relatively inactive, and are therefore not used as chemical reagents in organic synthesis. An exception to this is in the case of some of the cyclic forms. Ether does, however, have an industrial use as a solvent for gums, fats, and waxes.

First see ECOLOGY

Ethology

Next see COMPETITION AND ALTRUISM

The study of how and why animals behave as they do in their natural surroundings.

Why do birds sing? How do honeybees tell each other where to find food? How do parents and offspring recognize each other? These are among the classic questions to which the branch of biology called ethology has provided convincing answers, as it explores the intricacies of courtship, mating, feeding, navigation, social organization, and communication among animals, from single-celled to human.

Underlying these engaging puzzles are broader questions at the heart of ethology: How do inheritance and learning interact to shape behavior? How has behavior evolved? How applicable to humans are findings about how other animals function?

To explain behavior, ethologists traditionally focus on evolution, genetics, and instinct.

**Konrad Lorenz
(1903-1989)**

Further Reading
Ardrey, Robert, *The Territorial Imperative* (1997); Benyus, Janine, *The Secret Language and Remarkable Behavior of Animals* (1998); De Waal, F. B. M., *Good Natured* (1996); Dugatkin, Lee Alan, *Cheating Monkeys and Citizen Bees* (1999); Tinberger, N., *Curious Naturalists* (1984).

Naturalist James L. Gould has described it as "the heritable, genetically specified neural circuitry that organizes and guides behavior." Much of human behavior will be explicable by the same mechanisms, ethologists expect, because evolution will have caused similar successful behavioral strategies to have been retained, across the continuum of the animal world, which includes man. Generally speaking, ethology's approach has been in conflict with that of psychology, which explained many of the same phenomena as a result of learning or culture, favoring laboratory experimentation over observation in nature.

Roots. Like much of modern biology, ethology can be traced to the Darwinian revolution of the late-nineteenth century, which explained how natural selection resulted in animals' adaptation to their environment and saw man as a part of nature rather than a special creation. Darwin's theories helped expand the study of animals from descriptive natural history to a science explaining and predicting behavior across the realm of living things.

Three scientists were central to that conversion. Karl von Frisch (1886–1982), who explored how animals gain information, is best known for discovering that honeybees use a complex dance to tell others in the hive where they have found food. Konrad Lorenz (1903–1989), an Austrian zoologist like von Frisch, won his reputation as the father of ethology by first noting many of the basic mechanisms of behavior and by developing often-controversial theories about instincts and drives that set the agenda for ethology for years to come. Niko Tinbergen (1907–1989), a Dutch-born zoologist who often collaborated with Lorenz, was a pioneer of experimental ethology, designing simple and powerful experiments that have become models in the field. The three shared a 1973 Nobel Prize.

Senses. One of the tenets of ethology is that animals must be understood in their world, including their sensory world, which may be very different from ours. This was illustrated by von Frisch's discovery that bees see ultraviolet light. A bee-pollinated flower that to us looks pale and monotone, to a bee can look as bold as a sunflower, centered with a dark bull's-eye that marks the spot for pollen or nectar. Von Frisch and his students later found that bees also can detect the sun-centered polarization of UV light, can smell carbon dioxide, and can hear sounds humans can't. The world as an animal perceives it is sometimes called its "Umwelt."

Releasers. A key concept of ethology is that behavior may be triggered by sign stimuli or "releasers," simple signals that "release," or stimulate, a specific response. For instance, during breeding season a male robin will attack any red object that intrudes into his territory even if the object does not otherwise resemble a male robin. These sign stimuli are believed to correspond to specific sensory receptors in the animal.

Nature vs. Nurture. Untangling the relationships between innate and learned behavior has been one of the central problems of ethology. It has become apparent that in many cases apparently innate behavior—hunting or nest-building, for instance—can be perfected only if an animal imitates a role model or learns by trial and error. At the same time, many learned behaviors seem at least partially programmed, in that they always occur in a set sequence of steps or only at a certain point in an animal's life cycle. The acquisition of language in humans is one such example.

In recent decades, many ethologists have given greater attention to social behavior and relationships, especially in the study of higher animals, chiefly primates. They have pointed out ape and monkey behavior that appears to show thought, emotion, planning, awareness of others' feelings, and even self-awareness, with what appear to be striking parallels to features of human society. Traditionally, ethology has been wary of such claims about cognitive processes in animals, regarding them as misleadingly anthropomorphic. But some, such as Frans de Waal, a cognitive ethologist who studies primates, are embracing that approach. "Provided that it is based on intimate knowledge and translated into testable hypotheses," de Waal wrote, "anthropomorphism is a very useful first step toward understanding a psychology similar to and almost as complex as ours."

Related areas to be considered are AGGRESSION AND TERRITORIALITY; CONDITIONING; INSTINCT; NAVIGATION. *Other aspects of ethology are discussed in* COEVOLUTION; EVOLUTION; NATURAL SELECTION; REPRODUCTIVE STRATEGIES. *Related material can be found in* EMOTIONS; EXTINCTION; POPULATION ECOLOGY; SPECIATION; SYMBIOSIS.

First see SPACE

Euclidean Geometry

Next see NON-EUCLIDIAN GEOMETRY

Euclidean geometry is the branch of mathematics devoted to describing figures on a plane. It was first codified by the Greek mathematician Euclid sometime around 295 B.C.E. For a man who played such an important role in intellectual history, we know surprisingly little about Euclid. Born sometime after 347 B.C.E., he died sometime before 287 B.C.E.; he taught in the city of Alexandria in Egypt.

Elements. Euclid did not derive all of plane geometry, but in his book titled *Elements* he collected and codified hundreds of years' worth of theorems and proofs that had been written down by Greek, Babylonian, and Egyptian mathematicians be-fore him. His great contribution was to collect work from far-flung sources which contained miscellaneous theorems and results and to put them together in a single, coherent, logical system.

Some parts of geometry were developed well before Euclid, of course. Understanding this branch of mathematics has played a crucial role through the ages for architects, surveyors, and others involved in designing and building edifices or tracts of land. We know, for example, that the Egyptians had developed an approximate formula for π (the circumference of a circle divided by the diameter—approximately 3.14159) long before Euclid's time. Thus, Euclid played the role of a summarizer and codifier of previous knowledge, although he may well have added some work of his own as well.

Starting Points. Euclid's *Elements* begins by defining some basic terms: point, line, and circle. He then follows with a set of postulates, which (in modern language) say that:

1. only one line can be drawn between two points;
2. two different lines can share at most one point;
3. it is possible to draw a circle with any radius centered at any point;
4. all right angles are equal to each other;
5. two lines perpendicular to a third line are parallel to each other.

Any figure drawn on a two-dimensional plane can be derived from these definitions and postulates. A large number of theorems about the properties of figures can then be proven. For example, a standard exercise in high school geometry involves proving that in a triangle, the sum of the angles is 180 degrees—a Euclidean theorem.

The Fifth Postulate. While Euclid's postulates, however, seem to be self-evidently true, they do not necessarily hold up in all mathematical systems. For example, the fifth postulate seems pretty clear. If you have two lines perpendicular to a third, and you tilt one of the two slightly, the two original lines will eventually cross. But consider lines on the surface of a sphere, such as the lines of latitude on the Earth, and particularly about a triangle made up of two lines of latitude extending from the pole to the equator and the stretch of equator between them. Each of these lines meets the equator at a 90-degree angle. Consequently, in this particular triangle, the two angles at the equator already add up to 180 degrees, and the remaining angle has not yet been taken into account. This means that for triangles on a convex surface like Earth, the sum of the angles is more than 180 degrees. In other words, there is one location—the surface of a sphere—where Euclidean geometry simply does not work. The reason for this is implicit in the discussion so far—Euclidean geometry applies only to a flat plane, and the surface of Earth is not a plane. In fact, if small geometrical figures, such as those that are needed to survey a new building or a highway, are being measured, then the surface of Earth is flat enough for Euclidean geometry to apply. But surveyors who lay out large tracts of land often have to allow for the fact that the Earth is not flat and then make the appropriate correction.

It wasn't until the nineteenth century that mathematicians developed consistent systems of non-Euclidean geometries; in the twentieth century, these geometries were found to have interesting physical applications. Perhaps the most striking example of this was the discovery of general relativity by Albert Einstein. He envisioned space-time as a four-dimensional surface, and used the complex geometrical system developed by Georg Riemann, the nineteenth century German mathematician who was one of the pioneers of non-Euclidean geometry. By using this sort of mathematics, Einstein gave provided the best current theory of gravitation.

Influence. But Euclid had yet another important influence, one reaching beyond mathematics and not often mentioned. He organized his book in such a way that he would first state a theorem and then provide a proof. The book has a pattern of theorem-proof, theorem-proof, throughout. Because the *Elements* was so widely studied, scientists from the Middle Ages on have felt that they, too, had to present their work in this form. Even in a modern scientific paper, the presentation is often done in such a way that the conclusions follow in a logical pattern from some beginning hypothesis.

In point of fact, no scientist ever works this way. The process of science is one of stumbling and correcting, and then stumbling again. (Neils Bohr, one of the founders of quantum mechanics, once said, "You achieve progress only after you have made all possible mistakes.") Consequently, the real serendipitous human process of science gets lost in the formal Euclidean presentation found in science textbooks.

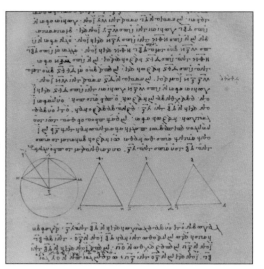

The study of Euclid's *Elements* was an essential part of scientific training right up to the modern period. Above, a medieval text containing a proof of a Euclidean theorem.

Background material on geometry can be found in FUNCTION; SETS AND GROUPS; SPACE. *More details can be found in* DIFFERENTIAL GEOMETRY; TOPOLOGY; VECTORS AND TENSORS. *More information on particular aspects of the subject is contained in* FRACTALS; KNOTS; NON-EUCLIDEAN GEOMETRY. SEE ALSO SCIENTIFIC METHOD.

Further Reading
Calinger, R., *Classics of Mathematics* (1995); Gulberg, J., *Mathematics* (1997); Duren, Peter, *A Century of Mathematics in America* (1988); Laugwitz, Detlef, *Bernhard Riemann, 1826-1866: Turning Points in the Conception of Mathematics* (1993).

First see CELL

Eukaryotic Cells

Next see NUCLEUS, CELL

Living cells that contain a clearly defined nucleus.

Eukaryotic cells make up the vast majority of existing cells. Only bacteria and blue-green algae, which are members of the Moneran kingdom, are not included in this category.

The major difference between eukaryotic cells and the more primitive prokaryotic cells is the presence of a "true" nucleus and membrane-bound organelles. Eukaryotic cells have genetic material in the form of paired chromosomes bound up in various "packing" proteins. The chromosomes are separated from the rest of the cellular contents by a nuclear envelope, or membrane. Eukaryotic cells also contain several other internal membranes, separating the cytoplasm and its contents into various compartments. Prokaryotes, by contrast, have a single round chromosome, and their only membrane is the plasma membrane encasing the cell. (*See* CELL MEMBRANE.)

Contrasting Cells. Eukaryotic cells are typically much larger than prokaryotic cells. Although they contain many of the same organelles, as a general rule the eukaryotic version is larger and more complex than the prokaryotic one. The two types of cells perform many of the same metabolic activities and reactions, such as protein synthesis, photosynthesis, and cellular respiration. However, there are differences in the actual enzymes and molecules involved in these processes. (*See* PROKARYOTIC CELLS.)

Eukaryotic cells can be unicellular organisms, such as members of the Protist kingdom, or can make up multicellular organisms as seen in the animal and plant kingdoms.

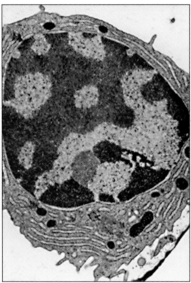

Eukaryotic cells are typified by a nucleus. What the containment of the nucleus adds to the functioning of the cell as carried out by the organelles is the subject of ongoing research.

First see SOIL CHEMISTRY

Eutrophication

Next see DESERTIFICATION

An accumulation of nutrients that gradually helps turn a lake from a clear, open body of water into a fertile green soup of vegetation and bacteria, then into a marsh or swamp, and finally into dry land.

Although eutrophication is natural and part of the normal aging process for lakes, it can be distorted and greatly accelerated by agricultural runoff, sewage, and other forms of pollution that add phosphorus and nitrogen to lakes and ponds. As a result, cultural or artificial eutrophication—as the pollution-driven version of the process is sometimes called—has become one of the most common environmental problems in the industrialized world. More than half the lakes in the United States are said to be affected by this problem to some extent.

Young Lakes. When lakes are young, they are usually oligotrophic, or poorly nourished. Algae, cyanobacteria, and plants are relatively sparse, so light can penetrate and photosynthesis can occur at relatively deep levels, making oxygen plentiful in the water. Such lakes are prized because they contain water that tastes and smells clean, they harbor desirable game fish such as trout, sturgeon, and pike, and they are perfect for swimming, boating, and fishing.

The Process. Normally, nutrients begin to accumulate in a young lake, which stimulates the growth of vegetation, algae, and bacteria. Increased photosynthesis and the action of bacteria on dead organic matter further increase dissolved nutrients, leading to further growth. Sediments are deposited on the bottom. The lake grows shallower, cloudier, and malodorous. The activity of bacteria and other organisms at the bottom decreases oxygen content there, until the depths can no longer support fish and other forms of aerobic life. Oxygen content is reduced near the surface of the lake as well, so trout are asphyxiated and replaced by fish that tolerate lower oxygen levels. The lake has become eutrophic—from the Greek for "well nourished"—and biologically more active, but less useful to humans. As the lake grows ever shallower, the process is accelerated through positive feedback until the lake no longer exists. (*See* HYDRAULIC CYCLE.)

This process can take thousands of years under normal conditions, but human activities speed it up drastically, causing huge blooms of algae or cyanobacteria. Nitrogen, phosphorus, and other nutrients flow into water in runoff from fertilizers and agricultural animal wastes; they leach or are dumped in with treated sewage and phosphate-containing detergents. In addition, clear-cutting of forests greatly increases natural runoff. (*See* WASTE DISPOSAL.)

Man-Made Causes. Cultural eutrophication can also occur in saltwater settings, causing low-oxygen "dead zones." In one famous case, the manure from large-scale duck farming on Long Island in the 1940s and 1950s caused not only a blossoming of phytoplankton in the Great South Bay, but a change in the kind of organisms making up the plankton. The new species were indigestible to the region's bluepoint oysters, and the local oyster industry was destroyed.

By the 1960s, eutrophication was seen as a widespread problem in North America and Europe; in the Great Lakes, it wiped out some forms of commercial fishing. A series of experiments on test lakes in Ontario in the 1960s and 1970s showed that adding phosphorus seemed to be the key step in causing runaway eutrophication in lakes. In estuaries, fixed nitrogen seems to be the key factor. It also became apparent that lakes could recover when major sources of pollution were eliminated. Since then, environmental regulations have improved water quality in North America. (*See* WATER POLLUTION.)

First see ADAPTATION

Evolution

Next see NATURAL SELECTION

Broadly speaking, evolution deals with the process by which the earth went from being a hot, rocky, lifeless ball in space to a planet teeming with a diversity of life forms. The process of evolution can be conveniently thought of as taking place in two stages: (1) chemical evolution, the process by which inorganic materials came together to form the first living things, and (2) evolution by natural selection, the process by which the descendants of that living thing came to be the life that we see on Earth today.

Chemical Evolution. In 1956, Harold Urey and Stanley Miller, scientists at the University of Chicago, did an experiment that was to revolutionize our thinking on the origins of life. What they did was to fill a closed system with materials that they believed had been present in Earth's early atmosphere—water, hydrogen, methane, ammonia, and other chemicals. They heated the resulting liquid (to simulate evaporation under the sun) and subjected it to electrical sparks (to simulate the effects of lightning). In a few weeks, the fluid had turned a milky brown in color. Upon analysis, they found that a large number of amino acids had formed in the fluids. Amino acids are the basic building blocks of proteins, which are one of the fundamental molecules necessary for life.

This experiment marked an important milestone, because it showed that it was possible that materials, like amino acids, which we normally associate with living things, can be formed by natural process from non-living things.

Aftermath of the Experiment. It is no longer believed that the so-called Miller-Urey process is the one that actually operated on the newly formed Earth, but the general idea that there were natural chemical processes that produced the beginnings of life has persisted. In fact, we now know that amino acids can be formed in many different kinds of environments, even in deep space. They are routinely found in meteorites, and scientists believe that they will be found in the cores of comets as well. Scientists have also been able to use analogs of the Miller-Urey process to produce not only amino acids, but all of the molecules normally found in living systems, including short stretches of DNA. Thus, there seems to be no problem

The theory of evolution has faced many challenges in the last century and a half. One has been the question of how life could arise from inanimate matter (though this is not strictly a problem for evolutionary theorists). Above, the apparatus for Stanley Miller's famous "origin of life" experiment, which showed that glycine, a simple amino acid, could have been formed in an early form of a proposed Earth atmosphere. In the years since, the experiment and its conclusions have become less relevant to the question of the origin of life.

in producing the basic materials from which life can be constructed in atmospheres like that of early Earth.

The next step, which involved the assembly of these materials into something like a primitive living cell, is still the subject of intense research and debate. There are many different theories as to how this could have happened, but as yet there is no consensus as to what actually occurred. Theories being considered are as follows:

Tidal Pools. Materials formed by Miller-Urey experiments were concentrated in tidal pools until they reached the critical mass needed to drive the chemical processes of life.

RNA World. The first important molecules were not proteins, but the molecule known as RNA (ribonucleic acid), a cousin of DNA. These molecules have been shown to be capable of acting as catalysts for important chemical reactions.

Clay World. Natural electrical charges on the surfaces of clay could have held molecules together while they formed into living systems.

Bubble World. Fatty molecules, called lipids, formed by the Miller-Urey process formed bubbles on the surface of the ocean, with each bubble containing whatever chemicals happened to be inside it. Some of these chemicals were capable of self-replication, and eventually became primitive cells.

This list is by no means all-inclusive, but it gives some idea of current thinking on this subject. At the moment, the "RNA world" theory seems to have a slight edge over the others, but the resolution of this issue is a long way off. In any case, the end result of chemical evolution was the formation of an enclosed blob of chemicals, which could take in materials from its environment, run chemicals that reproduced its materials, and then undergo reproduction by division. These were the first cells.

Natural Selection. As soon as there is more than one living thing in an environment, the principle of natural selection can begin to operate. This principle was discovered by Charles Darwin in his famous book, *On The Origin of Species*, published in 1859. Its basic premises are two rather simple facts about living things. In any population there will be differences between individuals that allow some to exploit the resources in the environment more efficiently than others. In addition, resources are always limited, so individuals are always in competition with one another for survival.

The basic idea behind natural selection is that some individuals in a population will have a variation that allows them to survive better than their colleagues. This variation might involve their ability to bring nutrients to the cell wall, (something that would have been very important for those first few cells). It may involve being able to run fast (which might be important to an antelope on the plains of Africa), or just the abil-

Alfred Russel Wallace (1823–1913)

ity to digest a particular kind of food more efficiently. On the average, individuals that have this property are more likely to survive to adulthood and reproduce than individuals that do not. This means that in the next generation, there will be more offspring with this characteristic than in the last one, and, over time, all members of the population will eventually share this trait.

It is important to remember that natural selection does not work by changing individuals. If the advantage we are talking about is a particular digestive enzyme, you were either born with the genes for that enzyme or you were not, and nothing can change that. The point of natural selection is that over long periods of time, it is more likely that organisms with that enzyme will have offspring to whom they pass on the trait. Over long periods of time, the population will come to be dominated by descendants of the offspring, and the others will simply die out.

The point of evolution by natural selection is that as soon as living things appear on Earth, competition and natural selection begin. Even among those first cells, some would be more efficient at bringing in materials from the environment, and some would be more efficient at operating in cold climates than others; these would migrate towards the poles. Eventually, there will be many different types of cells. In the same way, natural selection has produced an enormous variety of living things on Earth.

It is important to realize that though we speak of the "theory of evolution," the fact that we use the word theory in no way implies that there is uncertainty about the reality of natural selection having occurred. We also speak of a "theory of gravity," for example, but that does not mean that if you jump out of a window you might not fall. The evidence for natural selection falls into three classes:

The Fossil Record. The remains of ancient life forms, preserved in stone, give us an increasingly detailed view of how life actually developed. We can now trace the fossil record back to thriving single cell bacterial communities that lived on Earth 3.5 billion years ago.

The Evidence of DNA. Almost all living things share the same genetic code. In fact, you can think of living things as simply being differ-

ent books written in the same language. The longer it has been since two living things have had the same ancestor, the more the DNA differs. Scientists now routinely analyze the DNA of living things to reconstruct the history of the family tree.

Vestigial Organs. The most striking single piece of evidence for DNA involves organs in living things that do not contribute to their survival, and which may often harm them. The human appendix is a good example of this. It is hard to imagine how such organs could exist except as remnants of things which were once useful and are on the verge of disappearing.

Human Evolution. Human beings, like every other animal and plant on Earth, evolved through the process of natural selection. Even though we now know this to be true, it took a long time before people began to seriously consider that Darwin's theory could be applied to our species as well as to any other.

Today, two separate lines of evidence help to unravel the evolution of human beings: (1) the fossil record of early human beings and their ancestors, and (2) the analysis of DNA in modern humans from different parts of the world.

The fossil record is the easier of the two to interpret because there is something very real and immediate about a fossil skull. Unfortunately, throughout most of our history we were not very numerous. Consequently, there is not a great deal to work with in interpreting our fossil record.

The oldest known human fossil (that is, the oldest known fossil of a member of the hominid family) is *Australopithecus ramidus*, found in Ethiopia. It was a small animal, probably the size of a modern chimpanzee, and had a brain capacity similar to that of a newborn baby or a modern great ape. It did, however, walk upright. It was a member of the same family as human beings, but it was of a different genus and species.

"Lucy." The most famous human fossil, of the species *Australopithecus afarensis*, was named Lucy by its discoverers (after the Beatles' song "Lucy in the Sky with Diamonds"). This is an almost complete skeleton of a young girl who lived about 3.5 million years ago in what is now

A dramatic support for the theory of evolution is the appearance of striking biological specimens with unique adaptations suited to their individual biomes, but spread across the globe. One such family of mammals is the anteater, represented by the South American anteater; the African aardvark; the Australian echidna (far right); and the Asian pangolin (near right). Each has adapted to a specific environment, which has extended even into differences in the manner in which each species gives birth.

Ethiopia. Lucy walked upright, but probably had hair like a modern chimpanzee. She was a member of a family group, and members of her species existed for a long period of time in Africa.

Other members of the genus *Australopithe-*

cus lived in Africa after her. The members of one group were large and had very heavy jaws, probably because they ate a diet of nuts and other heavy vegetation. The other group was rather light boned. The genus *Australopithecus* died out about 1.5 million years ago.

Pre-Humans. The first member of the genus *Homo* (the genus in which modern humans belong) is *Homo habilis* ("man, the toolmaker"). They walked upright, had larger brains, and were known to make tools by chipping stones. They lived in Africa about 2.5 million years ago. Perhaps the most widespread of the early fossils was *Homo erectus* ("man, the erect"). *Erectus* had a brain about twice the size of Lucy's and probably stood over five feet tall. *Erectus* left Africa and settled as far away as China and Indonesia. In fact, most of the celebrated fossils of early man (such as Peking man and Java man) were members of this species.

Modern Humans. The first modern human beings, which are normally called Archaic *Homo sapiens*, appear in Africa between 100,000 and 200,000 years ago. One can trace a direct line of descent from the Cro-Magnon people that invaded Europe about 35,000 years ago to modern man. Current thinking is that Neanderthal man does not figure in our direct line of descent, but was a collateral cousin who went extinct about 35,000 years ago, probably as a result of being pushed out of the livable space by the expanding Cro-Magnons.

This story is what has been pieced together from the fossil record. It is partly correct in general, but will be modified (particularly around the early points) by new discoveries.

**Charles Darwin
(1809–1882)**

Left, an 1890 illustration of the HMS *Beagle*, with Darwin aboard, passing the Straits of Magellan, with Mt. Sarmiento in the distance.

DNA Evidence. The DNA evidence for human evolution comes from the DNA of modern human beings. The basic idea is that the more different the particular strands of DNA are between two people, the longer is it since they shared a common ancestor. DNA analysis of human beings all over the world seems to indicate that modern human beings started in Africa, perhaps leaving some time in the last few hundred thousand years, perhaps more recently. Thus, the story of the DNA compliments in many ways the story of the fossils.

One great controversy that persists in our understanding of human ancestry involves exactly when human ancestors left Africa. The DNA evidence indicates very strongly that this was a very recent event, perhaps no more than 100,000 years. The fossil record, on the other hand, shows very little of the kind of discontinuities one would expect had *Homo erectus* left at one time, and then been replaced at a later date by *Homo sapiens*. It is likely that when the full story of human evolution is known, it will turn out to be much more complicated than a simple single migration out of Africa. More than likely, there were several such migrations and counter migrations over a period of 100,000 years in which our ancestors spread from their home in Africa to be found in every corner of the globe.

OBSERVATIONS

Neanderthals and Cro-Magnons

Fossils of anatomically modern humans were discovered in 1868 in the Cro-Magnon Cave in France. Some of these early modern humans show primitive skeletal characteristics, like large brows and teeth, which may be holdovers from interbreeding with Neanderthals. Otherwise they are not physically distinguishable from humans living today. Cro-Magnons exhibited a complex culture and social organization with sophisticated tools. Paradoxically, the fossil evidence points to the fact that the average cranial brain size of Neanderthal man was larger (by 15 percent) than Cro-Magnon man's.

Neanderthals disappeared from the fossil record approximately 30,000 years ago. They may have evolved into modern humans or, most likely, became extinct due to competition with a new species. Anatomically modern humans appear to have arisen outside Europe, possibly from Africa. It is thought that they coexisted with their more primitive forebears for several thousand years.

Further Reading
Darwin, Charles, et al., *The Portable Darwin* (1993); Fortey, Richard, *Life: A Natural History of the First Four Billion Years of Life on Earth* (1998); Gould, Stephen J., *Ontogeny and Phylogeny* (1985); Gould, Stephen J., *The Flamingo's Smile* (1987); Jones, Steve, *The Cambridge Encyclopedia of Human Evolution* (1995).

Background material on evolution can be found in LIFE, DEFINITION AND ORIGIN OF; BIRDS, EVOLUTION OF; FOSSILS; NATURAL SELECTION; SPECIATION. *More details can be found in* CAMBRIAN DIVERSIFICATION OF LIFE; HOMINIDS; HOMO SAPIENS; NEANDERTHAL. *Relevant information is contained in* DINOSAURS, EXTINCTION OF; EXTINCTION; PALEOECOLOGY. *See also* BIODIVERSITY *and* CO-EVOLUTION.

First see QUANTUM MECHANICS

Exclusion Principle

Next see QUANTUM ELECTRODYNAMICS

The Pauli exclusion principle is one of the basic axioms of quantum physics. It is valid for electrons, protons, neutrons, and other elementary particles, but not for all particles. The particles to which the principle applies are called fermions; those to which it does not apply are called bosons. This would mean that the properties of a collection of fermions are radically different from those of a collection of bosons.

Several Formulations. The exclusion principle states that if two elementary particles of the same type are in the same region of space, they must differ in at least one observable property—that is, they must occupy different quantum states. To state it another way, the exclusion principle says that any wave function involving several identical particles must change sign when the coordinates of any identical pair are interchanged.

The principle was first stated in 1925 by Swiss physicist Wolfgang Pauli to explain why electrons in an atom do not all fall into the lowest energy state. This principle is the fundamental key to the internal structure of atoms. When the exclusion principle is combined with other principles of quantum mechanics, it explains why the electrons in an atom are distributed in their various orbits. The electron structure of atoms is described in terms of orbitals. Orbitals, in turn, are arranged in shells. Each orbital is able to accommodate one or two electrons. These orbitals are described in terms of quantum numbers, which are designated n—the principal quantum number—l—the azimuthal quantum number—and m—the orbital magnetic quantum number. Therefore, it is possible to describe a well-defined series of energy shells, each of which can accommodate a maximum number of electrons that correspond to increasing energy and increasing distance from the nucleus.

While the energy shell picture is derived from the application of theories such as the exclusion principle, its reality has been demonstrated by experiments in which atoms have been probed by x rays or electrons. The observed chemical and physical properties of the elements can be explained by the electron structures obtained through the application of the exclusion principle and the forces that modify it.

For example, when the exclusion principle is applied to clouds of free electrons, it enables physicists to explain the properties of metals, and when it is applied to the interactions between the protons and the neutrons that make up the atomic nucleus, it explains many of the properties of atomic nuclei. (*See* QUANTUM MECHANICS *and* QUANTUM ELECTRODYNAMICS.)

First see GENE

Exons and Introns

Next see DNA

Exons, introns, operons, and transposons all refer to specific base sequences along a DNA molecule, but each has a very different function.

A gene is a segment of DNA beginning with a sequence known as the promoter region and ending with a terminator region. A structural gene contains information for the assembly of a particular protein. This information is "transcribed" to form a molecule of messenger RNA (mRNA) which is in turn "translated" to form a protein. The product of a regulatory gene controls the expression of structural genes, either allowing transcription to take place or else blocking it. (*See* DNA; GENE; GENETICS.)

Exons and introns are segments found within genes. Exons are the segments that correspond to the "useful" part, whereas introns are "nonsense" segments interrupting the main body of a gene. Introns are "spliced out" of the sequence during post-transcription modification and are no longer present when the mRNA is translated to form the actual protein. It is unknown why introns exist, or why they are only present within eukaryotic DNA and not prokary-

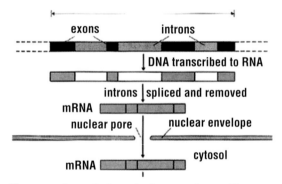

Above, a schematic for a single gene. Some of its material is useful and other serves merely as a place holder.

otic (bacteria and blue-green algae) DNA. A current theory proposes that perhaps introns are vestigial remnants of our evolutionary past.

Operons. Operons are the formal assemblies of regulator genes that control gene expression, turning it "on" or "off" as needed. The best-known is the lac operon, which contains the genetic code for the enzymes that digest lactose. It is necessary only to produce these enzymes when lactose is present. In the absence of lactose, the inhibitor, or repressor protein, binds to a part of the gene sequence that causes the promoter region to be "blocked" as well. Therefore, transcription cannot occur and the genes are "off." When lactose is present, it binds to the inhibitor, preventing it from blocking anything. Transcription can occur, so the genes are "on."

The lac operon model is an example of positive feedback regulation, in which genes are normally "off" unless a regulator protein turns them "on." Other operons exhibit negative feedback regulation in which the genes are normally "on" unless a regulator protein turns them "off." There are also operons that allow variable amounts of gene expression to occur.

Transposons. Transposons are segments of DNA able to insert themselves into new locations along the gene sequence. The transposon does not need to be carried by a virus or other vector, but can move directly from one site to another site. Transposons may be a major source of mutations, as they can cause deletions or inversions within a sequence, or can even cause the host sequence to move to another location. Some transposons are related to retroviruses; they carry their genetic material in the form of RNA and insert DNA versions of it into a host cell.

First see PROGRAM, COMPUTER

Expert Systems

Next see ARTIFICAL INTELLIGENCE

Expert systems can be traced to 1956, when Allan Newell and Herbert Simon invented Logic Theorist, a program to prove symbolic logic problems. Twenty years later, Edward Shortliffe developed MYCIN, a diagnostic program which proved to be more accurate than most human physicians; it soon led to programs like HEADMED, for diagnosing psychiatric problems; PROSPECTOR, which helps geologists find ore deposits; and R1, which helps configure VAX computers. Today, expert systems formulate schedules for flight crews, diagnose auto engine problems, process credit card applications; some even manage an entire factory.

Methods. Expert systems work in two major ways. Early systems used information synthesized from interviews with hundreds of acknowledged experts in the field; the developers of MYCIN used the expertise of more than 500 diagnosticians to develop their question sequence. Other systems use the root-and-branch method of sorting and identifying primary components; these systems are derived from early military programs such as AEGIS, where threat identification and response selection had top priority. (*See* ARTIFICIAL INTELLIGENCE.)

Benefits. The benefits of expert systems can be wide-ranging. At Nippon Steel in Japan, a Quality-Design Expert System addresses such customer demands as quality, product size, materials, and delivery time, improving design cycle time by 85 percent and accuracy by 30 percent. IBM's Logistics Management System schedules, controls, and monitors its Vermont semiconductor plant, improving output by 35 percent and saving ten million dollars in capital costs. A Pennsylvania Blue Cross unit cut its audit time for claims from one week to one hour with a system called PlanTracker; credit approval from Dun & Bradstreet now comes in three seconds instead of three days, thanks to the CCH-ES credit risk management system.

First see OXIDIZING AGENTS

Explosives

Next see COMBUSTION

Substances that can undergo very rapid combustion or another reaction that releases hot gases, whose rapid expansion is accompanied by a high-speed shock wave that can destroy nearby objects.

The earliest known explosive is gunpowder, invented in China in the tenth century and reinvented in the West in the thirteenth century by Roger Bacon, an English scholar and scientist. Gunpowder consists of about 75 percent potassium nitrate or sodium nitrate, 15 percent charcoal, and 10 percent sulfur. Today, it is used primarily to ignite other explosives and in fireworks. Gunpowder is classified as a low explosive, because its chemical transformation when it is ignited by a spark or flame, is relatively slow. A well-known low explosive is black powder, also called blasting powder, which has been used in fuses and in mining, to break rock and ore into workable fragments. Black powder has largely been replaced by smokeless powder, a gelatinous substance.

Another class of explosives consists of primers or initiators, which are extremely sensitive to heat, flames, friction, or blows, and detonate without burning. Primers (also called primary explosives) include nitrogen sulfide, silver acetylide, nitrogen chloride, and fulminate of mercury. These compounds are commonly used in detonators or blasting caps to start the detonation of less sensitive explosives. A detonator is made by enclosing the primary explosive in a cylindrical capsule, along with an ignition charge and a small amount of a more powerful explosive. Blasting caps are set off by a spark from a time fuse, by a jolt of electricity, or by an impact.

TNT. These detonators are used to set off the most powerful group of explosives, the high explosives. These are less sensitive than the primary explosives; if a small amount of a high explosive such as trinitrotoluene (TNT) is exposed to a flame, it can burn without exploding. In order to achieve the most powerful release of energy, a high explosive is often mixed with a small amount of a more sensitive explosive, called a booster. When a high explosive is detonated, it has an impressive shattering effect called brisance. In addition to TNT, some widely used high explosives are picric acid, dynamite, blasting gelatin, nitroglycerin, guncotton, and ammonium nitrate.

Extinction

First see EVOLUTION

Next see BIODIVERSITY

The fossil record of life goes back many hundreds of millions of years. In that record, one thing stands out: animals that were around in the past are no longer here. In fact, paleontologists estimate that 999 out of 1,000 species that have existed on this planet have gone extinct. The average life of a species seems to be between 3 and 5 million years, at which point the species either evolves into something else or disappears from the fossil record. Looking at the history of extinction, two general types emerge:

Background Extinctions. In general, the fossil record shows that about 10 percent of the species around at the beginning of any 10 million-year period will not be there at the end. There are many causes for this kind of steady background extinction. Probably the most important are changes in climate. For example, the rain forests of the tropics are currently the major source of biodiversity on the planet, and many species are disappearing because of human activity. But there were times in the past when there have been no rain forests, since they appeared only when the continents are aligned in a general north-south direction. When rain forests disappeared in the past, species dependent on the rain forest environment became extinct. Similar extinctions occurred when sea levels changed, when temperatures went up or down, or when deserts appeared or disappeared.

Mass Extinctions. There appear to have been many episodes in the history of the Earth when large numbers of species went suddenly extinct—meaning, in time frames, anywhere from thousands of years to a few weeks. The most spectacular mass extinction took place about 65 million years ago at the end of what is known as the Cretaceous period. This involved the demise of the dinosaurs, but it also involved the demise of almost 70 percent of the species living on the Earth at the time. We now believe that this particular extinction was caused by the impact of a giant asteroid on the the Earth.

This was not, however, either the most recent or the biggest mass extinction on record. The biggest mass extinction took place 285 million, at the end of what scientists call the Permian period. In this mass extinction, over 80 percent of the species disappeared. It is believed that this mass extinction was not caused by an asteroid, but by some kind of catastrophic climate change, perhaps involving a major change in the dynamics of the oceans. Presently, the theory of this particular extinction has not been clearly resolved.

Extinction History. There are generally thought to have been five large mass extinctions

Artist's depiction of an asteroid colliding with Earth, an event that seems to have occured several times in Earth's history.

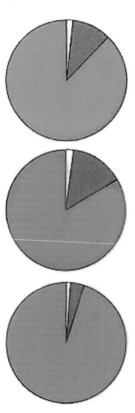

An inventory of species of (from top) birds; mammals; and reptiles. The full circle represents the total number of species (about 4,700 for mammals and reptiles; twice that for birds); the orange slice the number threatened with extinction; the white slice those that have become extinct in the course of recorded history.

over the past 500 million years, with about 7 minor ones interspersed between them. They seem to have occurred roughly every 25 million years or so. The theories as to why they occur range from recurring comet bombardments to periodic changes in the circulation of molten rock deep inside the Earth.

Today, many species are threatened with extinction due to human modifications of the biosphere. It is not generally possible to compare modern extinction rates with those discovered in the fossil record. Scientists discussing modern extinctions are almost invariably referring to the extinctions of insects, which compose the largest number of species on earth. The fossil record of insects is incomplete and no data exists on what their normal rates of extinction are. On the other hand, the majority of the fossils that have been studied are of marine invertebrates—clams, mussels, and the like. Their fossil record sheds light on extinction cycles that may have included a wide range of life on Earth.

First see GENETICS

Extranuclear Inheritance

Next see DNA REPLICATION

The nucleus, which controls and directs all cell activities, contains the majority of the DNA found within a cell. Genes are segments of DNA that begin with a specific sequence, called the promoter region, and end with another specific sequence called the terminator region. The genes are arranged within structures called chromosomes. (*See* DNA.)

Eukaryotic cells contain paired chromosomes, whereas prokaryotes have a single round chromosome. In addition, prokaryotes contain extrachromosomal elements known as plasmids, which are small circular "bits" of DNA. Plasmids are self-replicating, and their number remains constant from generation to generation. Plasmids can either exist as separate units or can be integrated into the main chromosome. Once integrated, they are referred to as episomes, although the terms episomes and plasmids are often used interchangeably. Plasmids may be "transmitted" from one cell to another, thus allowing genes to be exchanged. Because of the genetic variation involved, the transfer of plasmids can be viewed as a type of sexual reproduction in these primitive cells.

Until recently, it was believed that the nucleus was the only organelle that contained DNA. Mitochondria, the energy-producing structures of the cell, were the first "non-nuclear" organelles discovered to have their own DNA. This DNA codes for various proteins important in the production of energy, and unlike the nuclear variety is inherited exclusively from the mother. Other organelles found to contain DNA are chloroplasts, the site of photosynthesis, and centrioles, which play a role in nuclear division in animal cells.

First see LIFE, DEFINITION AND ORIGIN OF

Extraterrestrial Life

Next see ASTEROIDS AND METEORS

The possibility that a form of life—possibly with intelligence—exists somewhere else (and possibly in many locations) in the universe.

The possibility that life may exist elsewhere in the universe has been considered seriously in nearly every culture in human history, and the the notion that such beings may possess an intelligence of some kind has generally not been rejected. Virtually every religion contains teachings that populate the ethereal regions of heaven with sentient beings, and myths abound in every culture regarding visits to this planet by beings from elsewhere. Ironically, the rise of science in the past four centuries has made the idea that there is intelligent life elsewhere in the universe a fringe notion, fit for the tabloids and the unbalanced. This is mainly due to the realization of the enormous distances that would have to be traversed by an intergalactic traveller and the difficulty an intelligent being would encounter communicating to Earth across the vast expanse of space. (*See* UNIVERSE.)

Several factors, however, give credence to the notion that life in some form, and possibly with intelligence of some kind, exists elsewhere. First, improved methods of observing the heavens have made it possible to detect matter in distant space that is not emitting stellar radiation. These observations support the idea that planetary systems sufficiently similar to our own are not at all uncommon. There may well be a great many planets in every galaxy in the right orbital range to their suns to support life. Even systems with protective outer planets and satellites capable of bearing the brunt of cometary impacts that would threaten life—as Jupiter and the moon are thought to have protected Earth—may be relatively common occurrences.

Second, current understanding of biological processes suggests that molecules of a certain complexity will organize and develop structures and functions that inevitably lead to a form of life. Life, in other words, may be the ultimate organizing principle of inanimate matter.

The Drake Equation. In 1961, Frank Drake, an astronomer at the Green Bank, West Virginia, radio telescope, devised an equation for estimating how many observable civilizations (N) exist in our Milky Way galaxy:

$$N = (R) \, (f_p) \, (n_e) \, (f_l) \, (f_j) \, (f_c) \, (L),$$

where R is the number of stars born in the Milky Way each year; f_p is the fraction of those stars with planetary systems; n_e is the number of "Earthlike" planets suitable for life in the typical solar system; f_l is the fraction of those planets on which life develops; f_j is the fraction of those planets where that life develops intelligence; f_c is the fraction of those planets where an intelligent species develops the ability to communicate by radio; and L is the average lifetime of a communicating civilization in years. Extensive searches for radio signals from extraterrestrial civilizations, however, have revealed no candidates within 1,000 light years of the earth. (*See* INTERSTELLAR SPACE TRAVEL.)

First see NERVOUS SYSTEM

Eyes and Vision

Next see SENSORY MECHANISMS

Despite innumerable variations, eyes can be grouped into three major categories. Simple light receptors, common among invertebrates, perceive light but do not form visual images. Compound eyes, characteristic of insects and crustaceans, form faceted images and can perceive details of movements too rapid for vertebrates to see. Vertebrate eyes, which provide sharp images, are often likened to cameras with a lens, adjustable aperture, and changeable focus. Vertebrate vision—the perception of visual images—takes place in the brain.

The simplest eyes are clusters of photoreceptor cells on the surface of the body in such invertebrates as starfish and jellyfish. More commonly, the cells are recessed to form an eye cup. Although they do not form images, they do allow an animal to move toward or away from light. Many lizards have a light receptor—a "third eye," called the parietal eye—on the backs of their heads; it seems to play a role in light-associated behavior, such as thermoregulation and diurnal patterns of activity.

Compound eyes are made up of tube-shaped units called ommatidia. The giant eye of a dragonfly contains more than 20,000 facets; an ant's eye contains only a few. At the top of each ommatidium is a lens and crystalline cone that is attached to seven to nine elongated receptor cells. Running the length of the receptor cells near the center of the unit is the rhabdom, an area of light-sensitive pigments arranged in so many layers that the unit absorbs light more efficiently than vertebrate eyes. Some facets within the eye may be specialized to perceive specific col-

Structure of the human eye.

Further Reading
Davies, P. C. W., *The Fifth Miracle: The Search for the Origin and Meaning of Life* (1999); Drake, Frank, *Is Anyone Out There?: The Scientific Search For Extraterrestrial Intelligence* (1994); Harrison, A., *After Contact: The Human Response to Extraterrestrial Life* (1997); Sagan, Carl S., *Intelligent Life in the Universe* (1998); Sagan Carl S., *Contact* (1997).

ors, ultraviolet light, or polarized light.

Light Path. In vertebrate eyes, light enters through the cornea (the transparent curved connective tissue on the front of the eye) and then through the pupil, the opening in the iris (the pigmented, muscular tissue that opens and closes to regulate incoming light). The light passes through the lens, which is suspended just behind the pupil. In mammals, as well as some birds and reptiles, tiny muscles can change the shape, and therefore the focus, of the lens, depending on the distance of the object being viewed. In fish, amphibians, and other reptiles, the lens changes focus by moving forward or back, as in a camera. This focusing is called accommodation.

The light is focused on the retina, a mem-

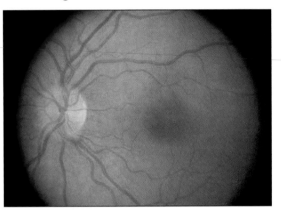

Right, the retina of the human eye.

brane composed of receptor and nerve cells on the inner back of the eyeball. There are two types of receptors. Rods, which produce poorly defined, black-and-white images, are very sensitive to light and can form images in dim settings. Cones, which need bright light to function, produce sharp images as well as color vision. Each cone is sensitive to red, blue, or green; the degree to which different cones are stimulated allows perception of a full range of color.

The human retina contains about 100 million rods and 5 million cones. The cones are concentrated within the macula, the part of the retina that serves the central 10 degrees of vision. A small pit within the macula, called the fovea, provides the best visual acuity, but serves less than 2 degrees of the visual field.

Rods are sometimes concentrated beside the fovea. Due to rods' sensitivity to dim light, stargazers often can see a faint star when they look at it slightly peripherally. Rods can see what the cones of the fovea cannot.

Compared to humans, many birds and some reptiles have relatively larger eyes, a higher proportion of cones to rods, faster accommodation, and two foveas. As a result, they have superior daytime visual acuity, as well as excellent color vision. Deep-water fish, nocturnal animals, and many other mammals lack color vision.

Both rods and cones contain chemicals that decompose when exposed to light, exciting the nerve cells in the retina. In humans, the array of nerve cells is tremendously complex, with six basic kinds—and more than 30 subtypes, involved even before the optic nerve leaves the eye. Some of these cells are inhibitors; they ensure sharp visual borders by preventing excitatory signals from spreading. Others may be involved at only specific instants during stimulation or may respond only to movement in a specific direction. Visual pathways from the cones, involving larger neurons and nerve fibers, provide faster conduction of signals to the brain than other pathways from the rods.

In humans, conscious vision takes place in the visual cortex of the occipital lobe of the brain, with visual information analyzed along two major pathways. One deals with the three-dimensional position, motion, and gross form of objects; the other with detail and color. In addition, pathways lead from the eye to older areas of the brain, which deal with reflex movements of the eye and circadian rhythms that are tied to

Background material can be found in LIGHT; NERVOUS SYSTEMS; SENSORY MECHANISMS. *Advanced subjects are developed in* JAUNDICE; LOCOMOTION; PREDATION. *Other aspects of this subject are covered in* GENETIC DISEASES; LASER SURGERY; SLEEP.

Further Reading

Chalkley, Thomas, *Your Eyes* (1982); Sinclair, Sandra, *How Animals See: Other Visions of Our World* (1987); Srinivasan, Mandyam V., *From Living Eyes to Seeing Machines* (1995); Weale, Robert Alexander, *Focus on Vision* (1983).

THE CUTTING EDGE

Admired from Afar

What do ancient mosaics, Impressionist paintings, and the works of modernist Chuck Close have in common? All of them are composed of visible blocks of color, whether paint or tile, that can only be seen as a picture by standing at a distance; up close, their images dissolve into individual bits of shape and color. The reasons for this phenomenon are optical blur and the perceptual threshold. Some pictures require that the viewer be far enough away that the image bits blur into one another before the image becomes visible. More precisely, a viewer must be at a distance more than 200 times the average width of the component "mark" —the piece of tile or the brush stroke; otherwise, one sees only flat paint or stone. One should not approach closer than four feet to a mosaic made from quarter-inch tiles and one should view Chuck Close's paintings from across the room.

Faults, Folds, and Joints

First See GEOMORPHOLOGY

Next See GEOSYNCLINE

Faults, folds, and joints are geological features of the Earth's crust. A fault is a fracture in the crust, where adjacent blocks of stone formations have shifted relative to one another. While faults occur in every type of rock, they are most noticeable when they cut across and displace identifiable layers in sedimentary or metamorphic rocks. The abrasion caused as blocks move against one another can produce grooves called sickenslides.

Faults can extend for hundreds of miles. Perhaps the most famous is the San Andreas Fault, which is 600 miles long, from the Mojave Desert to the Pacific Coast, north of San Francisco. It was a sudden shift of this fault that caused the San Francisco earthquake of 1906.

Folds are curvatures in layers of rocks, generally found in rock formations that were originally horizontal and produced by stresses in the crust. The angle of deformation of folds ranges from very small to extremely contorted; their size ranges from a few inches to many miles. When folded rocks erode, the result is a series of parallel ridges and valleys, such as those that can be observed in the Appalachian Mountains.

Joints are smoothly curved fractures in a rock. Joints can be small or up to thousands of feet long. Hundreds of joints may appear in a single outcropping of rock. A joint system consists of two or more sets of joints that are arranged in characteristic patterns—concentric, radial, etc. The jointing of rock formations is a major factor in such geological changes as weathering and erosion. The movement of the rock at right angles to this fracture can produce an open joint, or fissure. If the movement of the rocks of a joint is parallel to the surface of the fractures, the resulting break is classified as a fault. (*See* EARTHQUAKE.)

Fermat's Last Theorem

First See Algebra

Next See Number Theory

More than 2,500 years ago, the Greek mathematician Pythagoras discovered a relationship between the sides of a right triangle that has become one of the best-known laws of higher mathematics: $a^2 + b^2 = c^2$, or the sum of the squares of the two shorter sides of a triangle will equal the square of the hypotenuse. There are indeed an infinite number of whole number solutions to this formula. (*See* GEOMETRY.)

No one, however, was ever able to discover for certain whether there were any solutions to the Pythagorean formula when higher powers than squares are involved: $a^n + b^n = c^n$. Most early mathematicians suspected that there were, in fact, no solutions to Pythagoras's formula for higher powers. Pierre Fermat (1601–1665), a French mathematician, wrote a note in the margin of a book on arithmetic written by Diophantus of Alexandria in the third century C.E.: "I have a truly marvelous demonstration of this proposition, which this margin is too narrow to contain." Alas, three centuries of mathematicians struggled—and failed—to reconstruct Fermat's "marvelous demonstration."

Proving "Fermat's Last Theorem" became the greatest challenge in mathematical number theory. Some mathematicians came to believe that the proof Fermat had in mind was actually invalid, and that was why he never pursued the matter. In 1908, Paul Wolfskehl even put up a prize of 100,000 German marks, payable to anyone who could solve the devilish puzzle.

End of the Quest? Finally, in 1994, Princeton University mathematician Andrew J. Wiles proved Fermat's last theorem. He worked for eight years, mastering three separate bodies of mathematical knowledge, to demonstrate that there was no integral solution to the original Pythagorean formula when n was greater than two.

Despite the enthusiasm with which his proof was met, there are some mathematicians who claim that, even if Wiles' proof stands up, Fermat still has the last laugh, because Wiles' inductive, indirect proof could not be the one so delicately hinted at by Fermat more than 300 years ago.

Further developments in the field are discussed in ALGEBRA; NUMBER; SETS AND GROUPS. *More details can be found in* DIFFERENTIAL GEOMETRY; FUNCTIONS; NUMBER THEORY. *Additional relevant information is contained in* CATEGORY THEORY; GÖDEL'S THEOREM.

A marginal note (possibly an idle boast) written by Pierre de Fermat, above, sent mathematicians on a 300-year quest. Below, Andrew Wiles in 1994.

Further Reading
Aczel, Amir D., *Fermat's Last Theorem: Unlocking the Secret of an Ancient Mathematical Problem* (1997); Ribenboim, Paulo, *13 Lectures on Fermat's Last Theorem* (1979); Ribenboim, Paulo, *Fermat's Last Theorem for Amateurs* (1999); Singh, Simon, *Fermat's Enigma: The Epic Quest to Solve the World's Greatest Mathematical Problem* (1998); Van Der Poorten, Alf, *Notes on Fermat's Last Theorem* (1996).

Ferromagnetism

First See METAL

Next See MAGNETISM

The tendancy of a collection of atoms in certain metals to align in parallel lines, creating the effect of a magnetic field.

The key property of a ferromagnetic material is that, although it is weakly magnetic in its natural state, the application of a relatively small magnetic field rapidly and strongly magnetizes the material to its saturation point, a level that varies with temperature. At the Curie temperature—a point that varies with the material—it just as rapidly loses its magnetization as the atoms begin vibrating too rapidly.

The first theory to account for the phenomenon of ferromagnetism (known since antiquity) was propounded by Werner Heisenberg in 1928, based on the earlier discovery by Wolfgang Pauli that electrons spinning in the same direction will undergo electrostatic repulsion unless they are relatively widely separated. Ferromagnetism occurs in certain materials because the repulsive force pushing apart the atoms of such very dense metals causes the electrons to line up. (*See* ATOM; ELECTRON.)

Alignment of Charges. The alignment of ferromagnetic charges is also controlled by the crystalline structure of the specific metal. Because iron crystals are arranged in cubes, the magnetic charge tends to align with the edges of these cubes; however, these crystals are randomly arrayed within a given block of iron. It is for this reason that magnets are usually made of iron alloys, in which the crystals have been rolled or annealed in order to line up in nearly the same direction.

Modern uses of magnetic materials rely on the theory of ferromagnetism. This theory, developed by Louis Eugène Felix Néel in 1948, states that certain substances can be rendered magnetic only at very restricted temperatures, displaying no magnetism either above or below that point. Digital information can be stored in magnetic memory storage devices made from such materials at a very high density of 20 billion bits, the equivalent of four optically recorded CD-ROMs, per square inch.

Background material can be found in CONDUCTORS AND RESISTORS; ELECTRIC CURRENT; MAGNETISM. *Further developments in the field are discussed in* INDUCTION; MAGNETIC FIELD OF THE EARTH; METAL. *Special topics in this area are found in* MOTORS AND GENERATORS; PIEZOELECTRICITY; SUPERCONDUCTOR.

First See ELEMENTARY PARTICLES

Feynman Diagrams

Next See QUARK

Graphical representations of the way nuclear and subnuclear particles interact with one another.

Feynman diagrams are named for their developer, the American physicist Richard P. Feynman. In relativistic quantum field theory, particles can interact with external fields or with each other through the emission and absorption of virtual particles, which are not directly observable but which enable the phenomenon to occur.

Feynman diagrams have two purposes. One is to guide the calculations that are made about

Richard P. Feynman (1918–1988). Feynman's influence in the world of physics and science was considerable, both as a theoretician and as an educator.

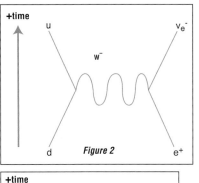

Figure 2

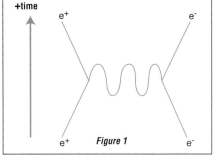

Figure 1

Figure 3

Further Reading

Feynman, Richard. *QED: The Strange Theory of Light and Matter* (1988); Kreimer, Dirk, *Knots and Feynman Diagrams* (1999); Mattuck, Richard D., *A Guide to Feynman Diagrams in the Many-Body Problem* (1992); Schweber, Silvan, S., *QED and the Men Who Made It* (1994); Veltman, Martinus, *Diagrammatica: The Path to Feynman Rules* (1994).

these interactions. Another is to give a physical picture of the interaction or process being studied. Use of Feynman diagrams makes it possible to determine that all the contributing factors in a given interaction have been counted. Each diagram has a specific integral—the sum of changes—associated with it.

A simple example in quantum electrodynamics is the interaction of an electron and a positron, illustrated in *Figure 1*. Reading from the bottom up, an electron (e^-) and a positron (e^+) begin in an initial state, then scatter each other into a final state with the exchange of a virtual photon, creating the final electron-positron pair. However, for the purposes of calculation, it is usually more convenient to think of Feynman diagrams in terms of momentum rather than in terms of coordinate space. The rules of Feynman diagrams associate specific functions with each line and vertex, specify signs for the particles, and require conservation of energy and momentum at each vertex.

Feynman diagrams offer an advantage in relativistic field theory because a given diagram can represent a number of processes. *Figure 2*, for example, shows a down quark and a positron interacting by exchanging a W^- particle and then decaying into a positron (e^+) antineutrino pair. The process depicted in *Figure 3* is a down quark decaying into a W^- particle and then creating an electron-antineutrino pair. Feynman realized that all three processes were theoretically allowed (and they have all been observed), but he also saw that the *Figure 3* was equivalent to *Figure 2* if a positron is looked at as an electron moving backwards in time.

Feynman diagrams have proven to be more than simple schematics for possible (or impossible) subatomic reactions. They are also useful mathematical tools for making difficult calculations in quantum physics.

Background informatin on Feynman diagrams is discussed in QUANTUM MECHANICS; ELEMENTARY PARTICLES; TIME. *Advanced subjects are developed in* QUANTUM ELECTRODYNAMICS; NUCLEAR FORCES; *Additional relevant information on Feynman diagrams is contained in* ACCELERATOR, PARTICLE; STANDARD MODEL.

First See REFLECTION AND REFRACTION

Fiber Optics

Next See TELECOMMUNICATIONS

The transmission of light and images through plastic fibers that have very high indexes of refraction.

Fiber optic systems grew out of research in semiconductors. Light is inherently a better carrier of speech and radio waves than electricity, because it oscillates faster and thus transmits information more efficiently. But light is easily blurred, distorted, or even blocked altogether, while electricity flow through copper wire is nearly impervious to such problems. Nonetheless, a single four-and-a-half pound spool of optical fiber can carry the same number of messages as 16,000 pounds of copper wire.

Semiconductor research focused attention on quartz, which is a silicon oxide: in theory, a quartz crystal could transmit light pulses almost indefinitely. However, it was only when silicon for transistors and microchips began to be produced with fewer than one flaw per billion that fiber optics became practical.

Eventually, researchers found that by mixing germanium oxide with silicon oxide they could achieve fibers capable of carrying a light pulse 150 miles without amplification. Large cylinders of carefully prepared glass, called preforms, are heated above 2,000° Celsius, then drawn out into fibers and surrounded with a reflective cladding that will ensure against a loss of any of the signal over great distances. A single preform may yield six miles of fiber optic cable. (*See* TELECOMMUNICATIONS.)

Applications. The first fiber optic cable was used in 1977 in Chicago, where one and a half miles of glass fiber was used to connect a single office building with two offices of Bell Telephone. AT&T installed TAT-8, its first fiber optic trans-Atlantic telephone cable, in 1988. It was capable of carrying forty thousand calls at once. In comparison, TAT-1, laid in 1956, could handle a mere 51 calls. Because copper remains an efficient conductor and costs far less than fiber optics, manufacturers are developing higher operating efficiencies, approaching the level of one gigabyte per second.

Optical fiber scopes are used in medicine, where they are called endoscopes or laparoscopes, and in aircraft and spacecraft manufacture, where they are used to inspect for hidden flaws. Larger bundles of optical fibers, called image conduits, can transmit large images, while tapers and inverters can change both the size or orientation of the image at the same time.

Industry-wide applications have been regulated through the adoption of a synchronous optical network, or Sonet, which serves as the standard for all fiber optics.

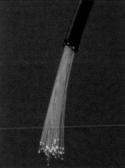

Top, a coil of fiber optic cable seen under utra-violet light. Bottom, a single cable often contains many separate fiber optic filaments, allowing multiple signals to be transmitted simultaneously.

First see PLASTIC

Fiberglass

Next see FIBER OPTICS

Fiberglass is a form of glass that is made when glass is drawn or blown into extremely fine fibers. These fibers retain the tensile strength of glass and yet remain very flexible. The most commonly used raw material for fiberglass is quartz, a form of silica that is the chief constituent of sand. Quartz is resistant to attack by almost all chemicals and can be extracted very easily when it is in the molten state. In most cases, the molten glass from which fiberglass is made is forced through a platinum plate with very fine openings. On the far side of the plate, the fine fibers of glass that emerge are united without being twisted, and are wound on a suitable spindle. (*See* SYNTHETICS.)

Mats of fiberglass, or glass wool, are formed from shorter fibers that radiate in a variety of random directions. These fibers are bonded together with a thermosetting resin, a high molecular-weight kind of glue. Fiberglass has a number of applications today; it is often used in automobile bodies and insulating materials.

First see SOLVATION AND PRECIPITATION

Filtration

Next see CHROMATOGRAPHY

The process of separating one substance from another by means of a filter.

The molecular structures of a mixture's components must be different enough to allow one substance to pass easily through the filter, while the other one is retained. There are two main types of filtration; gravity filtration and vacuum filtration. (*See* LIQUID.)

Gravity filtration is used to remove small solid particles from a liquid. The process involves folding filter paper to form a fluted filter that is moistened and placed into a funnel. The solution is then poured through the filter. Any solids left behind in the filter itself results in a pure liquid sample. It is sometimes necessary to add an inert substance known as filter-aid to the mixture in order to prevent very fine grains from passing through the paper filter or clogging its pores. (*See* OSMOSIS.)

Vacuum filtration is used to remove crystalline solids from solvents. A different type of funnel is used, and the paper filter is not fluted. In addition, a vacuum pump is utilized to keep the crystals from going through the holes in the filter and to hold the filter paper tightly against the funnel. Unlike gravity filtration, where the liquid portion of the mixture is the key substance for recovery and purification, vacuum filtration aims to recover the crystals.

First see INVERTEBRATES

Fish

Next see GILLS

Fish are the most primitive of the five classes of vertebrates, animals with a backbone. The category of fish excludes "seafood" such as lobsters, shrimp, crabs, and clams, as these animals are all invertebrates.

Most fish are characterized by the presence of gills and the absence of lungs. However, some animals other than fish, such as amphibians, have gills, and some fish have lungs in addition to their gills. Gills—membranes rich in small blood vessels or capillaries—are designed to extract oxygen from water, just as lungs extract it from air. "Water-breathers" need oxygen just as much as "air-breathers" do. When water is forced over the gills, carbon dioxide diffuses from the blood into the water at the same time that oxygen from the water diffuses into the capillary. As opposed to the mammalian circulatory system, oxygenated blood returning from the gills mingles with deoxygenated blood returning from the rest of the body.

Fish are "cold-blooded" (ectotherms), meaning they cannot maintain a consistent body temperature. Their temperature remains very close to that of their environment. Different species of fish are adapted to either fresh or salt water, in addition to specific water temperatures. Some fish, like salmon, spend the majority of their lives in the ocean, but return to the freshwater streams in which they were hatched in order to spawn.

Reproductive System. The majority of fish are egg-layers. Females lay hundreds, if not thousands, of eggs that are then born fertilized by the male. A few species are born live; eggs are fertilized internally, and the female gives birth to the young, or "fry." Some fish can even change from female to male, depending on the needs of the population.

There are four main divisions of fish:

Agnatha—jawless fish, including lamprey and hagfish;

Acanthodians and Placoderms—armored fish, now extinct;

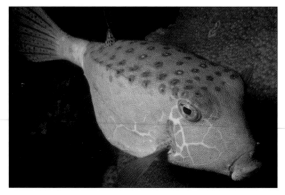

Chondrichthyes—cartilaginous fish, including sharks, skates, and rays;

Osteichthyes—bony fish with covered gill slits and scaly skin.

DISCOVERIES

Coelacanth

One of the most famous "fossils" ever uncovered was alive when found: the coelacanth. The family tree of the coelacanth goes back about 350 million years. Found in a fisherman's net off the coast of Madagascar in 1938, the coelacanth was soon identified as *latimeria chalumnae*, thought to be extinct for 60 million years. It is about five feet long, weighs more than 100 pounds, and is covered with deep-blue scales. Researchers were able to photograph coelacanth in the 1980s, but by 1995 their population had decreased significantly; ironically, only a few decades after being found, the coelacanth may now be in danger of extinction (or may already be extinct).

Further Reading
Goodson, Gar, *Fishes of the Atlantic Coast: Canada to Brazil, Including the Gulf of Mexico, Florida, Bermuda, the Bahamas, and the Caribbean* (1985); Moyle, Peter B., *Fishes: An Introduction to Ichthyology* (1995); Paxton, John R., *Encyclopedia of Fish-es* (1998); Stiassny, Melanie, *Interrelationships of Fishes* (1998).

Further developments in the field are discussed in OCEANS; RESPIRATORY SYSTEMS; OSMOSIS. *Advanced subjects are developed in* GILLS; UNDERWATER EXPLORATION; EVOLUTION. *Elementary aspects of this subject are covered in* ETHOLOGY; OCEANOGRAPHY.

Fish are popularly conceived of as thin and flat, but the box fish, left, has much the appearance of a land animal.

First see NUCLEAR FORCES

Fission, Nuclear

Next see NUCLEAR POWER

The splitting of an atomic nucleus into at least two fragments.

Nuclear fission was discovered in 1938, when physicists added a neutron to the nucleus of uranium, then the heaviest known element. They found that new elements were produced that were about half the size of uranium; the nucleus had split into two parts.

Nuclear fission results from the properties of the nuclear force that holds the protons and neutrons of a nucleus together. This force is strongly attractive at very short distances. Normally, all the protons and neutrons in a nucleus are held together close to one another. But if the balance of force is changed, then the nucleus will break apart. (*See* ATOM.)

Fission can be triggered artificially by bombarding uranium nuclei or the nuclei of some lighter elements with neutrons, gamma rays, or high-energy particles. Once the bombarded nucleus breaks up, its fragments fly apart, propelled by the strong repulsive force of the positively charged protons, which are no longer close enough to feel the attraction of the nuclear force. The splitting of a large or heavy atomic nucleus also results in the liberation of free neu-

Left, spent nuclear fuel elements at France's La Hague facility spend 2 years submerged in a special storage tank. The blue light they emit is known as the Cerenkov glow.

trons. These neutrons and the fragments of the nuclei collide with the nuclei of neighboring atoms. The result can be a chain reaction, in which the fissioning of nuclei in a mass of uranium atoms continues as more nuclei fission, releasing products that cause fission in their turn. If a chain reaction of fissions is allowed to occur very rapidly, the result will be a violent release of energy, as in an atomic bomb. If the fission is kept under control, the result will be a steady production of heat, which can be put to use turning a turbine in a generating plant to produce electricity.

Related areas to be considered are ATOM; ENERGY; TRANSURANIC ELEMENTS. *More details can be found in* RADIOACTIVITY; NUCLEAR POWER; ENERGY, EQUIVALENCE OF MASS. *More information on particular aspects is contained in* FUSION, NUCLEAR; BREEDER REACTOR; NUCLEAR WEAPONS.

First see PLANT

Flower

Next see GERMINATION

The flower is the reproductive organ of a plant. In most cases, it bears both male pollen and female ovules, as well as mechanisms that prevent self-pollination. It often displays enticements—in color, shape, scent, or nectar—to lure insects, birds, or bats to its center so they will carry pollen off to fertilize other members of its species. Once its own egg is fertilized, a flower typically develops into a fruit enclosing a seed, which in turn encloses a growing plant embryo.

Structure. The typical flower consists of four parts: pistil; stamen; petal; and sepal—all

Above, the process of nuclear fission.

Further Reading
Gottfried, Kurt, et al., *Concepts of Particle Physics* (1987); Graetzer, Hans, S., *The Discovery of Nuclear Fission* (1981); Heyde, Kris, L.G., *Basic Ideas and Concepts in Nuclear Physics: An Introductory Approach* (1994); Jung, Robert R., et al., *Brighter Than a Thousand Suns: A Personal History of the Atomic Scientists* (1970); Wagemans, Cyriel, ed., *The Nuclear Fission Process* (1991).

set on top of the receptacle, the enlarged top of the stem.

The pistil, the female organ, is found in the center of the flower. It consists of a rounded ovary, containing ovules, with a stalk or style rising above it capped by the stigma, a furry or rough-surfaced knob that catches pollen. The stamens—the male organs—surround the pistil. They consist of two-lobed anthers, each lobe housing a pollen sac, atop a stalk called the filament. When pollen, usually from another flower's stamen, is deposited on the stigma, it grows a pollen tube down through the style and into the ovary, where one of the pollen's sperm cells fertilizes the egg cell, which has developed from the ovule. (*See* SEXUAL REPRODUCTION.)

The pistils and stamens are surrounded by petals, collectively called the corona, which typically attract potential pollinators. Surrounding the petals is a ring of sepals, collectively called the calyx. Usually green and leaflike, the sepals protect the closed bud. Together the petals and sepals are called the perianth.

Methods of Pollination. The wind is a careless pollinator, wasting much of the energy-rich pollen it scatters, but insects, birds, bats, or reptiles can be more reliable, visiting one or only a few species of plants. As a result, plants have evolved a breathtaking array of devices to enlist their services.

Most common among insect-pollinated plants are tissues that secrete nectar deep within the flower, so the insect must brush by the anthers on its way to feed, picking up pollen on its body. Petals often bear markings pointing the way to the nectar; these are sometimes visible only in ultraviolet light, to which insects are sensitive. Many flowers tailor their structures to attract specific species; some European orchids, for instance, emit the pheromone of a female species of bee in order to attract the male bee.

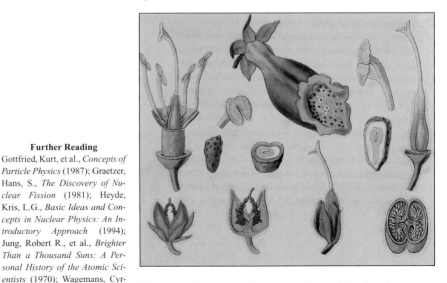

Above, a diagram and cross-sections of the foxglove flower from *Ladies' Botany* by John Lindley, 1834

First see LIQUID

Fluid Mechanics

Next see AERODYNAMICS

The study of fluids and gases at rest and in motion.

Fluid mechanics can be divided into hydrostatics, the behavior of liquids at rest; hydrodynamics, the behavior of liquids in motion; and aerodynamics, the behavior of gases in motion.

Hydrostatics. Hydrostatics is important in the construction of dams, storage tanks, underwater tunnels, and other structures in which fluid behavior is a necessary consideration. It takes into account the forces exerted by a liquid in all directions, not just the downward gravitational pull, such as the upward force exerted on a submerged object that causes bouyancy. The downward force exerted by a liquid on a unit of area at a given level of submergence is called hydrostatic pressure. This pressure is always exerted perpendicularly to the submerged surface. The product of this pressure and the area of the submerged surface is expressed as the total hydrostatic force, F, whose value is $F=pA$, where p is the hydrostatic pressure and A is the area of the submerged surface. Pressure varies directly with the depth of submersion and the weight-density of the liquid.

Fluid pressure is not affected by the shape of the container holding the fluid. The pressure of a confined liquid is transmitted to all parts of the container, a principle known as Pascal's law that is applied in the design of such devices as the hydraulic brake and the hydraulic press.

Hydrodynamics. Hydrodynamics is the study of fluid flow and fluid friction, or viscosity. In the case of a steady, uniform flow, the velocity of the fluid stream and its size and shape, are the same at every point of the channel in which the fluid is flowing. However, since the same amount of fluid must flow through narrow as well as wider regions in a given unit of time, if the width of the channel varies, the velocity of the fluid stream varies inversely with the cross-sectional area of the channel. An increase in the velocity of a fluid is accompanied by a decrease in pressure, a phenomenon that was explained in the eigtheenth century by Daniel Bernoulli.

Bournelli's principle explains that because the water pressure between them is decreased, two ships that pass each other at close range and high speed are in danger of collision. The principles of hydrostatics are applied in the design of the turbine, in which the momentum or pressure of a moving liquid produces a torque that causes the rotation of the turbine; the rotation is transformed into electrical energy.

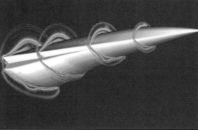

Computer-simulated model of air flow around a hypersonic aircraft, a critical step in preparation for the modeling of the sub-orbital X–33 aircraft.

An early fluorescent lamp bears a striking resemblance to its incandescent counterpart.

Aerodynamics, the study of the motion of gases, is most often applied to the study of air and the motion of solid bodies in it. Aerodynamic lift is the upward force exerted by a body as it moves through the air, while the force that opposes the motion of such a body is called aerodynamic drag. The major practical concern of aerodynamics is the motion and stability of aircraft. Internal aerodynamics deals with the flow of gases through ducts, compressors, fans, and other devices.

First see ENERGY

Fluorescence

Next see LIGHT

The emission of light upon absorption of energy.

Fluorescence and phosphorescence are both types of luminescence. Fluorescence lasts only as long as energy is being supplied, whereas phosphorescence continues even after the energy source has been removed. Incandescence refers to light emission due to heat exposure.

Fluorescent materials give off light because of their atomic structure. Electrons of an atom are arranged in discrete energy levels surrounding the nucleus, with each level having a predetermined amount of energy. When an electron absorbs additional energy, it becomes "excited" and literally jumps to a higher level. The excitement does not last long, however; the electron loses the additional energy and drops back to its original location. The extra energy is given off in the form of visible light, or, in some cases, as ultraviolet or infrared.

The phenomenon of fluorescence was first explained by a British scientist, Sir George Stokes, in 1852, although it had been observed for hundreds of years prior to this. Fluorescent materials include solids, liquids, and gases, and are now used in such devices as light bulbs, television screens, and electron microscopes.

First see MINERAL

Foliation and Lineation

Next see METAMORPHIC ROCK

Foliation and lineation are different but related geological phenomena that result in some types of geological structures. Foliation is a kind of layering occurring in rocks of metamorphic origin that generally produce alignment and segregation of the minerals they contain into bands. In the case of fine-grained metamorphic rocks such as slate, foliation is caused by the segregation or replacement of the mineral constituents making up the original version of the metamorphic rock; it is particularly conspicuous if the constituents of the rock differ in color. Foliation can also develop along flat rock structures produced by the flow of igneous rocks, along the bedding of sedimentary rocks, or along rock structures of ancient origin.

Lineation refers to the linear arrangement of mineral deposits and other structures in the Earth's crust described according to their geographical direction and horizontal plane. The form of such a linear structure is expressed by such characteristics as its dip or its plunge, the angle it makes with the horizontal, and the orientation in which it descends. There are several characteristic arrangements of linear structures. For example, if the poles of planes are tangential to a folded surface, and if they are plotted on a stereographic net, they will fall on a single grand circle. The pole to this circle will correspond to the axis of the fold. Such a diagram is called a "pi diagram." Mutual relationships can be distinguished in the arrangement of linear structures on a plane surface. They include parallel, orthogonal, and oblique relationships.

First see NUTRITION

Food Science

Next see DIGESTION REGULATION

Food science deals with the composition of foods, how they are used by animals and plants, and their effects on health. Foods consumed by animals contain water, carbohydrates, proteins, fats, minerals, and vitamins. Water is both common and essential, playing an important role in nearly every function of an animal's body. It is involved in the regulation of body temperature, nutrient and oxygen transportation, and waste removal. A person requires eight eight-ounce glasses of water daily.

Carbohydrates. Carbohydrates are found primarily in breads, cereals, fruits, and vegetables. Chemically, they are starches—complex carbohydrates—and sugars—simple carbohydrates. During digestion, complex carbohydrates are broken down into simple sugars.

Proteins. Proteins are large molecules composed of sub-units called amino acids. Some amino acids are produced in the human body, but others—the essential amino acids—are not. Meat, eggs, fish, milk, and cheese provide necessary amounts of essential amino acids; other foods, such as vegetables, cereals, and beans do not provide the same optimal mixture of essential amino acids as protein of animal origin, so the proper combinations must be consumed in order to meet the body's needs. Nevertheless, a properly planned vegetarian diet can meet the body's demand for protein.

Fats. Fats exist in various forms and are found in a variety of foods of animal origin, including meat, poultry, and fish, and in plants. Fats may be in liquid form, as in the case of cooking and salad oils, or solids, such as meat fat, butter, milk, and vegetable shortening. Chemically, fats are classified by the molecular structure of their building blocks, the fatty acids, which in turn can be classified as either saturated or unsaturated. Saturated fatty acids do not have double or triple bonds between their atoms and do not undergo further reactions. They usually are solid at room temperature, while unsaturated fats are liquid. Saturated fats have traditionally been used for processed foods because they are less likely to turn rancid; unsaturated fats are transformed into saturated fats by hydrogeneration, which fills out their molecular structures. However, foods containing saturated fats can raise blood levels of cholesterol, thus increasing the risk of heart disease.

Vitamins. Vitamins are organic compounds needed in small amounts to maintain health. Vitamin A is present in green leafy vegetables, tomatoes, carrots, and some fats and oils; vitamin A deficiency causes night blindness and a rare disease called xerophthalmia. Vitamin B_1, or thiamine, is found in cereal grains, while vitamin B_2, or riboflavin, is found in milk, eggs, and green leaves. Vitamin B_{12} is found in liver and other animal products. Vitamin C, or ascorbic acid, is found in oranges and other fresh fruits and vegetables. Vitamin C deficiency causes scurvy. A vitamin D deficiency causes the bone-deforming disease rickets; once common in Victorian slums, it has almost been eliminated today.

The energy needs of both humans and animals are calculated in terms of calories, which are units of heat. One calorie is the amount of heat needed to raise the temperature of one gram of water by one degree Celsius at one atmosphere of pressure. Dieticians and food scientists commonly work in units called units of kilocalories, or Calories; one Calorie equals 1,000 calories. A man or woman weighing 150 pounds will use body energy at the rate of 65 Calories an hour to watch television. That same man or women requires some ten to 15 times that amount of Calories to walk up a flight of stairs for the same amount of time.

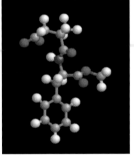
Molecular model of the artificial sweetener aspartame.

OBSERVATIONS

Artificial Sweetness

Food science has come to rely on artificial sweeteners, such as saccharine (discovered by accident in 1897) and aspartame (developed in 1967). These products are much sweeter than natural sugar, so much smaller quantities are used when baking; this changes the density of the finished cake, or the texture of the cookie. Food scientists are searching for a natural sugar that would be indigestible, comparable to the indigestible fat substitute, Olean. A sugar that had a different physical conformation would still cause taste buds to react, but would not be digested by the enzyme that breaks down sucrose, and thus would not add weight to the body.

Force

First see ACCELERATION

Next see NEWTON'S LAWS

A physical agent or any operative agency that affects the status of, or brings about a change in, the motion or momentum of a body.

In dynamics, where the concept was originally applied, force is defined as a physical agent that causes a change of momentum, measured by the rate of change in time of a body's momentum. In dynamics, force is a vector quantity; both its magnitude and its direction must be known. If the speeds in a physical system are much lower than the speed of light, a force can be defined as being proportional to the mass (m) of a body and to the acceleration (a) that is produced by the force acting on the body. Thus, a force (F) can be expressed as $F = ma$.

In static systems, force is defined as a physical agent that produces an elastic strain in a body. A static force can be equated to a dynamic force by allowing a weight to produce a strain in a body and then having the weight fall under the influence of gravity.

From these initial conceptions of force, the term has been applied to describe any operating agency. Examples are electromotive force, magnetomotive force, and coercive force.

An electromotive force is one that is generated by a running motor or by an inductive element of an electric circuit in which the current increases with time.

A magnetomotive force is one that exists in any magnetic circuit, such as those created by a magnet or a coil of wire carrying a current. Magnetomotive force is analogous to electromotive force; the magnet or coil of wire corresponds to the battery, and thus provides magnetomotive force as the battery provides electromotive force. The strength of magnetomotive force depends on the dimensions and material of the magnetic circuit.

A coercive force is one caused by magnetism. When a bipolar magnet is placed in a magnetic field, it experiences a torque that is proportional to the intensity of the field and the sine of the angle between the axis of the magnet and the direction of the magnetic field.

Special Forces. There are several other special forces. An impressed force is any external force that acts on a particle in a dynamical system. Such a force can be separated into the external impressed force and the internal constraint force created by that impressed force. An example of such a system is a ball hanging on a string in a gravitational field. The weight of the ball is the impressed force, and the tension that it produces in the string is the constraint force.

Tangential Forces. A tangential force is one

The four forces of Nature. Above, the force that maintains a solid is electromagnetic; below, the weak nuclear force unleashed by an atom bomb; bottom, the strong nuclear force at work in the heart of a black hole; below, right, the force of gravity that brings the skier back to Earth.

Further Reading
Davies, P. C. W., *The Forces of Nature* (1990); Davies, P. C. W., *Superforce* (1990); Grigaryev, V., *The Forces of Nature* (2001); Jammer, Max, *Force* (1999); Stommel, Henry M., *An Introduction to the Coriolis Force* (2000).

that is associated with a wheel or disk. It always acts perpendicular to the radius of the disk. Examples of tangential force include the frictional force between a rolling wheel and the surface on which it rolls, and that of a belt on a pulley and the wheel that turns the belt.

A restoring force is the elastic force that acts on part of a mechanical system when that system is displaced from equilibrium (is out of balance). The restoring force acts to return the system to equilibrium. In simple systems, the restoring force is linear—it is proportional to the first power of the distance by which the system has been displaced. For more complicated systems, the restoring force may be proportional to the square of the distance, or to a higher power of the distance.

An attractive force is one that acts to attract a particle or some other body. Simple examples are the force that a magnet exerts on a piece of iron and the attraction that the Earth exerts on an apple falling from a tree. (The apple exerts its own attractive force on the Earth, but that force is very small.) (*See* NEWTON'S LAWS.)

Stress. Another form of force is stress. Stress is a condition of change that occurs in an elastic material, caused by an external force, such as the force exerted on a bed by someone who lies down on a mattress. The measure of stress is the ratio of force to area and can be expressed in pounds per square inch or kilograms per square meter.

Thermal stress, the internal resisting force that arises in a body because of temperature changes, is yet another form of stress; Examples of this type of force are the expansion of bridges in hot weather, and the expansion of a balloon, also because of heat, as a result of an increase in pressure of the gas inside it.

Related areas to be considered are FRICTION; MECHANICS; NEWTON'S LAWS. **Advanced subjects are developed in** ELECTROMAGNETIC FORCE; GRAVITY; ROTATIONAL MOTION. **More on particular aspects of this subject is contained in** AERODYNAMICS; MAXWELL'S EQUATIONS; NUCLEAR FORCES; VECTOR.

First see ELECTROPHORESIS

Forensic Science

Next see DNA

Forensic science involves the use of several scientific disciplines in the procurement of evidence in criminal matters. Methods such as fingerprinting, blood and speech analysis, and the increasingly popular DNA testing are all part of this field.

Foundations. Forensic scientists are able to do their work knowing one thing for certain: all contact leaves some sort of trace. Trace evidence such as hairs and fiber are easily detectable through the use of a microscope. However, keeping up with the latest advances in research greatly increases the scientist's chance of success. The scanning electron microscope is one such advance. It allows the scientist to see objects invisible to the regular microscope. It can also detect x-rays emitted by surface elements, allowing the scientist to identify individual particles and differentiate between different types of bullet residue. This links ballistics, the study of projectiles, to forensic science.

Current Cases. Anyone vaguely familiar with the O.J. Simpson trial has heard about DNA testing. DNA testing, or DNA fingerprinting, requires the DNA patterns from both the suspect and the crime scene in order to establish (or eliminate) a link between the two. This technology has proven invaluable in cases of murder and rape, and in establishing parentage. The "prints" taken from these tests can be scanned into a computer and cataloged in an effort to link a suspect to multiple crimes. For instance, a suspect's DNA sample is taken and run through the computer. If it matches samples taken from a past crime scene, the link has been established.

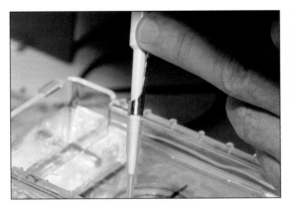

Special topics in this area are found in BLOOD TYPE; DNA; CHROMATOGRAPHY. *Advanced subjects are developed in* POLYMERASE CHAIN REACTION; ELECTROPHORESIS. *More information on particular aspects of this subject is contained in* EXPERT SYSTEMS; RADIOCHEMISTRY. *DNA fingerprinting is discussed in the entry* DNA.

First see GEOLOGICAL TIME SCALE

Fossil

Next see EVOLUTION

Fossils are remnants left behind by creatures that lived long ago. Fossils are usually found in layers of sedimentary rock composed of sediment carried by rivers into the sea. The sediment is formed by the erosion and weathering of rocks into smaller particles. Under water pressure, the material in the sediment becomes "cemented" together. A fossil can be the petrified or preserved organism itself or an impression left in mud or other soft material that gradually hardened into rock.

Formation. Fossils are formed in a number of ways. Petrification refers to the process in which an animal or woody plant is covered with sediment. Minerals replace the hard parts of the bones or wood, and the sediment is changed into sedimentary rock. Changes in the Earth's surface, such as earthquakes, volcanic eruptions, and erosion bring the fossils closer to the surface, enabling their discovery. Carbonization is the process in which decaying tissues leave behind a thin black film of carbon in the shape of the organism.

The process of fossilization is responsible for our knowledge about long-dead creatures. Below, a fossil of an archeopteryx.

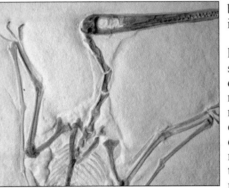

Occasionally, footprints or leafprints left in soft mud or sand are preserved. As the soil dries up, it changes into sedimentary rock. Sometimes animals buried in mud form casts or molds. As the organism decays, its place is taken by minerals, which leave a cast of the original animal in the surrounding rock.

Many preserved bodies of prehistoric creatures have been discovered. The skin and tissue of mummified bodies, such as those buried in sand, are preserved by desiccation. The La Brea tar pits in Los Angeles contain skeletons of animals trapped in tar. Many ancient insects and microorganisms were trapped in tree resin which gradually hardened into amber. Whole wooly mammoths were discovered encased in ice in Siberia, where the intense cold prevented bacterial decay. The Alpine "Iceman," believed to be approximately 6,000 years old, was found in 1991 in much the same condition.

The oldest fossils, normally found in the lowest strata, are those of microorganisms believed to have lived approximately 3 billion years ago. The oldest animal fossils discovered are invertebrates that lived 700 million years ago. The oldest vertebrate fossils are primitive fish that lived 500 million years ago.

The ages of rocks and the fossils they contain are determined by a variety of methods:

The methodologies of forensic science are among the routine procedures of the modern biology laboratory, but they continue to be challenged by the legal establishment.

Further Reading
Batten, Jack, *Mind over Murder: DNA and Other Forensic Adventures* (1997); Browning, Michael, *Dead Men Do Tell Tales: The Strange and Fascinating Cases of a Forensic Anthropologist* (1995); Evans, Colin, *The Casebook of Forensic Detection* (1988); Rhine, Stanley, *Bone Voyage: A Journey in Forensic Anthropology* (1998); Zonderman, Jon, *Beyond the Crime Lab: The New Science of Investigation* (1998).

Carbon Dating. A relatively rare isotope of carbon, C_{14}, found in the atmosphere, combines with oxygen to form carbon dioxide, which is then incorporated by living plants. C_{14} decays to an isotope of nitrogen, N_{14}. After the plant dies, no new C_{14} is taken in. The proportion of C_{14} to N_{14} therefore indicates how long it has been since the organism died.

Rate of Sedimentation. Some types of sediment turn into sedimentary rock at the rate of one foot in 900 years. Age can thus be determined by measuring the thickness of a stratum of rock.

Ocean Salinity. The salinity of marine fossils increases over time because rivers flow into the oceans carrying dissolved salt.

Lessons. Transition fossils are creatures that combined characteristics of two major groups, providing a glimpse of the evolutionary process. For example, the archaeopteryx had the skin and teeth of reptiles and the feathers of birds, a strong argument for the theory that some dinosaurs evolved into birds.

Fossils also help show how climate and landscape have changed over millions of years, based on the type of plants and animals found in different areas. For instance, many deserts were once under water because they have yielded fossils of sea creatures.

Fossils also provide support for the theory of plate tectonics, by which all the continents were once one large land mass referred to as Pangaea. Dinosaurs first appeared 240 million years ago, and dinosaur fossils have been discovered on all of the continents. By the time early mammals began appearing 200 million years ago, the continents had begun to separate, as evidenced by the distinct differences among the mammalian fossils of each continent.

Most fossils are collected in fragments and must be reconstructed to come up with a whole specimen. Many years often elapse between the discovery of a particular fossil and its proper identification and the determination of its place in the established evolutionary time line. Fossils, however, were not always identified as being the remnants of past lives. The first Neanderthal fossils, unearthed in Germany in 1856, were first believed to have been the deformed bones of present-day humans.

Further developments in the field are discussed in EVOLUTION; GEOLOGICAL TIME SCALE; STRATIGRAPHY. *Advanced subjects are developed in* BIOSTRATIGRAPHY; EXTINCTION; PALEOECOLOGY. *More information on particular aspects is contained in* CAMBRIAN DIVERSIFICATION OF LIFE; DINOSAUR; HYDROCARBONS. *See* BIRDS, EVOLUTION OF *for a discussion on fossil evidence of a bird-dinosaur connection.*

An ichthyosaur. This creature became extinct 66 million years before the age of the dinosaurs.

Although reliance on fossil fuels has declined a bit over the past two decades, they are still the world's major source of energy.

Further Reading
Attenborough, David, *Digging Dinosaurs: The Search That Unraveled the Mystery of Baby Dinosaurs* (1996); Donovan, S.K., *The Adequacy of the Fossil Record* (1998); Doyle, Peter, *Understanding Fossils: An Introduction to Invertebrate Palaeontology* (1996); Fortey, Richard, *Fossils: The Key to the Past* (1994); Mayr, Helmut, *A Guide to Fossils* (1996); Rich, Patricia V., *The Fossil Book: A Record of Prehistoric Life* (1997).

First see ENERGY

Fossil Fuel Power

Next see ENERGY, ALTERNATIVE

A fossil fuel power plant converts energy from coal, oil, or natural gas to electrical energy by burning it. Fossil fuel-generating plants are usually built on a large scale to provide electrical power to a large number of users. A typical fossil fuel plant consists of facilities to process and handle fuel; a combustion furnace to burn the fuel, producing and superheating steam; a steam turbine; and an alternator and accessory pieces of equipment for plant protection and for the control of electrical voltage, power flow, and frequency. The steam produced by burning the fuel is fed into a turbine, which transforms mechanical motion into electric power by turning a coil of wire in an electric field.

Environmental considerations require careful control of the emissions from a fossil fuel plant. Emissions of sulfur oxides and particulate matter are of major concern. Cooling towers or ponds are often required for dissipation of waste heat from the plant. Since fossil fuels are nonrenewable resources, efforts are under way to develop other forms of energy production, such as solar, tidal, and thermal power.

FUEL CONSUMPTION PERCENTAGE COMPOSITION

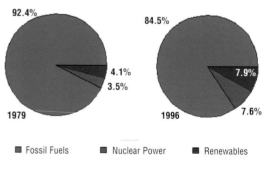

92.4% 1979 4.1% 3.5%

84.5% 1996 7.9% 7.6%

■ Fossil Fuels   ■ Nuclear Power   ■ Renewables

The foundations of the subject are discussed in HYDROCARBON; PETROLEUM DISTILLATION; PETROLEUM PROSPECTING. *More details can be found in* AIR POLLUTION; GEODETIC SURVEY; REMOTE SENSING. *Advanced subjects are developed in* ENERGY, ALTERNATIVE; NUCLEAR POWER.

First see FUNCTION

Fourier Analysis

Next see CALCULUS

Fourier analysis refers to solutions of partial differential equations based on the Fourier series, according to which every function can, within certain limits, be expressed as the summation of a series of trigonometric operations (sine and cosine functions); thus, time and frequency are intimately, and predictably, related. This analysis has made possible solutions to problems in many fields, including cardiology, cryptography, data compression, elasticity, heat transfer, holography, geophysics, and spectrum analysis.

History. The Fourier series was developed by French mathematician Joseph Fourier (1768–1830). Fourier had wanted to be a soldier, but his working-class origins disqualified him from an officer's position; he settled for teaching mathematics at his old military school. There he developed revolutionary ways of treating problems that to that point had been considered insoluble; but when he submitted his ideas to the French Academy of Sciences in 1807, his work was rejected. Again, his lack of the proper credentials had prejudiced observers against him. Nevertheless, Fourier persisted, and submitted a paper in 1811 that won a special prize, but again the Academy refused to publish it. Finally, in 1822, Fourier published his work by himself as *The Analytical Theory of Heat*. This time the work was accepted, and he was elected to the Academy. Two years later, he succeeded in having his prize-winning paper published in the Academy's *Proceedings*.

Uses. The most common use of Fourier series analysis is in electronics. Any electrical waveform—and therefore any data flow—can be expressed as a basic direct current, modified by a series of sine and cosine waves of a certain frequency, plus the harmonics associated with that frequency. Since a sine wave and cosine wave are 90 degrees out of phase (or "orthogonal"), every added Fourier wave is independent of every previous addition. This principle allows one to add depth and richness to music by adding resonant harmonics, for example. Another common use of Fourier analysis is for the analysis of very large numbers in computer applications such as weather modeling, encryption, and virtual reality. By treating very large numbers as signals, technicians can decompose them into frequency bands, which can then be multiplied with far fewer steps. The result is a new signal, which when inverted and reprocessed comes out as the numerical product of the original numbers.

First see FUNCTIONS

Fractal

Next see CHAOS AND COMPLEXITY

A mathematical language and an approach for describing shapes, forms, and patterns that look the same when magnified.

Fractals and fractal geometry refer to a quality found often in nature. For example, a magnified view of a leaf on a tree may show the same pattern as that of the entire branch, and the branch may in turn show the same pattern as the entire tree.

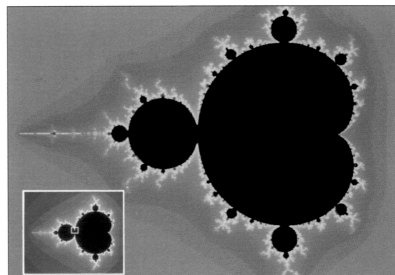

The word fractal, from the Latin *fractus*, meaning "broken," was coined in 1975 by the mathematician Benoit B. Mandelbrot to denote highly irregular shapes and mathematical functions that still displayed some sort of orderliness, however slight. Euclidean geometry and the theory of smooth functions describe regular shapes and patterns such as lines, planes, and very smooth surfaces. Fractal geometry is a method of dealing with the many complicated shapes and forms that exist in nature.

Fractal concepts are used to describe mathematically a wide range of phenomena and processes of scientific and practical importance in such diverse fields as biology, geology, physics, chemistry, engineering, mathematics, computer graphics, art, music, and motion picture technology. One of the most important scientific results of fractal geometry has been the recognition that a single fundamental process or mathematical law can give rise to many radically different shapes or outcomes with the same basic fractal properties. That these very rough and irregular shapes and different phenomena can be analyzed mathematically at all is one of the more remarkable developments of the modern age.

Self-Similarity. A fractal is a shape or pattern made of parts similar to the whole in some way. Magnifying a fractal yields a larger object but of similar (if not identical) shape. From this fact one may expect that many of the properties of a fractal are the same at any magnification and will exist at all scales. This is an idealization—an idealized extension of what is observed to be true at a simple level—and points to some possible limitations and pitfalls of fractal thinking.

A common example of a fractal phenomenon is a coastline. A coastline is a rough curve that often looks the same at a wide range of length scales (the same might be said of a mountainside or any terrestrial feature). It is a ragged edge when looked at from space at a distance of

Above, a graphic representation of the Mandelbrot set, an image created by plotting a function (in this case, by computer). It is remarkable because the basic image design is identical when a portion of the image is enlarged. When the small area in the red box is magnified (inset), one sees a fresh image identical to the large original. An area where fractals have found important applications is in the theory of systems that develop chaotically.

Benoit Mandelbrot emigrated to the United States in 1958. It was there that he published his landmark paper on the fractal nature of the English shoreline, the first indication that fractals may have practical applications.

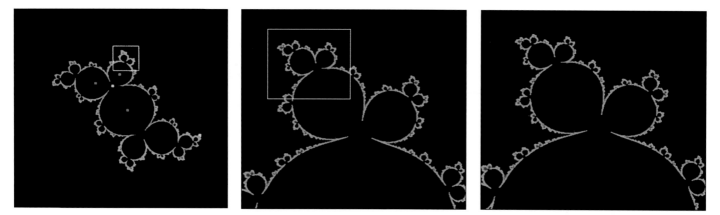

Zero in on a segment of a fractal image—and one finds the same fractal image. Above, a portion of a fractal image is magnified and yields another image that can be enlarged to reveal the same image. The images above have been made the same size. How should these three images be placed and read so that they progress in the proper order? (Answer: The two images on the left should be interchanged and then the images read from left to right.)

Above, the beginning stages of a Sierpinski gasket.

thousands of miles, yet it has the same winding and ragged shape when one walks along it on a beach. When looked at closely, say, from a few millimeters, it has the same basic shape.

When presented with two pictures of a coast, one taken from far away and one taken close up, one would have great difficulty telling which is which (and that is something for which movie makers are grateful, since that allows them to use models of battlefields on small patches of earth and still look convincing). This lack of a characteristic length is the most basic property of a fractal and is called self-similarity or the property of scale invariance.

Regular and Random Fractals. Fractals come in two basic varieties: regular and random. Regular fractals are created like a jigsaw puzzle by joining together similar shapes in a prescribed way. A simple example is the Sierpinski gasket, so called because when fully developed the shape resembles a plumbing rubber gasket.

A Sierpinski gasket is composed of regular shapes—squares or triangles. One starts with a single triangle, say, and then adds two triangles in triangular fashion. In successive steps, each shape formed is treated as a unit and is placed in triangular fashion. This process can be continued forever to create a very large pattern made up of triangles and triangular holes. Since the repeating pattern is always in the shape of a triangle with a large triangular hole in the center, this object is a self-similar fractal, having the same basic shape and geometrical features at any scale of magnification.

By contrast, fractal shapes and patterns found naturally are usually random (or "stochastic," meaning determined by statistical probability) fractals. This is because the fractals of nature form as a result of the action of irregular forces. For example, the flow of a river is rarely even and smooth because it flows over uneven terrain and through earth of varying densities. Examples of random fractals in nature are clouds, coastlines, mountains, polymer chains, colloidal suspensions, and rubber and gel polymers.

Much of the attention currently given to fractals is in the area of physical systems involving random fractals. For example, a fractal is formed when manganese dioxide crystallizes against the face of white limestone, a process that, in some cases, takes millions of years. Since crystal growth is controlled by the diffusion process, this random fractal structure is similar to many other natural patterns formed by a diffusion-like process.

Application of Fractals. Fractal concepts have been applied to a wide range of scientific and engineering problems because many phenomena in chemical reactions, electrical phenomena, biological growth, and fluid flow are subject to the same basic mathematical equations. Fractals have played a major role in research and development of polymer chemistry and materials science, particularly in developing the alloys required for stealth aircraft or for space travel. The phenomenon of "percolation," which signals the onset of flow or conduction in a random system, has been fully described only by fractal theory.

An area where fractals have found important applications is in the theory of what is popularly called chaos. It is now believed that the basic character of phenomena in biological, chemical, mathematical, and physical systems is nonlinearity. Nonlinear systems differ from linear systems in that they respond very sensitively to small stimuli and slight changes in input parameters, producing unpredictable and chaotic behavior. Linear systems, by contrast, react in a manner commensurate with the magnitude of the stimulus and in a very orderly and predictable way.

An important mathematical element of the theory of chaos is the Mandelbrot set. This set is generated by the simplest nonlinear mathematical operation—the squaring of an input number—yet it has a surprisingly rich and complex geometrical structure.

History. An early form of fractal was suggested by Swedish mathematician Helge von Koch (1870–1924). The so-called Koch curve was presented initially as an example of a continuous curve that is nowhere differentiable (an oddity in calculus). The Koch curve is the simplest form of regular fractal. German mathematician Felix Hausdorff was the first to notice this in 1919, and developed the early theory of fractals. Russian mathematician A. S. Besicovitch extended Hausdorff's work and applied it to thermodynamic systems.

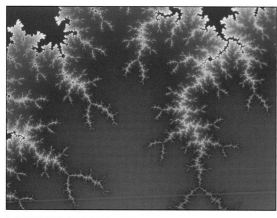

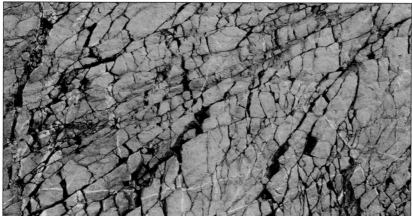

An image from the Julia set (top) shows many similarities to the fracture lines of a cracked piece of the stone (bottom).

Benoit Mandelbrot, a Polish-born mathematician who emigrated to the United states in 1958, published a series of studies beginning in 1961 on the fluctuations of the stock market and compared these fluctuations to the turbulent motions of fluids and to the distribution of galaxies in the universe. A 1967 paper by Mandelbrot showed that coastlines are fractals, and in 1975 he coined the word fractal and established fractals as a serious discipline. Physicists, such as Ilya Prigogine, have been able to apply fractal methods to nonequilibrium thermodynamic systems that formerly defied mathematical description. (*See* CHAOS AND COMPLEXITY. *Also see* SOLAR SYSTEM *AND* WEATHER FORECASTING *FOR APPLICATIONS.*)

Further Reading
Barnsley, Michael, F., *Fractals Everywhere* (1993); Briggs, John, *Turbulent Mirror: An Illustrated Guide to Chaos Theory and the Science of Wholeness* (1990); Mandelbrot, Benoit, B., *Fractal Geometry of Nature* (1988); Peitgen, Heinz-Otto, *Chaos and Fractals* (1992); Pickover, Clifford A., ed., *Fractal Horizons: The Future Use of Fractals* (1996).

First see ELECTROMAGNETIC WAVES

Frequency Modulation (FM)

Next see RADIO AND TELEVISION BROADCASTING

Frequency modulation (FM) was the second form of wireless communication developed, after amplitude modulation (AM). Although both forms of communication allow the transmission, reception, and reproduction of sound, FM is superior in many ways, particularly where clear reception and accurate reproduction are at a premium. Although it occupies greater bandwidth, allowing fewer transmission sources per unit of frequency allotted, FM has become the medium of choice for most applications.

In contrast to AM transmissions, which increase or decrease the magnitude of the carrier wavelength to modulate sound, FM transmissions increase or decrease the frequency in order to modulate sound, thus remaining free of distortion either from overmodulation or from static. However, the bandwidth required for such a transmission will include multiple harmonics of the modulating wave, both above and below the carrier frequency; therefore FM carrier frequencies must be very high compared to the frequency of the signals transmitted—at least 25 Megahertz (MHz). While commercial AM radio frequencies occupy the 570–1570 kHz band, FM radio frequencies occupy the 88–108 MHz band, some one hundred times higher.

FM transmissions display an additional freedom from static interference, since the ratio of signal to noise in the output of an FM receiver is geometrically, rather than arithmetically, proportional to frequency deviation, improving even more as bandwidth is increased. However, since the signal increases as bandwidth increases, a better technique is to employ negative feedback. This technique is especially useful in satellite communication, where power supplies are limited and a multiplex system must carry numerous channels without distortion.

CONTROVERSY

Commercializing FM

Although J. R. Carson developed the theory of frequency modulation in 1922, it was E. H. Armstrong who obtained the first patent for the process in 1933. Armstrong then tried and failed in a series of attempts to commercialize FM, being opposed strenuously by RCA and other existing radio powers, whose capital infrastructures were built around AM broadcasting. RCA's strategy (used successfully earlier by Ford and by Curtis against the Wright brothers in aviation) was to overwhelm Armstrong with lawsuits. Although he won them all, his will was broken; he died before FM became a commercial success.

First see FORCE

Friction

Next see LUBRICATION

The resistance to motion that occurs between two touching surfaces when one slides over the other.

When force is applied to move a surface, it is opposed at first by static friction, which prevents movement until enough force is applied. The point at which motion occurs is called the point of "limiting friction." Friction increases with the force that presses the two surfaces together, but it is affected very little by the area of the surfaces that are in contact. For any pair of surfaces, there is a constant, called the coefficient of friction, which is defined as the limiting friction divided by the force on the surfaces. The work done in overcoming friction is converted to heat.

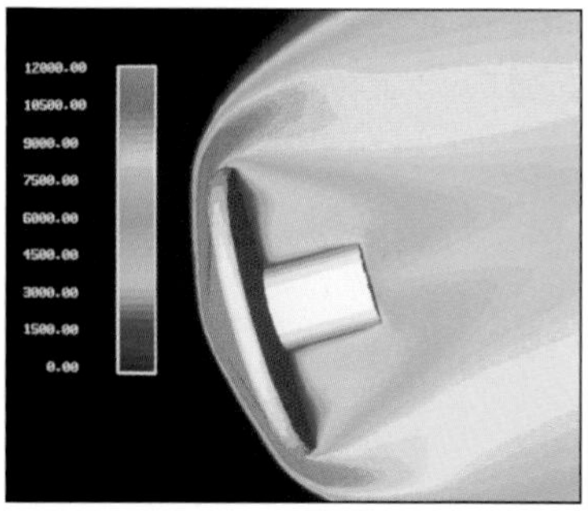

The exact mechanism of friction is not known, but it is believed to be due to electrical forces. The classic laws of friction were formulated by the French scientist Coulomb in the late 18th century. (*See* SOLID STATE PHYSICS.)

Rolling friction is considerably less than sliding friction, and so ball bearings and roller bearings are used in machinery. Friction is also reduced by lubrication, which substitutes contact separated by a lubricating film for surface-to-surface contact. (*See* HEAT; ENTROPY.)

Computers are now being used to model the effects of friction, as in the computer simulation shown above, which depicts a simulation of a Mars vehicle encountering the red planet's atmosphere.

First see SEED

Fruit Structure

Next see GERMINATION

When an egg cell in the ovary of a flowering plant has been fertilized, it becomes encased in a seed, and the carpel containing the ovary develops into a fruit that protects and helps to disperse the seed. The fruit may also contain accessory structures of the flower. In apples and pears, for instance, the core develops from the carpel, while the rest of the fruit develops from the fused bases of sepals, petals, and stamens.

Fruit in the botanical sense include not only apples and oranges but also grains of wheat, rice, corn, nuts, bean pods, tomatoes, cucumbers, olives, and peppers.

The enlarged carpel-derived wall of a fruit is called the pericarp and may have three layers: the exocarp (skin), the mesocarp (flesh), and the endocarp (core or stone). Drupes, such as peaches and plums, have a hard endocarp. Berries, including grapes and blueberries, have a thin skin and no endocarp. Pomes, such as apples, have an endocarp core and a remainder formed from accessory structures.

Two Groups of Fruit. Although we commonly think of fruits as fleshy and juicy, like those mentioned above, most fruits are dry. They are usually divided into two groups. Dehiscent fruits, which include peas, beans, and other legumes, dry out and burst open upon maturity in order to scatter their numerous seeds. Indehiscent fruits, which usually have a single seed, do not open. These include grains, sunflower "seeds," and hazelnuts.

Even fruits that do not burst can help disperse their seeds. Many have hooks, spines, wings, or fringe to cling to animals or ride the wind. Others grow sweet and change color as they ripen, a signal that attracts animals and birds who eat the fruit and later in their travels regurgitate or pass the seeds in their feces.

First see SETS AND GROUPS

Functions

Next see CALCULUS

Functions are ways of talking about the relations between two (or more) variables. Given two sets of numbers—which may be real or complex, exponential or trigonometric—a function defines a correspondence between the numbers in the first set, called the domain, and the numbers in the second set, called the range, such that every number in the domain yields a unique number in the range. A function defines an action, or an operation, performed on one number that turns it into a second number. The number in the domain is known as the independent variable, while the number that is produced in the range is known as the dependent variable.

Categories of Functions. There are five different categories of functions, depending on the kind of operation performed on the domain number: linear functions; exponential functions; algebraic or quadratic functions; trigonometric functions; and polynomial functions. All functions can be added, subtracted, multiplied, and

CONTROVERSIES

Making the Grade

The development of computers has made the manipulation of functions much less onerous. Many integrated software packages contain spreadsheet programs, which are merely automatic function calculators. Once one has programmed the specific relation desired between cells of the spreadsheet, changing the independent variable will change all dependent variables in the other cells. This allows the computer user to examine a wide range of potential effects: how a rise in interest rates may affect the cost of a loan, how a rebate program may increase the number of auto sales, or how well a student has to do on subsequent tests in order to achieve a desired final grade.

divided; a function obtained by dividing one function into another is called a rational function. Most functions can also be combined to obtain a function of a function, in what is called the composition of functions. This last operation becomes especially important in calculating differential equations.

Many functions create sequences of numbers that have practical value, such as the harmonic sequence, which contains the reciprocals of the arithmetic sequence: 1, 1/2, 1/3, and so on; or the Fibonacci sequence, in which each term after the second is the sum of the two previous terms: 1, 1, 2, 3, 5, and so on. Analysis of sequences leads to theories about how to compute their sums, such as in the sequence containing reciprocal powers of two: 1/2, 1/4, 1/8, and so on; the sum of this sequence approaches, but never quite reaches, 1. The sum of a sequence is denoted by the Greek letter sigma (Σ); in integral calculus it is denoted by the old German form of the letter "s"—$\int$.

History. Although scientists used some functions intuitively in the course of their computations for many centuries, the theory of functions—the idea that actions have predictable consequences, which can be codified and therefore manipulated—was first promulgated in the 17th century. The word "function" was first used by Gottfreid Leibniz in 1673. In 1822, Joseph Fourier (1768-1830) introduced the revolutionary concept that every function could be interpreted as the sum of an equivalent sine sequence; this notion, which is now called the Fourier series in his honor, has led to the solution of functions far too complex to solve directly.

Background material can be found in EUCLIDIAN GEOMETRY; NUMBER; SETS AND GROUPS. *Further developments in the field are discussed in* CALCULUS; FOURIER ANALYSIS; VECTORS AND TENSORS. *Special topics in this area are found in* FRACTALS; INTEGRAL CALCULUS; VARIATIONAL CALCULUS.

First see LIFE, DEFINITION AND ORIGIN OF

Fungus

Next see GYMNOSPERMS

The members of the kingdom Fungi used to be considered plants. They might more reasonably be viewed as antiplants, however, a mirror image that makes possible the organic cycle of creation and destruction. Plants, through photosynthesis, turn simple inorganic compounds into organic compounds—food. Fungi cannot perform photosynthesis. Instead, like bacteria, they break down organic matter—living or dead—and release carbon, nitrogen, and other atoms for recycling by plants. Plants produce oxygen. Fungi and nearly all bacteria produce carbon dioxide. Plants build up biomass. Fungi and bac-

Fungi range in size from the microscopic, below, to giant mushrooms several yards in diameter.

Further Reading
Berlinski, David, *A Tour of the Calculus* (1997); Dunham, William, *Journey Through Genius: The Great Theorems of Mathematics* (1991); Gleason, Alan, *Who Is Fourier? : A Mathematical Adventure* (1995); Gullberg, Jan, et al., *Mathematics: From the Birth of Numbers* (1997); Hoffman, Paul, *Archimedes' Revenge: The Joys and Perils of Mathematics* (1997).

teria decompose it, ridding the planet of its endless supply of dead animals and plants. Without either side of the cycle, the planet would be uninhabitable.

In their structure, too, fungi differ from plants. Except for yeast, which are single cells that reproduce by budding, fungi are multicellular, with elongated cells forming rapidly growing branched filaments called hyphae.

Cell walls in fungi are often absent or perforated, so cytoplasm is continuous. Fungal cell walls are composed not of cellulose, as plants' are, but of chitin, the polysaccharide that forms the exoskeletons of insects and crustaceans. As a result, fungi excrete cellulose-destroying enzymes. Fungi are generally either saprophytic—feeding off dead matter—or parasitic.

Reproduction. Fungi reproduce both asexually, through spores, and sexually, when hyphae of opposite mating types—generally designated by plus and minus signs—come into contact. In either case, the haploid stage of the life cycle, with each cell containing only one set of chromosomes, is usually dominant. The specifics of reproduction, including some unique arrangements, vary and help define the main divisions of fungi. These divisions are the zygomycetes, with less than 1,000 species, including the common black bread mold Rhizopus; ascomycetes or sac fungi, with an estimated 30,000 species, including yeast, truffles, and many food-spoiling molds; and basidiomycetes, with 16,000 species, including mushrooms, toadstools, puffballs, and the rusts and smuts, which are plant pathogens. Another division, the deuteromycetes or *Fungi Imperfecti*, includes 17,000 heterogeneous species whose mode of sexual reproduction is either not known or not used in their classification.

Fungal Diseases. Although individual species attack specific targets, as a group fungi attack almost every substance—wood, cloth, paper, jet fuel, paint, photographic film—including all sorts of crops and processed food. Fungi are the major cause of plant diseases. More than 5,000 species attack economically valuable plants, causing such diseases as corn smuts, wheat rusts and ergots, rice blast, Dutch elm disease, and chestnut blight.

In humans, fungi cause a wide variety of illnesses. The most common are skin infections, such as athlete's foot and ringworm, and mucosal infections, such as vaginal candidiasis (commonly called a yeast infection) and oral candidiasis, or thrush. Systemic fungal infections can be more severe or even fatal, especially in persons who are required to have long-term antibiotic treatment or who are taking drugs to suppress the activity of the immune system, as in AIDS treatment.

Along with their great destructive power, fungi also serve as life savers: they have been a source of many important antibiotics, including penicillin and Cyclosporine, the immune suppressant that revolutionized organ transplantation in the 1980s. As yeasts and molds, fungi are indispensable in the making of bread, beer, wine, and many cheeses. (*See* ANTIBIOTICS.)

Their service to plants is almost universal. About 80 percent of all vascular plants have mutually beneficial relationships, called mycorrhizae, with fungi. Typically, the fungus' hyphae, which are underground, penetrate the cells of the plant's roots, forming as much as 20 percent of the plant's root mass. The hyphae draw minerals, especially phosphorus, from a larger area of soil than the plant's roots can reach, causing more vigorous growth than in plants grown experimentally in fungi-free soil. The fungus, in turn, gets carbohydrates from the plant.

In another kind of fungal alliance, fungi grow symbiotically with photosynthetic microorganisms—green algae and cyanobacteria—to form lichen. Lichen grow slowly and inexorably in some of the world's most difficult spots, from deserts to windswept Arctic rocks. They can live thousands of years and routinely tolerate dry periods. (*See* MICROBIOLOGY.)

First see NUCLEAR FORCES

Fusion, Nuclear

Next see NUCLEAR POWER

A kind of nuclear reaction in which the nuclei of atoms of low atomic number, such as hydrogen and helium, fuse to form a heavier nucleus, releasing a substantial amount of energy in the process.

Nuclear fusion is the energy source of the sun and other stars, and has already been achieved in weapons, creating extremely powerful bombs. However, the design and operation of a power-generating fusion reactor are still under development. Since the nuclei of the two atoms that are to be fused both have positive electrical charges, there is a strong repulsive force between them that can be overcome only if the nuclei have very high kinetic temperatures, on the order of millions of degrees.

These temperatures are achieved in the sun and other stars because of the compressive forces created by their huge masses, where fusion reactions are self-sustaining. The reacting atoms at the temperatures inside a star are in the form of a plasma, in which the nuclei of the atoms and their electrons have become separated. A great deal of research is currently being done on several varieties of fusion reactor. The basic problem with controlling a fusion reaction involves finding a way to contain the extremely hot materials. One method involves trapping the plasma, which contains the hydrogen atoms, in a

Above, the 100-trillion-watt particle beam fusion accelerator II, the first machine to have the potential to ignite a controlled thermonuclear fusion reaction in a laboratory setting, as seen in the Sandia National Laboratories of Albuquerque, New Mexico, on its first firing, December, 11, 1985. It was considered the most powerful particle beam accelerator in the world at that time.

magnetic field, then squeezing the field lines together while the temperature of the material is raised. The largest fusion devices, known as tokomaks, contain the plasma in a large doughnut-shaped cylinder and use pulses of electromagnetic radiation to heat the plasma until the particles are moving fast enough to overcome the electrostatic repulsion and fusion begins. It has been demonstrated that fusion will take place in such devices, but they still do not produce more energy from the fusion than is required to run the machine.

Another avenue of approach involves the use of lasers. In this technique, a small frozen pellet of deuterium is blasted from all sides with high intensity laser beams. The outer layer of the pellet is vaporized and this process compresses the material in the interior, raising its temperature and pressure until fusion begins.

Most observers feel that the development of a commercially viable fusion reactor will not occur before the middle of the twenty-first century. Efforts in the area of "cold fusion"—fusion reactions at room temperature—while having some theoretical basis, have proven even less productive, though wild claims to the contrary have taken the world by storm.

Further Reading
Close, Frank, *Too Hot to Handle: The Race for Cold Fusion* (1991); Fowler, T. Kenneth, *The Fusion Quest* (1997); Herman, Robin, *Fusion: The Search for Endless Energy* (1990); Miyamoto, Kenro, *Plasma Physics for Nuclear Fusion* (1989); Post, Charles J., *Atomic and Molecular Physics of Controlled Thermonuclear Fusion* (1984).

Elementary aspects of this subject are covered in ENERGY; FISSION, NUCLEAR; NUCLEUS, ATOMIC. *More information on particular aspects of nuclear fusion is contained in* HAZARDOUS WASTE DISPOSAL; NUCLEAR POWER; PLASMA PHYSICS. *Additional relevant information is contained in* ENERGY, ALTERNATIVE; SOLAR ENERGY SYSTEMS; SPACECRAFT.

Gaia Hypothesis

Next see ECOLOGY

The Gaia hypothesis holds that the Earth is one highly integrated, self-regulating ecosystem, with multiple internal control systems that keep the chemical composition of the air and ocean stable and the temperature moderate, making life possible on the planet. Living organisms, particularly microbes and plants, play the major role in maintaining this constant, favorable environment, or homeostasis.

This theory, named for the Greek Earth goddess, was advanced in the 1970s by James Lovelock, a British physical scientist and engineer, and Lynn Margulis, a microbiologist. It resembles an approach outlined in the 1950s by Alfred Redfield.

Without the early and continuing activities of plants and microbes, according to Lovelock and Margulis, Earth would be nearly as hot as Venus. Its atmosphere—now 79 percent nitrogen and 21 percent oxygen, with far less than 1 percent carbon dioxide–would resemble the atmosphere of Mars and Venus—predominantly carbon dioxide, with a little nitrogen and little or no oxygen.

Scientists today commonly accept the idea that microbes and other organisms played important roles in creating our environment and continue to affect the chemistry of ocean and atmosphere. But the Gaia hypothesis that the biosphere is a controlled, or cybernetic, system is less widely shared. Any such control system would have to involve a staggering number of feedback loops and other interactive processes.

Next see MILKY WAY

Galaxy

First see NEBULA

The matter of the universe—stars, dust, nebulae, and the like—is not spread randomly though space. Instead, it is concentrated in large structures called galaxies, each containing many millions or billions of stars, and each separated from its neighbors by distances that are very large compared to the sizes of the galaxies themselves. (*See* SPACE.)

Discovery. The discovery that matter in the universe is collected into galaxies was made by American astronomer Edwin Hubble in 1927. Until then, astronomers had been aware of extended patches of light in the sky called nebulae (from the Latin word for cloud), but had not been able to ascertain whether these nebulae were part of our own Milky Way or were distant "island universes." Working at Mount Wilson Observatory in California, which had at that time the largest telescope in the world, Hubble was able to distinguish individual stars in some of these nebulae. He was particularly interested in Cepheid variables—stars that varied in brightness, becoming alternately brighter or dimmer over a period of weeks or months. The time it takes to go through this cycle is related to the amount of energy the star is pouring into space. By comparing the amount of light received in the telescope to the total energy output determined from the brightening and dimming cycle, Hubble was able to show that the Cepheid variables in other galaxies were millions of light years away. Since the Milky Way is, at most, a hundred thousand light years across, these Cepheid variables had to be located in separate galaxies. Since then, literally billions of galaxies have been observed in telescopes.

Structures. Most galaxies in the universe are sedate and homey places like our Milky Way. At the center of each galaxy is a bulge consisting of very tightly packed groups of stars. This is the nucleus of the galaxy. At the center of the nucleus of our galaxy (and probably most other galaxies) is an enormous black hole—perhaps one million times the size of the sun. Moving outward, we come to the "spiral arms." These are regions of the galaxy in which stars have formed recently, and therefore appear very bright. Stars form in the spiral arms from clouds of dust and interstellar gas, and the entire galaxy rotates in space like a giant pinwheel.

Moving still farther away from the center, we reach a region where the stars are no longer shining, but in which thin clouds of hydrogen gas rotate with the galaxy. In this region, the effects of "dark matter" begin to become important. Scientists know that at least 90 percent of a galaxy like the Milky Way is composed of matter that does not interact with light, but that still exerts gravitational force. We can tell it is there by watching the way that its gravity affects things that we can see, such as the hydrogen gas.

Other Forms. Not all galaxies are like the Milky Way, however. Some are elliptical in shape, like giant footballs floating in space. Others are small, irregular things, like the dough left on a cookie tray after all the cookies have been cut. A small percentage of galaxies are "active galaxies," violent places, wracked by great explosions and the release of enormous amounts of energy. These range from radio galaxies which, as the name suggests, emit intense radiation in the radio part of the spectrum, to quasars, the brightest objects known. It is believed that at the center of each of these active galaxies is a black hole much larger than the one at the center of the Milky Way, and that the energy that is emitted by them is released by matter falling into them. (*See* MILKY WAY.)

The question of exactly how galaxies formed remains a major puzzle in modern cos-

Above, galaxies come in various forms: top, Andromeda, a galaxy similar to our own; middle, a spiral galaxy; bottom, a ring galaxy.

Galaxies are assembled throughout the universe in clusters. Below, details of the cluster at right in the constellation Orion, each showing millions of stars.

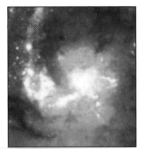

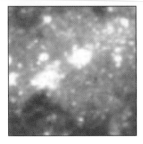

mology. The basic problem is that galaxies appear to have formed very quickly after the Big Bang, much too quickly for the formation to have been a matter of simple gravitational attraction between the parts. Today, the problem of galaxy formation is leaving the realm of theory, because with modern telescopes scientists can see much further out into space. Looking great distances in the cosmos is the same as looking backwards in time, since the light we see from a galaxy that is, for example, 12 billion light years away, was emitted 12 billion years ago, when the galaxy was much younger than it is now. Using information from these telescopes, scientists expect to be able to unravel the mystery of how galaxies formed in the first place.

THE CUTTING EDGE

Sizing Up Galaxies

The size of galaxies can be measured in a number of ways. There is a close relationship between the luminosity of a galaxy and its size—the larger the galaxy, the more luminous it is. For nearby galaxies, astronomers can measure their brightness to determine their position. Elliptical galaxies, for example, are brightest at the center, with brightness decreasing with distance from its center. The decrease in measured brightness is roughly equal to the square of the distance of the observing astronomer from the center of the galaxy. The structures of disc galaxies can be studied in the same way and can give information about characteristics other than distance from the Earth. For example, astronomers can use their observations to help determine the kind of stars that exist in a galaxy, how many of them there are, and when the stars of the galaxy were formed. The masses of galaxies can be determined either by measuring the movement of the stars and gases within them or by observing their motions in gravitationally-bound groups.

Further Reading

Green, James, A., *Galaxy Formation* (1996); Lightman, Alan, *Ancient Light: Our Changing View of the Universe* (1993); Merrifield, M., *Galactic Astronomy* (1998); ; Tayler, Roger J., *Galaxies: Structure and Evolution* (1993).

The foundations of the subject are discussed in GLOBULAR CLUSTER; STAR; TELESCOPE. More details can be found in MILKY WAY; NEBULAE; RADIO ASTRONOMY; UNIVERSE. Advanced subjects are developed in BIG BANG THEORY; INTERSTELLAR MEDIUM; QUASAR. See also HERTZSPRUNG-RUSSELL DIAGRAM AND UNIVERSE, EVOLUTION OF FOR MORE ON STELLAR EVOLUTION.

First see NUMBER THEORY

Game Theory

Next see ERROR ANALYSIS

The study of human and physical relations considered as a series of probabilistic events.

Game theory, first developed by John von Neumann (1903–1957), posited that every decision can be reduced to a series of choices, or strategies, which are designed to maximize the return, or "winnings," for the player. Games are usually considered under two aspects: the zero-sum game and the nonzero-sum game. In a zero-sum game, for every winner there is an equivalent loser; in a nonzero-sum game, on the other hand, all parties are capable of gaining, although there is still typically a discernible winner.

Long and Short Run. In its simplest form, a game has two players, each of whom has perfect information about the game and its payoffs, who choose from a finite set of strategies in order to reach a stable equilibrium. An example might be craps, in which players go to a casino and roll two dice, receiving seven dollars each time the dice add up six and paying six dollars each time the dice total seven. The players know that there is a 16.7 percent chance of a seven, but only a 13.9 percent chance of a six, and therefore the players will be returned only 97.1 percent of their money in the long run. But because all games are based on experience rather than on probability, players continue to crowd casinos, hoping that their rolls of the dice will beat the odds in the short run.

In other games, it is necessary to adopt a mixed—as opposed to a pure, or single—strategy; the child's game of rock-paper-scissors is a good example. If one consistently chooses a single move, one's opponent can counter by consistently choosing the appropriate countermove; thus only by varying one's pattern can one hope to achieve equilibrium.

Most such games are based on a minimax strategy, in which the goal is to minimize the potential loss if the opponent chooses the least favorable strategy. In a zero-sum game, one player will not settle for less than the known minimum expectation, but the other player is motivated to hold that gain to the minimum. In a nonzero-sum game, however, limiting the opponent's gain does not necessarily lead to the best result for oneself, so that defensive motives tend to give way to a cooperative approach, in which appropriate moves by both (or all) players lead to the greatest total payoff.

The classic example of the difficulty in achieving cooperation is a puzzle known as the Prisoner's Dilemma, in which a player who "defects" against other players gains a temporary advantage, but in which cooperation leads to a superior overall result.

First see PLANT

Gametogenesis

Next see SEED

The development of gametes in plants starts with a spore mother cell. The mother cell is diploid, meaning it has two sets of chromosomes, one from each parent. It divides through meiosis, producing four daughter cells that are haploid, having only one set of chromosomes. In addition, the mother cell's chromosomes usually exchange some of their parts during meiosis. This process, called crossing over, generally ensures that none of the four daughter cells is genetically identical to its parent or to another daughter.

In seed-bearing plants, the spores are either female (with a megaspore mother cell producing megaspores) or male (with a microspore mother cell producing microspores). In angiosperms, the flowering plants that constitute most terrestrial vegetation, the megaspore mother cell is contained in an ovule in the flower's ovary. Of the four daughter megaspores, three usually deteriorate. The fourth divides through mitosis until there are eight nuclei arranged in two groups of four. One nucleus from each group migrates to the center; these polar nuclei, as they are called, form a binucleate central cell. One cell near the micropyle, the opening of the ovule, develops into the egg, the female gamete. This eight-nucleate, seven-celled embryo sac constitutes the female gametophyte.

In angiosperms, four groups of microspore mother cells develop in the anthers of a flower, each enclosed in a pollen sac. They divide meiotically, each producing four haploid microspores. These then divide mitotically, forming a generative cell and a tube cell. In most species, the pollen grain—the male gametophyte—is released at this point, and each generative nucleus later divides to produce two sperm. In some species, the generative nucleus divides before the pollen is released. After pollination, the tube cell grows down to the egg, producing a pathway for the sperm. (*See* REPRODUCTIVE STRATEGIES.)

First see Blood

Gamma Globulin

Next see Antibodies

One of three molecularly similar proteins found in human blood serum (the other two are alpha and beta globulin).

Gamma globulin has been shown to contain the greatest concentration of antibodies, the protective molecules produced by the body when it is invaded by a foreign substance, and thus can be effective in producing immunity to certain diseases, because its antibodies will attack the infectious agents, viruses, fungi or bacteria, that cause the disease. For example, gamma globulin can be given by injection to a patient to treat measles, mumps, rubella, and infectious hepatitis shortly after exposure to the disease. It is obtained from the blood of someone who has been exposed to the infectious agent. Gamma globulin usage has declined greatly due to the development of vaccines against most of these diseases, but it is still used successfully when necessary. (*See* IMMUNE RESPONSE.)

First see COSMIC RAY

Gamma Ray

Next see X-RAY AND GAMMA RAY ASTRONOMY

Gamma rays originally were discovered in excited atomic nuclei that gave up energy as they passed to a lower energy state. Today, the term is applied to all high-frequency radiation of a certain wavelength between ten kilovolts and ten megavolts; it is characteristically highly penetrating. Several inches of metal are needed to reduce the intensity of gamma rays to half their original level. Gamma rays are emitted plentifully by particle accelerators and can be studied by a variety of spectrometers. Most of them convert gamma-ray energy into charged particles, such as electrons, for further study.

Many high-energy processes in astrophysics produce gamma rays. One such phenomenon is the gamma-ray burst, intense concentrations of bursts which last only a few seconds and occur in space. These gamma rays produce electron-photon cascades in Earth's atmosphere, which astronomers can then study.

In astronomy, gamma rays can be studied by satellites that orbit above the ray-absorbing atmosphere. A gamma-ray telescope on such a satellite can consist of a sandwich of sodium-iodide and cesium-iodide, which converts gamma radiation into positrons and negatrons that can then be studied in detail to get information about possible emitting sources.

Above, an array of mirrors ten meters in diameter, for collecting and focusing gamma rays. A human hand is reflected in all of the mirrors.

First see MOLECULE

Gases, Behavior of

Next see LIQUEFACTION

The behavior of gases is described by physical laws that date back to the seventeenth and eighteenth centuries. The gaseous phase of matter is the one in which the molecules of the substance are most loosely bound to one another. It is this loose binding that allows gases to expand to fill any container, be compressed easily, diffuse through porous barriers, and intermix with one another. The laws describing gas behavior relate the temperature, pressure, and volume of an ideal gas, which is conceived as one whose molecules occupy negligible space and have negligible forces between them, and whose collisions between themselves and the walls of their container are perfectly elastic.

Universal Equation. Boyle's law, discovered in 1662 by Robert Boyle, states that the pressure (P) of a given mass of gas that is held at a constant temperature is inversely proportional to the volume (V) of the gas; stated another way, it says that P multiplied by V is always a constant quantity. Charles' law, which was put forward by J. A. C. Charles, a French scientist, in the late seventeenth century, states that the volume of a fixed mass of an ideal gas that is held at a constant pressure at a temperature of 0° Celsius expands by a constant fraction of its volume for each one-degree increase in temperature. This can be expressed in several formulas; one is $V = kT$, where V is volume, T is temperature and k is a constant.

This law was perfected by another French scientist, Joseph Gay-Lussac, and so is sometimes known as Gay-Lussac's law. A third law states that the pressure of a gas that is kept at a constant volume is directly proportional to the thermodynamic temperature of the gas. The three laws can be combined in what is called the universal gas equation, the expression of which is $pV = nRT$, where n is the amount of gas in the specimen being considered and R is the universal gas constant, which has the value 8.314 joules per kelvin-mole.

These gas laws were established by experiments using real gases, such as oxygen and hydrogen. However, these real gases do not obey the ideal gas laws exactly, because there are small forces that act between the molecules of a gas, and the collisions are not completely elastic.

The gas laws are obeyed best when a gas is held at a high temperature and a low pressure. The ideal law of gases itself is not perfect. For example, it does not take into account the forces between the gas molecules or the volume occupied by the molecules of gas; according to the law, at an infinitely great pressure, the volume of a gas would become zero.

The enormous sphere of a liquefied natural gas tank (above), towers over workers at a General Dynamics plant near Charleston, South Carolina. Tanks such as this one are fitted into tanker ships and transported around the country.

Further Reading
Allaby, Michael, *Air: The Nature of Atmosphere and the Climate* (1992); Kerrebrock, Jack L., *Aircraft Engines and Gas Turbines* (1992); McNair, Harold M., *Basic Gas Chromatography* (1997); Shu, Frank H., *The Physics of Astrophysics: Gas Dynamics* (1992); Zucker, Robert D., *Fundamentals of Gas Dynamics* (1995).

Plants and Gas Exchange. Gas exchange in plants makes possible two reciprocal processes. Photosynthesis, in which water, carbon dioxide and light energy are used to produce carbohydrates, releases oxygen as waste into the environment and stores energy. Respiration or metabolism, in which the carbohydrates are broken down to fuel the work of the organism, absorbs oxygen and releases carbon dioxide, water, and energy. Of these, photosynthesis is of far greater importance: it is estimated that each year Earth's plants produce many billions of tons of organic matter and oxygen above what they use up in respiration. Virtually all organisms depend for life, either directly or indirectly, on photosynthesis.

Most of the gas exchange in both processes takes place in leaves, whose waxy epidermis is broken by up to 60,000 microscopic openings per square centimeter. These pores, called stomata, allow photosynthesis to occur by giving carbon dioxide direct access to the mesophyll, the internal tissue of the leaves. Respiration is less dependent on the stomata, because oxygen is better able than carbon dioxide to penetrate the epidermis of the leaf.

The layer of mesophyll near the stomata is composed of loosely arranged cells, filmed with water and surrounded by intercellular spaces. The gas exchange takes place in these cells, the gases first dissolving before they enter the cell. The thin, flat leaves present an enlarged surface area over which gas exchange can occur, and the structure of the mesophyll, with its many free-standing cells, greatly multiplies that area. For their mass, plants have a much larger surface area for gas exchange than animals do in their lungs. This is necessary for adequate photosynthesis because carbon dioxide is present in the air in much lower concentrations than oxygen.

The performance of the stomata reflects the leaf's trade-off between allowing carbon flow and preventing water loss through transpiration. Each stoma is ringed by two bean-shaped guard cells. When the guard cells swell with water, they pull apart, opening the stoma and allowing carbon dioxide to enter and water to leave. When water leaves the guard cells, they grow flaccid and move back together, closing the stoma, slowing photosynthesis, and conserving water. The amount of water and sunlight are the most crucial factors in regulating this behavior. For instance, in most plants, stomata open only when photosynthesis is taking over during the day and close at night, even though nighttime water loss is negligible.

Elementary aspects of this subject are covered in LIQUID; MOLECULE; SOLID. *More information on particular aspects is contained in* BROWNIAN MOTION; PHASE. *Relevant information is contained in* CHROMATOGRAPHY; NOBLE GASES.

First see QUANTUM MECHANICS

Gauge Theory

Next see GROUP THEORY

A quantum field theory put forward to explain fundamental interactions, such as the strong and weak forces, gravity, and electromagnetism.

Gauge theory describes quantum phenomena using symmetry groups to describe the fields and potentials of fundamental interactions. Such groups have a series of elements, A, B, C, etc. There is a law of composition called multiplication for each set of elements—for example, AB or ABC. Two elements of a group are said to commute if AB = BA. If all the elements of a group commute, the group is "Abelian." If they do not, the group is "non-Abelian." The distinction between Abelian and non-Abelian groups is fundamentally important to gauge theory.

The interaction between particles is explained in gauge theories by the interchange of particles such as intermediate vector bosons or gauge bosons. Examples of gauge bosons are the photons of quantum electrodynamics, the gluons of quantum chromodynamics, and the W and Z bosons of the electroweak theory.

Most bosons that mediate the fundamental forces are required to have no mass. The absence of mass allows different gauge transformations to occur at different points in spacetime. These gauge degrees of freedom can be used to describe some of the degrees of freedom of a gauge field, a description that requires massless particles. The consequence is that any theory that calls for the existence of particles without mass signals the existence of a gauge symmetry. This principle predicts that both the photon and the gluon have no mass. (*See* Z-BOSON)

Gauge theory is still being developed, and further explanations of the basic forces and elementary particles can be expected.

First see GENETICS

Gene

Next see DNA

Genes, our hereditary blueprints, are segments of DNA that specify the sequence of amino acids that form a particular protein. Genes are located on chromosomes, which are complex arrangements of DNA and protein, within the nucleus of the cell.

There are two genes for a particular trait—one inherited from each parent. An allele is the form a gene may take, either dominant or recessive. The genotype is the set of genes found in an organism. The phenotype is the physical expression of those genes. If two dominant alleles are present, the genotype is homozygous dominant and follows the dominant phenotype. If two recessive alleles are found together, the genotype is homozygous recessive and follows the recessive phenotype. If one dominant allele is found with one recessive, resulting in a hybrid, the genotype is heterozygous and follows the dominant phenotype. It is impossible to determine by simple physical observation if an individual with the dominant phenotype is heterozygous or homozygous dominant. In some gene pairs, inheritance exhibits incomplete dominance, which means that the heterozygous has a unique phenotype, distinct from either the homozygous dominant or the recessive.

Genes and DNA. On the molecular level, genes are actually segments of DNA that contain information for the construction of a particular protein. The "one-gene–one-polypeptide" theory states that each gene is highly specific, corresponding to a single protein. In many cases, several genes work in concert, each responsible for a particular segment of a complex protein. Such a genetic unit is referred to as a cistron.

DNA is shaped in a double helix, composed of two long strands. A gene is found along one or the other strand of the DNA duplex, and begins with a specific sequence known as the promoter region and ends with the terminator region. A structural gene contains information for the amino acid sequence of a protein. This information is "transcribed" to form a molecule of messenger RNA (mRNA) which is in turn "translated" to form a protein. The product of a regulatory gene controls the expression of structural genes, either allowing transcription to take place or else blocking it.

Exons and introns are segments found within genes. Exons are the segments which correspond to the "useful" part, whereas introns are non-coding segments interrupting the main body of a gene. Introns are "spliced out" of the sequence during post-transcription modification and are no longer present when the mRNA is

---

OBSERVATIONS

The Eyes Have It

Want eyes in the back of your head? The day may come when such "unnatural" variations are possible, if not necessarily desirable. Scientists in Switzerland activated a gene in fruit fly embryos that controls eye development—only they activated it in leg cells, antenna cells, and at other sites. The result was fruit flies with eyes all over their bodies. It is a long way from fruit flies to humans, and the time and effort needed to genetically engineer individual sites would be enormous, but a mammal was cloned only two decades after the first work on recombinant DNA. The ethical questions raised by our growing ability to perform such genetic feats must be resolved soon if we are to use genetic engineering responsibly.

translated to form the actual protein. It is unknown why introns exist at all, or why they are only present within eukaryotic DNA and not prokaryotic (bacteria and blue-green algae). A current theory proposes that perhaps introns are vestigal remnants of our evolutionary past.

Gene Regulation. Each cell in the body contains exactly same genes as every other cell, yet the cells in one type of tissue are quite different from the cells elsewhere. How can this be? The answer lies in which genes are active at any given time. When a gene is "on," it is being transcribed and its protein is being produced. When it is not being transcribed, it is "off." In the early stages of development, a single fertilized egg divides rapidly to form a ball of cells, which in turn differentiate into distinct cell layers from which the various organ systems arise. All of the genes are turned on "full blast." Gradually, with specialization, certain genes are permanently switched off, whereas others remain on. Still others are turned on or off as needed. The formal assemblies of regulator genes that control gene expression are known as operons. Control of gene expression, or regulation, can occur either during transcription or translation. Those two stages in turn are made up of other steps, initiation, elongation, and termination, any of which can be affected by various regulating factors. Control at the transcription level usually involves interfering with or helping the RNA polymerase identify and bind to the promoter region of a gene. Control at the translation level usually involves interfering with or helping the mRNA bind to the ribosome.

Prokaryotic Genetics. In prokaryotes, small primitive cells such as bacteria, gene regulation is normally achieved through negative control, with a repressor protein preventing gene expression from occurring. In eukaryotes, organisms whose cells have a membrane-bound nucleus containing DNA, gene regulation usually involves positive control, although negative regulation exists as well.

Structural genes in prokaryotes are arranged in clusters, with one promoter region for the whole set of genes. Eukaryotic genes are found individually with their own promoters.

In eukaryotes, the RNA polymerase enzymes do not recognize the promoter regions directly. Transcription factors recognize characteristic sequences within the promoter region and bind the enzyme to it. For different enzymes, individual factors can be used alone or in combination.

The promoter region of a eukaryotic gene may be stimulated by the presence of enhancers, sequences similar to the promoter region located at a distance either "upstream" or "downstream."

Autogenous regulation means the protein product regulates the expression of the gene responsible for its production. Some proteins

Identical twins—seen in the hologram above—have the same set of genes. Scientists have exploited this phenomenon in order to determine how great a part genetics plays in human development.

Further Reading

Bishop, Jerry E., et al., *Genome: The Story of the Most Astonishing Scientific Adventure of Our Time—The Attempt to Map All the Genes in the Human Body* (1992); Jones, Steve, *The Language of Genes: Solving the Mysteries of Our Genetic Past* (1995); Klug, William S., *Concepts of Genetics* (1997); Lewin, Benjamin, *Genes VI* (1997); Shapiro, Robert, *The Human Blueprint: The Race to Unlock the Secrets of Our Genetic Script* (1992); Wills, Christopher, *Exons, Introns, and Talking Genes: The Science Behind the Human Genome Project* (1991).

regulate at the translation level, by targeting the mRNA and preventing it from binding to the ribosome. The level of protein synthesis is also important in regulating gene expression. It usually affects elongation of the transcription process.

Gene Amplification. Gene amplification refers to the production of additional copies of a gene. The additional material can be found as either intrachromosomal (within a segment of the chromosome) or extrachromosomal (outside the chromosome entirely) DNA. Extra-chromosomal DNA is called unstable, as it tends to disappear within a few generations. Extra copies of genes are not necessarily functional. However, the more copies there are, the more likely the gene is to be expressed.

The causes of gene amplification are still being studied. One theory is that additional copies are formed during mitosis, the replication of all chromosomes to ensure that both "daughter" cells formed by cell division receive a complete set. During this time, additional replication can occur during recombination (exchange of segments) between chromosomes.

Some genetic diseases, like Huntington's disease, are thought to be caused by the presence of repeating segments at the end of chromosomes. The severity of the disease appears to be linked to the extent of repetition.

Gene Flow. When fertile individuals migrate from one group to another within a species, they change both the gene pools of the population that they left behind and the one they have joined. This transfer of genetic material, called gene flow, reduces the differences between separated populations. Without it, populations would grow increasingly distinct, eventually forming separate species. By encouraging diversity, gene flow—along with random mutation, genetic drift, and natural selection—helps make evolution possible.

In plants, gene flow often involves gametes, such as sperm in pollen blown by the wind, or zygotes in seeds carried by wind or water to a new home. In humans, gene flow has been facilitated by migrations and wars, with their dislocations of large numbers of people.

Related matters are discussed in CELL; CHROMOSOME; NUCLEUS, CELL. *Other aspects of the subject are discussed in* DNA; GENETIC CODE; GENETICS. *Additional related material can be found in* DNA REPLICATION; EXTRANUCLEAR INHERITANCE; MUTATION, GENETIC. *See also* EXONS AND INTRONS; EUKARYOTIC CELL; PROKARYOTIC CELL.

First see EQUIVALENCE PRINCIPLE

General Relativity

Next see UNIVERSE, LARGE-SCALE STRUCTURE OF

The general theory of relativity is a theory of gravity formulated by Albert Einstein in 1915 that appears to offer a better explanation of gravitational phenomena than are provided by other theories. In the general theory, Einstein extended his work on the special theory of relativity to include systems that are under acceleration. He pictured the universe in terms of a four-dimensional space-time continuum in which the presence of mass causes a curvature of space, thus creating a gravitational field. This challenged the Newtonian conception of gravity, which described it as a force exerted instantly by a body on another body at any distance, that force being proportional to the mass of the bodies. Instead, Einstein proposed the idea of a gravitational field, composed of lines of gravitational force similar to the lines of magnetic force that exist around a magnet. The orbits of celestial bodies are determined by the conditions in that field, just as the positions of iron filings are determined by the lines of force in a magnetic field.

One basic postulate of the general theory is the principle of covariance. This says that space-time can be described by a set of differential equations that have the same form in all coordinate systems. Another basic principle is the principle of equivalence, which says that the effects of inertial forces and of gravity are the same.

Predictions. Einstein's theory predicted a number of astronomical phenomena that allowed the theory to be tested. One prediction concerned the perihelion of Mercury, its closest approach to the sun. The observed advance of Mercury's perihelion differed slightly but significantly from the value predicted by Newton's theory. The value predicted by the general theory of relativity agreed with astronomical observations. In recent decades, Einstein's predictions of planetary movements have been verified by radar observations of the Earth and Venus.

Another prediction was the existence of a gravitational red shift, in which the light emitted by a very massive body would be shifted toward the lower end of the visual spectrum.

The general theory also suggested that light reaching Earth from the stars would be deflected slightly as it passed through the gravitational field of the sun. The bending was twice as great as was predicted by Newton's theory of gravity. Measurements during total solar eclipses, when light from stars close to the sun become visible, have verified this prediction.

Gravity Waves. General relativity also predicts the existence of gravitational radiation. Such gravity waves, theoretically expected to be very weak, have not yet been detected. However,

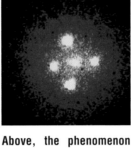

Above, the phenomenon known as an "Einstein Cross" (named after the discoverer of general relativity, Albert Einstein). It shows a single distant quasar's image four times as the light from the quasar is bent by an intervening galaxy in a configuration known as an Einstein lens.

Right, a "perfect" sphere from a gyroscope at Stanford University's Applied Physics Laboratory. The device was designed to determine the relationship between gravity and electromagnetism—a part of Einstein's theory of general relativity.

Albert Einstein (1879–1955).

there is some evidence for their existence from observations of stellar objects. Any system that radiates gravitational energy must lose a very small amount of energy. Observations of a binary pulsar system in the 1970s showed that the rotation of the two bodies around each other was in fact slowing by a fraction of a second a year, confirming general relativity's predictions within an accuracy of one percent.

Cosmology and Relativity. Einstein's general theory of relativity has a number of implications for cosmology (the study of the nature, origin, and evolution of the universe). The relativistic cosmological model can be said to start with the equation for the Hubble constant, which describes the present rate of expansion of the universe in terms of length, time, and mass. The best measurements indicate that the universe is expanding at a rate between 50 and 95 megaparsecs per second (a parsec is 3.2616 light years; a megapersec is one million parsecs).

General relativity can thus be used to describe the age of the universe. In classical general relativity, the origin of the universe is traced back to a singularity in the distant past, a time when the currently observed expansion of the universe began. That time is in the neighborhood of 12 to 14 billion years ago; the precise time is unknown because the present rate of expansion is not known with exactitude. A test of the accuracy of the predictions made by general relativity would depend on a better knowledge of this rate of expansion.

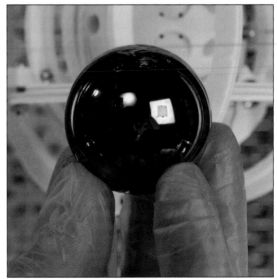

The rate of change of the expansion rate can also be expressed in terms of general relativity. This rate of change is expressed in the "acceleration parameter," which fixes the relativistic corrections to the observed sizes and numbers of galaxies in terms of the red shift, the change in electromagnetic frequency caused by expansion of the universe. In principle, the acceleration parameter can be measured. But until recently, it had not been possible to measure it accurately enough to determine the age of the universe to within a factor of two.

Cosmological Constant. Another factor that can be included in general relativity is the cosmological constant, an antigravitational force that Einstein proposed and then abandoned, calling it his "biggest mistake." Einstein included the cosmological constant as a counterforce to the attractive force of gravity in his gravitational field equations in order to allow the existence of a stable, homogeneous universe. He abandoned it when the expansion of the universe was discovered. The cosmological constant has been revived in recent years by some theorists because of observations indicating that the expansion of the universe may be accelerating.

Left, model of a black hole warping the space around it in a process known as "frame dragging." The process, with its signature bursts of plasma from the core, has been observed several times throughout the universe.

An open model of the universe in terms of general relativity would mean steady, continuing expansion. This unlimited expansion has been described as the heat death of the universe, because the stars and galaxies would eventually exhaust their energy supplies; it is opposed to the "Big Crunch," which pictures the expansion of the universe slowing and eventually reversing, until the universe is limited to a single point in space, presumably the one at which the Big Bang is said to have begun.

Direct measurements of the mass density of the universe thus far fall short of the predictions made by Einstein. Recent measurements suggest that the expansion of the universe is actually accelerating, indicating an open future for the universe.

Related discussions can be found in EQUIVALENCE PRINCIPLE; GRAVITY; SPACE; SPACE-TIME. *Other aspects of the subject are discussed in* BIG BANG THEORY; NEUTRON STAR; SPECIAL RELATIVITY. *Related material can be found in* UNIVERSE, LARGE-SCALE STRUCTURE OF; SYMMETRY IN NATURE; UNIVERSE. *See also* GALAXY *and* UNIVERSE, EVOLUTION OF.

Further Reading

Bernstein, Jeremy, *Cosmological Constants: Papers in Modern Cosmology* (1986); Foster, James, *A Short Course in General Relativity* (1998); Geroch, Robert, *General Relativity from A to B* (1981); Misner, Charles W., *Gravitation* (1973); Thorne, Kip S., *Black Holes and Time Warps: Einstein's Outrageous Legacy* (1995); Wald, Robert M., *Space, Time, and Gravity: The Theory of the Big Bang and Black Holes* (1992); Weinberg, Steven, *Gravitation and Cosmology: Principles and Applications of the General Theory* (1972).

First see GENETIC DISEASES

Gene Therapy

Next see GENETIC ENGINEERING

Gene therapy is the idea that a genetic disease can be cured by replacing a defective gene causing a disease with a normal gene. Significant barriers must be overcome to make gene therapy a reality, but two possible mechanisms appear promising. One involves the direct introduction of foreign, or exogenous, DNA—the material of genes—into defective cells. Cells are capable of absorbing very large molecules such as DNA without breaking them down into smaller molecules. In this process of absorption, the outer membrane of the cell pinches inward around the large molecule that is to be absorbed. The resulting bubble, called a vesicle, migrates through the outer regions of the cell and ultimately deposits its contents in the cell nucleus, where the genes reside. This process is called pinocytosis. If normal DNA from a human or other source could be delivered to the nucleus by this method, it probably would become part of the cell's genetic material, overcoming the ill effects of an abnormal gene.

DNA Delivery. A second mechanism for gene manipulation, occuring frequently in nature, involves the delivery of exogenous DNA into the cell by viruses. The viruses that would be used in this method are the simplest of organisms. A virus consists of a single strand of DNA or RNA, which is surrounded by a coat or jacket made of protein. To reproduce, a virus requires a host organism. The hosts available to different viruses include the whole range of cells from simple bacteria to humans. In a typical virus infection, the protein coat of the virus becomes enmeshed in the cell membrane of the host cell. The DNA or RNA of the virus is then released into the cell, where it makes its way to the nucleus and joins the host DNA. Using the molecules of the host cell as raw material, the viral DNA directs its own reproduction and the synthesis of new protein coats. In a short period of time, the material of the host cell is converted into thousands of new viruses. The cell membrane bursts and the new viruses are released, thereby infecting neighboring cells.

Instances in which exogenous viral DNA becomes incorporated into the genetic material of the recipient cell are known as transductions. This kind of genetic modification has been known to occur in bacterial cells for a number of years, but has also been observed in the cells of mammals. One of the most extensively studied viruses in this area is SV-40, whose viral DNA becomes physically integrated into the chromosomal DNA of the recipient cell during the transduction process. For application to the treatment of human genetic disease, viral transduction would require the laboratory production of innocuous viruses. These viruses would co .tain the DNA sequences necessary for the synthesis of the protein that is missing or defective in a given genetic disease. Once this DNA would be incorporated into the host cell DNA, it would start producing the normal protein through the usual cell processes.

Genetic modification of human cells by either method, direct transformation with native DNA or transduction with viral DNA, is regarded as a real possibility. In the laboratory, some genetically determined properties of the fruit fly Drosophila have been changed after the eggs of one strain of Drosophila were treated with DNA extracted from other strains of Drosophila. While eventual use of gene therapy to treat human disease seems inevitable, the practical problems that stand in the way of routine gene therapy will almost certainly take years to overcome.

THE CUTTING EDGE

Gene Therapy of ADA

Gene therapy was first attempted in 1990 on a child who could not produce the enzyme adenosine deaminase (ADA), needed for immune system development. White blood cells were removed from the child and retrovirally altered to produce ADA, then returned to the child's bloodstream. A retrovirus is encoded in RNA instead of DNA; when combined with an enzyme called reverse transcriptase in the new host cell, it converts to DNA, joining with the DNA of the host. To ensure that the RNA/transcriptase combination does not overwhelm the child's system, the section of the retrovirus that would allow it to reproduce is cut out. More than a hundred children with ADA deficiency have been successfully treated in this manner.

Background material for gene therapy can be found in DNA; GENETICS; GENOME, HUMAN. *More details about this subject can be found in* CLONING; KARYOTYPING; TRANSCRIPTION. *Fundamental aspects of this subject are covered in* DNA SEQUENCING; GENETIC ENGINEERING; RECOMBINANT DNA. *See also* CYSTIC FIBROSIS; MULTIPLE SCLEROSIS; PARKINSON'S DISEASE *for specific applications.*

First see GENE

Genetic Code

Next see DNA

Our genes control every aspect about us—what we look like, how we behave, and what can go wrong. On the molecular level, a gene is simply a segment of DNA that contains information for constructing a particular protein. In many cases, several genes work in concert, each responsible for a particular segment of a complex protein. Different chemical reactions take place within a cell, based upon which proteins are being produced at any given time, and it is these chemical reactions which affect our characteristics on a "macro" level.

When unraveled, the genetic code consists of a string of repeating letters A, G, T, and C. These letters represent nucleic bases, the main components of DNA. The basic unit of a nucleic acid is the nucleotide, which in turn consists of a sugar molecule, a phosphate group (PO_4), and one of four nucleic bases: adenine (A), guanine (G), cytosine (C) and thymine (T). The nucleotides form a chain consisting of alternating sugar and phosphate groups forming a "backbone" with the bases protruding off the sugar molecules. There are approximately 3 billion bases in the human genome.

Building Blocks. DNA consists of two such polynucleotide chains running "antiparallel," or in opposite directions. The famous "double helix" shape of DNA is actually a twisted version of the "ladder" formed by the two chains, with the "sides" of the ladder formed by the alternating sugars and phosphates, and the "rungs" consisting of pairs of bases, known as Watson-Crick base pairs after their discoverers, James Watson and Francis Crick. The pairs are held together with hydrogen bonds, relatively weak forms of inter-molecular bonding, in order to facilitate the "unzipping" of the DNA in order to perform its functions. Adenine is paired with thymine (in DNA) by means of two hydrogen bonds. The guanine-cytosine pair is held together by three hydrogen bonds.

Delineating the Gene. A gene is found along one or the other strand of the DNA duplex. It begins with a specific sequence known as the promoter region and ends with the terminator region. A structural gene contains information for the amino acid sequence of a protein. This information is "transcribed" to form a molecule of messenger RNA (mRNA), which is in turn "translated" to form a protein. The product of a regulatory gene controls the expression of structural genes, by either allowing transcription to take place or by blocking it.

Background material can be found in DNA; GENETICS; GENOME, HUMAN. *Further details on the genetic code can be found in* EXONS AND INTRONS; GENETIC DISEASES; NATURAL SELECTION. *Elementary aspects of this subject are covered in* ADAPTATION; GENE THERAPY; GENETIC ENGINEERING.

Further Reading
Judson, Horace Freeland, *The Eighth Day of Creation: Makers of the Revolution in Biology* (1996); Murphy, Michael P., *What Is Life? The Next Fifty Years-Speculations on the Future of Biology* (1997); Olby, Robert C., *The Path to the Double Helix: The Discovery of DNA* (1994); Sayre, Anne, *Rosalind Franklin and DNA* (1978); Watson, James, D., *The Double Helix: A Personal Account of the Discovery of the Structure of DNA* (1981).

First see GENETICS

Genetic Diseases

Next see GENE THERAPY

Genetic diseases are disorders caused wholly or in part by one or more faults in the genetic material in human cells. The normal complement for a human cell is 46 chromosomes, in 23 pairs.

There is one pair of sex chromosomes, which are named for the shape they appear to have under the microscope. A female has two X chromosomes while a male has one X and one Y chromosome. All the other chromosomes are called autosomes. A number of genetic disorders are caused by defects in one or more of the genes included in the chromosomes. These are further classified as unifactorial disorders, which are caused by a defect in a single gene or pair of genes, and multifactorial disorders, which are caused by more than one gene. Genes control the manufacture of proteins such as enzymes that carry out many of the functions of individual cells and organs. If the genetic material is flawed, abnormal proteins or abnormal amounts of proteins may be produced, causing a disorder. (*See* PROTEIN; CHROMOSOME.)

Such abnormal genetic material must be present in all the cells of the body. This means that the abnormal material must have been present in either the sperm cell or the egg cell that it fertilized. This can happen in two ways: through inheritance—the defect was present in the egg from the mother or the sperm from the father, or both; mutation—a normal gene becomes abnormal because it is not reproduced perfectly. Mutations are usually caused by outside influences, such as radiation.

Chromosomal abnormalities occur in about one out of every 200 babies born. Most of these abnormalities are the result of an error in the process by which a cell divides and produces new cells. Others are caused by the presence of one or more extra chromosomes, or by the absence of part of a chromosome. One of the best-known chromosomal disorders is Down's syndrome, which causes mental retardation and other abnormalities.

There are many unifactorial genetic disorders. They often are divided into two groups: sex-linked disorders, caused by a defect of a gene in a sex chromosome, X or Y, and autosomal disorders, caused by defects in one of the other chromosomes. There is a further subdivision of autosomal disorders. Some are dominant, meaning that the disorder occurs if there is an abnormal gene in one chromosome. Others are recessive, meaning that the same abnormal gene must be in both chromosomes. When an individual who carries a dominant gene for a disorder has children, each child has a 50 percent chance of inheriting the abnormal gene.

Multifactorial genetic disorders include some fairly common conditions such as diabetes and schizophrenia. Multifactorial disorders that make themselves apparent at birth include clubfoot and cleft palate. In recent years, many married couples have undergone testing and obtained genetic counseling if a genetic defect is known to be present in one or both families. This has helped reduce the incidence of genetic diseases. (*See* BIRTH; GENETIC ENGINEERING.)

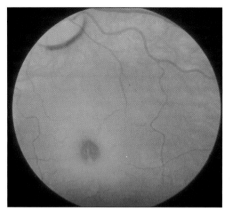

Tay-Sachs disease is an autosomal recessive disease, primarily affecting the nervous system. A macular cherry-red spot appears in the eye (above), with a lipid deposit in the retinal ganglion cells, usually resulting in blindess.

Sickle cells in the blood of a patient with sickle cell anemia.

First see GENE

Genetic Engineering

Next see GENE THERAPY

Engineering can require two distinct types of understanding; one derives from a long familiarity with the way a particular system behaves, the other from an understanding of the basic properties of the systems which make it behave the way it does. For example, the men who built the medieval cathedrals in Europe knew, through long experience, what materials would stand up, but knew nothing about stress and strains and properties of materials. On the other hand, someone building a modern skyscraper would begin from an intimate knowledge of the materials going into the building and the way these would respond to different circumstances.

Engineering with DNA. Genetic engineering involves the manipulation of stretches of DNA known as genes. These genes contain the blueprint for specific proteins to be made by the cell, and each protein runs a specific chemical reaction in the cell. In a sense, human beings have been practicing genetic engineering for a long time. Cattle breeders, for example, developed a rough-and-ready way of improving the qualities of their stock through selective breeding. They are analogous to the medieval cathedral builders. The latter half of the 20th century, however, saw a major change in the way we understand living things. We are currently beginning to understand how living things work at the level of the atom and the molecule. Modern genetic engineering is an attempt to put that to use. Modern genetic engineers are analogous to the skyscraper builders.

The ability to perform genetic engineering depends on one important fact about the chemistry of living things. All living things on earth—from the smallest microbe to the largest whale—use the same code in their DNA. In a sense, you could think of different living things as books written in the same alphabet. This means that the DNA of one living thing can be "read" by any other living thing—just as a sentence of the English language can be read by any literate person. (*See* DNA.)

Micromanipulation. Over the last several decades, biochemists have learned how to cut individual genes out of one strand of DNA and insert them into another. For example, in human

DNA there is a gene that codes for the protein insulin. In the human body, this gene is expressed only in the pancreas. Malfunctions in the working of this gene lead to diabetes, and one way of treating some types of diabetes is by administering added insulin. Medicinal insulin used to be obtained by collecting insulin from the pancreases of pigs. This was a somewhat tedious practice, and it also created problems for some patients who had allergies.

Insulin. In the 1980s, however, a new technique was developed. The gene for insulin was taken out of human DNA and put into the DNA of a bacterium called *E. coli* (a very common bacterium that resides in the human intestine). Vats of these bacteria were grown. The net result was a large tankful of bacteria, each of which was producing insulin. In this way, the insulin could be harvested from bacteria in much the same way that we obtain milk from cows. Virtually all commercial insulin used today is a product of genetic engineering.

Universality of DNA. Because all living things use the same genetic code, there is no restriction on where a gene comes from or the host into which it is implanted. Almost 1,000 different kinds of genetically engineered plants have been tested in the field. Genes from arctic bacteria that secreted a kind of antifreeze to protect them from the cold have been put into strawberries to make them frost resistant. Recently, people have even talked about putting genes from bacteria into foods like potatoes and bananas to stimulate the human immune system to produce antibodies. In this way, instead of going to the doctor for treatment, one would eat a medicinal banana. This technology, when fully developed, is expected to play a major role in improving public health in developing countries.

Gene Therapy. There is also a major research effort under way aimed at changing the DNA in living human beings. This technique goes by the name gene therapy. The first successful gene therapy was carried out at the National Institute of Health in 1990. Blood cells from patients with a rare blood disease caused by a single malfunctioning gene were engineered to have a healthy gene, then allowed to multiply. When they were reinserted into the patients, they "took" and the patients were cured.

Cystic Fibrosis. Another example of genetic engineering in living humans involves cystic fibrosis. The most common form of this disease has been identified as a defect in a particular gene on chromosome seven. Modern therapies for cystic fibrosis involve inserting this gene into a relatively mild virus and spraying it into the respiratory tracts of people with the disease. In some cases, it appears that the virus carries the gene into the cells and inserts it into the

patient's DNA. When that happens, the patient starts producing the proper proteins and the symptoms of the disease are alleviated.

Most research in this area today is centered on finding the right mechanism for inserting the new gene into the DNA of a functioning cell. Some problems include finding the right virus to carry the gene to a specific cell, finding ways for the virus to enter the cell; and finding ways to ensure that the new gene is inserted into the right stretch of the cell's DNA. There are several hundred gene therapy protocols now being tested in hospitals around the United States.

Background material for genetic engineering can be found in DNA; GENETIC CODE; GENETICS. *Further details on the subject can be found in* CLONING; GENOME, HUMAN; IMPRINTING, GENETIC. *More information on particular aspects is contained in* GENE THERAPY; LINKAGE, GENETIC; RECOMBINANT DNA.

First see GENE

Genetics

Next see GENETIC DISEASES

The study of heredity.

The goal of every organism is to produce offspring, thereby ensuring the preservation of its own kind. Some living things undergo asexual reproduction. This type of reproduction involves only one parent and by necessity all of the offspring are genetically identical to each other and to their parent. Sexual reproduction involves two parents, each of whom contributes half the genetic material, resulting in variation among the offspring.

Gregor Mendel. The science of genetics began in the mid-1800s with Gregor Mendel, an Austrian monk. Mendel was in charge of the monastery gardens and began to notice patterns of inheritance among the plants. From these observations he developed two main principles. The first principle stated that there are two genes for a particular trait—one inherited from each parent. An allele is the form a gene may take, either dominant or recessive. The dominant allele is usually denoted by a capital letter, the recessive by a lower case. For example "T" denotes the dominant allele for height, tall, and "t" denotes the recessive allele for height, short. The genotype is the set of genes found in an organism. The phenotype is the physical expression of those genes.

If two dominant alleles are present, TT, the genotype is homozygous dominant and follows the dominant phenotype. If two recessive alleles are found together, tt, the genotype is homozy-

Further Reading
Aldridge, Susan, *The Thread of Life: The Story of Genes and Genetic Engineering* (1996); Grace, Eric, S., *Biotechnology Unzipped; Promises and Realities* (1997); Lyon, Peter, *Altered Fates: Gene Therapy and the Retooling of Human Life* (1995); Rudolph, F., B., *Biotechnology: Science, Engineering, and Ethical Challenges for the Twenty-First Century* (1996).

Gregor Johann Mendel (1822–1884).

gous recessive and follows the recessive phenotype. If one dominant allele is found with one recessive, Tt, resulting in a hybrid, the genotype is heterozygous and follows the dominant phenotype as well.

It is impossible to determine by simple physical observation if an individual with the dominant phenotype is homozygous dominant TT or heterozygous Tt. In some gene pairs, however, the inheritance exhibits incomplete dominance, in which the heterozygous has a unique phenotype, distinct from either the homozygous dominant or recessive.

Second Law. Mendel's second law is the law of independent assortment; the inheritance of the genes for one trait does not affect the inheritance of another. For example, the height of a plant does not determine its color as well.

Mendel's work was largely ignored for the next 50 years, until scientists identified chromosomes and worked out the details of cellular reproduction. Then Mendel's forgotten laws were seen to correspond directly with the events of meiosis that causes the production of the sperm and egg. Both of these gametes or sex cells contain only half the chromosome number of a regular cell, so they have to unite to form a zygote with the correct number of chromosomes. (*See* CHROMOSOME.)

Sometimes, however, there is more than one set of genes responsible for a particular trait. This is known as polygenic inheritance, an example of which is human eye color. The color of the iris is determined by the amount of pigment present. The more pigment, the darker the color, like brown or black, and the less pigment, the lighter the color, usually blue or gray. Two pairs of genes are responsible: one to produce the pigment, and the other to deposit it in the proper site. This explains why there are so many different eye colors, and how two blue-eyed parents can have a brown-eyed child.

Multiple Allele Inheritance. Another type of inheritance is called multiple allele inheritance, in which there is only one pair of genes responsible for the trait, but there are more than just two alleles. An example of this is human blood groups, which are caused by the presence of a specific antigen, or protein. Mendel's law of independent assortment is not always valid. The human genome contains approximately 30,000-40,000 genes, all of which are contained in only 23 pairs of chromosomes. Logically, there must be several genes found together on the same chromosome. Since a whole chromosome is inherited as a unit, genes located on the same chromosome must be inherited together. Gene linkage obviously disrupts independent assortment. Depending upon which alleles are found together on the same chromosome, only certain combinations of traits will result.

Gene linkage can be reversed during the early stages of meiosis. When the chromosome pairs are lined up next to each other, they often "cross over," whereby segments of chromosomal material are exchanged between pairs. Gene linkage will still exist, but the linkage involves different alleles than before.

Based upon the genotypes of the parents, the genotypes and phenotypes of the offspring can be predicted. In order to figure out these probabilities, punnet squares are used. First the possible gene combinations of the parents are determined, then, with the punnet square, a display matrix is set up to all possible combinations. (*See* PROBABILITY.)

In addition to types of inheritance caused by autosomal genes, those located on the 22 pairs of non-sex chromosomes, there are also types of inheritance caused by the single pair of sex chromosomes in each cell. In humans, females have two X chromosomes and males have one X and one Y. The Y chromosome only carries a few genes, mostly related to the perpetuation of the

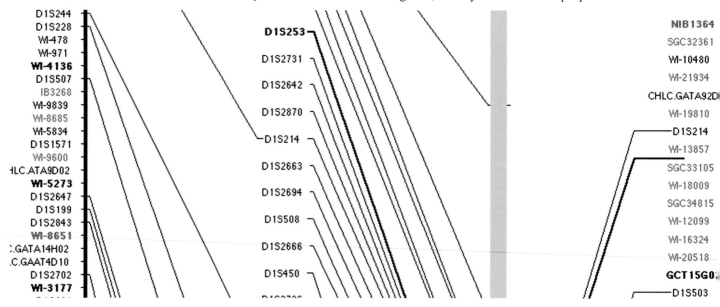

Y chromosome. Sex-linked characteristics are caused by genes carried on the X chromosomes.

All eggs carry an X chromosome. Half of all sperm carry an X, and half Y. If an X sperm combines with an egg, the resulting zygote will be XX and female. If a Y sperm combines with an egg, the zygote will be XY and male. Fathers always pass on a Y chromosome to a son and an X chromosome to a daughter. Therefore, they cannot pass on sex-linked characteristics to their sons, only to their daughters. Mothers pass on an X chromosome to all of their offspring and can therefore pass on sex-linked characteristics to a child of either sex.

Sex-Linked Traits. Common human sex-linked characteristics include hemophilia and color blindness. They are recessive traits, meaning they will only occur if there are no dominant genes involved. A woman can be homozygous dominant, heterozygous, or homozygous recessive. If she is homozygous dominant, she will be completely normal. If she is heterozygous, she has one dominant allele and one recessive. The dominant allele means she will not exhibit the condition, but she has a recessive allele which can be passed on to her offspring. If she has two recessive genes, she will exhibit the condition.

In contrast, a male has only two possibilities. Either he carries a dominant allele on his single X, or else he carries a recessive allele. If the allele is dominant, he is normal. If it is recessive, he has the condition.

Nature vs. Nurture. Genes determine every aspect of an individual, both physical and mental. However, the environment in which the genes are expressed also plays an important role. The pendulum swings back and forth each year in the "nature vs. nurture" debate over which is the more important determinant of the characteristics and behavior of an organism. The most sensible approach, however, gives them equal importance.

Related areas include ADAPTATION; GENETIC CODE; NATURAL SELECTION. *Advanced subjects are developed in* COMPLEMENTATION AND ALLELISM; MUTATION, GENETIC; SEX LINKAGES. *Advanced information on particular aspects is contained in* EXTRANUCLEAR INHERITANCE; HARDY-WEINBERG LAW; IMPRINTING, GENETIC.

First see DNA

Genome, Human

Next see DNA SEQUENCING

The Human Genome Project is an international effort to obtain a complete, detailed picture of the genetic material that is found in every human cell and that determines all the characteristics of human beings. In the United States, the project was begun in 1990 and is coordinated by the National Center for Human Genome Research, a part of the Department of Health and Human Services. Internationally, the coordinating body is the Human Genome Organization (HUGO) based in Europe.

Basic Structure of the Human Genome. The human genome is made up of molecules of DNA, deoxyribonucleic acid, which in turn consists of sub-units of four molecules called bases —adenine, cystine, guanine and cytosine. Each molecule of DNA consists of two intertwined strands. The genetic material of the human cell is contained in 23 pairs of molecules called chromosomes. The DNA in the chromosomes of a single human cell is six feet long and carries information for the production of 100,000 proteins. A stretch of DNA that carries the information for one protein is called a gene.

Two Maps. In the genome project, scientists developed two kinds of chromosome maps. One of them is a genetic linkage map, based on the way a disease is inherited in families. By studying how frequently a given disease and

Further Reading
Appleyard, Bryan, *Brave New Worlds: Staying Human in the Genetic Future* (1998); Gould, Laura L., *Cats Are Not Peas: A Calico History of Genetics* (1996); Leach, David R.F., *Genetic Recombination* (1996); Rifkin, Jeremy, *The Biotech Century: Harnessing the Gene and Remaking the World* (1999); Russel, P. J., *Genetics* (1997).

The mapping of the human genome is a long and complicated process. Below is a map of a portion of chromosome 16. Represented is .01 percent of the chromosome's genetic material.

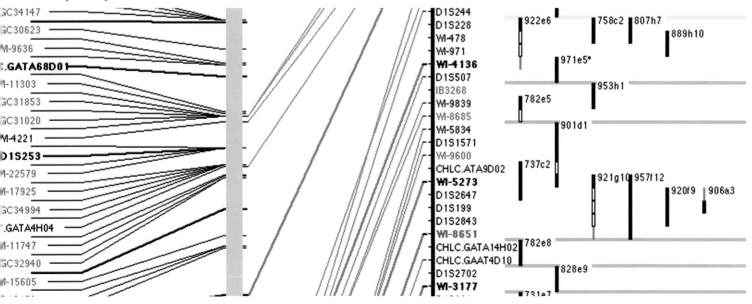

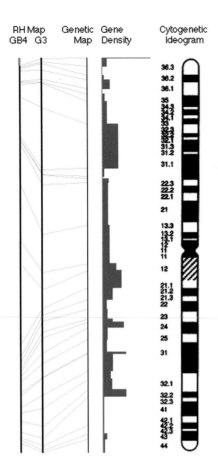

RH Map Genetic Gene   Cytogenetic
GB4 G3 Map   Density   Ideogram

Left, each segment of each chromosome is analyzed for its biochemical composition and for its genetic contribution.

be realigned in the order in which they originally occurred in the chromosome. By knowing which segments lie next to each other, scientists can make a map showing the location of each segment on the chromosome. The pieces can then be used for further studies, such as locating the position of genes or sequencing DNA.

DNA Sequencing. Sequencing is a critical part of the genome project. The order of the subunits in the DNA of a gene determines the genetic information that the gene carries. To determine how a gene works or malfunctions, molecular biologists must interpret the language that a gene uses to instruct the cell to make a given protein. The anatomy of a gene consists of two parts. One is the coding region, which serves as the blueprint for a protein. The other consists of the regulatory regions that act to turn on a gene when the protein that it makes is needed. The DNA that codes for proteins may make up as little as five percent of the entire human genome. Researchers also expect to learn about the role of the rest of the DNA, which some scientists believe plays an important part in the overall organization of chromosomes and the regulation of gene activity.

Project Schedule. Automated methods have made sequencing a fast and reliable process. A first draft of the complete human genome was finished in 2001, a few years ahead of schedule. The results almost certainly will revolutionize our understanding of the human organism as well as the manner in which doctors practice the art of medicine. It is well to remember, however, that these are but the first steps of a long journey.

other traits are inherited together over several generations, scientists can gauge the location on a chromosome and the approximate order of the genes. Until recently, only the genes that are responsible for easily visible traits could be mapped by genetic linkage, which severely limited the use of the technique. The recently developed tools of molecular biology have given biologists better methods of constructing chromosome linkage maps. For example, molecular biologists can use markers, unique segments of DNA that can be followed from one generation to the next, as landmarks for a genetic map. These markers do not play a role in disease but can be used to find the location of a gene that causes a disease. Linkage mapping depends on "crossing over," which occurs during sex cell formation and results in the exchange of genes between two chromosomes. Genes that are closer together are less likely to cross over than those that are farther apart.

A second kind of chromosome map is a physical map, which gives the actual distance in the number of bases between the genes on a chromosome. There are several different physical maps, which have different levels of detail or resolution. The most useful physical maps rely on techniques that cut chromosomes into large fragments of DNA. These fragments are then cloned in the laboratory. By means of a variety of techniques, the cloned segments of DNA can

CONTROVERSIES

Whose Genome?

With the human genome project complete, the prospect of its potential commercial application looms large. Who will profit from this enormous base of knowledge, and how? The question of patent rights over genome discoveries, particularly their relevance to complementary DNA (cDNA), was first raised in 1991. By 1999, more than 5,000 patent applications had been filed for partial gene sequences, and 1,500 had been granted by the U.S. Patent and Trade Office. Although many of these discoveries are offered freely to researchers, at least one company, Human Genome Services, has reserved all rights on its patents, arguing that it cannot hope to recover the huge development costs of gene-based medicines without government support of such exclusivity.

Further Reading
Bishop, Jerry E., *Genome* (1992); Kevles, Daniel, J., *Code of Codes: Scientific and Social Issues in the Human Genome Project* (1993); Shapiro, R., *The Human Blueprint: The Race to Unlock the Secrets of Our Genetic Script* (1992).

Background material can be found in GENE; GENETIC CODE; GENETICS; *and* MUTATION. *More details can be found in* DNA; DNA SEQUENCING; *and* RNA. *More information on particular aspects is contained in* GENETIC ENGINEERING; GENE THERAPY; CANCER; MUTAGENS AND CARCINOGENS; POLYMERASE CHAIN REACTION (PCR); *and* RECOMBINANT DNA.

First see CARTOGRAPHY AND SURVEYING

Geodetic Survey

Next see EARTH

The effort to determine the configuration of the surface of the Earth over a large area, taking the Earth's curvature into account.

Geodetic surveying is done by a series of successive approximations. An international agreement has set the shape of the Earth as an oblate spheroid whose radius at the equator is 6,378.3 kilometers and whose radius from pole to pole is 6,356.91 kilometers. The difference between the two radiuses, one part in 298, is known as the oblateness of the Earth. Once the overall shape of the planet has been established, surveys are conducted over its great arcs, with observations of stars made at many points to determine the exact longitude and latitude. The observed values are then compared to Earth's assumed oblateness.

The Geoid. Large-scale differences can be used to define a better conventional spheroid, while local differences can be used to find the shape of a second idealized body, the geoid. This geoid is an imaginary sea-level surface of the Earth that is extended by imaginary canals under the land surface. The geoid is then used as a base from which surveys can be made of elevations in the land surface and the ocean floor. Over the past 40 years, orbiting satellites have provided powerful tools for geodetic surveys.

First see EARTH

Geological Time Scale

Next see GEOLOGY, ARCHAEOLOGICAL

The branch of geology which deals with the geological time scale, measured in millions and billions of years, is called geochronology. At the beginning of the 20th century, standard geology books gave the age of the Earth as one million years. By the 1920s, the estimate increased to 500 million years. It is now recognized to be well over four billion years.

Several principles are used to establish the overall geological time scale: the principle of uniformitarianism, which states that geological processes occur steadily over many years; the principle of superposition, which states that in a sequence of sedimentary rocks, the youngest layers are on top; and the principle of intrusion, which states that a layer of rock that intrudes into another layer is younger than the intruded-upon rock. Fossils found within rock layers can also be used as indexes to the age of sedimentary rocks. More recently, studies of radioactive elements have helped establish the geological time scale.

The geological time scale can be expressed in chart form. Such charts were first developed during the nineteenth century and have been refined

as newer methods of geological science were developed. (*See* GEOLOGY, ARCHAEOLOGICAL.)

The earliest period on such a chart is the Precambrian, which is estimated to have begun more than 4.5 billion years ago, as the Earth was formed from a cloud of solar dust. The Precambrian period lasted nearly four billion years, and witnessed the extensive development of land forms. The next period, the Cambrian, began about 600 million years ago and lasted perhaps 500 million years. One of the features of the Cambrian period was the invasion of the North American continent by seas; another was a generally mild and uniform climate.

The following period, the Ordovician, lasted about 75 million years and was distinguished by extensive mountain building in northeast North America. The Ordovician was followed by the Silurian period, which also lasted about 75 million years, and by the Devonian period, which began about 400 million years ago and ended about 350 million years ago. The Devonian period was succeeded by the Mississippian period, from 345 to 310 million years ago; by the Pennsylvanian, from 310 to 280 million years ago, and by the Permian, from 280 to 230 million years ago.

The time from the Cambrian period to the Permian period is called the Paleozoic era. It was succeeded by the Mesozoic era, which lasted until about 65 million years ago and is divided into the Triassic, Jurassic, and Cretaceous eras. We now live in the Cenozoic period, which is divided into the Paleocene, Eocene, Oligocene, Miocene, Pliocene, and Pleistocene eras, the last beginning "only" 1 million years ago.

First see GEOLOGICAL TIME SCALE

Geology, Archaeological

Next see FOSSILS

Geological archaeology deals with the dating of Earth materials and events, in both absolute and relative terms. The key development in the history of geological archeology was the acceptance in the early nineteenth century of the principle of uniformitarianism, or constancy of geological processes, which says that the same forces have acted in the same way over billions of years on the features of the Earth.

By extrapolating current geologic processes into the past, scientists began to understand that many features and materials of the Earth were hundreds of thousands, millions, or even billions of years old. For example, by using the current rate of soil deposition, scientists estimated that about 6.5 billion years had been required for the layers making up the Eocene Green River shales to be deposited to their depth of more than 2,000 feet. (Modern methods of stratigraphy have more recently dated the early eocene to

CENOZOIC ERA					MESOZOIC ERA					PALEOZOIC ERA					PRECAMBRIAN ERA			
Millions of Years Ago	Duration (in millions of Years)	Period	Epoch	Age	Millions of Years Ago	Duration (in millions of Years)	Period	Epoch	Age	Millions of Years Ago	Duration (in millions of Years)	Period	Epoch	Age	Millions of Years Ago	Duration (in millions of Years)	Eon	Era
NOW		NEOGENE (TERTIARY)	HOLOCENE		70	80	CRETACEOUS	LATE	MAASTRICHTIAN	260	40	PERMIAN	LATE	TATARIAN / KAZANIAN	750	2,000	PROTERZOIC	LATE
			PLEISTOCENE	CALAMBRIAN					CAMPANIAN	280			EARLY	KUNGURIAN / ARTINIKIAN / SAKMARIAN	1000			
5			PLIOCENE L/E	PIACENZIAN / ZANCLEAN	80				(several)	300	80	CARBONIFEROUS (MISSISSIPPIAN PENNSYLANIAN)	LATE	KASIMOVIAN / MOSCOVIAN / BASHKIRIAN	1250			MIDDLE
			MIOCENE L	MESSINIAN / TORTONIAN	90				CENOMANIAN	320			EARLY	SERPUKHOVIAN / VISEAN / TOURNAISIAN	1500			
10					100			EARLY	ALBIAN	340					1750			
15			MIOCENE M	SERRAVALLIAN / LANGHIAN	110				APTIAN	360	45	DEVONIAN	LATE	PAMENNIAN / FRASNIAN	2000			EARLY
20			MIOCENE E	BURDIGALIAN / AQUITANIAN	120				BARREMIAN				MIDDLE	GIVETIAN / EIFELIAN	2250			
25		PALOGENE	OLIGOCENE L	CHATTIAN	130			NEOCOMIAN	HAUTERIVIAN / VALANGINIAN	380			EARLY	EMSIAN / SIEGENIAN	2500			
30					140				DERRIASIA	400	40	SILURIAN	LATE	PRIDOLIAN / LUDLOVIAN	2750	1,500+	ARCHEAN	LATE
35			OLIGOCENE E	RUPELIAN	150	65	JURASSIC	LATE	TITHONIAN / KIMMERIDGIAN / OXFORDIAN	420			EARLY	WENDLOCKIAN / LLANDOVERIAN	3000			
40			EOCENE L	PRIASONIAN / BARTONIAN	160					440	65	ORDOVICIAN	LATE	ASHGILLIAN / CARADOCIAN	3250			MIDDLE
45					170			MIDDLE	CALLOVIAN / BATHONIAN / BAJOCIAN / AALENIAN	460			MIDDLE	LLANDEILIAN / LLANVIRNIAN	3500			
50			EOCENE M	LUTETIAN	180					480			EARLY	ARENGIAN / TREMADOCIAN	3750			EARLY
55			EOCENE E	YPRESIAN	190			EARLY	TOARCIAN / SINEMURIAN / HETANGIAN	500					4000			
60			PALEOCENE L	SELANDIAN	200					520	80	CAMBRIAN	LATE	TREMPEALEAUAN / FRANCONIAN / ORESBACHIAN				
65			PALEOCENE E	DANIAN	210	40	TRIASSIC	LATE	NORIAN	540			MIDDLE					
					220				CARNIAN	560								
					230			MIDDLE	LANDINIAN / ANISIAN	580			EARLY					
					240			EARLY	SCYTHIAN									

around 50 million years ago.)

At the beginning of the twentieth century, John Joly divided the total amount of salt in the ocean by the amount that was added yearly by rivers and streams. He concluded that the age of the oceans was in the neighborhood of one million years, an assumption based on the beliefs that the addition of salt has been unchanged during geological time and that the oceans have lost no salt over that time. At about the same time, the British scientist Lord Kelvin estimated that the Earth was no more than 40 million years old.

Those estimates were determined to be decidedly too low after the discovery of natural radioactivity. Radioactive elements such as uranium decay at a steady rate to produce stable elements. By comparing the amount of the radioactive element with the amount of the product element in a substance, it is possible to determine the age of the substance once the half-life—the amount of time needed for the decay of the radioactive element—is known (for uranium-235, the half-life is 4.5 billion years). Radioactive carbon-14, which has a half-life of 5,568 years, can be used to accurately determine the age of organic materials up to about 70,000 years. In minerals containing radioactive uranium and thorium, the amount of helium or of lead can be measured to determine their age. Both methods have their drawbacks. The helium

The division of Earth's history (above) is based on the presence of discernably distinct layers in the geological record.

Further Reading
Compton, R. R., *Geology in the Field* (1985); Lambert, David, *Field Guide to Geology* (1997); Levin, Harold L., *Contemporary Physical Geology* (1990); Lutgens, Frederick K., *Essentials of Geology* (1997); Skinner, Brian J., *The Dynamic Earth: An Introduction to Physical Geology* (1995).

method must be used only in minerals from which helium has not escaped, while the lead method cannot be used in minerals that had a large percentage of lead content when they were originally formed.

Background material can be found in EARTH; EVOLUTION; PLATE TECTONICS; STRATIGRAPHY; RADIOCHEMISTRY. *Advanced subjects are developed in* SEDIMENTARY ROCK GEOLOGY; UNIFORMITARIANISM. *Special aspects of this subject are covered in* EARTHQUAKE; GEOMORPHOLOGY; SEISMOLOGY. *See also* HOMO SAPIENS *and related entries on paleontology.*

First see GEOLOGY, ARCHAEOLOGICAL

Geomorphology

Next see FAULTS, FOLDS, AND JOINTS

The study of the surface features of the Earth, focusing largely on their origin and development.

Geomorphology is closely related to physiography, which covers much of the same subject matter, but includes oceanography and climatology, the study of the Earth's climate and oceans. Geomorphologists explain topographic features in terms of three major geological processes: weathering; diastrophism; and igneous activity, or volcanism.

Three Processes. Weathering has produced the clay, gravel, sand, and boulders that make up a great part of Earth's surface. Weathering occurs as rock that was underground is exposed to the air by the erosion of the rock that covers it. This exposed rock tends to expand slightly, which causes the formation of fractures that can be penetrated by water. Freezing of the water during cold weather then can accelerate the breakup of the rock. Weathering can also occur by chemical reactions involving the oxygen, carbon dioxide, and moisture of the air.

Diastrophism is the overall process by which the Earth's crust is deformed. The diastrophic forces that act parallel to the Earth's surface produce the folded and faulted geological structures seen in mountain areas. In geology, folds—curvatures in layered rocks—are generally associated with sedimentary rocks, those that usually have horizontal layers. The degree of folding ranges from barely noticeable to extreme contortion and crumpling. In faulting, adjacent blocks in the Earth's surface shift with respect to one another. Faults occur in most types of rock, and are most evident when cut across and displaced in clearly visible layers of rock.

The forces of diastrophism often act at right angles to the surface of Earth and cause parts of the crust either to become uplifted or to subside from the original surface level. It is these forces of diastrophism that result in the elevation of large areas of flat terrain to form plateaus, or the depression of long, narrow areas beneath the oceans to form the oceanic deeps.

Volcanism. Volcanism—the eruption of magma or molten rock—can produce a number of geological features. For example, the solidified rocky material in the pipe of a volcano that has become inactive can be exposed by erosion, forming a towerlike mass.

Another aspect of the Earth studied in geomorphology is erosion. There are five agents of erosion on Earth—underground water; aboveground streams; wind; waves and currents; and glaciers. Over long periods, these agents wear down the large relief features of the Earth's surface. In the process, they produce many smaller-scale features, such as valleys, river deltas (caused by the deposit of soil at the mouth of a river), sand bars, and dunes.

Since all the forces that change the appearance and nature of the surface of Earth are still active, geomorphology is a never-ending and continuously dynamic branch of geology.

Background material on geomorphology can be found in CONTINENTS, FORMATION OF; GEOLOGICAL TIME SCALE; PLANET, INTERIOR OF. *More details can be found in* GEOLOGY, ARCHAEOLOGICAL; SEDIMENTARY ROCK GEOLOGY; STRATIGRAPHY. *Additional relevant information is contained in* GEOSYNCLINE; PETROLOGY; MINING TECHNOLOGY.

First see GEOLOGY, ARCHAEOLOGICAL

Geosyncline

Next see GEOMORPHOLOGY

A large basin or concave fold in the rock strata in the Earth's crust that has subsided slowly over long periods of geological time.

In the Earth's crust, thick layers of sediment have accumulated in folds, to depths of as much as several thousand feet. The term was coined in the nineteenth century by J. D. Dana, a geologist studying the origin of the Appalachian Mountains. Like many other mountain ranges, the Appalachians are composed of a sequence of thick folded and faulted sedimentary rocks. Dana defined a geosyncline as a sediment-filled depression that had been formed by lateral compression. Another geologist, Emile Haug, emphasized the importance of Dana's theories in relation to the geological activity that led to the formation and evolution of the Alps.

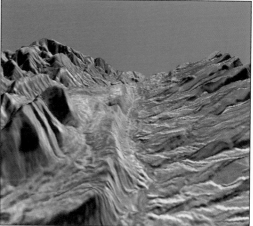

Above, a geosyncline in the Himalayas, a rich collection site for sediments and material from many geological ages.

Geological studies of the major island arcs, such as the East Indies and West Indies, indicate that the ocean deeps in front of these arcs represent geosynclines that were not filled with sediments in the process of their formation. A basin that contains a preponderance of ordinary continental-shelf deposits such as sandstone and shales is called a miogeosyncline, while one in which the dominant rocks include basalt and graywacke is called a eugeosyncline. The term "geosyncline" has fallen out of use by geologists in recent years and has been replaced by these latter terms for the appropriate geological features.

First see ENERGY

Geothermal Energy

Next see ENERGY, ALTERNATIVE

The generation of electrical power from the stored heat in the Earth's crust.

In the natural generation of geothermal energy, existing emissions of steam or hot water from sources like geysers, fumaroles, or underground reservoirs are harnessed to generate steam at high pressure, which then drives a conventional turbine electricity generator. Natural geothermal power generation is mainly limited to volcanic regions of the Earth, such as Italy, Japan, New Zealand, Russia (at Kamchat-ka), Iceland, and the United States (in California and Hawaii).

A geothermal power plant (above) uses water to convert heat energy to electricity.

Artificial, or drilled, geothermal energy requires the development of methods to drill very deep holes, more than 24 inches in diameter, to a depth of at least 50,000 feet. Drilled geothermal power is based on the observation that the temperature in the Earth's crust increases by 1.5 degrees Fahrenheit for every 100 feet of depth. This means that at a depth of 50,000 feet, the temperature of rocks in the crust would be about 800 degrees Fahrenheit. A 24-inch-diameter encased hole that was drilled to this depth would have an effective heat-transfer area of about 40,000 square feet. Water sent down such a hole would absorb this heat, and then could be returned via an insulated pipe.

Geothermal energy has two important advantages over its energy rivals. A geothermal power plant costs two-thirds of a fossil-fuel plant and half of a nuclear plant. Furthermore, geo-thermal plants do not pollute the air as oil or coal plants do and, unlike a nuclear plant, there is no risk of radiation exposure. What environmental impact a geothermal plant might have is still under investigation. (*See* FOSSIL FUEL POWER PLANT.)

First see SEED

Germination

Next see DORMANCY

The formation of a seed is usually followed by a period of dormancy. Once dormancy is broken, germination or sprouting begins with the seed beginning to hydrate itself. Most mature seeds are intensely dry, with water making up only five to 20 percent of their weight. But during imbibation, they may absorb 10 or more times their weight in water. As a result, cell membranes and other structures within the cell assume their normal size and shape.

The hydration activates enzymes in the seed and new enzymes are synthesized to begin digesting stored food. The food stores, contained either in the cotyledons or in the endosperm, consist largely of water-insoluble starch molecules. These are enzymatically converted to soluble sugars to fuel the cell enlargement and cell division that begins in the embryo.

The rate of respiration in the cells, barely detectable in dry seeds, jumps with the rapid water intake and remains stable until the emergence of the root, when it increases sharply again. To maintain the level of respiration required for growth, an adequate supply of oxygen is necessary, which explains why water-logged soil can "drown" a seed. (*See* SEED.)

Germination occurs once the embryonic root, or radicle, emerges from the seed coat to anchor the incipient seedling. By the time the shoot unfurls, the root system is already established and has begun absorbing water and minerals from the soil. (*See* SOIL CHEMISTRY.)

In some dicots, such as the garden bean, the hypocotyl—the portion of the stem below the cotyledons—elongates and bends, forming an arch. When the hook breaks through the surface of the soil, it straightens, pulling the cotyledons into the air. The first true leaves emerge from beneath the hood of the cotyledons, which eventually wither and drop off as the food they hold is used. In other dicots, such as peas, it is the epicotyl—the portion of the stem above the cotyledons—that elongates and arches; the cotyledons remain underground. Similarly, in monocots such as grass seedlings, the coleoptile—the sheath enclosing the embryonic leaves—breaks through the soil, but the cotyledon remains buried. (*See* GAMETOGENESIS.)

First see DISEASES, THEORY OF

Germ Theory

Next see DISEASES, INFECTIOUS

The belief that contagious diseases are caused by microorganisms that enter the body.

Germ theory was raised and rejected for centuries before it was finally proven in the late 19th century. Credit for the development and proof of the theory in its modern form usually goes to Louis Pasteur, the French chemist who was a pioneer of microbiology, and Robert Koch, a German physician who isolated the microbes that cause tuberculosis and cholera. Joseph Lister, the British surgeon who demonstrated the theory's practical importance by using antiseptic in the operating room, was a key figure in gaining acceptance for the theory.

Pasteur, who did his work from the 1850s to the 1880s, showed that living microbes, then called ferments, caused alcoholic fermentation and that good wine contained yeast while sour wine contained rod-shaped bacteria. He demonstrated that sour wine could be prevented, by heating the juice, cooling it, and then introducing ferments from good wine. Besides showing that specific microbes bring about specific chemical changes, Pasteur demonstrated that microbes generate only their own kind, disproving the possibility of spontaneous generation.

Early Vaccination. Anthrax was the first disease seen in humans that was shown to be caused by a specific microorganism, through the work of Casimir-Joseph Davaine in 1863. In 1876, Koch isolated the rod-shaped organism in a pure culture. Pasteur, who had created a vaccine against chicken cholera in 1877, created an anthrax vaccine in 1881, the first effective bacterial vaccine for humans.

Koch, who started out as a country doctor,

developed methods of growing individual types of bacteria in the laboratory, eventually settling on a culture medium of agar, which is still used today. His techniques made possible such an explosion of microbial knowledge that by 1900 almost all major bacterial pathogens had been described. Building on the work of his teacher Jacob Henle, Koch also formulated a set of criteria for proving that a specific bacterium causes a specific disease. With some modifications, Koch's postulates, as they are called, are still in use today. They are:

1. The organism must be found in diseased animals but not in healthy ones;
2. The organism must be isolated from diseased animals and grown in a pure culture away from the animal;
3. When the culture is inoculated into a healthy animal, the animal develops the disease;
4. The organism must be isolated from the experimentally infected animal.

Viruses, which were identified later than bacteria, cannot be cultured, so Koch's postulates do not apply to them directly. Similar principles, however, are used in verifying viral pathogens. (*See* DISEASE, THEORY OF.)

The gills of the box fish, above, are located just behind its forward fins. In most fish, the breathing and digestive intake apparatus are separate; by contrast, in most land animals, both breathing and ingestion begins at the mouth.

OBSERVATIONS

The Myth of Spontaneous Generation

The idea that tiny particles, alive or not, cause disease had been raised sporadically in print since 100 B.C.E. It competed with ideas that epidemics represented divine punishment or a demonic force, or that contagious disease was caused by bad air or "miasma." This debate was intertwined with the question of spontaneous generation—whether living organisms can arise from inorganic matter, as was widely believed, or must be generated by their own kind. Many of the experiments that laid the foundation for the germ theory were aimed at disproving the theory of spontaneous generation. For instance, Pasteur showed that when broth is boiled it remains free of microbes unless microbes in the air are allowed to contact it. A cruder version of these experiments had been done 200 years earlier by Lazzaro Spallanzani.

First see FISH

Gills

Next see BREATHING REGULATION

Gills are a highly efficient respiratory organ shared by a wide range of aquatic animals. In their simplest form, they may be little more than bumps on the skin of a starfish or flaps jutting out from the sides of marine worms. At their most highly developed, and most familiar, form in fish, they are intensely convoluted structures in which a large surface area is exposed to water, facilitating the gas exchange—the pickup of oxygen and removal of carbon dioxide—that is

the main function of all respiratory systems. In fish, they also play important roles in excretion and osmoregulation, maintenance of the salt and fluid balance in the body.

Origins. Gills seem to have evolved independently many times in the animal kingdom. It has been theorized that they originated as ciliated food-collecting organs in ancient invertebrates and eventually evolved a respiratory function.

With an ability to extract up to 80 percent of the oxygen from water—compared to the human lung's ability to extract about 60 percent of the oxygen from air—fish gills are considered the most efficient respiratory organ known to vertebrates. Such efficiency is necessary because water carries far less oxygen than air, and oxygen diffuses much more slowly in water.

Structure. Most fish have four gill arches on each side of the head, protected by a hard covering called the operculum. Each arch bears two comblike gill filaments. Stacked across each tooth of those combs are tiny parallel lamellae, thin folds of gill mucosa in which the gas exchange occurs. The lamellae are essentially sacs of flowing blood, with internal pillar cell posts to support their thin walls. Only a cell or two separates the blood flowing in the lamellae and the water flowing over their surface.

"Breathing." The blood and water flow in opposite directions. This countercurrent exchange system maximizes diffusion of oxygen from the water to the blood by ensuring that, at every point on the lamellae, the water has a higher oxygen concentration than the blood. By the time water leaves the lamellae, it is has already given up most of its oxygen. However, the blood it encounters at that point is just entering the lamellae; it has picked up no oxygen yet and is even lower in oxygen than the blood. Therefore, the gradient favors diffusion from water to blood. Conversely, when blood is about to leave the lamellae, it has already picked up a significant amount of oxygen. But the water it meets, which is just entering the gill, has its full load of oxygen, so the gradient again favors diffusion from water to blood.

The gills are also central to solving fishes' osmotic problems. The body fluids of freshwater fish are more concentrated than the water around them. As a result, osmosis causes them to take in water and lose salt. To maintain their fluid balance, they absorb salt through the gills and excrete large amounts of watery urine.

Saltwater fish have the opposite problem. Their body fluids are less concentrated than the water around them, so they constantly lose water and gain salt. To maintain their fluid balance, they excrete salt through special chloride cells in the gills and drink large amounts of water. The gills also serve to excrete most nitrogenous wastes that result from protein metabolism. (*See* AMPHIBIANS; FISH. *Also see* BREATHING REGULATION; CIRCULATORY SYSTEMS; LOCOMOTION IN ANIMALS.)

First see GEOLOGICAL TIME SCALE

Glaciers

Next see ICE AGE

A large mass of ice, consisting mostly of recrystalized snow, that moves on a land surface.

The location of glaciers is closely related to the altitude of the snowline, the lowest level of perpetual snow, which can vary from sea level in areas near or in the polar regions to 20,000 feet or more near the equator. The mass of ice in a glacier moves steadily downward from the region of its origin. The volume and length of a glacier depends on the speed of that flow, which brings ice into areas of higher temperature, the rate at which it accumulates snow above the snowline, and the amount of ice lost by melting and evaporation. (*See* CLIMATOLOGY)

Above, the remnants of the Pas Moraine glacier, which covered all of northwest Manitoba in the last ice age.

Size and Shape. Glaciers have many different shapes, depending on the thickness of their ice and the configuration of the land on which they lie, although geologists generally recognize three major types. One is the valley glacier, which is long and narrow. Another is the piedmont glacier, which exists on lowlands and whose ice is renewed by the flow of valley glaciers. The third kind is the ice sheet, a cakelike body that covers a large surface. Most glaciers are the valley type, because the snow that accumulates on mountains crystallizes and moves down through valleys that have been cut by streams. Though most glaciers are small, there are notable exceptions, such as the 125-mile-long and 75-mile-wide Beardmore Glacier in the Antarctic. (*See* MOUNTAIN FORMATION.)

Glacier Formation. The formation of glacier ice takes place under the weight of fresher, overlying snow. When the ice of a glacier becomes about 200 feet thick, it begins to flow downward under the pressure of its own weight. The flow of glacier ice is different from the flow of a liquid. The ice melts partially and then refreezes; meanwhile, individual ice particles roll downward. The rate of movement of a glacier can vary widely, from a fraction of an inch to tens of feet per day. Under some circumstances, this ice flow can be uneven and can cause the formation of crevasses, open cracks that may be as deep as 100 feet or even more.

Glaciers cause erosion of the ground under them, partly by the abrasive action of glacier ice and partly because the moving ice plucks rocks—some of them very large—from the surface. Most of these rocks are eventually broken into small bits by the grinding, breaking, and crushing that occurs within the glacier.

Glaciers are sensitive to changes in temperature, and there has been a steady reduction in their size over the past few decades as Earth grows warmer. Today, more than 95 percent of the total area of Earth's glaciers is in Antarctica and Greenland. The other five percent consists of thousands of glaciers, most of them small, distributed worldwide. (*See* ICE AGE.)

First see AIR POLLUTION

Global Warming

Next see FOSSIL FUEL

Global warming is a potentially harmful consequence of human activities, which derives from the greenhouse effect. Earth's atmosphere is semi-transparent to visible radiation from the sun. About 50 percent of the sun's radiation reaches the surface of the Earth and is absorbed by it. The surface of the Earth radiates the rest of that solar energy—consisting of radiation in the infrared wavelength region—back into space. Fortunately, the water vapor and carbon dioxide in the Earth's atmosphere are strong absorbers of energy in these wavelengths. Thus, the reradiated energy is trapped between the Earth's surface and the edge of the atmosphere a few miles above it. This trapped energy helps to raise the temperature both of the Earth's surface and of the air in the lower atmosphere, making the planet habitable to humans, animals, and plants. Eventually, the trapped radiation is radiated back into space, keeping the the Earth's temperature at a constant level.

However, this natural temperature balance is being changed by the emission into the atmosphere of carbon dioxide, caused by the burning of fossil fuels such as coal and oil, and by the emission of other gases that absorb solar radiation. These other gases include chlorofluorocarbons (CFCs) such as Freon, which is used in refrigerating equipment and as an aerosol propellant; nitrous oxide, released into the atmosphere from nitrogen-rich agricultural fertilizers; and methane, produced by the decomposing organic matter in sewage. (*See* AIR POLLUTION.)

Venus Model. The greenhouse effect is evident on Earth's sister planet, Venus, which is 28 percent closer to the sun. There, the water levels built up in the upper atmosphere did not condense and fall as precipitation, as happens on Earth, because Venus is so much closer to the sun. Instead, water molecules at high altitudes were broken into hydrogen atoms (which escaped into space) and oxygen atoms, many of which formed heat-trapping carbon dioxide molecules. As a result, Venus has always had a surface temperature of well over 800° Fahrenheit.

Awareness of the possibility of an enhanced greenhouse effect on Earth grew in the 1960s when a small but steady rise in global temperatures over the past century, coincident with the world's greatly enhanced industrial activity, was noticed. In the decade to come, some have predicted a steady rise of a small percentage of a degree a year—enough to have a significant influence on the Earth and its inhabitants. Others dispute this claim.

Some effects of a global temperature rise may be beneficial, for example, increasing the very low winter temperatures in polar regions. Since the Earth was considerably warmer in the distant past when dinosaurs flourished, causing a rich growth of vegetation that became deposited to form fossil fuels, it is possible that higher temperatures could raise plant productivity in the future. But melting ice could raise sea levels to a point where some coastal areas would become flooded. And higher temperatures in normally warm regions, such as the southern United States and sub-Saharan Africa, could make them unfit for human habitation.

First see STAR

Globular Cluster

Next see INTERSTELLAR MEDIUM ("DARK MATTER")

A group of older stars that are close enough to each other to be physically associated.

Globular clusters typically contain between a thousand and a million stars and are roughly spherical. The stars in a globular cluster tend to be very old, about 10 billion years of age, and have low abundances of heavy elements.

Star clusters were first identified by the ancient Greeks. Large compilations of globular clusters were made in the seventeenth century by Edmund Halley and in the eighteenth century by Charles Messier. In the early twentieth century,

Harlow Shapley, at the Mount Wilson Observatory, showed that there is a distinct class of stars in these clusters—the RR Lyrae stars, the light output of which pulsates regularly, often with a period of 12 hours. The period of pulsation and the brightness of these stars is related, and so Shapley was able to use that relationship, together with the measurements he made of the velocity and position of the stars, to determine that the globular clusters have a spherical distribution around the center of the galaxy (and also that the sun is somewhat away from the center of the galaxy). (*See* GALAXY.)

Distance Indicators. Later it was discovered that stars in the most distant of the globular clusters appear to be redder than the nearer stars. This finding led to the discovery of interstellar dust, which causes the reddening, and also helped astronomers make better determinations

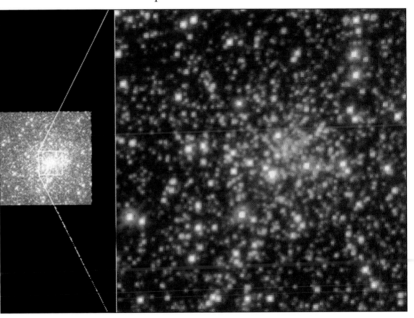

A closer look at the globular cluster M13 in Hercules, some 22,500 light years away, shows it to contain over half a million stars. Clusters are not distributed evenly throughout the universe, but are themselves aggregated into "superclusters."

of the distances from Earth to objects in the galaxy. In recent years, astronomers have discovered many more globular clusters in the halos of galaxies outside our own, and have increased the use of globular galaxies as indicators of distance in the universe. (*See* NEBULA.)

Observations of the colors, motions, and brightness of cluster stars were used in the 1940s to test models of the evolutionary pathway of stars. Astronomers reasoned that when stars are formed at the same time, the most massive ones will burn faster and evolve more rapidly toward the red giant stage. It would thus be possible to use the luminosity and temperature of the brightest stars in a cluster to find the mass of the most evolved star, and thus determine the age of the cluster. Observations of globular galaxies from spacecraft began in the late 1960s with the orbiting of the OAO-2 spacecraft, and are continuing with the Hubble telescope. (*See* HERTZSPRUNG-RUSSELL DIAGRAM.)

Glycolysis

First see METABOLISM

Next see DISTILLATION

Respiration—the enzymatic breakdown of glucose into carbon dioxide and water—is the chief source of energy to cells. Through a series of chemical reactions, the energy is usually stored in molecules of ATP (adenosine triphosphate), a compound that releases energy in amounts small enough to be efficiently used by cells. (*See* ATP.)

Aerobic respiration, which requires oxygen, and anaerobic respiration, which does not, begin with a series of reactions called glycolysis, in which a glucose molecule is split into two molecules of pyruvic acid, with a net gain of two molecules of ATP. Hydrogen released during glycolysis is picked up by a hydrogen acceptor molecule, NAD (nicotinamide adenine dinucleotide).

If oxygen is present, the pyruvic acid undergoes complete oxidation through three more stages—the Acetyl Co-A step, the Krebs cycle and the electron transport chain—which occur within the mitochondria and produce many more molecules of ATP. (*See* RESPIRATORY SYSTEMS.)

If oxygen is not present, the hydrogen released during glycolysis is transferred back to the pyruvic acid as part of the anaerobic process of fermentation. In yeast and most plant cells, this produces ethanol (ethyl alcohol) and carbon dioxide in the process of alcoholic fermentation, which underlies the making of bread and alcoholic beverages. In many bacteria, fungi, and animal cells, the pyruvic acid undergoes lactic fermentation, resulting in the formation of lactic acid. This process makes possible the manufacture of most cheeses and yogurt. The buildup of lactic acid is also responsible for muscle pain that occurs in humans during heavy exercise when the oxygen supply is inadequate.

Further Reading
Casti, John L., *Gödel* (2000); Davis, Martin, *The Undecidable* (1965); Dawson, John W., *Logical Dilemmas* (1994); Hintikka, J., *On Gödel* (1999); Smullyan, R., *Forever Undecided* (1989); Wang, Hao, *A Logical Journey* (1996).

Above, Kurt Gödel leans against a tree, posing for a picture with Albert Einstein.

Gödel's Theorem

Next see SCIENTIFIC METHOD

Despite its astounding scientific successes, the twentieth century witnessed the growth of uncertainty as a philosophical principle. In the physical sciences, Heisenberg's uncertainty principle left observers unable to measure both position and velocity at the same time. In the social sciences, analysts using statistical reasoning are left with an irreducible margin of error in every conclusion. And in logic, Gödel's theorem showed that no system—whether linguistic or mechanical—can have both syntactic and semantic completeness.

Every formal system must have a syntax—symbols, operations, and underlying logic—that controls what constitutes an acceptable statement in that system. Mathematical symbols include numbers, parentheses, and operands—the signs of the basic operations (+, -, X, /). Mathematical operations are also controlled by certain logical rules, such as that operations in parentheses are performed first, no quantity can be both equal to and not equal to another quantity, etc. With these syntactical matters, however, there also stand semantic questions of meaning and truth. Every such agreed-upon meaning may be called a theorem of mathematics.

In 1931, the German mathematician Kurt Gödel published a paper "On Formally Undecidable Propositions in Principia Mathematica." This paper was an attempt to clarify certain ambiguities in classical physics, particularly needed since the publication of Einstein's theory of relativity. The heart of Gödel's argument was his assertion that the above process of constructing theorems hides a fundamental flaw: one can always construct a syntactically "true" statement that is not a semantically valid theorem.

The second stage of Gödel's theorem appeared in 1934, when he published a general theory of recursive functions—those which can be computed by a finite, but exceedingly long, series of discrete mechanical steps. As a result, it became possible to determine not only whether a problem can be solved, but also whether one cannot be solved; recently, recursive theory was used to prove "The Four-Color Problem," showing that a map printed in no more than four colors could successfully avoid having same-color sectors border one another.

Thus the general statement of Gödel's theorem that "every formal system of a certain complexity [what Gödel called "interesting systems"] will contain statements that are undecidable." That is, any statement one constructs to define the consistency of a system is never provable within that system. But then any statement one constructs to define Gödel's theorem will also be unprovable by it, and so on.

Background material can be found in ALGEBRA; NUMBER; SETS AND GROUPS. *Advanced subjects are developed in* FERMAT'S LAST THEOREM; NUMBER THEORY. *Foundational aspects of this subject are covered in* CATEGORY THEORY; CHAOS AND COMPLEXITY; SCIENTIFIC METHOD.

First see NUCLEAR FORCES

Grand Unification Theories (GUT)

Next see THEORIES OF EVERYTHING

Combining the strong, weak, and electromagnetic interactions into a single gauge theory—a quantum field theory with a single symmetry group.

Grand unification theories, or GUTs, are based on the belief that all nuclear interactions merge at very high energies. The theories also predict that the proton will decay into other particles at these high energies. It has not yet been possible to verify these predictions, since the energies at which they come into play are much greater than those that can be obtained with existing particle accelerators. But even if such energies could be achieved, the time of decay of the proton that is predicted by different GUTs varies greatly, making verification difficult.

Supersymmetry. Some GUTs also involve the principle of supersymmetry, which can be applied both to bosons and to elementary particles, such as protons and fermions. The simplest supersymmetry theories say that each boson has a corresponding fermion partner, and thus that every fermion has a corresponding boson partner. The fermion partners of existing bosons are named by replacing the "-on" at the end of the boson particle name or by adding "-ino," creating such names as the gluino, the photino, and the zino. The boson partners of existing fermions are named by adding s to the beginning of the name of the fermion, creating such names as the selectron, the slepton and the squark. The infinities that cause problems in relativistic quantum field theories are lessened in supersymmetry theories, since the infinities of bosons and fermions cancel one another.

Plausibility. Supersymmetry theories are considered plausible for several reasons. One is that the masses of the fundamental scalar fields—those that do not depend on direction—are not sensitive to the fine details of the theories at very high energies. Another is that supersymmetric quantum field theories are believed to have more manageable behavior than other quantum field theories.

Local theories of supersymmetry also suggest that there is a connection between supersymmetry transformations and space-time transformations. This connection implies that it might be possible to unify the gravitational force with both the strong and electroweak forces using these theories of local supersymmetry. As of now, however, scientists have not been able to obtain any experimental evidence that would validate supersymmetry. If supersymmetric partners of the known quarks, leptons, and gauge bosons do exist, their masses must be greater than 20 GeV.

Background material can be found in FORCE; SCIENTIFIC METHOD; SYMMETRY IN NATURE. *Advanced subjects are developed in* QUANTUM ELECTRODYNAMICS; STANDARD MODEL; THEORIES OF EVERYTHING. *More information on particular aspects is contained in* GAUGE THEORY; QUANTUM MECHANICS; STRING THEORY.

Isaac Newton (top, 1642–1727) and Albert Einstein (1879 –1955).

A gravity map of the moon shows the presence of mountain roots, indicative of seismic and volcanic activity that once made the moon geologically more active.

Further Reading
Hooft, Gerard 'T, *In Search of the Ultimate Building Blocks* (1996); Kaku, Michio, *Hyperspace* (1995); Lederman, Leon, *The God Particle* (1994); Peat, F. David, *Superstrings: And the Search for the Theory of Everything* (1989); Weinberg, Steven, *Dreams of a Final Theory* (1994).

First see NEWTON'S LAWS

Gravity

Next see GENERAL RELATIVITY

The attractive force exerted by Earth on any mass, from a feather on the Earth to the moon 240,000 miles away.

Gravity can be distinguished from gravitation, which is the force of attraction between any two masses. Both gravity and gravitation are described by the laws developed by Isaac Newton, which state that every particle of matter attracts every other particle with a force that is proportional to the product of the masses and to the inverse square of the distance between them ($F=Gm_1m_2/r^2$, where m_1 and m_2 are the masses of two bodies, r is the distance between them, and G is the gravitation constant, which is sometimes called the Newton constant).

Newton himself did not know the value of G. It was determined toward the end of the 18th century by Henry Cavendish, a British scientist who used an instrument called a torsion balance to measure the attractive force between two masses. Cavendish placed two small metal balls at the end of a lightweight rod suspended horizontally from a vertical quartz fiber. He then brought two larger spheres near the small ones, rotated the transverse rod, and measured the angle at which the fiber was twisted. The value of the gravitation constant is now known to be 6.670×10^{-8} ($\pm$ .005) dyne cm²/gm². Thus, the attraction between two masses of one gram each that are one centimeter apart is 6.670×10^{-8} dynes.

1st Operational Lunar Data Gravity Map

Near side	**Far side**

6
5
4
3
2
1
0
-1
-2
-3
-4
-5
-6
Acceleration (mgal)

Action at a Distance. Newton described gravitation as action at a distance. In the 19th century, British scientist Michael Faraday developed a new concept on the basis of experiments with magnetism. Faraday introduced the concept of a field, describing it as a medium that is filled with lines or tubes of force. In Faraday's terms, the intensity of a gravitational field, E, is the

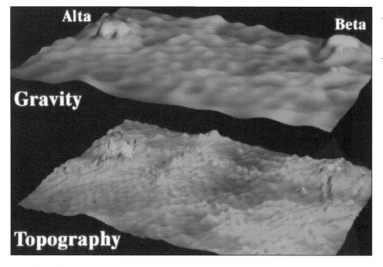

Alta · Beta · Gravity · Topography

Magellan's on-board gravitometric sensors mapped Venus as its radar sensors mapped the topography. Gravity anomalies at Alta Regio and Beta Regio (above) are the most pronounced on the planet, indicating them to be sites of mantle upswelling. The correspondence between gravity and topography is much greater on Venus than on Earth, indicating that geological features on Venus are more closely linked to fluid motions of the mantle.

force that is exerted on a unit of mass that is placed in the field—mathematically, $E = F_m$. Faraday's definition of gravitation is identical with those given for the strength of electrostatic and magnetic fields.

The Earth's gravitational pull is directed toward its center at any point on the surface. However, the weight of a body on the Earth's surface is a little less than the gravitational pull exerted by the Earth, because the Earth's rotation creates a centrifugal force that reduces the gravitational pull. For standardization, an international agreement has set the acceleration caused by gravity at any point on the Earth's surface at $g = 980.665 \text{ cm/sec}^2$.

Equipotentials. One can imagine a number of imaginary lines in space around Earth joining points of equal gravitational attraction called equipotentials. No work is done if any mass moves around the Earth on an equipotential path. However, if a mass is moved above or below an equipotential, work is done along a line extending above or below an equipotential called a gradient. Legend has it that Isaac Newton conceived the idea of a gravitational gradient when he was hit by an apple falling from a tree.

The concept of gravity has changed in the twentieth century as a result of Einstein's theory of general relativity, according to which any mass deforms the space around it. This assumption led him to propose that the path of a ray of light would be affected when it passed through the gravitational field of a very massive body. Measurements of starlight that passes close to the sun has confirmed Einstein's proposal. Einstein also proposed that a body in acceleration would emit gravitational waves with the velocity of light, but this prediction has not yet been confirmed.

Further Reading
Bergmann, Peter G., *The Riddle of Gravitation* (1993); Misner, Charles, W., *Gravitation* (1973); Morinigo, B., *Feynman Lectures on Gravitation* (1995); Strathern, Paul, *Newton and Gravity* (1998); Weinberg, Steven, *Gravitation and Cosmology: Principles and Applications of the General Theory of Relativity* (1972); Wheeler, John Archibald, *A Journey Into Gravity and Spacetime* (1990).

Background material can be found in FORCE; EQUIVALENCE PRINCIPLE; KEPLER'S LAWS; WEIGHT. *Advanced subjects are developed in* INTERSTELLAR MEDIUM. *Additional relevant information is contained in* GENERAL RELATIVITY; PLANET; FORMATION OF.

First see PERIODIC TABLE OF THE ELEMENTS

Group IV Elements

Next see CARBON

The elements found in group IV on the Periodic Table include carbon, silicon, germanium, tin, and lead. Unlike many of the other families of elements, these atoms do not exhibit a family resemblance in terms of properties or behavior. The only thing they have in common is the presence of four electrons (negatively charged particles) in their outermost (valence) energy levels.

Carbon and silicon are both non-metals. However, because of their proximity to the divide between metals and non-metals, they exhibit some metallic properties. For example, graphite, a form of carbon, is a good conductor, and silicon has a lustrous sheen just like a metal.

Carbon atoms form covalent bonds in which electrons are shared between atoms and may do so with up to four partners at a time. These bonds may be single, double, or triple depending on how many pairs of electrons are being shared. Carbon has the ability to form long-linked chains and rings called hydrocarbons that are the basis of organic chemistry.

Silicon, the second most abundant element in Earth's crust, is also capable of forming compounds called silicanes, which are analogous to hydrocarbons. Another group of silicon polymers are silicones, in which the silicon atoms are interspersed with oxygen. Silicones are chemically inert, water repellent, good insulators, and stable in the presence of heat. For these reasons, silicone gels have long been used as implants in the human body, particularly breast and muscle implants.

Tin and lead are metals that form ionic bonds (electrons are gained or lost) and lose electrons to become cations or positively charged ions. They are then attracted to the non-metals, which have gained their electrons and become anions, or negatively charged ions. Tin and lead, unlike most other metals, are able to form two types of cations, those with a charge of +2 (2 electrons are lost) and those with a charge of +4 (4 electrons are lost). This increases tremendously the number of compounds they are able to form. (*See* METAL; ORGANIC COMPOUNDS.)

First see SETS AND GROUPS

Group Theory in Physics

Next see QUANTUM MECHANICS

Group theory is a set of symmetry principles that brings order to the classification of elementary particles. Since the pi meson was discovered in 1947, the number of known hadrons has grown steadily (a hadron is an elementary particle—such as a proton, neutron, and pion—that interacts through the strong nuclear force). Thus far, more than 400 hadrons have been identified.

The first stage in applying group theory to hadrons is to group them in isospin multiplets, which distinguishes between hadrons that differ in electromagnetic properties but are otherwise identical; an example of such a pair is the proton and the neutron. Then another factor called the hypercharge Y, which is closely related to strangeness, can be applied. Hypercharge Y was introduced by physicist Murray Gell-Mann, who in 1962 discovered how to merge the isospin and the hypercharge into a new symmetry group called SU(3). The SU(3) symmetry has successfully predicted the existence of previously unknown elementary particles and with the help of other theorems can be used to predict many physical properties of elementary particles, such as their magnetic moments, mass differences, and various modes of decay.

Quarks. Not long after SU(3) was introduced, Gell-Mann and others proposed that all the known hadrons could be regarded as bound states of three even more elementary building blocks—quarks and their antiparticles. But the discovery of new particles has caused theorists to enlarge the model. In 1974, they proposed the existence of the charmonium family, whose properties are understood by the existence of a new quantum number, called charm. The existence of charm demands the existence of a fourth quark. In 1977, another new family, the upsilon, was described. It requires the existence of another quark, the bottom quark.

The Standard Model. Quarks are said to emit and absorb massless particles called gluons. Two characteristics of elementary particles, charge and flavor, are conserved in the quark-gluon interactions. By joining these quark-gluon interactions to the electroweak interaction, physicists have arrived at what is called the Standard Model. In this picture, quarks and leptons are closely related source particles, and the photon, the gluon, and other particles of the weak interactions are described as field or force particles. In another development, Gell-Mann and others have proposed that the electromagnetic current and the weak current can be included in SU(3).

Studies of group theory and the elementary particles are continuing. Newer developments include the development of grand unification theories, or GUTs, that include all the elementary forces. Meanwhile, existing group theory has had great success in describing elementary particles and their interactions.

Background material can be found in SETS AND GROUPS; ELEMENTARY PARTICLE; QUANTUM MECHANICS; *Advanced subjects are developed in* QUANTUM ELECTRODYNAMICS; QUARKS; STANDARD MODEL; AND STRING THEORY. *See also* SYMMETRY IN NATURE; GRAND UNIFICATION THEORIES (GUT); THEORIES OF EVERYTHING.

First see PLANT

Growth Regulation in Plants

Next see PLANT HORMONE

Growth in plants is regulated by many factors, including the interplay of hormones and other chemicals, the presence of light or darkness, changes in temperature, and the workings of the organism's biological clock.

Plant hormones, produced in the apical meristems of shoots and other actively growing parts, are effective in minute amounts. Five kinds have been fully identified: auxins, cytokinins, gibberellins, abscissic acid, and ethylene. Hormones cause a wide range of effects in different plants, different tissues, or different stages of development. In general terms, auxin causes growth by elongation of cells and promotes fruiting. Cytokinins cause growth by cell division, promote bud formation, and delay the aging of leaves. Gibberellins are involved in breaking dormancy, causing stem elongation, and promoting fruiting. Ethylene promotes ripening of fruit, and abscission causes the dropping of fruit, leaves, and flowers from a plant. Abscissic acid promotes dormancy and helps prevent excessive water loss.

Hormonal Triggers. One of the most important chemical factors in growth regulation is phytochrome. Like hormones, this blue pigment affects almost every stage of plant development from seed germination to flowering to breaking of dormancy to senescence.

Phytochrome, in a form called Pr, has been found to absorb the red light (600-700 nm region) that promotes germination, and then to convert to Pfr, which absorbs the far-red light (720-760 nm) that inhibits germination, and converts back to Pr.

In normal sunlight, red light exceeds far-red, so most phytochrome is in the Pfr form. During darkness, Pfr reverts to the Pr form. This two-sided system is believed to work in conjunction with a complex biological clock that is thought to be reset at dawn and dusk, perhaps by the changing ratio of Pr and Pfr. In any case, plants can measure the duration of night, an ability that controls the onset of flowering in many species, as part of the phenomenon called photoperiodism.

Short-day plants, which include asters and chrysanthemums, flower when the day is shorter than some specific length, which means they usually flower in fall. Long-day plants, which include lettuce and wheat, flower when the day is longer than a specific length, usually in summer. Intermediate-day plants, which include some grasses, flower when the day is neither too long nor too short. Day-neutral plants, which include

The environment in which hydroponic systems grow seems as important as the nutrient delivery system. Right, wheat grown in a chamber lit by red LED lights and low-pressure sodium lamps. The experiment is being conducted by NASA in anticipation of the nutritional needs of very long space voyages.

Further Reading

Bryant, John A., *Plant Cell Proliferation and Its Regulation in Growth and Development* (1998); Fosket, Donald E., *Plant Growth and Development: A Molecular Approach* (1994); Wareing, P. F., *The Control of Growth and Differentiation in Plants* (1978).

roses, sunflowers, and tomatoes, flower irrespective of day length; they mostly originate in tropical regions, which do not have seasons of varying day length. Despite the names of these categories, it is the night length, not the day length, that is crucial to photoperiodism. If a long-day (short-night) plant is exposed to light for even a few minutes in the middle of a long night, it will bloom as if the night had ended. (*See* TROPISM.)

Phytochrome is also involved in sensing competition from neighboring plants. Foliage absorbs red light and transmits far-red light, so the ratio of red to far-red in the sunlight that reaches a leaf can indicate whether the leaf is shaded by other foliage. That, in turn, affects growth patterns, from the elongated stems often seen in shaded plants to the reduced photosynthetic capacity of leaves that grow in the shade.

Like light, temperature influences growth in many ways. Each plant generally has a minimum, optimum, and maximum temperature for growth. Specific temperature patterns may be required to initiate germination or flowering, as well as the induction or breaking of dormancy. One of the most common of these patterns is vernalization, in which plants must experience a certain period of low temperatures in order to bloom. (*See* PLANT.)

First see SEED

Gymnosperm

Next see EVOLUTION

The earliest seed-bearing plants were the gymnosperms, whose name means "naked seed." Rather than being encased in fruit, as the seeds of angiosperms are, gymnosperm seeds lie exposed on the surface of sporophylls, the cones or other

organs that give rise to the reproductive cells.

Today about 720 species of gymnosperms survive, compared to more than 200,000 species of angiosperms, the flowering plants that dominate the plant world. The gymnosperms, mostly trees whose fossil record reaches back 290 million years to the late Carboniferous period, are classified into four divisions. The most important and familiar, the conifers, include about 550 species, among them the pines that make up great swathes of forest in North America, Europe, and Asia. Firs, spruce, hemlock, cedars, junipers, yew, and redwoods also belong in this venerable class. (*See* GAMETOGENESIS.)

Conifer Growth. In most conifers, male and female cones grow on the same tree. Among pines, small male cones 0.4 to 1.5 inches long cluster on lower branches in the spring, when they release four-celled pollen grains—as many as hundreds of millions of grains from a single tree. Female cones, which are much larger and have ovules at the base of each scale, grow on the higher branches of the same trees. After pollination, the female cone's scales grow together to protect the ovule. Over the next 15 months, the ovule produces two to six structures called archegonia, each bearing an egg, and a pollen tube grows from a pollen grain to an archegonium, enabling fertilization to occur. Two sperm travel down the tube; one unites with the egg, the other degenerates. The seed coat develops and a thin layer of the cone scale becomes the wing that helps disperse the seed when the cone scales open and the seed is shed, usually in the second autumn after pollination.

Cycads. The other groups of gymnosperms have little in common. The cycads—slow-growing, palmlike plants and trees—appeared at least 320 million years ago and flourished along with the dinosaurs in the Mesozoic. Today, they number about 100 species, including the so-called sago palm, and grow in tropical and subtropical regions. Their pollen and seed cones do not grow on the same tree, and insects appear to play a role in pollination. The gnetophytes include about 70 diverse species grouped in three genera: Gnetum, which includes tropical trees and vines; Ephedra, desert shrubs with scalelike leaves; and Welwitschia, unusual southern African plants whose stem is a shallow, woody cup that hugs the ground and bears two leaves that grow throughout the plant's 100-year lifespan. (*See* REPRODUCTIVE STRATEGIES *and* BIODIVERSITY.)

First see CHARGE AND CURRENT

Hall Effect

Next see ELECTROCHEMISTRY

The development of a voltage across a flat material that carries an electric current when that material is placed in a magnetic field perpendicular to it.

The Hall Effect was discovered in 1879 by Edwin H. Hall of Johns Hopkins University. He placed a strip of gold leaf that carried an electric current in a magnetic field and found that the points exactly opposite to each other at the ends of the strip revealed a difference in electric potential. Hall spent the rest of his life studying that effect, and many of the terms in the field bear his name. He found that if the current-carrying material is iron, cobalt, zinc, or antimony, and the magnetic field is directed downward, the drop in electric potential occurs on the right side of the material; the effect is said to be positive. In gold, silver, bismuth, copper, platinum, aluminum, and nickel, the drop in potential occurs on the left and is said to be negative. The difference in electric potential depends on the intensity of the magnetic field and the current density. It is called the Hall coefficient. A negative current is due to the flow of electrons, while a positive current is due to the flow of holes. (A hole represents the absence of negative charge in a solid, and it behaves as if it is positively charged.) Hall mobility is the measure of the movement of electrons or holes in a semiconductor caused by the Hall effect.

First see PERIODIC TABLE OF THE ELEMENTS

Halogens

Next see DENTISTRY

Group VIIA on the Periodic Table, second from the right, is also known as the halogen family. Halogens are the most reactive of all the nonmetal elements because they are only one electron away from a full valence shell and are extremely "anxious" to obtain it. The halogens are quite electronegative, meaning they strongly attract electrons and have no trouble "grabbing" an electron from a passing metal atom. With the additional electron, the atom is no longer neutral but is transformed into a negatively charged ion, or anion, that will be attracted to any positive ions around.

The halogen family includes the elements fluorine, chlorine, bromine, and iodine. Although they share many chemical properties, these elements are quite different from one another. For example, chlorine is a gas at room temperature, whereas iodine is a solid.

The halogens form ionic bonds when combined with metal atoms, since they are extremely electronegative. All of the halogens are diatomic, meaning they are so eager to form bonds that they will pair up with another atom of their own kind in the absence of anything else available. For this reason, it is impossible to find any halogen as an individual atom.

Halogens are often added to hydrocarbons as functional groups. In this capacity they have a variety of functions and uses, although chlorofluorocarbons (CFCs) have been found to have a detrimental impact on the environment and their use is being phased out.

Chlorine is used as a disinfectant and germicide, particularly for fresh produce and municipal water supplies. Fluorine is added to the water supply of many communities, as fluoridated water has been found to have a beneficial effect on dental health.

Iodine is used as a topical disinfectant and also as a reagent to indicate the presence of starch in a substance. Since iodine is a solid, it is usually dissolved in alcohol (forming a tincture) and then diluted with water before use.

Halogens are also used in the manufacture of light bulbs and produce an exceptionally bright light. These bulbs, which tend to become hotter than standard incandescent bulbs, have recently been redesigned to reach only about 300° Fahrenheit instead of the earlier 900°F.

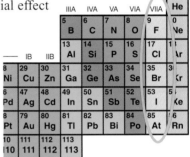

Above, the position of the halogens on the Periodic Table of the Elements.

First see GENETICS

Hardy-Weinberg Law

Next see POPULATION ECOLOGY

A population consists of members of the same species living in the same immediate location. The gene pool contains all possible alleles (the form that a gene may take, either dominant or recessive) for a particular trait present within a population. The gene pool, or more precisely, the gene frequencies—the percentage of each allele within the gene pool—remain constant from one generation to the next provided that it contains a large population—random mating is present, but there are no mutations or migrations in or out of the population. The Hardy-Weinberg law of genetic equilibrium expresses this idea mathematically with the formula $p^2 + 2pq + q^2 = 1$, where "p" represents the frequency of the dominant allele and "q" represents the frequency of the recessive allele. For a particular trait, there are three possible genotypes:

1. Homozygous dominant—two dominant alleles, represented as p^2;

2. Heterozygous—one dominant one recessive, represented as pq;

3. Homozygous recessive—two recessive alleles, represented as q^2;

Using a punnett square (an algebraic matrix to ensure all possible combinations)

$$\begin{array}{c|cc} & p & q \\ \hline p & p^2 & pq \\ q & pq & q^2 \end{array}$$

yields the following equation: $p^2 + 2\,pq + q^2 = 1$

The Hardy-Weinberg law was developed in the early twentieth century by mathemetician G. H. Hardy, and physician W. Weinberg. It is important to note that most populations do not meet the necessary criteria for genetic stability. However, many populations have stable frequencies for certain alleles over several generations. The Hardy-Weinberg Law is used in population genetic studies to examine the frequency of recessive alleles or the percentage of the population carrying at least one recessive allele for a particular trait. (*See* GENETICS.)

First see WATER POLLUTION

Hazardous Waste Disposal

Next see NUCLEAR POWER

Hazardous waste disposal involves two discrete processes: isolation of wastes, typically by geologic disposal; and destruction of wastes, typically by incineration or high-intensity discharge. Hazardous wastes as defined by the Environmental Protection Agency may contain any of 90 different chemicals that have been proven toxic, carcinogenic, mutagenic, or teratogenic; they are further categorized by their ignition rate, corrosiveness, and chemical reactivity.

Hazardous wastes were for many years treated like sanitary waste—compacted, confined to a restricted area, and covered over to some extent. The results, especially in areas with strong groundwater flow, were disastrous; leachate from chemical wastes stored in the Love Canal area of Niagara Falls contaminated homes up to a mile from the dump site. In its 1984 survey, the EPA found 15,000 uncontrolled hazard-ous waste sites, although few posed direct threats to the public.

Landfills. Landfills for hazardous materials are sited on natural clay surfaces, preferably in dry climates, and defend against groundwater contamination with the installation of an impermeable cover, bottom liner, and system of drainage pipes within the waste storage structure. Nevertheless, the Office of Technology Assessment has declared that complete protection is not possible. Thus, some method of treating hazardous wastes must be joined with containment. The most common method is bioremediation, in which natural bacteria or fungi are added to the waste materials and, after sufficient nutrients are pumped through the waste, inert compounds like carbon dioxide and water are produced.

Another method of waste disposal, prac-

Further Reading
Meyer, Eugene, *Chemistry of Hazardous Waste Management* (1997); Wagner, Travis P., *The Complete Guide to Hazardous Waste Regulations* (1999); Woodside, Gale, *Hazardous Materials and Hazardous Waste Management* (1999).

ticed for many years by petroleum producers who found themselves with unwanted byproducts of distillation, is deep-well injection. Unlike a production well, in which the drill bit turns inside a larger well pipe, injection tubing in a waste-disposal well must be surrounded by high-pressure inert fluid to prevent the waste from exiting before the appropriate stratum. Rock formations must be carefully chosen to contain the waste either above, or below, fluids naturally occurring in the rock. Salt domes several miles beneath the surface have also been employed.

The extreme toxicity of many wastes, such as PCBs containing dioxin, chemical weapons, and dust containing heavy metals, necessitates more thorough methods of treatment to ensure that the wastes are within tolerable levels before burial or injection. For this reason a rotary kiln incinerator has been used, which can achieve much higher temperatures than either conventional or even pyrolytic incinerators. But some wastes need to be heated at least to 1,250°C for several seconds in an oxygenated airflow, a demand the rotary kiln cannot effectively meet.

For these wastes, an electric discharge can be used, eliminating the need for oxygenation. One such method of incineration is glow or corona discharge, which applies a technology used for ozone manufacture to dispose of power station flue gases, such as sulfur dioxide and nitrogen oxide; even dioxins might be destroyed using such corona discharges. Arc discharges are the second method of waste disposal, using a high-intensity plasma torch which can produce

Sites where toxic waste barrels are dumped (above) are often plagued by leaching and overflow problems.

extremely high temperatures. Arc discharge plants are used to destroy PCBs, hospital wastes, heavy metal slags, and dust—even automobile tires. A benefit of such processes is that much of the residue is vitrified, so that it can be stored in landfills without the threat of secondary leaching. Electric discharges offer destruction efficiencies greater than 99 percent.

Hazardous waste disposal still faces intense controversy. For example, the U.S. Navy stores 23 million pounds of napalm, left over from the Vietnam War, at a facility in San Diego; the substance—a mixture of gasoline, benzene, and polystyrene—was banned by the United Nations in 1972, but the Navy never worked out a satisfactory disposal method. In 1994, the Navy seemed to have succeeded, with a plan that involved shipping the napalm by tank car halfway across the United States to a plant in East Chicago, Indiana, where it would be blended with other chemicals to produce an industrial fuel; but protests over both the method of shipping and the disposal method itself have left that plan unresolved seven years later. A revised timetable promises completion of napalm processing in 2001. (*See* AIR POLLUTION *and* DIOXINS.)

First see CIRCULATORY SYSTEMS

Heart

Next see ANGIOPLASTY

A muscular pump in vertebrates that drives blood to pick up oxygen in lungs or gills and then to deliver it, along with nutrients and other elements, to cells throughout the body.

The heart is composed of striated muscle that contracts automatically when exposed to the proper blood chemistry. Its rhythmic beat is regulated by the autonomic nervous system.

Structure. Birds and mammals—including humans—have a double-circuit heart that functions much like two separate, side-by-side pumps, each with two chambers. On the right side of the heart, blood moves from the right atrium to the right ventricle, which pumps it through the pulmonary artery to the lungs to be oxygenated in a process called pulmonary circulation. When the blood returns to the heart, it enters the left atrium before moving to the left ventricle where it is then pumped out again, this time with greater force. The blood is forced through the ascending aorta and out to the body in a process called systemic circulation. Within the heart, the oxygen-depleted and oxygen-rich blood do not mix, ensuring that a high concentration of oxygenated blood, needed to support the high metabolism of warm-blooded animals, reaches tissues throughout the body.

In these animals, the two atria contract simultaneously, followed a fraction of a second later by the two ventricles. The heartbeat is stimulated by impulses from sympathetic nerve fibers that accelerate heart action, and parasympathetic nerve fibers that slow action. The nerve impulses are received in the sinoatrial node, or S-A node, the heart's "pacemaker"—a small mass of tissue on the wall of the right atrium. A wave of excitation spreads from the S-A node through the atria and to the atrioventricular node, or A-V node, located in the wall between the right atrium and ventricle. This node sends excitatory impulses throughout the ventricles.

Special arteries and veins, called the coronary circulation, supply oxygen-rich blood to the heart muscle itself and return the depleted blood to the right atrium.

Heart Size. In general, the smaller the animal, the more contractions per minute. In humans, it is normally 55 to 90 beats a minute. Shrews, the smallest mammals, may have a heart rate 100 times greater. Reptiles and amphibians have left and right atria but only a single ventricle. The mixing of oxygenated and unoxygenated blood is minimized, however, by certain anatomical features. In the conus arteriosus, the last chamber of the amphibian heart, a spiral valve properly directs the two streams of blood; in reptiles, a partial wall divides the ventricle. (*See* AMPHIBIANS; MAMMALS; *and* REPTILES.)

In fish, the heart has a single circuit. With the ventricle supplying the main pumping action, blood moves through a linear series of chambers—the sinus venosus, atrium, ventricle, and bulbus or conus arteriosus—and out to the gills to be oxygenated. It continues on to the rest of the body without first returning to the heart for a pumping boost. As a result, it circulates under low pressure, but the gills oxygenate the blood efficiently enough to compensate.

Heart Disorders. Disorders of the heart are the leading causes of death in the United States. The major cause of heart disease in adults is impaired blood supply. The coronary arteries, which supply blood to the heart muscle, gradually become narrower because of atherosclerosis, a condition in which deposits called plaques form on the inner linings of the arteries. These plaques consist of cholesterol, low-density lipoproteins, and clumps of blood platelets. When they grow to block most or all of the flow in an artery (the result can be angina pectoris, pain in the chest and arms or jaw due to a lack of oxygen for the heart muscle), or a myocardial infarction (heart attack), in which part of the heart muscle dies. About one million Americans (more men than women) suffer heart attacks each year, and about a third of them die from the attack or from subsequent complications.

The range of other heart disorders starts with congenital defects, structural abnormalities of the heart that result from errors of development. They include septal defects (malformations of the heart muscle) and abnormalities of the valves that control the flow of blood from one heart chamber to another. Another general form of heart disorder is cardiomyopathy, a disease of the heart that reduces blood circulation by reducing the force of heart contractions.

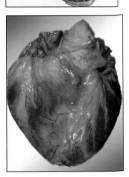

An illustration (above, top) depicts the outer structure of the heart. The different types of tissue in a human heart (above, bottom) are distinct in color and texture. Fatty tissue is yellow and smooth while muscle is a deep red with striations.

Replacement heart valves for humans (above) are made by attaching pericardium tissue from a calf to a plastic core.

Infectious disease of the heart include endocarditis, an infection of the heart valves that can occur in persons whose hearts have been damaged. Rheumatic fever, for example, can cause deformation of any of the heart valves, resulting in dangerously reduced blood flow.

Other kinds of heart disease include arrythmia, an abnormal pattern of heartbeat; heart block, in which the contractions of the upper and lower parts of the heart are not properly synchronized; heart failure, in which the heart simply cannot pump enough blood to meet the body's needs; and cor pulmonale, a failure of the right side of the heart that results from lung diseases such as emphysema.

Tumors of the heart muscle are not common, but they can occur. The most common tumor is a myxoma, which is benign rather than malignant and grows inside one of the chambers of the heart. While some malignant sarcomas can develop in the heart tissue, the more common kind of cancer that affects the heart results from the spread of cells from a malignancy elsewhere in the body, such as the breast or lung, to the heart. These metastases, as they are called, can grow within the heart muscle or the pericardium, the sac that surrounds the heart, but rarely affect the heart valves.

Further Reading
American Heart Association, *Your Heart: An Owner's Manual* (1995); American Heart Association, *American Heart Association Guide to Heart Attack Treatment, Recovery, and Prevention* (1998); Debakey, Michael, E., and Gotto, Antonio, *The New Living Heart* (1997); Ewing, Douglas C., *A Patient's Guide to Coronary Bypass Surgery and Its Aftermath* (1996).

Special topics in this area are found in BLOOD; CIRCULATORY SYSTEMS; SURGERY. *Advanced subjects are developed in* BLOOD PRESSURE; HOMEOSTASIS; NON-INFECTIOUS DISEASE. *Additional aspects of this subject are covered in* ANGIOPLASTY; ORGAN TRANSPLANTATION; STRESS.

First see TEMPERATURE

Heat

Next see ENTROPY

Until the early nineteenth century, heat was believed to be a substance, gas or fluid, called "caloric," said to flow from object to object. Heat today is known to be a form of energy that passes from a body at a relatively high temperature to a body at a lower temperature. Heat equals increased motion of the molecules that make up a substance. The thermal properties of matter include specific heat, thermal conductivity, thermal convection and latent heat. (*See* THERMAL REGULATION.)

Specific Heat. The amount of heat required to produce a specified increase in temperature in a unit mass of a substance is called the specific heat of that substance. The units used for specific heat are the gram and the calorie. Specific heat indicates the ratio of the heat that is absorbed to the increase in temperature for a given substance in comparison to a standard

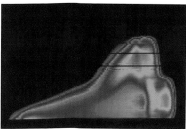

Heat profile of the Space Shuttle, showing increased temperature at the wings.

substance, most often water, which has a high specific heat. For example, the specific heat of acetone is 0.5, meaning that half as much heat is needed to achieve a set temperature rise in a given mass of acetone as is needed for an equal mass of water. The specific heats of most liquids and solids remain constant over a wide range of temperatures. But the specific heats of gases are changed not only by the temperatures at which they are measured but also by the conditions of measurement. Gas contained in a balloon that can expand has a higher specific heat than a gas

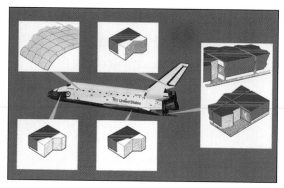

The ceramic tiles used on the Space Shuttle are designed to withstand extreme temperatures encountered in different parts of the hull.

in a rigid container that does not allow expansion, because some of the heat absorbed by the gas is convected into the expansion, rather than an increase in temperature.

Conductivity. Thermal conductivity is the quantity of heat transmitted in a unit of time across a unit of mass for a given change in temperature. There are several mechanisms of thermal conductivity. One is the increased movement of atoms and molecules caused by an increase in temperature, which causes the atoms and molecules to jostle one another. Another mechanism depends on the fact that good conductors of heat, like good conductors of electricity, have active electrons. In substances that are electrical insulators, on the other hand, imperfections limit not only electrical conductivity but also heat conductivity.

Convection. Thermal convection is the transfer of heat by the circulation of a liquid or gas. An example is the quick heating of a kettle of water when a flame is applied at the bottom. Water is not a good conductor of heat, but as water is warmed at the bottom of the kettle, it becomes less dense and rises. Cold water sinks, to be warmed in turn. The heating coil of a radiator system and a gasoline engine are cooled by circulation caused by thermal convection; in the engine, the circulation may be increased by a small rotary pump.

Latent Heat. There are several kinds of latent heat. The latent heat of fusion is the amount of heat needed to convert a unit of mass of a substance from a solid to a liquid state while the substance remains at the same temperature. The latent heat of sublimation is the amount of heat needed for the conversion of a substance from a solid to a gas while the temperature remains unchanged. The latent heat of vaporization is the amount of heat needed to cause the evaporation of a given mass of liquid.

Further developments in the field are discussed in ENERGY; GASES, BEHAVIOR OF; TEMPERATURE. *More details regarding heat can be found in* ENTROPY; THERMODYNAMIC CYCLES; THERMOMETRY. *Additional relevant information is contained in* PHASE; REFRIGERATION; THERMODYNAMICS.

First see BLOOD

Hemophilia

Next see GENETIC DISEASES

An inherited blood disorder that is caused by lack of a blood protein, called factor VIII, essential to the blood-clotting process.

Hemophilia is the result of an inherited faulty factor VIII gene; it occurs almost always in males. About one in every 10,000 males born in the United States has hemophilia. An affected man transmits the gene only to his daughters. They are carriers and can pass the gene to their daughters, who also become carriers, and their sons, who can develop the disease.

Hemophiliacs can suffer frequent bleeding episodes, in which blood leaks into their joints and muscles. These episodes usually begin during childhood and can cause deformities of the knees, ankles, and other joints. Internal bleeding can also occur frequently; even a tooth extraction can set off a bleeding episode. These can be controlled by infusions of factor VIII, given immediately after bleeding starts. Until recently, most hemophiliacs did not survive childhood, but the availability of factor VIII infusions has lengthened life expectancy considerably.

The AIDS epidemic caused problems with the use of factor VIII, which used to be obtained from large pools of blood given by up to 5,000 donors. Many hemophiliacs became infected with the AIDS virus during the early years of the epidemic, but blood is now routinely screened to detect the virus, and synthetic blood factors have been developed. (*See* AIDS.)

First see VIRUS

Herpes

Next see VIRAL DISEASES

A term used to describe many viral infections that cause an eruption of small blisters on the skin.

Most herpes infections are caused by the herpes simplex virus, of which there are two forms:

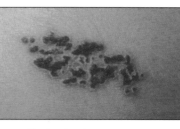

Lesion of herpes zoster (shingles).

Further Reading
Fuchs, Hans, U., *The Dynamics of Heat* (1996); Granger, Robert, *Experiments in Heat Transfer and Thermodynamics* (1994); Pobell, Frank, *Matter and Methods at Low Temperatures* (1996); Zemansky, Mark, *Heat and Thermodynamics* (1981).

Below, an electron micrograph of the Herpes simplex virus.

HSV1 (type 1) and HSV2 (type 2). HSV1 most often causes infections of the mouth, face, and lips, while HSV2 most frequently causes infections of the genital area; it can also cause infections acquired by babies at birth. The viruses are spread by direct contact with the blisters that they cause or with the fluid within them.

Most people acquire the HSV1 virus early in life, but it often causes no detectable symptoms. It can be activated from time to time, however, causing problems such as cold sores, which erupt around the mouth. These eruptions can be caused by an elevation in body temperature resulting from exposure to the sun or from fever. HSV1 can also cause a finger infection called a herpetic whitlow, whose major symptom is an eruption of extremely painful blisters. HSV1 infection is most dangerous in persons with AIDS or those who are taking drugs to suppress the immune system; the infections can then be fatal. HSV2 is the usual cause of genital herpes, which produces painful blisters on the sex organs.

First see STAR

Hertzsprung-Russell Diagram

Next see UNIVERSE, EVOLUTION OF

The Hertzsprung-Russell diagram was developed early in the twentieth century by American astronomer Henry Norris Russell and Danish astronomer Ejnar Hertzsprung as a way to display the relationship between the absolute magnitude, or brightness, of stars and their spectral class or color index. Brightness is usually shown on the y-axis, top to bottom, and spectral class on the x-axis, left to right. The y-axis thus represents the energy output of a star and the x-axis represents its surface temperature. Most of the stars in a Hertzsprung-Russell diagram fall into a broad band running from the top left to the bottom right of the graph. These are called main-sequence stars; our sun is one of them. The sun can be found near the center of the main sequence band, just to the right of the center of the diagram.

Main Sequences. The main sequence band represents stars converting hydrogen to helium through nuclear reactions in their cores. Stars found off the main sequence shine for some other reason, such as burning hydrogen in regions outside their cores, burning other elements, showing the effects of gravitational contraction, or radiating residual heat into space. The location of a star on the main sequence thus indicates both its mass and its energy generation process.

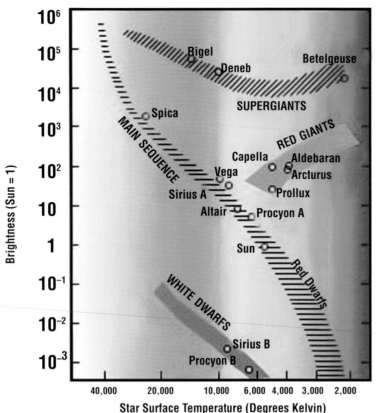

Brightness (Sun = 1)

10^6	
10^5	Rigel
	Deneb
10^4	Betelgeuse
10^3	Spica SUPERGIANTS
10^2	MAIN SEQUENCE RED GIANTS Capella Aldebaran
	Vega Arcturus
10	Sirius A Prollux
	Altair Procyon A
1	Sun
10^{-1}	Red Dwarfs
10^{-2}	WHITE DWARFS
10^{-3}	Sirius B
	Procyon B

40,000 20,000 10,000 6,000 4,000 3,000 2,000

Star Surface Temperature (Degrees Kelvin)

Above, the Hertzsprung-Russell diagram, plotting the evolution of stars.

The other classes of stars identified on the Hertzsprung-Russell diagram include:

Red Dwarfs. Red dwarfs are cool stars found in the main sequence. However, the masses of red dwarfs are much less than that of the sun. They are found at the bottom right end of the main sequence. Their colors range from orange to red. The nearest star to the sun, Proxima Centauri, is a red dwarf.

Red Giants. Above and to the right of the main sequence, red giants have masses that are about the same as that of the sun. Red giants are stars that have already passed through the main sequence stage, so that most of the hydrogen in their cores has been converted to helium. They are now burning hydrogen to helium in a shell just outside their cores.

Red Supergiants. These are very large, cooler stars with masses several times that of the sun. They are found in the upper right-hand corner of the diagram. Red supergiants have evolved well beyond the main sequence stage, so the nuclear reactions that take place within them are forming elements heavier than carbon. Red supergiants eventually will explode, becoming Type II supernovas.

Blue Giants. Blue-white in appearance, blue giants have masses many times that of the sun. A blue giant is still in the main sequence, burning hydrogen in its core. They are found in the uppermost left-hand corner of the diagram. One conspicuous blue giant is Alkaid, the star at the end of the handle of the Big Dipper.

Blue Supergiants. These are massive stars that have left the main sequence, having burned most of the hydrogen in their cores. They are brighter than the blue giants, and so lie toward the left of the diagram. One blue supergiant is Rigel, the brightest blue-white star in the constellation Orion.

White Dwarfs. These small dense stars, the masses of which are about 1.4 times the mass of the sun, are found to the left of the diagram, well below the main sequence. A white dwarf is in the last stage of stellar evolution. Nuclear reactions that release energy are no longer taking place in their cores. Instead, they are growing cooler, their surfaces are dimming, and eventually they will become invisible to observers.

Bare Spots. There are some regions of the Hertzsprung-Russell diagram that are bare, with few or no observed stars. This does not necessarily mean that there are no stars with the brightness and temperature needed to occupy these regions. There may well have been stars with these values that displayed their brightness and temperature for only brief periods, so that astronomers on Earth have had little chance to observe them.

Background material can be found in GALAXY; MILKY WAY; NEBULAE; STAR; SUN. *Further developments in the field are discussed in* BROWN AND WHITE DWARFS; GLOBULAR CLUSTERS; NOVAS AND SUPERNOVAS; RED GIANT STAR. *Special topics in this area are found in* INTERSTELLAR MEDIUM *and* UNIVERSE.

First see WELDING

High-rise Construction

Next see ARCHITECTURAL ENGINEERING

The principles of high-rise construction began to be established toward the end of the nineteenth century with the development of high-strength building materials. As early as 1885, engineers and architects had learned how to use girders made of steel to make an internal building frame of columns, beams and shelf angles, arranged to carry thin external walls made of materials that did not bear any load, such as glass. This technique soon became known as skyscraper construction. Advances in design that were introduced in the following decades included wind-bracing of frames, increased vertical framing, welding of building elements, and the use of pre-fabricated panels for walls, making it possible to raise the height of skyscrapers to 1,000 feet or more. (*See* HIGHWAY ENGINEERING.)

Major advances have also been made in the use of concrete as a building material. The development of reinforced concrete at the turn of the twentieth century made it possible to utilize it as the basic element of the internal frames of taller buildings. In the decades that have fol-

At far left, 78 stories up, construction workers finish the roof and spire of the Central Plaza Building on Hong Kong Island. The complex pattern that a highway crossover exhibits can be seen in the photograph to the left.

lowed, reinforced concrete has been used in flat-slab construction, in which beams are not necessary. Reinforced concrete is also used to make slender arch ribs, thin shells and plates for construction purposes. These applications have made it possible for architects to design building vaults and domes that have very wide, clear spans made of shells that can be only a few inches thick. These advances have produced the modern high-rise structure, which gives an appearance of extraordinary lightness and delicacy in buildings that are in reality much more massive than the bulky-looking masonry structures of past centuries. (*See also* CONCRETE.)

First see AUTOMOTIVE DESIGN

Highway Engineering

Next see ARCHITECTURAL ENGINEERING

Higway engineering involves the design and construction of main arteries built to carry heavy, nonstop traffic. This field of engineering goes back to the ancient Romans, who built extensive networks of roads and made highway engineering a part of city planning. Roman roads were essentially walls that were horizontal rather than vertical. They had bottom and top layers of closely fitted stone blocks, with loose, rubble-like fill between them. A network of roads radiated from Rome to every part of the Roman Empire.

After Rome fell, road engineering remained static until the eighteenth century, when French roads consisting of flat stones that were piled on one another, and that thus could be easily displaced by heavy wagons, were replaced by highways that had foundations of stones set on edge and held in place by strong stone curbs. Above this foundation were several layers of crushed stone that were arched so that water would run off them into gutters on each side of the road.

Great Britain assumed the leadership in highway engineering in the nineteenth century. One of the great names of British road-building was John Loudon McAdam, who developed surfacing that consisted of compacted layers of broken stone; "macadam" is still a term that is commonly used in highway engineering.

Turnpikes. In the United States, the first important surfaced road was the 62-mile-long Lancaster Turnpike built between 1792 and 1794 in Pennsylvania, with a broken-stone surface. But the era of railroad building opened, and so highway engineering became a neglected enterprise for half a century. Toward the end of the nineteenth century, however, the need for new and better roads was created first by the popularity of the bicycle and then by the arrival of the automobile. The first modern highway system was the German Autobahn, constructed in the 1930s and still in use today. In the United States, the Interstate highway system was begun in 1953 and finally completed in 1997.

The concern of highway engineers includes the layout of roads and their curves, rises, and falls, ensuring that the cars remain stable at all times, and that drivers have a clear line of sight. Highway surfacing materials are constantly being improved. The surface of a highway must be designed to sustain the weight of the heaviest vehicles expected to travel on it and to bear up for long periods of time under the continuous friction of the wheels of those vehicles. The surface must also resist the deterioration that can be caused by expansion in the heat of summer and contraction in the cold of winter.

Background material can be found in AUTOMOTIVE DESIGN; CARTOGRAPHY AND SURVEYING; GEODETIC SURVEY; HIGH-RISE CONSTRUCTION. *Advanced subjects are developed in* BRIDGE DESIGN; SOIL CHEMISTRY. *More information on particular aspects is contained in* ECOLOGY; HYDRAULICS; WELDING.

First see VIRUS

HIV (Human Immunodeficiency Virus)

Next see AIDS

Human immunodeficiency virus, or HIV, is the infectious agent that causes AIDS, acquired immunodeficiency syndrome. HIV infection can be contracted by unprotected sexual activity, by sharing unsanitary drug needles, and through blood transfusion—although recently, the latter has become increasingly rare due to careful screening. Once it enters the body, HIV attaches itself to the T-lymphocytes, cells that coordinate the attack of the body's immune defense system against infectious bacteria and viruses. Once inside the lymphocytes, HIV takes over the cells' genetic apparatus, so that multiple copies of HIV are produced. After they multiply inside one lymphocyte cell, the new HIVs come out of the cell and infect other lymphocytes. The immune system tries to overcome this cycle of infection by producing antibodies, but it cannot succeed because HIV continues to reproduce itself, destroying lymphocytes, and eventually weakening the body's defenses to the extent that it can no longer fight off ordinary infectious agents that would not otherwise be a serious threat. (*See* IMMUNE RESPONSE.)

The signs and symptoms of HIV infection include persistent fatigue, night sweats, unexpected weight loss, chronic diarrhea, persistent white spots on the tongue, blotches inside the mouth or nose, and difficulty with speech, memory, concentration, or coordination. Untreated, HIV infection can cause death in a brief period of time. Several drugs now can be used to treat HIV infection, but the virus and AIDS continues to spread. The World Health Organization estimates that more than 40 million people worldwide are infected with HIV, and that about two million of them are residents of the United States. (*See* AIDS.)

First see LYMPHATIC SYSTEM

Hodgkin's Disease

Next see AUTOIMMUNITY

A malignancy of the lymphoid tissue of the lymph nodes and the spleen, which are important parts of the body's immune defense system.

The cause of Hodgkin's disease is unknown. It is rare, with only three cases diagnosed for every 100,000 Americans every year. Most often, the first symptom is enlargement of lymph nodes, generally those in the neck or the armpits. The major symptoms of Hodgkin's disease are caused by a gradual reduction in the effectiveness of the body's immune defense system. Increasing impairment of the body's immune response can turn an infection that normally is easily handled into a life-threatening condition. Treatment—most effective if the disease is detected early—includes radiation therapy and anticancer drugs.

With early detection and treatment, up to 80 percent of patients survive for five years or more.

Right, the making of a laser hologram—in this instance, of the skull of the Taung child—for use on a magazine cover. Holography offers the possibility of stereoscopic motion pictures and television (but not the only possibility; see CRYSTAL).

First see LASER AND MASER

Holography

Next see INTERFERENCE

A method of recording and displaying a three-dimensional image, using the coherent light of a laser.

Holography was first developed by Dennis Gabor in 1948, before lasers were available, and has flourished in the era of laser light. Whereas an ordinary photograph records just the various intensities of light falling on a scene, a hologram records information about both the intensity and phase, the ups and downs of light waves. The phase condition requires that the light be coherent in two ways, temporally and spatially. Temporal coherence requires monochromatic light; spatial coherence requires the light to travel in a straight line.

Process. To make a hologram, two beams of coherent light are used. One falls directly on a photographic plate or film. The other strikes the object or scene that is being recorded and then falls on the film. The result is a series of interference patterns. In ordinary light, the film appears to be gray and almost featureless. But when the film is

Above, identical twins pose together for a holographic picture.

illuminated by a beam of coherent light (preferably from the original source), two images are formed: a real image behind the film or photographic plate, and a virtual image. Both are three-dimensional. It is possible to look around an object in the foreground of the hologram and see what is behind it.

Causes. This three-dimensionality is made possible by the information stored in the interference patterns. These consist of alternating bright and dark lines called fringes. The reason why a hologram appears gray in ordinary light is that these fringes are too small for the eye to see. When coherent light strikes the fringes, it is diffracted so that the original object becomes visible.

Holograms can be classified according to the material on which the interference pattern is recorded, the orientation of the recording light beams, and the optical system needed to record and reconstruct the hologram. Sometimes holograms are classified as thick or thin. A thick hologram produces a single reconstructing beam, and a thin hologram can produce several beams.

Applications. The largest commercial application of holography is in nondestructive testing. Holograms are also used to store digital images and data, for image processing, for precise interferometric measurements, and for pattern recognition.

For example, a hologram can be used to perform the same functions as lenses and prisms. If a hologram is made from a plane wave and a spherical wave, it can produce the same kind of image as a positive lens. Some of these holographic optical elements, as they are called, are used to display cockpit instrument information on the visors of pilot helmets. They also allow chemists to move virtual atoms and molecules about as they design new drugs in virtual space.

Background material on holography can be found in INTERFERENCE; LIGHT; MIRRORS; OPTICS; PHOTOGRAPHY, CHEMISTRY OF. *Further developments in the field are discussed in* LASERS AND MASERS; POLARIZED LIGHT. *Special topics in this area are found in* CD-ROM; FIBER OPTICS; VIRTUAL REALITY.

First see CELL

Homeostasis

Next see THERMAL REGULATION

The maintenance of a relatively steady internal state within a cell, organism, or larger biological system by intrinsic regulatory mechanisms.

Homeostasis is necessary to preserve physical conditions favorable to life in the face of wild external fluctuations and a hostile environment.

Homeostasis is a central concept in animal physiology. Homeostatic mechanisms were first described in mammals, because they are able to maintain their body temperature within a relatively narrow range, allowing cells to function efficiently. Another important element in homeostasis is osmoregulation, which preserves a stable fluid environment by controlling the concentration of water, sodium, potassium, and other solutes within the organism.

In organisms, the typical homeostatic system involves negative feedback, in which deviation from the "setpoint," or norm, triggers a corrective action. Such systems usually operate only within certain tolerance limits. If the limits are exceeded, positive feedback may take over, increasing the deviant conditions to fatal levels.

Plant and animal populations are sometimes said to exhibit homeostasis in their tendency to fluctuate in size around a mean. When populations become too dense, competition, starvation, disease, and immigration tend to correct the balance, much as a negative feedback system would in an organism.

The term *homeostasis* is also used to describe the stability seen in ecosystems, which frequently can resist stress (an ability termed resistance stability) or recover quickly from damage (resilience stability). The ability of the biosphere as a whole to maintain stability in its atmosphere and oceans is a key concept of the Gaia theory, which holds that the planet is one integrated, homeostatic, self-regulating system.

The foundations of the subject are discussed in ADAPTATION; BIODIVERSITY; OSMOSIS; ECOLOGY. *More details can be found in* COEVOLUTION; NITROGEN AND PHOSPHOROUS CYCLES; PREDATION. *Advanced subjects are developed in* EUTROPHICATION; GAIA HYPOTHESIS; POPULATION ECOLOGY.

First see EVOLUTION

Homo Sapiens

Next see AUSTRALOPITHECUS

Modern humans belong to the species *Homo sapiens* and the hominid family, which diverged from the primate order millions of years ago. A creature known as *Ramapithecus*, which originated in Africa approximately 17 million years ago, may be the common ancestor of both apes and humans, though recent genetic studies indicate that it split off from the evolutionary branch that leads to modern humans.

Human origins and evolution are studied-based on the evidence provided by the fossil record. Characteristics of the skull used to distinguish between apes and humans include the location of the hole for the spinal cord; the angle at which the spinal cord enters the skull, the angle of the face in relation to the spine, the size of the cranial cavity, and the forehead structure.

Earliest Hominids. The first recognizable hominids appeared in Africa around 4 million years ago. They were Australopithecines, a very primitive creature that was still more advanced than an ape. The best-known fossil of an *Australopithecus afarensis* is known as Lucy, and is thought to be between 3 and 4 million years old.

Other species of Austalopithecines have been found in East and South Africa. *Australopithecus africanus* lived in southern Africa between 3 and 2.5 million years ago, was about five feet tall and had a rounded skull and larger brain capacity than *Australopithecus afarensis*.

Further Reading
Chiras, Daniel D., *Human Biology: Health, Homeostasis, and the Environment* (1995); Hardy, Richard Neville, *Ecosystem Homeostasis* (1984); Hardy, R. N., *Homeostasis* (1986); Langley, Lee, *Homeostasis: Origins of the Concept* (1990).

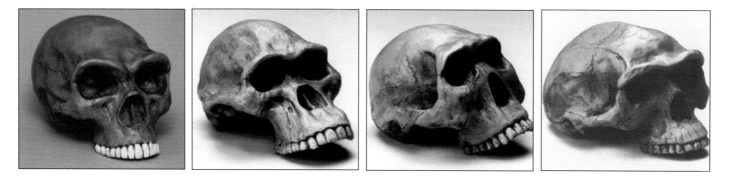

Assembling a credible picture of the development of the human species has been a difficult undertaking. Above, from left and going back in time: skull of a large, robust, fully bipedal hominid with heavy bone structure, indicating strong musculature; skull of a bipedal hominid with similar bone structure to a modern human but different musculature, probably a holdover from earlier forms; skull of *Australopithecus afarensis*, the first creature that can lay claim to being human; skull of *Homo erectus*, marking a turning point in primate evolution.

Australopithecus robustus appeared between 2.2 to 1.4 million years ago. *Australopithecus robustus* was even larger than *Australopithecus africanus*. There are questions about descent relationships between the two groups: some paleontologists believe *Australopithecus robustus* evolved from *Australopithecus africanus* in a separate line of descent from humans; others think humans did not evolve from any of the Australopithecines.

All species of *Australopithecus* walked upright, as indicated by their skeletal structures. They had relatively long arms, which may have been an adaptation to a tree-dwelling life.

CONNECTIONS

Apewoman?

Lucy was a member of the species *Australopithecus afarensis* and exhibited characteristics of both apes and humans. Lucy was only about 39 inches tall. Her skull and face were very apelike but her hip and leg bones provide evidence for upright locomotion. The skull was much larger than that of an ape, indicating a larger brain, but there is no evidence of tool use. The Lucy fossil proves, however, that brain size of early humans increased after the development of the ability to stand upright.

Between 2.2 and 1.5 million years ago, a new genus, *Homo*, appeared. The earliest species was *Homo habilis*, whose name means "handy human." Fossilized remains of *Homo habilis* were discovered by members of the famous Leakey family of scientists in East Africa in the early 1960s. *Homo habilis* is believed to be the first humanlike species to make tools.

Change in the Weather. At around the time of the appearance of *Homo*, the climate changed, becoming cooler and dryer. The forests gave way to open grasslands, which may have led to the evolution of *Homo* over earlier forms.

Approximately 1.5 million years ago *Homo habilis* was "replaced" by *Homo erectus*, a much larger-brained specimen. *Homo erectus* was the first widely distributed hominid.

The first fossil of *Homo erectus* was found on Java in 1891, and was known as "Java Man." Other fossils were found in China, near the city of Peking (now Beijing), as well as in Europe, the Middle East and Africa. It was first thought that *Homo erectus* originated in Asia, but the Asian fossils are "younger" than the *Homo erectus* fossils found in Africa.

Recent study of some of the Asian fossils suggests that *Homo erectus* arrived in eastern Asia within only a few hundred thousand years of arising in Africa. The migration and dispersal may have been driven by the changing climate.

Homo erectus survived until 300,000 years ago. During that time, the species remained relatively unchanged physically. The skeleton still had features similar to both apes and humans. The bones were thicker and heavier than human ones, and the skull had a low forehead, no chin, and large teeth. As its name implies, *Homo erectus* walked upright, but with a more striding gait than any earlier species. Its brain capacity was nearly that of modern humans.

Homo erectus groups manufactured large flaked stone tools like hand axes and may have used fire. They were nomads, moving from one site to another to obtain food and other materials as needed. Later hominids, from 1.6 million years ago, exhibited territory scavenging, in which small resource locales were used simultaneously instead of sequentially.

The Neanderthals. The next major species arose by the end of *Homo erectus*' time period and may have coexisted with them briefly. Formally called Neanderthals, after a valley in Germany where the fossilized remains were first discovered in 1856, they were archaic *Homo sapiens* who lived in Europe and Asia during the Ice Age, between 130,000 and 35,000 years ago.

Neanderthals were more robust and much stronger than the modern humans who replaced them. They were about five feet tall and had thick skulls, sloping foreheads, heavy brow ridges, and protruding jaws with large teeth that may have been used as tools. Their cranial capacities were larger than those of modern humans.

Neanderthals were nomadic hunter-gatherers who lived in caves. They used hand-held

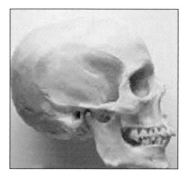

tools made of bone and stone and wore animal skins. They used fire. They exhibited ritual activity such as burial of the dead. They do not appear to have been able to articulate many vowels. Neanderthals disappear from the fossil record approximately 30,000 years ago. They may have evolved into modern humans or simply become extinct due to competition with the new species.

Cro-Magnon. Anatomically modern humans appear to have arisen outside Europe, possibly originating in Africa. They may have coexisted with their more primitive forebears for several thousand years. Fossils of these humans, formerly called Cro-Magnon, were discovered in 1868 in the Cro-Magnon Cave in France. Some of these early modern humans show primitive skeletal characteristics, like large brows and teeth, which may be holdover characteristics from interbreeding with Neanderthals. Otherwise they are not physically distinguishable from humans living today.

Race. As populations of humans settled specific areas and became relatively isolated from each other, certain physical characteristics became more pronounced. This gave rise to what were formerly called races. Gene pool divisions, however, produce many more numbers of human groups than the "traditional" races.

In recent years, travel, migration, and intermarriage have broken down many of these barriers. As geographic isolation becomes more and more a thing of the past and gene pools intermingle, it has become even more evident that all humans, despite physical differences, are members of the same species. Some want to cast the net of the human family even wider to include chimpanzees, who share 98 percent of their DNA with us and are the closest living relatives to humans. Some include them in the human genus as well, as *Homo troglodytes*.

Elementary aspects of this subject are covered in EVOLUTION; ICE AGE; PRIMATES. *Additional information on particular aspects is contained in* ADAPTATION; AUSTRALOPITHECUS; NATURAL SELECTION. *Relevant information is also contained in* FOSSIL; LIFE, DEFINITION OF; NEANDERTHAL.

Richard Leakey with a reconstructed skull of *Homo habilis*, above. Left, skull of *Homo erectus*.

Edwin Hubble (1889–1953) at the eyepiece of the telescope at the Mount Wilson Observatory in Pasadena, California.

Further Reading
Jones, Steve, *The Cambridge Encyclopedia of Human Evolution* (1992); Lewin, Roger, *Bones of Contention* (1997); Lewin, Roger, *The Origin of Modern Humans* (1998); Napier, John, *Hands* (1993); Stanley, Steven, *Children of the Ice Age* (1998); Stringer, Christopher, *African Exodus: The Origins of Modern Humanity* (1997); Tattersall, Ian, *Becoming Human: Evolution and Human Uniqueness* (1998).

First see DOPPLER EFFECT

Hubble Constant

Next see UNIVERSE, LARGE-SCALE STRUCTURE OF

The relationship between the rate at which the stars and galaxies are moving away from Earth and the distance of those stars and galaxies from the Earth.

The Hubble constant is named for American astronomer Edwin Hubble, who formulated the rule in the 1920s.

Hubble originally calculated the value of the constant to be 550 kilometers per second per megaparsec. (A megaparsec is one million parsecs; one parsec is 19.16 million million miles.) He based his estimate on the observations that astronomers had made of the red shift, the lengthening of light waves caused by a star's movement away from Earth. Calculating backward from the value of the Hubble constant gives a time when all the matter of the universe was at a central point and its expansion began. That time is the age of the universe, which Hubble calculated to be two billion years.

In recent decades, other astronomers have recalculated the value of the Hubble constant. Hubble's value was based on observations of Cepheid variable stars and assumed that all those stars had the same relationship between the period of time during which their light and their brightness varied. More recent studies have found that the relationship is different for Cepheids in the spiral arms of galaxies and those in globular clusters. Recent measurements with the Hubble Space Telescope place the Hubble constant at 70 kilometers per second per megaparsec, which puts the lifetime of the universe at about 12 billion years.

First see GENETIC DISEASES

Huntington's Disease

Next see GENE THERAPY

A relatively rare genetic condition in which there is degeneration of the basal ganglia, an area of nerve cells in the brain.

Huntington's disease, often called Huntington's chorea, results in involuntary, jerky, rapid movements of the body and progressive deterioration of mental function. The disease has an autosomal pattern of inheritance; it is caused by a single abnormal gene. The incidence is low, with only five cases for every 100,000 people. The symptoms of Huntington's disease can appear in childhood, but such an early onset is uncommon. Most often, symptoms began to appear at the age of 35 or later. This late onset means that a person who carries the flawed gene often has had children, who then have a 50 percent chance of inheriting that gene. (*See* GENETICS.)

The chorea can affect the arms, trunk, and face, causing facial twitches and grimaces and an overall clumsiness of movement. The effects on the brain can result in changes in personality and behavior, as well as irritability, loss of memory, and overall apathy.

It is only in recent years that advances in genetic medicine have made it possible to determine whether a child of a person with Huntington's disease has inherited the abnormal gene. That determination can now be made with more than 95 percent accuracy. A person who carries the gene but has not yet shown symptoms of the disease can undergo genetic counseling. There is no treatment for the disease, but drugs such as chlorpromazine can help reduce the involuntary movements. (*See* BRAIN.)

First see CORIOLUS FORCE

Hurricanes and Tornadoes

Next see WEATHER

Hurricanes and tornadoes are different kinds of atmospheric disturbances. A hurricane is a cyclonic storm that originates over a tropical ocean, with winds at speeds of at least 74 miles an hour. Hurricanes are called "ty-phoons" when they occur over the western Pacific Ocean and "cyclones" when they occur over the Indian Ocean. A tornado, in sharp contrast, is a violently circulating column of air that extends downward from a thundercloud and usually has a diameter of several hundred yards.

Hurricanes. Hurricanes usually form near the equator during the summer and autumn and

Above, the cloud pattern of Hurricane Luis, April 1996, shows the pressure sinkhole at the eye of the storm.

often move far westward before they turn northward and accelerate into the westerly wind belt of the middle latitudes. The energy source for a hurricane is the latent heat of condensation released when warm, moist air rises into the cloud system around the center of the hurricane. At their most forceful, wind speeds of over 150 miles per hour and barometric pressures as low as 26.35 inches of mercury have been measured near the centers of hurricanes.

The strongest winds and heaviest rains usually are found in a zone that forms a ring around the center of the hurricane. Inside this ring, which can be up to 25 miles in radius, is the well-known eye of the hurricane. The eye is a region at the very center of the storm in which there is less cloudiness, much lower wind speeds—perhaps 20 miles per hour—and little or no rain. Outside the central ring there is a region in which squalls and thunderstorms occur, often in spiral-shaped bands. The most significantly destructive wind and weather conditions of a hurricane are found almost entirely inside the area covered by the spiral bands.

Tornadoes. On a local scale, tornadoes are a more destructive atmospheric phenomenon. A tornado can be recognized by the funnel cloud that is formed consisting of small water droplets cooled and condensed by the low pressures near the center of the tornado. Some tornadoes never reach the ground. They can oscillate upward and downward before they do touch down. The wind speed of a tornado may be in the neighborhood of 300 miles per hour.

Most tornadoes produce a loud roaring noise, which has been compared to the buzzing of billions of bees or the roar of many jet aircrafts. This noisy, whirling column of air may last only a few minutes, but that may be enough time for great destruction to be caused in its path. The air pressure at the center of a tornado is extremely low; buildings in the path of the tornado may literally explode because of the sudden drastic reduction of air pressure.

Right, satellite photo of Hurricane Elena in the Gulf of Mexico, heading toward the Mexican coast in September, 1985.

Tornadoes have been observed on all continents; they are common in the United States, occuring frequently in the spring months in the Central Plains. There are about 150 tornadoes in an average year in the United States, and more than 200 persons each year suffer injuries caused by them. Residents of regions in which tornadoes are most common often have underground shelters to which they retreat for protection when a storm approaches.

Related areas to be considered are Atmosphere; Climatology; Weather. *Other aspects of the subject are discussed in* Remote Sensing; Wind and Clouds. *Related material can be found in* Coastal Engineering; Ocean Currents; Paleoclimatology.

Further Reading

Davidson, Keay, *Twister: The Science of Tornadoes and the Making of an Adventure Movie* (1996); Faidley, Warren, *Storm Chaser: In Pursuit of Untamed Skies* (1996); Longshore, *Encyclopedia of Hurricanes, Typhoons, and Cyclones* (1998); Pielke, Roger, A., *Hurricanes: Their Nature and Impact on Society* (1998); Rosenfeld, Jeffrey O., *Eye of the Storm* (1999).

First see Liquid

Hydraulics

Next see Fluid Mechanics

The applied science that deals with the flow of water and other liquids.

Hydraulics is one of the oldest applied sciences, dating back to antiquity. Most recently, it has become a branch of the newer field called the general mechanics of fluids.

Three Principles. One of the basic principles of hydraulics is continuity, which states that the mean velocity at which a fluid flows is inversely proportional to the size of the cross-section of the stream; in other words, a fluid will flow at a higher speed in narrower sections of a stream.

Another principle of hydraulics is conservation of momentum, which states that the external force exerted on a liquid in a given region of the stream equals the rate at which the momentum of the liquid changes as it passes through that region. Momentum is determined by multiplying the mass of the fluid by the speed at which it flows. The momentum principle means that if a liquid flow changes either its speed or its direction, that change must be due either to the force of gravity or the pressure exerted on the liquid

by the boundary of the passage through which it is flowing.

A third principle of hydraulics, energy, states that the rate at which the kinetic energy of a flowing liquid changes is equal to the rate at which work is done on it. Kinetic energy is defined as half the mass of the liquid multiplied by the square of its velocity, and work is determined by multiplying the force of the liquid by the distance it moves. The energy of a flowing fluid is usually expressed by the Bernoulli equation, named for the eighteenth-century Swiss scientist who developed it.

History. The principles of hydraulics have been applied for many centuries in such devices as hydraulic machines, which are run by the pressure or motion of a liquid. These machines go back to the Archimedes screw. The same prinicple was in use even earlier to raise water for irrigation in Egypt. Modern hydraulic machines include the impulse wheel, the reaction turbine, and the centrifugal pump. The impulse wheel is driven by a jet of water at high pressure. Because of the extra pressure, the impulse wheel can deliver much more power than the water wheel, which was widely used in past centuries and remains in use in some nonindustrialized societies.

In a reaction turbine, a series of nozzles admits water around the edge of the wheel that is to be turned. This allows for the generation of a great deal of power. At the Hoover Dam for example, some hydraulic devices of this type generate 115,000 horsepower.

A centrifugal pump is operated by setting up a variation of the pressure in a rotating fluid—usually expressed as centrifugal force. In a centrifugal pump, water or another fluid is propelled by a device called an impeller, which has vanes that drive the water out of a nozzle. Centrifugal pumps are used when high liquid pressure is needed as, for example, in pipelines.

Engineering. Hydraulic engineering is important in the control of natural water flow for industrial or domestic water supples, irrigation and drainage, and sewage disposal. Hydraulics is also applied to flood prediction and control, the construction and maintenance of harbors, and the generation of electric power.

Because the flow of water is very complex, hydraulic engineers often use scale models to help them design specific systems or structures. The simplest hydraulic applications involve hydrostatics, systems in which liquids are not in motion. Hydrostatic systems can include dams, and the principles of hydrostatics can also be applied to systems in which water or another liquid has minimal motion, such as structures that are immersed in water or float on it. In many ways, hydraulics is as essential to our modern society as it was to the ancient Egyptians. (*See* Dams *and* Coastal Engineering.)

First see ORGANIC COMPOUND

Hydrocarbon

Next see PETROLOGY

Among the simplest organic compounds, containing only carbon and hydrogen.

Hydrocarbons may be as small as one carbon atom in length or extend to thousands of atoms. All the atoms are held together by covalent bonds in which electrons are shared between the atoms. The majority of hydrocarbons consist of relatively long chains of linked carbon atoms with hydrogen atoms attached on the sides to ensure that each carbon has a total of four bonds.

If there are only single bonds (one pair of shared electrons) between adjacent carbons, carbons on the end of the chain will have three hydrogen atoms attached while middle carbons will have only two. Hydrocarbon chains containing only single bonds are said to be saturated. If any carbons in the chain are connected by double or triple bonds (two or three pairs of shared electrons), the corresponding number of hydrogens will go down and the chain is unsaturated.

In addition to being either saturated or unsaturated, hydrocarbons may be straight or branched chains. The latter have minichains extending from the main chain or root. Both these types are called open-chain or aliphatic hydrocarbons. Chains may also be cyclic, with the end carbons bonding to each other to create a closed structure. (*See* BOND, CHEMICAL.)

Hydrocarbons may contain exclusively carbon and hydrogen, or incorporate other elements as well, such as oxygen, nitrogen, and various members of the halogen family. All these extra attachments are referred to as functional groups. The smallest hydrocarbons (fewest number of carbons) are gases at room temperature, whereas long chains are solids. Those of intermediate length are liquids. The boiling and melting points of all hydrocarbons increase as the molecules become larger. (*See* HALOGENS.)

Fuels. All hydrocarbons undergo combustion and therefore make good fuels. The most abundant hydrocarbon fuels are petroleum and natural gas. Petroleum can be refined by various methods to produce gasoline, kerosene, various other fuels, and oils. Complete combustion in the presence of oxygen will result in the hydrocarbons being transformed into carbon dioxide and water. Incomplete combustion results in the production of carbon monoxide, which is toxic, and elemental carbon, commonly known as soot. (*See* PETROLEUM DISTILLATION *and* FOSSIL FUEL POWER.)

Polymers. All hydrocarbons are capable of polymerization, in which smaller units are combined to form larger, more complex molecules known as polymers. (*See* POLYMERS.)

The *Hindenburg* disaster of 1937 put an end to the use of hydrogen in lighter-than-air flight. Helium, an alternative gas (which was available at the time of the crash), turned out not to be cost-effective for passenger aviation.

The five most important series of hydrocarbons are alkanes, alkenes, alkynes, alkadienes, and aromatic compounds. There are no functional groups on any of these series.

Alkanes, also known as the paraffin series, contain only single bonds between the adjacent carbons. Alkenes, known as the olefin series, have a double bond between one pair of carbons present in the chain; all of them are oily liquids. The alkynes, or acetylene series, have a triple bond between one pair of carbons present in the chain. Alkadienes contain two pairs of carbon atoms that are linked by a double bond, although these two sets of double bonds are usually not adjacent to each other. They are used as raw material to make synthetic and natural rubber.

The aromatics are all derivatives of benzene, a molecule consisting of six carbon atoms and six hydrogen atoms. The carbon atoms form a ring with alternating double and single bonds between them. Many of these molecules have quite distinctive odors (hence their name) and are the starting points for synthesizing dyes, explosives, aspirin, sulfa drugs, and plastics. (*See* AROMATIC COMPOUNDS; SYNTHETICS.)

First see PERIODIC TABLE OF THE ELEMENTS

Hydrogen

Next see FUSION, NUCLEAR

Hydrogen, a gas at room temperature, is the simplest of the naturally occurring elements. All other atoms have a nucleus containing protons (positively charged particles) and neutrons, with electrons (negatively charged particles) orbiting in discrete energy levels. The hydrogen atom, however, consists of only one proton and one electron. Despite hydrogen's structure, it is far from simplistic and certainly not unimportant. Hydrogen makes up less than one percent of Earth's crust, oceans, and atmosphere, but ten percent of the human body.

Uniqueness of Hydrogen. Hydrogen does not belong to any specific family of elements on the Periodic Table, although it is often depicted

as if it were a member of group IA, the alkali metals, which have only one electron in their outermost energy level. However, hydrogen is most definitely not a metal. Hydrogen shares something else with helium; a helium atom consists of two protons and two neutrons; in thermonuclear fusion, two hydrogen nuclei regularly fuse together to form helium. This is the reaction which powers the stars and by which they produce energy. Fusion is also the basis of certain types of nuclear weapons.

Heavy Water. Isotopes are atoms of the same element that have different numbers of neutrons and consequently different atomic masses. The most common form of hydrogen has no neutrons. However, a second isotope, deuterium, has one neutron. A third form, tritium, has two neutrons. Each of those isotopes has a heavier atomic mass than does "regular" hydrogen, but reacts chemically in much the same way. Heavy water contains deuterium in place of hydrogen. In terms of taste, color, and odor, it is indistinguishable from regular water. Heavy water was formed as an early step in the experiments which led to the development of nuclear weapons. The isotopes of hydrogen are also used as "tracers" to determine the fate of various atoms and compounds in the course of chemical reactions, as they are easily identified by means of their heavier masses.

Hydrogen Bond. Hydrogen is one of the diatomic elements, atoms which will pair up with another atom of their own kind in the absence of anything else with which to bond. Hydrogen is capable of forming either covalent bonds, in which electrons are shared between atoms, or ionic bonds, in which one atom gains electrons while the other loses them. Since hydrogen has only one electron, it can form only one bond at a time. (*See* ELECTRON.)

The type of bond hydrogen forms depends largely on the other atom involved, and on the relative electronegativity values. Electronegativity measures how strongly an atom attracts electrons—its own as well as those belonging to another atom. If the difference between the respective values is relatively small, the bond will be covalent. If the discrepancy is greater, the more electronegative element will monopolize the electrons. The result is a polar bond, which is a covalent bond with a hint of ionic character. If the difference is too large, the bond will be ionic. Hydrogen, with a low electronegativity value, tends to lose its electron and form a cation, or positively charged ion. When hydrogen is involved in a polar bond, it is attracted to negative charges on nearby molecules, thus creating hydrogen bonding between adjacent molecules.

Water. Hydrogen is often found together with oxygen. The most obvious example is water, H_2O, in which two hydrogen atoms bond with one oxygen. These bonds are polar, which gives water many of its unique and important properties such as surface tension and the ability to act as a solvent. (*See* WATER.)

Ubiquity of Hydrogen. Hydrogen is found in many important compounds, among them organic molecules. In a sense, the hydrogen atoms are used to insure that each carbon atom has its maximum number of bonds. A saturated hydrocarbon chain has a maximum number of hydrogen atoms, as there are only single bonds (one shared pair of electrons) between the adjacent carbons. In unsaturated chains, because of the presence of double or triple bonds (two or three shared pairs of electrons) between carbons, fewer hydrogens are used.

A functional group found in many organic compounds is the hydroxyl group (OH). It is covalently bonded to hydrocarbon chains to form alcohols; it is also an important part of the carboxyl group (COOH), which is used to combine smaller subunits to form polymers. The hydroxyl group also plays a role in acid base chemistry. An acid is defined as a molecule that has a hydrogen ion (H^+) as its cation. Since the hydrogen atom minus its electron is essentially just a lone proton, an acid is known functionally as a proton donor. Correspond-ingly, a base that has the hydroxide ion (OH^-) as its anion is known as a proton acceptor.

Background material can be found in ACIDS AND BASE; ALCOHOL; ATOM; PERIODIC TABLE. *More details can be found in* ISOTOPE; SUN; WATER. *Additional aspects of this subject are covered in* FUSION, NUCLEAR; HYDROCARBON; HYDROLOGIC CYCLE.

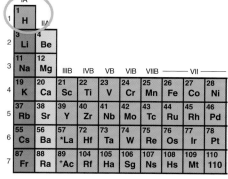

Above, the position of hydrogen in the Periodic Table of the Elements.

Further Reading
Farndon, John, *Hydrogen* (1999); Hoffmann, Peter, *The Forever Fuel* (1987); Jeffrey, George, A., *An Introduction to Hydrogen Bonding* (1997); Peoppel, *Atlas of Galactic Hydrogen* (1995); Rhodes, Richard, *Dark Sun: The Making of the Hydrogen Bomb* (1995); Scheiner, Steve, *Hydrogen Bonding* (1997).

First see WATER IN LIVING CELLS

Hydrologic Cycle

Next see EUTROPHICATION

The process by which the waters of Earth circulate between the land, the oceans, and the atmosphere.

The hydrologic cycle can, in some cases, be short and direct—for example, when water evaporates from the ocean and falls as rain in the next few hours. It can also be long and complex, as when rain falls on land and passes through several phases. Some of the water may evaporate quickly. Some of it may run through small streams into rivers and then to the sea, where it evaporates to begin the cycle again. Some of it may be absorbed by plants, eventually evaporating from the surfaces of those plants. As ground water, it may be absorbed in a different way by plants, being taken up by their root systems.

While there are many pathways in the hydrologic cycle, most of those paths lead to the

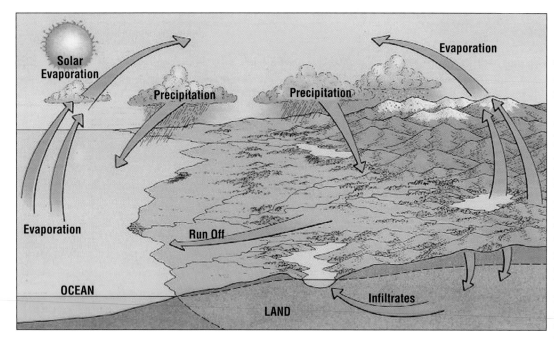

seas. On the globe as a whole, nearly 80 percent of water falls as precipitation on the seas. The water that falls on the land can follow many different paths; the amount that runs off, evaporates, or seeps into the ground can vary widely depending on the nature of the region in which it falls. In the United States, from 10 percent to 50 percent of rainfall runs off at once, another ten percent to 30 percent evaporates, and 40 percent to 60 percent is absorbed by the soil. One way or another, plants use about 15 percent to 30 percent of the rainfall.

Background material can be found in ACID RAIN; ECOLOGY; SOIL CHEMISTRY. Advanced subjects are developed in EUTROPHICATION; HOMEOSTASIS; WATER IN LIVING CELLS. Additional relevant information is contained in DEFORESTATION; DESERTIFICATION; GAIA HYPOTHESIS; NITROGEN AND PHOSPHOROUS CYCLES.

The hydrologic cycle is probably the most critical cycle to the continuation of life on Earth—but also the most delicate. Slight variations in evaporation, precipitation, and infiltration rates could, when multiplied across a global ecosystem, have a profound effect on life.

Further Reading
Averett, Robert C., *Chemical Quality of Water and the Hydrologic Cycle* (1987); Berner, Elizabeth Kay, *Global Environment: Water, Air, and Geochemical Cycles* (1994); Browning, K. A., *Global Energy and Water Cycles* (1999); Smith, David, *The Water Cycle* (1990).

First see SOIL CHEMISTRY

Hydroponics

Next see GROWTH REGULATION IN PLANTS

A technique by which plants are grown without soil.

Hydroponics, also known as soilless culture, is an outgrowth of the laboratory techniques used by plant physiologists, in which plants are grown with their roots immersed in a liquid solution containing the mineral salts that provide the nutrients plants ordinarily obtain from soil.

In one hydroponic technique, the plants are placed on a wire screen that holds a matrix of peat or a similar material, with their roots extended downward into the solution below. In

Further Reading
Dekorne, James B., *The Hydroponic Hothouse: Low-Cost, High-Yield Greenhouse Gardening* (1992); Nicholls, Richard E., *Beginning Hydroponics: Soilless Gardening* (1990); Resh, Howard M., *Hydroponic Food Production: A Definitive Guidebook of Soilless Food-Growing Methods* (1995); Savage, Adam J., *Hydroponics Worldwide: State of the Art in Soilless Crop Production* (1985)

another method, the plants are grown on a thin layer of sand or gravel, in a shallow tank into which a solution containing the necessary nutrients is pumped.

In hydroponics, as in ordinary agriculture, the plant obtains carbon, oxygen, and hydrogen from air and water. The major elements needed for plant growth are nitrogen, phosphorus, sulfur, potassium, calcium, and magnesium. Other elements that plants need in small amounts include iron, manganese, boron, copper, zinc, and molybdenum. In ordinary farming, the plant obtains these from the soil. In hydroponics, a variety of chemical compounds containing the necessary elements in the best proportion are added to the water, which is otherwise kept as pure as possible—either as distilled water or as rainwater. The resulting solution is replaced by a fresh one periodically, and some elements, notably iron, must be added from time to time.

Yields. With proper management, hydroponically grown plants can give yields as good as those obtained by conventional agriculture. The raising of crops by this method, however, is economically competitive only under special circumstances. For example, some flowers now are being grown successfully using hydroponic methods. In theory, at least, hydroponic farming could be done in regions where the soil is very infertile but where the climate is suitable to farming, or in very rocky regions. Hydroponic techniques have also been used successfully on some of the coral islands of the Pacific Ocean.

In Space. Hydroponic farming has also been proposed as a method for providing food crops in space exploration. When (and if) a manned colony is established on the moon, or a voyage lasting for years is made to explore the outer regions of the solar system, the hydroponic techniques proven to be successful on Earth could then be transferred to the weightless or low-gravity conditions of space travel.

Further developments in hydroponics are discussed in PLANT; SOIL CHEMISTRY; WATER IN LIVING CELLS. More details can be found in GERMINATION; PHOTOSYNTHESIS; SEEDS. Elementary aspects of this subject are covered in CALVIN-BENSON CYCLE; GROWTH REGULATION IN PLANTS; PLANT HORMONES. See also SPACECRAFT.

Ice Age

Next see PALEOCLIMATOLOGY

A glacial period lasting approximately 100,000 years. Ice ages occur during glacial epochs, which last from 20 to 50 million years.

The earliest known ice age occurred 2.3 billion years ago. The most recent ice age occurred during the Pleistocene epoch. It began 2 million years ago and ended 11,500 years ago.

Many theories have attempted to explain the climatic alternation between ice ages and interglacial periods. Changes in climate have been linked to continental movements as well as to changes in the inclination of the Earth's rotational axis. The most widely accepted theory involves changes in the Earth's orbit around the sun that affect the distribution of energy, driving the climate in and out of ice ages.

During the late Cretaceous to early Tertiary, 40 to 80 million years ago, the climate had generally higher temperatures. During the Paleocene and Eocene periods, approximately 55 million years ago, there was abundant year-round precipitation. However, by the end of the Eocene, there was a major decline in the annual mean temperatures. In the middle Tertiary, rapid change occurred with a decrease in temperature. Major climatic deterioration occurred within just 1 to 2 million years.

Glaciers began forming in Antarctica 38 million years ago and grew rapidly. By 13 million years ago, the Antarctic ice sheet had fully formed. Seven million years ago ice sheets began forming in North America, Europe, and Asia, covering vast areas within just a few million years. It is this period that is often referred to as *the* Ice Age.

Glacier Depth. The Pleistocene glaciers reached depths of almost two miles. The ice flowed outward under pressure of its weight. It left its mark on the ground by carving out rivers, lakes, and valleys, and sculpting mountain ranges. Moraines are mounds and ridges of soil and rock left behind when the glaciers eventually receded and melted.

The main ice sheet center in North America was near Hudson Bay in Canada, but the glaciers extended as far south as the valleys of the Missouri and Ohio rivers. In Europe the ice sheets reached down into what are today northern Germany and Moscow.

The glacier retreats occurred less than 20,000 years ago. Today only Antarctica and Greenland are still covered by glaciers.

In the last ice age, the climate was not all snow and ice. There was permafrost—soil permanently frozen past a certain depth; only the top layers ever thawed. However, the long spring was mild and wet and was followed by a brief, hot summer. Winter was very long and cold. Further north, there was less snow as the glaciers absorbed most of the available moisture. Nearest the vast ice sheets, the cold was very intense and very dry.

Animal Life. The abundant Ice Age animal life was well adapted for the extreme cold. Woolly layers of long hair and fur were grown over thick layers of insulating fat. Creatures like mammoths were found very near the ice, away from the deep snows that covered up their foraging grounds and could trap the animals themselves. Rapid plant and animal growth occurred during the spring and summer seasons in preparation for the long winter.

Archaic *Homo sapiens*, formerly known as Neanderthals, were the dominant form of human in Europe and Asia during most of the Ice Age. Neanderthals were nomadic hunter-gatherers who lived in caves. They used hand-held tools made of bone and stone and wore animal skins. They used fire and exhibited ritual activity such as burial of the dead. It is unknown if they had speech. Some research based on skull structures seems to indicate that Neanderthals did not have a spoken language.

Humans Appear. Towards the end of the Ice Age, anatomically modern humans appeared, possibly originating in Africa. They may have coexisted with their more primitive forebears for several thousand years. These humans, formerly called Cro-Magnon, also used animal skins and stone tools, but were more advanced than their primitive ancestors. Cro-Magnons exhibited a complex culture and social organization with use of sophisticated tools.

Further developments in the field are discussed in EXTINCTION; FOSSIL; GLACIER. *More details regarding ice ages can be found in* HOMO SAPIENS; OCEAN, ORIGIN AND EVOLUTION OF; PALEOCLIMATOLOGY. *Additional relevant information is contained in* NEANDERTHAL; PALEOECOLOGY.

Above, the extent of the glacial ice sheet in the north polar region during the ice age of the late Pleistocene epoch.

Further Reading
Erickson, Jon, *Glacial Geology: How Ice Shapes the Land* (1996); Erickson, Jon, *Ice Ages* (1990); Imbrie, John, *Ice Ages: Solving the Mystery* (1986); Powell, L., *Night Comes to the Cretaceous: Dinosaur Extinction and the Transformation of Modern Geology* (1998); Stanley, Steven M., *Children of the Ice Age* (1998).

First see METAMORPHIC ROCK

Igneous Rock

Next see GEOMORPHOLOGY

Rocks formed from lava or magma.

Igneous (from the Latin for "fire") rock geology deals with the kind of rock that forms from the molten matter that is called lava when it is on the surface and magma when it is below ground. Those igneous rocks that form below the surface and are exposed later by erosion or faulting are called intrusive rocks, while those that form on the surface are called extrusive rocks.

If the formative magma or lava was more than half composed of silica, the resulting igneous rock is called sial; if the composition was less than 50 percent silica, the igneous rock is called sima. In general, sial is lighter in color, less dense, and has a coarser texture than sima. Intrusive rock is generally sial and extrusive rock is generally sima, but there are exceptions to this rule. Geologists often use the term sial to refer to the rock layers underlying continents and sima to refer to the layers under oceans. (*See* CONTINENTS, FORMATION AND EVOLUTION OF.)

Texture. The texture of igneous rock generally is determined by the way in which it solidifies. If the solidification process takes place slowly, the various elements making up the magma or lava crystallize one after another, in an order determined by the complexity of their molecular structures. The first minerals to crystallize are those with the simplest structures, such as olivine in the ferromagnetic group and anorthite in the feldspar group. The last mineral to crystallize usually is quartz, which is composed entirely of silicon and oxygen. As crystals form, they either separate from the magma or lava or react with the remaining liquid rock to form different crystals. (*See* CRYSTALS.)

Slow cooling of magma, which generally occurs at greater depths, usually produces the largest crystals, and thus the most coarsely grained rock. Igneous rocks that form on the surface from lava usually cool very quickly, so that small crystals are formed. The resulting rock has a very fine grain or no grain at all; obsidian is formally classified as a glass. If the lava is simatic, the rock that forms usually will be basalt, a fine-grained rock rich in ferromagnetic material. If the lava is sialic, it will be andesite, a fine-grained rock poor in ferromagnetic material and feldspar. Most lava is basalt, but in some areas of the continents where orogeny—mountain-making—is in the process of occurring, a great deal of andesite is found. Other varieties of igneous rock, based on their feldspar content and other characteristics, include limburgite, rhyolite, tachyte, phonolite, kimberlite, and hornblendite. (*See* VOLCANO.)

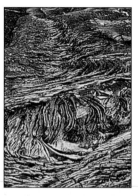

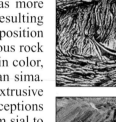

Above, (top) dense rock formations found in mountainous regions give rise to the striking structure of igneous rock formations. Bottom, bands of obsidian volcanic glass formed by hydrocarbon sedimentary deposits crushed in the aftermath of a lava flow.

First see ANTIBODIES

Immune Response

Next see IMMUNIZATION AND VACCINATION

The system of the body designed to protect it from invasion by foreign substances or organisms.

The essence of an immune system is its ability to distinguish between "self" and "non-self": what belongs in the body and what does not. It is believed that this recognition system occurs by detection of antigens or protein "markers" on the surface of cells.

The skin is the body's first line of defense against infection. If it remains unbroken, it is a solid barrier that nothing can penetrate. The regular body openings are lined with mucus or other materials such as wax to wash away or trap any particles that enter. However, if a break occurs in the skin, resulting in a cut or sore, invaders can easily enter into the bloodstream and from there travel anywhere in the body.

The body reacts to infection with either nonspecific or specific responses. There are three main nonspecific responses:

—inflammation: blood vessels in the infected region dilate, and the capillary walls become more permeable. This results in more fluid entering body tissues and the entire area exhibiting redness and swelling;

—fever: body temperature increases above normal in order to put any invading bacteria or viruses at a metabolic disadvantage;

—increased white-cell count: white blood cells are designed to destroy invading germs and bacteria. When an infection is present, the number of white cells circulating in the bloodstream sharply increases. Depending on the specific type of cell, some are able to consume from 20 to 100 bacteria during their lifespan.

Responses. Specific responses involve the action of highly specialized types of white blood cells, called T- and B-lymphocytes. T cells are responsible for cellular immunity by destroying foreign cells. There are many different types of T cells, with each variety capable of responding to a specific type of antigen. When the antigen is detected, those specific lymphocytes become activated or sensitized. They increase in size and divide rapidly to form hundreds of cells.

Some of the newly formed cells are killer T cells, which directly destroy invaders. Some become helper T cells, which enhance responses, and others are suppressor T cells, which inhibit defenses several weeks after the infection is over. A few sensitized T cells will remain in the lymph nodes as "memory cells" in the event that the antigen is discovered again at a later date.

B-lymphocytes are responsible for antibody immunity. Sensitized B cells also divide rapidly in response to a particular antigen. Most of the new cells differentiate into plasma cells, which produce antibodies. Others become memory cells and behave in a similar fashion to their T cell counterparts. Unlike T cells, B cells never leave the lymph nodes; only their antibodies circulate in the bloodstream.

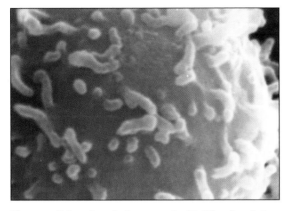

Above, a B-lymphocyte is covered with bits of an infectious invader, stimulating an immune response.

Antibody Types. Antibodies are also called immunoglobulins. They react with antigens according to shape but do not require a perfect fit in order to form an antigen-antibody complex. There are five different classes of antibodies: G, M, A, D, and E. In humans, 75 percent of antibodies belong to the G class.

The formation of an antigen-antibody complex has one of three results: it inactivates, but does not destroy, the antigen; it makes the antigen more susceptible to killer T cells; or it results directly in the destruction of the antigen.

After the infection is over, some antibodies remain in circulation at a much lower concentration called basal level.

Types of Immunity. Active immunity is when an individual has been exposed to an antigen and develops antibodies in response. Exposure to the antigen may come about as a result of having a disease, or receiving a vaccine against it. Many viral diseases, such as measles, mumps, diphtheria, hepatitis, and chicken pox, can now be prevented by receiving an inoculation. The shot contains weakened versions of the virus, or antigens from its protein coat, which stimulate the body's immune system. Vaccinations are given in a set schedule during childhood, and periodic boosters are sometimes required several years later to ensure continued immunity against the viral agent.

Passive immunity is when an individual receives someone else's antibodies against a disease. This causes temporary protection against the illness but will not result in permanent immunity. The most common example of passive immunity is in a newborn baby. The infant receives antibodies from the mother during pregnancy, and for the first few months the baby is protected against various diseases. More antibodies are transmitted through breast milk. However, the antibody levels eventually drop and the child must be exposed to the antigens and develop his or her own antibodies for permanent immunity.

Another instance of passive immunity can occur when a person has been exposed to a disease for which he or she does not have immunity and the contraction of which would be dangerous for the individual at that time. An injection of gamma globulin may provide temporary immunity for several weeks. However, this method is not foolproof, and the individual may still contract the disease, albeit in a milder form.

The immune system also produces various antiviral substances. The best known of these is interferon, which stimulates cells to produce other antiviral proteins to prevent the production of more viruses within host cells.

Allergy. An allergy is an example of the immune system getting "carried away." An allergen is a substance that is treated as a harmful antigen in certain individuals. The immune system unleashes a full response, including inflammation, redness, and swelling.

In individuals with hay fever, pollen is mistaken for an antigen. Immunoglobulin E is released from sensitized plasma cells. These antibodies combine with mast cell receptors in the nasal passages. The mast cells release histamines that cause the blood vessels to dilate and increase their permeability. This, in turn, causes congestion, increased fluid output, and "scratchy" feelings in the respiratory pathways, and often the eyes and ears as well. Antihistamine drugs tone down this response by counteracting the effects of the histamines. (*See* ALLERGY.)

The allergen can be a food or other chemical, but the result is the same. Sometimes the immune response can be so severe, it can become life-threatening—the air passageways can become blocked, or the swelling can reach dangerous proportions. Other allergic responses include nausea, vomiting, and the appearance of hives, which are raised itchy bumps on the skin.

Diseases. Autoimmune diseases represent a variety of conditions and diseases that interfere with immune system functions. In some cases, the immune system begins to attack normal body tissue, somehow mistaking it for invading antigens. In other diseases, most notably AIDS, the immune system itself is attacked and weakened, thereby leaving the body open to invasion by opportunistic infections.

Related areas are discussed in GAMMA GLOBULIN; MONOCLONAL ANTIBODIES. *Advanced subjects are developed in* AUTOIMMUNITY; B-LYMPHOCYTE; BLOOD TRANSFUSION; LUPUS; LYMPHATIC SYSTEM; MAJOR HISTOCOMPATIBILITY COMPLEX (MHC); T-LYMPHOCYTE. *Other aspects of this subject are covered in* AIDS; HIV; IMMUNIZATION AND VACCINATION; IMMUNOASSAY.

Below, the nodes of the lymphatic system play a crucial role in the body's immune defenses.

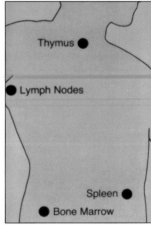

Further Reading
Cunningham, Madeleine W., *Effects of Microbes on the Immune System* (2000); Mims, Cedric, *The War Within Us* (2000); Nowak, Martin A., *Virus Dynamics: Mathematical Principles of Immunology and Virology* (2000).

Immunization and Vaccination

First see IMMUNE RESPONSE

Next see DISEASES, INFECTIOUS

Immunization refers to any process in which an organism becomes capable of combating a disease; vaccination involves inducing immunity by introducing a mild form of the disease.

Immunization and vaccination—the terms today are used interchangeably—involve the use of vaccines to protect against infection. A regular vaccination schedule has been set up for children in the United States.

Delivery System. Immunization generally is done by giving an individual a weakened, harmless form of the infectious agent for a given condition—enough to arouse the body's immune system to set up defenses against the disease, but not enough to cause any serious symptoms of disease. The first vaccine, against smallpox, was developed in the 1790s by William Jenner, a British researcher who observed that farm workers who had contracted cowpox, a mild disease affecting cattle, were resistant to smallpox. Jenner used a form of cowpox to give immunity against smallpox. The work was greatly extended by French scientist Louis Pasteur, who worked on vaccines against cholera, human anthrax, and rabies.

Today in the United States, the first vaccination, against the liver disease hepatitis B, is often given in the first month of life. Children who do not receive the anti-hepatitis series of shots in infancy must receive it before adolescence. At two months of age, children are vaccinated against diphtheria, pertussis (whooping cough), tetanus, and *Haemophilus influenzae* type b, which can cause meningitis. The vaccine against diphtheria is given as a series of five shots; a booster shot should be given every 10 years thereafter. The tetanus toxoid vaccine is also given in a series of five shots. Some children may have a reaction against the pertussis component of the DPT vaccine, and it should not be given to children older than 6.

Vaccination against poliomyelitis, a disease that causes paralysis, is usually administered orally at 2 months, 4 months, and 18 months of age; the vaccine may be given at 6 months if polio is prevalent in the area. A single combination vaccine is generally used for immunity against mumps, rubella (German measles), and measles. The vaccine is usually given after one year of age.

Immunization against the infectious agent *Haemophilus influenzae* Type b is recommended for children, with the vaccine given at 2, 4, 6, and 12 months of age; it is also recommended for all persons who are at risk of contracting the

disease. The vaccine against rabies is given to anyone who is bitten by an animal suspected of carrying this deadly disease. The initial shot is given on the day the bite is incurred, with subsequent injections 3, 7, 14, and 28 days later. A protective injection of rabies vaccine is recommended for persons who are traveling to areas where rabies is common, such as some parts of South America.

Travel Advisories. A variety of vaccines are recommended for travelers who are visiting different parts of the world. For example, a live virus vaccine against yellow fever is advised for individuals who are visiting areas of South America or Africa where the disease is widespread. A live virus vaccine is available at specialized yellow fever vaccination centers. This vaccination should be repeated every 10 years. Immunization against bubonic plague is advised for travelers to areas where the disease can still be found.

Bubonic plague vaccine is given in three shots, a month or more apart. This vaccine is not currently available in the United States and so must be obtained in the country being visited. A vaccine against typhoid is available for persons traveling to countries where the disease can be encountered. It is a live vaccine taken by mouth and is effective for up to five years.

By contrast, vaccination against cholera, a disease caused by unsanitary living and cooking conditions, is not recommended, although a vaccine is available. The vaccine is effective for only a few months and is only 50 percent effective. Scrupulous cleanliness and careful choice of food and drink are the best defenses. In recent years, a vaccine against acquired immune deficiency syndrome (AIDS) has been a major goal of biomedical researchers. The hope is that a vaccine will become available within a decade, to protect against the virulent disease.

Influenza. The most devastating epidemic in history—worse in terms of sheer numbers than the Black Death of the Middle Ages or the AIDS epidemic—was the influenza (flu) epidemic of 1918, which killed between 20 million and 40 million people worldwide in the winter of 1918–1919. In the month of October, nearly 200,000 Americans died; the flu struck so quickly that people became sick and died overnight. Currently, the virus is under check, but a repetition of 1918 is always a possibility; flu shots should be a considered seriously for the elderly and for people with weakened immune systems.

Further developments in immunization and vaccination are discussed in IMMUNE RESPONSE; INFECTIOUS DISEASES; PHARMACOLOGY. *Advanced subjects are developed in* CHICKEN POX; MEASLES; POLIOMYELITIS; SMALLPOX; TETANUS. *Important aspects of this subject are covered in* EPIDEMIOLOGY; SYMBIOSIS, COMMENSALISM, AND PARASITISM.

Top, William Jenner; bottom, Jonas Salk.

Further Reading
Chaitow, Leon, *Vaccination and Immunization: Dangers, Delusions and Alternatives* (1996); Dudgeon, J.A., *Immunization: Principles and Practice* (1990); Hurniston, Sharon G., *Vaccinating Your Child: Questions and Answers for the Concerned Parent* (2000); Jenner, E., *Vaccination Against Smallpox* (1996); O'Shea, Tim, *The Sanctitu of Human Blood: Vaccination is Not Immunization* (2000).

First see IMMUNE RESPONSE

Immunoassay

Next see ANTIBODIES

A laboratory technique used to diagnose infectious disease by analyzing a patient's blood for the presence of a protein associated with a given condition.

Antigens are proteins on the surface of a bacterium, virus, or allergy-causing substance that cause the body's immune system to produce protective proteins called antibodies. Each antibody is specific for a given antigen, and an immunoassay may also be used to look for such a protein in a patient's blood. In addition, immunoassays are used to look for other molecules associated with illness, such as hormones.

The principle behind the use of an immunoassay is that for each specific antigen there is a specific antibody. If individual molecules of these two proteins come together, they will bind closely to each other. An antibody will bind only with a specific antigen, and vice versa. Immunoassays include the enzyme-linked immunoabsorbent assay (ELISA) and the radioimmunoassay, both of which are used in the diagnosis of infectious diseases. Other immunoassays include RAST, the radioallergosorbent test, and RIST, the radioimmunosorbent test, which, respectively, are used to diagnose allergies and to measure concentrations of specific hormones in the blood.

Procedure. To perform an immunoassay, the first step is to prepare the interior of a test tube or the surface of a laboratory plate by covering it with the specific protein, either an antibody or an antigen, that will react with the antigen or antibody present in the blood of the person tested.

In the ELISA test for the HIV virus that causes AIDS, for example, small amounts of antigenic proteins from HIV are used to line the interior of a test tube. The lined surface is then exposed to a sample of blood plasma from the individual being tested. If the antibody or antigen that is the object of the test is present in the plasma, it will stick to the coated surface of the test tube or plate. The surface or plate is then washed and a chemical is added binding to the protein that is the object of the test. This chemical is linked to an enzyme called peroxidase in the ELISA test, or to a radioactive isotope in a radioimmunoassay. The excess chemical is then washed away, and if the enzyme that is the ob-ject of the test is present, either peroxidase or radioactivity will be left on the surface or test tube.

Peroxidase is detected by adding a chemical that makes it change color. Radioactivity is measured by a gamma counter. RIST is slightly different, because the blood serum that is being tested is mixed with a solution containing a

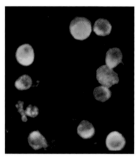

Fluorescent probes are used in an immunoassay (above) as an alternative to radioactive probes.

radioactive sample of the substance at which the test is aimed. A reduction in radioactivity after the test is done indicates that the substance being tested for was in the blood serum sample. The greater the reduction, the higher the concentration of that substance.

First see GENE

Imprinting, Genetic

Next see GENETICS

Refers to the differences in physical traits in a particular organism depending on which parent contributed the genetic material.

An organism has two copies of a gene for a specific trait, located on paired chromosomes. Normal human body cells, called somites, contain 46 chromosomes arranged in 23 pairs. One pair is made up of two sex chromosomes; the others are autosomes, the "regular" chromosomes. Gametes, the sex cells, have only one chromosome from each pair. This is because sperm and egg unite to form the new organism, with each contributing half the genetic material. Therefore, one chromosome from each pair comes from the mother, and one from the father.

Parentage. It was previously believed that, with the exception of sex-linked characteristics, the genes of which are carried only on the sex chromosomes, it did not matter which parent contributed which gene for a particular trait. It was also believed that both copies were equally active and important in determining the phenotype, the physical expression of the trait. Research has disproved both of these theories.

In an "imprinted region," only one copy of a gene is expressed. The other copy has been inactivated and is "genetically silent." The inactivation occurs only in the chromosomes inherited from a parent of one sex, but not those inherited from the other.

Genetic imprinting appears to be a way of regulating gene expression. Studies have shown that both maternal and paternal genetic materials are essential for normal development and that the different parental contributions produce different phenotypes. (*See* SEX LINKAGES.)

Lyon Hypothesis. Inactivation of a chromosomal region is part of the Lyon hypothesis, which states that one X chromosome in each body cell becomes inactivated early in the development of a normal female. This inactivation is random, allowing some cells to express the genes on the maternally inherited X chromosome, and others to express the genes on the paternally inherited X chromosome. The result is a mixture of traits.

In terms of phenotype, genetic imprinting has results similar to uniparental disomy, the presence of two copies of a gene from one parent, and none from the other. Uniparental disomy has been linked to several diseases, and is believed to have its origins in another genetic "mistake" called nondisjunction. Nondisjunction is when homologous chromosomes fail to separate during gamete formation. A gamete may result that has both chromosomes of the pair, instead of just one. If that gamete, whether sperm or egg, is used for reproduction, the chromosome will be present in triplicate. This condition, called trisomy, may involve either the sex chromosomes or the autosomes.

Uniparental disomy is believed to result from an initial case of trisomy followed by the loss of the other parental chromosome. Uniparental disomy is a useful tool for locating imprinted regions, by showing what occurs when the active genetic material from one parent is missing.

Background material on imprinting can be found in CHROMOSOME; DNA; GENE; GENETICS. *Further details can be found in* DIFFERENTIATION, CELLULAR; DNA REPLICATION. *More information on particular aspects is contained in* GENE THERAPY; MUTATION, GENETIC; TRANSCRIPTION.

First see MAGNETISM

Inductor

Next see ELECTRIC CIRCUIT

A device commonly used to obtain a high but intermittent voltage from a low and steady source of electricity, such as a battery.

A schematic diagram for a transformer, a type of inductor. The diagram clearly demonstrates the wrapped iron core.

An inductor is based on the principle of induction, in which an electric charge is produced by the presence of a magnetic field. One part of an inductor is a wire coil of relatively few turns that has a core of soft iron. This coil, called the primary, is connected to a battery and to a device that regularly interrupts the flow of current from the battery to the coil. The regular interruption of current flow creates a variation in the magnetic field around the primary coil. This allows the transmission of electromotive forces to the secondary coil, which is made of many turns of fine wire wound on the same core. The secondary electromotive force is reversed at every make and break of the primary coil.

The performance of the inductor can be improved by placing a capacitor across the terminals of the device that regularly reverses the direction of current flow. Induction coils are used to operate Geissler and x-ray tubes, but the largest use at present is in the operation of automobile engines; in that use, the induction coil is called a spark coil. Similar devices are used to produce the voltage change that enables radio to be powered by low-voltage batteries. (*See* MOTORS AND GENERATORS *and* TRANSFORMERS.)

Further Reading
Kilbourne, Edward D., *Influenza* (1987); Kolata, Gina Bari, *Flu: The Story of the Great Influenza Pandemic of 1918 and the Search for the Virus That Caused It* (2001); Krug, R. M., *The Influenza Viruses* (1989); Pyle, Gerald F., *The Diffusion of Influenza* (1986); Ramen, Fred, *Influenza* (2001).

First see VIRUS

Influenza

Next see DISEASES, INFECTIOUS

An infection of the respiratory tract caused by a number of different viruses. Symptoms include chills, fever, head and muscle aches, and general fatigue.

The three main classes of influenza virus, commonly known as the flu, are classified A, B, and C. The C virus is genetically very stable, so that a single attack makes the immune system provide antibodies that prevent future attacks, and causes only a mild, coldlike illness. The A and B viruses cause more severe illnesses, and both can have genetic mutations that produce new strains, thus evading the body's immune protections resulting from previous infections. The A influenza virus is most variable, with new strains coming into existence unpredictably from year to year. Such A virus strains were responsible for the worldwide outbreaks of influenza that occurred in 1918 (the Spanish flu), 1957 (the Asian flu), and 1968 (the Hong Kong flu).

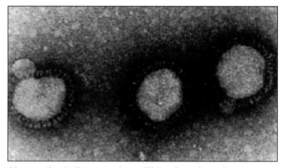

Above, the influenza virus. This virus has shown a remarkable ability to adapt through mutation and to develop virulent new strains.

Infection. An influenza infection usually starts with a cough, chest pains, and fever. Respiratory symptoms continue for a week, leaving the patient weak but able to recover. Older persons may experience life-threatening bacterial infections. Influenza vaccines are widely available but have a protection rate of about 65 percent and provide protection for only a short time. Immunization must be repeated every year, just before the start of the winter influenza season. Treatment consists largely of bed rest, with drugs to relieve aches and pains. Older and weaker patients can benefit if the drug amantadine is given at the onset of infection.

Related subjects are discussed in DISEASES, INFECTIOUS; PNEUMONIA; VIRUS. *Advanced subjects are developed in* IMMUNIZATION AND VACCINATION; RESPIRATORY SYSTEM. *Further information on particular aspects of influenza is contained in* COMMON COLD; EPIDEMIOLOGY; VITAMINS AND MINERALS.

First see TELESCOPE

Infrared and Ultraviolet Astronomy

Next see UNIVERSE, LARGE-SCALE STRUCTURE OF

The branch of astronomy that gathers information about objects in the universe by observations of electromagnetic radiation whose wavelengths are longer than those of visible light.

Infrared observations are valuable in the study of the earlier history of the universe because objects such as the galaxies are moving away from Earth at such great speeds that much of their light radiations are "red-shifted" out of the visible range. The luminosity of even some nearby galaxies is greater in the infrared than in the visible light frequencies. While many infrared observations have been made from ground-based observatories, observations made from spacecraft have two advantages. First, they eliminate the distorting effects caused by the absorption and emission of electromagnetic radiation in Earth's atmosphere. In addition, spacecraft infrared telescopes can be shielded and cooled to temperatures near those of liquid helium, which reduces background radiation by a millionfold. It is thus possible to study protogalaxies, which are in the early stages of star formation; galaxies that emit mainly infrared radiation; and haloes of

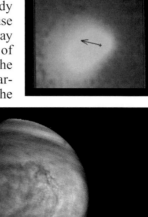

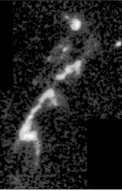

Infrared and ultraviolet astronomy provide an oppotunity to see a wider variety of astronomical phenomena. From top: Halley's Comet; a star-forming region in a distant galaxy; two images of Earth at infrared (left) and ultraviolet; an arm of spiral galaxy M81 in the constellation Ursa Major. At left is a schematic of an infrared orbiting observatory.

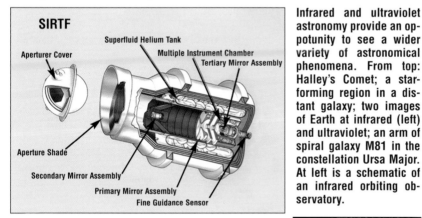

SIRTF

Aperturer Cover
Superfluid Helium Tank
Multiple Instrument Chamber
Tertiary Mirror Assembly
Aperture Shade
Secondary Mirror Assembly
Primary Mirror Assembly
Fine Guidance Sensor

galaxies whose emissions are dominated by those of infrared-rich dwarf stars.

Ultraviolet astronomy can be used to study the planets of the solar system. For example, such observations have indicated the presence on Mars of widespread hazes in the planet's atmosphere which are not normally visible in ordinary light observations. Observations of galaxies and nebulae have indicated the presence of stars of unusually high temperatures emitting intense ultraviolet radiation. Sometimes this ultraviolet radiation is converted into visible light, as happens in the Orion nebula.

First see DENTISTRY

Ingestion

Next see DIGESTION

The process by which living organisms take in food.

The feeding behavior of animals is usually closely related to their means of locomotion, defense, and sometimes reproduction. A medium or large land carnivore is usually fast enough to chase down its prey, which it tears into chunks and swallows, while a sedentary creature like the clam merely opens its shell and lets minute particles of food wash in.

In the Sea. Many aquatic animals are, like the clam, filter feeders, with the mucus-coated gill acting as the filter to screen food out of the water, as well as extract oxygen. Food is then carried to the mouth by beating cilia. More active filter feeders swim forward with their mouth wide open; long, fringed gill rakers hang into the throat from their gill arches to provide a larger filter for food. (*See* FISH; GILLS.)

The weightiest of the filter feeders are the baleen whales, which have hundreds of ribbonlike plates of horny baleen hanging from their top jaws to filter out krill, the tiny crustaceans that provide their main nourishment. The humpback whale gulps in about 81 cubic yards of water at a time, then raises its throat to force the water out through its baleen.

Many fish, including perch and carp, are suction feeders. They inhale prey by means of a powerful pump formed when the throat and jaw move suddenly to expand the volume of the head by as much as 40 percent. Ingestion is lightning fast, taking as little as one hundredth of a second.

On Land. Ingestion among land animals relies largely on tooth and tongue. The projectile tongue that unrolls at high speed and pinpoint accuracy captures prey for many frogs, salamanders, and chameleons. A variety of birds and mammals use the tongue to root out insects.

Carnivores use bladelike teeth to bite, tear, and crush food, while fruit- and nut-eaters have crushing teeth in which a projection on one tooth rubs against a depression on an opposing tooth. Although birds lack teeth, avian predators use talons and beaks to tear flesh. Insect-eating birds generally swallow their prey whole, while grain- and nut-eating birds grind their food in gizzards that form part of the stomach.

Spiders and other arachnids are fluid feeders that liquify the tissue of their prey with digestive secretions before sucking them up. Many insects, including mosquitoes and fleas, feed on blood and have both piercing and sucking mouth parts; another large group of insects, including grasshoppers and beetles, bite and chew.

Of all forms of ingestion, perhaps none is as dramatic, or grotesque, as the swallowing of large prey whole. Snakes are famed for this. Some can swallow whole eggs three times the diameter of their heads because their jaws can separate and move sideways. During the long, slow swallowing of giant prey, the snake's epiglottis sticks out of its mouth so that it can continue to breathe while it eats. (*See* PREDATION *and* POPULATION ECOLOGY. *Also see* DIGESTIVE SYSTEMS *and* DIGESTION REGULATION.)

First see CHEMICAL FORMULA

Inorganic Compound

Next see ELECTRONEGATIVITY

Any compound not containing carbon and hydrogen.

Chemistry is divided into two main categories: organic chemistry, which involves compounds containing both carbon and hydrogen, and inorganic chemistry, which involves everything else. The only inorganic carbon compounds are carbonates and carbon oxides.

Characteristics. Unlike organic compounds, inorganic molecules do not form long complex polymers. All of inorganic chemistry concerns smaller compounds made up of just a few atoms. Organic compounds are held together by covalent bonds; electrons (negatively charged particles) shared between atoms. Inorganic compounds often contain ionic bonds, in which electrons are gained or lost. When a metal and a nonmetal combine, the resulting compound is ionic. When two non-metals combine, the compound is covalent. (Two metal atoms cannot bond with each other.) The driving force behind chemical bonds is so great that it is difficult to find atoms in nature in their pure elemental states.

Electron Movement. The electrons of an atom are located in energy levels extending outward from the nucleus. The basis of all chemical bonds is the "desire," or affinity, each atom has for a full valence shell, the outermost level that contains electrons. For most elements, the magic number is eight, also known as a stable octet because then the atom achieves its most stable energy state. With the exception of the noble gas family of elements, all atoms must obtain the electrons needed either by transferring electrons, by sharing them, or by some combination of those actions.

All inorganic reactions are based upon relative electronegativity values, which trace how strongly a particular atom attracts electrons. Nonmetals are much more electronegative than metals. Therefore, when a metal atom bumps into a nonmetal, it becomes the victim of a "mugging," losing its valence electron to the nonmetal. Up to three electrons can be obtained in this way. The nonmetal then has the additional electron it needs, and the metal is also content,

Further Reading
Cotton, F. Albert, et al., *Advanced Inorganic Chemistry* (1999); Cotton, F. Albert, *Basic Inorganic Chemistry* (1994); Greenwood, N. N., *Chemistry of the Elements* (1997); Karplus, Martin, *Atoms and Molecules: An Introduction for Students of Physical Chemistry* (1970); Miessler, Gary L., *Inorganic Chemistry* (1998).

because it has lost its extra electron(s). When the metal loses an electron, it becomes a cation or positively charged ion, and the non-metal becomes an anion or negatively charged ion. Their opposite charges cause them to be attracted to each other, and so they stay together as an ionic compound.

Two nonmetals will share valence electrons between them in order to have a full shell, thereby forming a covalent bond. Ideally, the sharing is done equally. However, if the disparity in electronegativity values between the two atoms is too great, one atom will monopolize the electrons, almost appearing to gain electrons while the other one will appear to lose them. This type of covalent bond, with an ionic character, is called a polar bond. Polarity results in localized areas of positive or negative charges within the molecule, known as apparent charges. If the ends of the molecule are oppositely charged, the molecule is called a dipole.

Polarity results in additional types of bonds between molecules, such as hydrogen bonding and van der Waals' forces, which are weak but still important. Water molecules are held together with hydrogen bonds (giving it many of its unique properties), as are the two chains that form a DNA double helix.

Diatomic Atoms. Some atoms are so eager to form bonds that they will bond with another atom of their own type if there is nothing else available. These atoms are diatomic and consequently are never found as individuals. The seven diatomic elements are hydrogen, oxygen, nitrogen, fluorine, chlorine, bromine, and iodine.

The two major types of reactions that produce inorganic compounds are oxidation and reduction. Oxidation refers to the loss of electrons and reduction to the gain of electrons. Since they always occur together, they are referred to as coupled redox reactions.

Special topics in this area are found in ACIDS AND BASES; CHEMICAL REACTIONS; PERIODIC TABLE. *Advanced subjects are developed in* CHEMICAL FORMULA; ELECTROCHEMISTRY; SALTS. *More information on particular aspects is contained in* HALOGENS; ORGANIC COMPOUNDS; RADIO CHEMISTRY.

First see GENETICS

Instinct

Next see ETHOLOGY

Genetically inherited, often nearly involuntary behavior shared by all members of a species.

Instinct and learning are often so intertwined that it is difficult to separate their contribution to behavior. Understanding their relationship has been one of the central and most controversial quests of ethology. In fact, some ethologists reject the terms instinctive or innate, referring instead to "species-specific" or stereotyped behavior. They argue that all behavior, no matter how automatic it seems, is influenced by environmental factors.

In many species and situations, it appears that animals are born with a rough form of a needed skill, such as hunting or nest building, but must learn, through practice or the example of others, to develop it to a normal level. It can be difficult, however, to distinguish between learning and maturation of innate skills. Even when learning is clearly involved, often it can occur only at a certain time in life or with a particular setting or stimulus.

To develop a normal song, for instance, many birds need to hear their species' song early in life, long before they can sing themselves. Many can learn only the song of their species, while some can learn the song of a foster parent if exposed to it at the right time. Experiments have shown that honeybees can remember the color of a flower, but only if they have seen it in the two seconds before they land on its petals. In terms of more complex learning, honeybees learn and use spatial maps.

Instinct Mechanisms. Sign stimuli or "releasers" are signals that "release," or stimulate, a specific response. For instance, newly hatched herring gull chicks seek food by pecking at the beaks of their parents. They identify these beaks not as a unit but by a number of separate sign stimuli—narrowness, verticality, back-and-forth movement (the parent gull swings its beak before feeding its young), and a red spot of color. By emphasizing these features, researchers can create a "supernormal stimulus"—a vertical dowel with red bands that is moved back and forth—that gull chicks will choose over their parents' beaks.

Complex, automatic behaviors, whether learned or innate, are said to be controlled by "motor programs," neural circuits that orchestrate muscles to move in the proper order and timing. The most extreme form of motor programs are largely inherited patterns of behavior that, once turned on, continue to the end even if changes in circumstance render them pointless, absurd, or counterproductive. These "fixed action programs" were described by pioneer ethologists Konrad Lorenz and Niko Tinbergen in the 1930s. One classic example is the egg-rolling behavior of the greylag goose. If the goose sees an egg outside the nest, she reaches her neck out and rolls it back with the underside of her beak. If someone removes the egg after the goose has started reaching, she will complete the sequence of motions, miming the egg retrieval.

Associative Learning. There are two main forms of associative learning. In operant conditioning, or trial-and-error learning, an animal learns by reward or punishment. In the classic example, a rat in a Skinner box (named for psychologist B.F. Skinner) pushes a lever by accident, gets a pellet of food and, through repetition, learns to push the lever intentionally. In the wild, this form of associative learning is seen, for instance, when birds use trial and error to learn the most efficient way of opening a new kind of seed. It also works adversely. Many animals—including some humans—will avoid a food for life if they become sick even hours after eating it for the first time. Rats will not only abstain from the food but somehow manage to teach the aversion to their young—a form of cultural learning that helps explain why they are so infamously hard to exterminate.

Classical Conditioning. The other form of associative learning is classical conditioning. In his famous experiment, Ivan Pavlov (1849–1936) rang a bell or flashed a light just before giving food to dogs. After some repetition, the bell or light by itself would trigger salivation in the dogs. Classic conditioning can teach animals to seek out conditions associated with food or to take defensive measures before danger is actually upon them.

A variety of animals use tools in the wild—once thought to be a uniquely human ability—although it's not clear whether these are primarily learned or genetically programmed skills. Primates learn the identities and social relationships of the many individuals in their group. In experiments, chimpanzees, monkeys, and pigeons have been taught to identify concepts such as "human being," "inside/outside," "same/different," and colors. Chimpanzees and sea lions have even been taught the basics of Aristotelian logic: If X=Y and Y=Z, then X=Z. Alex, an African grey parrot who was taught 70 words over 10 years by researcher Irene Pepperberg, could identify a characteristic—shape, color, or material—that two objects have in common.

Cultural Learning. In cultural learning, the young learn from others in their group—often to recognize food or enemies. One striking example of cultural learning involved an apparent stroke of insight A troop of macaques, being studied on a preserve in Japan, were fed with food dumped on a beach, where it got sandy. About 1953, one young female monkey, called Imo, started rinsing her sweet potatoes off in the water. Slowly this behavior spread—first to Imo's playmates and mother, then to other young macaques, then to older females, and finally to the older males, the highest status members of the troop. It took nine years for a majority of the 60-member troop to start using the technique.

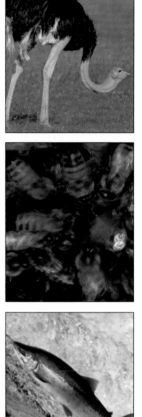

Instinctive Behavior.
The wild ostrich (above, top) buries its head when danger approaches. Bees (above, middle) are thought to communicate through a flying pattern known as the bee dance. Fish (above, bottom) will brave predators and impossible rapids (leading to certain death), driven by the instinct to reach their spawning ground.

Related material can be found in ADAPTATION; AGGRESSION AND TERRITORIALITY. Further details can be found in COEVOLUTION; COMPETITION AND ALTRUISM. Additional relevant information on instinct is contained in MEMORY; NAVIGATION; REFLEXES; REPRODUCTIVE STRATEGIES.

Further Reading
Darwin, Charles, *The Expression of the Emotions in Man and Animals* (1965); Lorenz, Konrad, *Behind the Mirror: A Search for a Natural History of Human Knowledge* (1978); Lorenz, Konrad, *On Aggression* (1997); Pinker, S., *The Language Instinct* (1995).

First see Conductors and Resistors

Insulator

Next see Electric Circuit

A material that does not transmit electric current.

Insulators are used to stop the flow of current or to prevent loss of electricity. One commonly used insulator in some electrical devices is ordinary air, which can prevent the jumping of current from one conductor to another. Another gas used as an insulator in electrical or electronic devices is sulfur hexafluoride. Solid dielectrics, or insulators, include ceramics, glass, plastics, paper, and mica. Liquid insulators include silicon oils, salt-free water, and a number of hydrocarbon compounds. The rubber coatings on wires in the home and the paper wrappings on radio capacitors and resistors are other examples of insulators. Each material is chosen for a specific application. (*See* CAPACITORS.)

Dielectrics do not conduct electricity because they do not have the free electrons or holes needed to carry a current. There are more complicated insulators that can consist of a material with an array of positive and negative charges that are arranged with a high degree of symmetry. When an electric current is applied to such a material, it causes the formation of a surface electric charge that is opposed by a field created inside the insulator. That field prevents the transmission of an electric current. The opposing field that is created inside the dielectric material is expressed in terms of a dielectric constant, which is the difference in electrical conductance between two plates when the plates are separated by the dielectric material or a vacuum.

Insulators are vital for high tension lines that must remain separated.

First see Function

Integral Calculus

Next see Calculus

One of two basic forms of calculus; whereas differential calculus seeks to find the derivative of a function, integral calculus seeks to find the sum of all these derivatives, thus defining the area under the curve of the function.

Calculus is vital to modern mathematics because nearly all functions are represented by curves, and classical geometry offers no formulas for finding the area inside a curve. Integral calculus offers a way to use the simplest formula for area, the formula for the area of a rectangle: $A = h \times w$. At first glance, this is impossible, because although one can find a width w for any function by measuring along the x-axis of a graph, its height h will not be constant because the upper border is curved. However, as one makes the width of the rectangle smaller and smaller, the upper border

Isaac Newton (1642– 1727).

approaches more and more closely to a straight line. At a certain point, when the width of each rectangle is infinitesimal, its area reaches a limit equivalent to that of an actual rectangle; to find the total area, all these rectangles are then added together, or integrated.

So far, integral calculus has been considered geometrically, but most sophisticated uses of integral calculus treat integration analytically. To approach it this way, it is necessary to discuss the derivative and the antiderivative. The basis of calculus is the derivative of a function. The first derivative of the function defines its instantaneous rate of change, and the second derivative defines its rate of change of that rate. Knowing these allows one to compute maximum and minimum values, and thus solve many real-world problems. But many natural phenomena are defined only by their rates of change; for example, gravity is expressed as an acceleration of approximately 9.8 m/sec^2. In order to find out what velocity an object will have at a given time, one must calculate the antiderivative; then, in order to determine its position at that time, one must calculate the second antiderivative. Antiderivatives are also used in economics, where they allow managers to move from a marginal cost function—which can vary wildly depending on the limits used—to the cost function, which is more accurate.

Fundamental Theorem. As the independent variable of a function increases by infinitesimal increments, the sum of the rectangles produced will also increase infinitesimally in proportion with the function; the antiderivative of the original function will be the area function. Thus an integral is an antiderivative of a function; conversely, if one takes the derivative of a function and then integrates the result, one will obtain the original function (plus, in some cases, a constant). This inverse relationship is called the Fundamental Theorem of Calculus.

Like much else in calculus, the integral was discovered by Gottfried Leibniz (1646–1716) and Sir Isaac Newton (1642–1727). They had been attempting to develop a differential calculus, in which functions are dissected into a series of infinitesimal intervals, each of which forms a rectangle whose base is the x-axis. In a manuscript note dated October 29, 1675, Leibniz first used the old form of the German letter s, ∫, to stand for the sum of these infinitesimal rectangles; it is the notation still used today.

The applications of integral calculus are wide ranging. Integration is used in astrophysics, economics, engineering, harmonics, and probabilistics. It can be used to find the bending strength of a steel I-beam, the "sweet spot" of a tennis racquet, the amount of concrete that will have to be poured on a spiral ramp, or the most efficient design for the cylinder heads in a new high-performance engine. (*See* CALCULUS.)

First see TRANSISTOR

Integrated Circuit

Next see COMPUTER, DIGITAL

A miniaturized electronic circuit produced on a single crystal of a semiconducting material.

Integrated circuits were first proposed in the 1950s as a way of gaining speed in electronic circuits. Once transistors had supplanted vacuum tubes, the next step was to eliminate as much as possible all electromechanical interfaces in a circuit; relays, solenoids, and other devices added size and weight, while costing time. If all necessary components could be fabricated out of semiconductor materials, then it should be possible to combine, or integrate, them in a single multifunctional component.

"Early" History. The first to achieve this feat was Jack St. Clair Kilby of Texas Instruments; in September 1958, he succeeded in integrating five components on a single germanium rod. A few months later, Robert Noyce of Fairchild Semiconductor accomplished a similar feat; later on, he would establish his own company, dedicated to the fabrication of semiconductor integrated circuit components: Intel.

Fairchild's development of the integrated circuit forged ahead because where Texas Instruments relied on a "mesa" transistor, in which the active layer of the semiconductor protruded above the surrounding base and therefore was vulnerable to contamination, Fairchild solved the problem of producing a "planar" transistor, in which the semiconductor surface was coated with a protective layer of silicon dioxide, etched away where it was necessary to make contact with the active layer. Furthermore, where wiring patterns had previously been projected onto the surface of the wafer by a silkscreen process, Fairchild used photolithographic techniques, able to distinguish features less than one thousandth of an inch across.

Using this new technique, Noyce could lay fine lines of aluminum atop the silicon dioxide, etch holes to connect them with the underlying active layer, and have as many transistors as he needed on a single wafer. As a result, Noyce was the first to secure a patent on what, in 1961, went on the commercial market as the Micrologic Element, containing the astonishing equivalent of two dozen transistors, resistors, capacitors, and diodes.

By 1965, there were 50 components per chip; by 1975, there were more than 64,000; and today there are more than a million. As the distance be-tween components shrinks, so does the time needed for calculations and the cost per component: Gordon Moore calculated that the complexity of integrated circuits has doubled—and the cost has been halved—every two years since their invention.

Future Growth. While pressure continues to pack ever more components on a single chip, in what is termed very large scale integration (VLSI), the real growth has come in application-specific integrated circuits (ASIC), designed to perform a given set of operations, whether it be an industrial security sensor-and-alarm unit or a digital signal processor for a home theater.

Further developments in the field are discussed in COMPUTER, DIGITAL; ELECTRIC CIRCUITS; P-N JUNCTION. *Advanced subjects are developed in* JOSEPHSON JUNCTION; SEMICONDUCTORS; TRANSISTOR. *Additional relevant information on integrated circuits is contained in* NANOTECHNOLOGY; OPERATING SYSTEM.

Further Reading
Augarten, Stan, *Bit by Bit: An Illustrated History of Computers* (1987); Campbell-Kelly, Martin, *Computer: A History of the Information Machine* (1997); Dermassa, Thomas A., *Digital Integrated Circuits* (1995); Kidder, Tracy, *Soul of a New Machine* (1995); Malone, Michael S., *The Microprocessor: A Biography* (1995); Mano, M. Morris, *Digital Design* (1991); Riordan, Michael, *Crystal Fire: The Birth of the Information Age* (1997).

An early integrated circuit by Fairchild, etched on silicon in the 1960s, would soon come to be regarded as an immense dinosaur of a bygone age.

First see DIFFRACTION

Interference

Next see X-RAY DIFFRACTION

The interaction of two wave motions, such as beams of light or water waves, when they cross each other at a glancing angle.

Waves reinforce each other at certain points and diminish or annihilate each other at other points. This interaction can give rise to unexpected effects, such as two beams of light combining to produce areas of darkness or two sound waves combining in such a way that no sound is heard over a small area.

Interference was first described in 1801 by Thomas Young, a British scientist, who noted its effect on light waves. At that time, the discovery provided strong evidence for the wave theory of light. In a device called Young's splits, light from a small source passes through a slit in a screen. The light that emerges from the slit is beamed at two slits on a second screen, so that the light that passes through them falls on a third screen. A series of parallel interference fringes is formed on this third screen. Where the waves reinforce each other, constructive interference is said to occur; where the maxima of one wave lies over the minima of the other, destructive interference is said to occur. Applying this formula to streams of electrons marked the beginning of quantum theory.

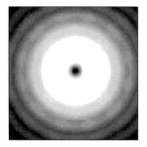

Circular interference patterns created by a Fresnel diffraction lens, above.

Further Reading
Fowles, Grant R., *Introduction to Modern Optics* (1989); Ingard, K.U., *Fundamentals of Waves and Oscillations* (1988); Keating, Michael P., *Geometric, Physical, and Visual Optics* (1988); Meyer-Arendt, J. R., *Introduction to Classical and Modern Optics* (1995); Park, David A., *The Fire Within the Eye: A Historical Essay on the Nature and Meaning of Light* (1997).

The sound produced by a vibrating violin string can produce what are called standing waves, which result from the interference between the wave traveling up the string from the bow and the wave that is reflected back down the string. The same kind of interference effect can occur in organ pipes. The technology is available today to exploit interference effects; for instance, noise-canceling headphones on an airplane trip effectively silence engine noise.

Related material can be found in LIGHT; OPTICS; WAVE. *Other aspects are discussed in* DIFFRACTION; QUANTUM MECHANICS. *Additional material can be found in* SPECTROSCOPY; WAVE-PARTICLE DUALITY.

First see IMMUNE RESPONSE

Interferons and Interleukins

Next see AIDS

Recently discovered molecules that are essential components of the body's immune system.

The interferon story began in 1957 with the discovery by two British scientists, Alick Isaacs and John Lindenmann, of a molecule produced by cells in response to infection by a virus. They found that the molecule, which they named interferon, did not kill viruses directly but instead prevented them from reproducing inside an infected cell.

Two decades later, other researchers found that interferon could slow the development of cancer in animals. That discovery led to the use of genetic engineering, in which a gene for a protein is isolated, cloned, and put into bacteria, which then produce large amounts of the protein for the production of interferon. Genetic engineering is now used for the production not only of the original interferon discovered by Isaacs and Lindenmann, but also of many other interferons that are used in the treatment of disease.

Three Kinds. It has been discovered that humans have three kind of interferons, classified as alpha, beta, and gamma, and these different interferons bind to different cell receptors. There are at least 15 alpha interferons that have been given official approval for treatment of various diseases. The first to get approval, in 1988, was an alpha interferon that is now used against hairy-cell leukemia, a relatively rare condition that affects about 2,000 Americans each year.

Interleukins. The first interleukins were discovered in 1972 by Byron Waksman and Igal Gery of Yale University. They grew the cells called macrophages in a broth, removed them and added T-lymphocytes, immune defense cells. They expected the T cells to die but found that a substance secreted by the macrophages caused them to multiply. That substance, originally called lymphocyte-activating factor, now is called interleukin-1.

Other interleukins were discovered in quick order; by 1989, six of them had been found. Interleukin-1 induces fatigue and sleep, which can be helpful during an illness. It also stimulates the multiplication of T-lymphocytes, a key class of cells in the body's immune defense system. Interleukin-2 has been found to increase the multiplication of T cells and their production of more interleukins. One property of interleukin-2 is to activate killer T cells, which may, in turn, destroy cancer cells.

An advance that was made possible by the use of interleukin-2 was the identification by Robert Gallo and colleagues at the National Cancer Institute of the first proven human cancer virus. Called HTTLV-1, the virus causes T cell leukemia. Interleukin-2 was also found by Gallo and a French team, headed by Luc Montagnier of the Pasteur Institute in Paris, as the cause of acquired immunodeficiency syndrome (AIDS). That discovery was possible because interleukin-2 stimulated the multiplication of T cells that are attacked by HIV. A third interleukin, IL-3, is made by lymphocytes and stimulates the multiplication of stem cells in the bone marrow.

Background material can be found in IMMUNE RESPONSE; VIRAL GENETICS; VIRUS. *Further developments in the field are discussed in* AUTOIMMUNITY; DNA REPLICATION; RNA. *Special topics in this area will be found in* GENE THERAPY; RECOMBINANT DNA; VIRAL DISEASES, EXOTIC.

First see DIESEL ENGINE

Internal Combustion Engine

Next see AUTOMOTIVE DESIGN

An engine in which the substances used to create heat are also used to perform work.

An internal combustion engine differs from an external-combustion system, such as a coal steampower plant, in which the heat created by burning fuel must be transferred from the burning chamber to create usable energy. The advantage that has made internal combustion engines so widely used is that they are lighter than external combustion engines and offer considerable flexibility in operating conditions. They are capable of a wide range of speeds and can be made to deliver any desired energy almost instantly with a single control.

Several methods can be used to get working energy from an internal combustion engine. One is to have the energy of combustion push a piston, as in an automobile engine. Another is to have the energy turn a rotating shaft, such as the propellor of an airplane or a ship. A third way is to expel the gases created by combustion through a nozzle, as in a jet engine.

Three Phases. There are three phases—three types of action—common to all internal combustion engines. The first is compression of a mixture of air and fuel (or in the case of a diesel engine, of air alone). The second is ignition and combustion of this mixture (in the case of the diesel, injection of fuel and ignition). The third is expansion, the first step in transferring the energy created by combustion out of the system to perform work.

Compression and expansion can be considered together. There are four general classes of compressors and expanders. One uses a piston in a cylinder, which is called a reciprocator because reciprocating motion is required. In this system, compression, combustion, and expansion take place in a single reciprocator, with the reciprocating motion being transferred by a rod-and-crank mechanism. This system is used in most automobile engines. A rotary-displacement engine is similar to a reciprocating engine but uses rotary motion.

A turbomachine, which is used in gas turbines, compresses and expands the working substance by passing it over closely spaced foils. The turbocompressors and turboexpanders used in these engines are classified by the general direction of the flow. The compressors and expanders are separate, which maintains a continuous flow through each of these components to be maintained.

A fourth kind of internal combustion engine has no moving parts but converts the kinetic energy of a flow stream to pressure. Some jet engines operate in this way. A mixture of fuel and air burns in a combustion chamber and the resulting gases are ejected through a nozzle, creating thrust. A ram-jet engine operates on this principle. Aircraft using ram-jet engines must move at high speeds, so that the air entering the engine has enough energy to allow ram compression to occur.

Compound Engines. Internal combustion engines can be designed to use two different methods of compression and expansion in series. These are called compound engines. One example is a free-piston engine. Combustion of the fuel takes place by compression. The resulting gases are transferred to two reciprocators, in which energy is made to do useful work.

Even a rocket engine can be regarded as an internal combustion engine. In a rocket, compression, combustion, and expansion can be compared to the same activities that take place in an air-breathing engine, such as an automobile engine. In any form, internal combustion engines continue to be primary providers of power to our industrial society. (*See* AIR POLLUTION; AUTOMOTIVE ENGINEERING; ENERGY; FOSSIL FUEL POWER; *and* HIGHWAY ENGINEERING.)

William Gibson, the sci-fi novelist who is credited with predicting the coming of the Internet and with coining the terms "internet" and "cyberspace."

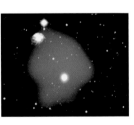

The ROSAT x-ray satellite observatory indicates that the three galaxies, NGC 2300, 150 million light years away, are in the midst of an immense cloud of dark matter, 1.3 million light years across.

First see TELECOMMUNICATIONS

Internet

Next see LOCAL AREA NETWORK (LAN)

During the the height of the Cold War, the Pentagon created the precursor of the Internet in order to provide leaders of government, the military, and science a means of communicating during and after a nuclear war. ARPANET, sponsored by the Pentagon's Advanced Research Projects Agency, was created in 1961 when computer scientists at UCLA linked their computer via telephone to a computer at the Stanford Research Institute, near Palo Alto. By the early 1980s, universities and research laboratories across the country joined this community of interconnected computers, increasing the size of ARPANET a hundredfold. (*See* LOCAL AREA NETWORK.)

In 1990, the the U.S. military relinquished control of the ARPANET project, and what was once the private domain of scientists and the U.S. government exploded into the public domain. As thousands of smaller networks joined the existing infrastructure of ARPANET, the Internet was formed, and became accessible to anyone with a computer and a telephone line. For the counterculture segment, led by people like novelist William Gibson, who is credited with coining the words "internet" and "cyberspace," this development was a sci-fi dream come true.

Operation. The Internet links millions of computers around the world through "gateway" computers, via telephone lines and fiber-optic cables. Information that is transferred across the Internet is assigned an electronic address, and is passed along from gateway to gateway until it reaches its destination. The absence of one central computer or command infrasructure regulating the flow of information between computers is a salient feature of the Internet.

The most popular means of information transfer are e-mail, newsgroups, chat rooms, and "web-browsing" or "surfing." The World Wide Web is a collection of multimedia files, a subset of the Internet, that computer users can view using a browser. These files, called web pages, or web sites, are provided by many sources.

First see NEBULA

Interstellar Medium ("Dark Matter")

Next see UNIVERSE, LARGE-SCALE STRUCTURE OF

Matter and radiation between the stars in a galaxy.

The interstellar medium is the matter and radiation that exist between the stars in a galaxy. Observations have found that this interstellar matter is found in spiral galaxies but not elliptical galaxies. Earth's galaxy is spiral, and most observations of interstellar matter have been made in our galaxy. The main constituent of interstellar matter is hydrogen, which is also the main constituent of stars.

At least 50 other molecules have also been detected in the interstellar matter, some as complex as ethanol and dimethyl ether. The mode of formation of these complex molecules is unknown. One possibility is that they form in chemical reactions on extremely small particles of matter in the interstellar medium. Interstellar matter also contains cosmic rays, which are high-energy particles such as protons. In our galaxy, this hydrogen is contained in a thin, flat disc, believed to have a spiral structure caused by the rotation of the galaxy.

The overall picture of interstellar matter structure is that of cool clouds in a mixed intercloud medium consisting of both warm and hot gases in a pressure equilibrium. The energy that heats and compresses interstellar matter originates from a combination of stellar winds and supernovas, exploding stars. The clouds are formed when shock fronts from such events compress and heat material that is initially cool. In addition to the known constituents of the interstellar medium, some astrophysicists say that it also contains dark matter of unknown content. The existence of dark matter would explain the fact that the observed amount of matter in the galaxy is not enough to account for the gravitational forces that are observed in the galaxy.

Elementary aspects of this subject are covered in GALAXY; HUBBLE CONSTANT; SPACE. *More information on particular aspects is contained in* BIG BANG THEORY; INFRARED AND ULTRAVIOLET ASTRONOMY; RADIO ASTRONOMY. *Additional relevant information is contained in* NUCLEOSYNTHESIS; UNIVERSE, LARGE-SCALE STRUCTURE OF.

First see UNIVERSE, LARGE-SCALE STRUCTURE OF

Interstellar Space Travel

Next see CRYOGENICS

Interstellar space travel poses an immense challenge because of the vast distances between our solar system and even the nearest stars. A one-way voyage to a nearby star in a spacecraft speeding at a million miles an hour would require about 3,000 years—the original crew of the spacecraft would never reach the destination unless special measures were taken.

One proposed measure would be to extend the life span of the crew by putting them in cold storage, freezing them so that their metabolic processes would be slowed drastically. While low-temperature preservation of human blood and sperm is now routine and microbes have been preserved for many years by freezing them, the preservation of a whole human being would require major advances in technology. The rea-

Above, among the most serious schemes for interstellar space travel are spaceships that "sail" through space by capturing sunlight (or laser light or atomic blasts) and achieve a significant fraction of the speed of light in two years. Such a ship would reach our nearest stellar neighbor in 22 years.

Further Reading
Bartusiak, Marcia, *Through a Universe Darkly: A Cosmic Tale of Ancient Ethers, Dark Matter, and the Fate of the Universe* (1993); Dyson, J.E., *The Physics of the Interstellar Medium* (1997); Holt, Stephen S., *After the First Three Minutes* (1991); Krauss, Lawrence M., *The Fifth Essence: The Search for Dark Matter in the Universe* (1992);

Further Reading
Howerton, B. A., *Free Space!—Real Alternatives for Reaching Outer Space* (1995); Pickover, Clifford, *Time: A Traveler's Guide* (1998); Sagan, *Carl, Pale Blue Dot: A Vision of the Human Future in Space* (1994); Schmidt, Stanley, *Islands in the Sky: Bold New Ideas for Colonizing Space* (1996).

son is that the human body contains a large amount of water. Freezing the body would cause serious damage to the cells of the body, both during the freezing process and during thawing.

Propulsion Systems. Current propulsion systems would not be adequate for such a mission. Using present-day technology, the amount of fuel that would be required would be impossibly great, even if all the mass of the fuel could be converted into energy, as is theoretically possible.

The complete conversion of mass into energy might be possible, on the other hand, if the fuel for the rocket of an interstellar space ship consisted of antimatter—that is, matter in which the normal positively charged protons of ordinary matter are replaced by negatively charged antiprotons and conventional negatively charged electrons are replaced by positively charged anti-electrons. Containment of antimatter would pose a problem, since both it and ordinary matter are annihilated when they come into contact. It is this reaction that would be used to propel an interstellar spacecraft.

One possible way to contain antimatter would be in a magnetic bottle, made of an intense magnetic field. Such bottles have been investigated in connection with experiments on controlled thermonuclear fusion. Another proposal is to use the atoms found in interstellar matter to provide propulsion for the spacecraft. An interstellar ramjet would require a large surface area measuring in the hundreds of square miles, to collect enough interstellar gas to propel the spacecraft; this would require more material than could be practically launched into space. One way of counteracting this problem would be to use magnetic fields rather than solid materials to serve as the ramjet intake.

Other Hazards. Another problem to address is the damage that could occur to a spacecraft and its crew traveling at close to the speed of light. At that speed, the impact of even small dust grains in interstellar space could cause great damage and could heat the interior of the spacecraft to temperatures that would literally fry the crew members. Again, the same magnetic deflection techniques used to gather fuel for the spacecraft could be used to deflect interstellar material capable of damaging the ship.

While the technologies for interstellar space travel seem unachievable today, it should be noted that travel to the moon was regarded as science fiction a century ago, and that technological progress is continuing in many areas applicable to the interstellar challenge.

Related areas to be considered are SPACE; SPECIAL RELATIVITY; UNIVERSE, LARGE-SCALE STRUCTURE OF. *Other aspects of the subject are discussed in* ROCKET; SPACECRAFT; TWIN PARADOX. *Related material can be found in* CRYOGENICS; EXTRATERRESTRIAL LIFE; PLANETS, FORMATION OF.

Invertebrates

First see BIODIVERSITY

Next see THERMAL REGULATION

Animals that lack a backbone, comprising eight of the nine phyla in the animal kingdom.

Invertebrates include a wide variety of creatures: among them are worms, jellyfish, slugs, clams, insects, and sponges.

Porifera. Sponges, phylum Porifera, are the most primitive invertebrates. They can be found in either salt or fresh water, but are sessile, anchored to the floor or to a rock. All of the porifera are filter feeders, meaning they strain out and digest the microscopic plankton and algae found in the water.

Coelenterates. Coelenterates are more advanced in that they consist of two cell layers and have a single body opening. This phylum includes jellyfish, hydras, and sea anemones, animals that sting and capture their prey. The basic body plan consists of a base with attached tentacles. The polyp form of coelenterates is oriented with the tentacles up, as in the hydra. Locomotion occurs as a series of "somersaults." The jellyfish represents the medusa form, in which the tentacles hang downward and beat back and forth for the animal to move.

Coelenterates are hermaphrodites; each organism contains both male and female sex organs. However, they do not self-fertilize; two animals get together in order to fertilize each other's eggs. Coelenterates also are cap-able of asexual reproduction in the form of budding.

Worms. The next three phyla consist of worms: platyhelminthes—flatworms whose bodies consist of three cell layers and contain some organ systems; nematodes—roundworms with more advanced organ systems and, for the first time, two body openings; and annelids—segmented worms such as the earthworm.

Most of the platyhelminthes, such as flukes and tapeworms, are parasites. However, planaria are free living. Some nematodes are parasites, including hookworms and pinworms, and some are free living. Annelids all live independently. Each segment is more or less self-sufficient, which is why an earthworm can be cut in half and each half wriggles. Annelids have a primitive circulatory system consisting of a dorsal (back) and ventral (belly) blood vessel, with "aortic arches" to serve as a heart. Their nervous system consists of a nerve cord. For a digestive system they have a crop, gizzard, and intestine. Respiration occurs through their moist skin, which is why the worms die if they dry out.

Mollusks. Mollusks are soft-bodied creatures with an "optional" hard shell for protection. This phylum includes the clam, octopus, and snail. These animals have gills and can be land or marine dwelling. The body consists of three basic parts: the headfoot for locomotion (which may include tentacles), the mantle, which secretes the shell, and the body, which contains the heart and other organs. Sessile creatures like clams and oysters are filter feeders.

Arthropods. Arthropods are the most numerous phylum in terms of species. All of these creatures have an exoskeleton, a hard outer shell consisting of a protein called chitin, and pairs of jointed legs. Depending upon whether they are land or marine creatures, respiration takes place by means of gills or spiracles, which are essentially air holes in the outer shell. Arthropods have an open circulatory system; blood is not contained within vessels but sloshes around inside the body cavity. Gas exchange and circulation are completely separate, which is why arthropods' blood is not red.

The three main classes of arthropods are:

—crustaceans, which include lobsters, crabs, and crayfish;

—arachnids, such as spiders, which have two distinct body regions and four pairs of legs;

—insects, such as grasshoppers, flies, and beetles (the most numerous); insects have three distinct body regions: head, thorax, and abdomen, and have multiple pairs of legs.

Echinoderms. Echinoderms include starfish and sand dollars. All of them are marine creatures and use gills for respiration. They have a spiny skin and an internal skeleton made of cartilage that serves to separate the body into distinct compartments. All echinoderms exhibit radial body symmetry. The nervous system of an echinoderm is advanced enough that these creatures are capable of regeneration. If a starfish loses an arm, not only will it regrow the missing limb, but the severed arm will grow a new body!

Chordates. The ninth phylum, chordates, includes both vertebrates and invertebrates. All chordates have gills during early development, as well as a notochord, the precursor to a backbone, and a neural tube, which is the precursor to a central nervous system.

The three main subphyla are:

—lancelets, which maintain a notochord and gills throughout life;

—tunicates, in which the notochord is lost at an early developmental stage (an example of a tunicate is the sea squirt); and

—vertebrates, in which a true backbone develops around the notochord.

The vertebrates include fish, amphibians, reptiles, birds, and mammals. All other animals are invertebrates.

The world of the invertebrates. Above, a purple jellyfish.

Background material can be found in ECOLOGY; EVOLUTION; FOSSILS. *More details can be found in* BIODIVERSITY; OCEAN BASINS; PHYLOGENY. *See also* GILLS; UNDERWATER EXPLORATION; OCEANOGRAPHY, *as well as* FISH; AMPHIBIANS; REPTILES.

Further Reading
Brusca, Richard C., *Invertebrates* (1990); Buchsbaum, Ralph, et al., *Animals Without Backbones* (1987); Morris, S. Conway, et al., *The Crucible of Creation: The Burgess Shale and the Rise of Animals* (1998); Pechenik, Jan A., *Biology of the Invertebrates* (1996); Waller, Geoffrey, ed., *Sealife: A Complete Guide to the Marine Environment* (1996).

First see BOND, CHEMICAL

Ion

Next see VALENCE

An atom or atoms with either a positive (cation) or negative (anion) charge.

An atom consists of three subatomic particles: protons, neutrons, and electrons. Both the positively charged protons and the neutral neutrons are located in the nucleus, whereas the negatively charged electrons are located in discrete energy levels outside. All atoms start out neutral, with an equal number of protons and electrons.

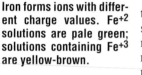

Iron forms ions with different charge values. Fe^{+2} solutions are pale green; solutions containing Fe^{+3} are yellow-brown.

Ionic Bonding. The outermost energy level that contains electrons is called the valence shell. All atoms "desire" a full valence shell to reach their most stable state. However, only the noble gases start out with a full shell. All others must steal, give up, or share electrons. If an atom that needs one more electron takes one from an atom that has one too many, both profit. This is the basis of ionic bonding.

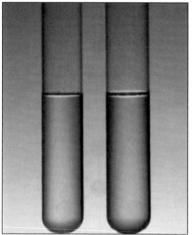

Nonmetals. Nonmetals are much more electronegative (strongly attract electrons) than metals. Therefore, when a metal atom bumps into a nonmetal, it loses its valence electron to the nonmetal. The nonmetal now has the additional electron it needs and the metal is also content, as it has a new valence shell, the previously second-to-last occupied energy level that already had a full complement of electrons. As a result of their mutual encounter, the metal has lost an electron and become a cation or positively charged ion, and the nonmetal has gained an electron, becoming an anion or negatively charged ion. Their opposite charges cause them to be attracted to each other and so they stay together as an ionic compound.

OBSERVATIONS

Pass the Salt...

A common example of an ionic bond forming between two atoms involves sodium and chlorine. Sodium, a metal, originally has one valence electron, and chlorine, a nonmetal, has seven valence electrons. Chlorine needs just one more electron to complete its shell and so will grab sodium's electron, transforming sodium into a cation (Na^{+1}) and itself into an anion (C^{-1}). Because of the limits imposed by ionization energy, it is easier for sodium simply to lose its lone valence electron rather than gain an additional seven. The resulting compound is sodium chloride (NaCl), more commonly known as table salt.

Ionic Compound. Atoms can gain or lose up to three electrons. The energy required to remove an electron from its original atom is called ionization energy. To remove the first electron from a neutral atom requires a small amount of energy. However, removal of a second electron demands much more energy as the atom is already positively charged and therefore holding its negative particles more tightly.

Some ions are monatomic, meaning they are single atoms that have become ions. Ions may also be polyatomic, consisting of more than one atom. Examples of polyatomic ions include NH_4^{+1} (ammonium), NO_3^{-1} (nitrate), SO_4^{-2} (sulfate) and CO_3^{-2} (carbonate). A polyatomic ion will behave exactly the same way as a monatomic ion in bonding situations.

All ionic compounds are neutral, because their component ions cancel out. If the numerical values of the cation and anion are equal from the outset, one of each is used, as in the case of sodium and chlorine. However, if the values are not equal, as in the case of aluminum (Al^{+3}) and sulfate (SO_4^{-2}), the "crisscross" method is used, in which the number charge of one ion becomes the subscript (number of ions used) of the other and vice versa. Therefore, the formula for aluminum sulfate is $Al_2(SO_4)_3$.

Ionic compounds include acids, bases, and salts. An acid is an ionic compound whose cation is hydrogen H^+, while a base is an ionic compound whose anion is the hydroxide ion OH^-. A salt is a compound that does not have H^+ or OH^- as one of its ions.

Ionic bonds are not as strong as covalent bonds, in which electrons are shared between atoms. However, they are still relatively strong. Ionic solids are solids whose crystal structure is made up of ions. The lattice or pattern consists of a seemingly infinite array of alternating cations and anions, giving the crystal a regular, ordered three-dimensional shape. Ionic solids have high melting and boiling points, because of the strength of these ionic bonds.

Ion Exchange. If the cation of one compound encounters the anion of another compound, they often form an entirely new ionic compound—this is an ion exchange reaction.

Ion exchange reactions are also referred to as displacements, as one ion is "displaced" by another in the compound structure. In a single displacement, only one ion moves, while in a double displacement, two ionic compounds trade ions between them, resulting in the formation of two new compounds.

Two particular types of ion exchange reactions are acid-base reactions and precipitation reactions. An acid is an ionic compound whose cation is H^+ and a base is an ionic compound whose anion is OH^-. When combined, the acid and base neutralize each other—the H^+ and OH^- combine to form water, and the other two ions, the acid anion and the base cation, combine to form a salt, a neutral ionic compound. This is an example of a double displacement, as two new compounds have beem formed.

In a precipitation reaction, two aqueous solutions react together to form a non-soluble solid. The solid is formed by a recombination of the ions of the two compounds that were originally dissolved. A precipitation reaction may be either a single displacement or a double displacement reaction.

Ionic Solids. The crystal lattice of an ionic solid consists of a seemingly infinite array of alternating cations and anions. This gives the crystal a regular, ordered three-dimensional shape such as a cube or a hexagon. The size of the individual crystals can be large or small, depending on the materials it is made of as well as the conditions under which the crystal formed. A powder consists of many tiny crystals.

Compared to molecular compounds, ionic compounds are made up of relatively few atoms and are roughly spherical in shape. Consequently, the pattern can be envisioned as closely packed spheres filling a particular volume. Since anions are larger than cations, the ionic crystal consists primarily of an arrangement of anions, with cations placed in the interstices or intervening holes. The attraction between the ions is strong, causing ionic solids to have high melting and boiling points.

Within the crystal, each ion is surrounded by a specific number of "neighbors" or oppositely charged ions to which it is attracted. The number of these neighbors is known as the coordination number. The higher the coordination number, the stronger the ionic bonds holding together the solid, due to the maximization of attractive forces.

The coordination number for sodium chloride, or table salt, is six, as each Na^{+1} is surrounded by 6 Cl^{-1} ions, and each Cl^{-1} ion is surrounded by 6 Na^{+1} ions.

Other Ionic Solids. Other ionic solids have different coordination numbers, such as zinc sulfide (ZnS), which has a coordination number of 4, and cesium chloride ($CsCl_2$), which has a coordination number of 8. Within the same crystal, a cation and anion do not necessarily have the same coordination number. For example, in calcium fluoride CaF_2, the coordination number for the calcium ion Ca^{+2} is 8 and for the fluoride ion is 4, meaning each calcium is surrounded by 8 fluoride ions and each fluoride is surrounded by 4 calcium ions.

Related areas to be considered are ATOM; CHARGE AND CURRENT; VALENCE. *Advanced subjects are developed in* ELECTRON AFFINITY; OXIDIZING AGENTS. *More information on particular aspects is contained in* BATTERIES AND FUEL CELLS; ELECTRONEGATIVITY; PLASMA PHYSICS. *For background, see* CHEMICAL FORMULAS *and* CHEMICAL REACTION.

Further Reading
Amaldi, G., *The Nature of Matter: Physical Theory from Thales to Fermi* (1982); Asimov, Isaac, *Atom: Journey Across the Subatomic Cosmos* (1992); Friedrich, H., *Theoretical Atomic Physics* (1998); Lisitsa, V. S., *Atoms in Plasmas* (1994); Stwertka, A., *The World of Atoms and Quarks* (1995); Wong, Cheuk-Yin, *Introduction to High-Energy Heavy-Ion Collisions* (1994).

First See CHEMICAL FORMULA

Isomerism

Next See SYMMETRY IN NATURE

The existence of two compounds with the same chemical formula.

A chemical formula specifies the elements and number of atoms in a molecule and was originally thought to be unique to an individual compound. Isomerism was first discovered in the 1820s by Liebig and Wöhler, when they were working with the compounds silver cyanate (AgNCO) and silver fulminate (AgONC). (*See* PHOTOGRAPHY, CHEMISTRY OF.)

Three types of isomers exist: structural, geometrical, and optical. Structural isomers have the same chemical formulas, but a different three-dimensional arrangement of the atoms. The same units, in the same amounts, are used to make entirely different things. In general, isomers usually have different physical and chemical properties.

Alkanes, simple hydrocarbons consisting of long chains of carbon atoms with attached hydrogen atoms, are found as various structural isomers. A molecule with five or more carbon atoms can be a straight chain, with all five atoms linked consecutively (this is known as a normal alkane) or it might have branched chains (these isomers are called derivatives). The number of possible isomers increases with an increase in the number of carbon atoms.

Well-Known Isomers. Glucose and fructose are a pair of well-known isomers. They are both simple sugar units, called monosaccharides, with the formula $C_6H_{12}O_6$. Glucose is found either in a straight chain form or as a hexagon-shaped ring structure made up of five of the six carbons with one carbon remaining outside the ring. Fructose is found as a pentagon-shaped ring made up of four of the carbons with two outside the ring.

Geometrical isomers differ in the arrangement of groups around the same central atom. The prefix *cis-* means two identical groups are adjacent to each other, and the prefix *trans-* means that the groups are across from each other, or at least not adjacent.

Optical isomers always occur in pairs known as enantiomers, which display the characteristic of handedness. They are nonsuperimposable mirror images of each other, a property known as chirality. The central atom around which the isomers are formed is known as the chiral center or stereocenter. Some compounds have more than one stereocenter around which the groups are arranged. Examples of enantiomers include the L- and D- forms of amino acids. Some stereoisomers differ from each other only in how they interact with polarized light. (*See* OPTICS.)

First see TRANSURANIC ELEMENTS

Isotope

Next see RADIOACTIVITY

Atoms of the same element that differ by the number of neutrons contained within the nucleus.

All atoms are identified in two ways: by the number of protons in their nuclei, also known as their atomic number, and by their mass, usually determined by adding together their protons and neutrons. Isotopes have different atomic masses, but their behavior regarding chemical bonds remains the same. All elements have more than one isotope. Some well-known examples of isotopes include hydrogen, carbon, and uranium.

Hydrogen. A regular atom of hydrogen has one proton in its nucleus, and no neutrons. Its atomic mass is one amu. Deuterium and tritium also have one proton in each of their nuclei, but deuterium contains one neutron and tritium contains two. Their atomic masses are 2 amu and 3 amu, re-spectively. "Heavy water" contains two atoms of deuterium in place of the hydrogens. It is indistinguishable from ordinary water (H_2O) by odor, color, taste, or smell. Only in terms of mass is there a difference. Heavy water was developed in one of the early experiments leading up to the development of nuclear weapons.

Carbon. The most common form of carbon has six protons and six neutrons in its nucleus. It is known as C_{12}, as it has a mass of 12 amu. A major isotope of C_{12} is C_{14} with 8 neutrons (mass = 14 amu). C_{14} is used in radiocarbon dating, a method used to date fossils and other excavated materials. C_{14} has a half-life of 5,730 years. C_{14} is used to date wood and cloth because only living plants maintain a constant C_{14} content in their molecules. Once the plant is dead, no more carbon is taken in so no new C_{14} is produced, and the C_{14} content begins to decrease.

Uranium. Ordinary uranium ($Z=92$, mass of 238 amu) is called U_{238}. Enriched or weapons-grade uranium is U_{235}. It is radioactive, meaning its atoms spontaneously give off alpha or beta particles (electrons) and gamma radiation (a high-energy photon of light). The typical fuels used in a nuclear reactor are U_{235} and plutonium (symbol Pu, $Z=94$). Plutonium is formed when U_{238} is transformed into yet another isotope, U_{239}, which then decays into Pu_{239}. Radioactive isotopes decay to form more stable isotopes either by electron loss or by electron capture or positron (a positively charged subatomic particle with the mass of an electron) emissions. Any time a nucleus decays, there is a loss of mass which results in a lower energy state and therefore greater stability for the atom.

Stability. In stable isotopes, the number of protons is never greater than the number of neutrons. It is believed that the excess neutrons "dilute" the positive charges of the protons and enable them to cling together more easily. Isotopes with even numbers of protons and neutrons have greater stability. The most stable nuclei have a mass of approximately 60 amu. The most stable nucleus is the iron isotope Fe_{56}.

Background material can be found in ATOM; PERIODIC TABLE OF THE ELEMENTS; VALENCE. *More details can be found in* LANTHANIDES; NOBLE GASES; RADIOACTIVITY. *Additional relevant information is contained in* RADIOCHEMISTRY; TRANSURANIC ELEMENTS.

First see SPACE

ISU (International Standard of Units and Measures)

Next see TIME, MEASUREMENT OF

The International System of Units and Measures (ISU or SI), used throughout the world, is different from the system commonly used in the United States. The ISU uses the meter as the unit of length, the liter as the unit of liquid or gas, and the kilogram as the unit of weight. One Amer-ican gallon equals 3.785 liters and one quart equals 0.914 liters. The kilogram (the symbol of which is kg) is defined as the mass of an international prototype, made of platinum and iridium, that is kept by the International Bureau of Weights and Measures at Sevres, near Paris.

A pound, by contrast, has traditionally been defined in terms of the gravitational force near Earth's surface. In relation to the ISU, one pound is formally defined as 0.45359237 kilograms; in practice, Europeans define a "metric pound" as exactly 500 grams. For measurements of length, a meter can be divided into decimeters (one-tenth of a meter), centimeters (one-hundredth of a meter), millimeters (one-thousandth of a meter) or into smaller units, each based on dividing the meter by increasing powers of 10. For weighing purposes, a kilogram can be divided into grams (one-thousandth of a kilogram) or milligrams (one-millionth of a gram). For liquid measurements, the liter can be divided into milliliters (one thousandth of a liter). One unit of force in the ISU is the newton, which is the force that is required to impart an acceleration of one meter per second to a mass of one kilogram.

Until 1959, Great Britain and the United States both used the same system of weights and measures. Britain adopted the ISU system that year, and the United States is now the only nation that does not use the ISU system. However, the units of weights and measures of the United States are defined in terms of their metric system counterparts. The administration of weights and measures in the United States is coordinated by the National Bureau of Standards.

Jaundice

First see LIVER

Next see BLOOD

A condition in which the skin and the whites of the eyes become yellowed because of an excess of bilirubin, a bile pigment, in the blood.

Jaundice can be a symptom of many disorders of the biliary system and the liver. There are three major types of jaundice—hemolytic, hepatocellular, and obstructive.

Hemolytic jaundice occurs when the body produces more bilirubin than the liver can process. Normally, bilirubin is formed when old red blood cells are broken down. It is then processed in the liver and is excreted in bile. Too much bilirubin can be produced by a number of adult conditions, such as hemolytic anemia, and in infants when the liver is not developed enough to do its job properly. Hepatocellular jaundice occurs when the transfer of bilirubin from the liver to bile is prevented by liver failure or hepatitis, an acute inflammation of the liver. Obstructive jaundice occurs when the flow of bile from the liver is prevented by one of several disorders that block the bile ducts. It can also occur when disease destroys the bile ducts.

The first step in treating jaundice is to discover the underlying problem that causes it, generally by examining accompanying symptoms. In hemolytic jaundice, for example, the color of both the urine and the feces will be normal, whereas in hepatocellular jaundice the feces will be normal but the urine will be dark. Blood tests, liver function tests, and ultrasound scanning are among the methods used to diagnose the underlying cause of jaundice so that it can be treated.

Jet Propulsion

First see PROPULSION

Next see AERODYNAMICS

The movement of a vehicle by means of a force that is produced by discharging a fluid or gas in the form of a jet in a direction opposite that of the motion.

In accordance with Newton's third law of motion, the rearward-moving jet of fluid or gas creates a reactive force that drives the vehicle forward. Jet propulsion can be seen in nature; the squid uses a kind of jet propulsion to push itself through water. Jet-propelled automobiles and boats have been developed but the main application of jet propulsion is in aircraft and spacecraft. The rockets that are used to launch spacecraft provide jet propulsion. Because they carry their own oxidant, which is needed to ignite the fuel, rockets can be used in space. On Earth, air-breathing jet engines are used. In the Earth's atmosphere, jet propulsion becomes more effi-

cient at higher altitudes, because the efficiency is inversely proportional to the density of the medium—in this case air—through which a body is flying.

In addition to rockets, major forms of jet engines include the pulse jet, the ramjet, and the turbojet. The pulse jet was invented in 1908 but first became widely known during World War II, when it was used to propel the German V-1 missiles that attacked England. The inlet end of the pulse jet has valves that normally are held by spring tension to block the flow of air out of the front end of the engine. They can be sucked inward to allow air to enter the engine. Its combustion chamber is downstream from the air flaps and has a fuel injection system and a spark plug. Behind the combustion chamber is a long exhaust duct. When the spark plug ignites a fuel-air mixture, there is a pressure surge that produces a flow of combustion products out of the exhaust duct of the engine. It is this flow that provides the thrust.

Ramjet. The ramjet is the simplest air-breathing propulsion system. In flight, the compression of the oxidant is achieved by the forward motion of the device as it flies through the atmosphere. This enables a ramjet to operate without a compressor and turbine. The system consists of an inlet diffuser, a combustion chamber in which the fuel is burned, and a jet nozzle through which the products of combustion are discharged. When it is used in guided missiles, the ramjet must be accelerated to its operating

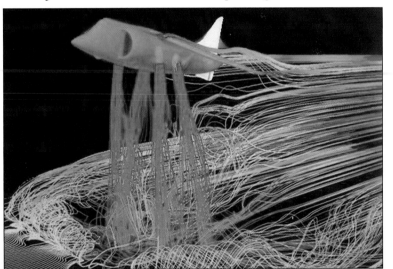

velocity before it can fly. In some missiles, a rocket is used to take off and accelerate the vehicle to the speed at which the ramjet can be operated. In aircraft, where many successive takeoffs and landings are desired, a turbojet engine can be used for this purpose. Ramjet engines are usually considered for use in vehicles that travel at two to eight times the speed of sound.

Turbojet. The turbojet and a similar engine, the turboprop, are used for aircraft propulsion.

Above, the computer-simulated jet propulsion profile of a Harrier jet, capable of a vertical takeoff, as is indicated by the jet discharge.

Developed in Germany in 1939, the turbojet operates on a kerosene-based fuel mixed with air and ignited in a combustion chamber. The expanding gases of combustion are directed at the blades of a turbine wheel. A shaft leads from the center of the turbine wheel to the front opening of the engine. The shaft drives a compressor that pushes air into the engine. The hot gases that pass the blades of the turbine pass through a constriction in the inner hollow tube leading to the exhaust nozzle of the engine. The gases expand through the nozzle, increasing in velocity, thus providing the thrust of the engine.

The jet prop or turboprop combines jet propulsion with propeller propulsion. The turboprop interposes another turbine wheel that is positioned just ahead of the exhaust nozzle. A shaft from this turbine leads to a propeller, which is turned to provide propulsion. After passing this stage, the gases pass out of the engine in jet fashion, with their energy reduced by the amount of energy needed to turn the propeller turbine.

THE CUTTING EDGE

Speed Racer

The next step in jet propulsion will be hypersonic flight, which begins at Mach 5. To achieve that speed, a supersonic combustion ramjet, or scramjet, will be needed. The problem is that a normal ramjet must slow down the air entering the engine so that combustion and expansion can take place within the engine. The Concept Demonstration Engine, burning hydrogen fuel and ignited by an additive called silane, has run successfully at outside speeds of Mach 6.8 using a revolutionary fuel injection system that actually shifts the injection site forward in the engine as speeds rise. Perhaps someday the hypersonic (and very costly) National Aerospace Plane will indeed fly.

Related areas may be found in AERODYNAMICS; COMBUSTION; PROPULSION. *More details can be found in* AIRCRAFT, SUBSONIC AND SUPERSONIC; HYDROCARBONS. *Additional relevant information is contained in* MISSILE; ROCKET; SPACECRAFT.

First see WEATHER

Jet Stream

Next see WIND AND CLOUDS

The high-speed, easterly wind band flowing from 20,000 to 40,000 feet above the surface of the Earth.

The maximum wind speed in a jet stream can be more than 250 miles an hour, but ordinarily the speeds are not that great. The speeds in the core of a jet stream average about 50 miles per hour during the summer months and about 100 miles per hour during the winter months.

Multiple Jet Streams. There are actually several jet streams. Each is about 300 miles wide and four miles deep. In the Northern Hemisphere, there are the polar jet stream and the subpolar jet stream.

The polar jet stream can extend completely around the hemisphere at times, but it can be discontinuous, and it varies from day to day. The subpolar jet stream occurs between 20 and 30 degrees of latitude, and also demonstrates variations in speed and continuity. There can be other jet streams as well; their number in each hemisphere will vary from week to week, and their paths will vary from day to day and season to season.

The polar jet stream occurs in the tropopause, the boundary between the stratosphere and the atmospheric layer next to it, the troposphere. The tropopause consists of several discrete, overlapping layers called leaves; the jet stream blows where the leaves of the tropopause overlap at different latitudes. The strong winds of the jet stream are generated in part by the strong temperature contrasts that are found in these regions of overlap. That is why El Niño, which warms the surface of the Pacific Ocean and thus the air passing over it, affects the jet stream's course. The jet streams were not discovered until World War II, when high-flying military pilots began to report unexpectedly strong winds at high altitudes.

Applications. Knowledge of the jet streams is used every day by pilots and meteorologists for flight planning and weather forecasting. Pilots of jet aircraft traveling east will fly in a jet stream, while pilots of aircraft flying west will plan their flight paths to avoid flying into it. The most pronounced areas of maximum jet stream wind speeds have been observed to occur across central Japan and over the northeastern United States.

Further Reading
Crumpsty, Nicholas, *Jet Propulsion: A Simple Guide to Aerodynamic and Thermodynamic Design and Performance of Jet Engines* (1998); Golley, John, *Genesis of the Jet: Frank Whittle and the Invention of the Jet Engine* (1998); Hill, Phillip Graham, *Mechanics and Thermodynamics of Propulsion* (1992); Hunecke, Klaus, *Jet Engines: Fundamentals of Theory, Design and Operation* (1998); Saarlas, Maido, *An Introduction to Aerospace Propulsion* (1996).

Right, a satellite photo of the jet stream as it leaves the North American coast and heads over the Atlantic towards Europe.

First see ELECTRIC CURRENT

Josephson Junction

Next see TRANSISTOR

A switch employed in low-temperature superconducting components.

Josephson junctions are composed of thin films of barium copper oxide, separated by an even thinner insulating barrier; they can also be formed between one thin film and an exceedingly fine stylus point. A promising technique deposits the film on an angled piece of lanthanum aluminate (an insulating material), achieving a Josephson junction where the crystalline deposit turns at a sharp angle. Each Josephson junction is superconductive at very low currents but at a critical value becomes resistive, so that electrons tunnel through the insulating barrier literally one at a time. The value of this switch lies in its incredible sensitivity, particularly as part of a superconducting quantum interference device (SQUID). Experimental SQUIDs have measured changes as small as 1 femtotesla (10^{-15} tesla) in a magnetic field and 1 femtoampere in a current, or a distance of 10^{-19} meters. This is less than three times the theoretical limit for accuracy established by Heisenberg's uncertainty principle. As an added advantage, the Josephson junction works at a temperature that can be sustained in commercial equipment, above $-321°$ Fahrenheit (the temperature of liquid nitrogen, the standard coolant).

The availability of Josephson junctions has created a new specialty, neuromagnetometry, which has already found applications in brain surgery and in monitoring fetal heartbeats. SQUIDs have also provided an order of magnitude increase in the sensitivity of aircraft metal inspection. Finally, Josephson junctions may be used as digital logic gates, opening the way for further computer speed and size improvements.

First see PLANET

Jupiter

Next see PLANETARY ATMOSPHERE

The fifth planet from the sun and by far the largest in the solar system—it is larger than all the other planets put together in both size and mass.

Jupiter has a mass nearly 317 times that of the Earth, and its volume is more than 1,300 times that of our relatively tiny planet. Because of its large surface area and high albedo—the percentage of light reflected by its surface—Jupiter is one of the brightest objects in the night sky; only the moon and the planet Venus appear brighter to Earth-based observers. Jupiter rotates very rapidly, with a period of less than 10 hours, and

Above, a thin-film Josephson Junction.

Right, Jupiter, its Great Red Spot visible at lower left. On July 16-22, 1994, over twenty fragments of comet Shoemaker-Levy 9 collided with the planet Jupiter. The comet had been discovered only a year earlier.

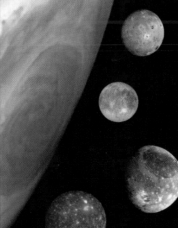

Above, Jupiter and its major moons (from top): Io; Europa; Ganymede; and Callisto.

so it is noticeably flattened at its poles. While the equatorial diameter of Jupiter is 88,700 miles, its polar diameter is just 82,800 miles. Jupiter's period of rotation is the fastest of all the major planets. The rotation period varies with latitude—it is fastest at the equator and slowest at the poles.

Jupiter revolves around the sun at a mean distance of 484 million miles, with one complete rotation taking 11.86 Earth years. The orbit of Jupiter is more elongated than that of Earth, so that, at perihelion, its closest approach to the sun, it is 47 million miles closer to the sun than at aphelion, the farthest distance from the sun. Jupiter's orbit is inclined about 1 degree to Earth's orbit.

Great Red Spot. Viewed through a telescope from Earth, Jupiter is seen to have a number of light and dark bands parallel to its equator, with red and brown shades predominating in the bands. The details of the bands change constantly, an indication that the markings are in the atmosphere of Jupiter, not on its surface. The most visible marking, the Great Red Spot, is about 30,000 miles long and 7,000 miles wide; its color and period of rotation change continually.

This semipermanent character of most of Jupiter's surface features, together with the variation of its rotation in different latitudes, high reflecting power, and low density—about one-quarter of Earth's density—indicate that Jupiter probably has a small solid core surrounded by a very thick atmosphere. One theory is that the atmosphere forms a compressed layer several thousand miles thick, with a thick layer of ice below it and a very small, inner rocky mass at the center of the planet.

Atmosphere. The Jovian atmosphere has been studied intensively, and the results indicate

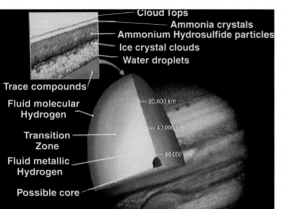

Cloud Tops
Ammonia crystals
Ammonium Hydrosulfide particles
Ice crystal clouds
Water droplets

Trace compounds

Fluid molecular Hydrogen

Transition Zone

Fluid metallic Hydrogen

Possible core

20,000 km
40,000
60,000

A cross-sectioned view of Jupiter. Space probes sent to Jupiter have confirmed that Jupiter has a ring over 35,000 miles above the cloud tops. It is over 4,000 miles wide, but only a half-mile thick, and lies on the equatorial plane.

that it consists mostly of molecular hydrogen, methane, and ammonia. Large amounts of helium are believed to be in the atmosphere, but there is no direct evidence of its presence. The temperature of Jupiter's surface is too low to be measured directly, but it is believed to be about 112 degrees Celsius above absolute zero.

Jupiter emits electromagnetic radiation in radio frequencies. The shorter wavelengths of these emissions are believed to originate from thermal activity, while the longer wavelengths are believed to arise from synchrotron radiation emitted by a belt of electrons trapped by Jupiter's magnetic field, similar to Earth's Van Allen belts.

Satellites. Jupiter has 12 known moons. The four largest and brightest of them were discovered by Galileo in 1610, and so are called the Galilean satellites. Two of these satellites are about the size of the Earth's moon, while the other two are about 50 percent larger. The planes of the orbits of the two inner satellites nearly match the plane of Jupiter's orbit. As a result, these satellites pass within the shadow of Jupiter or cast shadows on the surface of the planet at almost every revolution.

Observations of these satellites and the times of their eclipse and occultation led to the first determination of the probable speed of light. This determination was made in 1675 by the astronomer Olaus Roemer, who observed the discrepancy between the predicted time of the eclipse of a Jovian satellite and the actual time of its occurrence.

The outermost eight satellites of Jupiter are too small and faint to be observed from Earth except with very powerful telescopes; they were discovered as recently as the 1950s. Even with such telescopes, the four outermost can be seen only by taking photographs. It has been determined that these four satellites orbit the planet in a direction opposite to that of Jupiter's rotation. The motions of these outermost satellites are so greatly disturbed by gravitational interactions with the inner satellites that the problem they present in celestial mechanics has not been fully solved. Studies of Jupiter and its satellites are still ongoing.

Background material can be found in ASTEROID AND METEOR; PLANET; SOLAR SYSTEMS. *Advanced subjects are developed in* BROWN AND WHITE DWARFS; SATURN; URANUS. *More information on particular aspects is contained in* COMET; EXTRATERRESTRIAL LIFE; MARS; PLANET, FORMATION OF.

Further Reading
Barbieri, Cesare, *The Three Galileos: The Man, the Spacecraft, the Telescope* (1997); Beebe, Reta, *Jupiter: The Giant Planet* (1994); Hockey, Thomas A., *Galileo's Planet: Observing Jupiter Before Photography* (1999); Levy, David H., *Impact Jupiter: The Crash of Comet Shoemaker-Levy 9* (1995); Simon, Seymour, *Destination: Jupiter* (1998).

First see GEOLOGICAL TIME SCALE

Jurassic Period

Next see DINOSAUR

The period of geological time that began 210 years ago and lasted 70 million years. It is the middle period of the Mesozoic era.

The Jurassic period is known as the Age of Reptiles. The most famous of these, of course, were the dinosaurs. However, there were other creatures existing as well, such as crocodiles and their relatives. In addition, there were ichthyosaurs, plesiosaurs, and sharks in the ocean, along with various cephalopods, which are related to modern squid and octopi.

Not all dinosaurs belong to the Jurassic period. Triceratops and Tyrannosaurus rex lived in a later time. Jurassic dinosaurs include sauropods such as Diplodocus, Brachiosaurus, and Apatosaurus, as well as other plant-eaters like Stegosaurus. Carnivorous dinosaurs of the Jurassic period include Allosaurus. Dinosaurs are believed to be very similar to modern reptiles. They were egg layers and probably tended their young to some degree, had scales, and were mostly cold-blooded. (*See* DINOSAURS.)

A Jurassic period fossilized shrimp found in the Solnhofen Limestone pits of Bavaria, Germany.

The first birds are believed to have originated in this time period, including archaeopteryx, considered to be the first true avian. Most scientists accept the theory that birds evolved from dinosaurs; the debate centers mostly on which particular group gave rise to birds.

In terms of plant life, there were giant ferns, gingkoes, and other conifers, many of which have relatives present today. Flowering plants, however, had not yet evolved.

The name "Jurassic" comes from the Jura mountains, located on the border between France and Switzerland, where rocks dating from this time were first discovered. Many of our petroleum deposits are fossilized plants and animals from this period.

The Jurassic period was followed by the Cretaceous period, which ended 65 million years ago with mass extinctions, including the extinction of the dinosaurs. (*See* GEOLOGICAL TIME SCALE.)

Karyotyping

Next see DNA

A technique for examining the chromosomes of a given species.

Karyotyping is a technique for examining the chromosomes, the bodies in the nucleus of the cell that are made of deoxyribonucleic acid (DNA) and contain the genes. One method of making a karyotype starts with collecting blood, whose white cells contain chromosomes. A diluted solution of salt is added to the blood sample, causing the cells to swell so that the chromosomes separate. A stain is then added to make the chromosomes more visible. The sample is placed on a microscope slide, another glass slide or a cover slip is put over over the cells, and pressure is applied to the glass. This pressure squashes the cells, spreading the chromosomes out as far as possible. The chromosomes are then examined under a microscope, and photographs are taken of representative cells. Each photograph is then enlarged up to three or four thousand times. The resulting print is cut up by hand, so that each chromosome in the photograph can be isolated and mounted on paper. The chromosomes are matched in pairs—

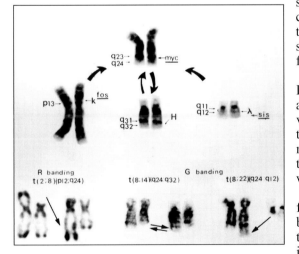

The karyotyping chromosome chart for the genetic disease Burkitt's lymphoma, showing the chromosomal defect responsible.

there are 23 pairs, or 46 chromosomes, in a human cell—and lined up according to size. The result is a picture that contains the 23 pairs, numbered according to size.

Classification of chromosomes is not always easy, because several of them are very close in size. Study of a karyotype can reveal basic chromosomal defects, such as an additional, missing, or misshapen chromosome. Karyotyping also reveals the gender of a fetus by displaying the sex chromosomes. (*See* AMNIOCENTESIS.)

Kepler's Laws

Next see NEWTON'S LAWS

In astronomy, the laws of planetary motion put forth by Johannes Kepler in 1609 and 1619.

Kepler's laws were a major step toward establishing the modern view of the solar system and the universe. The first two were published in *Astronomia Nova* (1609). They stated that (1) the planets circle around the sun in elliptical orbits, with the sun at one focus of the ellipse; and (2) the radius vector, the line drawn from the sun to a planet, sweeps out equal areas in equal times. Kepler's third law states that the square of the period of revolution of a planet is in direct proportion to the cube of the semimajor axis of its orbit. Kepler based his laws on the observations made by Tycho Brahe, for whom Kepler worked in Prague. Brahe had designed and constructed astronomical instruments that were far more accurate than any others in existence at the time, using the results of his observations to support the heliocentric theory of the solar system.

Although Kepler accepted the heliocentric theory, he was uncertain about the mechanism by which the planets remained in orbit around the sun, since he still subscribed to the Aristotelian concept that a continuing force had to be applied to keep a body in motion. He theorized that the sun exerted a force on the planets that "spread from the sun in the same manner as light."

Kepler's laws provided major support for Isaac Newton's theory of gravity, in that they agreed with his discovery that the sun's attraction varies inversely as the square of the distance of the planet from the sun and is proportional to the mass of the planet. Newton predicted that the third law was not quite accurate, a prediction that was borne out by very precise observations.

Applications. Kepler's laws, with the modifications made by Newton, today are known to be accurate for all the known celestial bodies in the solar system and elsewhere in the universe, including asteroids, comets, natural satellites such as the moon, and artificial satellites and double-star systems. In practical applications, the laws must be modified with respect to artificial satellites in orbit around the Earth, to take into account the effects of the outermost regions of the Earth's atmosphere, and the fact that the Earth is not a perfect sphere. More recently, Kepler's laws have been found to be accurate for electrons orbiting the nucleus of an atom.

Background material on Kepler's laws can be found in ACCELERATION; MECHANICS; SOLAR SYSTEM. *Advanced subjects are developed in* COMET; SATELLITE, PLANETARY. *Additional relevant information is contained in* CALCULUS; GRAVITY; NEWTON'S LAWS; SYMMETRY IN NATURE.

Johannes Kepler (1571–1630)

Further Reading
Koestler, Arthur, *The Watershed: A Biography of Johannes Kepler* (1965); Kozhamthadam, Job, *The Discovery of Kepler's Laws: The Interaction of Science, Philosophy, and Religion* (1993); Rosen, Edward, *Three Imperial Mathematicians: Kepler Trapped Between Brahe and Ursus* (1986); Stephenson, Bruce, *Kepler's Physical Astronomy* (1994); Voelkel, James R., *Johannes Kepler And the New Astronomy* (1999).

First see DIGESTION

Kidneys and Excretory Systems

Next see RESPIRATORY SYSTEM

Organs responsible for regulating the balance of water, salt, and other electrolytes in body fluids and for removing foreign chemicals from the cells.

The kidneys are the centerpiece of the execretory system in most vertebrates, even though the skin, respiratory, and digestive systems may also have excretory functions. In vertebrates other than fish, nitrogenous wastes are excreted through the kidneys. In mammals and amphibians, they are first converted to urea, a soluble compound. In birds and many reptiles, they are converted to uric acid, which can be concentrated almost into a solid. In fish, the kidneys have a smaller role. Most nitrogenous wastes are excreted as ammonia through the gills, which also regulate salt concentration.

Human System. In humans, two kidneys are located in the back of the abdominal cavity. They are made up of microscopic units called nephrons that filter blood and produce urine. Nephrons have several parts. A network of capillaries called a glomerulus sits inside a hollow structure called Bowman's capsule; together they form the renal corpuscle. The corpuscle is connected to a long tubule shaped like a backward N. It consists of the proximal tubule, the loop of Henle, the distal tubule, and the collecting duct. The duct of each nephron—the human kidney has a million of them—empties urine into the renal pelvis, the central cavity in the kidney, and a large duct carries it away. In mammals, this is the ureter that leads to the urinary bladder. Urine is stored in the bladder and released through the urethra, which empties through the penis in males and the vulva in females. In some animals, including birds and amphibians, the large duct empties into the cloaca, a chamber in which the digestive and genital tracts terminate. There the urine can be further concentrated before leaving the body through a vent.

The glomerulus acts as a mechanical filter of the blood, retaining cells, platelets, and proteins too big to pass through its pores. As the remaining filtrate passes through the nephron's tubules, most of it is reabsorbed and returned to the capillaries. In humans, for instance, 99 percent of the water and sodium and 50 percent of the urea may be reabsorbed. A complex process involving osmosis and ion pumps allows kidneys in mammals and birds to conserve water by producing urine far more concentrated than the

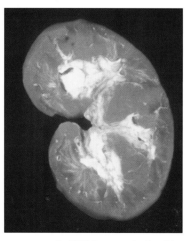

An MRI image of a healthy human kidney.

Further Reading
Cameron, J. Stewart, *Kidney Failure: The Facts* (1997); Greenberg, A., *Primer on Kidney Diseases* (1998); Rodman, John S., *No More Kidney Stones* (1996); Samir, I., *Kidney Physiology* (1997).

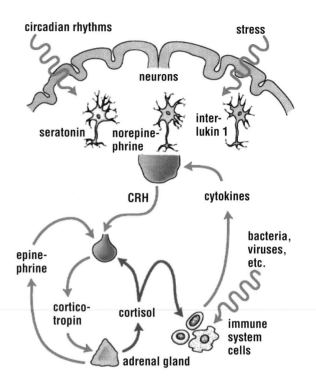

The adrenal-hypothalmus axis, one of several that respond to infection and trigger an immune response.

organism's blood plasma. The degree of concentration fluctuates with the body's needs for salt and water. (*See* DIALYSIS.)

Fish Systems. Fish face special problems of water and salt balance. Freshwater fish have blood and tissue fluids more concentrated than the water in which they swim. As a result, osmosis causes them to acquire water and lose salt through the gills and mouth. To maintain their fluid balance, they excrete large amounts of very watery urine, produced by the kidneys, and absorb salt through special cells in the gills.

Saltwater fish, by contrast, have body fluids less concentrated than seawater, and are constantly losing water and gaining salt, risking dehydration by osmosis. To counter this process, they drink almost constantly and excrete salt, again through special cells in the gills. Because their kidneys apparently cannot concentrate urine, they cannot excrete excess salt that way. Instead, their kidneys produce very little urine, conserving water.

First see EUCLIDEAN GEOMETRY

Knots

Next see TOPOLOGY

Knot theory began in the 1880s, as an outgrowth of early molecular theory. If the "ether" existed, then atoms would be "knots" in that ether. Therefore, scientists like P. G. Tait (1831–1901) and C. N. Little began to tabulate all possible forms of knots, believing they were uncovering the secrets of atomic structure in the process.

With the abandonment of the ether theory, interest in knot theory diminished. Then biochemists discovered that DNA was manipulated in nature by enzymes called topoisomerases, which use knotting techniques to interact and combine with the DNA. Almost simultaneously, physical chemists were learning that knot theory could be used to synthesize topological stereoisomers of known molecules, in which newly created geometric forms yielded new physical characteristics.

Geometry of Knots. A knot is a closed curve that crosses over itself at least twice. Because it deals with the deforming of surfaces, knot theory is a branch of topology. Two factor knots can be combined, by linking them at a point on the outside of each curve, to form their composition. A knot that cannot be analyzed as the composition of two other knots is, by analogy to number theory, called a prime knot.

Although there is a limited number of prime knots, an infinite number of different knot projections can be created by using Reidemeister moves, named after the German mathematician who in 1926 distinguished between actions that only change the appearance of a knot, and are therefore allowable, and actions that produce a different knot, and therefore should be avoided.

Knots are analyzed using the theory of tricolorability. If one changes the color of each string segment as it reaches a new undercrossing, then at every intersection three colors should be present—the base color, the new color, and the color of the crossing strand. Since there are no color changes in the circle, this theory provides proof that knots are distinct forms, rather than being just extremely tangled loops.

Knots are sorted in two ways. They can be divided into three categories: torus knots, or knots that can be drawn on an untwisted doughnut shape; satellite knots, or knots formed by twisting the torus itself into a knot; and hyperbolic knots, visualized using non-Euclidean geometry as the products of hyperbolic triangles. Finally, knots can be sorted according to Conway's notation or according to polynomials, first defined by J. W. Alexander (1928) and since extended by V. Jones and the HOMFLY group (1984). (*See* TOPOLOGY.)

First see METABOLISM

Krebs Cycle

Next see ADENOSINE TRIPHOSPHATE (ATP)

The third of four stages of aerobic respiration.

The Krebs cycle, also known as the citric acid cycle, describes the breakdown of glucose to produce energy in the form of adenosine triphosphate (ATP). The Krebs cycle begins with the end product of the previous stage, acetic acid—a 2-carbon compound. Overall, the following events occur during the Krebs cycle: transformation of the "carbon skeleton"; release of carbon dioxide; production of ATP, NADH, and FADH; and the reduction of carrier molecules.

The carbon compound undergoes the following changes: the 2-carbon acetic acid combines with a 4-carbon compound to produce a 6-carbon compound, citric acid. The citric acid loses one carbon in the form of carbon dioxide (CO_2) to become a 5-carbon compound. This molecule in turn loses another carbon in the form of carbon dioxide and then rearranges itself several times without the loss of any additional carbons to form a new 4-carbon and begin the cycle again. The cycle occurs twice due to the presence of two acetic acid molecules from the previous stage.

A link exists between the Krebs cycle and the urea cycle, which involves the synthesis of urea. Urea is formed as a way of removing ammonium ($NH4^+$), a waste product formed during the breakdown of amino acids. The two cycles share some of the same intermediary products, fumarate and aspartate.

Although the majority of ATP molecules are formed during the fourth stage of cellular respiration, enough energy becomes available in the Krebs cycle during the transformation from a 5-carbon compound to a 4-carbon compound to produce a molecule of ATP virtually instantaneously. ATP is produced by attaching a third phosphate group to adenosine diphosphate (ADP) with a special high energy bond.

At various points in the cycle, two carrier molecules, NAD^+ (niacin) and FAD (riboflavin) pick up hydrogen atoms and become reduced. These hydrogen atoms will be used in the fourth stage of cellular respiration, oxidative phosphorylation, to generate additional ATP molecules.

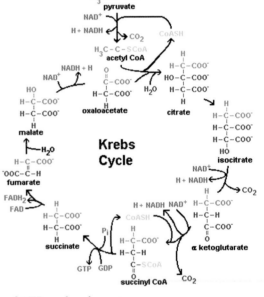

The Krebs cycle.

Related material may be found in ADENOSINE TRIPHOSPHATE (ATP); GLYCOLYSIS; MITOCHONDRIA. More details can be found in CELLULAR MEMBRANES; PROTEIN METABOLISM; WATER IN LIVING CELLS. Foundational aspects of this subject are covered in SECRETION, CELLULAR; TRANSPORT, CELLULAR.

Further Reading
Kay, J., *Krebs Citric Acid Cycle: Half a Century and Still Turning* (1987); Loewenstein, W. R., *The Touchstone of Life: Molecular Information, Cell Communication, and the Foundations of Life* (1999); Michal, G., *Biochemical Pathways: An Atlas of Biochemistry and Molecular Biology* (1999); Spallholz, J., *Nutrition: Chemistry and Biology* (1998).

Lanthanides

First see PERIODIC TABLE OF THE ELEMENTS

Next see TRANSITION ELEMENTS

A series of metallic elements, atomic numbers 57 to 71, also known as the "rare earths."

Lanthanides are found in the sixth period (row) of the Periodic Table. The first element is lanthanum, whose atomic number (Z) is 57. The next 14 elements following it are called the lanthanoid series. They are all classified as transition elements, or group B metals. The lanthanides appear below the main section of the Periodic Table in order not to make the table too long and disrupt the columns of group A elements. (*See* PERIODIC TABLE OF THE ELEMENTS.)

Orbital Overlap. Like the rest of the transition elements, the lanthanides exhibit orbital overlap, an interesting phenomenon in terms of the arrangement of their electrons (negatively charged particles). As in all atoms, the electrons are not located in the nucleus but orbit in discrete energy levels. Normally, electrons are arranged as close to the nucleus as possible and are located in the lowest orbitals available. By the time we reach the third energy level, however, the distances have grown so large that some of its orbitals overlap with those in level 4. Some of the level 3 orbitals are actually farther away from the nucleus than some of the level 4 orbitals; therefore, electrons are placed in level 4 although level 3 is not yet filled. Similarly, the energy level overlaps both the fifth and sixth levels. (*See* ELECTRON; VALENCE.)

The lanthanides are typical metals in terms of luster and conductivity. All of them tarnish readily and react well with water. The lanthanides are so similar to one another in properties and behavior it is difficult to distinguish one element from another or even to isolate them in a mixture. (*See* METAL; TRANSURANIC ELEMENTS.)

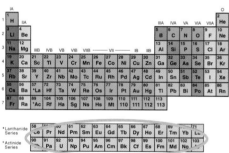

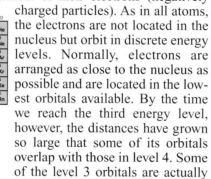

Above, the position of the Lanthanides in the Periodic Table.

Laparoscopy

First see FIBER OPTICS

Next see MEDICAL DIAGNOSTICS

A medical technique that allows direct visual observation of a woman's reproductive organs and can also be used to perform surgery.

To perform a laparoscopic examination, the patient is first anesthetized and an incision is made in the abdomen. The abdomen is then inflated with gas, and the laparoscope, a long metal tube with a lens and a light source at one end, is inserted through the incision. The physi-

cian can then examine the interior of the abdomen through the laparoscope. Sometimes a dye is injected through the cervix into the uterine cavity so that the physician can look for obstructions in the fallopian tubes. After the examination, the gas is expelled from the abdominal cavity and the incision is closed. The surgical procedures that can be performed through the laparoscope include tubal ligation, a surgical form of birth control; removal of an ovary, fibroid tissue, or the uterus; and cholecystectomy, removal of the gallbladder. For gallbladder removal, several incisions are made below the breastbone, near the navel and beneath the right side of the rib cage. Several instruments are then inserted through tubes placed in the incisions. One is a tiny video camera. Another is an instrument that allows the doctor to remove the gallbladder with a laser or an electric cutting device. This operation requires a general anesthetic and takes about one hour to perform. While conventional gallbladder surgery requires a hospital stay of several days, the laparoscopic technique can be done without hospitalization, although an overnight stay may sometimes be necessary. (*See* SURGERY.)

Laser and Maser

First see LIGHT

Next see HOLOGRAPHY

Devices for amplifying the intensity of a light beam or radiation by synchronizing the amplitudes of the constituent waves.

Laser is an acronym for light amplification by stimulated emission of radiation. Lasers operate in the infrared, visual, and ultraviolet regions of the electromagnetic spectrum. A maser is a similar device that operates in the microwave region of the electromagnetic spectrum.

Ordinary sources of light emit radiation in all directions, as photons are emitted by a thermally excited solid, such as the filament of a lamp, or electronically excited atoms, molecules, or ions. In a laser, the atoms, ions, or molecules are stimulated to emit photons of a given level by collision with a photon of the same energy level. To create this state of stimulated emission, a condition is created in the amplifying medium called population inversion, meaning that most of the atoms, ions, or molecules are in an excited state. A random emission of photons from one such atom or molecule can then trigger coherent emission from the others, amplifying the emission of the light.

This amplifying portion of the laser is enclosed within a resonator; the light is reflected back and forth between mirrors, while its intensity is amplified by further stimulated emission. One of the mirrors in the resonator is semitrans-

Laser Surgery

Next see SURGERY

Surgery performed by using the powerful light emitted by a laser to cut through human flesh.

Left, a typical holography lens bench. Lasers are an important area of research in space flight, where they are utilized for everything from long-range communication (below, top) to bonding coatings to ceramic tiles (bottom).

parent, and eventually a powerful, parallel monochromatic beam of light emerges from it. The light waves that emerge are parallel because those that do not bounce between the mirrors have escaped through the sides of the resonator.

Lasers can be solid, liquid, or gas devices. The population inversion needed by a laser can be induced by optical pumping by a light source as simple as a flashlight or by light from another laser, chemical reactions, or gas discharges. The light emitted by some lasers is powerful enough to cut through many solids. Lasers today are used in communications, printing, welding, surgery, and other fields.

Masers. Masers were developed in the 1950s and are used in atomic clocks and as amplifiers in radio astronomy, amplifying weak signals from space. In an ammonia gas maser, a beam of ammonia molecules is introduced into a vacuum chamber that has an uneven electric field. The pyramid-shaped ammonia molecules, with three hydrogen atoms at the base and a nitrogen atom at the apex, are excited to a higher energy level and are fed into a cavity that is fed with microwave radiation corresponding to the energy difference between the unexcited and excited molecules. This causes the amplification of the introduced radiation.

In a solid-state maser, molecules or atoms that are paramagnetic—having aligned magnetic moments—are placed in a magnetic field. The electrons of the atoms or molecules can be in two levels, depending on whether they are aligned with the applied field. An emission of microwaves is achieved by making sudden changes in the applied magnetic field. Solid-state masers achieve amplification over wider bands of radiation than gas masers.

Lasers are used in eye surgery to change the shape of the cornea, thereby correcting nearsightedness, far-sightedness and astigmatism (above, right).

The technique of laser surgery is often used for disorders of the eye. For example, one of the frequent applications of the technology is to treat diabetic retinopathy, which is caused by a reduction of the oxygen supply to the tissues of the retina because of the deterioration of the blood vessels common in diabetes. The laser is used to make a number of small burns in the periphery

of the retina, thus reducing the amount of retinal tissue requiring oxygen. The remaining retinal tissue then has a sufficient supply of oxygen. The burns caused by the laser reduce the visual capacity of the eye, but the reduction is not great because the affected tissue is not at the center of the visual field.

For severe cases of glaucoma, which causes a vision-damaging pressure increase in the eye, physicians use a technique called laser iridotomy. This procedure makes a small opening in the iris to reduce the glaucoma-caused pressure. Lasers can also be used for retinal detachment, reattaching the retina so that it does not die, thus preserving vision. Laser surgery is sometimes used as a follow-up to cataract surgery, clearing up a portion of the lens capsule that may have become cloudy after the operation. Newer lasers are being tried against different types of tumors that form around the eyes. (*See* EYES.)

Further Reading
Hawkes, John, *Lasers: Theory and Practice* (1995); Kock, Winston E., *Lasers and Holography: An Introduction to Coherent Optics* (1981); Siegman, Anthony, *Lasers* (1986); Silfvast, William T., *Laser Fundamentals* (1996); Townes, Charles H., *How the Laser Happened: Adventures of a Scientist* (1999).

First see PLANT

Leaf

Next see LIQUID TRANSPORT

The outgrowth on the stem of a plant and the primary organ of photosynthesis.

Amid their seemingly infinite variety of size, shape, color, and arrangement, leaves share a unity of function: they collect solar energy and transform it, along with carbon dioxide and water, into sugars that fuel their own lives and ultimately the lives of all organisms on Earth.

This invaluable function, photosynthesis, takes place in the leaf's flattened blade, or lamina, which is usually joined to the stem by a stalk, the petiole. Small leaflike appendages, called stipules, sometimes grow at the base of the leaves. Leaves that lack a petiole, growing directly from the stem, are said to be sessile. In most monocots, such as grasses, the base of the leaf forms a sheath, the coleoptile, that wraps the stem. In many plants, leaves are modified to form tendrils or spines.

Patterns. Leaves may be arranged in various patterns, including spiral or whirled, in which three or more leaves grow at the same node. The blade may be simple (undivided) or compound. Palmately compound leaves have leaflets all attached at a single point at the end of the petiole. Pinnately compound leaves have leaflets in pairs, with a row on each side of a stalklet called the rachlis.

Leaves are extensions of plant stems—collectively, the two organs form the shoot—with structural similarities. The vascular tissue, which carries water, minerals, and sugars within the plant, is continuous between the stem and leaf, where it forms the veins. In most dicot leaves, the veins form a netlike pattern with successively smaller veins branching from larger ones. In most monocots, the larger veins run parallel to the length of the leaf, with smaller veins interconnecting them.

Other Leaf Structures. Besides the veins, the other main regions of the leaf are the epidermis and the mesophyll. The epidermis, usually a single layer of transparent cells, covers the surface of the leaf and is sealed with a waxy cuticle that prevents water loss. Numerous microscopic openings in the epidermis, called stomata, allow gas exchange within the leaf, with carbon dioxide entering and oxygen leaving. They are also the site of the plant's water loss through transpiration. Guard cells around each stoma can close the opening when water loss becomes excessive. Stomata are concentrated on the lower surface of the leaf.

The mesophyll, located between the two epidermal layers, is where most photosynthesis takes place. It is composed of parenchyma cells,

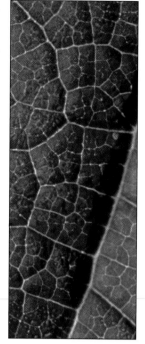

A close-up of a wild cucumber leaf (above) shows the capillary structures used for water transport in plants. These structures also provide rigidity to the leaf.

Further Reading
Galston, Arthur W., *Life Processes of Plants* (1994); Heldt, Hans-Walter, *Plant Biochemistry and Molecular Biology* (1998); Hoyt, Erich, *The Earth Dwellers: Adventures in the Land of Ants* (1997); Klucking, Edward P., *Leaf Venation Patterns: Myrataceae* (1988); Taiz, Lincoln, *Plant Physiology* (1998).

the most common kind of plant cells, set amid generous amounts of intercellular space, allowing a large cellular surface area in which gas exchange takes place.

In many plants, the mesophyll has two regions. Toward the upper side of the leaf is the palisade mesophyll, with barrel-shaped cells lined up in columns. These cells contain most of the leaf's chloroplasts, the bodies in which photosynthesis occurs. Toward the lower part of the leaf is the spongy mesophyll, where the cells are irregularly shaped and loosely arranged. In some plants, especially those adapted for arid conditions, palisade mesophyll is found on both sides of the leaf. In others, including corn and other grasses, the two regions are not distinguishable.

Adaptation. Leaves are commonly modified in response to environmental conditions. In many species, leaves on a single plant differ depending on whether they grow in sun or shade. Shade leaves are larger, thinner, with fewer well-defined mesophyll layers and fewer chloroplasts than sun leaves. As a result, in intense light, shade leaves cannot attain as high a rate of photosynthesis as sun leaves do, although in low light the leaves perform at similar levels.

Many other modifications are found in plants that grow where water is scarce. Beneath their epidermis, for instance, pine needles have a layer or more of thick-walled cells called the hypodermis, and their stomata are sunk below the surface of the leaf. In other species, leaves may be leathery or covered with hair, succulent and water-retaining, or nonexistent, with stems left to do the work of photosynthesis.

Further developments in the field are discussed in PHOTOSYNTHESIS; PLANT; ROOTS. *More details can be found in* GROWTH REGULATION IN PLANTS; PLANT HORMONES. *Additional relevant information is contained in* TROPICAL RAIN FOREST; TROPISMS IN PLANTS.

First see LIGHT

Lens

Next see OPTICS

A piece of transparent material with at least one curved surface that is used to direct and focus light in optical equipment.

Many lenses are made of glass, although molded plastic or crystalline materials are also used. A lens produces an enlarged or smaller image of a visible object by changing the direction of light rays emanating from the object. This bending occurs because light travels at different speeds in different mediums. When a ray of light passes from one medium to another—from air to glass, for example—that ray will be bent unless it is at an exact 90-degree angle to the surface of the new medium. The curved surface of a lens usually is a segment of a sphere (although this may not be true of eyeglass lenses). The center of curvature of a lens is the center of that sphere. The optical axis is the line that joins the two centers of curvature of a lens that is curved on both sides or, in the case of a lens with a single curved surface, the line through the center of curvature that is at a right angle to the uncurved surface. The optical center of a lens is the point on the optical axis at which entering light waves will pass in a straight line. The distance between the optical center of a lens and its principal focus is called its focal length. (*See* OPTICS.)

Kinds of Lenses. There are many kinds of lenses. A double convex lens, with two surfaces curved away from its center, causes light rays passing through it to converge, producing a real image—one that can be formed on a screen and is made by focusing the rays of light passing through the lens. A double concave lens, with two surfaces curving inward from its center, causes light rays to diverge, producing a virtual image—one that cannot be formed on a screen and can be seen only by the eye of an observer. A camera lens forms a real image, while the lens of a magnifying glass forms a virtual image.

Lens Limits. There is a limit to the focusing power of a single lens, called spherical aberration. This limit is not a result of any defect in the lens but of the inherent limitation on the ability of a spherical surface to refract light waves. Because light rays of different colors have different refractive characteristics, a single lens actually forms a number of images, one for each color of the light that passes through it—a phenomenon called chromatic aberration. There are several such aberrations in any lens. These cannot all be corrected in that one lens, but a large number of lenses in an optical system can be used to correct most or all of the aberrations. High-quality optical systems designed to produce exact images thus consist of many lenses of different shapes and refractive indexes.

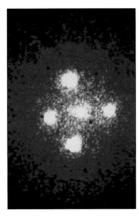

Above, an "Einstein cross" created by an Einstein lens—a focusing of the light from a distant light source by an intervening massive gravitational force.

First see BACTERIA

Leprosy

Next see DISEASES, INFECTIOUS

Also called Hansen's disease, leprosy is an infection caused by a series of bacteria (*Mycobacterium leprae*), resulting in major nerve damage.

There are two main types of leprosy—tuberculoid leprosy, a relatively mild form, and lepromatous leprosy, which is much more damaging. Persons with leprosy were once generally isolated in leper colonies because the disease was believed to be highly contagious. Research has disproved that belief, but some countries still isolate persons with the disease. The leprosy

An example of the effects of lepromatous leprosy is shown below. This Tanzanian woman's feet have been deformed by her body's reaction to the lepromatous bacterium.

bacterium is spread in droplets of nasal mucus, and a person carrying the bacterium can spread the disease only in the first stages of infection. The only people at risk of contracting leprosy are those who live in close contact with a leper.

Leprosy has a very long incubation period—it can be three to five years before destructive effects of the disease appear. Most of the damage is caused by an excessive reaction of the body's immune system to the bacteria. The first damage is done to the peripheral nerves of the muscles and skin. In later stages, the skin, hands, and feet become numb, and the muscles lose function. Treatment can be effective if it begins in the early stages of the disease; if left untreated, leprosy can lead to blindness and major disfigurement. The drug dapsone kills the leprosy bacterium, but it must be used quickly. Resistance to dapsone is growing, but other drugs are being developed. (*See* DISEASES, INFECTIOUS.)

First see NUCLEUS, ATOMIC

Leptons

Next see STANDARD MODEL

Subatomic particles that interact with the weak gravitational and electromagnetic forces, but not with the strong forces.

The weak force plays a role in beta decay, the process by which a radioactive atomic nucleus decays to a more stable form. The best-known lepton is the electron, which is a stable particle with a charge of -1. The two other known leptons with -1 charge are the muon and the tau, each of which decays in a lifetime measured in millionths of seconds.

For each lepton, there is an associated neutrino and antineutrino. The concept of the neutrino was developed in 1930 by Wolfgang Pauli to explain the apparent loss of mass seen when a particle undergoes beta decay. The concept was developed further in the 1930s by Enrico Fermi. In July 2000, the tau neutrino was the last known neutrino to be detected.

There is a law known as the law of lepton conservation, which says that leptons cannot be created or destroyed. According to the lepton conservation principle, leptons come in pairs. Each lepton pair consists of a charged lepton and a neutral neutrino. Each pair of leptons is called a generation. In each generation, the mass of the neutrino is much less than the mass of the lepton that carries a charge.

The exact nature of the weak interaction has not been fully developed. Studies designed to look further into the interaction are being conducted. The neutrino was first detected in 1956 by physicists at Los Alamos Scientific Laboratory using a large liquid scintillation detector near the laboratory's powerful fission reactor.

Physicists believe that the Earth is continually bombarded by neutrinos that carry a wide range of energies. They originated in a number of processes in the universe, including the "Big Bang" that created it, and collisions of protons in interstellar space. Because neutrinos reach Earth from places in the universe that are otherwise inaccessible, they potentially can provide us with information about such regions as the interior of stars. But they can be detected only by large systems using hundreds of thousands of tons of material, since any single neutrino can easily pass through Earth without interacting with any of the particles that make up the mass of the Earth.

Solar Neutrino Problem. Studies of the sun have led to what is known as the solar neutrino problem. Since the mass of the sun is known with great precision, the rate at which solar neutrinos are emitted can easily be predicted. However, the number of solar neutrinos registered by detectors is only about one-third of that predicted. Solutions to the solar neutrino problem have been proposed; none has been widely accepted.

Leptons spin = 1/2		
Flavor	Mass GeV/e^2	Electric charge
ν_ε electron neutrino	$<2 \times 10^{-4}$	0
ε electron	5.1×10^{-4}	-1
ν_μ muon neutrino	$<3 \times 10^{-4}$	0
μ muon	0.106	-1
ν_τ tau neutrino	$<4 \times 10^{-3}$	0
τ tau	1.784	-1

Catalog of known leptons.

THE CUTTING EDGE

Neutrino Hunting

An intense race is being run, in the pitch black vacancy of empty lead and zinc mines on opposite sides of the globe. At Japan's super-kamiokande, a 12.5 million-gallon tank of pure water detects not only electron neutinos, streaming from the sun, but also moon neutrinos, byproducts of collisions between cosmic rays and air molecules. The detector can record the direction of each neutrino, as well as its passage through the tank. Meanwhile, at the Sudbury Neutrino Observatory (SNO) in Ontario, Canada, a tank filled with heavy water, rich in deuterium isotopes, also records the neutrinos, hoping to detect them in sufficient quantities to help solve the puzzle of the universe's "dark matter." And a third detector, called BOREXINO, is about to begin operation in Italy. A Nobel Prize awaits the winners.

Meanwhile, physicists have not closed the door on the possible existence of other leptons. As no known law limits the existence of other leptons, there is a possibility that others may be found, such as those with zero spin.

Background material can be found in ELECTRON; ELEMENTARY PARTICLE; FORCE; NUCLEAR FORCES. *Further developments in the field are discussed in* BUBBLE CHAMBER; NEUTRINO; RADIOACTIVITY. *Special topics are found in* ACCELERATOR, PARTICLE; SUN; SYMMETRY IN NATURE. *See also* CONSERVATION LAWS IN NATURE.

Further Reading
Duff, Brian G., *Fundamental Particles: An Introduction to Quarks and Leptons* (1986); Halzen, Francis, *Quarks and Leptons: An Introductory Course in Modern Particle Physics* (1984); Pais, Abraham, *Inward Bound: Of Matter and Forces in the Physical World* (1988); Trefil, James, *From Atoms to Quarks* (1995).

First see BLOOD

Leukemia

Next see CANCER

The name given to several forms of cancer that cause a disorderly proliferation of abnormal white blood cells in the bone marrow.

There are several forms of leukemia. In acute leukemia, the disease develops rapidly and can be fatal in a matter of months if left untreated. Acute leukemia can affect the lymphoblasts, immature forms of the white cells called lymphocytes, or myeloblasts, immature forms of other white cells. The overgrowth of abnormal white blood cells reduces the production of red cells, normal white cells, and platelets, and can damage the brain, liver, spleen, and other organs.

Treatment. Treatment with anticancer drugs and transfusions of blood and platelets can be effective in saving lives, but they must be accompanied by antibiotics because the body becomes more vulnerable to infection. Chronic leukemia, which develops more slowly but is more likely to be fatal, is divided into chronic lymphocytic leukemia, in which the blood cells called lymphocytes multiply abnormally, and chronic myeloid leukemia, in which the white blood cells called granulocytes are those that show uncontrolled growth.

The incidence of all forms of leukemia in the United States is about 13 new cases per year per 100,000 population. Drug treatment and bone marrow transplantation, in which the abnormal cells are replaced by normal ones, have reduced the toll of leukemia, but life expectancy can be less than ten years after diagnosis for either form of chronic leukemia.

First see BLOOD

Leukocytes

Next see IMMUNE RESPONSE

Another name for white blood cells.

There are three major types of blood cells: leukocytes (white cells), erythrocytes (red cells), and thrombocytes (platelets). All three are formed in the bone marrow from stem cells, but they undergo different specialization routes and have vastly different functions and lifespans.

White blood cells are part of the immune system, the body's defense against invading foreign substances. Very few white cells are actually in circulation at any given time; the majority of them are sequestered in the lymph nodes awaiting a call to action. When the call does come, they rapidly enter the bloodstream, resulting in an elevated white cell count. Some types of cells, called macrophages, behave much as an amoeba does when confronted with prey—they engulf bacteria and digest them. Depending on the specific type of white cell, some cells are able to consume from 20 to 100 bacteria during their lifespan. White cells live seven to ten days.

Leukocytes are classified according to appearance. Granulated cells, those that have a grainy appearance when seen under the microscope, include eosinophils, basophils, and neutrophils, all of which absorb different types of dye and are grouped accordingly. Non-granulated cells include lymphocytes and monocytes. Lymphocytes are responsible for specific immunity against disease and are further divided into B cells and T cells, whose maturation process occurs in the thymus gland.

T cells. T cells are responsible for cellular immunity. There are many different types of T cells, with each variety capable of responding to a specific type of antigen. When the antigen is detected, those specific lymphocytes become activated, or sensitized, meaning that they increase in size and then divide rapidly to form hundreds of cells.

Some of the newly formed cells are killer T cells, which directly destroy foreign cells. Some are helper T cells, which enhance responses. Others are suppresser T cells, which inhibit defenses several weeks after the infection is over. A few sensitized T cells remain in the lymph nodes as memory cells in the event that the antigen is discovered again at a later date.

B Cells. B-lymphocytes are responsible for antibody immunity. When a specific type of B cell responds to its particular antigen, the sensitized B cells also divide rapidly. Most of the new cells differentiate into plasma cells, which produce antibodies. Others become memory cells and behave similarly to T memory cells. B cells never leave the lymph nodes; only their antibodies circulate in the bloodstream.

Other Blood Cells. Erythrocytes are the most numerous blood cells. Their appearance is similar to balloons that have been slightly squashed in the center. Red cells are not actually red, but pale yellowish pink. (Oxygenated blood is bright scarlet in color, whereas deoxygenated blood is dull crimson.) Red cells undergo a very complicated differentiation process, and by the time they are mature no longer contain a nucleus. Instead, they are "stuffed" with hemoglobin, a protein responsible for binding and releasing oxygen. An individual red cell may contain 265 million molecules of hemoglobin. Red blood cells circulate all over the body, picking up oxygen at the lungs and dropping it off at cells in the rest of the body as needed.

Red cells have an average life span of about 120 days. Immature red cells are stored in the spleen. At the end of its useful life, a red cell is degraded in the liver, and the heme portion of its hemoglobin, the iron-containing component, is stored to be used again in other cells.

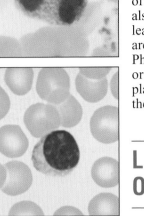

Top, blast cells—immature red and white blood cells—can be seen in bone marrow. At 500-times magnification, cell division can be seen in the center of the photograph. Bottom, a lymphocyte can be seen in the midst of red blood cells.

Thrombocytes are responsible for the formation of clots in the blood, to prevent excessive loss through hemorrhage. The formation of a clot, or thrombus, requires an intricate set of chemical changes and reactions to ensure that clots do not form needlessly. However, because of the accumulation of plaque and other materials, clots can and do form in major blood vessels, leading to the cessation of blood flow to vital areas, resulting in heart-attacks and strokes. Physically, thrombocytes resemble small saucers or plates, hence their more popular name, platelets. They have the shortest life span of all the blood cells, existing for just a few days.

First see ORGANIC COMPOUNDS

Life, Definition and Origin of

Next see EVOLUTION

Life is a difficult concept to define. No one disputes that a person is alive, or that an amoeba and a tree are. Yet life means something different when applied to each of those organisms. A unicellular organism such as the amoeba is alive, but can the same be said about a single cell from our own bodies? At what point is a human considered alive—as an individual egg or sperm cell, as a fertilized egg called a zygote, or as an embryo consisting of a handful of cells?

The characteristics of living things are easily distinguishable from non-living things:
—locomotion (generally self-actuating);
—response (varied and measured);
—nutrition (pursued);
—excretion (of waste material);
—gas exchange mechanism;
—growth (and development);
—reproduction (genomic); and
—adaptation (to altered environment).

Animals exhibit these characteristics in a different manner than do plants. Animals have muscles and often limbs to enable them to move. Plants do not "move," yet they do exhibit responses called tropisms. Phototropism refers to the leaves of a plant growing specifically towards light, and geotropism refers to the roots growing downward in response to the pull of gravity. These responses are consistently seen, even if the seed is planted upside down. An individual plant cannot relocate itself, but some species send out underground runners that enable them to spread or literally pop up in a different area. (*See* LOCOMOTION.)

Consumption of Nutrients. Animals are consumers and eat other organisms, whether plants or animals. They do this to obtain glucose, which is broken down by their cells for energy, as well as to acquire other needed nutrients. Plants do not "eat," but they do perform photo-

Life appears on the Earth in many forms. From top, a hydra, pitcher plants, a jellyfish, and an African elephant.

synthesis, which is the process of using light energy to produce the glucose they need. They obtain other necessary nutrients, such as minerals, from the soil and ingest them with water taken in by the roots.

Animals require oxygen to break down glucose. As a result of this process, called cellular respiration, they produce carbon dioxide, which must be released. Plants exchange their gases a bit differently; carbon dioxide is one of the raw materials required for photosynthesis and oxygen is a byproduct.

Reproduction. Reproduction can be sexual or asexual. Sexual reproduction requires two parents and results in genetic variation among the offspring. Asexual reproduction requires only one parent and all offspring are genetically identical to one another as well as to their parent. Depending on the species, animals can reproduce either sexually or asexually. Plants are capable of both methods as well. Flowers are the sex organs of higher plants. Asexual reproduction can be accomplished by means of spores or by vegetative propagation, in which a plant cutting is encouraged to grow into a new individual.

Both plants and animals are multicellular organisms and grow by producing more cells. Animals stop growing relatively early in their life span, after reaching a certain size. Plants continue growing all their lives, although they achieve the majority of their growth early on.

Adaptation. Animals are better at adapting than plants, because of their superior response mechanisms and ability to move. For example, a dog will pant when it is hot to release excess heat and shiver when it is cold. A plant caught in temperatures too low or too high will die. However, a plant whose normal habitat is the desert has as an adaptation a very thick waxy coating on its upper leaf surfaces in order to minimize water loss. (*See* EVOLUTION.)

Organisms, such as bacteria and protozoa, exhibit these life processes as well, but with a slightly different approach than animals or plants. As unicellular organisms, their method of reproduction is asexual, called binary fission, and consists of simply splitting in half. However, one form of protist, the paramecium, also exhibits a type of reproductive behavior that is considered sexual, as it involves two individuals and results in genetic variation.

Many functions occur simply as a result of diffusion, or transport across the cell membrane, such as gas exchange, nutrition, and excretion. Unicellular organisms have a structure known as a food vacuole, roughly analogous to a stomach, which digests anything brought into the interior of the cell. Some unicellular organisms are capable of photosynthesis.

Unicellular organisms have chemoreceptors on their exterior surfaces, enabling them to identify chemicals in their vicinity. They act on this information by moving towards beneficial objects and away from detrimental ones. For locomotion, many unicellular organisms are equipped with cilia, microscopic hairs, or flagella—"tails"—that propel them through liquids.

Cells. All living things are made up of cells. This raises a question in the case of viruses as to whether or not they are living organisms. Viruses are non-cellular; they consist simply of a piece of genetic material wrapped in a protein coat. Viruses are the ultimate parasite, incapable of performing any of the life processes on their own. Their modus operandi is to penetrate a host cell, shed their protein cover, and head straight for the nucleus of the cell. There they incorporate their own genetic material into that of the host and take over the machinery of the cell, forcing it to manufacture more viral particles. Eventually the host cell dies, or bursts open, releasing a swarm of new viruses.

Origins. One scientific theory regarding the origin of life on Earth is that conditions on the planet billions of years ago resembled a chemical "soup." As the outer crust cooled, gases escaped to form a primitive atmosphere consisting mostly of nitrogen, carbon dioxide, and water vapor. Ultraviolet radiation from the sun provided the energy necessary for these simple elements and molecules to begin forming more complex compounds, among them organic compounds such as amino acids, the "building blocks" of proteins.

The earliest life forms were actually chemical aggregates, also called coacervates. They incorporated other molecules for food. The aggregates became more complex and organized over time, eventually forming nucleic acids and becoming self-replicating. The ability to reproduce is the hallmark of living organisms, the lowest threshold for declaring that something is alive.

Some of the heterotrophs developed the ability to produce their own food—simple sugars—and became autotrophs or "self-feeders." As a result of photosynthesis, the amount of atmospheric oxygen increased, allowing for the development of eukaryotes, more "advanced" cells. Some of the more primitive "protocells" may have banded together to form the first eukaryotes. Evidence for this theory may be seen in the fact that eukaryotic cells contain several smaller structures bound in their own membranes bearing their own DNA that is not at all related to the cell's nuclear DNA. (*See* DNA.)

The theory further states that these primitive life forms evolved gradually over a period of 2 billion years into the complex organisms present today. The conditions of the early atmosphere have been duplicated in the laboratory, and organic molecules have been seen to form, as they must have as a preliminary step to becoming the early aggregates.

Despite some experimental evidence, however, there are still more questions than incontrovertible answers concerning the origins of life. There are also many vexing questions regarding the definition of life, as well as its beginning and its end.

CONTROVERSIES

Life From Space?

The origins of life on Earth are shrouded in mystery. Though a theory prevails, the difficulty in obtaining hard evidence hampers the search for proof. One of the most controversial theories holds that a life-containing planet might have been hit by a meteor, splitting the planet and sending bacteria-containing rocks careening through the universe. These bacteria were frozen by the low temperature of outer space and, when the rock crashed to Earth, they were thawed and became the ancestors of modern life. Recently, NASA researchers found a meteor originally from Mars, which some researchers believe contains fossilized bacterial structures, suggesting that life might once have existed on Mars.

The foundations of the subject are discussed in CELL; CONCEPTION; EVOLUTION; SUCCESSION. *Further details can be found in* BIRTH; ECOLOGY; REPRODUCTIVE SYSTEMS. *Advanced relevant subjects are developed in* ARTIFICIAL INTELLIGENCE; BIODIVERSITY; INTELLIGENCE; PROTEIN SYNTHESIS.

Further Reading
Cairns-Smith, Alexander Graham, *Seven Clues to the Origin of Life: A Scientific Detective Story* (1991); Davies, P.C.W., *The Fifth Miracle: The Search for the Origin and Meaning of Life* (1999); Lahav, Noam, *Biogenesis: Theories of Life's Origin* (1999); Morowitz, Harold J., *Mayonnaise and the Origin of Life* (1991); Thomas, Paul J., *Comets and the Origin and Evolution of Life* (1996).

First see WAVE

Light

Next see ELECTROMAGNETIC WAVES

The segment of the electromagnetic spectrum that is visible to the human eye.

The wavelengths of visible light extend from about 4,000 nanometers, in the extreme violet area, to 7,700 nanometers, in the extreme red area. (A nanometer is 10^{-9} of a centimeter.) The particle of light, and of other electromagnetic radiation, is the photon.

Classical Theories. The concept of light has evolved steadily over many centuries. In ancient Greece, there were two theories of light. One held that the eye emits streams of vision that interact with something emitted by luminous bodies in the presence of sunlight. Euclid originated the idea of light waves, saying that the eye emitted such waves. He applied his geometrics to problems of perspective by drawing diverging straight lines from the eye to the object being observed. Another theory said that luminous bodies give off layers of atoms. These atoms, as they travel through space, maintain the image of the surfaces of the emitting bodies and are detected when they enter the eye. Some centuries later, Ptolemy of Alexandria recorded experimental observations of the refraction that light undergoes when passing from one medium to another, as from air to water.

Wave Theory of Light. The classical theories, with variations on the themes, remained intact until as late as the seventeenth century. Proposals for a new kind of wave theory began to emerge at that time. Francesco Grimaldi, for example, studied shadows and said that light seemed to behave like waves in a liquid. Christian Huygens used a wave theory to explain reflection and refraction. But in 1704, Isaac Newton's *Optics* proposed a corpuscular theory of light, although he said in passing that light could consist of waves as well as corpuscles, and that when rays of light "impinge on any refracting or reflecting superficies, [they] must as necessarily excite vibrations in the ether, as stones do in water when thrown into it."

In the early nineteenth century, British scientist Thomas Young strengthened the wave theory of light in a series of experiments showing that when light from two narrow and closely spaced slits was beamed on a screen, an interference pattern—light and dark bands—was formed. Such bands could be formed only if light consisted of waves, Young said. His theory was neglected and attacked for years, until French scientist Augustin Fresnel showed that polarized light—light oriented in specific planes—required that light consist of waves.

Maxwell's Work. The great British scientist, James Clerk Maxwell, provided major support for the wave theory by proving mathematically that it is possible to have transverse waves whose energy is shared equally between fluctuating electric and magnetic fields, and that the velocity of light was the same as the velocity of other electromagnetic waves. When electric and magnetic constants were inserted into the equations that Maxwell had developed, the velocity calculated for the electromagnetic waves was found to be the same as the velocity of light. Assuming that light was an electromagnetic wave, the index of refraction for a transparent material—which is an optical constant—could be calculated from the material's dielectric constant, an electrical property. In 1887, Heinrich Hertz provided definitive proof of the wave nature of light by generating exactly the kind of waves that Maxwell had predicted, using an oscillating electrical discharge.

Quantum Theory. Yet the theory remained incomplete because no theory yet explained the entire spectrum of electromagnetic radiation, including light, that is emitted by a hot body. That problem was solved in 1901 by Max Planck, who introduced a radical new assumption: light is emitted from a hot body, such as a glowing rod of metal, not in continuous waves, but in packets of energy, or quanta. He proposed that the energy of each quantum of light is equal to the frequency of the light multiplied by a universal constant. The difference between Planck's quanta and Newton's particles of light was that the quanta were not presumed to be material particles, as Newton's particles were.

Einstein's Work. Einstein added to that theory by showing that light is not only emitted in quanta but is also absorbed in quanta. Einstein demonstrated that there seemed to be a particle-to-particle interaction between quanta of light that fell on a surface of photosensitive material and the electrons in that material. Einstein's and Planck's picture of the quantization of light required a change in the simple classical picture of an atom which said that the electrons orbiting an atomic nucleus could have a wide range of kinetic energies and orbital radii. But from the quantum point of view, the emission of radiation such as light always occurred in quanta. This could be explained only by assuming that when an electron emits energy, such as a light photon, its speed must change in a single jump. An entirely new kind of mechanics was required to describe atomic systems with such properties. This new type of description is called quantum mechanics.

Support for this quantum theory of light came from physicist Arthur Compton in the 1920s. Compton showed that under certain conditions electromagnetic radiation behaves like a stream of particles. Classic electromagnetic theory said that if a target was bombarded with electromagnetic radiation, it would emit radiation of the same frequency. Compton showed that, in fact, radiation of a different frequency (or a different kind of photon) was emitted. The best explanation was that the momentum of a quantum of light is equal to its energy divided by its velocity. (*See* QUANTUM MECHANICS.)

As it stands today, there is ample evidence for both the particle and the wave nature of light. Experiments involving interference, diffraction, or the polarization of light amply demonstrate its wave nature. But close observations of the emission and absorption of light, and of Compton scattering demonstrate the particle or corpuscular aspect of light. The dual nature of light thus appears to be firmly established in physics.

Elementary aspects of this subject are covered in ELECTROMAGNETIC WAVES; LIGHT, SPEED OF; WAVE. *More information on particular aspects is contained in* ELECTROMAGNETISM; FLUORESCENCE; LASER AND MASER. *Additional relevant information is contained in* MAXWELL'S EQUATIONS; REFLECTION, REFRACTION; PHOTOCHEMISTRY; PHOTOVOLTAIC TECHNOLOGY. *See also* SPECIAL RELATIVITY; LORENTZ-FITZGERALD CONTRACTION; MICHELSON-MORLEY EXPERIMENT.

Possibly the most important question for 20th-century science was asked by nine-year-old Albert Einstein in 1885, a year after the photo above was taken. The question: what does one see when one is riding on a beam of light?

Further Reading
Baierlein, Ralph, *Newton to Einstein: The Trail of Light: An Excursion to the Wave-Particle Duality and the Special Theory of Relativity* (1992); Bohren, Craig F., et al., *Clouds in a Glass of Beer: Simple Experiments in Atmospheric Physics* (1987); Hecht, Eugene, et al., *Optics* (1997); Park, David, *The Fire Within the Eye: A Historical Essay on the Nature and Meaning of Light* (1999); Zajonc, Arthur, *Catching the Light: The Entwined History of Light and Mind* (1995).

First see LIGHT

Light, Speed of

Next see SPECIAL RELATIVITY

The speed of light in a vacuum is approximately 186,300 miles (or 299,800 kilometers) per second. That is the speed not only of visible light but also of all electromagnetic radiation, and it is the ultimate speed: nothing travels faster than light. Light travels slower in water than in air as the light waves interact with molecules; it has been shown that the speed of light is slightly affected by gravitation. The ancients thought that light was instantaneous.

The first demonstration that light takes time to pass through space was made in 1675 by European scientist Olaus Romer. He observed that the eclipses of Jupiter by one of its moons appeared to be delayed when Earth was moving away from Jupiter and seemed faster when Earth was moving toward Jupiter. He proposed that the difference was due to the changing distances from Jupiter to Earth. Romer calculated that the time needed for light to travel the diameter of Earth's orbit around the sun was 22 minutes, an estimate that was five minutes too fast.

Relativity and the Michaelson-Morley Experiment. A key to establishing the theory of relativity was the Michelson-Morley experiment, performed in 1887, which implied that the measured speed of light does not change when the instrument measuring it moves. That experiment and others established that c, the speed of light, is unique and is a physical quantity of fundamental importance in nature. It is the maximum speed possible for the transfer of energy. It thus is part of a number of basic equations describing light, the most famous of which is $E=mc^2$.

Related areas to be considered are LIGHT; OPTICS; SPECIAL RELATIVITY. *Other aspects of the subject are discussed in* MICHELSON-MORLEY EXPERIMENT; TIME, MEASUREMENT OF. *Related material can be found in* DOPPLER EFFECT; ENERGY, EQUIVALENCE OF MASS AND; TWIN PARADOX.

First see WEATHER

Lightning and Thunder

Next see HURRICANES AND TORNADOES

Lightning is the discharge of atmospheric electricity that results in a flash of light. Thunder is the acoustic shock wave caused by the sudden expansion of air heated by a lightning discharge.

In a rapidly developing storm, clouds become electrically charged—positively at the top, negatively at the bottom. A cloud thus becomes a huge static electricity machine, with water drops carrying the charge, until the electrical stress becomes so great that there is a discharge of electricity between the charged surfaces of the same cloud, between two clouds, or between a cloud and the surface of Earth below it. Lightning flashes are often very long, sometimes several miles in length, and have been estimated to be four to six inches in diameter. Several flashes, each of very short duration, can follow one another in rapid succession, not quite following the same path, thus producing the effect of forked lightning.

Because light travels at 186,000 miles per second and sound at 1,100 feet per second, lightning flashes are seen and vanish before the rumble of thunder is heard. About three-quarters of the energy of a lightning flash is expended in heating the atmosphere around it. The air can suddenly reach a temperature of more than 10,000 degrees, so that a cylindrical shock wave is sent out, followed by a series of atmospheric fluctuations that reverberate through the air. These are heard as thunder. Thunder may be heard as far away as 25 miles from a lightning flash, although a ten-mile limit is more common.

Lightning can take the familiar form of a discharge to the ground (top), but it can also discharge into clouds (bottom) of lower potential.

Special topics in this area are found in ELECTRICITY; WEATHER; WIND AND CLOUDS. *Advanced subjects are developed in* HURRICANES AND TORNADOES; JET STREAM. *More information on particular aspects is contained in* AURORAS; FRACTALS; OZONE LAYER.

Technology and Stanford University. Both standing-wave and traveling-wave designs were used at first, but it became apparent that the traveling-wave linacs gave superior performance. The largest electron linac, designated SLAC, is a two-mile long machine operated by Stanford University. It can accelerate electrons to energies of 20 billion (GeV) electron volts.

The first proton linac was built in 1946 at the University of California at Berkeley. It was a standing-wave accelerator that used an array of electrodes, called drift tubes, whose length increased down the length of the accelerator, and which sped up the particle by applying an oscillating electric field. The largest existing proton accelerator is the LAMPF, Los Alamos Physics Facility linac at Los Alamos Scientific Laboratory. It can accelerate a beam of protons to final energies of 800 million electron volts (MeV).

Linacs are also used as particle generators for high-energy proton synchrotrons and as radiation sources for medical treatment and research. Linacs that use superconducting accelerator systems are being developed, thereby achieving high efficiency and continuous operation. Yet another advance is development of a proton or heavy-ion system, the Radio Frequency Quadropole (RFQ), which has resonant cavities with four specially shaped vanes that focus and accelerate a beam of low-velocity ions. The RFQ system is rapidly being adopted in the low-velocity section of ion and proton accelerators. Since research demands low-cost and reliable sources of radiation, manufacturing, and medicine, development of linac systems continues at universities and other research centers.

First see ACCELERATOR, PARTICLE

Linear Accelerator

Next see CYCLOTRON

An accelerator that propels charged subatomic particles by repeated applications of small electrical forces.

Particles in linear accelerators, or linacs, go through a series of cylindrical electrodes, gaining energy as they pass through each electrode. The spacing of the electrodes is designed to match the velocity of the particle that is being accelerated.

There are two kinds of linac: traveling-wave accelerators and standing-wave accelerators. In a traveling-wave linac, the lengths of the electrodes and the radio frequencies are adjusted in a way that provides an increase in velocity with each successive electrode. In a standing-wave linac, adjacent electrodes are strongly coupled, so that the particle is accelerated continuously.

Electron linacs were first developed in the late 1930s at the Massachusetts Institute of

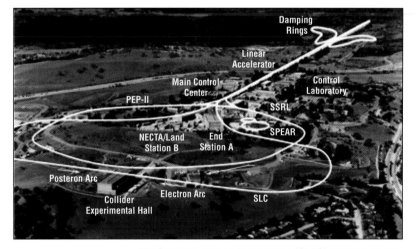

The Stanford Linear Accelerator (SLAC) facility, above, is one of the premier research laboratories in particle physics in the world.

Further Reading
Close, Frank, *The Particle Explosion* (1987); Humphries, Stanley, *Charged Particle Beams* (1990); Lee, S.Y., *Accelerator Physics* (1999); Pais, Abraham, *Inward Bound* (1988).

Background material can be found in ACCELERATOR; BUBBLE CHAMBER; ELEMENTARY PARTICLE. *Further details on the tools of particle physics can be found in* CYCLOTRON; STANDARD MODEL; SYNCHROTRON. *Relevant information is contained in* GRAND UNIFICATION THEORIES; SYMMETRY IN NATURE; QUARK.

First see GENE

Linkage, Genetic

Next see GENETICS

The association between two or more genes on the same chromosome.

There are approximately 30,000-40,000 human genes; they are responsible for all characteristics and traits. These genes are arranged within structures known as chromosomes. As there are only 46 human chromosomes (two are sex chromosomes; the others are called autosomes), several genes must be located together on the same chromosome.

Each individual carries two genes for a particular trait. During meiosis, the production of gametes such as sperm and eggs, homologous chromosomes separate from each other so that each resulting gamete has only half the chromosomes, and consequently half the genes, of a regular cell. Mendel's second law of genetic inheritance states that independent assortment occurs, meaning that the inheritance of a specific allele (the form a gene may take, either dominant or recessive) for one trait occurs independently of the inheritance of a specific allele for another trait. However, this is only true if the genes for the traits being studied are located on separate chromosomes. Genes present on the same chromosome must be inherited together.

Genetic linkage can be altered by means of a phenomenon known as crossing over. During the early stages of meiosis, when the chromosomes are pairing up, homologous chromosomes often exchange pieces of themselves. Genes for particular traits will still be found on the same chromosome, but the specific alleles that are inherited together may now be different. Crossing over occurs very frequently; in fact, the frequency is used as a tool to construct a genetic map of the chromosomes—the closer the gene loci, the higher rate of linkage in crossing over.

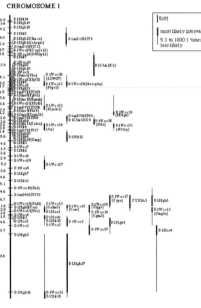

An integrated genomic map based on an analysis of three rat pedigrees. Comparison of maps identifies the specific traits determined by specific genes.

First see DIGESTION

Lipids

Next see METABOLISM

Lipids contain the elements carbon, hydrogen, and oxygen, and include fats, waxes, and oils. Lipids are a major component of cell membranes, and are used for protection. Leaf surfaces have a waxy coating called the cuticle that prevents excess water loss, the ear canal is also coated with wax in order to trap dirt and germs and prevent their entry into the body. In addition, fats are used for insulation purposes: the subcutaneous layer of fat developed by a baby during the last weeks of pregnancy, for example, enables it to maintain its body temperature. Fats are also a very efficient method of energy storage. One gram of carbohydrate, the usual energy source, yields four calories of energy, whereas one gram of fat yields nine calories of energy.

Fats. The basic subunit of a lipid is the fatty acid, which is essentially a hydrocarbon chain with a carboxyl group (COOH) on the end. The most common form of lipid is the triglyceride, which consists of glycerol, a 3-carbon chain, with three attached fatty acids. The fatty acids usually contain from 14 to 18 carbon atoms, although it is possible to have greater or fewer numbers. The types of bonds between the adjacent carbon atoms determine if the fatty acid is "saturated" or "unsaturated." If there are only single bonds (one shared pair of electrons)

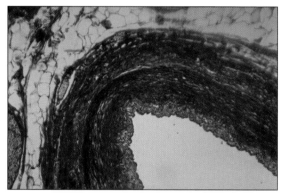

A cross-section micrograph of a blood vessel (above), shows a large artheroma—a lipid deposit—that can decrease blood flow.

between the carbon atoms, the fat is saturated. If there are double bonds (two shared pairs of electrons) or triple bonds (three shared pairs of electrons), then the fat is unsaturated. Depending on how many of these unsaturated bonds are present, the fat can be "monounsaturated" or "polyunsaturated." Saturated fats have higher melting points than unsaturated fats, which is why saturated fats are usually solid at room temperature.

Lipids are hydrophobic, meaning they are "water-hating," or insoluble in water. However, phospholipids also have a hydrophilic or "water-loving" portion, the phosphate group. Phospholipids are arranged in the cell membrane with their hydrophilic parts extended and the hydrophobic segments clustered together.

Cholesterol. Cholesterol belongs to a group known as steroids, all of which consist of a 4-carbon ring and a hydrocarbon "tail" extending outward. Many of them also contain the same functional group (OH) found in alcohols. Steroids are also insoluble in water.

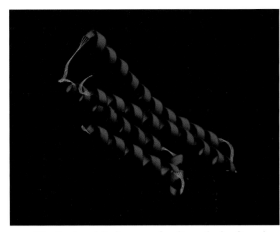

A three-dimensional computer model of an apolipoprotein is shown at left. A lipid combined with an apolipoprotein forms a lipoprotein. The green spiral ribbons are alpha-helix amino acid strings.

Cholesterol is known for its role in forming fatty deposits on the inner linings of the major blood vessels, increasing the risk of heart attacks and strokes. However, cholesterol also plays a regulatory role in the body regarding lipid metabolism. The "bad" type of cholesterol carrier is known as low-density lipoprotein (LDL); the "good" type is high-density lipoprotein (HDL). The ratio of HDL to LDL in the bloodstream is very important. Cholesterol is also found in cell membranes and is a major component of myelin sheath, the membrane wrapped around nerve fibers.

Guidelines. In 1993, the National Cholesterol Program published guidelines for the assessment of blood cholesterol levels. The guidelines say that an individual who is free of coronary artery disease should have a total cholesterol level of less than 200 milligrams of cholesterol per 100 milliliters of blood. A reading of between 200 and 239 milligrams per milliliter is classified as borderline hypercholesterolemia; individuals in this range are advised to avoid high-fat foods. Readings above 240 mg of cholesterol per 100 milliliters of blood are classified as hypercholesterolemia. In addition to dietary measures, drug therapy may be prescribed to reduce the level if it remains above 240.

As for LDL cholesterol, a reading greater than 160 milligrams per milliliter is classified as hypercholesterolemia. A reading between 130 mg per milliliter is borderline, while a reading of less than 130 mg is desirable. With HDL cholesterol, a higher level is desirable. If the reading is less than 35 milligrams per milliliter of blood, more exercise and weight reduction are advised even if total blood cholesterol levels are in the safe range. HDL cholesterol is regarded as desirable because it acts as a scavenger, decreasing the amount of LDL cholesterol.

Related areas to be considered are ALCOHOL; ORGANIC COMPOUND; WATER IN LIVING CELLS. *Advanced subjects are developed in* CARBOHYDRATES; DIGESTIVE CHEMISTRY; METABOLISM. *More information on particular aspects is contained in* ENZYMES; LYMPHATIC SYSTEM; NUTRITION.

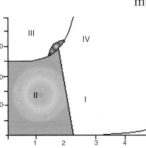

The phase diagram for helium. Pressure is plotted against temperature (in degrees Kelvin). Helium is a liquid in area I; a superfluid in area II; and a solid in area III. Instead of the usual triple point, helium has a fourth phase.

Further Reading
Chang, T.Y., *Intracellular Cholesterol Trafficking* (1998); Gunstone, Frank D., *The Lipid Handbook* (1996); Hemming, J., *Lipid Analysis* (Introduction to Biotechniques) (1993); Pond, Caroline M., *The Fats of Life* (1998); Spiller, Gene A., *Handbook of Lipids in Human Nutrition* (1995).

Further Reading
Goldman, Gordon Kenneth, *Liquid Fuels From Coal* (1972); Haywood, R. W., *Analysis of Engineering Cycles: Power, Refrigerating, and Gas Liquefaction* (1991); Schlosberg, Richard H., ed., *Chemistry of Coal Conversion* (1985); Whitehurst, D. Duayne, *Coal Liquefaction: The Chemistry and Technology of Thermal Processes* (1986).

First see GAS, BEHAVIOR OF

Liquefaction

Next see REFRIGERATION

The process of converting a gas to a liquid.

The liquefaction of gases can be achieved by lowering the temperature of a gas until it is at or below the condensation point, so that the gas condenses spontaneously. It can also be done by increasing the pressure, causing the molecules of the gas to come closer together, until the attractive forces between them are strong enough to cause condensation. But most common gases will not liquefy at room temperature no matter how high the pressure becomes. Nitrogen must be cooled to 154 degrees Kelvin (degrees above absolute zero), and hydrogen must be cooled to 22 degrees Kelvin.

Critical Temperature. Every gas has a characteristic maximum temperature, called the critical temperature, above which liquefaction is impossible no matter how high the pressure becomes. The minimum pressure that is required to liquefy a gas at its critical temperature is called its critical pressure. For example, the critical temperature of oxygen is 155 degrees Kelvin, and its critical pressure is 50.1 times normal atmospheric pressure, while the critical temperature of argon is 151 degrees Kelvin and its critical pressure is 48 times normal atmospheric pressure.

The existence of critical temperatures and pressures can be explained in several ways. Above the critical temperature, no amount of pressure can push the gas molecules close enough so that the attractive forces overcome thermal motion. Gases with small molecules, which have weak attractive forces, have very low critical temperatures, while gases with larger molecules, such as carbon dioxide, have higher critical temperatures. Another way to explain critical temperature is to imagine a liquid in a sealed container. While the liquid stays at the bottom of the container, its vapor phase fills the rest of the container. The division between the two phases is called a meniscus. If the temperature of the container increases, the vapor pressure increases as more of the liquid becomes a gas. When the temperature is high enough, all of the liquid becomes a gas. The meniscus disappears and the liquid and the gas become indistinguishable. The temperature at which this happens will be just above the critical temperature.

Topics related to liquefaction can be found in GASES, BEHAVIOR OF *and* LIQUID. *Advanced subjects are developed in* ENERGY; NITROGEN; REFRIGERATION. *Additional relevant information is contained in* ABSOLUTE ZERO; CRYOGENICS; PHASE; SUPERFLUID.

First see GAS, BEHAVIOR OF

Liquids

Next see LIQUID TRANSPORT

Molecules in a fluid state that are relatively incompressible.

An ideal liquid offers no permanent resistance to sheer stress and is completely incompressible. Such an ideal liquid would have a constant volume that would not completely fill any container having more volume than the liquid. Real liquids differ from this ideal picture because they are at least partially compressible. X-ray diffraction studies show that near the melting point—the temperature at which a solid becomes a liquid—the molecules of most liquids are arranged in a solid-like crystal form over very small volumes. This local short-range order means that the average molecule of a liquid is surrounded by molecules that occupy nearly the same relative positions as they would in a solid. Therefore, a liquid can be visualized as an imperfect crystal whose molecules have comparatively free movement; the energy required to move a molecule is not large compared to the thermal energy of the liquid. Several theories of the liquid state use this concept as their starting point.

Fluid Vacancy. One such model is the fluid vacancy concept. If one of every eight molecules were removed from a solid and the remaining molecules were put into rapid motion—for example, by heating them—the result would be a "gas" absorbed into a "solid." This model can be described by using a partition function that contains both a "solidlike" function and a "gas-like function," both expressed in terms of the difference between the volume of the substance in the solid state and in the liquid state, and with which the thermodynamic properties of the liquid can be calculated. The fluid vacancy theory has been used to calculate a number of properties of ordinary liquids, such as water, and also of metals and salts in the liquid state. A liquid has also been described as being composed of "nonpolar, symmetrical, compact molecules (that) have a structure of maximum randomness...There is no quasicrystalline or lattice structure, there are no holes of definite size or shape, no discrete molecular frequencies or velocities."

Another approach to the study of liquids is to observe their behavior as they are heated. When a layer of liquid is heated from below—as when a pot of water is put on the stove—convection currents are formed as the heated liquid on the bottom rises toward the top. Studies show that the onset of convection in a typical liquid is marked by the appearance of a regular array of hexagonal cells, with the liquid rising in the center of each cell and flowing near the edge of the cell. The appearance of these cells can be predicted by the Rayleigh number, which can be calculated with precision.

Another type of liquid is the associated liquid. Water, which is believed to contain groups of H_2O molecules caused by the formation of hydrogen bonds between those atoms, is an example. There are also polar liquids (a class to which water also belongs) that have dipole moments—slight electrical charges on the molecules. (*See* WATER.)

Further Reading
Caro, Paul, *Water* (1993); March, Norman H., *Atomic Dynamics in Liquids* (1991); March, Norman H., *Chemical Physics of Liquids* (1989); Outwater, Alice, *Water: A Natural History* (1997); Reid, Robert C., *The Properties of Gases and Liquids* (1987).

Background material can be found in GASES, BEHAVIOR OF; MOLECULE; SOLIDS. *Advanced subjects are developed in* LIQUID TRANSPORT; OSMOSIS. *More information on particular aspects is contained in* CIRCULATORY SYSTEMS; DIALYSIS; LIQUEFACTION.

First see FLUID DYNAMICS

Liquid Transport

Next see WATER IN LIVING CELLS

A system used by plants to replace water lost by transpiration in their leaves.

All sizable land plants are vascular, containing vessels for the transport of water, minerals, hormones, and food. These systems can move water at a meter a minute to heights as high as the tallest tree.

Nonvascular plants, including algae and bryophytes, tend to be very small or aquatic, relying on diffusion or other slow processes to transport liquid short distances.

Vascular Tissue. There are two main types of vascular tissue: xylem carries water and inorganic ions upward from the roots to the leaves; phloem carries carbohydrates down from the leaves where it is synthesized and up from the roots where it is stored. It also moves amino acids from older to younger areas. Some xylem cells form rays that allow lateral movement of nutrients from the phloem. Xylem and phloem occur

---

THE CUTTING EDGE

Liquid Crystals

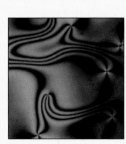

Matter is typically thought to exists in only three states: solid, liquid, and gas. Liquid crystals, however, exhibit characteristics of both solids and liquids. A liquid crystal (inset) demonstrates both a high level of order (as in solids) and the ability to form droplets and be poured (as in liquids). Liquid crystals are formed in two ways: thermotropic liquid crystals are created when a particular substance is heated. Lyotropic liquid crystals develop when substances are mixed together. Liquid crystals are used in calculators, digital watches, and television displays.

together in bundles. In leaves, the bundles run in the veins; in trees they form the rings that reflect the tree's age.

In flowering plants, xylem is composed of two specialized cells, tracheid and vessel elements, as well as parenchyma and sclerenchyma cells, more general plant cells. In mature xylem, all but the parenchyma cells have died, leaving only their cell walls as structure. In woody plants, the xylem helps support the stems; it forms almost all the wood in trees.

A number of theories have been offered over the years to explain what force can move liquid to the top of a 400-foot tree. This impressive phenomenon is now usually explained by the cohesion-tension theory (also called the transpiration theory, or the transpiration-adhesion-tension-cohesion theory). It is based on the fact that water molecules cohere to each other because of their hydrogen bonds and also adhere to the inside of a tube as long as the column of water is continuous and not broken by air.

As water is lost from the leaf's mesophyll cells by transpiration (a process that claims more than 90 percent of all water absorbed by plants), the water potential of the cells falls. As a result, they draw water from adjoining cells, which then draw water from the cells adjoining them, and so on. When this water-potential gradient reaches the xylem, it causes the cells next to the xylem to pull water from the column within the xylem, thus causing the entire column of water to rise. In other words, transpiration pulls the column of water up. The cohesive strength of such a column of water has been measured at about 300 atmospheres, while it is estimated to take only 30 atms to raise water to the top of a 400-foot tree. (*See* LEAF.)

Pressure-Flow Hypothesis. There is less agreement about the force that powers the phloem. The most popular theory, the pressure-flow hypothesis, is that sugars produced by photosynthesis are actively transported into phloem cells in the leaves (called the source). Water tends to diffuse into these cells because their sugar concentration is high. As the water enters, the turgor pressure of the cells rises and forces sugars out of the cells and into adjacent cells along the sieve tube. The cycle is repeated until the sugar-water reaches an area of growth where it is removed (the sink). With the sugar concentration down, water diffuses out of the cells and turgor pressure falls.

Background material on liquid transport phenomena can be found in GASES, BEHAVIOR OF; MOLECULE; LIQUIDS; WATER IN LIVING CELLS. *The mechanics of how liquid is transported into and out of cells is discussed in* CELL MEMBRANES; OSMOSIS. *More information on particular aspects of liquid transport is contained in* ELECTROPHORESIS; BLOOD; BLOOD PRESSURE; CIRCULATORY SYSTEMS; DIALYSIS; LIQUEFACTION.

Further Reading
Allnatt, A.R., *Atomic Transport in Solids* (1994); Logan, B. E., *Environmental Transport Processes* (1998); Millat, Jurgen, *Transport Properties of Fluids: Their Correlation, Prediction and Estimation* (1996); West, Ian C., *The Biochemistry of Membrane Transport* (1983); Yeagle, Phillip L., *The Membranes of Cells* (1993).

First see DIGESTION

Liver

Next see METABOLISM

The largest internal organ in vertebrates. Located in the upper abdomen, it has a variety of regulatory and storage functions.

The liver's tasks range from housekeeping—getting rid of toxins and spent red blood cells—to chemical production—keeping the body supplied with bile and with many plasma proteins, including the blood-clotting agents fibrinogen and prothrombin. Perhaps most strikingly, the liver orchestrates a shifting series of chemical changes that aim to preserve stable levels of sugar, fat, and amino acids in the bloodstream despite the vagaries of eating, exercising, and illness. The organism's attempt to preserve its chemical status quo, a process called homeostasis, relies heavily on the liver.

All carnivores and most other vertebrates have livers. Across species, the organ tends to have lobes, usually two. In humans, the liver is a wedge-shaped, red-brown organ with a larger right lobe and a smaller left one. Tucked under the diaphragm, it fills much of the upper abdomen, with its lower portions overhanging parts of the stomach and small intestine. When food is digested, nutrient-rich blood flows from the intestines into the liver through the portal vein, which branches into a network of tiny capillaries within the liver. There the blood is purged of a wide range of substances, including alcohol and many medications.

The blood is processed in other ways, as well. Laden as it is with nutrients, it is higher than normal in glucose (digested carbohydrates) and amino acids (digested protein). The liver removes most of the excess glucose, converting it into glycogen for storage on site. If the liver's glycogen stores are full—it can hold enough to supply about four hours' worth of glucose—it converts the glucose to fat, to be stored in adipose (fatty) tissue throughout the body. Because excess amino acids cannot be stored, the liver converts them into glucose, glycogen, or fat. As a first step, it must rid the amino acids of nitrogen, by means of a process called deamination, which produces ammonia. In humans, this is excreted as urea, a less-toxic compound. In other species, it may be excreted directly as ammonia or as uric acid.

Once this balancing of blood chemistry is complete, the blood leaves the liver through the hepatic vein, which leads to the vena cava and on to the heart. Conversely, if an organism has been expending energy without eating enough, the blood entering the liver will be low in glucose. In that case, the liver converts some of its glycogen stores back to glucose and adds it to the blood.

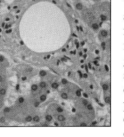

Above, epatocytes—liver cells—clustered around a central vein.

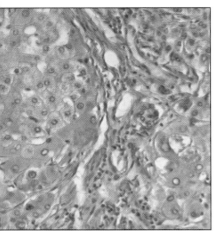

Liver cirrhosis is characterized by the presence of fibrous septa and regenerative nodules (above).

Further Reading
Askari, Fred K., *Hepatitis C, The Silent Epidemic* (1999); Francavilla, A., ed., *Liver and Hormones* (1987); Maddrey, Willis C., *The Liver* (1995); McCartney, Scott, *Defying the Gods: Inside the New Frontiers of Organ Transplants* (1994); Wilson, Michael A., *Modern Imaging of the Liver* (1996).

Role in Intestinal Digestion. The liver also has a direct role in digestion in the intestines. It produces bile from salts and pigments and from cholesterol, which it also makes. Bile, a greenish yellow fluid, emulsifies fat so that it can be digested by the enzyme lipase from the pancreas. It also aids in the transport of digested fat and serves as a vehicle for excreting bilirubin, the remains of destroyed red blood cells. Bile flows from the liver through the hepatic duct. This channel joins with the gallbladder's cystic duct to form the common bile duct that enters the duodenum, part of the small intestine. Between meals, bile goes up the cystic duct to the gallbladder, where it is stored and concentrated. When fatty foods enter the small intestine, the gallbladder contracts and empties into the duodenum.

> *Related material regarding the liver can be found in* BLOOD; DIGESTIVE SYSTEM; METABOLISM. *Additional details can be found in* BLOOD CLOTTING; DIGESTIVE CHEMISTRY; PANCREAS. *Further elementary aspects relevant to this subject are covered in* ADDICTIVE DISORDERS; ORGAN TRANSPLANTATION.

First see TELECOMMUNICATIONS

Local Area Network (LAN)

Next see INTERNET

The product of interconnections among individual personal computers.

Local Area Networks, LANs as they are usually known, can be configured in two basic ways: peer-to-peer networks, in which similar computers are simply connected by a serial cable linking their serial ports; and client-server networks, built around a network interface card, or NIC. Peer-to-peer networks are inexpensive and easy to set up, but can lead to information jams if several users need the same application, or if large files must be transferred. Client-server networks allow management and security to be centralized, allowing one to perform such useful functions as backing up all machines at once or duplicating applications.

Client-server networks may be interconnected according to any of three basic topologies—bus, star, and ring—each of which has advantages and disadvantages. A bus topology runs a single cable along a path linking all the client machines, with branches leading off the cable to individual units. This topology is unsuited for large networks, because the bandwidth of a single cable can easily be overloaded by high-volume use. A ring topology also uses a single cable, but the cable is looped, and each client machine must wait for a special signal, called a token, before it can access the server. A star topology requires a direct connection between each client and the server—hence the name, as such a network looks like a five- or six-pointed star; although more complicated, this arrangement centralizes the network more efficiently. Bus and star networks usually use an Ethernet connection, while ring networks must use the more expensive Token Ring method. Wireless LANs, using spread spectrum radio technology, are also available. (*See* INTERNET.)

First See NAVIGATION

Locomotion

Next See PREDATION

The ability to move from one place to another.

With the exception of a few invertebrates, like barnacles or oysters, that live anchored to a surface, all animals have evolved some way to move themselves through space in order to find food, elude predators, and in most cases, mate. The diversity in animal locomotion is extraordinary—from the jellyfish weakly contracting its bell in the water to the cheetah sprinting at nearly 70 miles per hour.

One-celled and small multicelled invertebrates are commonly moved in the water by the waving motion of hairlike projections; these are called cilia if they are short and numerous, or flagella if they are few and relatively long. More complex invertebrates have contractile tissue or outright muscles that allow them to move tentacles in swimming.

Four-legged Movement. Fish generally propel themselves through the water by the lateral, or side-to-side, undulation of the tail, the caudal fin, and the rear part of the trunk. The other fins serve to steer and stabilize the animal to prevent rolling and to control its angle of inclination, thus conserving energy. Tuna and other members of the mackerel family swim like whales, moving forward through dorsiventral, or up and down, undulation of the tail and rear portion of the trunk.

A bottle-nosed dolphin in motion. The dorsiventral (up-and-down) motion of the dolphin's tailfin is also a trait shared by several fish.

Tetrapods—four-legged animals or their descendants—variously swim, crawl, walk, run, hop, jump, dig, climb, glide, and fly. The modifications required by each form of locomotion varies, with flyers being among the most specialized of vertebrates.

To gain enough upward force to counter gravity, fly, and maneuver with stability, birds need great strength combined with light weight, firm trunks, and efficient use of power. Accordingly, they have light skeletons with air-filled bones, high metabolic rates, rapid digestion, and highly efficient respiratory systems, and they lack digits and teeth to save on weight. Their firm, compact bodies—with short, stiff trunks and many fused vertebrae—mean that thrust is transmitted from the wings to the body as a unit without twisting or flapping the body.

Predators or large herbivores tend to be runners, able to range over large areas or migrate seasonally in search of food and water. Most are built for speed, with relatively long leg bones that may be lengthened, in effect, by standing on the tips of the toes, as ungulates, or hooved animals, do. By comparison, the human foot, like those of monkeys and bears, is held with the heel flat on the ground. Such a plantigrade posture, as it is called, is characteristic of animals that walk well but are not great runners.

Snakes. Even legless snakes have evolved a variety of ways of moving. In the most common, lateral or serpentine undulation, the snake presses loops of its body against the sides of pebbles or other projections. In rectilinear movement, snakes bunch their belly plates together and then stretch out, pushing against the ground. In concertina movement, the snake forms S-shaped coils. It pushes downward with the back coils and thrusts forward with the front coils, then draws the back of the body forward. Finally, there is the rapid motion of sidewinding, used in sandy soil, in which the head and neck are thrust forward above the ground.

Special topics in this area are found in MUSCLE; NERVOUS SYSTEMS; SPACE. *Advanced subjects are developed in* BIRDS; CARTOGRAPHY AND SURVEYING; NAVIGATION. *Elementary aspects of this subject are covered in* INSTINCT; LUBRICANTS; PREDATION.

First see NUMBER

Logarithm

Next see STATISTICS

The index or exponent of a number to a specific base.

A logarithmic scale is used to graph values whose rate of change is more important than their absolute values. A conventional graph employs a grid whose units are equidistant from one another; this form of graph is useful to show

Movement is vital to living creatures; nearly all have to move to acquire sustenance.

Further Reading
Barre, Michael, *How Animals Move* (1998); Cordo, Paul, et al., eds., *Movement Control* (1994); McMahon, Thomas A., *Muscles, Reflexes, and Locomotion* (1984); Muybridge, E., *Horses and Other Animals in Motion* (1985).

constant change like that defined by the equation $y = ax + b$. As x grows, y grows proportionally, so the grid allows one to find the value of y simply by reading over to the appropriate x, then reading up (or down) to the corresponding point on the line. Information on a conventional graph can also be read as a vector, allowing geometric solutions to algebraic problems.

Many real-world situations, however, involve not constant changes but percentage changes: population, sales, career choices, disease rates, etc. In these cases, determining absolute values is less critical than identifying changes in value. Is population growth leveling off as a result of birth-control efforts? Are increases in sales keeping up with those by our competition? Which academic departments will need additional faculty members? Have our investments in cancer research paid off in lower disease rates and higher cure rates? For all questions of this type, a logarithmic graph is used to provide answers.

The spacing of the lines in a logarithmic grid is based not on unit differences, but on differences in the logarithm of the number being plotted. For common logarithms, that means the lines are spaced from 1, the zero logarithm, to 10, the identity logarithm, getting closer to one another as the value rises. A logarithmic grid may contain one complete cycle from 1 to 10, or be extended indefinitely; such grids are identified by the size of the stack, as "two-cycle," "three-cycle," etc. Most logarithmic scales are actually semilog grids, because the x-axis—which usually records change in time—remains arithmetic; however, sometimes it is necessary to use logarithmic scales for both axes, in which case the result is called a log-log grid. Paper preprinted with these different scales is widely available, colored with pale ink ("non-repro blue," for example) designed to disappear during copying so that the unconventional grid will not distract the reader. Most software programs also allow data to be recorded on various log scales, as well as on conventional grids.

Reading a logarithmic scale is no more difficult than reading a conventional scale, as long as one remembers the focus is on change, not simply on value. A vertical increase of 100 percent will be represented by the same distance on a log scale, no matter what the actual numbers involved. This is especially useful when one is dealing with large numbers, such as population figures or molecular activity, since a small percentage increase can sometimes produce an alarmingly large change: the birthrate may increase from 1.8 percent to 2.2 percent, but on a base of 5 billion people that will still result in a population growth of nearly 250,000 a day! On a conventional scale, population growth would look out of control; on a logarithmic scale, the slope of the line would be visibly less steep.

First see MICHELSON-MORLEY EXPERIMENT

Lorentz-Fitzgerald Contraction

Next see SPECIAL RELATIVITY

The Lorentz-Fitzgerald contraction was a hypothesis proposed by G. F. Fitzgerald and expanded by Hendrik A. Lorentz to explain the negative results of the Michelson-Morley experiment, which measured the speed of light along the path of Earth's orbit and at right angles to that path. Michelson and Morley expected to observe a difference in the speed of light in those two pathways, but saw none. Fitzgerald made the first attempt at explanation, saying that when a body moves through space, it experiences a compression or shrinkage of its mass in the direction of its motion. Lorentz then showed how that effect could be predicted on the basis of the theory of electromagnetics and the electrical constitution of matter. He deduced that when a body moves through space, its dimension parallel to the direction of motion should be reduced, and that the amount of reduction is dependent on its speed. For Earth, which travels at a speed of about 18.5 miles per second, the calculated reduction is one part in 200 million, or about 2.5 inches. That accounted for the Michelson-Morley result.

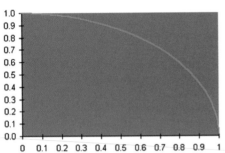

Apparent length of an object plotted against speed as a fraction of the speed of light, set equal to 1.

One of the first to grasp the full significance of the Lorentz-Fitzgerald explanation was Albert Einstein. When he formulated the special theory of relativity, Einstein proposed that the contraction of a body in motion is related to the speed of motion of the body as compared to the speed of light. Since the speed of motion of most objects is very small compared to the speed of light, the contraction can be observed only by specially designed instruments.

First see FRICTION

Lubricants

Next see AUTOMOTIVE DESIGN

Oils, fats, greases, and other chemical compounds that are put between moving parts of machines to reduce friction and wear.

Lubricants are needed because even the most carefully finished metal surfaces are covered with very tiny depressions and bumps, which tend to resist the movement of one surface over another. The application of a lubricant to these surfaces reduces the friction between them by covering them with a thin film of an oily substance. The two most important characteristics of a lubricant are its viscosity and its viscosity index. Viscosity can be defined as the measure of a lubricant's resistance to flow, or its thickness. The viscosity index is the relationship between the lubricant's viscosity and its temperature. A high index means that the viscosity of the lubricant will not change much as the temperature rises—an important factor for machinery whose parts generate high temperatures because of their rapid motion.

Early in the industrial age, animal fats or vegetable oils were used as lubricants. Most lubricants now are petroleum products, although vegetable lubricants, combining hydroxy fatty acids and vegetable oils, are recommended alternatives in "total loss" applications, such as oil sprayed on railroad tracks and wheels, where the use of petroleum would dump 300,000 gallons of non-degradable product into the environment. In many cases, artificial lubricants developed by chemists have replaced both natural and petroleum-based products. Ordinary bearings can work well with basic lubricants, but bearings that work at high speeds and under high loads require special lubricants, often the newly developed synthetic types.

First see GAS, BEHAVIOR OF

Lungs

Next see BREATHING REGULATION

Air-filled respiratory sacs used by almost all land vertebrates to bring in oxygen from the environment and exchange it for carbon dioxide to be expelled from the body.

Although lungs may be of varying complexity, they share certain characteristics: they provide a humid environment, moister than the outside air, to facilitate gas diffusion; they contain a rich supply of blood vessels to carry oxygen throughout the body; and unlike gills, the respiratory organs of fish, they are completely internal, with a passageway leading to the outside.

In amphibians and some reptiles, the lungs are often simple sacs, perhaps with a few internal ridges. But in mammals and birds, where they are most highly developed, they have evolved a richly subdivided inner surface, with many small folds and pockets providing a vastly increased surface area over which gas exchange can take place.

Humans have two large elastic cone-shaped lungs that lie within the chest, separated by the heart and a partition called the mediastinum. The right lung has three lobes; the left lung—smaller in many mammals to make room for the heart—has two. Air is drawn in through the nostrils, moves to the pharynx, the larynx, and down the trachea or windpipe, which divides into two bronchi, one leading to each lung. The bronchi branch into bronchioles, which keep branching until they end in tiny alveoli, air pockets that form the spongy inside surface of the lung. The alveoli walls are only one cell thick and are surrounded by dense networks of capillaries. Oxygen diffuses from the alveoli into the capillaries to be carried to the heart for circulation throughout the body; carbon dioxide diffuses from the capillaries into the alveoli to be exhaled. The process occurs across a large surface area. A single human lung may contain 300 million alveoli, with a surface area of 115 to 164 square feet.

Mammals. In mammals and birds, breathing relies on negative pressure. Air is drawn into the lungs when the air pressure in the chest falls below the atmospheric pressure. That occurs when the volume of the chest has been expanded by muscular contractions of the rib cage and diaphragm. Exhalation happens passively when the muscles relax, reducing chest volume, raising chest air pressure, and driving air out.

In mammals, breathing is tidal—air moves in and out of the lungs through the same route. The tidal volume, the amount of air moved by one normal breath, is about 500 milliliters. With effort, an additional 3,000 milliliters can be inhaled, and an additional 1,100 milliliters can be exhaled. After even the deepest exhalation, however, a reserve volume of about 1,200 milliliters remains in the lungs; without it, they would collapse. The vital capacity, a common measure of human lung function, is a total of all these volumes except reserve volume. In other words, it is the most a person can exhale after inhaling as much as possible.

Birds have lungs that are unique in structure, and more efficient at extracting oxygen than those of mammals. As a result, they can fly comfortably at low-oxygen altitudes that would leave mammals in a stupor. Besides a pair of compact lungs, birds have five or six pairs of large air sacs opening off the lungs, including some that penetrate into the bones.

The air sacs act as bellows, sending a continuous stream of air in a single direction through the lungs, in contrast to the tidal motion in mammals' lungs. When birds inhale, air goes from the bronchus to posterior air sacs. At the same time, air already in the lungs moves into anterior air sacs. When birds exhale, air moves from the posterior sacs into the lungs, while air from the anterior sacs is expelled from the body. So on both inhalation and exhalation, air moves through the lungs with no unexpelled reserve. Within the lungs are parabronchi, small tubes whose walls contain a network of air capillaries, each far smaller in diameter than mammalian alveoli and surrounded by blood capillaries. It is there that

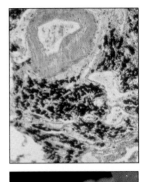

Bronchioles are the smallest tubes of the lungs (above, bottom). They bring air to the alveoli where gas exchange occurs. Lung tissue that has been polluted with coal dust particles (above, top) has been characterized as "black lung" tissue, and is associated with lung cancer.

Below, a male (at right) and female Lyme tick, though both can grow to several times their normal size after feeding on the blood of a host.

the exchange of oxygen and carbon dioxide takes place. Air sacs are seen in some lizards and snakes as well. Fossil evidence indicates that dinosaurs also had them.

First see IMMUNE RESPONSE

Lupus

Next see AUTOIMMUNITY

An autoimmune disease characterized by skin lesions.

Lupus erythematosus is an autoimmune disease in which the body's immune defense system attacks the connective tissues, such as tendons and cartilages, that hold the body structure together. For unknown reasons, lupus is nine times more common in women than in men, usually occurring during the childbearing years. Hormonal factors appear to play a part in development of the disease, and its occurrence can sometimes be tracked to a specific viral infection.

There are two forms of lupus. The more common type is discoid lupus erythematosus, DLE, which affects exposed areas of the skin. Less common but more dangerous is systemic lupus erythematosus, SLE, which attacks many parts of the body, including the kidneys and the joints, and is often fatal. DLE usually starts with the appearance of reddish, thickened circular areas of the skin, where scar tissue later forms. These scars can form on the face and the scalp and behind the ears, often causing permanent loss of hair. In SLE, a blotchy, red rash develops over the cheeks and nose (resulting sometimes in a wolf-like—or lupine—appearance), accompanied by sickness, fever, fatigue, nausea, pain in the joints, and loss of weight. Other SLE-caused problems can include anemia, kidney failure, arthritis, and inflammation of the membrane around the heart.

There are no specific treatments for either condition, but their symptoms can be ameliorated. For example, nonsteroidal anti-inflammatory drugs can reduce joint pains, and corticosteroids can be given for fever and neurological problems. Such treatments have lengthened the life expectancy for SLE sufferers to more than ten years after diagnosis.

First see DISEASES, INFECTIOUS

Lyme Disease

Next see PARASITE

Lyme disease is so named because it was first described in the town of Lyme, Connecticut, in 1975. It is caused by the bacterium *Borrelia burgdorferi*, which is transmitted to humans by the bite of a species of tick that usually lives on deer, but which can be carried by dogs. Most of the early cases of Lyme disease were first reported in the northeastern United States, but it has been found in other sections of the country and in other countries. The first sign of the disease is a small red dot that appears at the site of the tick bite. In many cases, that dot expands to form a reddened area several inches in diameter. The expansion is accompanied by symptoms that include headache, fever, lethargy, and muscle pains, and later by inflammation of the large joints, including the knees, accompanied by redness and swelling of those joints.

Lyme disease can be treated with antibiotics or, if the disease is diagnosed in an advanced stage, with nonsteroidal anti-inflammatory drugs and sometimes with corticosteroids. If the disease is not treated, the symptoms can continue for years, in cycles that last about a week. Symptoms gradually decline with time in most cases, disappearing after a few years and causing no permanent damage. However, there have been patients in whom complications affecting the heart (heart block) and the nervous system (meningitis) have occurred in cases where underlying Lyme disease was not treated.

First see CIRCULATORY SYSTEM

Lymphatic Systems

Next see IMMUNE RESPONSE

A secondary circulatory network for the immune system, producing, storing, and transporting bacteria-fighting white blood cells and helping to filter bacteria from the body's tissues.

In addition to being a secondary circulatory network for the immune system, the lymphatic system has other unrelated functions, including retrieving protein and excess fluid that has escaped the bloodstream and conveying digested fat into the bloodstream. Unlike blood circulation, lymphatic circulation moves in only one direction: from the tissues toward the heart.

All vertebrates have some form of lymph system. In birds and mammals, thin-walled lymph capillaries are found in almost all soft tissue They collect fluid and protein that have leaked out of the blood-bearing capillaries of the cardiovascular system. Once in the lymph channels, the fluid, a pale yellow liquid similar to blood plasma, is called lymph. It moves through the lymph channels by the contraction of nearby muscles, much as blood moves through veins. In mammals, lymph channels, like veins, have valves to prevent backflow. Eventually the lymph passes through a lymph duct and into a vein. In humans, lymph from the right upper part of the body drains through the right lymphatic duct into the right subclavian vein near the heart. Lymph from the rest of the body drains through the thoracic duct into the left subclavian vein.

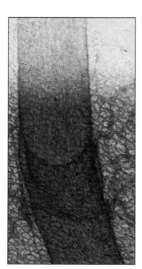

Above, a lymph vessel; the valve preventing backflow is barely visible.

Below, lymph node tissue, site of frequent skirmishes between the body's defenses and toxic invaders.

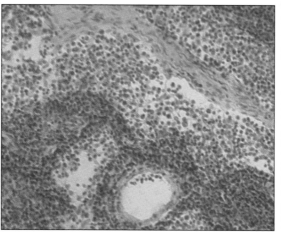

Further Reading
Eckstein, Gustav, *The Body Has a Head* (1982); Marieb, Elaine Nicpon, *Essentials of Human Anatomy and Physiology* (1999); Nuland, Sherwin B., *The Wisdom of the Body: Discovering the Human Spirit* (1997); Nuland, Sherwin B., *How We Live* (1998).

Lymphatic capillaries in the intestines, called lacteals because of their milky appearance, transport fat from the gut into the bloodstream. In humans, 80 to 90 percent of all fat absorbed from the intestines is transported by lymph.

Nodes. Lymph nodes are numerous in mammals, and are seen in some birds. In humans, these small oval capsules occur in clusters in the neck, underarm, inner elbow, abdomen, lower back, and groin. Inside the nodes is a mesh of connective tissue that filters the lymph for bacteria, dead cells, and other nondigestible particles. They contain lymphocytes, white blood cells that attack and destroy disease-causing microbes, as well as macrophages, large white blood cells that engulf microbes and debris. During an infection, nearby lymph nodes often are so taxed they become sore or swollen. Biopsy of lymph nodes serves as an important tool in diagnosing the spread of cancer, because cancer often metastasizes along the route of the lymph system.

In mammals, the lymphatic system includes other organs. The thymus, an organ in the chest that is active early in life, helps produce T-lymphocytes, which protect against viral infections and some cancers. The spleen, an organ suspended from the stomach, helps produce lymphocytes, filters blood, and destroys old red blood cells. The bone marrow helps create B-lymphocytes, which produce antibodies. Lymphoid tissue—lymphocyte-containing tissue that fights infection—is also found in the tonsils and adenoids, the liver, and in Peyer's patch (small nodules on the small intestine). Birds have an additional lymphoid mass called the bursa of Fabricius.

In frogs, lymph capillaries widen into sinusoids, which form large lymph reservoirs just under the skin. Fish, amphibians, and reptiles propel lymph through their vessels with the help of lymph hearts, pulsating swellings on the lymph vessels that contain striated muscle. Frogs have two pairs of lymph hearts, but other amphibians have dozens. As semiaquatic animals, amphibians have far more tissue fluid to move than do landlocked vertebrates. (*See* THERMAL REGULATION.)

Further developments in the field are discussed in CIRCULATORY SYSTEM; DIGESTIVE SYSTEM; LIPIDS. **More details can be found in** LEUKOCYTES; LIPIDS; NUTRITION. **Additional relevant information is contained in** CANCER; THERMAL REGULATION.

First see MAGNETISM

Magnetic Field of Earth

Next see PALEOCLIMATOLOGY

The magnetic field of Earth originates deep within the planet and extends far out into space. This magnetic field is believed to be produced by the flow of electric current in the core of Earth. It has been found to be an extremely dense fluid, probably molten iron, surrounding a small, solid center. The movements of the material in the core result from convection, most probably caused by the heat generated by radioactivity in the deep interior. These currents are believed to produce electric current much as a dynamo does, by electromagnetic induction. The resulting magnetic field is weak, with a strength of 70,000 nT at the magnetic poles to 25,000 nT on the magnetic equator. Anywhere on earth, a compass needle is easily deflected by even a small magnet.

The effect of the Earth's magnetic field is quite similar to the effect of a small dipole magnet placed at the planet's core. If such a dipole existed, it would be tilted about 11 degrees from Earth's axis of rotation.

The magnetic poles, the points on the surface where a needle points straight down, do not quite coincide with the axis of the inclined dipole, because the field is not exactly that of a dipole. The magnetic poles toward which a compass needle points are located about 1,200 miles from the North and South (geographic) Poles. The angle of declination, the deflection from true north of a compass needle, has been measured by sighting with a telescope along a suspended magnet. The angle of dip, the angle that a magnetic needle assumes in relation to the horizontal, is measured by suspending a magnet so that it pivots around its center of gravity. The angle of dip is horizontal at the magnetic equator, vertical at the poles, and has interim positions in between.

History. The existence of Earth's magnetic field was first demonstrated in 1600 by British scientist William Gilbert. Studies of the magnetic field over the past 1.5 billion years have shown that the field has deviated at times as much as 10 or 20 degrees from its present orientation. Its strength and polarity has also changed from time to time. Daily variations of magnitude can be measured today, and have been shown to result from atmospheric tides raised by the gravitational effects of the sun and the moon.

Related areas to be considered are CHARGE AND CURRENT; EARTH; ELECTRIC AND MAGNETIC FIELD. *Advanced subjects are developed in* PLANET, INTERIOR; PLANETS, FORMATION OF; SOLAR WIND. *Elementary aspects of this subject are covered in* AURORAS; ELEMENTARY PARTICLE; PLANETARY ATMOSPHERE.

First see ELECTRIC AND MAGNETIC FIELD

Magnetism

Next see ELECTROMAGNETISM

The force of interaction between two wires that carry electric currents, between two magnets, or between a magnet and a magnetic material. It results from electrical charge in motion on the atomic level.

Magnetism gets its name from Magnes, a shepherd in Asia Minor, who supposedly was the first to notice that there was an attraction between the iron crook he carried and bits of soil or ore that were naturally magnetic. This substance is called lodestone or magnetite. Deposits of magnetite found in Asia Minor were the first permanent magnets.

History. By 2700 B.C.E., the Chinese noted that magnetic material always pointed one way. This discovery led to the development of com-

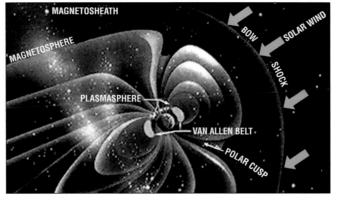

passes, which were simply magnetic needles suspended freely so they could point toward the north. The idea of magnetic poles was developed by Petrus Perigrinus in the thirteenth century. At the beginning of the seventeenth century, William Gilbert, an English observer, explained that magnets could serve as compasses because the Earth itself has magnetic action. Gilbert observed that like magnetic poles (north-north) repel each other and unlike magnetic poles (north-south) attract each other. Gilbert also noted that a single magnetic pole cannot exist; when a piece of magnetic material is broken, both have north and south poles. The law describing the force between two magnetic poles was discovered in the eighteenth century by several scientists, most notably Charles Augustine de Coulomb. Two magnetic poles attract or repel each other with a force that is proportional to the strength of their magnetic fields and the square of the distance between them.

Experiments establishing the relationship between electricity and magnetism were conducted in 1819 by Hans Christian Oersted. He noted that when a wire carrying an electric current is placed parallel to a compass needle, the needle swings until it is perpendicular to the

Magnetic field lines can be seen radiating between the (magnetic) north and south poles of the Earth in an artist's rendering, above left. Charged particles become trapped within these field lines, forming a magnetosphere. This magnetic field is believed to be a result of the high iron and nickel content of the Earth's molten core (top).

Left, Japan's Bullet Train rides on air as it is raised off the track by a repelling magnetic force.

direction of the current. The next year, André Marie Ampère showed that an electrically energized coil of wire acts as a magnet, and Dominique Arago showed that a a piece of iron can be magnetized temporarily and a piece of steel permanently by placing them inside a coil of wire carrying a current. Those discoveries led to the development of powerful electromagnets by William Sturgeon and Joseph Henry.

The discovery of the electron in the late nineteenth century led to the explanation of atomic magnetism as the result of the circulation of electrons around the atomic nucleus. Magnetism occurs in atoms where electron orbital motions and spins do not cancel one another out. Pierre Weiss proposed the existence of magnetic domains that consist of billions of subatomic magnets, with their separate magnetic moments joined together. Partial magnetism occurs when domains are partially oriented with respect to each other; complete magnetism occurs when the domains are completely aligned with an applied field.

Above, Michael Faraday. Faraday made many contributions to physics in the areas of electricity and magnetism. Faraday demonstrated that when a wire is exposed to a changing magnetic field, an electric current is generated in the wire, a phenomenon known as Faraday's Law.

CONTROVERSIES

Are There Magnetic Monopoles?

A magnetic monopole is a hypothetical entity that is the source of a magnetic field with only one pole, north or south. All known magnets are dipoles, with both north and south poles; if such a magnet is cut in half, both the two resulting magnets will have two poles. Classical and quantum electrodynamics describe magnetism as a byproduct of the motion, or circulation, of electric charge within a substance. This description explains the absence of single magnetic poles, since a single pole cannot be created by a circulating electric current. Nevertheless, electromagnetic theory says that magnetic monopoles can exist under certain circumstances.

Background material on magnetism can be found in CHARGE AND CURRENT; ELECTRICAL AND MAGNETIC FIELDS. *Further developments in the field are discussed in* ELECTROMAGNETIC FORCE; ELECTROMAGNETISM; INDUCTOR. *Special topics in this area are to be found in* AURORAS; COSMIC RAYS; MAGNETIC FIELD OF THE EARTH.

Further Reading
Lee, E.W., *Magnetism* (1984); Maxwell, James Clerk, *Treatise on Electricity and Magnetism* (1991); Tipler, Paul A., *Physics* (1998); Verschuur, Gerrit L., *Hidden Attraction: The History and Mystery of Magnetism* (1996).

First see IMMUNE RESPONSE

Major Histocompatability Complex (MHC)

Next see AUTOIMMUNITY

A set of genes producing proteins that allow the immune system to distinguish between self and non-self—between a person's own cells and those from any other source.

In the presence of foreign tissue, MHC proteins promote the two main kinds of immune response: attacks by antibodies and mobilization of T-lymphocyte cells to destroy the foreign tissue. The T cell reaction is the mechanism behind immune rejection, in which the body rejects a transplanted organ unless the immune system is suppressed by drug therapy. In addition, variations in the MHC have been found to influence susceptibility to many diseases.

Discovery. The genes for the major histocompatibility complex are located on the short arm of human chromosome 6. Its proteins were discovered in the 1950s when people who had had multiple pregnancies or blood transfusions—repeated exposures to foreign tissue—were found to have antibodies in their blood that reacted against proteins on leukocytes, white blood cells, from other people. The proteins targeted by these antibodies were called human leukocyte antigens (HLA), another term for human MHC proteins.

The natural role of MHC proteins is to bind with fragments of disease-causing microbes and present them to T-lymphocyte cells for attack. The process is extremely complex, but can be simplified this way: there are two types of MHC proteins. MHC-I is found on the membranes of most cells of the body. When a viral or bacterial protein, or antigen, enters a cell, MHC-I binds with it and carries it to the surface of the cell for presentation to a T cell. Eventually the proper T cell—one that recognizes the specific antigen—binds to both the antigen and the MHC-I protein and attacks the infected cell.

B Cells. MHC-II is found on the membranes of some immune system cells, including B-lymphocytes. The B cells produce antibodies, which bind with a particular viral or bacterial antigen. The antibody-antigen combination is taken into the B cell, where the antigens are removed and bound to MHC-II molecules. As before, the bound antigens are displayed on the cell surface for attack by a T cell. In either case, the antigens must bind with MHC proteins in order for the T cells to be effective.

The immune system recognizes the body's own tissue by the presence of self-antigens, cell-surface proteins that mark tissue as non-foreign. In addition to its other functions, several genes of the major histocompatibility complex are necessary for the production of self-antigens.

A great variety of MHC gene variants—called HLA types—have been identified in humans. Since the 1970s, it has become clear that these variations influence susceptibility to many diseases. Fully understanding the effects of HLA types on disease is the goal of much current research in immunology.

Most of the diseases linked to HLA types so far involve an autoimmune reaction, in which the immune system mistakenly attacks the body's own tissue as though it were foreign. These include rheumatoid arthritis, diabetes mellitus, psoriasis, and multiple sclerosis. The strongest association has been found with ankylosing spondylitis, a disease in which the spine

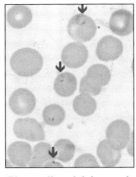

Plasmodium falciparum is the most common type of malaria (above). Arrows indicate infected cells.

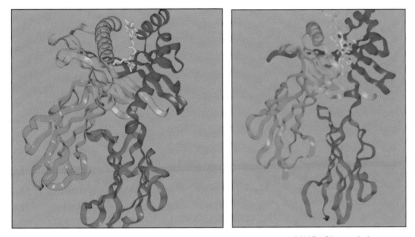

and large joints become inflamed. This illness, like some other rheumatic diseases, has been linked to the HLA-B27 variant. Among people of western European ancestry, about seven percent have HLA-B27, and it appears in 80 to 90 percent of patients with ankylosing spondylitis.

The foundations of the subject are discussed in GENETIC CODE; IMMUNE RESPONSE; KARYOTYPING. *More details can be found in* IMMUNIZATION AND VACCINATION; IMMUNOASSAY; ORGAN TRANSPLANTATION. *Advanced subjects are developed in* AUTOIMMUNITY; BIOSYNTHETICS; INTERFERONS AND INTERLEUKINS; LIFE, ORIGIN AND DEFINITION OF.

First see DISEASES, INFECTIOUS

Malaria

Next see PARASITE

A parasitic disease that is prevalent in the tropics and is spread by the bite of anopheles mosquitos.

Malaria is caused by parasites in the family of single-cell protozoa called plasmodium. Each parasite spends part of its life cycle in humans and part in anopheles mosquitoes. A person who contracts malaria will experience a range of symptoms that include a high fever and sometimes fatal complications affecting the kidneys,

MHC Class I is a membrane-spanning protein, divided into three globular domains (above, left). MHC Class II is also a membrane-spanning protein, but has four globular domains (above, right).

Further Reading
Kuby, Janis, *Immunology* (1997); Moulds, Joann M., *Scientific and Technical Aspects of the Major Histocompatability Complex* (1989); Parkham, Peter, *The Immune System* (2000).

the liver, the brain, and the blood. Symptoms such as chills, fever, and uncontrollable shaking appear when red blood cells infected by plasmodia break apart to release the parasites into the blood-stream. The symptoms of malaria usually appear a week or two after a person is bitten by an infected mosquito. Typically, there will be a first stage in which there is uncontrollable shivering, followed by a stage in which body temperature can reach 105 degrees, and finally, severe sweating that brings down body temperature until the next attack begins, which can be as soon as a day or two later.

Malaria is often treated with the drug chloroquine, which can eliminate the protozoa from the bloodstream. There have been an increasing number of choroquine-resistant cases, however. These cases can be treated with combination therapy that includes such drugs as quinine, pyrimethamine, and sulfadoxine. Visitors to malaria-ridden tropical areas are advised to take anti-malarial drugs for several days before their arrival, during their stay, and for several weeks thereafter. (*See* PARASITE.)

First see INSTINCT

Mammals

Next see PRIMATE

The most advanced order of vertebrates have the following characteristics in common: hair or fur covering the body and the production of milk from mammary glands to feed newborn offspring.

All mammals undergo internal fertilization, in which the egg is fertilized inside the female's body for better protection of the gametes. For development of the growing embryo, however, there is great variety. Some mammals, such as the duck-billed platypus and echidna (spiny anteater), lay shelled eggs. After incubation, the eggs hatch and the mother lactates—nurses her young. There is no nipple for the offspring to suck; the milk exits through ducts and the hatchlings lick it off the mother's skin. It is the lactation feature which causes these animals to be classified as mammals.

Other mammals exhibit at least some internal development. Marsupials, such as kangaroos, koalas, and opossums, give birth after a very short period of time. The newborns are wholly incapable of surviving on their own. Tiny, naked, and blind, they must wriggle their way into the mother's pouch, located on the external surface of the abdomen, and attach themselves to a nipple in order to gain nourishment. The newborn, called a joey, will spend the next several months in the pouch. Gradually, it grows larger and eventually begins leaving the pouch for short periods of time. By the time the joey is about a year old, it makes only occasional stops

Four examples of mammals (from top): a gorilla; a bottle-nosed porpoise; a mole rat (the only cold-blooded mammal); and an elephant.

in the pouch, which by this time is occupied by another, smaller sibling.

Placentals undergo complete internal development in the mother's uterus. The placenta consists of several tissues that provide a connection between the maternal bloodstream and the fetal one through the umbilical cord (which is cut at birth, thus forming the navel). All nutrients, minerals, oxygen, etc., that the developing fetus requires are obtained from the mother's blood. In exchange, fetal wastes and carbon dioxide are deposited into the mother's bloodstream for removal. The gestational period varies greatly according to species, from several weeks for small creatures, such as mice, to 22 months for whales. The human period of gestation is approximately 9.3 months or 280 days.

Mammalian Birthing. At birth, several species of animals are fully developed and can move about on their own. Primates, such as humans, are born relatively helpless; indeed, human babies can still be considered in the fetal stage until they are approximately nine months old. The reason humans are born so "early" in development has to do with the size of the cranium and the difficulty of passage through the birth canal. If the cranium is too large, the baby will not be able to negotiate its way out of the body, putting both mother and itself at risk.

All mammals are "warm-blooded" (endotherms); they are able to regulate a consistent body temperature, despite the external temperatures surrounding them. All mammals have lungs and take oxygen from the air.

Mammals have a four-chambered heart, consisting of two atria or "collecting" chambers and two ventricles or "pumping" chambers. The heart can really be considered two separate pumps, with the right side collecting deoxygenated blood returning from the rest of the body and sending it to the lungs to pick up oxygen, and the left side collecting the oxygenated blood from the lungs and sending it to circulate throughout the rest of the body.

Marine Mammals. Whales and dolphins are mammals, not fish. They are covered with hair, not scales, and nurse their young. While they can spend long periods of time under water, they must surface periodically. These creatures give birth under water, but the newborns swim immediately to the surface in order to breathe. To facilitate this, whales are normally born tail first, unlike humans, who are born head first in order to breathe, and for whom a foot-first presentation is considered a breech birth.

Further Reading
Gould, Edwin, *Encyclopedia of Mammals* (1997); MacDonald, David W., *The Encyclopedia of Mammals* (1995); Quammer, David, *Boilerplate Rhino: Nature in the Eye of the Beholder* (2001).

Elementary aspects of this subject are covered in DIGESTIVE SYSTEMS; EMBRYOLOGY; EVOLUTION; PHYLOGENY. *More information on particular aspects is contained in* ETHOLOGY; PRIMATES; REPRODUCTIVE SYSTEMS; SKELETAL SYSTEMS. *Additional relevant information is contained in* AGGRESSION AND TERRITORIALITY; CLONING; GENETIC CODE.

First see MEDICAL DIAGNOSTICS

Mammography

Next see CANCER

An x-ray procedure that is performed to detect breast cancer at an early stage.

Breast cancer screening procedures using mammography have reduced the death rate from the disease in women over the age of 50 by an estimated 30 percent. Mammography is done periodically because successful treatment of breast cancer depends on early detection of tumors when they are still small—less than a half-inch across. A tumor that is small may not be detectable with breast self-examination, which all women are encouraged to perform. Women should receive a baseline mammogram between the ages of 40 and 50; the procedure should be repeated every two to three years afterwards.

Mammography is also recommended to aid in the diagnosis of established breast cancer and to help plan treatment. The procedure uses only low-dose x rays. The breast may be x rayed from above or the side, or both; sometimes an angled view is taken. (*See* X RAY.)

Procedure. In the traditional method of mammography, the breast is placed against a plate and compressed between the plate and a plastic cover above it. This pressure is exerted to flatten the breast, so that the maximum amount of tissue can be imaged. In another method, the breast is allowed to hang freely and the x ray is taken from the side.

The mammogram image of a normal breast will show the milk ducts of the breast appearing as denser areas. To confirm a diagnosis of potential concern, a biopsy is performed, in which a tissue sample of an abnormal area is removed for microscopic analysis.

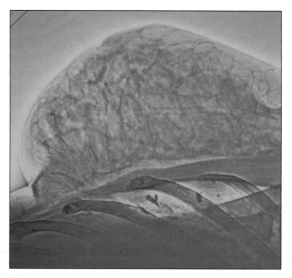

Above, a mammogram of a normal left breast. Possible tumors would appear as dark areas.

Mars

First see PLANET

Next see PLANETARY ATMOSPHERE

Mars, the fourth planet from the sun, is the only planet on which surface features can be seen from Earth. For hundreds of years, there was speculation that life might exist on Mars. In the 1870s, Italian astronomer Giovanni Schiaparelli made detailed drawings of Mars including a network of linear features that he called *canalli*, or channels. Many, including noted American astronomer Percival Lowell, interpreted the word to mean "canals," and drew the conclusion that they were the work of a Martian civilization. His theory has since been discredited. However, the speculation that water once flowed freely on the Martian surface has been supported by modern planetary probes.

As a Planet. The diameter of Mars at the equator is 4,213 miles, about 53 percent of Earth's equatorial diameter. Because Mars is

Though Mars is further from Earth than Venus, it is the only planet on which humans expect to land one day.

made of material that is less dense than that of Earth, its surface gravity is 38 percent of Earth's. A Martian day is 24 hours, 37 minutes, 22.6 seconds and a Martian year—the time for one orbit of the sun—is 686.9 days. Mars is tilted 24 degrees on its axis of rotation, almost the same tilt as the Earth's, and therefore it has seasons. These seasons are uneven in length because its orbit around the sun is eccentric, or oval—an eccentricity of 0.093, compared to the Earth's 0.017 eccentricity.

Mars has two moons, Phobos and Deimos, named for the mythological horses that drew the chariot of Mars, the Roman god of war. Curiously, the existence of the two moons of Mars was related in Jonathan Swift's book, *Gulliver's Travels*, in the eighteenth century—a flight of fancy that proved to be true. Both moons are believed to be captured asteroids.

Like Earth, Mars has polar ice caps. The southern ice cap is larger than the northern cap

because of the eccentricity of Mars' orbital path around the sun, which causes the planet to be farthest from the sun during the south polar winter. Water on Mars also exists as vapor in the atmosphere and probably as permafrost under the surface.

Mars has been extensively explored by American and Russian spacecraft, which have orbited the planet and landed on it. One American Pathfinder craft that landed on Mars was active as recently as 1998. These explorations have led to detailed maps of Mars with names for specific features, such as mountains, craters, and plains. A marsquake, measuring 2.8 on the Richter scale, was detected, which enabled astronomers to determine that the outer crust of the planet is 9.3 miles thick. The fact that the quake lasted only a few minutes indicated that water or ice is present in the crust.

Photographs show that the southern hemisphere of Mars has many volcanoes, including the largest to have been found in the solar system. There is a major rift system, Valles Marineris, that may be analogous to rift systems on Earth. Photographs show that in the northern highlands of Mars, there has been extensive erosion, while near the equator there have been major episodes of flooding. The planet's upper atmosphere consists mostly of carbon dioxide, with small amounts of nitrogen, carbon monoxide, argon, and nitrogen oxide.

Spacecraft on Mars all found the same reddish-brown soil (Mars has traditionally been known as the "red planet"), most likely caused by the mineral magnetite, made up of iron and oxygen. Planetary temperatures fell as low as –123 degrees Celsius at night.

Life on Mars. Soil samples were analyzed for the presence of organic molecules, but none were found. The absence of organic molecules is a strong indication that life has not existed on Mars, though the issue is far from settled. Astronomers speculate that if organic molecules once existed on Mars, they were destroyed by ultraviolet radiation from the sun, which reached the surface once the atmosphere was lost.

Related discussions are found in KEPLER'S LAWS; PLANET; PLANETARY ATMOSPHERE. *Other aspects of the subject are discussed in* JUPITER; PLANET, INTERIOR OF; SATELLITE, PLANETARY. *Regarding life on Mars, see* ASTEROIDS AND METEORS; EXTRATERRESTRIAL LIFE; LIFE, DEFINITION AND ORIGIN OF; SPACECRAFT.

Above, *Viking* lander explores the surface of Mars, gathering data.

Mars has been dubbed the "red planet" because of the distinct coloration of the soil (above, top). Mars Pathfinder—a remote-controlled rover—collected soil and rock samples for NASA (middle). Several face-shaped formations, like the crater discovered in 1985 (bottom), are optical effects of light and shadow.

Further Reading
Kiefer, Hugh H., *Mars (Space Science Series)* (1992); Raeburn, Paul, *Mars: Uncovering the Secrets of the Red Planet* (2000); Sheehan, William and Stephen James O'Meara, *Mars: The Lure of the Red Planet* (2001).

First see GAS, BEHAVIOR OF

Maxwell-Boltzman Distribution

Next see ENTROPY

Principle that describes the most probable distribution of the velocities of molecules in a gas.

The Maxwell-Boltzmann distribution principle was first described in 1860 by British physicist James Clerk Maxwell and was modified in 1877 by German scientist Ludwig Boltzmann, who added the effect of molecular collisions to Maxwell's calculations. The basic assumption of the principle is that the motion of molecules is completely random. It is impossible to say what velocity any particular molecule will have, but the range of velocities can be predicted.

Maxwell proposed that molecular speeds are distributed in a way similar to the familiar bell-shaped curve, which has a peak in the region of the average value and a sharp decline on either side of the peak. By promoting a statistical view of nature, Maxwell and Boltzmann helped to prepare for the twentieth-century view of the world. Newton's laws viewed the world as a machine whose characteristics could be described sharply and clearly. The modern view is that there is a certain randomness that cannot be eliminated from our picture of the world. Maxwell and Boltzmann helped to explain that randomness in mathematical terms.

CONTROVERSIES

Ludwig Boltzman

Ludwig Boltzmann (1844–1906) was a pioneer in the development of modern thermodynamics. In addition to his work on the laws of probability as applied to gases, he developed an equation relating the total energy of a gas to its temperature: $E = 1/2\ mu^2 = 3/2KT$, where T is the temperature in degrees Kelvin, and K is a constant, 1.3805×10^{-23} joules/Kelvin. In tribute, this constant is today known as the Boltzmann constant. However, his discoveries were never universally accepted during his lifetime, and in 1906 the depressed scientist committed suicide.

It might be thought that the continuing and random collisions of the molecules of a gas would result in every molecule having the same velocity. What Maxwell proposed is that even if two molecules with identical velocities collide, they will usually have different speeds as they career off after the collision.

Under some conditions, quantum effects must be considered and thus other statistics must be used, but the Maxwell-Boltzmann principle applies to most gases at high temperatures.

Verification. The first experimental verification of the Maxwell-Boltzmann principle was developed by Otto Stern and other physicists in the 1920s, using a hot wire of known temperature from which atoms of the metal's wire evaporated constantly in all directions. The wire was enclosed in a hollow cylinder with a slit that could be opened and shut quickly. The stream of metal atoms emerging from the slit produced a distribution pattern on a glass slide that could be studied in detail. The details of that pattern confirmed the velocity distributions predicted by Maxwell and Boltzmann.

Applications. In addition to describing the behavior of molecules of a gas, the Maxwell-Boltzmann principle can also be applied to the distribution of electrons and holes in many semiconducting materials, the distribution of optical phonons in a solid at low temperatures, and other solid-state systems. (*See* GAS.)

James Clerk Maxwell (1831-1879). Maxwell's contributions to many areas of physics were among the most important in the history of science.

First see ELECTROMAGNETISM

Maxwell's Equations

Next see GAUGE THEORY

The four fundamental equations of the physics of electricity, magnetism, radio waves, and light.

Maxwell's equations were derived by James Clerk Maxwell, a British theoretical physicist, in the 1860s. Maxwell built on the work of many other scientists, including Ampère, Coulomb, and Faraday, in developing his equations.

In each of the four equations, H stands for magnetic field strength, E stands for electric field strength, t stands for time, c stands for the speed of light, and $\partial/\partial t$ indicates partial differentiation with time. Div, an abbreviation for divergence, and curl, an abbreviation of rotation, are specific mathematical operations.

The first equation, div $E = 0$, states that in the absence of a charge, electric lines of forces cannot be created or destroyed. Maxwell pictured an electric field as a flow, and so the first equation says that in a given period of time and for a given space, as much electricity flows in as flows out.

The second equation, div $H = 0$, says the same thing about magnetic lines of force that the first equation says about electric lines of force, but in a more general sense: magnetic charges do not actually exist.

The third equation, curl $E = -(\partial/\partial t)H$, is a formula for Faraday's law of electromagnetic induction. It states that the limiting value of an electromagnetic force for each unit of area is proportional to the rate of change of H, the magnetic field, at a limit point P of the area, which means that a changing magnetic field creates an electrical field that is at right angles to the change in the magnetic field.

The fourth equation, curl $H = (\partial/\partial t)E$, states that a changing electric field produces a magnetic field, just as a changing magnetic field produces an electric field. Maxwell modified the fourth equation by adding another term, called the displacement current, $1/c\ (\partial/\partial t_t)E$. He added it for theoretical reasons; there was no experimental evidence supporting it.

Wave Equations. Working with these equations, including the displacement current, Maxwell derived what is called a wave equation. Wave equations were well known in other fields of physics but had never been applied to electricity and magnetism. The derivation of the wave equation allowed Maxwell to make two predictions. One was that there are electromagnetic waves. These waves had never been seen, but they were observed a few years later by H. R. Hertz, a German physicist who was following Maxwell's lead. These radio waves are of great practical importance today. To give just one basic example, they make television possible.

When Maxwell computed the speed of these electromagnetic waves, he found that they were almost identical with the speed of light. Maxwell then proposed that light itself is an electromagnetic wave, a proposal that was found to be correct. Maxwell thus included the study of light into the study of electricity and magnetism, which led to a unified theory combining magnetism and electricity. Maxwell's equations still are the basic theoretical tools for the study of electromagnetic waves and their applications.

> *Background material can be found in* ELECTRIC AND MAGNETIC FIELDS; MAGNETISM; VECTORS AND TENSORS. *Further details can be found in* CALCULUS; ELECTROMAGNETIC WAVES; ELECTROMAGNETISM. *Advanced aspects of this subject are covered in* GAUGE THEORY; GRAND UNIFICATION THEORIES; QUANTUM ELECTRODYNAMICS. *See also* LIGHT; WAVE-PARTICLE DUALITY.

First see DISEASES, INFECTIOUS

Measles

Next see IMMUNIZATION AND VACCINATION

A viral disease that usually occurs in childhood but can occur at any age.

Symptoms of measles—fever, a runny nose, sore eyes, and a cough—appear about ten days after infection. The red rash that is the most prominent symptom of measles appears three or four days later and starts to fade after an additional three or four days. Complications can include chest and ear infections, vomiting, diarrhea, and pain in the abdomen. It is very rarely fatal, except in children who have impaired

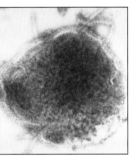
The rubella virus that causes measles.

Further Reading

Dunham, William, *Journey Through Genius: The Great Theorems of Mathematics* (1991); Dunham, William W., *The Mathematical Universe: An Alphabetical Journey Through the Great Proofs, Problems and Personalities* (1997); Guillen, Michael, *Five Equations That Changed the World: The Power and Poetry of Mathematics* (1995); Romanov, V.G., *Inverse Problems for Maxwell's Equations* (1994).

immune defenses, but one child in every 1,000 who is infected with the virus can develop encephalitis, a brain inflammation that may lead to mental retardation or death. Mild cases of measles can be treated with plenty of fluids and a drug such as acetaminophen to reduce fever. In some cases, antibiotics are given to treat secondary infections.

Measles was once an accepted part of childhood, but the development of a vaccine has virtually eliminated it in the United States. Children usually get a combined measles-mumps-rubella vaccine in their second year of life. The vaccine may cause some minor side effects, such as a low fever and a rash, but these effects disappear quickly. Despite the availability of the vaccine, some cases of measles still occur every year in the United States, and many cases are recorded in underdeveloped countries.

First see ACCELERATION

Mechanics

Next see FORCE

The oldest branch of physics, it deals with the forces that act on bodies both at rest and in motion.

Mechanics usually is divided into three main branches: dynamics, statics, and fluid mechanics. Dynamics is the branch that deals with bodies or systems that are in motion. It usually is divided into kinetics, which studies how applied forces change the path of an object in motion, and kinematics, which studies bodies in motion without referring to the forces that produce that motion. All these branches of classic dynamics are united at their core, since they all are governed by Newton's laws of motion.

Statics starts with Newton's first law of motion, which says that a body at rest will stay at rest and a body in motion will stay in motion when the total forces acting on that body equalize one another. Statics thus centers on identifying and evaluating the orientation and value of the forces acting on a body at rest. The practical application of statics is in engineering and construction. It is used to determine the stability of a structure—a building, a machine part, a dam—by analysis of the forces acting on that structure.

Fluids. Fluid mechanics deals with the behavior of a liquid or gas that is in motion. Fluid mechanics is used in a broad range of practical applications, including sewer systems, weather studies, and the design of supersonic craft. There are several categories of fluid flows. One deals with what is called the incompressible flow of an ideal fluid; the term applies both to fluids and gases. "Incompressible" means that the density of the fluid does not change. "Ideal" means that the fluid is frictionless—that is, it has no viscosity. These flows are described by

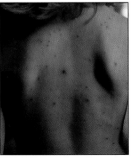
Above, measles spots can be seen on a child's back.

Bernoulli's laws, which say that when we look at a fluid in motion, the sum of the pressure, the square of the speed of flow, and the elevation of the fluid are constant along the path of flow. Any change in one factor causes a change in the others. For example, when a pipe that is carrying a fluid becomes narrower, the fluid flows faster, which means that its pressure drops.

Complex Fluids. Bernoulli's laws do not describe more complex fluid flow, however. For example, when the velocity of a fluid or gas is near or higher than the speed of sound, that fluid or gas is no longer incompressible. The density and temperature of such a compressible fluid can change considerably. In a supersonic fluid, for example, stationary or moving waves may be created, causing sudden jumps in pressure, density, and temperature—these are shock waves. When a fluid that has been flowing at a very high speed is slowed, its temperature can rise dramatically so that its atoms are ionized (they lose some of their electrons). The fluid can then conduct an electric current, and unusual chemical reactions can develop.

Further Reading

Cohen, I. Bernard, *The Birth of a New Physics* (1985); Goldstein, Herbert, *Classical Mechanics* (1980); Landau, L.D., *Course of Theoretical Physics: Mechanics* (1976); Marion, Jerry B., *Classical Dynamics of Particles and Systems* (1995); Szebehely, Victor G., *Adventures in Celestial Mechanics* (1998); Vogel, Steven, *Cats' Paws and Catapults: Mechanical Worlds of Nature and People* (1998).

> *Background material on mechanics can be found in* ACCELERATION; FORCE; NEWTON'S LAWS. *Further details can be found in* CORIOLIS FORCE; FRICTION; ROTATIONAL MOTION. *More on particular aspects of mechanic is contained in* FLUID MECHANICS; GRAVITY; PERPETUAL MOTION; SPECIAL RELATIVITY.

First see X-RAY

Medical Diagnostics

Next see CT AND PET SCANS

Diagnosis of a medical condition may involve a number of clinical techniques, but it always begins with the physician asking the patient to describe his or her condition. In many cases, this description, followed by a physical examination, may be enough. But often this first encounter provides the physician with a provisional diagnosis that must be proved or disproved by conducting specific tests. Today, there are a wide variety of tests available that can be applied depending on the provisional diagnosis.

Chemical Diagnostics. The physician may want to conduct one or more blood tests. In most routine examinations, blood testing includes a complete blood cell count, a chemistry group, and a test of blood lipids, or fats.

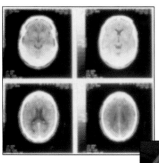

The development of sophisticated x-ray equipment, right, and the MRI (a less anxiety-producing label than the old NMR), above, has radically improved the field of diagnostics.

The blood cell count measures the number of each type of blood cell found in a given volume of blood. The count includes the number and kinds of white blood cells, the hematocrit, which is the percentage of the blood that is composed of red cells, and the number of platelets. The blood chemistry test can include an analysis of the electrolytes (sodium, potassium, chloride, and phosphorus), a test of blood sugar, a series of liver function tests that include a measurement of bilirubin, and tests for other chemicals such as uric acid, creatinine, and albumin, a major blood protein. The test for lipids can measure levels of total cholesterol, high-density lipoprotein cholesterol, and triglycerides, all of which are indicators of the risk of coronary artery disease.

Other blood tests include:

—sedimentation rate, which measures the rate at which red cells settle to the bottom of a tube (a faster-than-normal rate can indicate a number of problems, including infection, anemia, inflammation, and rheumatoid arthritis);

—coagulation tests, which measure the levels of the substances that control the rate of blood clot formation. These tests include measurement of partial thromboplastin time and prothrombin time. Abnormal results can identify not only blood-clotting disorders but also liver diseases. These tests are taken regularly by patients who use anticoagulant medications;

—enzyme tests, which can indicate abnormalities of specific organs (for example, abnormally high blood levels of certain enzymes can indicate liver disease or a heart disease, such as a myocardial infarction, or heart attack);

—thyroid tests which measure blood levels of hormones, such as thyroxine and thyroid-stimulating hormone (abnormal levels of a specific hormone help to pinpoint a given thyroid disorder); and

—arterial blood gas analysis, which measures the acidity of the blood and the amount of oxygen and carbon dioxide dissolved in it (this test differs from the usual blood test because it requires a local anesthetic and special measures are taken to make sure that the blood sample remains pure).

Fluid Analysis. Other chemical tests include synovial fluid analysis, which examines fluid secreted by the membranes lining the joints of the body. This test can help diagnose some kinds of arthritis, such as those caused by an infection or by gout. The test can be done in a hospital or at a doctor's office. A throat culture, in which a sample is taken from the back of the throat, helps diagnose an inflammation or infection of the throat caused by bacteria, viruses, or fungi. A cerebrospinal fluid analysis is done by spinal tap, or lumbar puncture, to help diagnose conditions ranging from meningitis to infections of the central nervous system to tumors.

Image Sensing. Image sensing methods of medical diagnosis include a variety of x-ray examinations. They range from mammograms, to detect breast cancer at an early stage; dental x rays, to determine whether and how much restorative work must be done; and barium x rays of the esophagus, stomach, and intestine. The barium x ray enables the doctor to detect whether there are ulcers, tumors, or other abnormalities of the gastrointestinal tract and small bowel.

The range of other x-ray examinations is very wide. It includes the CT, or computerized tomography, scan, in which a narrow beam of x rays is sent through the body to create an image of many soft-tissue organs and structures that are not shown by a conventional x-ray examination.

Magnetic resonance imaging (MRI) generates images of the head and body without using x rays. MRI uses a combination of magnetic fields and radio waves that result in images that are remarkably clear and can show cross-sections of the tissues or organs being examined.

Ultrasonography, or sonography, sends sound waves through the body at frequencies far too high to be detected by the human ear. The sound waves pass through the body and bounce

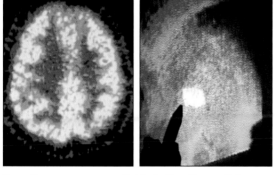

Two other resources available to the diagnostician are positron emission tomography (PET) scan, above, left; and ultrasonics, above, right.

back to a receptor that uses computer processing to create a moving image that is displayed on a video screen and can be photographed for further analysis. Ultrasonography is used to examine organs in the abdomen, including the gallbladder, liver, pancreas, kidneys, and spleen; those in the pelvis, including the uterus, ovaries, and prostate; as well as the thyroid, parathyroid, testicles, and breasts. This technology can also be used during pregnancy, so that the doctor can see the fetus in the uterus without exposing it to potentially damaging radiation. A sonogram of a fetus will show its position, size, and gestational age. It will also show whether there is a multiple pregnancy.

Radioscans. Radionuclide scans use small amounts of radioisotopes attached to substances that settle in various organs within the body.

These preparations can be given by inhalation, injection, or swallowing. Bone scans are used to diagnose cancer, infection, and the cause of unexplained bone pain.

A lung scan is most often used to detect a pulmonary embolism, the presence of a blood clot in the lung. A liver scan can detect cysts, abscesses, and tumors, while a radioactive iodine uptake test can help diagnose an overactive or underactive thyroid gland. There are also several newer radionuclide scans using preparations that localize in tumors, helping determine the presence and size of an abnormal growth. The variety and number of radionuclide scans is constantly increasing, as research develops new preparations that permit better diagnosis of specific suspected disorders.

Background material can be found in AMNIOCENTESIS; BLOOD; BLOOD PRESSURE; LIPIDS; MICROSCOPY; RADIOLOGY. *More details can be found in* CT AND PET SCANS; IMMUNOASSAY; NUCLEAR MAGNETIC RESONANCE (NMR). *Additional relevant information is contained in* GENE THERAPY; KARYOTYPING; LAPAROSCOPY.

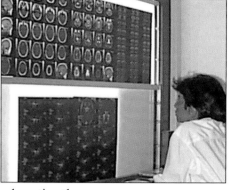

A new dimension in diagnostics was opened with computer-assisted (x-ray) tomography (CAT) scanning, in which the physician has access to virtually a complete three-dimensional view of the body.

Further Reading
Berner, Eta S., *Clinical Decision Support Systems: Theory and Practice* (1998); Brodin, Michael B., *The Encyclopedia of Medical Tests* (1997); Gaedeke, M.K., *Addison Wesley's Laboratory and Diagnostic Test Handbook* (1995).

First see CELL CYCLE

Meiosis

Next see MITOSIS

A stage of cell division in which the number of chromosomes in the cell is halved.

The cells of an organism can be divided into two types: somites, which are ordinary body cells, and gametes, also called sex cells or germ cells, which are sperm and eggs. Chromosome number, referred to as n, is unique to a particular species and consistent throughout all the cells of an organism. Human somites contain 46 chromosomes and are called diploid or $2n$, whereas gametes contain 23 chromosomes and are haploid or $1n$. Of these chromosomes, the vast majority are "regular" ones, known as autosomes, and only a single pair are the sex chromosomes X and Y. Females have two X chromosomes, while males have one X and one Y.

Somites undergo a process known as mitosis prior to cell division, in order to ensure a fixed number of chromosomes from one cellular generation to the next. Mitosis involves first copying each individual chromosome prior to cell division. The stages of mitosis begin with interphase, in which all the chromosomes are duplicated, and continues on to prophase, in which the structure of the nucleus slowly disappears.

During metaphase the chromosome pairs line up across the center of the cell preparatory to their separation in the next stage, anaphase, where each set is pulled towards an opposite pole of the cell. The final stage, telophase, sees the formation of two new nuclei and the eventual division of the rest of the cellular material (called cytokinesis). The end result is two diploid cells, identical to their parent cell and to each other.

The chromosomal requirements for gametes are different. Sexual reproduction is distinguished from reproduction of other cells by two factors: two parents, each of which contributes half the total genetic material; and genetic variation among the offspring. An organism begins life as a single cell, called a zygote, formed by the union of sperm and egg. In order to ensure that the zygote and its resulting descendant cells contain the proper number of chromosomes, the gametes must all be haploid. The process used to create them is called meiosis.

Meiosis differs from mitosis chiefly by having two cytoplasmic divisions, and by ultimately ending up with four haploid cells instead of two diploid ones. Each stage, with the exception of interphase, occurs twice. The events of each stage of meiosis are roughly analogous to their counterparts in mitosis. The primary or precursor cell undergoes interphase, prophase I, metaphase I, anaphase I, and telophase I, followed by cytokinesis. This results in the formation of two diploid secondary cells, each of which undergoes prophase II, anaphase II, and telophase II, followed by cytokinesis and the appearance of the haploid gametes.

Sperm Cell Production. Spermatogenesis refers specifically to the production of sperm cells. The precursor cell is called the primary spermatocyte; this cell undergoes the first part of meiosis, dividing at the end of telophase I to form two diploid secondary spermatocytes. Each secondary spermatocyte in turn undergoes the rest of meiosis. Telophase II ends with the formation of four haploid cells called spermatids. The spermatids eventually develop the physical characteristics of sperm, however, their chromosomal content is set at the end of meiosis.

Oogenesis refers specifically to the production of egg cells. The precursor cell is called the primary oocyte and undergoes the first stages of meiosis. However, unlike spermatogenesis, the cytoplasmic division at the end of telophase I is unequal, resulting in one relatively large diploid secondary oocyte and one much smaller diploid polar body. In terms of chromosomal content the two cells are equal; it is only their relative sizes that are different. The secondary oocyte continues the meiotic process. Telophase II once again shows an unequal cytoplasmic division, resulting in one haploid ovum, or egg cell, and one much smaller haploid polar body. The ovum is nearly the size of the original precursor cell, one of the largest cells in the body, almost visible to the naked eye. The haploid polar body simply disintegrates; it plays no role in reproduction. The diploid polar body present at the end of telophase I may ultimately divide into two haploid polar bodies, or it may disintegrate. Its "descendant" polar bodies also disintegrate.

All egg cells contain an X chromosome as their single sex chromosome. Approximately half of sperm cells contain X chromosomes, and the other half Y. The sex of a fetus is determined by which type of sperm reaches the egg first for fertilization. If the successful sperm has an X, the fetus is female. A sperm bearing a Y chromosome produces a male fetus.

THE CUTTING EDGE

Meiosis vs. Mitosis

Nearly all cell division takes place through mitosis, during which chromosomal material is distributed equally to both daughter cells, which are consequently identical. However, this process of division is inadequate for sexual reproduction—two cells must join their chromosomal material to produce a cell with the same number of chromosomes but that is genetically different from both parents. The generation of eggs and sperm cells involves meiosis, a two-step division that produces four cells, each containing half the chromosomal material of the parent cell; furthermore, the daughter cells are not identical. In fact, since there are 23 pairs of chromosomes in each parent cell, there are 8 million possible combinations for the egg, and 8 million for the sperm; that is why children of the same parents do not all look exactly like one another.

During prophase I, the chromosomes form "double pairs," known as tetrads or bivalents, which consist of four chromatids. The pairing of homologous chromosomes is called synapse and is frequently accompanied by "crossing-over," in which the chromosomes actually exchange pieces of themselves. This promotes more genetic diversity among the gametes.

Mistakes happen occasionally during meiosis as well. Nondisjunction is when homologous chromosomes fail to separate during meiosis. Trisomy is when a particular chromosome is present in triplicate, two from one parent and one from the other, as opposed to one from each. It may involve either the sex chromosomes or the autosomes. Abnormal numbers of sex chromosomes can result in conditions such as Turner syndrome, in which individuals have only one sex chromosome, an X, and are underdeveloped, sterile females.

Further Reading
Alberts, *Essential Cell Biology* (1997); Goodsell, David S., *The Machinery of Life* (1998); Pollack, Robert, *Signs of Life* (1995); Rensberger, Boyce, *Life Itself* (1997); Thomas, Lewis, *The Medusa and the Snail* (1995).

Background material on meiosis can be found in CELL; CHROMOSOME; DNA; NUCLEUS, CELL. *Advanced subjects are developed in* DNA REPLICATION; RNA; VIRAL GENETICS. *Elementary aspects of this subject are covered in* MITOSIS; PROKARYOTIC CELLS; REPRODUCTIVE SYSTEMS.

First see BRAIN

Memory

Next see INSTINCT

The ability to store and remember sensations and observations.

Psychologists have learned a great deal about remembering and forgetting over the last century, but the neurological mechanisms behind these crucial functions are only now beginning to emerge. While much remains obscure or unproven, it seems clear that memory is not a single faculty, but instead relies on an array of systems and subsystems in the brain.

The "standard model" of human memory, described in the 1980s, includes three main components. Sensory registers hold a memory for only about five seconds. Working memory (sometimes called short-term memory) lasts from seconds to hours and draws information from the environment and from long-term memory. It is crucial for planning and reasoning, allowing us to understand speech, do mental arithmetic, remember a phone number, or follow a map. Psychologist Alan Baddeley proposed that working memory included not only visual and verbal stores but also a "central executive" in the prefrontal cortex that controls the flow of information throughout the memory system, a concept that is not universally accepted. In recent years, tests on monkeys have suggested that working memory in general may be located in the prefrontal cortex, with shape and color registering in one part and location in another.

Long-term memory, the third component of the model, includes at least two systems. Implicit or procedural memory deals with how to do things—retaining motor skills and perceptual strategies that are unconscious, acquired through practice, and hard to forget. Explicit or declarative memory holds information on people, things, and places—material that is conscious, forgettable, and can be learned without practice. Other suggested categories include episodic, or autobiographical memory, and semantic memory.

Search for the Engram. The search for the engram or "memory trace"—a lasting change in the nervous system that represents a memory—has been one of neuroscience's major quests. For several decades scientists have thought that memory storage is likely to involve a strengthening of connections across synapses, the junctions where messages are transmitted from neuron to neuron in the brain. (*See* BRAIN.)

For the past twenty years, much attention has focused on one possible mechanism: long-term potentiation (LTP) in the mammalian hippocampus, a part of the brain thought to play a role in the transition between short- and long-term memory. In LTP, a high-frequency series of electrical impulses in a neural pathway increases the release of synaptic neurotransmitters, especially glutamate. This makes the neurons more likely to fire when stimulated hours or days later. In addition, LTP appears to trigger the growth of new synaptic connections, structural change that some think may be the basis of long-term memory. Since LTP was described in 1973, it has been seen to occur in many regions of the brain, and dozens of compounds have been shown to increase, reverse, or prevent it, raising hope that memory-enhancing drugs will be developed. But despite years of research, LTP's role in memory has not been proven; some researchers suggest it may generally facilitate memory but may not be essential to it.

In any case, it has been shown that a number of factors, including electrical stimulation and enrichment of living environments, can alter the function of neurons. At the same time, synaptic changes have been linked with memory in several well-studied invertebrates. In studies of the sea slug aplysia, for instance, Eric Kandel and his colleagues have found short-term memory correlates with increased release of a neurotransmitter at the synapse between a sensory and a motor neuron, while long-term memory appears to involve protein synthesis and the growth of new synapses. They have called this "a switch from a process-based memory to a structural-based memory." (*See* BRAIN.)

First see BRAIN

Meningitis

Next see DISEASE, INFECTIOUS

Inflammation of the meninges, the membranes that surround and protect the brain and the spinal chord.

Meningitis most often results from an infection caused by a virus, fungus, or bacterium. The infection usually originates elsewhere in the body and is carried to the meninges by the blood, although meningitis sometimes is caused by bacteria or viruses that enter the body through a fracture of the skull or from an infected sinus or ear. Viral meningitis is much more common than bacterial meningitis. It usually occurs during the winter months and most often is found in persons under the age of 30. Viral meningitis infections generally are mild, with symptoms that resemble those of influenza and that last only a week or two with no serious aftereffects.

Bacterial meningitis, by contrast, can be life-threatening and requires immediate treatment. Most cases occur in children. The most common form is meningococcal meningitis, which usually occurs in winter epidemics. The major symptoms are fever, nausea, vomiting, stiff neck, and headache. These symptoms can develop over a few hours, after which the patient

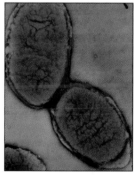

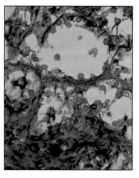

Top, the cryptococcus fungus that can infect the meninges through the lungs; bottom, the *Hemophilus influenzae* virus that infects the meninges (particularly in children) through the blood.

can lose consciousness. Bacterial meningitis is diagnosed by lumbar puncture, in which fluid is removed from the spinal cord for analysis. It is regarded as a medical emergency and is treated by giving large doses of antibiotics intravenously. Meningitis is not common; about 12,000 cases of viral meningitis and about 5,000 cases of bacterial meningitis are reported in the United States each year. The Hib vaccine protects against meningitis caused by the *Haemophilus influenzae* Type b bacteria and is routinely administered at around four months of age.

First see EMOTION

Mental Disorders

Next see SCHIZOPHRENIA

Mental disorders can be mild, such as a neurosis that does not affect judgment, or severe, such as a psychosis in which the individual loses touch with reality. Experts generally recognize three forms of psychosis: schizophrenia, manic-depressive illness, and organic brain syndrome.

Schizophrenia is the most common form of mental illness, with a lifetime prevalence of one percent. Its onset usually occurs between the ages of 15 and 25, generally later in women than in men. The incidence is the same in both sexes. Schizophrenia often begins slowly, with the individual becoming increasingly more withdrawn from daily life. Then there is an onset of delusions, false ideas that do not respond to reasoned argument (an individual may believe that he is Jesus Christ, for example), and hallucinations, which may appear as visual distortions or more often are experienced as voices that make comments about the individual's behavior or thoughts. Most schizophrenics also have impaired concentration or disordered thinking, and many must be hospitalized initially. Some can return to community life as their condition is brought under control by anti-psychotic drugs such as chlorpromazine.

Bipolar Illness. Manic-depressive illness is a condition in which the person may swing between depression and mania (bipolar illness) or suffer either depression or mania. Depression is much more common than mania. About one in ten men and one in five women will experience it at some point in life. Mania, by contrast, affects only about 1 in 125 people, striking men and women equally.

Hospitalization is often necessary in severe cases of manic-depressive illness. Depression can be treated by antidepressant drugs or electroconvulsive therapy (ECT). Manic symptoms can be controlled by drugs such as chlorpromazine and haloperidol, with lithium given to sustain remissions. At least 80 percent of manic-depressive patients are eventually able to return to normal living, often with the help of ongoing-

Further Reading
Diagnostic and Statistical Manual of Mental Disorders DSM-IV-TR (2000); Herman, Judith, *Trauma and Recovery* (1997); Karp, David Allen, *The Burden of Sympathy: How Families Cope With Mental Illness* (2001).

group, family, or individual therapy.

Organic brain syndrome is a physical condition that leads to a disturbance of intellect, consciousness, or mental functioning. The causes include degenerative conditions such as Alzheimer's disease, metabolic imbalances, infections, and the brain damage caused by an injury, a stroke, or a tumor. Organic brain syndrome can be chronic or acute. The effects of the acute form include slight, persistent confusion, disorientation, constant restlessness, hallucinations, and delusions. The chronic condition leads to a progressive, steady decline in memory, intellect, and behavior. Organic brain syndrome is treated by identifying its underlying cause and applying the appropriate treatment. In chronic cases, treatment may not be applied soon enough to prevent permanent brain damage.

Paranoid illness is often regarded as a fourth type of psychosis, although some psychiatrists classify it as a separate disorder. The central feature of paranoia is a persistent delusion, in some people a feeling of persecution, in others an exaggerated belief in their own power. Treatment with antipsychotic drugs often brings a return to normality, although results of drug treatment are generally less satisfactory for chronic paranoia.

Related areas to be considered are ADDICTIVE DISORDERS; BRAIN; EMOTIONS; MEDICAL DIAGNOSTICS. *More details can be found in* AGGRESSION AND TERRITORIALITY; ALZHEIMER'S DISEASE; AUTISM; MEMORY. *Basic aspects of this subject are covered in* NEUROTRANSMITTERS AND RECEPTORS; SCHIZOPHRENIA; STRESS.

First see SOLAR SYSTEM

Mercury

Next see SUN

Mercury, the nearest planet to the sun, is also the smallest planet, with an equatorial diameter of 3,031 miles. Its average distance from the sun is 36 million miles. It makes a complete orbit around the sun every 87.97 days, with one of the most eccentric orbits in the solar system. Its perihelion, or closest approach, brings it within 28.6 million miles of the sun, and its aphelion, or greatest distance, is 43.5 million miles.

For centuries, astronomers believed that a day on Mercury—the time for one complete rotation of the planet on its axis—was the same length as its year, so that Mercury always kept the same side facing the sun. That belief came under suspicion when astronomers at the University of Michigan detected thermal emissions from the dark side of Mercury, emissions that could not be detected if the dark side always faced away from the sun. Using the radio telescope at Arecibo, Puerto Rico, radar pulses were bounced off Mercury. Measurements of the frequency shifts caused by the planet's rotation showed that the true length of a Mercury day is 58.6 Earth days.

The Mariner Mission. The Mariner 10 spacecraft, which was sent to explore the inner planets in 1973 and 1974, scanned about one-third of Mercury's surface during a 127-month mission and sent back more than 5,500 pictures, which showed Mercury to be a rougher version of Earth's moon. The principal land forms on Mercury are craters and basins, but there are also long, sinuous cracks similar to the rilles of the moon and ridges with a length of several hundred miles. Mercury was found to have a very faint atmosphere, with a trace of helium, resulting from the decay of radioactive elements in the planet's crust. Mercury has no water.

The pictures indicate that Mercury underwent the same evolutionary sequence as the moon, with a formation period of about 600 million years that terminated with a major bombardment of planetoids, asteroids, meteors, and comets about 3.9 billion years ago. The most impressive feature in the pictures was a circular basin in the northwest quadrant of Mercury's sunlit hemisphere, at 30 degrees north and 195 degrees west in the grid system constructed by space agency astronomers. The basin was named Caloris, because it is situated in the region of Mercury that gets the maximum heat from the sun. Caloris is 839 miles in diameter and is rimmed by mountains rising 1.25 miles above the floor of the basin. There is a secondary range of mountains about 93 miles beyond the rim of Caloris. Astronomers have compared Caloris with Mare Imbrium, a basin on the moon that is believed to have been formed 3.9 billion years ago, when both Mercury and the moon underwent major bombardments.

Cratering. Beyond the secondary ridge of mountains around Caloris, the Mariner pictures showed plains that are cratered and have a series of radial valleys. Some valleys are 75 miles long and 10 miles wide. The valleys, ridges, and cracks seen around Caloris are believed to have originated from the impact that created the vast basin. That impact is also believed to have had a major effect on the side of Mercury opposite to Caloris, where there is a chaotic landscape of uneven hills; some of them are three to six miles wide and up to 5,000 feet deep. These features are believed to have been created by shock waves from the Caloris impact that traveled through to the opposite side of the planet. The craters observed in this region are similar to those seen on the moon and are believed to have undergone the same process of erosion caused by events such as the impact of small meteoroids and cosmic dust.

While there is no direct evidence of volcanic activity on Mercury, some astronomers believe that the planet's plains could have been created by very ancient volcanic flows. An alternative theory is that the plains consists of matter ejected as the result of huge impacts of the past.

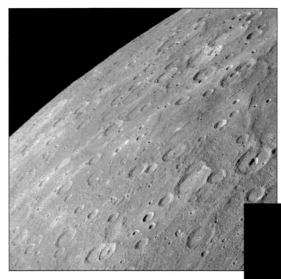

Below, a photomosaic of Mercury assembled from *Mariner 10* images taken in 1974. Left, a false-color image of the Mercury surface. The planet bears a striking resemblance to the moon.

Spacecraft measurements of the temperatures on Mercury found a daily high of more than 500 degrees Celsius at the equator, with lows of –210 degrees Celsius on the dark side. The planet was found to have an unexpectedly strong magnetic field. Although that field was only one percent as strong as the Earth's magnetic field, its existence had not been expected because of Mercury's slow rotation. Convection currents in Mercury's large iron core are probably responsible for this phenomenon.

> *Background material on Mercury can be found in* KEPLER'S LAWS; PLANET; SOLAR SYSTEMS; SUN. *Advanced subjects are developed in* GRAVITY; SOLAR WIND; SPECIAL RELATIVITY. *More information on particular aspects is contained in* PLANETS, FORMATION OF; SOLAR SYSTEMS; VENUS.

Further Reading
Chapman, Clark R., *The Inner Planets* (1987); Simon, S., *Mercury* (1998); Strom, R. G., *Mercury: The Elusive Planet* (1987); Vogt, G. L., *Mercury* (1996); Wilkinson, R., *A New Look at Mercury Retrograde* (1997).

First see ELEMENTARY PARTICLES

Mesons

Next see RADIOACTIVITY

Unstable subatomic particles that decay in a few billionths of a second by a variety of mechanisms.

Since mesons can decay by the strong, weak, or electromagnetic force, there is a relatively wide range of lifetimes. About 100 mesons are known to exist. Each meson consists of a quark-antiquark pair, bound together by the strong force. At least six quarks are thought to exist, arranged in pairs: up (u) and down (d), charm (c) and strange (s); top (t) and bottom (b). Mesons also carry a so-called flavor property, which is usually just the flavor of the heavier quark in the meson: strangeness (s), charm (c), bottomness (b), or topness (t). The quantum numbers of mesons are specified by the properties of the quarks of which they are made, and by their spin and orbital angular momentum.

Prediction. The existence of the lowest-mass meson, the *pi*-meson, was predicted a half-century ago by Japanese physicist Hideki Yukawa. He pictured it as the principal carrier of the nuclear force, an idea that today is regarded as highly simplified. Mesons do play a role in holding the neutrons and protons of an atomic nucleus together, but the exact nature of that role is still unknown.

Since mesons decay so quickly, their existence must be inferred by looking at peaks in the

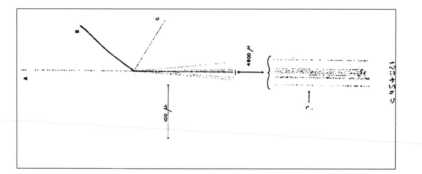

mass of the particles resulting from their decay. High-mass mesons that include either the up or down quark decay in a series of steps, which end with the appearance of a *pi*-meson. Mesons with the characteristics of strangeness, charm, or bottomness decay to form a K (sd), D (cd) or B (bd) meson as well as *pi*-mesons. A few mesons decay through the electromagnetic interaction; their lifetimes are intermediate between those of mesons that decay through the strong interaction and those that decay weakly.

The nature of mesons that have the same quantum number as the photon can be determined by experiments using an electron-positron storage ring. As the energy of these rings is increased to the range above 3 gigawatts, two peaks that indicate the presence of mesons are seen. If the energy is increased further, to 9 gigawatts, peaks that indicate the existence of three other mesons are seen. Mesons that have the same quantum number as the photon can be seen as energy peaks in electron-positron storage ring experiments involving electron-anti-electron interaction.

In the established theory of strong particle interactions, the mesonic particles called gluons, which carry the force between quarks, should interact strongly, and should stick together to form particles. These mesons are called glueballs. Because very high energies would be required, no glueball particle has yet been identified.

Background material can be found in COSMIC RAY; ELECTRON; ELEMENTARY PARTICLE. *Advanced subjects are developed in* BUBBLE CHAMBER; NEUTRINO; STANDARD MODEL; UNIVERSE, EVOLUTION OF. *Relevant information is contained in* RADIO ASTRONOMY; WIMP (WEAKLY INTERACTING MASSIVE PARTICLE).

Above, confirmation of the existence of mesons occured in 1950 in this record of high-energy proton-proton collision. The very short-lived meson requires very high energy just for the particle to make a track long enough to detect and measure.

Right, West Falkland Island off the Argentinian coast is a fragment of ancient Gondwana, a supercontinent that broke up in the Mesozoic era.

Further Reading
Benton, Michael J., *Basic Paleontology* (1997); Farlow, James O., *The Complete Dinosaur* (1999); Horner, John R., *Digging Up Tyrannosaurus Rex* (1995); Padian, Kevin (Ed.), *The Beginning of the Age of Dinosaurs: Faunal Change Across the Triassic-Jurassic Boundary* (1989).

First see PALEOZOIC ERA

Mesozoic Era

Next see CENOZOIC ERA

Era that began about 230 million years ago, at the end of the Paleozoic era, and ended about 70 million years ago, at the start of the Cenozoic era.

The Mesozoic is divided into three periods: the Triassic, at the beginning, followed by the Jurassic and the Cretaceous. Its name, from the Greek for meso, "middle," and zoa, "life," indicates the mixed flora and fauna that existed during the period. At the start, reptiles on land were the dominant animals, but mammals and birds later made their initial appearances. The continents of the Mesozoic era had assumed some elements of their present form, but shallow seas sometimes spread across their interiors. The climate then was apparently milder and more uniform than it is today, but there are geological traces of Mesozoic deserts and dead seas. Eastern North America was relatively stable dur-

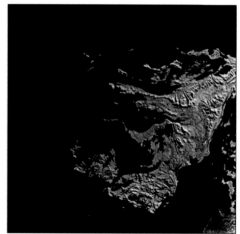

ing the early part of the Mesozoic, but lava from deep in Earth's crust worked its way up to create such formations as the Palisades, at the southern end of the Hudson River.

During the middle of the Mesozoic, the Sierra Nevada and Coast ranges were formed in western North America, and the formation of the Rocky Mountains began. In South America, the Andes Mountains began to rise. Australia, South America, and Africa were moving apart, as were North America and Europe, and the Atlantic Ocean formed. By the end of the Mesozoic era, the continents had largely assumed their present positions.

Related areas to be considered are EVOLUTION; FOSSIL; GEOLOGY, ARCHAEOLOGICAL. *Advanced subjects are developed in* CRETACEOUS-TERTIARY BOUNDARY; DINOSAURS; ICE AGE. *Relevant information is contained in* CAMBRIAN DIFFERENTIATION OF LIFE; DINOSAUR, EXTINCTION OF; JURASSIC PERIOD. *See also* PLATE TECTONICS *and* PANGAEA.

Metabolism

First see PROTEIN SYNTHESIS

Next see NUTRITION

The sum of all chemical reactions that take place within an organism.

Metabolism liberates energy from food so that it can be used to do the work of an animal, including muscular movement, hormone secretion, transport of key ions across cellular membranes, maintenance and repair of cell structures, and many other functions. Metabolism is a hallmark that distinguishes living from nonliving systems.

Two Processes. Metabolism has two aspects: catabolism, the energy-releasing breakdown of food-derived molecules like glucose and fatty acids, and anabolism, the energy-consuming synthesis of molecules. The bridge between these processes is the compound ATP (adenosine triphosphate), which stores liberated energy in conveniently small amounts and then releases it when needed by the body. If the energy transfers of the body are thought of as monetary transactions, ATP is the everyday currency used countless times a day in energy transactions. As long as adequate amounts of food are digested, the supply of ATP is endlessly reconstituted, like an automatic-teller machine ever restocked by consumers' deposits.

The Fuel of Life. ATP is present in all animal cells. It is composed of adenosine and three phosphate groups bonded in sequence. When the bond of the last phosphate group is broken, energy is released. What remains is ADP (adenosine diphosphate, or adenosine with two phosphate groups) plus inorganic phosphate. New ATP can be formed if enough energy is added to ADP and inorganic phosphate to bond a third phosphate group to the compound, a process called phosphorylation.

There are two forms of metabolism. Anaerobic metabolism, used by the earliest organisms and by some microorganisms today, does not involve oxygen. It is far less efficient in releasing energy than aerobic metabolism, in which oxygen plays a crucial role. Even with aerobic metabolism, a large portion of energy is dissipated as heat, rather than being stored in ATP for later use.

In aerobic metabolism, energy is transferred by oxidation and reduction, or redox. In oxidation, a substance loses electrons to another substance that has less electron pressure. Such a reaction is said to be exergonic, which means that it liberates energy. Oxidation in aerobic metabolism almost always involves hydrogen electrons, and the final acceptor of electrons is oxygen, with the end products being carbon dioxide (CO_2) and water (H_2O). In reduction, hydrogen electrons are transferred from oxygen to a substance that has more electron pressure, such as carbon. This reaction, which is said to be endergonic, requires energy, which it stores in the newly formed compound.

Below, the complexity of the metabolic pathways in the human body can be seen in its entirety.

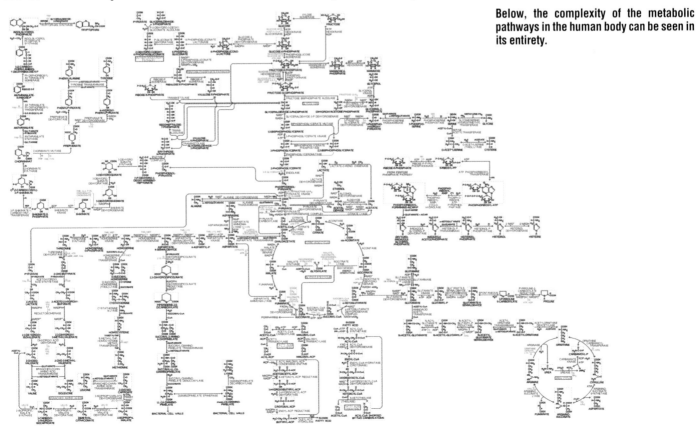

Metabolic Pathways. Within cells, metabolism takes place through metabolic pathways, precise sequences of chemical reactions. These orderly sequences are regulated by genetic and chemical controls. The catabolism of glucose, the breakdown product of carbohydrates, is usually portrayed as the model of this process. But the metabolic pathways of glucose intersect at many points with those of fat- and protein-derivatives, and all are part of one integrated system. The glucose molecule is split a little at a time, with small amounts of energy released at various points to form a molecule of ATP. Each molecule of glucose eventually yields 38 molecules of ATP. If the glucose had been completely oxidized in only one step, it would have had the opportunity to form only one molecule of ATP, with the rest of the energy lost to heat.

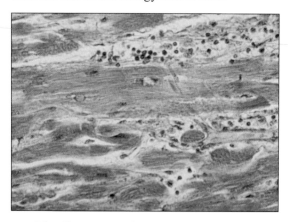

At left, the effects of hypokalemia (a metabolic disorder that results in reduced plasma levels of potassium) can be seen in cardiac muscle.

The first stage of metabolism is called glycolysis and is anaerobic. Through ten steps of chemical reaction, each catalyzed by at least one protein enzyme, a glucose molecule is split into two molecules of pyruvic acid. During glycolysis, two molecules of ATP are used to power the process and four molecules of ATP are formed, leaving a net gain of two molecules of ATP. In addition, four hydrogen atoms are formed. As will be seen later, the oxidation of hydrogen generates large amounts of ATP.

In the second stage of metabolism, which is aerobic, the pyruvic acid is carried into a mitochondrion, a structure in the cytoplasm of the cell, and oxidized into two molecules of acetyl-coenzyme A (acetyl-CoA). This releases four hydrogen atoms.

The third stage of metabolism is commonly called the Krebs cycle, after Sir Hans Krebs, the British scientist who worked it out in the 1940s; it is also known as the citric acid cycle or the tricarboxylic acid cycle. For each original molecule of glucose, two turns of the Krebs cycle are required. This yields two more molecules of ATP and 16 hydrogen atoms.

The fourth stage is the electron-transport chain, or respiratory chain, in which the previously formed hydrogen atoms are split into hydrogen ions and electrons and are eventually used to form water. During the final stage, a sequence of oxidative reactions called the chemiosmotic mechanism, a great deal of energy is released to form ATP.

The Human Energy Tally. Under optimal conditions in the human body, the final energy tally looks like this: For each molecule of glucose, six molecules of ATP and 24 hydrogen atoms are formed by the end of the Krebs cycle. Oxidation of the hydrogen releases 34 more ATP molecules, for a total of 38 ATP molecules. Each molecule of ATP stores 12,000 calories under the conditions of the human body (7,300 under standard conditions) for a total of 456,000 calories stored. That total represents 66 percent of the 686,000 calories released by complete oxidation of each molecule of glucose. The remaining calories become heat.

As mentioned earlier, the metabolisms of carbohydrates, fats, and proteins meet at many intersections. For instance, fatty acids undergo a process called beta oxidation that converts them into acetyl-CoA molecules and releases hydrogen. The acetyl-CoA molecules then enter the Krebs cycle and are finally oxidized by the same chemiosmotic oxidative system of the mitochondria that oxidizes glucose. When amino acids, the breakdown products of protein, are used for energy, they are also converted into compounds that can enter the Krebs cycle. Per gram, fat yields more than twice as much energy as carbohydrates or protein. The liver is a key organ in metabolism of both fats and proteins.

Because their metabolic pathways intersect, many amino acids can be converted into glucose or fatty acids. When carbohydrates are consumed in excess, they are converted to triglycerides, another component of fat, for storage in the fatty tissue of the body.

Special topics in this area are found in CARBOHYDRATE; DIGESTION; DIGESTIVE CHEMISTRY. *Advanced subjects are developed in* DIGESTION REGULATION; ENZYMES; WATER IN LIVING CELLS. *Elementary aspects of this subject are covered in* NUTRITION; PROTEIN METABOLISM; VITAMINS AND MINERALS.

Further Reading
Alberts, Bruce, *Essential Cell Biology: An Introduction to the Molecular Biology of the Cell* (1995); Coffee, Carole J., *Metabolism* (1997); Michal, Gerhard, *Biochemical Pathways: An Atlas of Biochemistry and Molecular Biology* (1999); Rensberger, Boyce, *Life Itself: Exploring the Realm of the Living Cell* (1998).

First see PERIODIC TABLE OF THE ELEMENTS

Metal

Next see ORGANOMETALLIC COMPOUNDS

An element, alloy or compound substance that is a good conductor of heat and electricity.

Metals make up the majority of the elements on the Periodic Table. Of the 92 naturally occurring elements, only 20 of them are nonmetals. The metal category includes not just the elements we commonly think of as metals, like gold, silver, copper, iron, and aluminum, but also elements such as sodium, calcium, and magnesium.

Metals are located on the left side of the Periodic Table and have certain characteristics in common. With the exception of mercury, they are solids at room temperature. They are all lustrous, shiny, or reflective. They are malleable, meaning they can be hammered into thin sheets, and they are ductile, meaning they can be formed into wires. Metals are good conductors of heat and electricity.

Metallic Bonding. The basis behind bonding is each atom's desire for a full valence shell, the outermost energy level that contains electrons. This promotes greater stability in terms of energy. An atoms that needs only a few additional electrons fills its valence shell by grabbing electrons from another atom. The advantage of such a transaction is clear for the former, but the latter atom also benefits. Its outermost shell is now empty, and, therefore, the previously next-to-last level that was already full becomes the new valence shell.

Metals are not very electronegative; they do not strongly attract electrons. In fact, they have trouble holding onto their own valence electrons. Metal atoms may lose up to three electrons at a time, being transformed into positively charged ions, or cations. Nonmetals, in contrast, are very electronegative and are transformed into negatively charged ions, or anions, as they gain additional electrons. The oppositely charged ions are attracted to each other and form an ionic bond.

Many of the properties of metals listed above are a direct result of these ionic bonds. The electrons, moving easily from one atom to another, become part of the whole metal crystal. They attract and hold the positive metal ions together. This metallic bond is what gives metals their hardness and ability to act as conductors. The attraction between electrons and ions continues even when the metal is deformed.

Metals readily combine with oxygen to form compounds known as oxides. These metal oxides are all base anhydrides—when water is added they will form compounds with a basic pH. An example is calcium hydroxide, more commonly referred to as lime.

Alkali Metals. The most reactive metals, the alkali metals, are those found all the way to the left on the periodic table. Alkali metals include lithium, sodium, and potassium. The next most reactive group, located next to them, are the alkaline-earth metals, which include magnesium and calcium. The farther they are to the right on the table, (and the closer to the non-metals), the less reactive metals become. This is because reactivity is affected by the amount of positive charge in the nucleus (due to the number of protons present) and the number of valence electrons. The more positive the nucleus, the more tightly it holds onto the valence electrons and consequently the less reactive the metal becomes. The greater the number of valence electrons, the more difficult it becomes to lose them. As one proceeds to the right on the table, atomic nuclei become larger and more positive, and the number of valence electrons increases.

Pure metals are often too soft or too brittle for many applications; therefore they are made into alloys. The first alloys formulated were substitutional alloys, in which atoms of a similar size intermix.

Elements located at the dividing line between metals and nonmetals are called metalloids, because they often exhibit properties of both. For example, solid iodine, a nonmetal, is lustrous; graphite, a form of carbon, conducts electricity. Other metalloids include boron, silicon, arsenic, and antimony.

Metallurgy. Metallurgy is the study and science of extracting and refining metals from their ores and shaping them into useful products.

The art of metallurgy can be divided into two separate areas: extractive metallurgy, which deals with the various chemical processes required for the extraction of metals from their ores; and physical metallurgy, which concentrates on the adaptation of metals for everyday use.

Most present-day machines, tools, and modes of transportation are products of the art of metallurgy. It is one of the world's oldest arts—iron samples have been discovered dating back to 4000 B.C.E., and the art of ironmaking was well known to the ancient Egyptians by the time of Ramses II (reigned 1290–1223 B.C.E.) Most of the advances before the fifteenth century in the field of metallurgy were introduced to Europeans by Arab craftsmen. Once established in Europe, metallurgy, specifically iron production, exploded, and iron became indispensible at the time of the Industrial Revolution.

The invention of the Bessemer process in 1856 (by British engineer Henry Bessemer) made steel affordable and led to the nonstop production of steel-related products. Advances have taken place in the production of steel, and we are more dependent on it and the field of metallurgy than ever. Products such as planes, trains, automobiles, and machines of every kind all necessitate the use of an art and basic technology that began almost 6,000 years ago.

Researchers have discovered that how an alloy is formed can be as critical as its makeup. Above, a micrograph of a nickel-copper alloy in which the solidification of the alloy was very controlled. Below, alloy layering creates composite materials with unusual (and sometimes desirable) properties.

Further developments in the field are discussed in ALKALI METALS; BOND, CHEMICAL; MOLECULE; PERIODIC TABLE OF THE ELEMENTS. *More details can be found in* ALLOY; ANNEALING; INORGANIC COMPOUND; WELDING. *Additional relevant information is contained in* CLUSTER; ATOM; ELECTROMETALLURGY; ORGANOMETALLIC COMPOUNDS.

Further Reading
Atkins, P.W., *The Periodic Kingdom: A Journey into the Land of the Chemical Elements* (1997); Cobb, Cathy, *Creations of Fire: Chemistry's Lively History from Alchemy to the Atomic Age* (1995); Emsley, John, *The Elements* (1998); Emsley, John, *Molecules at an Exhibition: Portraits of Intriguing Materials in Everyday Life* (1998); Gray, H. B, *Braving the Elements* (1995).

First see GEOLOGY, ARCHAEOLOGICAL

Metamorphic Rock

Next see GEOMORPHOLOGY

Rocks that have undergone change because of heat, pressure, or chemical action in the Earth's crust.

Metamorphic changes affect the mineral composition, texture, and structure of rocks. The minerals that make up most rocks have definite chemical compositions that remain stable only if conditions do not change. If these minerals are subjected to radically different conditions, they will tend to change into new chemical compositions that are stable under the new conditions. One example is anthracite coal, which is formed when bituminous coal is subjected to higher temperatures and higher pressures. The bituminous coal loses some volatile constituents and its carbon concentration goes down as it becomes anthracite coal.

Metamorphic rocks acquire distinctive physical as well as chemical compositions as they are formed. Most often a zone of metamorphic rock will show distinctive banding or foliation, partly because the rocks have been elongated by the pressure put upon the mineral particles of which they consist and partly due to a growth of new grains of minerals. A metamorphic rock that has banding that is coarse and crude is called a gneiss. One that has closer foliation and splits readily because there is a parallel arrangement of its flat or elongated mineral grains is called a schist. Slate is a kind of schist in which the mineral particles are too small to be detectable. Two kinds of metamorphic rock have no distinctive banding, although they retain some of their original sedimentary stratification. One of them is quartzite, formed when the grains in quartzose sandstone undergo crystallization and are cemented close together. The other is marble, which is formed by the recrystallization of limestone or dolomite.

Formation. Metamorphic rocks are formed by several different processes. One is contact metamorphism, in which igneous rock such as magma intrudes into other rock formations to form the bands typical of metamorphic rock. These bands are the results of alterations produced by the heat and other characteristics of magma. Zones in which contact metamorphism has occurred are often regions where a large variety of valuable ores can be found. The most common source of metamorphic rock formation, however, is regional metamorphism, which takes place well below Earth's surface. The process occurs very slowly, often because of different pressure zones within the crust. Other factors involved can include high temperatures, water pressure, and chemical properties of specific regions of the crust. (*See* GEOMORPHOLOGY.)

Above, rock formations tell a tale regarding the history of the Earth.

Above, a 1931 portrait of Albert Michelson, the first American scientist to win a Nobel Prize. He became a celebrity, performing his famous null-result experiment all over the world.

Further Reading

Bohm, David, *The Special Theory of Relativity* (1996); Feynman, Richard, *Six Not-So-Easy Pieces: Einstein's Relativity, Symmetry, and Space-Time* (1998); Resnick, Robert, *Introduction to Special Relativity* (1968); Rindler, Wolfgang, *Introduction to Special Relativity* (1991); Taylor, Edwin F., *Spacetime Physics: Introduction to Special Relativity* (1992);

First see LIGHT, SPEED OF

Michelson-Morley Experiment

Next see GENERAL RELATIVITY

The Michelson-Morley experiment, performed in 1887 by Albert Michelson and Edward Morley, set the stage for the ultimate development of the theory of relativity. The experiment was designed to measure the Earth's velocity through the ether, a medium that was then believed to pervade all of space and to be necessary for the transmission of electromagnetic radiation, such as light. Michelson and Morley used an interferometer, a device designed originally for measuring the frequency of electromagnetic waves. They expected to observe a shift in the interference fringes formed when the interferometer was rotated 90 degrees, which would show that the speed of light measured in the direction of Earth's motion through space was different from the speed of light at right angles to Earth's motion. They did not see such a difference in their first experiment and in several others that they performed in the following years. They interpreted the results as disproving the existence of the ether. The results also contradicted existing theory of stellar aberration, the apparent displacement in the position of a star resulting from Earth's rotation around the sun.

It was in response to the Michelson-Morley results that H. A. Lorentz and G. F. Fitzgerald proposed that the mass of a body moving through space is contracted in the direction of its motion. The Michelson-Morley experiment was given theoretical support by the special thory of relativity, which Albert Einstein introduced several years later.

Background material can be found in INTERFERENCE; LIGHT, SPEED OF; SPACE; WAVE; SPECIAL RELATIVITY. *Further developments in the field are discussed in* ENERGY, EQUIVALENCE OF MASS AND; LORENTZ-FITZGERALD CONTRACTION; TWIN PARADOX. *Special topics in this area are found in* GENERAL RELATIVITY; SPACE-TIME.

First see BACTERIA

Microbiology

Next see DISEASES, INFECTIOUS

The study of microorganisms and their activities.

Microorganisms (virtually by definition) can only be seen with a microscope. These unicellular organisms include bacteria, various protists, and fungi. All of these, together with viruses, can be referred to as microbes or germs.

It is important to emphasize the differences between the various organisms. Bacteria are cells known as prokaryotes. These cells are very primitive; they contain no membrane-bound organelles, and the various structures they do contain are as a rule small and simple in form. Protozoa and fungi are all euk-aryotes and are much more complex in terms of structure and organization. Viruses are not made up of cells at all. A virus simply consists of a piece of genetic material wrapped up in a protein coat.

Microbiology places a particular emphasis on structure, reproduction, physiology, metabolism, and identification of microorganisms. In addition, it investigates their distribution in nature, relationship to other life forms, beneficial and detrimental effects, and any physical or chemical changes caused in the environment.

Microorganisms have many characteristics that make them good subjects for the study of biological systems, biochemical as well as genetic. They are easily maintained in comparatively little space, grow rapidly, and reproduce quickly. Some species of bacteria can produce 100 generations within a single 24-hour period.

History. The history of microbiology can be said to have begun in the seventeenth century with Antony van Leeuwenhoek, the inventor of the first microscope, and his discovery of the existence of microscopic organisms. As early as the thirteenth century, Roger Bacon hypothesized that disease was produced by invisible living creatures, but he had no supporting evidence. By 1762, Anton von Plenciz was able to support with some empirical evidence that living things cause disease and that different germs are responsible for different diseases.

Pasteur. Before Louis Pasteur, microorganisms were studied in terms of their morphology, or shape, and classification in relation to higher life forms. It was Pasteur who investigated the involvement of microbes in chemical processes like fermentation, as well as their role in particular diseases such as chicken cholera and rabies. He popularized the idea of inoculations against a particular disease, inspired by the work of Edward Jenner, who used cowpox as a source for his vaccine against smallpox.

Koch and Lister. By the early 1900s, microbiology had become a fully developed field, thanks to scientists like Robert Koch, whose work proved that a specific organism can always be found in association with a specific disease, and that the organism can then be isolated and grown in pure culture. Koch also developed solid culture media, essential for growing microorganisms in the laboratory. In 1878, Joseph Lister produced pure cultures of bacteria. Around this time as well, the fields of soil microbiology and industrial fermentation were being developed.

Microorganisms are grown in a culture medium containing all of the required chemicals and nutrients. Different organisms need different materials for their particular metabolic reactions. Some cultures are solid, consisting of agar, whereas others are solutions. Some microbes require living host cells called tissue culture. Depending on the particular organism, the temperature and oxygen requirements may differ as well. Cultures are generally grown within incubators—special temperature-regulated chambers—in order to maximize growth. A pure culture consists of a single kind of microorganism. If there are two or more types of organisms within a culture, it is called mixed.

When working with microorganisms, it is important to maintain a sterile environment in order to avoid contamination from other cultures, or from microbes present in the air and on the surfaces of laboratory equipment.

Characteristics of Microorganisms. Before identifying and classifying microorganisms, their characteristics must first be determined: which nutrients and physical conditions are needed for their growth; the morphology, size, and arrangement of cells, and the metabolism and chemical processes that take place. In order to see the metabolic characteristics, cultures are grown in the presence or absence of a specific nutrient or chemical, then examined to see what changes have occurred. The chemical composition of the cell is also studied, as well as its proteins and special cell components. The cellular components can be separated by centrifuging; they then can be examined along with the DNA sequence.

Staining. Cell smears are often stained before being placed under the microscope to make it easier to see gross morphological characteristics as well as internal structures. There are multiple steps involved in the preparation of a "fixed" stained smear. The dyes used may be acidic, basic, or neutral. Acidic dyes stain basic cell components and basic dyes stain acidic components. Simple staining uses only one dye solution. The smear is "flooded" with dye for a specific length of time, the excess is then washed off and the slide blotted dry. The cells stain uniformly, although some parts have a greater affinity for the stain and will absorb more of it. Differential staining uses more than one dye or staining agent to see differences between cell parts or between different types of cells.

Bacteria Classification. Bacteria are classified as either gram-positive or gram-negative. Gram staining involves using several dyes in a specific order: crystal violet, iodine, alcohol (a decolorizing agent), and safranin. Gram-positive bacteria retain the crystal violet dye and appear purplish-blue in color, while gram-negative bacteria "lose" color when exposed to alcohol and therefore absorb the safranin and appear red. Gram staining is not used to classify other microorganisms.

Gram-negative bacteria contain a higher

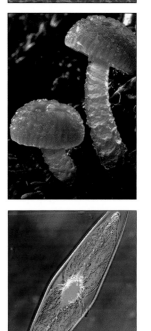

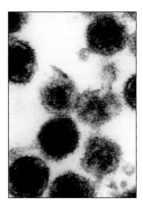

Above, four examples of the microbial world. From top: bacteria; fungi; algae; and (a controversial entry) viruses.

percentage of lipid than do gram-positive bacteria. Their cell walls are thinner, allowing them to be decolorized more easily. Gram-positive bacteria become dehydrated by the alcohol and their membranes lose permeability, "locking in" the original dye color. As they age, gram-positive organisms can lose their ability to retain crystal violet and will therefore "pick up" the safranin stain. This is called a gram-variable reaction.

Gram-positive bacteria are more susceptible to penicillin and less susceptible to disintegration by mechanical treatment or enzyme exposure. Gram-negative bacteria are more susceptible to antibiotics like streptomycin.

Another type of staining for classification purposes is acid-fast staining, which is used especially for mycobacteria. The specific dyes used are carbolfuchsin, acid-alcohol, and methylene blue. If the smear retains the carbolfuchsin, it appears red and the cells are called acid-fast. The cells are called nonacid-fast if they are decolorized by the acid-alcohol and subsequently pick up the blue dye.

Giemsa staining is used for locating rickettsia, organisms that are larger than a virus but smaller than a bacterium, within host cells. This staining method is also used to examine blood films for the presence of protozoa.

There are other special staining procedures used for specific structures within the cell, similar in method to gram- and acid-fast stains in terms of treatment with multiple staining agents and decolorizers. The structures exhibit different degrees of affinity for particular dyes.

Negative staining is when the whole suspension is treated with India ink and then spread across the slide in a thin film and allowed to dry. The cells will appear transparent against the dark background. This is particularly useful in studying the morphology of a cell, as fixing smears before staining and treating with other chemicals can distort its shape.

The field of microbiology has had an obvious impact on understanding and controlling disease, but it has also contributed a great deal to the study of molecular genetics. Most of what we know about genomes and the genetic control of cells has come from studying bacteria and other unicellular organisms. It is to be expected that microbiology will have an impact on other areas of scientific investigation as well.

The foundations of microbiology are discussed in BACTERIA; CELL; FUNGUS; MICROSCOPY. *Further details on microorganisms can be found in* GAMETOGENISIS; PROTISTA; VIRUS. *Advanced subjects in microbiology are developed in* EUTROPHICATION; GAIA HYPOTHESIS; GERM THEORY.

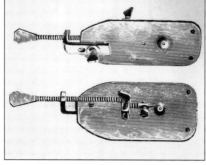

Top, Anton Van Leeuwenhoek's original microscope—a lens mounted between two metal plates. Middle, cork cells as seen through an early microscope. Bottom, Sir Alexander Fleming, discoverer of penicillin, looking into a microscope in his lab in London.

Further Reading
Henderson, Brian, *Cellular Microbiology: Bacteria-Host Interactions in Health and Disease* (1999); Heritage, J., *Introductory Microbiology* (1996); Heritage J., *Microbiology in Action* (1999); Lansing M. P., *Microbiology* (1998); Nester, E. W., *Microbiology: A Human Perspective* (1998).

First see OPTICS

Microscopy

Next see SCANNING TUNNEL MICROSCOPY

A microscope is an instrument used for forming enlarged, high resolution images. The term "micro" refers to a micron or micrometer, which is one-millionth of a meter (0.000039 inches).

The earliest microscopes were developed in the middle of the fifteenth century and were simple devices, consisting of only one lens, which magnified objects to make them appear from two to 20 times their original size. In the 1670s, Anton van Leeuwenhoek produced lenses capable of magnifying objects between 50 and 300 times. Today we would refer to these simple microscopes as magnifying glasses.

The first compound light microscope was invented in 1590 by Hans and Zacharias Janssen, two Dutch eyeglass makers. Their microscope consisted of a tube with a lens at each end. Early compound microscopes were more powerful than single lens instruments, but they produced distorted images.

In the 1660s, Robert Hooke, an English scientist, used a microscope to study samples of cork tissue. He discovered that the tissue consisted of regular boxlike structures, which he called cells. Thus the use of microscopes in studying cell structure and function was born. Shortly afterwards, Leeuwenhoek discovered microorganisms swimming about in pond water and named them "animalcules."

The compound light microscope can magnify objects up to 2,000 times their original size. It contains two lenses, an ocular or eyepiece which by itself has a magnification of ten times, and an objective lens placed near the specimen. A beam of ordinary light is used to illuminate the object, provided by a lamp or mirror that reflects light up and through the slide upon which the object is placed.

Specimens must be carefully prepared before viewing. A "wet mount" consists of a droplet of water containing the object, with or without a cover slip on top. Microorganisms, cells from living tissue, or inanimate objects may be viewed in this way. "Prepared slides" consist of "dead" matter carefully treated with various chemicals to preserve them. Dyes are added to make features more visible. The sample is then embedded in a block of wax and sliced very thin, less than tissue-paper thickness, by a device known as the microtone. The "shavings" are then placed on a slide and covered. Unlike wet mounts, preserved slides are permanent.

The stereomicroscope is used to study large specimens, beyond cellular level, and has an ocular and objective lens for each eye. This microscope provides a three-dimensional view of the specimen with a magnification of between

5 and 60 times. A "dissecting" microscope is an example of such an instrument, used to catch fine detail when studying the specimen. Geneticists also use these instruments while studying the physical characteristics of small organisms, such as fruitflies.

A phase contrast microscope is very useful for examining features inside living cells. The edges of cell structures bend light waves, contrasting with the unbent light waves elsewhere. This enables the viewer to see clearly the boundaries between the different cell parts.

Magnification refers to an increase in the apparent size of an object, whereas resolution refers to an increase in visible detail. Simply increasing magnification power ultimately leads to a picture in which everything resembles fuzzy dots and it becomes difficult if not impossible to see the separation of one small feature from another. The best objective lenses can only distinguish objects up to 0.2 microns apart. More advanced microscopes improve resolution as well as magnification power.

Electron Microscopy. An electron microscope uses a beam of electrons instead of a beam of light. The first microscope of this type was introduced in 1935 and has been much improved upon and refined since then. Electron microscopes provide high magnification and high resolution, but cannot be used on living organisms. The preparation method required for viewing kills living cells. In addition, the interior of the instrument contains a vacuum in which the beam of electrons travel.

The two types of electron microscopes are transmission electron microscopes (TEM) and scanning electron microscopes (SEM). In TEM, a beam of electrons is sent through the specimen. The SEM sends electrons across the specimen from left to right, in a process called scanning. The electrons "bounce off" in different directions, producing a three-dimensional view of the surface. Scanning electron microscopes are used to study DNA structures in great detail. In terms of magnification power, SEM can only produce images magnified up to 100,000 times, as opposed to TEM, which produces a magnification of up to 200,000 times.

Computer enhancement of magnification images further increases the usefulness of microscopy in studying biological material.

Elementary aspects of this subject are covered in LENS; LIGHT; MICROBIOLOGY; OPTICS. *More information on particular aspects is contained in* ELECTRON MICROSCOPY; MEDICAL DIAGNOSTICS. *Relevant information is contained in* CT AND PET SCANS; FORENSIC SCIENCE; SCANNING TUNNEL MICROSCOPY.

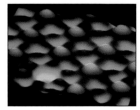

Above, top, the electron microscope used in many laboratories today is essentially unchanged since its initial development by Vladimir Zworykin. Above, bottom, SEM image of atoms.

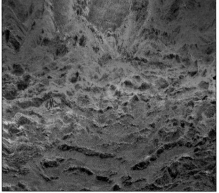

Microwaves find application in remote sensing, measuring the ocean currents characteristic of El Niño (above, right) or mapping the terrain of Venus (above) by the *Magellan* space probe.

Further Reading

Bai, Chunli, et al., *Scanning Tunneling Microscopy and Its Application* (1995); Lyman, Charles E., *Scanning Electron Microscopy, X-Ray Microanalysis, and Analytical Electron Microscopy* (1990); Rainis, Kenneth G. *Guide to Microlife* (1997).

First see ELECTROMAGNETIC WAVES

Microwave

Next see TELECOMMUNICATIONS

The portion of the radio spectrum with wavelengths between one millimeter (0.04 inches) and one meter (3.3 feet), corresponding to frequencies between 1,000 and 300,000 megacycles (MHz).

Microwave radiation is put to many practical uses, since it is relatively easy to build devices using its wavelengths. One example is radar equipment that gives precise information about the position and velocity of an aircraft or ship. Microwaves are also used in communication systems, for relaying telephone messages and television signals, for example. Because micro-

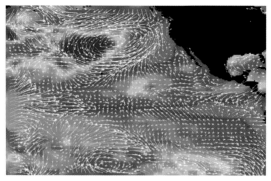

wave antennas can be built with great precision of direction, it is possible to use low-power, low-cost microwave transmitters, which makes possible the transmission of many signals simultaneously. In the home, microwaves are used in electronic ovens that heat food quickly.

Microwave spectroscopy is used to detect and interpret the transitions in the energy levels of molecules. Each molecule has a distinct energy-level diagram that depends on the masses of its atoms, the electron distribution, and the distance between particles. When electromagnetic radiation strikes a molecular sample, there may be transitions between energy levels that result in the emission of microwave radiation.

Analysis of microwave radiation provides information about the nature of a molecular sample. In astronomy, the study of microwave background radiation can provide information about the early stages of the universe. This background radiation is believed to have been emitted by the fireball, or "Big Bang," with which the universe is thought to have originated.

First see GALAXY

Milky Way

Next see UNIVERSE

The faint, shimmering band of stars that stretches in a great circle around the sky as seen from Earth.

The band in the night sky known to the Romans as Via Lactea outlines the central plane of the galaxy of which our sun is a part; it contains about 100 billion stars, half brighter and half dimmer than the Sun. Some of these stars are within a few hundred light-years of the sun; others are perhaps 20,000 light-years distant.

To astronomers, the Milky Way is a flattened spiral galaxy, whose circular diameter is about 100,000 light-years and whose maximum thickness in its central region is about 4,000 light-years. Compared to other such galaxies, the Milky Way is relatively flat, which astronomers explain by observations showing that it is rotating rapidly. The sun and most of the stars near it move around the center of the Milky Way at a speed estimated to be 170 miles per second, which means that the sun will complete one circuit in close to 250 million years.

Below, left, a visible light photo of the Milky Way. The dark markings are clouds of dark matter that obscure the structure of our galaxy. At right, Halley's comet (circled) passing in front of the Milky Way in a 1983 satellite photograph.

Structure. One feature of interest to astronomers is that the Milky Way has a spiral structure, resembling many spiral galaxies that are observed from Earth, such as the Andromeda Galaxy, which is about 2 million light-years distant from Earth. A great amount of evidence has been assembled to verify the spiral structure of the Milky Way. For example, studies of the distribution of relatively nearby gaseous nebulas and young stars—most with white-hot surfaces—show that they trace the same spiral structure seen in other spiral galaxies. In addition, studies of the absorption by interstellar gas of the visible light emissions of distant stars have helped to verify the spiral structure.

In the 1940s, American astronomer Walter Baade proposed that there are two basic star populations in the Milky Way. One population of stars, found mainly in the outlying regions of the Milky Way, consists of blue-white supergiant stars that are relatively young on the astronomical time scale—about 10 million to 100 million years old, only one percent of the age of the sun and the solar system. The second population consists of the much greater number of older stars, none of them very bright, a population that includes the oldest stars—perhaps 10 billion years old, twice the age of the sun. Baade's proposal has been accepted in general outline by astronomers, with some elaborations.

It is now believed that when the most massive stars formed from a cloud of almost pure hydrogen, they underwent rapid evolution and exploded as supernovas, returning some heavier elements to the interstellar gas. The next generation of stars that condensed from this gas consisted of hydrogen enriched with these heavier elements. The process of star evolution and formation continued until the creation of the present generation of young stars, which contain more of the heavier elements. The evolution of the Milky Way and its stars is still ongoing.

At the Center. The center of the Milky Way is believed to contain a black hole, with a mass of about one million suns. The recognition of that structure started with the radio astronomy observations of Karl Jansky, who found that there were strong radio emissions from the nucleus of the Milky Way, produced by high-speed electrons circling magnetic fields, which indicated the existence of a compact central object, the source of these electrons. Because visible light from the center of the Milky Way is absorbed by interstellar dust before it reaches the Earth, the composition of the center must be determined by infrared and radio observations. From these, it appears that material in the innermost spiral arm around the center of the Milky Way is expanding away from the center. At the very center, astronomers have identified a source of radio emissions of enormously high energy, but no larger than the solar system—it is presumed to be a black hole.

Further Reading
Bok, Bart Jan, *The Milky Way* (1981); Gilmore, Gerry, *The Galaxy* (1987); Paul, Erich Robert, *The Milky Way Galaxy and Statistical Cosmology, 1890-1924* (1993); Shuter, W.L.H., *Kinematics, Dynamics and Structure of the Milky Way* (1983).

Related material may be found in GALAXY; GRAVITY; STAR; TELESCOPE. *Other aspects of the subject are discussed in* BIG BANG THEORY; BLACK HOLE; X-RAY AND GAMMA-RAY ASTRONOMY. *Additional related material can be found in* HERTZSPRUNG-RUSSEL DIAGRAM; UNIVERSE, LARGE-SCALE STRUCTURE.

First see GEOMORPHOLOGY

Mineralogy

Next see CRYSTAL

The study of the physical and chemical characteristics of minerals, and of their origin and associations.

The principle areas of the discipline of mineralogy include the following:

Crystal morphology, or crystallography, is the study of the crystals in which minerals occur, with determination of crystal lattice structure made by such techniques as x-ray diffraction. Crystallography lists all crystals in one of six classes: cubic, in which all angles are at right angles and all sides are equal; tetragonal, in which all angles are right angles and the crystal has sides of two different lengths; orthorhombic, in which all angles are right angles and the crystal has sides of three different lengths; monoclinic, in which the crystal has sides of three different lengths and some of its angles are not right angles; triclinic, in which there are no right angles and there are three different lengths of sides; and hexagonal, in which the vertical sides of the crystal make right angles and there are two regular hexagonal faces.

Mineralogy also includes the determination of the chemical composition of minerals and the correlation of crystal lattice parameters with the chemical composition of minerals. Mineralogists also explore: physical properties such as density, hardness, and magnetism; the optical properties of minerals, such as the way in which they refract, reflect, and absorb light, generally using polarizing and reflecting microscopes; precise determination of the various isotopes of specific elements contained in minerals, often to a precision of parts per billion, which can help establish the age of a given mineral sample; determination of the specific gravity of a mineral by weighing it in and out of water; the testing of minerals for magnetism, magnetic polarity, and associated characteristics such as fluorescence, thermoluminescence, phosphorescence, and radioactivity; and the testing of minerals for tenacity, or brittleness. Most minerals are brittle, but some are malleable, ductile, or sectile, which means they can be cut by a knife and easily fashioned into sheets and wire.

Determinative mineralogy accomplishes the testing and identification of minerals by widely available techniques. One of these is the scratch test, which determines the hardness of a mineral. Hardness is classified on the basis of the Mohs scale, which lists ten degrees of hardness. The scale starts with talc, the softest, and proceeds through gypsum, calcite, fluorite, apatite, orthoclase, quartz, topaz, corundum, and diamond, the hardest.

The techniques and principles of mineralogy can be applied, with some minor modifications, to a number of allied fields. These include gemstone identification, the industrial production of glass and ceramics, and the production of abrasives and cements.

Background material can be found in ELEMENTS, DISTRIBUTION OF; IGNEOUS ROCK; METAMORPHIC ROCK; MINING TECHNOLOGY. *More details can be found in* GEOMORPHOLOGY; MINING TECHNOLOGY; SEDIMENTARY ROCK GEOLOGY. *Elementary aspects of this subject are covered in* MAGNETIC FIELD OF THE EARTH; PETROLOGY; SEISMOLOGY.

Coal mining still accounts for a large portion of the world's energy needs.

Further Reading
Schumann, *Handbook of Rocks, Minerals, and Gemstones* (1993); Schumann, *Minerals of the World* (1998); Sinkankas, J., *Field Collecting Gemstones and Minerals* (1995); Sinkankas, J., *Gemstones of North America* (1997); Zussman, J., *An Introduction to the Rock-Forming Minerals* (1992).

First see PETROLEUM PROSPECTING

Mining Technology

Next see EXPLOSIVES

Mining technology was first developed early in the history of mankind and was elaborated as civilizations grew. But the major impetus for modern mining technology came in the Industrial Revolution, which created a rising demand for coal. Today, mining technologies fall into three major categories—placer mining, open-pit mining, and underground mining.

Placer mining is the recovery of metals or ores from alluvial sands and gravels created by erosion over long periods of time. Gold is the most important product of placer mining, but it is also used to obtain tin, copper, platinum, copper, silver, bismuth, diamonds, and sapphires. In alluvial mining, the deposits are excavated and valuable minerals are separated by a sluice, an inclined trough with cleats at the bottom. A mixture of ore and water is dumped at the top of the sluice. As the ore moves down, the heavier minerals settle to the bottom and are trapped by cleats at the end of the sluice.

At the Surface. Open-pit mining is used when massive ore deposits lie close to the surface. Open-pit mining is distinguished from strip mining, in which horizontally extended deposits close to the surface are removed by power shovels after the rock that covers them is stripped away. Open-pit mining is similar in some respects to strip mining, but it uses drilling and blasting to break up the continuous benches or shelves (as they are called) in which the ore is found. The shelves and benches that have been excavated already are used as roads on which the extracting equipment and the trucks or railway cars removing the ore can ride.

Beneath the Surface. Underground mining is used for deposits that are too deep to be removed by open-pit methods. Horizontal tunnels called adits or drifts are drilled first to determine the size of an ore deposit, and then to haul away the recovered ore or coal. Vertical shafts are driven from the tunnels to reach deeper deposits, and adits are then cut to go into the deposits. The adits must be supported by timber, concrete, or steel to prevent cave-ins.

The two basic methods of underground mining are stoping, in which the ore deposit is drilled and blasted to loosen it; and caving, in which a slice or block of ore is undercut so that it caves in and breaks up. In general, caving is used for large bodies of low-content ore. Coal mining is more dangerous than other types because dangerous gases, including methane and carbon monoxide, tend to be associated with coal deposits. Coal is usually mined using continuous rippers connected to conveyer belts carrying the coal to transportation facilities.

First see REFLECTION, REFRACTION

Mirror

Next see HOLOGRAPHY

A smooth surface that reflects most of the light that falls on it.

In ancient Greece and Rome, mirrors were highly polished bronze surfaces. By the 16th century, Venetians were making and selling mirrors of glass, backed with an amalgam of tin and mercury. The mirrors we use today, made of glass coated with silver, were developed in Europe in the 1840s. Mirrors are defined by their shape, which determines the way they reflect light. (*See* LENS; OPTICS; *and* CAMERA.)

Plane mirrors, the ordinary household type, form an image that is the same size as the object being reflected but is reversed, with the right side of the object appearing on the left side in the image. It is called a virtual image because it is not formed directly by rays from the object, but by the extension of these rays behind the mirror.

A spherical mirror has a surface that is a section of a sphere. When the outer surface of the sphere is the reflecting surface, the mirror is convex; when the inner side is the reflecting surface, the mirror is concave. Convex mirrors always produce virtual images. Concave mirrors produce virtual images when the object is closer to the mirror than half its radius of curvature and real images when the object is farther away.

A paraboloid mirror is the kind found in astronomical telescopes, because it does not cause aberrations in the image it receives; it thus gives a sharp real image. Modern reflecting telescopes, such as the 200-inch instrument on Mount Palomar, use paraboloid mirrors.

First see PROPULSION

Missiles

Next see NUCLEAR WEAPONS

Unmanned, self-propelled devices that carry warheads through space, the atmosphere, or the ocean.

The principle components of a missile are its propulsion system, guidance and control system, and payload. The propulsion system generally is a rocket for a missile that travels through space or the upper atmosphere or an air-breathing engine for a missile that travels through the lower atmosphere; some missiles have a combination of the two.

The guidance system determines whether the missile is diverging from its preset path, and signals the control units to bring the missile back into the correct path. The missile payload can be ordinary explosives or, in the case of larger missiles, nuclear warheads.

Above, a technician's hand is reflected in the mirrors of the Gamma-Ray observatory.

Missiles, once used strictly for strategic purposes from afar, are increasingly being deployed in the field (above, in Europe) as tactical weapons.

Further Reading
Denoon, David B.H., *Ballistic Missile Defense in the Post-Cold War Era* (1995); MacKnight, Nigel, *Tomahawk Cruise Missile* (1995); Westrum, Ron, *Sidewinder: Creative Missile Development at China Lake* (1999); Zarchan, Paul, *Tactical and Strategic Missile Guidance* (1998).

Missile Types. There are a number of types of missiles. An unguided missile gets no instructions from the ground or an internal guidance system after it is launched. The V-2 rockets launched by the Germans in World War II were unguided missiles. Guided missiles have guidance systems that use GPS, digital computers, and radar to reach the target. Inertial guidance allows cruise missiles to fly within 100 feet of a changing terrain and hit their targets with 10-foot accuracy. Sometimes a missile's guidance system locks onto radiation or electronic waves emitted by the target, such as the signals sent out by a target aircraft or the reflection of a laser beam.

Missiles can also be classified as aerodynamic or ballistic. An aerodynamic missile carries large fins or wings to give it lift and a certain amount of maneuverability. Ballistic missiles rely entirely on their propulsion system for stability during their flight; in general ballistic missiles are powered by rocket engines.

Another way to classify missiles is by their range of flight; for example, the intercontinental ballistic missile, ICBM, can travel thousands of miles. Such an ICBM has several advantages over manned bombers for attacking enemy targets. It does not require a crew and is simpler to design because it is made for one-way travel. But despite major advances in guidance instrumentation, ICBMs cannot deliver their warheads as accurately as aerodynamic missiles. The United States still has approximately 700 ICBMs and 400 submarine-launched ballistic missiles in its active arsenal.

Antimissile Defense. Antimissile defense systems use smaller missiles that are faster to launch and are intended to meet an incoming enemy missile before it can explode over its target. The defensive missiles are controlled by radar systems that are aimed at the probable paths that enemy missiles will follow. The idea is to detect an enemy missile launch as soon as possible, using either ground-based or orbiting radar and other detection equipment, and then to send the protective missiles aloft as quickly as possible, exploding close enough to the enemy missile to disable it. THAAD missiles are the latest in this variety.

Background material regarding missiles can be found in AERODYNAMICS; PROPULSION; ROCKET. *More details can be found in* COMBUSTION; EXPLOSIVES; NAVIGATION. *More information on particular topics is contained in* AVIONICS; NUCLEAR WEAPONS; SPACECRAFT; WEATHER FORECASTING.

Mitochondria

First see CELL

Next see ADENOSINE TRIPHOSPHATE (ATP)

The sites of cellular respiration, which is the process of breaking down glucose to produce energy in the form of adenosine triphosphate (ATP).

Mitochondria are the "power plants" of the cell. Depending on its energy needs, a cell may contain anywhere from a few mitochondria to hundreds of them.

An individual mitochondrion is from two to ten microns in length, which makes it one of the larger and more prominent organelles. It has a double membrane covering, with the inner membrane containing many folds known as cristae. The purpose of the cristae is to provide more surface area in which the various enzymes and chemical reactions can function.

Cellular respiration is divided into four main stages, with each stage occurring in a different location in the mitochondrion. The first stage, called glycolysis, doesn't take place in the mitochondrion at all, but in the cytosol immediately outside. The second stage, the acetyl-CoA step, takes place in the outer membrane. The third stage, called either the Krebs or citric acid cycle, occurs in the space between the membranes. The fourth stage, known as either oxidative phosphorylation or the electron transport chain, occurs in the membranes of the cristae of the inner membrane. It is in the fourth stage that the majority of ATP are produced.

Mitochondrial DNA. Mitochondria were the first organelles other than the nucleus found to contain DNA. The genes in the mitochondrion contain a code for specific proteins used in the reactions for cellular respiration. Mitochondrial DNA (or mDNA) has a low mutation rate and is only maternally inherited, unlike nuclear DNA which comes from both parents. This makes mDNA ideal for use in population genetics, in which the degree of relationship between various animal or human populations is studied.

Lynn Margulis of the University of Massachusetts, Amherst, has hypothesized that both mitochondria and plastids such as chloroplasts originated as free-living prokaryotic cells that eventually formed symbiotic living arrangements with other similar cells to form the first eukaryotic cells. This would explain why these organelles contain their own specialized DNA.

Background material can be found in ADENOSINE TRIPHOSPHATE (ATP); CELL; METABOLISM. *More details can be found in* CELL CYCLE; CYTOPLASM; HOMO SAPIENS. *Additional relevant information is contained in* AUSTRALOPITHECUS; LIFE, DEFINITION AND ORIGIN OF; EXTRANUCLEAR INHERITANCE.

Further Reading
Darley-Usmar, V. M., *Mitochondria: DNA, Proteins, and Disease* (1993); Scheffler I. E., *Mitochondria* (1999); Thomas, L., *The Lives of a Cell* (1995); Tribe, M., *Metabolism and Mitochondria* (1976).

First see CHROMOSOME

Mitosis

Next see CELL CYCLE

The process of cell division that produces identical daughter cells.

Cells reproduce by binary fission—a "parent cell" divides into two smaller "daughter cells." All of the cellular material of the parent is split evenly between the offspring, including all organelles except for the nucleus, which contains the genetic material in the form of paired chromosomes. The chromosome number is unique to each species and is a constant within all of the cells of an organism. For example, each human body cell, or somite, contains 46 chromosomes. If the nucleus were simply split in half, the chromosome number would be halved with each successive cellular division.

Mitosis refers to the events that take place in the nucleus of the cell prior to cell division. A copy is made of every chromosome in order to ensure that each new daughter cell receives a complete set and no chromosomes are "lost" from one generation to the next. It is not enough simply to duplicate each chromosome; steps must be taken so each newly formed nucleus contains no duplicates and is not missing any chromosomes. Occasionally, however, mistakes do occur.

Mitosis takes place in distinct phases, each of which is marked by certain key events and follows a specific progression. The "choreography" is highly refined, and special structures exist to drive the chromosomes into their proper positions.

Stages. The first stage is called interphase, and it is during this time that the replication of all genetic material occurs. At this point, the chromosomal material, called chromatin, is

Pyruvate   **2 ATP**

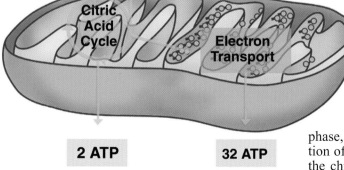

Citric Acid Cycle   Electron Transport

2 ATP   **32 ATP**

At left, the metabolic processes of the mitochondrion, the "power plants" of eukaryotic cells.

very long and thin, and resembles tangled strands of spaghetti, rather than distinct and separate chromosomes.

During the next stage, prophase, the chromosomes can be seen individually. Each chromosome is really two "sister chromatids" or homologous structures connected by a centromere. Observation of the nucleus at this time reveals pairs that appear simply to be milling about aimlessly. Meanwhile, the nuclear membrane is dissolving and a structure known as the mitotic spindle is forming. The spindle consists of a series of fibers made up of microtubules that extend between the poles of the cell. The centrosomes, organelles involved in cell division, contain microtubule organizing centers (MTOCs) and help to form and arrange the spindle fibers. It is the spindle fibers that direct the movement of the chromosomes in the next stages.

Metaphase, which follows prophase, is characterized by the lining up of the chromosome pairs across the center of the cell, caused by the "herding" efforts of the spindle fibers. The kinetochore is the part of the chromosome to which the spindle fibers attach. This is followed by anaphase, in which the centromeres holding together the sister chromatids split, allowing one chromatid from each pair to be pulled towards an opposite pole of the cell.

Finally, telophase occurs and the basic events of prophase are reversed: the spindle apparatus begins to disappear and a new nuclear membrane forms around each set of chromatids. Cytokinesis usually follows telophase, except in the case of a cell which has been undergoing the mitotic process in order to obtain multiple nuclei. Each stage of mitosis follows the previous one seamlessly. Some textbooks attempt to characterize a "late" phase of one stage as distinct from an "early" phase of the successive stage, but in reality it is difficult to do so.

The Cell Cycle. The cell cycle, which encompasses all of the stages of a cell's life, is made up of the phases G1, S, G2, and M. Newly formed cells begin at G1, in which they rapidly grow until they reach their full size and become specialized. Depending on the type of cell, and how many generations of division have already elapsed, the length of G1 is highly variable. It may be the entire lifespan, a brief period, or anything in between. In a rapidly growing animal, the cell cycle can repeat every 18-24 hours, with G1 lasting between six to eight hours.

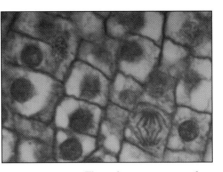

The chromosomes of a cell (at lower right, above) in a lily plant are condensed into chromatids; the cell is in the metaphase stage of mitosis.

Further Reading
Bowen, I.D., *Mitosis and Apoptosis* (1997); De Duve, Christian, *Blueprint for a Cell: The Nature and Origin of Life* (1991); Reider, Conly L. (Ed.), *Mitosis and Meiosis* (1998); Rensberger, Boyce, *Life itself* (1996); Thomas, Lewis, *The Lives of a Cell: Notes of a Biology Watcher* (1995).

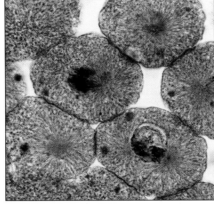

Above, a scanning electron micrograph shows whitefish eggs in the process of mitosis.

G1 is followed by S, or the synthesis stage, in which the genetic material is replicated as the cell prepares to divide. This stage encompasses interphase. S lasts only as long as is needed to copy all of the chromosomes, usually six to eight hours. G2 is a "gap" or pause in the events, lasting three to four hours. The rest of mitosis occurs during the M phase and usually occurs in less than an hour with no further interruptions.

The two key control points of the cell cycle are G1 and G2. At G1, a "commitment" is made to enter the replication cycle which then automatically leads into the S phase. At the end of G2, another "decision" is made to enter the rest of the stages of mitosis. Between the M of one cell cycle and G1 of the next is a period called G0 in which the cell can withdraw from the replication cycle or can re-enter it.

The actual activation events that occur are not well understood but are believed to involve various activator proteins.

Background material on mitosis can be found in CELL; CHROMOSOMES; KREBS CYCLE. *Advanced subjects are developed in* CALVIN-BENSON CYCLE; CELLULAR MEMBRANES; METABOLISM. *Elementary aspects of this subject are covered in* ENZYMES; TRANSPORT, CELLULAR; WATER IN LIVING CELLS. *See also* MEIOSIS *for a comparison between these two processes.*

First see ATOM

Molecule

Next see BOND, CHEMICAL

A collection of atoms chemically bound together in a certain way with a specified geometrical structure.

The smallest division of matter that still has a chemical identity is the atom. Chemists have known for a long time that most materials can be broken down into their constituent atoms, but that atoms cannot be broken down further without destroying their identity. Breakfast foods, for example, can be broken down into piles of atoms of carbon, hydrogen, oxygen, and other atoms, but if those atoms of carbon were taken apart, one would find protons, neutrons, and electrons, and would no longer have a chemical element.

As fundamental as atoms are, we generally have very little contact with them in our daily lives. Almost all of the chemicals with which we come into contact (including our own bodies), are made from molecules. The air we breathe, the material of this book, and the food we eat are all made up of molecules. A material made from a combination of different atoms is called a compound. All molecules are compounds, but not all compounds are molecules.

At the dinner table, for example, the sugar is made from molecules, as is the butter. The sugar molecules consist of two rings of carbon compounds joined together, and the butter consists of long chains of carbon compounds joined together. The reason that the butter can be spread with a knife is that, while the forces that hold atoms together in individual molecules is very strong, the forces between the molecules is relatively weak. Table salt, on the other hand, is a compound that is not a molecule, although it is made from sodium and chlorine atoms. In table salt, the sodium atoms donate an electron to the chlorine atom so that they both become electrically charged. It is the electrical attraction between the two ions (or charged atoms) that holds the crystals of salt together.

Organic Molecules. The most interesting class of molecules are the so-called organic molecules. It used to be thought that these molecules could only appear in living systems, but we now know that they can be synthesized as well. The main characteristic of organic molecules is that they involve chains of carbon atoms, which have four electrons in their outermost orbit. Every carbon atom in an organic molecule shares each of its four outer electrons, and it is the sharing of those electrons that creates the bond that holds the molecule together. Sometimes, as in methane (natural gas), each of the carbon atom's outer electrons is shared with one electron from a hydrogen atom. In other materials, however, such as hydrogen cyanide (HCN), a carbon and a nitrogen atom share three pairs of electrons (the extra electron on the carbon is shared with the hydrogen).

Although other atoms can form chains like carbon, none can form chains of such complexity. Atoms can be likened to a bunch of Lego blocks, where some have one connecting joint, some have two, some have three, and others have four. Just as a lot more can be made with the four-connector blocks than with those having a single connector, many more interesting chains can be made with carbon atoms than with other atoms.

Isomers. Molecules can be described by enumerating how many of each kind of atom is in the molecule. For example, water (H_2O) contains two hydrogen atoms for each oxygen atom.

In complex organic molecules, two different molecules can have the same number of carbon, hydrogen, and nitrogen molecules arranged in different patterns (much the same as a collection of Lego blocks, which can be arranged in many different ways). For example, gas has an octane rating. As the name implies, octane is an organic molecule that contains eight carbon atoms. When five of those carbon atoms are in a straight chain and the other three are on side branches, octane behaves very well in modern high compression engines. An octane rating of 100 signifies that the gasoline mixture in question behaves as well as a pure sample of five-chain octane. Oddly enough, octane molecules in which all the carbon atoms are in a chain behave poorly in engines, and hence have a low octane rating.

Two molecules that have the same atomic composition but a different structure are called "isomers" of one another. As the above example shows, different arrangements of the same set of molecules can produce materials with radically different properties.

The ability to synthesize molecules has had an enormous impact on human life. This is certainly true of materials like plastics, which are long carbon chains with other kinds of molecules attached. Hard plastics often contain chains with carbon rings interspersed at intervals along their length to give more rigidity. (Kevlar is an example of this kind of arrangement.) Other plastics are simply long single-stranded chains with an occasional nitrogen thrown in to link one chain to another (as in the case of nylon). It is hard to imagine a society without such synthetic molecules.

Background material can be found in ATOM; ELECTRO-MAGNETIC FORCE; PERIODIC TABLE OF THE ELEMENTS. *Advanced subjects are developed in* BOND, CHEMICAL; CHEMICAL REACTIONS; CRYSTAL; POLYMER. *More information on particular aspects is contained in* ACIDS AND BASES; INORGANIC COMPOUND; ORGANIC COMPOUND; SOLID.

First see IMMUNE RESPONSE

Monoclonal Antibodies

Next see ANTIBODIES

Laboratory-made versions of the protective molecules produced by the body's immune system.

Substances that are foreign to the body, such as the viruses and bacteria that cause disease, are recognized as invaders because they have molecules called antigens that are not found in the body. Antibodies are proteins that seek out the antigens and help to destroy them, protecting the body against disease.

Function. Antibodies have two useful characteristics. First, they are very specific—one kind of antibody attacks only one specific antigen. Second, some antibodies that are activated by a disease-causing invader remain active in the body, conferring resistance to that invader and the disease that it causes. Medicine takes advantage of this second characteristic by creating vaccines that arouse antibody activity but do not cause the disease. Monoclonal antibodies can be used not only to protect against disease but also to diagnose a variety of illnesses. Monoclonal antibodies are made by using cancer cells, which can reproduce themselves endlessly, and fusing them with normal mammalian cells that produce an antibody. This cell fusion produces what is

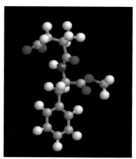

Two well-known and widely used compounds: aspartame (an artificial sweetener) and acetylsalicylic acid (popularly known as aspirin).

Further Reading
Atkins, P.W., *The Periodic Kingdom* (1997); Ball, Phillip *Designing the Molecular World* (1996); Emsley, John, *Molecules at an Exhibition* (1999); Greiner, Walter, *Nuclear Molecules* (1995)Kettle, Sidney Francis *Symmetry and Structure* (1995).

called a hybridoma, a cell that will produce antibodies continuously. These are called monoclonal antibodies because they come from one type, or clone, of a cell, the hybridoma. Antibodies that are produced by conventional techniques are derived from many kinds of cells, and so are called polyclonal. The antibodies produced by monoclonal cells are purer than those from polyclonal cells, and so are more effective at fighting infection and cause fewer side effects.

Background material can be found in ANTIBODIES; BLOOD; IMMUNE RESPONSE. *Advanced subjects are developed in* AUTOIMMUNITY; IMMUNIZATION AND VACCINATION; IMMUNOASSAY. *Relevant information is contained in* ANTIBIOTICS; B-LYMPHOCITE; GAMMA GLOBULIN; T-LYMPHOCYTE.

First see PROBABILITY

Monte Carlo Methods

Next see GAME THEORY

The use of probability to estimate the results of processes too complicated for complete analysis.

Monte Carlo methods were first employed by John von Neumann (1903–1957) and Stanislav Ulam (1909–1984) in the development of game theory, but now are used most often as sampling techniques in statistics.

An Example. Let us say the United States Forest Service is attempting to discover how many trees in the Northeast have been killed by acid rain. It would be impossible to actually count every dead tree, but it is possible to use a Monte Carlo method to sample the area in question. A satellite passes over the forest, and takes a picture enclosing a known area; then the picture is digitized, and a certain number of points are randomly chosen for examination. The proportion of points that reveal dead trees to total points chosen roughly equals the proportion of affected forest to the whole. Clearly, the greater the number of points examined, the greater the accuracy of the Monte Carlo estimate. This form of Monte Carlo method was used in assessing the damage caused on the Alaskan coastline by the *Exxon Valdez* oil spill. (*See* STATISTICS.)

The other use of Monte Carlo methods is in stochastic simulations, where a computer generates random numbers to produce data streams; these can be used, for example, to model the effects of the nuclear accident at the Chernobyl power plant. Such simulations use vast amounts of computer time and power, so they have given way in recent years to decomposed simulations, in which parallel processors work on linked aspects of the model, using interprocessor synchronization to achieve the effect of the more powerful brute-force method. The Department of Transportation uses such simulations when modeling the effects of changes in the Interstate Highway System. (*See* GAME THEORY.)

First see SOLAR SYSTEMS

Moon

Next see SATELLITE, PLANETARY

Earth's only natural satellite, it has a diameter of 2,160 miles, just over one-quarter of the Earth's, but a surface area that is about one-fourteenth of Earth's.

The moon's average distance from Earth is 239,000 miles; its nearest distance is 226,000 miles and its farthest distance is 252,000. The moon makes a full orbit around Earth in 27 days, 7 hours, and 43 minutes. It also rotates on its own axis, making a complete rotation every 27 days, so that it always presents the same side to Earth. But because there are slight variations, or librations, in the moon's movement, a total of 59 percent of its surface is visible to observers on Earth. Unlike the Earth, the moon has no magnetic field.

Orbit. The plane of the moon's orbit is at an angle of more than five degrees to the plane of Earth's orbit, so that the "new moon" is not exactly between Earth and the sun and the "full moon" does not entirely enter Earth's shadow. Eclipses occur as the moon comes between Earth and the sun or as Earth comes between moon and the sun.

Phases. The phases of the moon result from the fact that the moon reflects sunlight, and we on Earth see varying amounts of its illuminated surface. At the new moon, the illuminated phase of the moon is turned away from Earth, so we see nothing. At full moon, the hemisphere that faces the sun faces Earth, so we see a completely illuminated hemisphere. At the first or last quarter, half of the sunlit hemisphere is turned toward Earth, and that is the portion that is visible. The moon reflects about seven percent of the sunlight that strikes its surface.

The moon is the largest planetary satellite in the solar system in terms of its size relative to the planet that it orbits. The average density of the moon is 3.3 times the density of water, so that the gravitational pull on the surface of the moon is 16 percent that of Earth. The moon has no atmosphere, and until recently it was thought to have no water. Recently, water (in the form of ice) was detected toward the poles of the moon, which has raised hopes of establishing a human colony on the moon.

The moon has been mapped in detail, and its principal features have been recognized. These include the "maria," literally "seas" but actually smooth, dark plains, some a few hundred miles across; craters, which are circular, some very small and the largest more than 150 miles in diameter; mountains and mountain ranges, rising as much as six miles above the surface; clefts, or rills, cracks in the surface that can be several hundred miles long; and bright rays and bright streaks, some of them as long as 1,000 miles, which radiate from many craters.

Theories of how the major features of the moon's surface were formed involve the impact of asteroids or volcanic activity; some astronomers believe that both played a part.

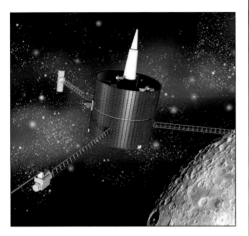

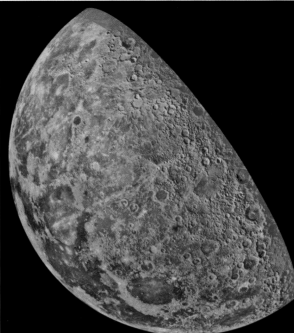

The importance of the moon for Earth is becoming more and more appreciated. In addition to protecting Earth from asteroid impact and churning up the sea with the tides (which is conducive to life), the moon may become an important source of elements such as helium. Far left, the Lunar Prospector Satellite surveyed the moon until 1999, when it was allowed to crash on the lunar surface. The moon was also the site of humankind's first foray into space. Below, Buzz Aldrin on the moon, photographed by Neil Armstrong, July 21, 1969.

OBSERVATIONS

Apollo's Legacy

Thanks to the *Apollo* missions, we now know a great deal about the moon's origin, composition, and age. It was probably created from debris ejected from Earth by some huge impact, and this discovery has led to the revelation that the Earth has been the target of several such impacts, the most recent of which wiped out the dinosaurs 65 million years ago. Its craters are also the products of subsequent impacts, not volcanism; however, the moon did have a molten interior for some time, because *Apollo* discovered oceans of hardened magma that are some two billion years younger than the main body of the moon. Thanks to an experiment that could only be done in the vacuum-surrounded gravity of the lunar surface, we know that Galileo was right: the time a body takes to fall is independent of its weight.

Related material may be found in KEPLER'S LAWS; PLANET; SATELLITE, PLANETARY. *Advanced subjects are developed in* ASTEROIDS AND METEORS; SOLAR SYSTEMS. *Additional relevant information is contained in* PLANETARY ATMOSPHERE; PLANETS, FORMATION OF.

Further Reading
Burnham, Robert, *Burnham's Celestial Handbook* (1983); Cherrington, Ernest H., *Exploring the Moon Through Binoculars and Small Telescopes* (1984); Harland, D.M., *Exploring the Moon* (1999); Lawrence, Fred, *Earth, Moon, and Planets* (1990).

First see REPRODUCTIVE SYSTEMS

Morphogenesis

Next see EMBRYOLOGY

The development of the shape and form of an embryo.

An organism starts out as a single cell, the fertilized egg known as a zygote. The zygote divides several times until a ball of cells, called the blastula, is formed. The blastula is a hollow structure, one cell layer thick. A portion of its cells makes up the embryo and the rest of the cells form the embryonic membranes which help provide the embryo with everything it needs.

The blastula develops into the gastrula, with two cell layers, through the process of invagination, an inward migration of cells. These cell layers are known as the ectoderm (outer) and endoderm (inner). A third cell layer, called the mesoderm, eventually forms between them through the same process. From these three cell layers arise all body systems and structures.

How do the cells "know" what kinds of tissue to develop into? Somehow, probably through chemical messengers, the cells "communicate" with each other. Tissues develop in certain ways based upon which other tissues are nearby. This process is known as embryonic induction. Experiments have shown that it is location which directs the development process. Early frog embryo cells have been "relocated," and cells that should have developed into eyes, upon being moved to the tail region, instead developed into tail tissue. Cells from the tail, upon being transplanted to the head, developed into tissue normally found on the head. (*See* DIFFERENTIATION.)

First see GAMMA RAY

Mossbauer Effect

Next see NUCLEAR FORCES

The absence of recoil by an atomic nucleus in a solid when that nucleus emits a gamma ray.

In a gas, a nucleus will recoil when it emits a gamma ray, just as a rifle recoils when it fires a bullet. That recoil reduces the energy of the gamma ray from its usual level, reducing the accuracy of measurements that are made with gamma rays. In 1957, R. L. Mossbauer discovered that because an atomic nucleus is held by strong forces when it is in a crystal solid, the energy of the recoil is shared by all the atoms in the crystal lattice, so that the energy of the emitted gamma ray is not affected. Mossbauer first observed the effect with a crystal of iridium 191; it has since been observed in crystals of many other atoms. One significant use of the Mossbauer effect has been to verify the theory of gravitation, which states that the energy of a gamma ray emitted by a nucleus at ground level on Earth will be different from the energy of a gamma ray emitted by the same nucleus at some altitude above Earth's surface. The Mossbauer effect has several useful applications. It has been applied to the study of the vibration of crystal lattices and of the internal magnetic field in iron. The same principle applies to the absorption of gamma rays by atomic nuclei, which is applied in Mossbauer-effect spectroscopy for studies in nuclear physics and solid-state physics.

First see ELECTRIC CIRCUIT

Motors and Generators

Next see ELECTRICITY AND ELECTRICAL ENGINEERING

Motors and generators combine to make up the basic electric power system of the world today. All electric motors and generators are based ultimately on two complementary principles discovered during the early 1800s, Ampère's law and Faraday's law. Ampère found that a current flowing at right angles to a magnetic field would undergo a motive force, while Faraday discovered that a conductor moving at right angles to a magnetic field would induce a current. Thus once one has established a magnetic field within a stator, or stationary element, the movement of a rotor within that field will produce electricity, and, correspondingly, the passage of an electric current through the field will make the rotor move—in the first case one has a generator, in the second case a motor. The first practical models of such devices were constructed by A. Pacinotti in 1863 and by Z.T. Gramme in 1873.

To manufacture such a device, a circular housing must be built, lined with either perma-nent or electromagnets so that a magnetic flux flows across the air gap inside; then an iron-core rotor, wound with copper wire, is inserted inside that flux. Then Faraday's law takes over: as the rotor turns, on one side the conductor is moving upward relative to the magnetic field, generating a current flowing towards the operator, while on the other side the conductor is moving downward, generating a current flowing away from the operator. As the rotor continues to turn, the conductor that has been moving upward through the flux cuts across the flux at shallower angles until it is parallel to the flux and no longer generating a current, then it starts to move downward, cutting across the flux at greater and greater angles until it is perpendicular again. Meanwhile, the conductor on the other side is undergoing exactly the same movement. Thus, although a continuous current is generated in each conductor, its strength will depend not only on the density of the magnetic flux, but also on the length of conductor that is perpendicular to the flux and the velocity of the conductor that is perpendicular to the flux.

Alternating Current Generators. The result of this strengthening and diminishing of the current flow is an alternating current in the shape of a sine wave, produced at the rate of one wave for each revolution of the rotor (or more for multiple windings). The resulting frequency of electricity was a matter of great controversy in the late 1800s.

Early water turbine generators ran at the relatively low speed of 250 rpm, resulting in a frequency of about 25 Hz; this was fine for industrial applications, but produced an annoying flickering of lights. Steam generators, meanwhile, operated at 8,000 cycles per minute, or 133.3 Hz; while this provided excellent domestic service, it could burn out motors. Eventually the compromise figure of 3,600 rpm, or 60 Hz, was reached. A second problem that had to be dealt with was the extreme variation in current of the sine wave. In order to regularize the current flow, electric generators have their stators wired together in three groups, each covering 60 degrees on each side; the result is a three-phase current, in which the peak voltage in each group is delayed by one-third of a revolution, so that over a full cycle the peak of one phase counteracts the valleys of the other two. Although this reduces effective power by $\sqrt{2}$, it smooths out the current flow so that it can be used.

Direct Current Generators. The first generators and motors were equipped with a commutator, which counteracted the variations in current and produced direct current. This form of electrical current was preferred, because it more closely resembled the current derived from batteries. Direct current motors are rugged, and hence are used in automobile cooling fans and starter motors, as well as in vehicles that need a

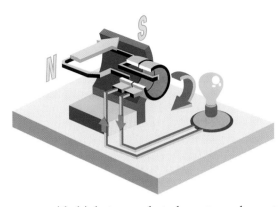

Left, an AC generator.

motor with high torque but do not need great speed; they also allow precise speed control, so these universal motors, as they are called, are commonly found in small domestic appliances and tools.

However, all other applications of electric motors use alternating current. There are two basic forms of AC motors, induction and synchronous. Induction motors, first developed by Nikola Tesla in 1888, rely on three-phase current flowing through the stator, creating a rotating magnetic flux. If the rotor is not moving, a large current is created in it, which in turn creates a mechanical torque; as the rotor speeds up, the induced current grows less and less until, when the rotor is moving at the same speed as the magnetic field, the torque of the rotor equals the torque of the flux. Induction motors thus run at set speeds based on the frequency of the input current, either 1800 or 1200 rpm. Linear induction motors have recently been developed for "mag-lev" train service and electromagnetic pumps, where no physical contact—and therefore no frictional wear and no potentially disastrous slippage—is involved.

Synchronous motors, as their name implies, display no such torque component, and thus have to be started mechanically; but once operating, typically in large-scale industrial applications, they improve overall power factors. Small synchronous motors called hysteresis motors run in exact accord with frequency, so they are used in tape recorders, clocks, and other applications where precise speed is vital. (*See* CIRCUIT, ELECTRICAL *and* ELECTRICAL ENGINEERING.)

First see FAULTS, FOLDS, AND JOINTS

Mountain Formation

Next see GEOSYNCLINE

Mountain formation can occur by several different processes. One such process is volcanic activity, which can produce several different types of mountains. For example, in Hawaii, Mauna Loa is a volcanic mountain made chiefly by the consolidation of lava flow from the mouth of the volcano. It is classified as a shield moun-

tain, as are other mountains produced by the same process. Another class of mountains can be formed as the outer layers of a volcano erode, leaving the lava that existed in the throat of the volcano. Yet another class, cinder-cone mountains, are built chiefly by the fall of material emitted during explosive activity of the volcano. Cinder-cone mountains generally have steep slopes, while shield mountains have lower, more gradual slopes. Another class is strato-volcano mountains, which are formed by alternating layers of ash and lava. Mounts Hood, Shasta, and Rainier on the West Coast of North America are examples of strato-volcanic mountains.

The greatest mountain ranges on Earth—the Alps, the Himalayas, the Andes, the Rockies, and the Appalachians—consist of folded and faulted mountains, which are made of broken and bent layers of rock produced by movements of Earth's crust. Movements of the crust squeeze these layers upward, creating mountain ranges. Two major geological processess involved in this kind of mountain formation are orogenic movements, in which layers of rock are mashed together, and epeirogenic uplifts, which push the layered material upward.

Another class, fault-block mountains, arise at the regions of Earth's crust where major blocks of crustal rock are broken apart. The forces that cause the breaks produce shearing surfaces that tilt the blocks upward. In the U. S., the Sierra Nevada range is an example of fault-block mountains; others are found in Africa and in the Rhine Valley of Germany.

Some mountains are formed by erosion that takes place over millions of years. Stone Mountain in Georgia and Mount Monadnock in New Hampshire are made of geological material that resisted the erosive processes eating away the surrounding ground. Geological studies show that mountain formation has occurred at every stage of Earth's history, and that mountains and mountain ranges have come and gone in the past. However, mountain formation has been a relatively rare occurrence, since during most of the history of the continents, the terrain consisted mostly of shallow seas and lowlands. Our current geological era, extending back millions of years, is thus an unusually active period of mountain formation.

Above, the Starlette satellite is covered with mirrors that reflect laser beams back to Earth. This provides super-accurate measures of variations in gravity. This data is used to determine the density of material beneath mountains, which in turn tells much about the formation of the mountains.

Related areas are discussed in GEOLOGICAL TIME SCALE; GRAVITY; PLATE TECTONICS; VOLCANO. *Further details can be found in* FOLDS, FAULTS, AND JOINTS; GEOSYNCLINE. *Elementary aspects of this subject are covered in* GEOMORPHOLOGY; GLACIER; SEISMICS. *See also* CONTINENTS, FORMATION OF.

Further Reading

McPhee, John, *Annals of the Former World* (2000); Ollier, Cliff, *The Origins of Mountains* (2000); Wessels, Tom, *The Granite Landscape: A Natural History of America's Mountain Domes, From Acadia to Yosemite* (2001).

First see NEURON

Multiple Sclerosis

Next see GENE THERAPY

Disease in which there is a destruction of segments of myelin, the substance that covers and protects nerve fibers in the spinal cord and brain.

The cause of multiple sclerosis (MS) is unknown, but it is believed to be an autoimmune disorder, in which the body's immune system mistakenly attacks its own tissue. The disease usually begins its onset in the early adult years. Its symptoms vary, depending on which nerves lose their protective cover. If these nerves are in the spinal cord, the disease can cause numbness, tingling, or a constrictive feeling in any part of the body, sometimes accompanied by stiffness. The arms and legs may feel heavy and weak. If nerve cells in the brain are attacked, the result can be dizziness, fatigue, muscle weakness, clumsy movements, vision difficulties, and slurred speech. These effects can continue for weeks or months, and their severity also can vary widely.

Some individuals have long periods free of ill effects, with only occasional attacks. Others can have gradual but steady deterioration, while in some cases there may be a steady, relentless progression of the disease. There is no single diagnostic test for multiple sclerosis. Several neurological tests may be done, including examination of a sample of fluid from the spinal cord and magnetic resonance imaging of the brain. Treatment can include the use of corticosteroid drugs to ease the effects of an acute attack and other drugs to control specific symptoms. Some patients can be helped by physical therapy, which can strengthen muscles.

First see VIRUS

Mumps

Next see PHARMACOLOGY

A viral disease that usually occurs during childhood.

Mumps' most prominent symptom is inflammation and swelling of the salivary glands on one or both sides of the face, although it can also cause facial pain, fever, headache, and difficulty swallowing for several days. The fever will subside after two or three days and the swelling will go down after a week to ten days. If mumps strikes a man after puberty, one or both of the testes may become inflamed. If a single testis is affected, it will shrink to smaller than normal. If both are affected, sterility may result in a very small percentage of cases. In rare cases, meningitis may occur, causing headache, drowsiness, and fever. If infection occurs, there is an incubation period of two to three weeks before symptoms appear. The mumps virus spreads from person to person in airborne droplets.

Treatment. There is an effective vaccine against mumps that usually is given in combination with vaccines for measles and rubella in the second year of life. The availability of the vaccine has drastically reduced the incidence of mumps. In the mid-1960s, before the vaccine became available, there were more than 150,000 cases of mumps each year in the United States. Today, there are only a few thousand cases annually. The incidence remains high in less developed countries, where the vaccine is not widely available. There is no specific treatment for mumps, but a child with the disease usually is given painkilling drugs and plenty of water to drink. (*See* DISEASE, INFECTIOUS.)

First see ADENOSINE TRIPHOSPHATE (ATP)

Muscle

Next see MUSCLE SYSTEMS

Tissue that shortens or contacts when stimulated and then returns to its original shape.

Skeletal muscle includes red and white muscle fibers. Red (or slow-twitch) fibers are relatively slow to contract and even slower to tire. In some cases, they simply maintain muscle tone. They gain their color from myoglobin, a hemoglobin-like molecule. White (fast-twitch) fibers contract rapidly but tire more quickly. In chickens, dark and light meat is composed of red and white muscle fibers, respectively. Like chickens, humans also have legs rich in red fibers, for standing, walking, and maintaining posture without fatigue, and upper limbs that show more white fiber, for quicker movements. Muscles in general are a mix of red, white, and intermediate types.

Skeletal muscles are composed of long, multinucleate muscle fibers, each made up of hundreds to thousands of myofibrils. Each myofibril is composed largely of two protein compounds: thick filaments of myosin alternate and overlap with thin filaments of actin. Striations are caused by light bands, called I bands, containing actin filaments; dark bands, called A bands, containing myosin filaments and the ends of the overlapping actin filaments; and Z discs, where the actin filaments attach. From one Z disc to the next is a sarcomere, the basic unit of muscle contraction. The myosin molecules in the thick filaments consist of a double helix with two free heads at one end. The protruding heads, called cross bridges, reach up toward the actin filaments.

Activity. Muscle contraction begins when an action potential or nerve impulse travels along a motor nerve to its ending on the muscle fibers, where the nerve secretes the neurotransmitter acetylchloline. As a result, sodium ions flow to the inside of the muscle fiber, creating an action potential in the fiber. This causes the sarcoplasmic reticulum to release large amounts of calcium ions into the myofibrils. The calcium stimulates the cross bridges of the myosin filaments to bend toward the actin, hook into it, and pull it, sliding the two kinds of filaments together so the overlap between them increases greatly. The energy for the contraction comes from the myosin heads' cleaving of ATP (adenosine triphosphate) to form ADP (adenosine diphosphate).

A similar interplay of myosin and actin filaments causes contractions in smooth muscle, but the components are arranged differently and the process is prolonged. Each single smooth muscle contraction lasts an average of one to three seconds, about 30 times as long as a single contraction of an average skeletal muscle. The stimulation mechanism is also different. Smooth muscle contractions may be stimulated by autonomic nerve fibers that secrete neurotransmitters near, but not directly into, the muscle fibers, as well as by hormones and by local factors, such as oxygen or carbon dioxide concentrations in nearby tissues.

Cardiac muscle includes atrial and ventricular muscle that contracts much like skeletal muscle, although for longer duration. In addition, cardiac muscle includes specialized excitatory and conductive fibers that contract only weakly.

Special topics in this area are found in MUSCLE SYSTEMS; NERVOUS SYSTEM; SKELETAL SYSTEMS. *Advanced subjects are developed in* ADENOSINE TRIPHOSPHATE (ATP); LOCOMOTION; METABOLISM. *Additional aspects of this subject are covered in* NEUROTRANSMITTERS AND RECEPTORS; PROTEIN METABOLISM; STEROID HORMONES.

First see MUSCLE

Muscle Systems

Next see LOCOMOTION

In many invertebrates, muscle fibers in the body wall are arranged in two layers: one longitudinal, one circular. When the longitudinal muscles contract, the animal's body shortens; when the circular muscles relax, its body lengthens. If the longitudinal muscles contract more on one side than the other, the body bends toward the contraction. This pattern is seen in animals as simple as the hydra, which does not have separate muscle cells but has contractile muscle fibers within the epithelial cells that form its two-cell thick body wall. The outer layer of cells, or ectoderm, contains longitudinal fibers, the inner layer, or endoderm, contains the circular contractile fibers. Other members of the phylum *Cnidaria* or *Coelenterata*, include jellyfish, which swim weakly by contracting and relaxing their contractile cells, and sea anemones, which

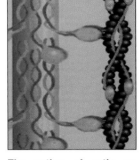

The action of actin on the myofilaments. The release of ATP-bound energy causes the troponin (brown ovals) to vibrate, shortening the fiber.

Further Reading
Field, Derek, *Anatomy and Human Movement: Structure and Function* (1998); Gray, Henry, *Anatomy of the Human Body* (1997); McMahaon, Thomas A., *Muscles, Reflexes, and Locomotion* (1984); Stone, Robert J., *Atlas of Skeletal Muscles* (1997).

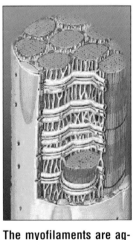

The myofilaments are aggregated into myofibral strands, which in turn compose a muscle fiber. Thus, muscles can only contract or relax, never expand—they can pull, but do not push.

have specialized muscles that allow them to contract their bodies tightly as a protective measure.

Complex Systems. More complex animals have a third, thicker layer of cells between the ectoderm and endoderm. This mesoderm forms the muscles, as well as other structures such as reproductive organs. Among the simplest of animals with mesoderms are planarians, small waterborne flatworms. Along with longitudinal and circular layers of muscles, flatworms have a tubular, complexly muscled pharynx that can be extended out through the mouth to feed on prey.

Invertebrates. Other invertebrates also rely on specialized muscles. The clam moves, albeit slowly, by extending its foot, anchoring it, and then contracting its foot muscles, dragging its body along. For protection, its shell is held tightly closed by two large muscles.

Segmented worms or annelids, such as earthworms, have circular and longitudinal muscle layers around a fluid-filled body separated into segments. The body fluid acts as a hydrostatic skeleton around which the muscles contract. The walls between the body segments, when compressed, prevent the fluid from merely moving into another part of the body, which would dissipate the force of the contraction. Instead, the force is concentrated within each segment. The worm can move by peristalsis: waves of contraction that ripple down its body, shortening one segment while lengthening another.

Most annelids, however, are not earthworms, but marine worms. In some cases, their bodies are too rigid to shorten and lengthen. Instead, some have extra muscles that flex the body wall for burrowing. The muscles also move parapods, footlike projections that stick out of the sides of each body segment and assist in swimming, crawling, and burrowing.

Arthropods, which include nearly a million described species of insects, crustaceans, and arachnids, have a tough, flexible external skeleton to which the muscles are attached. Rods of cuticle also extend into the body for muscle attachment. The muscles are grouped in bundles, rather than arranged in the continuous layers seen in annelids. They include longitudinal and circular muscles as well as others that run in various directions, allowing a wider range of movement. In arthropods, all muscles—even the muscles of the digestive system—are striated, which means they can contract rapidly. In many other invertebrates, all muscles are smooth, suited for slow contraction and endurance. In vertebrates, skeletal muscles are striated, but digestive-system and other visceral muscles are smooth.

Vertebrates. The skeletal muscle system in vertebrates opens the eyes, moves the legs, flaps the wings, raises the arms, and wags the tail. Working with connective tissue and bone, it makes possible virtually every externally oriented activity, from walking to mating to breathing.

Skeletal muscles in vertebrates are enmeshed in a web of connective tissue. The endomysium, which surrounds individual muscle fibers, is continuous with the perimysium, which divides the muscle into bundles of fiber. That, in turn, is continuous with the epimysium, which surrounds the overall muscle and merges with tendons, tough cords of collagen that attach the muscle to bone, and with fascia, loose connective tissues that link muscle to muscle and skin to muscle. This connective net helps shape the muscles and transmits their forces to the bones they move.

Another form of connective tissue, strong flat sheets called aponeuroses, anchor those muscles that do not connect to bone, such as some abdominal muscles in mammals. But in most cases, one end of the muscle, called the origin, is fixed to bone and is not free to move. The other end, called the insertion, is also attached to bone but is free to move.

Muscles can only pull and cannot push. To provide range of motion, muscles that bend a joint, as the biceps bend the elbow, are paired with muscles that straighten it, as the triceps do for the elbow. Opposing muscles are called antagonists. Muscles that supplement each other are called synergists. Most functional movements, such as walking or picking up an object, require the coordination of many muscle groups, and most involve the simultaneous contracting of antagonistic muscles.

Typically, one muscle group—called the prime mover—will contract strongly and be offset by a weaker opposing contraction. This provides fine-tuning of a motion. Antagonists also commonly work together to stabilize a joint; muscles in this role are called fixators. In many cases, bones work as levers with the joint as the fulcrum. In general, the force of a muscle is inversely related to the amount and speed of movement it causes.

First see MUTATION, GENETIC

Mutagens and Carcinogens

Next see CANCER

Mutagens are physical or chemical agents that can increase the rate of mutation in living cells. Carcinogens are agents capable of causing cancer.

The most important mutagens are chemicals and ionizing radiation, including x-rays and emissions from nuclear explosions, radioactive fallout, and other sources of radiation. The largest group of carcinogens are chemicals, among which are the polycyclic aromatic hydrocarbons that are found in tobacco smoke, soot, and tar fumes. Another major group of chemical carcinogens are the aromatic amines, used in the rubber and chemical industries. High-energy radiation, the class of mutagens mentioned

above, are also carcinogens. High doses of radiation can cause malignant changes in cells, causing them to divide endlessly. Even sunlight can be a carcinogen because of its ultraviolet radiation; over many years, exposure to sunlight can cause skin cancer.

Biological Carcinogens. There are several biological carcinogens. Some of them are viruses. For example, the papilloma virus is believed to be a cause of cancer of the cervix, while the hepatitis B virus has been linked to liver cancer. The cause of Burkitt's lymphoma, a cancer of the jaw and abdomen that occurs in African children, has been identified as the Epstein-Barr virus, while the cancer known as Kaposi's sarcoma is believed to be caused by the human immunodeficiency virus, HIV, which causes AIDS.

Among other infectious agents that are believed to cause cancer are *Schistosoma haematobium*, a blood fluke that is found in Africa and is responsible for the tropical disease schistosomiasis; it can also cause cancer of the bladder, the organ of the body where it lays its eggs. *Aspergillus*, a fungus that grows in stored grain and peanuts, produces a poison called aflatoxin, which has been implicated in liver cancer.

Carcinogenic Foods. Some common foods increase the risk of cancer. Salt-cured, smoked, and nitrite-cured foods, which include bacon, sausage, and ham, have been linked to a higher risk of cancer of the esophagus and cancer of the stomach. High-fat foods have also been linked to cancer of the prostate, colon, and rectum. Drinking large amounts of alcohol over a long period of time can increase the risk of liver cancer, while combining alcohol with either chewing or smoking tobacco increases the risk of cancer of the mouth, larynx, throat, and esophagus.

Known industrial carcinogens generally are banned, but their use may be allowed under careful controls if exposure to them is limited, as long as workers get periodic physical examinations and other protective measures. Substances that could be carcinogens are screened before they are allowed to be manufactured. One widely used test exposes a strain of bacteria to the suspected carcinogen to determine whether it causes possibly dangerous mutations. The substance can be tested further on animals to see whether it causes an increased incidence of abnormal growths; if it does, it is banned.

First see GENE

Mutation, Genetic

Next see DNA

A change in an organism's genes caused by a change in the organism's DNA.

A gene is found along one or the other strand of the DNA duplex. Each gene begins with a specific sequence known as the promoter region and ends with the terminator region. A structural gene contains information for the amino acid sequence of a protein. This information is "transcribed" to form a molecule of messenger RNA (mRNA), which is translated to form a protein. The product of a regulatory gene controls the expression of structural genes, either allowing transcription to take place or blocking it.

Spontaneous mutations are those that result during the normal course of cellular activities, or through some random interaction with the environment. The exact rate of spontaneous mutations, called the background level, is specific to a particular organism. Such mutations are relatively rare in nature.

Mutagens are compounds that increase the rate of mutation; the mutations they cause are called induced mutations. Mutagens modify a particular base of the DNA sequence, or are themselves incorporated into the nucleic acid chain. Many mutagens are in fact chemical "cousins" of the conventional DNA bases.

Point Mutations. Any base pair can undergo a mutation. A point mutation is a change in a single base pair. Either a chemical modification has occurred to transform one base into another, or the wrong base was introduced during DNA replication. Sometimes the mistake can be rectified by the removal of the modified or incorrect base. Ligase, an enzyme used to connect adjacent bases in the polynucleotide chain, removes incorrectly paired bases.

Point mutations fall into one of two categories:

Transition—the substitution of one pyrimidine for another, or one purine for another. The net effect is the replacement of a G-C pair with an A-T or, more commonly, vice versa;

Transversion—the substitution of a purine for a pyrimidine, or a pyrimidine for a purine. The net effect is the replacement of an A-T pair with a T-A or C-G, or vice versa.

Nitrous acid is a well-known mutagen. It can transform cytosine into uracil, a pyrimidine virtually identical to thymine that is found exclusively in RNA, never DNA. Once cytosine has been changed into uracil, the net effect is to replace a C-G pair with a T-A. Nitrous acid also works on adenine, deaminating it (removing an amino group) and thereby transforming adenine into guanine. The net effect is the substitution of an A-T pair with G-C.

Susceptibility to Mutations. Mutations frequently occur when an abnormal base is present. Some mutagens are analogs of normal bases and have structures which allow them to pair up with different partners. For example, bromouracil, an analog of thymine, can pair either with adenine or guanine. Mutation "hot spots" are base sites that are more susceptible to mutation, usually due to the presence of these abnormal bases. In general, susceptibility to mutation is proportional to the size of the gene.

A point mutation affects only one base, and therefore does not have far-reaching consequences in most cases. When DNA is used to make a particular protein, every three bases constitute a unit known as a codon, which signifies a particular amino acid. Therefore, a point mutation will at most affect one amino acid in the entire protein chain. However, sickle-cell anemia is an example of a change in just one amino acid in a protein chain that does have drastic consequences. The protein involved is hemoglobin, which carries oxygen within red blood cells. In sickle-cell anemia, the altered protein results in abnormal or "sickle-shaped" red blood cells, which tend to obstruct small blood vessels, leading to pain crises and organ damage.

Other Types. In some cases, as a result of a built-in redundancy in the code (more than one codon is used to signify a particular amino acid), there is no change in the protein product at all. "Leaky" mutations are mutations in which some residual function has been retained.

A frame-shift mutation involves insertions or deletions of bases within the DNA sequence. From the point of mutation onwards, every single codon, and therefore every single amino acid, has been affected. The resulting protein will be vastly different from what was intended. In many cases, there will be a severely truncated protein with only residual function.

A forward mutation inactivates a particular gene. It can be reversed by a "back mutation," which may consist of an actual reversal of the original mutation, or by what is known as a second-site reversion, which is a second mutation elsewhere that compensates for the first mutation. The second site affected may be in the same gene, or in another gene entirely.

The vast number of mutations are silent, that is, they cannot be detected with the naked eye. Of those that are noticeable, the vast majority are benign; of the small percentage that are not, some are fatal and others may be beneficial.

Within a multicellular organism, mutations that occur within somites, ordinary body cells, are not passed on to the next generation. Only mutations in the germ cells, sperm, and eggs have the potential of being inherited, and then only if the mutation is of a type that does not affect the viability of the sex cells and interfere with their ability to form a healthy embryo.

Sickle-cell anemia is the result of a mutation that impairs the ability of the red blood cells' hemoglobin to carry oxygen.

Further developments in the field are discussed in ADAPTATION; GENE; GENETIC CODE; REPRODUCTIVE SYSTEMS. *Further details regarding mutations can be found in* DNA REPLICATION; EVOLUTION; MUTAGENS AND CARCINOGENS. *Additional relevant information is contained in* AGING; ANTI-OXIDANTS; EXONS AND INTRONS; GENETIC DISEASE. *See also* RADIATION *and* INTERFERON AND INTERLEUKINS.

Further Reading
De Duve, Christian, *Blueprint for a Cell: The Nature and Origin of Life* (1991); King, John, *The Genetic Basis of Plant Physiological Processes* (1991); Rensberger Boyce, *Life Itself* (1996); Resnick, David, *Human Germline Gene Therapy* (1999); Thomas, Lewis, *The Lives of a Cell: Notes of a Biology Watcher* (1995).

Nanotechnology

First see MOLECULE

Next see ARTIFICIAL INTELLIGENCE

Nanotechnology's goal is to create machines nanometers in size able to manipulate individual atoms.

One nanometer is a billionth of a meter, the length of three or four atoms lined up in a row. Technicians using scanning tunneling microscopes and atomic force microscopes have taken some first steps: spelling out "IBM," using 35 Xenon atoms; constructing an abacus (non-functioning) three molecules thick; and forging Buckytubes, each a few nanometers in diameter. A tiny motor has been set in motion, although its torque was slight at best. However, these feats of nanoengineering have only been achieved in vacuums at temperatures just a few degrees above absolute zero. (*See* SCANNING TUNNELING MICROSCOPE; BUCKMINISTERFULLERENES.)

Scientists have defined two basic challenges that must be met for nanotechnology to become a viable technology: positional control and self-replication. Tiny rods of graphite have been produced, which can exert a force of 10 Newtons. But to work effectively, "tripods" and "crankshafts" must be built to allow precise positional control.

A single nanomachine, working on one molecule at a time, would take billions of years to make an object visible to the naked eye. With replication, however, many machines could work in parallel, greatly reducing the time required. Once self-replication has been achieved, scientists will turn to the creation of a super-miniaturized computer. An MIT researcher has already designed a dipole switch (the heart of a digital computer) built with only 90 atoms; if tools were only small enough.

Top, an abacus comprised of individual atoms; bottom, a microtubule made of "fullerened" carbon.

Further Reading
Crandall, B.C., *Nanotechnology: Molecular Speculations on Global Abundance* (1996); Gross, M., *Travels to the Nanoworld: Miniature Machinery in Nature and Technology* (1999); Regis, Edward, *Nano: The Emerging Science of Nanotechnology* (1996); Timp, G., *Nanotechnology* (1999).

Natural Selection

First see ADAPTATION

Next see EVOLUTION

One of the processes of evolution. Based on environmental conditions and demands, certain individuals have an inherent natural advantage over others—it is they who are "selected" to survive.

Rudyard Kipling explained how the giraffe got its long neck in his *Just So Stories*. Lamarck's theory of natural selection sounds very similar—the giraffe's neck gradually stretched as the animal strove to reach ever higher tree branches in order to eat the leaves, and this trait was passed on to the offspring. According to Darwin, there naturally existed two varieties of giraffe, those with long necks and those with short necks. As the leaves on the lower tree branches were consumed, the long-necked animals were able to continue feeding, whereas the short-necked ones could not and died of hunger. Long-necked animals therefore lived long enough to produce offspring, who resembled them, unlike their diminutive competitors.

The same phenomenon was seen with the pepper moth population in the North of England around the time of the Industrial Revolution. Originally, the population consisted mostly of gray moths, which were able to conceal themselves better on the light bark of the trees than black moths. But when soot darkened the tree trunks, the gray moths lost their camouflage and became "unfit." In the span of just 20 years in the late 1800s, the population changed to consist mostly of black moths.

Types of Selection. There are three specific types of natural selection: directional, in which evolution proceeds in a specific direction, e.g., towards longer necks; stabilizing, which eliminates the extremes of a trait and causes a reduction in the genetic variation within a population; and disruptive, the opposite of stabilizing, which favors extremes over the average.

Natural selection is an example of microevolution, in which conditions cause slow, gradual changes within a species. Macroevolution refers to the sudden appearance of a totally distinct species. Groups of organisms are subject to natural selection just like individuals, and a disfavored group, unable to compete, will be replaced by a group better suited to the environment.

The foundations of the subject are discussed in ECOLOGY; EVOLUTION; MUTATION, GENETIC. *Further details can be found in* ADAPTATION; COMPETITION AND ALTRUISM; POPULATION ECOLOGY. *Advanced subjects relating to evolution and natural selection are developed in* HOMO SAPIENS; PALEOECOLOGY; PHYLOGENY.

Navigation

First see Avionics

Next see CARTOGRAPHY AND SURVEYING

The science of finding the position, course, and distance traveled by any craft.

Navigational techniques historically include dead reckoning, piloting, celestial navigation, and electronic navigation. These have all been superseded mainly by navigation based on the Global Positioning System, which can be used to determine a location anywhere on Earth within a few feet.

Dead reckoning (the phrase derives from "deduced reckoning") is the oldest method. It consists of keeping track of the course of a ship or aircraft and the distance traveled from the last well-known position through frequent compass readings. The distance that has been traveled is obtained by multiplying the vessel's speed by the elapsed time of travel.

Piloting (or pilotage for aircraft) involves the frequent or continuous determination of position in relation to known geographical points. For vessels, piloting is practiced in confined waters or close to the shore in areas where aids to navigation, known landmarks, and features of the ocean floor are available. In the air, pilotage is done by observing the ground underneath and noting major features, such as towns and cities, railroads and lakes. Light beacons on the ground assist pilotage at night.

Celestial navigation is based on observations of the stars. To determine the vertical and horizontal positions of these celestial bodies, ship navigators use the marine sextant and the compass, while pilots use the bubble sextant and the gyrocompass. (A sextant consists of a fixed telescope pointed at the horizon and a radial arm carrying a mirror that is moved until the image of a fixed star or the sun appears in the mirror. The elevation of the star or the sun gives the latitude.)

Electronic navigation began with radio direction finders, followed by radar, loran, and similar distance-finding techniques. Radio direction finders are simply radio receivers with directional antennas that are used to find the direction of an antenna of known location that is transmitting a signal. More recently, electronic navigation using radio signals transmitted from the Global Positioning System are used to provide continuous, all-weather information available anywhere on the globe.

Navigation and Migration in Nature. The ability of animals to make their way across hundreds or thousands of miles of difficult terrain or open ocean, in many cases precisely locating a place they have never seen, is among the more amazing feats in nature. Yet migration—the periodic, usually seasonal, movement of animal populations to and from specific areas—is an important part of the life cycle of many species.

Migration is chiefly seen among birds, fish,

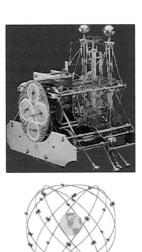

Top, the device built by Harrison (see "The Cutting Edge," below). Current methods for finding one's location employ a network of satellites, circling the globe in six orbital planes, comprising the GPS (Global Positioning System), bottom.

Further Reading

Dernay, Eugene, *Longitudes and Latitudes in the United States* (1986); Farrell, Jay A., *The Global Positioning System* (1998); Sobel, Dava, *Longitude: The True Story of a Lone Genius Who Solved the Greatest Scientific Problem of His Time* (1996); Toghill, Jeff E., *Celestial Navigation* (1988); Toghill, J. E., *Coastal Navigation* (1988).

marine mammals and large, hoofed land mammals, such as caribou and wildebeest, although the migration patterns of many mammals have been disrupted by human development. Migration is thought to have evolved as a way of maximizing an animal's food supply. It allows for seasonal food shortages caused by harsh weather and exploitation of rich temporary feeding ground—such as the Arctic summer's banquet of insect life—that would otherwise go unused.

Most migrating animals commute each year between a warmer range where they winter and a cooler range where they breed in spring. Their journey is triggered largely by seasonal changes in the amount of daylight; some animals prepare for it by building up body fat. In Africa, many animals move in accord with the cycle of wet and dry seasons. Among some sea creatures, including salmon, eels, and turtles, one cycle of migration takes years, sometimes a lifetime.

Many animal journeys seem impossibly strenuous. The Arctic tern, believed to make the longest commute in the animal kingdom, shuttles between the Arctic and Antarctic, a journey of 11,000 miles each way. It has been estimated that to equal the metabolic exertion of a Blackpoll warbler's flight from North to South America a human would have to run a four-minute mile for 80 consecutive hours.

Animal Navigation. Animals appear to use a combination of sensing and mapping systems that may vary among species, or they may navigate by preprogrammed dead reckoning. An example of the latter is the garden warblers in Germany. They head southwest for several weeks, then turn southeast until they reach their nesting and breeding ranges in Africa.

Animals have also been found to use a magnetic compass: they can sense the angle between the Earth's magnetic field and the horizontal plane. Since this angle is sharper at the magnetic poles and flatter toward the equator, it can serve as a way of gauging latitude. Loggerhead sea turtles, for example, know when to turn south as they ride the Gulf Stream from the Florida coast to the Sargasso Sea in the Atlantic. At a point off Portugal, they make a crucial turn, heading south toward their Sargasso feeding grounds rather than north into the fatally cold waters off England. In tanks fitted with artificial magnetic fields, hatchlings swam east when the magnetic field was at a 57-degree angle, as it is at the Florida beaches. When the angle hit 60 degrees—the angle of the Earth's magnetic field at the point of the crucial turn—they headed south.

Some animals act as if they always know their latitude and longitude. In one experiment, a sea bird called a Manx shearwater was taken from the coast of Wales, flown by jet to Boston and released. The bird made it home in 12 and a half days. How it did so remains a mystery. (*See* SENSORY MECHANISMS; UNDERWATER EXPLORATION.)

First see AUSTRALOPITHECUS

Neanderthal

Next see HOMO SAPIENS

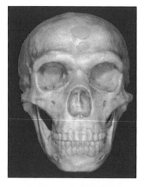

Archaic *Homo sapiens* who lived in Europe and Asia between 130,000 and 35,000 years ago, during the Ice Age. They appeared at the end of the time of an earlier hominid species, *Homo erectus*.

The archaic humans are called Neanderthal after the Neander valley in Germany (*thal* means valley), where fossilized remains were first discovered in 1856. Neanderthals were more robust and much stronger than modern humans. They were about five feet tall and had thick skulls, sloping foreheads, heavy brow ridges, and protruding jaws with large teeth that may have been used as tools. Their cranial capacity was even larger than that of modern humans.

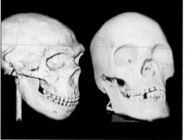

Neanderthals were nomadic hunter-gatherers who lived in caves. They used handheld tools made of bone and stone and wore animal skins. They used fire and exhibited ritual activity such as burial of the dead. It is unknown if they had speech. Some research based on skull structures seems to indicate that they did not have a spoken language; they had a limited ability to produce a wide variety of vowels.

Neanderthals disappeared from the fossil record about 30,000 years ago. These archaic humans may have evolved into modern humans, or may simply have become extinct due to competition with the new species.

Fossils of anatomically modern humans, formerly called Cro-Magnon, were discovered in 1868 in the Cro-Magnon Cave in France. Some of these early modern humans show primitive skeletal characteristics, like large brows and teeth, which may be holdovers from interbreeding with Neanderthals. Otherwise they are not physically distinguishable from humans living today. Cro-Magnons exhibited a complex culture and social organization with the use of sophisticated tools.

Anatomically modern humans appear to have arisen outside Europe, possibly originating in Africa. They may have coexisted with their more primitive forebears for tens of thousands of years. Whether Cro-Magnon and Neanderthal interbred is an open question.

Top, skull of *Homo sapiens neanderthalensis*, an early human that appeared between 40,000 and 100,000 years ago (reconstructed at bottom). Middle, what happened to Neanderthals (left skull) is still in doubt, and how they were supplanted by *Homo sapiens* (right skull) is a subject of current research.

Further Reading

Gooch, Stan, *The Neanderthal Question* (1989); Kennedy, Kenneth A. R., *Neanderthal Man* (1997); Shackley, Myra L., *Neanderthal Man* (1996); Shackley, Myra, *Still Living?: Yeti, Sasquatch and the Neanderthal Enigma* (1995); Solecki, Ralph S., *Shanidar; the Humanity of Neanderthal Man* (1992).

Elementary aspects of this subject are covered in EVOLUTION; GEOLOGICAL TIME SCALE; ICE AGE. *More information on particular aspects can be found in* AUSTRALOPITHECUS; FOSSIL; HOMO SAPIENS; PRIMATES. *Additional relevant information is contained in* EXTINCTION; NATURAL SELECTION; SPECIATION.

First See TELESCOPE

Nebula

Next See GALAXY

A nebula was originally defined by astronomers as a fixed, extended, fuzzy white haze that could be observed with a telescope. It is now defined as an interstellar cloud of gas or dust.

Many of the originally identified nebulae can now be resolved into clouds of stars or galaxies; they are sometimes referred to as extragalactic nebulae. The variety of nebulae includes gaseous nebulae, planetary nebulae, reflection nebulae, and dark nebulae.

Gaseous nebulae cannot be resolved into individual stars. They consist mostly of gas and dust that lie between the stars. Gaseous nebulae include the emission nebulae, such as the Orion Nebula and the Eta Carinae Nebula. When a very hot star rich in ultraviolet radiation is located in or very near a cloud of interstellar gas, this cloud becomes an emission nebula. These exceedingly large, tenuous gas clouds are composed mostly of hydrogen atoms (65 percent), helium atoms (making up most of the remaining 35 percent), and oxygen, calcium, sodium, potassium, and titanium (in traces).

The Orion Nebula is 1,500 to 1,600 light-years from the sun, with a main body that measures about 25 light-years across. It contains a mass of gas about 300 times greater than the mass of the sun. Observations by radio astronomers and special photographic equipment have shown that the Orion Nebula is an unusual-

The nebula above (the Horseshoe Nebula) is comprised of stars, gas, and dark matter that cover vast distances.

ly bright island in a vast gaseous complex, with a mass perhaps 100,000 times that of the sun and a diameter of at least 300 light-years.

The Orion Nebula and other emission nebulae shine by absorbing and re-emitting radiation from very hot blue-white stars. The hydrogen atoms in the nebulae absorb ultraviolet radiation from the stars, and split into protons and electrons. The visual radiation emitted by the nebulae results from the radiation given up by each electron as it drops back to a normal energy state. Studies of the radiation thus emitted indicate that a typical emission nebula contains about 1,000 atoms per square inch at its densest point.

To astronomers using small telescopes planetary nebulae appear as discs having some resemblance to the planets Uranus and Neptune. But these nebulae are far distant from the solar system. They are formed by an unusually bright zone that lies within a huge cloud of gas surrounding a hot blue star. The atoms in this cloud of gas absorb energy from the ultraviolet radiation emitted by the star, and then re-emit this energy as visible light. The most luminous gases in a planetary nebula are hydrogen and oxygen. Planetary nebulae are always connected with a star that has become a nova in the past, throwing off material in the process of undergoing a partial explosion. The planetary nebula consists of the material thrown off by the star. Planetary nebulae are usually symmetrical, forming an expanding shell around the central star. The Ring Nebula is an outstanding example.

Clouds of Dust. Reflection nebulae are clouds of cosmic dust that shine by reflecting light from a relatively cool star or group of stars embedded in the cloud. One example is the Pleiades star cluster, which has an associated cloud of cosmic dust. Inside this cloud, astronomers can make out delicately striped nebulous structures, seen on long-exposure photographs.

The spectrums of light emitted by reflection nebulae are similar to those of the stars embedded within them, with differences caused by the fact that the blue and red light wavelengths of the star are not reflected equally. In addition, the light from these stars is reddened considerably. Astronomers have used these color effects to determine the diameter of the cosmic dust particles of the nebulae; they are on the order of .00001 of an inch. The degree of reflectivity of the nebulae also indicates that the particles most likely are made of simple molecular combinations of hydrogen with carbon, oxygen, and nitrogen; they can be described essentially as tiny ice particles.

Dark nebulae are collections of tiny cosmic dust particles between stars. They do not emit light but are seen as dark markings across the bright parts of the Milky Way. One example is the Horsehead Nebula. Dark nebulae are of interest to astronomers because astronomers believe that they are in the process of condensing to form new stars.

Related material on nebulae will be found in GALAXY; STAR; UNIVERSE, LARGE-SCALE STRUCTURE OF. Other aspects of the subject are discussed in GLOBULAR CLUSTER; INTERSTELLAR MEDIUM ("DARK MATTER"); UNIVERSE, EVOLUTION OF. Additional relevant material can be found in HUBBLE CONSTANT; NOVA, SUPERNOVA; NUCLEOSYNTHESIS.

Top, the "Pillars of Creation" nebula (M16) in the constellation Serpens, is believed to be a spawning ground for stars. Bottom, the sagiattarius star cloud that includes two other nebulae: the Lagoon Nebula and the Triffid Nebula.

Above, Neptune, as seen by *Voyager 2*, glimmering blue in space because of its methane atmosphere.

Further Reading
Elmegreen, Debra Meloy, *Galaxies and Galactic Structures* (1998); King, Ivan R., *The Milky Way As a Galaxy* (1996); Malin, Stuart, *The Greenwich Guide to Stars, Galaxies and Nebulae* (1990); Milton, Simon, *Crab Nebula* (1993); Simon, Seymour, *Galaxies* (1991).

First see JUPITER

Neptune

Next see URANUS

Neptune, the eighth planet from the sun, is still something of a mystery because of its great distance from the Earth. But our knowledge has improved thanks to *Voyager 2*, which passed within 3,000 miles of Neptune in 1989. It is invisible to the naked eye and can only be seen as a "star" of the eighth magnitude through telescopes, with a fuzzy blue-green appearance due to the presence of large amounts of methane gas in its atmosphere. Neptune was discovered in the nineteenth century because the orbit of Uranus, its neighboring planet, deviated from its predicted orbit. Two astronomers, John Couch Adams in England and Urbain Leverrier in France, explained the deviations as the result of the gravitational effects of a then unknown planet. That planet, Neptune, was found in 1846 by the German astronomer Johann Galle.

Neptune makes a complete orbit around the sun every 165 years, at an average distance from the sun of 2.794 billion miles. Neptune has an extensive atmosphere made up mostly of hydrogen and helium, with some methane. The presence of methane has enabled astronomers to take pictures of the planet using infrared light, which is absorbed by that gas. Those pictures show bands of clouds in the middle latitudes and perhaps storms that are analogous to Earth's tornadoes. While the atmosphere is dense, with pressures approaching 200,000 times those of Earth's atmosphere, it constitutes only a small part of the mass of Neptune. Astronomical studies and experiments in laboratories indicate that Neptune is composed mostly of rock and ice. That ice is not pure water; it is believed to contain large amounts of ammonia and methane. The average density of Neptune has been calculated to be 2.29 times that of water.

Neptune rotates rapidly on its axis. Its magnetic field rotates once every 16.1 hours, while the cloud layers rotate anywhere from 12 to 18 hours. It has been estimated that the jet streams on Neptune reach speeds of 1,500 miles per hour. Because its magnetic field is tilted some 46 degrees from its axis, Neptune's climate is quite variable. It appears to undergo seasonal changes similar to those that occur on Earth, with large storm systems appearing and disappearing rapidly.

Another mystery about Neptune stems from the observation that the planet emits large amounts of energy in the form of infrared radiation. Neptune emits more than twice as much

First see CELLULAR AUTOMATA

Neural Network

Next see ARTIFICIAL INTELLIGENCE

Neural networks reflect the most successful strategy in the development of Artificial Intelligence. Also called "evolvable hardware," neural networks are designed to learn from their experience, becoming faster and "smarter" as time goes by. The secret lies in software that allows the computer to tackle several parts of a problem at the same time, shuttling data back and forth until a solution emerges—more or less what humans do. This is in sharp contrast to the "brute force" method used by most computer software, relying on a step-by-step approach that considers every possible consequence. Significantly, the "Deep Blue" computer that beat Gary Kasparov in a chess match was equipped with neural network capability, and thereby avoided the time-consuming consideration of unproductive moves that had doomed its predecessor in a previous match.

The theory of neural networks was set forth by Warren McCulloch and Walter Pitts in the 1940s, long before any practical use could be thought of. They recognized that human brains process information in two different ways: not only do they absorb data and manipulate it in their short-term memory, they also compare it to similar data contained in long-term memory.

Neural networks in current use employ pattern recognition software that enables them to spot anomalies: changes in credit card use that might signal a stolen card; uneven temperature patterns in a steel furnace; or indications that an x-ray may have revealed a tumor or lesion. Future neural networks may perform tasks as brutal as mining ore, or as delicate as sorting fruit.

> *Background material on neural networks can be found in* BRAIN; CELLULAR AUTOMATA; COMPUTER, DIGITAL. *More details can be found in* CONTROL SYSTEMS; ROBOTICS; SERVOMECHANISMS. *Additional relevant information is contained in* PARALLEL COMPUTING; PATTERN AND OCR RECOGNITION; SUPERCOMPUTER.

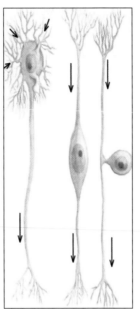

Above, three varieties of neuron design. From left, an efferant (motor) neuron; a bipolar hybrid (having qualities of motor and sensory neurons); an afferent (sensory) neuron. There are many others.

Further Reading
Jefferis, David, *Artificial Intelligence: Robotics and Machine Evolution* (1999); Lewis, F.L., *Neural Network Control of Robot Manipulators and Non-Linear Systems* (1999); Omidvar, Omid, *Neural Systems for Control* (1997).

First see CELL

Neuron

Next see NERVOUS SYSTEM

The nervous system is responsible for control of body activities. Nerves, brain, and spinal cord are all composed of specialized cells called neurons.

The main portion of a neuron is the cell body, with dendrites, fibers that resemble tree branches, projecting from one end. Extending from the cell body on the other side is a long fiber known as the axon, which also ends in branched fibers.

The message, or electrical impulse, received by the neuron originates at the dendrites and from there is carried to the cell body, the axon, and the axionic fibers. When the message reaches the end of the first neuron there is a space, called the synapse or synaptic gap, before the dendrites of the second neuron. The message itself does not cross the synapse. Instead, the nodes on the axionic fibers release a chemical called a neurotransmitter, which flows across the gap and touches the dendrites of the next neuron, causing the continuation of the impulse.

There are many different neurotransmitters. The most prominent ones include acetylcholine, serotonin, and dopamine. Parkinson's disease is a disorder caused by a shortage of dopamine.

Some neurons contain extra attachments on the axon called glial cells, which causes the message transmission to be speeded up. One type of glial cell is the Schwann cell, also called a myelinated sheath because it contains myelin, a type of lipid. Glial cells outnumber the neurons ten to one. The glial cells do not entirely cover the axon; there are small gaps between them called nodes of Ranvier. Transmission of the impulse is faster because it jumps from one node of Ranvier to the next, instead of proceeding along the entire length of the axon.

Nature of the Impulse. The impulse is electrical in nature. Ions contained within and around the neural membrane include sodium, potassium, and calcium, all of which are positively charged, and chloride, which is negatively charged. Before the impulse begins, the neuron is said to be in resting state or polarized. All the positive ions are outside the neural membrane, and all the negative ones are on the inside. To transmit the impulse, the ions cross over to reverse this pattern, resulting in a wave of depolarization. Once the impulse has passed, the neuron is completely depolarized, and it must be restored to a resting state to send a new impulse.

The sodium-potassium pump is the mechanism by which the neuron is repolarized. The ions are "pumped back" across the membrane to return to their original positions. The calcium ions are not pumped, but flow through special channels within the membrane.

The threshold is the minimum level of intensity an impulse must be at in order to be transmitted, approximately 0.5 microvolts. Below this level no impulse at all will be sent. The "All or None Law" states that an individual neuron must either be completely polarized or depolarized. There is no in-between state of "half-depolarization." Of course, different numbers of individual neurons may depolarize at any time.

Types of Neurons. There are three types of neurons: sensory to detect a stimulus; associative or connective to connect between sensory and motor neurons; and motor neurons to cause a response to a stimulus.

A stimulus is a message or signal from the external environment. A response is a reaction to the stimulus. If the response is automatic, or involuntary, it is called a reflex. What distinguishes a reflex from a voluntary response is the fact that the brain is not notified until after the fact. For example, when a person touches a hot stove, a sensory neuron in the fingertip detects the stimulus and sends a message to an associative neuron located in the spinal cord. The associative neuron in turn sends a message to a motor neuron in the finger, directing it to order a muscle fiber to contract, thereby causing movement. Only then does the associative neuron report to the brain what has transpired. The person finds that the hand have moved without the person having been aware of what was going on.

The connection between a motor neuron and a muscle fiber is called the neuromuscular plate. Electrical stimuli from the motor neuron is what causes the muscle fiber to contract.

Ganglions are clusters of cell bodies that coordinate incoming and outgoing impulses. Nerves are bundles of axons. Gray matter, found in the brain and spinal cord, also consists of clusters of cell bodies. White matter, present in the central nervous system, consists of the axon components of neurons.

> *Background material can be found in* CELL; CELLULAR MEMBRANE; EYES AND VISION; NERVOUS SYSTEMS. *Advanced subjects are developed in* BRAIN; NEUROTRANSMITTERS AND RECEPTORS; SENSORY MECHANISMS. *Further aspects of this subject are covered in* CHARGE AND CURRENT; CYSTIC FIBROSIS; EPILEPSY.

First see NEURON

Neurotransmitters and Receptors

Next see NERVOUS SYSTEM

Neurotransmitters are chemicals that are released by neurons for the purpose of carrying signals to neighboring cells. Receptors are the parts of cells that receive signals and convert them into nerve impulses.

In a neural pathway, an electrical signal is conveyed along a nerve cell's axon until the fiber ends in a multitude of tiny branches, each capped by a synaptic terminal. To be passed on to the next neuron—or to a muscle, gland, or other target organ—the signal must be conveyed across a tiny cleft. The vehicle of this passage is a neurotransmitter, a short-lived secretion that is released from the synaptic terminal of the first cell, binds to receptors on the next cell, and is quickly destroyed or pumped back into the terminals.

Synaptic connections are highly complex and sensitive. Because they are crucial to the processing of information—to thought, memory, emotion, and sensory perception—research has focused intensively on this area in recent years. Psychiatric disorders have been linked to lapses at the synapses; for instance, forms of depression and schizophrenia have been found to correlate with abnormal levels of the neurotransmitters serotonin and dopamine, respectively. The research has produced some of the most heavily used drugs in the U.S. The anti-depressant Prozac (fluoxetine hydrochloride) magnifies the effects of serotonin by delaying its reabsorption.

Besides serotinin and dopamine, common neurotransmitters in vertebrates include acetylcholine, which is involved in voluntary muscle movement; noradrenaline (also called norepinephrine), which increases heartbeat, blood pressure, and mental alertness; nitric oxide, endorphins, GABA (gamma-aminobutyric acid), glycine, and glutamate.

Neurotransmitters generally have either an excitatory or an inhibitory effect depending on the receptor. If the target cell is another neuron, it will either fire or not fire—its response is all or nothing—depending on whether it receives more excitatory or inhibitory impulses.

Not all synaptic connections are direct. Neuropeptides, which include serotonin and noradrenalin, use a "second-messenger" system. Instead of directly provoking a physiologic change in the target cell, they cause the cell to form a second messenger—usually cyclic AMP—which produces the response. Second-messenger systems generally cause longer-term changes in postsynaptic neurons; as a result they are thought to figure in memory and learning.

Synaptic connections can be shaped before they occur, by presynaptic inhibition or facilitation. In such cases, interneurons—neurons specialized for integrating inputs—release a neurotransmitter into presynaptic cleft. If this neurotransmitter is inhibitory, the presynaptic neuron releases less of its own neurotransmitter. If the neurotransmitter is excitatory, the presynaptic neuron will release more of its own transmitter. By this means, neural impulses from certain sources can be minimized or amplified.

> *Background material can be found in* CELL MEMBRANE; NEURON; NERVOUS SYSTEMS. *Advanced subjects are developed in* BRAIN; BREATHING REGULATION; REFLEXES. *More information on particular aspects is contained in* CONDITIONING; PARKINSON'S DISEASE; RETICULAR ACTIVATING SYSTEM.

Further Reading
Deecke, L., *From Neuron to Action* (1991); Juergen, Mai K., *Atlas of the Human Brain* (1997); Leigh, P. N., *Motor Neuron Disease: Biology and Management* (1995); Parasuraman, Raja, *The Attentive Brain* (1998); Williams, A.C. *Motor Neuron Disease* (1993).

Further Reading
Hanin, Israel, *Dynamics of Neurotransmitter Function* (1983); Masters, R. D., *The Neurotransmitter Revolution: Serotonin, Social Behavior, and the Law* (1994); Nicholls, D. G., *Proteins, Transmitters and Synapses* (1994); Restack, R. M., *Receptors* (1995).

First see TELESCOPE

Neutrino Astronomy

Next see ELEMENTARY PARTICLE

Neutrino astronomy requires special facilities because of the unusual qualities of the particle that is being studied. Neutrinos interact very

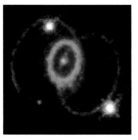

Left, the halo nebula, also known as Supernova 1987A, was a source of a neutrino burst.

weakly with matter and travel at essentially the speed of light. They are produced inside stars by the weak interactions that occur during nuclear fusion. Neutrinos thus offer an insight into the processes that occur inside stars and that are otherwise inaccessible to astronomers. But because neutrinos interact so rarely with matter, their detectors must have hundreds or thousands of tons of material. These detectors must be placed deep underground to avoid confusion between true neutrino events and interactions caused by cosmic rays and their secondary particles.

The first operating solar neutrino detector consisted of 100,000 gallons of perchlorethylene, a cleaning fluid, in the Homestead Gold Mine in Lead, South Dakota. The results were stated in terms of the solar neutrino unit (SNU), which includes a prediction of the expected production of neutrinos by interactions in the sun's interior. The observed SNU rate was about one-third the predicted rate, a difference not yet fully explained. A number of theories have been proposed; the most widely accepted involves subtle changes in neutrino identity during the journey from the sun to the Earth. Meanwhile, other neutrino detectors have been built, such as the Kamiokande II experiment in the mountains of Japan and a Russian facility using about 60 tons of gallium metal, located in the Caucasus Mountains, which permit neutrino astronomers to study interactions in distant stars and in our sun.

First see Nucleus, Atom

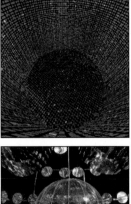

Top, computer-generated display of the detector configuration of the bubble chamber (bottom) of Gargamelle, the CERN freon-filled neutrino detector

Neutron

Next see Neutron Star

A neutral, uncharged atomic particle, the mass of which is 1.00898 on the standard scale in which the mass of an atom of oxygen-16 is 16.000.

Neutrons are found in the nuclei of all atoms except hydrogen, whose nucleus consists of a single proton, a positively charged nuclear particle. A neutron is slightly heavier than a proton. Outside an atomic nucleus, a neutron will decay in about 12 minutes into a proton.

Neutron excess is the difference between the number of neutrons in an atomic nucleus, its neutron number, and the number of protons in that nucleus. The neutron number is determined by subtracting the atomic number from the mass number. Atoms of the same element can have different neutron numbers; these are isotopes.

Discovery. The neutron was discovered in 1912 by a British physicist, James Chadwick. He bombarded the nuclei of the element beryllium with alpha particles, the nuclei of helium atoms, which he obtained from the element polonium. The bombardment caused the beryllium to emit neutrons. It has since been found that neutrons can be produced by a number of nuclear reac-

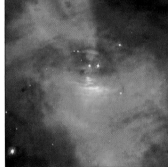

Above, the best pre-Hubble image of Supernova 1987A was not able to discern the halo effect.

Further Reading
Brown, Andrew P., *The Neutron and the Bomb: A Biography of Sir James Chadwick* (1997); Fernow, Richard Clinton, *Introduction to Experimental Particle Physics* (1989); Kane, Gordon, *Modern Elementary Particle Physics* (1993); Scheck, Florian, *Electroweak and Strong Interactions: An Introduction to Theoretical Particle Physics* (1996).

tions, such as those that occur in the fission of uranium atoms in power-producing nuclear reactors. The number of neutrons given off by the atoms in a reactor and entering a sphere of a given cross-section in a unit of time is the neutron flux density. A neutron will not cause the ionization of atoms as it passes through matter; it interacts with other atoms primarily by collisions and secondarily by magnetism.

Types of Neutrons. There is a variety of neutrons, classified by their energies. Thermal neutrons are those in thermal equilibrium. Their energy level is about 0.025 electron volts, which is about two-thirds of the kinetic energy of a molecule at a temperature of 15 degrees Celsius. Epithermal neutrons have higher energies, ranging from a fraction of an electron volt to about 100 electron volts. Slow neutrons, a less-defined class, have energies between those of thermal neutrons and those of epithermal neutrons. Intermediate neutrons are those with energies ranging from 100 to 100,000 electron volts. Fast neutrons are those with energy levels above 100,000 electron volts.

Other neutrons include prompt neutrons, which are released in the process of nuclear fission; and resonance neutrons, defined in terms of the resonance, or natural vibrational frequencies, of an atomic system. Delayed neutrons are emitted by the excited nuclei that are formed in any radioactive process, such as beta decay, or the reactions that occur in a nuclear reactor. Delayed neutron emission is possible only if the excitation energy of the nucleus that absorbs a neutron is greater than the neutron-bonding energy of that nucleus.

The Neutron Cycle. The neutron cycle is the average life history of a neutron in a nuclear reactor, starting with the fission of atoms and continuing until the neutron has been absorbed by another atom or has leaked out of the reactor. The number of neutrons in a reactor core increases with time; the increase is given by the formula $n^{(k-1)}$, where n is the number of neutrons in the reactor at the beginning of the cycle and k is the multiplication factor, defined as the ratio of the number of neutrons in one generation to the number in the preceding generation. If at least one of the neutrons produced by the fission of reactor fuel causes fission in another atom of the fuel, k is equal to or greater than 1, and a chain reaction will occur. Neutrons of a given range of velocities can be obtained by an instrument called a neutron velocity selector.

Background material on neutrons can be found in Atom; Electron; Nucleus, Atomic; Proton. Advanced subjects are developed in Accelerator, Particle; Elementary Particle; Nuclear Forces. Additional relevant information is contained in Isomerism; Neutron Star; Radioactivity.

First see NEUTRON

Neutron Star

Next see BLACK HOLE

The last stage in the evolution of a star that is about 20 to 40 percent more massive than our sun.

The size limit for the formation of a neutron star is called the Chandresekhar limit, after the Indian astronomer who discovered it. A star in this mass range is unstable and collapses to form a smaller object, which includes centers that become so dense that the electrons and protons in them combine to form neutrons. When the matter inside a star reaches a very high density, these neutrons exert what is called a degeneracy pressure, which means that their density determines the characteristics of the star. This ball of degenerate neutrons, the neutron star, will have a mass greater than that of our sun but a radius of less than ten miles, about the size of the island of Manhattan.

Astrophysicists in the 1930s described neutron stars as theoretical objects. The first neutron stars were discovered in the late 1960s in the form of pulsars, celestial bodies that emit radiation in brief, regular pulses. Jocelyn Bell, a British astronomer at Cambridge University, detected pulsars when she was investigating stellar sources of radio waves. The regular radio wave emissions from some bodies, Bell discovered, sounded like the ticking of a clock. The intensity of the beams could vary, but the pulses came at precisely timed intervals. Studies of a number of very fast pulsars showed that they are rapidly rotating neutron stars. Their pulses are produced because the magnetic poles of the neutron star are not aligned precisely with the rotational poles (the same is true of Earth). As the neutron star rotates, the beam of radiation sweeps around the sky.

Artist's rendering of an imploding neutron star.

Further Reading
Geroch, Robert, *General Relativity from A to B* (1981); Glendenning, Norman K., *Compact Stars: Nuclear Physics, Particle Physics, and General Relativity* (1996); Kenyon, I.R., *General Relativity* (1990); Ludvigsen, M., *General Relativity: A Geometric Approach* (1999); Meszaros, P., *High-Energy Radiation from Magnetized Neutron Stars* (1992) .

OBSERVATIONS

The Death Star

For 25 years, astronomers have been detecting intense bursts of gamma rays from outer space, lasting anywhere from a few thousandths of a second to more than a minute. Originally, scientists thought they were witnessing the effects of "starquakes," unstable events occuring on neutron stars somewhere in our galaxy. The Compton Gamma Ray Observatory, launched in 1991, showed that these bursts occur all over the universe, not just in the plane of our galaxy. Therefore, the bursts come from much farther away, and are inconceivably larger in intensity than previously thought. The new theory is that these bursts reflect the death of a neutron star or other mass sufficient to disrupt its degenerating pressure. Some scientists believe that such an event occuring near our solar system (say, within 300 light years) could be intense enough to disturb the gravitational balance of the solar system and possibly destroy the Earth.

Neutron-star pulsars are closely related to supernova explosions. The innermost part of the star is compressed to the point where a core the mass of which exceeds the Chandrasekhar limit is formed. The energy of this collapse blows the mass of the star into interstellar space, leaving an expanding cloud of gas visible on Earth.

Some aspects of neutron stars/pulsars remain unclear. For example, astronomers still do not understand precisely how the radio wave pulses are produced. Astronomers are working to develop methods of measuring the temperature, chemical composition, and other characteristics of neutron stars. Much information about neutron stars has come from measurements of the arrival time of their pulses. In one case, astronomers found a pulsar and a nonpulsating neutron star orbiting one another so closely that general relativity determined the characteristics of the orbit.

Related areas to be considered are GRAVITY; NEUTRON; NOVA, SUPERNOVA; STAR. *Advanced subjects are developed in* HERTZSPRUNG-RUSSEL DIAGRAM; NUCLEOSYNTHESIS. *Relevant information is contained in* BROWN AND WHITE DWARFS; INTERSTELLAR MEDIUM ("DARK MATTER"); X-RAY AND GAMMA RAY ASTRONOMY.

First see KEPLER'S LAWS

Newton's Laws

Next see MECHANICS

Newton's laws of motion, first stated by Sir Isaac Newton in 1686 in his book *Principia*, are the basis for mechanics, a branch of physics and engineering.

Newton stated the first law as: "every body persists in its state of rest or uniform motion in a straight line unless it is compelled to change that state by forces impressed upon it." Today, the law is commonly stated as: a body in motion tends to stay in motion, and a body at rest tends to remain at rest. While the idea seems obvious to us today, it went against a commonly held belief of that time, which was that when a body was in motion, a continued force was needed to keep it in motion.

Newton stated his second law as: "the change in motion is proportional to the motive power impressed and is made in the direction of the straight line in which the force is impressed." Newton's "motion" included not only the velocity of the body but also its mass; today we would call it momentum. We thus can say that the rate of change of momentum is equal to the force acting on a body, or that the force equals the mass of the body times the rate of change of velocity. Since the rate of change of velocity is commonly called acceleration, we have the familiar formula $F=ma$. This formula gives us the means for calculating the exact value of a force, by measuring the acceleration it produces on a body of known mass, or of calculating the value of a mass if we know the force applied to it and the acceleration produced by that force. There are actually two parts to the second law. One states that when different forces act on a body, the changes in momentum of that body are proportional to the forces that are applied. The second states that the change in direction caused by a force is the line of action of that force.

Newton stated his third law as: "to every action there is always an opposed and equal reaction, or the initial actions of two bodies upon each other are always equal and directed to contrary parts." Today we usually say that for every action there is an equal and opposite reaction. One implication of the third law is that a single particle, or body, that is totally isolated cannot exert a force or have a force exerted on it. Forces exist only as the result of interactions between two or more bodies, and the forces that are created act on both bodies. For example, when an apple falls from a tree to Earth, Earth is also attracted toward the apple. We could thus express the third law by saying that whenever two bodies interact so that body A experiences a force, then body B simultaneously feels an equally large force expressed in the opposite direction. The third law applies not only to gravity but also to magnetism and any other force.

Combining the Laws. If we look at the three laws, we can see that each one can be described in terms of the single formula $F=ma$. For example, in the case of the first law if there is no force acting on a body at rest or in motion, $F=0$ and so $a=0$. In the case of the third law, we can say that the momentum of a body consists of acceleration and reaction—as when a rocket takes off. The rocket goes up because it is propelled by the rearward action of the gases produced by burning its fuel, and those gases push the Earth away from the rocket. We do not notice the Earth's motion because it is much more massive than the rocket.

It was not until the twentieth century that it became necessary to modify Newton's laws for certain situations and systems. The laws still apply to the operations of bodies of normal size and normal speed, but are often not adequate to describe the motion of bodies moving near the velocity of light, or for the study of bodies the size of atoms or electrons. In these situations, systems based on the concepts of relativity (in the case of extremely fast velocity) or the postulates of the quantum theory (in the case of atomic and subatomic masses) must be used.

Related material on Newton's laws will be found in ACCELERATION; FORCE; FRICTION; KEPLER'S LAWS. *More details can be found in* CALCULUS; ROTATIONAL MOTION; VECTORS AND TENSORS. *Foundations of this subject are covered in* CENTRIFUGAL FORCE; GRAVITY; VARIATIONAL CALCULUS.

Isaac Newton (1642–1727)

Night-vision technology brings several innovative areas of research together to solve a narrow practical problem (and in this case, military) problem; this technology may, however, have much wider implications and applications.

Further Reading
Cohen, I. B., *Newton: Texts, Backgrounds, Commentaries* (1996); De Gandt, François, *Force and Geometry in Newton's Principles,* (1995); Dobbs, Betty Jo Teeter, *The Janus Faces of Genius: The Role of Alchemy in Newton's Thought* (1992); Hall, A. Rupert, *Isaac Newton:* (1996); White, Michael, *Isaac Newton: The Last Sorcerer* (1998).

First see SEMICONDUCTOR

Night-vision Technology

Next see ELECTRON EMISSION

Night-vision technology is based on electron emissions from surfaces, a feature of semiconductors. In the simplest form, photons of light enter a photovoltaic array of charge-coupled devices, where they stimulate electron flow; the amplified result is displayed on a screen or made visible through an eyepiece. The screen is colored green because the human eye can differentiate more shades of green than any other color.

Night-vision technology is usually split into three generations: Gen I, developed during the Vietnam War, employed this basic photocathode response; Gen II, developed in the 1970s, introduced a microchannel plate, a metal-coated glass disk with 2 to 6 million tiny holes or channels, which substantially multiply the electrons produced as part of a vacuum-insulated image

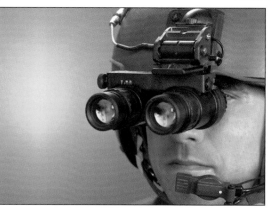

intensifier tube; and Gen III introduced gallium arsenide, which has greater sensitivity than silicon and allows extension of bandwidth into the near-infrared region. Modern night-vision scopes are so sensitive that they can be powered by a pair of AA batteries.

Night-vision image intensifiers are often combined with infrared sensors, employing lead selenide or lead sulfide detector arrays. Such detectors can operate at ambient temperature, or can be cooled to 220 degrees Kelvin and contained within a Dewar flask for maximum efficiency. For even greater sensitivity, indium antinomide can be used, but such detectors operate only at 77 degrees Kelvin (the temperature of liquid nitrogen), so their applicability is limited.

Night-vision technology has expanded from its original defense environment, where it found use both in low-level night flying and in tank sighting systems. Night-vision scopes were widely used during the Gulf War. Now security systems rely on night-vision cameras rather than bright lighting; hunters comb the wilds more effectively; and police pursue fugitives without endangering innocent bystanders.

Nitrogen

First see PERIODIC

Next see NITROGEN CYCLE

Nitrogen, a gas at room temperature, makes up approximately 79 percent of the Earth's atmosphere. The nitrogen content of the human body is about three percent. Nitrogen is the seventh element of the Periodic Table, located next to carbon, with which it shares some chemical properties.

An atom of nitrogen contains seven protons, seven neutrons, and seven electrons. The basis of all chemical bonds is the desire each atom has for a full valency shell, the outermost level that contains electrons. For most elements, the "magic number" is eight, also known as a stable octet, because with a full valency shell the atom is in the most stable energy state. Nitrogen has five electrons in its valency shell, so it attempts in various ways to obtain the electrons needed, usually by sharing them with another atom.

Nitrogen Bonding. Nitrogen forms only covalent bonds, in which electrons are shared between atoms. A nitrogen atom will form three bonds at a time, as this is how many electrons it needs to fill its valency shell. These bonds may be in the form of either single bonds (in which only one pair of electrons is shared), double bonds (two pairs of electrons), or a triple bond (three pairs of electrons). Nitrogen is a diatomic element, willing to pair up with another atom of its own kind in the absence of anything else. Diatomic elements are never found as individual atoms. Such molecular nitrogen can be liquefied and used as a refrigeration agent or in the technology of superconductivity.

Although nitrogen has the ability to form long-linked chains of atoms like carbon does, any molecule with two or more adjacent nitrogen atoms is rarely stable. Hydrazine, one such compound, is used as rocket fuel. Other related compounds are used as detonators for explosives.

Nitrogen easily forms chains and rings with carbon and is therefore a versatile and useful compound in organic chemistry. Nitrogen is chiefly found in amino acids, the building blocks of proteins, and in nucleic acids like DNA and RNA. (*See* DNA; RNA.)

There are 20 different types of amino acids, all of which differ by the structure of their side chains. One of the features all amino acids have in common is the presence of an amino group (NH_2) used to form polypeptide chains or proteins. Amino groups and related molecules, amides, are found in a variety of other compounds as well.

The basic sub-units of nucleic acids are nucleotides, which in addition to sugar molecules and phosphate groups contain nucleic bases, single- or double-ringed structures consisting of carbon and nitrogen. (*See* CARBON.)

Nitrogenous Waste. The basic metabolic activities of all organisms result in the formation of nitrogenous wastes. In lower animals this nitrogen is excreted in the form of ammonia. In higher animals, the nitrogen is incorporated into uric acid or urea excreted from the body in the form of urine. This nitrogen recirculates throughout the ecosystem in what is known as the nitrogen cycle. Some of the nitrogen deposits are used by plants and incorporated into their cells. Other nitrogen compounds are utilized by microorganisms, which allows the nitrogen to escape into the air. Finally, bacteria, known as nitrogen-fixers, transform atmospheric nitrogen into a form that can be redeposited in the soil.

Special topics in this area are found in GAS; NITROGEN CYCLE; PERIODIC TABLE OF THE ELEMENTS. *Advanced subjects are developed in* NITROGEN FIXATION; NITROGEN GROUP. *Additional relevant aspects of this subject are covered in* ATMOSPHERE; CRYOGENICS; OXYGEN GROUP.

Further Reading
Atkins, P.W., *The Periodic Kingdom* (1997); Lea, Peter J., *Plant Nitrogen* (2001); Smil, Vaclav, *Enriching the Earth* (2001); White, T.C.R., *The Inadequate Environment: Nitrogen and the Abundance of Animals* (1994).

First see NITROGEN

Nitrogen Cycle

Next see NITROGEN FIXATION

In ecosystems, materials essential to life are used again and again, cycling between organic and inorganic forms. Such cycles may be either gaseous, like the nitrogen cycle, with the atmosphere or oceans serving as a reservoir of the material, or sedimentary, like the phosphorus cycle, with rocks and soil as the main repository. Human activities have greatly altered the balance in both these cycles, turning nitrogen and phosphorus into pollutants.

Nitrogen makes up 79 percent of the atmosphere, but it must be fixed, or converted into a chemically usable form, before it can be used by organisms. A little of the fixation is done by lightning or volcanic activity. But about 90 percent of the work is done by three kinds of bacteria: symbiotic bacteria that live in root nodules on legumes and some other plants; aerobic bacteria that live in the soil; and cyanobacteria (also called blue-green algae) that live in aquatic ecosystems. The bacteria split the molecular nitrogen, N_2, into two atoms of N that combine with hydrogen to form ammonia, NH_3. Nitrifying bacteria in the soil convert the ammonia first to nitrite and then to nitrate, NO_3^-, which can be absorbed by the roots of plants. The plants convert the nitrate to amino acids consumed by animals. Bacteria and fungi decompose the animals' wastes, as well as dead animal and plant tissues, converting the nitrogen in them back to ammonia in the soil. The ammonia is then converted again into nitrite and nitrate. (*See* BACTERIA.)

Most nitrogen continues to cycle from ammonia to nitrates to amino acids to ammonia without returning to the atmosphere as gaseous N_2, but some does return. Denitrifying bacteria convert some nitrate to N_2 and release it into the air. This balances the N_2 removed from the atmosphere by fixation.

Agriculture, industry, and automobiles have raised the atmospheric levels of nitric oxides, which eventually lead to accumulations of ozone, a component of smog. Excess nitrogen also makes its way into aquatic ecosystems, upsetting their equilibrium.

In nature, available phosphate is far rarer than nitrogen. It enters the soil through the slow weathering of rocks and is absorbed by plants that turn it into organic compounds. Like nitrogen, it is returned to the soil through the decomposition of plants and the animals that eat them. Then it is recycled into plants again. Some phosphate leaves the ecosystem by precipitating out of water at the bottom of the ocean. Eventually it will be incorporated into rocks that may someday be uplifted to weather and return phosphorus to the system. But this is such a lengthy process that, in effect, there is a slow drain of available phosphorus out of the ecosystem.

Phosphorus, like nitrogen, is a major component of sewage and agricultural fertilizers. Phosphate pollution from runoff is a major cause of the algal blooms and reduced water quality that accompany eutrophication of lakes. By mining rock for phosphorus, which then gets washed to sea, humans have increased the amount of phosphorus lost to the oceans. Although that is not a practical problem for the foreseeable future, it does represent a distortion of the phosphorus cycle.

Further devlopments in the field are discussed in ATMOSPHERE; ECOLOGY; NITROGEN. *Advanced subjects are developed in* AIR POLLUTION; CHEMICAL REACTIONS; NITROGEN FIXATION. *Relevant information is contained in* EUTROPHICATION; HYDROLOGIC CYCLE.

Further Reading
Blackburn, T. Henry, *Nitrogen Cycling in Coastal Marine Environments* (1988); Raffaelli, Dave, et al., *Advances in Ecological Research* (1999); Smil, V., *Carbon-Nitrogen-Sulfur* (1986); Sprent, J.I., *The Ecology of the Nitrogen Cycle* (Cambridge Studies in Ecology) (1988).

First see NITROGEN

Nitrogen Fixation

Next see NITROGEN CYCLE

The process of converting atmospheric nitrogen, N_2, into nitrogen compounds, to be utilized by plants.

Nitrogen fixation results in the creation of ammonium (NH_4^+), an organic form of nitrogen that can be incorporated into various amino acids and protein compounds.

Nitrogen fixation can occur due to interactions between N_2 and other atmospheric gases with lightning, or by reacting nitrogen with hydrogen to get ammonia (NH_3). The majority of nitrogen fixation, however, occurs due to the activity of microorganisms like blue-green algae and Rhizobium bacteria that are in symbiotic relationships with legumes such as clover, peas, beans, and alfalfa.

Nitrogen fixation involves a process known as reduction, in which the nitrogen gains electrons. In most nitrogen-fixing bacteria, ferrodoxin, an electron carrier also used in photosynthesis, is the source of electrons for reduction. The enzyme that runs this process in cells has two main protein components: a reductase, which "empowers" the electrons used, as well as a nitrogenase, which uses the electrons to reduce the nitrogen. Each enzyme component contains an iron atom; the nitrogenase also contains molybdenum and is known as the MoFe protein.

Nitrogen fixation has beneficial effects beyond the legumes associated with the bacteria. Extra nitrogen is deposited into the soil for use by other plants as well. (*See* BACTERIA.)

First see NITROGEN

Nitrogen Group

Next see NITROGEN CYCLE

Group VA, also known as the nitrogen group, contains the following elements: nitrogen, phosphorus, arsenic, antimony, and bismuth. With both metals and nonmetals, there is a wide variation in the behavior and properties of the elements in this family.

All of these elements have five electrons in their outermost (valence) energy level, which affects the types of bonds they form. Atoms form bonds to fill their valence shells. A full valence shell means the atom is in its most stable energy state. Nitrogen and phosphorus are true nonmetals; they form covalent bonds in which electrons are shared between atoms. Arsenic and antimony are semimetals or metalloids; they exhibit both metal and nonmetal properties. Only bismuth is a true metal, and only bismuth forms ionic bonds, in which electrons are gained or lost. An atom of bismuth loses three of its valence electrons to become a positively charged ion, a cation, with a charge of +3.

Nitrogen is almost as important to organic chemistry as carbon. It is found as a component in many carbon rings and chains, particularly in the structures of proteins and nucleic acids. Nitrogen is one of the diatomic elements; it is so "eager" to form bonds that it will pair up with another atom of its own kind in the absence of anything else with which to bond.

Phosphorus is also an important element in biological systems. It is a major component in the phosphate ion (PO_4), which is an integral part of polynucleotide chains such as DNA and RNA. In addition, three phosphate groups are found in the molecule adenosine triphosphate (ATP), which is the energy "currency" of all cells.

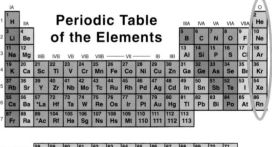

Periodic Table
of the Elements

Above and below right, the positions of the nitrogen group and the noble gases, respectively, in the Periodic Table.

Arsenic and antimony can exist as either molecular or metallic solids. A molecular solid is held together by weak attractive interactions between the individual molecules. A metallic solid is made up of atoms that are somewhat electron "deficient" and share electron density with several neighboring atoms of the same type. The solids formed by both arsenic and antimony have low atomic coordination numbers, meaning they have relatively low melting and boiling points due to a less stable structure.

Antimony, also known as stibium from its Latin root, is a soft black material that leaves a dark mark. It was used thousands of years ago as a cosmetic, in particular as mascara and eyeliner. Currently, antimony is used together with the element indium in an array camera on the Hale telescope, to photograph the regions around particular types of stars.

First see PERIODIC TABLE OF THE ELEMENTS

Noble Gases

Next see RADIOACTIVITY

The last group on the Periodic Table, located at the extreme right, is known as the noble gas family. This name probably stems from the fact that all of its members are chemically inert and were believed to be "too noble" to interact with other elements to form compounds. In reality, each of these elements has a full electron valence shell, and therefore has no "incentive" to form bonds with other atoms.

The members of this family include helium, neon, argon, krypton, xenon, and radon. They are all gases at room temperature. As previously stated, they have a full valence shell, which means eight electrons (a "stable octet") for all except helium, which, due to a smaller size, only requires two electrons to complete its valence shell.

Helium is well known for its property of being lighter than air and is consequently used in all manner of floating devices, from balloons to blimps and dirigibles. Although making up less than one percent of the Earth's atmosphere, helium can usually be found underground along with deposits of natural gas. The United States still maintains a strategic deposit of helium for military purposes. Helium is much more abundant in space than it is on Earth. All stars, including our sun, are composed of just two elements, hydrogen and helium, undergoing a process known as thermonuclear fusion in which the smaller hydrogen nuclei are fusing together to form helium. This is the reaction by which all stars act as the power units of the galaxy.

Glowing Neon. Neon is famed for its ability to glow when an electrical current passes through it. The gas is transformed into a supercharged state known as a plasma. Neon signs are simply colored glass or plastic tubes that contain neon gas and wires for conducting electricity. If the tubing were clear, the neon would still glow red-orange when charged. The strange atmospheric glow known as St. Elmo's Fire is the same phenomenon occurring naturally.

Krypton once had a very real prominent role in the world of measurement. In 1960, the General Conference on Weights and Measures defined the meter in terms of the number of waves of a particular wavelength of light emitted by krypton-86 atoms. This standard held until 1983, when the meter was redefined in terms of the speed of light.

The last element in this family, radon, is the only one that is radioactive. Radon exposure has been cited as a risk factor in developing lung cancer. Various regions of the country report higher than usual accumulations of this gas; homeowners are thus urged to test their properties.

Abundance on Earth. All of the noble gases can be found as trace elements (making up less than 1 percent) in the atmosphere. Therefore, the water in the Earth's oceans could not possibly come from icy comets or meteorites that struck the Earth during its early history. Meteorites contain much more xenon than is found on the Earth. If meteorites had delivered the water in the oceans, the atmosphere would contain nearly ten times as much xenon as it does.

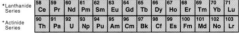

Periodic Table
of the Elements

Further developments in the field are discussed in BORON GROUP; ISOTOPE; PERIODIC TABLE OF THE ELEMENTS; VALENCE. *More details can be found in* RADIOACTIVITY; TRANSURANIC ELEMENTS. *Additional relevant information on this group of elements is contained in* GEOMORPHOLOGY; RADIATION, NATURAL; RADIOCHEMISTRY.

Further Reading
Asimov, Isaac, *The Noble Gases* (1989); Emsley, John, *The Elements* (1998); Greenwood, N.N., *Chemistry of the Elements* (1997); Greenwood, N. N., *Noble Gas and High Temperature Chemistry* (1990).

First see EUCLIDEAN GEOMETRY

Non-Euclidean Geometry

Next see TOPOLOGY

Non-Euclidean geometry stems from the basic human impulse to ask, "What if?" For more than 2,000 years, geometry was defined by the axioms set forth in Euclid's *Elements* (c. 300 B.C.E.): "a straight line constitutes the shortest distance between two points," and so on. The last of these axioms was the following rather complicated one, which became known as the axiom of Euclid: if a straight line *x-y* intersects two other straight lines, *a* and *b*, and the interior angles produced by the intersection on a given side of line *x-y* total less than 180 degrees, then the two lines *a* and *b* will themselves intersect on that side of *x-y*. This axiom is central to numerous better-known axioms, including every axiom dealing with parallel lines, and to all of Euclid's theories about the sum of angles in a triangle, similar triangles, trigonometric functions, and the circle. Reformulations of this axiom include the statements that, in a triangle, the sum of the angles equals 180° and that, for any given line and point, there is exactly one line passing through the point that is parallel to the given line.

Euclid's fifth axiom is neither as simple nor as intuitive as the other four axioms, and there followed two millennia of attempts to prove that the axiom of Euclid was a necessary result of the preceding four axioms. A number of such proofs were accepted and later proven to be false, and in the late 18th and early 19th centuries, mathematicians began to develop systems of geometry in which the axiom of Euclid did not hold.

Janos Bolyai (1802-1860), Nicholai Lobachevsky (1793-1856), and Carl Gauss (1777-1855) developed hyperbolic geometry, in which the sum of the angles in a triangle is less than 180°, or in which there can be more than one distinct line parallel to a given line. This can be envisioned by picturing a triangle drawn on a pseudosphere (shown top left). The lines—defined as the shortest distance between two points—appear curved, and the angles at the vertices of a triangle are clearly more acute than the same angles would be on a flat surface.

Riemann's Work. Georg Riemann developed spherical geometry, in which the sum of the angles in a triangle is more than 180°, or in which there is no line that is parallel to a given line. In this case, Euclid's fifth axiom is trivially true, as all lines eventually meet. The second axiom, however, which states that a line can be continued indefinitely or, alternatively, that given two points, only one distinct line can be drawn through those points, is not valid. To envision this, picture a triangle drawn on the surface of a sphere. The lines appear to curve outward, and the angles of the vertices are larger than they would be on a flat surface. Also, given two points on a sphere, there are an infinite number of lines between them that are exactly the same length. For example, if the Earth were a perfect sphere, all of the lines of longitude connecting the poles would be the shortest connecting lines.

Einstein's theory of "curved space," in which all lines in space eventually meet, is based on this form of non-Euclidean geometry. Thus, non-Euclidean geometry may be the geometry that describes the shape of the universe.

Over the next few decades, it was shown that these two types of non-Euclidean geometry were consistent and did not lead to any contradictions, thus establishing them as legitimate mathematical systems.

An Example. In non-Euclidean geometries, lines that are very short or triangles that are very small in relation to the curvature of the space they exist in look very much like Euclidean lines or triangles. Larger objects, however, show significant variance from Euclidean geometry. This is similar to how a small triangle drawn on the Earth appears to have angles equal to 180°, but a triangle joining, for example, San Francisco, New York, and Mexico City would have angles that are clearly greater than 180°.

On a sphere whose radius approaches infinity, known as a horosphere, lines approach Euclidean behavior; this provides a way of mathematically connecting Euclidean and non-Euclidean geometries. The power of non-Euclidean geometry lies not only in its theoretical brilliance, but also in the way in which it allows mathematicians to use geometry in ways never anticipated by classical geometers—such as spherical trigonometry or quantum astrodynamics—then return to conventional uses without distorting their results.

Top, a graphic representation of a pseudosphere, the mapping of a sphere onto a plane in non-Euclidean geometry. Above, an example of a spherical geometry.

First see OPTICS

Nonlinear Optics

Next see CHAOS AND COMPLEXITY

The study of the nonlinear response of a medium exposed to intense electromagnetic radiation.

A nonlinear interaction can change the polarization or propagation characteristics of electromagnetic waves, or can result in the generation of new electromagnetic waves whose frequencies may be different from those of the original radiation or may differ in some other respect—for example, having the same frequency but a different direction of polarization.

Applications. Nonlinear optical interactions have a number of practical uses. They can change or control some characteristics of laser radiation, including the duration of laser light pulses, their wavelength, their bandwidth, or the quality of the beam. Nonlinear optics is also used for high-resolution atomic and molecular spectroscopy, for materials studies, for information processing, to compensate for distortions caused by imperfections in optical material, and to modulate other optical beams.

These nonlinear interactions mostly occur in the range of electromagnetic radiation emitted by lasers, from the extreme ultraviolet to the far infrared, but some nonlinear interactions have been observed at wavelengths ranging from microwaves to x rays. The generation of a nonlinear optical interaction usually requires a very intense optical field, such as the light given off by lasers. But these interactions can occur at lower intensities; some were observed before laser light became available.

When an electromagnetic wave such as a light wave travels through a medium, it causes a polarization, the creation of an electric dipole moment, because the electrons and nuclei of the atoms of the medium vibrate in response to the wave. The frequencies of the vibrations of the induced polarizations and magnetizations are determined by a combination of the frequencies of the light waves and the properties of the medium. At low intensities of incident light waves, the induced polarizations and magnetizations are proportional to the electric or magnetic fields in the light, and so the response of the medium is said to be linear. Some well-known linear responses include Raman scattering, which involves molecular vibrations or rotations, and Rayleigh scattering, which involves diffusion, orientation, or density variations of molecules.

Nonlinear Responses. When the intensity of incident light is high enough, the response of the medium changes and ceases to be linear. Some of the resulting nonlinear interactions result from the unusually large motion of electrons and ions in the intense optical fields. Another kind of nonlinear response is caused by a change in a property of the medium caused by the intense incident light. For example, the refractive index of the medium may change, because the density of the medium is altered by the intense light or because of a temperature change.

Kerr Effect. Nonlinear interactions can be classified in several ways—whether they are caused by the electric or the magnetic field of the light, whether they change the propagation properties of the incident light, or whether they involve a transfer of energy into or out of the nonlinear medium. These classifications can overlap, so that examples of each such interaction can be found in the other categories. Some specific examples of these interactions include the Kerr effect, in which an electric field causes birefringence, a double refraction effect, which is proportional to the square of the strength of the electric field of the incident light; the Cotton-Mouton effect, which is birefringence caused by the magnetic field of the light; and the Pockels effect, which is birefringence that is proportional to the electric field strength (not to its square, as in the Kerr effect).

Most of the commonly observed nonlinear effects are driven by the electric field of the incident light. These interactions are classified first by whether they generate a light wave at a different frequency, which is called frequency conversion, or self-action, meaning that they affect the propagation of the incident light. The frequency-conversion reactions are further classified by whether or not they involve a transfer of energy. The self-action effects are classified by whether they change the spatial, temporal, or spectral distribution of the incident light and whether they affect its other properties. The study of nonlinear optics, for both purely scientific and practical purposes, continues at a high level.

Background material can be found in LENS; LIGHT; OPTICS. *Further developments in the field are discussed in* DIFFRACTION; PHONON; REFLECTION AND REFRACTION. *Special topics in this area are found in* LASER AND MASER; POLARIZED LIGHT.

First see STAR

Nova, Supernova

Next see NEBULA

Novas and supernovas are stellar explosions, but of different types. A nova is believed to originate in a binary star system, usually consisting of a red giant and a white dwarf, both representing advanced stages in the evolution of stars. Matter is transferred from the red giant to the white dwarf and accumulates on its surface until a thermonuclear explosion occurs. The brightness of the star system can increase by 1,000 to 10,000 times over a period of a few days. From ten to 15 novas are observed in the Milky Way each year. As many as 50 are believed to occur annually in our galaxy, but most of them cannot be observed because their light is absorbed by grains of dust in the space between stars. (*See* INTERSTELLAR MEDIUM.)

Supernovas are explosions that occur when stars burn up all their available nuclear fuel and their cores collapse catastrophically. Astronomers separate supernovas into two major groups, according to the spectrum of light they emit. Type I supernovas, so called because they were

Further Reading
Agrawal, Govind P., *Contemporary Nonlinear Optics* (1992); Agrawal, Govind P., *Nonlinear Fiber Optics* (1995); Boyd, Robert W., *Nonlinear Optics* (1991); Delone, Nikolai B., *Fundamentals of Nonlinear Optics of Atomic Gases* (1988).

Supernova SN1987A, observed in February 1987, was a major astronomical event. Below, the event was recorded in visible (top), infrared (right),and ultraviolet (left, middle) several times between March and September of that year.

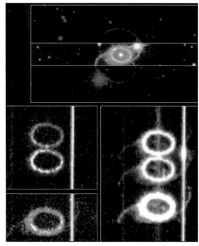

the first to be observed in detail in the 1930s, have broad spectral features that evolve with time in a pattern that is now well defined. An astronomer skilled in the study of such spectra can estimate the time that has elapsed since the maximum emission of light by the supernova. Type II supernovas, which were recognized in the 1940s, have nearly continuous spectra at the time of maximum light emission but develop broader features within a few weeks. The spectra of type II supernovas also evolve according to a standard pattern, but there are more individual variations than are seen in type I supernovas.

Both types of supernovas reach their maximum brightness in the sky two to three weeks after the explosion occurs. At their peak, type I supernovas are brighter than type II by about one magnitude. The light from a supernova fades slowly over a period of more than one year. Type II supernovas can be divided into II-L (for linear) and II-P (for plateau). Two-thirds of type II supernovas are II-P, whose light maintains a nearly constant brightness for perhaps 80 days. The light from a type II-L supernova will show an almost linear decline from its peak in the 80 days following its maximum brightness.

Supernovas appear to occur at a higher rate in spiral galaxies than in elliptical galaxies. In spiral galaxies, the rate of supernova occurrence is related to the color of the galaxy. Blue galaxies, which have a higher rate of recent star formation, have a higher rate of supernova occurrence. For all galaxies, the supernova rate is roughly proportional to the luminosity of the galaxy. The average interval between supernova events in a fairly large spiral galaxy, such as the one in which our sun exists, is about 20 years, an estimate based both on astrophysical calculations and on the observed incidence of supernovas over the centuries.

The foundations of the subject are discussed in Galaxy; Nebula; Red Giant Star. *More details can be found in* Hertzsprung-Russel Diagram; Interstellar Medium ("Dark Matter"); Neutron Star. *Advanced topics relating to novas and supernovas are developed in* Nucleosynthesis; Quasar; Radio Astronomy.

First see Nucleus, Atomic

Nuclear Forces

Next see Standard Model

Two forces are known to act within the nucleus of the atom. One is the strong force, which holds together the nucleons—protons and neutrons—that make up the nucleus. The other is the weak interaction, which is responsible for the beta decay of particles and nuclei.

Strong Forces. Knowledge of the strong interactions began with the classic experiments

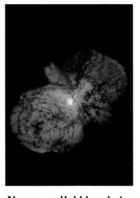

Above, a Hubble photograph of the star Eta Carinae amid the remnants of a supernova of long ago.

Above, the large white dot near the center of the image is the supernova of 1987, photographed on February 24.

Further Reading
Danziger, John, *Supernova Remnants and Their X-Ray Emission* (1983); Kafatos, Minas, *Supernova 1987a in the Large Magellanic Cloud* (1988); Kaler, James B., *Astronomy* (1997); Roger, R.S., *Supernova Remnants and the Interstellar Medium* (1988); Rubin, Vera C., *Bright Galaxies Dark Matters* (1996).

of Ernest Rutherford, which established that almost all the mass of the atom is concentrated in the nucleus. Since nuclei contain positively charged protons and neutrons that have no electric charge, it was evident that electrostatic repulsion would push the protons apart, unless it was countered by a strong attractive force. Studies of nuclear energy levels showed that this strong force was the same for neutrons and protons, and thus was independent of electric charge. Experiments also showed that the force between nucleons had a very short range, less than a trillionth of a centimeter, and that within this limited range the force was a thousand times stronger than electromagnetic forces.

In 1938, the Japanese physicist Yukawa proposed that this short-range strong force was produced by the exchange of a new kind of particle between nucleons. The existence of that particle was confirmed in 1948 by cosmic ray experiments. The particle, called the pi-meson (which exists in three charge states, +1, 0, and -1) was made the basis of the meson theory of strong interactions.

Meson field theory, however, was found to be inadequate to describe the strong interaction fully. Then, the development of particle accelerators made it possible to create beams of mesons and do scattering experiments with pi-mesons and protons. In the early 1950s, Enrico Fermi and his collaborators discovered a short-lived resonant state that could be considered a new kind of nucleon. Many other new particles have since been discovered.

Weak Forces. The weak interaction is many trillion times weaker than the strong interaction. An example of the weakness of this interaction is the neutrino, a particle that reacts with other matter only through the weak force. A single neutrino can pass through Earth with only one chance in a million that it will interact with any matter on Earth. Knowledge of the weak interaction has only been made possible because nuclear reactors and particle accelerators produce huge amounts of neutrinos, and by the fact that neutrinos make themselves known in a large variety of decay processes.

One such process is one by which a radioactive nucleus can decay, emitting neutrinos and electrons, called beta rays. In this decay process, a neutron of the nucleus is transformed to a proton. Examples of beta decay include the decay of cobalt-60 and the decay of potassium-40. Another such example is the decay of a neutron into an electron, a proton, and an antineutrino.

Standard Model. In the early 1970s, a new theory called the Standard Model showed that the weak interaction and the electromagnetic interaction are separate manifestations of one force, the electroweak force. This joining of the weak and electromagnetic forces was the first unification of different forces since Maxwell showed that electricity and magnetism are manifestations of the same force. Unlike the Fermi theory, the Standard Model does not require the neutrino to have zero mass. It is now known that the neutrino has a mass of about 35 electron volts, the electron neutrino has a mass that is less than ten electron volts, and the mu-neutrino has a mass of a quarter of an electron volt. Neutrino masses are of interest to astronomers, since they may provide the dark matter, the gravitational effect of which is evident in the universe but the source of which is not known.

Elementary aspects of this subject are covered in FORCE; LEPTON; NUCLEUS, ATOMIC. *More information on particular aspects is contained in* ELEMENTARY PARTICLES; RADIOACTIVITY; STANDARD MODEL. *Additional relevant information is contained in* ACCELERATOR, PARTICLE; GAUGE THEORY; QUARKS.

Further Reading
Cottingham, W.M., *An Introduction to Nuclear Physics* (1986); Coughlan, G.D., *The Ideas of Particle Physics* (1991); Satchler, George R., *Introduction to Nuclear Reactions* (1990); Williams, W.S.C., *Nuclear and Particle Physics* (1991).

First see MAGNETISM

Nuclear Magnetic Resonance (NMR)

Next see MEDICAL DIAGNOSTICS

Behavior of an atomic nucleus with a magnetic moment above zero that is in an external magnetic field as it absorbs a precise frequency of electromagnetic radioactive energy.

For NMR to occur, the nucleus must have a nonzero spin, so that it behaves as a small magnet. When the external magnetic field is applied, the magnetic moment vector of the nucleus processes in a conical motion around the direction of the field. Under quantum rules, only certain orientations are allowed. The hydrogen atom, which has a spin of 1/2, has two possible states when it is in a magnetic field. Each state has a slightly different energy level. Nuclear magnetic resonance of the hydrogen atom is caused by the absorption of radiation whose photon energy is the precise difference between these two levels. That absorption of energy causes a transition of the nucleus from a lower to a higher energy state. For most purposes, the difference between these energy levels is so small that the required frequency is in the radio band. The NMR effect varies with the strength of the magnetic field in which the nucleus is placed.

NMR can be used in a number of ways—for example, for the accurate determination of nuclear moments. It can also be applied in a sensitive magnetometer to measure the strength of magnetic fields. In medicine, it can be used to produce images of tissues and is known as MRI ("magnetic resonance imaging"). The main scientific application of NMR is in chemical analysis and structural determination, a field called NMR spectroscopy. The application is based on the knowledge that different atoms will absorb

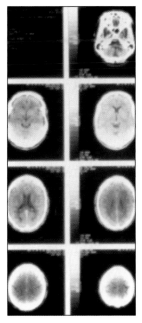

NMR brain scans (above) are capable of detecting microlesions that might escape x-rays.

electromagnetic energy at slightly different frequencies. If the frequency is fixed, the atoms will absorb energy differently in different magnetic fields. These effects are called chemical shifts. (*See* ATOM.)

Methods. There are two methods of NMR spectroscopy. In the method called continuous wave NMR, the sample being studied is subject to a strong magnetic field, which can be varied continuously over a small range. As the magnetic field is changed, transitions in absorption occur at different values, causing oscillations in the field, which are picked up by the detector.

In Fourier transform NMR, a fixed magnetic field is used and a high-intensity pulse of radiation that covers a variety of frequencies is beamed at the sample being studied. The signal that results is analyzed mathematically to obtain the NMR spectrum of the sample. Most commonly, NMR is aimed at hydrogen atoms that are part of a complex molecule. For example, ethanol—CH_3CH_2OH—will have an NMR spectrum with three peaks, each of which corresponds to a different environment of its hydrogen atoms. Other nuclei, including carbon-13, nitrogen-14 and fluorine-19, can also be used for NMR spectroscopy, although they are less abundant and have a lower magnetic moment than hydrogen.

Related material regarding NMR techology is to be found in ATOMIC SHELL MODEL; MAGNETISM. *Other aspects of the subject are discussed in* BRAIN; MAMMOGRAPHY; MEDICAL DIAGNOSTICS. *Additional material can be found in* CT AND PET SCANS; PETROLEUM PROSPECTING; RADIOLOGY.

First see FISSION, NUCLEAR

Nuclear Power

Next see HAZARDOUS WASTE DISPOSAL

Nuclear power is produced by reactors, systems that act as furnaces to convert into electricity part of the energy that is latent in certain atomic nuclei. The physical phenomenon that makes this conversion possible is nuclear fission, which occurs in uranium-235 (a naturally occurring element) and in the nuclei of some other very heavy elements. For example, the nucleus of an atom of uranium-235 will sometimes split in half when it is struck by a neutron. Two other nuclei, which can be produced artificially, also have this property of fission. One of them is uranium-233, produced by having a nucleus of thorium absorb a neutron. The other is plutonium-239, which is produced when a nucleus of uranium-238 absorbs a neutron without splitting. (*See* RADIOACTIVITY.)

The slower the speed of an incoming neutron, the greater the probability that the target nucleus will fission. (As a rule, slower-moving neutrons interact more with atomic nuclei because they spend more time in those nuclei.) When the fission of a uranium-235 nucleus does occur, the result is the creation of two medium-weight nuclei, which fly apart at great speed. These speeding fragments quickly collide with the nuclei of neighboring atoms, giving them additional kinetic energy and thus creating heat. That heat can then be converted to electricity. In a non-nuclear power plant, heat is produced by burning a fuel such as coal or oil, but a fission reaction produces a million times more heat than is obtained by combustion of a similar weight of coal or oil. The heat that is produced by nuclear fission is used in the same way as the heat of coal or oil, producing team-to-team turbines that generate electricity.

The uranium-containing core of a nuclear power plant produces a continuous supply of heat in a chain reaction. In a nuclear power plant, the fuel rods that contain the uranium also contain other metals, which are added to minimize corrosion and maximize the conductivity of the heat produced by nuclear fission.

In the core of a nuclear power plant, there are also control rods that prevent the chain reaction from getting out of hand. The number of free neutrons is controlled by inserting or withdrawing the control rods. If too many control rods are removed, the result can be an oversupply of neutrons and the melting of a fuel element. A nuclear reactor cannot explode like an atomic bomb, but it can release substantial amounts of radioactivity into the environment if such an accident occurs. This type of event occurred at Chernobyl, Ukraine, in 1986.

The reactor core will also contain a moderator, a material whose purpose is to slow down any high-speed neutrons that are emitted by fission fragments, thus increasing the probability that they will cause fission. Light substances are used as moderators because they enable a neutron to transfer a larger portion of its energy to other nuclei. Water is commonly used as a moderator; carbon or beryllium or other materials can also be used. The heat produced by fission is transferred to a boiler or turbine by a coolant, a gas or liquid that is pumped through the reactor.

One component found in all nuclear power plants is the reflector, a shell that surrounds the reactor core completely. The function of a reflector is to send back into the reactor core any neutrons that might otherwise leak out. A reflector must be made of a material that scatters but does not absorb neutrons. The materials used for moderators can also be used for reflectors.

Nuclear Waste. Nuclear waste and radioactive waste management are among the most pressing problems of the early 21st century. Nuclear waste includes spent fuel, contaminated portions of decommissioned reactors and weapons systems, ore refining byproducts, and miscellaneous high- and low-level waste. In theory, nuclear waste materials simply have to be stabilized and contained for a period sufficient to allow their radioactive elements to decay; at the end of that period the materials will be inert. In practice, plutonium waste would take 10,000 years—the entire length of human history—to lose only half its radioactivity, and at least forty more millennia to reach the inert stage.

Nuclear waste emits not only radiation but heat; during the first year a typical stainless steel canister of high-level waste will emit 22 kW of heat in addition to alpha and other particles. Fortunately, its heat generation rate will decrease by an order of magnitude in ten years, and again in a hundred years; similarly, its toxicity will decline by about three orders of magnitude within three hundred years, as short-lived materials decay. Thus contemporary storage decisions are based on a critical period of three to four centuries, followed by long-term storage of much more stable materials.

Dumping. In recent years, a great deal of nuclear waste has simply been dumped, usually in deep water. Off Russia's Arctic coast, at least thirteen naval reactors and 17,000 containers of liquid nuclear waste have been dumped into the Kara Sea; radioactive wastes have also been dumped at ten different sites in the Sea of Japan. Ironically, deep seabed disposal is a viable option, when managed with sufficient care. Waste must be encased in a needle-shaped projectile, designed to bury itself in deep strata of red clay in the ocean's abyssal hill regions; these regions are deep, undisturbed by currents, and have little or no life that might be disrupted. Test corings have revealed that these deep clays could safely absorb any radiation leakage, and that they have been undisturbed for millions of years. Deep-sea disposal remains under intense study.

On land, geologists have identified only a few potential waste sites that can be shown to have been both geologically inactive and not subject to groundwater infusion for at least ten thousand years. The only two such sites in the United States, at Yucca Mountain, Nevada, and Carlsbad, New Mexico, have been under preparation for nearly two decades. The Carlsbad site, officially called the Waste Isolation Pilot Project, is designed to store 5 million cubic feet of military waste 2,150 feet under the surface, in salt caverns which have remained undisturbed for 250 million years; it finally opened in 1998. Civilian wastes remain stored haphazardly, at above-ground sites around the world with a significant potential for deadly accidents.

Further Reading

Bodansky, David, *Nuclear Energy: Principles, Practices, and Prospects* (1996); Galperin, Anne L., *Nuclear Energy/Nuclear Waste* (1992); Grossman, Karl, *Cover Up: What You Are Not Supposed to Know About Nuclear Power* (1980); Morone, Joseph G., *The Demise of Nuclear Energy: Lessons for Democratic Control of Technology* (1989); Yaroshinka, Alla, *Chernobyl: The Forbidden Truth* (1995).

Background material can be found in ENERGY; FISSION, NUCLEAR; FUSION, NUCLEAR. *More details can be found in* ENERGY, ALTERNATIVE; HAZARDOUS WASTE DISPOSAL; WATER POLLUTION. *Elementary aspects of this subject are covered in* BREEDER REACTOR; NUCLEAR WEAPONS; POPULATION ECOLOGY.

Nuclear Weapons

First see FISSION, NUCLEAR

Next see FUSION, NUCLEAR

Weapons that generate massive explosive power by releasing the energy that holds protons and neutrons together in the atomic nucleus.

Fission bombs get their energy by tearing apart the nuclei of heavy elements, such as uranium or plutonium. Fusion bombs get their energy by squeezing together the nuclei of light atoms, such as deuterium. The complete fission of one pound of uranium would release as much energy as 9,000 tons of TNT, and complete fusion of one pound of deuterium would release as much energy as 26,000 tons of TNT. The first nuclear weapon was a uranium device that was exploded over Alamogordo, New Mexico, on July 16, 1945. The U.S. dropped a uranium bomb on Hiroshima on August 6, 1945, and a plutonium bomb on Nagasaki three days later, bringing World War II to a quick conclusion.

A fusion bomb initiates the melding together of a nucleus of deuterium, which consists of one proton and one neutron, with a nucleus of tritium, which has one proton and two neutrons. The combination is unstable. One neutron is expelled, and it and the remaining nucleus fly apart at high speeds, releasing a large amount of energy and starting a chain reaction that releases much more energy, all in a matter of seconds. To achieve such a reaction, it is necessary to overcome the force of repulsion that ordinarily exists. In the stars, where fusion reactions provide the energy, this is accomplished by the high pressures and temperatures that exist in their interiors. In hydrogen bombs, fusion is also accomplished by means of high temperatures. These temperatures are achieved by using a uranium bomb to act as a trigger. Thus, a fusion weapon consists of a uranium bomb at the core, which is surrounded by the light elements deuterium, tritium, and sometimes lithium, which produce the fusion reaction. In addition to the damage caused by their explosive power, nuclear weapons also cause damage by their tremendous heat and emission of lethal radiation. This radiation can spread over long distances, damaging areas far from the site of an explosion over a number of years.

Nuclear Winter. A theory first raised in 1982 claimed that, if a full-scale nuclear war were ever waged, thousands of nuclear explosions would raise enough dust and soot in the atmosphere to block sunlight for an extended period. Temperatures on Earth would fall by 20 to 25 degrees Celsius; many species would be obliterated, especially in tropical regions, and mass starvation of humans would sweep the globe, threatening extinction at worst and extinguishing civilization at best.

The nuclear winter theory was presented in 1983 in the so-called TTAPS report, named for the last initials of its authors, Richard P. Turco, Owen B. Toon, Thomas P. Ackerman, James B. Pollack, and Carl Sagan. The paper presented a range of scenarios, with the most devastating nuclear winter reserved for the most severe. The long-term consequences it predicted included not only cold and darkness, but heavy clouds of toxic gases, the worldwide distribution of radioactive fallout, and ravaging of the ozone layer, which now blocks deadly ultraviolet light from reaching Earth's surface.

The TTAPS report, advanced while the U.S.-Soviet arms race was still alive, undercut the notion that nuclear war could be winnable by any party. The theory outraged opponents of arms reduction, who argued that it was a scare tactic rooted in politics, not science.

Since the initial report, later models of nuclear war, making different assumptions and factoring in different variables, have led to a number of different scenarios. One alternate model, by Starley Thompson and Stephen Schneider, predicted a temperature decline of around ten degrees Celsius, rather than 20 to 25 degrees Celsius. This was dubbed by some to be nuclear autumn. While some political commentators implied the effect would be trivial, a ten-degree drop in temperature would represent extreme climatic change.

Background material can be found in EXPLOSIVES; FISSION, NUCLEAR; FUSION, NUCLEAR; RADIOACTIVITY. *Further details can be found in* ASTEROIDS AND METEORS; GAME THEORY; RADIATION DETECTOR. *More information on particular aspects is contained in* EXTINCTION; MISSILE; NUCLEAR POWER.

The development of nuclear weapons in the twentieth century is one of the less vaunted legacies of the science of the age.

Further Reading
Ehrlich, A. H., *Hidden Dangers* (1991); Falkenrath, R. A., *America's Achilles' Heel: Nuclear, Biological, and Chemical Terrorism and Covert Attack* (1998); Marinacci, B., *Linus Pauling On Peace* (1998); Winkler, A. M., *Life Under a Cloud: American Anxiety About the Atom* (1999).

First see CELL

Nucleic Acid

Next see DNA

Organic acid composed of a chain of nucleotides, found in the cell nucleus and occasionally in the cytoplasm of the cell.

There are two major types of nucleic acids: those responsible for carrying the hereditary information of the cell and directing cell activities, like deoxyribonucleic acid (DNA) and ribonucleic acid (RNA); and those used as energy "currency" within the cell, like adenosine triphosphate (ATP).

The basic unit of a nucleic acid is the nucleoside, which in turn consists of a sugar molecule, either ribose or deoxyribose, and one of five nucleic bases: adenine, guanine, cytosine, thymine and uracil. Adenine and guanine are both types of purines, which are double-ringed

Further Reading
Aldridge, Susan, *The Thread of Life* (1998); Behe, Michael J., *Darwin's Black Box* (1998); Frank-Kamenetskii, Maxim D., *Unraveling DNA* (1997); Niedle, Stephen, *The Oxford Handbook of Nucleic Acid Structure* (1999).

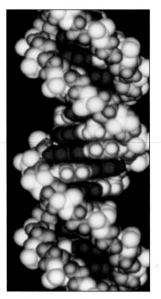

Above, a molecular model of DNA.

Below, a molecular model of RNA.

structures. Cytosine, thymine, and uracil are all types of pyrimidines, which are single-ringed structures.

Nucleosides that also have a phosphate group (PO_4) attached to the sugar molecule are called nucleotides. Individual nucleotides, those not incorporated into a polynucleotide chain, may have three adjacent phosphate groups linked to the sugar.

To incorporate a new nucleotide into the growing chain, the "incoming" nucleotide drops its outer two phosphate groups and forms a bond between its remaining PO_4 and the sugar molecule of the nucleotide preceding it in the chain. The polynucleotide chain itself consists of alternating sugar and phosphate groups forming a "backbone," with the bases protruding off of the sugar molecules.

DNA consists of two such polynucleotide chains running "antiparallel," or in opposite directions. The famous "double helix" shape of DNA is actually a twisted version of the "ladder" formed by the two chains, with the "sides" of the ladder formed by the alternating sugars and phosphates and the "rungs" consisting of pairs of bases, known as Watson-Crick base pairs after their discoverers, James Watson and Francis Crick. In Watson-Crick base pairs, a purine is always found together with a pyrimidine, in order to guarantee a uniform width throughout the DNA double helix. The pairs are held together with hydrogen bonds, relatively weak forms of intermolecular bonding, in order to facilitate the "unzipping" of the DNA so that it may perform its functions. Adenine is paired either with thymine (in DNA) or uracil (in RNA) by means of two hydrogen bonds. The guanine-cytosine pair is held together by three hydrogen bonds. (*See* BOND, CHEMICAL.)

Structural Contrast. In terms of structure, there are three major differences between DNA and RNA:

DNA is found as a duplex. RNA is primarily a single strand, though it can form a duplex by base-pairing along its own length, with another RNA strand or with a single DNA strand. DNA contains deoxyribose as its sugar and RNA contains ribose. DNA contains thymine and RNA contains uracil. Thymine and uracil are chemically identical, except that thymine has an additional methyl group (CH_3) attached to its ring.

ATP consists of ribose and adenine (the "adenosine") and three adjacent phosphate groups attached to the ribose. The third, PO_4, is attached with a pyrophospate bond, which acts as a temporary energy reservoir.

When energy is required, the third phosphate group is detached from the nucleotide, thereby transforming the triphosphate ATP into adenosine diphosphate (ADP). The process is easily reversible. ADP can be further broken down, by removal of yet another phosphate group, to form adenosine monophosphate (AMP). A special type of AMP, called cyclic AMP or cAMP, plays an important role in hormone-target cell interactions as well as in other cellular reactions.

> *Background material can be found in* CARBON; ORGANIC COMPOUNDS; PROTEIN SYNTHESIS. *More details can be found in* DNA; RNA; TRANSPORT, CELLULAR. *Relevant information is contained in* BIOSYNTHETICS; CYTOPLASM; LIFE, DEFINITION AND ORIGIN OF.

First see BIG BANG THEORY

Nucleosynthesis

Next see INTERSTELLAR MEDIUM ("DARK MATTER")

The formation of chemical elements by astrophysical nuclear processes.

Nucleosynthesis can take place in several ways. Cosmological, or primordial, nucleosynthesis took place very soon after the Big Bang, the cosmic explosion in which the universe was formed. The extremely high temperatures and densities that existed at the time of the Big Bang led to the formation of light elements, such as helium and hydrogen. Astronomical theorists have established that the production of elements heavier than helium would be impossible in the conditions that existed during the Big Bang. Nucleosynthesis in the time immediately following it, however, could have led to the formation of elements as heavy as lithium, atomic number 7.

Heavier Elements. The formation of the heavier elements takes place mostly inside stars, although some nucleosynthesis is possible in the explosion of supernovas. By far the greatest part of the active burning lifetime of a star is spent converting hydrogen, the lightest element, into helium, a process that releases the energy that makes the star shine. This process is accompanied and followed by nuclear reactions that lead to the production of the heavier elements. Less massive stars develop dense cores in which elements such as carbon, oxygen, neon, and magnesium can be formed. More massive stars have nuclear reactions in which elements as heavy as iron are built in a succession of stages:

Helium produces carbon and oxygen; two carbon nuclei, atomic number 6, produce one nucleus of neon, atomic number 10, and a nucleus of helium; two oxygen nuclei, atomic number 8, produce one nucleus of silicon, atomic number 14, and a nucleus of helium, or one nucleus of phosphorus, atomic number 15, and a proton. The nuclear burning of silicon leads to a complex series of photonuclear and charged particle reactions that result in the production of iron, atomic number 26, and other nuclei whose atomic numbers are just below that of iron.

Because the protons and neutrons that make up the nucleus of an iron atom are tightly bound to one another, further nuclear processing of the material inside stars is not possible. Instead, the formation of heavier elements occurs by a process of neutron-capture reactions. Production of the most neutron-rich isotopes of elements may take place in supernovas. A massive star that explodes into a supernova has a core of iron, with surrounding shells that are dominated by silicon, magnesium, oxygen, carbon, and helium, and an extended hydrogen envelope beyond them. Recent observations of supernova explosions have shown that heavier elements can be formed in them.

It is now believed that most heavier elements, up to uranium, are produced by supernovas and are ejected by the force of the explosion into space, where they eventually become parts of other stars and the planets orbiting those stars. (*See* UNIVERSE.)

First see NUCLEAR FORCES

Nucleus, Atomic

Next see QUARK

The positively charged center of an atom that makes up nearly all of the atom's mass.

The nucleus of an atom consists of protons and neutrons (except for hydrogen, the smallest atom, the nucleus of which is a single proton). These nucleons, as they are called, are about the same in mass but differ in electric charge. The proton carries a positive charge and the neutron carries no charge. The number of protons in the nucleus determines the element to which that atom belongs. It is designated by Z, the atomic number. The number of neutrons is designated by N, the neutron number, and the total number of nucleons is designated by A, the nucleon number or mass number. Atoms of the same atomic number can have different numbers of neutrons; they are called isotopes.

For example, the most massive atom in nature is uranium-238; its atomic number is 92 and its nucleon number is 238. Two other isotopes or uranium also exist in nature: uranium-235, nucleon number 235; and uranium-234, nucleon number 234 and neutron number 142.

Nuclear Forces. The nucleons of an atom are held together by the strong force, which is powerful enough to overcome the electrostatic repulsion between the like-charged protons but extends only over a very short distance, measured in billionths of a centimeter. The strong force is envisioned as an exchange of particles called virtual mesons, and is described by a gauge theory called quantum chromodynamics.

Nucleons also are subject to the weak force, which is responsible for the beta decay of particles and nuclei. The weak force has been found to be unified with the electromagnetic force, in the electroweak theory.

Liquid-Drop Model. Several models of the structure of the nucleus have been proposed. One of the first was the liquid-drop model, in which the nucleus was pictured as behaving like a drop of water, with the nucleons distributed evenly throughout the nucleus and existing in a state of constant motion, like the thermal motion of molecules in a liquid. In the liquid-drop picture, all the nucleons in the interior of the nucleus have about the same binding energy, while nucleons near the surface are less strongly bound. One of the great early successes of the liquid-drop picture was its use by Niels Bohr to explain the process of nuclear fission. This model still offers the best explanation of fission.

Nuclear Shell Model. A newer model pictures the nucleons as moving independently of one another. Each nucleon is assigned an orbital l, a spin s, and a magnetic quantum number m. These quantum numbers are used to describe the angular momentum of each nucleon as they move in the appropriate shells in the nucleus, just as electrons form shells around the nucleus. The evidence for the existence of such shells includes the existence of a larger number of isotopes of atoms of certain atomic numbers and neutron numbers. These "magic numbers" are 2, 8, 20, 28, 50, and 82 for both atomic numbers and neutron numbers and 126 for the neutron number.

The measure of the stability of an atomic nucleus is its binding energy, the energy that would be released if the nucleus could be formed directly by combining free neutrons and free protons. Among the stable nuclei that occur in nature, even-even nuclei, those with even numbers of both protons and neutrons, are much more common than odd-even nuclei.

Furthermore, only four stable odd-odd nuclei are known—in hydrogen, lithium, barium, and nitrogen. This preference for even-even nuclei is related to an extra-large binding energy that produces what is called a pairing force between individual pairs of protons and individual pairs of neutrons. This pairing force makes it more difficult to achieve the higher energy levels needed to cause the nucleus to fission. An odd-even nucleus, by contrast, has an unpaired nucleon that can produce excited energy levels more easily, while an odd-odd nucleus has both an unpaired proton and an unpaired neutron.

Background material relating to atomic nuclei can be found in ATOM; ELECTRON; NEUTRON; PROTON. *Advanced subjects are developed in* ATOMIC SHELL MODEL; ELEMENTARY PARTICLES; NUCLEAR FORCES. *Foundational aspects of this subject are covered in* GAUGE THEORY; GROUP THEORY IN PHYSICS; QUARKS; STANDARD MODEL.

Further Reading
Eichler, Jorg, *Relativistic Atomic Collisions* (1995); Howe, James, *Interfaces in Materials: Atomic Structure, Thermodynamics and Kinetics of Solid-Vapor, Solid-Liquid and Solid-Solid Interfaces* (1997); Reiss, H. R., *Radiative Processes in Atomic Physics* (1997); Yang, F., *Modern Atomic and Nuclear Physics* (1996).

First see EUKARYOTIC CELL

Nucleus, Cell

Next see MITOSIS

The nucleus is the "brain" of the cell and is responsible for directing all cellular activities. In eukaryotic cells, the nucleus contains paired chromosomes and is surrounded by a nuclear membrane that separates it from the rest of the cell contents. In prokaryotes there is no "true" nucleus; a single loop chromosome is present and not compartmentalized in any way.

Chromosomes contain genes made up of DNA, bound with an equal mass of proteins. A gene contains information that specifies the structure of a particular protein. When a gene is turned "on," its protein is produced. When the gene is "off," its protein is not produced. All body cells, called somites, contain the exactly the same genes. What differentiates one type of cell from another is a matter of which genes are turned "on" or "off." Determining which proteins are formed dictates what chemical reactions occur within the cell. All cellular activities can basically be defined in terms of what reactions take place and what do not.

The nuclear membrane, or envelope, is actually a double layer. The space between the outer and inner membranes is called the perinuclear space. Nuclear pores connect the two membranes and provide entry and exit sites for any materials transported in and out of the nucleus. The outer membrane faces the cytosol of the cell and is connected to the endoplasmic reticulum, which is a network of membrane tubes for intracellular transportation. The nuclear lamina is a network of protein fibers that organizes the structure of the nucleus. The interior of the nucleus is called the nucleoplasm.

The nucleus is the largest and most prominent structure of the cell, between five and ten microns in length. It may contain one or more nucleoli, which are "auxiliary" nuclei and are sites for the assembly of ribosomal and transfer RNA, used in protein synthesis.

Cell Karyotype. The karyotype of a cell is its chromosome pattern and number. During most of a cell's life, the nuclear contents are not seen as distinct pairs of chromosomes, but as a tangled mass of threads known as chromatin. Prior to cell division, all of the genetic material must be copied in order to ensure that each new "daughter" cell receives a full set of chromosomes. Mitosis is the process of replicating the chromosomes and forming two complete nuclei. Cytokinesis, the division of the cytoplasm and its contents, can then occur. If mitosis is not followed by cell division, the original cell is left with more than one nucleus. Some cells of the body, such as muscle cells, contain multiple nuclei, as do some unicellular organisms, such as paramecia.

Meiosis is the process used to ensure that gametes, sperm and eggs, contain nuclei with only half the number of chromosomes. Sperm and egg unite to form a zygote, which develops into the new organism. Half the chromosomes come from the maternal parent and half from the paternal. If sperm and egg started out with a complete set of chromosomes, the zygote would have twice the proper number.

Just as some cells have more than one nucleus, others may have no nuclei at all. Red blood cells contain a protein called hemoglobin and transport oxygen around the body. These cells undergo a very complicated maturation process as they become specialized. By the time a red cell is fully mature and functional, it has "lost" its nucleus. The reason for this is that red blood cells are essentially sacs crammed with hemoglobin (approximately 265 million molecules) and do not require a nucleus to dictate their activities. All a red blood cell has to do is be swept along with the current of the bloodstream. The hemoglobin in its interior alternately binds and releases molecules of oxygen.

Background material on cell nuclei can be found in CELL; CELL CYCLE; CYTOPLASM. *Advanced subjects are developed in* CELL MEMBRANE; CHROMOSOME; KARYOTYPING; TRANSPORT, CELLULAR. *More information on particular aspects is contained in* DNA REPLICATION; MEIOSIS; MITOSIS. *See also* EUKARYOTIC CELLS *and* PROKARYOTIC CELLS.

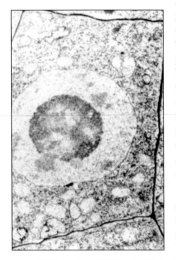

Above, a normal human cell—the cell nucleus can clearly be seen in the center of the cell, surrounded by the nuclear envelope.

Further Reading
Agutter, Paul S., *Between Nucleus and Cytoplasm* (1991); De Duve, Christian, *Blueprint for a Cell* (1991); Pollock, Robert, *Signs of Life* (1995); Strauss, Phyllis and Samuel Wilson, *The Eukaryotic Nucleus* (1990).

First see SETS AND GROUPS

Number

Next see NUMBER THEORY

A symbol used in counting or measuring.

Are we born with a sense of number already hard-wired in our brains? Recent research suggests rats possess a rudimentary ability to distinguish between "more" and "less." This ability to understand cardinal numbers, those obtained by one-to-one matching, is paralleled by the ability to understand ordinal numbers, those which exist in a sequence. Human beings, born with ten fingers, an equal number of toes, and a striking collection of symmetrical pairs of attributes —ears, eyes, nostrils, and so on—can be expected to develop number systems based on either a decadic or a binary base.

However, human history does not always confirm this seemingly basic idea. Some African tribes use three or four as their number base; many native American tribes and the Mayans used 20 as their base; and the ancient Babylonians had a number system based on 60. European number systems incorporate many of these nonstandard counting systems: in French, the word for 80 is *quatre-vingt*, or "four twenties," and the same number—"four score"—was memorably used by Abraham Lincoln. English also incorporates references to a duodecimal system (base 12), in words like "dozen" and "gross."

The foundation of counting in the western system, however, is the number 10. Some linguists believe that the very word "ten" is derived from an Indo-European root meaning "two hands," that "eleven" means "one left over," and that "hundred" means "ten times [ten]." One of the most important mathematical rules that children learn is that our number system is positional. In base ten, each position in a given numeral is filled by the corresponding power of ten:

$$4321 = 4 \times 10^3 + 3 \times 10^2 + 2 \times 10^1 + 1 \times 10^0.$$

Although this pattern is applicable to any number base, in some other system, such as the binary, most people find the equivalent to be much more difficult to decipher:

$$1000011100001 = (1 \times 2^{12}) + (1 \times 2^7) + (1 \times 2^6) + (1 \times 2^5) + (1 \times 2^0).$$

Numbers such as those written above are the result of developments covering thousands of years. The Hindu-Arabic numerals, which are used throughout the West, can be traced back only to around 800 C.E., and in published form only to 976; before that, the rules governing recording and manipulation of numbers—particularly large numbers—were simply arbitrary.

The recording of numbers in early societies was performed in two major ways: through the abacus, or counting board, in one of its many forms, or through the tally stick. The first of these is positional: one marks off parallel columns, each representing a separate power of ten, and then adds or subtracts counters in the appropriate columns to yield the desired number. The second is cardinal in nature, carving notches on a wooden rod to represent an agreed-upon rent, for example; when the rent is brought in and counted, the notches on the new tally are matched against those on the old tally. It was the burning of old tally sticks in the basement of the old English Houses of Parliament that led to the building's reduction to ashes in 1834.

Most early systems of numerals were based on simple grouping. Though they all used direct representation for 1, 2, and 3—Egyptian numerals employed the corresponding number of vertical lines, Chinese numerals employed horizontal lines, and the Mayans used dots—after that point the systems diverged; the symbol for ten could be an "X" (Roman), an upside-down "U" (Egyptian), a triangle (Greek), or a cross (Chinese). These were the only systems possible before the introduction of the zero.

Advent of the Zero. The Mayans were probably the first to use a symbol for zero in a positional system, although their number base was 20 and their numbers were written vertically rather than horizontally. The zero was then discovered independently in India and Persia, where it was written as the familiar circle, but with a dot in the center. The first writer to use it was the great Mohammed ibn Musa al-Khwarizmi, whose work *Al-Jabr wal-Muqabalah* gave the West a new word as well: "algebra." (*See* ZERO.)

The zero made its way to Europe most widely through the work of Leonardo Fibonacci, also called Pisano, whose *Liber Abaci* (Book of the Abacus) appeared in 1202, and John of Halifax, whose *Algorismus* (a corruption of al-Khwarizmi's name) appeared about 1250.

The concept of zero derives ultimately from transforming the act of counting into a linear act. Going from one to two is seen as walking, or moving one's finger, along a line in a certain direction—in Hindu-Arabic notation, from left to right. Going from one to zero, correspondingly, is seen as walking or tracing the path from right to left. The immediate corollary is the introduction of negative numbers as well, since extending one's path from zero one or more steps to the left leads one into negative territory: -1, -2, etc. At this point one can begin to develop algebra. (*See* ALGEBRA.)

Infinity. The second corollary is even more fascinating. As one walks along this number line, there will always appear another number in the distance; and when one reaches that number, another will appear, and so on. Thus, the concept of infinity is introduced into the concept of number. And of course this extension of the number line must be true in both directions, so negative infinity is discovered as well. This final visualization of the number line yields the entire set of natural numbers:

$$-\infty \,...\, -4 \; -3 \; -2 \; -1 \; 0 \; 1 \; 2 \; 3 \; 4 \,...\, \infty$$

These numbers, the integers, are the heart of mathematics. Their importance was articulated best by Leopold Kronecker (1823–1891): "God made integers; all else is the work of man." It is said that devotees of the Eleusinian Mysteries of ancient Greece, which counted among its high priests no less a figure than Pythagoras, actually worshiped numbers. Others, such as Albert Einstein, declared that "the series of integers is obviously an invention of the human mind."

First see NUMBER

Number Theory

Next see PROGRAM, COMPUTER

In the most famous application of number theory, mathematicians have sought to determine the characteristics of prime numbers. If a number can be divided only by one or itself, then that number is a prime number; if it has other divisors, it is called a composite number. Every composite number must therefore be the product

Further Reading
Clawson, Calvin C., *Mathematical Mysteries: The Beauty and Magic of Numbers* (2000); Clawson, Calvin C., *Mathematical Sorcery: Revealing the Secrets of Numbers* (1999); Conway, John Horton, *The Book of Numbers* (1997); Friedburg, Richard, *AN Adventurers Guide to Number Theory* (1994); Gazale, Midat J., *Number* (2000).

of some combination of prime numbers. Before computers, mathematicians slaved over the calculations necessary to produce tables of factors; J. P. Kulik of Prague (1773–1863) spent twenty years compiling a book listing all the factors of numbers up to 100 million.

Composite numbers can also be thought of as the sum of two factors. Leonhard Euler (1707–1783) was the first to theorize that a square number could be expressed as the sum of two squares. The question whether numbers could also be expressed as the sum of two higher powers became the subject of Fermat's Last Theorem, and was not proven until 1995.

As one might expect, the number of primes decreases as numbers grow larger; the prime number theorem was developed around 1800 to predict their frequency. This states that the number of primes before a given number x, termed $\pi(x)$, approaches $x / \log x$—or, as it is more commonly worded: $\lim \pi(x) / (x / \log x) = 1$. For the first million numbers there are 78,498 primes, while $(x / \log x)$ is 72,380; for the first 10^{14} (one hundred trillion) numbers, there are about 3.2 trillion primes, while $(x / \log x)$ is about 3.1 trillion; and so on. This theorem could not be proven using natural number theory until 1949.

The earliest group of number problems include Diophantine problems, so called because they were collected and published by Diophantos of Alexandria in the third century. Diophantine problems can still challenge the enthusiast; for example: "find two squares such that, when one forms their product and adds either number to it, the result is also a square."

Branches. An important branch of number theory is called geometric number theory, based on the special properties of the unit square lattice. This version of number theory substitutes counting the points in a specific region of a rectangular lattice for the arithmetic computation of a number. Lattice theory was first formulated by Hermann Minkowski in 1889, and extended by Hans Frederick Blichfeldt (an American mathematician) in 1914. Although lattice point theory sometimes seems far removed from classical number theory, the concept of "visibility" that is essential to geometric number theory turns out to relate directly to the concept of primes.

Because number theory deals with very large numbers, it has proven useful in fields as disparate as cryptography and graphic design, acoustics and chemistry. Random number generators, essential for efficient computer operations, often rely on number theory.

Further Reading
Chetwynd, Amanda, et al., *A Cascade of Numbers; An Introduction to Number Theory* (1998); Friedberg, Richard, *An Adventurer's Guide to Number Theory* (1994); Knopfmacher, J., *Abstract Analytic Number Theory* (1990); Koch, H., et al., *Algebraic Number Theory* (1997); Rose, H.E., *A Course in Number Theory* (1996).

Background material on number theory can be found in ALGEBRA; NUMBER; SETS AND GROUPS. Advanced subjects are developed in FERMAT'S LAST THEOREM; FUNCTIONS; LOGARITHM. Additional relevant information is contained in CATEGORY THEORY; COMPLEX NUMBERS; GÖDEL'S THEOREM.

First see METABOLISM

Nutrition

Next see DIGESTION REGULATION

The science that deals with the composition of foods, how they are used by animals—including humans—and their effects on health.

Good nutrition starts with an adequate supply of calories, or energy, from carbohydrates, fats, and proteins. Proteins also supply the amino acids, nitrogen-containing molecules. Proteins and other food elements supply minerals, such as calcium, phosphorus, potassium, sodium, chlorine, magnesium, iron, manganese, copper, iodine, cobalt, zinc, and fluorine. These must be taken in appropriate amounts. For example, an oversupply of sodium can lead to high blood pressure in susceptable individuals.

When the nutrients in food are digested, they are absorbed from the intestinal tract and distributed throughout the body in the blood. The carbon compounds found in carbohydrates, fats, and proteins play a major role in nutrition. They are used both to supply energy as they are metabolized and to build new body tissues. If there is an excess of these compounds, they are stored as fat. Since an excess of fat can be unhealthy, it is important to eat an adequate, but not excessive, amount of energy-supplying foods.

Requirements. Energy requirements differ according to body weight and levels of activity. For example, a man weighing 150 pounds burns just 65 calories per hour when he is asleep, but requires 1,100 calories per hour when engaged in moderate activity, such as walking up a flight of stairs. Some of the mineral elements absorbed from food are used to repair or build parts of the body, such as the bones. Others are required as parts of the system of enzymes, the molecules that carry out many of the functions of the body. Vitamins are essential parts of many enzyme systems, so that vitamin deficiency can lead to deficiency conditions. For example, a deficiency of vitamin C can cause scurvy.

Animals have their specific nutritional requirements, which they obtain from different sources. Carnivores such as lions and tigers are meat-eaters, while horses and related species consume grass and other plants. In turn, plants have their own nutritional requirements. They need 12 minerals, water, and carbon dioxide. The carbon dioxide is absorbed from the air, while other plant nutrients are absorbed from the ground through the roots. Most plants utilize the energy from sunlight to transform carbon dioxide into carbohydrates such as sugars, which then react with the water, oxygen, nitrogen, and sulfur in the plants to create carbohydrates, fats, proteins, and other carbon compounds that the plants need to grow and reproduce.

First see Plate Tectonics

Ocean Basins

Next see OCEANOGRAPHY

Bowl-shaped depressions found throughout the oceans. These basins are formed by tectonic movement and volcanic action, much as mountains are.

Ocean basins and ridges are among the most prominent underwater features on Earth. Perhaps the most noteworthy of the ridges is the Mid-Ocean Ridge, a 40,000-mile-long range of mountains that occupies the middle third of the South Pacific, Indian, and Atlantic Oceans. Some segments of the ridge are a few hundred miles wide; others can be as much as 3,000 miles wide. The height of different segments varies from 4,000 feet to as much as 12,000 feet above the floor of the adjoining basins.

Rift Valley. The most prominent features of the Mid-Ocean Ridge are the Rift Valley, the Rift Mountain, and the High Fractured Plateau, which form a strip 200 miles wide that runs through

Mitchell Basin
(N265090W)

both the Atlantic and Pacific Oceans. The Rift Valley, at the center of this strip, is bounded by the peaks of the Rift Mountains. These peaks rise 3,000 to 9,000 feet above the valley, then drop abruptly to the outward-located High Fractured Plateau, which lies in depths of 9,600 feet to nearly 11,000 feet on either side of the mountains.

The Mid-Ocean Ridge can be divided geologically into the crest provinces and the flank provinces. The crest provinces are geologically similar to the structures seen in the high plateaus of Africa. The flank provinces can be divided geologically into several steps, or ramps. These provinces have a geological structure that is similar to that of the ocean basins.

Origin Theories. There are different theories about the origin of the Mid-Ocean Ridge. One theory suggests that the ridge represents the geological debris left on the floor of the sea when the continents drifted apart. Another theory postulates that the ridge consists of sediments that filled the cracks that came into existence during the process of continental drift. The most widely accepted theory is that the Mid-Ocean Ridge is the result of geological tension, and that material is being added to the floor of the Rift Valley by rock flowing upward from the Earth's interior.

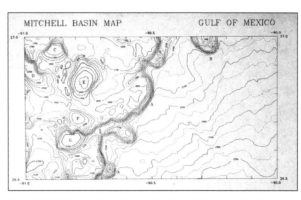

The NOAA's Exclusive Economic Zone Mapping Project maps portions of the oceans. Above, a standard map shows a portion of Sigsbee Escarpment in the Gulf of Mexico. Below, left, a 3-D map generated from the same kind of data used to create the standard map above.

Further developments in the field are discussed in EARTH, FORMATION OF; OCEAN CURRENT; OCEANS, ORIGIN AND EVOLUTION OF. *More details can be found in* OCEANOGRAPHY; SEISMOLOGY; UNDERWATER EXPLORATION. *Additional relevant information is in* PETROLOGY; SUBMARINE TECHNOLOGY; WAVES, OCEANIC.

Further Reading
Ballance, Peter F., *South Pacific Sedimentary Basins* (1994); Blondel, P., *Handbook of Seafloor Sonar Imagery* (1997); Geyer, Richard A., *CRC Handbook of Geophysical Exploration at Sea: Hard Minerals* (1992); Nicolas, A., *The Mid-Oceanic Ridges: Mountains Below Sea Level* (1995); Sinton, John M., *Evolution of Mid Ocean Ridges* (1989).

First see OCEAN BASIN

Ocean Current

Next see CLIMATOLOGY

The flow of water that results from forces such as the wind, differences in water density, and the Coriolis effect, caused by Earth's rotation.

Although ocean currents flow much slower than rivers, the amount of water they move is very great. For example, the Gulf Stream current is estimated to move as much as 90 million cubic yards of water per second in the vicinity of Chesapeake Bay. Current flows are measured by using such low-tech devices as the drift bottle, which is placed in a current with a note directed to the finder asking that it be returned with information about where and when it was found.

The major surface currents have a maximum depth of about 1,000 feet, shallower in the lower latitudes. Surface currents result directly or indirectly from wind forces, which not only move the surface layer of the water but also set up turbulence in water below the surface. Because of the Coriolis effect, the surface layer is deflected to the right of the wind direction in the Northern Hemisphere and to the left of the wind direction in the Southern Hemisphere.

Another form of ocean current is polar creep, in which water in the polar regions sinks and moves toward and past the Equator until it encounters even colder water and moves toward the surface. These convection currents are important to living things in the oceans; they carry dissolved oxygen to great depths and, when they move upward, carry life-supporting minerals toward the upper regions of the oceans.

Yet another current is the turbidity current, which consists of water made dense by the addition of mud or silt from the land. Turbidity currents are believed to be responsible for the deposit of sand and shells on the continental shelf at great distances from land masses.

Other Currents. Among the most notable currents are the Gulf Stream, which flows along the east coast of North America; the North Equatorial Current, which flows from Africa toward North America; the Canary Current, which flows south along the westernmost part of northern Africa; the Equatorial Current, which flows in the ocean between the southern part of Africa and Australia; the North Equatorial and South Equatorial Currents, which flow in opposite directions in the Pacific Ocean between Asia and South America; and the West Australian current, which flows along the northern coast of Australia.

In recent years, a number of currents have been found flowing at moderate depths in directions that are different from the direction of flow of the water above them, and the existence of currents at very great depths has been established by photographs that show current-caused ripples in sediments at the bottom of the sea.

Above, a simulated current is generated as a buoy streams from the bow of a test vessel in Puget Sound, Washington.

Above, the current line between greenish glacial meltwater and seawater is visible on the surface.

Below, right, a microwave-generated map of the Earth's oceans.

First see OCEAN, ORIGIN AND EVOLUTION OF

Oceanography

Next see UNDERWATER EXPLORATION

The scientific exploration and study of every aspect of Earth's seas and oceans.

Oceanography is a multi-faceted discipline that includes not only the water of the oceans and seas but also the sediments and rocks that lie beneath them, the interactions between their waters and the atmosphere, the movements of seawater, the plants and animals that live in the seas, the physics of the seas and of the sea floors, and the formation of beaches, shores, and estuaries.

Oceanography thus can be said to consist of the marine aspects of a number of scientific disciplines. Physical oceanography is the study of ocean waves, ocean currents, tides, the turbulence and mixing of ocean waters, and similar phenomena. Chemical oceanography examines a number of areas, such as: the elements that are essential nutrients of phytoplankton, the microscopic plants on which many ocean animals feed; trace organic substances in seawater; and the atmospheric gases and radioactive substances found in seawater. Geological oceanography studies the geological formations found under the seas, the building and erosion of beaches and other shore features, and sediments and their transport. Biological oceanography, or marine biology, studies the living creatures of the oceans and all the aspects of their existence.

History. The discipline of oceanography began in the middle decades of the nineteenth century. A crucial event in the history of oceanography was the raising in 1858 of one of the first submarine telegraph cables from the bottom of the Mediterranean. It was found encrusted with unknown living organisms, and marine biology was born of an effort to identify and understand them. In 1872, the British ship *Challenger* set out on a cruise that lasted for

OBSERVATIONS

The Voyage of St. Brendan

In the 6th century C.E., an Irish monk named Brendan had a vision that the Promised Land lay to the west, across the Atlantic Ocean. He built a 17-foot boat out of oxhides, caulked with beef tallow, and set sail to his destiny. After three years without a trace, Brendan returned with a spectacular story. He had sailed the North Atlantic currents all the way to North America—and returned to tell the tale. He took the Irminger Current north and west to Iceland, then the Greenland and Labrador Currents south past Canada, finally picking up the Gulf Stream for his voyage home.

Material related to ocean currents will be found in OCEAN BASINS; WAVES, OCEANIC; WINDS AND CLOUDS. *Advanced subjects are developed in* CONTINENTS, FORMATION OF; OCEANOGRAPHY; TIDES. *Basic aspects of this subject are covered in* CLIMATOLOGY; JET STREAM; SUBMARINE TECHNOLOGY; WEATHER.

Further Reading
Elsner, James B., *Hurricanes of the North Atlantic: Climate and Society* (1999); Kampion, Drew, *The Book of Waves: Form and Beauty on the Ocean* (1997); Pedlosky, Joseph, *Ocean Circulation Theory* (1996);

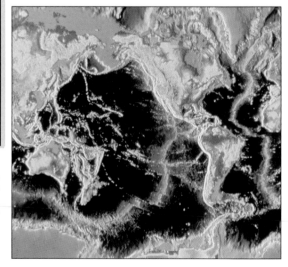

three and a half years, during which it circled the Earth and collected not only living creatures from the ocean floors but also rocks and sediments. More recently the descent in 1953 of French oceanographer Jean Picard to a depth of 10,000 feet in a specially designed underwater craft, the bathysphere, and the cruise under polar ice by the American nuclear submarine *Nautilus* in 1958 were great events of oceanography.

Today, there are important oceanographic institutes, laboratories, and university departments in every major nation, with perhaps a score of them in the United States alone. More than 20 oceanographic vessels are in operation, again from a number of countries. International cooperation by these institutions and ships is a well-established custom, fostered by the International Council for the Exploration of the Seas, which was established in 1901 to promote the study of the North Sea, and is further supported by several similar organizations.

Above, oceanographers deploy a conductivity-temperature-depth rosette.

TOOLS

Heavy Baggage

Most oceanographic studies are done on ships, including submarines, but oceanographers also use aircraft, shore stations, anchored buoys, and even ice islands to make their observations. The equipment on an oceanographic vessel includes some sonic detectors, instruments that can be lowered for miles on wires operated by winches, thermometers for measuring sea temperatures at various depths, nets and trawls for capturing fish and other living creatures, and so on, in an almost endless variety. An oceanographic vessel may tow a variety of instruments, such as instruments that measure the strength of the Earth's magnetic field and light meters that measure underwater visibility.

First see OCEAN BASINS

Oceans, Origin and Evolution of

Next see OCEANOGRAPHY

The origin of the oceans, which cover more than three-quarters of Earth's surface, dates back to Earth's formation 4.6 billion years ago. In the past, three possible theories have been suggested as to the sources of the water in the oceans, representing over 99 percent of the Earth's surface water. The first is that the water arrived as part of the icy coating of comets; the second that the water arrived as part of meteorites that struck the Earth, and the third that it separated out from the rocks of the Earth itself.

Further Reading
Calder, Nigel, *Comets: Speculation and Discovery* (1994); Levy, David H., *Comets: Creators and Destroyers* (1998); Sagan, Carl, *Comet* (1997).

To determine the correct theory, the composition of the atmosphere and seawater is studied. Using these methods, it has been determined that comets could not be the source for all of the ocean water. The ice in comets studied so far, namely Halley's and Hyakutake, contains twice as much deuterium, an isotope of hydrogen, than does seawater.

Meteorites are also unlikely as a source for all the water on Earth. Meteorites carry a lot of excess xenon, an inert gas that is relatively rare on Earth. If meteorites were the source of ocean water, Earth's atmosphere would contain nearly ten times as much xenon as it does. Comets do not contain high concentrations of xenon. However, a theory combining water from both sources—meteorites and comets—also presents difficulties, as there would still have to be more deuterium than is found in the oceans.

The best model is a combination of cometary water and water that was trapped in the Earth's rocks as the planet was formed. If some of the water vapor came from the local region of the solar nebula (a cloud of gas and dust surrounding the sun), it would be low enough in deuterium to "balance" the cometary amount.

Accretion. Earth, its oceans, and its atmosphere all evolved together. Water and other volatile compounds were probably released from Earth's rocks as the planet solidified. During the Earth's accretion phase (its accumulation and solidifying from smaller objects called planetesimals), kinetic energy was converted into thermal energy, causing the planet to grow extremely hot. Most of the water was probably present as liquid water trapped in clay or as separate hydrogen and oxygen atoms (from hydrocarbons and iron oxides), rather than as ice crystals.

Like the rest of the planet, the oceans are still evolving. For the last 4 billion years, there has been a continual exchange of volatile material such as water between Earth's surface (crust) and interior (mantle).

Plate tectonics have caused oceanic water to mix with material from the planet's interior. Volcanoes also release water and carbon dioxide to the atmosphere and to the ocean. Subduction of sediments rich in volatiles takes place in deep ocean trenches. The ocean crust sinks at these subduction zones and carries water and carbon dioxide back into the mantle.

Further developments in the field are discussed in OCEAN BASINS; OCEAN CURRENT; OCEANOGRAPHY. *Advanced subjects are developed in* PLANETARY ATMOSPHERE; UNDERWATER EXPLORATION; WINDS AND CLOUDS. *Background material on this subject is covered in* HYDROLOGIC CYCLE; WATER; WAVES.

First see CHARGE AND CURRENT

Ohm's Law

Next see ELECTRIC CURRENT

A rule devised by Georg Simon Ohm, a 19th-century German physicist, to formulate the relationship between the electric current passing through the material of an electrical circuit and the resistance of the material in the electrical circuit.

Ohm's law can be expressed as $R=V/I$, where R is the resistance in ohms, V is the potential difference of the circuit in volts, and I is the current in amperes. This simple relationship is based on the idea that a material that can carry an electric current contains mobile electric charges; it can be positively charged, negatively charged, or both. When the source of the voltage produces an electric field, these mobile charges move in the direction of the electric force that is exerted on them. In most cases, the mobile charges carrying the current are electrons, but the conventions of electricity were determined before atomic structure was understood. Thus, despite the physical direction of electron flow, current is said to flow out of the positive terminal of a battery that is connected to a circuit and into the negative terminal. (*See* ELECTRIC CIRCUITS.)

The basic statement made by Ohm's law is that the current in any circuit is proportional to the voltage that is applied to the circuit. The value of R, the resistance, depends on the material of which the circuit is made and varies with the temperature of the material. A pure metal whose temperature is drastically reduced usually has its resistivity lowered by many orders of magnitude. (*See* CONDUCTORS AND RESISTORS.)

A Model. A simple model helps to explain the behavior of materials that obey Ohm's law. In this model, electrons are envisioned as moving continuously, randomly, and with high velocities, colliding with atomic impurities or other imperfections in the lattice structure of the conducting material. When a potential difference is applied, it produces an electric field that accelerates the motion of the electrons. Some of the extra kinetic energy gained by the electrons is lost to the lattice every time a collision occurs.

Ohm's law has been found to be valid for metallic conductors over a wide range of conditions. It is valid to a lesser extent when applied to semiconductors and liquids that conduct electricity, and does not apply to the flow of electricity through gases or vacuum tubes. The resistance of semiconductors is midway between that of metals and of dielectric materials. The resistance of semiconductors is greatly affected by the addition of very small amounts of impurities. Ohm's law is extremely useful in the design and analysis of electric circuits made of many different kinds of material. (*See* SEMICONDUCTORS.)

First see GENE

Oncogene

Next see CANCER

A gene capable of transforming normal eukaryotic cells into cancerous ones.

Cancer is uncontrolled cell division, resulting when cells ignore the normal "brakes" imposed upon when and how often they can divide and increase rapidly in number at the expense of nearby cells. Often these cells are abnormal in terms of function as well.

Genes are segments of DNA responsible for the production of a particular protein. Any gene containing a product that stimulates a cell to divide uncontrollably is considered an oncogene. Oncogenes are mutated versions of proto-oncogenes, genes that play a role in normal cell division. Usually these genes are involved in making enzymes for mitosis (replication of all genetic material in the nucleus prior to cell division), growth factors, and other chemical signals. (*See* MITOSIS.)

Under Study. Examples of oncogenes currently being studied include ras genes and myc genes. Normal ras genes are signaled by growth factors to stimulate other proteins to be active. Mutant ras genes transmit instructions continuously, even in the absence of their growth factors. They are found in 25 percent of all human tumors, including carcinomas, offering a hopeful avenue of cancer therapy.

A myc oncogene alters the activity of transcription factors, which are used in the early stages of protein synthesis. The myc transcription factors normally are made only after stimulation by growth factors on the cell's surface. In individuals who have cancer, myc levels rise very high, even in the absence of these growth factors.

If a cell has one normal and one mutated gene, the oncogene is dominant. No oncogene by itself can cause cancer, but it can increase the rate of mitosis in its cell. Rapidly dividing cells are at an increased risk for further mutations. When a cell accumulates several active oncogenes (the critical number is believed to be around half a dozen), it loses control over its mitosis and becomes a cancerous cell.

Retrovirus. Some oncogenes, instead of arising from mutations in proto-oncogenes, are carried into a cell by a retrovirus (a virus that uses RNA as its genetic material instead of DNA). Oncogenes of retrovirus origin are called v-onc instead of the eukaryotic c-onc. A v-onc gene enables a virus to "transform" a specific type of host cell. It is believed that v-onc genes originate from RNA copies of c-onc genes and are expressed only at low levels, as opposed to v-onc genes, which are expressed at high levels. (*See* VIRUS.)

First see SOLAR SYSTEM

Oort Cloud

Next see COMET

The Oort cloud is believed by many astronomers to be the residence of a great mass of comets. Named for Jan H. Oort, the twentieth-century Dutch astronomer who proposed its existence, the Oort cloud is beyond the farthest planets of the solar system, at a distance estimated to be between 20,000 and 100,000 astronomical units (an astronomical unit is the distance from the Earth to the sun). The mass of the matter in the Oort Cloud may contain 100 thou-

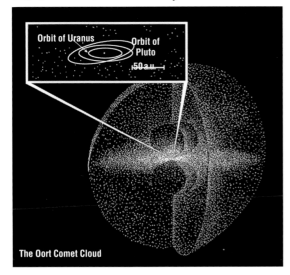

The Oort Comet Cloud

sand million comets and is a relic of the cloud from which the solar nebula formed. At the distance of the Oort cloud, the orbit of comets is subject to stellar perturbations, which propel a comet into the inner part of the solar system, where it can be seen by observers on earth.

Paths of Comets. Comets that leave the Oort cloud and enter the planetary region are either dynamically ejected into interstellar space, well outside the solar system and the Oort cloud, or are captured into short-period orbits that keep them in the solar system, as a result of the gravitational effects of Jupiter or Saturn. Comets that are trapped in short-period orbits gradually decay. Some of them form meteor streams; collections of dust particles that have a common orbit and that intersect the orbit of the Earth, giving rise to predictable annual meteor showers.

One theory explaining the source of the comets is that they may be icy planetesimals formed in the vicinity of Uranus and Neptune and then gravitationally ejected into the Oort cloud as a result of close

Further Reading
Oort, Jan Hendrik, *The Letters and Papers of Jan Hendrik Oort* (1997); Sagan, C., *Comet* (1997); Anderson, H.A., *Oort and the Universe* (1980).

Comets are observed to come to the solar system from all directions; therefore, it is believed that a giant sphere populated by comets surrounds the solar system. This sphere has been named the Oort Cloud after Jan Oort (below), who postulated its existence in 1950. Some comets come from closer in, a region of space called the Kuiper belt (bottom), located past the orbit of Pluto.

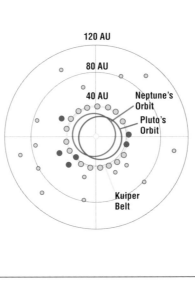

encounters with a planet. Another theory is that comets originated in orbits outside that of Pluto, the outermost planet. According to this theory, comets may be frozen, unaltered samples of the interstellar material out of which the solar system was formed.

Related areas to be considered are ASTEROIDS AND METEORS; COMET; SOLAR SYSTEMS. *More details can be found in* GRAVITY; JUPITER; PLANET. *More information on particular aspects is contained in* INTERSTELLAR MEDIUM ("DARK MATTER"); KEPLER'S LAWS.

First see COMPUTER, DIGITAL

Operating System

Next see PROGRAM, COMPUTER

The program that controls the basic functions and operations of a computer.

Computer operating systems occupy a vital place in computer operations. They must perform five basic functions: initializing the main hardware; providing basic routines for controlling peripheral devices; scheduling programs to run; managing and organizing memory; and maintaining system integrity. It must also communicate with users, typically through a shell interface, which can be either text-based, as in MS-DOS and UNIX, or graphical, as in Windows95 and MAC/OS. In addition to these kernel tasks, an operating system must exercise file management and task scheduling.

History. The earliest operating systems were of the batch type, allowing only one program to run at a time; in addition, input data could not be modified once a program had begun. The next generation of operating systems was interactive, so that data could be modified. Then came time sharing, first with multi-user capability and later with multi-tasking capability. Once these challenges had been met, the computer had effectively been transformed from a dedicated, single-purpose calculating machine to a flexible, multi-user system, one that could perform both text and numerical manipulations.

The first operating system that fit on a single floppy disk was achieved by Gary Kildall, whose CP/M (Control Program for Microcomputers) was developed in 1974. CP/M included a single-user file system, designed to prevent data loss and recover directory information.

In 1981, CP/M was adopted by the Microsoft Corporation for its own operating system and renamed MS-DOS. With its short filenames and rigid command structure, it proved decidedly inferior to the Apple Macintosh operating system introduced in 1982, which incorporated the first commercial graphical interface and mouse-driven menu controls. Nevertheless, like the inferior VHS system of videotape recording, MS-DOS achieved industry dominance through its multiplatform architecture and a contract with IBM. Microsoft has finally created a system that is almost as simple to use and as powerful as Apple's design with its Windows family of operating systems.

Many operating systems do not communicate well with other operating systems; for example, a program written for a Macintosh will not run in Windows. The operating system UNIX, first released in the late 1970s, is written in a programming language, C, that makes it usable with a variety of different systems. Also, UNIX easily handles multiple users working on it at the same time. Although many people find UNIX difficult to use because it is text-based and uses non-intuitive commands, its combination of portability and multitasking often makes it a system of choice for network servers.

Further Reading
Stallings, William, *Operating Systems: Internals and Design Principles* (1997); Tanenbaum, Andrew S., *Modern Operating Systems* (1992); Tanenbaum, Andrew S., *Operating Systems: Design and Implementation* (1997).

Background material can be found in COMPILER; COMPUTER, DIGITAL; PROGRAM, COMPUTER. *Further developments in the field are discussed in* ASCII; PARALLEL COMPUTING; SUPERCOMPUTER. *Special topics in this area are found in* ARTIFICIAL INTELLIGENCE; CONTROL SYSTEMS; EXPERT SYSTEM.

First see OPERATING SYSTEM

Operations Research

Next see GAME THEORY

The application of scientific methods and techniques to a decision-making process.

Whenever one is faced with a set of alternative courses of action, each of which leads to different results, one faces an operations research problem. There are two main methods of choosing among alternatives: mathematical models and stochastic processes. The major difference is that one can optimize mathematical problems; one can only satisfy stochastic, or probabilistic, problems.

The foundations of operations research were laid during the early years of the 20th century, when changes in technology, both industrial and war-related, demanded new tools. Early researchers studied methods of controlling submarine losses, of queuing telephone calls at early switchboards, and of replenishing business inventories. During World War II, groups like "Blackett's circus" employed physiologists, physicists, mathematicians, and geographers working together to coordinate England's defense plans. After the war, "think tanks" like the RAND Corporation were established to analyze American strategy and find the most effective combination of tactics. The method they developed, called linear programming, lies at the heart of modern management techniques.

Further Reading
Berlinsky, David, *The Advent of the Algorithm* (2000); Davis, Martin, *The Universal Computer* (2000); Hillier, Frederick S., *Introduction to Operations Research* (2000); Kim, Daniel H., *Itroduction to Systems Thinking* (1999); Nemhauser, G.L., *Handbooks in Operations Research and Management Science, 1: Optimization* (1994).

Linear Programming. In all operations research situations, the problem must first be formulated. What are the relevant variables? What are the inescapable constraints? What function is the solution designed to maximize? For example, a manufacturer faces numerous production variables related to many items: size of the projected market, availability of components, profit margins, and training and human resources costs. Linear programming works by transforming all these inequalities into equations. Then, so long as one has only two main variables, one can graph each equation to produce an irregular polygon; the vertex of the polygon that satisfies the Pareto criterion (the farthest upward and rightward on the graph) will be the optimal solution.

Real linear programming problems, of course, may have thousands of variables and constraints. Consider how many options must be faced by manufacturers of automobiles, computers, or clothing; for them, computer algorithms have been established to reach optimal solutions. One of the most important such algorithms is the matrix method. Other mathematical methods include geometric programming; dynamic programming, also known as the calculus of variation method; and back-propagation.

The other major category of operations research problems involves stochastic processes, which are distributed according to probability. In any industry where customer flow is important, managers rely on queuing theory. By analyzing changes in the load factor, a decision-maker knows when to open another check-out line or schedule another flight. A second major stochastic method is simulation, based on mathematical theories of probability and statistics. Sometimes it is possible to sample the actual population, as when a school district analyzes birthrate data in order to project needs 15 years in the future; more often, however, one must sample through random number generation. The third method is to use Markov chains, in which an initial matrix of transformations is established and then these assumptions are played out through a number of generations in a computer simulation; when a steady-state solution is reached, it represents an optimization.

Applications of operations research span the gamut of the modern world. It is used in production planning and staffing projections, to allocate raw materials and minimize waste, to design communication networks, to test system reliability, and to simulate client-server relations.

The foundations of the subject are discussed in DIFFERENTIAL EQUATIONS; OPERATING SYSTEMS; STATISTICS. *Further details can be found in* COMPUTER-AIDED DESIGN; ERROR ANALYSIS; GAME THEORY. *Advanced subjects are developed in* KNOTS; PARALLEL COMPUTING; SUPERCOMPUTER.

Optics

First see LIGHT

Next see LENS

Optics was originally defined as the branch of physics dealing with light and its interactions with matter. Now that visible light is known to be a segment of the electromagnetic spectrum, optics is the study of electromagnetic radiation with wavelengths longer than x-rays and shorter than radio waves.

Optics is usually divided into two fields. Physical optics emphasizes the wave and particle nature of light and related radiation; geometric optics regards light and related electromagnetic radiation as a mathematical abstraction.

Physical optics studies the behavior of light in specific media. Physiological optics, for example, is the study of vision, the sense that is triggered in humans and animals by changing light patterns. The eye is a very complex instrument. While the geometric aspects of vision are well understood—and are applied in optometry and ophthalmology—the links between vision and perception that allow formation of a mental image from an optical image are still being studied. One example is color vision. It has been understood as an optical phenomenon for nearly three centuries, since Isaac Newton demonstrated that the eye interprets the wavelengths of light in terms of subjective color. But the exact process by which the eye-brain combination performs this interpretation is still being researched actively. Similarly, the study of the perception of shapes, patterns, movements, and spatial relationships is a very active field of physiological optics.

History. Modern optics can be said to have been born in 1704, with the publication of Isaac Newton's *Opticks,* which explained that light actually consists of a mixture of all the colors in the spectrum. Each set of rays forming one colored patch in the spectrum was described by Newton as an individual entity, characterized by how it was affected when passed through a prism. Newton was able to explain many previously baffling phenomena, such as chromatic aberration, the formation of colored fringes when white light passes through glass.

Applications. Optics can also be used to study other electromagnetic radiation. For example, the flow of beams of electrons through a vacuum tube can be analyzed in terms of geometric optics. There are many electronic devices that are comparable to lenses, prisms, and other optical elements, used in the construction of quasi-optical devices, such as the electron microscope, which can view objects that are too small to be observed with a light microscope.

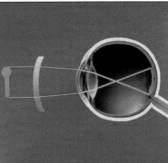

Above, lenses are used to change the eye's focal length, thereby correcting poor vision.

Further Reading
Bass, Michael, et al., *Handbook of Optics* (1994); Bohren, Craig F., *Absorption and Scattering of Light by Small Particles* (1998); Meardon, Susan L. Wymer, *The Elements of Fiber Optics* (1992).

The instruments used in optics are divided into two classes: those used for optical projection, such as the camera, and those used to aid natural vision, such as the microscope and the telescope. Optical projection instruments form a real image of an object on a screen or photographic plate, using a lens system or a mirror. Natural vision instruments depend on placing the eye of an observer so that it views an image formed by the optical system. A real image, one that produces a picture when projected on a screen, may or may not be formed in the interior of the instrument. But the virtual image created by the instrument, while it cannot produce a picture, is seen by the eye. Both types of optical instrument use an objective lens or mirror; in natural vision instruments, the final image is formed by an eyepiece, or ocular. A natural vision instrument usually has several stops, apertures that limit the cross section of the beam of light that can pass through it.

TOOLS

Adaptive Optics

Earth-based telescopes cannot approach the power of orbiting observatories—or can they? Adaptive optics is a technique that uses computers to determine the amount and direction of atmospheric distortion, then changes the optical path of the telescope ever so slightly to correct it. Since many modern telescopes employ multiple mirror systems, these changes are easily accomplished by adjusting the appropriate mirrors.

Elementary aspects of this subject are covered in LENS; LIGHT; MIRRORS; REFLECTION AND REFRACTION; WAVE. *More information on particular aspects is contained in* ELECTROMAGNETIC WAVES; HOLOGRAPHY; POLARIZED LIGHT. *Additional relevant information is contained in* FIBER OPTICS; LASERS AND MASERS; NONLINEAR OPTICS.

First see SURGERY

Organ Transplantation

Next see AUTOIMMUNITY

The replacement of a diseased organ with a healthy and compatible one obtained from another person.

Organ transplantation can also involve replacement of a tissue, notably in the case of corneal grafting, the first such operation to be performed. In this procedure, the tissue that covers the eyeball is replaced because it has become too cloudy to permit normal vision. Corneal grafting was done successfully early in the twentieth century because the cornea is not affected by the action of the body's immune system to attack and destroy foreign cells. The next attempt at organ transplantation came decades later, in the 1950s, when kidney transplantation was attempted. Most of the first attempts were unsuccessful because of the rejection problem. An exception was the first successful kidney transplant performed in 1955 at the Harvard Medical School. The organ was not rejected because it came from the recipient's identical twin. General organ transplantation became possible in the 1960s with the development of drugs to suppress the rejection process.

Christiaan Barnard. A milestone in organ transplantation was the first heart transplant, performed in Cape Town, South Africa, by Dr. Christiaan Barnard. The first immunosuppressant drugs were corticosteroids and anticancer drugs, but the field broadened considerably in the 1970s and 1980s with the introduction of cyclosporine, a more effective drug.

Another advance that promoted organ transplantation was the development of better methods for making sure that a donated organ is similar enough to the tissues of the recipient that the immune rejection response will be muted. Tissue typing is done by comparing the donor's and recipient's histocompatibility antigens, the proteins in and on the surface of cells that are recognized as foreign by another person's immune system.

Current State. Since the condition of the organ that is to be transplanted is important to the long-term success of the procedure, advanced techniques for preserving organs have been developed. After the organ is removed from the donor, it is washed in an oxygen-rich fluid and is kept cold to reduce the possibility of damage from lack of oxygen. The operation is done as soon as possible after the removal of the organ. The organs that are transplanted on a regular basis include the heart, the liver, the pancreas, and the kidney. In 1998, the first transplantation of a hand was reported.

Kidney transplantation is by far the most common procedure currently, in large part because donor organs are easier to obtain, since each person has two kidneys and can survive with only one. Even so, a recipient of a donor organ must almost invariably take drugs to suppress the immune response indefinitely. Because these drugs reduce the body's protection against infectious agents, organ recipients are more prone to infections, especially by fungi, and also have an increased risk of developing certain kinds of cancer.

Further Reading
Caplan, Arthur L., *The Ethics of Organ Transplants: The Current Debate* (1999); Pizer, H.F., *Organ Transplants: A Patient's Guide* (1991); Youngner, Stuart J., *Organ Transplantation: Meanings and Realities* (1996).

Background material relating to organ transplantation can be found in Autoimmunity; Heart; Immune Response; Kidney; Liver. *Other aspects of the subject are discussed in* Major Histocompatability Complex (MHC); Surgery. *Related material can be found in* Cloning; Organogenesis; Prosthesis.

First see Carbon

Organic Compounds

Next see Hydrocarbons

Compounds composed of chains of carbon molecules bonded to each other.

Organic molecules, such as carbohydrates, lipids, proteins, and nucleic acids, are the main structural components of cells and tissues. In addition, they are highly involved in all metabolic reactions and act as the fuel molecules of living systems. Also included as organic compounds are molecules that seemingly have no immediate connection to living things, such as fossil fuels, oils, waxes, artificial sweeteners, alcohols, plastics, rubber, and synthetic polymers and fibers.

All organic compounds have at least one of these five distinguishing features:

1. a tetrahedral shape for the molecule when carbon is bonded to four single atoms;

2. a tendency to form bonds with itself, leading to long chains of linked carbon atoms (known as polymers);

3. branched and cross-linked chains;

4. double and triple bonds, in which a carbon atom shares either two or three pairs of electrons with an adjacent atom (instead of just one pair), resulting in an unsaturated chain; and

5. a ring structure with alternating double and single bonds, known as delocalized aromatic bonds.

Bonds. All organic compounds are held together by covalent bonds, in which pairs of electrons are shared between the atoms involved. Covalent bonds are much stronger than ionic bonds, in which one atom gains electrons that the other atom has lost. Due to the stronger bonds holding them together, and the absence of free ions eager to bond with an oppositely charged entity, organic compounds undergo chemical reactions at a much slower rate than do inorganic compounds.

Typical organic molecules are nonpolar, meaning that the ends of an individual molecule have no electric charge. At room temperature they are either gases, liquids, or low-melting solids. They are held together by weak intermolecular forces known as van der Waals forces. This means that organic liquids have high vapor pressures, which accounts for their strong odors and low boiling points. Among the more prominent examples are vanilla, naphthalene (mothballs), and ether. Organic solids have low melting points relative to inorganic solids, ranging from room temperature to approximately 400 degrees Celsius.

Because they are nonpolar, organic liquids and solutions do not conduct electrical currents, nor are they soluble in polar solvents like water.

They do dissolve readily in nonpolar solvents. Two organic materials, acetic acid (vinegar) and ethyl alcohol, are themselves slightly polar and can dissolve in water, but these are exceptions.

Of the millions of known carbon compounds, only the carbonates and carbon oxides (numbering around 60,000) are classified as inorganic. Carbon fixation is the process by which inorganic carbon can be changed to the organic form. This transformation can be done in a laboratory, but it also occurs on a regular basis in nature, during the series of chemical reactions that make up the later stages of photosynthesis.

CONTROVERSIES

Organic Roots

The current misconception over the word "organic" has its roots in the history of scientific investigation. It was originally believed that organic compounds, or "compounds of life," could be produced only by living organisms or from their components. In 1776, Karl Scheele, a German scientist, sought to disprove this idea by making oxalic acid, an organic compound, by reacting sugar with nitric acid. His proof was not accepted because one of his reactants, sugar, came from a living thing. However, in 1828, another German scientist named Friedrich Wöhler, synthesized urea (an organic substance found in urine) by reacting together two inorganic compounds, ammonium chloride and silver cyanate. This was the first conclusive evidence that organic compounds could be produced outside of living systems.

Background material can be found in CARBOHYDRATES; CARBON; NUCLEIC ACIDS. *More details can be found in* ENZYMES; KREBS CYCLE; SOAPS AND DETERGENTS. *Elementary aspects of this subject are covered in* CYCLIC COMPOUNDS; HYDROCARBONS; PETROLOGY.

First see EMBRYOLOGY

Organogenesis

Next see GENOME, HUMAN

The development of bodily organs.

Organogenesis begins with a single cell, the fertilized egg known as a zygote. The zygote divides several times until a ball of cells, called the blastula, is formed. The blastula is a hollow structure, one cell-layer thick.

The blastula develops into the gastrula, with two cell layers, through the process of invagination, an inward migration of cells. These cell layers are known as the ectoderm (outer layer) and endoderm (inner layer). A third cell layer, called the mesoderm, eventually forms between them through the same process.

From these three cell layers arise all body systems and structures:
1. ectoderm—central nervous system, skin;
2. mesoderm—musculoskeletal, reproductive, endocrine, and excretory systems;
3. endoderm—digestive system, lungs.

Cells having the same structure and function and located in the same area compose a tissue. Tissues located together, with the same general function, compose an organ. Organs with related functionality compose a system. For example, individual cells of the same type that secrete a particular acidic enzyme together form a specific gastric tissue. Other tissues, whose cells secrete other digestive enzymes, together make up the stomach, which in turn is one of several organs of the digestive system.

How do the cells "know" what kinds of tissue to develop into? Somehow, probably through chemical messengers, the cells "communicate" with each other. Tissues develop in certain ways based upon what other tissues are nearby. This process is known as embryonic induction.

Experiments have shown that location directs the development process. Scientists have "relocated" cells of early frog embryos. Cells that should have developed into eyes, upon being moved to the tail region, instead developed into more tail tissue. Cells from the tail, upon being transplanted to the head region, developed into tissue normally found on the head.

First see ORGANIC COMPOUND

Organometallic Compounds

Next see COATINGS AND FILMS

Compounds in which an organic group is bonded directly to a metal atom.

The majority of the organic groups involved with organometallic compounds are alkyls (from the hydrocarbon series called alkanes) or aryls (aromatic hydrocarbons). All organometallic molecules decompose in water, but are soluble in various organic solvents like ethers and alkanes. They are extremely reactive and quite useful in the synthesis of other organic materials.

The most prominent organometallic compounds are those that contain any of the alkali metals (group IA on the Periodic Table), chiefly magnesium and lithium. They form specific types of salts—ionic compounds made up of a positively charged and a negatively charged ion. In this case, the alkali metal forms the cation (positive ion) and the organic component, called the carbanion, is the anion (negative ion).

The magnesium compounds are among the most important, particularly the alkyl magnesium halides. They make up the group of chemicals known as Grignard reagents, which are the basis of many synthesis reactions.

Some of the organometallic compounds are so reactive they will spontaneously burst into flame on contact with air. For this reason their reactions are generally carried out under inert atmospheres made up of nitrogen or helium.

There is a special category of organometallic molecules, called porphins, that are involved in some of the most basic cellular chemical reactions. Porphins are flat organic molecules that have a metal atom bonded in the center. For this reason they are known as chelating groups. When iron is the atom involved, the porphin formed is heme, which is found in the protein hemoglobin. Hemoglobin is a major component of human red blood cells and is used to transport oxygen around the body and to body tissues. It is the iron atom in the heme that actually binds the oxygen molecule and then releases it as needed.

A related molecule, the cytochrome, also has iron in its center. Cytochromes are used by cells during the combustion of organic molecules—carbohydrates and lipids—to produce energy in a process known as cellular respiration. This process takes place in a series of sequential chemical reactions. As energy is released, it is "harnessed" into a form of chemical energy that the cell can use, a molecule called adenosine triphosphate (ATP), which is the energy "currency" of the cell.

When an atom of magnesium is used in a porphin, the resulting molecule is chlorophyll, a light-sensitive pigment found in plants and used for photosynthesis, a process by which glucose is produced. (*See* METAL.)

First see FILTRATION

Osmosis

Next see CHROMATOGRAPHY

The diffusion of water across a cell membrane, either entering or leaving the cell.

Cell membranes, which separate the contents of the cell from the outside, are highly permeable to water. The specific direction in which the water molecules move depends on the concentration gradient. Water always crosses to the side with a higher concentration of solute.

The side of the membrane with the lower concentration of dissolved molecules is said to be hypotonic and the other side, with a higher concentration, is hypertonic. These terms refer to both the cell and its environment. If one is hypertonic, the other one must be hypotonic, and vice versa.

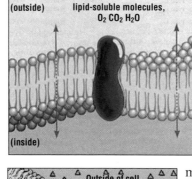

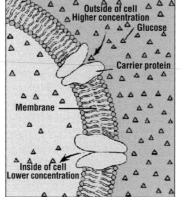

Cell membranes allow molecules to pass through them in different ways. Top, a lipid-soluble membrane allows lipids to diffuse in and out of the cell. Above, glucose is brought into a cell by carrier proteins which aid in keeping water in the cell against the osmotic gradient created by the high concentration of glucose outside the cell. Right, a diagram of a synthetic permeable membrane in operation.

Further Reading
Eisenberg, Talbert N., *Reverse Osmosis Treatment of Drinking Water* (1986); Pfeffer, Wilhelm, *Osmotic Investigations: Studies on Cell Mechanics* (1993); Ranney, Maurice W. *Desalinization by Reverse Osmosis* (1970).

When a cell is hypotonic in relation to its environment, the direction of water flow is out of the cell. Eventually the cell loses so much water it undergoes plasmolysis; it shrivels up and dies.

Balance. Just as losing water is harmful to the individual cell, so is the influx of too much water. A cell that is hypertonic in relation to its environment continually has water flowing into it. Eventually a "danger point" is reached, where the cell contains so much water it literally bursts. Animal cells are more susceptible to this fate than plant cells, because plant cells have larger and more numerous contractile vacuoles, organelles that remove excess water. Additionally, plant cells have a structure known as the cell wall surrounding the outer membrane. The excess water accumulates between the membrane and the wall, giving the plant cell a rigidity known as turgor.

Effect of Salt. The direction of water flow between hypotonic and hypertonic areas is also why a diet high in salt causes body tissues to retain water, leading to swelling. High salt intake can also lead to an increase in blood volume and, consequently, in blood pressure.

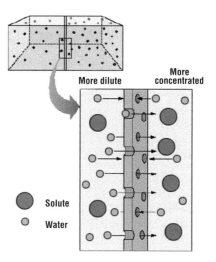

Isotonic means that both sides of the membrane have an equal concentration of solid particles, and therefore water moves freely in either direction. Bodily fluids such as tears are specifically designed to be isotonic in relation to the surrounding cells.

Background material can be found in FILTRATION; LIQUID; SOLVATION AND PRECIPITATION. **More details can be found in** CENTRIFUGATION; CHROMATOGRAPHY; SALTS; WATER IN LIVING CELLS. **More information on particular aspects is contained in** CELL MEMBRANE; LIQUID TRANSPORT.

First see INTERNAL COMBUSTION ENGINE

Otto Cycle Engine

Next see DIESEL ENGINE

The Otto engine is perhaps the most familiar internal combustion engine, since it powers most of today's automobiles and trucks. It was the first internal combustion engine. The original version of the engine was developed in 1876 by Nikolaus Otto, a German inventor. The first version used gas as a fuel, but the development of the oil industry at the end of the nineteenth century made possible a switch to gasoline as a fuel.

The conventional Otto engine is a four-stroke engine; it produces power on only one of those strokes. On the first stroke, a mixture of air and fuel is drawn through open valves by a descending piston. On the second stroke, the valves close and the piston rises, compressing the mixture of air and fuel, raising its temperature. At this point, ignition occurs. A spark, produced by a spark plug, ignites the mixture of air and fuel so that it burns and expands, pushing the piston down. This is the stroke that produces power. On the fourth stroke, an exhaust valve opens, the piston moves up again, and the gases consumed in the power stroke are expelled.

To get a continuous output of power, an Otto engine must have at least four pistons, whose ignition is timed in the correct sequence. Many of today's automobiles have engines with eight pistons. These automobile engines have their pistons, or cylinders, arranged in either a line or in a "V." (*See* AUTOMOTIVE DESIGN.)

First see REDOX REACTION

Oxidizing Agents

Next see ANTIOXIDANTS

Oxidation is a chemical combination with oxygen. It occurs every time a piece of fruit turns brown upon exposure to air, or when metal rusts. But beneath the surface of the physical changes, a chemical change is occurring as well, involving the electrons (negatively charged particles) of the reactant compounds.

The oxidation number, also known as the oxidation state, is the "charge" an atom has when it is part of an ion or neutral molecule. An atom in its elemental state (not part of a compound) has an oxidation number of zero. Oxidation refers to a loss of or decreased hold on electrons. Reduction is the opposite—a gain of or increased hold on electrons. These two processes must always occur together, maintaining the original total of the oxidation numbers, and are therefore known as "redox" reactions.

In every redox reaction, the oxidizing agent is the element that acts as an electron acceptor. It is the substance that becomes reduced and undergoes a decrease in its own oxidation number. The reducing agent is the element that acts as an electron donor. It is the substance that becomes oxidized and undergoes an increase in its oxidation number. The oxidation states verify that an electron transfer from one element to another has occurred.

Because oxygen is such an electronegative element (strong electron attractor), an atom that combines with it will become "oxidized"—it will lose electrons to the oxygen atom. The oxygen itself then becomes reduced.

Oxidation Numbers. The oxidation number of oxygen in most compounds is -2. Accordingly, in carbon monoxide (CO) and carbon dioxide (CO_2), the oxidation numbers of the carbon atoms are $+2$ and $+4$, respectively. In polyatomic ions (made up of more than one atom), there should be a "leftover," or net, charge that equals the charge of the ion.

Oxidizing agents are important in metallurgy, which is the process of separating a metal from its ore, and in electrochemistry, in which the redox reaction causes the production of an electric current. For example, lead is found in the form of galena (PbS). In a two-step process, the ore is first "roasted," or converted to its oxide. The oxidizing agent used is oxygen, which is reduced while the sulfur becomes oxidized. The lead oxide is then treated with carbon monoxide in a second redox reaction to free the metal.

Oxidizing agents are also involved in electrochemistry. The redox reaction causes the production of an electric current. To ensure that the current is directed through a wire, the oxidizing agent (electron acceptor) is separated from the reducing agent (electron donor).

Background material on oxidizing agents can be found in BOND, CHEMICAL; CHEMICAL REACTIONS; ORGANIC COMPOUNDS. *More details can be found in* ANTI-OXIDANTS; COMBUSTION; REDOX REACTION. *Additional relevant information is contained in* AGING; MUTATION, GENETIC; SOAPS AND DETERGENTS.

First see PHOTOSYNTHESIS

Oxygen

Next see RESPIRATORY SYSTEMS

Oxygen, the eighth element on the Periodic Table, is one of the most abundant elements. It makes up 49 percent of Earth's crust, oceans, and atmosphere, as well as 65 percent of the human body. Each oxygen atom contains eight protons, eight neutrons, and eight electrons.

Oxygen is essential for life. All living cells must perform a process called cellular respiration, in which they break down glucose in order to obtain energy for their metabolic activities. Most organisms are aerobes, meaning that oxy-

Further Reading
Arndt, Diether, *Manganese Compounds as Oxidizing Agents in Organic Chemistry* (1981); Lawless, Edward W., *Inorganic High-Energy Oxidizers: Synthesis, Structure and Properties* (1993); Nriagu, Jerome O., *Environmental Oxidants*.

gen is needed for these chemical reactions. The mirror image of cellular respiration is photosynthesis, in which plants produce glucose using energy from the sun. In addition, oxygen is liberated as a result of photosynthesis, which helps to maintain a constant level of this vital gas in the atmosphere. Together, cellular respiration and photosynthesis perpetuate the carbon cycle, in which carbon dioxide and oxygen are continually recirculated throughout the ecosystem.

Atomic Structure. Oxygen is one of the diatomic elements—atoms of these elements will pair up with another atom of their own kind in the absence of anything else with which to bond. Oxygen is capable of forming both covalent bonds, in which electrons are shared between atoms, and ionic bonds, in which one atom gains electrons while the other one loses them. Oxygen is very electronegative, meaning it strongly attracts electrons—its own as well as those that belong to other atoms. When oxygen is involved in an ionic bond, it will gain two electrons to become a negatively charged ion, or anion, with a charge of -2. When oxygen is covalently bonded, it often monopolizes the electrons being shared due to its greater electronegativity. This results in a covalent bond that has an ionic character and is called a polar bond.

A molecule that contains polar bonds has localized areas of accumulated charges, negative where the electrons have clustered and positive wherever the electrons are absent. These apparent charges are referred to as oxidation numbers, as they result from the electronegativity values of atoms involved in these special types of covalent bonds, even if oxygen itself is not present.

The most prominent oxygen-containing compound is water, H_2O. Water is an essential material for all living things and life processes.

Many of water's unique properties, such as surface tension and ability to act as a solvent, come as a direct result of the oxygen's high electronegativity, which in turn causes the water molecule to become a polar substance.

Most organic compounds contain oxygen. Oxygen is often found as a member of a functional group, such as hydroxyls (OH), found in alcohols, or carboxyls (COOH), found in organic compounds such as fatty acids (lipid components), amino acids (protein components), and nucleic acids (such as DNA and RNA). Carboxyl groups are used to combine smaller subunits into polymers. Oxygen atoms are also found in hydrocarbons known as aldehydes and ketones.

Acids and Bases. Oxygen also plays an important role in acid-base chemistry. An acid is defined as a molecule that has a hydrogen ion (H^+) as its cation, or positively charged ion. Because a hydrogen atom originally consisted of simply one proton and one electron (which is now missing), the H^+ cation is essentially a lone proton. Consequently, acids function as proton donors. Bases are defined as molecules that contain hydroxide ions (OH^-) as their anions. All bases function as proton acceptors, since their negative charge attracts the H^+ ion. The hydroxyl group found in many organic compounds enables them to function as either proton donors (by releasing the H from the OH group) or, alternatively, as proton acceptors, depending on the environmental pH.

Although a gas at room temperature, oxygen can be cooled sufficiently to be transformed into a liquid or solid. Liquid oxygen (called LOX) is one of the fuels used by the space shuttle and booster rockets.

Further Reading
Farndon, John, *Oxygen* (1988); Krauss, Stephen R., *Oxygen: Nature's Most Important Dietary Supplement* (1999).

Background material can be found in ATMOSPHERE; COMBUSTION; RESPIRATORY SYSTEMS. *Advanced subjects are developed in* ANTI-OXIDANTS; BREATHING REGULATION; NUCLEOSYNTHESIS. *Further aspects of this subject are covered in* BLOOD; OXIDIZING AGENTS; PALEOCLIMATOLOGY.

OBSERVATIONS

Diving and Breathing

How can mammals, who are incapable of drawing oxygen from water, dive to great depths and remain there for extended periods of time? Sperm whales can remain 3,000 feet below the surface for more than an hour; Weddell seals can swim one to two miles without coming up for air. Part of the answer is that sea-going mammals have a higher proportion of red blood cells, and nearly twice the ratio of blood to body weight, compared to humans. The other part is the dive reflex, which sharply reduces blood supply to muscles and other organs which can withstand oxygen deprivation, while maintaining vital oxygen supply to the brain, adrenal glands, and other critical areas. This reflex is also seen in humans who suffer near-drownings in very cold water, many of whom have been revived without long-term brain damage after more than 30 minutes under water.

First see OXYGEN

Oxygen Group

Next see SULFUR

Group VIA, also known as the Oxygen Group, contains the elements oxygen, sulfur, selenium, tellurium, and polonium. All of the members of this family have six electrons in their outermost (valence) energy level. However, there are variations among their properties and behavior due to the presence of both metals and nonmetals in this family. Oxygen and sulfur are nonmetals. Selenium and tellurium are metalloids, with properties of both metals and nonmetals. Polonium, a very rare radioactive element, is the only metallic element of this group.

Oxygen is a very electronegative element, meaning that it strongly attracts electrons. Oxygen can gain two electrons and become a negatively charged ion, or anion, and will consequently form an ionic bond. Oxygen can also form covalent bonds, in which electrons are shared between atoms. Due to its electronegativity, however, oxygen tends to monopolize the shared electrons, giving the bond an ionic character. These types of covalent bonds are known as polar bonds.

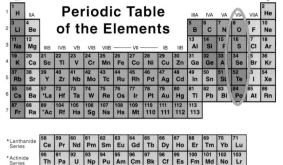

Periodic Table of the Elements

Oxygen forms many important compounds, known as oxides. In addition, chemical combinations with oxygen, called oxidation reactions, are very important for living systems as a means of producing energy.

Sulfur is quite similar to oxygen in the types of bonds it can form. Sulfur is found together with many of the transition elements as sulfide ores in Earth's crust.

Selenium exists as either a molecular solid or a metallic solid. A molecular solid is held together by weak attractive interactions between the individual molecules. A metallic solid is made up of atoms that are somewhat electron deficient and share electron density with several neighboring atoms of the same type. In both arsenic and antimony, the solids formed have low atomic coordination numbers, meaning they have relatively low melting and boiling points due to a less stable structure. Selenium as a mineral supplement to combat esophageal and stomach cancer has been the subject of a study in a high-risk Chinese population. The earlier results were encouraging, and follow-ups are continuing.

Tellurium crystallizes as a metallic solid and may also exist as a molecular solid.

First see ATMOSPHERE

Above, the place of the oxygen group on the Periodic Table of the Elements.

Ozone Layer

Next see CHLOROFLUOROCARBONS

A region of Earth's atmosphere that lies roughly ten to thirty miles above the surface of the Earth.

The ozone layer, or ozonosphere, contains a significant amount of ozone, a three-atom molecule of oxygen that has a characteristic odor of "clean air." It is formed when an electrical discharge passes through oxygen or when oxygen is irradiated by ultraviolet light. Near the Earth's surface, ozone is highly irritating and toxic to human beings even at concentrations of .12 parts per million. However, in the atmosphere, ozone ab-

Right, the differences in ozone concentration as seen from September to October 1993 by NASA's Total Ozone Mapping Spectrometer (TOMS).

Further Reading
Benedick, Richard Elliot, *Ozone Diplomacy: New Directions in Safeguarding the Planet* (1998); Hall, Stephen E., *Mapping the Next Millenium* (1992); Horel, John Dewitt *Global Environmental Change: An Atmospheric Perspective* (1996); Nilsson, Annika *Ultraviolet Reflections: Life Under a Thinning Ozone Layer* (1996).

sorbs solar ultraviolet radiation, shielding humans, animals, and plants on the Earth's surface.

UV-C rays strike oxygen molecules, creating ozone; meanwhile, UV-B rays strike ozone molecules, creating oxygen. Thus, the proportion of ozone remains constant at about eight parts per million, and ultraviolet rays are nullified. Because these reactions also give off heat, the ozone layer has an influence on climate and wind patterns as well.

Degradation. Recent years have seen increasing concerns that the ozone layer is subject to depletion by industrial chemicals, such as chlorofluorocarbons (CFCs), which are widely used as refrigerants, as aerosol propellants, and in the production of plastic foam products. Because they have long lifespans, chlorofluorocarbons migrate upward to the stratosphere, where chemical reactions cause their chlorine to be released. The result is a complex series of chemical interactions that eventually results in the destruction of atmospheric ozone. A major cause for alarm is the "ozone hole" in the atmosphere over Antarctica and the South Pole, where extreme cold conditions and long-lasting ice clouds lead to accelerated destruction of ozone during the Antarctic spring. (*See* CHLOROFLUOROCARBONS.)

In response to these concerns, a movement to ban the use of CFC was begun; since 1987 the Montreal Protocol on Substances that Deplete the Ozone Layer has been signed by 163 countries. While CFC production has been eliminated worldwide, some ozone-destroying chemicals, such as methyl bromide, continue to be used. The United States plans to phase out methyl bromide use by 2005. It is estimated that the ozone layer will be fully restored in about 50 years.

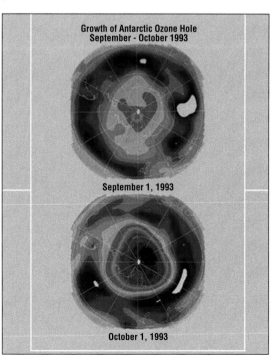

Growth of Antarctic Ozone Hole September - October 1993

September 1, 1993

October 1, 1993

P-N Junction

First see INTEGRATED CIRCUIT

Next see TRANSISTOR

P-n junctions form the basis of transistor technology; they describe the characteristics of semiconducting materials brought into contact with one another.

Above, an early point contact transistor—precursor to William Shockley's sandwich transistor.

The semiconductor industry grew out of efforts to make computers smaller and more efficient; ENIAC, built in 1945, took up more than 1,000 cubic feet, had more than 18,000 vacuum tubes, and produced 150 kilowatts of heat when in use. Not only did the vacuum tubes produce large amounts of heat and take up large amounts of space, they blew out at an alarming rate, crashing the system every time they did so.

The problem was that electrical energy flows best through conductors, typically metals, because these materials either attract electrons (p) or contain excess electrons (n); where there are no free electrons, electrical energy will not flow. Vacuum tubes were designed to exploit this characteristic. If two electrodes are set at opposite sides of the tube, one positive and one negative, electrons will flow across the gap only in one direction; thus, an alternating current can be rectified into a direct current. Furthermore, a very small current, induced in a third electrode midway between the primary ones, can control electron flow between the main electrodes; in this way a very small current, like that received by a radio antenna, can be amplified into a very large one, capable of powering the speakers.

The solution to the problems associated with vacuum tubes came from a team working on long-distance telephone communication at Bell Labs. In December 1947, William Shockley, John Bardeen, and Walter Brattain successfully demonstrated that by using semiconducting materials rather than metals, one could dispense with the bulky, fragile, heat-producing vacuum tubes and achieve the same effects of switching and amplification. They called their discovery a transistor. How did it work? Even as they refined and commercialized it, they did not fully know. The answer lies in the p-n junction.

Semiconductors. Semiconductors are not metals: they do not contain large numbers of free electrons. On the other hand, they are not insulators. Their electrons are not wholly taken up in rigid chemical bonds. Although they are crystals, and therefore share many characteristics with insulators, a small amount of energy will release free electrons from their lattice bonds; additionally, each electron that flows within the crystal leaves a "hole," or defect, behind, which is also free to travel within the lattice. The deliberate addition of impurities strengthens this effect. Phosphorus, arsenic, and antimony increase the number of free electrons, while

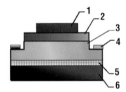

Above, a schematic of a GaN p-n junction. (1) palladium contact to p-GaN; (2) p-GaN layer; (3) n-GaN layer; (4) aluminum contact to n-GaN; (5) buffer layer; (6) H-Si substrate.

boron and gallium increase the number of defects. Thus, a semiconductor can contain regions that are electron-rich, or negatively charged (n), and, simultaneously, regions that are defect-rich, which act as if they are positively charged (p). (*See* SEMICONDUCTOR.)

Along the plane where two such regions touch, there will exist a p-n junction—a barrier for electrons flowing in one direction, but a gate for electrons flowing the other way, making up a rectifier. If a p-type layer is put between two n-type layers, one interface serves as the rectifier, while the other interface generates a current, making up an amplifier. With the creation of this n-p-n junction transistor, the modern electronic age was born. (*See* TRANSISTOR.)

First see CLIMATOLOGY

Paleoclimatology

Next see PALEOECOLOGY

The study of the Earth's climate in prehistoric times.

Paleoclimatology is studied indirectly, focusing on fossils of plants and animals and the sediments in which they are found. Stratigraphy—the study and dating of layers of rock in the Earth's crust—is an important complementary discipline. Paleoclimatology studies are also done on coral cores, ice cores, tree rings, pollen, and ocean and lake sediment.

During the late Cretaceous to the early Tertiary period (40–80 million years ago), the climate had generally higher temperatures. During the Paleocene and Eocene periods (approximately 55 million years ago), there was abundant year-round precipitation. By the end of the Eocene, there was a major decline in the annual mean temperatures. In the middle Tertiary, rapid change occurred, with a decrease in temperature. Major climatic deterioration occurred within just 1–2 million years.

Possible Causes. Changes in climate have been linked to continental movements as well as to changes in the inclination of Earth's rotational axis. Changes in the Earth's orbit around the sun affect the distribution of energy, driving the climate in and out of ice ages.

Ice ages generally last 100,000 years, with interglacial phases of 10,000 to 20,000 years. Ice ages occur during glacial epochs, which last between 20 and 50 million years. The most recent ice age occurred during the Pleistocene epoch. It began 2 million years ago and ended 11,500 years ago. As many as 18 separate ice ages may have occurred during the Pleistocene. Each ice age had warmer and colder time periods of different lengths, and the amount of ice varied.

The Quaternary Period. The focus of most paleoclimatology studies is the Quaternary period, the most recent geological interval, 1 to 2 million years ago. The period is unique for its

Paleoecology

Next see EVOLUTION

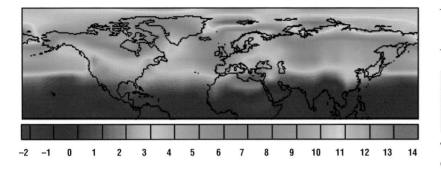

A branch of paleobiology, paleoecology is an attempt to recreate the geological conditions of past eras in order to understand the environment in which prehistoric plants and animals lived.

"oscillating climate," alternating between temperate interglacial phases and cold glaciated ones. It is also the interval of the Earth's history that saw the evolution of the human species.

The emergence and dispersal of the human species were linked to climatic conditions. In Africa, there was a shift toward more arid conditions about 2.8 million years ago due to the onset of Northern Hemisphere glacial cycles. Before that, the climate was relatively tropical and provided a good set of conditions for the early *Australopithecus* hominids, who were forest dwellers. The cooler climate caused a change in the habitat to more open plains; at about the same time the genus *Homo* emerged and appeared more suited to these conditions.

Rapid millennial climate changes occur too frequently to be a result of changes in Earth's orbit. Each cycle of the millennial oscillations begins with a temperature rise over Greenland in just decades or centuries. After 1,000 to 2,000 years of moderate temperatures, temperatures rapidly fall again and then begin to warm once more to begin the next cycle. We are currently in a warm period that began 11,000 years ago in the Holocene.

During the Pliocene, global temperatures, particularly at high latitudes, are believed to have been significantly warmer than today (above).

Below, a map shows estimates of the difference between the Pliocene and modern vegetation global albedo distribution. NASA scientists hope that studies of the Pliocene epoch will allow them to more accurately model global temperatures today.

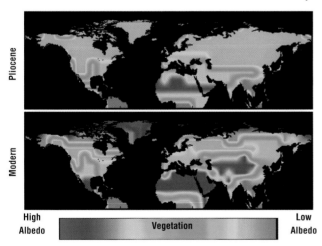

The structure and composition of ecosystems change as global conditions of atmosphere, oceans, and land change. Paleoecology seeks to reconstruct in as much detail as possible former patterns of distribution and abundance of individual organisms and populations, their physiology and relationships, and the paleogeography of the environment.

Methodology. Naturally, past ecosystems cannot be observed directly but must be inferred from fossils and the sediments in which they are found. Paleoecology is therefore limited to the study of past organisms that were preserved as fossils. (*See* FOSSIL.)

Descriptive paleoecology, in which the present is used to model the past, is the dominant approach to paleoecology. Descriptive paleoecology is divided further into paleoautecology, the study of individual organisms or species, their life history, and behavior; and paleosynecology, the study of groups of organisms associated with each other as populations, communities, or ecosystems.

Periods of relative equilibrium alternate with major changes like extinction and speciation. Processes affecting ecosystem structure through time include climatic change, rising and falling of sea levels, soil development, continental movements, meteor impact, volcanic eruptions, storms, habitat diversification, speciation, and extinction.

Paleoecology is also a bridge between ecology and evolution, since it studies the patterns of ecological organization and change over periods of time through which evolution occurred.

Evolutionary paleoecology studies the environments of extinct organisms and their effects on evolution. It examines the extent to which modern ecology accounts for structure, properties, and change within ancient communities. It also determines what ecological interactions are independent of species composition and time period and investigates long-term responses of ecosystems to changing conditions. It enables us to see how ecological relationships influence the evolutionary history of groups and organizations. (*See* PALEOCLIMATOLOGY.)

Questions in paleoecology currently being studied include how processes seen in modern ecology, such as competition between organisms and species, apply to longer periods of time. (*See* EVOLUTION; ECOLOGY.)

Background material can be found in ATMOSPHERE; CLIMATOLOGY; ICE AGE; WEATHER. *Advanced subjects are developed further in* GEOLOGY, ARCHAEOLOGICAL; ICE AGE. *More information on particular aspects is contained in* EXTINCTION; MAGNETIC FIELD OF THE EARTH; PALEOECOLOGY.

Further Reading
Cronin, Thomas M., *Principles of Paleoclimatology* (1999); Fagan, Brian M., *Floods, Famines, and Emperors: El Niño and the Fate of Civilizations* (1999).

First see FOSSIL

Paleozoic Era

Next see MESOZOIC ERA

The era that began 600 million years ago and extended until about 230 million years ago, at which point the Mesozoic era began.

The Paleozoic era gets its name from the fact that the first geological records of a large variety of living things are found in Paleozoic rock formations—in Greek, *palaeos* means "ancient" and *zoa* means "life." The Paleozoic is divided into the Cambrian period, at its beginning, and the Ordovician, Silurian, Devonian, Mississippian, Pennsylvanian, and Permian periods, which followed. The Paleozoic began with the spread of shallow seas across the existing continental land masses. It ended with the elevation of the major continental land masses.

Early Paleozoic rocks show traces of only aquatic living organisms, such as arthropods, annelid worms, snails, and clams. Land plants and animals—insects, amphibians, reptiles—evolved later. During the Paleozoic, North America and the other continents were stable and subsiding slowly, but at their margins they were changing more rapidly. Evidence such as the orientation of iron particles in Paleozoic rocks suggests that the continents were shifting relative to Earth's poles and each other. The presence of similar Paleozoic plants and animals in now-distant continents suggests that those continents were closer together then than they are now. While there is evidence of the existence of some glaciers, fossil findings and geological formations indicate that Earth's climate was milder then than it is today.

First see DIGESTION

Pancreas

Next see METABOLISM

A large gland with diverse functions, playing important roles in both the digestive and the endocrine systems of mammals.

Most of the cells in the pancreas, called acinar or alveolar cells, produce digestive enzymes that travel through one or two ducts into the intestines, where they help digest fats, carbohydrates, and proteins, as well as nucleic acids. The enzyme-producing cells are referred to as exocrine tissue, meaning their secretions travel outward through ducts. Interspersed with this tissue are the islets of Langerhans. These masses of cells—in clumps ranging from a few cells to a few hundred cells—are responsible for the endocrine function of the pancreas. They produce the hormones insulin and glucagon (or

anti-insulin), which are secreted into the bloodstream and regulate the uptake and use of glucose by cells throughout the body.

In many non-mammalian species, the exocrine and endocrine tissues tend to be separate, and one or both of these tissues may be diffused within other tissue, such as the intestinal wall, rather than forming a separate organ. In many fish, for instance, pancreatic tissue is scattered along the blood vessels of the digestive system. In birds, the pancreas is generally three-lobed and less compact than in mammals.

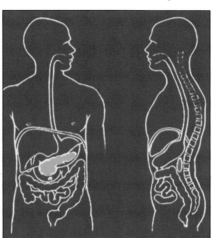

Above, front and side views of the body with the pancreas highlighted.

Anatomy. In humans, the pancreas is a pale pink, flame-shaped organ about five inches long, which lies horizontally in the upper part of the abdominal cavity. Its thicker end, called the head, is cradled in the curve of the duodenum, the part of the small intestine adjoining the stomach. It is linked to the duodenum by a main duct and, in some cases, an accessory duct. Its tail touches the spleen on the left side of the body.

The human pancreas, along with the intestinal glands, is the principal source of the enzymes that digest food. Pancreatic enzymes generally continue the digestive process that begins in the mouth or stomach and is completed by intestinal enzymes. The pancreatic enzymes include pancreatic amylase, which helps digest starch; lipase, which partially digests fat; trypsin and chymotrypsin, which break down proteins; and exopeptidases, which complete the digestion of proteins into free amino acids. The pancreas also produces nucleases—enzymes that help break down nucleic acids contained in food. The pancreatic juice, as the exocrine secretion is collectively called, also

OBSERVATIONS

Diabetes

The islets, or endocrine tissue, which make up only one percent of the mass of the human pancreas, include beta cells that secrete insulin. Insulin works in various ways to reduce the level of free glucose, or blood sugar. It encourages muscle and adipose (fatty) tissue to absorb more glucose from the blood, stimulates the conversion of glucose into glycogen for storage in the liver, and slows the breakdown of protein and fat, forcing cells to use more glucose for energy.

If the beta islet cells do not produce enough insulin, the result is the Type I form of diabetes mellitus, a chronic disease in which blood levels of glucose are abnormally high. In Type II diabetes, the beta cells still produce significant amounts of insulin, though generally less than normal, but the body fails to react properly to it, a condition called insulin resistance. Type II diabetes is far more common, accounting for 85 to 90 percent of all diabetes mellitus cases in the United States. It tends to be less severe and to occur later in life.

includes large amounts of sodium bicarbonate to neutralize stomach acid.

The digestive enzymes normally do not become activated until they enter the intestines. But if the pancreas is severely damaged, usually by alcoholism, or if a duct becomes blocked, usually by gallstones, the enzymes can begin digesting the organ itself, causing acute pancreatitis, a sudden, painful inflammation with severity that can range from mild to fatal.

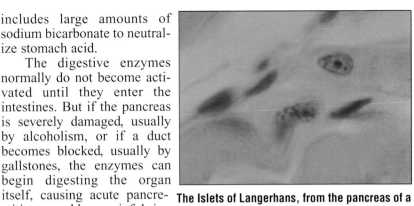

The Islets of Langerhans, from the pancreas of a monkey. The islets secrete hormones which regulate blood sugar levels.

Background material can be found in DIGESTION; ENDOCRINE SYSTEM; ENZYME. *Advanced subjects are developed in* DIGESTION CHEMISTRY; LIPIDS; PROTEIN METABOLISM. *Relevant information is contained in* CANCER; DISEASES, NONINFECTIOUS; PHARMACOLOGY.

Further Reading
Baumel, H., *Exocrine Pancreatic Cancer* (1986); Beger, Hans G., *The Pancreas* (1998); Misiewicz, J.J., *Diseases of the Gut and Pancreas* (1994); Toledo-Pereyra, L., *Pancreas Transplantation* (1988).

First see PLATE TECTONICS

Pangaea

Next see CONTINENTS, FORMATION OF

A supercontinent that existed in the early history of the Earth.

During the Paleozoic era, perhaps 500 million years ago, two recently formed continents, Gondwanaland in the Southern Hemisphere and Laurasia in the north, came together to form the universal land mass, Pangaea. The formation of Pangaea continued into the Mesozoic era. Parts of the major land mass were dispersed to the east of the supercontinent, close to India and Africa, which were then subarctic. These neighboring parts came together to form China, which was welded to the rest of the Asian land mass during the Triassic and Permian periods. Pangaea, meanwhile, was so vast and its mountains were so high that the flow of moisture-bearing air from the sea was limited, and extensive deserts formed.

Animal Migration. The continuity of the supercontinent enabled the dinosaurs to migrate easily across it. Pangaea began to break up about 150 million years ago. The crystalline basement rocks of eastern North America began to pull apart, opening a series of rift valleys that led to the formation of the Atlantic Ocean. Pangaea continued to break up over the next tens of

Below, the evolution of the continents, beginning with Pangaea in the top image.

Laurasia

Gondwanaland

200 million years ago

North America

South America   India

Australia

100 million years ago

Today

millions of years, splitting apart from east to west, as Africa split from what would become South America. The Atlantic Ocean widened, and the proto-Pacific Ocean narrowed somewhat. The continental motions that were the cause of the split and the formation of the continents that exist today still continue, with continent movements that are measured in inches per year.

Related areas to consider are CONTINENTS, FORMATION OF; GEOLOGICAL TIME SCALE; PLATE TECTONICS. *Advanced subjects are developed in* MOUNTAIN FORMATION; OCEAN BASINS; SEISMOLOGY. *Additional information is contained in* BIOSTRATIGRAPHY; EVOLUTION; GEOMORPHOLOGY.

First see LOCAL AREA NETWORK (LAN)

Parallel Computing

Next see SUPERCOMPUTER

Steps of an algorithm computed simultaneously; allowing for faster problem solving.

Parallel computer systems form the heart of all supercomputers. In order to gain greater speed, operations are broken down into component sections that can be worked on by different parts of the computer simultaneously. Since most computer programs are made up of short, repeated sections, called subroutines, several processors can work side by side, each one pursuing its own subroutines. In fact, the first supercomputers built by Seymour Cray contained four processors (in the CRAY-2) and as many as 16 (in the CRAY-3).

"Deep Blue." With the development of the microprocessor, it became possible to expand this process greatly, achieving what is now called massively parallel computing. Intel's Janus computer, introduced in 1996, combined 9,072 Pentium Pro microprocessors (later increased to 9,152), working in parallel in order to achieve the first teraflop machine, capable of processing one trillion operations per second. IBM, whose "Deep Blue" machine used parallel processing to defeat world chess champion Gary Kasparov in 1997, has designed a supercomputer that arranges 16 microprocessors in a single unit called a node and then runs 512 such nodes simultaneously; its theoretical speed reaches 10 trillion operations per second.

Consequences. The effects of these achievements in parallel computing are vast. Entire weather systems can be modeled, as can subatomic processes. In 1970, a Cray supercomputer succeeded in modeling 1,000 atoms as they interacted for a single nanosecond (one billionth of a second); the Janus system can track 100 million atoms for a microsecond (one millionth of a second). Future supercomputers will test nuclear devices or crash-test automobiles, sparing time, materials, and environmental consequences. To this end, Sandia National Laboratories has set up the Accelerated Strategic Computing Initiative (ASCI), whose goal is the development by 2004 of a massively parallel computer with a speed of 100 teraflops.

Achieving even higher speeds will necessitate new formats. One of the most promising is the subatomic computer, which replaces magnetic ones and zeros with quantum states in individual atoms. In this way an almost infinite number of "q-bit"-sized computers could be set to work simultaneously, giving incredible new power to the notion of massively parallel computing. But there appears to be a practical limit to such achievements, because memory latency—the tendency of demagnetized particles to retain their charge for a short time—prevents processor speed from exceeding a certain level.

As a result, the latest advances in parallel computing are not limited to supercomputers. Tera Computing recently released details of a fast computer system that uses only eight PCs in parallel and costs about $6 million—one-tenth the cost of large supercomputers. By running a smaller number of advanced 64-bit processors, this design gives promise of achieving nearly equivalent results, without the memory latency and programming difficulties of massively parallel supercomputers.

Related areas to be considered are COMPUTER, DIGITAL; OPERATING SYSTEMS; PROGRAM, COMPUTER. *Further details can be found in* CONTROL SYSTEMS; LOCAL AREA NETWORK; TELECOMMUNICATIONS. *Elementary aspects of this subject are covered in* INTERNET; OPERATIONS RESEARCH; SUPERCOMPUTER.

Further Reading
Murray, Charles J., *The Supermen: The Story of Seymour Cray and the Technical Wizards Behind the Supercomputer* (1997); Newborn, Monroe, *Kasparov Vs Deep Blue: Computer Chess Comes of Age* (1996); Tabak, D., *Advanced Microprocessors* (1994).

First see MICROBIOLOGY

Parasite

Next see MALARIA

An organism that lives on or in another (host) organism and depends on it for nutrition, often to the detriment of the host.

Parasitic diseases are caused by organisms that live on or in the human body, satisfying their nutritional needs by drawing on the body's blood, tissues or nutrients. Parasites are classified as ectoparasites, which live on the skin, or endoparasites, which live within the body.

Types. Common human ectoparasites include head lice, ticks, bedbugs, leeches, scabies mites, ringworm fungi, and wart viruses. Common endoparasites include tapeworms, flukes, roundworms, pinworms, hookworms, and protozoa, microscopic single-celled animals that cause infections and diseases such as giardiasis, trichomoniasis, and malaria.

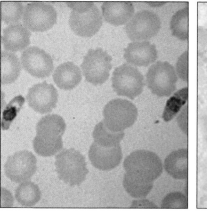

Above left, the parasite that causes malaria—*Plasmodium falciparum*—can be seen inside a human red blood cell. Another parasite is giardia (above, right), which infects the intestines of mammals.

Protozoa are in fact the simplest, most primitive type of animal. They are bigger than bacteria but still are of microscopic size. There are about 30 types of protozoa that are troublesome human parasites. These include the organisms that cause amebiasis and giardiasis, infections of the intestine that lead to diarrhea. Other human protozoa cause trichomoniasis, a sexually transmitted infection; toxoplasmosis, a disease acquired from cats; and insect-borne tropical diseases, including malaria, sleeping sickness, and leishmaniasis.

Several types of worms are human parasites. Some of them are microscopic, while others can be inches or even feet long. They fall into two main classes—roundworms, which have long, cylindrical bodies, and platyhelminths, which have flattened bodies. The platyhelminths are divided into cestodes, such as tapeworms, and trematodes, such as flukes. Worm infestations can be acquired by eating undercooked meat infected with worms, by contact with water or soil that is infested, and in situations where sanitation may be inadequate. Most worm infestations can be eliminated by antihelmintic drugs.

Both lice and leeches feed on human blood. There are three species of human lice—the head louse, *Pumanus capitis*; the body louse, *Pediculus humanus corporis*; and the pubic louse, or crab, *Phthirius pubis*. All of them have flattened bodies and grow to about an eighth of an inch in length. Different species of leeches can live on land or in water. All prefer warm climates.

Bedbugs are flat, wingless insects that are about a fifth of an inch long. They live in furniture, especially beds, but also can inhabit floors. They emerge at night to feed on human blood. Bedbugs rarely transmit disease, but their bites can become infected.

Scabies mites burrow into the skin, where they lay their eggs. A scabies infection is highly contagious. When the mites hatch, they can pass from an infected individual to someone who is standing close to him or her. This kind of infestation often can occur in adults during sexual intercourse. More often, however, scabies infections occur in infants and children. Adults who become infected are often in institutions where scabies mites have become endemic. A scabies mite infection causes intense itching, particularly at night. Scratching can lead to formation of sores and scabs. Scabies mite infection is treated with an insecticide such as lindane, which is applied to the skin below the head. If one person in a household is infected, treatment is recommended for all the other occupants.

Prevalence. Parasitic infections once were common in all countries and all classes. Modern sanitation has largely eliminated the problem in developed nations, although it persists in places where good sanitation is not practiced.

> *Special topics regarding parasites are found in* EVOLUTION; MICROBIOLOGY; SYMBIOSIS. *Advanced subjects are developed in* COEVOLUTION; ECOLOGY; MA-LARIA. *Foundational aspects of this subject are covered in* GAIA HYPOTHESIS; POPULATION ECOLOGY.

Further Reading
Behnke, Jerzy M. (Ed.), *Parasites: Immunity and Pathology: The Consequences of Parasitic Infection in Mammals* (1990); Ewald, Paul W., *Evolution of Infectious Disease* (1994); Thompson, S.N., et al., *Parasites and Pathogens of Insects: Pathogens* (1993).

First see NEURON

Parkinson's Disease

Next see NERVOUS SYSTEMS

> **A neurological disorder caused by damage to or degeneration of nerve cells in the basal ganglia, the regions of the brain that control signals to the muscles.**

Because of the degeneration associated with Parkinson's disease, the muscles become overly tense, resulting in tremors, joint rigidity, and slowed movement. The disease occurs most often in the elderly and is caused by the death of cells of the substantia nigra region in the base of the brain. These cells are responsible for the production of dopamine, a neurotransmitter that controls movement.

The first sign of Parkinson's disease is a light tremor that affects one hand, arm, or leg. As the disease progresses, both sides of the body are affected with weakness, stiffness, and trembling of the muscles. There may be shaking of the head, a fixed facial expression, and a permanent body stoop. Speech may be hesitant and slow, and handwriting often becomes very small. Patients often suffer from depression.

The disease is treated with drugs, which ease symptoms but do not stop its progression. The first drug that is tried is usually levodopa, which the body converts to dopamine. Other drugs that can be used include amantadine and bromocriptine. With no treatment, the disease causes severe weakness in 10 to 15 years, but drug therapy can delay or prevent that deterioration.

First see PRINTING

Pattern Recognition and OCR

Next see TURING MACHINE

> **An algorithm that allows previously defined patterns to be accurately distinguished in new and different situations. Patterns can be part of printed text, colors, handwriting, and audio data.**

Pattern and optical character recognition have become a major focus of computer development, both as ends in themselves and as key components in artificial intelligence. Once computers gain the ability to discriminate analog as well as digital inputs, true automation will become possible. But there have been numerous delays in perfecting either pattern or character recognition, due to the need for great processing power and sophisticated algorithms. Only recently have image, speech, and handwriting recognition become possible, with the development of statistical pattern recognition following close behind.

At first, it was thought that image recognition would not be difficult to achieve, given the relative ease with which fingerprint analysis and identification by humans had been achieved. But a face has many more significant features, and far more varied ones, than a fingerprint; only since 1995 have several state motor vehicle systems begun to store photographs of licensed drivers in digitized as well as analog form. When joined with statistical pattern recognition software for signature analysis, these new pattern recognition processes offer major advances in citizen identification.

OCR. Optical character recognition (OCR) has proven equally difficult. Although specially designed letters and numerals were incorporated into the software for computer scanners in the 1970s, recognition of handwriting has proven to be erratic at best. Apple's Newton electronic memo pad proved unable to read as many as 30 percent of the words inscribed on it, although increased processing power and improved software eliminated many of those bugs. One key to improvement has been the development of expert systems, which use context clues to discard all word choices that do not fit the sentence being constructed. A second key has been the use of digital signal processors, which filter out not only background "noise" but also stray markings that might make one letter pattern resemble another.

Vector Analysis. The next generation of pattern recognition software uses vector analysis. Instead of inputing data as scalar functions, this software reads changes in data from one input to the next, creating time functions of the data. This is especially important in such applications as air traffic control, where radar data must be analyzed to distinguish not only the altitude, speed, and heading of each aircraft, but also its type and classification of the aircraft's particular flight segment.

Applications. Applications of pattern recognition and OCR are widespread. Companies like Arkenstone and Kurzweil offer software for the disabled, including readers and scanners that read braille and printed texts and synthesize them into speech for the visually impaired. In 1997, a California company succeeded in perfecting computerized fingerprint identification, and in 1998, a patent was taken out for a device to scan the dealer's cards at the blackjack table—perhaps the first step in automating the most labor-intensive aspect of the casino business.

Further developments in the field of pattern recognition are discussed in CAMERA; OPTICS; RECORDING TECHNOLOGY. *More details can be found in* CONTROL SYSTEMS; DIGITAL COMPUTER; ROBOTICS. *Additional relevant information is contained in* COMPUTER-AIDED DESIGN; MEDICAL DIAGNOSTICS.

Further Reading
Caelli, Terry, *Machine Learning and Image Interpretation* (1997); Kurzweil, R., *The Age of Spiritual Machines: When Computers Exceed Human Intelligence* (1999); Yu, Francis T.S., *Optical Pattern Recognition* (1998).

THE CUTTING EDGE

Building Elements

Elements with very high atomic numbers have been created in the laboratory. In 1999, a team of Russian scientists created an atom with 114 protons and 184 neutrons, which survived for 30 seconds—a long time in comparison to element 118, which was created later that year, and which survived for less than one ten-thousandth of a second. This last element decayed into element 116, which decayed into 114, then into 112, and so on, down to element 106, seaborgium. It is believed that bombarding lead with ruthenium may yield element 126, the first element in "the island of stability" that may theoretically exist beyond element 124. Such an element should be quite stable, perhaps even useful.

ilar properties appear in the vertical columns of the table. These columns are known as subgroups; up to three subgroups can be gathered together to make a group. Most periodic tables have eight groups, although some consider Group VIII actually to be three separate groups. The Roman numbers at the heads of columns designate groups of elements; the A groups are

First see ATOM

Periodic Table of the Elements

Next see NUCLEUS, ATOMIC

A visual display of the periodicity of the physical and chemical properties of the elements.

As far back as the early nineteenth century, Johann Wolfgang Doebereiner discovered that there are triads, or triplets, of elements whose atomic weights are in arithmetic progression and which have similar properties. In the 1860s, when the atomic weights of many more elements had been determined, John A. R. Newlands reported a "law of octaves," which says that similar elements occur in intervals of eight. The first fairly complete periodic table was published in 1869 by Dmitry Mendeleyev based on his observations that the properties of elements vary periodically with their atomic weights. Mendeleyev left gaps in his periodic table corresponding to elements that were then unknown; he was able to predict their properties with great accuracy.

Today, it is understood that the periodicity of properties is due to the number and arrangement of the electrons in atoms. It is the atomic number—the number of protons in the nucleus—that determines the number of electrons, so the Periodic Table uses atomic number as the basis of its organization.

Forms of the Table. There are several forms of the Periodic Table today, but they all have major features in common. In a periodic table, the elements are arranged so that those with sim-

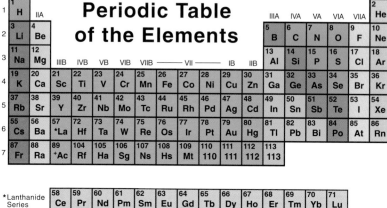

The Periodic Table.
All of the elements above Uranium (atomic number 92) do not occur naturally and are unstable. Elements have been produced with atomic numbers as high as 118, although that element broke down in a fraction of a second. An "Island of Stability" is predicted to begin again at element 126.

often called main groups, and the B groups are called transition elements.

A horizontal sequence of elements is known as a period, and a portion of a period or a group is sometimes called a family. Similar properties reappear when the elements have similar electron structures. For example, each of the alkali metals in Group IA—lithium, sodium, potassium, rubidium, and cesium—has one electron in its outermost shell. All of them have eight electrons in the next innermost shell, except lithium, which has an atomic number of 3 and therefore has only three electrons. The members of the alkali metal family tend to lose the outermost electron in chemical reactions. Intermediate properties can be predicted by a group's electron structure and place in the Periodic Table.

Properties. In some cases, the properties of elements in the rows are similar. One example is the horizontal group that begins with scandium, atomic number 21, and ends with copper, atomic number 29. Because these elements exhibit some degree of gradation in their properties, the group is called a transition series.

In two cases, the properties of some elements are so similar that they are extremely difficult to separate. One case is the lanthanum elements, which have lanthanum, atomic number 57, as their first member and lutetium, atomic number 71, as their last member. Another is the actinium elements, beginning with actinium, atomic number 89, and ending with lawrencium, atomic number 103. Both these groups are put in separate rows below the main Periodic Table, in order to preserve the similarity of the properties of the elements in the vertical columns.

More elements, with higher atomic numbers, are being added to the Periodic Table as science progresses. These elements have extremely short lives, decaying in fractions of seconds.

Background material can be found in ATOM; BOND, CHEMICAL; ISOTOPE. *Further developments in the field are discussed in* BORON GROUP; GROUP IV ELEMENTS; HALOGENS; NITROGEN GROUP. *Special topics in this area are found in* OXYGEN GROUP; TRANSITION ELEMENTS; TRANSURANIC ELEMENTS.

Above, magnets are mounted on a sliding mechanism on the inner wheel with their north poles facing out. On the outer cylinder the magnets on the left have their north poles facing out, while on the right side, the north poles face in. Thus, a torque is generat-ed on the inner wheel, which can theoretically be used to drive an external load.

Further Reading
Anderson, David L., *The Discovery of the Electron* (1981); Asimov, Isaac, *Atom: Journey Across the Subatomic Cosmos* (1992); Kelman, P., *Mendeleyev: Prophet of Chemical Elements* (1991).

First see THERMODYNAMICS

Perpetual Motion

Next see ENTROPY

The notion that a machine can produce more energy than it uses, or, alternatively, that it can do work without using or dissipating energy.

There are several kinds of perpetual motion machines, at least in theory; none of them works in practice, because such a machine would violate one of the laws of thermodynamics.

Types. Perpetual motion machines fall into three categories. One type of perpetual motion machine performs useful work without getting energy from any source, such as an engine that runs without fuel. Such a machine violates the first law of thermodynamics, otherwise known as the law of conservation of energy, which states that energy can be transferred from one system to another, but that there is no process by which energy can be created from nothing. Another kind of perpetual motion machine is one that converts energy completely into work, with no loss at all. It would differ from all existing cyclic machines, such as steam engines,

which do work by absorbing energy from a heat source, such as burning coal or oil, and releasing it at a lower temperature. A perpetual motion machine that released energy at the same temperature at which it entered would violate the second law of thermodynamics, which states that the complete conversion of energy into work is impossible; some energy must be spent in the process of doing work. Before the engine can be restored to the condition at the start of a cycle, some of the energy absorbed from the heat source must be transferred to a cold reservoir.

A third type of perpetual motion machine is one that does no work but continues to run forever, without any input of energy. Such a machine is impossible because some energy is always dissipated, usually as a result of friction. One modern device that approaches a perpetual motion machine is a superconducting ring, in which electric current can flow endlessly without an input of energy. This device is not a true perpetual motion machine, however, because energy must be expended to keep the ring material at the temperature necessary to make it superconducting. The fact that no workable perpetual motion machine has been developed despite centuries of effort is empirical evidence for the truth of the laws of thermodynamics.

Right, a perpetual motion machine proposed by Richard Feynman. Random collisions between the fins and the gas molecules turn the shaft, while a ratchet mechanism allows the cog to spin in only one direction. The problem with this example, like most failed perpetual motion machines, is that energy is lost through heat in the ratchet mechanism.

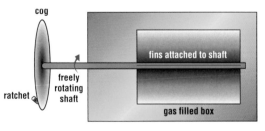

cog
fins attached to shaft
freely rotating shaft
ratchet
gas filled box

The foundations of the subject of perpetual motion machines are discussed in ENERGY; MECHANICS; NEWTON'S LAWS. *Further details can be found in* CONSERVATION LAWS IN NATURE; FRICTION; THERMODYNAMICS. *Advanced subjects are developed in* ABSOLUTE ZERO; ENERGY; SUPERCONDUCTOR.

First see DISTILLATION

Petroleum Distillation

Next see FOSSIL FUEL POWER

The separation of crude oil into chemically distinct hydrocarbons suitable for different purposes.

Petroleum distillation and cracking are two technologies for extracting usable products from crude oil. Distillation is by far the older technique, having been developed perhaps 2,000 years ago. In distillation, crude oil is heated in horizontal or vertical stills, vessels in which the liquid is evaporated.

In the nineteenth century, stills holding a few hundred barrels were used to obtain kerosene. It was soon discovered that if stills were run more slowly, heavier oils could be processed so that large molecules were split into smaller ones, producing large yields of kerosene. This was the first version of cracking. The lighter products, such as gasoline, obtained by this process were discarded as waste products until the automobile arrived in the first decade of the twentieth century. The products were purified by being washed with a small amount of sulfuric acid, sometimes followed by filtering through clay to improve the color and odor of the products.

The next development was the continuous battery still, in which a series of horizontal stills were interconnected. The undistilled oil flowed to stills that were progressively hotter, so that progressively heavier, and more valuable, products were produced. The "sweetening" of kerosene and gasoline—the elimination of odors by removing sulfur—came into use at about this time. In 1913, the Burton cracking process, in which a heavy distillate oil was heated under pressure, came into use; it doubled the yield of gasoline.

Pipe Stills. In the 1920s, continuous battery stills were replaced by pipe stills, with a capacity of many thousands of barrels a day. These stills heat crude oil rapidly in pipe coils and discharge the oil into vertical fractionating towers that are 100 feet or more in height.

In later decades, the size of oil treatment units grew progressively, until the units could handle tens of thousands of barrels a day. In the 1930s, gasoline quality was improved by thermal reforming, in which heavier fractions of the gasoline are cracked to obtained the desired products. A more recent technique is hydrotreating, in which the surplus hydrogen produced by hydroformers is used to treat stocks of oil at moderate temperatures and pressures.

Hydrocracking, another recently developed technique, proceeds by two main reactions: adding hydrogen to molecules that are too massive and too complex for gasoline and then cracking them to obtain the desired fuels. The process is carried out by passing oil feed and hydrogen at high pressure and moderate temperature—from 500 to 700 degrees Fahrenheit—into contact with a bifunctional catalyst, consisting of an acidic solid and a metal component that is hydrogenating. This produces gasoline with a high octane number. In general, hydrocracking is used as an adjunct to catalytic cracking.

Further Reading
Meyers, Robert A., *Handbook of Petroleum Refining Processes* (1996); Selly, Richard C., *Elements of Petroleum Geology* (1997); Watkins, Robert N., *Petroleum Refinery Distillation* (1991).

Elementary aspects of this subject are covered in DISTILLATION; FOSSIL FUEL POWER; HYDROCARBON. *More information on particular aspects is contained in* AUTOMOTIVE DESIGN; PETROLEUM PROSPECTING; PETROLOGY. *Relevant information is contained in* PLASTICS; SOAPS AND DETERGENTS; SYNTHETICS; TEXTILE SCIENCE.

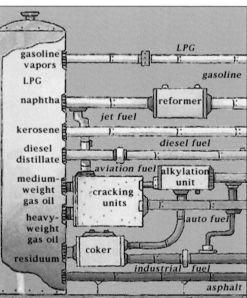

Above, a schematic of a distillation tower, where hydrocarbons can be separated from one another on the basis of their densities.

First see PETROLOGY

Petroleum Prospecting

Next see PETROLEUM DISTILLATION

The search for oil wherever it may be on Earth—on land or beneath the sea.

Petroleum usually occurs in sandstone or limestone, where geological upheavals have produced porous formations that occur between nonporous formations. These porous formations are formed by upthrusting or slippage. Pockets of natural gas are often associated with these oil deposits.

Surface deposits of oil were being used many centuries before the birth of Christ. In North America, seventeenth-century settlers found oil springs, and eighteenth-century maps indicated the location of oil fields in Pennsylvania and Ohio. The first successful oil well in North America was the Drake well, which was completed at Titusville, Pennsylvania, in August 1859; oil was found in it at a depth of 69 feet. Today, magnetometers and gravitometers are among the instruments used to detect sites that can be suitable for drilling. The analysis of soil for traces of hydrocarbons can also help to reveal underlying oil deposits. One important method of searching for oil is seismic surveying, in which an explosive charge is detonated on the surface and instruments record the shock waves generated by underground rock strata. Because the shock waves travel at different speeds in rock layers of different density and

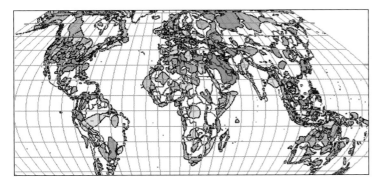

type, analysis of the shock wave patterns can disclose the likely location of oil deposits.

Until 1900, the method used to drill for oil was cable drilling, in which a drill bit on the end of a cable was raised and lowered in a hole. Rotary drilling, in which a bit is fixed on the end of a rotating drill pipe inside a casing, came into widespread use by the 1960s.

After it is drilled, a well may produce free-flowing oil because of high reservoir pressure generated by natural gas trapped with the oil or by the pressure of layers of water that lie above the oil. But it may ultimately be necessary to use pumping to get all of the recoverable oil out of a well.

Other methods used to retrieve all the recoverable oil from a well include fracturing the oil-bearing rock formation by using explosives; using acid to help dissolve the oil-bearing rock formation; pumping water, natural gas, or some other gas down one well to increase the production of oil from neighboring wells in the same rock formation; and pumping air down and creating a fire in the rock formation around one well to increase the flow from neighboring wells by heating their oil. Well over 80 percent of the active oil wells in the United States use one or more of these methods. Today, exploring and drilling for oil under the surface of the sea plays an integral role in petroleum prospecting.

Related material can be found in MINING TECHNOLOGY; PETROLOGY; SEDIMENTARY ROCK GEOLOGY. *Other aspects of the subject are discussed in* BIOSTRATIGRAPHY; HYDROCARBON; MINERALOGY. *Special subjects of related interest can be found in* BIOREMEDIATION; COASTAL ENGINEERING; ENERGY, ALTERNATIVE.

Above, a map depicting the world's recoverable petroleum in 1994. Areas in green have the highest recoverable futures and areas in purple have the lowest. Areas in white have virtually no recoverable futures.

Further Reading
Curtis, Doris M., *How to Try to Find an Oil Field* (1981); Jain, K.C., *Concepts and Techniques in Oil and Gas Exploration* (1982); Steinmetz, Richard, *The Business of Petroleum Exploration* (1992).

First see GEOLOGY, ARCHAEOLOGICAL

Petrology

Next see EARTH

The branch of geology that studies rocks—their origin, composition, alteration, decay, and placement.

Much of petrology is closely tied to geochemistry, the study of the chemistry and evolution of rocks and other materials of Earth. Most rocks are mixtures, or aggregates, of minerals. The composition of rocks generally has been defined by geologists. Some rocks, such as quartzite and marble, consist of a single mineral. Others, such as granite and basalt, consist of many different minerals, and others, such as coal and obsidian, consist not of minerals but of other substances, such as organic matter. Field studies are conducted to obtain information about rock units—their size, shape, composition, and internal structure. These studies are combined with laboratory investigations to learn about the time, manner, and environment of rock formation. The laboratory methods used include chemical analysis of rocks, microchemical tests, and a number of x-ray studies.

A closely related field is petrography, the systematic classification and description of rocks. Petrographers use the polarizing microscope, an instrument that allows them to examine thin sections of rocks, to determine the chemical composition of the individual minerals in a rock by measuring their optical properties.

First see MEDICAL DIAGNOSTICS

Pharmacology

Next see CHEMOTHERAPY

A branch of medicine, the aim of which is the discovery and testing of drugs.

Pharmacology deals with the molecular structure of medications, the ways in which they act in the human body, their side effects, and how they can be used to prevent or treat disease. Pharmacologists also engage in research to develop new drugs, to find new combination treatments using existing drugs, and to modify drugs to improve their effectiveness against diseases.

A drug can be defined as any chemical that affects the development or progression of a disease or that alters the activity of one or more organs of the body. In the past, drugs were derived from naturally occurring plants, minerals, and animals. In the modern era, drugs generally are made in the laboratory.

Developing New Drugs. One way to develop a new drug is to modify the molecular structure of an existing drug. Another is to obtain a likely compound and screen it for activity against one or more diseases or medical conditions.

All drugs used medically in the United States must have the approval of the Food and Drug Administration; the steps leading to approval generally take several years. The first step is use of a promising drug in trials on laboratory animals. If the drug passes this test, it then can be tested on a small number of human volunteers. The last and most important step is use of the drug to treat human patients. In these clinical trials, patients may get either the drug being tested or an inactive substance, called a placebo. Neither the patient who receives the drug nor the doctor who administers it knows which is being given to a specific patient, to avoid the psychological effects that can have a major impact on the physical health of a patient.

A drug generally is effective because it either stimulates or blocks a chemical reaction in the body. Some drugs act on outside agents; antibiotics, for example, block the reproduction of disease-causing bacteria. Other drugs act on the cells of the body, either by binding to a receptor molecule on the surface of a cell or by being absorbed into a cell, where the drug can change the processes going on within that cell. Some diseases or conditions require combination therapy, in which several drugs must be taken in a prescribed formula.

Side Effects. In addition to their desired effects, almost all drugs have adverse side effects. Some of these involve only a certain group of patients. For example, pregnant women are often are told not to take a drug because it can cross the placenta and interfere with the normal growth of a fetus. But most side effects are felt by many patients who take a drug. These side effects vary widely from drug to drug. In some cases, they can be slight enough to cause few, if any, symptoms in the patient. In other cases, the effects can be severe enough to have the physician cease to give the drug to a patient. In every case, the physician and the patient must consider the balance between the good a drug can do and the ill effects that it can cause.

Right, phase diagram of water. As the state of a quantity of water passes through "phase space" (the pressure vs. temperature diagram), a change in energy results in a change of state. At the borders, however, an additional increment of energy (added or removed) is required to cross into a new phase.

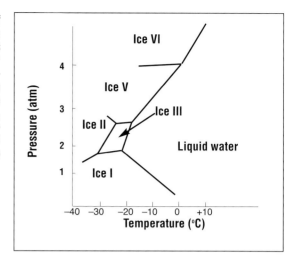

Further Reading
March, Norman, *Amorphous Solids and the Liquid State* (1985); Reid, Robert, *The Properties of Gases and Liquids* (1987); Wheeler, Lynde Phelps, *Josiah Willard Gibbs: The History of a Great Mind* (1998).

tem can remain in equilibrium only if both the temperature and the pressure are fixed.

Any variation in either temperature or pressure causes the proportion of phases in the system to change. The phase rule was derived by American chemist J. Willard Gibbs and is of great practical importance in studying complex systems such as metal alloys.

Background material regarding phase and phase changes can be found in GASES, BEHAVIOR OF; LIQUID; TEMPERATURE. *More details can be found in* CARNOT CYCLE; HEAT; THERMODYNAMIC CYCLES. *Advanced aspects of this subject are covered in* ABSOLUTE ZERO; LIQUEFACTION; LIQUIDS; REFRIGERATION.

First see GAS, BEHAVIOR OF

Phase

Next see THERMODYNAMIC CYCLES

A distinct physical state of matter.

Matter is generally said to have three phases: gas, liquid, and solid. Thus, a mixture of water and ice is a two-phase system. Changes of phase usually occur at set temperatures and are accompanied by changes in properties such as volume, specific heat, and electrical conductivity.

The phase rule is an equation for describing any system at equilibrium that contains several phases. The equation is $v = 2 + n - f$, where v represents the number of variables that can be altered and still have the system remain in equilibrium, n represents the number of components of the system, and f represents the number of phases of the system. For example, a system of water and water vapor has one component—water ($n = 1$)—and two phases—liquid and vapor ($f = 2$). Therefore, the number of variables v is 1; one can change only a single variable, such as temperature, and have the system remain at equilibrium. In a system containing water, vapor, and ice, $f = 3$ and $n = 1$, so $v = 0$; the sys-

---

First see INSTINCT

Pheromones

Next see REPRODUCTIVE STRATEGIES

Chemicals that an organism emits into the air that trigger behavioral or hormonal changes in another member of the organism's species.

In most cases, pheromones are a functional part of the act of reproduction: they may alert males to the reproductive readiness and location of females, as in moths; regulate the estrous cycle, as in mice; or stimulate copulation by males and nest-building behavior by females, as in rats. But pheromones can also signal danger or mark trails or food sources.

Communication. Pheromones are believed to compose the most primitive form of communication, serving life forms from slime molds to mammals. Its importance has been especially well studied in insects, some of which can perceive sex attractants emitted several kilometers away. The sex-attraction pheromone of female moths is so powerful that a pheromone-dampened piece of paper will draw hordes of males—none of whom will even notice a real female sequestered nearby in an airtight glass container.

Although pheromones are often referred to as perfumes or odors, it is believed that they are not detected by the animal's main olfactory system and, in humans at least, would not be consciously perceived as odors. Instead, in mammals, the main receptor in believed to be the vomeronasal organ (Jacobson's organ) in the nose, which is part of an accessory olfactory system.

In the 1990s, studies aimed at finding the vomeronasal organ, long thought to be vestigial or nonfunctioning in humans, found it to be a working human chemosensory organ that differs in some ways between men and women. In humans, the organ consists of paired epithelial structures adjacent to the nasal septum.

OBSERVATIONS

Human Nature

It was long suspected that pheromones were at work in humans, but it was not until the mid-1990s that experiments began to provide evidence of their presence. In one study, for instance, a putative pheromone applied to the vomeronasal organ caused changes in gonadal hormone secretion in men, as well as increased heart rate and decreased respiration. In another, researchers found that secretions wiped from women's armpits at different points of the menstrual cycle, then applied above the lips of other women, could alter the menstrual cycles of the recipients. This finding may explain why college roommates are more likely to have synchronized menstrual cycles than chance would predict.

Background material can be found in ENDOCRINE SYSTEM; REPRODUCTIVE SYSTEMS; SEX. *For more details in* COMMUNICATION IN NATURE; INSTINCT; REPRODUCTIVE STRATEGIES. *More information on particular aspects is contained in* CONDITIONING; PREDATION; SENSORY MECHANISMS.

Further Reading
Brown, R. E., *Social Odours in Mammals* (1985); Carde, R. T., *Insect Pheromone Research* (1997); Johnson, R. L., *The Secret Language: Pheromones in the Animal World* (1989); Mayer, M. S., *Handbook of Insect Pheromones and Sex Attractants* (1991); Stoddart, M. D., *Mammalian Odors and Pheromones* (1991); Van Toller, S., *Perfumery,* (1988).

First see SONICS

Phonon

Next see CRYSTAL

A quantum of the energy produced by the vibration of a crystal lattice or of an elastic medium, such as air.

A sound can be considered both as a wave in air and as a phonon. The concept of the phonon is analogous to that of the photon, which is a quantum of energy associated with an electromagnetic wave. The random heat motion that all atoms undergo in a crystal can be pictured as the result of a large number of waves that travel through the crystal. Classical theory says that the possible values of the energy content of the vibration of a crystal lattice are continuously variable. But quantum theory says that this energy content can have only a specific set of values. The energy of this quantum, or phonon, is expressed by the formula $(N + 1/2)hv$, where v is the frequency of the vibration and h is Planck's constant.

The concept of the phonon is useful in understanding the way that nonmetals conduct heat and electricity. In a crystal, phonons can interact with other excitations, particularly electrons. These electron-phonon interactions affect the paths of the electrons. In a metal, all the electrons interact with phonons. The study of electron-phonon interactions helps to explain why electrical conductivity varies with temperature. In semiconductors, electrons interact directly only with low-frequency phonons. At very low temperatures in nonmetal crystals, phonons can travel in straight lines from one surface of the crystal to the other, which means that heat conductivity varies with size and surface condition. (*See* HEAT; ELECTRIC CIRCUIT.)

First see LIGHT

Photochemistry

Next see PHOTOGRAPHY, CHEMISTRY OF

Chemical reactions triggered by light.

Silver halides are compounds consisting of silver and a member of the halogen family, such as fluorine, chlorine, bromine, or iodine. The silver atom and the halogen are held together by an ionic bond; the silver ion, with a charge of +1, and the halogen ion, with a charge of –1, stay together because of the attraction between their opposite charges.

All silver halides, with the exception of silver fluoride, are light-sensitive. To make photographic film, crystals of silver bromide ($AgBr$) are spread in gelatin on a film backing. Light from the camera image interacts with the silver bromide and makes it more sensitive to reduction, an electron gain, by a mild organic reducing agent like hydroquinone. The compound separates into metallic silver (Ag) atoms and bromide ions (Br^-). A negative film image is formed by the pattern of silver

Right, cross-section of double-coated photographic paper. The base is in blue, sandwiched between two sheets of adhesive, which are covered by a supercoat.

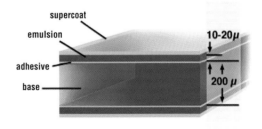

residue. Any unsensitized silver bromide grains are dissolved and washed away in a sodium thiosulfate solution during the development process.

Photoluminescence refers to the ability of some living organisms to produce light through biochemical reactions taking place inside their cells. Organisms capable of photoluminescence include fireflies and certain marine animals such as jellyfish. In response to a signal from its environment, the organism's cells fill with calcium ions, which bind to various molecules, especially a protein called aequorin. By binding to the calcium, aequorin gains energy, which it emits in the form of visible light, the source of the glow. The signal may be stress, as in the case of the jellyfish, or an impetus to find food or to mate, as in the case of fireflies.

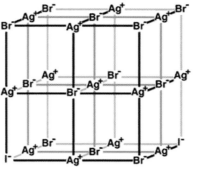

Above, a silver halide crystal lattice shows the locations of the ions of bromine, silver, and iodine.

in sodium thiosulphate, which removes any residual silver halides, or in an acidic salt such as ammonium thiocyanate, which stabilizes the image through the conversion of the silver halides to more stable compounds. The result is a negative image, which can then be used to expose similarly treated paper to achieve a positive print of the desired size.

A newer class of emulsions uses silver-behenate materials, which require much longer exposure times and are less stable. However, they can be processed without liquid; heated to between 116 and 127 degrees Celsius, the latent image becomes overt. Such emulsions are called dry silver films.

Dye Transfer. Yet another class is the dye transfer system, such as the Polaroid™ system, in which the ejection of the film chemically transfers the image from the image-forming layer to a previously transparent image-receiving layer. The image gradually forms on the top layer of the film sandwich, visible because the section of film that contained the reagent turns opaque white. Because exposure and viewing take place from the same side, a mirror optics system is required to correct the image.

Color Photography. Color photography is more complicated, because the silver halide emulsion has three layers, corresponding to the subtractive primary colors: yellow, magenta, and cyan, which record blue, green, and red, respectively. Each dye image is formed along with the silver image, producing a color negative; alternatively, reversal processing can be employed (with a re-exposure stage and a bleaching stage) to produce a direct color positive, as for slides.

The Kodachrome™ method of color processing, introduced in 1935, used a four-step method of development. After conventional black-and-white development had removed unexposed grains, each dye layer was developed

---

OBSERVATIONS

Old MacDonald Had a Farm...

Certain fungi are capable of emitting a phosphorescent glow, and recent experiments have begun to transplant genes for calcium-binding proteins like aequorin into various types of crop plants. Plants are known to exhibit an electrical response to stress; with the aequorin gene, a field of crops could glow as a distress signal when under environmental or insect attack, allerting farmers to act quickly to save their acreage.

Background material can be found in CAMERA; ELECTRON EMISSIONS; RECORDING TECHNOLOGY. *More details can be found in* AIR POLLUTION; CHLOROFLUOROCARBONS; PHOTOGRAPHY, CHEMISTRY OF. *Relevant information is contained in* PHONON; PHOTOSYNTHESIS; PHOTOVOLTAIC TECHNOLOGY.

Further Reading
Bryce-Smith, D., *Photochemistry* (1985); Coyle, James D., *Introduction to Organic Photochemistry* (1988); Neckers, D. C., *Advances in Photochemistry* (1995).

First see PHOTOCHEMISTRY

Photography, Chemistry of

Next see CAMERA

Since its inception, photography has been performed through the exposure of silver salts and halides to light, which reduces some of the silver to its metallic state. The plate or film is then immersed in a developing agent, which is also a reducing medium. Where metallic silver already exists because that area of the image was brightly lit, the agent catalyzes the speed of reduction, so that after a given amount of development those areas with a latent image have been fully reduced, while those areas that represent shadows in the original have been only slightly reduced. At that time, the image is washed either

---

TOOLS

Early Development

Color photography did not begin with Kodachrome™, or even with one of the processes developed at the turn of the 20th century. It began, apparently, with the painstaking work of Reverend Levi Hill of Westkill, New York. Around 1850, Hill began coating daguerrotype plates with as many as 20 coatings, including mercury nitrate, gold sodium thiosulfate, iodine monochloride, and chlorine; he developed them over mercury fumes. Hill published *A Treatise on Heliochromy* in 1856, but his process was too complex, and his results faded quickly when exposed to light. Hill died in 1865, displaying clear evidence of heavy metal poisoning.

successively. Simpler modern processes allow all three dye images to be produced in a single step.

Background material can be found in CAMERA; LIGHT; MICROSCOPY; OPTICS. *Advanced subjects are developed in* PHOTOCHEMISTRY; RADIO AND TELEVISION BROADCASTING. *Special aspects of this subject are covered in* DIODE AND PHOTODIODE; ELECTRON MICROSCOPY; PHOTOSYNTHESIS.

Further Reading
Anthony, John W., *Handbook of Mineralogy: Halides, Hydroxides, Oxides* (1997); Keller, Karlheinz, *Science and Technology of Photography* (1993); Carr, Kathleen Thormod, *Polaroid Transfers: A Complete Visual Guide to Creating Image and Emulsion Transfers* (1997).

First see CHLOROPLAST

Photosynthesis

Next see CALVIN-BENSON CYCLE

The process by which green plants obtain energy from the sun to produce glucose.

Glucose, a simple sugar, is used by all living things as a source of energy. The process of making glucose is called photosynthesis and is performed only by cells containing chlorophyll or other light-sensitive pigments. The "raw materials," or basic reactants, needed for photosynthesis are water and carbon dioxide (CO_2). The final products include oxygen, water, and glucose ($C_6H_{12}O_6$).

The electrons in the chlorophyll molecules are used to "harness" energy from the sun and convert it into Adenosine triphosphate, or ATP, which can then be converted into chemical energy by the cell. Electrons are arranged in discrete energy levels surrounding the nucleus of an atom. The farther away from the nucleus a particular electron is located, the more energy it has. Reduction and oxidation are two interrelated processes referring to the movement of electrons between entities. The substance that gains an electron is reduced, while the one losing it becomes oxidized. These processes occur simultaneously and are known as coupled redox reactions. They are highly exothermic, meaning they give off energy.

Light and Dark Reactions. The reactions of photosynthesis can be grouped into two major stages: the light reaction and the dark reaction. The light reaction can occur only in the presence of light, though not necessarily sunlight. The dark reaction does not require light.

The light reaction begins with Photosystem II, when light "hits" an electron in a specific chlorophyll molecule known as P680. The electron absorbs the light energy and becomes excited, meaning it has more energy than usual. The excited electron "jumps" to a higher energy level. Normally, the electron would immediately lose its additional energy and drop back down to its original position. However, it is met by an electron acceptor, Q, which sends the excited electron down a series of molecules known as a cytochrome chain. As the electron is passed from

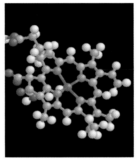

Above, a computer generated model of the molecule chlorophyll b. Below, right, a schematic of a chloroplast, showing the stroma, thylakoid, granum, and the intermembrane space surrounded by the inner and outer membranes.

one molecule to the next, a series of coupled redox reactions occurs. The energy is immediately used to make ATP. The unexcited electron settles into a different chlorophyll molecule, known as P700, leaving behind a "hole" in P680.

Photosystem I begins when a different electron in P700 also absorbs light energy and becomes excited. It too jumps to a higher energy level, where it is met by the electron acceptor Z. Z sends the excited electron down a ferrodoxin chain, where coupled redox reactions occur.

Meanwhile, back in Photosystem II, the ATP just formed supplies the energy used to split some water molecules into their component hydrogen and oxygen atoms. The oxygen is released into the air. One of its electrons is used to "plug" the hole in P680. The hydrogen atoms move over to Photosystem I, where they are picked up by the carrier molecule $NADP^+$ (which is the oxidized form of nicotinamide adenine dinucleotide phosphatase), along with the electron from P700 that went down the ferrodoxin chain and the energy that was released from the coupled redox reactions. The hydrogen and energy will be used to produce glucose in the dark reaction.

The major series of events that occur in the dark reaction are known as the Calvin cycle. CO_2 is reduced to organic carbon, a process known as carbon fixation. One molecule of CO_2 is "fed" into the cycle at a time. Three turns of the cycle produce a phosphoglyceraldehyde (PGAL) molecule with three carbon atoms, two of which can combine to form glucose. Therefore, the cycle runs six times in order to form a six-carbon sugar such as glucose. Plants that perform the Calvin cycle in this manner are called C_3 plants. In C_4 plants, carbon dioxide is initially accepted by a compound called phosphoenolpyruvate (PEP) to form a four-carbon organic acid.

Photosynthesis generally takes place during the day, when the stomata of the plant leaves are open, allowing gas exchange to occur. However,

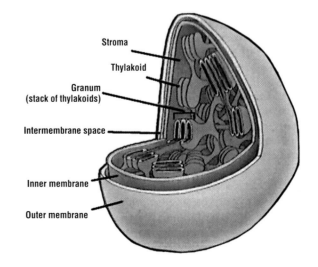

Stroma

Thylakoid

Granum
(stack of thylakoids)

Intermembrane space

Inner membrane

Outer membrane

some plants that live in arid climates have their stomata closed during the day and open at night. Carbon dioxide taken in during the night is converted to organic acids such as malic and isocitric acids. During the day, CO_2 is released from these acids and used in photosynthesis. This process is known as Crassulacean acid metabolism, or CAM, photosynthesis, after a family of plants in which it occurs.

Background material can be found in ADENOSINE TRIPHOSPHATE (ATP); CHLOROPLAST; PLANT. *Advanced subjects are developed in* CALVIN-BENSON CYCLE; FRUIT STRUCTURE; LEAF. *More information on particular aspects is contained in* ATMOSPHERE; CHLOROPLAST PIGMENTATION; HYDROPONICS.

Further Reading
Hall, David O., *Photosynthesis* (1999); Pessarakli, Mohammed, *Handbook of Photosynthesis* (1996); Volkov, Alexander G., *Plant Energetics* (1998).

First see PHOTOCHEMISTRY

Photovoltaic Technology

Next see CIRCUIT

The application of electron emissions from surfaces, as discovered by Max Planck and Albert Einstein in the early 1900s.

Early experimenters found that certain rare metals emit electricity when exposed to light, but they did not know why; nevertheless, the phenomenon was exploited for such applications as photographic exposure meters, using selenium cells. After the invention of semiconductor technology in 1947–1948, however, research became focused on the potential of these semiconducting crystals to transform sunlight into usable electric power.

Most contemporary solar cells are made of silicon or gallium arsenide; the latter offers higher operating efficiency, but at greater cost. In a typical arrangement, a panel of silicon one foot by four feet is covered by a collector grid of aluminum or molybdenum, laid on by photolithography.

Much research has gone into the development of thin film cells, using exotic compounds like copper indium. These films are flexible, so they can be arranged in parabolic sections, and they are easier to manufacture than solar plates.

Photovoltaic technology is still not directly competitive with other sources of electric power, although the cost of generating energy in this way continues to fall. The future of photovoltaic technology may lie in multijunction cells, in which each p-n junction will capture a different wavelength of solar radiation, allowing a greater amount of energy to be absorbed per cell.

Background material regarding photovoltaic technology can be found in ELECTRON EMISSIONS; LIGHT. *Advanced subjects are developed in* DIODE AND PHOTODIODE; FIBER OPTICS; P-N JUNCTION; PHOTOCHEMISTRY. *Relevant information is contained in* CAMERA; NIGHT-VISION TECHNOLOGY; PHOTOSYNTHESIS.

Further Reading
Markvart, Tomas, *Solar Electricity* (1994); Mazer, J. A., *Solar Cells: An Introduction to Crystalline Photovoltaic Technology* (1996); Treble, Fred C., *Generating Electricity from the Sun* (1991).

First see EVOLUTION

Phylogeny

Next see BIODIVERSITY

The study of taxonomy in an attempt to reconstruct the pattern of events leading to the distribution and diversity of life.

Classification, or taxonomy, is one aspect of phylogeny; there is a pattern of similarities among the various organisms that helps us to understand their evolutionary relationships. The broadest category is the kingdom, which is divided into various phyla.

Each phylum is divided into several classes, each class into different orders, each order into families, each family into genuses, and each genus into one or more species. In order to determine whether or not species are closely related, one must look for the following:

Homologous characteristics—body parts with the same general structure and function, e.g., a whale flipper and a human arm;

Interbreedability—the ability to mate and produce viable offspring, usually confined to a species but possible to some degree within a genus;

Life history—whether the species lays eggs or gives birth, how members feed their young, etc.;

Biochemical similarities—similarities in DNA, blood proteins, digestive enzymes, etc.

Phylogenetic trees represent our best current understanding, with closely related species grouped closer together and connected by lines leading to shared ancestors. In tracing living things back to the beginning, scientists believe that the earliest life forms were archaebacteria, primitive unicellular organisms adapted to live in the extreme conditions that existed at that time. Eventually, these gave rise to prokaryotes, cells lacking internal membranes, and eukaryotes, more "advanced" cells with internal membranes and compartmentalization.

Prokaryotes are considered to be among the oldest groups of organisms in existence. A current theory has it that the first eukaryotic organisms were actually collections of prokaryotes that "banded together" in symbiotic relationships to form more complex cells. Prokaryotes include all members of the moneran kingdom, such as bacteria and blue-green algae.

Four Kingdoms. There are four kingdoms of eukaryotes: protists, fungi, plants, and animals. Protists are unicellular organisms such as amoebae and paramecia. Fungi include molds and yeasts. Plants are either unicellular or multicellular and contain chlorophyll, which enables them to carry out photosynthesis, the process of using light energy to make simple sugars. Animals are all consumers, incapable of making their own food.

In terms of animal evolution, early life forms were very primitive. The Cambrian "explosion," a sudden, rapid diversification of life, saw the appearance of many types of invertebrates, which gradually gave rise to vertebrates, animals with backbones. Of the vertebrates, fish are the most primitive. Amphibians represent an "in-between" adaptation to life on land, existing as aquatic creatures with gills at the beginning of their lifespan and as terrestrial organisms with lungs for the latter part. Reptiles are the first to be totally adapted for life on land and are the most primitive amniotes, no longer needing to lay eggs in water.

Birds are more advanced amniotes, believed to have descended from dinosaurs (a prominent group of early reptiles). Mammals represent the highest degree of advancement, with internal development of the young and lactation afterward to care for them. Most mammals are adapted to life on land, but some, such as the whales and dolphins, represent a return to aquatic life.

Related areas to be considered are EMBRYOLOGY; EVOLUTION; GENETICS. *Advanced subjects are developed in* COMPLEMENTATION AND ALLELISM; MORPHOGENESIS; SUCCESSION. *Relevant information is contained in* GENETIC CODE; IMPRINTING, GENETIC; INVERTEBRATES; LINKAGE, GENETIC.

Further Reading
Grande, Lance, *Interpreting the Hierarchy of Nature: From Systematic Patterns to Evolutionary Process Theories* (1994); Martins, Emilia P., *Phylogenies and the Comparative Method in Animal Behavior* (1996); Novacek, Michael, *Extinction and Phylogeny* (1992).

First see CRYSTAL

Piezoelectricity

Next see ELECTROMETALLURGY

The conversion of mechanical energy to electrical energy caused by the deformation of a crystal lattice. Only certain types of crystals exhibit this effect.

Piezoelectricity is an effect that was discovered in 1880 by Pierre and Jacques Curie. If a crystal that does not conduct electricity and does not have a center of symmetry, such as quartz, is placed under stress, an electrical charge appears on its surface. Conversely, if an alternating electric charge is applied to such a crystal, it starts to vibrate, generating high-frequency sound waves. The piezoelectric effect was first put to practical use in World War I, when it was adapted for submarine detection systems. The high-frequency sound waves produced by a piezoelectric crystal pass through water but are reflected by any large underwater object, such as a submarine. The reflected sound waves are picked up by another piezoelectric crystal in the system. This crystal generates an alternating voltage that can be used to operate devices that determine the location of the object.

The magnitude of the piezoelectric effect is proportional to the strain or stress placed on the crystal. A quartz crystal of a given size has a natural frequency of expansion and contraction in the direction of the applied electric field; if the electric field alternates at the same frequency, the plate increases its vibrations, augmenting the piezoelectric effect. The piezoelectric effect is used widely in commercial systems such as loudspeakers, microphones, and frequency control devices in radio transmitters. Quartz is used in many such systems, because it has great mechanical strength and remains stable at temperatures over 100 degrees Celsius.

First see ENDOCRINE SYSTEM

Pituitary Gland

Next see AGGRESSION AND TERRITORIALITY

The controlling, regulator gland in the endocrine system of vertebrates.

If the endocrine system were an orchestra, the pituitary gland would be its conductor. Located at the base of the brain, this small, reddish-brown oval integrates signals from the brain with hormone feedback from the body to orchestrate the growth and hormonal activity of the thyroid gland, adrenal cortex, testes, ovaries, and mammary glands. In addition, through its secretion of growth hormone (somatotropin), the pituitary affects the metabolism, growth, and development of virtually every cell in the body.

Structure. The pituitary gland is divided into an anterior and a posterior lobe. Besides producing growth hormone, the anterior lobe (also called the adenohypophysis) produces prolactin, which stimulates milk production, and four hormones that stimulate other glands: thyrotropin, or thyroid-stimulating hormone (TSH); adrenocorticotropic hormone (ACTH), which stimulates the adrenal cortex; and follicle-stimulating hormone (FSH) and luteinizing hormone (LH), which stimulate the gonads.

The posterior lobe of the pituitary (also called the neurohypophysis) releases two hor-

OBSERVATIONS

Hormone Release

A stalk connects the pituitary gland to the hypothalamus of the brain, which produces releasing hormones that spur production of each of these pituitary hormones. The system—often called the hypothalamus-pituitary axis—is under feedback control. For instance, when the level of thyroid hormone in the blood gets low, the hypothalamus secretes thyrotropic-releasing hormone, which stimulates the anterior pituitary to secrete thyroid-stimulating hormone. This, in turn, spurs the thyroid to secrete more thyroid hormone into the blood. The higher thyroid hormone level inhibits the hypothalamus and the pituitary. When the thyroid-hormone level falls again, the inhibition dwindles as well, and the hypothalamus secretes more releasing hormone, starting the cycle once more.

mones. Oxytocin causes the uterus to contract in labor, and vasopressin (also called antidiuretic hormone) stimulates the kidneys to absorb more water, affecting fluid balance. These hormones are produced in the hypothalamus and stored in the posterior lobe until the hypothalamus triggers their release.

Further Reading
Belchest, Paul E., *Management of Pituitary Disease* (1984); Joffe, Russell T., *The Thyroid Axis and Psychiatric Illness* (1993); Melmed, S., *The Pituitary* (1994).

> *Related material regarding the pituitary gland can be found in* ENDOCRINE SYSTEM; NERVOUS SYSTEM. *Further details can be found in* BONE AND BONE GROWTH; BRAIN; ENZYMES. *Basic aspects of this subject are covered in* ADRENAL GLANDS; AGGRESSION AND TERRITORIALITY; METABOLISM.

First see DISEASES, INFECTIOUS

Plague

Next see ANTIBIOTICS

A bacterial infection that normally occurs in rodents but can be transmitted to humans by the bites of the rodent's fleas.

Often called bubonic plague, because it causes swollen lymph glands, or "buboes," the "black death" of the fourteenth century killed 25 million people in Europe. Another form of the disease, pneumonic plague, affects the lungs and is spread in droplets that are expelled by coughs. Better sanitation and antibiotics have greatly reduced the incidence and death toll taken by plague today. The first symptoms of the disease are fever, shivering, and severe headache that begin two to five days after infection. The buboes then appear, most often on the face but also in the groin, armpits, and neck. Without treatment, half of infected patients die.

Pneumonic plague causes severe coughing that not only spreads the disease but also produces strained breathing and bloody sputum. The disease is diagnosed by taking a fluid sample from a bubo, in the case of bubonic plaugue, or from sputum, in the case of pneumonic plague. The fluid is cultured in the laboratory to detect *Yersinia pestis*, the bacterium that causes the infection. Once diagnosed, plague is treated with antibiotics such as streptomycin, chloramphenicol, or tetracycline. Prompt treatment reduces the death rate to less than five percent.

In the United States, plague is still found in wild rodents, such as squirrels, in the West, and 10 to 50 cases are diagnosed each year, mostly in the spring and summer.

Further Reading
Benedict, Carol, *Bubonic Plague in Nineteenth-Century China* (1996); Butler, Thomas C., *Plague and Other Yersinia Infections* (1983); Cantor, Norman, *In the Wake of the PLague: The Black Death and the World it Made* (2001); Gottfried, R. S., *The Black Death: Natural and Human Disaster in Medieval Europe* (1985).

> *Special topics in this area are found in* DISEASE, INFECTIOUS; PARASITE; RESPIRATORY SYSTEM. *Advanced subjects are developed in* GERM THEORY; PHARMACOLOGY; VIRAL DISEASES, EXOTIC. *Additional aspects of this subject are covered in* DISEASE, THEORY OF; EPIDEMIOLOGY; IMMUNIZATION AND VACCINATION.

First see SOLAR SYSTEM

Planet

Next see PLANETS, FORMATION OF

A solid or gaseous body in orbit around a star.

A planet emits no light of its own but can reflect the light of a star. For most of human history, the only planetary system known was the solar system. However, that is changing, and planets have now been detected orbiting other stars.

Formation. When stars form out of the collapse of interstellar clouds, most of the material in the cloud ends up inside the star. In some cases (such as that of our own solar system), a small amount of the material in the original cloud stays in a flattened, spinning disk of debris centered around the newly forming star. It is the material in this so-called protoplanetary disk that provides the basic building blocks for planets.

As the star begins coalescing at the center of this system, heat and light from the newly formed star begin to change the nature of the material in the protoplanetary disk. Although all parts of the disk started out with similar chemical composition,in the area near the star, where temperatures are high, volatile materials such as helium and water become gases. The newly formed solar wind starts to blow them away, leaving only solid material behind. These bits of solid material bump and stick together, eventually aggregating into boulder-size objects called planetesimals. Swarms of planetesimals, in turn, collide and come together to form the beginnings of planets.

Inner Planets. The inner planets of our solar system—Mercury, Venus, Mars, and Earth—were formed in this way. Called the terrestrial planets, they are small, rocky objects orbiting close to the sun. Early in their history, they went through a period known as the Great Bombardment, when debris from the disk fell onto their surfaces in a fiery shower. The scars of this bombardment can still be seen in the craters on the moon and Mercury, but they have been weathered away on the other planets. The bombardment generated so much energy that the Earth melted through, allowing heavy materials like iron and nickel to sink to the center.

Outer Planets. Farther out, the story of the formation of the planets was different. The Jovian planets, named after Jupiter, formed from the original material of the protoplanetary disk. Consequently, Jupiter, Saturn, Uranus, and Neptune are gigantic compared to the terrestrial planets and are composed primarily of helium and hydrogen. They may have small, rocky cores like the terrestrial planets, but these planets do not really have surfaces. If one could descend into their atmospheres, one would encounter steadily higher pressures and denser layers of

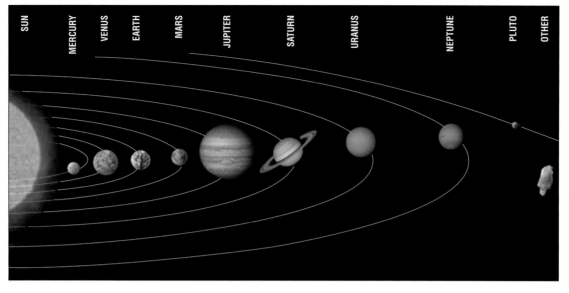

SUN · MERCURY · VENUS · EARTH · MARS · JUPITER · SATURN · URANUS · NEPTUNE · PLUTO · OTHER

Left, artist's rendering of all the planets in the solar system. Below, top, brown dwarfs are "failed stars" because they do not have enough mass to shine by fusion. Below, middle, sun-like stars and planets are forming inside Lynds 1551, an interstellar cloud of gas and dust. Using the VLA in New Mexico, it is believed protoplanets can be seen forming.

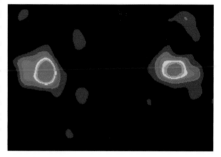

gas, which would fade imperceptibly into liquid. In the case of Jupiter, the largest of the planets in our system, the pressures were so high that they produced a core of solid metallic hydrogen.

The outermost planet in our system, Pluto, has always been something of an enigma. Its orbit is tilted with respect to the orbits of all the other planets, it has a highly eccentric orbit, and it is very small—about two percent of the mass of Earth. Some astronomers speculate that Pluto is actually a large planetesimal, the last survivor of a swarm of objects orbiting in the outer reaches of the solar system.

Discovering Planets. Because planets—even large ones—are small compared to their stars, and because they shine by reflected light, they are very hard to detect around distant stars. Astronomers find them by looking for a wobble. A star and a planet both move around a point between them called the center of mass. If they are imagined as being on two ends of a long stick, the point where a fulcrum would have to be placed to balance them would be the center of mass. Even though this point is well within the star, the fact is that the presence of a planet causes the star to wobble slightly in the sky. It is this slight wobble that astronomers can detect when they look at distant stars.

The first discovery of an extrasolar planet was made in 1994 by Alexander Wolszczan of Pennsylvania State University. The planets (there were actually three of them) circled a pulsar, the remains of a long-dead star. Then, starting in 1995, astronomers in Switzerland and California began discovering planets around normal stars. As might be expected given the definition of the center of mass, large planets are much easier to detect than small ones, because they produce a much bigger

wobble in the star. Also, planets close to the star produce bigger wobbles than do those farther away. It should come as no surprise, then, to learn that the first extrasolar planets detected around normal stars were bigger than Jupiter and very close to their stars —up to five times the mass of Jupiter and anywhere from .05 to 2.1 times as far from their stars as Earth is from the sun. The problem now is to explain how these so-called hot Jupiters could be close to their

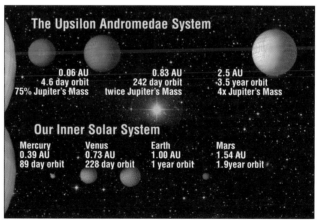

The Upsilon Andromedae System

0.06 AU / 4.6 day orbit / 75% Jupiter's Mass

0.83 AU / 242 day orbit / twice Jupiter's Mass

2.5 AU / 3.5 year orbit / 4x Jupiter's Mass

Our Inner Solar System

Mercury / 0.39 AU / 89 day orbit

Venus / 0.73 AU / 228 day orbit

Earth / 1.00 AU / 1 year orbit

Mars / 1.54 AU / 1.9year orbit

Left, astronomers at the High Altitude Observatory (HAO) found evidence of extrasolar planets orbiting the star Upsilon Andromeda—the first known multiple planet system orbiting a star similar to our own star, the sun.

stars, when theory says they have to form far away. The current best guess is that they formed farther out but for some reason have spiraled in toward their stars.

Further developments in the field are discussed in KEPLER'S LAWS; PLANETS, FORMATION OF; SOLAR SYSTEM. *More details can be found in* EARTH; PLANETARY ATMOSPHERE; SATELLITE, PLANETARY. *Additional relevant information is contained in* ASTEROIDS AND METEORS; ECLIPSE; PLANETARY RINGS.

Further Reading
Grossinger, Richard, *Planetary Mysteries* (1987); North, Gerald, *Advanced Amateur Astronomy* (1997); Zubrin, Robert, *The Case for Mars: The Plan to Settle the Red Planet* (1996).

First see PLANET

Planet, Interior of

Next see PLANETS, FORMATION OF

The interiors of the planets of the solar system differ widely in composition and density, suggesting a way of dividing the planets roughly into groups. One group consists of the four innermost planets, called the terrestrial planets because they all resemble Earth. These four planets—Mercury, Venus, Earth, and Mars—are composed primarily of silicate rock and iron. They are all believed to have cores made of nickel-iron, with mantles of solid rock above those cores.

Earth has a strong magnetic field, which is generated by convective motions in its liquid metal core. Venus, sometimes described as Earth's "twin planet," has no magnetic field, while Mercury and Mars have very weak magnetic fields. One theory about why Venus lacks a magnetic field is that it is due to the very slow rotation of the planet, which completes a rotation once every 243 days and thus does not have convective currents in its the interior.

The Giants. The two giant planets, Jupiter and Saturn, have deep atmospheres that extend nearly to their centers and consist largely of hydrogen. Astronomers believe that the interior of Jupiter consists almost completely of hydrogen, but with some helium as well. Jupiter is believed to have other, less abundant elements in its interior, but these elements are believed to be deep inside the planet, most likely in a rocky core. Saturn is unique in the solar system because it is the only planet whose density is less than that of water.

Like Jupiter, Saturn has a surface that appears to be a top deck of clouds. Its interior is believed to be a multilayered ball composed of hydrogen and helium. Saturn is believed to have a rocky core like Jupiter, a core that is small in terms of the planet's size but that nevertheless has 15 to 20 times the mass of the Earth. The rocky cores of Jupiter and Saturn are believed to have gravitationally gathered in the lighter elements that were blown outward from the sun as the solar system formed.

Outer Planets. Observations of the mean densities and sizes of the next outermost planets, Uranus and Neptune, indicate that they consist largely of rock and water ice. Both are believed to have cores of silicates and iron, with an ice layer above the core. The ice on the surface of these planets is believed to include large amounts of ammonia and methane.

Little is known about the interior composition of Pluto, the outermost planet. Its density as measured by astronomers indicates that it is composed almost entirely of water-ice and frozen gases.

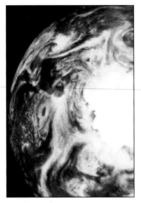

Below, a satellite photograph of the Earth. Cloud formations are clearly visible against the dark blue of the oceans.

Above, NASA's *Pathfinder* rover captured this true-color photograph of the horizon of Mars. The blue-gray color of the sky is in stark contrast to the deep red color normally seen.

First see ATMOSPHERE

Planetary Atmosphere

Next see VENUS

The atmospheres of the planets in the solar system were formed during the planets' creation. Several effects, including the heat created by the impact of material on the growing planets, caused the release of gases trapped in the solid material, a process called volatile outgassing. The oxidation state, and hence the chemical composition of this outgassed volatile material, depended on the structure and composition of the solids forming the planet—in particular, on the presence or absence of iron in the upper layers of the new planet. The planets in which the greater part of their iron migrated to the core would have outgassed volatiles consisting mainly of water vapor and carbon dioxide—about the same as the composition of present-day emissions from volcanoes. The atmospheres of these planets would have formed very quickly.

Starting from the innermost planet, Mercury is believed to have virtually no atmosphere. Measurements made by the Mariner 10 spacecraft, which flew by Mercury three times in 1974 and 1975, found that the surface atmospheric pressure was less than a trillionth of Earth's, with helium as the major constituent. Venus, the second planet from the sun, has been found by space probes to have an atmosphere that is more than 90 percent carbon dioxide, with less than 1 percent oxygen and up to 1.6 percent water vapor.

Earth and Mars. Earth's atmosphere is 78.09 percent nitrogen, with 20.95 percent oxygen and smaller amounts of argon, carbon dioxide, neon, krypton, xenon, methane, and hydrogen. The water vapor content of its atmosphere varies from 0.2 to 0.4 percent by volume; the atmosphere is considered to be part of the hydrosphere, the watery part of Earth. Mars, Earth-like in many ways, has been found by space probes to have an extremely thin atmosphere, less than 1 percent that of Earth's. Its upper atmosphere consists mainly of carbon dioxide, with small amounts of nitrogen, argon, carbon monoxide, and nitrogen oxide.

The two next planets, the giants Jupiter and Saturn, have similar atmospheres. Space probes have found that Jupiter's atmosphere is 82 percent hydrogen, 17 percent helium, and 1 percent other gases. The Jovian atmosphere is deep—so deep that at its lower boundary, 596 miles below the uppermost layer, the hydrogen becomes liquid. The atmosphere of Jupiter is in continual, turbulent motion. One of the most noticeable features of the Jovian atmosphere is the Great

Red Spot, which is 24,000 miles across. The atmosphere of Saturn also consists largely of hydrogen, with about 11 percent helium. Space probes have photographed light and dark belts and circulating storm regions. A thick haze at lower levels hides the features of the planet.

Both Uranus and Neptune, the next outermost planets, appear greenish through telescopes, a coloring caused by the presence of large amounts of methane gas in their atmospheres. Uranus has a layer of compressed hydrogen and helium above the methane layer; so does Neptune, which also has a thin, variable upper-atmosphere haze. Pluto's atmosphere contains some methane and perhaps nitrogen or argon.

Background material regarding planetary atmospheres can be found in ATMOSPHERE; GASES, BEHAVIOR OF; GRAVITY; PLANET. *Further developments in the field are discussed in* COMET; MARS; SOLAR SYSTEMS; VENUS. *Special topics in this area are found in* PLANETS, FORMATION OF; SATELLITES, PLANETARY.

First see ELECTRIC AND MAGNETIC FIELD

Planetary Magnetic Field

Next see PLANET, INTERIOR OF

Planetary magnetic fields, or magnetospheres, have been found to exist around Earth, Mercury, Jupiter, Saturn, Uranus, and Neptune. Earth's magnetosphere is formed by an interaction between the magnetic field resulting from the dynamo effect of its metallic inner core and the solar wind, the continuous, supersonic outward flow of charged particles, mostly electrons and protons, from the sun's corona. Within Earth's magnetosphere, spacecraft have detected bands of radiation, the Van Allen belts. There are two of these belts, about 2,000 and 10,000 miles from Earth's surface. Mercury's magnetic field was something of a surprise. Although Mercury has a metallic core, no magnetic field was expected to exist, because the planet's slow rotation was expected to produce no dynamo effect.

Outer Planets. The magnetospheres of the outer planets are predominately caused by rapid planetary rotation. For Jupiter, the injection of heavy molecules such as sulfur dioxide into the atmosphere by the planet's volcanoes provides the major source of charged particles. The injected molecules are ionized, and the ions are then accelerated by the electric field induced by Jupiter's rotation. The resulting magnetosphere extends far from the planet—up to three or four astronomical units. The heavy ions eventually escape into the solar wind. The magnetospheres of the other outer planets are much weaker than the magnetosphere of Jupiter, because the planets do not have major sources of charged particles.

Further Reading
Durrant, C.J., *The Atmosphere of the Sun* (1988); Kliore, A., *The Mars Reference Atmosphere* (1982); North, Gerald, *Advanced Amateur Astronomy* (1997).

First see SATELLITE, PLANETARY

Planetary Rings

Next see SATURN

Planetary ring systems have been detected around at least three of the four outermost planets of the solar system. They come into existence because the tidal gravitational forces from large planets such as Jupiter and Saturn perturb and even destroy most bodies orbiting the planets. Once such a body comes closer to the planet than a certain distance, called the Roche limit, these gravitational forces rip it apart, creating a swarm of small objects going around the planet in a common orbit. From a distance, this swarm appears as a ring.

Rings of Saturn. The most famous rings in the solar system are those of Saturn, which were first observed by Galileo Galilei. The outer ring is called the A ring, and the ring inside it is the B ring. Between them is the Cassini division, named for the seventeenth-century Italian astronomer Giovanni Cassini. More powerful modern instruments have identified a D ring, inside the C ring, and F, G, and E rings farther out than the A ring.

The rings of Uranus were discovered by accident, because they occluded the light from a distant star that was passing behind the planet as seen from Earth. The rings of Jupiter were detected by a *Voyager* space probe. These rings orbit the planet at a distance of 35,500 miles above its clouds and are less than 19 miles thick.

Neptune has two rings, one narrow and bright, the other wider and dim. (*See* JUPITER; NEPTUNE; SATURN.)

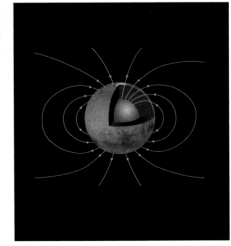

Above, left, the F-ring of Saturn in false color. At right, a diagram of Earth's magnetic field.

First see SOLAR SYSTEM

Planets, Formation of

Next see PLANET, INTERIOR OF

The formation of the planets of the solar system is believed to have begun in a region of dense, cool interstellar gas and dust clouds. The mass of this complex of clouds and gas was probably in the range of 1,000 to 100,000 times the mass of the sun. Over a period of perhaps 10 million years, at least one supernova explosion occurred in that complex. The shock wave from such a supernova explosion would compress and trigger the collapse of a number of small cloud fragments; several of these explosions may have occurred. Each pre-solar cloud fragment collapsed into a flattened disk, so that angular momentum was pumped outward and mass was pumped inward by the resulting large-scale turbulent motions. These motions were maintained by the conversion of gravitational energy into heat. The inner regions of this flattened disk, inside the current orbit of Mercury, are believed to have reached temperatures that were high enough to vaporize all the interstellar dust.

Inner Planets. In the realm of the four innermost planets—Mercury, Venus, Earth, and Mars—temperatures were high enough to permit a kind of equilibrium between the solar-composition nebular gas and dust grains but not high enough to vaporize the major elements, so rocky planets formed in that region. Farther out from this inner belt, maximum temperatures were lower, so that pre-solar grains of interstellar organic matter could continue to exist. The high concentration of these grains led to the formation of the asteroids, in what astronomers now know as the asteroid belt.

When the sun ignited and began to emit energy, the grains of solid material began to come together, slowly forming planetesimals. After perhaps 200 million years, about 200 of these lunar-size bodies, and many of smaller size, would have formed. Slowly, many of these planetesimals joined one another, a process of accretion that led to the formation of the planets over a period of perhaps 100 million years. The process of accretion and planetary formation would occur most quickly near the sun, where the density of solid material would be greatest. Each growing planet would gather in solid material from great distances.

It is estimated that 25 percent of Earth's mass came from the vicinity of Venus or Mars, the two neighboring planets, and that the ratio for the other planets is about the same. A very small proportion of the mass of each planet is believed to have come from even greater distances. This material is believed to be the predominant source of the volatile elements of the planets. Even after the major period of accretion and planetary formation, volatile material would be added to the new planet by the bombardment of bodies rich in volatile materials, such as carbonaceous asteroids and ice-bearing comets.

OBSERVATIONS

The Fire Within

"It may be that at one time our sun, that quiet and well-behaved body, had a large companion that rapidly consumed its store of hydrogen and ended as a supernova. Or it may be that the debris of a nearby supernova explosion mingled with the swirl of interstellar dust and gases from which the sun and its planets were condensing. There is no other credible explanation of the great quantity of exploding atoms still present on Earth. We stand on fallout from a vast nuclear explosion. Within our bodies, no less than three million atoms rendered unstable in that event still erupt every minute, releasing a tiny fraction of the energy stored from that fierce fire of long ago." —J. E. Lovelock, *Gaia* (1979)

Further Reading
Kaler, James B., *Astronomy* (1997); Silk, Joseph, *The Big Bang* (1988); Zeilik, M., *Astronomy: The Evolving Universe* (1997).

The foundations of the subject of the formation of the planets are discussed in GEOLOGICAL TIME SCALE; GRAVITY; PLANET. *More details can be found in* GEOLOGY, ARCHAEOLOGICAL; INTERSTELLAR MEDIUM ("DARK MATTER"). *Advanced subjects are developed in* IGNEOUS ROCK; SEISMICS.

First see GAIA HYPOTHESIS

Plant

Next see FLOWER

Kingdom whose members contain chlorophyll and are capable of forming glucose by photosynthesis.

Plants are referred to as producers or autotrophs (literally, "self-feeders"). Glucose is the universal food source, and organisms that cannot produce their own supply of glucose must consume other organisms that are producers. Plants are therefore the first "link" in virtually every food chain in the Earth's ecosystem.

Plants provide another useful material as well: oxygen. During photosynthesis, plants take in carbon dioxide and give off oxygen. Plants can be small, unicellular organisms such as algae, or multicellular, complex structures such as trees. (The vast majority of photosynthesis occurring in the world is due to the action of the microscopic algae. They, not the tropical rain forests, are truly the lungs of the planet.)

Categories. Plants are divided into two categories, based on whether or not they contain vascular tissue, which is circulatory tissue consisting of xylem and phloem. Xylem is made up of hollow tubes for the transport of water and minerals. Phloem is used for the transport of glucose. Plants that lack vascular tissue must be relatively close to the ground in order to access ground moisture, and are therefore limited in size and complexity compared to vascular plants.

Cacti, like the *Agave parasana* above, thrive in dry, high-altitude climes but suffer in the wet winters of the United States.

Lower plants, such as moss, do not contain specific tissues and structures such as roots, stems, and leaves. They are made up of a few cell layers in which transport takes place by diffusion from one cell to the next. In terms of reproduction, they exhibit what is called alternation of generations, in which one generation reproduces sexually, the next asexually. The sexual generation is called the gametophyte generation (from gamete, meaning a "sex cell"). Sperm are produced in a structure known as the antheridium and swim through a thin film of moisture to fertilize the eggs, located in the archegonium. The zygote grows up to be the sporophyte generation, which, true to its name, produces spores. Each spore in turn develops into another gametophyte.

Higher plants all contain roots, stems, leaves, and either flowers or cones. Vascular tissue is found throughout these plants. The primary function of the roots is to absorb water and minerals from the soil, and they also anchor the plant in the ground. Stems provide structure and support to the plant and serve as a major "thoroughfare" connecting the roots and the leaves. Most, if not all, of the photosynthesis takes place within the leaves.

Reproduction in Higher Plants. Flowers are the sex organs of plants. The female portion is known as the pistil or carpel, and the male portion, which produces pollen, is the anther. Reproduc-tion involves what is called double fertilization. Pollination is the transfer of pollen from the anther to the pistil. A single pollen grain contains two nuclei, a sperm nucleus and a tube nucleus. The tube nucleus "digs" a tunnel down the length of the pistil until it reaches the ovary, where the egg cells are found. The sperm nucleus fertilizes the egg to form a zygote. The tube nucleus in turn fertilizes a structure called the embryo sac to form an endosperm. The endosperm is the stored food for the plant inside the seed.

Angiosperms and Gymnosperm. Higher plants are further divided into angiosperms, or flowering plants, and gymnosperms, or nonflowering plants (such as conifers). Angiosperms produce seeds enclosed within a fruit (which was the ovary of the flower containing the egg cells), and gymnosperms produce "naked" seeds in cones. The angiosperms are further divided into monocots and dicots and differ as to the basic seed symmetry, the type of root system, the distribution of vascular tissue within the stem, the vein pattern of the leaves, and the number of leaves and flowers per cluster.

Elementary aspects of this subject are covered in CHLOROPLASTS; FLOWER; FRUIT STRUCTURE; SEED. *More information on particular aspects is contained in* GERMINATION; PHOTOSYNTHESIS; PLANT HORMONES. *Further information is in* CALVIN-BENSON CYCLE; GROWTH REGULATION IN PLANTS; ROOTS.

A sampling of the plant kingdom. From top, an illustration of a *rosa gallica regalis*; pitcher plants; a Venus flytrap; and a field of black-eyed Susans.

Further Reading
Bazzaz, Fakhri A., *Plants in Changing Environments* (1996); Crawley, Michael J., *Plant Ecology* (1996); Gardiner, A., *Modern Plant Propagation* (1995).

First see PLANT

Plant Hormones

Next see PHOTOSYNTHESIS

Higher plants are composed of specialized tissues—leaves, stems, roots, and reproductive organs—whose growth and functioning are regulated largely by hormones, in coordination with external factors such as light, day length, and gravity. Plants do not have special hormone-producing organs, like the endocrine glands of animals. Instead, their hormones are produced mainly in the plant's actively growing parts, such as the developing fruit or the apical meristems of shoots, the perpetually embryonic cells at the tips of stems.

Some hormones are active in the tissue that produced them as well as in other tissues to which they are transported. Plant hormones are notable for being effective in minute amounts and for causing a wide range of effects in different tissues or at different stages of development.

Categories. Five kinds of plant hormones have been fully identified. They are auxins, cytokinins, gibberellins, abscissic acid, and ethylene. In addition, researchers have amassed evidence suggesting the existence of a flowering hormone, but it has not been identified and some attribute its presumed effects to a combination of known hormones.

In 1881, Charles Darwin and his son Francis published results of experiments on grass and oat seedlings that first suggested the existence of a plant growth hormone. In 1926, plant physiologist Frits W. Went proved its existence and named it auxin, from a Greek word for growth. It was soon identified as indoleacetic acid (IAA), a substance found in many natural sources, including human urine.

Auxins appear to regulate the basic plant growth process, causing young, cube-shaped cells to elongate as they mature and, in conjunction with other substances, regulating the rate of cell division. They are also thought to be involved in maintaining the polarity of the plant, its top-vs.-bottom organization. Their own slow movement is also polar, toward the base in stems and leaves, and toward the tip in roots. In most plants, auxins trigger the rapid growth of the ovary, which produces fruit after fertilization. When applied commercially to certain plants, they can cause fruiting without fertilization, producing seedless tomatoes, cucumbers, and eggplants.

Synthetic auxins are used as herbicides to kill broad-leaf weeds, by distorting their growth patterns while sparing grass and grains. These herbicides include the widely used 2,4-D, as well as 2,4,5-T, which has been banned in the United States. Both these auxins were found in Agent Orange, the defoliant used in the Vietnam War.

Cytokinins. Discovered in the 1950s, cytokinins balance auxin in several ways. They promote cell division, as opposed to cell elongation; the formation of buds, as opposed to the formation of roots; and the growth rather than the inhibition of lateral buds. Cytokinins also delay the aging of leaves. The most active naturally occurring cytokinin is a compound called zeatin, first isolated from corn.

Since gibberellin was isolated in the 1930s by T. Yabuta and other researchers, more than 80 variants have been identified, the best studied being gibberellic acid (also called GA_3). Gibberellins can often break seed and bud dormancy; in many seeds, they are also involved in converting starch reserves to readily usable sugars. They cause stem elongation: their most dramatic effect, when applied artificially, is to cause dwarf mutants to grow to normal heights. They can also cause fruiting of unfertilized plants, including species that do not respond to auxin.

Ethylene, a gas, can occur naturally in plants or from a fungal infection or a wound. It causes fruit to ripen and leaves, flowers, and fruit to drop from the plant, in a process called abscission.

Abscissic acid is an inhibitor that promotes seed and bud dormancy and in other ways helps prepare a plant for winter. In addition, it stimulates the closing of the stomata, the openings in the leaves, when a plant begins to lose too much water through transpiration.

First see ION

Plasma Physics

Next see FUSION, NUCLEAR

Branch of physics that deals with the behavior of highly ionized gases in which the number of free electrons and the number of positive ions are nearly equal.

Plasmas exist in interstellar space and in the atmospheres of stars such as the sun. On Earth, they are created in discharge tubes, in experimental thermonuclear reactors, and, in everyday life, in fluorescent lamps and neon lights. A gas approaches the plasma state at a temperature of about 3,500 degrees Fahrenheit and becomes fully ionized at temperatures of 15,000 degrees Fahrenheit and higher. At these temperatures, the random movements of the atoms are so violent that their collisions jar their electrons loose, creating the plasma. A fluorescent tube does not reach such high temperatures because the plasma particles collide continuously with the walls of the tube, cooling them.

Because the particles in a plasma carry electrical charges, the behavior of a plasma differs in many respects from that of an ordinary gas. For example, one phenomenon is plasma oscillation, an oscillation of the electrons of the plasma. To make a plasma electrically neutral, there has to

Bright purple streams of plasma can be seen in this plasma reactor (right) at NASA's Ames Research Center. High voltages of electricity at both the left and right electrodes ignite the gas in the center tube, which burns at a temperature above 15,000 degrees Fahrenheit.

be a positive background to balance the negative charge of the free electrons. This positive background causes a charge disturbance, which the electrons move to screen. But the electrons overshoot, are pulled back, overshoot again, and so on. Thus, the charge density of a plasma is described by a simple harmonic motion, the periodic oscillation of the electron, which is called the Langmuir frequency, named for the American physicist Irving Langmuir, who analyzed plasma oscillations in the 1920s.

Production. A number of methods of producing plasma on Earth for scientific or other purposes have been developed. One method is ohmic heating, which is produced by passing an electric current through a gas. Another method is magnetic compression, in which an increasingly strong magnetic field is applied to a gas, compressing it and raising its temperature. Another method is to subject the gas to a shock wave, causing a very large and sudden increase in pressure. The leading edge of the shock wave has the normal speed of sound, but the following portions are even faster, because the speed of sound increases in a compressed gas. The magnetic pumping method produces a plasma by applying a rapidly oscillating magnetic field.

Applications. Plasmas have some important applications in physics and chemistry. For example, a method called plasma-assisted vapor deposition is used to deposit a thin film of material on a substrate, the surface of a material, and is important in the manufacture of electronic devices.

Plasma techniques are also used for etching, in which patterns are created on substrates. One important example is the use of carbon tetrafluoride to etch silicon for electronic purposes. In dry etching, a plasma is created by applying an electric field to a gas. Pressure is increased at

Natural Plasmas in the Universe

Center of the Sun
Sun's Photosphere
Sun's Chromosphere
Sun's Corona
Solar Wind (near Earth)

Interstellar Space
  H I Regions
  H II Regions

Intergalactic Space

Earth
  Outer magnetosphere
  Plasmasphere
  Ionosphere

Some metals

the same time to provide additional energy to the electrons that are freed by the electric field. The electron temperatures become high enough to break chemical bonds in the substrate.

Other applications include plasma synthesis, in which plasmas are used to drive or create chemical reactions; the creation of new polymers by the ionization of a monomer gas; and the use of plasmas in such electronic devices as microwave sources, welders, analytical instruments, and laser tubes.

Material related to plasma physics can be found in ELECTROCHEMISTRY; ELECTRON; ION; STAR; SUN. *Other aspects of the subject are discussed in* PLANETARY MAGNETIC FIELD; SOLAR WIND. *Additional related material can be found in* AURORAS; INTERSTELLAR MEDIUM ("DARK MATTER").

Further Reading
Baumjohann, W., *Basic Space Plasma Physics* (1996); Goldston, R. J., *Introduction to Plasma Physics* (1995); Manheimer, Wallace, *Plasma Science and the Environment* (1996).

First see HYDROCARBON

Plastics

Next see SYNTHETICS

Organic materials that are made synthetically by polymerization—linking molecules together—and that can be formed into a variety of products.

The principal material incorporated in a plastic is called a resin; "plastic" refers to the product made from the resin by incorporating other materials, such as coloring matter, antioxidants, plasticizers, and fillers. The first plastic was celluloid, which was made in the United States in 1869 by John Wesley Hyatt. The widespread use of celluloid was hampered because it cannot easily be molded and is flammable. Thus, the real era of plastics can be said to have begun in 1907, when Bakelite was created. Named for its creator, Leo H. Baekeland, Bakelite is manufactured from phenol and formaldehyde. Bakelite products are stable, strong, and resistant to corrosion and heat, and so were quickly available in great abundance.

There are several varieties of plastics. Thermoplastics consist of long-chain molecules and can be softened by heat, so that they can be molded into many shapes. Thermosetting plastics are much more rigid than thermoplastics, because their polymer chains are cross-linked; they are shaped permanently once they have been set in a mold.

Some resins that are used to manufacture plastics are natural materials, such as shellac, cellulose, and rosin, but the great majority of resins are synthetic materials. The substances that are added to the resin to give the plastic its desired qualities—hardness, resistance to abrasion, resistance to shock—are called fillers. They include asbestos, glass fibers, and even wood flour. Substances added to a plastic or a resin to make it more pliable and workable are

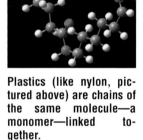

Plastics (like nylon, pictured above) are chains of the same molecule—a monomer—linked together.

called plasticizers. The oldest plasticizer is camphor, which was used to turn the brittle substance pyroxylin into celluloid. In the plastic manufacturing process, materials called lubricants can be added to the resin formulation or to the mold to prevent sticking, while antioxidants can be added to promote the chemical stability of the plastic product. Catalysts, which speed chemical combination, and stabilizers, which protect the plastic against heat, sunlight, and the like, are also part of the manufacturing process.

Polymerization. The properties of a plastic can be determined by varying the method of polymerization. One example is Plexiglas™, which is a polymer made of methyl methacrylate. A number of chemicals can be added to the molding powder, creating different plastics. If the monomer is not made into a polymer in such a way, it can be added to water-based paints to give them desired properties.

In addition to developing new plastic compositions, researchers have also done work on the structure of plastics. Cross-linking, for example, creates products that are harder and more resistant (although less flexible) by making chemical bonds between the polymer chains. The more cross-links that are created between the chains, the harder and less flexible the end product is. The degree of hardness and flexibility can be controlled very precisely.

Chain rigidity is another effect used to control the properties of plastics. Just as large or complex groups attached to an atom prevent its free rotation, adding bulky molecules to molecular chains that are ordinarily flexible makes the end product stiffer and raises its softening point.

THE CUTTING EDGE

Growing Plastic

Researchers at Stanford University have genetically engineered plants to produce plastic. Taking mustard plants, they insert genes to have them encode three enzymes that will synthesize PHB (polyhydrobutyrate) in the plants' chloroplasts, where the process will not interfere with plant growth. As much as 20 percent of the dried plant is PHB. Admittedly, PHB is not a very useful plastic, lacking the strength and flexibility of other plastics. But processing does recover half the plastic material, and even the PHB that decomposes produces methane gas, which can be captured and burned. Furthermore, PHB is a degradable plastic, a feature that is becoming ever more important.

Further Reading
Meikle, J. L., *American Plastic: A Cultural History* (1997); Strong, A. Brent, *Plastics: Materials and Processing* (1996); *Plastics Handbook,* (1994).

Background material can be found in HYDROCARBON; MOLECULE; POLYMER AND POLYMERIZATION. *More details can be found in* FIBERGLASS; SYNTHETICS; TEXTILE SCIENCE. *Specific aspects of this subject can be found in* BIOREMEDIATION; CERAMICS; COATINGS AND FILMS.

First see EARTH, FORMATION OF

Plate Tectonics

Next see EARTHQUAKE

The geological theory that views the Earth's crust as a series of semirigid plates that are in motion relative to one another.

At the boundaries where two large plates meet, one is subducted, or forced under, the other. In the middle of the oceans, this activity results in ocean trenches—long, narrow V-shaped depressions that usually run parallel to coastal mountain ranges on the continents or to midoceanic arcs of volcanic islands. When two lighter continental plates meet, subduction does not take place, and more complicated processes occur, mainly orogeny, or mountain building.

Plate tectonics, first proposed in the 1960s, states that these plates move at a rate of about 80-100 inches per century. The plates are thousands of miles across but only 50-75 miles thick. They are jammed together so tightly that the individual plates cannot move freely. Instead, they jostle one another, an activity that generates earthquakes and volcanoes. The major boundaries between plates are thus defined by a map showing the epicenters where earthquakes most often occur.

Plate tectonics views the continents as a relatively insignificant amount of Earth's mass, representing no more than half of one percent. A greater percentage is represented by the mafic oceanic lithosphere, the ocean crust, and the Earth's rocky outer mantle, which lies beneath it. Rock from this lithosphere descends regularly beneath the continents or the thin oceanic crust into the athenosphere, at a recycling rate of about 110 million years. In the athenosphere, this rock may be remelted and returned to the surface, where it becomes the building material for volcanic-island arcs, such as the island chains of the western Pacific Ocean, or arcs on the edges of continents, such as the Andes mountains. While the plates of the continents are believed to be over 1 billion years old, this constant activity of the oceanic crust means that areas like the Pacific Rim are no more than 180 million years old.

In the United States, the great San Francisco earthquake of 1906 is attributed to the fact that the northwestward motion of the Pacific plate had been resisted along the line of the San Andreas fault. A sudden end to that resistance caused the abrupt movement of the Pacific plate and the plate adjoining it, resulting in the earth-

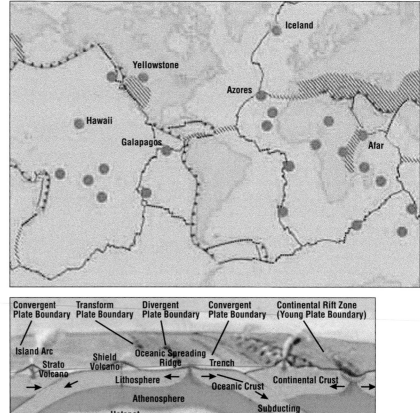

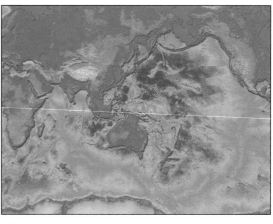

Above, top, world map showing locations of selected hotspots. Above, cross-section of the Earth's crust at the three kinds of plate boundaries.

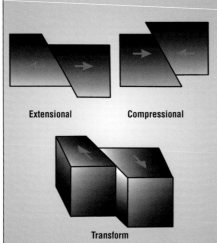

Above, a false-color satellite image of Earth, showing the ocean ridges and basins where tectonic activity is most prominent. Left, schematic of the three kinds of plate movements.

quake. A series of earthquakes in mid-America that began in Missouri in 1811 and lasted for the following 15 months is attributed to similar abrupt plate movements.

Background material regarding plate tectonics can be found in GEOLOGICAL TIME SCALE; PLANETS, FORMATION OF; SEISMICS. *Further details can be found in* VOLCANO; EARTHQUAKE; SEISMOLOGY. *Additional relevant information is contained in* PETROLEUM PROSPECTING; PLANET, INTERIOR OF; UNDERWATER EXPLORATION.

Further Reading
Keller, Edward A., *Active Tectonics: Earthquakes, Uplift, and Landscape* (1996); Moores, E. M., *Tectonics* (1995); Twiss, R. J., *Structural Geology* (1992).

First see SOLAR SYSTEM

Pluto

Next see OORT CLOUD

Pluto, the smallest planet in the solar system, is also the most distant from the sun (although its orbit sometimes brings it nearer to the sun than Neptune, the next outermost planet). Recent estimates put the diameter of Pluto at about 1,400 miles, which means that it is substantially smaller than Earth's moon. Its mass is estimated to be one-fifth that of Earth's moon. Pluto was discovered in 1930 by Clyde Tombaugh at the Lowell Observatory in the United States.

The mean distance of Pluto from the sun is 3,700 million miles, or 39.5 astronomical units (an astronomical unit is the distance from the earth to the sun). Pluto has the most eccentric orbit of any of the planets, and the inclination of its orbit, 16 degrees, is more than twice as great as that of any other planet. Pluto is also inclined to its own orbit, being tilted 112 degrees so that it lies on its side, like Uranus. Pluto actually comes closer to the sun than Neptune at perihelion; the orbits of the two planets at present do not come close to intersecting, but there is a possibility that they may intersect in the future and may have intersected in the past, a possibility that has caused some astronomers to speculate that Pluto may once have been a moon of Neptune—it is about the size of the Neptunian moon Triton—and that it escaped to become an independent planet.

Charon. Pluto has a moon of its own, named Charon. But because Charon is so large in relation to Pluto—it has a diameter of about 1,000 miles—Charon and Pluto are often considered to be a double-planet system. Charon moves around Pluto in an orbit that is equal to the rotational period of the planet, so that an observer on the Pluto who could see Charon would see it at the same position in the sky at all times.

At its brightest, Pluto as seen from Earth is only a 15th-magnitude object, so it can be seen only with a large telescope. It is yellowish and reflects very little light, indicating that it probably has a rough surface and an atmosphere that is transparent or extremely thin. The observed brightness of Pluto has been found to vary regularly as its orbital position changes. These variations have enabled astronomers to estimate the length of the day on Pluto at 6.38 Earth days. Because the amplitude of the variations has changed steadily over the past 20 years, it is believed that Pluto has an equatorial region that

Further Reading
Mechler, Gary, et al., *Planets and Their Moons* (1995); Stern, Alan (Ed.), *Pluto and Charon* (1998); Zeilik, Michael, *Astronomy: The Evolving Universe* (1997).

Below, the *Pluto Kuiper Express* mission is designed to fly by and make studies of the planet Pluto and its satelite Charon in 2012. It will then fly further on to the Kuiper Belt.

Above, Pluto and Charon as seen by the Hubble Space Telescope. The pair are sometimes dubbed a "double planet" because of their similar sizes.

is darker than its poles, which may have ice caps made of frozen nitrogen. Evidence for the existence of these polar caps has come from spectroscopic and infrared observations that are consistent with the existence of a substantial Plutonian atmosphere of methane gas, with patches of methane frost on the planet's surface. Pluto manages to hold this atmosphere because its relatively large rocky core gives it a density of more than 2 grams per cubic centimeter, much higher than any of the other outer planets.

Background material can be found in KEPLER'S LAWS; PLANET; PLANETS, FORMATION OF. *Advanced subjects are developed in* NEPTUNE; PLANETARY SATELLITES; URANUS. *Elementary aspects of this subject are covered in* COMET; OORT CLOUD; INTERSTELLAR MEDIUM ("DARK MATTER").

First see RESPIRATORY SYSTEMS

Pneumonia

Next see BREATHING REGULATION

An inflammation of the lungs that can be caused by any of a number of viruses and bacteria.

Pneumonia can be a complication of any serious disease and is one of the leading causes of death in the United States. There are two major types of the disease: lobar pneumonia and broncho-pneumonia. In lobar pneumonia, one lobe, or section, of one lung is affected at first. Broncho-pneumonia starts as an inflammation of the bronchi and bronchioles, the airways of the lung, and then spreads to other lung tissues. Pneumonia is most often caused by a virus or a bacterium, although some cases, in persons with deficient immune systems, can be caused by fungi, yeasts, or protozoa, notably *Pneumocystis carinii* in people with AIDS. The most common cause of bacterial pneumonia is *Streptococcus pneumoniae,* although the disease can also be caused by *Haemophilus influenzae, Legionella pneumonophila* (Legionnaires' disease), and *Staphylococcus aureus.* (*See* DISEASE, INFECTOUS.)

Bacterial pneumonia is usually treated with antibiotics. There are no drugs to treat viral pneumonia, but antibiotics may be given to prevent bacterial infection of the lungs. The signs and symptoms of pneumonia include fever, chills, and shortness of breath. Chest pain can be felt when the disease causes pleurisy, an inflammation of the membrane that lines the chest cavity and lungs. In cases where pneumonia is mild, patients can be treated at home, but hospitalization is often required for serious cases. While most patients recover in two weeks, elderly or debilitated persons may fail to respond to treatment. Pneumonia is the sixth leading cause of death in the United States.

First see NUTRITION

Poison and Toxicology

Next See DIOXINS

A poison is a substance that can cause injury, impairment, or death to a living organism; toxicology is the study of poisons, including their preparation, chemical composition, effects on the body, and antidotes.

Further Reading
Anderson, Gerald L., *The Gas Monitoring Handbook* (1999); Hodgson, Ernest, *Introduction to Biochemical Toxicology* (2001); Steingraber, Sandra, *Living Downstream* (1998).

Poisons can enter the body by a number of routes. They can be swallowed, inhaled, injected under the skin, as in the case of an insect sting or snakebite, or absorbed through the skin. (The term "toxin" is often used interchangeably with "poison", but toxins are specifically poisonous proteins that are produced by some bacteria, by some animals, such as snakes, and by some plants.)

Some poisons originate inside the human body, which happens with such disorders as liver failure or kidney failure. Poisoning is classified as acute or chronic. In acute poisoning, a large amount of a poisonous substance enters the body or is produced in the body in a brief period of time. In chronic poisoning, there is a gradual accumulation of a poisonous substance over a relatively long period of time.

There are many substances, liquid, solid, and gaseous, that can be poisonous to humans. These include a number of compounds of copper, lead, arsenic (which is a poison itself), antimony, selenium, barium, mercury, thallium, and fluorine. Some extremely poisonous substances include soluble metal cyanides, isocyanic acid esters, cyanogen, hydrogen cyanide, some glucosides, alkaloids, many organic substances that contain nitrogen and sulfur, yellow phosphorus, and chromates. Some poisons are also very corrosive to the skin. These include phenol, hydrochloric acid, sodium hydroxide, bromine, concentrated nitric acid, and concentrated sulfuric acid. Among the gases that are poisons, some that are especially hazardous are carbon monoxide, nitrogen tetroxide, chlorine, bromine, cyanogen, and cyanogen chloride. (*See also* POLLUTION.)

Poisons act in specific ways, generally by interfering with the work of key enzymes within the body. For example, heavy metals such as mercuric chloride or barium nitrate react with thiol groups, chemicals that are essential to the functioning of many enzymes.

Carbon monoxide is an exception to this rule of poison-enzyme activity. Instead of acting primarily on enzymes, carbon monoxide ties up the hemoglobin molecule that carries oxygen from the lungs to the cells of the body through the blood. When a carbon monoxide molecule becomes attached to a hemoglobin molecule, the hemoglobin can no longer transport oxygen.

Poisons have their practical uses. Some gases that are poisonous are used to fumigate rooms or foods. Many solid poisonous substances are used, in powder form or in solution, as insecticides, germicides, fungicides, weed killers, or rodent killers. (*See* FOOD SCIENCE.)

In human poisoning, there can be a number of telltale symptoms. These include burns and redness around the mouth, which result from drinking poisonous liquids; a smell of chemicals on the breath; and stains, burns, or odors on the skin. If such symptoms appear, the best advice is to telephone the local Poison Prevention Center immediately. Toxicologists have developed standard treatments for the most common household poisons. (*See* FORENSIC SCIENCE.)

First see LIGHT

Polarized Light

Next see LASER AND MASER

Light with a vibration pattern that exhibits a preference in orientation.

In ordinary, unpolarized light, the electric field of the light vibrates in all directions perpendicular to the direction in which the light is propagated. When light is reflected or transmitted through certain substances, the electric field can be confined to one direction. The light is then said to be plane-polarized. The plane of plane-polarized light can be rotated by making it pass through certain other substances. The molecules of these substances are not symmetrical, so they can exist in mirror-image form. One form rotates the light in one direction, the other rotates it in the opposite direction.

There are other kinds of polarization. If the electric vector of the light describes a circular helix around the direction of propagation with a frequency that is the same as the frequency of the light, it is said to be circularly polarized. The magnitude of the vector is constant in circularly polarized light. If the vector rotates around the direction of propagation and the amplitude changes, the light is said to be elliptically polarized.

Polarized light is common in nature. For example, the light from a rainbow is polarized, and light from a blue sky and light reflected from smooth water surfaces such as those of lakes is partially plane-polarized. While the human eye is not sensitive to it, the eyes of many insects and crustaceans are; they orient themselves in relation to the direction of polarization.

Background material can be found in ELECTROMAGNETIC WAVE; LIGHT; OPTICS. *Advanced subjects are developed in* DIFFRACTION; LENS; PHONON. *More information on particular aspects is contained in* PHOTOGRAPHY, CHEMISTRY OF; QUASICRYSTAL.

Poliomyelitis

First see MUSCLE

Next see IMMUNIZATION AND VACCINATION

A viral infection that affects the central nervous system, causing paralysis.

Poliomyelitis, once commonly called infantile paralysis, is an infectious disease that has virtually been eliminated in the United States and Europe by development of effective vaccines. Polio, as it is usually called, can be caused by three related viruses. In about 85 percent of cases, a polio infection causes no symptoms at all. In the other cases, there will be a fever, sore throat, and headache, sometimes accompanied by vomiting, all of which disappear after a few days. In a small percentage of cases, however, a serious illness develops, marked by inflammation of the protective tissues of the brain and spinal cord, a high fever, and a headache and stiffness of the neck and back. There is no treatment for this illness, and some patients experience extreme paralysis of the muscles of the legs and trunk. When the virus strikes the brainstem, the disease can be fatal. Two kinds of polio vaccine are available. Inactivated polio vaccine contains dead viruses and is given by injection. Oral polio vaccine contains strains of viruses that are alive but that are harmless for people with healthy immune systems.

Polymer

First see ORGANIC COMPOUNDS

Next see PLASTIC

Substance composed of large complex molecules formed by joining together smaller sub-units into long chains.

The process by which monomers are combined to form polymers is called polymerization; depending on the molecule, a polymer may consist of several hundred or even thousands of monomers. Because of their size, polymers are also referred to as macromolecules.

Polymers may be divided into two broad categories, naturally occurring and synthetic molecules. The natural polymers include carbohydrates, lipids, proteins, and nucleic acids.

Natural Polymers. The monomer of a carbohydrate is called a monosaccharide; the polymer is a polysaccharide. Examples of monosaccharides include glucose and fructose, which are simple sugars. Polymers of glucose include starch and cellulose—the fiber component of all plant structures. Cotton is an example of a naturally occurring polysaccharide.

Lipids include fats, waxes, oils, and steroid molecules such as cholesterol and some of the sex hormones. Some of the most common lipids are triglycerides, the monomers of which are fatty acids. Fatty acids are a type of hydrocarbon, a long linked chain of carbon atoms with attached hydrogens, with a carboxyl group (COOH) at the end. The identity of the lipid depends on the number of carbons in each of its fatty acids and whether or not the chain is saturated (linked exclusively by single bonds).

All of the previously mentioned polymers contain only the elements carbon, hydrogen, and oxygen. The more complex polymers, such as proteins and nucleic acids, incorporate other elements, such as nitrogen, sulfur, and phosphorus, as well.

The basic monomer of a protein is the amino acid, of which there are 20 different types. All amino acids share the common features of an amino group (NH_2), as well as a carboxyl group. The amino acids are linked to form a polypeptide chain. Proteins include a vast number of types of molecules, including hormones, enzymes, and muscle tissue. Wool and silk are protein polymers.

Synthetic Polymers. Many of the synthetic polymers are various types of plastics and textiles, formed from repeated units of small hydrocarbons or amides (subunits containing nitrogen). Examples include Teflon™, Plexiglas™, Lucite™, polyurethane foam, nylon, and polyester.

Synthetics are formed by addition reactions, which involve simply adding together monomers that automatically connect to each other, or by condensation reactions, in which a molecule of water or alcohol must first be removed in order to allow the formation of bonds between the individual monomers.

Regardless of a polymer's type or category, all of them have certain characteristics and behavior in common. At high temperatures, a polymer is often a viscous liquid in which the molecular chains have mobility relative to each other. At lower temperatures, some regions within the polymer may form regular crystalline structures. Alternatively, at very low temperatures, the molecular chains may freeze in an irregular pattern.

Background material on polymers can be found in BOND, CHEMICAL; CHEMICAL FORMULA; MOLECULE. *Advanced subjects are developed in* FIBERGLASS; PLASTICS; SYNTHETICS. *Additional relevant information is contained in* ALLOY; CERAMICS; QUASICRYSTAL; TEXTILE SCIENCE.

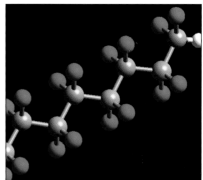

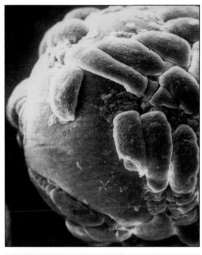

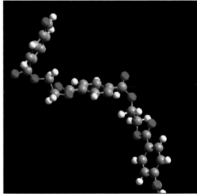

Above, Top, a molecular model of Polytetrafluoroethylene—Teflon—is similar to polyethylene terephthalate (PET) shown at bottom. A space shuttle experiment involved the generation of polymers in the zero gravity of outer space (middle).

Further Reading
Allcock, Harry, *Contemporary Polymer Chemistry* (1990); Grosberg, A. Lu, *Giant Molecules: Here, There, and Everywhere...* (1997); Morawetz, Herbert, *Polymers: The Origins and Growth of a Science* (1995).

Further Reading
Clewley, Jonathan P., *The Polymerase Chain Reaction* (1995); McPherson, M.J., *PCR: From Basics to Bench* (2000); Rabinow, Paul, *Making PCR: A Story of Biotechnology* (1997).

First see DNA SEQUENCING

Polymerase Chain Reaction (PCR)

Next see FORENSIC SCIENCE

A technique for creating a large sample of DNA—suitable for testing and research—from an unsuitably small sample.

In addition to the sequence that is to be multiplied, PCR requires an adequate supply of the four sub-units that make up DNA—adenine, guanine, thymine, and cytosine. It also requires two kinds of primers, which are short DNA chains to which new subunits can be added. Each of the two primers is identical to a short stretch of one end of the DNA chain that is to be reproduced. A final requirement is a supply of DNA polymerase, an enzyme that acts as a catalyst in the reproduction of DNA.

The first step in PCR is to make a solution containing the DNA fragment to be multiplied, the primers, and the nucleotides. The solution is heated for two minutes. Heating causes the two strands of the DNA molecule to come apart. The primers then become attached to the appropriate ends of the strands.

After the solution is cooled, the polymerase is added. This enzyme causes the reproduction of the DNA fragment that has the two primers at each end, and the cycle of heating and cooling is repeated after two minutes. As new strands of the DNA fragment are produced, they serve as templates for more strands, so that the supply of the DNA fragment doubles every time the sequence of the procedure is repeated, usually at intervals of two minutes. After 20 cycles, the original fragment of DNA has been multiplied a millionfold.

Applications. PCR was developed in the 1980s by scientists at the Cetus Corporation in Berkeley, California. PCR can be used to detect the existence of a defined sequence in a sample of DNA, a sequence that is delineated by the location of the two PCR primers.

PCR is especially useful in detecting the mutations that are responsible for a number of genetic diseases, including Duchenne muscular dystrophy and Lesch-Nyhan syndrome.

PCR permits the diagnosis of a gene defect using the DNA from only a single cell of the affected individual. If that cell is obtained from a fetus carried by a woman who has already borne a child with a genetic disease, it is possible to determine whether the fetus is carrying the abnormal gene. If a cell is obtained from each of the parents before pregnancy, it is possible to determine their risk of bearing another affected child. PCR thus opens a new field of genetic diagnosis.

Basic aspects of this subject are covered in DNA; GENE; DNA REPLICATION. *More advanced discussions can be found in* DNA SEQUENCING; CLONING; RECOMBINANT DNA. *Applications of PCR are discussed in* FORENSIC SCIENCE; GENE THERAPY; GENETIC ENGINEERING; *and* GENOME, HUMAN.

First see CHROMOSOME

Polyploidy

Next see MEIOSIS

A genetic condition in which there are two or more sets of chromosomes in a gamete, where the normal amount is one.

Chromosome number, referred to as n, is unique to a particular species and consistent throughout all the cells of an organism. Human somites, ordinary body cells, contain 46 chromosomes (arranged as pairs) and are called diploid, or $2n$. Somites undergo mitosis prior to cell division, whichensures a fixed number of chromosomes from one cellular generation to the next. Gametes, the sex cells, contain 23 chromosomes and are haploid, or $1n$. Of these chromosomes, the vast majority are "regular" ones, known as autosomes, and only a single pair are the sex chromosomes X and Y. Females have two X chromosomes, while males have one X and one Y.

The chromosomal requirements for gametes are different. An organism begins life as a single cell, called a zygote, formed by the union of sperm and egg. In order to ensure that the zygote and its resulting descendant cells contain the proper number of chromosomes, the gametes must all be haploid. The method used to create them is called meiosis—the process of cell division in which the number of chromosomes is divided in half.

Sometimes, however, mistakes occur during meiosis. Nondisjunction occurs when homologous chromosomes fail to separate. The resulting gametes have too many chromosomes and are called polyploid. If those gametes are used in reproduction, trisomy, the presence of a particular chromosome in triplicate, may result. It may involve either the sex chromosomes or the autosomes. Abnormal numbers of sex chromosomes can result in conditions such as Turner syndrome, in which individuals have only one sex chromosome, an X, and are underdeveloped, sterile females. Klinefelter's syndrome results from having three sex chromosomes, XXY. Individuals with this condition are sexually underdeveloped males with slight mental retardation. (*See* GENETIC DISEASES; GENETICS.)

Trisomy 21, having an extra entire chromosome 21 or just a piece of it, results in Down's syndrome. (*See also* AMNIOCENTESIS.)

First see ECOLOGY

Population Ecology

Next see AGGRESSION AND TERRITORIALITY

The study of how animal or plant populations grow and shrink, how their numbers are distributed, and how they respond to competition, predation, and other pressures.

In comparing separate populations, or following changes in one population over time, ecologists try to determine several key measurements. These include natality, or birthrate; mortality, or death rate; immigration and emigration; population density; and age structure and distribution. The most common pattern of distribution in nature is clumping, with groups of individuals scattered within a habitat. Less commonly, distribution is random or uniform, with individuals evenly spaced. The latter usually reflects territoriality in animals.

Growth Models. Some populations grow exponentially until they outstrip their resources and crash, with their numbers cut sharply by starvation, disease, or emigration. The population may end in extinction or it may recover, either to grow exponentially again or to hover at some level below its peak. Exponential growth patterns form a J-shaped curve. They tend to occur when individuals enter a new area where there is little competition for resources.

Another theoretical model of growth is the S-shaped, or sigmoid, curve formed by a logistic growth pattern. As population density increases, so does competition for resources and other forms of density-dependent negative feedback. Mortality or emigration increases, and fertility may decline. The growth rate is reduced until the population size levels off as it approaches the carrying capacity, designated K. This is the theoretical upper limit for a population, the greatest number of individuals that can be sustained by a habitat. (*See* COMPETITION AND ALTRUISM.)

In nature, such a perfect, self-limited S-curve is hard to find. More typically, there is a time lag before negative feedback slows population growth. Growth outpaces resources, leading to a population drop. Over time, such a pattern leads to fluctuations, large or small, around the carrying capacity.

Populations are limited not only by density-dependent factors, such as increased competition and diminishing resources, but by density-independent factors, such as weather, fire, and loss of habitat.

Survivorship Curves. To better understand population dynamics, ecologists plot survivorship curves, which reflect what portion of the population will still be alive at various ages. There are three basic patterns. In Type I, seen in humans and other large mammals, most individuals live until old age, when the mortality rate rises sharply. In Type II, seen in some birds and some invertebrates, the mortality rate is constant at all ages. In Curve III, typical of fish, invertebrates, and many plants, the mortality rate is extremely high at the very beginning of life, but individuals who survive the early risks are likely to live to old age. (*See* BIRTH.)

Population Interaction. Besides studying the dynamics of separate populations, population ecology also focuses on how populations of different species interact and affect each other's growth and well-being. Major types of relationships between populations in-clude competition, in which each population limits the other; predation and parasitism, in which one party feeds off the other; commensalism, in which one species benefits but the other is not harmed; and mutualism, in which both parties profit from the relationship. (*See* ETHOLOGY; PREDATION.)

First see INSTINCT

Predation

Next see ECOLOGY

The interplay between the hunter (predator) and the hunted (prey) in nature.

Predation is among the most fundamental processes in nature. Rare is the organism that does not have its place on one side of the equation or the other. In fact, except for organisms that make their own food (chiefly plants), all living creatures can be said to engage in some form of predation.

Broadly defined, predation can include parasitism, although ecologists usually give separate treatment to that even more intimate relationship. In parasitism, the eater lives in or on its prey and feeds off it without killing it outright. In ordinary predation, the predator is free-living and kills and consumes its prey at one sitting. Herbivory—the consumption of plants—is a form of predation. Herbivory is often parasitic, as when birds or insects inhabit a tree or plant and eat small bits of it over a lifetime.

Adaptations. Predation has produced a range of remarkable and effective adaptations for both offense and defense. These include armor, spikes, noxious chemical defenses, and camouflage and other forms of cryptic coloring. Many adaptations are believed to be the result of coevolution, in which a change in one species acts as a selective force on another species to which it is linked.

Related material can be found in AGGRESSION AND TERRITORIALITY; ECOLOGY; ETHOLOGY; INSTINCTS. *Advanced subjects are developed in* ADAPTATION; BIODIVERSITY; COEVELUTION; POPULATION ECOLOGY. *Additional relevant information is contained in* PARASITE; REPRODUCTIVE STRATEGIES; SYMBIOSIS.

Above, the populations of some predators such as the gray wolf—*Canis lupis*—and the northern spotted owl—*Strix occidentalis*—are declining at an alarming rate.

Further Reading
Hummel, Monte, *Wild Hunters: Predators in Peril* (1992); McGowan, Christopher, *The Raptor and the Lamb: Predators and Prey in the Living World* (1997); Schaller, George B., *Serengeti Lion: A Study of Predator-Prey Relations* (1976).

First see MAMMALS

Primates

Next see ETHOLOGY

Primates are primarily arboreal or tree-dwelling animals that probably evolved as an offshoot of Cretaceous insectivores. Members of the primate order include lemurs, monkeys, and apes, as well as human beings. The major primate specializations include: a grasping hand with opposable thumb (the big toe is also opposable in most primates); some claws replaced by nails; a prehensile tail; a shortened snout and flattened face with both eyes directed forward; overlapping fields of vision, resulting in depth perception; and only one pair of nipples, located on the thorax (chest) instead of the abdomen.

"Primitive" features of primates include: a flat-footed gait, a large clavicle, or collarbone, central wrist carpal, and generalized dentition or tooth type; such tooth patterns are usually indicative of an omnivorous diet.

Primates are divided into two groups: prosimians, or "lower" primates, which include tarsiers, lemurs, and lorises; and anthropoids, or "higher" primates, which include monkeys, apes, and humans. Anthropoids are further divided into platyrrhini (South American monkeys and marmosets) and catarrhini (Old World monkeys, apes, and humans).

Differentiating Primates. Platyrrhines and catarrhines are differentiated on the basis of direction of the nostril openings. Platyrrhines nostrils are open to the side, whereas the nostrils of the catarrhine open downward. Both have heads located at right angles to the vertebral column, with the eyes close together and directed forward. The cerebral hemispheres are maximally developed. There are 32 teeth in the permanent set. All primates usually produce only one offspring at a time. Platyrrhines include capuchins, spider monkeys, and howler monkeys. Howlers have an enlarged hyoid bone and larynx, which enable them to make screeching cries.

Catarrhines are further divided into cercopithecoids (baboons, mandrills, and rhesus monkeys) and hominoids (which include gibbons, orangutans, gorillas, chimpanzees, and humans).

Old World monkeys are usually larger than their New World counterparts and do not have prehensile tails. In some primates, including humans, the tail is evident only in the embryonic stage of development. The "special" characteristics are believed to be adaptations for life in the trees. Grasping hands with opposable thumbs would bestow a distinctive advantage, as would long arms with flexible wrist joints, allowing hand rotation in a full semicircle, and shoulder joints that permit movement in many directions.

There is great variation in species among primates. From top: black spider monkey; chimpanzee; gorilla; and Gelada baboon.

Further Reading
Cheyney, Dorothy L., *How Monkeys See the World: Inside the Mind of Another Species* (1992); Savage-Rumbaugh, E. Sue, *Apes, Language, and the Human Mind* (1998); Tomasello, Michael, *Primate Cognition* (1997).

Gibbons and orangutans are the only apes that live in trees. Gorillas spend their waking hours on the ground and sleep in trees at night. All apes can stand upright and walk for short distances on their hind legs, although their hip and leg bones are not designed for true bipedalism. With the exception of orangutans, apes live in highly developed social groups. Most of them use sounds to communicate.

Reproduction. Primates generally bear only one offspring at a time and provide extended care and nurturing of their young. This care extends for a longer period than in other mammals. Among monkeys and apes, newborns emerge from the birth canal head first, with the face pointing upward, as opposed to human infants, who are born with the face pointing downward.

All primates have an estrus cycle that governs their reproductive lives. This period of "heat" lasts about three to five days and occurs only when the female is ovulating. Some monkeys and chimpanzees exhibit genital swelling. Females will mate only during this short time period but may mate with all the adult males in the area. The human estrus is referred to as the menstrual cycle, but humans have lost the combination of physiology and behavior associated with ovulation. (*See* REPRODUCTIVE SYSTEMS.)

The most outstanding feature of primates is the highly developed brain, particularly the frontal lobes of the cerebral hemispheres. Primates have brains larger in relation to overall body size than other animals. However, the human brain is larger than any other primate's.

Posture. The most important human anatomical characteristic is an upright posture with the head held erect. Unlike other primates, the human foot is designed for standing and walking upright instead of for grasping.

Early hominids were already quite different from their primate "cousins." Close to 4 million years ago, *Australopithecus* already exhibited an S-shaped curve in the vertebral column, which allows for an erect posture. As hominids became more advanced, the facial angle became less acute and the teeth smaller. The frontal lobes of the cerebrum enlarged, causing an enlarged braincase and a more prominent forehead.

Eventually, eyebrow ridges were reduced and the nose became more prominent. The arms became shorter in proportion to the legs, and the foot arch appeared. Humans also developed articulate speech.

Related material may be found in EMBRYOLOGY; ETHOLOGY; MAMMALS. *Further details can be found in* HOMO SAPIENS; REPRODUCTIVE STRATEGIES. *More information on particular aspects of primates is contained in* AGING; DIGESTIVE SYSTEMS; PHYLOGENY.

Printing

First see PHOTOGRAPHY, CHEMISTRY OF

Next see PATTERN RECOGNITION AND OCR

Printing and image reproduction technology have changed dramatically in recent years. For centuries the only stable forms of image reproduction relied on animal or vegetable dyestuffs, in either a water- or an oil-based medium. Whether it was an Egyptian craftsman decorating the walls of Queen Hatshepsut's temple, a medieval scribe copying a manuscript with India ink on parchment, or an Impressionist artist recreating on canvas the fields of his or her imagination, the technology was essentially the same. The liquid medium instigated capillary action, which drew the colored pigments into the pores of the stone, the underlayer of the animal skin, or the fibers of the canvas; when the medium dried, the pigments remained.

The Printing Press. The introduction of mechanical technologies did not change this basic process; it merely increased the efficiency with which pigment was transformed into an image. The printing press allows many pages of letters or imagery to be reproduced at one time; the lithograph and its successor, the photo-offset printer, accept a liquid medium over part of their surface while remaining dry elsewhere, then transfer the image in the same way; the typewriter and its successor, the ink-jet printer, transfer ink one letter or one line at a time from a storage medium (ribbon or reservoir) to paper.

The introduction of electrostatic printing in the late 1940s made "Xerox" a popular term. This first truly new method of reproducing images employs the photoelectric effect to produce areas that are ionized and areas that are neutral, corresponding to letters and spaces, or to shadows and highlights. First, the image is exposed to a bright source of light; the white areas reflect the light, stimulating the photoelectric effect, while the dark areas do not. Second, the ionized areas attract tiny particles of toner, while the corresponding neutral areas attract none; finally, the toner is heated to its melting point, fusing with the paper.

Laser Technology. The next revolution in image reproduction came around 1970, with the introduction of laser technology. The first printing systems to incorporate lasers merely used their powerful beams to incise traditional photo-offset plates; the "second wave" incorporated photographic technology, by using the laser to expose a silver film emulsion that serves as a mask over the conventional offset plate. The most recent developments use the thermal imaging power of the laser. This technology, like xerography before it, has several significant advantages: Because it does not rely on silver-based emulsions, it can be used in normal room light, and because it is dry, processing time and "hazmat" (hazardous materials) risks are minimized.

Color Printing. Similar advances have been made in color printing. The bulk of color printing relies on relatively traditional ink-jet techniques, whether ejected in a continuous stream or in rapid impulses. An-other, a so-called "dry" technique, still relies on an aqueous interface between a donor sheet and the final image. However, a third technique, called dye sublimation, appears to be a significant advance. Eliminating the aqueous interface, this process uses heat to boil off dye colorant from the donor sheet onto the receptor sheet, where the vapor condenses, or sublimes, back into solid form; this process therefore promises true dry color printing.

Photocopiers and many printers use tiny charged particles (above) to generate the different colors on a printed page.

> Special topics in printing technology are found in COMPUTER GRAPHICS; LASER AND MASER; PATTERN RECOGNITION AND OCR. *Advanced subjects are developed in* CD-ROM; RECORDING TECHNOLOGY; TELECOMMUNICATIONS. *Basic aspects of this subject are covered in* CRYPTOGRAPHY; INTERNET.

Further Reading
Collin, P.H., *Dictionary of Printing and Publishing* (1998); Hall, David D., *Cultures of Print: Essays in the History of the Book* (1996); Remer, Rosalind, *Printers and Men of Capital: Philadelphia Book Publishers in the New Republic* (1996).

Probability

First see STATISTICS

Next see MONTE CARLO METHOD

Probability is a conceptualization of the physical world, in which a mathematical model provides an abstraction of events against which we can judge real events. When a coin is flipped in the real world, it can land either on heads or on tails, and no one can predict which way a given coin will land after a given flip; but when a coin is flipped in the world of probability there is a one-in-two-chance that it will land on heads, and an equal chance that it will land on tails. Similarly, there is a one-in-six-chance that any given number will show on a probabilistic die. It is not even necessary that every chance be equal—there is, in fact, twice as great a probability that two dice will total seven as that they will total ten—but the sum of all probabilities connected with a given event must equal one.

Probabilities are generally not additive. That is, if the probability of heads is one out of two, and one flips the coin twice (performs an experiment consisting of two trials), the probability of getting heads at least once is not two out of two, but three out of four, as the possible outcomes are HH, HT, TH, and TT. The same pattern is found in the genetic transmission of dominant and recessive traits. If two parents each have brown eyes and carry the recessive gene for blue eyes (Bb), there is a three in four chance that a child will have at least one gene for blue eyes and a one in four chance that the child will receive two recessive genes.

Conditional Probability. Often one is interested in a conditional probability—that is, the probability of a given state of affairs as modified by additional knowledge. For example, consider a 99.9 percent accurate medical test used to discover a genetic condition affecting one person in a thousand. If it is given to one million people, what is the probability that someone who tests positive for the condition actually has it? Nine hundred and ninety-nine people who have the condition will test positive for it, but so will 999 people who do not have the condition but obtained a false positive on the test. So the conditional probability of having the condition after testing positive for it is 999 out of 1998, or 50 percent. In the case of some rare conditions, the conditional probability even after a positive test result is still only three to four percent.

Understanding conditional probability allows one to calculate the posterior probability of a given result through a formula known as Bayes' Theorem, after Thomas Bayes, the eighteenth-century mathematician who first devel-

---

OBSERVATIONS

Happy Birthday to You . . . And Me?

How many people would have to be in a room before one reaches a 50-percent probability that two people share the same birthday? An unsophisticated guess might be that one needs 182 people, since there is only a 1 in 365 chance of any selected person's sharing a birthday with any other selected person. But a little more thought reveals that a third person has two people to match birthdays with, a fourth person has three potential matches, and so on. The probability model needed, called the cell model, is central to quantum mechanics. Once one determines the probability of the complement, the remainder must be the desired answer. The formula for determining this probability is thus:

$$P = 1 - [(365 \times 364 \times 363 \ldots \times (365 - \{n-1\}) / 365n]$$

After a few trials, it becomes clear that P reaches 51 percent when n is only 23; by 30 it passes 80 percent.

---

oped it. This theorem is widely used in the interpretation of statistics, where the measurements one really needs have not been made, or cannot be made, such as predicting the outcome of a contested election. A given voter may state a preference for one candidate over the other, but the election will be influenced by the voter's likelihood to change preference, the voter's likelihood actually to go to the polls and vote, etc. That is why even the best polls include a wide margin of error, often more than the final margin of victory.

Further developments in the field of probability are discussed in NUMBER; SETS AND GROUPS; STATISTICS. *More details can be found in* ERROR ANALYSIS; FOURIER ANALYSIS; POPULATION ECOLOGY. *Relevant information is contained in* CHAOS AND COMPLEXITY; FEYNMAN DIAGRAM; HARDY-WEINBERG LAW.

Further Reading
David, F.N., *Games, Gods and Gambling: A History of Probability and Statistical Ideas* (1998); (1998); Lowry, Richard, *The Architecture of Chance: An Introduction to the Logic and Arithmetic of Probability* (1989).

First see COMPUTER, DIGITAL

Program, Computer

Next see COMPILER

A set of instructions that tells a computer to perform a specific series of operations on a certain group of data and to signal the completion of those operations by a specific output.

The most compact computer programs are those that minimize unique instructions and maximize loops or subroutines, which can be repeated many times. For example, suppose you want to measure electrical current over a period of time. You could write a program to tell a computer to count (operation) 360 cycles of electrical current (data) and at the completion of that count to add one to the minute section of the clock (output) and then resume the count (loop); when the minute count reaches 60, the computer adds one to the hour section, restores the minute count to zero, and resumes; when the hour reaches 12, the computer restores both counts to zero, switches from AM to PM (or vice versa), and resumes.

Early Programs. The earliest computers did not have programs; they were wired to perform a certain predetermined group of calculations. Once the calculations were solved, the computer had to be rewired, a process that could take several days, in order to perform the next calculation. Later, programs were composed of individual computer operations. The first modern programming languages, ALGOL, COBOL, and FORTRAN, were developed in the late 1950s, both to enhance the ability of computer programmers to develop ever more complex software and to enable those who were not experienced programmers to experience a more natural interface with what was already intimidating equipment.

Each of the early programming languages displayed strength in its particular specialty. For example, ALGOL and FORTRAN were developed for scientific applications and therefore relied heavily on algebraic expressions operating on floating-point numbers expressed in scientific notation; however, file access in these languages was primitive, and decimal arithmetic was practically ignored, making them unsuitable for commercial applications. Pascal, a later programming language derived from ALGOL, was initially touted as a "universal" language but foundered on the same grounds. COBOL, meanwhile, offered the commercial facilities but lacked scientific and technical features. In 1960, PL/I was created by a committee of IBM users, attempting to combine the best features of these first three languages; PL/I led to Multics, which eventually produced UNIX, which became a major operating system of the 1980s.

One important thrust of development was the effort to design natural-language programs. Among the earliest and most popular of these was BASIC, developed in the 1970s; those who were totally inexperienced with computers could design, run, and interpret simple experiments and operations.

Object-Oriented Programs. The dominant force in contemporary programming is object-oriented (O-O) programs. In most programs, code—sequences of instructions—and data—what the instructions operate on—are deliberately kept separate, so each can be modified without affecting the other. But in O-O programming, the two are enclosed together in a "black box," which receives messages and which emits messages in response; the interface is the operation.

There are many advantages of O-O programming. When it becomes necessary to change the program—and the one constant in computer programming is that programs will change—one merely replaces the "box" with a new one, avoiding the unintended consequences that are the bane of the programmer's life. New programs can inherit the entire repertoire of the original program, components or classes, thus saving development time, minimizing program length, and avoiding "bugs."

Major O-O languages include C++, Smalltalk, and Java. C++ is derived from the powerful traditional language C; Smalltalk introduced run-time binding, which means that users don't have to know anything about the objects they are manipulating; Java mates the syntax of C++ with Smalltalk's virtual machine, creating a powerful program that will run on any platform, even through a Web browser.

> *Related material in the field of computer programming can be found in* ALGORITHM; COMPUTER, DIGITAL. *Advanced subjects are developed in* EXPERT SYSTEM; OPERATING SYSTEM; TURING MACHINE. *Fundamental aspects of this subject are covered in* ARTIFICIAL INTELLIGENCE; INTERNET; NEURAL NETWORK.

First see CELL

Prokaryotic Cells

Next see BACTERIA

Much smaller and simpler precursors of eukaryotic cells. The major difference is their lack of a "true" nucleus and other membrane-bound organelles.

The nucleus of a eukaryotic cell consists of paired chromosomes surrounded by a nuclear membrane. Prokaryotes have a single round chromosome, which is "suspended" in the cytoplasm, not "walled off" by any barrier. It is, however, tightly coiled, which allows the replicator chromosomes to separate. Therefore, a prokary-

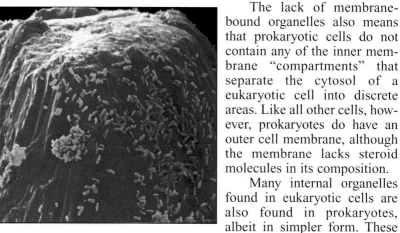

Tiny rod-shaped (bacillus) bacteria are much smaller than the head of a pin (above).

Further Reading
Lawlor, Steven C., *The Art of Programming: Computer Science With C* (1995); Luger, George F., *Artificial Intelligence: Structures and Strategies for Complex Problem Solving* (1997); Stiller, R.J., *Asunder: An Unauthorized History of the Origins of Java Programming Language* (1996).

otic cell can divide without the necessity of first undergoing an elaborate procedure of mitosis. The chromosome is copied, and then cytokinesis, the division of cytoplasm, occurs.

Prokaryotes reproduce by binary fission, in which the cell divides in half. Some organisms also reproduce by budding, in which fragments of the cell are "broken off" and grow into new individuals. In the absence of mutations, all offspring are genetically identical to each other and to their parent. Growth occurs rapidly, and a population can double every 20 minutes.

The lack of membrane-bound organelles also means that prokaryotic cells do not contain any of the inner membrane "compartments" that separate the cytosol of a eukaryotic cell into discrete areas. Like all other cells, however, prokaryotes do have an outer cell membrane, although the membrane lacks steroid molecules in its composition.

Many internal organelles found in eukaryotic cells are also found in prokaryotes, albeit in simpler form. These include ribosomes, the site of protein synthesis, and cilia and flagella, which are used for locomotion. A prokaryotic cell wall is made of protein, not cellulose like its eukaryotic counterpart.

Metabolic Differences. There are also subtle differences in many metabolic activities, such as protein synthesis and cellular respiration, due to the absence of membrane-bound organelles. Lack of mitochondria means cellular respiration occurs in the cytoplasm (and sometimes at the membrane) instead of within a specific organelle. Photosynthetic prokaryotes lack plastids such as chloroplasts, yet have sites for photosynthesis in their outer membrane folds.

Bacteria and blue-green algae are the best-known representatives of prokaryotes. All prokaryotes are unicellular organisms, although many species are organized into colonies.

Prokaryotes are believed to be among the oldest group of organisms in existence. It is also believed that the first eukaryotic organisms were actually collections of prokaryotes, which "banded together" in symbiotic relationships to form more complex cells. This would also explain the existence of membrane-bound organelles in eukaryotes and their absence in prokaryotes.

Further Reading
Cotterill, Sue, *Eukaryotic DNA Replication: A Practical Approach* (1999); Lengeler, Joseph W., *Biology of the Prokaryotes* (1999); Sadava, David E., *Cell Biology: Organelle Structure* (1993).

> *Background material on prokaryotic cells can be found in* ARCHAEBACTERIA; CELL; EUKARYOTIC CELL. *Further developments in the field are discussed in* BACTERIA; CELL CYCLE; VIRUS. *Special topics in this area are found in* EXTRANUCLEAR INHERITANCE; LIFE, DEFINITION AND ORIGIN OF; VIRAL GENETICS.

First see LOCOMOTION

Propulsion

Next see JET PROPULSION

The conversion of chemical energy in fuel to create enough thrust, or mechanical power, to overcome air resistance and the force of gravity.

Propulsion systems for aircraft originated before the development of airplanes. As early as the 1850s, steam engines fueled with coal were used to drive the propellers of lighter-than-air dirigibles. Steam engines were too heavy for heavier-than-air aircraft, which became possible only with the development of the internal combustion engine.

A number of propulsion systems are currently used for a variety of aircraft. Some use their energy to drive an air screw, a rotating propeller that pushes against the air in one direction and thus drives the aircraft in the opposite direction. A variation on this theme is the helicopter, which uses a vertically rotating propeller to both provide lift and direct the aircraft. Other engines accelerate a mass of gases in one direction, creating a jet that moves the aircraft in the opposite direction.

The first engines were water cooled, but that was replaced by air cooling through thin metal fins around the cylinder heads. A few diesel engines were adapted for use in aircraft, but they were not widely used.

Jet Engines. In the 1940s, jet engines began to replace propeller engines because they offered greater efficiency. In a turbojet, a special fuel, more like kerosene than like gasoline, is ignited in a combustion chamber. The expanding gases that are created by ignition turn the blades of a turbine wheel, which provides part of the power, and are then expelled through the rear of the engine, providing most of the power. A turbojet engine both turns a propeller and develops thrust. A ramjet engine is essentially a long tube through which air flows. The air that comes in at the front of the tube is compressed when it passes through a narrow part and mixed with fuel. Ignition of the air-fuel mixture creates a powerful jet that propels the aircraft.

Rockets. Rocket engines, unlike internal combustion and jet engines, do not draw oxygen from the atmosphere; they carry their own air supply, often in the form of liquid oxygen. The first rocket-propelled aircraft was flown in 1928 by American inventor R. H. Goddard.

Further Reading
Hunecke, Klaus, *Jet Engines: Fundamentals of Theory, Design and Operation* (1998); Stine, G. Harry, *Handbook of Model Rocketry* (1992); Sutton, George P., *Rocket Propulsion Elements: An Introduction to the Engineering of Rockets* (1992).

The foundations of the subject are discussed in COMBUSTION; LOCOMOTION; ROCKET. *Further details can be found in* INTERNAL COMBUSTION ENGINE; JET PROPULSION; SPACE SHUTTLE. *Advanced subjects in propulsion technology are developed in* INTERSTELLAR SPACE TRAVEL; MISSILE; SPACECRAFT.

First see HORMONE

Prostaglandins

Next see REPRODUCTIVE SYSTEM

A class of chemically related substances found in almost all tissues of the human body.

Prostaglandins have a wide range of hormone-like effects on local tissue. They can cause dilation and, less important, constriction of the blood vessels; stimulation of smooth muscle in the intestines, the bronchial tree, and the uterus; and resorption or formation of bone cells under various circumstances. They are also involved in the inflammatory response and may help cause fever, which could explain why aspirin, which blocks prostaglandin production, also reduces fever. (*See* PHARMACOLOGY.)

Prostaglandins have a number of prominent effects on the reproductive system. Their levels rise in follicular fluid just before ovulation and are thought to have a role in the rupture of the follicle that lets the ovum emerge. Prostaglandins induce uterine contractions when given to pregnant women and are produced naturally during labor. They can also cause abortion when adminstered in the uterus or vagina in the second trimester and are given orally, along with mifepristone (RU-486), to cause early abortion. Nonetheless, under natural conditions, prostaglandins are not believed to trigger the onset of labor but are thought to be part of an inflammatory response to the trauma of cervical dilation.

Prostaglandins seem to play an important role in regulating bone cell metabolism. They are thought to contribute to the bone resorption (or dissolution) seen with prolonged immobility and to the bone formation that accompanies weight-bearing stress on the skeleton.

First see SKELETAL SYSTEMS

Prosthesis

Next see CYBERNETICS

An artificial replacement for a missing or diseased part of the body.

Examples of prostheses include an artificial breast that might be implanted after mastectomy (removal of a cancerous breast) and a glass eye that can be inserted after removal of a diseased or injured eye. Probably the most common kind of prosthesis is an artificial arm or leg that is fitted to replace all or part of a limb that has been amputated or that has failed to develop. A mold that is made from the stump of the missing limb is used to make a socket into which the top of the prosthesis can be fitted closely and comfortably. Such a socket can be made from plastic, leather, or wood. It is attached to the stump of the missing limb by straps or by suction. The main part of an artificial limb that replaces the lower leg, forearm, upper arm, or thigh is called an extension. It consists of an inner strut that is covered with foam rubber shaped to match the corresponding part of the natural limb and has an outer shell made of metal, leather, or wood. (*See* MEDICAL DIAGNOSTICS; SURGERY.)

First see ORGANIC COMPOUND

Protein

Next see PROTEIN METABOLISM

Polymers composed of amino acids linked by peptide bonds; among the most complex molecules found within a cell.

Proteins, which contain the elements carbon, hydrogen, oxygen, nitrogen, and sulfur, are among the most complex molecules found within a cell. Proteins are the "building blocks" of the cell, forming membranes and other basic cellular components and structures. Collagen, hair, silk, wool, horns, nails, and feathers are examples of fibrous proteins. Antibodies, which fight infection; enzymes, which regulate cellular reaction; and hormones, which regulate body processes, are also types of proteins. Proteins also function as transport molecules, such as the hemoglobin that carries oxygen in red blood cells, and as gene regulators, which cause genes to be turned "on" and "off" as needed.

Amino Acid. The basic unit of a protein is an amino acid. There are 20 types of amino acids, consisting of a central carbon atom, an attached hydrogen atom, a carboxyl (COOH) group, an amino (NH$_2$) group, and a side chain. Amino acids differ from each other by the structure of their side chains, which can be as small as a single hydrogen atom, as in the amino acid glycine, or as long as a hydrocarbon (a long linked chain of carbon atoms with attached hydrogens), as in alanine.

An "average" protein contains several hundred amino acids. There are several thousand different proteins, each of which is "coded for" by a particular gene.

Amino acids are formed within cells, using sugars as the starting materials. Animals are able to synthesize only some of the amino acids needed, using ammonia as a nitrogen source. The amino acids that cannot be synthesized, called the essential amino acids, must be obtained through diet. The eight essential amino acids for adult human beings are lysine, tryptophan, threonine, methionine, phenylalanine, leucine, valine, and isoleucine. Meat and eggs are examples of "perfect" proteins, meaning they include all of the essential amino acids. Certain foods, like grains and beans, complement each other in terms of amino acid content, and when eaten together form a complete protein diet.

The Ribosome. The site of protein synthesis in the cell is the ribosome. Two amino acids held together by a peptide bond form a structure known as a dipeptide. Three or more amino acids form a polypeptide chain. The sequence of amino acids in the polypeptide chain, known as the primary structure, determines the final physical form of the mature protein molecule. However, protein structure is actually more complex than just a string of amino acids. Interactions between the side chains of adjacent amino acids, causing looping, coiling, and folding, produces secondary protein structure.

These interactions bring originally nonadjacent amino acids into close proximity with each other, allowing their side chains to interact as well, which results in further distortions in the polypeptide chain, producing the tertiary structure. The interactions between two or more polypeptide chains result in quaternary structure, the final stage of protein structure.

Categories of Shapes. Protein shapes can be divided roughly into four categories: globular, or irregularly shaped; spherical, or hydrophobic ("water-hating"), which limit their exposure to the aqueous environment of a cell; helical, which are held together with hydrogen bonds; and beta pleated sheets, which are the long loops of polypeptide chain held together by "sulfur bridges," bonds between sulfur atoms on neighboring cysteine side chains.

Hemoglobin. Proteins are highly specific, both in function and in structure. Hemoglobin is the protein responsible for binding oxygen and transporting it around the body. Hemoglobin consists of four polypeptide chains: two "alpha" chains and two "beta" chains.

In addition to its polypeptide chains, hemoglobin, like many other proteins, contains a prosthetic group that enables it to perform its job. The prosthetic group is heme, which contains an atom of iron bonded by amino acids to form a porphin ring. It is the iron atom that actually binds the oxygen molecule.

A mature red blood cell contains approximately 265 million molecules of hemoglobin. The substitution of a single amino acid in its structure can result in the condition known as sickle-cell anemia, in which the red blood cells are deformed and may clog small blood vessels. When red blood cells are broken down, the heme portion of the hemoglobin is stored in the liver and "recycled" in new hemoglobin molecules.

Elementary aspects of this subject are covered in CARBOHYDRATES; NUCLEIC ACID; ORGANIC COMPOUNDS. *More information on particular aspects of proteins is contained in* BOND, CHEMICAL; DIGESTIVE CHEMISTRY; PROTEIN METABOLISM. *Additional relevant information is contained in* METABOLISM; PROTEIN SYNTHESIS; STEROID HORMONES.

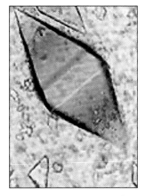

Above, a sweet-tasting protein crystal—thaumatin—isolated from an African plant. It was chosen for use as a commercial sweetener because of its potency and stability over an unusually large pH range.

Further Reading
Angeletti, Ruth Hogue, *Proteins: Analysis and Design* (1998); Smith J.L., *Protein Structure-Function Relationships in Foods* (1994).

First see PROTEIN

Protein Metabolism

Next see PROTEIN SYNTHESIS

Amino acids, the building blocks of proteins, are involved in a variety of metabolic activities. The basic structure of an amino acid consists of a central carbon atom surrounded by a hydrogen atom, an amino group (NH_2), a carboxyl group (COOH), and a hydrocarbon side chain.

Excess amino acids are not stored or excreted, but are instead converted into other compounds. The amino groups are removed in a process called deamination. The remaining "carbon skeleton" is converted into fatty acids, ketones, glucose, or some of the intermediary products of the breakdown of glucose.

The amino groups are first turned into ammonium (NH_4^+). In aquatic animals and most invertebrates, the NH_4^+ itself is excreted. In birds and reptiles, the ammonium is converted into uric acid, and in most other animals, it is converted into urea. Urea is synthesized in the urea cycle, which was the first cyclic metabolic pathway to be discovered.

The urea is formed by cells and "dumped off" into the bloodstream, from which it is later removed by the kidneys. Urea is ultimately excreted from the body in the urine. The removal of ammonium and its related compounds is important, as high levels of NH_4^+ in the blood are toxic. The toxicity is caused by a decrease in the rate of formation of adenosine triphosphate (ATP), the energy "currency" of cells. The brain, in particular, is highly vulnerable to decreases in ATP levels.

First see PROTEIN

Protein Synthesis

Next see DNA

The building of specific proteins required by a particular organism.

Protein synthesis begins in the nucleus, with DNA. A gene is a segment of DNA that codes for, or specifies, the amino acid sequence of a particular protein. A gene is found along one or the other strand of the DNA duplex; it begins with a specific sequence known as the promoter region and ends with the terminator region.

The "major players" in protein synthesis are the coding strand of DNA, known as the template; the messenger RNA (mRNA) molecule, which conveys the information from the nucleus to the ribosomes; and the transfer RNA (tRNA) molecules, which transport the amino acids.

Stages. Protein synthesis occurs in two major stages: transcription, which is the formation of mRNA from the DNA template; and translation, the interaction of mRNA, tRNA, and amino acids and ribosomes to form the polypeptide chain. Transcription begins when an enzyme called RNA polymerase settles on the promoter region of the gene and causes the double helix to "unwind." The RNA polymerase matches up nucleotides to pair with the exposed DNA bases along the entire length of the gene until it reaches the terminator region. Another enzyme, ligase, links the new nucleotides together to form the RNA chain. Only one strand of the DNA duplex is copied, and then the duplex re-forms. The RNA base sequence is complementary to the DNA template and is almost identical to the noncoding strand.

Primary Transcript. The RNA molecule formed at the end of transcription is called the primary transcript. Further "editing" before translation involves the addition of a methylguanine (mG) "cap" and a polyadenine "tail," as well as the removal of introns ("nonsense" sequences of bases) and splicing together of the ends of exons (the "useful" parts of a gene). Post-transcription modification does not occur in prokaryotic cells (bacteria and blue-green algae) but does occur in eukaryotic cells. (*See* DNA REPLICATION.)

Translation begins when the mRNA reaches the ribosomes, which always work sequentially in groups known as polysomes. Each ribosome starts at the beginning of the mRNA strand and works its way down until the entire strand has been translated. (*See* DNA; RNA.)

The ribosome separates into upper and lower halves. Once the mRNA attaches to the lower half, the first tRNA, carrying its amino acid, settles into a specific ribosomal "niche" called the "P" site. Then the ribosomal halves reunite, and the next tRNA, carrying its amino acid, settles into another niche, called the "A" site. A bond forms between the first amino acid, held by the tRNA in the P site, and the second amino acid, held by the tRNA in the A site. The first tRNA exits, leaving its amino acid behind. The ribosome shifts over, causing the remaining tRNA, which is holding the growing poly-peptide chain, to occupy the P site and allowing a third tRNA, carrying a third amino acid, to settle into the A site. Once again, a bond is formed between the amino acids, followed by the exiting of the tRNA from the P site and a ribosomal shift. (*See* TRANSCRIPTION.)

Each three bases of the mRNA make up a codon, signifying a particular amino acid. The lower portion of the tRNA, at the opposite end to where the amino acid is attached, has a complementary set of three bases, called the anticodon. Base-pairing between the codon and anticodons enables the tRNA to recognize its designated location.

A codon "calls for" one particular amino acid, yet most amino acids can be signified by more than one codon. In addition, there are three specific "start" codons. When a particular codon has no corresponding anticodon, translation immediately stops.

In eukaryotes, the mRNA is not immediately broken down; it lasts for several hours and is usually translated by multiple polysomes. In prokaryotes, however, as soon as the last ribosome in the polysome begins translation, an enzyme begins to degrade the mRNA. By the time the translation process is completed, the mRNA has been completely broken down.

Related areas to be considered are DNA; METABOLISM; NUCLEIC ACID; PROTEIN. *Other aspects of the subject are discussed in* CATALYST; DNA SEQUENCING; PROTEIN METABOLISM. *Additional related material can be found in* KREBS CYCLE; POLYMERASE CHAIN REACTION (PCR); SURFACE CHEMISTRY.

Further Reading
Clark, Brian F.C., *The Genetic Code and Protein Biosynthesis* (1992); Moldave, Kivie, *RNA and Protein Synthesis* (1981); Watson, James D., *The Double Helix: A Personal Account of the Discovery of the Structure of DNA* (1998).

First see GEOLOGICAL TIME SCALE

Proterozoic Era

Next see EVOLUTION

One of the earliest stages of the Earth's history. It began about 2 billion years ago, after the Archaean era, and was followed by the Cambrian era.

The early period of the Proterozoic era was a time when vast bands of iron formed, bands that today provide the large majority of our iron sources. These banded iron formations consisted of thick iron-containing layers between iron-poor layers of soil and rock. The sources of this iron were volcanic activity and weathering. The Proterozoic witnessed the first periods of glaciation, on a continental and perhaps a global scale. It was also the period of the formation of the first continents. The iron particles that are found in Proterozoic rocks point in directions other than to the existing magnetic poles; it is thus believed that the continents of that time may have shifted position as well as changed their shapes.

While little is known about the composition of the atmosphere or the seas during the earliest eons of Earth's existence, it is believed that the amount of oxygen in the atmosphere increased, as did the amount of water on the Earth's surface and the salt content of the oceans. The physical environment of that era was therefore much different from that of the Earth we inhabit. It is pictured as an Earth with small, barren continents, shallow seas, and a poisonous atmosphere that was bombarded regularly by ultraviolet radiation from the sun. While modern animals and plants could not exist in such an environment, these conditions favored the appearance and evolution of early living things. (*See* LIFE.)

The large organic molecules from which living things are made came into existence during this era. As for the atmosphere, the first geological layers that indicate the presence of oxygen

The kingdom Protista is believed to be a holdover from the Proterozoic Era. Above, a spirochete.

in the air appeared about 2.2 billion years ago. By 1.9 billion years ago, the amount of oxygen in the atmosphere had increased enough to shield the Earth's surface from ultraviolet radiation. (*See* OZONE LAYER.)

First see CELL

Protista

Next see MICROBIOLOGY

Kingdom consisting of a heterogeneous grouping of one-celled organisms and multicelled relations.

The diverse members of the kingdom Protista do not have the distinctive characteristics that define members of the kingdoms Animali, Plantae, or Fungi. As a result, the boundaries of this kingdom are in dispute. (*See* CELL.)

Despite these disputes, the grouping is widely agreed to embrace one-celled organisms such as protozoa, including amoebas and paramecia; slime molds; water molds, including *Phytophthora infestans*, which caused the Irish potato blight of 1846; chytrids; euglenoids; single-celled algae such as dinoflagellates, which cause red tide; and trypanosomes, flagellated parasites that live in the blood and cause African sleeping sickness. Most authorities limit the kingdom to eukaryotic organisms, those that have a membrane-bounded nucleus, thus barring bacteria. Some biologists think the category should include all eukaryotic algae, even the large, multicellular brown and red algae that form the familiar seaweeds. Others classify these algae as plants or assign brown algae to a more recently proposed kingdom called Chromista.

Because they are so diverse, protists show a variety of modes of life. Algae are photosynthetic; protozoa and slime molds ingest food; euglenoids—which are variously considered algae or protozoa—include species that use each of those means of nutrition. Many protists have flagellae with which they swim, although the multicellular protists usually do not move. Reproduction also varies, but it typically involves both cell division and sexual processes.

First see NUCLEUS, ATOMIC

Proton

Next see ELECTRON

An elementary particle with a positive electrical charge, found in the nucleus of every atom.

A single proton comprises the nucleus of hydrogen, the lightest element. On a scale in which the mass of the carbon-12 atom is 12, the proton has a mass of 1.00726. Its mass is 1,386 times the mass of an electron and slightly less than the mass of a neutron, the other particle found in atomic nuclei. The proton carries a positive electric charge that is equal to the negative charge on the electron.

The existence of the proton was proposed as early as 1816 by William Prout, an English scientist who said that all atomic masses might be multiples of the mass of hydrogen. Toward the end of the nineteenth century, a number of scientists, including J. J. Thomson in England, J. B. Perrin in France, and Eugen Goldstein and Wilhelm Wien in Germany, found proof of the existence of protons and established their mass and electrical charge by studying positively charged hydrogen ions in discharge tubes. When the existence of the neutron was discovered in 1932 by William Chadwick, it became evident that all atomic nuclei consist of protons and neutrons.

In the atomic nucleus, there are so-called "magic numbers" of protons. A magic number of protons indicates a nucleus that is especially stable. The magic numbers for protons (and neutrons) are 2, 8, 20, 50, and 82.

Accelerated protons have been used to produce and investigate nuclear reactions and interactions. The proton thus has played a major role in the development of nuclear theory. Laboratories in many countries today use proton accelerators, which can achieve energies of millions or billions of electron volts in their studies of atoms and their nuclei. One well-known type of proton accelerator is the cyclotron, which uses radio-frequency energy to accelerate particles.

The proton is a stable particle, but some grand unification theories of physics propose that it will eventually decay. The lower limit of a proton's lifetime is many billions of years, and no evidence of proton decay has yet been found.

Proton beams are emitted by the sun. The sun emits a steady flow of protons and other particles, called the solar wind, as well as bursts of protons associated with solar flares. Protons also are trapped in planetary magnetic fields.

First see RADIO ASTRONOMY

Pulsar

Next see BINARY STAR

A stellar object that emits sharp, rapid bursts of electromagnetic radiation—either radio waves or x-rays.

Pulsars are believed to be neutron stars, which have the mass of the sun but have collapsed to spheres less than ten miles in radius. The first to be discovered were radio pulsars, identified in 1968 by the British astronomers Anthony Hewish and Susan Jocelyn Bell. X-ray pulsars were identified a few years later. More than 400 pulsars have since been discovered. Both types of pulsars rotate rapidly. In radio pulsars, this rotation pulls charged particles from the surface

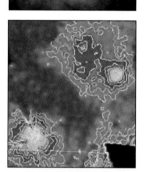

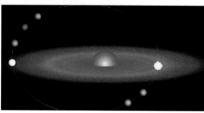

From top: Susan Jocelyn Bell, one of the discoverers of the pulsar effect; the crab nebula; the N175B pulsar; an artist's rendering of the inclined orbit of a pulsar around a circumstellar disk. When the pulsar passes through the disk, it absorbs matter causing it to emit bursts of energy.

Further Reading
Blandford, R. D., *Pulsars As Physics Laboratories* (1994); Kaler, James B., *Astronomy* (1997); Smith, Francis Graham, *Pulsars* (1976).

of the pulsar. The radio wave emissions are believed to be sent out as beams that sweep the sky like the beam from a lighthouse. The neutron stars of x-ray pulsars are believed to be in orbit around a companion star, which transfers mass to the neutron star. This influx of mass is heated to millions of degrees, which causes the emission of x rays, again in a beam that sweeps the sky. The fastest known radio pulsar, the Millisecond Pulsar, emits a burst every 1.558 milliseconds, which is close to the maximum rotation rate that is possible before an object would fly apart. The fastest known x-ray pulsar is the crab pulsar, located in the center of the crab nebula; it emits a burst every 33.1 milliseconds. A more typical pulsar emits a burst on the order of once every second.

Formation. Pulsars are believed to be formed in supernova events, explosions that occur when stars have used up all their available nuclear fuel. All the known radio pulsars are slowing down, as their rotational energy is consumed. X-ray pulsars are different; the period between emissions may increase over a year and then decrease. Radio-wave pulsars all seem to be single stars, unlike x-ray pulsars, which are binary systems. Pulsars are distributed evenly in the sky; in the Milky Way galaxy, for example, most of the detected pulsars are in the disc of the galaxy, where most of the galaxy's stars are located. The distance to pulsars can be estimated by the observed dispersion of their beams as they travel through interstellar space. Radio waves interact with the small number of electrons in space, which causes a sharp pulse to be smeared out. Since astronomers have a good estimate of the concentration of electrons in space, they can determine the approximate distance of a pulsar by the amount of smearing that takes place. The closest pulsars are estimated to be about 80 parsecs from Earth (a parsec is 3.261 light-years); some are estimated to be as distant as 55,000 parsecs.

Theories about the origin and nature of pulsars continue to evolve. The exact process by which their bursts of electromagnetic waves are produced is still not fully known, and several models have been proposed to explain it. The exact nature of the relationship between supernova events and the formation of pulsars is being further investigated.

Background material can be found in GALAXY; STAR; NEUTRON STAR; UNIVERSE, LARGE-SCALE STRUCTURE OF. *More details can be found in* BINARY STARS; RADIO ASTRONOMY; TELESCOPE. *Elementary aspects of this subject are covered in* EXTRATERRESTRIAL LIFE; NOVA, SUPERNOVA; QUASARS.

First see QUANTUM MECHANICS

Quantum Electrodynamics

Next see QUANTUM STATISTICS

The study of the properties of electromagnetic radiation and the ways in which that radiation interacts with charged particles, expressed in terms of quantum mechanics.

Quantum electrodynamics (QED) stands in relation to classical theories of electricity and magnetism as quantum mechanics relates to classical Newtonian mechanics. Quantum mechanics is a part of a more general theory—quantum field theory—that describes the strong interactions between the neutrons and protons in the nuclei of atoms in terms of the meson fields that are thought to be responsible for these interactions.

In quantum electrodynamics, the electromagnetic field that exists at every point in space and at each moment of time is characterized by two vectors, the electric field vector and the magnetic field vector. Both of these vectors are components of a single entity in space-time, an asymmetric tensor. The fields described by these vectors are defined in terms of the force that acts on each unit charge at a given place, moving with a given velocity.

The differences in effects between quantum electrodynamics and classical electrodynamics generally are so small that they are barely observable. Nevertheless, physicists have measured the effects of QED accurately, verifying the theoretical structure on which the subject is based. The most important of these effects is the Lamb shift, first described by Willis Lamb. This small displacement of some of the quantized energy levels in the hydrogen atom shows that the magnetic moment of the electron is slightly greater than was predicted by elementary theory. (*See* GRAND UNIFIED THEORY (GUT).)

First see WAVE-PARTICLE DUALITY

Quantum Mechanics

Next see QUANTUM ELECTRODYNAMICS

The word "quantum" comes from the Latin for "so much" or "bundle." "Mechanics" is the old term that describes the study of motion. Quantum mechanics, therefore, is the study of the motion of objects that come in "bundles" or discrete particles.

Quantum mechanics is a branch of science that began developing in the early twentieth century; it deals with the motion and interactions of matter at the atomic and the subatomic level. At this level, everything does indeed come in little bundles. Particles have certain masses and electrical charges, and even quantities like energy or the position of an electron's orbit can have only certain specified values. An electron may be found at a distance A from its nucleus, or at a distance B, but it cannot be found anywhere between A and B. The radial position of the electron, in other words, is quantized.

The world of the quantum differs from the world of our ordinary experience in three ways:

It is impossible to know certain quantities related to quantized objects simultaneously.

When one looks at a familiar object like a table, one is, in fact, taking part in a rather complex process. Light from some source—a light bulb or the sun—hits the table and is reflected to

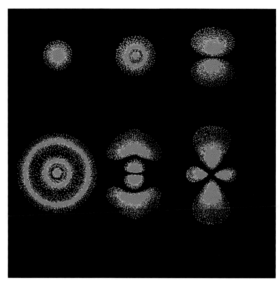

the eye, which then detects it. We do not normally think about things this way because the light does not affect the table greatly. To look at an electron, however, one would still have to go through the procedure of bouncing something off of it. But because the world of the atom is quantized, the thing that bounces off the electron is going to have to be comparable in energy to that of the electron itself. This means that the act of detecting the electron must necessarily change it. Therefore, there are certain things that we cannot know about subatomic particles. For example, we cannot know both the position and the velocity of a particle at the same time. If we know exactly where it is, we cannot know how fast it is moving, and if we know how fast it is moving, we cannot know where it is. This relationship is the essence of what is known as the Heisenberg uncertainty principle.

In the world of the quantum, all descriptions become statistical.

There is an important distinction between familiar objects and the kind of objects found in the subatomic world. Because every measurement must affect the object being measured, we cannot talk realistically about what that object is doing between measurements. Thus, if an electron is moving from point A to point B, it cannot be measured at any point in between. Any mea-

Left, probability density plots of the first six hydrogen atomic orbitals (clockwise from top left), 1s, 2s, 2P_0, 3s, 3P_0, 3d_0. The typical interference pattern for light (below) is duplicated for electron beams at the double slits in the metal sheet at left.

Richard P. Feynman, one of the foremost expositors of quantum electrodynamics (also known as QED).

surement will change the electron, and it will behave differently than it would have had it not been measured. What this means is that between measurements, objects in the quantum world have to be described by probabilities or "wave functions." This does not mean that one cannot predict what quantum objects will do—we do so routinely—it means that the kinds of descriptions we get will not be the same in the quantum world as they will be in our large-scale world.

Events in the quantum world cannot be pictured in ordinary ways.

The quantum world sometimes seems bizarre. We are used to living in a world of normal-size objects moving at normal speeds. All of our intuition—our sense of how the world should operate—is based on our experience with such objects. However, many apparent paradoxes can arise in quantum mechanics if we try to picture what electrons are doing as if they were baseballs or waves in the ocean. An electron may inexplicably change its identity from a particle to a wave, depending on how it is being measured. Or we may find that it will "know" how an experiment is going to turn out before that experiment is actually conducted. In all of these cases, if one remembers that nothing in our experience has prepared us to deal with these kinds of objects, it will become apparent that the paradox is not a paradox at all, but simply a result of our unfamiliarity with the subatomic world.

Background information on the field of quantum mechanics can be found in ATOM; BLACK BODY RADIATION; BROWNIAN MOTION. *Further details can be found in* ATOMIC SHELL MODEL; ENERGY; SCHRÖDINGER'S EQUATION. *Additional relevant information is contained in* QUANTUM ELECTRODYNAMICS; QUANTUM STATISTICS; UNCERTAINTY PRINCIPLE. *See also* BELL'S INEQUALITY; EQUIVALENCE PRINCIPLE; WAVE-PARTICLE DUALITY.

First see QUANTUM MECHANICS

Quantum Statistics

Next see SUPERFLUID

The statistical description of a system of particles that obey the rules of quantum mechanics rather than the rules of classical mechanics.

In quantum statistics, the energy levels of particles on the atomic level are quantized—that is, they are restricted to certain energy levels. Quantum statistics is a variation of statistical mechanics, which uses statistical methods to describe the average properties of complicated physical systems. In the nineteenth century,

The future of quantum mechanics was laid out at the famous series of Solvay Congresses in Brussels, the first held in 1911. Below, participants in the fifth Solvay Congress, held in 1927. Included were Einstein (front row, center), Max Planck and Marie Curie (second and third to Einstein's right); Dirac (over Einstein's right shoulder); Bohr (right end of second row); Schrödinger (back row, center); and Heisenberg (three from Schrödinger's left).

Further Reading
Catellani, E., *Interpreting Bodies: Classical and Quantum Objects in Modern Physics* (1999); Omnes, Roland, *Understanding Quantum Mechanics* (1999).

Further Reading
Bogoliubov, N.N., *An Introduction to Quantum Statistical Mechanics* (1994); Khinchin, Alexsandr I., *Mathematical Foundations of Quantum Statistics (1998);* Schulman, L.S., *Time's Arrows and Quantum Measurement* (1997).

Ludwig Boltzmann used this classical method to give a picture of the second law of thermodynamics, which describes the limitations on the conversion of heat into work. In particular, Boltzmann gave a statistical description of many of the properties of gases.

The application of Boltzmann's statistics to the motion of individual particles in such a system requires substantial revision under quantum mechanics. There are two forms of quantum statistics, the Bose-Einstein statistics and the Fermi-Dirac statistics, which describe the behavior of different groups of particles. The elementary particles that obey the Bose-Einstein statistics are called bosons and have values expressed in whole integers. The elementary particles that obey the Fermi-Dirac statistics are called fermions and have half-integral values in the calculations applied to them.

Fermions. Electrons, protons, and neutrons are fermions. The fact that electrons are fermions plays a major role in the Pauli exclusion principle, which explains the behavior of electrons in atoms and the Periodic Table of the Elements; it also explains the distinction between solids that conduct electricity and those that are not conductors.

For these particles, the quantum mechanical wave function describing the state of a system is symmetrical; for a system of bosons, the wave function is antisymmetrical. "Symmetrical" in this context means that the value of the function does not change if the coordinates of two particles are interchanged; for antisymmetrical particles, the sign of the function is reversed in such an interchange.

In two-space dimensions, there can be particles or quasi-particles whose statistics are midway between bosons and fermions. These particles are called anyons. For anyons that are identical, the wave function is neither symmetrical, with a value of +1, nor antisymmetrical, with a value of –1. Instead, the wave function of an anyon fluctuates continuously between +1 and –1. The existence of anyons has been proposed as a possible mechanism for high-temperature superconductivity.

The relation between the spin and the quantum statistics of particles is given by the spin-statistics theorem, which states that half-integer spins can be quantized consistently only if they obey the Fermi-Dirac statistics, while whole-integer spins can be quantized consistently only if they obey the Bose-Einstein statistics. This theorem, proved by Wolfgang Pauli in 1940, helps to explain why the wave functions for bosons are symmetrical and the wave functions for fermions are antisymmetrical.

Related material can be found in MAXWELL-BOLTZMANN DISTRIBUTION; QUANTUM MECHANICS; UNCERTAINTY PRINCIPLE. Advanced subjects are developed in ABSOLUTE ZERO; CRYOGENICS; ENTROPY. Further aspects of this subject are covered in EXCLUSION PRINCIPLE; GROUP THEORY IN PHYSICS; SUPERFLUID.

First see ELEMENTARY PARTICLES

Quarks

Next see STRING THEORY

Subatomic particles that play a major role in the strong interaction, binding together the protons and neutrons of the atomic nucleus.

The strong interaction, as the name implies, is strong—about 100 times stronger than the electromagnetic interaction—but is effective only over very short distances, much less than the radius of a typical atomic nucleus.

The proton and neutron are classified as hadrons; a hadron is any particle that responds to the strong force. According to a concept first advanced by Murray Gell-Mann in 1964, all hadrons are made of smaller particles, quarks. The proton and the neutron, which are also classified as baryons, consist of three quarks. Unlike protons and electrons, which carry integral (but opposite) charges, quarks have charges that are fractions of the charge on the electron, either +2/3 or –1/3 of the electron charge.

Quarks are said to occur in six flavors (a term that has nothing to do with taste). In this classification, the up, or u, quark has a +2/3 charge; the down, or d, quark has a –1/3 charge; the charmed, or c, quark has a charge of +2/3; the strange, or s, quark has a charge of –1/3; the top, or t, quark has a charge of +2/3; and the bottom, or b, quark has a charge of –1/3. For every flavor quark there is an antiquark, with an opposite electric charge. For example, the up antiquark has a charge of –2/3.

The proton consists of three quarks, *uud*, with charges of +2/3, +2/3 and –1/3, which equals +1. The neutron quark structure is *udd*, which gives it no charge.

Color. The Pauli exclusion principle says that no two identical particles in a system, such as quarks in a hadron, can have an identical set of quantum numbers. To satisfy this principle, the concept of color has been added to the six flavors of quarks. Each flavor of quark is said to occur in the three primary colors of red, green and blue, while each antiquark has the complementary colors of cyan, magenta and yellow. ("Color," like flavor, has no connection with the everyday meaning of the word.) The use of color as well as flavor means that there are 18 quarks and 18 antiquarks. The theory governing the combination of quarks to form hadrons is called

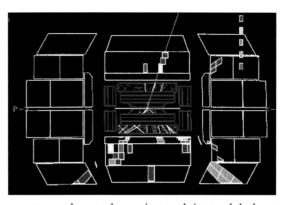

quantum chromodynamics and is modeled on quantum electrodynamics. To form a hadron, the combination of colors should always yield white—either by mixing one primary color with its complementary anticolor or by mixing three primary colors, as is true of baryons.

Gluons. The strong charge between quarks is said to occur by the exchange of gluons (so called because they hold quarks together), which have no rest mass and no electric charge, but which do have a color charge. Each gluon has one color and one anticolor. Thus, there are nine color-anticolor combinations, but one is excluded because it is equivalent to white.

A quark can change its color through an interaction. Each such color change is accompanied by the emission of a gluon, which is absorbed by another quark. The color of the absorbing quark changes as a result. For example, when a red quark changes to green, it emits a gluon with the colors red and antigreen. When this gluon is absorbed by a green quark, the green of that quark and the antigreen of the gluon annihilate each other, so that the second quark then turns to red acquired from the gluon. There is no net change in the overall quark system, because there is still one red quark and one green quark after the interchange. In the larger picture, all hadrons remain white, even as quark colors move from point to point. Thus, the strong force maintains the integrity of the nucleus.

Neither quarks nor gluons have yet been identified in experiments, although some physicists have reported evidence of the fractional electron charges that would be carried by unattached quarks. Nevertheless, the quark theory as a whole is supported by ample circumstantial evidence. Some theorists believe that quarks cannot exist as isolated particles, because they would have enormous potential energies when separated from one another—energies so great that the quarks making up a hadron would be much more massive than the hadron.

Further developments in the field are discussed in BARYONS; ELEMENTARY PARTICLE; NUCLEAR FORCES; QUANTUM MECHANICS. **For advanced discussions, see** ACCELERATOR, PARTICLE; STANDARD MODEL. **Special aspects of this subject are in** GAUGE THEORY; GRAND UNIFICATION THEORIES (GUT); STRING THEORY.

Below, the track in the bubble chamber at CERN that first indicated the existence of quarks. Left, current systems use computerized reconstructions of the events recorded in a bubble chamber; the computers even interpret the events before any researcher sees them.

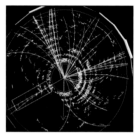

Further Reading
Close, F.E., *The Cosmic Onion: Quarks and the Nature of the Universe* (1986); Halzen, Francis,, *Quarks and Leptons: An Introductory Course in Modern Particle Physics* (1984); Heath, Helen F., *Physics in Collision* (1998).

Quasar (Quasistellar Object)

First see GALAXY

Next see UNIVERSE

Believed to be the most distant objects in the universe, quasars emit visible light, radio waves, and other forms of electromagnetic radiation.

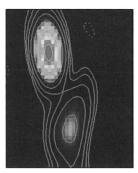

The emission of radiation by a quasar can vary by large amounts and on short time scales. On astronomical photographs, quasars appear to be near-normal stars, but studies of their light emissions have found sizable red shifts, indicating very rapid movement away from Earth. Such a red shift would indicate a distance of 10 billion light-years. The first quasars were observed in 1961, and more than 3,000 of them, with a variety of characteristics, have been identified in the universe. They appear to be associated with the early stages of the evolution of galaxies. Most quasars are found in the nuclei of spiral galaxies.

Further Reading
Swarup, G., *Quasars* (1986); Thorne, Kip S., *Black Holes and Time Warps: Einstein's Outrageous Legacy* (1994).

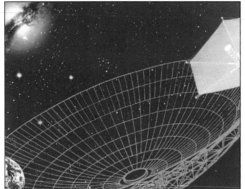

Theories and Models. Most astronomers believe that the high red shifts can be explained by the expansion of the universe. The exact nature of quasars, however, is unknown. One theory is that a quasar is a massive black hole—a huge object that has collapsed under its own gravitational weight, and that gathers in material from the stars and gases surrounding it. But the way in which the collapse of a black hole leads to the generation of the high-energy particles typical of a quasar has not been worked out.

Satisfactory models exist for the ionized gas that produces the broad emission lines of a quasar. They are believed to originate in a broad band of clouds that surrounds the central energy source of the quasar. The gas in these clouds is thought to be ionized, to exist at very high temperatures, and to have very high densities of electrons. The chemical composition of these clouds seems to be the same as that of our sun.

In addition to their broad emission lines, quasars also can emit narrow emission lines caused by "forbidden" transitions between energy states of common elements, transitions that are not permitted by the ordinary rules of quantum mechanics. These forbidden lines have been observed to remain constant for many years and are believed to originate in the extremely rapid motion of outflowing gas. The exact mechanism of their production remains unclear. (*See* INTERSTELLAR MEDIUM ("DARK MATTER").)

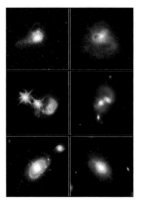

Top, a radio image of a quasar 30 billion light-years from Earth, taken with the Very Long Base Interferometry (VLBI) Space Observatory Program (middle), a U.S.–Japan project involving placing a radio telescope in orbit and using it in co-ordination with Earth antennae to create a "telescope larger than the Earth." Bottom, Hubble images of quasars.

What are They? The relationship of quasars to the galaxies that contain them is a controversial subject in astronomy. It is not clear whether quasar formation precedes, follows, or is an alternative path to the formation of galaxies. Some studies have found that high red-shift quasars may be associated with galaxies that have lower red shifts. These studies may require a revision of the generally accepted theory about the origin of quasar red shifts.

Related areas to be considered are GALAXY; INFRARED AND ULTRAVIOLET ASTRONOMY; PULSAR. *Advanced subjects are developed in* BLACK HOLES; UNIVERSE, LARGE-SCALE STRUCTURE OF. *More information on particular aspects is contained in* HUBBLE CONSTANT; NOVA, SUPERNOVA; RADIO ASTRONOMY; VERY LARGE ARRAY (VLA).

First see CRYSTAL

Quasicrystal

Next see X-RAY DIFFRACTION

A solid that exhibits some of the features of a traditional crystal—symmetry and a regular arrangement of atoms or molecules—but that lacks a unit cell.

A normal crystal can be defined by three values, corresponding to its three-dimensional periodicity; a quasicrystal demands five or six vectors, called Miller indices, to be adequately defined. They are usually grouped according to their "quasiperiodic" structure, typically decagonal, dodecagonal, or icosahedral. Quasicrystals are proving useful because their magnetic and elastic properties are greater than those of crystals, particularly at high temperatures.

Quasicrystals can be grown in the same way as normal crystals but will display a more complex structure. An icosahedral quasicrystal may have a triacontahedral shape—that is, thirty different faces—and may consist of an icosahedron nested inside a pentagon dodecahedron, inside another icosahedron, inside a "soccer ball," inside a third icosahedron, totaling 117 atoms.

The applications of quasicrystals are just beginning to be developed. A frying pan coated with quasicrystal instead of Teflon™ is just as non-stick, but is safe for metal utensils. Composites made with quasicrystals are tougher, and last longer, than silicon carbide composites. Quasicrystal powders have extremely low coefficients of friction, so they are now being used as dry lubricants. And because of their electromagnetic properties, quasicrystals are being used in thermoelectric films.

Special topics in this area are found in BOND, CHEMICAL; CRYSTAL; SOLIDS. *Advanced subjects are developed in* INORGANIC COMPOUND; POLYMER AND POLYMERIZATION. *More information on particular aspects is contained in* DIAMOND; MINERALOGY; NANOTECHNOLOGY.

Rabies

Next see DISEASES, INFECTIOUS

Rabies is an acute and almost always fatal viral disease that strikes the nervous system, causing coma, paralysis, and usually death. It is most commonly spread to a human by the bite of a rabid dog, but it can also be transmitted by the bite of any rabies-infected animal, domestic or wild. Immunization is possible, and almost always prevents the disease if it is given within two days after a person is bitten.

Symptoms. If protective measures are not taken, symptoms of rabies can appear in a few days or up to months later, with an average time of four to eight weeks. The first symptoms are low-grade fever, headache, and loss of appetite. They are followed by hyperactivity and loss of orientation, sometimes accompanied by seizures. There can be intense thirst, but the patient often cannot drink because of painful throat spasms, which is why the disease is sometimes called hydrophobia. A lapse into coma and death can occur in as little as three days after the appearance of symptoms.

Radar

Next see SONAR

A method of detecting the position and location of distant objects, such as ships and aircraft.

In addition to its well-known use as a detector of objects, radar is used for navigation and guidance, through the emission and detection of electromagnetic radiation whose wavelength is in the centimeter range. Its name derives from the phrase originally used to describe it, radio detection and ranging. The heart of a radar system consists of a transmitter that sends out a beam of radio-frequency radiation, often in pulses, through a movable aerial. If the beam strikes an object such as an aircraft, a part of its energy is reflected back to the aerial, which sends it to a receiver so that it can be amplified and the location and size of the object can be determined. The signal, or echo, caused by that reflection results in a sudden rise in the output of the detector, usually on a cathode-ray tube.

Calculations. The distance d to the object is calculated by the time t needed for the radar pulse to reach the target and be reflected back, using the formula $d = ct/2$, where c is the speed of light. In some radar systems, the distance is measured by using the Doppler effect, the apparent change in the frequency of a wave that results from the relative motion between the source of the wave (the object that reflects the radar beam) and the detector.

Radiation Detector

Next see RADON

Radiation detectors come in a variety of forms. The oldest group consists of gas-filled counters, which are still used extensively in nuclear science. Gas-filled counters take advantage of ionization, the removal of electrons from atoms, which can be achieved directly by charged particles such as electrons or protons.

Two Arrangements. There are two basic arrangements used in ionization detectors. One of them is the parallel-plate configuration, in which an electric field is maintained between two electrodes. The electrons and positrons that appear along the pathway of a charged particle or a photon, a unit of light, will move toward the two electrodes, causing an electric current to flow in the circuit connecting the electrodes. The current will increase as the applied electrical potential increases, until it reaches a limiting value, called the saturation current. This value is proportional to the intensity of the source.

When the rate of arrival of ionizing radiation is too low to permit the measurement of the current, or when scientists want to determine the energy distribution of particles, the ionization chamber may be operated in what is called a pulse mode. This creates a situation in which electrons, which are negatively charged, are collected rapidly; however, positively charged ions, which move about a thousand times more slowly than the electrons, can complicate the measurement. The pulse circuits thus are usually designed to respond only to the electron collection portion of the pulse.

As the applied voltage of a counter is raised beyond the region at which an ionization chamber becomes saturated, the electrons that are produced acquire enough energy to produce additional ionization of the gas in the counter. Proportional counters are widely used because they are easy to design and are stable in operation. The solid-state equivalent of a gas-filled ionization chamber uses a semiconductor. Semiconductor detectors have become increasingly important in radiation detector technology in recent years, and the field is developing rapidly.

The scintillation counter uses a material that scintillates—emits photons—when struck by radiation. Other more specialized radiation detectors include the Cerenkov counter, which measures the electromagnetic radiation emitted when a charged particle passes through a trans-

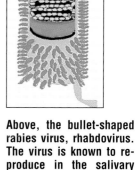

Above, the bullet-shaped rabies virus, rhabdovirus. The virus is known to reproduce in the salivary glands of the host.

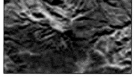

Above, false color satellite radar images of Earth.

parent material at a velocity greater than the velocity of light; the spark chamber, used primarily for high-energy physics experiments, which detects the track of ionization produced by the passage of a charged particle; and dielectric track detectors, which use solids such as mica, glass, or a polymer film to record the trail of radiation damage left by a particle as it passes through the detector. (*See* SCINTILLATORS.)

First see RADIOACTIVITY

Radiation, Natural

Next see RADIATION DETECTOR

The natural background radiation that bathes everything on Earth has two sources. One is the cosmic radiation that falls on earth from space. The other is the radiation given off by naturally radioactive elements that exist in Earth's crust.

Cosmic radiation can be described as primary and secondary. Primary cosmic radiation consists of nuclei of the most abundant elements. Protons, which make up the nuclei of hydrogen atoms, are by far the largest part of cosmic radiation, but electrons, positrons, neutrinos and gamma ray photons are also part of cosmic radiation. The energy of these individual particles ranges between 100 million electron volts and several billion electron volts.

The sources of primary cosmic radiation are not fully known, but the sun is believed to be the principal source of those particles with energies of up to about 10 billion electron volts. The cosmic particles whose energies are higher are believed to originate mostly in our galaxy, but the highest-energy particles are believed to come from other galaxies. As these particles enter the earth's atmosphere, they collide with the nuclei of oxygen and nitrogen in the air, causing the production of secondary cosmic rays. This secondary cosmic radiation consists of elementary particles and gamma-ray photons. A single high-energy particle can produce a shower of secondary particles.

Earthly Sources. The natural radioactivity that is emitted from the crust of the earth comes almost entirely from the chemical elements whose atomic number ranges between 81 (thallium) and 92 (uranium). Physicists have determined that only three of the naturally occurring radioactive elements whose atomic number is greater than 80 are long-lived enough to remain radioactive at this time of Earth's evolution. One of them is thorium-232, whose half-life is greater than 10 billion years. Another is uranium-238, whose half-life is about 4.5 billion years. The third is uranium-235, with a half-life

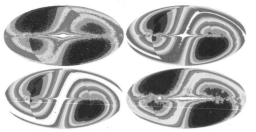

Thermal emission maps, such as those above, are used by NASA scientists to study the background radiation in the universe. However, one must find ways to subtract the "noise" of the background from the signal, so as to better study the object being viewed.

of about 700 million years. All the other radioactive elements in the earth's crust, some 40 of them, are daughter products of successive generations that derive from these three elements. One of them, radon, has become a matter of concern among homeowners. (*See* RADON.)

Decay. These naturally radioactive elements can decay in several ways, giving off different kinds of background radiation. For example, a nucleus of uranium-238 can emit an alpha particle—a helium nucleus containing two protons and two neutrons—and be converted to a nucleus of thorium-234. Or it can fission into two roughly equal parts of various sizes with the emission of different forms of radiation, such as a beta particle (an electron, with a negative charge), or gamma rays, high-energy electromagnetic radiation. Measurements of background radiation can be made with instruments such as the Geiger-Mueller counter, whose core is a positively charged wire surrounded by a negatively charged wire; the device counts the number of subatomic particles or electrons emitted by a specimen of material.

First see TELECOMMUNICATION

Radio and Television Broadcasting

Next see FREQUENCY MODULATION

Radio and television broadcasting has made it possible to disseminate information throughout the world. Both operate by transmitting electromagnetic waves through the air (they move equally well through empty space), originally through the making and breaking of a sparking circuit, but today through the modulation of a carrier wave. These waves are then received, the signal is discriminated from background noise, and the modulations are interpreted as voice, music, and image. (*See* ELECTROMAGNETIC WAVES.)

Although work had been done throughout the nineteenth century on electromagnetism, it was not until 1895 that a young Italian researcher, Guglielmo Marconi, succeeded in transmitting a coherent signal across more than a few meters of empty space. Development came rapidly after that; by 1901 Marconi could send a telegraphic signal across the Atlantic Ocean, and in 1912, a program of music was broadcast from the top of the Eiffel Tower.

Early radios worked through amplitude modulation, in which modifications in the strength of the carrier wave yielded coherent voices or music; this type of broadcast is subject to static distortion, but is capable of long-range transmission. Most radios today also work through frequency modulation, invented by F. H. Armstrong in 1933, in which the frequency of the carrier wave is modulated rather than its amplitude. Although this type of broadcasting takes up more bandwidth and is not capable of long-range transmission, its high signal-to-noise ratio makes it virtually static-free.

Once the principle of sending an electromagnetic signal through air or space had been established, it was possible—at least in theory—to extend that signal's complexity by adding image to sound. (*See* RECORDING TECHNOLOGY.)

Television. In 1920, a Russian emigré named Vladimir Zworykin began research into the transmission of visual images via modulated electrical signal. He patented an iconoscope, or transmitter, in 1923, and a kinescope, or receiver, a year later; by 1929, he had added color transmission. Asked by Robert Sarnoff, president of RCA, how much it would cost to perfect his system, Zworykin optimistically replied, "About $100,000." In actuality, it cost 500 times that, and took nearly 20 years.

Television broadcasting depends on the photoelectric effect. In a transmitter, light is focused onto a set of photoreceptor cells, and their varying charges are measured by a rapidly scanning electron beam and turned into a broadcast signal. In a conventional receiver, the signal is transformed back into a scanning electron beam, which bombards bands of fluorescent material—modern television receivers have 525 lines of such material—30 times a second. The material fluoresces in different colors, which blend to create images.

Recent advances in television include: HDTV (high-definition television), which improves picture sharpness by "interlacing" areas between the lines to match bordering images; digital signal processing, which yields crisper images than analog curves; and thin-screen displays, such as the liquid crystal displays in some portable computers and plasma display panels, which create images with 900,000 pixels.

CONTROVERSIES

Who Invented Radio?

Edwin H. Armstrong (1890–1954) was a pioneer in radio technology, but he never saw its final triumph. Armstrong invented the system of frequency modulation (FM) in 1933, only to find RCA wholly committed to amplitude modulation (AM). Determined to show the superiority of his system, Armstrong invested $300,000—this in the middle of the Great Depression—and built his own FM station in Alpine, New Jersey. Although he succeeded in persuading General Electric, Westinghouse, and other second-rank companies of FM's value, he could not even get RCA to pay royalties on his invention; in 1948, he was forced to sue for his rights. RCA deliberately dragged out the case, driving Armstrong into bankruptcy and, in 1954, he committed suicide. A few years later, all his lawsuits succeeded, and FM became the dominant medium of radio.

First see TELESCOPE

Radio Astronomy

Next see X-RAY TELESCOPE

The study of radio-frequency radiation that is emitted by stars and other celestial bodies.

Radio astronomy began in 1932 when an American astronomer, Karl Jansky, detected radio waves originating outside the Earth's atmosphere. The instrument used in radio astronomy is the radio telescope, of which there are many types. The simplest consists of a steerable, paraboloidal dish that receives incoming signals and reflects them to the center, or principal focus, of the dish, where they are amplified up to 1,000 times. These signals, or waves, are then converted to a lower frequency and transmitted to a detector and display unit for study.

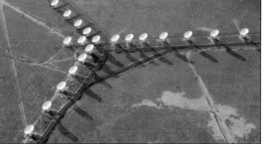

Above, the Very Large Array (VLA) observatory located in California, uses as many as 26 radio dishes arranged in a Y to achieve the same reception as a much larger, linear array.

Because the radio waves that arrive at the focus must be completely in phase, the surface of the receiving dish must be constructed with great accuracy. For example, a dish with a diameter of 100 meters must be accurate to one millimeter if it receives radio waves whose wavelength is one centimeter. There are mechanical limits on the size and precision of such antennae, and so an array of antennae is usually linked together to form an interferometer. Radio interferometry connects an array of relatively small aerials by cable to simulate a very large dish aerial. All but the smallest steerable radio telescope dishes are made from metal mesh, so the wind can pass through them without disturbing their aim. A few very large radio telescope dishes have been built on the surface of the Earth to overcome the stability problem, but these dishes cannot be aimed toward the variety of radio sources that can be studied with movable dishes.

Radio astronomers study thermal emissions, which arise from the interaction of charged particles in the ionized gas of a star. Hundreds of sources of thermal emissions have been identified in the Milky Way. They are signposts for massive hot stars, since the gas in these stars is ionized and therefore emits radio waves. Also studied is synchrotron radiation, which is generated by high-energy electrons moving in a magnetic field. This is also called nonthermal emission because its intensity is not related to the temperature of the emitting body but rather to the strength of the magnetic field and the number and energy distribution of the electrons in the field. The focus of the investigation of radio

Above, the world's largest radio telescope is located in remote Arecibo, Puerto Rico.

emissions includes quasars, radio galaxies, and the remnants of supernovas. The sources of radio galaxy and quasar emissions are generally outside our solar system. These emissions are divided into two categories: one from extended structures and the other from compact structures. Extended structures are usually associated with other galaxies, but sometimes come from quasars. Most compact sources are identified with the nuclei of active galaxies or with quasars.

The Milky Way galaxy generally emits synchrotron radiation. An all-sky map of the galaxy's radio emissions at a frequency of 408 megahertz has been made by using three of the world's largest parabolic reflectors. The map shows intense emissions in a band at the center of the galaxy, with reduced emissions in outer regions—but with some bands of intense activity extending out from the center.

Galaxy Content. Radio emissions from hydrogen, the most abundant element in the universe, are studied to obtain information about our galaxy, other galaxies, and the universe as a whole. Data from these studies, coupled with information on the red shifts of visible emissions, have established the existence of large-scale voids—regions that have significantly less matter than is found in normal galaxies. One focus of research is whether these regions contain non-emitting, or "dark," matter.

Radio astronomy has identified more than 80 molecular species in dense clouds that exist in interstellar space. This result has led to the creation of a new field of astronomy—astrochemistry. Studies indicate that interstellar space is rich in carbon, as Earth is, but that many exotic molecular species exist in space that are not found on Earth. Study of these molecules is playing an important role in explaining how stars form from interstellar gases.

Related areas to be considered are INFRARED AND ULTRAVIOLET ASTRONOMY; TELESCOPES. *More details can be found in* HUBBLE CONSTANT; VERY LARGE ARRAY (VLA) TELESCOPE. *Relevant information is contained in articles on* INTERSTELLAR MEDIUM *and* X-RAY AND GAMMA RAY ASTRONOMY.

Particle emissions

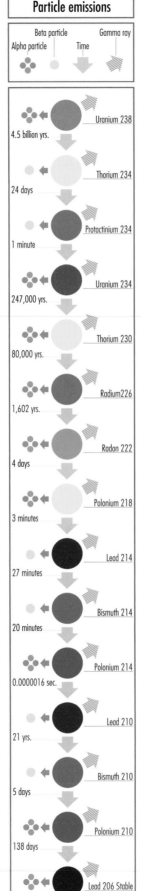

Beta particle	Gamma ray
Alpha particle	Time

- Uranium 238 — 4.5 billion yrs.
- Thorium 234 — 24 days
- Protactinium 234 — 1 minute
- Uranium 234 — 247,000 yrs.
- Thorium 230 — 80,000 yrs.
- Radium 226 — 1,602 yrs.
- Radon 222 — 4 days
- Polonium 218 — 3 minutes
- Lead 214 — 27 minutes
- Bismuth 214 — 20 minutes
- Polonium 214 — 0.0000016 sec.
- Lead 210 — 21 yrs.
- Bismuth 210 — 5 days
- Polonium 210 — 138 days
- Lead 206 Stable

First see TRANSURANIC ELEMENTS

Radioactivity

Next see SCINTILLATOR

The emission of energy by certain types of matter. The energy emitted can be detected either as particles or as radiation.

Radioactivity was first described in 1896 by the French physicist Henri Becquerel, who was investigating the phosphorescence of some compounds of uranium. Becquerel found that uranium itself and all the compounds containing uranium emit radiation; the amount of radiation emitted was proportional to the number of uranium atoms in the material he was investigating.

In 1899, the British physicist Ernest Rutherford identified two forms of the emitted radiation. In 1900, the French physicist Philippe Villard identified a third form. These three forms are now known as alpha radiation, beta radiation, and gamma radiation. Alpha radiation has been found to consist of helium atoms, which carry a positive charge and are emitted at very high velocities. Beta radiation consists of electrons, which carry a negative charge and are also emitted at high velocities. Gamma radiation consists of photons, high-energy units of electromagnetic radiation. Gamma rays are emitted at the speed of light and are highly penetrating and potentially damaging; thick layers of lead are necessary to shield them completely.

It was Rutherford who first identified radioactivity with the spontaneous disintegration of atoms. Rutherford also established that the rate at which the radioactive emission of a preparation decreases is exponential with time. This characteristic is used to define a basic characteristic of a radioactive substance, the half-life, which is the length of time required for half of the atoms in the preparation to decay.

Natural Radioactivity. In nature, radioactivity is observed in chemical elements whose atomic numbers—the number of protons in their nuclei—range between 81 and 92; there are only a few exceptions to this rule. Since the Earth is several billion years old, any radioactive substance found in its crust today either must have a very long half-life or be a radioactive daughter that is constantly being produced by a parent with a very long half-life. Only three naturally occurring radioactive elements whose atomic number is greater than 80 are long-lived enough to meet this definition. One of them is thorium, another is the isotope uranium-235, and the third is uranium-238. All the other naturally occurring radioactive substances, some 40 of them, are products of these three elements.

After Rutherford formulated the modern model of the atom in 1911, it became evident that radioactivity arises in the nucleus of the atom. When such a nucleus emits an alpha particle, it loses two protons, so the resulting daughter atom has an atomic number that is two less than the number of the parent atom. Similarly, the daughter product of an atom that emits a beta particle has an atomic number that is one more than that of the parent atom.

Artificial Radioactivity. Artificial radioactivity was first described in 1934 by Jean-Frédéric Joliot and Marie Curie, French scientists. Their discovery has been used to create hundreds of radioactive atoms. A distinction is often made between this "artificial" radioactivity and the "natural" radioactivity of elements found in the Earth's crust, but there is no practical difference between these two manifestations of radioactivity. Radioactive nuclides that are produced in the laboratory can have atomic numbers as high as 101; any nuclide with an atomic number over 92 is called a transuranic element. Many laboratory-made radioactive nuclides have atomic numbers that range between 60 and 65; most of them emit alpha particles. (*See* ATOM; RADIATION DETECTOR; RADIATION, NATURAL.)

First see ISOTOPES

Radiochemistry

Next see MEDICAL DIAGNOSTICS

The chemical study and application of radioactive isotopes and their compounds.

Radionuclide, or nuclear, scans are imaging processes that use small amounts of radioactive "tracers" known as radioisotopes. A dye containing these materials is injected in or swallowed by a patient. Special instruments are used to detect the presence of these chemicals as they are distributed throughout the body, enabling a physician to distinguish between normal and abnormal tissues and to diagnose injuries undetectable by conventional x-rays. The imaging process and its interpretation fall under the category of medicine known as radiology, or its subspecialty, nuclear medicine.

There are many types of scans that involve radionuclides. All make use of a specific radiopharmaceutical and a gamma camera is used to record pictures of the radiation pattern within the body. Bone scans involve the use of a radiopharmaceutical known as technetium-99m disphosphate. A "hot spot" represents an accumulation of the chemical and indicates the presence of an abnormality. Liver and lung scans operate in much the same way.

The radioactive iodine uptake (RAIU) test determines whether thyroid function is normal. The patient ingests a solution containing radioactive iodine, and because iodine is an element that is normally used by the thyroid gland, the solution will be "taken up" readily.

Below, William Roentgen and one of the first radiograms ever produced—of his wife's hand (inset).

Above, Marie Curie working in her lab, and her husband Pierre Curie (inset).

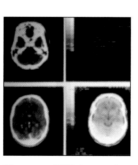

Above, a CAT (computerized axial tomography) scan shows doctors different "slices" of the brain.

Gallium screening uses the radiopharmaceutical gallium-67, which collects at sites of infection or inflammation and in tumors.

Cardiology also makes use of radiochemistry. Thallium imaging is used to locate areas of heart damage or regions that do not get sufficient blood flow. Radionuclide angiography shows how well the heart is functioning. Blood is removed from the body and mixed with the radiopharmaceutical to allow the cells to ab-sorb the chemical. The cells are then injected back into the body and their progress is followed.

First see X-RAY

Radiology

Next see MEDICAL DIAGNOSTICS

The medical specialty that obtains information about the interior of the body without breaking through the skin, but by using various radiations.

Traditionally, radiology relied almost entirely on x-rays, but radiologists now use a variety of technologies, including ultrasound, magnetic resonance imaging (MRI), and radionuclide scanning. Radiologic techniques can be used to guide needles and catheters into different parts of the body for treatment. This is done by a subspecialty called interventional radiology.

X-ray technology is based on electromagnetic radiation of extremely short wavelength, discovered by Wilhelm Roentgen in 1896. X-rays can be used to obtain images of bones, organs, and other tissues. Low doses of x-rays are passed through the body, and the images (or shadows) that result are visualized on film or on a fluorescent screen. X-rays must be used with care, because they can damage healthy tissue. But because they do the most damage to cells that are dividing rapidly, they can be used to treat cancerous tissue.

Medical x-rays are produced by bombarding a tungsten target with electrons. The tube that produces the x-rays is surrounded by a lead casing, which permits the rays to travel only in a carefully controlled beam. The patient is positioned to provide the clearest view of the body part that is being examined. If a hollow or fluid-filled part of the body is being examined, a special contrast medium can be injected to improve the image that is obtained. When film is being used, it is positioned in a cassette that is placed in line with the beam. The shortest possible exposure time is used, sometimes only a fraction of a second. The x-ray film is then developed and is analyzed by the radiologist.

A form of x-ray examination called tomography can produce a cross-sectional image, or slice of an organ or other body part. Tomography can be combined with computer processing to get extremely detailed images.

Other Techniques. Magnetic resonance imaging (MRI) is a technique in which the patient is exposed to short bursts of a powerful magnetic field. This magnetic field causes the hydrogen atoms inside the body to line up parallel to each other—normally, they point in all directions. A pulse of radio waves is administered to knock the hydrogen atoms out of alignment and the magnetic field is applied again. The hydrogen atoms produce a detectable radio signal as they go back into alignment. This signal is detected by magnetic coils in the MRI detector, and they are processed by computer to produce an image based on the strength of the signals generated by different body tissues. MRI is particularly useful in studies of the brain and the spinal cord and is also applied to studies of the heart and major blood vessels, since it can give images of blood flow, soft tissues, and joints such as the knee.

Above, proton beam therapy is used to selectively target tumors in the brain's tissue.

Further Reading
Aiver, Ness, *All You Really Need to Know About MRI Physics* (1996); Gurley, Laverne T., *Introduction to Radiologic Technology* (1996); Thomas, A.M. (Ed.), *The Invisible Light: 100 Years of Medical Radiology* (1995).

Further developments in the field are discussed in MEDICAL DIAGNOSTICS; MICROWAVE; X-RAY. *Advanced subjects are developed in* CT AND PET SCANS; MAMMOGRAPHY; NUCLEAR MAGNETIC RESONANCE (NMR). *Additional relevant information is contained in articles on* AMNIOCENTESIS; CANCER; RADIOCHEMISTRY; ULTRASONICS.

First see RADIOACTIVITY

Radon

Next see AIR POLLUTION

A radioactive gaseous element, the atomic number of which is 86 and atomic weight of which is 222.

Radon is classified as an inert gas because it does not take part in chemical reactions with atoms of other elements. Radon and two isotopes are formed when radium is exposed to air. Radon was discovered in 1900 by F. E. Dorn, who studied the radioactive properties of radium bromide. Another physicist, André Debierne, isolated one of the isotopes, actinon, in 1903.

Medical Applications. Radon-222 has medical uses, because it emits both beta rays and gamma rays. One use of radon is to implant it in the body in capsules that are used to destroy rotted body tissue, tissue that has been injured by radiation, and some forms of cancer.

Radon is being replaced in medicine by other radioactive elements, such as cobalt-60 and cesium-137, but radon is still useful in scientific research. Since it is inert and does not react with other elements, radon moves freely through a variety of tissues. It can thus be used as a tracer in biological research of tissue absorption of chemicals and in studies of gas flow.

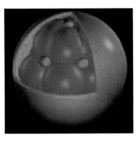

Above, a computer model of the radon molecule; protons (red) and neutrons (purple) can be seen in the nucleus.

First see LIGHT

Raman Effect

Next see DIFFRACTION

The Raman effect, discovered by the Indian physicist C. V. Raman in 1918, occurs when light of a single frequency is beamed through a transparent substance. The result is a shift in wavelength, so that the light is scattered in several frequencies, not just the frequency of the original beam. The most intense part of the scattered light is of the same frequency as the original beam, but a significant portion experiences a change in frequency. The scattered, low-intensity "Raman light" is the result of an exchange of energy between the photons of light from the original source and the molecules of the substance through which it passes. Some photons absorb energy from the molecules of the substance and emerge with a higher frequency; some give up energy in the molecular collision and emerge with a lower frequency.

Uses. The Raman effect can be used to study the structure of the molecules of the material through which the light is beamed. If that molecule consists of N atoms, the number of vibrational modes of motion it has when struck with light is $3N - 6$ for a three-dimensional molecule, $3N - 5$ for a linear molecule. Some of the new beams will have a change in electric moment; they can be observed in infrared frequencies. Others will remain in visible light frequencies. Thus, a full range of spectroscopic studies will provide a complete picture of the reflecting molecules. Raman was awarded the Nobel Prize in 1930 for his discovery.

First see DNA

Recombinant DNA

Next see GENETIC ENGINEERING

A hybrid DNA that is produced by joining pieces of DNA from different sources.

Recombinant DNA was developed in 1973 as a method of snipping a fragment of DNA from one genome—the complete genetic material of an organism—and splicing it into (recombining it with) another genome. The fragments of DNA are cut out of the first genome by using restriction enzymes, which are proteins that bind to and cut DNA at specific sites.

Identifying the location of the sequence to be recombined depends in large part on having a physical map of the genome; a physical map consists of a linear array of DNA fragments that span the full length of the chromosome containing the desired stretch of DNA. Once the stretch to be reproduced is identified, the restriction enzymes that will cut at the desired site are used to obtain the desired fragments. These fragments can then be separated from the rest of the chromosome by a method called pulsed-field gel electrophoresis, which uses alternating electric fields to cause the fragments to move through the gel to a site where they can be collected. This method allows the separation of DNA fragments containing as few as 10 and as many as 10 million base pairs. Once they are separated, the fragments can be inserted into genetic elements such as plasmids, which are entities that contain DNA but exist independently of the chromosomes and are found in bacteria and other organisms. As the plasmids reproduce themselves, the isolated fragments of DNA are also reproduced. It is thus possible to build up a library of genetic material from any number of sources, ranging from human cells to viruses that cause cancer.

Ethical Concerns. The possible dangers of reproducing, or cloning, such genetic material were recognized quickly. A scientific conference was held in 1975 at the Asilomar Conference Center in Monterey, California. The recommendations made at that conference led to the formation of a Recombinant DNA Advisory Committee within the National Institutes of Health to administer a set of government regulatory guidelines concerning the cloning of cancer viruses. Similar bodies have been created in Europe.

Recombinant DNA technology is now widely used in medicine and industry. The first drug produced by recombinant methods to gain government approval for general use was insulin, which until then was obtained from the pancreases of pigs and cows. Human growth hormone, which until then had to be isolated from cadavers, also won approval. Recombinant DNA technology is used not only for such lifesaving purposes but also for such applications as the improvement of a detergent enzyme and genetically engineering food, and its uses continue to expand.

Related areas to be considered are CLONING; DNA; GENE; KARYOTYPING. *Advanced subjects are developed in* DNA SEQUENCING; GENETIC CODE; GENETIC ENGINEERING. *Relevant information is contained in* BACTERIAL GENETICS; GENE THERAPY; GENOME, HUMAN; POLYMERASE CHAIN REACTION (PCR); VIRAL GENETICS.

First see ACOUSTICS

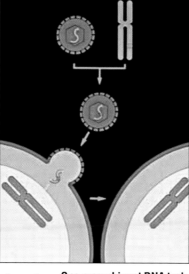

One recombinant DNA technique involves using a restriction enzyme to cut a specific piece of DNA from a chromosome. It is then "re-combined" with bacterial DNA and inserted into a plasmid, which serves as the transport vector.

Further Reading
Emery, A.E.H., *An Introduction to Recombinant DNA in Medicine* (1995); Read, A. P., *Human Molecular Genetics* (1997); Watson, J. D., *Recombinant DNA* (1992).

Recording Technology

Next see CD-ROM

The recording of sounds and images for reproduction at a later time has been an important technology throughout human history, from the prehistoric cave drawings in France to the cameras and sound equipment of the digital age.

Sound Recording. The story of sound recording technology involves the development first of analog methods and more recently of digital methods of recording and reproducing sound. The beginnings can be traced to 1876, when Alexander Graham Bell and Thomas Edison were simultaneously working on mechanical methods for reproducing speech and music. Bell's study of the deaf had led him early on to the idea of the vibrating diaphragm as the closest analogy to the human ear. He employed that form for the earpiece of his telephone, but was unable to produce a diaphragm microphone and instead used an electrode floating over a bowl of mercury to produce the necessary changes in current. Edison, however, was able to provide a working microphone not only for the telephone but also for his own invention, the phonograph. The microphone caused vibrations in an etching tool, which incised the appropriate waveforms on the surface of a wax cylinder (later, a disc became the standard form); when a needle traversed the waveforms, its vibrations caused the diaphragm to reproduce the original sound.

This process remained little changed for a century, although electrification allowed the vibrations of the phonograph needle to be electrically amplified and played back through much larger diaphragm speakers. An additional analog method of capturing sound was invented in the 1940s as a complement to the phonograph. Instead of incising the waveforms on a vinyl disk, it became possible to capture them on magnetized tape, which could then be played back through the same sensors used for recording. These tape recordings, which could be packaged on open reels or in cassettes, had two advantages. They could be erased and recorded many times without mechanical wear; and since they were not read by mechanical means, their signal-to-noise ratio was much higher.

Since the 1980s, it has become possible to transform the analog signals captured on magnetic tape into digital form, achieving greater dynamic range while reducing background noise even further. At first, only recording was digitized, but with the development of compact discs, sound can also be digitally reproduced.

Image Recording. The history of image recording technology goes back 10,000 years, when early humans took naturally occurring pigments from earth, mixed them with animal fats or the water and oils present in natural perspiration, and created images on cave walls. However, these images were not very accurate reproductions of visual perceptions, nor did image-recording gain dramatically in subsequent millennia, until the invention of the camera obscura, or "dark chamber," during the Renaissance. If one pierces the wall of a small chamber, on the wall opposite the pinhole will be projected an inverted picture of the scene outside.

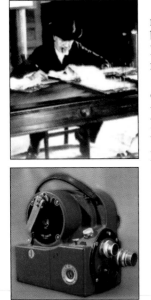

Top, Thomas Alva Edison works at his desk. He was a pioneer in sound recording technology. Above, the RCA Victor sound camera, introduced in 1935, was the world's first 16-mm sound-on-film camera.

Thus half the challenge—capturing the light reflected off exterior objects inside a "black box"—had been met; the other half of the challenge—fixing that image permanently, and thus making it portable—remained unsolved until 1839, when two different processes were developed almost simultaneously. The more exciting was the daguerreotype, developed by J. N. Niépce and L. J. M. Daguerre. When exposed to the fumes of potassium iodide, silver on a copper plate was transformed into silver iodide, a chemical compound sensitive to light. After exposure, the silver that had received light rays combined with mercury fumes to create a white amalgam, representing illuminated areas of the picture; silver that had not received light remained dark, representing the shadowed areas. This process produced beautiful, accurate daguerreotypes, but they could not be reproduced.

The other photographic invention was the calotype, developed by W. H. F. Talbot, which also relied on the effect of sunlight on silver iodide. Talbot, however, developed his images with gallo-nitrate of silver, which produced dark areas where the image was light, and light areas where the original was in shadow—a negative. This process was capable of producing multiple images, even manipulated images. By 1884, George Eastman had developed a way to layer the reactive emulsion on a long strip of celluloid, which could be backed with paper and inserted as a roll into a small cube, with an inexpensive glass lens on the opposite face and a shutter mechanism in between: the box camera (called a "Kodak" because the word could be pronounced in every known language) was introduced in 1888.

Television. Around 1923, a Russian émigré to America, named Vladimir Zworykin, succeeded in developing a third way to fix the image captured through a lens. Using an array of tiny photovoltaic cells, which would emit a current proportional to their exposure to light, he created the iconoscope, or television camera. By combining these bits of information into a single signal and projecting it onto an equivalent screen of phosphorescent dots, he created the kinescope, or picture tube.

Holography. The fourth, and most recent, method of capturing an image, is holography. A laser beam is split in two, and while one beam bounces incoherently off the subject, the other returns to the receiver still coherent. The result is a pattern of interference fringes between the two beams, which captures all significant information about the subject.

Further Reading
Huber, David Miles, *Modern Recording Techniques* (1995); Luther, Arch C., *Video Recording Technology* (1999); Watkinson, John, *An Introduction to Digital Audio* (1994).

Special topics in this area are found in ACOUSTICS; MAGNETISM; SOUND. *Other aspects of the topic are discussed in* CD-ROM; ELECTRICITY AND ELECTRICAL ENGINEERING; RADIO AND TELEVISION BROADCASTING. *More information on particular aspects is contained in* FIBER OPTICS; FREQUENCY MODULATION; HOLOGRAPHY; TELECOMMUNICATIONS.

First see STAR

Red Giant (Star)

Next see HERTZSPRUNG-RUSSELL DIAGRAM

A star in the later stages of stellar evolution.

A star of medium size, such as Earth's sun, burns hydrogen in its early years, fusing the nuclei of this most abundant element to form helium and creating the energy that makes the star shine. This fusion process usually takes place in the core of the star; temperatures in the outer layers are generally too low to allow fusion to occur. After eons, the hydrogen in the core of the star is converted completely to helium.

As hydrogen burning comes to an end, the pressures and temperatures in the core decrease, because there is not enough gas and radiation pressure to keep the core in its former state of equilibrium. The pull of gravity now becomes greater than the push of pressure, and the core contracts. This heats not only the core but the layer above the core. The hydrogen in that layer ignites, providing the fuel for another period of fusion. As the hydrogen in this layer burns, the radiation it creates puffs up the star's outermost layers, so that it increases greatly in size. The expansion of the gases in the star's outer layer has a temperature-reducing effect, so that the cool stellar atmosphere shines with a red or orange color. The star is now a red giant.

Structure. A cross section through a red giant shows that it has a dense center that is tenuous and turbulent. The star is constantly expelling its contents into space. There is a furious outpouring of energy from the shell that is still burning hydrogen, and so the outermost part of the red giant remains in seething convective motion. Most of the volume of the star consists of this convective envelope. A typical red giant

Above, the Egg Nebula is located 3,000 light-years from the Earth. A pair of "searchlight" beams —ejected stellar matter from a dying star—criss-crossed by bright arcs is captured by NASA cameras.

has a diameter 100 times greater than that of our sun, with only half its mass. Eventually, the surface temperature of the red giant will increase as fusion activity creates carbon and oxygen from helium. The surface temperature of the star increases, so that its color becomes yellow or white and it ceases to be a red giant.

Spectroscopic observations show that red giants have strong winds that can cause them to vent as much as 50 percent of their total mass into space. One prominent red giant, Arcturus, in the constellation Boötes, is shedding matter at a rate that will cause it to lose a mass equal to that of our sun in 100 million years, a small fraction of the time that the average star spends in the red giant stage. The most rapid example of mass loss is the red giant Zeta Ophiura, which is losing the equivalent of 5 million solar masses every year. Our sun eventually will become a red giant, but not in the immediate future. Astronomers estimate that it will reach that stage of evolution 5 billion years from now. (*See* SUN.)

First see CHEMICAL REACTION

Redox Reaction

Next see OXIDIZING AGENT

The combination of oxidation and reduction—the loss and gain of electrons, respectively. The two actions must always occur together, with one atom or compound losing electrons that the other gains.

In every redox reaction, the oxidizing agent acts as an electron acceptor, becoming reduced and undergoing a decrease in its own oxidation number. The reducing agent acts as an electron donor, becoming oxidized and undergoing an increase in its oxidation number. The oxidation states verify that an electron "transfer" from one element to another has occurred.

Because oxygen is such an electronegative element (strongly attracts electrons), an atom that combines with it will become "oxidized"— it will lose electrons to the oxygen atom. The oxygen itself becomes reduced. It is important to note, however, that not all redox reactions involve, or need to include, oxygen; all that is necessary is for one substance to gain electrons and the other to lose them. (*See* COMBUSTION.)

Redox occurs every time there is an electron transfer between reactants. Redox reactions are usually exothermic, meaning energy is released. Batteries make use of redox reactions to convert chemical energy to electricity. Oxidation occurs at one electrode and reduction at the other, causing a flow of electrons. Redox reactions are also involved in biological processes such as cellular respiration, the means by which cells obtain energy, and photosynthesis, the production of glucose. (*See* METABOLIC PATHWAYS.)

First see MIRROR

Reflection, Refraction

Next see DIFFRACTION

Reflection is the turning back of all or part of a beam of particles or waves at the boundary between two media. Refraction is the change of direction of a wave when it passes obliquely from one medium to another medium in which its speed of propagation is different.

Reflection occurs when any wave motion—of light, of sound, of water—encounters the interface between one medium and another. For example, when a beam of light traveling through air strikes a polished surface, such as a mirror or a polished metal surface, all or most of it will be reflected. If it strikes a smooth, transparent surface such as a pane of glass, only a small fraction of it will be reflected. The directions of the incoming and reflected beams are usually measured from the normal of the reflecting surface—that is, from the right angle to that surface. The laws of reflection state that the incident ray, the reflecting ray, and the normal to the reflecting surface all lie in the same plane, and that the angle at which the beam strikes the surface equals the angle at which it is reflected.

The portion of the light that is reflected from a surface is a function of, among other factors, the smoothness of the surface, the angle of incidence of the light, and the polarization of the light. When light strikes a rough surface, the reflection will be scattered, in a process called diffuse reflectance. A smooth surface gives a better reflection, called specular reflectance.

Refraction. In refraction, the change in direction of a wave occurs because that wave travels at different speeds in the two media. For example, the speed of light in glass is about one-third slower than in air, and the speed of light in water is one-quarter less. The change in speed that occurs in such a case is specified by the refractive index, which is the ratio of the speed of light in the two media. The refractive index for light is about 1.33 for water, 1.5 for air, and 1.0003 for light passing from a vacuum into air.

If a beam of light strikes a transparent surface at an oblique angle, the beam will be bent sharply. Snell's law, stated in 1621, relates the angle of incidence, i, the normal to the surface, r, and the refractive index of the medium, n, in the formula $n = \sin i / \sin r$. When light travels slower in a medium than in air, n is greater than 1 and r is less than 1, meaning that the light ray is bent toward the normal.

Background material can be found in LENS; LIGHT; MIRROR; WAVE. *Further developments in the field are discussed in* INTERFERENCE; OPTICS; POLARIZED LIGHT. *Special topics in this area are found in* ELECTROMAGNETIC WAVES; FIBER OPTICS; SONAR.

Above, mirrors used in the gamma ray observatory are designed to exacting specifications in order to direct reflected gamma rays precisely at the detector.

First see NEURON

Reflex

Next see INSTINCT

A simple, specific, unlearned response to a stimulus.

Among invertebrates, reflexes make up a good portion of all behavior, alowing animals to pull away from danger and reach toward food, for instance. In higher animals, where learned behavior dominates, reflexes still play an important role; they can pull the body away from pain before it has registered in the brain; they coordinate complex actions such as walking; and they form the basic pathways of the autonomic system, the unconscious nervous system that ennervates the heart, blood vessels, respiratory, digestive, reproductive, and excretory systems.

Reflexes vary in complexity. The simplest common reflex pathway is the kind that causes a coelenterate such as the hydra to pull back a tentacle. For this, only two cells are required. One neuron acts as both sensory receptor and conductor of information. The other cell is the effector cell, which stimulates the motion of the tentacle. The reflex has only one input, one pathway, no processing, and no central control. Slightly more complex pathways involve a receptor cell and a separate conductor cell.

In vertebrates, even the simplest reflex arcs involve the central nervous system, specifically the spinal cord. One example is the familiar withdrawal reflex, in which a person jerks a hand back from a flame. Sensory neurons run from the hand to the spinal cord. Their cell bodies are in a spinal ganglion just outside the spinal cord. The axons enter the cord and synapse with motor neurons. The motor neurons' axons run to the muscles. If the stimulus is strong, it may not only stimulate the flexor muscles to pull the arm up but can also inhibit the extensor muscles that would push it down.

The knee-jerk reflex commonly tested by doctors is a stretch reflex that is part of the system for maintaining equilibrium. When the doctor uses a rubber hammer to tap the patient's patellar tendon below the kneecap, stretch receptors register this as added weight and the quadriceps muscle stretches to compensate. This information is sent to the spinal cord, where it is conveyed both to the brain and to motor neurons. The motor neurons tighten the muscles—the extensors that pull the leg up—to adjust for the perceived added weight.

Further Reading
Garcia, George E., *Handbook of Refraction* (1989); Korsch, Dietrich, *Reflective Optics* (1991); Smith, A. Mark, *Descartes' Theory of Light and Refraction: A Discourse on Method* (1987).

The foundations of the subject are discussed in BRAIN; CONDITIONING; INSTINCT; NERVOUS SYSTEM. *More details can be found in* ADAPTATION; RETICULAR ACTIVATING SYSTEM (RAS); SEXUAL STRATEGIES. *Advanced subjects are developed in* AGGRESSION AND TERRITORIALITY; ENDOCRINE SYSTEM; PHEROMONES; PREDATION.

First see HEAT

Refrigeration

Next see CRYOGENICS

The science of cooling a substance or area and keeping it at a temperature below that of the surrounding atmosphere or environment.

To reduce the temperature of a substance or area, heat must be removed from it and transferred elsewhere. This heat removal is usually achieved by causing a change of phase in the material used as the refrigerant. The most recognizable kind of phase change is the melting of ice, which requires the removal of heat from the atmosphere or medium surrounding the ice. The limit on this method is the melting point of ice.

The Refrigeration Cycle. Mechanical refrigeration systems usually change a liquid into a gas, then change it back to a liquid. One example of such a system is the compression refrigeration cycle, which uses an evaporator, a compressor, an expansion valve and a condenser. In this kind of refrigerator, the substance used as the refrigerant, a volatile liquid, is put into an evaporator, where it boils, thus extracting heat from the refrigerator. The refrigerant, now a gas, goes into a compressor, where its temperature and pressure are raised. The compressed refrigerant then goes into a condenser, where its heat is dispersed to the exterior surroundings. The refrigerant now is a liquid. It goes into a storage vessel and then to an expansion valve, where it expands to become a gas and begin the cycle again. The refrigerants most often used in such a system are ammonia, sulfur dioxide, or a member of the chemical family called haloalkanes.

A refrigerator based on the vapor-absorption cycle has no moving parts. Its energy is supplied in the form of heat, by either a gas burner or an electric heater. The refrigerant, most often ammonia, is first liberated from a water solution and moved through the evaporator into a separator, where heat separates the ammonia from the water. The ammonia vapor then goes into a condenser, where it cools and becomes liquid, giving off its latent heat. The liquid ammonia is mixed with hydrogen gas, which carries it through the evaporator; evaporation of the ammonia absorbs heat. The hydrogen and ammonia then enter the absorber, where the ammonia dissolves in water to begin the cycle again. (*See* CARNOT CYCLE.)

Other systems can be used for different purposes. For example, refrigeration on a small scale can use the Peltier effect, the change in temperature that occurs when an electric current passes through the junction of two different metals or semiconductors. The direction of the current determines whether the temperature is raised or lowered. (*See* CRYOGENICS.)

First see CELL CYCLE

Regeneration

Next see DNA REPLICATION

The process in which any part that has been severed from a body grows back to its original form.

An example of regeneration with which all beach-goers are familiar is the starfish. When a starfish loses an arm, not only does the animal grow a new arm, but the severed limb can actually grow a new body. However, in order to regenerate, the limb must be connected to at least a piece of the central body portion.

Many years ago, pearl divers in the Pacific Ocean, determined to reduce the number of starfish that were depleting their prized oyster beds, embarked on a program whereby every time a diver encountered a starfish, he cut it into pieces and threw the pieces back into the water. After some time, it became clear that the starfish population, instead of being reduced, was actually increasing.

Regeneration can be viewed as a type of asexual reproduction, akin to vegetative propagation, the process in which a plant grows from a cutting. Something about the starfish nervous system, possibly a neurotransmitter or chemical messenger, enables the regeneration to take place. The process is still not completely understood and the phenomenon is being studied for possible applications in treating human trauma victims.

First see CARTOGRAPHY AND SURVEYING

Remote Sensing

Next see PHOTOGRAPHY, CHEMISTRY OF

The gathering and recording of information about Earth's surface, using techniques that do not require actual contact with the object or the area that is being observed.

The techniques of remote sensing include aerial photography, multispectral imagery, and radar. Remote sensing is generally carried out from aircraft and from satellites orbiting Earth.

One major field of remote sensing is photogrammetry, the application of photographic principles to the science of cartography, or mapmaking. Photogrammetry generally consists of taking pictures of a special area of the surface of the Earth. These photographs are used to form an overall picture of a large area or to make a map of that area.

The images used in photogrammetry most often are taken from aircraft. To perform aerial photographs, the aircraft is kept as close as possible to a predetermined altitude while a series of exposures are taken. When a very large area is to be mapped, several photograph-taking flights are made in opposite directions. Photographs of adjacent areas must overlap to be suitable for mapmaking.

Other forms of remote sensing rely on electronic systems. These methods include radar and loran. A radar system consists of a combined transmitter and receiver with a rotating antenna and a display console that indicates the distance and direction of any object that reflects the transmitted radio waves back to the receiver. Radar can also be used for the remote sensing of meteorological events and features, such as precipitation and clouds.

A loran system combines transmitting equipment on the ground with special receivers on a seagoing vessel that measure the differences in the times at which the transmitted signals are received, thus allowing ships to locate their positions on the basis of these time differences. The most recent form of remote sensing is provided by signals that are transmitted from satellites orbiting Earth. Some of these signals can be used to provide continuous, all-weather information that is readily available to any point on Earth with the necessary equipment. Photographs taken by orbiting satellites have provided overall maps of the Earth and of other bodies in the solar system, including the moon and the planet Mars.

Multispectral imaging, as the name implies, uses electronic transmissions at a variety of frequencies to study an area or object. Infrared imaging, or photography, came into existence as early as 1880. Some modern infrared imaging systems use films that are sensitive to a very narrow range of wavelengths. These generally are applied to such purposes as aerial photography.

The Hubble Space Telescope (HST), above, is a satellite put into Earth orbit by NASA to view distant regions of the universe more accurately.

CONTROVERSIES

Eye in the Sky

The ultimate tool of remote sensing is the reconnaissance, or spy, satellite. The first American spy satellites were launched in 1960, collecting pictures (the Corona series) or radar intelligence (the GRAB series) and relaying the results to Earth-bound scientists. In 1962, the Russians sent up a succession of converted Vostok capsules, performing equivalent functions. Modern reconnaissance satellites take two forms: photo intelligence and signals intelligence. The advanced KH-11 satellite, with its 100-inch mirror, is like a Hubble telescope aimed at Earth; although it cannot really read a license plate, it could distinguish one falling off its vehicle.

Elementary aspects of this subject are covered in MICROSCOPY; RADIO ASTRONOMY; TELESCOPE. *More information on particular aspects is contained in* CARTOGRAPHY AND SURVEYING; INFRARED AND ULTRAVIOLET ASTRONOMY; RADAR. *Additional relevant information is contained in* NEUTRINO ASTRONOMY; SONAR; X-RAY AND GAMMA RAY ASTRONOMY.

Further Reading
Asrar, Ghassem (Ed.), *Theory and Applications of Optical Remote Sensing* (1989); Danson, F. Mark, et al. (Eds.), *Advances in Environmental Remote Sensing* (1995).

First see REPRODUCTIVE SYSTEMS

Reproductive Strategies

Next see ETHOLOGY

The animal world demontrates a dizzying variety of mating systems and rituals; some moths spend 12 hours in a single act of copulation, presumably to prevent a second mating that might displace the sperm. When male lions take over a pride, their pheromones can cause miscarriage in pregnant females, leaving them ready to bear the young of the new males sooner. Many male insects offer a gift of food to the female, to be consumed during mating. Among praying mantises, the male himself is the sacrifice; mating is completed by the eating of his head. In leks—small territories each occupied by a single male during mating season—one male gets most of the chances to reproduce; so-called satellite males often lurk nearby to waylay and mate with females who are on their way to the central male. In some species, these lurkers have even evolved to look different from other males. In at least one fish species, all the young are born female; the oldest female changes sex when the male of the group dies.

Current theory is that each sex's level of parental investment in its young influences the mating strategy of the species. In most mammals, the female invests much more heavily, gestating the fetus, lactating, and protecting the newborn. The female, therefore, has a greater interest in seeing that each mating is likely to result in successful offspring. As a result, she tends to choose her mate—as Darwin first observed in 1871—and males compete to be chosen. They may vie with each other through fighting or ritualized combat, or they may try to win the favor of females directly. In any case, the contest is thought to give rise to sexual dimorphism, physical disparity between male and female, as males evolve larger size, elaborate plumage, manes, or horns. Many such showy elements seem to have no survival value beyond increasing the male's attractiveness to the female. The male, in this scenario, invests and risks little in mating. But the more he mates, the better his chances of passing on his genes. This leads to the form of polygamy called polygyny, in which one male mates with several females, usually in an ongoing association.

Most mammal species are polygynous, although some are monogamous, meaning they breed and remain together as a pair to raise their offspring, although each may occasionally try to mate outside the pair bond.

Bird Behavior. Monogamy is the rule among birds, where it is seen in 90 percent of species. The parental investment of male and female is more nearly equal, since in most cases, the male is as well equipped as the female to incubate and feed the young. In fact, feeding the young adequately usually requires both parents. Females are believed to choose their mates largely on the basis on their territories—bigger territories promise more abundant food for future offspring.

Further Reading
Bagemihl, Bruce, *Biological Exuberance: Animal Homosexuality and Natural Diversity* (1999)' Eberhard, William G., *Female Control: Sexual Selection by Cryptic Female Choice* (Monographs in Behavior and Ecology) (1996); Steen, Edwin B., *Human Sex and Sexuality* (1988).

Background material can be found in ETHOLOGY; REPRODUCTIVE SYSTEMS; SEX, BIOLOGY OF. *More details can be found in* INSTINCT; PHEROMONES; POPULATION ECOLOGY. *Elementary aspects of this subject are covered in* ADAPTATION; COMMUNICATION IN NATURE; COMPETITION AND ALTRUISM; NATURAL SELECTION.

First see SEX, BIOLOGY OF

Reproductive Systems

Next see REPRODUCTIVE STRATEGIES

Systems that allow an organism to produce other organisms similar to itself.

Reproduction is one element that distinguishes living from nonliving things. It involves more than just sex or procreation, however. It is a stab at immortality, an attempt to ensure that part of us lives on after we are gone. That part is our genetic material, the complex chemical known as DNA that determines who and what we are. Genes are passed from one generation to the next; in organisms with sexual reproduction, they are shuffled and reshuffled throughout the general population.

Two Types. The two basic forms of reproduction are asexual and sexual. Asexual reproduction requires only one parent, whereas sexual reproduction requires two. In the absence of any mutations, all of the offspring formed by asexual reproduction are identical to each other and to their parent. With sexual reproduction, there is genetic variation among the offspring because each one receives half its genes from one parent and half from the other.

Asexual Reproduction. The five basic methods of asexual reproduction are binary fission, budding, spores, vegetative propagation, and regeneration.

Binary fission, literally "to split in half," is how unicellular organisms such as bacteria and amoebas reproduce. Each parent cell produces two identical "daughter" cells. In addition, bacteria undergo a process that can be categorized as sexual reproduction, as it involves genetic recombination among different cells. Bacterial genes are found along a single round chromosome. In addition to this, there are smaller rings of DNA known as plasmids. Plasmids are easily replicated and can be transferred from one bacterium to another. In this way, specific traits can be spread among a population.

Paramecia, also unicellular, undergo a form of sexual reproduction known as conjugation.

Top, the hydra reproduces asexually, by budding a replica of itself on its stem. Above, the seahorse, is unusual in that the male of the species carries his offspring in a pouch until they are able to swim on their own.

Two paramecia can "hook up" at a structure known as the oral groove. Once attached, a "bridge" forms between their nuclei and allows for the exchange of genetic material. Separated, the two organisms now display new genes, although no new individuals have been formed.

Budding is found in organisms such as yeast and other fungi, as well as in primitive animals like the hydra. Unequal cell division occurs in a specific area of the organism. The smaller cells "pinch off" to form an independent creature. Spores are similar to seeds, except that they are produced asexually. Many types of fungus, such as molds, reproduce via spores, as do plants such as ferns.

Vegetative propagation refers to the ability of a plant cutting to sprout roots and develop into a new plant on its own. It is in some ways similar to regeneration, a phenomenon seen in starfish. If a starfish loses an arm, it has the ability to regrow the missing limb. Even more amazing, however, is the ability of the severed limb to regrow a new body.

An unconventional form of asexual reproduction is cloning. Cloning refers to the stimulation of a somite, an ordinary body cell, to develop into a new organism. The cell thus used can be a fetal or nonspecialized cell, or an "adult" cell that is already specialized. To date, a variety of animals have been cloned in the lab, including mammals, although the method is still far from perfected.

Sexual Reproduction. Gametes, or sex cells, are the agents of sexual reproduction. Males produce sperm and females produce eggs, or ova. The sperm and egg combine to form a zygote, a fertilized egg, which develops into the new organism. Each parent contributes equally to the genetic content of the zygote. However, the majority of the cellular contents come from the egg, as it is many times the size of the sperm. An unfertilized egg cell can, under certain circumstances, develop into a new organism, a process called parthenogenesis.

Plant Reproduction. Some organisms have the ability to reproduce both sexually and asexually. Lower plants, such as moss and ferns, exhibit what is called "alternation of generations" in which one generation reproduces sexually, the next asexually. The sexual generation is called the gametophyte generation (from "gamete"). Sperm are produced in a structure known as the antheridium and swim through a thin film of moisture to fertilize the eggs located in the archegonium. The zygote grows up to be the sporophyte generation, which, true to its name, produces spores. Each spore in turn develops into another gametophyte generation.

Flowers are the sex organs in higher plants. The female portion is known as the pistil or carpal, and the male portion, which produces pollen, is the anther. Reproduction involves what is known as double fertilization. Pollination is the transfer of pollen from the anther to the pistil. A single pollen grain contains two nuclei, a sperm nucleus and a tube nucleus. The tube nucleus grows a tunnel down the length of the pistil until it reaches the ovary, where the egg cells are found. The sperm nucleus fertilizes the egg to form a zygote. The tube nucleus in turn fertilizes a structure called the embryo sac to form an endosperm. The endosperm is the stored food for the developing plant inside the seed.

Animal Reproduction. In animals, sexual reproduction can be divided into two parts: fertilization and development. Both can occur either internally, inside the female's body, or externally.

The basic equipment for reproduction for males includes an organ where sperm are produced and a method for transferring the sperm to the eggs. Sperm are produced in the testes and, depending upon the species, are transferred through a variety of adaptive structures, such as a cloaca in amphibians and birds and a penis in reptiles and mammals. Females produce eggs in ovaries. In some animals, the ovaries are distinct from the oviducts, the tubes through which the eggs journey on their way to encounter the sperm (either internally or externally). Mammals further require a uterus in which the offspring can develop.

Some species of animals are hermaphrodites, meaning that they have both ovaries and testes. These species are not, however, self-fertilizing.

Two Basic Strategies. Reproduction involves a tremendous investment of energy by an organism. The goal is to leave as many offspring as possible. This can be accomplished in one of two ways: either by expending energy in producing large numbers of gametes and offspring, in the hope that at least some will survive to adulthood, or by producing only small numbers of gametes and expending energy in protecting and nurturing them to adulthood.

Most fish lay eggs. Females lay hundreds, if not thousands, of eggs that are then fertilized by the male. A few species bear live offspring in which the eggs are fertilized internally and the female gives birth to the fry. In seahorses, the female deposits her eggs in the male's pouch. He then fertilizes the eggs and protects them until they hatch. Technically, the male is not "pregnant" nor does he give birth, although it certain-

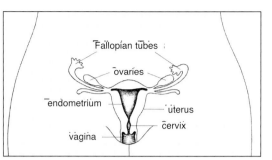

Above, the human female reproductive system.

Below, the human male reproductive system.

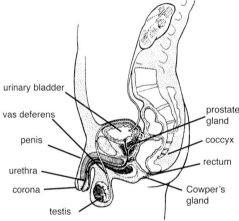

ly appears to be quite close. In other species of fish, sex is a highly flexible characteristic. Some fish can change from female to male, depending on the needs of the population.

Amphibians also undergo external fertilization and development. However, the eggs are fertilized as they are expelled by the female. The eggs are camouflaged for protection, with the coloration matching the surroundings, darker against the bottom of the pond and lighter toward the surface.

Reptiles and birds undergo internal fertilization, with external development. The newly fertilized eggs are encased in a shell before being expelled. In birds, the calcium-based shell is brittle, whereas in reptiles the shell consists of a tough leathery membrane. Birds incubate their eggs in the nest and care for the fledglings afterward. Reptiles cover their nests with dirt or other material to provide warmth and protection. Depending on the species, they may or may not care for the young after they hatch.

Mammalian Reproduction. Mammals can be egg-layers, such as the duck-billed platypus or echidna, or they can be marsupials or placentals. All three undergo internal fertilization. Marsupials, such as kangaroos or opossums, have a very brief gestation period in the uterus. The offspring are born very small, hairless, and blind and complete their development in a maternal pouch. The development is thus partially internal and partially external. As their name implies, placentals utilize a special set of tissues known as the placenta to provide nutrients and oxygen for the organism during the long uterine gestation. All mammals lactate and care for their offspring (to one degree or another) after giving birth.

Related areas to be considered are ASEXUAL REPRODUCTION; REPRODUCTIVE STRATEGIES; SEX, BIOLOGY OF. *Other aspects of the subject are discussed in* ETHOLOGY; MAMMALS; PHEROMONES. *Related material can be found in* AGGRESSION AND TERRITORIALITY; GENETICS; POPULATION ECOLOGY; SEX LINKAGE.

Further Reading
Demoya, Armando, *Sex and Health* (1993); Elgin, Kathleen, *The Human Body: The Female Reproductive System* (1992); Elgin, Kathleen, *The Human Body: The Male Reproductive System* (1993).

First see AMPHIBIANS

Reptiles

Next see JURASSIC PERIOD

One of the five classes of vertebrates. Representatives of this class include lizards, turtles, snakes, and alligators. All reptiles are land animals, with lungs, dry, scaly skin, and claws.

Unlike the more primitive amphibians, reptiles undergo internal fertilization in order to ensure better protection for the gametes. The female then lays her eggs in a nest. Like birds, which are believed to be their descendants, reptiles lay shelled eggs. Unlike birds, the reptile's shell is not brittle but is a tough, leathery membrane. The female reptile does not incubate her eggs directly; she usually covers them with dirt or sand, both to keep the eggs warm and to protect them from predators.

Body Temperature. Reptiles are cold-blooded (ectotherms), meaning they cannot maintain a consistent body temperature. Their temperature is very close to that of their environment. As a result, reptile metabolism increases and slows down depending on the external temperatures. Desert-dwelling reptiles usually huddle in burrows to conserve body heat during the chill of the night. During the heat of the day their temperatures soar, so they are quiescent at this time as well. They emerge to hunt in the cool of the evening or the early morning.

All reptiles have an internal skeleton, consisting of bone and cartilage. The shell of a turtle is simply an outgrowth of bone from the vertebral column. Turtles are among the more primitive reptiles. Their hearts consist of three chambers (like amphibians) with two atria, or collecting chambers, and one ventricle, or pumping chamber. Turtles are the only reptiles that have no teeth, but they do have very powerful jaws.

Lizards and Snakes. Lizards are considered the most versatile of all the reptiles. Their musculature allows them to be extremely agile, and many of them are very quick at running, jumping, and climbing. Some are capable of gliding in the air as well. All lizards have a third eyelid, called a nictitating membrane, and some have transparent eyelids called spectacles. Lizards vary greatly in size; the largest, the Komodo dragon found in Indonesia, can reach nearly ten feet in length. Some lizards are herbivores, and others are carnivorous.

Snakes are considered to be lizards that have lost their limbs over time and have developed other methods of locomotion, using the muscles of the body wall to slither. Some marine snakes give birth to live young instead of laying eggs.

Advanced Reptiles. Crocodiles and alligators represent the most advanced reptiles and are believed to be survivors from the Mesozoic period. They have a four-chambered heart with complete separation between the oxygenated and the deoxygenated blood. Crocodiles can be distinguished from alligators by their slender snouts and an enlarged tooth in the lower jaw that can be seen even when the mouth is closed.

Dinosaurs, extinct for 65 million years, are believed to have shared many characteristics with modern-day reptiles.

Further Reading
Callaway, Jack M., Nicholls, E. L. (Eds.), *Ancient Marine Reptiles* (1997); Frank, Werner, *Boas and Other Non-Venomous Snakes* (1989); King, F. Wayne, *The National Audubon Society Field Guide to North American Reptiles and Amphibians* (1979).

Background material can be found in BIRTH; INVERTEBRATES; JURASSIC PERIOD; MAMMALS; THERMAL REGULATION. *Further details can be found in* AMPHIBIANS; EVOLUTION; FOSSIL. *More information on particular aspects is contained in* DINOSAUR; DINOSAUR, EXTINCTION OF; ETHOLOGY; SPECIATION.

First see LUNGS

Respiratory Systems

Next see METABOLISM

Systems that provide an organism with the ability to take in oxygen and get rid of carbon dioxide.

While respiratory systems differ in nature and complexity, they generally reflect the aquatic origins of animal life. Most involve a moist, protected environment with a large, thin-walled surface area and a dense network of blood vessels. This arrangement allows dissolved gases to diffuse across short distances into the blood for transport throughout the body.

In aquatic creatures, respiration generally occurs through gills or skin, organs directly exposed to the oxygen-bearing water that surrounds them. In land animals, which generally have evolved thick body coverings to prevent fluid loss, the organs are internal—lungs in most vertebrates, tracheas in insects. Amphibian respiration varies, but can employ the skin as well as gills or lungs. (*See* FISH.)

Insect Respiration. The respiratory systems of insects are unusual among land animals in that they involve little or no transport by blood. The system is composed of many small tubes, called tracheas, that branch into tiny tracheoles and carry air directly to each cell, where it diffuses across cell membranes. The air enters the tubes at paired openings called spiracles in the sides of the thorax and abdomen. Some of the tracheas widen into air sacs. Although most of the air movement occurs by diffusion, muscle movement pumps the air sacs, increasing air circulation during periods of activity.

Many small aquatic invertebrates, such as hydra and flatworms, have no special respiratory tissue or organs. With body walls only two or three cells thick, respiratory exchange occurs across the whole body surface.

Most complex aquatic animals—with or without spines—have gills. These range from the footlike flaps called parapodia, seen in many marine worms, to the pair of thin gills hanging in the mantle cavity of clams, to the most familiar version: the finely subdivided filaments on the side of fishes' heads. Fish gills must be extremely efficient at extracting oxygen, since the gas makes up less than half a percent of seawater, compared to 21 percent of air. Most fish pump water across their gills by muscular movement. Some, including mackerel and tuna, lack the musculature and instead force water through by swimming with their mouths open.

Respiration in Land Animals. Lungs are seen in land snails, as well as in some ancient species of fish, most amphibians and all reptiles, birds, and mammals. In birds and mammals, where they are most highly developed, their

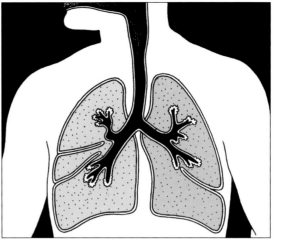

The human lung (left, in purple), has the largest surface area of any organ in the body, equal to that of a full-size tennis court. Below, brochioles are the smallest tubes of the lungs; they bring air to the alveoli sacs, where the oxygen-carbon dioxide exchange takes place.

inner surface is greatly subdivided to boost the area over which gas exchange can occur.

In the human respiratory system, air enters through the nostrils into the nasal cavities, where it is warmed, moistened, and filtered for dust. It moves to the pharynx, through an opening called the glottis and on to the larynx or Adam's apple, the voice box in humans and many other animals. Air continues down the trachea or windpipe, which divides into two bronchi, one leading to each lung. The bronchi branch into bronchioles, which continue to branch until they end in tiny alveoli or air pockets, surrounded by capillary networks. The alveoli, which form the spongy inside surface of the lung, are where the gas exchange takes place. (*See* GAS EXCHANGE.)

First see BRAIN

Reticular Activating System (RAS)

Next see MUSCULAR SYSTEM

The system that monitors all sensory signals bound for higher regions of the brain and all motor signals moving downward through the body.

The reticular activating system (RAS) is based in the reticular formation, a mass of densely interconnected neurons and nerve fibers that run through the brain stem of the medulla and midbrain and up into the thalamus. Its level of activity—and therefore the level of activity of the whole brain—largely reflects incoming sensory signals. Cutting off important sensory nerves can reduce brain activity almost to coma levels, while pain signals, on the other hand, activate the brain. (*See* BRAIN *and* NERVOUS SYSTEMS.)

The RAS's nerve fibers connect it to the cerebrum, cerebellum, various cranial nuclei, and the spinal cord. Activating these parts of the nervous system is one of its main functions, allowing animals to be alerted to changes in their environment, from the presence of a predator to the proximity of food. Brain stem RAS neurons project to the cortex primarily through relay nuclei in the thalamus that have a stimulatory influence on the cerebral cortex. The excitation can involve positive feedback: when the cerebral cortex becomes activated by thought or mo-tor processes, it sends signals to the RAS, which in turn sends more excitatory signals back to the cerebral cortex. This system encourages cerebral activity to increase, leading to an awake mind.

The RAS also has important inhibitory functions. It selectively suppresses—as well as enhances—sensory information on its way to the cortex, screening the huge amount of sensory data, much of it irrelevant, bombarding the brain. Similarly, the RAS inhibits some and enhances other motor commands sent by the cortex to the body. In other words, the reticular activating system plays a central role in determining what an animal will be aware of and how it will respond to that awareness. (*See* INSTINCT.)

First see DISEASES, INFECTIOUS

Rheumatic Fever

Next see HEART

Rheumatic fever is a disease that produces inflammation of various tissues in the body, most notably the heart valves. It generally follows an infection with some strains of streptococcal bacteria. It may be caused when the bacteria somehow induce the body's immune defense system to mount an attack against its own tissues.

Rheumatic fever most often occurs in children between the ages of 5 and 15 and can be prevented if streptococcal throat infections are treated quickly with antibiotics such as penicillin. The symptoms of rheumatic fever are fever accompanied by pain, with inflammation and swelling of one or more joints. The heart can be damaged in one of several ways. The most common damage is thickening and scarring of the mitral valve, which governs the flow of blood from one heart chamber to another. The valve can become narrow and may leak. Surgery to replace it with an artificial valve or one from an animal donor is often necessary. (*See* HEART.)

First see CELL

Ribosomes

Next see NUCLEUS

The sites of protein synthesis within the cell.

Ribosomes work together, in groups called polysomes, to translate the instructions for protein assembly. Multiple copies of a protein are manufactured by the cell as a result.

Ribosomes are made up of protein and ribosomal RNA (rRNA). They are very small indi-

vidually, compared to other organelles, yet make up approximately 10 percent of the total proteins in bacteria. A single bacterium contains around 20,000 ribosomes.

Protein synthesis involves an interplay between the messenger RNA (mRNA), which dictates the sequence of amino acids for the protein and transfer RNA (tRNA), molecules that bring in the amino acids. The ribosome provides an environment in which the mRNA and tRNA can come together in the proper manner.

Structure and Function. The structure and function of ribosomes varies depending on whether they are found in a prokaryotic cell (bacteria and blue-green algae) or a eukaryotic cell (everything else). Eukaryotic ribosomes are larger than prokaryotic ones, yet have fewer ribosomes per polysome. In both types of cells, the ribosome is spherical and separates into two functional units. The ribosome contains certain key active sites, P, A, and E, which are essential for its activity.

Ribosomes not involved in protein synthesis exist as a "pool" of separate halves. The lower half, which is the smaller of the two, is where the mRNA strand latches on. The first tRNA, carrying its amino acid, settles into the partial P site, and the two halves of the ribosome reunite. A second tRNA, carrying another amino acid, settles into the A site. The two adjacent amino acids form a bond, thus forming the first link of the polypeptide chain that will become a protein. The first tRNA then exits from the ribosome through the E site, leaving the growing polypeptide chain attached to the second tRNA. The ribosome "shifts over," leaving the remaining tRNA in the P site and the A site vacant for an incoming tRNA. The process repeats until the entire mRNA strand has been translated.

The ribosomes within the polysome follow each other, one after the other, down the entire length of the mRNA. Often multiple polysomes work on the same area. In prokaryotes, the last ribosome is immediately followed by an enzyme whose job is to break down the mRNA strand. By the time translation is completed, the mRNA no longer exists.

The majority of ribosomes within a eukaryotic cell are associated with other cellular structures, such as the endoplasmic reticulum, which is the "transportation network" within the cell, or the microtubules that make up the cytoskeleton, the internal scaffolding of the cell.

For background material, see PROTEIN; PROTEIN SYNTHESIS; DNA; DNA SEQUENCING; RNA. **Related material can be found in** CELL; CELL CYCLE; NUCLEUS, CELL. **Advanced subjects are developed in** CYTOPLASM; MITOSIS; TRANSCRIPTION; TRANSPORT, CELLULAR. **More information on particular aspects of this subject is contained in** ENDOPLASMIC RETICULUM AND GOLGI APPARATUS **and** MITOCHONDRIA. **Also, see** POLYMERASE CHAIN REACTION (PCR).

RNA

First see DNA

Next see TRANSCRIPTION

Ribonucleic acid (RNA) is one of the most important chemicals of heredity. Like its relative, DNA, it is a polymer, a long linked chain of individual units called nucleotides. Each nucleotide is in turn made up of a sugar molecule, a phosphate group and one of four bases: adenine (A), guanine (G), cytosine (C), and uracil (U). Adenine and guanine are both types of purines, which are double-ringed structures. Cytosine and uracil are types of pyrimidines, which are single-ringed structures. The polynucleotide chain itself consists of alternating sugar and phosphate group forming a "backbone," with the bases protruding off the sugar molecules.

DNA consists of two such polynucleotide chains running "antiparallel," or in opposite directions. They are held together by hydrogen bonding between the bases. A purine is always found together with a pyrimidine, in order to guarantee a uniform width throughout the DNA double helix. Adenine is paired either with thymine (in DNA) or uracil (in RNA) by means of two hydrogen bonds. The guanine-cytosine pair is held together by three hydrogen bonds.

RNA and DNA. There are three major structural differences between DNA and RNA:

1. DNA is found as a duplex. RNA is primarily a single strand, although it can form a duplex by base-pairing along its own length, with another RNA strand or with a single DNA strand.

2. DNA contains deoxyribose as its sugar, and RNA contains ribose.

3. DNA contains thymine, and RNA contains uracil. Thymine and uracil are chemically identical except that thymine has an additional methyl group (CH_3) attached to its ring.

Types. There are three types of RNA: messenger RNA (mRNA); transfer RNA (tRNA); and ribosomal RNA (rRNA). All of them play important roles in the business of genetic control of a cell and, consequently, the entire organism.

Messenger RNA is the "go-between" for genes and proteins. A gene is a segment of DNA that begins with a promoter region and ends with a terminator region, the sequence of which dictates the precise order of amino acids needed to make a particular protein. The DNA is located in the nucleus of the cell, and protein assembly takes place in the cytoplasm. The DNA is unable to leave the nucleus; in fact, it would be unwise to allow the "master copy" to be used on a regular basis. Therefore, a molecule of mRNA, which has all of the information of the gene, is produced; and mRNA leaves the nucleus and travels into the cytoplasm.

The formation of mRNA from the DNA template, or coding strand, is called transcription. Transcription begins when an enzyme called RNA polymerase settles on the promoter region of the gene and causes the double helix to unwind. The RNA polymerase matches up nucleotides to pair with the exposed DNA bases along the entire length of the gene until it reaches the terminator region. Another enzyme, ligase, links the new nucleotides together to form the RNA chain.

The RNA base sequence is complementary to the DNA template and is almost identical to the noncoding strand. The RNA molecule formed at the end of transcription is called the primary transcript. Further "editing" involves the addition of a methylguanine (mG) "cap" and a polyadenine "tail," as well as the removal of introns ("nonsense" sequences of bases) and splicing together of the ends of exons (the "useful" parts of a gene). Post-transcription modification does not occur in prokaryotic cells (bacteria and blue-green algae) but does occur in eukaryotic cells.

The second half of protein synthesis, known as translation, begins when the mRNA reaches the ribosomes, the organelles responsible for the assembly of proteins. Ribosomes always work sequentially in groups, known as polysomes. Each ribosome begins at the "head" of the mRNA strand and works its way down until the entire mRNA has been translated.

Amino Acids. The mRNA specifies the amino acids, but tRNA does the actual work of bringing them in. A molecule of tRNA is shaped roughly like a cloverleaf. The loops of the strand form its four arms. At one end of the molecule, there is an attached amino acid, and at the other is a specific sequence of three bases called an anticodon. The anticodon is complementary to the codon of mRNA, a three-base sequence that calls for a particular amino acid. It is by means of this base-pairing that the tRNA recognizes where to bring its amino acid. Each tRNA is specific for only one type of amino acid.

As its name implies, rRNA is a major component of the ribosomes and helps the mRNA and tRNA "settle in" to their proper positions, as well as providing the additional factors needed for protein synthesis.

In eukaryotes, the mRNA is not immediately broken down; it lasts for several hours and is usually translated by multiple polysomes. In prokaryotes, however, as soon as the last ribosome in the polysome begins translation, an enzyme begins to degrade the mRNA. By the time the translation process is completed, the mRNA has been completely broken down.

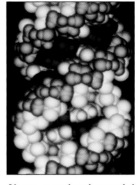

Above, a molecular model of RNA, the nucleic acid involved in translating genetic material and instructions into protein. RNA is chemically similar to DNA, with uracil replacing thymine around the bases.

Background material can be found in DNA; NUCLEIC ACID; RIBOSOMES; TRANSCRIPTION. *Advanced subjects are developed in* CELL CYCLE; DNA REPLICATION; PROTEIN SYNTHESIS. *Elementary aspects of this subject are covered in* EXONS AND INTRONS; GENETIC CODE; MUTATION, GENETIC. *See also* VIRAL GENETICS.

Further Reading
Eggleston, D. S.; *The Many Faces of RNA* (1998); Moldave, K., *RNA and Protein Synthesis* (1981); Lyon, Jeff, Gorner, Peter, *Altered Fates: Gene Therapy and the Retooling of Human Life* (1995).

First see TURING MACHINE

Robotics

Next see ARTIFICIAL INTELLIGENCE

The study of computer-controlled machines and the tasks they are capable of performing.

Robotics was an artistic creation before it was a creation of technology. In 1920, Karel Capek (1890–1938), a Czech playwright, wrote *RUR*, the first work to use the term "robots." In the late 1940s, Isaac Asimov wrote a series of science fiction tales based on what he called "The Three Laws of Robotics." Half a century later, Hollywood entered the robotics arena, creating characters like "Robbie, the Robot," R2-D2, the Terminator, Screamers, and countless other friends and foes to humankind. Despite its image in popular culture, robotics in the real world has proven to be far more serious, and far more productive.

The first true robots were fairly simple. Built by Joseph Engelberger in 1961, the Unimates, as they were called, were basically mechanical arms with electronic memories; once guided through their routines—tending metal-casting machines, spot welding, or paint

spraying—they could duplicate their original motions indefinitely, without regard to heat, fumes, or boredom. In 1978, Unimation introduced a robot able to handle and assemble small parts that, along with Milacron's T-3 robot, gained a foothold in the automobile industry. By 1985 there were 200,000 robots in use around the world, and by 1996 there were half a million, the majority of them in Japan.

The two challenges to robotics are vision and judgment. Intelligent robots must display skills in three separate aspects of vision: voice recognition, natural language processing, and image recognition. In other words, when a

Further Reading
Caudill, Maureen, *In Our Own Image: Building an Artificial Person* (1990); Nolfi, Stefano, *Evolutionary Robotics* (2000); Yoshikawa, T., *Foundations of Robotics: Analysis and Control* (1990); Malcolm, D. R., *Robotics: An Introduction* (1988).

Left, Cog, created by Rodney Brooks of the MIT Artificial Intelligence lab, can navigate its environment and pick up and manipulate objects on its own.

Below, engineers at NASA test-fire the redesigned Space Shuttle Solid Rocket Booster for the first time since the 1986 *Challenger* accident.

human passenger says, "Park here," a robot driver must: (1) recognize the words, (2) translate the two one-word commands into the act of parking a vehicle in an appropriate parking space, and (3) recognize a parking space and maneuver into it without hitting anything.

Second, robots must react to changes in their situation, whether through programming in Thematic Abstraction Units or through neural networks. This aspect is primarily a function of software development, the basis of artificial intelligence. In an excellent example of what robots are capable of, a robosurgeon at Guy's Hospital in London routinely performs prostate surgery; other robots work in shipyards, in nuclear power plants, and even as sheep shearers.

Robotic Futures. Alternatively, the future of robotics may lie in telepresence—the use of robots as skilled hands for remote human operators. This aspect of robotics connects to the developing science of virtual reality, in which a human operator equipped with a video headset and remote manipulation tools can achieve the goal of the ancients, "action at a distance." We already see this process at work in undersea and outer space exploration, where such successes as the finding of the *R.M.S. Titanic* and the analysis of the Martian surface were carried out first not by human daredevils but by capable (if sometimes inconsistent) robots.

Background material can be found in ARTIFICIAL INTELLIGENCE; COMPUTER, DIGITAL; TURING MACHINE. *Advanced subjects are developed in* CONTROL SYSTEMS; EXPERT SYSTEMS; SERVOMECHANISMS. *More information on particular aspects of robotics is contained in* ALGORITHM; NANOTECHNOLOGY; NEURAL NETWORK; VIRTUAL REALITY.

First see JET PROPULSION

Rocket

Next see MISSILE

A projectile or vehicle powered by an engine that generates thrust via a jet of hot gases.

A rocket operates through the principle expressed in Newton's third law of motion: for every action, there is an equal and opposite reaction. Jet engines operate on the same principle, but they differ from rockets because jet engines use oxygen from the atmosphere to achieve combustion. A rocket carries its own oxygen in addition to fuel and thus can function in outer space, where there is no air.

History. Rockets are mentioned in Chinese literature as early as the thirteenth century. The modern era of rocketry is often dated to the early twentieth century, when a

Russian mathematics teacher, Konstantin Tsiolkovsky, wrote about the significance of exhaust velocities and proposed the use of liquid fuels, such as hydrogen, instead of the black powder that was then in common use. The American pioneers of rocket technology were Robert H. Goddard, who worked on rockets from 1920 to 1940, and Theodore von Karman, who in 1937 began work at the California Institute of Technology. That work resulted in the establishment of the Jet Propulsion Laboratory, the first major rocket laboratory. Rockets became prominent during World War II, when they were used in such missiles as the German V-2, and became even more prominent with the opening of the space age, in which they provide the essential technology for getting into outer space.

Structure. The core unit of a rocket is the combustion chamber, where fuel and oxidizer, an oxygen-containing compound, burn to create high temperatures and pressure. The combustion chamber is connected to a nozzle through which the combustion products escape, creating thrust. The simplest rocket engines consist of just a combustion chamber and a nozzle, but more complex engines are needed for most missiles and space vehicles.

Whatever the equipment or payload that a rocket carries, the largest portion of its weight and volume consists of the propellant, which is the major determinant of the overall performance of the rocket. The capability of the propellant is described by its specific impulse, which is the number of pounds of thrust that are produced for each pound of propellant consumed per second. Typically, the chemical propellant used in a rocket has a specific impulse of about 250. The velocity that a given vehicle can achieve depends on the specific impulse of its propellant and the fraction of the total weight of the vehicle that consists of propellant; more propellant means a higher velocity.

Fuels. A chemical rocket fuel can be a liquid, such as hydrazine, a solid, or a combination of liquid and solid. Liquid rocket fuel is mixed

Above, Robert H. Goddard —father of modern rocket propulsion—was the first not only to envision exploration of space, but also to endeavor to make it a reality.

Further Reading
Jensen, Gordon E. (Ed.), *Tactical Missile Propulsion* (1996); Hujsak, E., *The Future of U.S. Rocketry* (1994); Harland, D. M., *The Space Shuttle: Roles, Missions and Accomplishments* (1998).

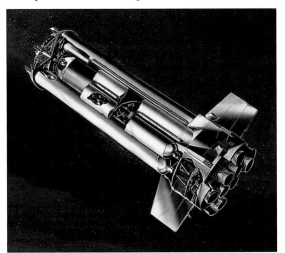

Left, a cutaway view of the V-2 rocket's engine component. Above, a V-2 awaits its launch at White Sands, New Mexico, in 1946. The V-2 was developed by Dr. Wernher von Braun, who came to the U.S. at the end of World War II to continue his research.

with the oxidizer, such as liquid oxygen, by an injection process in the combustion chamber. To make a solid rocket fuel, the fuel and the oxidizer are first mixed together in liquid form. They then harden to form a solid mass. To obtain the velocities needed to send a meaningful payload into outer space, rockets using propellants with this range of specific impulse generally must have several units. Multistage rocket systems are now in common use. As each stage ceases fire and is jettisoned, the next stage begins its burn, so that the acceleration becomes increasingly greater.

While other rocket systems have been proposed and experimented with, such as nuclear powered rockets and the electromagnetic rocket, which achieves thrust by expelling ions (charged particles) chemical rockets remain the basic systems used to send vehicles into orbit around the Earth or into outer space.

Special topics in this area are found in JET PROPULSION; MISSILE; PROPULSION. *Advanced subjects are developed in* COMBUSTION; SPACECRAFT; SPACE SHUTTLE. *More information on particular aspects of rocketry is contained in* INTERSTELLAR SPACE TRAVEL *and* SPACE STATION. *See also* NUCLEAR WEAPONS *and* SUBMARINE TECHNOLOGY.

First see SOIL CHEMISTRY

Roots

Next see LIQUID TRANSPORT

The parts of plants that absorb water and nutrients and that serve as anchors for plants in the soil.

Roots are far more extensive in surface area than the part of the plant that is visible aboveground. Underground roots grow either in a fibrous system of numerous thin roots, as in grasses, or in a taproot system with the first-formed root remaining dominant, as in dandelions. In some flowering plants, such as carrots and parsnips, the taproot is the part of the vegetable that is eaten.

Aerial Roots. Many plants have aerial roots. Some figs germinate in the branches of other trees and send down strangler roots that kill their host. Some trees and even corn plants grow "prop roots" that sprout from the lower portion of their stem or trunk and enter the ground, propping up the stem. Generally, roots that grow from a stem or another nonroot structure are called adventitious roots.

Typically, in flowering plants, underground roots do most of their absorption in the root hair zone just behind the growing tip of the young rootlet. The root hairs, specialized epidermal cells, provide a vast surface area for absorption. Beneath the epidermis, which is one cell wide, is the cortex, a wider area that stores starch. In older roots, the cortex and epidermis may be largely replaced by a corky periderm. Beneath the cortex are the thin layers of the endodermis and the pericycle; the pericycle can sprout secondary roots. The endodermis and pericycle ring the central portion of the root, which is filled with bundles of vascular tissues—xylem and phloem. (*See* LIQUID TRANSPORT IN PLANTS.)

In many cases, plant roots have permanent alliances with other organisms that help them absorb more nutrients. The best known of these partnerships is the one between legumes and the bacteria of the genus Rhizobium that live in nodules specially formed for this purpose on the plant's roots. The bacteria fix airborne nitrogen, making it biologically available to the legumes and freeing them from dependence on nitrogen-containing compounds in the soil. (*See* SEEDS.)

Many forest trees and fungi form alliances called mycorrhizae. The fungus acts like fine roots, absorbing nutrients, especially phosphates, into the tree. Orchids are especially dependent on mycorrhizae; in nature, they will not germinate without them. (*See* FUNGUS.)

First see ACCELERATION

Rotational Motion

Next see CENTRIFUGAL FORCE

The process that occurs when all of the parts of a body move in a circle around a common axis with a common angular velocity.

An ordinary top that a child sends spinning is an everyday example of gyrorotation. This rotational movement can be defined as free, as in the case of Earth spinning on its axis, or constrained, as in the case of a top or a flywheel.

A rotating body such as a top is said to move with a uniform angular velocity if a radius drawn from the axis of rotation to any point on the body sweeps through equal angles in equal periods of time. This angular velocity can be expressed in several ways: as degrees per second, revolutions per second or minute, or radians per second (1 revolution equals 2π radians). In mathematical terms, we can say that the angular velocity of a rotating body is equal to the rate of change of its angular displacement in a given period of time. The linear speed of a point on a rotating object such as a top is related to its

Right, twirling ice skaters use the conservation of angular (rotational) momentum to control spin. Placing arms and legs out and spinning builds up angular momentum. When arms and legs are brought in, the skater twirls faster to maintain the same angular momentum.

angular velocity and the radius of the top; linear speed equals radius times angular velocity. Thus, when a top is in gyromotion at a steady speed, points on its outer edge are moving faster than points near its center.

Tops. In a rigid body such as a top, there are three mutually perpendicular lines about which the body will rotate without a continuously applied force. These are called the principal axes of the body. Usually, there is only one line about which, in the absence of friction, the top will rotate permanently. That line is the principal axis through the center of mass of the top, the line that has the largest moment of inertia. When a body such as a top rotates, that rotation is affected by precession, which means that the body may wobble—something that is clearly observed in the case of a spinning top. What happens in precession is that the axis of rotation slowly describes a cone. At any instant, the motion of the axis of rotation is at right angles to the direction of the applied force.

Gyros. Gyromotion can occur when a body at rest is given a sudden push along a line that does not lie on its center of mass. The body begins to rotate on what is called its axis of instantaneous rotation, which lies beyond its center of mass and is perpendicular to the force that sets it into motion. The axis of instantaneous rotation is only temporary; the rotation quickly is transferred to an axis that lies through the body's center of mass.

Related areas include ACCELERATION; FORCE; MECHANICS. *Advanced subjects are developed in* CENTRIFUGAL FORCE *and* CORIOLUS FORCE. *Relevant information for rotational motion is contained in* FLUID MECHANICS; PERPETUAL MOTION; PLANETS, FORMATION OF.

Salts

First see ACID AND BASE

Next see CHEMICAL REACTION

An ionic compound whose cation is not H$^+$ and whose anion is not OH$^-$.

All ionic compounds have two parts: a positively charged ion, called a cation, and a negatively charged ion, called an anion. When an atom's electron number changes, the atom is transformed into an ion.

Whenever a metal combines with a nonmetal, that bond is ionic. The nonmetal atom is more electronegative (strongly attracts electrons) than the metal atom, resulting in the nonmetal becoming an anion and the metal a cation. These two oppositely charged entities are now attracted to each other and will remain together to form a compound.

Table Salt. The classic example of an ionic bond formed between two atoms involves sodium and chlorine. Sodium, a metal, originally has one valence electron, and chlorine, a nonmetal, has seven valence electrons. Chlorine grabs sodium's electron, transforming sodium into a cation (Na^{+1}) and itself into an anion (Cl^{-1}). The resulting compound is sodium chloride, NaCl, more commonly known as table salt. However, a salt in the chemical sense need not include sodium.

A salt is neither an acid nor a base; it has a neutral pH. All ionic compounds are electrically neutral because their charges cancel out. If the numerical values of the cation and anion are equal from the outset, one of each is used, as in the case of sodium and chlorine. However, if the values are not equal, as in the case of aluminum (Al^{+3}) and sulfate (SO_4^{-2}), the crisscross method is used, in which the number charge of one ion becomes the subscript (number of ions used) of the other and vice a versa. Therefore, the formula for aluminum sulfate is $Al_2(SO_4)_3$.

Aside from simply combining ions, salts can be formed in a variety of ways. The most common method is when an acid reacts with a base. They neutralize each other, meaning the H+ of the acid and the OH$^-$ of the base combine to form water. The remaining ions, the base cation and the acid anion, combine to form a salt.

The salt of an acid is the anion of a particular acid with a different cation. For example, H_2SO_4 is sulfuric acid. Replacing the hydrogen with sodium gives Na_2SO_4, sodium sulfate. Replacing the hydrogen with magnesium produces $MgSO_4$, magnesium sulfate. The salt of one acid can combine with another acid to result in a new acid and a new salt, simply by switching around cation-anion pairs.

Salts of an acid are often used in preparing buffer solutions, which are chemicals added to a solution to ensure that the pH remains constant.

Since salts include such a large variety of compounds, it is difficult to characterize them as a group in terms of behavior and properties. However, all salts dissociate (separate) in water, producing their original ions.

Related areas to be considered are ACID AND BASE; INORGANIC COMPOUNDS; WATER. *More details can be found in* ACID RAIN; BLOOD PRESSURE; CATALYST; TITRATION. *Advanced aspects of this subject are covered in* CYSTIC FIBROSIS; TRANSPORT, CELLULAR; WATER IN LIVING CELLS.

Further Reading
Wood, Stephen, *Conquering High Blood Pressure: The Complete Guide to Managing Hypertension* (1997); De Caro, Giuseppe, *The Physiology of Thirst and Sodium Appetite* (1986); Kraus, B., *Complete Guide to Sodium* (1991).

Satellites, Planetary

First see SOLAR SYSTEM

Next see MOON

Planetary satellites such as Earth's moon formed at the same time as the planets, about 4.6 billion years ago. The sun, the planets, and their satellites formed from a disk-shaped rotating cloud of gas, the protosolar nebula. The difference in the temperatures at which the contents of that nebula condensed accounts for the differences in composition of the satellites. Since there was a downward temperature gradient from the center of the nebula, only materials with high melting temperatures solidified in the central, hotter portion of the nebula—silicates, iron, aluminum, titanium, and calcium. The moon is made up primarily of these materials.

Beyond Mars. Further out, beyond the orbit of Mars, carbon, silicates, and organic molecules condensed to form a class of asteroids, the carbonaceous chondrites. Similar carbonaceous material is found on the surface of Phobos, on several of the satellites of Jupiter and Saturn, and perhaps on the satellites of Uranus.

Moving out from the region of the asteroids, temperatures of formation were low enough to allow water to condense and remain stable. Thus, the satellites of Jupiter consist primarily of a mixture of ice and silicates, except for Io, which apparently lost all of its water. On the satellites of Neptune and Pluto, the temperatures of formation were low enough for other volatile

Not all planetary satellites in the solar system have the round "planetary" shape of Earth's moon. Left, the Martian moons Phobos (at right) and Deimos (at left) are seen in montage comparison (in the same scale) with the asteroid Gaspra (top), a rock some ten miles long.

substances, such as nitrogen and carbon monoxide, to exist in both liquid and solid form. In general, the satellites that formed in the inner region of the solar system are denser than those in the outer region because they retained less volatile material.

As the evolution of the solar system continued, the small grains that formed were joined together by electrostatic forces. Collisions between these particles led to the formation of larger bodies, or planetoids. These in turn experienced gravitational collapse, which formed mile-sized planetesimals. The largest of these

Earth's remarkable moon has a greater interaction with our planet than any other moon in the solar system has with its planet. This unique configuration—in that the moon protects Earth from a great many asteroid impacts—may be one of the factors that would have to be duplicated for life to exist on other planets.

satellites swept up much of the remaining material around the planets, creating a smaller number of larger satellites. One important factor was that such a satellite cannot be formed at Roche's limit, the distance at which the tidal forces exerted by the planet become greater than the internal cohesive forces of the satellite. Rings such as those surrounding Saturn and Uranus probably contain debris from such satellites.

Solar System. Starting from the innermost part of the solar system, Mercury is not known to have any satellites. Neither is Venus, the second planet from the sun. Earth has just one, the moon. Mars has two, Deimos (the innermost) and Phobos. Jupiter has four major satellites, Ganymede, Callisto, Io, and Europa, and ten smaller, more distant ones. The larger, closer satellites of Saturn are Titan, Rhea, Iapetus, Dione, Tethys, and Enceladus. There are at least 16 others, the outermost being Telesto and Calypso. Uranus has 5 major satellites, Oberon, Titania, Ariel, Umbriel, and Miranda, and 10 smaller ones, while Neptune has 6, the largest of which are Triton and Nereid. Pluto, the outermost planet, has one moon, Charon, which is so large in relation to the size of Pluto that some astronomers consider that the bodies form a two-planet system.

Further Reading

Atreya, S.K., *Origin and Evolution of Planetary and Satellite Atmospheres* (1989); Rothery, D. A., *Satellites of the Outer Planets: Worlds in Their Own Right* (1992); Stewart, J., *Moons of the Solar System* (1991).

Special topics in this area are found in EARTH; ECLIPSE; MOON; PLANET; SOLAR SYSTEM. *Advanced subjects are developed in* COMET; JUPITER; PLANETARY RINGS; PLUTO; SATURN. *Additional aspects of this subject are covered in* ASTEROIDS AND METEORS; BINARY STARS; KEPLER'S LAWS.

First see JUPITER

Saturn

Next see PLANETARY RINGS

Saturn, the second largest planet in the solar system and the sixth from the sun, is most noted for its colorful rings. It is unusual in other respects, however. Saturn is the planet whose mass has the least density; just 71 percent that of water. Most of the mass of the planet consists of liquid hydrogen, and it is believed to have a compressed, rocky core. While Saturn has a volume that is 770 times that of Earth, its mass is only 95.2 times that of Earth. Saturn rotates rapidly, so that a point on its equator completes a rotation every 10 hours and 40 minutes. As a result, it is considerably flattened. The polar radius of Saturn, 33,555 miles, is 3,933 miles less than its radius at the equator.

Orbit. Saturn completes a circuit around the sun every 29.46 years. Its orbit around the sun is affected by the gravitational pull of Jupiter, so that its distance from the sun varies from 9 to 10.9 astronomical units (an astronomical unit is the distance from Earth to the sun). The visible surface of Saturn consists of clouds, with bands parallel to its equator. These bands are similar to those seen on Jupiter but are less prominent and less variable in color and intensity.

Rings. Saturn's rings were determined to be separate structures, rather than a single band, in the seventeenth century by the Dutch astronomer Christian Huygens. The individual rings were thought to be solid disks until 1895, when astronomers determined that they must consist of small pieces of matter. Solid rings could not exist so close to such a large mass as the planet; gravitational forces would tear them apart.

For centuries, Saturn was thought to have just three rings, designated A (the outermost), B and C (the innermost). The area between rings A and B was called the Cassini division, for Giovanni Cassini, the French astronomer who first described it. The A ring was later found to have a gap, called Enke's division, named for the German astronomer Johann Enke. Other rings have been discovered over the years. The E ring, for example, lies beyond the A ring. In recent decades, the *Pioneer 11* spacecraft has detected two more rings, F and G, lying between the E rings. High-resolution photographs taken by a later *Voyager* spacecraft showed that the F ring actually consists of three separate ringlets. Other spacecraft have found that the classical A, B, and C rings consist of hundreds of ringlets consisting of ice particles, some of which are circular and some elliptical in shape.

Satellites. Saturn has ten major moons, whose distances from the planet range from 51,900 to 8 million miles and whose orbital periods range from 18 hours to 550 days. Other,

First see MICROSCOPY

Scanning Tunnel Microscopy (STM)

Next see ELECTRON MICROSCOPE

A sensing technology for studying the properties of material surfaces on the atomic scale.

The scanning tunnel microscope was invented by Gerhard Binning and Heinrich Rohrer, who were awarded the 1986 Nobel Prize for their achievement. The microscope takes advantage of the fact that electrons will tunnel between an extremely sharp tip—one that may end in a single atom—and the nearby surface of a material. The distance between the tip and the surface must be very small—about ten angstroms. At this distance, the wave functions of atoms on the surface and the electrons will overlap. Electrons will then pass from the tip to the surface, causing a current to flow. In a scanning electron microscope, the position of the tip is controlled very precisely, and as the tip is moved slowly

smaller moons have been detected by spacecraft sent from Earth. The largest moon, Ti-tan, has a diameter of 3,000 miles and is the only planetary satellite in the solar system that is known to have an atmosphere. That atmosphere consists mostly of nitrogen and to be 60 percent denser than Earth's atmosphere. (*See* MOON.)

Exploration. Spacecraft have found that Phoebe, the outermost of Saturn's other moons, has a retrograde orbital motion (it orbits from east to west) and has characteristics indicating that it might be a captured asteroid. Phoebe has a diameter of 137 miles and spins on its axis once every 9 hours. Another moon, Iapetus, has been found to have the greatest range of reflectivity of any body in the solar system, with its brightest areas reflecting 50 percent of the sunlight falling on them. Hyperion is a moon whose cratered, irregular shape is believed to be due to bombardment by meteorites and asteroids. Astronomers studying data from space probes have concluded that the brighter moons of Saturn appear to be more highly evolved than the darker ones, which tend to have more irregular shapes.

Radio Emissions. Like Jupiter, Saturn emits radio signals, which originate in the planet's magnetosphere. This strong magnetic field is also probably the cause of the "spokes" visible in Saturn's B ring: these are believed to be dust levitated above the ring by electrostatic energy. Like Jupiter, Saturn's atmosphere has high-speed jet streams. Studies of a dominant easterly jet stream have found that the winds of Saturn are not confined to the upper clouds but extend deep into the planet's atmosphere.

Above, Saturn has 18 known moons and many other "shepherd" moons —large chunks of matter that orbit at the edges of the planet's rings and maintain the ring's shape. The false-color image of the rings highlights the Cassini division (gap).

Right, with magnification strengths in the millions, STM not only reveals atom-size configurations, but permits manipulation for possible nanotechnology application.

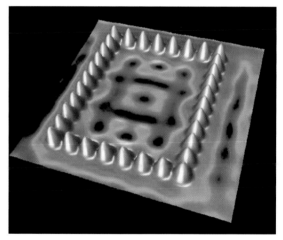

over the individual atoms of the surface, there are very small fluctuations in the tunneling current. A computer records the changes in the height of atoms on the surface, creating an image on a graphics screen. This image shows the number and position of the individual atoms making up the surface. It is thus possible to study the atomic makeup of surfaces of such materials as semiconductors, where differences in atomic composition and structure can be important. Scanning electron microscopes can also be used to study large biological molecules by depositing them on flat surfaces.

Further developments in the field are discussed in JUPITER; PLANETARY RINGS; SOLAR SYSTEM. *More details can be found in* PLANETS, FORMATION OF; RADIO ASTRONOMY. *Additional relevant information is contained in* NEPTUNE; PLANETARY ATMOSPHERES. *See also* NEMESIS HYPOTHESIS.

Further Reading
Batson, R. M., *Voyager 1 and 2, Atlas of Six Saturnian Satellites* (1985); Washburn, M., *Distant Encounters: The Exploration of Jupiter and Saturn* (1993); Cooper, H. S. F., *Imaging Saturn: The Voyager Flights to Saturn* (1990).

Background material can be found in ATOM; ELECTRON MICROSCOPY; MICROSCOPY. *Further developments in the field are discussed in* CELL; CELL CYCLE; NANOTECHNOLOGY; PIEZOELECTRICITY. *Special topics in this area are found in* NUCLEUS, CELL; RIBOSOMES; X-RAY DIFFRACTION.

First see BRAIN

Schizophrenia

Next see MENTAL DISORDERS

The most common form of psychotic illness—includes disturbed thinking and abnormal emotional reactions and behavior among its symptoms.

By some estimates, the worldwide incidence of schizophrenia is as high as 1 percent. There is a genetic factor to the condition; close relatives of patients have a 10 percent greater risk of developing schizophrenia. The disease usually begins between the ages of 15 and 25, later in women than in men. An individual may slowly become more withdrawn, losing drive and motivation, although the onset may be rapid in some cases.

Delusions and hallucinations often occur. The hallucinations usually take the form of voices that comment on the individual's behavior or thoughts, while the delusions may cause the patient to believe that he or she is someone else—Jesus Christ or Franklin Roosevelt, for instance. In most cases, patients lose the ability to think and reason coherently, which results in muddled and disjointed speech. The major form of treatment is antipsychotic drugs such as chlorpromazine, often accompanied by psychotherapy. The patients may be hospitalized when the condition is diagnosed, but most are able to leave the hospital, living either at home or in specialized housing. Only one schizophrenic in ten suffers lifelong, severe impairment, and three patients in ten eventually return, with treatment, to complete normalcy.

First see WAVE-PARTICLE DUALITY

Schrödinger's Equation

Next see QUANTUM MECHANICS

Schrödinger's equation is used in wave mechanics, the part of quantum mechanics in which a subatomic particle, an atom, or a molecule is described both as a particle and a wave. The equation was formulated by the German physicist Erwin Schrödinger in 1926, shortly after French physicist Louis de Broglie proposed the hypothesis that all particles have wave properties.

The Schrödinger equation measures this wave function for a subatomic particle or a system made up of a number of particles. Although the equation does not have any immediate physical significance, it does describe the probability of finding such a system in any prescribed position at any given time. That probability is generally said to be expressed as the square of the wave function of the particle or system, an interpretation that was originated by Max Born. The Schrödinger equation differs from the equations used in classical—nonquantum—physics in that

it does not give precise results. But it does allow the calculation of the probability that a given event on the subatomic level will occur.

One of the more interesting predictions of the Schrödinger equation is that certain quantities on the subatomic level are not continuous but are discrete—that is, they are seen only in certain fixed values.

Applications. The Schrödinger equation can be applied to systems described by classical physics, such as the motion of the planets. In these cases, there is an infinitesimal difference between the results of classic equations and the Schrödinger equation. On the atomic and subatomic levels, however, classical theories are useless, whereas the Schrödinger equation gives results that agree closely with observations made in experiments.

In recent years, computers have been used to perform calculations using the Schrödinger equation for the electronic configurations of large atoms, which have many electrons circling their nuclei, and to calculate the properties of the chemical bonds in multiatomic compounds.

The Schrödinger equation may also be viewed as an application of the principle of complementarity, which says that a single model—wave or particle—may not be adequate to explain all the observations made of atomic and subatomic systems in various experiments.

Further Reading
Gribbin, John, *Schrödinger's Kittens and the Search for Reality* (1995); Gribbin, John, *In Search of Schrödinger's Cat* (1984); Moore, Walter, *Schrödinger: Life and Thought* (1989).

The foundations of the subject are discussed in QUANTUM MECHANICS; WAVE-PARTICLE DUALITY. *More details can be found in* QUANTUM ELECTRODYNAMICS; UNCERTAINTY PRINCIPLE. *Advanced subjects are developed in* DIFFERENTIAL EQUATIONS; EQUIVALENCE PRINCIPLE; QUANTUM STATISTICS.

First see UNIFORMITARIANISM

Scientific Method

Next see THEORIES OF EVERYTHING

Scientific method describes the techniques that are applied to the study of phenomena in the world around us. While methods and techniques vary widely in different areas of science, they generally conform to a set of basic principles. One is that every scientific hypothesis or rule must be supported by evidence obtained by observations. Those observations must be repeatable by any scientist and must be observable by a large number of persons. Any scientific hypothesis can be changed if new observations using different methods give different results.

Conclusions. One major part of the scientific method consists of the rules that are used to draw conclusions from the data that are gathered by observations. In the early stages of any science, these rules generally classify observed phenomena into broad classes. The next step is

Erwin Schrödinger (1887–1961). Schrödinger was even more disdainful of convention than Einstein. He was often refused admittance to conferences where he was the principle speaker because of his tramp-like attire.

the development of techniques by which the phenomena can be measured and the development of mathematical equations, or laws, that describe the phenomena. A scientific law starts out as a hypothesis that is based on existing knowledge, often through a firsthand acquaintance with nature or information acquired in the laboratory—although chance also plays an important role. Albert Einstein noted that in his younger days at the Polytechnic Institute in Zurich, "I worked most of the time in the physical laboratory, fascinated by the direct contact with experience."

Inspiration also plays a role and usually leads to a belief about the kind of information that will be given by an experiment or set of experiments. These ideas may be modified as experimentation goes on, and new ideas can be invented. When Galileo did his work, for example, he could apply the new idea of acceleration to the analysis of his experimental findings.

Developing Hypotheses. Finally, there is the development of a hypothesis through deduction or induction based on experimental results. This hypothesis can lead to new experiments that are more specific, controlled, and directed toward testing of the hypothesis. The eventual result of these experiments can be a scientific law that explains observed phenomena—Newton's law of gravity or Einstein's law of relativity, for example. These laws can lead to newer hypotheses, which can lead to newer laws, and so on in a never-ending process.

Thus, scientific method is not a rigid set of rules that guarantee success, but a general set of procedures, the success of which depends greatly on the perceptions and abilities of individual scientists. At the heart of the method is the principle that any scientific finding, hypothesis or theory must be subjected to verification by tests that any qualified observer can perform.

Elementary aspects of this subject are covered in BIG BANG THEORY; SYMMETRY IN NATURE; UNIFORMITARIANISM. *More information on particular aspects is contained in* FEYNMAN DIAGRAM; GÖDEL'S THEOREM; MAXWELL'S EQUATION. *Relevant information is contained in* CHAOS AND COMPLEXITY; EQUIVALENCE PRINCIPLE; GRAND UNIFICATION THEORY (GUT); NEWTON'S LAWS; THEORIES OF EVERYTHINGS (TOE).

Further Reading
Harris, Errol E., *Hypothesis and Perception: The Roots of Scientific Method* (1996); Carey, Stephen S., *A Beginner's Guide to Scientific Method* (1997); Wilson, Edgar Bright, *An Introduction to Scientific Research* (1991).

First see RADIOACTIVITY

Scintillator

Next see RADIATION DETECTOR

Detector of light emitted by a material as an electrically charged particle passes through it, exciting the electrons in the atoms of the material into more energetic orbits.

Scintillators are among the most frequently used particle detectors in nuclear physics laboratories. The electrons emit electromagnetic radiation, mostly in the form of visible light, as they fall back into their equilibrium orbits. These so-called excited states last less than a millionth of a second and emit light impulses that are too faint to be detected without amplification.

A scintillator uses a photomultiplier tube to detect the original electromagnetic radiation. The photomultiplier tube consists of a faceplate that is covered with a material that emits electrons when it is struck by light and an electron multiplier, which is a series of metal plates with electric fields between them. The emitted electrons are accelerated from one plate to the next, dislodging electrons from each plate, thus multiplying the number of electrons. After about eight plates, there is a stream of moving electrons that makes up an electrical current large enough to be measured. A short electrical pulse from the multiplier is an indication that a charged particle has passed through the scintillator. Instruments called image intensifiers can then be used to take photographs of the track of the charged particle. (*See* RADIATION DETECTOR.)

First see CELL

Secretion, Cellular

Next see ENZYME

The production of a material for use outside the cell in which it is formed.

A gland is a group of secreting cells all working together to form the same product. All glands are composed of epithelial tissue (the same type of cells that make up skin and the inner linings of organs and blood vessels) that has adapted to produce a particular chemical product.

Glands are classified as either exocrine or endocrine, depending on whether or not they have ducts leading from the gland to the site where its product is sent. Exocrine glands contain ducts.

Examples of exocrine glands include apocrine (sweat) and sebaceous (oil) glands. Both of these are found in the dermal layer of skin, and their ducts lead to the surface of the epidermis. Sweat (mostly water, along with minute amounts of dissolved salts and urea) is part of the body's plan for maintaining a constant temperature and providing a way to eliminate excess heat from the body. Oil is necessary to keep skin moist and lubricated.

Mammary glands are actually modified sweat glands. Lactation is the production of milk within the mammary glands due to the influence of hormones such as prolactin and oxytocin, both produced by the hypothalamus.

Digestion. All of the digestive organs are exocrine glands. In the mouth, three salivary glands, the sublingual, submaxillary, and parotid, produce saliva. Many different digestive enzymes are produced by the stomach, liver, pancreas, and small intestines. The stomach also secretes hydrochloric acid to "activate" one of its enzymes, as well as hormones that regulate the process.

Food does not enter the interior of the liver and pancreas. Bile produced by the liver and stored in the gall bladder, as well as pancreatic enzymes, are transported to the small intestine through ducts. The pancreas has an endocrine function as well. Some of its cells, called the islets of Langerhans, produce hormones responsible for regulating blood glucose levels.

Mucus glands are found in much of the digestive and respiratory tracts, as well as in the urogenital system. They produce mucus for lubrication purposes, as well as to "trap" dirt and germs and prevent their further entry into the body. The cells of the auditory canal produce ear wax and the lachrymal glands of the eyes produce tears for much the same reason.

Endocrine glands do not contain ducts. Their products must reach their designated sites by traveling through the bloodstream. The products of the endocrine glands are all hormones. A complicated system exists to enable the hormone to recognize its target site. Some endocrine glands such as the pituitary produce hormones that in turn control the formation and secretion of hormones by other glands.

Further Reading
Rensberger, Boyce, *Life Itself: Exploring the Realm of the Living Cell* (1996); de Duve, Christian, *Blueprint for a Cell: The Nature and Origin of Life* (1991); Alberts, Bruce, *Molecular Biology of the Cell* (1994).

Related areas to be considered include CELL; CELLULAR MEMBRANES; TRANSPORT, CELLULAR. *Other aspects of the subject of bodily secretions are discussed in* DIGESTION; ENZYME; METABOLISM; NUTRITION; OSMOSIS. *Additional related material can be found in* ALLERGY; CHLOROPLAST; IMMUNE RESPONSE; MITOCHONDRIA.

First see SOIL CHEMISTRY

Seed

Next see GERMINATION

The reproductive structure of higher terrestrial plants (gymnosperms and angiosperms).

The formation of seeds is the defining characteristic of the higher terrestrial plants, the angiosperms (flowering plants) and the gymnosperms (chiefly, conifers). In angiosperms, the seed is enclosed in a fruit; in gymnosperms, it drops naked from the female cone. The seed contains the plant embryo and, in most cases, a surrounding endosperm that supplies its nutrition. The seed protects the embryo from desiccation and other calamities, allowing it to lie safely dormant through winter or drought.

In angiosperms, the seed is formed from the female gametophyte or embryo sac, which contains the egg cell. One sperm fertilizes the egg; another sperm combines with two polar nuclei to produce the primary endosperm nucleus. The zygote divides to form an embryo, which consists of one or two cotyledons or seed leaves, an embryonic stem (the epicotyl and hypocotyl) and the radicle, the precursor to the roots. The endosperm nucleus also begins dividing until the endosperm fills the space around the embryo. The integuments, one or two envelopes around the embryo sac, develop into seed coats. Usually they thicken and become leathery or hard, although some seeds have papery coats. Some angiosperms, such as peas and beans, absorb the endosperm and store food for germination in their own fleshy cotyledons. A few seeds contain another tissue, the perisperm, which also plays a nutritive role. In angiosperms, a fruit develops around the seeds.

Conifers. In conifers, which are the most common form of gymnosperm, the embryo, which can contain two to many cotyledons, is surrounded by the cells of the female gametophyte, which contain food, and by a seed coat formed from the integument. Often, it takes a year after pollination for fertilization to occur and then months for the seeds to mature and be released by the cones. In some species, the cones never open; their scales must either decay or be touched by fire in order to free the seeds.

Dispersal. The dispersal of seeds is crucial to the survival of species, and innumerable strategies have evolved to speed their journey. Many seeds are specialized to catch the wind, from the fluffy parachutes of dandelions to the winged seeds that spin from so many trees, both angiosperm and gymnosperm. Dehiscent fruits, which include peas and beans, dry out and rupture, casting their seeds to the wind. Others, like coconuts, travel by water. Many seeds have special features, like burrs or hooks, to catch the fur of animal couriers. The seeds of many South African plants come coated with eliasome, an oily substance valued by ants, who carry the seeds underground, eat the coating, and leave the seeds to germinate, safe from predators.

The most obvious seed packages are edible fruits that take on the colors, scents, and sweet taste of ripeness when the seeds within have matured. Once swallowed by animals, they are carried off and eventually planted elsewhere with the animals' feces. Since many of the seeds will be destroyed in the digestive tract, the benefits of being consumed have to be substantial. In the case of acacia trees in East Africa, those eaten by animals are far more likely to germinate than those left on the ground, apparently because the seeds are colonized by beetles and the animal's digestion kills the beetle eggs. Still, in other cases, seeds have evolved to prevent animal consumption by having hard shells or poisonous contents. Strychnine, for instance, comes from the seeds of an Indian tree. (*See* PLANT; SEXUAL REPRODUCTION IN PLANTS.)

Seismics

First see PLATE TECTONICS

Next see SEISMOLOGY

The study of the geological activity of the upper layers of the Earth.

The motion of the upper layers of the Earth can be divided into three components: vertical movements, east-west movements, and north-south movements. By measuring these three components, geologists can obtain a complete description of any motion of the ground.

The instrument that is basic to seismics is the seismograph, which detects and records the seismic waves that are produced by Earth's motions. Most seismograph systems have three components: a transducer that converts the mechanical motion of the ground into an electrical signal, transmittable over large distances; a second transducer that converts the transmitted signal into a mechanical motion that is recorded on paper or on a computer screen; and the recorder or computer that stores this information.

The seismic waves detected by this instrument are classified as compressional, or P, waves, which are propagated in vertical directions; shear, or S, waves, which are propagated perpendicular to the P waves; and surface waves, which have the lowest velocity and whose force decreases rapidly with depth. In general, the velocity of both compressional and shear waves increases with their depth in Earth and varies according to the composition of the rock formations through which they pass. (*See* EARTHQUAKE; PLATE TECTONICS.)

Seismology

First see SEISMICS

Next see EARTHQUAKE

The science that deals with the properties, location, and occurrence of earthquakes, and with the generation, propagation, and effects of their seismic waves.

Most earthquakes occur in two elongated regions. One of them, the circum-Pacific belt, passes around the Pacific Ocean. About 80 percent of the energy released by earthquakes is accounted for in this belt. The second seismic belt runs eastward from the Mediterranean region through Asia. The two belts meet at one point, at the Celebes. There is a less active earthquake belt consisting of the mid-ocean ridges, which include the mountains that lie under the centers of the Atlantic, Indian, and South Pacific Oceans.

Causes of Earthquakes. Most earthquakes are believed to be caused by the sudden release of the energy created by strains in the Earth's crust, but some have other causes, such as volcanic activity, meteor impacts, the collapse of major caves, or abrupt changes in the circulation pattern of magma, the liquid rock that is found inside the Earth's crust. Seismologists have determined that most earthquakes occur because of the horizontal displacement of two sides of a vertical fault in the crust. Movements of these transcurrent faults are believed to be the most common mechanism for the quakes that occur near the surface in the circum-Pacific belt.

Scales. Seismology measures earthquake intensity in two ways. One is the Mercalli scale, which designates an earthquake that is felt by very few people and has no destructive effect on building structures as degree I, while an earthquake that causes major destruction, visible ground motion, and accelerations exceeding those of gravity is designated degree XII. The Richter scale measures earthquakes on a logarithmic scale. The smallest earthquakes have a magnitude of 0, while the largest have a magnitude of 8.5.

Most earthquakes occur at a depth of about 20 miles, and the frequency of their occurrence decreases with depth. Another classification used by seismologists lists earthquakes as shallow-focus, occurring within about 45 miles of the surface; intermediate-focus, occurring between 45 and 180 miles beneath the surface; and deep-focus, occurring up to about 400 miles below the surface. Deep-focus earthquakes occur only in the circum-Pacific belt.

Most large earthquakes are preceded and followed by a series of tremors called foreshocks and aftershocks. Earthquakes can be preceded and accompanied by audible, low-pitched sounds that are produced by compressional and shear waves near the surface of the ground. Sometimes, a series of small earthquakes of about the same magnitude occur in one region over a relatively short period of time; this is called an earthquake swarm.

Tools. The most basic tool used in seismology is the seismograph, which records ground motion in visible form. The ground motion traced by the seismograph can be resolved into three components: vertical, east-west, and north-south. By measuring these three components, seismologists can obtain a complete description of the ground motion. Any single seismographic station can locate the center and time of origin of an earthquake by measuring the time intervals between the arrival of the various phases of the earthquake. (*See* EARTHQUAKE.)

Increased seismic activity is recorded (above) during an eruption of Mount St. Helens.

Background material can be found in EARTHQUAKE; GEOLOGY, ARCHAEOLOGICAL; SEISMICS. *More details on seismology can be found in* FAULTS, FOLDS, AND JOINTS; PLATE TECTONICS; STRATIGRAPHY. *Foundations of this subject are covered in* CONTINENT, FORMATION OF; GEOSYNCLINE; GLACIER.

Further Reading
Bolt, B. A., *Earthquakes* (1999); Doyle, H. A., *Seismology* (1996); Vernon, R. H., *Beneath Our Feet: The Rocks of Planet Earth* (2001); Wyss, M., *Earthquake Prediction—State of the Art* (1997).

First see CONDUCTORS AND RESISTORS

Semiconductors

Next see P-N JUNCTIONS

Crystalline solids whose electrical conductivity is midway between that of a conducting material such as copper and an insulating material such as wood.

The unit of conductivity is the siemens. In formal mathematical terms, a conducting material will have a conductivity of up to 1 billion siemens per meter, an insulating material will have no conductivity at all, and a semiconductor will have a conductivity of perhaps 100,000 siemens per meter. Semiconductors have become of great economic value because of their use in chips in computers and other modern electronic devices. They are many times smaller and much more reliable, and they require much less energy than the old-fashioned vacuum tubes that they have replaced.

Because the atoms in a crystalline solid such as germanium or silicon overlap, the orbitals of the electrons that circle their nuclei overlap, so that the individual energy levels of the electrons are spread out into energy bands. The outermost electrons of the atoms form what is called the valence band. Conduction occurs in semiconductors because when they are in an electrical field, there is a movement of electrons in the conduction band that lies beneath the valence band, and a movement of empty spaces, called holes, in the valence band. (A hole behaves as though it is an electron with a positive charge.) Thus, electrons and holes are known as the charge carriers of a semiconductor.

Metals and Metalloids. A prominent property of metals is that they are good conductors. This is because in a metal crystal the electrons are mobile and move easily from one atom to another in a sea of electrons. They attract and hold the positive metal ions together. This is known as a metallic bond, and the electron movement is called metallic conduction.

Metalloids are elements that exhibit properties of both metals and nonmetals. Non-metals do not conduct currents and are known as insulators because they impede the flow of electrons. The metalloids silicon and germanium are called semiconductors as they are an intermediate form between the metallic conductors and the nonmetallic insulators.

A semiconductor can carry a current if energy is provided to help the valence electrons jump outward from their energy level, mimicking the metallic sea of electrons. As the temperature is increased, so is the conductivity of these elements, in contrast to metals whose conductivity decreases with added heat.

The conductivity properties of semiconductors have made them vital to the shrinking of computer parts and of mother boards (above).

Types of Semiconductors. An intrinsic semiconductor is one in which the concentration of charge carriers is typical of a pure, or almost pure, sample of the material. In an intrinsic semiconductor, electrons jump to the conduction band from the valence band because of thermal excitation, or heat. Each electron that makes the jump leaves a hole in the valence band, and so the charge carriers of an intrinsic semiconductor consist of equal numbers of electrons and holes.

An extrinsic semiconductor has impurity atoms that are added to the original material. Thus, the type of conduction that takes place in an extrinsic semiconductor depends on the number and valence of the impurity atoms that have been added.

For example, the atoms of both germanium and silicon have a valence of four. If impurity atoms with a valence of five, such as antimony, arsenic, or phosphorus, are added, there will be one extra electron for each atom that is available for conduction, and such materials will have electrons as the majority of carriers. These are called n-type conductors, because electrons have a negative (n) charge. If impurity atoms with a valence of three are added, such as boron, aluminum, indium, or gallium, one hole per atom is created. These are called p-type conductors, because holes are regarded as having a positive (p) charge.

Diodes. The basic structure of the semiconductor devices used in modern electronic equipment is the semiconductor diode. A diode consists of a silicon crystal that has been "doped" in such a way that half of it is p-type and the other half is n-type. At the junction between these two halves, there is what is called a depletion layer, where electrons from the n-type material have filled holes in the p-type material. This depletion layer creates a barrier that tends to keep the remaining electrons in the n region and the holes in the p region. But a positive electric potential put on the p region will reduce the strength of this barrier. Thus, the holes in the p region can flow to the n region, and electrons in the n region can flow to the p region. The diode is said to be forward biased. In such a case, there will be a good flow of current across the barrier.

By contrast, placing a negative bias on the p region will increase the height of the potential barrier, so that there will be only a very small current of minority electrons from the p region to the n region. Control of current flow can thus be accomplished with very little expenditure of electrical energy.

Background material can be found in CHARGE AND CURRENT; CONDUCTORS AND RESISTORS; DIODE AND PHOTODIODE; ELECTRIC CURRENT. *More details on semiconductors can be found in* CRYSTAL; ELECTRICITY AND ELECTRICAL ENGINEERING. *More information on particular aspects of semiconductors is contained in* NIGHT-VISION TECHNOLOGY; P-N JUNCTIONS.

Further Reading
Hazen, Mark E., *Exploring Electronic Devices* (1997); Horowitz, Paul, *The Art of Electronics* (2000); Sze, S. M., *High Speed Semiconductor Devices* (1990).

Sensory Mechanisms

First see NERVOUS SYSTEMS

Next see EYES AND VISION

Mechanisms used by an animal or living organism to gain information about its surroundings.

Touch. The sense of touch, like that of hearing, is a response to mechanical stimuli. It is generally considered to include the sensations of pressure, vibration, pain, and temperature.

Animal skin contains a variety of touch receptors, ranging from naked nerve endings to different kinds of sense capsules containing modified nerve endings. The best-known of these sense capsules is the Pacinian corpuscle, a pressure sensor.

Any movement of a hair on the body stimulates nerve fibers at its base. This receptor, called the hair end-organ, detects movement on the body's surface or initial contact with the skin. In humans, Meissner's corpuscle perceives the same aspects of touch but is present in large numbers on the nonhairy parts of the body, including the touch-sensitive lips and fingertips. The expanded tip tactile receptor, also found in abundance in the lips and fingertips, is sensitive to continuous touch rather than initial contact.

Smell and Taste. The senses of smell and taste both rely on chemoreceptors that form bonds with certain chemicals. Smell, the least understood and the most primitive of the major senses, seems to have been highly developed in the earliest vertebrates. Part of the brain originally devoted to olfaction evolved in humans into the limbic system, which controls emotions, and smells in modern humans have a unique capacity to arouse visceral sensations of pleasure or disgust. In humans, smell receptors also are important in the perception of taste; if the olfactory system is disabled, if only by a cold, food can lose its flavor.

Olfactory cells, organized in the olfactory epithelium of the nasal cavity, contain hairlike cilia that provide the receptor surface. In air-breathing vertebrates, these are interspersed with Bowman's glands, which provide mucus to keep the epithelium moist. An odorant binds with a receptor protein in a way that multiplies its ability to excite the receptor. As a result, many animals can perceive a single molecule of some substances, although each kind of animal is more sensitive to some odors than to others. Even humans, who are not known for olfactory sensitivity, can perceive methyl mercaptan (the odorant added to natural gas) at a density of only one 25-billionth of a milligram per milliliter of air. It is not known exactly how odors are distinguished, but it appears there may be 1,000 primary odors, each with its own class of receptor.

By contrast, there appear to be only four primary tastes—sweet, sour, salty, and bitter—which combine to form a range of tastes. In insects, taste receptors are found on the sensory hairs of the feet, as well as on the mouthparts. Among mammals, the receptors, called taste buds, are found primarily on the tongue. While they are specialized—humans taste sweet and salt most easily with the taste buds on the front of the tongue, sour at the sides, and bitter at the back—each taste bud can sense all four tastes to some extent. Each taste bud is composed of 30 to 50 epithelial cells, with tiny hairs, or microvilli, that provide the receptor surface, entwined by a network of nerve fibers.

Material on hearing and sight is covered in the entries EARS AND HEARING *and* EYES AND VISION, *respectively. Related areas to be considered are* BRAIN; NERVOUS SYSTEMS; NEURONS. *Advanced subjects are developed in* COMMUNICATION IN NATURE; REFLEXES; REPRODUCTIVE STRATEGIES; PHEROMONES. *More information on particular aspects is contained in* ALLERGY; MEMORY; NAVIGATION.

Further Reading
Kruger, Lawrence, *Pain and Touch* (1996); Farbman, Albert I., *Cell Biology of Olfaction* (1992); Beauchamp, Gary K. (Ed.), *Tasting and Smelling* (1997).

Servomechanisms

First see CONTROL SYSTEMS

Next see ROBOTICS

Servomechanisms are self-correcting, automatic control mechanisms designed to compare actual measurements with their preplanned values, and to take certain prescribed actions to reduce the difference to zero. If a ship deviates from its intended compass heading, servomechanisms in the steering gear move the rudder in the appropriate direction until the correct heading is restored; the autopilot in an airplane works more complexly, since it has to control speed, altitude, roll, pitch, and yaw. (*See* CONTROL SYSTEMS.)

The term "servomechanism" was first used during World War II, when military technology demanded close coordination among different systems. Scientists at MIT developed a fire-control system for antiaircraft guns, in which radar input directly controlled a high-speed aiming motor on the gun; similarly, Germany's V-2 rocket employed a gyroscopic servomechanism to measure changes in attitude and velocity, adjust the steering vanes, then cut off the engine at the appropriate moment.

Servomechanisms are integral to modern control systems. Whether the system is activated by deviations from plan or by simple time-sequence, the actual opening and closing of valves, switching of circuits, and shifting of materials are all performed by servomechanisms.

A recent development in servomechanisms is servopneumatics. Electronically controlled, these units can perform many motion-control functions efficiently and cheaply, while matching electric motors in accuracy and reliability.

First see NUMBER

Sets and Groups

Next see GROUP THEORY

Modern set theory covers a range from the most basic concepts in mathematics to some of the most sophisticated. Yet even the most complex theory is grounded in this fundamental: a set is a collection of objects. These objects must have something in common, and that common property is defined as follows:

A = {x | x has property P}

This basic definition reads, "A is the set of x, such that x has the property P." So long as a given set A is not an empty set (so long as it contains at least one member), a second set, B, can be constructed, which contains some of the members of A and no members that are not members of A. In such a case, B is called a subset of A, denoted AB. Finally, if both A and B are subsets of a larger set S, then the set A∪B, called A union B, contains all elements in A or B or both; correspondingly, the set A∩B, called A intersection B, contains all elements in both A and B. If the intersection of two sets is empty, the two sets are said to be disjoint.

For instance, a deck of cards contains 52 members, containing many different subsets, among them colors, suits, numbers, and face cards. If A = {card | card is a heart}, containing 13 members, and B = {card | card is a face card}, containing 12 members, then A∪B = {card | card is either a heart or a face card}, containing 22 members, and A∩B = {card | card is both a heart and a face card}, containing only 3 members.

These first operations are analogous to addition and subtraction; the operation analogous to multiplication is called the product of two sets, or the Cartesian product. Each member of set A is paired with each member of set B, rather than actually being multiplied by it; the result is therefore a vector, which can be traced on a Cartesian grid and treated according to the rules of analytic geometry. Two sets may also be related by mapping, in which every item in set A is assigned to a corresponding item in set B. Such operations are usually denoted by lower-case Greek letters. The mapping of a set's Cartesian product back into that set is called a binary operation, and it is the heart of group theory.

Groups. Groups are formed from a set and a binary operation (in which performing the operation on two members of the set results in a member of the same set); the two together constitute a groupoid. If the groupoid satisfies the associative law, then it is a semigroup. A semigroup with an identity in which every element has an inverse constitutes a group. For scientific purposes, the properties of a group can be determined more precisely than the properties of a

particular subject; a symmetrical molecule has a symmetry group of a greater order than a less symmetrical molecule. Mathematicians typically work on groups such as small-order groups, abelian groups, divisible groups, or free groups.

History. Set theory proper was invented by Georg Cantor in a series of articles he wrote between 1874 and 1897. His major contribution was to extend the conclusions reached earlier with regard to finite sets into the realm of infinite sets, a concept previously rejected; his most severe critics claimed that he was violating the sacred precepts of religion, as well as those of mathematics. Although set theory has yet to produce specific applications, its ramifications have transformed modern mathematics.

TOOLS

Theory of Sets

The heart of Cantor's theory of sets is the membership relation: given an object x and a set A, either "x is a member of A" or "x is not a member of A." Cantor added to that the principle of extension—a set is totally determined by its members—and the principle of abstraction—any property, or combination of properties, may serve to define a set. Therefore, rather than seek arithmetical parity among sets, Cantor's theory seeks equivalence among them.

Background material on sets and groups can be found in ALGEBRA; FUNCTIONS; NUMBER. **More details can be found in** CATEGORY THEORY; FRACTAL; NUMBER THEORY. **Additional relevant information is contained in** GAME THEORY; GROUP THEORY IN PHYSICS; KNOTS; TOPOLOGY.

Further Reading
Roitman, Judith, *Introduction to Modern Set Theory* (1990); Goldrei, Derek, *Classic Set Theory: A Guided Independent Study* (1996); Cameron, Peter J., *Sets, Logic and Categories* (1999).

First see REPRODUCTIVE SYSTEMS

Sex, Biology of

Next see REPRODUCTIVE STRATEGIES

Sexual reproduction, as opposed to asexual reproduction, requires two parents, each of whom contributes half of the chromosomes, which carry the genes. This allows for genetic variation among the offspring, as opposed to identical clones of either parent. Greater variety is advantageous for a species because a recombination of genes may see the appearance of an organism that is better suited to the demands of its environment. A population of genetically identical individuals is at great risk of being completely wiped out by a single threat, such as a virus, or a sudden loss of the food supply.

Agents of Reproduction. Gametes, or sex cells, are the agents of sexual reproduction. Males produce sperm and females produce eggs.

The sperm and the egg combine to form a zygote, a fertilized egg, which develops into the new organism. Each parent contributes equally to the genetic content of the zygote. However, the sex is determined by the sperm. In humans, there are two sex chromosomes; XX for females and XY for males. All eggs carry an X chromosome, whereas half of the sperm carry X and half Y. Sex depends on which type of sperm reaches the egg first.

The basic "equipment" for males includes an organ where sperm are produced and a method for transferring the sperm to the eggs. Sperm are produced in the testes and, depending on the species, are either deposited over the eggs outside the female's body or released inside through a variety of adaptive structures, such as a cloaca in birds and a penis in reptiles and mammals. Females produce eggs in ovaries. In some animals, the ovaries are distinct from the oviducts, the tubes through which the eggs journey on their way to an encounter with sperm. Mammals further require a uterus in which the offspring can develop. (*See* REPRODUCTIVE SYSTEMS.)

In most animals, with the exception of primates, mating cycles only occur once or twice a year, in specific seasons. This brief period of time sees a flurry of activity, in which multiple acts of intercourse take place. Sperm and egg are only viable for a limited amount of time, and therefore the chances must be maximized.

Other Than Animals. Sex is not the exclusive purview of the animal kingdom. Flowers are the sex organs in higher plants. The female portion is known as the pistil or carpal, and the male portion, which produces pollen, is the anther. Pollination, the transfer of pollen from the anther to the pistil, ultimately results in seed formation within the ovary, which becomes the fruit. Lower plants, such as moss and ferns, exhibit what is called alternation of generations, in which one generation reproduces sexually, the next asexually. The sexual generation is called the gametophyte generation (from "gamete"). Sperm swim through a thin film of moisture to fertilize the eggs. The zygote grows up to be the sporophyte generation, which produces spores. Each spore develops into another gametophyte generation.

All unicellular organisms undergo a type of asexual reproduction known as binary fission. However, bacteria also undergo a process that can be categorized as sexual reproduction, as it involves genetic recombination among different cells. Paramecia, another unicellular organism, undergo a form of sexual reproduction known as conjugation. Two paramecia can join at a structure known as the oral groove. Once attached in this manner, a "bridge" forms between their nuclei and allows for the exchange of genetic material. Once separated, the two organisms now display "new" genes, although no new individuals have been formed.

First see CHROMOSOME

Sex Linkage

Next see GENETICS

The tendency for certain genetic characteristics to occur in one sex only.

Genes, the basic units of heredity, are arranged within structures called chromosomes. Human cells contain 46 chromosomes. Of these, 44 are "regular" chromosomes, known as autosomes. The remaining pair are the sex chromosomes.

Females have XX as their sex chromosomes, and males have XY. During meiosis, the production of sperm and eggs, homologous chromosomes separate from each other, so that each resulting gamete has only half the chromosomes, and consequently half the genes, of a regular cell. All eggs carry one X chromosome. Approximately half of all sperm carry an X chromosome, the other half Y.

The genes found on the X chromosomes are responsible for what is known as sex-linked characteristics. (Y chromosomes carry very few genes, most of which are concerned with simply replicating the Y chromosome.) Among these traits are male-pattern baldness, hemophilia, and color blindness. These conditions are all recessive—they are present only in the absence of any dominant alleles. Females, who have two X chromosomes, have a better chance of having at least one dominant allele and escaping the conditions than do males, who only have a single X chromosome and therefore a single allele for the trait. A female who has one dominant allele and one recessive is called a carrier. She herself does not have the condition, but she may pass it on to her offspring.

Pattern of Inheritance. The pattern of inheritance of sex-linked traits tends to be from mother to son and from father to daughter. A male inherits his X chromosome from his mother. If she is a carrier, her son has a 50 percent chance of receiving the recessive allele. If she has the trait, he has a 100 percent chance, and if the mother is completely "normal," there is no chance of the son having the trait. In all situations, it is irrelevant what allele the father has on his X chromosome, because he can pass only a Y chromosome on to his son.

For a female to have a sex-linked trait, she must inherit the recessive allele from both parents. If her mother is a carrier and her father has the condition, she has a 50 percent chance of having it. She will certainly have at least one recessive allele. If her mother has the condition and her father is "normal," she may be a carrier, but it will not be possible for her to have the condition herself. (*See* CYSTIC FIBROSIS; GENE; KARYOTYPING.)

First see PLANT

Sexual Reproduction in Plants

Next see SEED

Sexual reproduction in plants is often described as the alternation of meiosis and fertilization, which produces a life cycle called alternation of generations. In most land plants, almost all cells are diploid, which means they have two sets of chromosomes, one from each parent. A diploid cell—the megaspore mother cell, if it is female, or the microspore mother cell, if it is male—divides through the process of meiosis. This results in four daughter cells, the megaspores or microspores. These spores are haploid, having only one set of chromosomes. In addition, during meiosis, the chromosomes usually exchange some of their parts. This process, called "crossing over," generally ensures that none of the four daughter cells is genetically identical to its parent or to the other daughter cells.

In animals, haploid cells produced by meiosis develop directly into gametes, the egg and sperm. However, the life cycle in plants is more complicated. The haploid spores divide through mitosis, the usual process of cell division. In ferns and lower plants, the spores are all of one type, not distinctly male and female. They develop into haploid plants that look very different from the diploid version of the same species. The haploid plants, which are called gametophytes, produce the gametes. In seed-bearing plants, the haploid cells do not develop into independent organisms but become gametophytes contained within the diploid plant. The female gametophyte is an egg-bearing embryo sac; the male gametophyte is a sperm-producing pollen grain.

Zygote Formation. When two gametes unite in fertilization, they merge their chromosomes to form a diploid zygote. The zygote develops into a diploid plant called a sporophyte, which will produce megaspore and microspore mother cells to start the cycle again. So alternation of generations refers to alternations between gametophytes, which result from meiosis and produce gametes, and sporophytes, which result from fertilization and produce spores.

The evolution of plants shows a trend toward dominance of the sporophytes, which benefit from their diploid condition. With two copies of each gene, for instance, they are more likely to function normally even if one copy of a gene is damaged.

In the more primitive land plants, such as bryophytes (mosses, liverworts, and hornworts), the gametophyte is dominant, and the smaller sporophyte often depends on it for nutrition. In mosses, for instance, the familiar "leafy" plant is the gametophyte. The sporophyte, which grows from it, consists of a tiny globe—the spore-bearing sporangium—on a slender stalk.

In ferns, the two stages of the life cycle produce two independent plants. The sporophyte is the familiar fern, which bears powdery, rust-colored sporangia on the underside of its fronds. The sporangia release spores that develop into heart-shaped gametophytes called prothallia.

In most non–seed-bearing plants, the gametophytes need a wet environment to survive, and the sperm, which have threadlike flagella, must swim through a film of moisture to fertilize the egg.

Seed Plants. In seed plants, by contrast, the gametophyte generation is drastically reduced in size and complexity and is dependent on the sporophyte, which is larger, more complex, and more fully adapted to terrestrial life. The sperm are not flagellated and do not need water for transport. Encased in pollen grains, their precursors can travel through the air. The sperm finally reach the egg for fertilization through a pollen tube that grows out of the pollen grain.

Gymnosperms, seed plants that do not bear fruit, show this pattern. In the most common gymnosperm, the pine tree, the mature female gametophyte consists of several thousand cells, including two eggs, and the male gametophyte consists of a four-celled pollen grain that produces two sperm and a pollen tube. They develop on female and male cones, respectively.

In angiosperms, the flowering seed plants that dominate terrestrial vegetation, the gametophytes are even further reduced. The female gametophyte generally consists of seven cells, including one egg. The male gametophyte is a pollen grain with two haploid nuclei that produces two sperm and a tube.

In angiosperms, sexual reproduction is intertwined with the flowering and fruiting that, to humans, are among the greatest glories of the plant world. At the center of the flower is the ovary; within the ovary is the ovule that contains the megaspore mother cell that will eventually give rise to the egg. Standing above the ovary on slender stalks are the anthers; these bear the microspore mother cells that will eventually produce the pollen grains. The colorful petals attract insects that will carry pollen from one bloom to another, setting the stage for fertilization. After fertilization, the ovary develops into fruit; the ovule, with the embryo inside it, becomes the seed. (*See* PLANT; SEED.)

Further Reading
Rieder, Conly L. (Ed.), *Methods in Cell Biology: Mitosis and Meiosis* (1999); Raghavan, Valay-amghat, *Developmental Biology of Fern Gametophytes* (1989); Allard, Robert W., *Principles of Plant Breeding* (1999).

Background material can be found in ASEXUAL REPRODUCTION; FLOWER; PLANT. *Advanced subjects are developed in* DNA REPLICATION; ECOLOGY; GENETICS; SEED. *More information on particular aspects is contained in* FRUIT STRUCTURE; GERMINATION; HARDY-WEINBERG LAW.

First see BLOOD

Sickle Cell Disease

Next see GENETIC DISEASE

Sickle cell disease is an inherited form of anemia that occurs mostly in Africans or persons of Mediterranean descent. Their red blood cells have a reduced capacity for carrying oxygen because they contain an abnormal form of hemoglobin, called hemoglobin S. A person must inherit two genes for hemoglobin S, one from each parent, to have sickle cell anemia. Someone who has a single hemoglobin S gene has sickle cell trait, usually shows no symptoms, and also has some protection against malaria. The hemoglobin S gene distorts red cells into a sickle shape, which gives the disease its name. The red cells are fragile and cannot pass easily through small blood vessels, so their presence causes hemolytic anemia.

The first symptoms, which appear in the first year of life, include jaundice, fatigue, shortness of breath, and headaches. There can be sickle cell crises, which are brought on by infection, cold weather, or a number of other causes, resulting in pain and damage to the kidneys, lungs, or intestines. There can be brain damage from seizures or a stroke. Sickle cell disease has no cure, but it can be treated with folic-acid supplements.

First see BONE AND BONE GROWTH

Skeletal Systems

Next see MUSCULAR SYSTEM

Systems of rigid or semirigid structures that provide a framework for the body and points of attachment for the muscles.

Arthropods—the insects and crustaceans that make up the animal kingdom's largest phylum—have an exoskeleton, an external skeleton that covers all their muscles and organs. Like a vertebrate's internal skeleton, it is jointed and parts of it work with the muscles as a lever—in the legs, for instance. The exoskeleton is composed of chitin, a polysaccharide secreted by the epidermis. Unlike the vertebrate skeleton, which grows and is remodeled, the exoskeleton must be shed and replaced to allow growth.

Other invertebrates, such as earthworms, have a hydrostatic skeleton—a semifluid body that acts as a skeleton by resisting compression. Combined with muscular contractions, it lets a worm inch forward by peristalsis. Vertebrates may have hydrostatic skeletons in their boneless appendages, such as their tongues.

Vertebrates have endoskeletons composed of bone and cartilage, tissue formed by the deposit of minerals on a framework of collagen fibers. Cartilage, which is softer and less brittle, forms the skeleton of the embryo. Some animals, including sharks and skates, retain cartilage skeletons throughout life, but in most species, bone replaces cartilage as the animal matures. Only a few patches of cartilage will remain—on the tips of some bones and, in humans, in the external ear and nose.

Bones meet at joints. At movable, or synovial, joints such as the shoulder or knee, the opposing ends of the bones are covered with hyaline cartilage, which is especially smooth, and the bones are bound together by ligaments, bundles of collagen that are continuous with the periosteum, the fibrous membrane around the bone. The joint is enclosed by a fibrous capsule lined with synovial membrane that secretes synovial fluid, a lubricating substance.

At cartilaginous joints, which allow only limited movement, the bones are united by cartilage and kept aligned by fibrous joint capsules without any synovial membrane. Mammalian vertebrae are joined this way; the linking cartilage is in the form of intervertebral disks.

In the third type of joint—the fibrous or sutured joint—bones are joined at an irregular seam, and movement is impossible. Such joints are seen in the roof of mammals' skulls.

Skeleton. Vertebrate skeletons have two components: the axial skeleton includes the skull, vertebral column, ribs, and sternum; the appendicular skeleton includes the legs, arms, fins, wings and their pectoral and pelvic girdles.

The skull has several functions: it provides a protective case for the brain and special sense organs (eyes, ears, and nose), houses the feeding mechanism, and encloses part of the respiratory system. From fish to mammals, skulls show an evolutionary trend toward having fewer bones.

The vertebral column, the center of the skeleton, is a semiflexible rod that is a protective sheath for the spinal cord. In fish, the body is hung from the vertebral column, which moves only side to side. In four-legged animals, the column moves up and down, an arch to suspend the body over the ground between the limbs.

Ribs curve off from the vertebral column. In mammals, ribs are usually found in the trunk and normally—as in humans—number 12 pairs.

In the appendicular skeleton, the pectoral (shoulder) and pelvic (hip) girdles support the appendages. In fish, the pectoral girdle is attached to the skull. In humans and most other mammals, it consists of the clavicle and the scapula, while the pelvic girdle consists of three bones that fuse together. The limbs of tetrapods show great consistency among species—the forelimb is composed of humerus (upper arm), radius and ulna (forearm), carpals (wrist), metacarpals (palm), and phalanges (digits). The lower limb bones are the femur (thigh), tibia and fibula (shank), tarsal (ankle), metatarsal (instep), and phalanges.

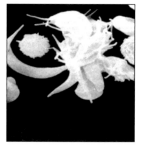

Normal red blood cells undergo sickling, but only after they have delivered oxygen to the remote reaches of the body. People suffering from sickle-cell anemia have a single amino acid substitution (valine for glutamic acid) in the hemoglobin in their red blood cells, which causes the early sickling, and consequent altering, of the cell shape (above).

First see BRAIN

Sleep

Next see STRESS, PSYCHOLOGICAL

The biological and behavioral state of natural unconsciousness that occurs at regular intervals.

There are significant body changes during sleep, which include lower blood pressure, lower body temperature, a reduced heart rate, and a slower rate of metabolism. Sleep provides an opportunity to dream. There is some evidence that dreaming is a positive factor in mental health, although the exact reason why people dream is unknown. One possibility is that dreaming allows a person to sort out feelings, impressions, and ideas and that dreams provide clues to a person's everyday concerns. It is believed that dreams occur only during periods of deep sleep called rapid eye movement (REM) sleep, in which there are active movements of the eyeballs. These periods occur four or five times a night and last about 20 minutes each. During REM sleep, the brain consumes great amounts of oxygen and has an increased flow of blood.

The changes in brain activity that take place during sleep are studied with an EEG, an electroencephalograph, which records the minute electrical impulses that are produced by the activity of brain cells. Brain waves are good indicators of the depth of sleep, and tiny electrodes that are attached to the scalp can record these waves. During waking periods, there are rapid and complex wave forms that are superimposed on slower alpha waves, which have a frequency of 8 to 12 seconds. During deep sleep, this pattern is replaced by delta waves, which are slower and simpler and have a frequency of 4 to 5 seconds. The EEG shows that there is an alternation between deep sleep and lighter sleep throughout the night.

There are frequent changes in the position of the body during sleep but generally not during the periods of REM sleep. An area of the brain that appears to be critical in controlling sleep is the hypothalamus. When this brain region is destroyed in animals, they can sleep for days and remain drowsy for many weeks. Nerve impulses from the body's sensory receptors reach the hypothalamus by passing through another part of the brain, the reticular formation. Activation of the reticular formation appears to eliminate sleepiness, while decreased activity in the reticular formation seems to promote sleep.

Background material can be found in BRAIN; CIRCULATORY SYSTEM; NERVOUS SYSTEMS. *Advanced subjects are developed in* METABOLISM; STRESS; THERMAL REGULATION. *Additional information is contained in* MENTAL DISORDERS; NEUROTRANSMITTERS AND RECEPTORS; NUTRITION.

Further Reading
Dement, William C., *The Promise of Sleep* (1999); Goswami, Meeta (Ed.), *Psychosocial Aspects of Narcolepsy* (1992); Empson, J., *Sleep and Dreaming* (1994).

First see VIRUS

Smallpox

Next see IMMUNIZATION AND VACCINATION

An extremely infectious viral disease that begins with flulike symptoms, then causes a rash and blisters.

Smallpox is transmitted from person to person by touch and other means. It starts as a bout of an influenza-like disease and soon causes a rash that spreads all over the body and develops into blisters full of pus. These blisters develop crusts, and when they disappear, they leave the deep, pitted scars that give the disease its name. In earlier eras, smallpox was often fatal, killing up to 40 percent of those who contracted the infection. Those who survived often suffered complications that included pneumonia, severe kidney damage, and blindness.

No effective treatment for smallpox was ever developed, but the disease was vanquished by a worldwide vaccination program. The eradication program was possible because there were no animal carriers of the smallpox virus, infected humans could pass the virus to others only for a brief period during their illness, and infected persons were easily detected. The vaccination program was concluded in 1980, when the World Health Organization officially declared that smallpox had been eradicated. Vaccination programs have been discontinued in most countries because one possible side effect of the vaccine is encephalitis. Certificates of smallpox vaccination, which once were required for international travel, are no longer needed.

As far as is known, the smallpox virus now exists only at the U.S. Centers for Disease Control in Atlanta and at a research institute in Moscow, where small amounts are kept for study and for use in case an outbreak should unexpectedly occur.

First see MOLECULE

Soaps and Detergents

Next see SALTS

Soap and detergents are known for their ability to remove stains from other materials. Water is a polar substance, meaning one end of the molecule has a slight positive charge and the other end has a slight negative charge. Most stains, such as grease, are nonpolar, so water alone cannot wash away stains completely. A soap or detergent molecule has a unique feature in its composition: one end of the molecule consists of a nonpolar material called a surfactant, which dissolves in other nonpolar materials, and the other end is polar and can dissolve in a polar solvent like water. The soap molecule is easily carried off by water, dragging the stain with it.

Soap is made of fat and a strong base such as sodium hydroxide, more commonly known as lye. The ingredients are heated together and a layer of soap forms. The chemical reaction that produces the soap is called saponification. Other materials are then added to give the product the desired texture, strength, and fragrance.

Detergents. Detergents are similar to soaps in composition and function, but they have an advantage in that they penetrate stains better, dissolve more readily in cold water, and do not leave deposits or residue soap scum.

The first synthetic surfactant for detergents was developed by the German scientist Fritz Gunther in 1916. By 1933, the first detergents for household use were sold in the United States. The earliest detergents were derived from petroleum products and were not biodegradable, meaning they could not be broken down in sewage treatment plants and so caused a surface foam on lakes and rivers. In 1965, a new biodegradable surfactant was developed, preventing the unsightly residue.

Since the 1970s, detergents no longer contain phosphates because these contribute to water pollution by causing a massive overgrowth of algae.

Related material on soaps and detergents can be found in HYDROCARBON; MOLECULE; ORGANIC COMPOUNDS. *Advanced subjects are developed in* CHEMICAL FORMULA; COATINGS AND FILMS; SYNTHETICS. *Relevant information is contained in* CATALYST; TEXTILE SCIENCE; WATER POLLUTION.

---

in different kinds of soils. For example, quartz is predominant in the soils of humid regions, while nonquartz mineral content is high in the soils of subhumid and arid regions. But the proportions of different mineral species vary from soil to soil; feldspars are common in the glacier-formed soils of southern Canada, while the glacier-derived soils of warmer regions have a high content of the mineral muscovite.

Many small particles of soil, both organic and mineral, have negative electrical charges. These charges are balanced by the presence of cations, positively charged ions, near the surface of these particles. These balancing ions are called exchangeable cations.

Acidity. Another important aspect of soil chemistry is acidity. Any soil with a pH of less than 7 is classified as acidic. Acid pH usually is caused by the presence of hydrogen and aluminum ions. Soils with a pH of less than 4 are rarely found.

The soils of dry areas often contain large amounts of salts, classified according to their ability to conduct electricity. Because salted soils are not good for farming, they are often reclaimed by the removal of excess salt through leaching and by ion-exchange techniques.

Further Reading
Bohn, Hinrich L., *Soil Chemistry* (1985); Sposito, Garrison, *The Chemistry of Soils* (1989); McBride, Murray B., *Environmental Chemistry of Soils* (1994).

Related areas to be considered are HYDROLOGIC CYCLE; PLANT. *More details can be found in* BIODIVERSITY; GERMINATION; HYDROPONICS; SEED. *Elementary aspects of this subject are covered in* LIQUID TRANSPORT; NITROGEN FIXATION; ROOTS.

First see NITROGEN CYCLE

Soil Chemistry

Next see HYDROPONICS

Soil chemistry is the study of the chemical properties of earth materials that support plant life. The composition of soils varies over a very wide range. For example, peats and mucks may contain as much as 95 percent organic matter, carbon-based materials that are derived from living things; any soil containing more than 20 percent organic material is classified as organic. In contrast, most upland soils contain 95 percent or more of such minerals as oxides of iron, hydrogen, silicon, and aluminum.

The chemical composition of any particular soil varies with depth, while organic content decreases sharply with depth. Clay and oxide minerals tend to accumulate in deeper layers; their aluminum oxide and iron oxide content tend to be higher in deeper layers, while the silicon oxide content is lower.

Minerals in soils are derived from rock and other formations and are broken down into simpler minerals by both physical and weathering processes. Primary mineral contents vary widely

Above, rows of solar energy panels at the ARCO Solar-Photovoltaic power plant in Hesperia, California, which has been in operation since 1983.

First see ENERGY

Solar Energy Systems

Next see ENERGY, ALTERNATIVE

Built to capture the energy in sunlight and transform it into usable electric power.

Three methods can be used to generate solar-electric power. One such method is the solar-thermal distributed receiver system (STDS). A second is the solar-thermal central receiver system (STCRS). The third is the photovoltaic system (PVS).

In the STDS, solar energy is absorbed over a large area that is covered with one of two kinds of collectors—flat-plate collectors or parabolic trough concentrators. Both use the heat they collect to turn electricity-generating turbines. A flat-plate collector operates at turbine inlet temperatures of 120 degrees to 260 degrees Fahrenheit. A parabolic trough concentrator focuses the sunlight it receives on a heat pipe that carries a working fluid. It can achieve temperatures of 300 degrees to 530 degrees Fahrenheit at the turbine inlet. Because a higher temperature means higher efficiency and less land to be covered by collectors, the parabolic trough concentrator can generate more electricity, but it is a more expensive system because the piping and coating needed for such a system are costly.

In the STCRS, sunlight is concentrated on a receiver by a large number of heliostats, mirrors that are mounted so that they follow the sun through the day. The receiver is a heater that is located on top of a tower. There can be a number of heaters in a system, each serving a certain collector area. The power output achievable by one such module depends on the area of the array of collectors; this area also determines the height of the tower on which the receiver is mounted. The horizontal distance of the mirror that is furthest from the foot of the tower is about twice the height of the tower; this height can range from 250 to 500 yards.

In the photovoltaic system, solar cells are used to generate electricity. These solar cells are spread over a large area, as in the STDS, to collect as much sunlight as possible. The output of a photovoltaic system is direct-current electricity. This is advantageous if the electricity is to be transmitted over a long distance, since power losses are less than with the transmissions of alternating current. The principal advantages of the photovoltaic system over the other solar power systems are that it does not require moving parts and it does not need cooling equipment. Its major disadvantage is its low efficiency, generally converting only about 20 percent of the sunlight it receives into electric power, about half the efficiency of the STCRS.

Special topics in the area of solar energy are found in ENERGY; SOLAR WIND; SUN. *Advanced subjects are developed in* ENERGY, ALTERNATIVE; FOSSIL FUEL POWER. *Elementary aspects of this subject are covered in* GEOTHERMAL ENERGY; POPULATION ECOLOGY. *See also* NUCLEAR POWER.

First see BINARY STAR

Solar System

Next see EXTRATERRESTRIAL LIFE

A star (such as our sun) and all the bodies orbiting it.

Because the sun is a very ordinary star, one might assume that many other stars have planetary systems similar to our own. A variety of theories have been proposed to explain the formation of planetary systems, and generally they apply equally well to other stars as to the sun.

The most widely accepted theory of solar system formation is the nebular hypothesis, first proposed in the seventeenth century by French astronomer Pierre Laplace. Laplace surmised that a star and planets would form from a large, slowly contracting mass of matter. As the contraction continued, the angular velocity of the

Below, a montage of the planets. From upper left, Mercury (image taken by *Mariner 10*); Venus (*Magellan*); Earth and Moon (*Galileo*); Mars (*Viking*); Jupiter; Saturn; Uranus; and Neptune (*Voyager*). (No spacecraft has visited Pluto as yet.)

Further Reading
Boer, Karl, *Advances in Solar Energy* (1998); Markvart, Thomas (Ed.), *Solar Electricity* (1994).

mass increased; when the centrifugal force pulling the mass apart became greater than the gravitational force holding it together, a ring of matter split off. As the angular velocity of the parent mass continued to increase, more rings split off. Laplace pictured these successive rings condensing to form the major planets of the solar system.

As the planets formed, the same process of condensation and splitting resulted in the formation of satellites such as the moon. Meanwhile, the central mass, representing the great bulk of matter in the system, condensed until the forces within it became great enough to cause thermonuclear reactions, creating a star.

Laplace's general idea, that a cloud of matter in space contracted to form a star and planets, is still widely accepted. However, it is now thought that, instead of rings forming and collapsing into planets, planets developed from a disk of gases and dust rotating around a developing star. Near the star, material clumped together to form boulder-sized objects called planetesimals, which then came together to form small, rocky planets like Earth and Mars. Farther out, where the warmth of the sun had not vaporized materials like hydrogen and helium, this core was covered by a huge sphere of these elements, resulting in gas giants similar to Jupiter and Saturn.

Images from the Hubble Space Telescope have revealed disks of dust around many young stars, lending support to this hypothesis.

Other Theories. In the early twentieth century, other theories were proposed, although these are not currently accepted. One was the tidal friction theory, which claimed that two stars brushing past one another could cause the ejection of enough material to form planets. This theory was questioned on the basis of astronomical calculations that indicate that the material pulled from a star by such a collision would dissipate rather than form planets.

First see SUN

The Quest for New Planets

A number of methods are being employed in the search for planets around other stars. Since 1995, astronomers have deduced the presence of planets from perturbations in a star's velocity, an extremely indirect search method. Now, the Hubble Space Telescope is watching for flickers of light from nearby stars, direct results of planets passing across their faces. A French satellite, Corot, is to be launched in 2001 to monitor 25,000 stars for such evidence. A Space Interferometry Mission, planned by NASA for 2005, will be able to find planets the size of Saturn or Neptune. Planets the size of Earth remain very difficult to identify.

The planetesimal hypothesis, proposed early in the twentieth century by T. C. Chamberlain and F. R. Moulton, claimed that the passage of a nearby star caused an immense tidal surge toward that star and a lesser one away from it. The matter freed by the larger tidal surge formed major planets, while the matter freed by the small surge formed smaller planets.

Age of the Solar System. Studies of the abundance of radioactive isotopes in the solar system indicate that it formed about 4.5 billion years ago. As far as can be determined, the orbits of the planets have been stable over that period, and major changes in the positions of the planets have not occurred. It is therefore assumed that similarly stable systems have formed around stars whose characteristics resemble those of the sun.

Other Solar Systems. It is believed that the physical conditions that resulted in the creation of our planetary system are prevalent in many observed instances of star formation, and that the characteristics of many of those star systems are basically similar to the characteristics of our own, indicating possible planetary development. To date, planets the size of Jupiter or greater have been found around 18 stars. One star, Upsilon Andromeda, has three such planets, two orbiting at about the same distances as Venus and Mars.

The ability to visit such systems is a more difficult problem to solve. The Terrestial Planet Finder, scheduled for 2010, and the Life Finder, scheduled a decade after that, should help us learn more.

Further developments in the field are discussed in PLANET; SUN; UNIVERSE, LARGE-SCALE STRUCTURE OF. *Further details can be found in* EXTRATERRESTRIAL LIFE; SATELLITES, PLANETARY; TELESCOPE. *Additional relevant information is contained in* LIFE, DEFINITION AND ORIGIN OF; OORT CLOUD; RADIO ASTRONOMY.

Above, the deformation of Earth's magnetic field by the solar wind.

Further Reading
Akasofu, S.I., *The Solar Wind and the Earth* (1987), Burch, J.L., *Solar System Plasmas in Space and Time* (1994); Buti, B., *Advances in Space Plasma Physics* (1986).

Further Reading
Weissman, Paul R., McFadden, Lucy-Ann, (Eds.), *Encyclopedia of the Solar System* (1998); Lewis, John S., *Physics and Chemistry of the Solar System* (1997); Greeley, Ronald, *The NASA Atlas of the Solar System* (1996).

Solar Wind

Next see COMET

A continuous outflow of plasma from the top of the solar atmosphere that penetrates beyond Earth to the reaches of the solar system.

The solar wind consists mostly of protons and electrons with a density of ten particles per cubic centimeter, at a temperature of 100,000 degrees Kelvin, moving at a speed of several hundred miles per second. The particles in the solar wind gain their energy from the high temperatures in the solar corona, the outer part of the sun's atmosphere. The gravitational field of the sun is not strong enough to hold these particles in place, and so they flow outward in every direction, dragging with them solar magnetic field lines.

Fluctuations of the solar wind occur during the 11-year sunspot cycle, from blast waves caused by a solar flare and from waves and turbulence in the outflow. The solar wind is the medium by which many effects of the sun are transported to Earth. For example, flare-associated shock waves can cause magnetic storms and auroras in Earth's atmosphere. Recent studies show a possible connection between the solar wind and weather on Earth.

Background material on the solar wind can be found in COMET; MAGNETIC FIELD OF THE EARTH; PLASMA PHYSICS; SUN. *Further developments in the field are discussed in* AURORAS; ENERGY, ALTERNATIVE; LEPTONS; NEUTRINO ASTRONOMY. *Special topics in this area are found in* INTERSTELLAR MEDIUM ("DARK MATTER"); INTERSTELLAR SPACE TRAVEL.

First see LIQUID

Solids

Next see CRYSTAL

One of three stages of matter. They are distinguished from liquids and gases because they tend to retain their shape and volume.

On the atomic and molecular level, most solids have a crystalline or near-crystalline structure; the individual atoms, ions, or molecules of a solid are arranged in a repeated pattern, at least over small volumes.

One distinguishing feature of solids is that they have definite melting points. In the boundary region between solids and liquids, there is a group of noncrystalline materials that do not quite fall into either class, such as glass and tar. Such materials do not have definite melting points, but grow increasingly soft and less viscous as they are heated. Even when they are at temperatures that are low enough for these materials to show the properties that are normally associated with solids, they tend to change shape when they are subjected to small, sustained forces. For example, a long glass rod that is supported only at each end will bend in the middle under its own weight over a time measured in weeks, although it cannot be bent much before it breaks. (*See* GLASS.)

Solid State Physics. Solids are the subject of solid-state physics, which is the study of the arrangement of atoms in rigid structures and the relations among the properties of these atoms, the structure in which they are arranged, and the properties and phenomena of the entire assembly. Until the 1920s, solid-state physics was regarded basically as identical to crystallography, since the major topic it studied was the arrangement of the atoms in the solid crystal. Now it is known that some solids are not crystalline.

In a crystal of table salt, for example, sodium and chlorine atoms are arranged alternately with perfect regularity. In window glass, a typical noncrystalline solid, an atom of silicon in the glass is likely to be surrounded by one arrangement or another of oxygen, another atom in the glass. There is no regular arrangement of silicon and oxygen atoms over long distances in a piece of window glass.

The properties of a solid can be structure-insensitive or structure-sensitive. Structure insensitive properties, such as the density of a solid or its melting point, do not depend greatly on impurities or imperfections in the crystalline structure of the solid. The structure-sensitive properties of solids, by contrast, are the most technologically important. For example, the electrical conductivity of a nonmetallic crystalline solid such as silicon or magnesium oxide can be increased by a factor of thousands or even millions when chemical impurities are incorporated in the crystals—a change that is of obvious importance in such fields as electronics.

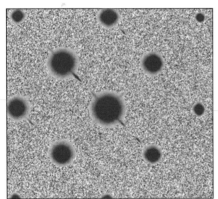

Above, the regular lattice structure of a metallic alloy.

Further Reading
Holden, A., *The Nature of Solids* (1992); Tanner, B. K., *Introduction to the Physics of Electrons in Solids* (1995); Keer, H.V., *Principles of the Solid State* (1993).

The foundations of the subject of solids are discussed in BOND, CHEMICAL; METAL; MOLECULE. *Further details can be found in* COVALENT SOLID; GLASS; LIQUID; PHASE; PLASMA PHYSICS; SALTS. *Advanced subjects are developed in* CLUSTER, ATOMIC; CRYSTAL; QUASICRYSTAL.

First see FILTRATION

Solvation and Precipitation

Next see CENTRIFUGATION

A solution consists of one material, known as a solute, dissolved within another substance, known as a solvent. Solutes can be solids, liquids, or gases. Solvents can be either liquids or gases. Aqueous solutions, in which water is the solvent, are the most common. All solutions are translucent and transparent.

The Example of Air. An example of a gaseous solution is air, which is a mixture of different gases. Nitrogen, the most abundant of the atmospheric gases, is considered to be the solvent. Gas can also be a solute in an aqueous or other liquid solvent, as is the case with carbonated soda in which the solute is carbon dioxide.

Solubility—referring to how much solute can be dissolved in a certain amount of a particular solvent—depends upon the nature of the solute and solvent involved, the temperature, and, in the case of a gaseous solute, the pressure. With the exception of a gaseous solute, the higher the temperature, the more solute will dissolve. With gaseous solutes, the opposite effect occurs; increased pressure increases the solubility of a gas.

A solubility curve shows the optimal temperature for maximum solute dissolution in a particular solvent. A solution is said to be unsaturated when it contains less solute than it possibly can at a particular temperature. A saturated solution contains the maximum amount of solute.

Solution Rates. Rate of solution, referring to how quickly the solute will dissolve in the solvent, depends on the size of the individual solute particles, the temperature, whether or not stirring occurs, and the amount of solute previously dissolved. The smaller the solute particles, the more surface area is exposed to the solvent, and therefore the more easily the particles will dissolve. Increased temperature means an increase in the solute particles' kinetic energy, which increases the rate at which they mix with the solvent. Stirring accomplishes the same thing. The more solute already dissolved, the longer it takes to dissolve additional solute.

Precipitation. Precipitation refers to a particular type of chemical reaction between two liquids or aqueous solutions. A solid product is formed that is not soluble in the liquid in which it is contained. The precipitate particles eventually settle to the bottom of the test tube or can be "spun down" by means of a centrifuge, leaving the rest of the solution clear. A precipitation reaction is actually just an ion exchange, in which two ionic compounds separate into their individual ions and "switch partners," resulting in the formation of new compounds.

Elementary aspects of this subject are covered in ACIDS AND BASES; ION EXCHANGE; LIQUID; OSMOSIS. *Further information on particular chemical procedures is contained in* ABSORPTION; CENTIRFUGATION; CHROMATOGRAPHY; FILTRATION. *Additional relevant information is contained in* CHELATION; ELECTROPHORESIS; TITRATION.

Sonar

First see SOUND

Next see SONICS

A method of locating underwater objects by sending and receiving short intensive pulses of sound.

Sonar is similar in principle to radar, which uses pulses of electromagnetic radiation. Radar is not effective underwater, but sound waves travel both farther and faster in water. The sound waves of a sonar system are transmitted and received by a transducer, an instrument that changes energy from one form to another. The active element in a sonar transducer is usually a resonant device that is similar in principle to a loudspeaker. Its sound waves can be produced by oscillating electric or magnetic fields. The active element of a transducer can be a piezoelectric crystal, a ferromagnetic ceramic, or a diaphragm that is driven electromagnetically.

Because the distance that sound travels through water varies with the frequency of the sound, different frequencies are used for different purposes. High-frequency sound waves are used to detect objects within a few hundred yards of the sonar set, while lower-frequency sounds can detect objects that are many miles away. One consideration of sonar detection is that sound velocity in water varies with temperature and pressure. The denser water at lower depths of the ocean can direct sonar waves downward too steeply, so that no echo is received. Although sonar was developed originally for military purposes, such as locating enemy submarines, today it is used by fishing crews to locate schools of fish, to measure water depths for undersea maps, and to measure the thickness of ice in the polar regions.

Sound

First see WAVE

Next see SONAR

A vibration in any elastic medium—air, water, or ground—that can be heard by the human ear.

Sound is informally defined as a vibration in any elastic medium—air, water, or ground—that can be heard by the human ear. More formally, sound is any continuous or pulsing vibration of a medium that carries energy outward from its source; it may or may not be audible. Thus, a body that vibrates in a vacuum does not create sound, since there is no air or other medium to carry the vibration. In air or water, sounds result from the expansion and compression of molecules caused by the sudden movement of some object, such as the vocal cords or a cymbal. This movement generates a wave in which molecules of the medium oscillate backward and forward, transmitting the sound. Sonics is the study of sound.

Velocity. The velocity of sound in any medium is determined by the elasticity and density of that medium. Sound travels faster in liquids than in gases such as air and fastest of all in solids. Its speed is about 1,130 feet per second in air (at 70 degrees Fahrenheit), 4,800 feet per second in seawater, 16,000 feet per second in steel, and 18,000 feet per second in quartz. Compared to these other materials, air is not a very good transmitter of sound. The explosion of a pound of TNT may be heard a mile away in air, but it can be heard for hundreds or thousands of miles in water. In formal terms, the acoustic impedance of solids and liquids, the product of density and velocity, is thousands of times greater for liquids and solids than for gases.

As it travels away from a single source, a sound diminishes by the law of inverse squares. The coefficient that describes the attenuation of sound is a function of the frequency of the sound; higher frequencies die away faster.

Measures. There are several measures of sound. One is its quality, which can range from the pure tone emitted by a tuning fork, which emits a single frequency, to the harmonically related tones emitted by a musical instrument to the noises of traffic or heavy surf. Another is intensity, or loudness, which is defined as the number of watts per square centimeter that fall on a surface that is perpendicular to the beam of sound. The unit of intensity is the decibel (db), and a tenfold increase increases the level by 1 db. An opera singer produces an intensity level of about 70 db at a distance of 3 feet. Sound becomes painful to the human ear at about 120 db. (*See* ACOUSTICS.)

Frequency, or pitch, is another measure of sound. Both high and low frequencies require more intensity to be heard at the same loudness as middle frequency sounds. The human ear is most sensitive to sounds in the range of 3,000 to 4,000 cycles per second. Younger people hear sounds ranging from about 20 to 20,000 cycles per second. Older people generally do not hear higher frequencies as well as younger people do.

Air and most liquids transmit sounds of any frequency with the same velocity, so that complex sounds do not disperse as they travel. And at ordinary loudness levels, the response in air, liquids, and other media is linear, meaning that the waves of different frequencies do not affect one another. This is not necessarily true of the human ear.

Human Perception. Because the human ear has a nonlinear nature, it can hear lower frequencies of sound only if higher frequencies are also present. This phenomenon can cause some unusual effects. If a sound of 440 cycles per second (such as the tone emitted by the A string of a violin) is put into an amplifying system that is arranged so that it does not reproduce any sound under 1,000 cycles per second, a human listener will still hear the tone of 440 cycles per second. This effect occurs because an A string has higher harmonics that are multiples of 440 cycles. The human ear hears those harmonics and recreates the original tone. This phenomenon is exploited by manufacturers of inexpensive loudspeakers. Such equipment generally does not reproduce bass sounds well, but the ear of the listener supplies them.

In the atmosphere, turbulence and strong winds tend to distort and dissipate sound waves. Thus, a warm, windy afternoon would not be a good time to attend an outdoor concert (unless the listener is close to the music); a clear, cold night would permit better listening at a distance.

Further Reading
Backus, John, *The Acoustical Foundations of Music* (1977); Newby, H. A., *Audiology* (1992); Elmore, William C., Heald, Mark A., *Physics of Waves* (1985).

Background material on sound can be found in DOPPLER EFFECT; PHONON; WAVE. *Other aspects of the subject are discussed in* ACOUSTICS; EARS AND HEARING; SONAR. *Related material can be found in* RECORDING TECHNOLOGY; TELECOMMUNICATIONS; ULTRASONICS. *See also* NOISE AND NOISE CONTROL.

First see NEWTON'S LAWS

Space

Next see SPACE-TIME

The vast area that exists beyond Earth's atmosphere.

We intuitively conceive of space as that which separates physical objects from each other. From a scientific point of view, there are two questions that you can ask about space. The first is how to measure it—how much is there? The second concerns its physical properties—what is it?

Measurement. The task of standardizing the measurements of space or, equivalently, the measurements of distance has throughout history been the task of governments. For example, we know that the Romans defined distance in terms of leagues, which were 1,500 standard paces of the Roman legions (the modern league is 3 miles). During the great medieval trade fairs in Champagne, France, the marshall of the fair kept an iron rod of a certain length. Every bolt of cloth sold at the fair had to be at least as wide as that rod—bolts that did not measure up could not be sold. In the Magna Carta, one of the founding documents of the modern democratic state, the king is required to see that there shall be standard measures of corn, wine, and ale throughout the kingdom.

Most measurements of length were based on a rough-and-ready human scale. A yard is roughly the distance from the tip of the nose to the fingers of your outstretched hand, while an inch is about the length of the last joint of a man's thumb. The foot was defined to be the average length of the feet of a group of men who came outside of Westminster Abbey on a certain day. Each country had its own units and its own traditional systems, a situation that became more difficult as international commerce grew.

In 1875, the industrial nations of the world entered into the "Treaty of the Meter," in which they agreed to keep a common set of standards based on the metric system. In 1889, the meter was defined to be the distance between two marks on a platinum/iridium rod kept in a vault at the International Bureau of Weights and Measures near Paris. Other industrialized countries kept copies of the official meter in their own vaults. (In the case of the United States, this was the National Bureau of Standards—now the National Institute of Standards and Technology—in Washington.) From time to time, these copies were taken to Paris for comparison.

However, having only one standard became more of a problem as industry demanded access to it more and more. The system became less and less useful. Finally, in 1960, the definition of the meter was changed. At that point the International Conference of Weights and Measures redefined a meter to be 1,650,763.73 wavelengths of a certain color of light emitted by the krypton atom. With this standard, anyone with a moderately well equipped lab and krypton gas could easily reproduce a length standard, and it was no longer necessary to keep a standard rod in Paris. This rod with the marks on it was consigned to a museum. In 1983, following the development of atomic clocks and extremely accurate time measurements, the meter was redefined again, this time as the distance that light travels in a vacuum in 1/299,792,485 of a second. Thus, the meter is now defined in terms of the second, and perhaps should no longer be considered a fundamental unit.

What Space Is. As to the second question, the constituents of space—the history of human thought has been somewhat circuitous. The Greek philosophers did not see how there could be pure emptiness (what we would today call a vacuum). Consequently, they postulated the existence of a substance called ether that was supposed to permeate space. This notion remained part of the scientific repertoire well into the nineteenth century, even though people knew about vacuums and could produce them at will. It was not, in fact, until 1887 that two scientists at the Case School of Applied Science Institute (now part of Case-Western University) in Cleveland did an experiment that showed once and for all that there is no such thing as ether. They argued that if ether really existed, then as Earth moves around the sun, it should be subject to a constantly changing "ether wind" in much the same way that someone in a moving car will feel the wind even on a still day. This "ether wind" would be expected to change the way that light behaved in their apparatus from one part of the year to the next. When no such change was detected, they concluded that space really was a vacuum after all.

Today, we understand that the vacuum is not simply the absence of everything but is a dynamic system. According to quantum mechanics, even in empty space, particle-antiparticle pairs can pop up out of nothing and be annihilated again without violating any physical law. Occasionally, one of these pairs appears next to an electron or a photon, and its presence can be detected. This was first done in the 1960s and is now a routine procedure.

Thus, the question "What is space made of?" leads to a dynamic picture of the vacuum and, ultimately, to the fundamental particles that make up the universe.

> Background material on space may be found in UNIVERSE; STAR; GALAXY; PLANET; NEBULA. Other aspects of the subject are discussed in UNIVERSE, LARGE-SCALE STRUCTURE OF; SATELLITE, PLANETARY; MOON; SPACE-TIME. Additional related material can be found in SPACECRAFT; SPACE SHUTTLE; SPACE STATION. See also VACUUM; ZERO.

First see ROCKET

Spacecraft

Next see INTERSTELLAR SPACE TRAVEL

A vehicle launched from Earth that is put in orbit around Earth or sent to another planet.

The theoretical principle of the launching of a satellite was expressed in the seventeenth century by Sir Isaac Newton. He showed that if a projectile is thrown in a direction parallel to the surface of the Earth, the distance it travels before falling to the ground increases with the force of the throw, and that if the force is strong enough, the projectile will never fall to the ground but will stay in orbit around the earth as an artificial satellite. An even stronger throw, Newton said, would cause the projectile to escape entirely from the gravitational pull of the Earth. The escape velocity for such a projectile is about 25,000 miles per hour.

Work of Tsiolkovsky. The first major step toward putting Newton's theory into practice was taken at the beginning of the twentieth century, when a Russian scientist, Konstantin Tsiolkovsky, claimed that rockets could be used to achieve the velocity needed to place a spacecraft in orbit or send it away from Earth. To achieve orbit around Earth, a satellite must first be sent up from Earth to its orbital location and then must be given the exact velocity needed to place it in permanent orbit. This double operation cannot be achieved by a single initial push—from a cannon, for example—because the heat generated as it passes through the atmo-

The *Lunar Excursion Module* (LEM), shown above with Buzz Aldrin descending onto the moon, and used on several Apollo missions, is the only true spacecraft yet employed by humankind. It qualifies as a spacecraft because it landed on a celestial body—and then took off into space.

Further Reading
Lewis, R. S., *The Voyages of Columbia: The First True Spaceship* (1984); Tribble, A. C., *The Space Environment: Implications for Spacecraft Design* (1995); Hartunian, R. A., *Reusable Launch Vehicle: Technology Development and Test Program* (1996).

sphere would cause it to burn up. Therefore, several rockets, or stages, are needed, first to get the vehicle off the ground and then, after it passes through the denser part of the atmosphere, to achieve orbital velocity. The lifetime of a satellite in orbit depends on its distance from Earth at perigee, the lowest point in its orbit. If the perigee of a satellite is less than 110 miles, its life in space is less than 2 weeks. Greater perigees mean longer lives; a satellite with a perigee of 499 miles will orbit for several hundred years.

Sputnik I was launched by the Soviet Union on October 4, 1957, and stayed in orbit for 82 days. The second artificial satellite was *Sputnik II*, which went into orbit on November 3, 1957, and orbited Earth for 162 days. It carried a passenger, a dog named Laika. The first U.S. satellite, *Explorer I*, was sent into space on January 31, 1958, in an orbit high enough to keep it in orbit for more than 7 years. The second American satellite, *Vanguard I*, was sent into orbit on March 17, 1958, with an anticipated life in space of hundreds of years. The first communications satellite, Telstar, was put into orbit by the United States in July 1962. Thousands of satellites have been orbited since then, for a variety of purposes, including communication, surveillance, and weather observation. In 1998, there were an estimated 2,500 satellites orbiting Earth, most of them for commercial purposes.

Humans in Space. The first manned spacecraft was launched by the Soviet Union on April 12, 1961. The spacecraft, *Vostok I*, made a single orbit around Earth in 1 hour and 48 minutes, carrying the cosmonaut Yuri Gagarin. The first American manned spacecraft, *Friendship 7*, was orbited on February 20, 1962. It made three orbits around the earth, carrying astronaut John Glenn, in a flight that lasted just short of 5 hours. On July 20, 1969, *Apollo II* became the first spacecraft to take off from Earth, land on another body, and return its crew to Earth, when it landed at Tranquility Base on the moon. The United States, Russia, and 13 other nations are now collaborating on the *International Space Station*, a permanent orbiting manned spacecraft. A mission to Mars is also planned.

Among the many highlights of space travel have been the first unmanned craft to reach the moon, *Ranger VII*, which made impact on July 28, 1964; the first soft landing of a spacecraft on the moon, *Lunar IX*, which sent back nearly 8,000 pictures after its landing in March 1965; and the first landing of astronauts on the moon, which occurred in the Apollo program in 1969.

> Background material on spacecraft can be found in MISSILES; JET PROPULSION; PROPULSION; ROCKET. Further discussion may be found in AVIONICS; SPACE SHUTTLE; SPACE STATION. Special topics relating to spacecraft are discussed in INTERSTELLAR SPACE TRAVEL.

First see ROCKET

Space Shuttle

Next see SPACECRAFT

A United States space system that can carry both astronauts and satellites into orbit around Earth.

The *Space Shuttle* is the only American space vehicle currently in use, designed for manned flight. Unlike earlier spaceships, which were designed for a single use, the shuttle can return to Earth and be ready for another flight in a relatively short period of time. The shuttle has three main units: the orbiter, the external tank and two solid rocket boosters. Each of the booster rockets has a thrust of 2.6 million pounds. The orbiter is the unit of the shuttle that carries the crew and payloads into orbit. It is 121 feet long, has a wingspan of 79 feet, and weighs about 150,000 pounds. It is about the size and weight of a DC-9 commercial jet aircraft.

Payloads. The orbiter can carry a payload of up to 65,000 pounds into orbit. This payload is contained in a cargo bay that is 60 feet long and 15 feet in diameter. The orbiter has three main liquid rocket engines of its own. Each of these engines has a thrust of 470,000 pounds. The fuel for these engines is carried in an external tank that is more than 150 feet long and nearly 30 feet in diameter and holds more than 1.5 million pounds of propellants—liquid hydrogen and liquid oxygen. The external tank is the only part of the shuttle system that is not reusable.

Mission Profile. A typical mission for the shuttle can last from 7 to 30 days. For missions that take it in an east-west orbit, the shuttle is launched from the John F. Kennedy Space Center in Florida. For north-south orbits, the launching site is Vandenberg Air Force Base in California. At the moment of launch, the shuttle's two main engines and boosters ignite simultaneously to lift the spacecraft off the launching pad. At a predetermined moment, the two solid rocket boosters separate from the orbiter. They release parachutes that carry them to the sea, where they are recovered for reuse. The orbiter jettisons the external propellant tank just before entering its orbit. The release is designed to let the external tank break up over a remote area of the ocean.

As it circles Earth, the orbiter uses its orbital maneuvering system, a set of small rockets, to adjust its path and to steer it toward any rendezvous it may have in space. When the mission is over, this system slows the shuttle for its return to Earth. On its reentry to Earth's atmosphere, the shuttle can maneuver as much as 1,250 miles to the right or left of its original entry path. To shield the shuttle and its astronaut occupants

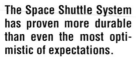

The Space Shuttle System has proven more durable than even the most optimistic of expectations.

from the intense heat of reentry, a special insulating material is used, which can survive temperatures up to 2,300 degrees Fahrenheit. The shuttle can land on runways at the Kennedy Space Center or at Vandenberg Air Force Base. Its landing speed is about 208 miles per hour.

Planning for the shuttle began in the 1970s. The basic design was determined by 1972, and flights began in the 1980s. One of the major missions of the shuttle in the first years of the twenty-first century is to carry into orbit the components and supplies for construction of the *International Space Station*, a cooperative effort of 15 nations to create a permanent manned presence in Earth's orbit.

Background material on the shuttle program can be found in JET PROPULSION; MISSILE; PROPULSION; ROCKET. *Further details can be found in* GRAVITY; SPACECRAFT; SPACE SHUTTLE. *More information on particular aspects is contained in* INTERSTELLAR SPACE TRAVEL; SPACE STATION.

Further Reading
Harland, D. M., *The Space Shuttle: Roles, Missions and Accomplishments* (1998); Lewis, R. S., *The Voyages of Columbia* (1984).

First see SPACECRAFT

Space Station

Next see INTERSTELLAR SPACE TRAVEL

A manned spacecraft designed to remain in geosynchronous orbit around Earth.

In the early history of space exploration, most of the space stations were orbited by the former Soviet Union (now Russia). The first Soviet space station, *Salyut 1*, was launched in 1971 and stayed in orbit for less than a year. It was followed by a series of *Salyut* space stations, ending with *Salyut 5*, which stayed in orbit for about one year. Two second-generation Soviet space stations were then orbited: *Salyut 6*, which stayed in orbit from 1977 to 1982, and *Salyut 7*, which orbited from 1982 to 1991, although its last crew left in 1986. During this time, the United States orbited several *Skylab* stations. One of them set a record by keeping a crew in orbit for 84 days in 1974. *Salyut 6* extended the record by keeping a crews in orbit for 96 days.

That record was extended by *Salyut 7*, whose longest crew stay time was 237 days. Cosmonauts from France and India worked aboard the *Salyut 7*, and 13 *Progress* spacecraft delivered more than 25 tons of equipment, tools, and supplies to it.

The Mir Station. The third-generation Russian spacecraft *Mir* (Russian for "peace") went into orbit in 1986 and was designed to be the first permanent station. Russian cosmonauts lived aboard *Mir* continuously for more than 9 years, and crew members from Afganistan, Austria, Great Britain, Bulgaria, and a number of other nations joined them for varying periods of time. *Mir* was finally abandoned in 1999, and was allowed to enter Earth's atmosphere and disintegrate in 2001.

In the mid-1990s, 15 nations, including the United States and Russia, agreed to build and orbit the International Space Station. It is designed to have living and working space equal to that of two Boeing 747 jumbo jetliners. There will be six laboratories, with a crew of up to seven members. Power will be supplied by solar cells, and atmospheric pressure in the station will be maintained at 14.7 pounds per square inch, the same as on the surface of the Earth. New supplies and new crews will be brought up periodically by spacecraft of cooperating nations. The station will have an emergency return vehicle, originally a Soviet *Soyuz* spacecraft and later a new vehicle developed by the United States, designated *X-38*.

> *Background material can be found in* Rocket; Space Shuttle. *More details can be found in* Gravity; Remote Sensing. *Relevant information is contained in* Interstellar Space Travel; Spacecraft.

First see Space

The U.S. space station mission *Skylab* (above) was followed by more sophisticated configurations like Russia's modular *Mir* space station, which eventually became an international effort. The future of and the need for space stations are still being debated.

Further Reading
Harland, David M., *The Mir Space Station: A Precursor to Space Colonization* (1997), Linenger, Jerry, *Off the Planet: My Five Months Aboard the Space Station Mir* (1999), Bizony, Piers, *Island in the Sky: Building the International Space Station* (1996).

Space-Time

Next see Special Relativity

A term for the relativistic geometry that includes the three dimentions of space and adds the fourth dimension of time.

In classical Newtonian physics, time and space are considered to be separate entities, and so observations of whether two events occur simultaneously or at different times are regarded as instinctive and obvious. But in Albert Einstein's concept of the physical universe, which is based on a system of geometry devised by H. Minkowski, space and time are regarded as interlaced. This means that two observers who are in motion relative to one another could have different observations about whether two distant events occur simultaneously. Minkowski's geometry identifies an event as a world point in a four-dimensional system of space and time.

Before Einstein proposed his special theory of relativity, the motion of objects relative to one another was not believed to have an effect on the time coordinates of those objects. We can say that the world was considered to have three-plus-one dimensions, rather than four dimensions. What Minkowski observed was that the basic equations of the special theory of relativity belong to a four-dimensional space-time that can be regarded as flat. A point moving in space is a world line in space-time, which can be compared to a line tracing the changing price of a stock on a graph. A burst of light that is sent out from an origin traces a three-dimensional light cone in time-space. It is only the events that occur within this cone that can be described as occurring earlier or later than the event represented by the burst of light from the origin. An event that occurs outside the light cone can appear to have occurred earlier to one observer and later to another observer. Therefore, such an event can neither be a cause of the event at the origin nor be affected by that event.

General Relativity. With the introduction by Einstein of the general theory of relativity, space-time became both more physical and more abstract. It is more abstract because it is related to a system of nonlinear differential equations that do not have a single solution. It is more physical because the space-time geometry participates in the dynamic physical processes of the universe. Thus, astrophysicists try to find phenomena in the heavens that will help them identify the geometrical properties that define physical space-time.

Various solutions of the equations proposed by Einstein give us a number of models of possible physical geometries. To define the specific space-times that are needed for these geometries, we must first consider that in curved space-time, a single set of time-space coordinates cannot cover an entire segment of space-time. Instead, coordinate patches are needed. Where these patches may overlap, differential transformation functions are used to relate the respective coordinates. Because of the curvature, there usually are no symmetries that can help pick out a preferred set of coordinate systems, such as the Euclidean system we use to define ordinary three-dimensional space. This means that the coordinates that are used do not have an intrinsic geometrical or physical meaning, as three-dimensional coordinates do. As a result, we must define physically meaningful quantities in a way that is independent of the coordinates.

Most specifically, the concept of space-time must be understood without reference to any system of coordinates. In its simplest form, a given space-time is a four-dimensional "manifold" (a generalized version of Euclidean space). We want the manifold to be continuous, so that every neighborhood has an infinite number of points, and we want to be able to distinguish these points from one another. In the abstract, a space-time system might not be physically reasonable. Nevertheless, while there are alternatives to the Einstein theory, recent observations have produced results that are within one percent of the predictions made by Einstein.

For example, it was the Einstein equations that predicted the existence of black holes, were discovered many decades later with precisely the properties hypothesized.

Background material can be found in MICHELSON-MORLEY EXPERIMENT; SPECIAL RELATIVITY. *Advanced subjects are developed in* GENERAL RELATIVITY; SPECIAL RELATIVITY. *Fundamental aspects of this subject are covered in* INTERSTELLAR SPACE TRAVEL; LORENTZ-FITZGERALD CONTRACTION; TWIN PARADOX.

First see LIGHT, SPEED OF

Special Relativity

Next see MICHELSON-MORLEY EXPERIMENT

A theory formulated by Albert Einstein that states that some laws of nature appear the same to all observers, no matter what their velocity is.

The special theory of relativity was Albert Einstein's response to the Michelson-Morley experiment, which showed that the speed of light is the same in all directions. It had been assumed that the speed of light would be different in different directions because Earth's velocity as it passed through the ether would affect it. Special relativity says that if light has a particular velocity in respect to a given observer, it has the same velocity relative to all observers who are in uniform motion with respect to that observer, whether they are traveling in the same direction or not. Breaking away from classical Newtonian physics, Einstein demonstrated that such phenomena as the speed of light could be described without knowing the velocity of the laboratory doing the study with respect to the rest of the universe. Another way to express this is to say that the equations of electrodynamics have the same form in all systems in which the equations of mechanics are valid.

The principle of the invariant speed of light had a number of revolutionary consequences for the concepts of space and time. One of those consequences is the contraction of an object's length as it approaches the speed of light. Suppose that we measure the length of a rod that, in relation to our own motion, is traveling at a very high speed in one direction and the length of a rod that is attached at a right angle to the first. We will find that the length of the second rod is unchanged but that the length of the first rod has

**Albert Einstein
(1879–1955)**

Further Reading
Davies, P. C. W., *About Time: Einstein's Unfinished Revolution* (1996); Friedman, Michael, *Foundations of Space-Time Theories: Relativistic Physics and Philosophy of Science* (1986); Thorne, Kip S., *Black Holes and Time Warps: Einstein's Outrageous Legacy* (1994).

Further Reading
Aczel, Amiel, *God's Equation* (2001); Folsing, Albert, *Einstein: A Biography* (1998); Miller, Arthur I., *Albert Einstein's Special Theory of Relativity: Emergence (1905) and Early Interpretation (1905–1911)* (1997); Thorne, Kip S., *Black Holes and Time Warps: Einstein's Outrageous Legacy* (1994).

contracted and that the amount of the reduction in its length is proportional to its speed.

Time Dilation. Another consequence of the invariant speed of light is time dilation. Suppose two flares are set off a few seconds apart. An observer who is moving away from the flare-setter will not measure the time between them as the same interval measured by the flare-setter; the difference in time is related to the rate of motion of the observer in relation to the flare-setter. Thus, time cannot be conceived of as being independent of a given observer; it is related to the frame of reference of each observer. In Newtonian physics, a complete description of an object can be given by measuring length, height, and width. In relativistic physics, time must be included in the description; it is necessary to describe a space-time continuum. The equation describing time dilation is known as the Lorentz transformation; this effect has been observed in the behavior of the subatomic particles called mesons.

Relativity's changes in the concepts of time and space made it necessary to change the laws of dynamics, especially as they concern a body in motion. When we consider the mass of a body, we generally describe its weight. But we can also think of that mass in terms of the energy that must be expended to stop the body when it is in motion. The heavier the body, the more energy is required to stop it, and the faster a body moves, the more energy is required to stop it as well. Another way to say this is that the mass of a body is increased by the amount of kinetic energy picked up from its speed.

Einstein expressed this idea in several formulas that related the mass of a body at rest to the mass of a body in motion. The best known of these formulas is $E = mc^2$, where E is energy, m is mass, and c is the speed of light. Einstein regarded this formula as the most important consequence of the special theory of relativity.

Today, it is a basic principle of nuclear physics and elementary-particle physics and is applied in many sciences, such as astronomy, where the principle explains the energy produced by the sun and other stars. The application of the principle during World War II led to the development of the atomic bomb. The principle is used in the production of nuclear weapons and in electricity-generating nuclear reactors, where uranium and other fuels are transformed into electrical energy.

Background material on special relativity can be found in LIGHT, SPEED OF; MICHELSON-MORLEY EXPERIMENT; SPACE-TIME. *Advanced subjects are developed in* ENERGY, EQIVALENCE OF MASS AND; LORENTZ-FITZGERALD CONTRACTION. *More information on particular aspects is contained in* EQUIVALENCE PRINCIPLE; GENERAL RELATIVITY; TWIN PARADOX.

First see ADAPTATION

Speciation

Next see EVOLUTION

The emergence of a new species in the course of, and as a consequence of, evolution.

A species is defined as a group of organisms that is capable of interbreeding and producing fertile offspring. Despite their vast differences in size and appearance, a St. Bernard and a miniature poodle can mate and produce a litter of pups. They are different breeds of dog but members of the same species, *Canis familiaris*. A horse and a donkey, however, are not the same species. The offspring of a female horse and a male donkey is a mule, which although physically hardy, is usually sterile.

Horses, donkeys, and zebras are all members of the same genus (the category encompasses several species) called *Equus*. The hybrid offspring of a zebra and a horse is a zebroid, and the offspring of a zebra and a donkey is called a zonkey. These species do not interbreed in nature. The sterility of the offspring is thought to be due to a difference in chromosome number. Horses have 64 chromosomes, donkeys 62, and zebras between 38 and 46. However, in 1984, and again in 1987, a mule named Krause gave birth to a colt (the father was a donkey). Krause and her colts have 63 chromosomes. Other closely related species can interbreed in captivity, like the wolf and the dog, and the lion and the tiger (the offspring of this pair is a liger). The offspring are either sterile or manifest severe disabilities either physically or in terms of personality and stability.

Interbreeding. Sometimes individuals from two different species do interbreed in nature. However, if this occurs only under limited circumstances, there are not enough "intermediate" individuals to blur the boundaries between species. Behavioral differences usually separate the species to such a degree that there are very few "mixtures," not enough to guarantee that these individuals will actually cross paths and mate in turn. A species is maintained by keeping potential mates of other species from meeting or mating. Differences in habitat and food supply can be enough to keep organisms separate in nature, even if they are capable of interbreeding in captivity.

Emergence of New Species. Speciation is the formation of a new species. Geographic isolation can lead to genetic isolation within a few generations, as is thought to have occurred with the grizzly bear (*Ursus arctos horribilis*) and the polar bear (*Ursus maritimus*). Once individuals become isolated, the gene pool shrinks and the variation among the population decreases. Over time, the shuffling and reshuffling of the same

Further Reading
Stuessy, Tod F., *Evolution and Speciation of Island Plants* (1998); De Beer, Gavin R., Sir, *Charles Darwin* (1976); McMenamin, Mark A. and Dianna L., *The Emergence of Animals: The Cambrian Breakthrough* (1990).

genes results in individuals with distinct physical characteristics, vastly different from the individuals from whom they became separated. Adaptive radiation then sets in, in which the members of a species adapt to a variety of habitats. Each finds a special niche and is able to establish itself with less competition for resources and therefore the possibility of producing more offspring. In this manner, the polar bear developed a unique coloration and diet as distinct from that of its grizzly cousin.

Related areas to be considered are EVOLUTION; GENETICS; PHYLOGENY. **Advanced subjects are developed in** ADAPTATION; BIODIVERSITY; BIRDS, ADAPTATION OF. **Additional information on particular aspects is contained in** EXTINCTION; MUTATION, GENETIC.

First see DIFFRACTION

Spectroscopy

Next see X-RAY SPECTROSCOPY

The study of spectra as they relate to atoms or molecules in a solid, liquid, or gaseous phase.

The spectrum of visible light, known by the acronym of R O Y G B I V and ranging from red to violet (through orange, yellow, green, blue, and indigo), is produced when white light is passed through a prism. Visible light, however, is just a small part of electromagnetic radiation, which includes gamma rays, followed by x-rays, ultraviolet (UV), visible light, infrared, radar, microwaves, and radio waves.

A bright-line spectrum is a set of bright lines produced when the light emitted by a glowing substance, such as a star or a heated chemical compound, is passed through a prism. Each element produces a unique bright-line spectrum, helping to determine the composition of a substance.

Applications. In addition to its astronomical applications, spectroscopy is used in the lab to provide structural information on many compounds, particularly organic compounds (those that contain both carbon and hydrogen). The various types of spectroscopy include ultraviolet (UV) spectroscopy, visible spectroscopy (VS), infrared (IR), nuclear magnetic resonance (NMR), and mass spectroscopy (MS). Often, multiple methods are used in combination.

All molecules have electronic energy levels, vibrational energy levels, and rotational energy levels. Electronic transitions are higher energy than vibrational-rotational changes. Transitions between rotational levels appear in the microwave region of the spectrum, between vibrational levels in the infrared region, and between electronic levels in the visible and ultraviolet regions. Depending on the energy originally absorbed and the type of photon emitted, different spectroscopy methods are used. As can be expected, UV and VS are used for molecules absorbing energy within their electronic energy levels, and IR is used for different vibrational and rotational transitions within the same electronic state.

UV and VS, which use an instrument known as a spectrophotometer, are used for molecules that contain one or more double or triple bonds between adjacent carbon atoms. They are most useful when those "unsaturated" bonds are adjacent to each other. UV and VS also provide useful information on structures that are aromatic (rings of carbon atoms linked by alternating double and single bonds).

IR also uses a spectrophotometer. This method is used to determine the various types of functional groups (atoms other than carbon or hydrogen attached to the hydrocarbon chain) in a molecule.

NMR involves the realignment of the spins of atomic nuclei in a magnetic field due to energy absorption. A type of NMR known as proton magnetic resonance spectroscopy (PMR) can determine the presence and location of alkyl (hydrocarbon) groups and aromatic rings. Another type, carbon-13 magnetic resonance (CMR), provides information on carbon-containing functional groups.

MS, which uses an instrument known as a mass spectrometer, involves bombarding the molecule with high-energy particles, such as electrons, that cause it to fragment into smaller molecular ions that are then identified on the basis of their mass. MS is used to determine the structure of most organic molecules. This method also gives a very accurate molecular weight of the compound.

Further Reading
Ebdon, L., *An Introduction to Analytical Atomic Spectrometry* (1998); Ferraro, John R., *Introductory Raman Spectroscopy* (1994); Silfvast, William T., *Laser Fundamentals* (1996).

Background material on spectroscopy can be found in DIFFRACTION; LIGHT. Advanced subjects are developed in BIG BANG THEORY; HUBBLE CONSTANT; X-RAY SPECTROSCOPY. Additional relevant information is contained in HERTZSPRUNG-RUSSELL DIAGRAMS; NUCLEAR MAGNETIC RESONANCE.

First see ELEMENTARY PARTICLE

Standard Model

Next see GROUP THEORY

Theory comprising two notions: matter is composed of particles called quarks and leptons; the forces that act between particles are produced by the exchange of other kinds of particles called "gauge" particles.

A useful analogy to understand the Standard Model is to think of a building. The quarks and leptons are like the bricks in the building—they are the units from which the structure is made. The gauge particles are like the mortar—what holds the building together. Quarks are the particles that make up the so-called hadrons, the particles that exist in the nuclei of atoms. There are six known quarks, which are given the fanciful names of up, down, strange, charm, top, and bottom. For example, the proton is made from three separate quarks—two up quarks and one down quark. Physicists speak of quarks as coming in three families—up and down in the first, strange and charm in the second, and top and bottom in the third. Each of these 6 "flavors" of quarks comes in 3 different varieties, which physicists call "colors," so there are 18 different kinds of quarks in all. (*See* QUARK.)

Leptons are particles that do not participate in the nuclear maelstrom. The most familiar lepton is the electron, which exists in orbit around the nucleus and is therefore an integral part of the atom. There are two other particles, called *mu* and *tau*, which are like the electron but heavier. The rest of the leptons are particles called neutrinos, which carry no electrical charge and have no mass. There are three neutrinos, one each associated with the electron, *mu*, and *tau*, respectively. Thus, as with the quarks, there are six leptons, arranged in three families.

The modern view of forces is that they are associated with the exchange of particles between two objects. To understand how this could be so, imagine two skaters approaching each other on an ice rink, with one skater throwing a bucket of water at the other as they pass. Each skater will recoil when this happens, and we would say that a force had acted between them. Clearly, that force would be associated with the exchange of the water. In just the same way, forces between elementary particles are associated with the exchange of different kinds of gauge particles.

The Four Forces. There are four forces in nature. The force that holds quarks together in the elementary particles—the so-called strong force—is associated with the exchange of a family of eight particles called gluons (because they "glue" the quarks together). The electrical force that, among other things, keeps electrons in orbit around the nuclei of atoms, is associated with the exchange of the photon (the same particle that carries light and other electromagnetic radiation). The weak force, which is responsible for some kinds of radioactive decay, is associated with a family of particles called heavy vector bosons, which are denoted by the letters W and Z. Whereas the gluons and photons have no mass, the W and Z are quite heavy—up to 80 times as massive as the proton. The fourth force, gravity, is not incorporated into the Standard Model but is thought to be associated with the exchange of a particle called the graviton.

Unification. The Standard Model predicts that at high enough energies, the weak and electromagnetic forces will unify. To understand this prediction, imagine that there are two sets of skaters in this example, one exchanging a bucket of water, the other a bucket of antifreeze. At temperatures below freezing, the forces associated with the exchanges will appear different because one will involve the exchange of a liquid, the other of solid ice. But if the temperature is raised above freezing, the nature of the exchanges (and the forces associated with them) will be the same, since they will both involve an exchange of a liquid. In the same way, the Standard Model predicts that at high enough energies, the nature of the weak and electromagnetic reactions will be the same.

As part of this unification process, the theory predicts that at these high energies, it becomes possible to produce the W and Z particles in the laboratory. When this prediction was confirmed in 1983, the Standard Model became widely accepted. The model also predicts that the strong and the electromagnetic-weak forces will be unified at energies much higher than those available in current machines.

The Origin of Mass. The Standard Model does not answer all questions about the nature of matter. For example, it does not explain why particles have the masses they do, nor, as mentioned above, does it incorporate gravity. There are theoretical attempts to extend the model to solve these problems. In some versions of the Standard Model, the question of why particles have the masses they do is resolved by the presence of another particle known as the Higgs boson (named after Scottish physicist Peter Higgs). In these versions of the theory, the Higgs particles are like a magnetic field permeating space, and each individual particle is like a different magnet. Just as different magnets will interact with a given magnetic field with different strengths, different particles will interact with the Higgs bosons with different strengths, and this interaction produces different masses. The search for the Higgs particle is one of the major goals of experimental physics.

Theories of Everything. The extensions of the Standard Model to incorporate gravity involve new theoretical ideas. The problem is to create a theory that treats all four forces in the same way. Such theories are sometime referred to (only half-jokingly) as "Theories of Everything." Such a theory would, in a sense, incorporate all fundamental knowledge of the universe. Finding such a theory is one of the major goals of contemporary theoretical physics.

Related areas to be considered are ELEMENTARY PARTICLE; NUCLEUS, ATOMIC; PROTON. *More details can be found in* ELECTRON; GROUP THEORY IN PHYSICS; NUCLEAR FORCES. *Foundational aspects of this subject are covered in* ACCELERATOR, PARTICLE; GAUGE THEORY; QUARKS.

Above, the Eagle nebula.

The Hubble Space Telescope (HST) provides what is thus far the deepest view of galaxies, such as the one below.

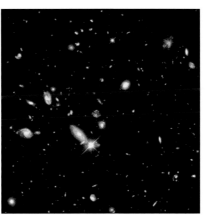

Further Reading
F. Halzen, Alan D., *Quarks and Leptons: An Introductory Course in Modern Particle Physics* (1984); Greene, Brian, *The Elegant Universe* (1999); Nambu, Y., *Quarks: Frontiers in Elementary Particle Physics* (1985); Trefil, J., *From Atoms to Quarks* (1999).

First see SUN

Star

Next see HERTZSPRUNG-RUSSELL DIAGRAM

A sphere of gas, mainly hydrogen and helium, that creates its own heat and light by nuclear reaction.

Stars may seem eternal, but in fact they are not: they are born, live out their lives, and die like everything else in the universe. Although the lives of stars are long compared with human history, that does not change the fact that stars are not eternal.

Stars are born in large clouds of gas and dust floating in space. In such clouds, there are always places where, by chance, matter is packed more densely than elsewhere. Such places serve as nuclei for the formation of stars—they pull in neighboring material, get bigger, pull in more material, and so on. The mutual gravitational force between parts of the cloud breaks the cloud into a series of contracting spheres centered on those nucleation points. In all likelihood, each of those collapsing clouds will become a star.

As a sphere of gas and dust collapses, the density and temperature at the center will start to climb. Eventually, the temperature reaches the point where collisions between atoms tear electrons loose, and the material becomes what scientists call a plasma—a material in which positively charged nuclei (especially protons) and negatively charged electrons wander around freely. As the temperature increases, these particles move faster and collide more violently, finally getting close enough together for nuclear reactions to take place. In a series of three separate reactions, four different protons in the plasma come together to create a single nucleus of helium in a process called fusion. The final helium nucleus and other particles created in this series of reactions have less mass than the original four protons. This mass deficit, via Einstein's famous equation $E = mc^2$, is converted into energy, which heats the center of the star and sets up a pressure that counteracts the inward pull of gravity. The contracting cloud stabilizes, and the energy radiates into space in the form of light. A star has been born.

Since protons, the primary fuel of these nuclear reactions, constitute the nuclei of hydrogen atoms, this process is called hydrogen burning. Depending on their size, stars can stay in their hydrogen burning stage for different lengths of time. The sun, for example, has been burning hydrogen for about 4.5 billion years and will continue to burn it for another 5.5 billion.

Small stars that do not have to burn much fuel to stave off the relatively weak force of gravity may burn feebly for a hundred billion years. On the other hand, stars 10 to 50 times more massive than the sun have to burn fuel at a prodigious rate to stave off collapse, so they only last for a few tens of millions of years. Ironically, stars with the most fuel have the shortest lives.

Eventually, every star will use all of its available hydrogen. What happens next depends on how big the star is, but all stars have this in common: with the hydrogen gone, a star tries to find another strategy to stave off the inward pull of gravity.

For stars of moderate size, like the sun, the endgame is relatively short. As the hydrogen in the core becomes depleted, the star starts to contract. This raises the core temperature until it reaches the point where helium nuclei can fuse to form carbon. This process, by which the "ashes" of one nuclear fire become the fuel for the next, is a recurring theme in stellar evolution. During this helium burning, the outer layer of the sun cools off and expands. The sun swells up until its outer surface actually extends past the current orbit of Earth, becoming what astronomers call a red giant.

When the helium is used up, the collapse starts again. For stars like the sun, the temperature at the core is insufficient for carbon burning, so there is no way to use fusion to overcome the inexorable pull of gravity. The sun will keep contracting until it is about as big as Earth. At this point, the sun will stabilize as a kind of cooling cinder in space or a white dwarf. Stars with masses up to eight times that of the sun follow this red-giant-to-white-dwarf sequence.

Larger stars go through a different (and more spectacular) endgame. In these stars, the temperature in the core is high enough to start carbon burning. These reactions go successively through silicon and magnesium until they produce iron. Iron is the most tightly bound nucleus in nature, which means that it cannot produce energy in fusion reactions. The star has run out of ways to fight off gravity.

As iron accumulates in the core, the electrons keep the star from collapsing, just as they do for a white dwarf. Eventually, the pressure reaches the point where the electrons in the plasma are forced into the protons in the iron nuclei. Deprived of the electrons to counteract gravity, the core, undergoes a catastrophic collapse until the neutrons can no longer be forced together and it rebounds. The outer layers hit the rebounding core and a titanic explosion occurs. Shock waves rip through the star, blowing all the outer materials into space. This is a supernova.

The final result of this scenario is an expanding cloud of material that contains all of the elements in the Periodic Table (elements heavier than iron are made in the final explo-

sion) and a small rotating core of solid neutrons. This neutron star will be only about ten miles across and rotating rapidly. On Earth, it is detected as a pulsar, a source of rapid pulses of radio waves in the sky.

However, if the star is more than 30 times as massive as the sun, even the neutrons cannot stave off the final collapse. Instead, it will continue on until the star leaves a black hole as its legacy—the ultimate triumph of gravity.

Special topics in this area are found in BINARY STAR; GALAXY; RED GIANT STAR; SUN. **Advanced subjects are developed in** BROWN AND WHITE DWARFS; ECLIPSE; HERTZSPRUNG-RUSSELL DIAGRAM. **Fundamental aspects of this subject are covered in** BLACK HOLE; INTERSTELLAR MEDIUM ("DARK MATTER"); NEUTRON STAR.

Further Reading
Greene, Brian, *The Elegant Universe* (1999); Thorne, Kip S., *Black Holes and Time Warps: Einstein's Outrageous Legacy* (1994); Tirion, Wil, *The Cambridge Star Atlas* (1996).

First see PROBABILITY

Statistics

Next see GAME THEORY

A set of methods used to bring order and insight to numerical information.

Because statistics involves arithmetic and algebraic manipulation of data, it is often a messenger unjustly blamed for the message (or an object of suspicion when the message is not to the recipient's liking).

Statistics offers a way of learning about populations by examining samples—whether random or matched—and arranging the data about them in terms of measurement, rank-order, or category. Once the data are arranged in grouped frequency distributions, they can be graphed to reveal the most important characteristic of statistical analysis, the measure of central tendency visible in the peak of the normal curve. There are three such measures: the mean (often written as $\bar{x}$), the median, and the mode. The algebraic sum of all deviations from the mean, or average, is zero; correspondingly, the percentile deviation from the median is (ideally) zero. In a symmetrical distribution, these measures will be identical, but in a skewed distribution, the mean will always fall toward the longer side of the curve; therefore, the median is a preferred measure in a skewed distribution, whereas the mean is preferred when the most stable measure is needed.

Shape of the Curve. The next important tools of statistics are those that describe the shape of the curve: the variance and the standard deviation. The variance is obtained by squaring all deviations from the mean, then adding them and dividing the total by the size of the sample; that is, the variance is the mean of the squared deviations, or the mean square. The standard deviation is the square root of the variance. A sample that displays a small standard deviation will be grouped more compactly around the mean than a sample displaying a large standard deviation, but all curves will generally stretch three standard deviations on either side of the mean.

The statistical model that makes best use of these manipulations of data is the normal curve, the product of the normal probability distribution. The normal curve contains 68.26 percent of its population within one standard deviation of the mean, and 95.44 percent of its population within two standard deviations. This curve allows one to move between statistical data and probability, since probability in a normal curve is the ratio of the area under a given part of the curve to the total area.

Therefore, the power of a statistical test is affected by three variables: the power decreases according to the size of the subject population; it increases according to the size of the sample used; and it increases with the magnitude of the difference between the norm, or null hypothesis, and the observed mean.

When more than one variable must be considered at a time, as when a new drug is being considered and potential variables range from the age and sex of the patient to the size and frequency of the dosage, the focus of the analysis shifts from the standard deviation back to the variance, or mean square. A factorial study is performed, using both additive and nonadditive combinations of data, to discover both the main effects of the variables and their interactions. Such tests are termed "parametric," since they require the estimation of at least one population parameter. However, there are also nonparametric, or distribution-free, techniques. The most important of these is the chi-square technique, which compares observed frequencies with expectations; others include the median test, the U test, and the signed-rank test.

Further developments in the field are discussed in NUMBER; PROBABILITY; SETS AND GROUPS. *Further details can be found in* ERROR ANALYSIS; GAME THEORY; MONTE-CARLO METHOD. *Additional relevant information is contained in* LOGARITHM; MAXWELL-BOLTZMANN DISTRIBUTION; NUMBER THEORY.

Further Reading
Freedman, D., *Statistics* (1997); Goldberg, Samuel, *Probability* (1987); Wagner, Susan, *Introduction to Statistics* (1992).

First see ALLOY

Steel

Next see HIGH-RISE CONSTRUCTION

An alloy of iron with varying proportions of carbon and small quantities of other elements.

Steels with more than 11 percent chromium are called stainless steels. They do not rust or stain and are therefore used in otherwise difficult environments. Carbon steels have three kinds of crystal structure: ferrite, a body-centered cube;

austenite, a face-centered cube; and cementite, an orthorhombic crystal. Another kind of steel, pearlite, is a mixture of ferrite and cementite arranged in parallel plates. In the nineteenth and early twentieth centuries, steel was made by the Bessemer process (named for its developer, British engineer Sir Henry Bessemer), in which pig iron is loaded into a furnace, air is blown into the base of the furnace, and the desired amount of carbon is added. Impurities such as phosphorus and manganese are removed as slag, and the steel is then poured out.

The Bessemer process was replaced by the open-hearth process, which uses a shallow open furnace heated by burning gas. Most steels today are made by the basic-oxygen process. Molten pig iron and scrap are put into a tilting furnace similar to the kind used in the Bessemer process. Oxygen is then blown onto the surface of the molten metal through a water-cooled lance. The advantage of the basic-oxygen process is that it allows a large proportion of scrap—up to 30 percent—to be recycled into new steel.

First see ENDOCRINE SYSTEM

Steroid Hormones

Next see LIPID

Hormones are chemical messengers that establish communication between various parts of the body. They are synthesized by specialized tissues known as glands and travel through the bloodstream until they reach their specific target sites, the areas at which they exert their effect and control. The target cell contains specialized receptors on its plasma membrane, which enables the hormone to "recognize" its designated work site. Hormones can be small molecules derived from amino acids, such as epinephrine and thyroxine; large peptides such as oxytocin and insulin; or steroid molecules such as the sex hormones. Hormones work by regulating pre-existing processes instead of creating new ones. They affect the rate of enzyme or protein synthesis, the rate of enzymatic catalysis, or the permeability of cell membranes.

Some examples of the better-known hormones produced by the human body are human growth hormone (HGH) and follicle-stimulating hormone (FSH) produced by the pituitary gland; oxytocin and anti-diuretic hormone (ADH) produced by the hypothalamus; glucocorticoids, mineralocorticoids, and epinephrine (adrenaline) produced by the adrenal glands; insulin and glucagon produced by the pancreas; thyroxine and calcitonin produced by the thyroid; parathyroxine produced by the parathyroid; estrogen and progesterone produced by the ovaries; and testosterone produced by the testes.

HGH targets the long bones of the arms and legs. FSH, estrogen, and progesterone all regulate a woman's reproductive cycle; testosterone is the male sex hormone. Oxytocin increases blood pressure. ADH targets the kidney and regulates water balance in the body. Mineralocorticoids, parathyroxine, and calcitonin affect mineral metabolism. Glucocorticoids, insulin, and glucagon regulate blood glucose levels. Epinephrine and thyroxine speed up heart rate and overall metabolism, enabling the body to go into "fight or flight" mode during periods of stress.

For many hormones, such as epinephrine and glucagon, a second molecule known as cyclic adenosine monophosphate (cAMP) is necessary in order to cause the desired reaction. When the hormone arrives at its target site, it binds to a specific receptor in the cell membrane instead of entering the cell. The formation of this complex stimulates production of an enzyme known as adenylate cyclase, which in turn increases the amount of cAMP present within the cell. The cAMP acts as the "second messenger," causing the actual change.

Steroid hormones are all derivatives of the cholesterol molecule. The five major classes are

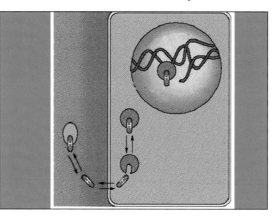

Right, the action of a steroid hormone in affecting gene expression. Such substances can stimulate muscle and bone growth but can also have deleterious side effects.

glucocorticoids, mineralocorticoids, progestagens (e.g., progesterone), androgens (e.g., testosterone), and estrogens. The primary effect of steroid hormones is on gene expression rather than on enzyme activity. These hormones must enter their target cells to exert their effects.

Prostaglandins are a group of fatty acids (the "building blocks" of lipids) that affect a variety of physiological processes and modulate the action of hormones. The effect of a specific prostaglandin varies from one cell to another as opposed to a hormone whose action is uniform. Prostaglandins are found in menstrual and seminal secretions. They cause muscular contractions and also increase inflammation.

Further Reading
Moudigil, V.K., *Recent Advances in Steroid Hormone Action* (1988); Moudgil, V.K., *Steroid Hormone Receptors: Basic and Clinical Aspects* (1994); Sheridan, Peter J., *Steroid Receptors and Disease* (1988).

Background material on steroid hormones can be found in ENDOCRINE SYSTEMS; MUSCLE; ORGANIC COMPOUNDS. *Further developments in the field are discussed in* BLOOD; CHEMOTHERAPY; CIRCULATORY SYSTEM. *Special topics in this area are found in* ALLERGY; ARTHRITIS AND RHEUMATISM; PROSTAGLANDINS; PHARMACOLOGY.

First see GEOLOGICAL TIME SCALE

Stratigraphy

Next see BIOSTRATIGRAPHY

The study of layered rocks or strata.

Stratigraphy deals with the description and naming of units of rock, the determination of their relative ages, and their correlation with rocks found in many other different areas. The earliest stratigraphic observations were made in the seventeenth century by Nicolaus Steno, who established several of the basic principles that govern the field. Steno observed that in a given series of rock layers the oldest layers must be those at the bottom, a rule that is known as the principle of superposition. Steno also observed that sediments usually are found as horizontal layers, a rule that is known as the principle of horizontality. Since Steno's time, it has been found that sheets of sediment usually extend continuously over extensive areas and that these layers wedge out against the sides of the basin in which they are deposited, a rule that is called the principle of original continuity. The principle of superposition is used to establish the relative ages of rock strata.

Works of Smith. New principles of stratigraphy were established in the nineteenth century by William Smith, a British canal engineer, who observed that the age of fossils found in rock layers could be used to correlate layers in which the lithology, or rock characteristics, were similar. It was soon learned that a definite series of assemblages of fossils existed and that at least some parts of this series could be found in many different locations, a rule called the principle of faunal succession. Before the expression of this principle, rocks could be correlated only if they were found in the same depositional basin, where the beds of rocks were continuous. This principle allowed for correlations to be made between separate basins, even though the beds of rock in those basins were not continuous, and to establish stratigraphic zones, with each zone being characterized by a distinct assemblage of layers that distinguished it from zones under it and above it.

Modern Stratigraphy. Today, the first goal of a stratigrapher investigating a new area is to construct a map showing the various kinds of rock that are exposed in that area and the distribution of those rocks. A field study of the rocks of the area is then undertaken, in which note is made of their lithology, the order of the beds in which they are found, and the structure of those beds. The rocks then are classified, usually on the basis of lithographic units. Rock formations can be lumped together to form a group or subdivided into members. In any given area, the rocks may preserve a continuous record, which indicates that they were laid down in essentially uniform deposits, or the layers may be discontinuous and incomplete.

Once such a map is completed, cross sections are constructed to determine the complete structure of the area being studied. With both the cross sections and the map, the geological history of the area can be reconstructed. The rocks of this area can be correlated with those of neighboring areas by lithostratigraphic correlations, which includes their lithological and stratigraphic characteristics. If the rock layers contain fossils, these fossils can be used to correlate the stratigraphic characteristics with those of other areas in which similar fossils are found. The basic unit of such a study is a zone. One or more zones can constitute a stage, several stages make a series, and two or more series make a system.

The foundations of the subject are discussed in GEOLOGY, ARCHAEOLOGICAL; METAMORPHIC ROCK. *More details can be found in* CRETACEOUS-TERTIARY BOUNDARY; GEOMORPHOLOGY; UNIFORMITARIANISM. *Advanced subjects are developed in* FOSSIL; GEOLOGICAL TIME SCALE; GLACIER; PETROLOGY.

Further Reading
Jackson, K.C., *Textbook of Lithology* (1970); Mutch, T., *Geology of the Moon: a Stratigraphic View* (1991); Tarbuck, E. J., Lutgens, F. K., *The Earth* (1998).

First see BRAIN

Stress, Psychological

Next see MENTAL DISORDERS

The cumulative force or forces that disturb a person's feeling of healthy mental and physical condition.

Stress can be experienced in response to a wide range of forces, physical or mental, that affect daily functioning. These include significant life events such as the death of a loved one, a divorce or a birth in a family with troubled finances, and physical violence. When such a stressful condition exists, the body responds by increasing the production of some hormones, most notably cortisol (also called hydrocortisone) and epinephrine (also called adrenaline). The results can be an increase in the speed and force of the heartbeat, a change in blood pressure, and changes in metabolism and physical activity. While these changes can be beneficial, when they reach a certain level they can disrupt the individual's ability to respond to challenges.

Continued stress often leads to both mental and physical symptoms. The mental symptoms include anxiety and depression. The physical symptoms can include indigestion (dyspepsia, in medical language), heart palpitations, and muscle aches and pains.

Post-Traumatic Stress. One kind of stress, called post-traumatic stress disorder, is a response to a specific stressful situation. This disorder can result from experience of a natural disaster, such as a fire or earthquake, or a serious personal trauma, such as physical violence or rape. When the disorder occurs in a military person involved in combat, post-traumatic stress disorder is called shell shock or battle fatigue. The symptoms of this condition include recurring dreams of the event that has caused it, a feeling of isolation, loss of concentration, and disturbed sleep. These symptoms can appear immediately after the stress-causing event or several weeks or months later. Most people can recover with the help of psychological counseling and emotional support, but some extremely severe experiences, such as military combat, imprisonment, rape, and confinement in a concentration camp during World War II, can cause lifelong problems.

Treatment. One way to counter the effects of stress is to utilize one or several relaxation techniques, which are methods designed to release muscular tension and achieve a state of calm. These techniques can be active or passive. In active relaxation, persons are taught to tense and then relax all the muscles of the body, usually starting with the head and moving down successively. In passive relaxation therapy, individuals experiencing stress are taught to clear the mind of every thought and to concentrate on a single phrase or sound.

In both active and passive relaxation therapy, there is a strong emphasis on controlling the rate of breathing, since hyperventilation (shallow, rapid breathing) can worsen feelings of anxiety. Biofeedback training is often used to help persons under stress achieve relaxation. Study has shown that traditional methods of achieving concentration, such as yoga and meditation, employ methods that are similar to those of relaxation training.

Further Reading
Goodwin, Donald W., *Anxiety* (1986), McGuigan, F. J., *Encyclopedia of Stress* (1999), Rowh, Mark, *Coping With Stress in College* (1989).

Background material regarding stress is covered in AGGRESSION AND TERRITORIALITY; BRAIN; NERVOUS SYSTEM. *More information on particular aspects is contained in* BLOOD PRESSURE; MENTAL DISORDERS; SLEEP. *Further nformation is contained in* ADDICTIVE DISORDERS; DISEASE, THEORY OF; NUTRITION.

First see QUARK

String Theory

Next see THEORIES OF EVERYTHING

Theory that replaces the idea of elementary particles as points with a conception of them as lines or loops.

The quantum theory of particles as points breaks down at extremely high energies or extremely short distances, where gravitational forces become strong enough to be comparable to the electromagnetic and nuclear forces that act between subatomic particles, opening the way for the string picture. Strings can occur in two topologies, open and closed. Open strings are pictured as segments that have two free ends, while closed strings are loops, with no free ends.

Given states of a particle are envisioned as standing waves that form on such a string.

Three Theories. There are three major string theories. In Type I string theory, there are both open and closed strings that have no specific orientation. In Type II string theory, there are closed strings only; this is also true of heterotic theory, the third in the field. These string theories lead to superstring theory, which is a unified theory of the fundamental interactions of basic particles pictured as superstrings whose length is measured in millionths of a meter and whose energies are measured in many billions of electron volts, far beyond the capability of any feasible particle accelerator.

The strings that are associated with the elementary particles called bosons, whose spin is expressed as integers, are consistent only with quantum theories that envision a 26-dimension space-time. Strings that are associated with fermions, particles whose spin is expressed in half-integers, are envisioned as existing in 10-dimensional space-time.

Consequences. One consequence of superstring theory is the prediction of the existence of the graviton, a particle or quantum of energy that is exchanged in a gravitational interaction. Gravitons have not been observed; they are postulated to travel at the speed of light and to have zero rest mass and charge. Thus, superstring theory includes a quantum theory of the gravitational interaction. There is no direct evidence for the existence of superstrings, but many of their features are compatible with the experimental observations of elementary particles. For example, the theory predicts the existence of particles that do not conserve parity, one property of the wave function of an elementary particle.

The space-time trajectory of a string is a two-dimensional surface called a world sheet. The world sheets of Type I strings can be very complicated; they are less complicated for Type II and for heterotic strings. These have a single fundamental interaction that can be described by a portion of the world sheet called a pants diagram. When this diagram is intersected by a plane that represents a slice in time, two closed strings are seen. If the surface is intersected by by a second time slice, just one closed string is seen. It is believed that the two closed strings approach and touch one another and join to form the single string.

The ultimate expression of string theory may potentially require a new kind of geometry, perhaps one involving an infinity of dimensions.

Background information for string theory can be found in ELEMENTARY PARTICLE; NUCLEAR FORCES; QUARKS. *Other aspects of the subject are discussed in* BOSON; GAUGE THEORY; GRAND UNIFICATION THEORY (GUT). *Additional related material can be found in* ACCELERATOR, PARTICLE; THEORIES OF EVERYTHING.

Further Reading
Greene, Brian, *The Elegant Universe* (1999); Gribbin, John, *Schrödinger's Kittens and the Search for Reality* (1995); Gribbin, John, *The Search for Superstrings, Symmetry, and the Theory of Everything* (1998).

First see OCEANOGRAPHY

Submarine Technology

Next see UNDERWATER EXPLORATION

Submarine technology has depended in large part on the development of propulsion systems. Specifically, the arrival of nuclear power has enabled construction of submarines that can remain submerged almost indefinitely. The first submarine of record, a craft with a wooden frame that was covered by greased leather, was built in 1620 by Cornelius Drebbel, but the real era of the submarine began in 1776, when David Bushnell, an American inventor, built the one-man submarine *Turtle*, which was powered by hand and used against British warships during the Revolutionary War. During the Civil War, the Confederacy manufactured several submarines. None of these crafts was effective as a warship.

The modern era of the submarine can be said to have begun in 1869, when Jules Verne described imaginary submarines that proved to be amazingly predictive of future vessels. In 1880, a major advance in propulsion technology was made by an American, the Reverend G. W. Barrett, who built a steam-powered submarine. A decade later, John P. Holland, an American inventor, built the first truly successful submarine, named the *Holland*, which was launched in 1898. This vessel, and others designed by Holland and another American inventor, Simon Lake, used gasoline engines for propulsion when they were on the surface and electric motors when they were submerged.

Nuclear-powered submarines armed with nuclear warheads, such as the Trident, above, formed a critical part of the strategic arsenal of both the United States and the Soviet Union during the Cold War.

The World Wars. Submarine technology took great strides forward during the two World Wars. Perhaps the most effective submarines were the German U-boats, the first to use snorkels, specialized breathing tubes, to supply air to their engines. Nevertheless, none of the submarines used by either side in the World Wars could remain submerged for a very long time, because they required oxygen for their engines. That handicap was overcome by the development of nuclear propulsion systems in the 1950s. The first nuclear-powered submarine was the *Nautilus*, which entered service with the U.S. Navy in 1955 and made a pioneering voyage under the polar ice cap in 1958.

Modern submarines generally have double hulls, with tanks for fuel and ballast between the inner and outer hulls. Submarines submerge by flooding the ballast tanks with water from the ocean, and surface by pumping the water out of the tanks. Submarines are equipped with inertial guidance systems that measure changes in the vessel's speed and direction, so that they can navigate without coming to the surface. In addition to their use as military vessels, submarines now are utilized for scientific observations of the underwater environment.

First see ECOLOGY

Succession

Next see HOMEOSTASIS

A progressive series of changes in the type and number of organisms in a particular habitat.

There is not much diversity in the early stages of succession. Succession begins with a pioneer community that "colonizes" an environment and makes it more hospitable to other types of organisms. If the pioneer community is successful, conditions may change enough that relative newcomers to the area are better adapted than the original "settlers." Eventually, the pioneers are replaced by organisms that could not have lived there under the early conditions. The climax is reached when a community is established that contains no potential ecological niches that can be filled by any new species or filled better than by the organisms already present.

Primary succession begins with a lifeless habitat, for example, bare rock. Lichen, which is really two organisms, a fungus and an alga living together in a mutually beneficial relationship, settles in. As the lichen thrives, other lichens begin to grow. The old ones die and are broken down, adding to the mineral deposits on the rock. Gradually, enough soil builds up that primitive plants such as moss begin to grow. The soil accumulation continues with weathering of the rock, along with the decay of plant material and the increase of mineral deposits. Eventually, further evolved plants begin to grow in the area. The original lichen have by this time been completely replaced. As plant life flourishes and becomes more varied, animals can establish themselves in the area as well.

Secondary succession begins with a pre-existing community within a particular habitat. A new organism invades and gradually replaces the original creatures. (*See* POPULATION ECOLOGY.)

First see PERIODIC TABLE OF THE ELEMENTS

Sulfur

Next see FOOD SCIENCE

The 16th element on the Periodic Table. Each sulfur atom has 16 protons, 16 neutrons, and 16 electrons.

Sulfur's chemical behavior is roughly analogous to that of oxygen because it is located in the same family of elements (beneath oxygen on the Periodic Table) and has the same number of valence electrons. Sulfur is a nonmetal and can form either ionic bonds (electrons are gained or lost) or covalent bonds (electrons are shared between atoms). When combined with a metal, sulfur forms an ionic bond, and when joined with another nonmetal, the resulting bond is covalent.

Sulfur forms strong bonds with those elements known as transition metals and the heavier metals. Many metals in the Earth's crust are found as sulfide ores, which contain lead, sphalerite, which contains a mixture of iron and zinc, and cinnabar, which contains mercury.

Pure sulfur in its elemental state (not part of a compound) exists as a solid at room temperature, a yellowish powder. It has two principal

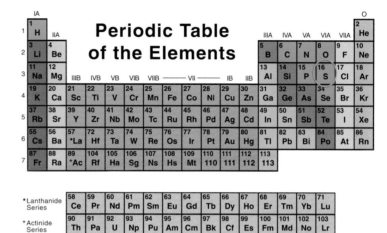

allotropes as well as two minor ones. Allotropes are interatomic structures of the same element that have different physical and chemical properties. The two principal allotropes of sulfur consist of rings made up of eight sulfur atoms each. Of the two minor allotropes, one is a ring of six sulfur atoms and the other is a helical chain of sulfur atoms.

Sulfur is found in a variety of compounds that have very vivid colors and/or odors. Sulfur dioxide, targeted by the Environmental Protection Agency, the EPA, as one of six major pollutants, is one of the principal components of acid rain. It is also the compound that gives rotten eggs their characteristic odor. Gunpowder, the earliest explosive material developed, is a mixture of sulfur, potassium or sodium nitrate, and charcoal. When the sulfate ion (SO_4^{-2}) combines with hydrogen, the resulting product is sulfuric acid, one of the most powerful acids known. (*See* ACIDS AND BASES.)

Above, the position of sulfur on the Periodic Table shows why it shares many properties with oxygen above it on the table.

Background material can be found in BOND, CHEMICAL; PERIODIC TABLE OF THE ELEMENTS; WATER POLLUTION. *More details can be found in* AIR POLLUTION; HYDROCARBONS; PETROLEUM DISTILLATION. *Elementary aspects of this subject are covered in* MINING TECHNOLOGY; SALTS; SOIL CHEMISTRY.

Further Reading
Malone, Leo J., *Basic Concepts of Chemistry* (1996); Szward, M. (Ed.), Prager, Jan C., *Environmental Contaminant Reference Databook* (1997).

Sun

First see STAR

Next see SOLAR WIND

The star nearest to the Earth and consequently the easiest star to study. It is a giant ball of gas floating freely in space; it is the source of all energy and is responsible for all life on our planet.

Like all stars, the sun formed when a cloud of interstellar gas and dust began to collapse because of the mutual gravitational attraction among its parts. For the sun, this process started about 4.5 billion years ago. As the contraction went on, the gas at the center got hotter and hotter, until electrons were stripped from their atoms. Soon, the interior of the sun was a roiling mass of electrons and protons (the nucleus of hydrogen, the simplest and most common atom). Eventually, these protons moved fast enough so that they overcame their electrical repulsive force and actually made contact. When this happened, the protons fused to form a new nucleus. This collision was the first step in a set of nuclear reactions that converted four of the wandering protons into a single nucleus of helium. This atom (and the rest of the particles created in this chain of reactions) has less mass than the four initial protons, and the difference, via the famous equation $E = mc^2$, was converted into energy. This energy heated up the center of the sun, creating a high pressure that halted the collapse of the gas cloud. It streamed out through the body of the star and into space, bathing the newly forming planets around it in light.

Today, the sun is still consuming hydrogen and creating helium to generate its energy. Astronomers estimate that some 4.5 million tons of hydrogen are needed to keep the sun going each second. The energy starts out from the center, carried by fast-moving particles and radiation. About two-thirds of the way out, the temperature and pressure of the sun drop to a point where hot gases rise in great streams toward the surface—in this so-called convection zone, the sun literally boils. This massive churning brings the energy to the photosphere, the part of the sun from which light is emitted, and from there another 8 minutes brings it to the Earth. Astronomers estimate that it takes more than 30,000 years for the energy to make this trip from the sun's center, which means that the energy in the sunlight seen today was generated about the time Neanderthals walked the Earth.

The Photosphere. Looking down into the sun is a little like peering into a murky pond. One can see only a little way—around 100 miles. Light emitted at greater depths undergoes collision and absorption as it moves toward the surface, and the light we actually see comes only from this thin outer layer, which is called the pho-

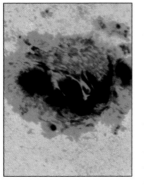

From top: the McMath Solar Telescope; image of the sun with sunspots (appearing as dots on a white circle); a sunspot on the surface of the sun.

tosphere. The temperature of the sun's photosphere is 5,800 degrees Kelvin, and the light it emits contains all the colors of the visible spectrum, from red to violet, as well as invisible ultraviolet and infrared radiation. (Ultraviolet radiation is responsible for sunburn.) (*See* INFRARED AND ULTRAVIOLET ASTRONOMY.)

Outside the photosphere is a thin atmosphere of hydrogen gas known as the chromosphere, which can be seen during solar eclipses as a bright red ring. Outside that is the thinner and hotter solar corona, whose light is normally obscured by sunlight scattered by Earth's atmosphere, but which can also be seen during eclipses. The corona fades out into the solar wind, a stream of particles (mainly protons and electrons) that blows out into the solar system. At the orbit of Earth, these particles move with speeds up to 500 miles per second.

The sun has a magnetic field, which averages about half the strength of that on Earth. Unlike Earth, however, different parts of the sun rotate at different speeds, with regions near the equator moving faster than those near the poles. This fact, plus the fact that the sun's magnetic field reverses every 11 years, gives rise to the sunspot cycle.

Sunspots. Regions of unusually high magnetic field appear as dark sunspots on the solar surface. After the solar magnetic field reverses, there is a period when the sun shows relatively few sunspots. As the rotation proceeds, however, the differential movement of the solar material twists the magnetic field, producing more and more sunspots until the solar field reverses and reforms itself, at which time the process starts all over again. Magnetic effects associated with periods of high sunspot activity make radio communication more difficult on Earth.

If sunspots are viewed as magnetic storms on the sun's surface, then solar flares would be analogous to thunder and lightning in an earthly thunderstorm. These are intense bursts of radiation and particles that are created by disturbances in the solar magnetic field and then move out into space. Solar flares occur unpredictably and quickly—even the biggest flares take only a few minutes to develop. They constitute a danger to spacecraft, often destroying detectors on craft in orbit around Earth.

Background material regarding the sun can be found in FUSION, NUCLEAR; SOLAR SYSTEM; STAR. *More details can be found in* ECLIPSE; NEUTRINO ASTRONOMY; NUCLEOSYNTHESIS; SOLAR WIND. *More information on particular aspects of this subject is contained in* INFRARED AND ULTRAVIOLET ASTRONOMY; MILKY WAY; SOLAR ENERGY SYSTEMS.

Further Reading
Markvart, Tomas (Ed.), *Solar Electricity* (1994); Phillips, Kenneth J. H., *Guide to the Sun* (1995); Spolter, Pari, *Gravitational Force of the Sun* (1994).

First see Computer, Digital

Supercomputer

Next see Parallel Computing

Traditionally defined as computers that can perform more than ten times as fast as ordinary computers.

The first supercomputers were designed to run at a speed of 20 megaflops—20 million floating-point operations per second—at a time when high-quality microcomputers could only reach 0.5 megaflops; the first true supercomputer, the CRAY-1, reached 100 megaflops. Today, when home computers can run that fast, the challenge has been to create supercomputers capable of more than 1 teraflop—a trillion or more operations per second.

History. The supercomputer was the brainchild of Seymour Cray, whose quest for massive computational power began when he was designing computers for the Control Data Corporation in the 1960s. The CDC 6600, delivered in 1964, employed ten 12-bit peripheral processors, each with its own 4K memory. Thus, it was the first computer to exploit parallel processing. Cray left CDC, founded Cray Research in 1972, and shipped the first CRAY-1 supercomputer four years later. With the development of parallel computer systems, it was no longer necessary to focus on freestanding monoliths, and processor companies like Intel soon entered the supercomputer market.

Obstacles. The main challenge in making a supercomputer lies in the length of its internal wiring. Although electrons travel 186,000 miles in a single second, which seems exceedingly fast, when the aim is to perform more than a trillion operations in that time, electron travel over individual wires adds a significant time lag. Cray achieved great improvements in speed by designing his supercomputers as circles in order to keep the maximum length of any wire below 4 feet in the CRAY-1, below 16 inches in the CRAY-2, and a mere 3 inches in the CRAY-3. Then, a second problem arose: all those electrons flowing through all those densely packed wires produced a tremendous amount of heat, which could disable the entire system. Cray solved that problem by immersing his computers in a liquid coolant, Fluorinert.

Cray's first supercomputers operated using vector processing, in which operations are broken down into component sections that can be worked on by different parts of the computer, as opposed to scalar processing, in which operations must be broken down into their smallest digital parts. Soon, this technique gave way to a much more complex development, massively parallel processing, in which problems are broken down in the programming stage into simultaneous smaller problems, which can be worked

Nearly one-third of the 5,500-pound bulk of the Cray-2 (left) consists of fluorocarbon coolant liquid, which flows continuously through the supercomputer's circuitry.

on in parallel rather than in series. Although this produced major programming headaches, it led to incredible breakthroughs in speed and power. The CRAY-2 used four processors, and the CRAY-3 sixteen; Intel's Janus supercomputer uses 9,152 Pentium-6 microprocessors to achieve over 1 trillion operations per second.

Applications. With supercomputers, calculations that approximate the complexity of the real world can be attempted: air flowing over an airplane wing; the development and movement of a hurricane; the explosion pattern of a nuclear bomb. At the Max Planck Society in Germany, a Cray supercomputer has even simulated the development of the universe—10 billion years in 3 days, in a time-lapse series of 28 megabytes for each image. Since the universe is 10 billion light-years across, at that level of detail the smallest thing visible is a cluster of ten galaxies, but with supercomputer power doubling every 18 months it will not be long before Earth comes into focus as well.

Background material can be found in Computer Digital; Operating System; Parallel Computing. *More details can be found in* Expert Systems; Operations Research; Weather. *Additional relevant information is contained in* Accelerator, Particle; Computer-Aided Design; Robotics.

Further Reading
Crichlow, Joel M., *An Introduction to Distributed and Parallel Computing* (1996); Mullin, L. M.R., *Arrays, Functional Languages, and Parallel Systems* (1991); Murray, C. J., *The Supermen: The Story of Seymour Cray and the Technical Wizards Behind the Supercomputer* (1997).

First see Conductors and Resistors

Superconductor

Next see Solid

A phenomenon whereby the resistance of a wire vanishes as the wire is cooled to absolute zero.

As electrons move through a conductor, they occasionally collide with an atom of the conductive material, disrupting electron flow and creating heat; these collisions are the source of electrical resistance. However, by cooling the conductor drastically, one slows the electrons down so they have fewer collisions; eventually, if one cools the material enough, electrical resistance disappears. This phenomenon was first discovered by H. K. Onnes in 1911, when he cooled mercury to 4.153 degrees Kelvin.

All metals were found to display properties of superconductivity. However, a relatively weak magnetic field could disrupt the effect. The phenomenon was considered to be of merely theoretical value. In the 1950s, a group of niobium compounds was found to display superconductivity at 18 to 19 degrees Kelvin, a temperature more easily reached. About the same time, John Bardeen, Leon Cooper, and J. R. Schreiffer developed the BCS Theory, which explained how superconductivity worked (they received the Nobel Prize for their work in 1972).

During the next decades, uses of superconductivity were perfected, including powerful electromagnets and magnetic resonance imaging (MRI)—a crucial modern medical imaging tool. But the demands of working at very low temperatures kept the applications minimal. Then, in 1986, J. G. Bednarz and K. A. Müller discovered a ceramic compound of barium, lanthanum, copper, and oxygen that reached superconductivity at 35 degrees Kelvin; within a year, similar compounds were developed with a critical temperature of about 95 degrees Kelvin, allowing liquid nitrogen to be used as the coolant. Research has continued, and there was even hope in the early 1990s that superconductivity at room temperatures had been discovered; but the experiment could not be duplicated.

Background material on superconductors can be found in CHARGE AND CURRENT; CONDUCTORS AND RESISTORS; SOLIDS. *Advanced subjects are developed in* CERAMICS; CRYSTAL; FERROMAGNETISM. *Elementary aspects of this subject are covered in* ACCELERATOR, PARTICLE; SUPERFLUID.

Further Reading
Hazen, Robert M., *The Breakthrough: The Race for the Superconductor* (1988); Van Duzer, Theodore, *Principles of Superconductive Devices and Circuits* (1999); Kadin, Ellen M., *Introduction to Superconducting Circuits* (1999).

First see VISCOSITY

Superfluid

Next see ABSOLUTE ZERO

Term used to describe the unusual behavior of helium when it is cooled to a fraction of a degree above absolute zero.

When the isotope helium-4 is cooled at atmospheric pressure, it becomes a normal liquid, called liquid helium I, at a temperature of 4.216 degrees Kelvin. If the helium is cooled further, to 2.178 degrees Kelvin at atmospheric pressure (its lambda point), it changes to liquid helium II. This is called a superfluid because it has virtually no viscosity (the drag that other fluids experience), so that it can flow almost without resistance. It also has a very high heat conductivity.

The result is a set of highly unusual properties. For example, the superfluid will flow upward over the edge of a container, will escape from a test tube through a thin, invisible film of liquid covering the glass wall and collecting in drops at the outside of the tube. It will also display the fountain effect, in which the fluid will spray out of a capillary.

Superfluid behavior is sometimes explained comparison with the behavior of a solid. The sound waves that pass horizontally and vertically through a solid are said to correspond to phonons and rotons in the case of the superfluid. Phonons are defined as sound waves that travel longitudinally, while rotons are defined as a different kind of wave, not quite comparable to the sound waves of a solid, because a liquid cannot support vertical sound waves. Equations derived by using these expressions have successfully explained the behavior of the superfluid helium-4 up to a temperature of 1.6 degrees Kelvin.

Two phenomena that are closely connected with superfluidity are mechanocaloric and thermomechanical effects. The first of these produces a drop in the temperature of liquid helium when it passes in superflow through a very narrow channel. The second is seen when two samples of liquid helium are connected by a narrow channel and one sample is heated. Contrary to what one might expect, the unheated helium sample then flows toward the heated sample.

Background material regarding superfluids can be found in ABSOLUTE ZERO; NOBLE GASES; PHASE. *Advanced subjects are developed in* ENTROPY; QUANTUM MECHANICS; VISCOSITY. *More information on particular aspects is contained in* CRYOGENICS; QUANTUM STATISTICS.

First see CATALYST

Surface Chemistry

Next see ENZYME

Many chemical processes take place on a solid surface. The study of these surfaces, their physical properties, and their role in catalyzing various chemical reactions is known as surface chemistry.

A solid surface may act as an anchor for chemical reactants. In this type of reaction, the surface provides a physical foundation upon which the chemical reactants come together, at the proper angles, in order to react. Heterogeneous catalysts are solids that increase the rate of chemical reactions because of their surface properties. The most common examples are metals, metal oxides, metal sulfides, and salts. They are used to catalyze reactions of gases or liquids on their surfaces. Catalysis by metal complexes has industrial applications in the production of pharmaceuticals, hydrometallurgy, and waste-treatment processes. Many biochemical reactions in living cells are catalyzed by metal-enzyme systems, such as the cytochrome molecules used in cellular respiration.

The first step in a surface-catalyzed reaction is the diffusion of the chemical reactants onto the solid surface. The molecules must then be adsorbed, or made to adhere to the surface. The molecules being adsorbed are known as the adsorbate, and the solid surface is referred to as the substrate. The adhesion may involve chemisorption, the formation of actual chemical bonds between the reactants and the surface molecules, or there may be another "connection" that involves no chemical bond formation, called physisorption. Once the adsorption has occurred, the chemical reaction takes place. Afterward, the products are desorbed, meaning their attachment to the surface is broken, and the products revert back to the gas or liquid phase.

The speed of a surface-catalyzed reaction depends on the rate at which reactions occur between adsorbed molecules on the surface of the catalyst but is also affected by the rate of adsorption of the reactants and desorption of the products.

The structure of the surface metals, such as surface symmetry, electrical characteristics, surface chemical reactivity, and the amount of each type of surface exposed, all affect the adsorption and reactivity of the reactants. The most stable surfaces have a high surface atomic density and contain surface atoms with a high coordination number, which is the number of nearest "neighbors" in a crystal lattice.

Background material on surface chemistry can be found in BOND, CHEMICAL; CATALYST; MOLECULE. *Advanced subjects are developed in* ABSORPTION; CLUSTER, ATOM; ELECTROCHEMISTRY AND ELECTROPLATING. *Additional relevant information is contained in* CHROMATOGRAPHY; VIRTUAL REALITY.

Further Reading
Adamson, Arthur W., *Physical Chemistry of Surfaces* (1997); Birdi, K.S. (Ed.), *Handbook of Surface and Colloid Chemistry* (1997); Delchar, T. A., *Modern Techniques of Surface Science* (Cambridge Solid State Science Series) (1994).

First see MEDICAL DIAGNOSTICS

Surgery

Next see LASER SURGERY

The branch of medicine that is chiefly concerned with direct physical intervention to remove or repair damaged, diseased, or deformed tissues of the body.

Many of the basic principles of surgery were established in the sixteenth century by a French physician, Ambrose Paré. The use of antiseptics to prevent infection was pioneered by Joseph Lister, a nineteenth-century British surgeon who used carbolic acid as an antiseptic. Blood transfusions became possible in the opening years of the twentieth century, when an Austrian pathologist, Karl Landsteiner, identified the major ABO blood groups. The era of transplant surgery opened in 1955, when American surgeons performed the first successful kidney transplant.

Above, laser surgery (performed here on the eye) offers microcontrol of the cutting blade.

In the modern era, surgery has become more complex, so that the field has been split into a number of specialities. More than ten such specialties are now recognized in the United States. For example, otolaryngology deals with the ear, larynx, and the upper respiratory tract. Colon and rectal surgery deal with the large intestine. Neurosurgery is concerned with the nervous system, which includes the brain, the spinal cord, and the nerves. Urological surgery deals with the components of the urinary system—the kidneys, ureter, bladder, and urethra—and the male reproductive system. Thoracic surgery deals with the structures within the chest cavity, but it has been further divided, so that cardiovascular surgery is now concerned only with the heart and major blood vessels.

Until the 1940s, almost all surgical procedures used scalpels (specialized knives) and were limited to the removal of diseased or damaged tissues. The field has expanded broadly in the decades since then, both in the kinds of surgical procedures that can be performed and in the instruments that are used to perform them.

Two New Fields. Prominent examples of new fields of surgery are transplants and implants. Transplants face two challenges: the difficulties involved in the replacement of a malfunctioning organ with a healthier one, and those involved in preventing the body's immune system from attacking and rejecting the transplanted organ. The first problem has been overcome by a number of improved surgical techniques. The second has been attacked by the development of effective drugs that reduce the rejection process without suppressing the body's defenses against infection. Transplant surgery today is limited in many cases only by the availability of donor organs. (*See* ORGAN TRANSPLANTATION.)

An implant must meet several requirements. It must not provoke an attack by the immune system and it must be durable enough to last for many years. In addition, there must be a method of securing it firmly in the proper position and the operation must be done without causing an infection. These challenges have been overcome in many cases, so that damaged heart valves now are replaced by plastic valves or by valves taken from an animal or a human donor, and damaged hip joints, eye lenses, blood vessels, and other body parts are replaced routinely by implants.

Enhancing Surgical Skills. While surgery once was done with the naked eye, recent decades have seen the implementation of microsurgery, in which surgeons use a specially designed microscope and extremely small instruments to perform a variety of procedures. Microsurgery has been used to reattach fingers, toes, and complete limbs that have been severed in accidents, to repair damage to the eye or ear, and to rejoin tiny blood vessels when reconstructive surgery is done. Meanwhile, the laser has joined the scalpel as a surgical instrument. A laser produces a narrow beam of light that is intense enough to cut through tissue. It has the advantage of cauterizing the blood vessels of those tissues as it cuts, so that excessive bleeding is avoided. Lasers can remove skin blemishes such as birthmarks, and they also are used in many procedures for the eye, especially those done on the retina.

Background material for surgery includes BLOOD TRANSFUSION; MEDICAL DIAGNOSTICS; RADIOLOGY. *Advanced subjects are developed in* ANGIOPLASTY; BIRTH; LASER SURGERY. *Additional relevant information is contained in* ANTIBIOTICS; CHEMOTHERAPY; ORGAN TRANSPLANTATION.

First see ECOLOGY

Symbiosis

Next see PARASITE

From the Greek for "living together," a term that refers to a close and long-lasting association between organisms of two species.

The most common forms of symbiosis are parasitism, in which one species benefits at the expense of the other; commensalism, in which one species benefits and the other is substantially unaffected; and mutualism, in which both species benefit. Ecologists often distinguish between obligate mutualism, in which the two partners cannot live without each other, and facultative mutualism, in which the relationship is not essential for survival.

Although these are useful categories, symbiosis occurs along a continuous spectrum of gain and pain, and specific relationships between species can be difficult to classify, in part because benefits may not be clear. In addition, as symbiotic partners evolve, so does the nature of their relationship. In parasitism, for instance, natural selection usually tends to reduce the damage done by parasite to host, ensuring the long-term survival of both parties. As a result, the heaviest damage occurs when a new, more virulent form of parasite arises or when an old parasite happens upon a new host population.

Symbiosis is extremely common among animals, plants, insects, and microorganisms. Mutualistic relationships are especially widespread, and some of them play a key role in maintaining life on earth. Bacteria that can fix nitrogen—convert atmospheric nitrogen to a form usable by cells—make plant growth possible. Some of these bacteria live symbiotically, forming nodules on the roots of legumes. Their host, in turn, supplies them with high-energy compounds.

Most higher plants have mutually beneficial relationships called mycorrhizae with fungi whose filaments form as much as 20 percent of the plant's root mass. The fungi draw minerals

Further Reading
Rutkow, Ira M., Md., *American Surgery: An Illustrated History* (1997), Schirmer, Bruce D. (Ed.), *Ambulatory Surgery* (1998).

Below, slime mold.

Further Reading
Knutson, R. M., *Furtive Fauna: A Field Guide to the Creatures Who Live on You* (1996); Mahler, M. S., *The Psychological Birth of the Human Infant: Symbiosis and Individuation* (1989); Sapp, J., *Evolution by Association: A History of Symbiosis* (1994).

from a larger area of soil than the plant's roots can reach, allowing the plants to survive in poor soil or to thrive in average soil. The fungi, in turn, get their food from the plant, which manufactures carbohydrates through photosynthesis.

Flowering plants also often have mutualistic relationships with nectar-eating insects that pollinate the plants and with fruit-eating birds or animals that disperse their seeds.

Mutualism. Mutualism can involve mammals, as well. Cows and other ruminants have a mutualistic relationship with bacteria that live in their rumen and digest the cellulose in their plant diet. And bacteria that live in the human intestines keep humans supplied with vitamin K, which is essential for blood clotting.

Commensalism. Commensalism, with its one-sided benefit, can be seen among sea creatures. Sea worm burrows and shellfish frequently provide shelter and leftover food to smaller worms or crustaceans, with no apparent payoff. Certain fish and shrimp get similar benefits by living among the tentacles of normally predatory sea anemones.

Like mutualism, parasitism is common, especially among insects. Parasites range from bacteria and fungi to protozoa, worms, and insects. Unlike most predators, parasites often have evolved specialized life cycles that limit them to feeding on only a few species. Their life cycles may require residence in a succession of hosts; for instance, the protozoa plasmodium, which causes malaria, alternates between the anopheles mosquito and humans in order to survive.

Among humans, parasites cause many diseases that devastate and kill millions in the developing world. Malaria alone is estimated to account for 1 million to 2 million deaths and 200 million to 300 million cases a year. Human also serve as hosts to ectoparasites, larger organisms such as lice, ticks, and mites that live on or in the skin.

Background material on symbiosis is to be found in COEVOLUTION; COMPETITION AND ALTRUISM; ECOLOGY. *More details can be found in* ETHOLOGY; PARASITE; PREDATION. *Advanced aspects of this subject are covered in* BIODIVERSITY; DISEASES, INFECTIOUS.

First see CONSERVATION LAWS IN NATURE

Symmetry in Nature

Next see STANDARD MODEL

To say there is symmetry in nature means that the laws of nature do not change when coordinates are reflected, as in a mirror. This rule is always observed when we create a mathematical description of ordinary states in the everyday world, but symmetry rules can be violated on atomic and subatomic levels.

To appreciate symmetry in space, extend the thumb of the right hand, then extend the forefinger, and point the middle finger at a right angle to the forefinger. The three fingers then mark the three axes of direction, x for the thumb, y for the forefinger, z for the middle finger. By convention, physics describes the world we live in as a right-handed world. We can create an exactly opposite but equally symmetrical world by using the same three fingers of the left hand.

Parity. In the world of quantum mechanics, the concept of space reversal that retains symmetry is called parity. A subatomic system is described mathematically by a wave function, and both theory and observation demand that parity remains constant (or is "conserved") even if a system changes its state.

Electric charge symmetry also exists. Electromagnetic theory would remain unchanged if, for example, we described the negative charge on an electron as positive and the positive charge on a proton as negative. On the atomic and subatomic scale, charge symmetry is an integral part of quantum theory: for every statement about a particle with a positive charge, there is a corresponding statement for a particle with a negative charge. One concept derived from this is that for every particle, there is a corresponding antiparticle.

Antiparticles have been observed, and they behave exactly as theory predicts—except in the case of some weak interactions between particles and systems. Parity may not be conserved in such interactions.

If we look at parity, charge, and time on the atomic scale, we find that their product remains symmetrical. Therefore, if all three symmetries are reversed, the physical behavior of the system will remain the same: this is the essence of the CPT (charge-parity-time) theorem.

Special topics in this area can be found in CONSERVATION LAWS IN NATURE; SCIENTIFIC METHOD; STANDARD MODEL. *Advanced subjects are developed in* GENERAL RELATIVITY; GROUP THEORY IN PHYSICS; MAXWELL'S EQUATIONS. *Further aspects are covered in* CHAOS AND COMPLEXITY; FRACTAL; THEORIES OF EVERYTHING.

First see NEURON

Synapse

Next see ALZHEIMER'S DISEASE

Junction between two nerve cells across which a nerve impulse is transmitted.

Synapses form the basic communication system of the body, the basis for perception, motor action, and learning. Since the average neuron makes about a thousand synaptic connections, and there are about a billion neurons in the brain, the number of synaptic connections that are possible has been estimated at somewhere between 10^{18}—itself a very large number—and 1,000,000,000! (factorial), a number greater than the total number of atoms in the universe.

Synapses operate either electrically or chemically, allowing neurons to communicate over relatively large distances. Electrical synapses appear in both nerve cells and muscle cells, such as the heart and other smooth muscles. Although most synapses transmit information in both directions, some allow transmission unidirectionally—a voltage potential in one direction travels one pathway, but a potential in the other direction activates a different pathway.

Chemical synapses typically occupy larger spaces between cells, 20 or 30 nanometers instead of 3 or 4 nanometers in electrical synapses. A membrane on one side of the synapse releases a neurotransmitter into the intercellular space; the chemical diffuses through the space and ultimately binds to a receptor on the membrane on the other side, altering its electrical conductance and allowing electrical current to flow. As might be expected, this process is somewhat slower than direct electrical transmission, but it covers substantially greater space.

Some synapses operate through the release of neurotransmitters that excite the function of the receptor cell; the best known of these is acetylcholine (ACh). Others operate through inhibition, such as gamma aminobutyric acid (GABA). To prepare for the next impulse, most neurotransmitters are reabsorbed into the neurons that released them.

Further Reading
Hayflick, Leonard, *How and Why We Age* (1994); Penrose, Roger, *The Emperor's New Mind* (1989); Penrose, Roger, *Shadows of the Mind: A Search for the Missing Science of Consciousness* (1994).

Further Reading
French, A.P., *Introduction to Quantum Physics* (1978); Greene, Brian, *The Elegant Universe* (1999); Gribbin, John, *The Search for Superstrings, Symmetry, and the Theory of Everything* (1998).

Further developments in the field are discussed in BRAIN; NERVOUS SYSTEM; NEURON. *More details can be found in* CONDITIONING; MEMORY; NEUROTRANSMITTERS AND RECEPTORS. *Additional relevant information is contained in* ALZHEIMER'S DISEASE; LOCOMOTION; REFLEX.

First see ACCELERATOR, PARTICLE

Synchrotron

Next see CYCLOTRON

A ring-shaped subatomic particle accelerator that is used both for the study of subatomic particles and for the production of radiation.

Particle beams from synchrotron accelerators can be used in medical treatment, in medical and biological research, and in physics. The name of the synchrotron is derived from the way in which particles are accelerated: a beam of particles is kept in step with an oscillating radio-frequency acceleration voltage as the particles circle the accelerator ring. In a typical synchrotron, a particle will travel millions of miles in an evacuated pipe only a few inches in diameter.

The phase stability that makes the synchrotron possible was discovered in the 1940s by V. I. Veksler, a Soviet physicist, and E.M. McMillan, an American physicist who proposed the name of the machine. McMillan designed an electron synchrotron with a beam energy of 300 MeV (million electric volts), built at the Lawrence Berkeley Laboratory in California.

Fermi Lab and CERN. One of the largest synchrotrons in operation is the proton accelerator at the Fermi National Accelerator Laboratory in Illinois. It is more than four miles in circumference. An even larger synchrotron is in operation at the CERN Laboratory in Switzerland. These synchrotrons reach energies of 500 GEV, nearly 2,000 times the power of McMillan's original machine.

Synchrotrons can accelerate electrons or protons. An electron synchrotron uses a laminated ring-shaped magnet to provide a guide field for the accelerated particles; the magnetic field is pulsed regularly. Synchronous electrons are accelerated in each cycle of the magnetic field.

A proton synchrotron also uses a ring magnet that is pulsed regularly. The acceleration of the protons requires an applied frequency that increases greatly during the acceleration cycle. The ions in such accelerators are preaccelerated to energies of several MeV. The proton synchrotrons that have achieved the highest energies use the alternating gradient principle, which requires magnets built to create wedge-shaped gaps that face alternately inward and outward around the orbit. The result is strong transverse focusing, which compacts the beam strongly.

Synchrotron radiation is the electromagnetic radiation that is emitted when a charged particle that is moving at relativistic velocities, velocities close to the speed of light, are accelerated further. It is called synchrotron radiation because it was first observed in this type of electron accelerator. For example, relativistic electrons that are passing through a uniform magnetic field move in circular orbits and also emit synchrotron radiation. Since the production of synchrotron radiation results from the interaction of an electron with a magnetic field of known strength, the energy distribution of emitted radiation can be easily calculated, and so sources of synchrotron radiation can be used as radiometric standards over a wide range of light spectra. Thus, synchrotron radiation in the x-ray frequencies is used in protein crystallography.

Background material can be found in ACCELERATOR, PARTICLE; ELECTROMAGNETIC FORCE; ELEMENTARY PARTICLE. Further developments in the field are discussed in BUBBLE CHAMBER; SCINTILLATOR; SPECIAL RELATIVITY. Special topics in this area are found in CYCLOTRON; LINEAR ACCELERATOR; NUCLEAR POWER.

Further Reading
Margaritondo, G., *Introduction to Synchrotron Radiation* (1988); Marr, Geoffrey V., *Handbook on Synchrotron Radiation* (1987).

Further Reading
Demir, A., *Synthetic Filament Yarn* (1997); Warner, S. B., *Sew the New Fleece: Techniques With Synthetic Fleece and Pile* (1995).

First see PLASTICS

Synthetics

Next see POLYMER

Any materials composed of chemical elements not synthesized by the cellular process of a living entity.

In 1910, when the Count Hilaire de Chardonnet discovered that cellulose from cotton or tree pulp could be made into a resin that captured the feel of silk, he began a process of development that now offers consumers Gore-Tex shells and Polartec liners that combine total insulation and water resistance with breathability and light weight. Synthetic fibers give tennis players a bigger sweet spot to hit, police officers a greater chance to survive criminal attack, and astronauts a permanent space station.

Rayon and its related fiber acetate are rather crude fibers, and significant water pollution is associated with their manufacture, but they continue to be used today in products that need high fluid absorbency, from diapers to cigarette filters. The first true synthetic fiber was nylon, derived from Wallace Carothers' discoveries of petroleum-based polymers, introduced in 1939. Nylon was an essential element in the winning of World War II, used in tires, ropes, tents, parachutes, and stockings.

The 1950s saw rapid development of fiber technology, leading to fibers like polyester, acrylic, and olefin; these third-generation fibers began to show specialized features, such as "wickability" and abrasion resistance. Later generations saw the introduction of high-strength fibers like Aramid, used in Kevlar and Nomex, and Novoloid, used in astronauts' flight suits. The latest fibers, such as PBI and Sulfar, are completely fireproof and resistant to both thermal and chemical breakdown; these fibers are made from boron, carbon, and similar materials. (*See* BOND, CHEMICAL.)

Environmental Issues. Synthetic fibers are not problem-free. Environmentalists have raised questions about the unregulated disposal of fibers that will never degrade; polyesters often contain chlorine, raising questions about both production and use. Carpets made with synthetic fibers and artificial glues have been associated with a wide range of allergic reactions; some contain volatile organic compounds, proven to be carcinogenic (cancer-causing), are suspected of being teratogenic (causing birth defects) as well.

The foundations of the subject are discussed in HYDROCARBON; MOLECULE; PLASTICS; POLYMER. *More details can be found in* CYCLIC COMPOUNDS; EPOXIES; ORGANOMETTALIC COMPOUNDS. *Advanced subjects are developed in* EXPLOSIVES; HAZARDOUS WASTE DISPOSAL; SOAPS AND DETERGENTS.

First see IMMUNE RESPONSE

T-lymphocyte

Next see B-LYMPHOCYTE

One of two major classes of the white blood cells that are the principal actors in the body's immune defense system against foreign invaders.

When organisms, like bacteria and viruses, that contain foreign molecules called antigens invade the body, they activate the immune system to produce either T-lymphocytes or B-lymphocytes. The T-lymphocytes are activated in the thymus gland. They attack antigens directly, while B-lymphocytes attack them by producing defensive proteins called antibodies. The immunity against dangerous invaders that is provided by T- lymphocytes is referred to as cell-mediated, because the reaction that occurs between the foreign antigen and the immune system cell takes place on or within the cells. (*See* IMMUNE RESPONSE.)

These immune system cells respond to the antigens of malignant origin, such as cancer, and to some infections caused by viruses and bacteria. The T-lymphocytes are also important in the rejection of foreign tissue and are thus a barrier to organ transplants. When a T-lymphocyte is aroused by the presence of a foreign antigen, it makes substances called lymphokines. These molecules protect the body by arousing scavenger cells called macrophages to attack and engulf bacteria. The kind of immunity that the T-lymphocytes produce is thus called cellular immunity, in contrast to the humoral immunity of the B cells. (*See* B-LYMPHOCYTE.)

First see RADIO AND TELEVISION

Telecommunications

Next see INTERNET

Communication over a distance through electronic means.

Telephone communication was invented by Alexander Graham Bell in 1876 and has remained essentially unchanged since. An electromechanical microphone transforms sound vibrations into a modulated electrical signal, which is sent along a branched circuit that has been switched to access a single desired receiver; when it reaches that receiver the signal is transformed back into sound waves by an electromechanical speaker.

Recent decades have seen two significant changes in telecommunications. Telephones have been made much more efficient by the introduction of fiber optics, which can carry as much as one gigabit of information per second. These cables carry telephonic communications that have been digitized, so that many calls can travel over a single cable. Each analog signal is sampled 8,000 times per second, then converted to an eight-bit binary number; the resulting 64,000 bits per second are compressed and sent in packet form.

Cellular Technology. Telephones have also been made more convenient through the introduction of cellular technology, which transforms the spoken voice into a radio signal, picked up by transmission/receiver units (cells) located between half a kilometer and two kilometers from one another; the signal is then sent by a combination of land line and satellite to the cell where the receiver is located (cellular telephones signal their location), where the original digitizing process is reversed. In many developing countries, cellular telephones now provide the bulk of telephone service.

New systems of low-altitude satellites provide broad cellular coverage using phased array antennas, which combine directionality with freedom from interference, and several forms of multiple access, such as frequency division, time division, and code division.

The foundations of the field of telecommunications are discussed in ELECTRIC CIRCUIT; ELECTROMAGNETIC WAVES. **Further details can be found in** CONTROL SYSTEMS; RADIO AND TELEVISION BROADCASTING. **Advanced subjects are developed in** LOCAL AREA NETWORK (LAN); NEURAL NETWORK.

Further Reading
Dodd, Annabel Z., *The Essential Guide to Telecommunications,* (1997); Irwin, James H., *The Irwin Handbook of Telecommunications* (1993); Muller, Nathan J., *Desktop Encyclopedia of Telecommunications* (1998).

First see OPTICS

Telescope

Next see RADIO TELESCOPE

An optical instrument that magnifies distant objects.

Optical telescopes collect visible radiation from distant objects in space. They have two mirrors or lenses, a larger and a smaller, and are classified by the size of the larger mirror or lens. Optical astronomical telescopes fall into two main classes. One class is that of refracting telescopes, which use a converging lens to collect light. The resulting image is magnified by the eyepiece—a lens of short focal length.

The first refracting telescope was built in 1608 by Hans Lippershey in Holland. It was used the next year for astronomical studies by Galileo Galilei, who used a diverging lens as the eyepiece. This Galilean telescope was improved by Johannes Kepler, who substituted a converging lens for the eyepiece. This type of optical telescope is still used for astronomical studies, primarily by amateur astronomers. Because this telescope produces an upside-down image, an additional lens or mirror usually is added to obtain an upright image.

A second type is the reflecting telescope, which was first developed by Isaac Newton in 1668. This reflecting telescope used a concave mirror to collect and focus light, with a small

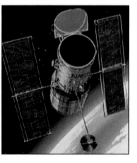

Above, artist conceptions of the Hubble Space Telescope (HST) after being deployed by the *Discovery* Space Shuttle. The aperture door (bottom) is open as it views the universe from high above the Earth's atmosphere.

secondary mirror, at a 45-degree angle to the first, to reflect the light into an eyepiece that magnified the image. Variations on this theme include the Gregorian telescope, developed by James Gregory in the seventeenth century, and the Cassegrainian telescope, developed by N. Cassegrain, also in the seventeenth century, which have different secondary optical systems.

Other types of optical instruments include catadioptric telescopes, which use both lenses and mirrors. One such instrument is the Maksutov telescope; another is the Schmidt camera, which has a correcting plate of complex spherical shape that is close to the center of curvature of the principal mirror. The Schmidt telescope is used primarily to take photographs of astronomical objects. The Palomar Sky Study, celebrated among astronomers, used a 48-inch Schmidt telescope on Mount Palomar in California to photograph the entire northen sky on 935 pairs of 14-inch square plates.

Astrophotography. Photographic plates were the first devices used to record telescopic images. But they have relatively low sensitivity to light and so it is difficult to determine accurate intensities of stars and other objects from them.

A newer class of detectors are photoelectric devices, which convert light to electrical signals. A photomultiplier tube converts an incoming photon, a unit of light, into an electron, whose intensity is then amplified a millionfold within the tube. These tubes are 100 times more efficient than a photographic plate.

Telescope Mounting. Astronomical telescopes must be mounted sturdily, because the least vibration spoils the image. They must also be mounted so that they can be pointed in every direction above the horizon. The largest telescopes use one variety or another of equatorial mountings, with which the telescope can be rotated in every direction. The large telescopes are moved by coarse drives for an initial setting, slow-motion drives for finer settings, and guidance and graduated circles that show the celestial coordinates of the object to be viewed.

The large reflecting telescope is the symbol of twentieth-century optical astronomy, although a 36-inch reflector was put into operation in 1895. A 60-inch reflecting telescope became operative at Mount Wilson in 1908, and telescope sizes grew after that until an 82-inch McDonald telescope went into operation in Texas in 1939.

Hale Observatory. Perhaps the most famous optical telescope is the 200-inch instrument on Mount Palomar, completed in 1948 and called the Hale Telescope, after George Ellery Hale, the astronomer who was primarily responsible for its construction. The Hale telescope weighs 500 tons, yet moves smoothly on oil-pad bearings. Still larger optical telescopes are found

Further Reading
Barbee, Jay, *A Journey Through Time: Exploring the Universe With the Hubble Space Telescope* (1995); Hitzeroth, Deborah, *Telescopes: Searching the Heavens* (1991); Naeye, R., *Through the Eyes of Hubble: The Birth, Life, and Violent Death of Stars* (1997).

Above, the open dome of the 100-inch telescope at Las Campanas Observatory in Chile.

at the Keck Observatory in Hawaii, with mirrors that are more than 30 feet across. This, and most other modern telescopes, like those at Cerno Tololo Observatory in Chile, are made with numerous smaller mirrors to prevent distortion and overcome atmospheric interference.

The foundations of the subject are discussed in LENS; LIGHT; MIRROR; OPTICS. *More details can be found in* RADIO ASTRONOMY; UNIVERSE; HUBBLE CONSTANT. *Advanced subjects are developed in* INFRARED AND ULTRAVIOLET ASTRONOMY; VLA TELESCOPE; X-RAY AND GAMMA RAY ASTRONOMY.

First see HEAT

Temperature

Next see THERMODYNAMICS

A concept that describes the flow of heat from one object or area to another.

That the concept of temperature should be defined only in relative terms—something can have a temperature only if there is something else in the universe that has a temperature—comes as no surprise; many physical properties make sense only as relative measures. But temperature has the additional requirement that there be something else in the universe that has a different temperature, so that there would be a flow of heat from one entity to the other. Indeed, our experience is that when we touch something that is exactly body temperature, we feel no sensation of hot or cold.

Quantifying temperature by assigning numbers of degrees has been practiced for only the past 300 years. The discovery in 1756 that ice does not change temperature when it melts is credited to Joseph Black, the Scottish chemist. This gave rise to the concept of a phase change as a substance changed from one state to another because of a flow of heat to or from it.

Thus, a thermometer records no change even though heat is flowing, and conversely it records a temperature change during an adiabatic expansion or compression of a gas even though no work is being done to or on the gas. From this it is clear that temperature is a kind of physical fiction, a convention that allows us to talk about what an object is likely to do when put in contact with another.

So ephemeral is this notion of temperature, that one version of a law attributed to Nernst, known as the "zeroth" law of thermodynamics, is that temperature is a useful concept.

Temperature Scales. The two most widely used scales are those devised by Fahrenheit and Celsius, both defining a degree by dividing their thermometer scales between the freezing and boiling of water, Fahrenheit choosing 32 and 212 as the end-points; Celsius choosing zero and 100. The conversion factor in going from

Fahrenheit to Celsius is thus to add 32 and multiply by 9/5. A third scale by Kelvin begins at "absolute zero" (where a gas presumably would come completely to rest), and uses the Celsius degree; the Rankine scale does the same but uses Fahrenheit degrees.

Background material on temperature is located in ENERGY; GASES, BEHAVIOR OF; HEAT. *More details can be found in* ENTROPY; MAXWELL-BOLTZMANN DISTRIBUTION; REFRIGERATION. *Advanced aspects of this subject are covered in* ABSOLUTE ZERO; BLACK BODY RADIATION; THERMAL REGULATION.

Further Reading
Liptak, Bela G., *Temperature Measurement* (1993); Kittel, Peter, *Advances in Cryogenic Engineering* (1998); Shachtman, Tom, *Absolute Zero* (1999).

First see DISEASES, INFECTIOUS

Tetanus

Next see IMMUNIZATION AND VACCINATION

A destructive infection of the central nervous system caused by infection of an open wound by spores of a bacterium, *Clostridium tetani.*

Tetanus has virtually been eliminated in the United States by the DPT—diphtheria, pertussis, tetanus—vaccine that is given routinely in childhood with booster shots every ten years, but a few dozen cases are reported every year in unimmunized persons. Worldwide, several hundred thousand persons are infected each year. Tetanus can cause the death of newborn infants in underdeveloped countries if the spores contaminate the stump of the umbilical cord.

The bacterial spores can multiply rapidly if they enter body tissues that are poorly supplied with blood. As they multiply, they produce a toxin that acts on the nerves that control the muscles. The most common symptom of tetanus is stiffness of the jaw; the disease is sometimes called lockjaw. There can also be stiffness of the muscles of the back and abdomen and contraction of facial muscles that causes a fixed grimace. Muscle spasms that can affect the larynx and chest wall can develop, causing breathing difficulties that may require a tracheotomy. With proper treatment, most patients will recover completely. (*See* ANTIBIOTICS AND ANTISEPTICS.)

First see SYNTHETICS

Textile Science

Next see SOAPS AND DETERGENTS

Textile science refers to fibers, filaments, and yarns and the products that are made from them by weaving, spinning, knotting, knitting, felting, and other processes of interlacing and twisting. Textile science deals with both natural fibers, such as cotton, silk, wool, jute, and flax, and artificial fibers. These are subdivided into cellulosics, such as rayon, and synthetics, such as nylon, polyesters, and polyacrylics.

In the early years of the twentieth century, textile science dealt almost entirely with fibers of natural origin. The first artificial fiber, rayon, became available during the 1930s and was immediately put to widespread use. A large number of artificial fibers have been introduced in recent decades. Most of them are manufactured from synthetic organic (carbon-based) compounds. While artificial fibers have achieved great success, natural fibers account for a majority of the textiles produced world-wide.

The basic processes and machines for converting fibers into yarns and fabrics have not changed greatly over the decades. First, fibers are separated, cleaned, blended, and made parallel. They are then made into rope-like strands, which are twisted into yarns. Finally the yarns are interlaced to make fabrics, which may then undergo a finishing process.

Artificial Fibers. The artificial fibers that are in use today fall into many different categories. Acrylics, such as Orlon and Arilan, are long-chain polymers composed of mostly acrylonitrile units, which are combinations of three small carbon-based molecules. Polyesters, such as Dacron and Fortrel, are composed mostly of esters that contain both an alcohol sub-unit and carbon-containing subunits. Rayon is built on a framework of regenerated cellulose. Fluorocarbons such as Teflon are long-chain carbon molecules that also contain fluorine. Spandexes such as Lycra are long-chain polymers that consist largely of polyurethane subunits. An olefin such as Prolene or Reevan is a long-chain synthetic molecule that consists predominantly of ethylene, propylene, or chemically similar subunits.

New fibers and new methods of treating them to make them more useful are constantly being developed. One example is the emergence of wash-and-wear treatments, which allow cotton fabrics to be used in ways that were not possible before. Chemical processes can be used to impart not only crease resistance but also fireproofing properties, stain resistance, and shrink resistance.

First see GRAND UNIFIED THEORY (GUT)

Theories of Everything

Next see STRING THEORY

Term describing the attempt by physicists to develop a theory that describes and explains all four forces of nature, including gravity, in terms of a single force.

As opposed to Grand Unified Theories (GUT), which aspire to provide an explanation of three of the four fundamental forces of nature—electromagnetism, the weak nuclear force, and the strong nuclear force—Theories of Everything (TOE) include gravity, thus encompassing all of the known natural world.

History. The desire to unify the natural world under a single principle goes back (at least) to ancient Greece when philosophers speculated about what one substance might make up the entire universe. As the phenomena of the natural world were more carefully observed, it became clear that various forces existed, so that by the nineteenth century, a great many forces were recognized by the scientific community.

A breakthrough occurred in the nineteenth century when James Clerk Maxwell demonstrated that the electric force and magnetism were two manifestations of a single force: electromagnetism. In the twentieth century, the cause was taken up by Albert Einstein, who spent some thirty years working on a "unified field theory" that would combine gravity and electromagnetism. Einstein failed, and it was fortunate that he did, because he was unaware of the character of the weak nuclear force and the strong nuclear force; a successful theory that failed to account for them would have been inadequate.

This points out a possible flaw in the entire enterprise of devising a Theory of Everything: a theory that encompasses all of the known natural forces can be expected to encounter difficulties when new phenomena are discovered for which the theory has not made room.

TOE Today. One current theory that lays claim to being a Theory of Everything is String Theory, a view of the world that has all matter and particles consisting of "strings" of many dimensions, the vibrations of which account for the fundamental forces and constants. Though the theory has many supporters in the physics community, it is short on verifiable predictions and even shorter on providing a satisfying image to which the human mind can relate.

There is also the feeling among some that such a theory is doomed to failure and that any theory must be an abstraction that brings order to a bed of confusion and chaos. Just as the kinetic theory of gases introduced several simplifying assumptions to show that the orderly behavior of a gas was the consequence of the random motions of molecules in a chaotic microscopic dance, so must any theory about the world at so fundamental a level be an abstact idealization that overlooks complicating aspects of the reality. In other words, a valid and successful physical theory will—and must—be incomplete in some important way. In spite of this, much genius of the physics community is expended on the creation of a unifying TOE, which is a testament to how powerful an idea it is.

Background material can be found in FORCE; SCIENTIFIC METHOD; STANDARD MODEL. *More details can be found in* GRAND UNIFICATION THEORIES (GUT); STRING THEORY. *More information on particular aspects is contained in* GROUP THEORY IN PHYSICS; SYMMETRY IN NATURE; QUANTUM ELECTRODYNAMICS.

Further Reading
Greene, Brian, *The Elegant Universe* (1999); Gribbin, John, *The Search for Superstrings, Symmetry, and the Theory of Everything* (1998); Pagels, H., *Perfect Symmetry* (1985).

First see CIRCULATORY SYSTEM

Thermal Regulation

Next see HOMEOSTASIS

The maintenance of body temperature in animals.

The process of temperature regulation varies fundamentally depending on whether or not an animal is endothermic—warm-blooded. To maintain an elevated body temperature despite generally cooler surroundings, mammals and birds rely on their hypothalamus to set an optimal temperature, their metabolism and muscular exertion to produce heat, their circulatory system to distribute or dissipate it, and their skin, fur, feathers, or fat to conserve or radiate it.

Most animals, however, have a body temperature that fluctuates with their surroundings. These creatures—fish, amphibians, reptiles, and invertebrates—are commonly called cold-blooded, although biologists prefer the terms poikilothermic (of variable temperature) or ectothermic (externally heated). Their metabolic rates and activity levels slow as temperatures fall, giving them a narrower range of habitat than mammals and birds. But to a lesser degree, they, too, can regulate their temperature. This may involve behavior—a lizard picks up heat by lounging on a warm rock—or special mechanisms, such as the heat-producing organ near the eye of a swordfish that warms its brain during deep dives. Perhaps most commonly, however, it involves changes in blood-flow patterns similar to those seen in endotherms.

Methods. Thermoregulation in mammals and birds relies on manipulation of the circulatory system. By constricting or dilating small blood vessels in various parts of the body, an animal can direct blood-borne heat to parts of the body that need it or get rid of the heat by radiation through the skin.

One key to this process is countercurrent exchange: arteries that carry warm blood out from the core of the body lie next to veins that bear colder blood in from the periphery. Much of the heat transfers from the arterial blood to the venous blood so that the core of the body remains warm. Countercurrent exchange also can help cool key parts of the body, particularly the brain, to prevent overheating. In hot settings, for instance, many cats and dogs use panting or shallow breathing to cool blood in the capillaries of the nose. The cool blood then flows into a carotid rete, a network of capillaries, where it flows past hot arterial blood bound for the brain, cooling it off.

As the examples above indicate, although endothermic animals are often described as maintaining a constant body temperature, their temperature can vary from one body part to another. Arctic animals, in particular, often let their limbs grow cold in order to keep their core temperature high. In humans, the core temperature is normally 37 to 38 degrees Celsius, but parts of the brain and liver are often slightly warmer and the skin is often cooler. Nor are all endotherms' temperatures constant over time. Maintaining an elevated body temperature in a cold climate requires an animal to metabolize a large amount of food. In such settings, many endotherms hibernate, with their bodies maintained at low core temperatures.

Human Thermal Regulation. In humans, the thermoregulatory center in the hypothalamus of the brain controls core temperature. Neurons there receive signals from two pathways. One is from neurons connected to cold and warm receptors in the periphery. The other reflects the temperature of the blood in the hypothalamic region. The hypothalamus is involved in constricting or dilating blood vessels as well as in causing sweating and shivering. When these means are not enough to maintain core temperature, the thermoregulatory center sends signals to the cerebral cortex so a human can take other steps, such as huddling up for warmth, seeking a warmer place, or putting on warm clothes.

Background material can be found in HEAT; HOMEOSTASIS; TEMPERATURE. *Further details can be found in* CIRCULATORY SYSTEM; METABOLISM; OXIDIZING AGENTS. *Additional relevant information is contained in* MAMMALS; THERMOMETRY; WATER IN LIVING CELLS.

First see CARNOT CYCLE

Thermodynamic Cycle

Next see PHASE

An arrangement by which one form of energy is partially converted to another form.

Every thermodynamic cycle requires a working substance, usually a gas or vapor, a mechanism in which the processes or phases of the cycle are done in sequence and a thermodynamic sink.

Sequence. The general sequence of events in a thermodynamic cycle starts with a compression process, in which the working substance undergoes an increase in pressure and density. Thermal energy is added from fossil fuels, solar radiation, or the energy from fissioning atoms. This is followed by an expansion process, in which the system does its work, and then by the transfer of the unused thermal energy to the surroundings.

Since some heat is always unused in a thermodynamic cycle, so that the efficiency of a heat engine is never 100 percent. The first and most notable attempt to outline a method of determining the efficiency of any heat engine was made in 1824 by a French engineer, Nicolas Leonard Sadi Carnot (1796-1832).

Further Reading
Gisotfe, Carl V., *The Hot Brain* (2000); Heinrich, B., *The Hot-Blooded Insects* (1993); Marchand, Peter J., *Life in the Cold* (1996); Shitzer, Abraham, *Heat Transfer in Medicine and Biology* (1985).

Further Reading
Duffy, J. E., *Auto Engines Technology* (1993), Hills, R. L., *Power from Steam: A History of the Stationary Steam Engine* (1993).

Carnot Cycle. Carnot is credited with describing the cycles of an ideal engine. This simple cycle is today called the Carnot cycle.

The Carnot cycle is most easily applied to a gas passing through engine components such as cylinders with pistons and heat exchangers. To start, the gas is compressed adiabatically, meaning that it is isolated from heat exchanges with the surroundings, so that its temperature increases. In the next step, the compressed gas is brought into contact with a heat reservoir. That contact makes the gas expand, converting some of its heat into work. The gas then comes in contact with a heat reservoir at a lower temperature and is compressed so that it eventually has the same pressure, volume, and temperature that it had at the beginning of the cycle. A heat engine such as a steam engine that operates on this cycle is called a Carnot engine.

In such an engine, the working substance alternates between the liquid and vapor stages. Another kind of thermodynamic cycle is the gas power cycle. The gas power cycle is particularly suited to engines of relatively small weight and relatively small power output, such as the engines used in automobiles.

Other Cycles. The Otto cycle is the model for such engines. After an intake stroke, the gas is adiabatically compressed. It then receives heat in the form of a spark-initiated combustion and expands adiabatically against a piston, thus doing work. The engine then rejects the unused heat, which is passed through an exhaust valve. There are four steps in the Otto cycle. Two of them involve heat but no work; the other two involve work but no heat.

A diesel engine is similar to the gasoline engine, except that it operates at very high compression without spark ignition. After intake, air is compressed adiabatically until its temperature exceeds the ignition point of the fuel, which is injected at such a rate that its consumption and expansion of volume occur at approximately constant pressure. After the expansion moves the cylinder, the unused heat is exhausted as in the Carnot cycle.

The Brayton cycle is the model for the operation of a gas turbine. In the first step of the cycle, air is drawn into the compressor and is compressed adiabatically. In the next two steps, the air is mixed with fuel in the turbine's combustion chamber and receives heat at a constant pressure. Adiabatic expansion then occurs and drives the turbine. In the final step, heat is ejected at a constant pressure.

Background material on thermodynamic cycles can be found in HEAT; TEMPERATURE; THERMODYNAMICS. *Advanced subjects are developed in* CARNOT CYCLE; GASES, BEHAVIOR OF; REFRIGERATION. *Other aspects of this subject are covered in* AUTOMOTIVE DESIGN; INTERNAL COMBUSTION ENGINE.

First see HEAT

Thermodynamics

Next see ENTROPY

The science that studies phenomena in which temperature changes play an important role.

The science of thermodynamics is based on the four laws of thermodynamics, which have been derived experimentally.

The Four Laws. The first law of thermodynamics is the law of conservation of energy. It starts with the assumption that any isolated system anywhere in the universe has a measurable quantity of energy, its internal energy. This is the total amount of energy, kinetic and potential, of the atoms and molecules of the system that can be transferred in the form of heat. The internal energy of a system can be changed only if the system is no longer isolated. In that case, internal energy can be transferred by a change of mass of the system, a gain or loss of heat by the system, or work done on or by the system. The first law states that for any process, the difference between the heat, Q, that is applied to the system and the work, W, done by the system equals the change in the internal energy, U, of the system. One consequence of the first law is the impossibility of perpetual motion, which envisions a machine that can work forever with 100 percent efficiency or can do work without an input of energy. The effort to make a perpetual-motion machine went on for centuries, until its impossibility was accepted as a consequence of the laws of thermodynamics.

The fact that a substance can be cooled by expanding it or heated by compressing it is an illustration of the first law of thermodynamics. A given change in the energy of the system can be accomplished by several different combinations of heat and work. Work alone thus can be equivalent to heat—in compression the addition of heat, in expansion the reduction of heat.

The second law of thermodynamics concerns the direction that a process involving energy can take. One statement of this law is that the entropy of an isolated system always increases with time. Entropy is a measure of the disorder of the system. Another statement of the law is that the heat of a system can never be transformed completely into work. Yet another is that natural processes involving heat are irreversible and occur spontaneously in one direction only. The second law implies that time has a definite direction, pointing from the past to the future. Thus, we could never observe time going backward, since we would be going backward along with time. Rudolf Clausius, a 19th-century German scientist, stated the second law in two sentences: the energy of the universe is constant; the entropy of the universe tends toward a maximum.

CONTROVERSIES

The Heat Death of the Universe

One of the more provocative applications of thermodynamics views the entire universe as an isolated system. Since the second law of thermodynamics says that the entropy of such a system always increases, a time is envisioned when the disorder of the universe will have become total, so that it will die an "entropy death." This heat death of the universe has been a matter of debate among astronomers and physicists, as it has not been known whether the universe will continue to expand or whether it will collapse under the force of gravity in a "Big Crunch." Recent observations have indicated that the expansion of the universe is accelerating, thus indicating indefinite expansion and increasing entropy.

The third law of thermodynamics concerns absolute zero, the temperature at which all movement caused by heat stops. That temperature is minus 469.67 degrees on the Fahrenheit scale and minus 273.15 degrees on the Celsius scale. The third law states that it is impossible to reach absolute zero in a finite number of operations by any procedure. Some experiments have reached temperatures within a fraction of a degree of absolute zero, but the third law says that the ultimate goal cannot be reached.

There is another law of thermodynamics, usually called the zeroth law. It states that if two systems are in thermal equilibrium with a third system, then all three systems are in thermal equilibrium with each other. This law is the foundation of the concept of temperature.

Real World Thermodynamics. While the laws of thermodynamics are essential in the interpretation of natural and industrial processes, thermodynamic studies in the real world require a knowledge of the thermodynamic properties of the substances being studied. These properties must be measured directly by thermodynamic methods or derived from methods used in other branches of physics.

Thus, the laws of thermodynamics provide tests that can be used to assay the consistency of measurements of properties relating to specific substances, or methods of evaluating measurements of other properties. The laws of thermodynamics also provide a general framework for other branches of physics that deal with the thermodynamic properties of substances and systems. Just one such application is the kinetic theory of gases, which is applied to explain the phenomena of heat and pressure.

Further Reading
Fuchs, H. U., *The Dynamics of Heat* (1996); Stephan, K., *Heat and Mass Transfer* (1998); Van Wylen, G., *Fundamentals of Classical Thermodynamics* (1985).

Background material on thermodynamics can be found in ENERGY; ENTROPY; HEAT; TEMPERATURE. *Advanced subjects are developed in* ABSOLUTE ZERO; CONSERVATION LAWS IN NATURE. *Further information on particular aspects of this subject is contained in* MAXWEL-BOLTZMANN DISTRIBUTION; SUPERCONDUCTOR; SUPERFLUID. *See also* THERMAL REGULATION.

First see TEMPERATURE

Thermometry

Next see CALORIMETRY

The measurement of temperature and changes in temperature.

A number of materials and techniques are used in the measurement of temperature, depending on the range of temperatures that is being measured and the degree of accuracy required in the measurement. All thermometers make use of one or another property of a substance that changes as the temperature changes. Liquid-in-gas thermometers, for example, utilize the expansion or contraction of a liquid, often mercury or alcohol that is colored with a dye. Such a thermometer has a glass bulb that is filled with the liquid and is attached to a partially filled capillary tube. As the temperature rises or falls, so does the level of the liquid in the tube, which has a temperature scale imprinted on it. A liquid-in-gas thermometer is not as accurate as a gas thermometer, which measures changes by the expansion or contraction of the gas. A bimetallic thermometer uses two different metals that expand or contract at different rates, so that a pointer is moved around a dial as the temperature changes. Single metals, such as platinum, nickel, or copper, are used in resistance thermometers, which measure the changes in electrical conductivity caused by temperature changes.

Thermocouples. Another kind of thermometer is the thermocouple, which consists of a rod made of two different wires of metal or semiconducting material, the ends of which are welded together. One end of the rod, called the measuring junction, is exposed to a substance at the temperature that is being measured. The other end, the reference junction, is kept at a known temperature. The temperature difference between the two ends causes a thermoelectric or semiconducting force to be generated in the rod, and that force is measured by a voltmeter to determine temperature changes.

Acoustic Thermometry. An acoustic thermometer measures temperature by the change in the speed of sound transmission through a gas that occurs as the temperature changes. Such a thermometer usually consists of an acoustic resonator whose speed of sound transmission is determined by studying a standing wave pattern in the gas. A noise thermometer measures the changes in electrical resistance, or noise, of a metal. Extremely low temperatures can be measured by the gamma ray anisotropy thermometer, which relies on the changes of orientation of the magnetic moments and gamma ray emissions of molecules that occur at these temperatures.

Modern thermometry began in the early seventeenth century with attempts at precise

Above, a calorimeter.

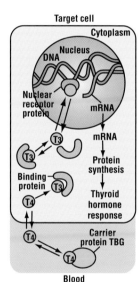

Above, the thyroid cycle.

temperature measurements. Today, thermometry uses the International Temperature Scale, which sets certain fixed temperature reference points. The latest resulted in a scale designated ITS-90. The accuracy of a given thermometer can be determined by comparing its results with the ITS-90 scale.

First see ENDOCRINE SYSTEM

Thyroid Gland

Next see AGGRESSION AND TERRITORIALITY

An endocrine gland found in vertebrates, it traps small amounts of iodine consumed in food and water and coverts it into thyroid hormones.

Thyroid hormones control the metabolic rate in all body tissues; they raise the level of oxygen consumption; increase body temperature and glucose absorption; and affect the metabolism of carbohydrates, proteins, and lipids. Along with growth hormone from the pituitary gland, they promote skeletal development. Without them, the ovaries and testes fail to mature. In some amphibians and reptiles, they are needed for metamorphosis and molting. (*See* METABOLISM.)

Except for fish, which usually have scattered thyroid follicles, all vertebrates have either a single thyroid, as in snakes and turtles, or a pair of glands, as in most other vertebrates. Humans have a single bow-tie-shaped gland—two lobes joined by a band of tissue called the isthmus—that hugs the front of the trachea, just below the larynx. Each lobe is normally about an inch wide by 1.5 inches high, but when deprived of dietary iodine, the gland can grow prodigiously, producing a large goiter.

Within the gland, thyroid follicles combine ionized iodine with the amino acid tyrosine to produce two nearly identical hormones—thyroxin or T4, a peptide containing four atoms of iodine, and Tri-iodothyronine or T3, which contains three atoms of iodine and is more biologically active. Collectively called thyroid hormone or TH, they are the only important iodine-containing compounds found in higher animals. Unlike most endocrine glands, the thyroid stores large amounts of its hormones; turnover is relatively low. (*See* ENDOCRINE SYSTEMS.)

Like the adrenal glands, the thyroid is regulated by the pituitary-hypothalamus axis. When the thyroid hormone level in the blood is low, the hypothalamus in the brain secretes thyrotropic releasing hormone, or TRH. This stimulates the anterior pituitary gland to release thyrotropic hormone (also called thyroid-stimulating hormone or TSH). This, in turn, stimulates the thyroid to release more thyroid hormone.

Hyperthyroidism—excessively high levels of TH—causes high blood pressure, high body temperature, loss of weight, irritability, muscular weakness, and protrusion of the eyeballs. It is often treated by partial destruction of the gland through surgery or the use of radioactive iodine.

Low TH Levels. Hypothyroidism—low levels of TH—can cause mental and physical lethargy. Iodine deficiency, once a common cause of the condition, and of goiters, has been eliminated in much of the world since the advent of iodized salt early in this century. When the condition is caused by malfunction of the gland itself, it can be treated with TH. But if untreated at birth, hypothyroidism can cause cretinism, in which size, intelligence, and sexual development are all stunted. (*See* MORPHOGENESIS.)

In mammals, the thyroid has an additional role. In conjunction with the parathyroid glands, it helps regulate calcium in the blood, which is essential for muscle contraction, nerve conduction, and enzyme function. (*See* BLOOD.)

Interspersed among the thyroid follicles in the thyroid gland are parafollicular cells, or C cells, which synthesize the hormone calcitonin. In most vertebrates, the calcitonin-producing cells are found in separate glands, called ultimobranchial glands, but in mammals, these merge with the thyroid during embryonic development.

Parathyroid Glands. Calcitonin lowers the concentration of calcium in the blood by enhancing the movement of calcium into the bones. Its powerful antagonist, which raises calcium levels in the blood, is parathyroid hormone, or PTH, produced by the parathyroids. These small glands are seen in virtually all vertebrates except fish, with one or two pairs found near or embedded in the thyroid or thymus. In humans, two pairs are embedded in the back of the thyroid.

PTH raises calcium levels in several ways. It stimulates the bones to release calcium, it acts on the kidneys to reduce the calcium excreted in urine, and it causes the kidneys to activate vitamin D, which increases calcium absorpton in the gastrointestinal tract. (*See* KIDNEYS AND EXCRETORY SYSTEMS.)

First see OCEAN CURRENT

Tides

Next see COASTAL ENGINEERING

The periodic rise and fall of the oceans or other large bodies of water, and of land as well.

The principal cause of tides is the gravitational pull of the moon, but the gravitational pull of the sun also is a contributor. For land, the maximal tidal movement is measured in inches—about 23 inches at the maximum. Water tides vary greatly depending on location. In the Mediterranean, for example, tidal rises and falls are very small. In the Bay of Fundy, by contrast, the difference between high tide and low tide can be as much as 50 feet. Because of the strong influence of the moon, the interval between one high tide

Further Reading
Cartwright, David Edgar, *Tides: A Scientific History* (1999).

Above, low tide reveals the oyster beds of Chincoteague, Virginia. In pools such as these, with the daily sequence of seawater and sun, life may have arisen in the early atmosphere of the Earth.

and the next is 12 hours and 25 minutes, the time it takes for the moon to make half a complete orbit around the Earth. The highest tides of the month, called the spring tide, occur twice each month, when the gravitational forces from the sun and moon are acting together. The lowest tides, the neap tides, occur when the gravitational pulls of the sun and moon are acting at right angles to each other. There are a number of other phenomena that contribute to the timing and degree of tidal movement. These include the rotation of the Earth, the revolution of the Earth-moon system around the sun, and the revolution of the sun-Earth system, and even the gravitational pull of some of the larger planets.

The difference between the time of high tide that is calculated from the movement of the moon and the actual observed time is known as the "establishment of the port." These are listed in tide tables. The values that are obtained for ports that are only a few miles apart can be quite different, because of the configuration of the coastline between the two areas.

Tidal Energy. The movement of water and land that is embodied in the tides represents an expenditure of energy. A large part of this energy must come from the rotation of the Earth. The tides can be pictured as dragging on the Earth as it turns. The net result of the tides should thus be a reduction in the rate of the rotation of the Earth, and thus a lengthening of the day. Scientists have made considerable efforts to determine whether this is happening, but the effect is too small to have been observed.

Background material can be found in EARTH; MOON; OCEAN CURRENT; OCEANS, ORIGIN AND EVOLUTION OF. *Advanced subjects are developed in* COASTAL ENGINEERING; ENERGY, ALTERNATIVE; OCEAN BASINS. *Additional relevant information is contained in* LIFE, DEFINITION AND ORIGIN OF; OCEANOGRAPHY.

Time

First see SPACE

Next see SPACE-TIME

Time can be defined in several ways—as the instant at which an event occurs, as a duration, or as the succession of events.

Our everyday timekeeping is based on the Earth's rotation. Astronomers use the concept of sidereal time, which is based on the apparent rotation of stars around the Earth, or ephemeris time, which is based on the Earth's orbital motion.

Physical concepts of time include:

Solar Time. The moment when the sun reaches its highest point in the sky is defined as local apparent noon, the moment when the sun reaches its lowest point is local apparent midnight, and the difference between two such midnights is one apparent solar day. But time as measured by the movement of the sun is not uniform. In the winter months, the Earth is closer to the sun and thus moves more rapidly than it does in the summer months, so the apparent solar day is shorter. To obtain a uniform length of the day, the concept of a "mean sun," which moves at a uniform rate, is used.

Sidereal time. The Earth's orbital motion around the sun causes an apparent westward shift of the position of stars in the sky from night to night. This means that the length of a day as measured by the position of a given star is about 3 minutes 56 seconds shorter than the solar day. Sidereal time is based on the vernal equinox, which occurs in March. Sidereal time is the angular distance from the vernal equinox eastward to the celestial meridian of the observer, which means the local hour angle of the vernal equinox. Zero hours in sidereal time occur at the upper transit of the vernal equinox, 12:00 at the lower transit. Slight variations in the sidereal day are averaged out to produce a mean sidereal day. Sidereal time and solar time coincide once a year, when the sun arrives at the autumnal equinox, in September.

Ephemeris Time. The rotation of the Earth can vary unpredictably, probably due to movements of mass in the interior of the planet. Astronomical observations are precise enough to show that these rotational variations in turn cause variations in both mean solar and sidereal time. Therefore, these time systems are not adequate for the most precise astronomical observations.

Ephemeris time is a more precise and uniform measure that is based on observations of the revolution of the moon around the Earth. While the motions of the Earth and moon may not be uniform, an extremely accurate time system is obtained by calculating the variations in these motions. The fundamental unit of time in the ephemeris system is the ephemeris second, which is defined as 1/31,556,925.9747 of the tropical year at noon on December 31, 1899. In practice, one ephemeris second is very nearly equal to one second of solar time. Astronomical events are predicted in ephemeris time but are recorded in solar time; the exact ephemeris time of an event is calculated several months after its occurrence.

Standard Time. Because actual local time can differ even in communities that are close to one another, a system of standard time has been adopted, which sets the time within given geographical areas. The reference meridians for this system are spaced 15 degrees apart in longitude, beginning with the meridian that runs through Greenwich, England. The difference in time between two adjacent zones is exactly one hour.

The boundaries of these time zones can be ad-justed in accordance with political, geographic, or economic boundaries. For zones west of Greenwich, time is earlier than Greenwich mean time; for zones to the east, time is later than Greenwich mean time. Accurate time signals based on this system are broadcast regularly by observatories in a number of nations. In the United States, these signals are broadcast by the U. S. Naval Observatory.

Background on the the subject of time can be found in ACCELERATION; SPACE; TIME, MEASUREMENT OF. *Advanced subjects are developed in* LIGHT, SPEED OF; SPACE-TIME; SPECIAL RELATIVITY. *Additional relevant information is contained in* BIG BANG THEORY; GEOLOGICAL TIME SCALE; NAVIGATION; TWIN PARADOX.

Further Reading
Greene, Brian, *The Elegant Universe* (1999); Gribbin, John, *Schrodinger's Kittens and the Search For Reality* (1995); Thorne, Kip S., *Black Holes and Time Warps: Einstein's Outrageous Legacy* (1994).

First see TIME

Time, Measurement of

Next see NAVIGATION

Time can be measured by the recurrence of any periodic event, such as the daily rotation of the Earth, the swing of a pendulum, or the vibrations of atoms in a crystal. Ordinary timekeeping, called solar time, is based on the Earth's rotation on its axis and its rotation around the sun. Astronomers use sidereal time for their observations, as measured by the apparent daily revolution of stars in the sky.

Measuring Solar Time. Solar time can be measured in several ways. Local apparent noon is the time when the sun reaches its highest point in the sky over a given area, and local apparent midnight is the time when the sun reaches its lowest point in regard to that area. The interval between two such midnights is one apparent solar day, which is the time that is measured by a sundial. But the time as measured by the sun is not uniform. Earth is closer to the sun during January and February, and it moves more rapid-

Above, Harrison's super-accurate clock was made to solve the problem of determining longitude.

ly during those months than it does in June and July, when it is furthest from the sun. Thus, the eastward motion of the sun against the stars is faster in December and January, so the length of the day (as opposed to daylight) is greater during those months. In addition, since the sun's motion is along the ecliptic, at an angle to the celestial equator, this tends to make the day longer when the sun is near the solstices and to make it shorter when the sun is at the equinoxes.

Mean Time. To get a uniform system of time measurement, the concept of mean time was introduced. Mean time is measured by a fictitious body, the mean sun, which is said to move eastward around the celestial equator once a year, at a uniform rate. The moment when the mean sun crosses the lower branch of the meridian of an observer is zero hours local time, and when the mean sun crosses the upper branch of that meridian, it is local mean noon, or 12 o'clock. The difference between mean time and apparent time is called the equation of time. It is the angular distance between the hour circles of the mean sun and the real sun.

But if local times were used in all communities, even those that are close together would have slightly different times. To obtain some uniformity of time, nations have adopted what is called standard time over land areas and zone time over ocean areas. In the United States, for example, Eastern Standard Time is measured by the 75th meridian. The reference meridians are spaced 15 degrees apart, with the 0 meridian running through Greenwich, England.

Daylight Savings Time. To extend the amount of daylight into the evening hours of the summer, many nations and communities have adopted daylight savings time, in which the clock is set ahead one hour in the springtime and turned back one hour in the autumn.

The speed of the rotation of the Earth is subject to irregular and unpredictable changes, probably because of activity within the depths of the Earth. In recent years, observations by astronomers have become precise enough to show that these changes cause variations in mean solar and sidereal time. Thus, these time systems are not precise enough for the most delicate and refined astronomical observations. Ephemeris time, a more precise and uniform measure, is used for these purposes. Ephemeris time is obtained from observations of the revolution of the moon around the Earth. The result is the ephemeris second, which is defined as 1/31,556,925.9747 of the tropical year in progress at noon on December 31, 1899.

Further Reading
Bedini, Silvio A., *The Pulse of Time: Galileo Galilei, the Determination of Longitude, and the Pendulum Clock* (1992); Greene, Brian, *The Elegant Universe* (1999); Thorne, Kip S., *Black Holes and Time Warps: Einstein's Outrageous Legacy* (1994).

Related amaterial can be found in EVOLUTION; GEOLOGICAL TIME SCALE; SPACE-TIME; TIME; WAVE. *More details can be found in* NAVIGATION; SYMMETRY IN NATURE. *Fundamental aspects of this subject are covered in* CRYSTAL; ELECTROMAGNETIC WAVE.

First see ACIDS AND BASES

Titration

Next see CHROMATOGRAPHY

The process by which the concentration of an acid or base solution can be determined experimentally.

An acid is any compound that dissociates (separates) in water to produce H^+ ions, while a base is any compound that dissociates in water to produce OH^- ions. When an acid and a base of equal concentration are brought together in equal amounts, a neutral compound known as a salt is produced, while the H^+ and OH^- ions combine to form water.

In titration, a solution of known concentration, called the standard solution, is used to neutralize a specific volume of a second solution whose concentration is unknown. An acid-base indicator is used to identify when neutralization has occurred. The indicator used is phenolphthalein, which is colorless in the presence of an acid or neutral substance, and a bright purple in the presence of a base. (*See* ACIDS AND BASES.)

The standard solution is added to the unknown until a change in color occurrs, showing that the number of H^+ ions is now equal to the number of OH^- ions. This is known as the endpoint of the titration. The volume of standard solution used is measured and used to calculate the concentration of the unknown solution, based on the volume of unknown solution that was neutralized.

First see EUCLIDEAN GEOMETRY

Topology

Next see NON-EUCLIDIAN GEOMETRY

The branch of mathematics concerned with the study of surfaces: specifically, those properties that remain unchanged when a surface is distorted.

Topology is neither metric—concerned with lengths and angles—nor quantitative. It was first developed by René Descartes (1596–1650) and Leonhard Euler (1707–1783), who each discovered an equation that links the vertices (V), edges (E), and faces (F) of every simple polyhedron: $V - E + F = 2$. According to this formulation, a tetrahedron is topologically identical to a cube, which is identical to an octahedron, which is identical to a dodecahedron, which is identical to an icosahedron; and all these faceted shapes are identical to a sphere, or solid of genus 0. Such related figures are termed isotopic. However, figures which are pierced by voids, or holes, belong to a different category.

A worker in a doughnut shop may make hundreds of doughnuts in a given day, but no two doughnuts may ever be identical: their weight, inside and outside diameter, and composition will fluctuate according to the properties of the mixing bowl, the twist of the worker's hand, even the temperature of the oven. But for a student of topology, these differences do not matter; every doughnut the worker produces is simply a torus, or solid of genus 1. Every shape with a single hole that pierces it completely is a torus. Therefore if the doughnut were deformed, by extending one side and hollowing it out, the result would be a coffee cup (with a handle), but the coffee cup would be a torus just like the doughnut. Such surfaces are called homeomorphic, because one can cut them, deform them, then glue them back together to form a topologically identical surface; this is perhaps the aspect of topology which differs most from classical Euclidean geometry. Likewise, the two-handled sugar bowl on the counter of the doughnut shop can be deformed into a coffeepot, with a handle on one side and a spout on the other; each will be a solid of genus 2.

Genus of a Surface. The genus of a surface is defined by the number of Jordan curves which can be drawn on its surface without cutting into discrete parts. These simple closed curves are named after the French theorist Camille Jordan (1838–1922). Any line drawn on a sphere cuts it into two parts, so the genus of the sphere is 0; any two lines will cut a doughnut into separate parts, so its genus is 1; and so on. If the genus number of a surface is given by p, then Euler's original equation can be adapted to any surface, not just simple polygons: V - E + F = 2 - 2p.

Most surfaces have two sides, even though in many cases the second side is the inside. In such cases, where the figure is closed, if each side is painted a different color the two colors never touch. In other cases, such as a doughnut with one bite taken out of it, the surface has a boundary curve where the colors do meet. (These are called the surface's boundary characteristics). However, in 1865 Augustus Möbius discovered that a surface could be one-sided by cutting out a long strip of paper, twisting one end 180 degrees, and taping the ends together. The resulting Möbius Strip has only one surface, and only one edge; and because a cut made down the center line of the strip adds an edge, but does not cut the strip, it is of genus 1.

Orientation. The final important characteristic to be considered in topology is orientation. Since nearly all surfaces are two-sided, they are orientable according to which side the observer happens to be viewing: in a closed figure, inside or outside; in a figure with a boundary curve, which side of the boundary one chooses to focus on. But a Möbius Strip has only one side, and therefore is nonorientable; so is the Klein bottle. By answering the following three questions, one can completely determine the homeomorphic type of any surface: what is its Euler character-

istic? Is it orientable? How many boundary characteristics does it have?

Topology has many contemporary applications. Jordan curves are used in computer graphics programs to determine which parts of a design to color. Seat belts are often given a half twist, turning them into Möbius Strips, in order to equalize wear across all sides and edges. And quantum field theory, a branch of theoretical physics, relies on a figure from topology called a three-manifold for its definition of the spatial universe.

Further Reading
Dunham, William, *Euler the Master of Us All* (1992); Gaukroger, S., *Descartes: An Intellectual Biography* (1995); Maunder, C.R.F., *Algebraic Topology* (1996).

> *Further developments in the field of topology are discussed in* EUCLIDEAN GEOMETRY; SETS AND GROUPS; SPACE. *Further details can be found in* NON-EUCLIDEAN GEOMETRY; SYMMETRY IN NATURE; VECTORS AND TENSORS. *Additional relevant information is contained in* DIFFERENTIAL GEOMETRY; FRACTALS; KNOTS.

First see DNA

Transcription

Next see DNA REPLICATION

The process by which proteins are constructed from their m-RNA blueprints.

The assembly of amino acids into a protein is performed by organelles known as ribosomes, which are located in the cytoplasm of the cell. However, protein synthesis really begins in the nucleus, with the DNA. A gene is a segment of DNA which "codes for," or specifies, the amino acid sequence of a particular protein. A gene is found along one or the other strand of the DNA duplex, and begins with a specific sequence known as the promoter region and ends with the terminator region. (*See* GENE.)

The major elements in protein synthesis are the coding strand of DNA, known as the template, the messenger RNA molecule (mRNA), which conveys the information from the nucleus to the ribosomes, and the transfer RNA molecules (tRNA), which transport the amino acids. (*See* RNA.)

Protein synthesis occurs in two major stages: transcription, which is the formation of mRNA from the DNA template, and translation, the interaction of mRNA, tRNA, and ribosomes to form the polypeptide chain.

The basic unit of both DNA and RNA is the nucleotide, which in turn consists of a sugar molecule, a phosphate group (PO_4), and one of 5 nucleic bases: adenine (A), guanine (G), cytosine (C), thymine (T), and uracil (U). Thymine is found only in DNA, and uracil is found only in RNA. The polynucleotide chain consists of alter-

Tryptophan

Tryptophan-tRNA

Anticodon

mRNA

Tryptophan codon

Above, a schematic representation of mRNA translation.

nating sugar and phosphate groups forming a "backbone" with the bases protruding off the sugar molecules. When two strands come together, they "match up" according to specific base pairs: A-T, A-U, and G-C.

The Process. Transcription begins when an enzyme called RNA polymerase settles on the promoter region of the gene and causes the double helix to "unwind." The RNA polymerase matches up nucleotides to pair with the exposed DNA bases along the entire length of the gene until it reaches the terminator region. Another enzyme, ligase, links the new nucleotides together to form the RNA chain.

Only one strand of the DNA duplex is "copied," and then the DNA duplex re-forms. The RNA base sequence is complementary to the DNA template and is almost identical to the noncoding strand.

The RNA molecule formed at the end of transcription is called the primary transcript. Further "editing" before translation involves the addition of a methylguanine (mG) "cap" and polyadenine "tail," as well as the removal of introns (nonsense sequence of bases) and splicing together the ends of exons (the useful parts of a gene). Post-transcription modification does not occur in prokaryotic cells (bacteria and blue-green algae), but does in eukaryotic cells. (*See* PROTEIN SYNTHESIS; RNA, MESSENGER.)

Further Reading
Herman, Stephen L., *Delmar's Standard Guide to Transformers* (1996); McPherson, George, *Introduction to Electrical Machines and Transformers* (1990).

First see INDUCTOR

Transformer

Next see ELECTRICITY AND ELECTRICAL ENGINEERING

A device that changes an alternating curent of one voltage into one of another voltage, without changing the current's frequency.

Transformers are a vital link in the distribution of electrical power and in audio and video signal processing. The AC transformer used today works by a process of induction; that is, a current of electricity flowing through a coil of wire induces a magnetic field, or flux. That magnetic flux in turn induces a current of electricity in a second coil of wire. According to Faraday's law, the voltage induced by a magnetic flux is directly proportional to the number of coils of wire subject to that flux. Therefore, to increase the voltage in a circuit one runs the original current through a transformer having a primary winding with only a few turns, but a secondary winding with many turns.

Efficiency. There are numerous efficiency losses in transformer use. The iron core around which the windings are laid is itself subject to induction, and must therefore be made out of a series of thin sheets, laminated with insulation between; even then some eddy-current losses remain present. Because the current reverses its

flow continually, the magnetic flux alternates its direction, producing magnetic hysteresis. These two losses make up the core loss, to which must be added the copper loss, resulting from resistance in the windings.

Signals. The second major use of transformers is in signal processing, where they must transfer complex waveforms rather than the simple sinusoidal currents induced in ordinary transformers. Audio and video transformers must be designed to much tighter specifications than power transformers, because they respond to signal voltages delivering frequencies ranging from 10 to 100,000 Hertz, and because miniaturization leads to a relatively high proportion of iron and copper in a limited space, affecting impedance. Nevertheless, video transformers typically operate at efficiencies of 99.98 percent. Signal transformers must carry a resistive load at all times, to limit distortion caused by hysteresis, variation in reactance, or overcoupling.

First see P-N JUNCTION

Transistor

Next see INTEGRATED CIRCUIT

An electronic component capable of regulating a current passing through it using semiconductor material.

The transistor came about as a response to the weaknesses of vacuum-tube technology. The first true computer, ENIAC, contained more than 18,000 vacuum tubes, each of which took up space, emitted heat, and failed at an alarmingly high rate. No real progress in electronics could be made until something was invented to take the place of tubes and the whole electro-mechanical technology of which they are a part.

The difficulty was that tubes are immensely useful. They turn alternating current into direct current, making them rectifiers. With the addition of a third electrode, which controls the flow be-tween the two main electrodes, they also serve to control and to amplify electric currents.

The breakthrough came from a team working on long-distance telephone communication at Bell Labs. In December 1947, William Shockley, John Bardeen, and Walter Brattain successfully demonstrated that, by using semi-conducting materials rather than metals, one could dispense with the bulky, fragile, heat-producing vacuum tubes and achieve the same switching and amplification effects. They called it a transistor.

Structure of a Transistor. The heart of the transistor was a crystal of germanium, deliberately laced with a tiny amount of impurities, which opened up spaces for the movement of free electrons, and of their corresponding "holes," throughout the crystal. Such electrons and holes might only exist for a fraction of a sec-

Above, an early P-N Junction, forerunner of the transistor.

ond, but in that time they could easily travel from one part of the crystal to another, carrying a current. As they traveled, they would meet a barrier known as a p-n junction, created by juxtaposing two semiconductor materials laced with slightly different impurities, which acted exactly like a vacuum tube rectifier; bouncing off that barrier, they would flow through another interface, where they stimulated even greater current—exactly like a vacuum tube amplifier. The invention would win all three researchers the Nobel Prize in 1956.

By 1958, production difficulties with germanium led to the development of silicon transistors, coated with a protective layer of silicon dioxide; and with a smooth surface to work on researchers soon created a planar, or surface-effect transistor, whose components were connected by fine aluminum lines laid directly on the coating and connected to the electrical activity below through tiny etched holes. From here it was a short leap of inspiration, achieved almost simultaneously by Jack Kilby and Robert Noyce, to place several transistor units on a wafer of silicon, even to add a few capacitors and resistors as well. Thus the integrated circuit was born.

Planar Transistor. The planar transistor also enabled re-searchers to perfect the field-effect transistor, in which a voltage applied to a tiny aluminum "gate" laid on the surface created a current in the silicon below, thereby controlling the lateral current just as the third electrode in the vacuum tube had. This transistor, technically called an insulated-gate transistor, is commonly called a MOSFET after the metal-oxide-silicon structure of the instrument; it is currently the standard component of high-speed random-access computer memories.

Future Transistors. Future transistor developments appear to lie in two directions: further miniaturization, and new materials. One area of research that combines both potentials is thin-film polymer transistors, based not on silicon but on an organic molecule called dihexylsexithiophene.

The other promising area is, ironically, a metallic transistor, based on the spin properties of ferromagnetic elements; recent experiments have shown that electron spin can induce similar spin orientation in a non-conducting substrate, comparable to the "tunneling" effect of a MOSFET, a condition that would be inherently stable until reversed by an external magnetic field. (*See* MAGNETIC FIELD OF THE EARTH.)

Background material on the transistor can be found in DIODE AND PHOTODIODE; ELECTRIC CIRCUIT; P-N JUNCTION. *Further developments in the field are discussed in* ELECTRIC CIRCUIT, APPLICATIONS OF; INTEGRATED CIRCUITS. *Special topics in this area are found in* JOSEPHSON JUNCTION; RECORDING TECHNOLOGY; TELECOMMUNICATIONS.

Further Reading
Feldman, James M., *The Physics and Circuit Properties of Transistors* (1990); Libes, Sol, *Repairing Transistor Radios* (1991); Shur, Michael, *Introduction to Electronic Devices* (1995).

First see PERIODIC TABLE OF ELEMENTS

Transition Elements

Next see METAL

Also known as the transition metals, they lie between groups IIA and IIIA on the Periodic Table. Beginning in the fourth row and continuing through the seventh, they also include the lanthanide and actinide series.

The transition elements include many of the more "familiar" metals such as gold, silver, iron, copper, zinc, mercury, and platinum. All of these metals exhibit an interesting arrangement of their electrons. As in all atoms, the electrons are not located in the nucleus but "orbit" in discrete energy levels. Each principal energy level contains a specific number of sublevels, and each sublevel contains a specific number of orbitals. Normally, electrons are arranged as close to the nucleus as possible and are located in the lowest orbitals available. In the transition elements, however, level 4 orbitals fill up with electrons even while some level 3 orbitals farther away from the nucleus remain empty. This is called "orbital overlap."

All of the transition metals have just one or two electrons in their valence energy levels. Like the "A group" metals, the transition elements will lose their valence electrons and form cations, or positively charged ions, and be involved in ionic bonds. Transition metals, however, are not as reactive as these "A group" metals.

Transition metals exhibit the same properties as the "A group" metals, namely being lustrous, malleable, ductile, and good conductors of heat and electricity. Many of our most important metallic compounds and alloys contain transition elements. (*See* METAL.)

CONTROVERSIES

Ghost Writing

The chemistry of compounds formed with transition metals is very complex. Many of them are very brightly colored and can change color according to their energy state. One interesting application involves the compound cobalt chloride, used to make "invisible" ink. The solution is pale pink and therefore difficult to see on paper. However, when heated, the ab-sorbed energy causes the removal of water from the compound and the ink turns a bright blue. The addition or removal of water changes the geometry of the compound and therefore its light absorption properties.

First see CELLULAR MEMBRANES

Transport, Cellular

Next see OSMOSIS

The movement of particles in and out of a cell by diffusion and osmotic processes.

Materials follow a concentration gradient, meaning they travel from an area of higher concentration to an area of lower concentration until there is an equal amount on both sides of the membrane.

The ability of a particle to diffuse depends upon the following properties: size, charge, and solubility, a result of the physical makeup of the membrane itself. A membrane consists of a double layer of proteins and lipids, which are large organic molecules with various charged groups attached. The spaces between the component molecules are called pores. Smaller particles can cross the membrane more easily than larger ones as they have a better chance of slipping through the pores and around the constituent molecules. If a particle has an electrical charge, it can only cross the membrane in an oppositely charged area. If it attempts to cross at an area of identical charge, it will be repelled.

Other Transport Mechanisms. Other forms of transport are used in cases when the desired result is not equilibrium, or when the molecules are too large to cross on their own. Passive transport, also known as facilitated diffusion, involves the use of carrier molecules, usually membrane proteins, to "piggyback" materials across. The carrier grabs hold of its passenger and then flips over. The part originally facing the outside environment of the cell is now on the interior and entry into the cell has been achieved. Active transport is similar, but requires the use of energy, as materials are being moved against the concentration gradient. Endocytosis refers to the bulk transport of materials into a cell, and exocytosis refers to moving them out.

Osmosis. Osmosis is the movement of water across a membrane. Water molecules travel to whichever side has a higher concentration of solid particles that have dissolved. The area with the higher concentration is said to be hypertonic in relation to the other side. The side of the membrane with the lower concentration of particles, which loses water, is said to be hypotonic. Isotonic means that both sides of the membrane have an equal concentration of solids, and therefore water will move freely in either direction.

Further Reading
Bray, Dennis, *Cell Movements* (1992); de Duve, Christian, *Blueprint for a Cell: The Nature and Origin of Life* (1991); Rensberger, Boyce, *Life Itself: Exploring the Realm of the Living Cell* (1996).

The foundations of the subject of cellular transport are discussed in CELLULAR MEMBRANES; OSMOSIS; WATER IN LIVING CELLS. *Further details can be found in* LEAF; LIPIDS; PLANT; PROTEIN; ROOTS. *Advanced subjects are developed in* ADENOSINE TRIPHOSPHATE (ATP); CYSTIC FIBROSIS. *See also* METABOLISM.

First see PERIODIC TABLE OF ELEMENTS

Transuranic Elements

Next see RADIOACTIVITY

Chemical elements, all synthetic, with an atomic number of 93 or more.

The elements on the Periodic Table are arranged in order of increasing proton number, also known as the atomic number (Z). The number of the other two subatomic particles, neutrons and electrons, can vary from atom to atom even within the same element. The electron number changes as atoms gain or lose electrons in the process of forming chemical bonds. Atoms of the same element which have different numbers of neutrons, and consequently different atomic masses, are called isotopes.

Uranium (Z = 92) is the last and largest of the naturally occurring elements. All subsequent elements, known as the transuranic elements, are synthetic.

Since 1940 scientists have had the ability to produce elements by the process of nuclear transformation, in which one element is changed into another. Nuclear transformation occurs when one element is bombarded with either alpha particles (helium nuclei consisting of two protons and two neutrons) or small nuclei from C_{12} or N_{15} atoms (common isotopes of carbon and nitrogen, respectively). For example, neptunium (symbol Np, Z = 93) is produced by bombarding the most common form of uranium, known as U_{238}, with a neutron. The uranium is changed into its isotope U_{239}, which then decays into Np_{239} (Z = 93) and one loose electron. Plutonium (symbol Pu, Z = 94) is formed when U_{238} is transformed into U_{239}, which then decays into Pu_{239}. Plutonium and another uranium isotope, known as U_{235}, are the typical fuels used in a nuclear reactor.

All of the transuranic elements are unstable. Their atoms spontaneously give off alpha or beta particles (electrons) and gamma radiation (a high energy photon of light). The instability of the elements increases with the atomic number. Some of them, like element 105, only last for a few seconds after being synthesized. All current versions of the Periodic Table go at least as far as element 118, which has been produced but broke down in a fraction of a second. Scientists are attempting to reach a projected "Island of Stability," beginning at element 126.

Many of the transuranic elements have colorful names quite different from the naturally occurring elements, most of whose names have Greek or Latin roots. They pay tribute to scientists or even laboratories that have contributed to important discoveries: curium (after the Curies), fermium (Enrico Fermi), and einsteinium (Albert Einstein) to name a few.

Tropical Rain Forest

First see BIODIVERSITY

Next see PHARMACOLOGY

Teeming with species and tangled with vegetation, tropical rain forests have become synonymous with biodiversity under siege. Although they cover only a small fraction of the Earth's surface, they are estimated to contain at least half of all known animal and plant species. In an area of the Peruvian rain forest that measures just over two acres, 283 species of tree have been found, and a single rain forest may be home to as many butterflies as the entire United States. Since World War II, however, logging, farming, and mining operations have killed millions of acres of rain forest, almost certainly destroying many species that were found nowhere else. Although estimates of the rate and extent of the destruction vary, the loss of substantial portions of the Earth's most productive and complex ecosystems has raised deep concern.

Tropical Soil. One of the ironies of rain forest destruction is that despite their lush growth, tropical rain forests generally have poor soil. They thrive because they efficiently recycle necessary nutrients within their own biomass—their flora and fauna—rather than storing them in the soil, as in North American forests. But when the tropical rain forest is cut or burned down, the remaining soil becomes unproductive for agriculture within a few years.

Tropical rain forests are generally found in equatorial regions that get more than 240 cm of rain a year—Central America, the Amazon region of South America, western and central equatorial Africa, Malaysia and other parts of southeast Asia, Madagascar and other islands.

Stratification. Typically, rain forests are stratified. Two layers of trees—one 50 to 80 yards high, one slightly shorter—together form an almost unbroken canopy of green crowns. Beneath it grow layers of shorter trees, shrubs, seedlings, herbs, and ferns. Rainforests are notable for their tree-dwelling plants, or epiphytes, that grow high above the ground on trunks, branches, and even leaves. These range from mosses and algae to orchids. The forest floor is typically dark—in a Malaysian rain forest only two to three percent of outside light reaches the floor—and thickly matted with shallow roots. Many of the larger trees are supported by buttresses, planklike props that grow from their roots up to their lower trunk. (*See* PLANT.)

Tropical Cycles. Many of these features aid in the recycling of nutrients. The matted roots, with their many fine feeders, draw in nutrients from fallen leaves because they can leach into the soil. They may also prevent the loss of some nitrogen into the air. The algae and lichen grab nutrients from rainfall and fix nitrogen. The

Above, the sun shines through the plant canopy of a rain forest in New Zealand. This important rain forest has been explored even less than the rain forest in Brazil.

Further Reading
Jacobs, Marius, *Tropical Rain Forest: A First Encounter* (1988); Sharp, Ilsa, *Green Indonesia: Tropical Forest Encounters* (1994); Vandermeer, John, *Breakfast of Biodiversity: The Truth About Rain Forest Destruction* (1995).

trees have thick bark and waxy evergreen leaves that prevent loss of water and nutrients.

Diversity. Tropical rain forests support a diversity of animal and insect life, including insectivorous, carnivorous, and fruit-eating birds and bats, squirrels and sloths that live in the trees, and larger herbivore mammals, including the Asian elephant, that live on the forest floor. They are the home of most primates in the world—from the lemurs of Madagascar to the African chimpanzees to the many small New World primates. The rain forest is heavily dependent on bees, beetles, moths, bats, and birds to pollinate its plants and on birds, bats, and primates to disperse the seeds of its fruit.

Background discussion of the tropical rain forest can be found in BIODIVERSITY; ECOLOGY; PHARMACOLOGY. *More information on particular aspects is contained in* DEFORESTATION; GAIA HYPOTHESIS; GLOBAL WARMING. *Additional relevant information is contained in* COEVOLUTION; EXTINCTION; POPULATION ECOLOGY.

First see PLANT

Tropism

Next see PLANT HORMONES

Bending or turning responses to external stimuli caused by changes in growth patterns.

The best known tropisms are phototropism, in which plant shoots bend toward the light, and gravitropism, a response to gravity in which roots grow downward (positive gravitropism) and shoots grow upward (negative gravitropism) even if a seedling is placed on its side. Another common form is thigmotropism, a response to contact, such as tendrils wrapping themselves around a support. Among other stimuli that some scientists think elicit tropic responses are temperature, chemicals, trauma, electricity, darkness, and geomagnetic forces.

Went-Cholodny. For many years, phototropism was explained by the Went-Cholodny theory, developed through the study of coleoptiles, the pale sheaths around the shoots of young monocot grasses. It held that when light hits the tip of the coleoptile from one side that side produces less of the growth hormone auxin. As a result, the shaded side grows more as cells there elongate, causing the plant to bend toward the light. Later experiments suggested that auxin production was not decreased on the lighted side, but instead that auxin was actively transported from the lighted to the shaded side.

More recently, however, experiments on sunflowers and other dicot seedlings with green stems have cast doubt on this explanation. In such plants, growth appears to be inhibited on the lighted side, but not stimulated on the shaded side. Some researchers have identified substances that seem triggered by light and appear to serve as growth inhibitors. Some plant physiologists, however, think the Went-Cholodny theory still holds for coleoptiles and other pale monocot seedlings. In green-stemmed dicots, these physiologists think, the transport of auxin, along with growth inhibitors, may be involved in phototropism in some more complex interplay.

The operation of gravitropism is no clearer. There is evidence that gravity may register in plants through the movement of heavy bodies, or statoliths. These bodies are believed to be amyloplasts, which contain starch granules and are found in special cells of the root cap, as well as in other parts of plants. It appears that when amyloplasts settle to the bottom of root-cap cells, they trigger the release of calcium. The calcium is thought either to play some role in the distribution of hormones, including auxin and the inhibitory hormone abscisic acid, or possibly to serve as a growth inhibitor itself. (*See* PLANT HORMONES. *Also see* ADAPTATION; INSTINCT.)

First see BACTERIA

Tuberculosis

Next see DISEASES, INFECTIOUS

An infectious disease of the lungs or other organs caused by *Mycobacterium tuberculosis* bacteria.

Tuberculosis is spread in airborne droplets produced by coughs and sneezes. When the bacteria enter the lungs, they form an infected zone called a focus that the body's immune system can control, leaving only a scar. But in about five percent of cases, the infection spreads to other parts of the body, a condition called miliary tuberculosis. In other cases, the bacteria can become dormant, sometimes reviving years later.

Tuberculosis accounted for a quarter of deaths in mid-19th century Europe. Better living quarters and treatment have reduced the toll substantially in developed countries, but tuberculosis is still a major medical problem in underdeveloped regions. Over one third of the world's population is currently infected with the organism that causes tuberculosis. At least 100 million people have active cases of the disease. Tuberculosis is the world's leading infectious killer, responsible for two million deaths per year.

The main symptoms of tuberculosis include a cough that is often bloody, chest pain, fever, sweating, shortness of breath, and weight loss. Diagnosis is confirmed by a chest x-ray and tests of the sputum and the skin for the infectious agent. Treatment starts with a combination of antibiotic drugs, such as isoniazid and rifampin; they may be given for periods of up to a year. Persons in high-risk groups may be given BCG vaccination, but it is usually not recommended.

First see ALGORITHM

Turing Machine

Next see VON NEUMAN MACHINE

The Turing Machine was developed in 1936 by Alan Turing (1912–1954), an English mathematician who had been trying to refute the assertion by David Hilbert, a German mathematician, that any mathematical problem could be solved by an appropriate automatic machine. For his rebuttal, Turing had a double challenge: first, he had to define whether all mathematical functions were computable; second, he had to determine whether any machine could be "intelligent" enough to perform such computations. For the second challenge, therefore, Turing had to invent a computer.

The only computers in existence in the 1930s were analog computers, capable of analyzing only a very limited number of real-world problems such as tidal flows and electrical currents. Furthermore, the digital computers invented during the next decade would all be single-function machines, requiring disassembly before they could be used for a new problem. Turing assumed that any machine capable of proving complex mathematical theorems must have an equally complex algorithm, or set of operating instructions—in short, a program. Turing himself never accomplished the feat of building such a machine; although his Colossus computers built during World War II were the fastest computers ever built at the time, they could perform only a single function.

Turing's Essay. In his influential essay, "On Computable Numbers, with an Application to the Entschei-dungs Problem," Turing described with remarkable prescience a modern computer, with data entered on paper tape (magnetic tape was not yet invented) and "scanned" by the machine; the machine he envisioned would accept input from the tape, store it in a series of binary on/off switches, create output, use this preliminary result as fresh input, and overwrite the first output with the final result just as a real computer does. He then demonstrated that such a machine would be far more powerful than any yet built; but it could not solve every mathematical problem, thus he refuted Hilbert's theory.

During World War II, Turing devoted his efforts to breaking German codes. He oversaw the construction of a series of Colossus computers designed exclusively for breaking German codes, as part of what has come to be called the "Enigma" project. After the war, Colossus continued to be used against the Russians.

In 1950, Turing returned to the theory of computers, in a further attempt to probe their limitations. This time he focused on the interface between computers and their human operators, analyzing the effects of communicating through keyboards rather than through direct physical contact. He asked at first whether one could tell if the person at another keyboard was a man or a woman; then, in what has come to be called the Turing Test, he asked if a person could distinguish, after a five-minute keyboard interview, whether a human or a computer had been at the other end of the connection. Modern expert systems are often tested against Turing's standard;

Further Reading
Herken, Rolf, *The Universal Turing Machine: A Half-Century Survey* (1989); Hodges, Andrew, *Turing: The Great Philosophers* (1999); Kurzweil, Ray, *The Age of Spiritual Machines* (1999).

Alan Turing (below, bottom) demonstrates the DISR Ace Pilot (below) at the British National Physical Laboratory in 1950.

Further Reading
Folsing, Albrecht, *Albert Einstein: A Biography* (1998); Greene, Brian, *The Elegant Universe* (1999); Thorne, Kip S., *Black Holes and Time Warps* (1994).

the movie *Blade Runner* was based on the implication of Turing's theory, that our "humanness" is not quite as unique as we like to think.

FBackground for the Turing machine can be found in ALGORITHM; COMPUTER, DIGITAL; PROGRAM, COMPUTER. *Other aspects of the subject are discussed in* COMPILER; OPERATING SYSTEM; PATTERN RECOGNITION AND OCR. *Additional relevant material can be found in* ARTIFICIAL INTELLIGENCE; COMMUNICATION IN NATURE. *See also* LIFE, DEFINITION AND ORIGIN OF.

First see SPECIAL RELATIVITY

Twin Paradox

Next see LORENTZ-FITZGERALD CONTRACTION

A consequence of Einstein's theory of relativity which states that two twins can grow older at different rates if their speed of travel is different and great enough.

This apparent paradox arises because the theory of relativity says that a clock that is in motion runs slower than a clock that is at rest. According to Einstein, this also means that biological processes, such as heartbeat or cell aging, are also slowed in an organism that is in motion. The slowing of a clock in motion has been verified by experiment and observation, but there is no direct experimental verification of the twin paradox.

The calculations behind the twin paradox assume that one twin (A) stays at home while the other (B) takes a rocket trip to a distant destination. At the current speed of rockets, the age difference between the twins would be so small as to be unmeasurable, but if speeds close to that of light—186,000 miles per second—were attained, the stay-at-home twin might be many years older than the traveling twin.

The twin paradox can lead to some unusual results. Suppose that each twin sends the other a happy birthday message, with the messages dated according to each twin's observed calendar. If a round trip by one twin in such a distant voyage takes 50 years, while the trip by the other twin takes 40 years, the second twin will return to Earth ten years younger than the first twin.

Background material can be found in LIGHT, SPEED OF; TIME; SPECIAL RELATIVITY. *Further details can be found in* SYMMETRY IN NATURE; TIME, MEASUREMENT OF. *Fundamental aspects of this subject are covered in* GENERAL RELATIVITY; INTERSTELLAR SPACE TRAVEL.

First see SOUND

Ultrasonics

Next see AMNIOCENTESIS

The study and use of sound waves whose frequency is at least 20,000 cycles per second.

Ultrasonic waves are produced by a large number of devices, which go by the general name of transducers. The original transducers were mechanical devices called whistles and sirens. A whistle uses a high-speed jet of gas or liquid; a siren uses high-speed jets of compressed air that strike a rapidly rotating plate. Today there is a wide variety of nonmechanical transducers, such as those that use the piezoelectric effect to transform electrical energy into mechanical energy that produces the ultrasonic waves.

High-intensity ultrasonic devices today have a number of practical applications. They are used to homogenize milk, to clean cooking ware, to test materials for flaws, and to degrade complex polymers into simpler materials. Underwater ultrasonic devices are used to measure ocean depths and, in sonar devices, to detect objects ranging from schools of fish to submarines. Sonar takes advantage of the fact that sound waves travel farther and faster in water than in air. Industrially, ultrasonic devices are used for soldering, welding, fatigue-testing, and machining. In the laboratory, ultrasound transducers are applied to speed chemical reactions and improve their yield and to break up biological samples, for study and to extract their natural products. (*See* SONAR.)

First see WAVE-PARTICLE DUALITY

Uncertainty Principle

Next see QUANTUM MECHANICS

First formulated by Werner Heisenberg in 1927, it states that it is impossible to simultaneously know both the position and momentum of a subatomic particle with complete certainty.

The principle is based on the supposition that an observation of such a particle must always affect either the position or the momentum of the particle being observed. For example, to determine the position of an electron with great accuracy, a short wavelength of light must be used. But this kind of light wave has a large quantum of energy, and so the state of motion of the electron will be changed when the light wave encounters it. If a longer wavelength of light is used to avoid this change in momentum, then the measurement of the position of the electron will be less accurate. The uncertainty principle states that the greatest accuracy possible in such a measurement is given by Planck's constant h, which is on the order of ten to 27 metric units.

In the everyday world, the limit of accuracy is so small that it can safely be ignored. Even on the molecular level, there are ways to increase the accuracy of measurements—for example, by carrying out the measurement on a large number of subatomic particles or molecules and averaging out the results. But detailed information about specific events, such as the movement of an electron from one orbit to another in an atom, must always remain uncertain.

First see OCEANOGRAPHY

Underwater Exploration

Next see SUBMARINE TECHNOLOGY

Underwater exploration and salvage was once limited to unmanned instrument packages such as the bathysphere, a hollow steel instrument-carrying sphere that was lowered by cables from a surface ship. That began to change in the 1940s, when the French oceanographer Auguste Picard developed the bathyscape, which included a spherical passenger cabin that was suspended beneath a flotation hull. The bathyscape dived and came back to the surface by emtying and filling the flotation hull. It had battery-powered motors that gave it a degree of mobility. Today's manned underwater exploration vehicles range from one-person craft to vehicles like Alvin, a three-person craft used in the *Titanic* exploration. (*See* SUBMARINE TECHNOLOGY.)

Today, standard oceanographic equipment, carried by manned submersibles, includes bottles and thermometers that can collect water samples and measure temperatures at all depths, and a number of devices for obtaining biological specimens and sediment samples from the ocean floor. These include heavy tubes that can punch out segments of the ocean floor, dredges that scrape samples of rock, heat probes to measure ocean-bottom temperatures, plankton nets for collecting small living oceanic creatures, and trawls for collecting larger, free-swimming organisms. Echo sounders are used to obtain profiles of the ocean floor.

Vehicles. The majority of underwater exploration today is carried on by unmanned craft of two kinds: remotely operated vehicles (ROV) and autonomous underwater vehicles (AUV). The best known user of ROV technology is Robert Ballard, who discovered the *Titanic* in 1985–1986, the *USS Yorktown* in 1995, and two ancient Phoenician vessels in 1998. Ballard uses a linked pair called Medea and Jason; Medea surveys the site, then Jason moves in with its high-intensity lights and television cameras for close-ups. ROVs are limited by their umbilical connections, decreasing their range, but they can remain on site for several days at a time. The new alternative is the free-ranging AUV, such as MIT's Odyssey, which can dive nearly four miles and range over 170 miles of seabed, following a pre-programmed search and recording the results.

Much exploration still relies on the oceanographic vessel, which carries both wet and dry laboratories. A wet laboratory is located near the winches that run water-collecting bottles out and back to the ship, to measure the chemical properties of the recovered water and to examine the biological and geological samples that the bottles collect. Dry laboratories can make underwater sound measurements, get specifics on the variations of the Earth's magnetic and gravitational fields in different locations, and make seismic measurements of the thickness of the Earth's crust at different underwater locations.

Positioning. It is important that oceanographic vessels be positioned precisely to make their measurements and collections. In recent years, the accuracy of positioning has been greatly improved by the introduction of satellite navigation systems. Computer analysis of the data collected by such systems allows a ship's position to be known within a few hundred yards while it is in motion and to several hundred feet when it is stationary. Such exact positioning is even more important for salvage efforts, since it allows a ship to come extremely close to the object of salvage.

Not all oceanographic work is done at sea. Vessels bring many samples of water, soil, and biological specimens back to their home bases, where laboratories can conduct extended and extensive studies that may not be possible on board ship.

Background material on underwater exploration can be found in BUOYANCY; OCEANOGRAPHY; SUBMARINE TECHNOLOGY. *More details can be found in* FISH; OCEAN BASINS; TIDES; WAVES, OCEANIC. *More information on particular aspects is contained in* PETROLEUM PROSPECTING; PLATE TECTONICS.

First see SCIENTIFIC METHOD

Uniformitarianism

Next see GEOLOGY, ARCHAEOLOGICAL

A geological principle that claims that all of the processes that take place on the Earth's surface today are identical to those which took place in Earth's past.

Uniformitarianism and catastrophism were two conflicting theories about the geology of the Earth and the formation of its major features. Catastrophism, the earlier theory, was replaced by uniformitarianism in the nineteenth century. Catastrophism proposed that the Earth's mountain ranges, deep valleys, rugged highlands, and other features had been created by sudden, great convulsions, or cataclysms—a word derived from the Greek words for "downward" and

Further Reading
Ballard, Robert D., *Discovery of the Titanic: Exploring the Greatest of All Lost Ships* (1998); Blot, Jean-Yves, *Underwater Archaeology: Exploring the World Beneath the Sea* (1996); Marx, Robert F., *The History of Underwater Exploration* (1990).

Further Reading
Huggett, Richard, *Catastrophism: Asteroids, Comets and Other Dynamic Events in Earth History* (1998); Palmer, T., *Controversy: Catastrophism and Evolution, The Ongoing Debate* (1999); Tarbuck, E. J., *The Earth: An Introduction to Physical Geology* (1998).

"washing away," as in floods. The implication of the word was that it was floods and other sudden events such as earthquakes that had produced most of the Earth's surface features. That belief was consistent with the Great Flood described in the Bible and with existing observations of earthquakes and volcanic eruptions. The first challenge to catastrophism came in 1795, when the British scientist James Hutton published *The Theory of the Earth*. That book was largely ignored, however, and acceptance of uniformitarianism began only when another British scientist, John Playfair, published *Illustrations of the Huttonian Theory of the Earth*, in 1802.

The major event in acceptance of the theory was the publication in 1820 by Sir Charles Lyell of *Principles of Geology*, which added a mass of evidence based on studies of fossils and their indications of the age of the geological deposits in which they were found.

Smith and McClure. Because uniformitarianism says that the geological processes that created the Earth are still continuing, its predictions can be tested to some extent by current geological observations. At the time, however, it required a drastic revision in some basic beliefs, such as the age of the Earth, because it said that such processes as mountain formation take place over millions of years. The defense of uniformitarianism required painstaking field work to assemble data on the Earth's structure and its evolution. One major contribution was made by a British civil engineer, William Smith, who played a significant part in establishing the belief that fossils are major indicators of the relative ages of sedimentary rock formations. Smith published the first geological map of England in 1815. That was six years after the first geological map of the United States was published, by William McClure.

Well into the nineteenth century, however, there still were some significant opposition to uniformitarianism. One of them was the French scientist Georges Cuvier. While he published studies of fossils from the biologist's point of view that became the foundation of the science of paleontology, Cuvier defended catastrophism for all of his life. But many other scientists offered explanations of the formation of mountains, continents, and other major geological features based on uniformitarian principles. One such classic publication was *The Origin of Continents and Oceans*, by Alfred Wegener, a German scientist, which proposed the theory of the continental drift, which says that major parts of the Earth's crust are in constant movement.

Background material on uniformitarianism can be found in GEOLOGY, ARCHAEOLOGICAL; SCIENTIFIC METHOD. *More details can be found in* CONSERVATION LAWS IN NATURE; SOLAR SYSTEMS. *Additional relevant information is contained in* ASTEROIDS AND METEORS; EXTINCTION; EXTRATERRESTRIAL LIFE.

Universe

First see BIG BANG THEORY

Next see HUBBLE CONSTANT

All of space and everything in it.

Large-Scale Structure. Concepts of the large-scale structure of the universe have changed over the centuries, as new astronomical information became available. In ancient Greece, the universe was described as a crystalline celestial sphere that surrounded the Earth. Pythagoras wrote of the moon, sun, and planets as being carried on separate transparent spheres that were inside a larger celestial sphere. This picture explained why the position of the planets changed in regard to that of the stars.

That view was challenged in 1542 by Nicolaus Copernicus, who placed the sun at the center of the universe, with the Earth and the other planets revolving in orbits around the sun. In this Copernican theory, the stars were at an almost infinite distance from the Earth.

The picture of the universe continued to evolve when Galileo made the first telescopic observations of the universe. Galileo reported that the Milky Way was made of stars that were individually too small to be seen by the naked eye. Galileo's observations led to the realization that the stars are in fact suns. In 1750, the British astronomer Thomas Wright proposed that our sun is part of a great system of stars, the galaxy. Five years later, Immanuel Kant proposed that there were other "island universes," or galaxies, in space. Later in the eighteenth century, William Herschel made systematic counts of stars. In addition to confirming Wright's proposal, Herschel also developed a picture of the Earth's galaxy as a giant disk of stars several thousand light-years in diameter, with the sun near the center of the disk.

Twentieth Century. In the early twentieth century, Harlow Shapley observed the distribution in space of globular clusters of stars, which contain tens of thousands of stars, and concluded that our galaxy is far larger than had been supposed. (Recent observations put its diameter at about 100,000 light-years.) Shapley also showed that our solar system is not at the center of the galaxy, but lies about two-thirds of the distance from its center. Today, the best estimate is that our galaxy contains about 100 billion stars and that the galaxy is rotating at the rate of one rotation every two billion years.

In 1924, Edwin Hubble demonstrated that there are billions of galaxies in the universe, some as close as a few hundred-thousand light-years away, some billions of light-years distant. Many of these galaxies are associated with strong sources of electromagnetic radiation such as quasars, which are believed to originate in explosive events.

Clusters. Galaxies tend to exist in clusters. Our galaxy is a member of the cluster called the Local Group, which has about a dozen members. Other clusters contain hundreds or even thousands of galaxies, and have diameters of several million light-years. More recent studies have found that the universe consists of even larger units of matter, collections that are tens of millions of light-years in diameter. These collections of matter include many galactic clusters, groups of galaxies and individual galaxies, as well as intergalactic matter.

Clusters of stars fall into two classes, open and globular, names based on their shape. About 120 globular clusters of stars, each with tens of thousands of stars, have been routinely observed. These globular clusters tend to be concentrated around the center of our galaxy, but well away from its plane. These star clusters generally lie within 10 to 15 degrees of the plane of the Milky Way.

Some galactic clusters, such as the Hyades and a double cluster in Perseus, are close enough to the Earth that their motion in respect to other clusters can be measured and their distance can be determined. For example, the Hyades are about 40 parsecs from the sun. (A parsec is about 3.26 light-years.) Because their distance is known, the absolute magnitudes of the stars and the ratio of their spectral type to their magnitude in these galaxies can be measured. These measurements have shown that these clusters are made up of younger stars.

All of these galaxies and clusters of galaxies are moving away from each other, in a universal expansion that is believed to have begun perhaps ten billion years ago. Most astronomers believe that this expansion will continue indefinitely.

Evolution. The evolution of the universe has been a matter of conjecture and debate in the astronomical community for nearly a century. The central fact that scientists grapple with is the universe's expansion, which was detected in the 1920s by the red shift, the shift in the frequency of light waves toward the red, or longer, end of the spectrum.

The Big Bang theory, proposed by the American physicist George Gamow, proposes that the universe started as a single point in space about 14 billion years ago and has been expanding steadily ever since. The theory also believes that the mass of the universe is constant, and thus the density of matter in the universe is decreasing steadily. A variation on that theme is

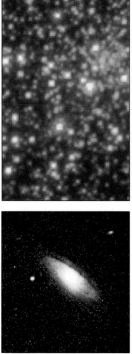

Top, a very distant globular cluster as seen by the Hubble Space Telescope. Above, the disk shaped Andromeda galaxy, the closest large galaxy to our own, but four times as massive as the Milky Way. Below, The Crab Nebula.

the inflationary Big Bang, which says that the universe should contain a critical density of matter, just enough to slow its expansion and eventually bring it to a halt, over billions of years. Astronomers describe the condition of critical density as omega equals one. If there is too little mass, so that omega equals less than one, the universe would expand forever. If omega equals more than one, the universe eventually would contract and collapse of its own weight, in what its proponents call the big crunch. Current measurements indicate that the expansion of the universe is accelerating, indicating an indefinitely continuing expansion.

Unorthodox Evolutionary Theories. An alternative to the Big Bang theory is the pulsating universe theory. This states that while the universe is now ex-panding, the rate of expansion is slowing, so that expansion eventually will stop, and the universe will contract for a time until a period of expansion begins again.

Another theory proposes a steady-state universe, in which the density of matter is supposed to remain the same despite expansion, because new matter is constantly being created. This theory, which was first proposed by the British astronomer Fred Hoyle, asserts that all the parts of the universe should have an identical appearance. However, observations of sources of radio waves outside our galaxy indicate that the number of these sources increases as astronomers look further into space, or backward in time, and so the steady-state universe has few proponents.

The Cosmological Constant. The most recent observations made by astronomers indicate that the expansion of the universe appears to be accelerating. That accelerating expansion could be explained by a repulsive force, the opposite of gravity, that is called the cosmological constant. The existence of the cosmological constant was first proposed by Albert Einstein to fill in what he regarded as a gap in his general theory of relativity. According to that theory, the universe must either expand or contract over time. But Einstein, like most scientists of his time, assumed that the universe was neither expanding nor contracting. He proposed the cosmological constant as a repulsive force that would counteract the force of gravity and thus make the universe stand still.

Einstein abandoned the cosmological constant after the American astronomer Edwin P. Hubble described the expanding universe in 1929. It has now been revived to explain the observed acceleration of the expansion of the universe. Other astronomers studying supernovas—stars or star systems that explode and expand—have said that their observations support the existence of the cosmological constant or some other force pushing galaxies apart. One consequence of an acceleration in the expansion

Further Reading
Grutsch, William A., *1001 Things Everyone Should Know About the Universe* (1999); Livio, Mario, *The Accelerating Universe: Infinite Expansion, the Cosmological Constant and the Beauty of the Cosmos* (2000); Moore, Patrick, *Atlas of the Universe* (1998); Padmanabhan, T., *After the First Three Minutes: The Story of Our Universe* (1998); Trefil, James, *The Dark Side of the Universe* (1989); Trefil, James and David H. Levy, *Other Worlds* (1999).

Below, a color composite of Uranus, recorded by *Voyager 2* on January 25, 1986, as the spacecraft left the planet to continue on to Neptune. The photo was taken when *Voyager* was about 600,000 miles from the surface of the planet. Uranus retains the pale blue-green color seen by ground based instruments, even at this extreme angle.

of the universe would be an increase in the life of the universe of perhaps one billion years. And the existence of the cosmological constant or other repulsive forces could help explain the formation of galaxies.

Background material on the evolution and structure of the universe can be found in BIG BANG THEORY; MILKY WAY; UNIVERSE, EVOLUTION OF. *Advanced subjects are developed in* GALAXY; GENERAL RELATIVITY; GLOBULAR CLUSTER. *Fundamental aspects of this subject are covered in* INTERSTELLAR MEDIUM ("DARK MATTER"); INTERSTELLAR SPACE TRAVEL.

First see NEPTUNE

Uranus

Next see PLUTO

Uranus, the third largest planet in the solar system, is the seventh from the sun. Its mass is 14.5 times that of the Earth. Its average distance from the sun is 1,783 million miles, but that distance varies by as much as 166 million miles. Uranus is classified as one of the giant planets of the solar system, but it is considerably smaller than the two other giant planets, Jupiter and Saturn. Its diameter is about 31,000 miles, which is more than four times greater than that of the Earth, but its mass is only 14 times greater than that of the Earth. Like Jupiter and Saturn, Uranus has a low density of 1.30 times the density of water. Uranus is flattened at the poles, a flattening that is caused by its rapid rotation of 17 1/4 hours. Its axis of rotation is at an angle of 98 degrees to the plane of the solar system (the Earth's axis is 23 degrees off the plane), which has led some astronomers to say that the planet goes around the sun "lying on its side."

Moons. Uranus has five major satellites and many minor ones, the latest one discovered in 1999. All the satellites move in almost circular orbits that are retrograde to the planet's motion. Uranus also has ten narrow rings closer to the planet, perhaps the remains of satellites caught within Roche's Limit. (*See* PLANET.)

Orbit. It takes Uranus more than 84 years to make one complete rotation around the sun, moving at a velocity of just 4.25 miles per second. That sluggishness means that each of the seasons on Uranus is more than 21 years long. Its surface temperature is only 58 degrees Kelvin. Uranus was discovered in 1781 by William Herschel, the British astronomer; it is barely visible to the naked eye of a skilled observer. The planet has a series of belts around its equator, which are greyish in color. Its atmosphere consists mostly of hydrogen and helium. (*See* SOLAR SYSTEM.)

Vacuum

First See ATMOSPHERE

Next See INTERSTELLAR MEDIUM ("DARK MATTER")

A space in which there is an extremely low gas pressure, with very few atoms or molecules present.

A perfect vacuum would contain no atoms or molecules, but in practice such a vacuum cannot be created because all the materials that would surround such a space have a finite vapor pressure, which means that they expel some atoms or molecules into the space. Vacuums are described as high or low, depending on how close they come to a perfect vacuum. The primary requirements for a vacuum are a well-sealed space and an efficient pump. (*See* FLUID MECHANICS.)

Pumps. The three main classes of pumps used for vacuum work are mechanical, ejector, and diffusion pumps. They are rated by the vacuum they can produce in a closed system and their capacity, the amount of gas they can move in a given time. Mechanical pumps, usually of the rotary type, have a moderately high capacity and can produce low vacuums. Diffusion pumps can produce higher vacuums, while ejector pumps, which have a high capacity but cannot produce high vacuums, are often connected with one of the other kinds of pump for vacuum work. Because it is essential to avoid leaks when making a vacuum, great attention is paid to the basic working parts of vacuum pumps—their gaskets, joints, seals, valves, and connecting lines. Devices for detecting any leaks are also an essential part of a vacuum pump system, and so are gauges for measuring the exact pressure in the resulting vacuum.

Valence

First see CHEMICAL FORMULA

Next see ELECTRONEGATIVITY

The outermost energy level that contains electrons is called the valence shell, and the electrons within it are known as valence electrons.

Electrons are the negatively charged particles arranged in discrete energy levels outside the nucleus. Each level is associated with a particular amount of energy, with levels farther away from the nucleus higher in energy than inner levels. Each level can contain a maximum number of electrons. Inner levels are filled first.

An atom is in its most stable energy state when the valence shell is "full," or contains its maximum number of electrons. This "magic number" is eight electrons, known as a "stable octet" (except for the elements hydrogen and helium, which due to their much smaller size have a maximum of only two electrons). With the exception of the noble gas elements, atoms do not naturally have a full valence shell. They attempt to achieve this state either by gaining additional electrons, or losing them in order to empty the level, thereby bestowing the status of "valence shell" on the previously next-to-last level which already has a full complement of electrons. The need to obtain a full valence shell leads atoms into forming chemical bonds, in which only valence electrons are involved.

Different atoms form different types of bonds. A metal atom will form an ionic bond with a nonmetal atom. The atom which gains electrons is a nonmetal; the atom losing them is a metal. Two nonmetal atoms form a bond by sharing electrons, known as a covalent bond. Two atoms can share up to three pairs of electrons between them at a time.

Covalently bonded molecules are made up of more atoms and are therefore larger than ionic compounds. Consequently, their molecular geometry is more complex. The three-dimensional molecular structures of covalent compounds can be predicted from the number of electron pairs. The model used is known as Valence Shell Electron Pair Repulsion (VSPER), and is based upon the idea that all electrons, being negatively charged, will repel each other if crowded too closely together. The structure around an atom is therefore determined by minimizing repulsions between electron pairs. Bonding and nonbonding pairs of electrons are positioned as far apart as possible. (*See* BOND, CHEMICAL.)

Variational Calculus

First see CALCULUS

Next see SCHRÖDINGER'S EQUATION

A specific branch of calculus that deals with the specifics of maxima and minima of geometrical forms.

The calculus of variations can be traced back to classical times, when early mathematicians studied how to maximize or minimize geometrical shapes. The most famous of these isoperimetrical problems, as they are called, was the story of how Princess Dido claimed the land that would become Carthage. Told she could have as much land as would fit in an oxhide, she cut the hide into very thin strips, tied the strips together, and ran her perimeter on a curve along the seashore.

This intuitive solution to a maximization problem remained the standard until the 17th century, when Isaac Newton first worked on the differential calculus. One of the problems Newton considered was the movement of a curved shape through water; the solution of such problems, he said, "may be of use in the building of ships." However, with calculus still in its formative stages, Newton could not determine how to minimize a ship's drag. Over the course of the next century, it became clear that Newton's problem was closely related to another problem left unsolved by Galileo, concerning gravitational acceleration, and to a classic problem in optics. All these problems sought to maximize an area or minimize a time; although these are precisely the solutions which integration and differentiation are designed to solve, more sophisticated methods were necessary.

History. Much of the groundwork of the calculus of variations was completed in the 18th century. In 1744, Leonhard Euler (1707–1783) published an entire book dedicated to finding maxima and minima, defining such basic shapes of modern mathematics as the cycloid and the catenary in the process. In an appendix, Euler attempted to extend his discoveries to all of dynamics, through what he called the principle of least action. Then in 1760, Joseph-Louis Lagrange (1736–1813), using double integrals, discovered how to maximize or minimize any surface with a fixed boundary; this last operation is essential to modern engineering design and manufacture, from forging cylinder heads to electroplating. Lagrange also reformulated Newton's second law of motion into a set of simultaneous differential equations, freeing it from external coordinate systems and forces.

During the course of the 19th century, the calculus of variations proved useful in areas ranging from astrophysics to physical chemistry. More recently, the calculus of variations has been instrumental in rocket motor design, electrical switching circuitry, and game theory. An offshoot called lag differential equations has also been developed, which focuses on operations in which there is a time lag between the input and the response; minimizing the effects of such time lags is important in complex feedback systems ranging from production facilities to computers.

Background material on variational calculus can be found in FUNCTION; MECHANICS; NEWTON'S LAWS. *Advanced subjects are developed in* CONSERVATION LAWS IN NATURE; INTEGRAL CALCULUS. *Additional information on particular aspects is contained in* SCHRÖDINGER'S EQUATION; QUANTUM

First see ACCELERATION

Vectors and Tensors

Next see MECHANICS

Vectors are quantities that include both a scalar and directional component. Tensors are generalized vectors with more than three components.

The notion of vectors is an ancient one; philosophers as far back as Aristotle knew that a force can be represented as a line segment whose length is proportional to its magnitude, and that

Further Reading
Bobylev, N.A., *Geometrical Methods in Variational Problems* (1999); Fox, Charles, *An Introduction to the Calculus of Variation* (1988); Kinderleher, David, *An Introduction to Variational Inequalities and Their Applications* (2000); Weinstock, Robert, *Calculus of Variations* (1974).

such forces can be added according to the parallelogram law. Galileo used this law in his work on planetary motion. However, not all mathematical problems can be tackled in a geometrical manner; what was required for much of physics was an algebraic method that would be able to incorporate vector theory.

Hamilton's Work. At the beginning of the 19th century, mathematicians like Gauss suggested that complex numbers could be used to achieve such algebraic vectors. The difficulty lies when one tries to add a third dimension, so that one can represent forces acting on a real body. The solution was achieved by William R. Hamilton (1805–1865), the greatest English mathematician after Newton: add not one but two components, representing two additional axes, so that each vector is represented by a scalar quantity plus three vector parts i, j, and k. Hamilton called the result a quaternion.

Quaternions. Hamilton's quaternions did not fulfill all the criteria of classical algebra; for example, vector multiplication was not commutative. This deliberate violation of a basic "rule" would open the way for later violations of many of mathematics' sacred cows, most notably non-Euclidean geometry such as that proposed by Georg Riemann (1826–1866). It also opened the way for physical applications of Hamilton's theory, first by James Clerk Maxwell in his *Treatise on Electricity and Magnetism* (1873), then by Josiah Willard Gibbs (1881), and Oliver Heaviside (1893). All three of these physical scientists dropped the scalar part of Hamilton's quaternion entirely, leaving a pure vector: $\mathbf{v} = a\mathbf{i} + b\mathbf{j} + c\mathbf{k}$.

The resulting algebra of vectors can be transformed into a calculus of vectors, by substituting functions for the scalar quantities: $\mathbf{v}(t) = a(t)\mathbf{i} + b(t)\mathbf{j} + c(t)\mathbf{k}$. Such an equation traces a curve in three dimensions, which can be analyzed by both differential and integral means. In fact, this had been the approach to vectors taken by Hermann Grassmann (1809–1877), who published *The Calculus of Extension* in 1844.

Grassmann's theory of vectors in multidimensional space, and the calculus based on it, became essential in the development of modern physics. Grassman's work was brought to light by Gregorio Ricci-Curbastro (1853–1925) and Tullio Levi-Civita (1873–1941); they clarified Grassmann's ideas, and published what they called an *Absolute Differential Calculus*, which would be invariant whether the coordinate structures being used were two-dimensional, three-dimensional, or n-dimensional.

Invariance means that every component transforms according to consistent laws as the frame of reference is changed; therefore, if two tensors are equivalent in one frame of reference, they will remain consistent when shifted to another frame of reference.

Twentieth-Century Applications. This calculus provided a crucial mathematical tool for Albert Einstein (1879–1955) in expanding his special theory of relativity, first published in 1905. Einstein's special theory had demonstrated that every observer perceives the universe from a unique perspective on the space-time continuum, due to his or her velocity and position; yet for a general theory of relativity, the universe which each observer perceives had to display invariant basic laws. Ricci's tensor calculus was essential to the development of Einstein's theory. In his 1916 paper on the general theory of relativity, Einstein attributed his success to Ricci and Levi-Civita's technique, calling it tensor analysis.

Tensor Analysis. The non-Euclidean geometry developed by Riemann also proved amenable to tensor analysis, and provided a second crucial component for Einstein's theory, the theory that space was curved; this aspect was worked out by Levi-Civita a year later, leading to the paradox that still characterizes for many people the "contradiction" of modern physics: parallel lines can never meet in Euclidean geometry, but in Riemann geometry—where they are vectors on a curved surface—they can and do intersect. However, scientists today often rely on this paradox, assuming a curved Riemann space within an otherwise traditional Euclidean universe thereby resolving problems which could not be tackled otherwise.

Tensor analysis has become highly useful in modern technology. When used to model electrical charges and currents, it allows electrical engineers to design more efficient capacitors or smaller semiconductor circuits. Because of its close relation to hydrodynamics, tensor analysis is integral to ship design; and petroleum engineers rely on tensors to determine pipeline shapes, dimensions, and flows.

Background material on vectors and tensors can be found in CALCULUS; FORCE; MECHANICS. *Advanced subjects are developed in* NEWTON'S LAWS; SPACE-TIME. *Additional relevant information is contained in* MAXWELL'S EQUATION; SPECIAL RELATIVITY. *Vectors are also important tools in* ELECTROMAGNETISM; MECHANICS; *and in* ARCHITECTURAL ENGINEERING.

Further Reading
Hankins, Thomas L., *Sir William Rowan Hamilton* (1991); Wrede, Robert C., *Introduction to Vector and Tensor Analysis* (1972).

First see SOLAR SYSTEM

Venus

Next see PLANETS, FORMATION OF

Venus, the second planet from the sun and the Earth's closest planetary neighbor in the solar system, is in some respects very similar to the Earth. Its diameter at the equator is 7,519 miles, about the same as the Earth's, and its density is 95 percent that of the Earth. It has an iron core and a molten mantle like the Earth, but it has no magnetic field. Venus is the second-brightest object in the evening sky (after the moon) and has played a major role in astronomical discoveries. In the seventeenth century, Galileo observed that Venus orbits the sun, a major step toward establishing that the sun, not the Earth, is the center of the solar system. In the eighteenth century, the British astronomer Edmund Halley used observations of Venus to help calculate an accurate distance of the Earth from the sun.

Surface Features. Because the surface of Venus is hidden by dense clouds, its period of rotation was difficult to determine. In the 18th century, the Italian astronomer Giovanni Schiaparelli said that its period of rotation was the same as the period of its revolution around the sun, 225 days. His estimate was accepted until 1962, when radar scans established the period of rotation as 243.1 days, and also that its rotation is retrograde—Venus turns from east to west (the Earth rotates from west to east). Because the retrograde rotation of Venus is slower than its period of revolution around the sun, each day lasts 58.5 Earth days, and the length of the night on Venus is the same.

Exploration of Venus. Because Venus comes within 26 million miles of the Earth every 19 months, many planetary probes have been sent to it, providing a detailed picture of Venus and its atmosphere. The United States sent several *Mariner* probes during the 1960s, the *Pioneer* orbiter and probe in 1978, and *Magellan* in 1990. The Soviet Union sent a series of *Venera* probes, which were the first to land on Venus and to return photos. *Magellan* completed a detailed radar map of the planet's surface and a gravity field map of subsurface features.

The Venetian Atmosphere. Atmospheric observations show a layer of smog more than nine miles thick at the top of the atmosphere,

Above, cloud-covered Venus as photographed by *Mariner 10*, from about 300,000 miles, in 1974.

A computer-generated radar map of the topography of Venus. It shows, for the first time, the exact location of unusual rough areas which are thought to be mountains. The data was recorded using the Radio telescope at Arecibo, Puerto Rico.

which is 96 percent carbon dioxide. Clouds of sulfuric acid race on winds as high as 250 miles an hour in a band 30 to 35 miles above the surface of Venus. Wind speeds lessen at lower altitudes, and the atmosphere is virtually stagnant at altitudes below six miles. The high-altitude smog layer disappears and reappears; cloud layers and wind patterns also change with time. At the surface, pressures are 90 times that on Earth, equal to pressures 3,000 feet deep in our oceans.

Venetian Volcanism. Temperatures on Venus are too high to allow the existence of any form of life. The mean temperature at the surface is 453 degrees Celsius, high enough to melt lead, and at least two active lava flows raise the temperature even higher. Nearly two-thirds of the surface consists of rolling plains of lava, dotted with craters and calderas. About 16 percent of the planet consists of low-lying basins, similar to the maria, or seas, found on the moon. Two elevated regions, the size of continents, were disclosed by radar reflections, one of which contains active volcanos. The largest volcano is Gula Mons, a shield volcano three miles high. An even more striking feature is Maxwell Montes, a peak rising more than ten miles above mean surface level. (One would say sea level, but the seas boiled away long ago.) Several large impact craters also mark Venus's surface, including Crater Mead, 170 miles in diameter, the impact of which was so great that debris was spread as far as 310 miles away.

Background material regarding Venus can be found in MERCURY; PLANET; SOLAR SYSTEMS; SUN. Advanced subjects are developed in PLANETARY ATMOSPHERE; PLANET, FORMATION OF. Additional relevant information is contained in GLOBAL WARMING; MICROWAVE; RADAR; VOLCANO.

First see VIRUS

Viral Diseases, Exotic

Next see AIDS

Exotic viruses differ in important ways from the well-known viruses that cause such diseases as measles, hepatitis, and poliomyelitis. Many exotic viruses are slow viruses, in that symptoms develop many years after the initial infection.

An Example. One example is the JC virus, which is formally classified as a human papovavirus. This virus causes a rapidly progressing central nervous system condition called progressive multifocal leukoencephalopathy, which is commonly associated with disorders of the body's reticuloendothelial system such as leukemia and lymphoma, but it may also occur in other diseases in which the body's immune defenses are depressed, such as AIDS. The onset of this disease may be gradual, but once it becomes established, death is at most six months away. The virus attacks the brain, usually causing progressive impairment of mental function. The JC virus can be detected in brain tissue, but no treatment for this viral infection has been found to be effective.

New exotic viruses appear rarely, but their appearance can be very dangerous. The outstanding example of this principle is HIV, the virus that causes AIDS, which was regarded as an exotic virus when it first appeared. (See DISEASES, INFECTIOUS.)

First see VIRUS

Viral Genetics

Next see HIV

The study of the heredity, variation, and evolution of biological viruses.

Viruses, the ultimate parasites, are not made up of cells, and some dispute that they are even living organisms. It is clear, however, that viruses posses a genome, albeit small, of their own. A virus is essentially a piece of DNA or RNA, wrapped in a protein coat. Viruses are incapable of surviving on their own; they require a host cell to help them carry out every life process, including reproduction. Different viruses have different "preferred" host cells. Some infect human cells, some other animals, some plants. Still others, called bacteriaphages, infect bacteria. (See BACTERIA; VIRUS, BIOLOGICAL.)

Viral Infection. Upon infection of the host cell, the virus sheds its outer "wrapper" and goes directly to the nucleus where it incorporates its own nucleic acids into the host genome. It then proceeds to take over the "machinery" of the cell, forcing it to produce more and more viral particles. Eventually, the host cell bursts and the new viruses stream out, in search of new hosts.

The virus may be dormant for a while within the host cell. It may even exit, often dragging with it some host genes. In this manner, viruses may act as "vectors" for transmission of genes from one cell to another, when the virus proceeds to infect a second cell.

Further Reading
Cattermole, Peter, *Atlas of Venus* (1997); Marov, Mikhail Ya., *The Planet Venus* (1998); Trinh, Xuan Thuan, *The Birth of the Universe: The Big Bang and After* (1993).

Certain gene therapies are being studied, in which the method of transmission of the desired gene into a cell is through the medium of a virus. For example, cystic fibrosis is a genetic disease which affects the human respiratory system. Individuals with this condition produce copious amounts of a thick, dry mucus, which clogs their lungs and promotes infection and scarring of the tissue. They lack a copy of the "good" gene. It is possible to take an influenza virus, remove the genes which would make it cause disease and add the "good" human gene. The virus proceeds to "infect" its preferred host cell, in the respiratory system, and once it enters, it incorporates the new genes into the host cell. The result is a restored cell. So far, there has been limited success. A lower percentage of "infected" cells than expected was found to have incorporated the new gene, and the percentage of those cells in which the new gene is active is even smaller. However, this method has promise for the future.

Viral Genome. The viral genome seems to function and be replicated in the same manner as that of cellular organisms. The actual number of genes is very small. Double-stranded DNA types contain the most genes, and even their number is less than 300. Contrast this with the human genome which is estimated to contain approximately 30,000-40,000 genes. Some viral genomes consist of a single nucleic acid molecule. The virus only carries the genetic information that it needs to produce proteins in which to package its genome, and for functions that can't be performed by the host cell.

Viroids. Viroids are small circular molecules of RNA that have been found to cause certain plant diseases. They lack the protein coating of "full-fledged" viruses, or virions. Viroid RNA does not seem to be "translated" into proteins, and it is unknown how viroid RNA replicates itself and how it affects its host cells.

Prions. Related to viruses and viral genetics are prions, protein molecules which contain no DNA or RNA component whatsoever. Prions are the cause of "mad cow disease," known as bovine spongiform encephalopathy, as well as similar human diseases, such as Creutzfeldt-Jacob syndrome and kuru. How they function is currently under investigation.

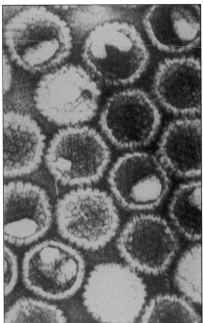

Above, an electron micrograph of the herpes simplex virus.

Further Reading
Andrewes, Christopher Howard, *The Natural History of Viruses* (1967); Fields, Bernard, *Genetically Altered Viruses and the Environment* (1986); Kaplitt, Michael G., *Viral Vectors: Gene Therapy and Neuroscience Applications* (1995).

Background material on viral genetics can be found in GENETICS; MICROBIOLOGY; VIRUS. *Further details can be found in* AIDS; HIV; LIFE, DEFINITION AND ORIGIN OF. *Elementary aspects of this subject are covered in* DISEASES, INFECTIOUS; IMMUNIZATION AND VACCINATION; VIRAL DISEASES, EXOTIC.

First see COMPUTER, DIGITAL

Virtual Reality

Next see COMPUTER GRAPHICS

An advanced form of computer animation in which the user is placed in a simulated environment.

Virtual reality is associated most often with modern computer games, in which one dons goggles and a glove in order to make oneself more part of the action. But virtual reality systems encompass far more than shoot-'em-up gaming. At the Ames Research Center in California, one can walk on Mars—or at least a digitized version of the site where the *Viking 2* lander obtained the data in 1976. And at the Defense Advanced Research Projects Agency (DARPA) in Virginia, tank commanders and crews fight the Gulf War over again—sometimes with startlingly different results.

History. Virtual reality simulation had its beginnings with the first analog computers, such as the *Link* flight trainer, a simulated airplane cockpit mounted on hydraulic pistons to provide the illusion of movement in three dimensions. As digital computers advanced, it became possible to provide visual simulation as well; the Center for Simulated Marine Operations in New York offers training in maneuvering supertankers through confined, crowded waters from a virtual ship's bridge, offering views of competing ship traffic in all directions. Fusions of real and virtual space, such as the Heads-Up Display on jet fighters, were developed in the 1970s. Such augmented reality systems are now in operation at Boeing and McDonnell Douglas.

Virtual reality is also available on the World Wide Web, through a Virtual Reality Modeling Language equivalent to 2-D Hyper Text Markup Language. Users equipped with a VRML browser are able to view and make use of 3-D graphics technology without buying their own workstations or special software.

But the true power of virtual reality is its promise for a complete simulated experience. Aldous Huxley, in his *Brave New World*, foresaw "feelies," or motion pictures that offered tactile feedback with special handsets, and olfactory feedback with timed-release aromas. The closest researchers have come to this is the Head-Mounted Display (HMD) and the DataGlove, which offer entrance directly into a virtual scene that provides visual, aural, and force feedback directly to the user. The HMD, invented by Ivan Sutherland, contains two miniature computer screens presenting binocular perspective on the scene, magnified to fill the field of view. The DataGlove, invented by Thomas Zimmerman and Jaron Lanier, senses finger movements and, perhaps more importantly, it also offers resistance—the first step towards true tactile feedback.

Applications. The applications of a fully functioning VR device would be widespread. Doctors could operate on patients hundreds of miles from a hospital, as long as a robot device was present to perform the actual cutting and suturing. Work with dangerous substances, such as toxic chemicals or nuclear wastes, could be done with absolutely no risk to humans. Even in its incomplete stage, VR has found hundreds of real-world applications. Problems difficult to visualize in two dimensions but clear in three, common in telecommunications or molecular biology, have become relatively easy to resolve; VR is used to teach skills in areas ranging from forestry to driving, surgery to factory management.

Finally, researchers have developed virtual humans able to simulate performance in real space, or at least in CAD space. Transom Jack tests whether real people will be able to manipulate components, or access parts for service, before an actual factory or weapon system is constructed. When fitted with a motion-tracking device, the virtual figure becomes fully functional.

Special topics in this area are to be found in COMPUTER, DIGITAL; COMPUTER GRAPHICS. *Advanced subjects are developed in* ARTIFICIAL INTELLIGENCE; PATTERN RECOGNITION AND OCR. *Important applications of this technology are covered in* INTERNET; ROBOTICS; SUPERCOMPUTER.

First see DISEASES, INFECTIOUS

Virus, Biological

Next see VIRAL DISEASES, EXOTIC

Minute particles that consist of a genome inside a protein coat and often an outer envelope of lipids and protein.

Unlike bacteria, viruses are not cells and cannot perform any activity until they enter a host cell. Once they attach to specific receptors on a host cell, the viral genome enters the cell and commandeers its apparatus to synthesize viral proteins and nucleic acid molecules that are assem-

Left, hand movements are interpreted and integrated into the scene that the user sees in the stereoscopic glasses.

Further Reading
Bertol, Daniela, *Designing Digital Space: An Architect's Guide to Virtual Reality* (1996); Harrison, D., *Experiments in Virtual Reality* (1996); Stuart, R., *The Design of Virtual Environments* (1996).

Below, a computer-generated model of the capsid proteins of the adenovirus.

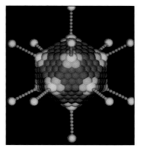

bled into new virus particles. When these leave the cell, they often take with them a piece of the cell membrane as their outer envelope. The complete virus particle is called a virion.

Viral Diseases. Viruses cause many lethal human diseases, including polio, influenza, rabies, hepatitis, hemorrhagic fevers, encephalitis, and the great scourge of our time, AIDS (acquired immune deficiency syndrome). They are also responsible for a range of illnesses that are less frequently fatal but cause widespread suffering: the common cold, measles, mumps, chicken pox, rubella, genital and oral herpes, mononucleosis, and many respiratory and gastrointestinal illnesses. Some viruses either cause or are cofactors in causing cancer, including cervical cancer, liver cancer, and some forms of leukemia and lymphoma.

Pathology. Viruses do their damage in a number of ways. So-called cytopathic viruses kill the host cell either shortly after infection occurs or much more gradually. Other viruses transform host cells causing them to become malignant. Some viruses trigger an immune response so severe it causes disease. HIV, the human immunodeficiency virus that causes AIDS, destroys the immune system itself. Most viruses cause a short, acute illness, but some can lie latent for years. Like bacteria, some are spread by coughing or sneezing, some by contaminated food or water, some by sexual contact.

Vaccination. Many viral diseases can be prevented by vaccination. Smallpox was first attacked by this means at the end of the 18th century, more than 100 years before the cause of the disease was identified. But unlike bacterial diseases, which are largely curable with antibiotics, no viral illness currently can be cured by treatment, if cure means clearing all of the viruses from the body. Genital herpes, however, can be effectively suppressed by drugs for long periods of time. Recent advances in AIDS treatments raise hopes that they, too, may soon achieve long-term viral suppression. (*See* VIRAL GENETICS.)

Mutation. Viruses have proven so difficult to treat in part because they have a genius for mutation that can allow them to evade recognition by the immune system or develop resistance to anti-viral drugs. Many viruses, including HIV, are prone to mutation from errors of replication and can evolve significantly in a short period of time. Influenza is notorious for undergoing genetic changes that force frequent re-engineering of the flu vaccine; it is also marked by occasional larger shifts, called genetic reassortment or antigenic shift, that can incorporate elements from bird flu viruses and cause worldwide epidemics. (*See* MUTATIONS, GENETIC.)

At the same time, viruses have become invaluable tools for study of basic biochemical processes and for genetic engineering. Because of their ability to integrate into host cell DNA, they can serve as vehicles to transfer genes from one organism to another. Vaccinia, the virus used in smallpox vaccine, is frequently used for this purpose.

Status of Viruses. Because they are inert outside a host cell without any means of metabolism or replication, but have genes and undergo replication within a host, viruses are variously considered nonliving, living, or denizens of some gray area. Some biologists suggest it is more useful to think of them as being active or inactive rather than alive or dead.

It is generally thought that viruses were derived from cellular genetic material and that even today they can insert themselves only into the cells of species similar to those from which they were derived. Thus there are distinct animal viruses, which include those attacking humans; plant viruses, and bacteriophages, which insert themselves only into bacteria.

Viruses are not included in the taxonomic kingdoms of life. Virologists, however, have their own classification system, based partly on the kind of RNA or DNA in the viral genome, usually a single molecule including from a handful to several hundred genes. The nucleic acid may be double-stranded or single-stranded DNA that is circular or linear, or it may be RNA, which is usually single-stranded and linear. Among the virus families are picornaviridae, which includes polio; paramyxoviridae, which includes measles and mumps, and herpesviridae.

Retroviruses. Retroviruses are unique. These viruses, which include HIV, have a genome consisting of two identical single-stranded RNA molecules, which means they have two copies of each gene. They also carry with them an enzyme called reverse transcriptase. Through a process called reverse transcription, the enzyme converts the RNA into double-stranded DNA, which is then incorporated into the genome of the host cell. This virus-derived DNA, termed the provirus, replicates with the cellular DNA during cell division. The provirus may also code for viral enzymes which allow it to be transcribed back into RNA and reproduce itself.

Some retroviruses, called transforming or oncoviruses, can cause acute leukemia or sarcomas by incorporating cancer-causing genes into the host's genome. Other retroviruses, such as HTLV-I (human T cell leukemia virus), cause cancer less frequently and only after years of infection.

Viruses are far smaller than bacteria, generally requiring an electron microscope to see their structure. Their existence was first suspected in the 1890s when a tobacco pathogen, later identified as the tobacco mosaic virus, made it through porcelain filters that screened out bacteria, which had been recently discovered. Over the next 20 years, similarly small human pathogens were identified, but their nature was not

Further Reading
Andrewes, Christopher Howard, *The Natural History of Viruses* (1967); Horowitz, L. G., *Emerging Viruses: AIDS and Ebola: Nature, Accident or Intentional?* (1996); Jenner, E., *Vaccination Against Smallpox* (1996).

clarified until the 1930s when the tobacco mosaic virus was purified and precipitated as crystals, behavior more like that of a chemical than an organism. When the crystals were redissolved, they still caused disease in a tobacco plant.

Further developments in the field are discussed in AIDS; DNA; HIV; RNA. *Additional details on viruses can be found in* LIFE, DEFINITION AND ORIGIN OF; TRANSCRIPTION; VIRAL DISEASES, EXOTIC. *Additional relevant information is contained in* ENCEPHALITIS; IMMUNIZATION AND VACCINATION; INTERFERONS AND INTERLEUKINS. *See also relevant entries on* BACTERIA; FUNGUS; GERM THEORY; MICROBIOLOGY; PROTISTA.

First see COMPUTER, DIGITAL

Virus, Computer

Next see PROGRAM, COMPUTER

A software program that is designed to enter and modify the behavior of a legitimate piece of software and reproduce, ideally without changing the outward size or structure of the original.

Some viruses, particularly the early ones, existed only to reproduce, and therefore were considered harmless, until such a virus caused the great Internet crash of November 1988. Robert Morris's virus was intended merely to penetrate each computer attached to the Net—at the time there were only about 6,000—and implant itself; it was never intended to do anything, just demonstrate by its existence the hacking power of its creator. Unfortunately for Morris and for the Net, the virus continued to reproduce within each computer system. Within seconds, infected computers were overwhelmed by viral reproductive activity. The cost of this "harmless" virus was later estimated at $98 million.

How a Virus Works. Viruses can work in three different ways. They can attack the startup (or boot) software, remaining invisible because they do their work before antivirus scans are activated; they can attack the operating system, typically making an exact copy of the system software—except that the virus is now written into that copy; or they can attack application programs, such as word processors and spreadsheets.

The first two methods were most common in the early days of computing, when computers had to be started by inserting a floppy disk. The last route is now the most common, as people download infected programs; the most cunning viruses attach themselves to macros, or templates, and thus normally remain invisible.

The ability of software to distort or even destroy computer memory was first noted at Bell Labs in 1959, but it was not combined with the ability to reproduce until 1974. The recipe for writing viruses remained a relative secret until 1983, when Ken Thompson gave a speech to the Association for Computing Machinery on the subject; the next year *Scientific American* published an article on viruses. By 1986, as many as half a million computers had been infected by a virus. (*See* PROGRAM, COMPUTER.)

Defenses. Most computer users now routinely employ antivirus software—which work in two ways. They can scan existing software for size, format, and date of last change, reacting to viruses which have penetrated normal security measures. Alternatively, they can work actively, scanning all incoming data for segments known to be virus-related and then issuing a warning, but this method leads to false alarms. A third method is being pursued by researchers, based on the human antibody system, in which "virtual T cells" roam the computer, alerting the operating system to potential malignancies.

Background material regarding computer viruses can be found in COMPUTER DIGITAL; OPERATING SYSTEM; PROGRAM, COMPUTER. *Further developments are discussed in* LOCAL AREA NETWORK (LAN). *Special topics in this area are found in* CRYPTOGRAPHY; INTERNET; OPERATIONS RESEARCH.

First see LIQUID

Viscosity

Next see FLUID DYNAMICS

The resistance to flow that is exhibited by liquids and gases.

While a solid substance that is subjected to an external force can reach a static equilibrium, a liquid or fluid can reach such an equilibrium only if there is some sort of flow. In a gas, viscosity arises from the motion of the gas molecules; in a liquid, the attraction between molecules is the important factor. To some extent, a liquid can be regarded as a solid that is very elastic. The viscosity of a liquid is in inverse proportion to the mobility of its molecules; for example, since the attraction between molecules of alcohol is less than that between the molecules of oil, alcohol is less viscous than oil. Typically, the viscosity of a liquid will decrease rapidly as the temperature increases, and will increase as the pressure increases.

In the metric system the unit of viscosity is the poise, which is the force in dynes that is required to move one square centimeter of a substance across the top of a layer that is one centimeter thick at a rate of one centimeter per second. The orderly viscous flow of a liquid is described as laminar, or sheet-like, while a disorderly flow is described as turbulent. In engineering the measure of the viscosity of a fluid is the time required for a given amount of that fluid to flow through the standard-sized hole of an instrument called a viscometer.

Further Reading
Atkins, Derek, *Internet Security: Professional Reference* (1997); Cohen, Fredrick B., *A Short Course on Computer Viruses* (1994); Ludwig, Mark A., *The Giant Black Book of Computer Viruses* (1998).

First see NUTRITION

Vitamins and Minerals

Next see COMMON COLD

Vitamins are chemically unrelated organic substances that are essential in chemical reactions in the body, though only trace amounts of them are required in the diet; minerals are natural substances that are also part of a healthy diet.

Among the functions in which vitamins participate are the processing of carbohydrates by the body and the production of blood cells, hormones, chemicals of the nervous system, and the genetic molecules, deoxyribonucleic acid (DNA) and ribonucleic acid (RNA).

Thirteen vitamins have been identified. They are classified as fat soluble and water soluble. The fat-soluble vitamins are A, D, E, and K. Vitamins A and D are usually present in the body in large amounts, with stores in the liver sufficient for six months. Vitamin K is stored in small amounts, good for a few days, while vitamin E may be stored in amounts sufficient for several weeks. Vitamin A, or retinol, is essential for the integrity of the body's tissues and is the molecular precursor for rhodopsin, the pigment of the retina of the eye. Vitamin A deficiency can adversely affect many of the body's organs.

Vitamin D, or calciferol, is an essential factor in calcium metabolism, which explains its importance in bone growth and maintenance. Vitamin E, or tocopherol, is believed to play a role in maintaining the tissues of the blood cells and the nervous system and is an antioxidant agent. Vitamin K is essential for the production of blood-clotting factors, and is used medically to treat blood-clotting disorders. The water-soluble vitamins are C and the various B vitamins.

Vitamin C, or ascorbic acid, plays a role in many of the body's metabolic pathways, as well as in the healing of tissue injuries, in the formation of blood cells and in the growth of both bone and tissue. A deficiency of vitamin C causes the disease scurvy, and can be prevented by eating citrus fruit rich in vitamin C.

The important members of the vitamin B group include B_1, or thiamine; B_2, or riboflavin; B_6, or pyridoxine; and B_{12}, or cyanocobalamin. This vitamin is essential for all cells, playing an especially important role in blood cells, the lining of the intestinal tract, and the proper functioning of the nervous system. Other B vitamins include niacin, a collective name for two molecules, nicotinic acid and nicotinamide, which are essential for carbohydrate metabolism; and folic acid, an essential factor in the production of the nucleic acids, as well as biotin, choline, inositol, and para-aminobenzoic acid, or PABA.

Minerals. The minerals are divided into macrominerals, which are needed in large

Linus Pauling (1901-1994), was a leading proponent of the health benefits of massive doses of vitamin C.

amounts by the body, and microminerals, or trace minerals, of which only small amounts are needed. Among the macrominerals, calcium, phosphorus, and magnesium are important in the development and continuing health of the bones and teeth. Potassium is an essential ingredient of the muscles, and sodium helps regulate the body fluids. An oversupply of sodium can increase the amount of some body fluid, leading to high blood pressure; public health authorities therefore recommend against use of too much salt, which contains sodium. The microminerals resemble vitamins in that the body requires them only in relatively small quantities. They include iodine, iron, zinc, copper, fluoride, selenium, and manganese. While a healthy diet generally provides enough minerals, doctors prescribe supplements for people with special needs.

Further Reading
Griffith, H. Winter, *Vitamins, Herbs, Minerals & Supplements: The Complete Guide* (1998); Heiby, Walter A., *The Reverse Effect: How Vitamins and Minerals Promote Health and Cause Disease* (1988); Sultenfuss, Sherry Wilson, *A Woman's Guide to Vitamins and Minerals* (1995).

The backgrounds of the subject of vitamins and minerals are discussed in DIGESTION; NUTRITION; METABOLISM. *More details can be found in* CHEMOTHERAPY; DIGESTION REGULATION; PHARMACOLOGY. *Advanced subjects are developed in* BONE AND BONE GROWTH; COMMON COLD; JAUNDICE.

First see TELESCOPE

VLA (Very Large Array) Telescope

Next see RADIO ASTRONOMY

A telescope configuration formally described as an unfilled-aperture telescope.

The Very Large Array (VLA) Telescope System at Socorro, New Mexico, is especially important to planetary radio astronomers because of its higher resolving power in the reception of radio signals from astronomical sources. Filled-aperture radio telescopes only have a single reflector, so their resolving power is far less than is need-

The VLA Telescope System in Socorro, New Mexico.

ed for adequate resolution of the disks of the planets. For example, a radio telescope antenna with a diameter of 100 meters operating at a wavelength of 10 centimeters would have a resolving power of perhaps 3.44 arc minutes. The angular diameters of Jupiter and Venus are about 1 arc minute, and so a much larger antenna—or a group of coupled antennas—would be needed to study them. (*See* RADIO ASTRONOMY.)

The VLA has a resolving power for radio signals that is equivalent to that of the largest ground-based optical telescopes. It consists of 27 antennas, each 25 meters in diameter (an effective aperture of 7,500 square meters), on a Y-shaped baseline, of which each leg is 21 kilometers long. The antennas are mounted on tracks, so that it is possible to tailor the configuration of the telescope for individual observations of specific astronomical radio-emitting bodies. The telescope supports observations of spectral lines, continuum, and polarization of radio waves at four different wavelengths, 1.3, 2, 6, and 16 to 20 centimeters. The VLA can measure the brightness distribution of radio emissions across most of the planets at its shortest wavelengths of operation, distinguishing between the radio emissions of the planet itself and those of any satellites, or moons, that it may have. The VLA can also be used in conjunction with radio wave observations by spacecraft, further increasing its resolving power and its value to astronomers. (*See* INTERFEROMETER.)

First see PLATE TECTONICS

Volcano

Next see SEISMICS

A vent in the surface of the Earth through which molten or solid rock and hot gases are erupted.

The molten rock that flows from a volcano is called lava; while it is beneath the surface it is called magma. Volcanoes emit lava at a temperature of 600 to 1,200 degrees Celsius. As lava cools, it forms an igneous rock that is also called lava. Rock that erupts violently from a volcano is called pyroclastic rock. It is formed as the pressure on the liquid rock, or magma, inside a volcano is reduced as it nears the surface. The result can be explosive, as gases trapped in the magma expand rapidly. Such violent reactions often shatter the volcanic rock into small fragments, building layers of volcanic tuff.

Some volcanoes emit vast amounts of flood basalt rocks, which build up thick accumulations that can cover thousands of square miles with deposits. The Columbia River plain of Oregon, Idaho, and Washington is such an area. Volcanoes also emit steam, carbon dioxide, and chlorine, which often form dense clouds about the volcanic rift.

SIMULATIONS OF STRATOSPHERIC VOLCANIC AEROSOL CLOUDS

El Chichon (April 1982)   Mt. Pinatubo (July 1991)

The shape of the volcanic hill that forms as lava is emitted depends on the nature of the materials that the volcano emits and the violence of the eruption. One volcano structure is the cinder cone, which is formed of coarse fragments emitted during explosive eruptions. These volcanoes have a cup-shaped crater near the summit, and often have vents in their sides through which lava may flow. One example is Mount Vesuvius in Italy. Another type of volcano, the shield volcano, is formed by eruptions from a number of openings and fissures. As the lava escapes, it forms a broad, slightly dome-shaped hill that resembles a warrior's shield. Mauna Loa in Hawaii is a shield volcano. A third type, the composite volcano, is the most common. A composite volcano structure consists of alternating layers of lava flows and pyroclastic rock. Mount Fuji in Japan is such a volcano. Sometimes the cone of a volcano can collapse as the magma below it retreats, so that a depression, or caldera, is formed. Crater Lake in Oregon is the result of such a volcanic collapse.

Most of the volcanoes that are active today are concentrated in two major belts. One of them circles the Pacific Ocean, and the other runs from the Mediterranean Sea to Indonesia and New Guinea. The two belts coincide with the younger mountain chains of the Earth and also with the most active earthquake belt.

Elementary aspects of this subject are covered in PLANET; PLANETS, FORMATION OF; PLATE TECTONICS; SEISMOLOGY. *Additional information on particular aspects is contained in* CONTINENTS, FORMATION OF; EARTHQUAKE; SEISMICS. *Relevant information is contained in* FAULTS, FOLDS, AND JOINTS; GEOTHERMAL ENERGY; PETROLOGY.

Scientists model the effects of the ash and dust explosively thrown into the atmosphere by erupting volcanos. Top, a comparison of the effects of the 1982 El Chicon and 1991 Mt. Pinatubo eruptions. Above, Mt. St. Helens erupts.

Further Reading

Aspray, William, *John von Neumann and the Origins of Modern Computing* (1991); Glimm, James, *The Legacy of John Von Neumann* (1990); Poundstone, W., *Prisoner's Dilemma; John Von Neumann, Game Theory and the Puzzle of the Bomb* (1993).

Further Reading

Decker, R., *Volcanoes* (1997); Fisher, R. V., *Volcanoes: Crucibles of Change* (1998); Sieh, K. E., *The Earth in Turmoil: Earthquakes, Volcanoes, and Their Impact on Humankind* (1998).

First see ALGORITHM

Von Neumann Machine

Next see TURING MACHINE

Von Neumann machine is a term applied to any electronic digital computer with a stored, programmable memory that operates in serial mode. The term is a tribute to the impetus John von Neumann gave to computer development in 1945, when he wrote a report on the EDVAC, summing up work on the first "very high speed automatic digital computing system." In this report, von Neumann not only gave legitimacy to the electronic computer but worked out its theoretical underpinnings as well.

Von Neumann saw that an effective computer needed six different components: 1) a central arithmetical unit, where the basic operations were actually performed (the modern processor); 2) a central control unit, where the arithmetical operations were scheduled; 3) a memory unit (modern RAM); 4) a means of receiving input (a keyboard); 5) a means of displaying output (a monitor); and 6) a recording device (a printer). However, no computer had yet been built that met all these criteria.

John Mauchly and J. Presper Eckert had recently developed a mercury delay storage line, which could hold a thousand bits of binary data —enough to store both the information the computer was designed to process, and the control information that told the processor what to do. Von Neumann added a critical bit, the variable-address code. By allowing the computer to move data from one area to another, variable addressing freed it from the need for constant human oversight and made it useful.

Ironically, although von Neumann's vision of a serial computer led to tremendous advances in speed and simplicity of operation, modern computer design stresses parallel processing more heavily, because of its greater flexibility and closeness in structure to the human brain.

Background material may be found in ALGORITHM; PROGRAM, COMPUTER. *Other aspects of the subject are discussed in* COMPUTER, DIGITAL; OPERATING SYSTEM; TURING MACHINE. *Additional related material can be found in* ARTIFICIAL INTELLIGENCE; CYBERNETICS; ROBOTICS.

First see ACIDS AND BASES

Water

Next see HYDROLOGIC CYCLE

A molecule of water consists of two hydrogen atoms chemically bonded to one atom of oxygen.

Water, one of the necessary ingredients for life, is one of the most abundant substances on our planet. Water covers more than three-quarters of the Earth's surface and makes up between 50 to 95 percent of the weight of any functioning living system. Most of the Earth's water is in the form of salt water, with 75 percent of the fresh water existing in the form of ice or snow in the polar regions.

The oxygen atom forms a covalent bond, sharing electrons, with each hydrogen. However, because the oxygen is much more electronegative (strongly attracts electrons) than either of the hydrogens, it ends up "monopolizing" all of the electrons. These bonds, in which the electrons are shared unequally, are called polar bonds. The oxygen atom, where all of the electrons are clustered, thus has a slight negative charge, while the hydrogen atoms, where the electrons are absent, have a slight positive charge. The water molecule has thus become a dipole (or polar molecule), a molecule with oppositely charged ends.

Hydrogen Bonding. Many of the unique properties we associate with water derives from its polarity. Adjacent molecules form hydrogen bonds with each other. This means that a hydrogen atom on one water molecule, being slightly positive, is attracted to the slightly negative (oxygen) end of another molecule. Individual hydrogen bonds are relatively weak, but collectively quite strong. Every single molecule in a glass of water is interconnected to every other water molecule nearby. The boiling point of water, is therefore much higher than it would be in the absence of hydrogen bonding. Hydrogen bonding also produces surface tension, wetting ability, and capillary action.

Surface Phenomena. Surface tension is evident to anyone who has ever seen an insect skimming along the surface of a puddle or filled a glass above the rim. Surface tension is due to the cohesion of the water molecules, which causes the molecules to form a "skin" on the surface of the liquid. Both capillary action and the ability to make things wet are due to the ability of water molecules to cling to other materials. In contrast, water-resistant materials repel the water molecules, causing them to "bead up" or cling only to other water molecules. Capillary action is seen when water rises up tubes or through layers of soil. It is sometimes called imbibition when the water is "drawn up" by a plant or animal tissue.

Vaporization is the same thing as evaporation, a change from liquid water into gas. Vaporization occurs when rapidly moving molecules break loose from the surface of a liquid and enter the air. Water has a high heat of vaporization, due to the hydrogen bonding connecting the adjacent water molecules. Evaporation requires a great deal of energy, drawn from the surrounding air molecules. Therefore, evaporation has a cooling effect on the immediate environment.

Solid Water. Ice is water in a solid state. As the temperature of a liquid drops, its density increases. Although water freezes at zero degrees Celsius, its density is greatest at four degrees Celsius. As the temperature is lowered, the water molecules get closer and closer together until each molecule has formed hydrogen bonds to four other molecules in an open lattice framework. Once that point is reached, the water expands again. Therefore, solid water takes up a greater volume than liquid water, explaining why ice floats on the surface of liquid water. If water contracted as it froze, as most materials do, bodies of water would freeze from the bottom up. In the case of ponds and rivers, this would be quite detrimental to any aquatic life. Instead, a layer of ice on top of the pond helps keep the water below it in a liquid state.

Ice and snow act as temperature stabilizers because of their high heat of fusion, the energy needed to melt them. When ice melts, the energy required comes from the immediate environment. When the water in turn freezes to form ice, the energy is released back into the environment.

Water Chemistry. Water is involved in many types of chemical reactions, as either a reactant or a product. In addition, most essential metabolic reactions require a background environment of water in which to occur.

Water is known as the universal solvent, because its polarity makes other materials readily dissolve in it to form solutions. When an ionic compound, such as salt, is dropped into water, the positive and negative ions making up the compound separate from each other. Instead of reuniting, the positive ions find themselves attracted to the negatively charged ends of the water molecules, while the negative ions find themselves attracted to the positively charged ends of the water molecules. This insures that the compound stays dissolved. Substances that dissolve readily in water are called hydrophilic (water-loving) and substances that do not dissolve in it, such as most organic compounds, are hydrophobic (water-fearing).

When substances are dissolved in water, they further lower the temperature at which water freezes. This is why salt is often placed on roadways and pathweys in wintertime to prevent any surface water from freezing and coating the roads with slippery ice.

The water molecule itself can dissociate (separate) to form H^+ and OH^- ions, which are the basis of acid-base chemistry. An acid is any compound which produces H^+ ions in solution and a base is any compound that produces OH^- ions in solution. The entire pH scale, which measures the relative acidity or basicity of a substance, is based upon the dissociation of water.

The Water Cycle. The water cycle describes how water circulates throughout the environment. Accumulations of water on land evaporate into the air. Water vapor in the air eventually condenses to form clouds. When a critical point is reached, the clouds discharge their moisture as precipitation, either in the form of rain or snow. The majority of the precipitation falls into the oceans, as oceans cover most of the Earth's surface. The water which does fall on land is ultimately pulled back into the oceans by gravity. Some water percolates down through the soil and porous rock into what is called the zone of saturation, or water table.

Water in Living Cells. Water is the background environment in which all cellular reactions takes place and is absolutely essential for life. Cytoplasm, the jelly-like substance which fills cells, is mostly water. Depending on the type of tissue and its age, its water content can be anywhere from 50 to 90 percent. Excessive loss of water leads to plasmolysis; the cell shrivels up and dies.

Some 60 percent of the body weight of an adult human male is water. For a female, the figure is 50 percent and for an infant it is 75 percent. Water is distributed within the body as intracellular fluid, e.g. cytoplasm, extracellular fluid such as blood plasma, and interstitial fluid that collects between cell layers.

Osmosis refers specifically to the diffusion or movement of water across a membrane. The water molecules travel in the direction of whichever side has a higher concentration of solid particles. The area with the higher concentration is said to be hypertonic in relation to the other side. Water continually moves to the hypertonic area, which is why high concentrations of salt cause water retention, while the side of the membrane with the lower concentration of particles is said to be hypotonic. Isotonic means that both sides of the membrane have an equal concentration of solids and therefore water will move freely in either direction.

Cells contain organelles, known as contractile vacuoles, whose job is to remove excess water from the cell. When a cell is hypertonic in relation to its environment, water continually flows in. The cell soon reaches a "danger point" where it is so filled with water it will literally burst. Animal cells are more susceptible to this fate than plant cells for two reasons. Plant cells have larger and more numerous contractile vacuoles to deal with the increased presence of

water. Also, plant cells have cell walls surrounding the outer membrane. Excess water accumulates between the membrane and the wall, giving the plant cell a rigidity known as turgor.

Interstitial fluid results from the seepage and collection of water between layers of cells. This water is not permanently lost however; it is returned to circulation via the lymphatic system. Excessive accumulation of fluid in the body tissues results in a condition known as edema, or swelling. This can also result due to blockage of the lymph ducts.

Background material can be found in BUOYANCY; LIQUID; PHASE; WATER IN LIVING CELLS. *More details can be found in* FLUID MECHANICS; HYDROLOGIC CYCLE. *Fundamental aspects of this subject are covered in* CYTOPLASM; DAMS; SUBMARINE TECHNOLOGY.

First see WATER

Water Pollution

Next see HYDROLOGIC CYCLE

Water pollution is dangerous because, although water is abundant, 99.7 percent of it is unavailable for human use and consumption, as it is locked in icecaps, stored too deep under the ground to be accessible, or too saline. Developed countries like the United States need a great deal of water for processes like industrial cooling; our annual water demand is about 700 cubic kilometers, or roughly the entire flow of the Mississippi River, which breaks down to 2,000 gallons per person per day.

Each of the main uses of water tends to pollute it. Irrigation, which accounts for nearly two-thirds of the water use in this country, leads to contamination of fresh water lakes and rivers by fertilizers and salts. Factories and power generators need enormous amounts of cooling water, which produces both contamination and thermal pollution. Finally, home use introduces pathogens into the water, in the form of human and other organic wastes.

Agriculture. Irrigation produces three different types of pollutants: nutrients, salts, and pesticides. Nutrient pollution is a major offender. Runoff of irrigation water leaches fertilizer into streams and lakes, stimulating the growth of algae and consequently reducing dissolved oxygen below viability levels in a process called eutrophication.

Irrigation also leads to an increase in the level of salts in runoff, both through evaporation of water from storage reservoirs and through the leaching of salts from the soil. As irrigation water is reused, its salinity increases. Irrigation also introduces pesticides into the water, and thence into the food chain. Along the Rio Grande, the rate of dissolved solids rises nearly eight times as water volume decreases while salt load increases.

Further Reading
Baird, Donald J., *Aquaculture and Water Resource Management* (1996); Kegley, Susan E., *The Chemistry of Water* (1997); Waggoner, P. E., *Climate Change and U.S. Water Resources* (1990).

Industry. Industrial contamination of water takes four forms: heavy metal contamination, oxygen-demanding wastes, volatile organic compounds, and thermal pollution. Heavy metals, such as arsenic, bismuth, chromium, manganese, and mercury, have threatened waterborne life downstream from many industrial sites. The worst case of heavy metal pollution was the mercury contamination of the area around Minamata, Japan, which led to poisoning in those who ate fish from the bay. Heavy metal contamination continues to occur; for example, 751 tons of heavy metals were dumped into the Bohai Sea off China in 1989.

Oxygen-demanding wastes, found in municipal effluents and near food processing plants, reduce the amount of dissolved oxygen in the water, threatening fish and other aquatic life while allowing noxious odors, tastes, and colors to accumulate. Waste water treatment plants are often graded on their ability to reduce biochemical oxygen demand, or BOD.

Volatile organic compounds, such as vinyl chloride and tetrachloroethylene, are used as solvents in many industrial processes; they are all either directly toxic or known carcinogens. Although because of their volatility they can usually be removed by aeration, even low concentrations in groundwater can be deadly. Finally, thermal pollution can kill all life in the affected water, since oxygen demands rise quickly as water temperature increases.

Home Use. Pathogens, or disease-causing organisms, are the form of water contamination that most directly affects us in everyday life. Before chlorination, which began in the United States in 1908, epidemics of cholera and typhoid were unavoidable; 90,000 people died in 1885 when a storm forced Chicago's sewage output directly into its drinking water. The problem was remedied by a civil engineering project that reversed the course of the Chicago River.

Even today, as many as fifteen million children die each year from diarrheal diseases. Water-borne contaminants range from giardia, which in 1998 threatened Sydney, Australia's drinking supply, to helminths, parasitic worms that infect 200 million people with schistosomiasis and guinea worm.

The problems of water pollution have been addressed by a series of actions over the past 30 years, both on the national and international level. In the United States, the Clean Water Act of 1970 began the process of controlling pollution, and the National Pollution Discharge Elimination System continues that process.

Further Reading
Abel, P.D., *Water Polution Biology* (1997); Lewis, Scott Alan, *The Sierra Club Guide to Safe Drinking Water* (1997); Symons, James M., *Plain Talk About Drinking Water: Questions and Answers About the Water You Drink* (1997).

Background material regarding water pollution can be found in COASTAL ENGINEERING; HAZARDOUS WASTE DISPOSAL; WATER; *Advanced discussions of particular subjects can be found in* BIOREMEDIATION; EUTROPHICATION; HYDROLOGIC CYCLE. *See also* SOIL CHEMISTRY.

First see LIGHT

Wave

Next see ELECTROMAGNETIC WAVES

A periodic disturbance in a medium such as air or water, or a field such as an electromagnetic wave.

The chief characteristics of a wave are: wavelength, the distance between successive points of equal phase of the wave; amplitude, the maximum difference of the disturbance, often measured from wave trough to peak; frequency, the number of complete disturbances, or cycles, in unit time, usually expressed in hertz, cycles per second; and speed of propagation, the distance covered by the wave in a unit of time. The velocity of propagation of a wave is found by multiplying the wavelength by the frequency. Sound is carried through air by a wave in which the molecules of air oscillate parallel to the direction of the sound. Electromagnetic waves, such as light or radio waves, result from oscillations of an electromagnetic field. Waves carry energy and momentum with them, just as solid objects do. The dual wave and particle concept of matter and forces—in which objects such as electrons and forces such as electromagneticsm can be described as both particles and wave functions, depending on how they are being measured—is a basic tenet of quantum mechanics.

The properties of waves include reflection, the return of all or part of a wave when it strikes a surface or encounters a change in medium; refraction, a change in direction when a wave passes from one medium to another (as when a light wave passes through a lens); diffraction, scattering of a wave when it strikes an object whose size is comparable to the wavelength; and interference, the cancellation or reinforcement of one wave by another that is out of phase.

Types of Waves. In a transverse wave the disturbances are at right angles to the direction of propagation. Thus something floating on the surface of water will move up and down but will barely move horizontally as the waves pass under it. In a longitudinal wave, such as a sound wave, particles are alternately compressed and separated as the wave passes through them. Sound traveling through air is an example of a longitudinal wave.

Solids can transmit transverse or longitudinal waves because of their rigid structure. Liquids can transmit transverse waves across their surface and longitudinal waves. Gases can transmit only longitudinal waves.

Polarized waves result when transverse waves at different angles to each other hit a grating or other arrangement that allows only one orientation of waves to pass through. Some sunglasses reduce glare by polarizing sunlight.

Damped waves are those whose amplitude

decreases with time or whose total energy decreases by transfer of some energy to other portions of the wave spectrum. Periodic waves are those in which the disturbance is repeated at equal intervals of time at each point in space. Stable waves are those whose amplitudes do not change with time. Unstable waves are those whose amplitudes increase with time or whose total energies increase as they draw energy from their environment.

Standing waves are waves in which the points of zero and maximum amplitude—the nodes and antinodes—appear to be stationary. They result when identical waves traveling in opposite directions are superimposed on each other. Progressive waves are those that move relative to a fixed coordinate system in a liquid. They are distinguished from stationary waves, which have no such relative movement.

There are a number of other wave descriptions that are of practical applications in describing terrestrial or other phenomena. Surface waves occur on the boundary separating two fluid phases, often a liquid and a gas or vapor of low density. They are called ripples if surface tension is the controlling force in their motion or gravity waves if gravity is the controlling force. Meteorologists describe some disturbances in the lower atmosphere as cyclonic waves, and use the term "easterly waves" to describe the wave-like disturbances that occur within easterly-moving weather systems. The term "tidal wave" is used to describe waves in the sea produced by seismic or thermal effects. Ionospheric waves in radio or television are electromagnetic waves that are reflected by the earth's ionosphere.

Background material regarding waves can be found in INTERFERENCE; LIGHT; POLARIZED LIGHT; SOUND. *Further details can be found in* DIFFRACTION; ELECTROMAGNETIC WAVES; MICHELSON-MORLEY EXPERIMENT. *Additional information on particular aspects of waves is contained in* WAVE-PARTICLE DUALITY; WAVES, OCEANIC.

First see LIGHT

Wave-Particle Duality

Next see SCHRÖDINGER'S EQUATION

The concept that subatomic particles have, under certain conditions, a wave aspect, while waves that carry energy have, under certain conditions, a particle aspect.

The model that is used to describe a subatomic entity depends on the specific properties that are being studied. For example, waves of electromagnetic radiation can also be pictured as particles called photons, which can be regarded as massless units with energy hf, where h is the Planck constant and f is the frequency of the wave in hertz, or cycles per second. Similarly,

Further Reading
Bartusiak, Marcia, *Einstein's Unfinished Symphony: Listening to the Sounds of Space-Time* (2000); Davis, Julian L., *Mathematics of Wave Progression* (2000); Elmore, William C., *Physics of Waves* (1985).

Gentle waves, such as the ones that lap the shoreline of Hawaii (above), are a key factor in ecosystems throughout the world.

Further Reading
Backus, John, *The Acoustical Foundations of Music* (1977).

electrons can be regarded either as particles or as waves. The principle of wave-particle duality, was stated by Louis de Broglie in the early 1920s and verified in the mid-1920s.

In general, fundamental entities with a rest mass that is not zero are usually described as particles. But quantum mechanics is based on a wave description of matter. The idea expressed by de Broglie was based on the knowledge that electromagnetic radiation already had been shown to have properties of both waves and particles. De Broglie extended that idea to say that any particle with a measurable rest mass could also manifest wave properties, and that the wave or particle nature of such a particle could be determined under different experimental conditions. Experiments in which an electron beam was directed at a crystalline solid were carried out soon afterward, and by the mid-1920s, sufficient evidence had been collected to make wave-particle duality an accepted theory. Wave-particle duality is true not only for subatomic particles but also for larger structures.

First see DIFFRACTION

Waves, Oceanic

Next see TIDES

A swell or ridge of water that is almost always formed by winds, but can also be caused by seismic events.

Waves are measured by their height from the trough to the crest; their distance from crest to crest, and their period, the time interval between the passage of two crests at a given point. All of these depend on the wind—its strength, the length of time that it has been blowing, and the distance it has been blowing over the water, called the fetch. When waves travel out of the area where the wind has created them, they become longer and lower with distance, until they may be several hundred feet long but with heights so small that they can be detected only by instruments.

The motion of the particles of water in a wave are affected by the depth of the water in that area of the ocean. In deep-sea locations, each particle of water has a circular motion—forward, down, backward, and up. Thus, there is no net movement of these particles of water, but there is movement of the form of the wave. As a wave goes into shallower water near the shore, the circular movement of the particles of water becomes more flattened, forming an ellipse rather than a circle. The length of the wave decreases, and the height of the wave increases, but the period does not change.

When a wave breaks on a beach, its water plunges forward precipitously at a point where the depth of the water on the beach is the same as the height that the wave had in deeper water.

When the water reaches the shore, it produces wash, water that flows up on the beach, and then backwash, the water that flows back down the beach into the ocean. The water that flows back to the sea can be concentrated in streams called rip currents, which can extend hundreds of feet out to sea. The pulls felt by a swimmer—the undertow—consist of backwash and rip currents.

The height of ocean waves rarely is greater than 60 feet, although waves of more than 100 feet have been recorded. However, height and other aspects of ocean waves are difficult to measure precisely because there usually are several trains of waves of different heights moving in different directions at any given point. One method of measuring wave dimensions is to measure the surface level of the ocean by using a bottom-fixed measuring device such as a long staff that records the changes in water pressure that result from the passage of waves. The most destructive kind of wave, the tidal wave (or tsunami), occurs when the ocean floor is moved by underwater earthquakes or volcanic activity. (*See* EARTHQUAKE; VOLCANO.)

Further Reading
Kampion, D., *The Book of Waves: Form and Beauty on the Ocean* (1997); Komar, Paul D., *Beach Processes and Sedimentation* (1997); Sorensen, R. M., *Basic Wave Mechanics: For Coastal and Ocean Engineers* (1993).

> *Background material can be found in* CLIMATOLOGY; OCEAN CURRENT; TIDES; WAVE. *More details can be found in* OCEANOGRAPHY; SUBMARINE TECHNOLOGY. *Additional relevant information is contained in* EVOLUTION; UNDERWATER EXPLORATION.

First see ATMOSPHERE

Weather

Next see WIND AND CLOUDS

The condition of the atmosphere at a specific time and place; whereas climate refers to the general conditions over time.

Weather depends primarily on the movement of the atmosphere. On a global basis, the primary factors affecting the movement of the atmosphere are the heat supplied by the sun, and the rotation of the Earth. If the Earth did not rotate, then the main circulation of the atmosphere would result from the fact that the sun heats the tropics more than the poles. Cool air would descend over the poles, flow along the surface to the tropics, then rise as warm air to return to the poles. In the Northern Hemisphere, the prevailing winds would blow from north to south.

Climatic Cells. Because of the Earth's rotation, the general circulation is broken up into three distinct cells. From the equator to the tropics, the "trade winds" blow from east to west. At mid-latitudes, the "prevailing westerlies," blow from west to east. These are the winds that normally move weather systems across the United States. Finally, in the tropics, the winds once again blow from east to west.

While the rotation of the Earth and solar heating determine the large-scale conditions of the atmosphere, on the scale of continents weather is controlled by large air masses—a thousand miles across and miles high—that require several days to cross a continent. Winds tend to flow into regions of low pressure in a spiral pattern because of the Coriolis force. The inflow is counterclockwise in the Northern Hemisphere, clockwise in the Southern. Air flowing into a low pressure area near the surface rises, cooling as it does so. When the temperature drops to the point where water can no longer remain in vapor form, it condenses out and clouds form. This is why low pressure areas are often associated with bad weather, cloudiness, and precipitation. In high pressure areas, on the other hand, air tends to enter at the top and move toward the surface, so that the relative humidity of the air is low.

Moving air masses can produce various kinds of severe storms.

Thunderstorms. These storms develop when warm moist air rises quickly, so that a great deal of heat is released as the water vapor condenses. The heat released in this way produces more updraft, more moist surface air being pulled into the nascent storm, and more heat release. Thus, the storm feeds on itself and builds up dark, towering thunderheads. These clouds can reach 11 miles into the atmosphere, and winds can reach 60 miles per hour.

Tornadoes. These funnel-shaped wind storms are associated with the instabilities in thunderstorms. The funnel develops from the strong updrafts in the thunderhead, which in some storms narrow and turn downward. The storm itself is just rapidly moving wind, which is invisible, but is made visible by dirt, debris, and water vapor carried in it. About 800 tornadoes strike the United States each year, and wind speeds can exceed 300 miles per hour.

Hurricanes. A large-scale storm that derives its energy from the warm ocean surface is called a hurricane if its wind speeds exceed 74 miles per hour. They start as ordinary low pressure storms over warm ocean areas. Hurricanes in the Atlantic typically start off the coast of Africa, then move westward with the trade winds. As the storm develops, the water evaporating from the surface is pulled upward into the storm, where it rises, condenses, and releases heat. Once they strike land or move north, they lose their source of energy and disperse.

Damage from hurricanes results from high wind, but other effects can cause damage as well. The most important of these is called the storm surge. The air pressure at the center of the

The mathematics involved in a comprehensive model of the Earth's weather pattern is so complex that scientists are not sure if they will ever be able to generate such a model.

hurricane is very low, which causes the sea level at that point to rise. The water at the center of the storm can be as much as 30 feet above normal, and this surge comes ashore with the storm.

This type of storm is called a hurricane in the Atlantic and a typhoon in the Pacific, and is sometimes called a cyclone in Australia.

Monsoon. During the summer in India, the land warms quickly. Rising warm air pulls in moist air from over the oceans. Thus, the summer is a time of humidity and heavy rain. In the winter, the ocean is warmer than the land, and cool, dry air is pulled from the Himalayas. Thus, the winter is characterized by cool, cloudless weather; the summer is referred to as the monsoon season.

El Niño. During normal times, winds in the central Pacific blow toward the west, and the warm surface water of the ocean piles up in the western part of the ocean. As a result, cold waters well up off the coast of South America, carrying nutrients from the depths and nourishing abundant marine life. Periodically, the warm surface waters slosh toward the east and the winds reverse, piling the warm water against the South American coast. The warm waters usually appear around Christmas, which explains the name of this weather phenomenon ("El Niño" is Spanish for "Christ Child"). El Niño events come every five to seven years, and have been around for hundreds of years at least. During an El Niño, weather patterns change around the world, with heavy rainfall and flooding in many areas of North and South America.

Forecasting. Weather forecasting is the application of the principles of meteorology to the prediction of the future state of the atmosphere for a given area. These predictions usually include temperatures, pressures, clouds, and precipitation and may also include other elements of special concern to a region, such as air pollution levels in a city. Accurate forecasting requires the collection and analysis of very large amounts of data that are gathered not only at the Earth's surface but also by balloons and orbiting satellites. The purpose of the analysis is to delineate weather systems that cover large or small regions. In the United States, meteorological observations are gathered through an international cooperative effort several times a day over the northern hemisphere. The observations are assembled and fed into computers that analyze them for predicted wind, temperature, and air pressure patterns. Meteorologists today also can study pictures of large-scale weather systems sent to the Earth by satellites.

The modern method of forecasting, called numerical prediction, builds on the inertia of atmospheric wind systems—when they are in motion, they tend to stay in motion in the same direction. One of the most important computations made is that of wind patterns at about 20,000

feet, which have a great influence on weather conditions. Once a predicted wind map is printed out, a meteorologist can interpret, modify, and expand the computer-made prediction, based on past experience. Weather charts produced by this method will show the expected position of fronts, air masses, and air pressures, and can be filled out to show cloud patterns and other elements of the weather.

To make an accurate weather prediction for a small area, such as a city, small-scale weather phenomena are important. For example, an early winter map showing a cold north wind over the central plains of the United States will also show clear or only partly cloudy skies over that region. But the same wind pattern on the eastern shores of the Great Lakes—in the area of Buffalo, New York, for example—may cause a heavy snowfall, because the air has picked up a great deal of water as the wind passes over the lakes. Therefore, separate forecasts must be made for each region, in addition to the larger-scale forecast.

Long-range Forecasting. Long-range forecasting, a field that started in the 1940s, is important in economic terms. These forecasts are naturally less detailed than daily predictions, but they can give the broad trends that are expected over the near future—for example, for the next five or seven days, with an emphasis on temperature and precipitation.

A longer-range prediction is the 30-day forecast. These forecasts do not attempt to make a detailed breakdown of future weather conditions, in either time or space. What the 30-day forecast does provide is a prediction of the average or prevailing conditions that are expected, in terms of departures from the normal conditions in a region. The emphasis in such a longer-term forecast is on such major factors as a large increase or decrease in temperature, the possible paths of major storm systems, and upper-air wind patterns.

Forecasts for even longer periods are usually based on the climatological records for a given region. Such forecasts are bound to be accurate to some degree—for example, they will say that the winter will be colder than the summer—but they can involve a good deal of plain guessing, as in the case of the year-long forecasts made in some almanacs.

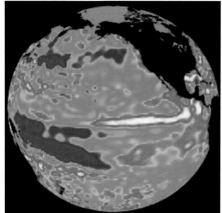

Above, satellites have been used extensively to track the El Niño effect, seen from 1997 to 1998. The false color images allow visualization of the pressure gradients caused by the fast moving winds, allowing one to attempt to predict the direction of movement of the storm.

Background material on weather can be found in ATMOSPHERE; CLIMATOLOGY; JET STREAM. Advanced subjects are developed in HURRICANES AND TORNADOES; LIGHTNING AND THUNDER; OCEAN CURRENT. Fundamental aspects of this subject are covered in CHAOS AND COMPLEXITY; DESERTIFICATION; GLOBAL WARMING. See also ACID RAIN; CHLORFLUOROCARBONS; OCEAN-ATMOSPHERE INTERACTION.

Further Reading
Abrahamson, Dean E., *The Challenge of Global Warming* (1989); Laskin, David, *Braving the Elements: The Stormy History of American Weather* (1997); Strzepek, Kenneth M., *As Climate Changes: International Impacts and Implications* (1995).

First see GRAVITY

Weight

Next see FRICTION

Weight is the result of the gravitational pull exerted by a massive body on a body of smaller mass, such as the pull exerted by the Earth on a person or object on its surface or nearby in space. Weight is proportional to the masses of both bodies and to the distance between them. On Earth, weight is also affected by the planet's rotation; the centrifugal force of that rotation reduces weight somewhat.

Thus, an object that weighs 100 pounds at the North or South Pole weighs 99.67 pounds at the equator, because the surface of the Earth is farther from its center at the equator and the centrifugal force of the Earth's rotation is greater, reducing the object's weight. And because the mass of the moon is much smaller than the mass of the Earth, an object that weighs one pound on Earth weighs about one sixth that on the moon. The weight of an object on Earth decreases with both altitude and with depth below the surface.

Measurement. Weight is not to be confused with mass, which is a measure of the quantity of material as it relates to an application of force. In the system of measurement used in the United States, the pound is a basic unit of weight. The basic unit of mass is the slug, which is defined as a mass which, when acted upon by a force of one pound, accelerates toward the Earth at a rate of one foot per second per second. Such a mass that falls freely near the Earth's surface accelerates at a rate of about 32 feet per second per second, so we can say that the weight of a slug is 32 pounds.

In the metric system of measurements, used in most of the world outside the United States, the units of weight are the gram and the kilogram. One kilogram equals 1,000 grams or about 2.2 pounds. A force such as gravity that accelerates one gram or one kilogram to an acceleration of one meter per second per second is a newton; a force that accelerates one gram or one kilogram to an acceleration of one centimeter per second per second is a dyne.

"Weightlessness" in Space. The weightlessness of astronauts in orbit around the Earth is caused mainly by the centrifugal force created by the spacecraft's rotation around the planet. When a spacecraft goes into interplanetary space, it is virtually weightless because of its distance from any planet or other mass that could exert a strong gravitational pull on it.

Further Reading
Narlikar, Jayant V., *The Lighter Side of Gravity* (1996); Shoemaker, Robert W., *All You Need to Know about the Metric System for Everyday Use* (1992); Thorne, Kip S., *Black Holes and Time Warps: Einstein's Outrageous Legacy* (1994).

Background material on weight can be found in EQUIVALENCE PRINCIPLE; FORCE; GRAVITY. *Advanced subjects are developed in* ACCELERATION; GENERAL RELATIVITY; INTERSTELLAR MEDIUM ("DARK MATTER"). *More information on particular aspects is contained in* FRICTION; SPACE STATION; WEAKLY INTERACTING MASSIVE PARTICLES (WIMPS).

First see ALLOY

Welding

Next see ELECTROCHEMISTRY

A method of joining two metals by fusing them by one or another solid-state process.

Two metal surfaces will form a strong bond if the surfaces are clean and are brought into close enough contact. Since most metal surfaces are covered by a layer of oxide or a similar material, the first step in welding is to remove that layer or form a new surface by cutting or deforming the metal to be welded. In gas welding, an oxyacetylene or oxyhydrogen torch is then used to create the weld. Arc welding uses the heat that is generated by an electric arc to join the metals. Atomic-hydrogen arc welding combines gas welding and arc welding.

Fusion welding may be done by using burning gas, pressure, electric current, or more modern methods such as electron beams or lasers. In solid-state welding, heat is not always needed to remove the oxide film from the surfaces of the metals to be joined. There are also some cold welding methods. One of them is vacuum welding, in which the two surfaces that are to be joined are kept free from contamination in a vacuum chamber, and form a bond when they are brought into contact. Vacuum welding became a nuisance during early space flights, since some pieces of equipment would become welded together in the airless environments of outer space. Diffusion bonding and roll bonding are other examples of solid-state bonding processes.

First see ELEMENTARY PARTICLE

WIMP (Weakly Interacting Massive Particle)

Next see INTERSTELLAR MEDIUM ("DARK MATTER")

A type of matter postulated by astronomers as a reason for their inability to detect more than 90 percent of the mass of the universe predicted by calculation.

The existence of missing mass in the universe first became evident in the 1970s when astronomers began measuring the speeds at which clouds of hydrogen orbit the centers of spiral galaxies, and determined that there had to be a large but invisible source of gravitational attraction in the outer reaches of the galaxies. Further evidence for the missing mass was provided by observations of gravitational lensing. Light from distant galaxies that reaches the Earth is sometimes distorted by the gravitational pull of intervening galaxies. Analysis of the distortions of this light allows one to calculate the mass of these galaxies; these show that much of their mass cannot be accounted for.

The Neutrino Solution. One candidate for the missing mass is the neutrino, billions of which shoot through the universe. The neutrino is currently assumed to have no mass. If it is found to have even a tiny mass, that could solve the problem. Another proposed candidate are MACHOs, short for massive compact halo objects, that could range in size from small brown dwarf stars to massive but invisible stars. Teams of astronomers in the United States and abroad have been looking for changes in the brightness of distant stars that could be caused by MACHOs, but the search for the existence of enough MACHOs to account for all the missing mass has thus far been unsuccessful.

Detecting WIMPs. As their name implies, WIMPs are difficult to detect because, unlike other particles, they rarely engage in interactions with other matter. WIMP-detection devices put into action in recent years look for other characteristics. One instrument, for example, uses crystals that are maintained at temperatures near absolute zero and thus might be able to detect a tiny pulse of heat that a WIMP might emit.

The problem with WIMP detectors is that they might be overwhelmed by known particles, such as debris from the decay of radioactive particles around the apparatus, or by cosmic rays. The United Kingdom Dark Matter Collaboration, UKDMC, operates a scintillation detector housed in the deepest mine in Europe, in northern England, where signals from cosmic rays are at a minimum. It consists of a 6-kilogram crystal of sodium that is monitored by two light-detecting photomultipliers. Other experimenters used small droplets of liquid Freon as detectors.

Background material on WIMPs can be found in ELEMENTARY PARTICLE; GRAVITY; STANDARD MODEL. *Advanced material can be located in* INFRARED AND ULTRAVIOLET ASTRONOMY; INTERSTELLAR MEDIUM; RADIO ASTRONOMY. *Further information is to be found in* HUBBLE CONSTANT; NEUTRINO ASTRONOMY; UNIVERSE, LARGE-SCALE STRUCTURE OF.

First see ATMOSPHERE

Wind and Clouds

Next see WEATHER

The air in motion over the Earth and the visible masses of condensed water droplets that are suspended in the atmosphere.

Winds are caused primarily by the unequal heating of the Earth by the sun, which results in pressure changes over the globe. Another cause is the Coriolis force, the deflection of air due to the rotation of the Earth. Yet another is the friction

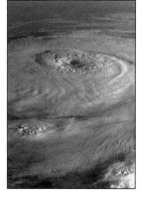

Above, the circling cloud pattern around the central eye—the unmistakable earmarks of a hurricane.

Further Reading
Barnett, R. Michael, *The Charm of Strange Quarks* (2000); Griffin, John, *Q is for Quantum* (1999); Hooft, Gerald H., *In Search of the Ultimate Building Blocks* (1996); Schramm, David N., *From Quarks to the Cosmos* (1995).

Further Reading
Day, John A., *Peterson Guide to Clouds and Weather* (1998); Ludlum, Dr. David M., *Clouds and Storms* (1995); Robinson, Trevor, *The Amateur Wind Instrument Maker* (1981).

between the Earth and the lowest layer of air, which slows down air motion near the surface. In the Northern Hemisphere, winds blow clockwise around regions of high pressure and counterclockwise around regions of low pressure; these directions are reversed in the Southern Hemisphere. Because the frictional effect of the surface decreases with height, wind speed generally increases with altitude. The effects of friction usually are not felt above an altitude of 2,000 to 3,000 feet. This altitude is lower over water and smooth ground and higher over rough terrain.

On most days, winds near the ground are characterized by gusty, turbulent motions that result from surface obstructions such as terrain features, trees, or buildings. In addition, a form of gustiness called clear-air turbulence has been detected in the upper atmosphere. Large variations in wind speed are often associated with the jet streams, narrow ribbons of high-speed winds that blow toward the east in the middle latitudes, at heights of 20,000 to 40,000 feet.

Clouds are formed when air that contains water vapor rises. The air expands because of the lower pressure that exists at higher levels in the atmosphere. This expansion causes the air to cool, until its temperature falls below the dew point. The vapor that the air carries then condenses into a very large number of tiny water droplets, which become visible as a cloud.

Clouds can form a sheet that extends over hundreds of miles, indicating a region where air is rising. These are called stratiform or layer clouds. Sometimes clouds are scattered over the sky in isolated puffs and heaps, separated by spaces. These clouds are formed by irregular rising currents of air, and are called cumulus. The widespread layer clouds that are associated with bad-weather systems often consist of several layers that extend up to 30,000 feet or more, with separations of clear air that can be filled in as rain or snow develops.

Storm Clouds. The approach of a storm may be heralded by the appearance of high, thin clouds at an altitude of 20,000 feet, known as cirrus clouds. These clouds may thicken to form a continuous thin sheet, called cirrostratus. The clouds then may thicken to hide the sun, partially or completely; this thicker layer is called altostratus. There are a variety of other cloud forms that have been classified and studied by meteorologists for many decades.

Background material on wind and clouds is in ATMOSPHERE; HYDROLOGIC CYCLE; WEATHER. *More details can be found in* CLIMATOLOGY; LIGHTNING AND THUNDER. *Advanced aspects of this subject are covered in* AERODYNAMICS; HURRICANES AND TORNADOES.

First see ELECTROMAGNETIC WAVES

X ray

Next see MEDICAL DIAGNOSTICS

Electromagnetic radiation of extremely short wavelength—about one ten-thousandth the wavelength of visible light.

X rays were discovered in 1895 by Wilhelm Roentgen, who was working with a Crookes tube (today called a discharge tube), a glass tube containing two electrodes. Kept at very low gas pressure, it can produce cathode rays and other discharges. Roentgen noticed that a nearby fluorescent screen glowed when cathode rays struck it, and that the same effect occurred even when the tube was encased in a cardboard box. X rays were first thought to be completely different from light, but in 1911 Max von Laue established that they, like light, were electromagnetic waves. X rays were put to work almost immediately when Roentgen noted that they could penetrate matter, including the human body, and produce an image; physicians were soon doing x-ray studies of their patients. (*See* MEDICAL DIAGNOSTICS.)

X rays are generated whenever high-speed electrons going through an evacuated tube strike a target, such as a metal plate. The energy lost by the electrons in the collision is then emitted in the form of short wavelength electromagnetic radiation. Early x-ray tubes consisted of a flat or concave cathode that emitted electrons and a metal anode that emitted x rays. The modern x-ray tube, invented by W. D. Coolidge, uses a hot wire to emit electrons and a massive tungsten or molybdenum anode; the tube can reach an electric potential of a million volts or more. X rays today have a wide range of uses, from medical diagnosis and treatment to the study of materials and the universe.

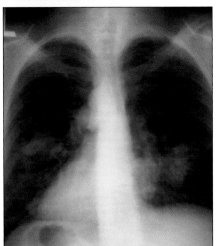

The discovery of x rays by Wilhelm Roentgen (top) has allowed doctors to see the inside of the human body, enabling them to diagnose diseases such as lung cancer (above) without invasive surgery.

First see DIFFRACTION

X-ray Diffraction

Next see DNA

The study of the atomic and molecular structures of crystalline substances through the use of x rays.

X-ray diffraction is an example of the spreading or bending of waves as they pass through an aperture or around the edges of a barrier. The diffracted waves then interfere with one another, producing regions of reinforcement and weakening. The phenomenon of diffraction was first observed with visible light in the seventeenth century and provided proof for the wave nature of light. X-ray diffraction by a crystal was discovered in 1912, a discovery that confirmed that x rays are a kind of light, or electromagnetic radiation. The nineteenth-century British scientist William Bragg formulated the modern principle governing x-ray diffraction, and used it to determine the atomic arrangement of many crystals, thus establishing the modern science of crystallography.

A crystal can be described as a number of planes of atoms that are evenly spaced, comparable to a succession of mirrors that are not completely reflecting. When x rays of one wavelength are beamed at such a crystal, the fraction of the beam that is reflected by the top plane will be reinforced by the fractions of the beam that are reflected by the other planes, but only if the additional distance that the other fractions must travel is an exact multiple of the wavelength of the x rays. The atomic arrangement of the crystal can thus be inferred by using Bragg's law. The diffraction pattern produced when x rays pass through a crystal consists of a pattern of spots on a photographic plate that can be interpreted to learn the structure of the particular crystal. (*See* X RAY; CRYSTAL.)

First see X RAY

X-ray and Gamma-ray Astronomy

Next see GAMMA RAY

The study of the very short-wavelength and very high-energy electromagnetic radiation that is emitted by objects in the cosmos.

Most observations in x-ray and gamma-ray astronomy must take place in outer space, because the detectable radiation, for the most part, does not reach the surface of the Earth. The first solar x-ray emissions were detected in 1948, and the first nonsolar x-ray source was detected in 1962. A series of satellites launched between 1970 (UHURU) and 1977 (HEAO), made a sky survey that cataloged about 800 x-ray sources. The distribution of these sources in the sky shows two components. One is distributed along the plane of the Earth's galaxy (the Milky Way), and the other, outside that plane, indicates emitters outside the galaxy.

Galactic x-ray sources include compact x-ray binaries, which are two-member star systems; supernova remnants, which often contain x-ray-emitting neutron stars and pulsars; and the coronas, or outermost layers, of stars. Sources of x rays outside our galaxy include the centers, or nuclei, of other galaxies, most of which contain massive black holes; and clusters of galaxies, whose x-ray-emitting region can extend over diameters of a million light-years or more. One striking feature observed by satellites is the existence of a strong background of x-ray emissions believed to originate in the distant universe. Some astronomers believe that this x-radiation originates from matter between the galaxies, while others believe that it is the total sum of emissions from a variety of specific celestial bodies.

The gamma rays observed by astronomers are emitted by energetic interactions that take place inside stars and galaxies, on their surfaces, and in their immediate vicinity. The direction of gamma rays indicates the nature of their sources, while the energy fluxes, or changes, and time distribution of gamma rays give information about the properties of the objects that emit them. Gamma-ray lines can be studied to identify the nuclear reactions, in which they originated, the temperature of those reactions, and the motions of the bodies in which the reactions take place.

One interesting phenomenon in this branch of astronomy is the gamma-ray burst. Such a burst lasts only a few seconds, during which it is the strongest source of gamma rays in the sky. The sources of gamma rays include pulsars that emit radiation in brief, precisely timed and repetitive pulses; black holes; and, outside our galaxy, other galaxies, supernova remnants such as the Crab Nebula, and radio galaxies. There are also diffuse gamma-ray emissions, similar to the x-ray background emissions in the universe.

Above, an array of mirrors ten meters in diameter, for collecting and focusing gamma rays. A human hand is reflected in all of the mirrors.

Special topics in this area are found in Radio Astronomy; Telescope. *Advanced subjects are developed in* Galaxy; Nova; Supernova; Universe. *Other aspects of this subject are covered in* Interstellar Medium ("Dark Matter"); Neutrino Astronomy.

First see X Ray

X-ray Spectroscopy

Next see Spectroscopy

Also known as x-ray crystallography, it is a method used to determine the structures of crystals and other solids.

X-ray spectroscopy is related to microwave spectroscopy and electron diffraction. It shows the bond angles and bond distances of substances, and has been used to determine absolute

Further Reading
Aschenbach, B., *The Invisible Sky: Rosat and the Age of X-ray Astronomy* (1998); Hirsh, Richard F., *Glimpsing an Invisible Universe: The Emergence of X-ray Astronomy* (1983).

stereostructures (how light is rotated) for some optically active compounds. This method was also used to prove the structure of DNA as postulated by James Watson and Francis Crick.

A technique known as x-ray photo-electron spectroscopy (XPS) is being used in cancer research. XPS allows close investigation of the molecules that coat a particular surface. In the past, XPS has been used to improve the way that conventional high explosives combine with binder substances, allowing them to be molded into particular shapes. This method is now being used to study the molecules that coat the surface of a particular tumor-marker known as mucin, to figure out a correlation between the molecular pattern of its surface and an immune system response. Two other forms of spectroscopy, nuclear magnetic resonance and mass spectroscopy, are being used to study mucin structure as well.

First see Virus

Yellow Fever

Next see Viral Diseases

Yellow fever is a viral disease that is transmitted by mosquitoes in warm areas of the world, such as Central America, South America, and Africa. It gets its name because in severe cases it causes jaundice, which makes the skin of the patient turn yellow. Incidence of the disease has been reduced greatly by eradication of *Aedes aegypti* mosquitoes, which carry the virus, in many populated areas, and by development and use of a vaccine. Many countries where yellow fever is still prevalent require a certificate of vaccination before a traveler is allowed to enter.

A single injection of the vaccine provides protection for at least 10 years and does not cause serious reactions. When infection does occur, there is an onset of fever and headache three to six days later, often accompanied by nausea and nosebleed. Many patients recover after three days, but others can go on to higher fever, headache, and pain in many parts of the body. The liver and kidneys may suffer severe damage that causes jaundice and kidney failure, which may be followed by agitation, delirium, and death. The disease is fatal in about ten percent of cases. There is no effective drug treatment for yellow fever, although one attack provides lifelong immunity.

First see QUARK

Z-Boson

Next see GAUGE THEORY

A particle that, together with the W particles, carries the weak nuclear force.

The Z-particle, or Z-boson (symbolized by Z^0, to indicate its lack of electrical charge) is the particle that carries the weak nuclear force from quark to quark, just as photons carry the electromagnetic force from charged particle to charged particle. Like other bosons, it does not obey the exclusion principle, and does not even obey a conservation law—bosons are created and annihilated by the millions virtually everywhere and virtually constantly. Every time a light is turned on, billions of photons are created and then disppear when they are absorbed by atoms.

The Z-boson has a mass of about 96 times that of a proton, a spin of one, and a lifetime of 10^{-26} seconds. Several enduring difficulties are associated with the Z-particle. One is why it has mass at all. Its fellow boson, the photon, is massless and some theoretical considerations demand that it also have zero mass. Another has to do with the relative absence of Z-particles in our experience. Why do we not experience them the way we experience photons? Z-particles were first detected at CERN in 1983. (*See* ELEMENTARY PARTICLES; NUCLEAR FORCES.)

Further Reading
Trefil, James, *From Atoms to Quarks* (1994); Trekil, James, *Introduction to the Strange World of Particle Physics* (1998); Watkins, Peter, *Story of the W and the Z* (1986).

First see MAGNETISM

Zeeman Effect

Next see QUANTUM MECHANICS

The splitting of the spectral lines from a light source when that source is placed in a magnetic field. The phenomenon is caused by the effect of the magnetic field on the orbitals of the electrons in the source.

The Zeeman effect, predicted by Hendrick Lorentz in the 1890s and discovered by Pieter Zeeman in 1896, is a very important tool for analyzing spectral lines of elements in the laboratory and of distant celestial objects. Much of what is known about the magnetic fields of the sun and stars is the result of analysis of the Zeeman splitting of their spectral lines. (*See* MAGNETISM *and* ELECTROMAGNETIC FORCE.)

Normal Zeeman Effect. The normal Zeeman effect can be explained in classical terms and entails the splitting of the spectral lines into two or three lines depending on whether the observer is parallel or perpendicular to the magnetic field. If a magnetic field is applied to an electron, the electron in its orbit is speeded up by the magnetic field in one direction and retarded in the other, with the result that the spectral line emitted by the electron has a

Further Reading
Barrow, John D., *The Book of Nothing: Vacuums, Voids and the Latest Ideas About the Origins of the Universe* (2001); Kaplan, Robert, *The Nothing That Is: A History of Zero* (1999); Siefre, Charles, *Zero: The Biography of a Dangerous Idea* (2000).

companion line on the other side. (*See* ATOM *and* ELECTRON; SPECTROSCOPY.)

Anomalous Zeeman Effect. Continued application of magnetic fields to spectral lines soon indicated that for systems more complicated than a simple electron orbiting a nucleus, other explanations would be required. This gave early indication that something like a quantum theory would be necessary. The effect of the magnetic field on the electron itself gave rise to the quantum mechanical concept of spin. The spectrum for sulfur was particularly given to these anomalous effects, and the successful explanation of its anomalies was an early triumph of the quantum theory. (*See* QUANTUM MECHANICS.)

The Zeeman effect has been applied in many variations and to many substances: molecules, crystals, and even the nucleus itself. Each has required greater resolution of the spectral lines as the splitting becomes finer and finer. Similar effects are observed when simple electric fields are applied to atoms, in which case the effect is known as the Stark effect.

First see SETS AND GROUPS

Zero

Next see NUMBER

The null element of a mathematical system.

The invention of zero ranks as one of the greatest contributions to the science of mathematics. The positional system of number notation required an element for the unoccupied position. The Babylonians used such a system with a base 60 number system; later the Hindus and Chinese used a base-ten system. The symbol for zero was introduced by the Babylonians and adopted a thousand years later by the Indians. It came west with the Arabs as part of the Arabic number system. (*See* NUMBER.)

As a number rather than a simple placeholder, however, zero is a relatively new concept. It was seen early to have special properties: any number added to zero is the same number (zero is the identity under addition); any number multiplied by zero is zero.

Leonardo Fibonacci in the thirteenth century was the first westerner to theorize about zero. The subtlety of the concept of zero is seen by the fact that mathematicians both east and west had a clearer concept of negative numbers, and much earlier, than of the number zero.

It is difficult to imagine any mathematics taking place without the zero. For example, when a polynomial equation of the nth degree equals zero, the statement gives rise to the question of the n roots of the equation, a central question in the field of algebra. (*See* ALGEBRA.)

INDEX

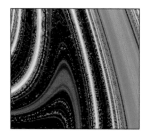

Entry titles are in bold and in color: blue for mathematics and the physical sciences; green for life sciences and medicine; red for technology. The color index entries thus constitute a table of contents for the work.

Alternate or partial article titles, and article titles that appear as sub-entries, are black bold. (For example, "Linear accelerator" is black bold when it appears as a sub-entry under "Accelerator, particle". The subject of special relativity is discussed in "Special Relativity," the title of an entry, but a black bold index entry appears under "Relativity, special.")

Italicized numbers indicate illustrations.

Amino acids, 343
  biosynthesis of, 65
  in **Proteins**, 201, 405, 406
  synthesis of, 187
  Transcription of, 483-84
Ammonium, 344
Amniocentesis, 35, *35*,
Ampère, Andre Marie, 297-98, 326
Amphibians, 36, *36*, 385, 425
Amplitude modulation (AM), 207, 414, 415
Anaerobic metabolism, 311
Analog computer, 37, *37*
Anatomy
  Adrenal glands, 16-17, *17*
  Aging and, 19-21
  Blood, 68-69
  Bones and bone growth, 72, *72*
  Brain, 73-76, *74*, *75*
  Circulatory systems, 108-9, *109*
  Digestive systems, 141-44, *141-43*
  Endocrine system, 175-76, *175*
  Eyes, 193-94
  Hearts, 239-40, *239*
  Kidneys and excretory system, 276, *276*
  Livers, 291-92, *292*
  Lungs, 294-95
  Lymphatic systems, 296, *296*
  Muscles, 328-29
  Muscle systems, 329-30
  Nervous system, 336-37
  Organogenesis, 365
  Organ transplantation, 363-64
  Reproductive systems, 424-25
    human, *424*, *425*
  Respiratory systems, 427, *427*
  Skeletal systems, 445
  teeth, 136
  Thyroid glands, 479-80
    see also Biology; **Diseases**; Medicine
Angioplasty, 38, 38
Angiosperms (flowering plants), 38, *38*, 391
  Gametogenesis and, 213
  Gymnosperms distinguished from, 236
  mutualistic relationships between
    insects and, 470
  Seeds of, 438
  Sexual reproduction in, 444
Animals, 283-84, 384-85
  Amphibians, 36, *36*
  anatomy of
    Digestive systems of, 143-44
    Eyes of, 193-84
    Hearts of, 239-40, *239*
    Lungs of, 294
    Nervous systems of, 238-39
    Skeletal systems of, 445
  aquatic
    Fish, 198, *198*
    Gills on, 229
  behavior of
    Aggression and territoriality, 19
    Communications among, 116-17, *117*
    Competition and altruism among, 117-18
    Conditioning of, 123
    Ethology, 183-84
    feeding behavior, 259-60
    Predation among, 399, *399*
  Birds, 65, *65*

Evolution of, 66, *66*
Birth of, 66-67, *66*
during **Cambrian diversification of life**, 83
Cancer in, 85
Digestion by, 140-41
Dinosaurs, 144-45, *145*
  Extinction of, 146
during **Ice ages**, 253
Ingestion by, 259-60
Instincts of, 260-61
Invertebrates, 267
Life, definition and origin of, 283-85
Locomotion of, 292-93, *292*, *293*
Mammals, 299-300
Metabolism of, 311-12
Navigation by, 333, *333*
Nutrition for, 356
Pheremones, 380-81
photoluminescent, 382
Population ecology of, 399
Primates, 400, *400*
Reflexes in, 422
reproduction of
  Biology of Sex in, 442-43
  Cloning of, 111
  Conception among, 122-23
  Reproductive strategies of, 425-26
  Reproductive systems of, 424-25
Reptiles, 426
respiration in, 427
Sensory mechanisms of, 441
Thermal regulation by, 476-77
  see also **Ethology**
Annealing, 38-39
Annelids, 267, 329
Anthrax, 228
Anthropoids, 400
Anthropology
  Australopithecus, 53-54, *54*
  Homo Sapiens, 245-47
  Neanderthals, 334, *334*
    see also **Homo Sapiens**
Antibiotics, 39-40, *39*, 103, 148
  Bacteria resistant to, 58
Antibodies, 40, *40*
  in **Gamma globulin**, 213
  in **Immune response**, 255
  Immunoassays of, 257
  Major histocompatability complex and, 298-99
  Monoclonal, 323-24
  produced by **B-lymphocytes**, 57
  produced by **T-lymphocytes**, 473
Anti-depressant drugs, 174
Anti-derivatives (mathematics), 82
Antidiuretic hormone (ADH), 461, 462
Antigen-presenting cells, 41
Antigens, 70
Antimatter, 41
Antimony, 345
Antioxidants, 39
Antiparticles, 41, 471
Antiseptics, 39, 469
Apodes, 36
Apollo 11 (spacecraft), 453
Apomixis, 47
Aquatic life
  Algae, 27-28, *27*, *28*
  Fish, 198, *198*

Entry titles are in bold and in color: blue for mathematics and the physical sciences; green for life sciences and medicine; red for technology. Alternate or partial article titles, and article titles that appear as sub-entries, are black bold.

Italicized numbers indicate illustrations.

Karyotyping of, 275
in **Mitochondria**, 321
as **Nucleic acid**, 351-52
in **Polymerase chain reactions**, 398
in **Protein synthesis**, 406
Recombinant DNA, 418-9, *419*
Replication of, 153-54, *154*
RNA distinguished from, 429
Sequencing of, 154
Transcription of amino acids into proteins by, 483-484
in **Viruses**, 500
DNA fingerprinting, 152-53, 203
DNA hybridization, 153
DNA replication, 153-54
DNA sequencing, 154
Doebereiner, Wolfgang, 376
Dolphins, 300
Doppler, Christian Johann, 155
Doppler effect, 60, 155, *155*
Dormancy, 155, 228
Dorn, F.E., 418
Down's syndrome (trisomy 21), 35, 107, 220, 398
Drebbel, Cornelius, 464
Drug dependence, 15
Drugs; *see* **Pharmacology**
Dust Bowl, 136
Dwarf stars, 78-79, 242
Dynamics, 202, 303-4
relativity and, 456

Entry titles are in bold and in color: blue for mathematics and the physical sciences; green for life sciences and medicine; red for technology. Alternate or partial article titles, and article titles that appear as sub-entries, are black bold.

Italicized numbers indicate illustrations.

Ears and hearing, 156, *156*, 451-52
Earth, 157-58, *157*
Archaeological geology on age of, 226
Atmosphere of, 48-50, *50*, 388
Cartography and surveying of, 89, *89*
Coriolis force on, 126
Eclipses visible from, 159, *159*
Gaia hypothesis on, 211
Geodetic surveys, 225
Geomorphology of, 227
Geothermal energy from, 227-28
Glaciers, 230, *230*
Global warming of, 230-31
Gravity of, 234
interior of, 388
Magnetic field of, 297
Moon of, 324-25, *325*
Oceans of
  basins, 357, *357*
  currents, 357-58, *358*
  Oceanography, 358-59, *358, 359*
  origin and evolution of, 359
  waves, 507-8
Remote sensing of, 423
Water on, 504-5
  see also Geology
Earth metals, 31

Earthquake, 158-59, *158, 159*
on **Mars**, 301
Plate tectonics and, 394, *395*
Seismology of, 439
Eastman, George, 420
Echinoderms, 267
Eckert, J. Presper, 503
Eclipse, 159, *159*
E.coli (*Escherichia coli*) bacteria, 58, 221
Ecology, 160-61
Acid rain, 12-13, *13*
Biodiversity, 62-63, *63*
Paleoecology, 371
Population ecology, 399
Succession, 465
Symbiosis in, 470
of **Tropical rain forests**, 487
Ecosystems, 160
Gaia hypothesis on, 211
Homeostasis in, 245
Paleoecology of, 371
Succession within, 465
Tropical rain forests, 487, *487*
Ectoparasites, 374, 470
Edison, Thomas, 163, 419
Egg cells, 424, 425
during **Conception**, 122-23, *123*
X chromosomes in, 223, 306, 443
Ehrlich, Paul, 113-14
Eilenberg, Samuel, 91
Einstein, Albert, 437
Bose-Einstein statistics by, 73
on **Brownian motion**, 79, 171
cosmological constant proposed by, 493
einsteinium named after, 486
Equivalence principle, 179, 182
General relativity, 217-18
on **Gravity**, 234
on **Light**, 286
on **Lorentz-Fitzgerald contraction**, 294
Michelson-Morley experiment and, 314
Non-Euclidean geometry used by, 185, 346
on **Numbers**, 355
on photoelectric effect, 168
Space-time in universe of, 455-56
on **Special relativity**, 456, 496
Twin paradox and, 489
Electric and magnetic fields, 161-62, *161*
Electromagnetism, 166-67
  see also **Magnetic fields**
Electric circuit, 162
Applications of, 162-63
Capacitors in, 86
Conductors and resistors in, 123-24
Currents and charges in, 99-100
Diodes and photodiodes in, 146
Inductors in, 258
Insulators in, 262
Integrated circuits in, 263, *263*
Ohm's Law, 360
Semiconductors in, 440, *440*
Transistors in, 484-85
  P-N junctions in, 370, *370*
Electric circuits, applications of, 162-63
Electrical engineering; *see* **Electricity and electrical engineering**
Electricity and electrical engineering, 163-64
Analog computers used in, 37

Gametogenesis, 213
Gamma globulin, 213
Gamma ray astronomy, 512-13
Gamma ray, 166, 213, *213*, 416
  Mossbauer effect and, 326
Gamow, George, 493
Ganglions, 341 Ganymede (satellite of
    Jupiter), 434
Gargrin, Yuri, 453
Gases
  Behavior of, 214
  Charles's Law of, 9
  Diffusion in, 140
  Fluid mechanics of, 200
  Hydrogen, 250-51, *251*
  Maxwell-Boltzmann Distribution on, 302
  Nitrogen, 343
  Noble gases, 345, *345*
  Oxygen, 368
  Phase changes of, 380
  Radon, 418
  Viscosity of, 501
Gases, behavior of, 214
Gastrulas, 173, 325
Gauge theory, 215
Gauss, Karl Friedrich, 119, 139, 495
Gay-Lussac, Joseph, 214
Gel **Electrophoresis**, 170
Gell-Mann, Murray, 172, 235, 411
Gels, 114
Gene, 215-16, *216*
  Alleles, 119
  for **Altruism**, 118
  in **Cell nucleus**, 354
  on **Chromosomes**, 107-8
    Karyotyping of, 275
  DNA in, 151-53
    Electrophoresis of, 170
    Exons and introns on, 190-91, *190*
    Replication of, 153-54, *154*
    Sequencing of, 154
  Embryology and, 173
  Extranuclear inheritance and, 192-93
  Gene therapy, 218-19
  Genetic code of, 219
  Genetic engineering of, 220-21
  Linkages between, 288
  Major histocompatability complex, 298-299
  Oncogenes, 85, 150, 360
  Sex linkages of, 443
Gene amplification, 216
Gene flow, 216
Gene pools, 457
Gene regulation, 216
Gene therapy, 218-19, 221
General relativity, 217-18, *217, 218*
  Black holes in, 68
  Equivalence principle in, 182
  Space-time in, 455
Generators and motors, 326-27
Genetic code, 219
Genetic diseases, 148, 219-20, *220*
  caused by gene amplification, 216
  Cystic fibrosis, 133-34, *133*
  Down's syndrome, 35
  Gene therapy for, 218-19
  Hemophilia, 241
  Huntington's disease, 247-48

Polymerase chain reactions to detect, 398
Sickle cell disease, 445
  see also **Mutations, genetic**
Genetic engineering, 220-21
  E.coli (*Escherichia coli*) bacteria used for, 58
  Viruses used for, 500
Genetic imprinting, 107, 257-58
Genetic linkages, 107, 222, 288
  mapping, 224
Genetics, 221-23, *221, 222*
  Attenuation, 52
  of **Bacteria**, 58
  Biodiversity, 62-63, *63*
  Cloning, 111, *111*
  Complimentism and allelism in, 119
  DNA, 151-53
    Electrophoresis of, 170
    Exons and introns on, 190-91, *190*
    Replication of, 153-54, *154*
  Emotions and, 174
  Ethology and, 183-84
  Extranuclear inheritance and, 192-93
  Genes, 215-16, *216*
  genetic algorithms, 30
  Genetic code, 219
  Hardy-Weinberg law, 237-38
  of immune system, 55
  Imprinting in, 257-58
  Instincts and, 260-61
  of **Mitochondria**, 321
  Mutations, 330-31
    Mutagens and, 330
  Transcription in, 483-84
  Viral, 497-498
Genome, human, 223-24, *224*
Genotypes, 221
Geochemistry, 172, 379
Geochronology, 225
Geodetic survey, 89, 225
Geogrphics Information Systems (GIS), 121
Geological time scale, 225
  climate changes over, 370-71
Geology
  Archaeological, 226-27
  Biostratigraphy, 64
  Catastrophe theory in, 90-91
  Continents, formation of, 124-25, *125*
  Crystals, 130
  Earth, 157-58
  Earthquakes, 158-59, *158, 159*
    Seismology of, 439
  Faults, folds and joints, 195
  Fossils and, 203-4, *203*
  geochemistry, 172
  Geodetic surveys, 225
  Geological time scale, 225
    Archaen era, 42
    Cambrian, 83
    Cenozic era, 96
    Cretaceous-Tertiary Boundary, 128, *128*
    Ice ages, 253, *253*
    Jurassic period, 274, *274*
    Mesozoic era, 144, 310
    Paleozoic era, 372
    Permian period, 192
    Proterozoic era, 407
    Quaternary period, 370-71
  Geomorphology, 227

Halley, Edmund, 116, 231, 496
Halley's comet, 116
Halobacterium, 42
Halogens (Group VIIA), 237, *237*
Hamilton, William R., 495
Hansen's disease (**Leprosy**), 281
Haploid cells, 444
Hardy, G.H., 238
Hardy-Weinberg law, 237-38
Harmonic sequence, 208
Harrison, John, 333
Haug, Emile, 227
Hausdorff, Felix, 206
Hazardous waste disposal, 238-39, *238*
  Bioremediation for, 64
  of **Dioxins**, 146-47
  nuclear, 350
HDTV broadcasting, 415
Head-Mounted Display (HMD), 498
Hearing and ears, 156, *156*
Heart, 239-40, *239*
  Rheumatic fever of, 428
  transplantation of, 364
Heart disease, 149
Heat, 240-41, *240*
Heaviside, Oliver, 495
Heavy water, 251, 270
Heisenberg, Werner, 129, 196
  Uncertainty principle of, 232, 409, 490
Helium, 251, 345
  near **Absolute zero**, 9
  as **Superfluid**, 468
Helmholtz, Herman von, 138
Hemodialysis, 137
Hemoglobin, 445
Hemophilia, 241
Henle, Jacob, 229
Henry, Joseph, 165, 298
Herbivores, 160, 399
  digestion by, 143
  among **Dinosaurs**, 145
Hermaphrodites, 425
Herpes, 241
Herschel, William, 492, 493
Hertz, Heinrich R., 286, 303
Hertzsprung, Ejnar, 241
Hertzsprung-Russell diagram, 241-42, *242*
Hess, V.F., 126
Heterogeneous catalysts, 468-469
Hewish, Anthony, 408
Hidden-variable theories, 60
Higgs, Peter, 459
Higgs particles, 459
High-density lipoprotein (HDL), 289
High Fractured Plateau, 357
High-rise construction, 242-43, *243*
Highway engineering, 243, *243*
Hilbert, David, 488
Hill, Levi, 382
Hiroshima (Japan), 351
HIV (Human Immunodeficiency Virus), 21-22,
  149, 243-44, 497, 499
  Encephalitis caused by, 174
Hodgkin's disease, 244
Holland, John P., 464
Holland (submarine), 464
Holography, 244-45, *244*, 420
Homeostasis, 245

Homo erectus, 189, 245-47
Homo habilis, 189, 245
Homologous characteristics, 384
Homo Sapiens, 245-47, *246-47*
  Aging of, 19-21
  Australopithecus, 53-54, *54*
  Bacteria and, 57-58
  Birth of, 66-67
  Blood types among, 70
  Chromosomes of, 107
  Conception among, 122
  Evolution of, 188-89
  Human genome of, 223-24
  Neanderthals, 334, *334*
  Parasites of, 374-75
  Pheromones and, 381
  as **Primates**, 400
  Sleep by, 446
    see also Anatomy
Hooke, Robert, 316
Hopper, Grace, 118-19
Hormones
  ACTH (adrenocorticotrophic hormone), 16-17
  cancer and, 103
  estrogen, 174
  insulin, 372
  pituitary, 385-86
  Plant, 235, 391-92
  produced by **Endocrine system**, 175-76
  produced by **Thyroid gland**, 479-80
  Steroid hormones, 461-62, *462*
Howard, Henry Eliot, 19
Hoyle, Fred, 493
Hubble, Edwin, 60, 211, 247, 492
Hubble constant, 97, 217, 247
Hubble expansion, 60
Hubble Space Telescope, 448, 449
Human genome, 223-24, *224*
Human Genome Project, 107, 223
Human growth hormone (HGH), 461, 462
Human immunodeficiency virus; *see* **HIV**
Humans; *see* **Homo Sapiens**
Huntington's disease, 247-48
Hurricanes and tornadoes, 248-49, *248*, 508-9
Hutchinson-Gilford progeria, 21
Hutton, James, 491
Huxley, Aldous, 498
Huygens, Christian, 139, 285, 434
Hyatt, John Wesley, 393
Hydraulics, 249
Hydrocarbon, 250
  Aldehydes, 27
  Alkyl halides, 31-32
  Aromatic compounds, 43
  during **Combustion**, 115
  Cyclic compounds, 132
  Petroleum, 378-79
Hydrodynamics, 200
Hydrogen, 250-51, *251*
  Hydrocarbon, 250
  in **Organic compounds**, 364-65
Hydrogen bombs, 351
Hydrogen bonds, 71, 127, 151, 504
Hydrologic cycle, 251-52, *252*
Hydrometallurgy, 167
Hydroponics, 252
Hydrostatics, 200
Hyperion (satellite of Saturn), 435

Hypersonic flight, 272
Hyperthyroidism, 479-80
Hypothalamus (brain), 175-76, 385
Hypothyroidism, 480

Iapetus (satellite of Saturn), 434, 435
IBM Corp., 373
Ice, 504
  in **Glaciers**, 230
  organisms preserved in, 203
Ice age, 253, *253*
  Paleoclimatology and, 370-71
Igneous rock, 254, *254*
Image reproduction technology, 401
Images
  Cameras to record, 84, *84*
  Computer graphics for, 121
  computer recognition of, 375-76
  in **Electron microscopy**, 169
  Fiber optics to transmit, 197
  Holography for, 244-45, *244*
  in **Mirrors**, 320
  Photography for, 381-83
  Printing, 401
  Recording technology for, 419-20
  from **Telescopes**, 473-74
Image sensing diagnostics, 305
Imaginary numbers, 119-20
Immortal cells, 94
Immune response, 254-55, *255*
Immune system
  Antibodies, 40, *40*
  Antigen presenting cells, 41
  B-lymphocytes in, 57
  diseases of, 150
    AIDS, 21-22, *21*, *22*
    Allergies, 32-33, *32*
    Autoimmunity, 54-55
    Hodgkin's disease, 244
    Lupus, 295
    Multiple sclerosis, 328
  Immune response by, 254-55, *255*
  Interferons and interleukins in, 264
  Leukocytes in, 282-83, *283*
  Lymphatic system and, 296
  Major histocompatability complex, 298-299
  Monoclonal antibodies and, 323-24
  organ transplants rejected by, 469
Immunization and Vaccination, 256
  against **Chicken pox**, 103
  against **Measles**, 303
  against **Mumps**, 328
  against **Poliomyelitis**, 397
  against **Rabies**, 413
  against **Smallpox**, 446
  against **Tetanus**, 475
  against **Viruses**, 499
  against **Yellow fever**, 513
  antigens in, 40
Immunoassay, 257
Immunoglobulins (**Antibodies**), 40, 57, 255
Impact Theory of Extinction, 146
Impressed forces, 202
Imprinting, genetic, 107, 257-58
Incubation periods, 149
Inductor, 258
Infantile paralysis (**Poliomyelitis**), 147, 149, 395
Infectious diseases, 148-49

AIDS, 21-22, *21*, *22*
  HIV and, 243-44
Antibiotics for, 39-40, *39*
Chemotherapy for, 103
Chicken pox, 103
Common cold, 116
Encephalitis, 174-75
Epidemiology of, 181
Germ theory of, 228-29
of **Hearts**, 240
Immune response to, 254-55
Immunization and vaccinations against, 256
Immunoassays to diagnose, 257
Influenza, 258
Leprosy (Hansen's disease), 281
Lyme disease, 295-96
Malaria, 299
Measles, 303, *303*
Meningitis, 307-8
Mumps, 328
Plague, 386
Pneumonia, 395
Poliomyelitis, 397
Rabies, 413
Smallpox, 446
Tetanus, 475
Theory of, 147-48
Tuberculosis, 488
Infective arthritis, 44
Inflammations, 40, 254
Influenza, 149, 258, *258*
Infrared rays, 166
Infrared spectroscopy (IR), 457, 458
Infrared and ultraviolet astronomy, 259, *259*
Ingestion, 259-60
Inheritance
  extranuclear, 192-93
  Genes for, 215-16
  Genetic imprinting and, 257-58
  Genetic linkages in, 288
  Genetics, 221-23
    see also **Genetics**
Inorganic compound, 260
Insects, 267
  diseases spread by, 148
  Extinctions of, 192
  feeding behavior of, 259
  mutualistic relationships between plants
    and, 470
  respiration in, 427
Instinct, 260-61
Insulator, 262
Insulin, 372
Integral calculus, 81, 82, 262
Integrated circuit, 263, *263*, 485
Intel Corp., 373
Interbreeding, 384, 457
Interference, 263-64
Interferon, 255
Interferons and interleukins, 264
Internal combustion engine, 265-66
  Diesel engines, 137-38, *138*
  Otto cycle engines, 367
Internal energy, 177
International Conference of Weights and
  Measures (1960), 452
International Council for the Exploration of the

Entry titles are in bold and in color: blue for
mathematics and the physical sciences;
green for life' sciences and medicine; red for
technology. Alternate or partial article titles,
and article titles that appear as sub-entries,
are black bold.

Italicized numbers indicate illustrations.

Transition elements, 485
Welding, 510
Metamorphic rock, 314
Meteorites, 48, 146, 359
Meteorology
  Acid rain, 12-13
  Atmosphere, 48-50, *50*
  Jet stream, 272, *272*
  Weather and, 508-9
    see also Climatology; Weather
Meteors, 47-48, *47*
Meter, Treaty of the (1875), 452
Metric system, 452
    see also International Standard of Units
      and Measures
MHC; *see* Major Histocompatability Complex
Michelson, Albert, 294, 314
Michelson-Morley experiment, 286, 294,
    314, 456
Microbes, 147, 314
Microbiology, 314-16
Microevolution, 332
Microorganisms
  Infectious diseases caused by, 148-49
  Microbiology of, 314-16
    see also Bacteria; Viruses, Biological
Microphones, 419
Microscopy, 316-17, *316*
  Electron microscopy, 169, 317
  Microbiology using, 315
  Scanning tunnel microscopy, 435, 435
Microsoft Corp., 362
Microsurgery, 470
Microwave, 317, *317*
Microwave spectroscopy, 317
Mid-Ocean Ridge, 357
Migrations, 333
Milky Way, 211, 318, *318*, 416, 492
Miller, Stanley, 187
Millikan, Robert A., 126, 167
Millisecond Pulsar, 408
Mineralogy, 318-19
Minerals (geological)
  Diamonds, 137, *137*
  Petrology of, 379
  in soils, 447
Minerals (nutritional), 501-2
  Calcium, 81
Mining technology, 319, *319*
Minkowski, Hermann, 356, 455
Minsky, Marvin, 45
Mir (space station), 455
Mirror, 320
Missiles, 320, *320*
Mississippian period, 223, 372
Mitochondria, 93, 321, *321*
  Extranuclear inheritance in, 193
Mitosis, 94, 134, 305, 321-22, *322*
  Chromosomes copied in, 107-8
  Meiosis distinguished from, 306
Möbius, Augustus, 483
Möbius strips, 483
Mohorovicic Discontinuity (Moho), 157-58
Molecular compounds, 100-101
Molecular crystals, 130
Molecule, 322-23
  in gases, Maxwell-Boltzmann Distribution on,
    302

Polymers, 397, *397*
Proteins, 405, *405*
  see also Chemicals and chemistry
Molina, M., 104
Mollusks, 267
Momentum, 249
  law of conservation of, 124
Monoclonal antibodies, 323-24
Monogamy, 426
Monsoons, 509
Montagnier, Luc, 264
Monte Carlo Methods, 324
Montreal Protocol on Substances That Deplete
    the Ozone Layer (1987), 104, 369
Moon, 324-25, *325*
  Apollo 11's trip to, 453
  Eclipses of, 159
  Gravity on, *233*
  Tides and, 480
Moore, Gordon, 263
Morley, Edward, 294, 314
Morphogenesis, 325
Morris, Robert, 500
Morse, Samuel F.B., 163
MOSFET (transistor), 485
Mossbauer, R.L., 326
Mossbauer effect, 326
Motion
  Acceleration, 10
  Brownian motion, 79
  Newton's Laws of, 341-42
    second law of motion, 138
  Perpetual motion, 377, *377*
  Rotational motion, 432, *432*
Motors and generators, 326-27
Moulton, F.R., 448
Mountain climates, 110
Mountain formation, 327
Mount Palomar (California), 474
MRI; *see* Magnetic resonance imaging
MS-DOS (operating system), 362
Mucus glands, 438
Multiple sclerosis, 328
Mumps, 328
Murgulis, Lynn, 321
Muscle, 328-29
Muscle systems, 329-30
Mutagens and carcinogens, 330, 331
Mutation, genetic, 330-31
  Complimentism in, 119
  Genetic diseases caused by, 220
  Mutagens and, 330
  Polymerase chain reactions to detect, 398
  by Viruses, 499
Mutualism, 160, 470
Myers, Norman, 63

Nagasaki (Japan), 351
Nanotechnology, 332
Napalm, 239
National Institute of Standards and
Technology (Washington), 452
Natural radiation, 414, *414*
Natural radioactivity, 416-17
Natural selection, 187-88, 332
Nautilus (submarine), 464
Navigation, 332-33, *333*
  Radar used for, 413

nuclear, 353
Atomic clusters, 112
Atomic shell model, 51-52
Atoms, 50-51
Electron affinity, 168
Electrons, 167-68, *167*
Elementary particles, 170-72, *171*, *172*
Fission, 198-99, *199*
Fusion, 210
Gamma rays, 213, *213*
Group theory of particles, 234-35
law of conservation of charge and, 124
Mossbauer effect, 326
of **Natural radiation**, 414
Neutrons, 340
Standard model of, 458-59
String theory, 463-64
Uncertainty principle, 490
Optics, 363, *363*
Non-linear optics, 346-47
Perpetual motion, 377, *377*
Phase changes, 380
Plasma physics, 392-93, *392*
Quantum mechanics, 409, *409*
Bell's inequality, 60
Equivalence principle, 182
Gauge theory, 215
Relativity
Equivalence of energy and mass, 179
General, 217-18
Grand unification theories, 232-33
Michelson-Morley experiment and, 314
Special, 456, *456*
of **Solids**, 449-50
of **Space**, 452-53
Symmetry in, 471
of **Temperatures**, 474-75
Theories of everything, 475-76
Thermodynamics, 478
Entropy and, 179
of **Time**, 481
tools and equipment for
accelerometers, 10, *10*
Bubble chambers, 79, *79*
Cyclotrons, 132-33, *133*
Linear accelerators, 287
Particle accelerators, 10-11, *10*
Radiation detectors, 413-14, *413*
Scintillators, 437
Spectroscopy, 457-58
Synchrotrons, 471-72
Thermometry, 479
VLA (Very Large Array) telescope, 502
X-Ray diffraction, 512
of **Vacuums**, 494
Wave-Particle Duality in, 507
of **Waves**, 506-7
Interference between, 263-64
see also Astronomy
Phytochrome, 235, 236
Picard, Auguste, 490
Picard, Jean, 359
Piezoelectricity, 385
Piloting, 333
Pioneer series (spacecraft), 434, 496
Pitts, Walter, 337-38
Pituitary gland, 385-86
Placental mammals, 300

Placer mining, 319
Plague, 148, 256, 386
Planck, Max, 67, 168, 286
Planck's constant, 490
Planetary nebulae, 335
Planet, 386-87, *387*
Atmospheres of, 388-89, *388*
Earth, 157-58, *157*
Moon of, 324-25
formation of, 390, 448-49
interiors of, 388
Jupiter, 273-74, *273*, *274*
magnetic fields of, 389, *389*
Mars, 301, *301*
Mercury, 308-9, *39*
Neptune, 335-36, *336*
Pluto, 395, *395*
Rings of, 389, *389*
Satellites of, 433-34, *433*, *434*
Saturn, 434-35, 435
in **Solar system**, 448-49, *448*
Uranus, 493
Venus, 496-97, *496*, *497*
Planet, interior of, 388
Planetary atmosphere, 388-89
Planetary magnetic field, 389
Planetary rings, 389
Planets, formation of, 390
Plant, 283-84, 384, 390-91, *390*, *391*
Angiosperms, 38, *38*
Fungi distinguished from, 209
gas exchange and, 214
gene flow in, 216
Growth regulation in, 235-36, *236*
Hormones of, 391-92
Hydroponics, 252
Leaves, 280
Liquid transport by, 290
mutualistic relationships between **Fungi** and, 470
Photosynthesis in, 383-84, *383*
Calvin-Benson cycle in, 83, *83*
Chloroplast pigmentation in, 105, *105*
Chloroplasts and, 104-5, *104*
phototropism of, 487-88
Population ecology of, 399
relationships between **Fungi** and, 210
reproduction of
Asexual, 46-47, *47*
Dormancy in, 155
Flowers, 199, *199*
Fruit structures, 208
Gametogenesis, 213
Germination of, 228
Gymnosperms, 236
Seeds, 438
Sex in, 443
Sexual, 444
Roots of, 431-32
Soil chemistry for, 447
see also Botany
Plant hormones, 391
Plasma (blood cells), 57, 69
Plasma physics, 392-93, *392*
Plasmas (physics), 392
at beginning of universe, 61
in **Solar wind**, 449
Plasmids, 58, 192
Plastics, 393, *393*

Pheremones and, 380-81
of **Plants**, 391
  Angiosperms, 38
  Asexual, 46-47
  Dormancy in, 155
  Flowers for, 199, *199*
  Fruit structure for, 208
  Gametogenesis, 213
  Germination in, 228
  of **Gymnosperms**, 236
  Seeds, 438
  Sexual, 444
Polyploidy in, 398
of **Prokaryotic cells**, 403
Sexual, 442-43
Reproductive strategies, 425-26, *425*
of **Birds**, 65
Pheremones and, 380-81
in **Plants**, **Seeds** in, 438
Reproductive systems, 424-25
human, *424*, *425*
  Amniocentesis, 35, *35*
  Prostaglandins in, 404
Reptiles, 385, 426
Dinosaurs compared with, 144
reproduction by, 425
Resins, 393
Resistance (electrical), 162
Resistors and conductors, 123-24
Respiration, 427
Breathing regulation in, 76-77
Gills for, 229
Glycolysis in, 232
Krebs Cycle in, 277
in **Plants**, 214, 228
  cellular, 284
Respiratory systems, 427, *427*
Breathing regulation by, 76-77
Gills in, 229
Lungs in, 294-95
Restak, Richard, 174
Restoring forces, 202
Restriction enzymes, 418-19
Reticular activating system (RAS), 427-28
Retroviruses, 500
Rh blood factor, 70
Rheumatic fever, 428
Rheumatism, 44
Rheumatoid arthritis, 44
Ribonucleic acid; *see* RNA
Ribosomal RNA (rRNA), 428, 429
Ribosomes, 428, 483
Ribozymes, 180
Ricci-Curbastro, Gregorio, 495, 496
Richter scale, 159, 439
Riemann, Georg, 139, 495, 496
Rift Mountains, 357
Rift Valley, 357
Right-hand rule, 166
Rings of planets, 389, *389*, 434
of **Saturn**, 434, 435
of **Uranus**, 493
RNA (ribonucleic acid), 187, 429
as **Cyclic compound**, 132
DNA distinguished from, 151-52
as **Nucleic acid**, 351-52
in **Protein synthesis**, 406
Transcription of amino acids into proteins by,

483-84
viroids, 498
in **Viruses**, 500
RNA polymerase, 406, 484
Roads, 243
Robotics, 44-46, *45*, 430, *430*
Rocket, 430-31, *430*, *431*
Jet propulsion for, 271
Missiles, 320, *320*
Propulsion by, 404
used to put satellites into orbit, 453
Rocks, 125
of **Archaen era**, 42
chemical composition of, 172
Faults, folds and joints in, 195
Foliation of, 200-201
Igneous, 254, 254
measuring age of, 226
Metamorphic, 314
Petrology of, 379
Stratigraphy of, 462-63
Volcanic, 502
  see also Geology; **Minerals**
Roemer, Olaus, 274
Roentgen, Wilhelm, 164, 417, 512
Rohrer, Heinrich, 435
Romer, Olaus, 286
Roots, 431-32
Rotational motion, 432, *432*
Rowland, S., 104
Russell, Henry Norris, 241
Rutherford, Ernest, 50, 171, 348
Radioactivity discovered by, 416, 417

Sagan, Carl, 351
Salamanders, 36
Salts, 433
table salt, 268
Salyut series (space stations), 454-55
San Andreas Fault (California), 195
Sarnoff, Robert, 415
Satellites
artificial, 453
  astronomical, 512
  communications, 473
  reconnaissance, 423
Satellites, planetary, 433-34, *433*, *434*
of **Jupiter**, 274
of **Mars**, 301
Moon, 324-25, *325*
of **Neptune**, 336
of **Saturn**, 434-35
of **Uranus**, 493
Saturn, 434-35, *435*
Atmosphere of, 389
Interior of, 388
Rings of, 389, *389*
Satellites of, 434
Saurischians, 145
Scabies, 374-75
Scanning tunnel microscopy (STM), 435, *435*
Scheele, Karl, 365
Schiaparelli, Giovanni, 301, 496
Schizophrenia, 308, 436
Schmidt telescopes, 474
Schneider, Stephen, 351
Schröedinger, Erwin, 436, *436*
Schröedinger's equation, 436

Scientific method, 436-37
  Operations research and, 362
Scintillation counters, 413
Scintillator, 437
Sea-horses, 425
Secretion, cellular, 437-38
Seed, 438
  Dormancy of, 155
  Germination of, 228
  in Gymnosperms, 236
Seismics, 439
  used in Petroleum prospecting, 378-79
Seismographs, 439
Seismology, 439
Selenium, 369
Self-induction, 165
Semiconductors, 440, 440
  Diodes and photodiodes, 146
  P-N junctions in, 370, 370
Semmelweis, Ignatz, 39
Senses, 441
  Brain activity and, 74-75
  Hearing, 156, 156
  Reticular activating system for, 427-28
  Vision, 193-94
Sensory mechanisms, 441
Sequencing of DNA, 154, 224
Servomechanisms, 441
Sets and groups, 442
  Category theory and, 91
Set theory (mathematics), 126, 442
Sex, biology of, 442-43
Sex chromosomes, 107, 219-20, 223, 305, 443
  abnormalities of, 306
  Linkages on, 443
  Polyploidy in, 398
Sex hormones, 103
Sex linkage, 223, 443
Sexual dimorphism, 426
Sexually transmitted diseases, 148
Sexual reproduction, 424-25, 442-43
  of Fungi, 209
  in Plants, 444
Sexual reproduction in plants, 444
Shapley, Harlow, 231, 492
Shelly, Mary, 44
Shockley, William, 146, 370, 484
Shortliffe, Edward, 191
Sickle cell disease, 445
Side effects of drugs, 380
Sidereal time, 481
Sierpinski gaskets, 206
Silicon, 234
Silurian period, 225, 372
Silver halides, 381-82
Simon, Herbert, 191
Simpson, O.J., 203
SIRF (Space Infrared Telescope Facility), 9
Skeletal muscles, 328-30
Skeletal systems, 445
Skin, 147, 254
  Herpes, 241
  Jaundice of, 271
  Parasites on, 374
  sense of touch in, 441
Skinner, B.F., 123, 261
Skylab series (space stations), 454
Sleep, 76, 446

Small intestines, 141, 144
Smallpox, 147, 256, 446, 499
Smalltalk (programming language), 403
Smell, sense of, 441
Smith, William, 462, 491
Snakes, 293, 426
Snell's law, 421
Snow, 504
  in Glaciers, 230
Soaps and detergents, 446-47
Sodium chloride (table salt), 268
Software; see Programs, computer
Soil chemistry, 447
Solar Eclipses, 159, 159
Solar energy systems, 178, 178, 447-48
  Photovoltaic technology for, 384
Solar flares, 466
Solar system, 448-49, 449
  Asteroids and meteors in, 47-48, 47, 48
  Comets in, 115-16, 116
  Formation of planets in, 390
  Kepler's laws of, 275-76
  Moon (Earth's), 324-25, 325
  Oort cloud, 361, 361
  Planets, 386-87, 387
  Sun in, 466, 466
    see also Planets
Solar-thermal central receiver system (STCRS),
  178, 448
Solar-thermal distributed receiver system (STDS),
  178, 447-48
Solar time, 481-82
Solar wind, 449
Solids, 449-50
  Adsorption on, 17-18
  Covalent solids, 127-28
  Crystals, 130, 130
  ionic, 269
  Phase changes of, 380
  Surface chemistry of, 468-69
Solid state physics, 450
Solubility, 450
Solvation and precipitation, 450
Somites, 134, 257, 305
Sonar, 451
Sonics, 451
Sonography (ultrasonography), 305
Sound, 451-52
  Acoustics, 13
  in communications between animals, 117
  Doppler effect and, 155, 155
  Ears and Hearing for, 156, 156
  Phonons, 381
  Recording technology for, 419, 419
  Reflection and Refraction of, 421
  Ultrasonics, 490
  used in Sonar, 451
    see also Speed of sound
Space, 452-53
  origins of life in, 285
  Vacuums in, 494
Spacecraft, 453
  Avionics for, 56
  Infrared and ultraviolet astronomy from, 259
  for Interstellar space travel, 266
  Mars explored by, 301
  Mercury explored by, 309
  SIRF (Space Infrared Telescope Facility), 9

Ultrasonics, 490
Ultrasonography (sonography), 305
Ultraviolet and infrared astronomy, 259, *259*
Ultraviolet light, 166
Ultraviolet rays, 369
Ultraviolet spectroscopy (UV), 457, 458
Uncertainty principle, 232, 409, 490
Underground mining, 319
Underwater exploration, 490-91
  Sonar for, 451
  Submarine technology for, 464-65
Uniformitarianism, 491
  Catastrophe theory versus, 90-91
  in **Geological time scale**, 225
  necessary for **Archaeological geology**, 226
Universe, 492-93, *492*
  Big Bang theory, 60-62, *60, 61*
  "entropy death" of, 478
  Entropy in, 179
  Galaxies, 211-12, *211, 212*
  General relativity and, 217-18
  Kepler's laws of, 275-76
  Quasars in, 412
UNIX (operating system), 402
Upsilon Andromedae (star), 449
Uracil, 351
  in **DNA**, 151
  in **RNA**, 429
Uranium, 486
  Isotopes of, 270
  natural radioactivity of, 416
  Nuclear power from, 349-50
Uranus, 493
  Atmosphere of, 389
  Interior of, 388
  Satellites of, 434
Urea cycle, 277, 406
Urey, Harold, 187
Uterotonins, 67

Entry titles are in bold and in color: blue for
mathematics and the physical sciences;
green for life sciences and medicine; red for
technology. Alternate or partial article titles,
and article titles that appear as sub-entries,
are black bold.

Italicized numbers indicate illustrations.

Vaccinations and immunizations, 256
Vacuum, 452-53, 494
Vacuum distillation, 151
Vacuum filtration, 197
Valence, 260, 494
Valence Shell Electron Pair Repulsion
  (VSPER), 494
Van Allen belts, 389
Van der Waal's bonds, 71
Van der Waals forces, 127-28, 130
Vanguard I (artificial satellite), 453
Vaporization (evaporation), 504
Variance, 460-61
Variational calculus, 494-95
Varicella; *see* **Chicken pox**
Vectors and tensors, 495-96
Vegetative propagation, 424
Veksler, V.I., 472

Venera series (spacecraft), 496
Venus, 496-97, *496, 497*
  Atmosphere of, 230-31, 388
  Interior of, 388
Verne, Jules, 464
Vertebrates, 267, 385
  Amphibians, 36, *36*
  Birds, 65
  Eyes and Vision in, 193-94
  Fish, 198, *198*
  Lymphatic systems in, 296
  Mammals, 299-300
  Muscle systems in, 329-30
  Nervous systems of, 337
  Primates, 400, *400*
  Reflexes in, 422
  Reptiles, 426
  Skeletal systems of, 445
Vestigial organs, 188
Vietnam War, 147
Villard, Philippe, 416
Viral diseases, 147-49, 499
  antiviral drugs for, 103
  cancer as, 330
  Chicken pox, 103
  Common cold, 116
  Encephalitis, 174-75
  Exotic, 497
  Herpes, 241
  Measles, 303, *303*
  Meningitis, 307-8
  Mumps, 328
  Pneumonia, 395
  Poliomyelitis, 397
  Rabies, 413
  Smallpox, 446
  Yellow fever, 513
    see also **Infectious diseases**
Viral diseases, exotic, 497
Viral genetics, 497-498, *498*
Viroids, 498
Virtual reality, 498-499, *499*
Virtual Reality Modeling Language (VRML), 498
Virus, biological, 229, 315, 499-500
  as **Carcinogens**, 330
  Exotic Diseases caused by, 497
  Genetics of, 497-498
  HIV, 21-22, 243-44
  Influenza, 258
  as parasites, 160
  used in **Gene therapy**, 218
Virus, computer, 500-1
Viscosity, 200, 501
  of **Lubricants**, 294
Visible light, 166
Visible spectroscopy (VS), 457, 458
Vision and eyes, 193-94
  Light visible to, 285-86
  Night-vision technology and, 342, *342*
Vitamins and minerals, 201, 356, 501-2
VLA (Very Large Array) telescope, 502, *502*
Volcanism, 227
Volcano, 502-3, *503*
  Cretaceous mass extinction linked to, 146
  Mountain formation by, 327
Volta, Alessandro (count, Italy), 59
Voltage, 59
Vomeronasal organ, 381

Credits and acknowledgments

T: Top; B: Bottom; TM: Top Middle; BM: Bottom Middle; R: Right; L: Left.

9- T: CORBIS/Charles O'Rear; M,B: Tony O'Hara. 10- TL: Douglas Heyman; BL: NASA; BR: Fermilab. 11- T:Fermilab; TR: SLAC. 12- Tony O'Hara. 13- T(2): CORBIS/Ted Spiegel; B: NJPAC. 15: TR: Eleanor Kwei. 16- 3M Inc. 17- NIH. 18- NASA. 19- BL: Eleanor Kwei. 20-T: CORBIS/Michael T. Sedam; M: NASA. 21- BL: NIH; BR-CDC. 22- CDC. 23- T (4): NASA; B: Douglas Heyman. 24- BL: NASA; MR: Douglas Heyman. 25- T,B: NASA. 26- B: CORBIS/Historical Picture Archive. 27: M: Wayne P. Armstrong; B: CORBIS/Owen Franken. 28- M,B: Wayne P. Armstrong. 29- CORBIS/Archivo Iconografico, S.A. 32 T: CORBIS/Jim Zuckerman; BM: CORBIS/Studio Patellani; B: Stan Marsh. 33- M: NASA; B- CORBIS/Paul A. Souders. 34- B: John Heuser M.D., Washington University School of Medicine. 35-Tony O'Hara; BL: NIH. 38: Tony O'Hara; B: CORBIS/Fritz Polking; Frank Lane Picture Agency. 39- T: CORBIS/Lester V. Bergman. 40- T: Mike Clark, Cambridge University. 42- BR: NASA. 43- T: CORBIS/Paul A. Souders; BL: CORBIS/Owen Franken. 44- T: Rodney Brooks, MIT; BL: NIH. 46- NASA. 47- TL: CORBIS/Stephen Frink; TR: CORBIS/Science Pictures Limited; BR: CORBIS/Charles O'Rear; M: NASA. 48- NASA. 51- TL: Tony O'Hara; TR: Courtesy of Purdue University and Digital Instruments, Veeco Metrology Group, Santa Barbara, CA. 52- BR: CORBIS/ Dennis di Cicco. 53- TL: NASA. 54- TL: CORBIS/Bettmann. 55- TR John Heuser M.D., Washington University School of Medicine. 56- TL Daimler-Chrysler; BR: NASA. 57- TR: CORBIS/Charles O'Rear; BL: CORBIS/Lester V. Bergman. 58- T: NASA; B: CORBIS/Lester V. Bergman. 59- TR, TL Daimler-Chrysler. 60- BL: CORBIS/Roger Ressmeyer; BR: NASA. 61- NASA; 62- NASA. 63- TL, TR: CORBIS/Gary Braasch. 64- M: CORBIS/John Farmar; Ecoscene. 65- T:ORBIS/Jamie Harron; Papilio; TM:CORBIS/Ralph A. Clevenger; BM: CORBIS/Kevin Schafer; B: CORBIS/Joel W. Rogers. 66- T: CORBIS/Sally A. Morgan/ Ecoscene; B: CORBIS/David Reed. 67- T: Douglas Heyman; M, B: NASA. 68- NASA. 69- T: NIH; M: CORBIS/Jim Zuckerman. 71 T, M, B: Douglas Heyman; 72- B: NIH. 74- L(2)- Marcus Raichle M.D., Washington University School of Medicine; R: CORBIS/Lester V. Bergman. 75- NIH. 76- T: DOE; B: CORBIS/Charles O'Rear. 78- M,B: NASA. 80- T: CORBIS/Bettmann; B: NASA. 83- T: Douglas Heyman. 84- B: Olympus of America Inc. 85- T,B: NIH. 86- B: Douglas Heyman. 87- Douglas Heyman. 88- BR: Douglas Heyman. 89 T, M: USGS; B: NASA. 90- T: Douglas Heyman. 93-B: NIH. 97- NASA. 98- TL(3): CORBIS/Jack Fields; CORBIS/David Muench; CORBIS/William James Warren;. 99- T: Douglas Heyman. 103- NIH. 104: TL: CORBIS/Joseph Sohm, ChromoSohm Inc. 109- T: NIH. 110- T: NASA. 111- T: CORBIS/AFP; M: CORBIS/Ted Spiegel. 112- Perdue University and Digital Instruments, Veeco group, Santa Barbara, CA. 113- CORBIS/James L. Amos. 114- B: NASA. 115- CORBIS/Jim McDonald. 116- T(3): NASA; B: CORBIS/Roger Ressmeyer. 117- TR: CORBIS/ James L. Amos; R: CORBIS/Chinch Gryniewicz, Ecoscene. 120- M: Apple Computer, Inc.; BR: IBM, Inc. 121- NASA. 122- CORBIS/Science Pictures Ltd. 124- NASA. 126- BL USGS; BR: NASA. 127- T, M: NASA; B: SLAC. 128-T, B: CORBIS/Jonathan Blair. 130- M: CORBIS/Roger Ressmeyer. 133- T: CORBIS/Jim Sugar Photography; BM: CORBIS/Bettmann; B: Barbara Lipp. 134- BL: NIH. 135- T: CORBIS/Charles and Josette Lenars; B: CORBIS/Marc Garanger. 136- NASA. 137- T:CORBIS/Bettmann; B: CORBIS/Hulton-Deutsch Collection. 138- Barbara Lipp. 139- CORBIS/Lester V. Bergman. 142-Barbara Lipp. 145- T, BM, BR: CORBIS/Jonathan Blair; BL:CORBIS/Jim Zuckerman. 146-T:CORBIS/Tom Bean; TM:CORBIS/Kevin Schafer; BM: CORBIS/Dean Conger. B: NASA. 148- M: NIH; B: CORBIS/Lester V. Bergman. 149- B: CORBIS/ Catherine Karnow. 151- T: CORBIS/Digital Art; M:NIH; B: CORBIS/Bettmann. 152- NIH. 153- CORBIS. 157- T(3): NASA. 158- T: USGS; B: NASA. 161- T: CORBIS/Bettmann; B: Douglas Heyman. 162- CORBIS. 165- Xerox Technology Corp. 169- B:Perdue University and Digital Instruments, Veeco Metrology Group, Santa Barbara, CA. 170-Jeffrey L. Rotman/CORBIS. 171- T: SLAC. 172- Eleanor Kwei. 173- Eleanor Kwei. 178- TL: CORBIS/Philip James Corwin; TR: CORBIS/Joseph Sohm; ChromoSohm Inc.; BL: CORBIS/Joseph Sohm, ChromoSohm Inc.; BR: CORBIS/Joseph Sohm; ChromoSohm Inc.. 181- CORBIS/Phil Schermeister. 184- Betmann/CORBIS. 185- Archivo Iconographico/CORBIS. 188-T: Hulton- Deutsh Colleciton/CORBIS; BL: Peter Johnson/CORBIS; BR: Paul A. Souders/CORBIS. 189- T: Michael Nicholson/CORBIS. 196-(3) illustrations, Douglas Heyman. 197- T: CORBIS/Charles O'Rear; B: CORBIS/Lawrence Manning. 198-B: CORBIS/Stephen Frink. 199- T: CORBIS/Roger Ressmeyer; M: Tony O'Hara; B: CORBIS/Michael Maslan Historic Photographs. 200-T: NASA; B:PV Scientific Instruments, Inc. 202- T: CORBIS/Hulton-Deutsch Collection; M:CORBIS; B: NASA; L: CORBIS/Ken Redding. 203- M: CORBIS/Sally A. Morgan/Ecoscene; B:CORBIS/Jeffrey L. Rotman. 204-T: CORBIS/Jonathan Blair ; B: DOE. 207- T: CORBIS; B: CORBIS/Bill Ross. 208-CORBIS/ Roger Ressmeyer. 210-CORBIS. 211- NASA. 212- NASA. 213: CORBIS/Roger Ressmeyer. 214- CORBIS/James L. Amos. 216- CORBIS/The Purcell Team. 217- T:CORBIS/Jim Sugar Photography; B: NASA. 218- NASA; 220- T:CORBIS/Dr. Charles J. Ball. 227- CORBIS. 228: CORBIS/Joseph Sohm; ChromoSohm Inc. 229- T:CORBIS/Stephen Frink. 230- NASA.

231- NASA. 233- NASA. 234: USGS. 236- NASA. 238- CORBIS/Ted Spiegel.
239- B: CORBIS/Nathan Benn. 241- B: CORBIS/ Lester V. Bergman. 243- TL: CORBIS/Derek M.
Allan/Travel Ink.; TR: CORBIS/Yann Arthus-Bertrand. 244- TR: CORBIS/Jonathan Blair;
B: Corbis/The Purcell Team. 246- TR: CORBIS/Christopher Cormack. 248- NASA. 249- CORBIS/
Bettmann. 250- CORBIS/Bettmann. 253- USGS. 254- B: CorbisCORBIS/James L. Amos. 255- NIH.
257- NIH. 258- TR: CDC. 259- NASA. 262- T: CORBIS/Schenectady Museum, Hall of Electrical
History Foundation. 263- BL: Texas Instruments. 265: M: Barbara Lipp; TM, B: NASA.
266: NASA. 267- T:CORBIS/Brandon D. Cole. 271- NASA. 272- NASA. 273- M, B: NASA.
274- MR: CORBIS/James L. Amos. 275: R:NIH; B: CORBIS/Seth Joel. 277- T: CORBIS/Lester V.
Bergman; B: Tony O'Hara. 279- TL, TM, BM: NASA; L: CORBIS/Charles O'Rear.
280- CORBIS/Gary Braasch. 281- T: NASA; B: CORBIS/Paul Almasy; 283- T,B: CORBIS/Lester V.
Bergman. 285- NASA. 287- NASA. 289- CORBIS 291- B: CORBIS/Lester V. Bergman.
292- TL: CORBIS/Lester V. Bergman; BR: CORBIS/Amos Nachoum. 293- T: CORBIS/Tom
Brakefield; M: CORBIS/Stuart Westmorland; B: CORBIS/Staffan Widstrand. 295- T: CORBIS/Lester
V. Bergman; M: CORBIS/Lester V. Bergman; B: CDC. 296- T,B: CORBIS/Lester V. Bergman.
297- B: NASA. 298- T: CORBIS/Bettmann; B: CORBIS?. 300- T: CORBIS/Karl Ammann;
TM: CORBIS/Amos Nachoum; BM: CORBIS/Jeffrey L. Rotman; B:CORBIS/Galen Rowell;
R:CORBIS/Lester V. Bergman. 301- NASA. 303- T: CORBIS/Bettmann; M: CORBIS/Lester V.
Bergman; B:CORBIS/John Heseltine.304- NIH. 305- NIH. 307- T,B: CORBIS/Lester V. Bergman;
309- NASA. 311- M: CORBIS/Bettmann; B: USGS. 312- CORBIS/Lester V. Bergman. 313- Office of
Scientific Research, U.S. 314- M: CORBIS/Gary Braasch; B: CORBIS/Bettmann. 316- T:CORBIS/
Bettmann; M: CORBIS/Lester V. Bergman; B: CORBIS/Bettmann. 317- MR, B: NASA. 318- NASA.
319- CORBIS/Larry Lee. 320- B: CORBIS/Yves Debay; The Military Picture Library. 321- Eleanor
Kwei. 322- T: CORBIS/Lester V. Bergman; B: CORBIS/Lester V. Bergman. 325- NASA.
334- BR: NASA. 335- NASA. 336- NASA. 339- NASA. 340- T,M: Princeton University; B: NASA.
341- NASA. 342- B: NASA. 347- NASA. 348- NASA. 349- NIH. 352- NIH. 354- NIH. 357- NASA/
USGS. 358- B: NASA. 361- T,B: NASA; M: CORBIS/Jonathan Blair. 369- T: NASA. 370- B: Douglas
Heyman. 371- NASA. 373- T: CORBIS/ Lester V. Bergman. 376- T: Vincent Arnone. 377- B: Douglas
Heyman. 378- DOE. 379- USGS. 380- T: Vincent Arnone. 387- NASA. 388- NASA. 389- NASA.
391- T:P.J. Redouté; TM:CORBIS/Hal Horwitz; BM: CORBIS/Bill Ross; B: CORBIS/Patrick Johns.
392- T: NASA. 394- T, TM, BM: USGS; B: Douglas Heyman. 395- NASA. 395- M: NASA.
399: U.S. Fish and Wildlife Service. 400- T: CORBIS/Tom Brakefield; TM: CORBIS/Nigel J.
Dennis/ABP; BM: CORBIS/Karl Ammann; B: CORBIS/Charles Philip. 408- TM,BM,B: NASA.
411- Fermilab. 412- NASA. 413- M, B: NASA. 414- NASA. 416- M: Vincent Arnone.
417- BM, B: NIH. 418- T: NIH. 419- NIH. 420- B: NASA. 424- NIH. 425- T: NIH; B: CORBIS/Lawson
Wood. 427- NIH. 430- T: Rodney Brooks, Artificial Intelligence Lab, MIT; B: NASA. 431- NASA.
432- M: CORBIS/Neal Preston. 433- NASA. 434- NASA. 435- T, M: NASA. 440- IBM Research, Inc.
448- NASA. 453- CORBIS/Digital image 1996 CORBIS; Original image courtesy of NASA.
454- NASA. 455- NASA. 456- CORBIS/Bettmann. 459- NASA. 466- CORBIS/Bettmann. 469- NIH.
473- NASA. 480- TR: CORBIS/James L. Amos. 487- CORBIS/ Buddy Mays. 492- NASA.
493- NASA. 496- CORBIS/Bettmann. 497- CORBIS/Bettmann. 498- CORBIS/Lester V. Bergman.
499- T: NASA; B: NIH. 503- T: NASA; M: CORBIS; B: USGS. 508- NASA. 509-NASA.

**The publishers and producers of this encyclopedia gratefully acknowledge the generous
assistance of the Corbis Archives, the National Cancer Institute, and NASA in assembling
much of the illustration program of this work.**